CAMBRIDGE
AND CO

E
J. DIGGLE   N. HOPK
M. D. REEVE   D. N. S   R. J. TARRANT

44

SOPHOCLES: ELECTRA

SOPHOCLES

ELECTRA

EDITED WITH INTRODUCTION
AND COMMENTARY

BY

P. J. FINGLASS

Lecturer in Classical Studies, University of Nottingham
Fellow of All Souls College, Oxford

CAMBRIDGE
UNIVERSITY PRESS

CAMBRIDGE UNIVERSITY PRESS
Cambridge, New York, Melbourne, Madrid, Cape Town,
Singapore, São Paulo, Delhi, Tokyo, Mexico City

Cambridge University Press
The Edinburgh Building, Cambridge CB2 8RU, UK

Published in the United States of America by Cambridge University Press, New York

www.cambridge.org
Information on this title: www.cambridge.org/9780521292580

First published 2007
Reprinted with corrections 2010
First paperback edition 2011

A catalogue record for this publication is available from the British Library

ISBN 978-0-521-86809-9 Hardback
ISBN 978-0-521-29258-0 Paperback

For my parents

CONTENTS

CONTENTS

PREFACE

The DPhil thesis with which this work began dealt with lines 251–870 of the play. My supervisor was Gregory Hutchinson: his wide learning, industrious scholarship and patient encouragement were of incalculable benefit to me. Jasper Griffin and Peter Wilson supplied useful comments on an early draft of part of the thesis; while my examiners, Christopher Pelling and James Diggle, also made numerous suggestions for improvement. I am grateful to Professor Diggle for his encouragement to submit my work to the Cambridge Classical Texts and Commentaries series, and to the Syndics of the Cambridge University Press for accepting it.

The entire commentary has been read by Sir Hugh Lloyd-Jones, Malcolm Davies, James Diggle, Michael Reeve, Donald Russell, Martin West and Nigel Wilson. Professors Diggle and Reeve have also examined my introduction, text, apparatus and appendices. Roger Dawe has provided helpful comments on individual passages. My sections on lyrical metre were improved through the advice of Laetitia Edwards (Parker), while Peter Thonemann supplied me with useful information on epigraphy. Christopher Collard communicated to me some unpublished remarks by Eduard Fraenkel on the messenger scene, which are included as an appendix. I am grateful to him, and to Professor L. E. Fraenkel and the President and Fellows of Corpus Christi College, Oxford for allowing it to be published in this way. Nigel Wilson kindly lent me a microfilm of K, while Jane Beverley, Malcolm Davies, Torsten Meissner and John Waś gave me permission to refer to their unpublished Oxford DPhil theses. Through the good offices of Guido Avezzù and Harm Pinkster I was able to consult the collection of Sophoclean conjectures gathered by Liny van Paassen of the University of Amsterdam in the 1970s. The officers of the Press have provided invaluable assistance throughout, especially my commissioning editor, Michael Sharp, and my copy-editor, Muriel Hall. I have also received assistance of various kinds (especially in tracking down obscure books) from Winfried and Ria Bühler, Almut Fries, Molly Guinness, Birke Häcker, Hannah Mason, David Saunders, Liesbeth Schuren, John Simmons, and Mary-Rose Wyles. I would also like to thank the staff of the Bodleian, Sackler, Taylorian and Corpus Christi College libraries in Oxford, the British and Maughan libraries in London, the University and Wren libraries in Cambridge, the Brotherton library in Leeds, the Staatsbibliothek and the library of the Faculty of Classical Philology at the Freie Universität in Berlin, the Thuringer Universitäts- und Landesbibliothek in Jena, the Herzog August Bibliothek in Wolfenbüttel, and the Dipartimento di Linguistica Letteratura e Scienze della Comunicazione at the Università degli Studi in Verona. My gratitude to all those who have helped me is keenly felt. Scarcely can any young person have had so many great scholars criticise his work with such care and with such beneficial effect.

It is a pleasure to mention here the three educational institutions of which I have been a member. Between 1990 and 1997 I began to learn first Latin and then Greek at King Edward's School, Birmingham under the sure guidance of Stan Owen, Philip Lambie, George Worthington, Lawrence Evans and James Stone. My time as an undergraduate at St. John's College, Oxford (from 1997 to 2001) was equally happy, blessed as I was with Malcolm Davies, Nicholas Purcell and Donald Russell as my tutors, and with an atmosphere wholly congenial to intellectual pursuits. Since November 2001 I have been a Fellow by examination at All Souls College, Oxford. There I have been able to continue my studies in ideal surroundings, free from many of the difficulties, financial and otherwise, which can afflict the graduate student. I am especially grateful to my college academic advisors: Martin West, who has ever been willing to discuss a multitude of problems, and Jim Adams, who has been

PREFACE

a constant source of advice and encouragement. It is a privilege to call these two men colleagues.

Scribebam Oxoniae   P. J. F. F.
in Collegio Omnium Animarum
die festo Sancti Patricii, anno Domini MMV

INTRODUCTION

1 DATE

There is no solid external evidence for the date of Sophocles' *Electra*. Scholars have generally placed it towards the end of his career, on the basis of perceived similarities with *Philoctetes* and *Oedipus at Colonus* (securely dated to 409 and 401 respectively). All three plays are centred on an isolated figure who has endured many years of lonely torment as the consequence of some outrage perpetrated on him or her in the distant past. During the course of the play this figure becomes the victim of an intrigue-plot, but manages to overcome his or her enemies to obtain a long-desired consummation. The prologues of each play show further similarities (1–85n.), while the increased use of *antilabe* and broken-up lyric dialogue found in each of the dramas also constitutes a distinctive shared feature (823–70n.). On these similarities see further Vögler (1967) 86–100.

None of this proves that *Electra* is a late play. A poet is free to employ similar material at different stages in his career; and the experience of the dating of Aeschylus' *Supplices* should make a classicist wary about placing too much weight on stylistic evidence. Nevertheless, even taking account of these caveats, the similarities do appear extensive enough to make it most unlikely that *Electra* was first performed before, say, 430. It is tempting to go further and say that the play must belong still closer to *Philoctetes*, say after 415. But such precision is not warranted by the evidence. S. could easily have experimented with plays of this type rather before the late 410s. Putting *Electra* as close as possible to the other two plays undoubtedly gives us a tidier picture of Sophocles' *oeuvre*: but in the chronology of Attic tragedy the tidy answer is not always right.[1]

[1] Lloyd-Jones's dictum 'after a hundred and fifty years of doctoral dissertations, people who confidently claim to *know* the date of Sophocles' *Electra* or

This uncertainty hampers attempts to decide whether the play was written before or after Euripides' *Electra*. Indeed, the date of the latter is also unknown. Most scholars (cf. e.g. Denniston's edition, pp. xxxiii–xxxiv) used to date it to 413, because of supposed allusions to a relief expedition sent by Athens to Sicily in that year (1347–8; cf. Thuc. 7.20.2, 7.42.1), as well as to a distinctive handling of the Helen myth explicable only as a foretaste of Euripides' own *Helen* to be performed in the following year (1280–3). The 413 dating was preferred even though the chronology obtained by counting the number of resolutions in the iambic trimeter (which steadily increase from the 420s onwards) suggested a rather earlier date.[2] But Zuntz (1955) 64–9 demonstrated that neither of the criteria used to date the play to 413 stands up to scrutiny. Vögler (1967) 52–85 attempted to re-establish the case for 413, but his work has rightly been criticised by Lloyd-Jones (1969b). Zuntz's case is now widely accepted. We have no reason to put the play outside the period suggested by the resolution chronology, namely *c.* 422–16 (cf. Zuntz (1955) 69–71).

The limitation to this period is less helpful than we might have hoped. Sophocles' play may date to after 416, but as we have seen, it could well be rather earlier than that. Furthermore, resolution chronology is not a flawless tool: for example, the Euripidean play with the highest resolution rate is *Orestes*, even though that play is not his last. This uncertainty means that the evidence does not allow even a provisional decision.

Trachiniae are living in a private world' ((1964a) 372 = (1990a) 275 = E. Segal (1983) (ed.) 54; Lloyd-Jones's italics) remains as true as ever. For an attempt to give an absolute date to the play on the basis of alleged reference to it in Euripides' *Helen* see 59–66n.

[2] On this see Zieliński (1925) 133–240, Ritchie (1964) 260–3 and Dale's edition of Euripides' *Helen*, pp. xxiv–xxviii. Cropp and Fick (1985) 5 provide the most up-to-date table of resolution rates. Zieliński's work marks an important advance over previous attempts to use these statistics (for which see Ceadel (1941) 66–7), since he shows how the placing of different shapes of resolved words also changes consistently over time.

This has not prevented many attempts to assert priority for one play over the other on other grounds, chiefly through the comparison of shared features. For some scholars the more developed or elaborate example of a common element must be the later; for others, the handling of a motif in the later play must seem inorganic, out of place or simply trivial compared with its treatment in the former. It is not hard to see how these approaches, neither of which is more valid than the other, could produce diametrically opposed results from the same material.[3] Our problem is especially recalcitrant to this kind of analysis because so many features shared between the two dramas have a common origin in Aeschylus' *Choephori* (see section 2 of this Introduction). Differences between the *Electra* plays are often better understood as the result of different responses to Aeschylus than as the later *Electra* reacting to the earlier, whatever the order in which they were performed.

The debates outlined above have had an unfortunate consequence for interpretation of the plays. When investigating a feature shared between the two dramas, scholars have tended to search for signs of immaturity, inappropriateness or some other fault in one of the plays, in order to provide evidence for relative dating. As a consequence, little effort has been directed at attempting to understand the varying treatments of such features on their own terms. Yet in dealing with the works of two of the great classical poets, it is not unreasonable to begin from the assumption that a given characteristic of their plays is composed for some poetic purpose. Differences between their work will then reflect not incompetence or derivativeness, but rather the diversity of their artistic aims. My attempts to compare the two plays (cf. e.g. 254–309n., 262–4n., 612–33n., 892–919n., 911–12n., 1398–1441n.) are based on this assumption. Rather than treating the plays as 'a tilting-ground for contests fought in the

---

[3] For specific examples and further criticisms of such reasoning see Jebb's edition, pp. liii–lvi, and Vögler (1967) 16–51.

heavy armour of well-trained chronologists' (Fraenkel on Aesch. *Ag.* 826), I try to use comparisons between them as a means of bringing out the distinctive characteristics and aims of Sophocles' drama. This approach remains valid whichever play came first: and indeed, in the end the question of priority may be less important than it first appears.[4]

2 THE STORY BEFORE SOPHOCLES[5]

Es ist als wenn Sophokles sagte 'ich habe die Choephoren nicht vergessen, aber ich mache es anders'.

Fraenkel (1962) 22 n. 1; cf. Wilamowitz (1974) 70

In writing his *Electra* Sophocles could scarcely fail to take account of Aeschylus' *Choephori*, which also deals with Orestes' revenge. Unsurprisingly, various motifs and patterns are common to both plays. Both begin with the return of Orestes to his homeland, prompted by an oracle from Apollo at Delphi. After a speech from Orestes Electra enters from the *skene*. In each play Clytemnestra has an ill-omened dream which prompts her to send her daughter to make offerings at the tomb of Agamemnon. Before the daughter can carry out her instructions, however, she encounters a sibling, who quickly realises that the dream bodes ill to Clytemnestra. As a consequence Clytemnestra's orders are not carried out: instead, her children beg for Agamemnon's assistance against his former consort. Each play contains a plot to

---

[4] This is not to deny that from the perspective of the literary historian it would be of interest to know which play came first, and thus (for example) who had the idea of focussing the action on Electra. But the effect on our interpretation of each drama would be surprisingly small. So for example, Clytemnestra and Aegisthus are presented with considerable sympathy in Euripides, but with near-total hostility in Sophocles (cf. 289–92n., 516n., 584–94n., 612–33n., 1398–1441n., 1442–1504n.). It matters little for our understanding which treatment came first. What is important is that the difference exists, a difference which has implications for our view of Electra and of her struggle in each play.

[5] The following does not pretend to be a full account of the pre-Sophoclean myth in literature and art. For an excellent brief survey see Garvie's edition of Aeschylus' *Choephori*, pp. ix–xxvi.

overcome Aegisthus and Clytemnestra by deception, and in each this takes the form of a false report of Orestes' death. The news of this 'death' leads to an emotional reaction from Clytemnestra, who welcomes the bearer of the tidings inside the *skene* as a guest. Aegisthus later appears, having heard the supposed good news: his arrival is swiftly followed by his dispatch by Orestes.

This bare summary gives some idea of the importance of *Choephori* for Sophocles' play. But alongside these basic similarities are a number of significant differences. Some are differences of omission. For example, the monumental *kommos* at Agamemnon's tomb which forms the centrepiece of *Choephori* plays no part in Sophocles' drama. So too the importance attached to the wider Argive *polis* in Aeschylus is considerably attenuated in Sophocles (see Introduction, section 4). Other differences involve the emphasising of aspects of the story undeveloped by Aeschylus. So whereas in the earlier tragedy Electra is a minor figure, forgotten half-way through the drama, in Sophocles she so predominates that 'der eigentliche Inhalt des Gedichts sind die πάθη der Heldin' (Schadewaldt (1926) 57). Electra, not Orestes as in Aeschylus, intercepts Clytemnestra's offerings to the dead Agamemnon, and is roused to new optimism by the account of Clytemnestra's dream. Chrysothemis and the Paedagogus, who do not even appear in *Choephori*, also play an important part in Sophocles' work.

But perhaps the most fundamental change occurs with Sophocles' handling of the recognition scene. His Electra does not identify her brother until 1221–2, some thousand lines later than the corresponding part in Aeschylus' play (212–45). She had received indications of her brother's presence more than three hundred lines earlier, but had steadfastly refused to believe them. Orestes then enters, but it is still over a hundred lines before Electra recognises him. Before that can happen, she delivers a moving lament for the brother standing next to her, and then engages in an emotional stichomythia with Orestes which eventually concludes in his self-revelation. This climactic moment is followed by a joyous lyric dialogue (1232–87). The emotive impact of the recognition is subsequently recapitulated in a less intense form in Electra's recognition of the Paedagogus (1346–63). The prominence given to the recognition far exceeds anything in Aeschylus' play. No longer a brief episode which soon makes way for the more important business of the *kommos*, it becomes a central moment of the drama, in which Electra's power of emotional expression is most vividly demonstrated.

The delay in the recognition of Orestes also allows Electra to be taken in by the deception plot. This too is much more elaborate than its Aeschylean model, involving as it does one of the most exciting messenger speeches in extant tragedy. But perhaps its most memorable aspect is its impact on Electra, whom it plunges into new depths of grief and suffering. An early recognition as in Aeschylus would thus have denied us the extremes of despair and joy which Electra shows during this central section of the play. Sophocles' decision to use the same basic set of story elements as Aeschylus, but to put them together in a quite different manner, turns out to be crucial to the individual character of the play.[6]

This departure from the Aeschylean version is signalled soon after the start of the play. Immediately before the entry of Electra at 86 the possibility is raised that Orestes will wait to hear his sister's laments. This is exactly what he does at the start of *Choephori*. But the possibility is raised only to be emphatically rejected by the Paedagogus. This decisive intervention sets Sophocles' plot on a very different course from that of Aeschylus. It programmatically stresses that although Sophocles is using Aeschylean material, his treatment of it will differ from his predecessor's. Fraenkel's famous comment on this passage (cited above as the epigraph to this section) applies no less to the play as a whole than to this episode.

---

[6] A prevailing fault in Winnington-Ingram's influential article of 1954–5 (expanded in 1980) is its emphasis on the Aeschylean character of Sophocles' play with little attention to the real and significant differences between the two dramas.

Excessive concentration on the Aeschylean background can blind us to the crucial significance of earlier poetry for the play. Stesichorus' *Oresteia*, for instance, is likely to have had an impact on Sophocles' drama, but our fragments of this work are too small to allow a proper comparison. Exiguous as they are, they do tell us that Clytemnestra's dream and the lock in the recognition scene both have Stesichorean precedent. If we had more of Stesichorus' work, then further aspects of Sophocles' play which we now label 'Aeschylean' might in fact turn out to have a more ancient pedigree. We can also find traces of material from various epics (cf. Davidson (1990b) 407). The *Cypria* appears to be the source for the number of Agamemnon's daughters (157n.) and Agamemnon's boast after killing the stag (569n.), while the number of Menelaus' children might be from the *Cypria* or from Hesiod (539n.).

But the most significant epic allusions are to Homer. Many of these have been catalogued and analysed by Davidson (1988); cf. also Di Benedetto (2003) 122. Prominent examples include the Paedagogus' opening speech (which owes much to Athena's words to Odysseus after his arrival on Ithaca in *Odyssey* 13 (1– 85n.)), Electra's condemnation of Chrysothemis (which evokes the language of Achilles (341–68n.)), the description of the chariot race (which is heavily influenced by *Iliad* 23 (680–763n.)), and the opening of the third episode (cf. *Od.* 23.1–84 (871–91n.)). On a structural level, the νόστος ἀναγνώρισις μηχάνημα pattern which so dominates the play (as it does other tragedies, such as Aeschylus' *Choephori* and Euripides' *Cresphontes* (see Harder's edition, pp. 14–17)) has its literary origins in Homer's account of Odysseus. Odyssean allusions are especially common with reference to the story of Orestes. These begin right from the opening of the play, when we learn that like Homer, but unlike Stesichorus, Pindar and Aeschylus, Sophocles has set the story of the vengeance in Mycenae. Other programmatic echoes (cf. 3n., 9n., 14n.) all establish this connexion from early on: so too does the parodos, where we learn that Agamemnon was killed at a feast

7

as in Homer,[7] not in his bath as in Aeschylus (and Euripides). Neither the location of the play nor the manner of Agamemnon's death is of particular thematic importance in Sophocles' play: he could just as easily have gone along with the Aeschylean version of events. His choice to return to the Homeric account, and to make this clear in the early part of his drama, thus represents a further prominent distancing from Aeschylus. It also suggests that Orestes' vengeance will lack the ethical complications prominent in Aeschylus but not in Homer: this, however, will turn out to be only partly correct.

3 GOOD SPIRITS?

Scholars who have written on Sophocles' *Electra* can generally be divided into two opposing camps. The 'optimists' argue either that Sophocles presents the matricide as an ethically justified act, or that his treatment simply does not raise any moral questions. The 'pessimists', on the other hand, take a much darker view of the vengeance, and a correspondingly less sympathetic view of Electra and Orestes.

The optimistic view dates back to A. W. Schlegel, and held sway during the nineteenth century (cf. Davies (1999a)). It is prominent in the influential commentary of Sir Richard Jebb, and received its most memorable summary in Murray's description of the play as a 'combination of matricide and good spirits' (his translation of Euripides' *Electra*, p. vi). The 'pessimistic' interpretation of the play starts to become fashionable in the first part of the twentieth century, particularly through the work of Sir John Sheppard (cf. (1918), (1927)). From the middle of the century it constitutes the dominant scholarly trend, with important articles by Winnington-Ingram (1954–5), Friis Johansen (1964) and C. P. Segal (1966) all taking a dark view of the play and its heroine. This approach is reflected and further intensified in the 1973 commentary by Kells. More recently there has been a

---

[7] This account may also have been found in the *Nostoi*: see 193–200n.

move in the opposite direction. Two works which appeared in 2001 – March's commentary and MacLeod's monograph *Dolos and Dike in Sophocles'* Elektra – both present a much more positive view of Electra and the matricide.[8]

This crystallisation of academic opinion into two separate camps has had a generally deleterious effect on the interpretation of the play. It often seems as if on deciding to write about Sophocles' *Electra*, scholars quickly make up their mind whether they are optimists or pessimists. With that decision made, they go through the play and force every episode into their preferred *schema*, without stopping to ask whether the drama might be too complicated a work to submit to such Procrustean practice. The commentaries by Kells and March are particularly at fault here. Both of these scholars will grasp at any interpretation, however absurd, if it will only support their case.[9]

My commentary takes neither an 'optimistic' nor a 'pessimistic' line. Rather than assign myself a label and then try to argue away those uncomfortable scenes which do not fit it, I have attempted to analyse each episode on its own terms. In some cases my views are close to those of the optimists (e.g. in the parodos or the recognition scenes), while in others they sit more easily alongside those of the pessimists (e.g. at the very end of the play). Sometimes elements of both trends must be taken into account if we are to understand a given episode properly (most notably in the *agon*). This is not a 'pick and mix' approach to interpretation, but the only means of coming to terms with this complicated and multiform drama.

In particular, the final part of the play presents us with a far less sympathetic Electra than in, say, the parodos; and correspondingly the portrayal of the last moments of Clytemnestra and Aegisthus is far more unsettling than we might have been

---

[8] Many other articles could have been cited here, but few do more than restate the positions held by the writers of the important works listed above. For more details see MacLeod (2001), which is especially valuable as a doxography for the play.

[9] For a recent critical assessment of March's commentary see Wright (2005).

expecting from the presentation of these characters earlier in the work. Careful preparations have been made for this shift, most notably in the *agon*, where Electra's victory had been tempered by a use of arguments which would easily recoil against her own future conduct (cf. 577–83n.). Yet the effect is still striking, especially given the joyous atmosphere of the immediately-preceding recognition scenes, which had appeared calculated to distract our attention from the potentially troubling business of matricide, and thereby to ensure a happy and confident ending. Interpretation of the climax of the play is vitiated by interpolation: but as far as can be made out, Sophocles has deliberately eschewed any attempts at a satisfying conclusion which ties up all loose ends. The different aspects of the presentation of Electra's character and of the killings which she supports leave us in the end with more questions than answers.

4 LEAVING OUT THE *POLIS*?[10]

Aeschylus' *Oresteia* is profoundly concerned with the impact of the dynastic troubles of the house of Atreus on the wider Argive community.[11] Sophocles' play, by contrast, has little to say on this subject: Griffin indeed goes so far as to claim that 'as for the present or future state of the *polis* of Argos, our attention is never directed to them' ((1999b) 80). The focus of the play lies on Electra herself and her fluctuating emotions, and there is a corresponding lack of emphasis on the community as a whole.[12]

Yet Griffin goes too far by asserting that the πόλις is never important for Sophocles' play. For through the course of the drama we do encounter occasional brief references to the wider

---

[10] The argument in this section is a summary of the more extensive treatment of this subject in Finglass (2005c).

[11] For references see Griffith (1995) 76–8.

[12] Cf. Griffin (1999b) 77–82, Knox (1983) 7–10. MacLeod (2001) adopts a radically new approach by arguing that the πόλις is all-pervasive, and that the actions of Electra and Orestes are informed by a commitment to its distinctive values. However, her case is never properly supported by the evidence of the text.

community. The prologue begins with the Paedagogus pointing out to Orestes the various sights of the locality (1–10). In her prayer to Apollo Clytemnestra is concerned that Electra might reveal her words to the city unless she conceals her true intentions (641–2). Electra describes to Chrysothemis the enthusiastic reaction of the community to her prospective act of tyrannicide (976–85); then at the climax of the recognition-scene she turns to the chorus and calls to it with the words ὦ πολίτιδες, an emphatically public mode of address (1227n.). The chorus itself invokes the πόλις at that other climactic moment, the killing of Clytemnestra (1413–14). Then at 1458–63 Aegisthus pompously asserts his authority over the citizen community during what turn out to be the dying seconds of his régime.

Brief though they are, many of these references occur at moments of great significance: the opening of the play, Clytemnestra's pivotal prayer, Electra's recognition of Orestes, the killing of Clytemnestra, the final moments of Aegisthus. Had Sophocles wanted to deny the πόλις any importance, he would hardly have given such prominence to the few political references which the play possesses. Indeed, he could easily have eliminated the πόλις from his play altogether. It is worth considering whether he had some purpose, however circumscribed, in referring to it.[13]

Taken together, these references form a consistent picture: Clytemnestra and Aegisthus are feared and hated by the Mycenaeans, whereas Orestes and Electra can count on their support. They hint at a broader reality behind the actions of the play which adds extra significance to the events of the drama. Electra's determined support for her brother will have consequences beyond the limits of her immediate family. Yet the mentions of the πόλις are brief enough not to divert our attention from the 'feminine emotion and heroic pathos' (Griffin (1999b) 82) which

[13] Cf. Davies's comment on Karl Reinhardt's discussion of the Judgement of Paris in the *Iliad*: 'in particular, while showing in a superlatively convincing manner why the Judgement is not alluded to more often, he does not try to explain why it has to be mentioned at all' ((1981) 57).

form the main focus. Sophocles thus deepens the significance of his work without compromising his fundamental aim of concentrating on Electra. This requires a delicate balancing act on his part, involving deft and intricate control over his material. Avoiding the extremes of a play dominated by the *polis* and a play which never touches on the *polis*, he takes a middle course in which the Mycenaean polity constitutes a feature with a limited but definite dramatic purpose.

5 PRODUCTION

The *skene* represents the palace of Agamemnon at Mycenae. Eisodos B leads to Agamemnon's tomb; eisodos A is used for entrances from elsewhere in the territory of Mycenae. Outside the *skene* building there is a statue representing Apollo Agyieus with an altar in front of it (635n.).

The πρωταγωνιστής played Electra, the δευτεραγωνιστής Orestes and Clytemnestra, and the τριταγωνιστής the Paedagogus, Chrysothemis and Aegisthus. Pylades and the attendants were played by mutes. Alternatively, the δευτεραγωνιστής could have played Chrysothemis too (cf. Marshall (1994) 58), but this gives him many more lines than the τριταγωνιστής.

2	Orestes, the Paedagogus and Pylades, probably with attendants, enter from eisodos A.
85	Orestes, the Paedagogus and Pylades, probably with attendants, exit via eisodos B.
86	Electra enters from the *skene*.
121	The chorus enters from eisodos A.
324	Chrysothemis enters from the *skene*.
471	Chrysothemis exits via eisodos B.
516	Clytemnestra enters from the *skene*, with at least one attendant.
660	The Paedagogus enters from eisodos B.
803	Clytemnestra and the Paedagogus exit via the *skene*.
871	Chrysothemis enters from eisodos B.

1057	Chrysothemis exits via the *skene*.
1098	Orestes, Pylades and at least two attendants enter from eisodos B.
1326	The Paedagogus enters from the *skene*.
1375	Orestes, Pylades and the Paedagogus (and attendants?) exit via the *skene*.
1383	Electra exits via the *skene*.
1398	Electra enters via the *skene*.
1422	Orestes and Pylades enter from the *skene*.
1428	Aegisthus is seen coming along eisodos A.
1436–41	Orestes and Pylades go into the *skene*.
1442	Aegisthus enters from eisodos A.
1466	Orestes and Pylades enter from the *skene* with the body of Clytemnestra on the *ekkyklema*.
1504	Orestes and Pylades force Aegisthus inside the *skene*, perhaps followed by Electra.

From 86 to 1383 and then from 1398 to the end Electra is on stage. After the chorus's arrival she is confronted by a series of figures: first Chrysothemis and Clytemnestra from the *skene*, both of whom provoke an argument with her, and then by the Paedagogus, Chrysothemis and Orestes from eisodos B, each of whom is bringing news of Orestes which each time is misinterpreted by Electra. After the recognition of her brother, her exit at 1383 expresses her unity of purpose with Orestes as he goes forward with his mission. It also movingly reverses her previous determination, prompted by the false news of her brother's demise, to remain outside until death (817–19). Her final exit into the *skene*, if that is what happened, would mark a similarly important stage in her recovery. 'Throughout the play her changing emotions and circumstances are interwoven with the scenic space' (Taplin (1989) 104).

6 THE TEXT

Few areas of classical studies have attracted more attention from scholars over the last five hundred years than the textual

13

criticism of Sophocles.[14] Yet few remain as controversial. This is partly because of the unique difficulty of Sophocles' style: as Lloyd-Jones put it, 'no other author reveals such subtle nuances, and no other goes so far in bending language to his will' ((1983b) 171). In addition, collations of the important Sophoclean manuscripts have only recently been published. We owe these collations to Roger Dawe, who not only made this vital information available for the first time, but also provided a wholesale reassessment of the importance of individual manuscripts for the establishment of the text. By demolishing the stemma advocated by Alexander Turyn (cf. Turyn (1952)), which had previously won widespread agreement, and by demonstrating the value of manuscript groups dismissed by Turyn as mere repositories of Byzantine conjecture, Dawe left us with an open recension in which the truth can, in theory, lie anywhere. Even isolated good readings may on occasion reflect unique preservations of the truth.

Since Dawe's work in the 1970s there have been important complete editions of Sophocles by Dawe himself and by Lloyd-Jones and Wilson. Dawe's three successive editions were characterised by a readiness to employ conjectural emendation, including many emendations of his own. While sometimes his conjectures hit the mark (cf. 1296n.), often they fail to convince, and the edition is that much the poorer (see the reviews of Lloyd-Jones (1978), (1986) and West (1978b)). There was thus a real need for a new edition which would take account of Dawe's manuscript work, while at the same time adopting a more judicious attitude to textual criticism.

This need was in part satisfied by the Oxford Classical Text of 1990, which presented a text of the seven plays that differed from Dawe's in more than a thousand places (conveniently set out in Renehan (1992) 374–5). Often these differences mark definite improvements on the text offered by Dawe, and as a result the

---

[14] For a brief account of this scholarly activity see Ll-J/W, *Sophoclea*, pp. 1–6.

OCT has since become the standard edition of the plays. Yet many of Ll-J/W's decisions have attracted considerable criticism from other scholars;[15] and in the course of my research I have found myself disagreeing with their text rather more often than I expected when I began.

All readings of L are taken from the facsimile (Thompson and Jebb (1885)). The OCT is often incorrect or incomplete in its citations of this, the most important witness to the text. Often only the reading of L^{pc} is recorded even when L^{ac} can be determined, while at 425 L is mis-cited outright (see n.). Papathomopoulos (1993) 87–8 points out some of these mistakes: his list contains numerous errors of his own and must be used with caution (cf. Ll-J/W, *Second Thoughts* p. 144), but several of the mistakes which he alleges are real enough. Dawe, by contrast, is much more accurate. In one place a new reading in L unnoticed by Dawe and Ll-J/W lends important manuscript support to a convincing conjecture, which here for the first time is adopted into the text (128n.).

My readings of K are all taken from a microfilm kindly lent to me by Nigel Wilson. Since its redating by Wilson (1983) 167–8, this manuscript is surpassed only by L and Λ in importance for the constitution of the text of Sophocles. The collation published in Metlikovitz (1890) is generally accurate, though I have silently corrected several errors. The OCT is sparing in its citation of K: given its status, I have preferred to cite it regularly.

For other manuscripts I rely chiefly, though not exclusively, on Dawe's collations (*STS* vol. ii).[16] There seemed little point in redoing his fundamental work (so also Ll-J/W, *Second Thoughts*

---

[15] For a list of reviews of the OCT see Ll-J/W, *Second Thoughts* p. 10, adding now Dawe (2002–3).

[16] Other sources include the following: Scheltema (1949) for Λ; Purgold (1802) 117–47, N. G. Wilson (1977), (1987) for J; Damiralis (1888) for Jg; Kopff (1993) 156–7, Turyn (1952) 169 for S; N. G. Wilson (1977) 169 for Wa; Peppink (1934) for Wb; Ll-J/W (OCT) for Ta; Soteroudes (1977–8) 399 for the Gnomologium Vatopedianum (Vat. gr. 36).

p. 145), while the harvest from the manuscripts which remain uncollated is likely to be slight. I have, however, collated Zf and Zg from microfilms and cite them occasionally.[17] I have been generous in my citations of the Suda and Eustathius, important sources for the text. With all manuscripts, I have not normally recorded corrections made by a hand other than that of the original scribe or scholiast.

Two subjects over which manuscripts enjoy relatively little authority are metrical colometry and orthography. My metrical analyses ignore the transmitted colometries, which provide no evidence for the colometry of Sophocles' text (cf. L. P. E. Parker (2001)). In orthographical matters I have not hesitated to prefer the evidence of inscriptions or grammarians where this can be shown to be an improvement on the spellings offered by the mediaeval tradition. In this I have been especially influenced by Threatte's *Grammar of Attic Inscriptions* and West's Teubner Aeschylus.

I have attempted to track down the precise locations of all the conjectures which I cite. These details are normally included in the commentary: when a conjecture is not discussed there, I have included its location in an appendix instead. I have tried to correct as many misattributions as possible, though doubtless many remain. A bare reference to the name of an editor (e.g. Turnebus, Fröhlich, Bergk) means that the conjecture is found in the text or apparatus of their edition. Where an editor produced more than one edition I have generally indicated the relevant work by a superscript (e.g. Nauck[3]).

---

[17] Zf shows an affinity with the **a** group: it agrees with manuscripts of this group against the rest of the tradition (or by far the greater part of it) at 42, 52, 279, 528, 676, 890, 956, 985, 1141 and 1456. Zg shows an affinity with the **t** group: it agrees with manuscripts of this group against the rest of the tradition (or by far the greater part of it) at 10, 56, 345, 373, 428, 466, 533, 721, 754, 771, 998, 1099, 1113 and 1473. But Zg is not simply a Triclinian manuscript: at 855, 1063, 1389, 1414, 1417, 1436 and 1437–41 it agrees with the rest of the tradition against Triclinius.

7 RECEPTION

Recent scholarship has produced some useful accounts of the reception of the play in modern times, especially with reference to the dramas of Hofmannsthal and Richard Strauss. See especially Lloyd-Jones (1989) = (1991) 151–71, Davies (1999b), E. M. Hall (1999a), Paduano (2002), Avezzù (2002) (ed.) and Hall and Macintosh (2005) 152–82.

TEXT AND CRITICAL
APPARATUS

INDEX SIGLORUM

---

[1] An image of this papyrus is available online via the Advanced Papyrological
Information System (APIS) website.

CODICES AD LIBITUM CITATI

Bb	Londinensis Harl. British Library 5744, saec. xv
Δ	Laurentianus conv. soppr. 41, saec. xiv
J	Jenensis Bos. q. 7, saec. xv ex.
Jg	Atheniensis Ἐθνικὴ Βιβλιοθήκη 1059, saec. xv
S	Vaticanus Urbinas gr. 141, saec. xiv
Wa	Ambrosianus E 103 sup., saec. xiii (ca. 1275)
Wb	Vaticanus gr. 1332, saec. xiii
Wc	Vindobonensis phil. gr. 281, saec. xv
Zf	Parisinus gr. 2884, ann. 1301
Zg	Laurentianus 32.2, saec. xiv in.
	Monacensis gr. 334, saec. xv
	Monacensis gr. 507, saec. xiv–v[2]
	Parisinus gr. 2794, saec. xiv
	Parisinus gr. 2820, saec. xv
	Vaticanus gr. 40, saec. xiii–iv
	Vaticanus gr. 45, saec. xv
Gnom.	Gnomologium Vatopedianum, Athous Μονὴ Βατοπεδίου 36, saec. xii[3]

LIBRORUM FAMILIAE[4]

l	consensus codicum LΛK
r	consensus codicum GR
a	consensus codicum ADXrXsZr

[2] This codex is the 'Aug. c' of several previous editions. It was transferred from Augsburg to Munich in 1806 (cf. Turyn (1944) 26–7).

[3] The Gnomologium Venetum, Marcianus gr. 507 (saec. xii) is a copy of this Gnomologium (cf. Longman (1959) 133).

[4] These abbreviations are used differently from in the Oxford Classical Text. In that edition their presence in the apparatus means that two or more of the relevant manuscripts have the reading in question. Here they always reflect the unanimous testimony of the original readings of all the relevant manuscripts. This lessens the bulk of the apparatus, without denying useful information to the reader. Note also that the manuscripts which are here designated **p** do not form a unified group: this label is used simply to save space.

p consensus codicum CFHNOPV (1–493, 602–1014), CHNOPV (494–601), CFHNOPPaV (1015–1510)

t consensus codicum TTa

TEXTUS ET APPARATUS SIGLA CETERA

Q^1 lectio in Q a scriba scripta
Q^r lectio in Q a rubricatore scripta
Q^2 lectio in Q ab alia manu scripta
Q^{ac}, Q^{pc} Q ante / post correctionem
Q^x Q ante vel post correctionem (incertum utrum)
Q^s lectio in Q supra lineam scripta
Q^{gl} glossema in Q, vel lectio quasi glossema adscripta
$Q^{\gamma\rho}$ varia lectio cum γρ. in Q adscripta
Q^m Q in margine
[] delenda censeo
< > inserenda censeo
† † corruptela non sanata
coni. coniecit
* littera obscura

CANTICORUM SIGLA

∪ syllaba brevis
— syllaba longa
× syllaba anceps
ᴗ syllaba brevis in elemento longo
∪∩ duae breves ex resolutione in loco principi
∴ longa ex contractione in loco bicipiti
∪̳ brevis in stropha, longa in antistropha
∪̳̄ longa in stropha, brevis in antistropha
∪∪̳ duae breves in stropha, longa in antistropha
∪∪̳̄ longa in stropha, duae breves in antistropha
:: mutatio personae
| finis vocabuli

‖	finis periodi
⦀	finis strophae

ad	adoneum (—∪∪—×)
asclep	metrum asclepiadeum (××—∪∪——∪∪— . . .)
an	metrum anapaesticum (∪∪—∪∪—)
an∧	——— pro metro anapaestico
anacr	versus anacreonteus (∪∪—∪—∪——)
cho	choriambus (—∪∪—)
cho dim	versus ——×——∪∪— quem alii 'choriambic dimeter', alii 'wilamowitzianum', alii 'polyschematist' vocant
cho enneas	—∪∪—∪—∪——
cr	creticus (—∪—)
D	—∪∪—∪∪—
δ	dochmius (×——×—)
da	dactylus (—∪∪)
dodr	dodrans (—∪∪—∪—)
e	—∪—
glyc	versus glyconeus (××—∪∪—∪—)
hδ	hypodochmius (—∪—∪—)
ia	metrum iambicum (×—∪—)
∧ia	—∪— pro metro iambico
ia∧	∪—— pro metro iambico
∧ia∧	—— pro metro iambico
iambel	versus iambelegus (∪—∪—∪—∪∪—∪∪—)
io	metrum ionicum (∪∪——)
ith	versus ithyphallicus (—∪—∪——)
lec	lecythium (—∪—×—∪—)
mol	molossus (———)
pher	versus pherecrateus (××—∪∪——)
pherᶜ	versus pherecrateus choriambo auctus (××—∪∪——∪∪——)
reiz	versus reizianus (×—∪∪——)
tr	metrum trochaicum (—∪—×)
tel	versus telesilleus (×—∪∪—∪—)

ΣΟΦΟΚΛΕΟΥΣ ΗΛΕΚΤΡΑ

TA TOY ΔΡΑΜΑΤΟΣ ΠΡΟΣΩΠΑ

Παιδαγωγός
Ὀρέστης
Ἠλέκτρα
Χορὸς ἐπιχωρίων παρθένων
Χρυσόθεμις
Κλυταιμήστρα
Αἴγισθος

ΚΩΦΟΝ ΠΡΟΣΩΠΟΝ

Πυλάδης

ΣΟΦΟΚΛΕΟΥΣ ΗΛΕΚΤΡΑ

ΠΑΙΔΑΓΩΓΟΣ

[῏Ω τοῦ στρατηγήσαντος ἐν Τροίᾳ ποτὲ]
Ἀγαμέμνονος παῖ, νῦν ἐκεῖν' ἔξεστί σοι
παρόντι λεύσσειν, ὧν πρόθυμος ἦσθ' ἀεί.
τὸ γὰρ παλαιὸν Ἄργος οὑπόθεις τόδε,
τῆς οἰστροπλῆγος ἄλσος Ἰνάχου κόρης·   5
αὕτη δ', Ὀρέστα, τοῦ λυκοκτόνου θεοῦ
ἀγορὰ Λύκειος· οὑξ ἀριστερᾶς δ' ὅδε
Ἥρας ὁ κλεινὸς ναός· οἷ δ' ἱκάνομεν,
φάσκειν Μυκήνας τὰς πολυχρύσους ὁρᾶν,
πολύφθορόν τε δῶμα Πελοπιδῶν τόδε,   10
ὅθεν σε πατρὸς ἐκ φονῶν ἐγώ ποτε
πρὸς σῆς ὁμαίμου καὶ κασιγνήτης λαβὼν
ἤνεγκα κἀξέσωσα κἀξεθρεψάμην
τοσόνδ' ἐς ἥβης, πατρὶ τιμωρὸν φόνου.
νῦν οὖν, Ὀρέστα καὶ σὺ φίλτατε ξένων   15
Πυλάδη, τί χρὴ δρᾶν ἐν τάχει βουλευτέον·
ὡς ἧμιν ἤδη λαμπρὸν ἡλίου σέλας
ἑῷα κινεῖ φθέγγματ' ὀρνίθων σαφῆ
μέλαινά τ' ἄστρων ἐκλέλοιπεν εὐφρόνη.
πρὶν οὖν τιν' ἀνδρῶν ἐξοδοιπορεῖν στέγης,   20
ξυνάπτετον λόγοισιν· ὡς ἐνταῦθ' †ἐμὲν†
ἵν' οὐκέτ' ὀκνεῖν καιρός, ἀλλ' ἔργων ἀκμή.

---

1 del. Haslam   στρατηγήσαντος] L^γρ H^gl τυραννήσαντος   5 post τῆς
add. τ' Blaydes   10 τε] δὲ t   11 φονῶν Dindorf: φόνων codd.   13
κἀξεθρεψάμην] καί σ' ἐθρεψάμην ΣB ad Hom. Il. 9.485   15 om. L (add.
L^im): Ὀρέστα . . . Πυλάδη del. Nauck   16 βουλευτέον] –ετον Porson
19 habent Π' et codd.: del. Schoell   20–2 habent Π' et codd.: del. Schenkl
(20 iam Nauck, ἐνταῦθ'. . . ἀλλ' iam Schwerdt)   21 ξυνάπτετον] –εον Zf,
coni. Toup   ἐμὲν LKADXsOt: ἐσμὲν cett.: ἵμεν Dawes

27

ΟΡΕΣΤΗΣ

ὦ φίλτατ' ἀνδρῶν προσπόλων, ὥς μοι σαφῆ
σημεῖα φαίνεις ἐσθλὸς εἰς ἡμᾶς γεγώς.
ὥσπερ γὰρ ἵππος εὐγενής, κἂν ᾖ γέρων,   25
ἐν τοῖσι δεινοῖς θυμὸν οὐκ ἀπώλεσεν,
ἀλλ' ὀρθὸν οὖς ἵστησιν, ὡσαύτως δὲ σὺ
ἡμᾶς τ' ὀτρύνεις καὐτὸς ἐν πρώτοις ἔπῃ.
τοιγὰρ τὰ μὲν δόξαντα δηλώσω, σὺ δὲ
ὀξεῖαν ἀκοὴν τοῖς ἐμοῖς λόγοις διδούς,   30
εἰ μή τι καιροῦ τυγχάνω, μεθάρμοσον.
ἐγὼ γὰρ ἡνίχ' ἱκόμην τὸ Πυθικὸν
μαντεῖον, ὡς μάθοιμ' ὅτῳ τρόπῳ πατρὸς
δίκας ἀροίμην τῶν φονευσάντων πάρα,
χρῆ μοι τοιαῦθ' ὁ Φοῖβος ὧν πεύσῃ τάχα·   35
ἄσκευον αὐτὸν ἀσπίδων τε καὶ στρατοῦ
δόλοισι κλέψαι χειρὸς ἐνδίκου σφαγάς.
ὅτ' οὖν τοιόνδε χρησμὸν εἰσηκούσαμεν,
σὺ μὲν μολών, ὅταν σε καιρὸς εἰσάγῃ,
δόμων ἔσω τῶνδ', ἴσθι πᾶν τὸ δρώμενον,   40
ὅπως ἂν εἰδὼς ἧμιν ἀγγείλῃς σαφῆ.
οὐ γάρ σε μὴ γήρᾳ τε καὶ χρόνῳ μακρῷ
γνῶσ', οὐδ' ὑποπτεύσουσιν ὧδ' ἠνθισμένον.
λόγῳ δὲ χρῶ τοιῷδ', ὅτι ξένος μὲν εἶ
Φωκέως παρ' ἀνδρὸς Φανοτέως ἥκων· ὁ γὰρ   45
μέγιστος αὐτοῖς τυγχάνει δορυξένων.
ἄγγελλε δ' ὅρκον προστιθείς, ὁθούνεκα

28 τ] δ' KˢG: om. ACV: non legitur L   ἔπῃ] ἔσῃ P, ΣL   33 πατρὸς]
πατρὶ LᵃᶜKCˢ   35 τοιαῦθ' ὁ codd. plerique, Suidas iv. 824.4, Eustathius
751.58, 1179.39: τοιαῦτα Oˢ, coni. Blomfield: τοιαῦτα δ' ὁ C   37 ἐνδίκου
Lange: –ους codd.   41 σαφῆ] σαφῶς POˡˢ   42 χρόνῳ μακρῷ] inverso
ordine DXrXs et Suidas ii. 574.12   43 ὑποπτεύσουσιν codd. plerique et
Suidas ii. 574.12–13: –σωσιν V, coni. Turnebus: –ουσιν GXrᵃᶜZr, fort. Fᵃᶜ
ἠνθισμένον codd. et Suidas ii. 574.13: ἠκισμένον Bergk   45 Φωκέως Bentley: –εὺς codd.   ὁ vel ὅ codd.: ὃ Erfurdt   47 ὅρκον Reiske: –ῳ codd.:
–ους Zakas

τέθνηκ᾽ Ὀρέστης ἐξ ἀναγκαίας τύχης,
ἄθλοισι Πυθικοῖσιν ἐκ τροχηλάτων
δίφρων κυλισθείς· ὧδ᾽ ὁ μῦθος ἐστάτω·   50
ἡμεῖς δὲ πατρὸς τύμβον, ὡς ἐφίετο,
λοιβαῖσι πρῶτον καὶ καρατόμοις χλιδαῖς
στέψαντες, εἶτ᾽ ἄψορρον ἥξομεν πάλιν,
τύπωμα χαλκόπλευρον ἠρμένοι χεροῖν,
ὃ καὶ σὺ θάμνοις οἶσθά που κεκρυμμένον,   55
ὅπως λόγῳ κλέπτοντες ἡδεῖαν φάτιν
φέρωμεν αὐτοῖς, τοὐμὸν ὡς ἔρρει δέμας
φλογιστὸν ἤδη καὶ κατηνθρακωμένον.
τί γάρ με λυπεῖ τοῦθ᾽, ὅταν λόγῳ θανὼν
ἔργοισι σωθῶ κἀξενέγκωμαι κλέος;   60
δοκῶ μέν, οὐδὲν ῥῆμα σὺν κέρδει κακόν.
ἤδη γὰρ εἶδον πολλάκις καὶ τοὺς σοφοὺς
λόγῳ μάτην θνήσκοντας· εἶθ᾽, ὅταν δόμους
ἔλθωσιν αὖθις, ἐκτετίμηνται πλέον·
ὡς κἄμ᾽ ἐπαυχῶ τῆσδε τῆς φήμης ἄπο   65
δεδορκότ᾽ ἐχθροῖς ἄστρον ὣς λάμψειν ἔτι.
ἀλλ᾽ ὦ πατρῷα γῆ θεοί τ᾽ ἐγχώριοι,
δέξασθέ μ᾽ εὐτυχοῦντα ταῖσδε ταῖς ὁδοῖς,
σύ τ᾽, ὦ πατρῷον δῶμα· σοῦ γὰρ ἔρχομαι
δίκῃ καθαρτὴς πρὸς θεῶν ὡρμημένος·   70
καὶ μή μ᾽ ἄτιμον τῆσδ᾽ ἀποστείλητε γῆς,
ἀλλ᾽ ἀρχέπλουτον καὶ καταστάτην δόμων.
εἴρηκα μέν νυν ταῦτα· σοὶ δ᾽ ἤδη, γέρον,
τὸ σὸν μελέσθω βάντι φρουρῆσαι χρέος.

---

52 λοιβαῖσι LKpJZc^{pc}t et Eustathius 692.58: λοιβαῖς τε L^sGR^sa: λοιβαῖς
τὸ Suidas iv. 810.14   55 del. Schoell   που KaCFHOPVt^{γρ}: μοι
L^{ac}rNZcT   56 κλέπτοντες] θνήσκοντες t   57 φέρωμεν G: –οιμεν cett.
61 del. Steinhart   μέν G^{pc}ADXrZrHN^{ac}PVt: μὲν ὡς lrXsCFOZc et
Suidas iii. 300.14, iv. 546.24   63 δόμους Kap: –οις L^{ac}ΛrZc et Suidas ii.
552.9   65 ὥς vel ὣς LGNZcZf: ὡς cett.   66 δεδορκότ᾽ codd. et Suidas
ii. 334.14: δεδυκότ᾽ H^{γρ}   73 μέν νυν] μὲν νῦν l: νῦν μὲν N: μὲν GA

νὼ δ' ἔξιμεν· καιρὸς γάρ, ὅσπερ ἀνδράσιν   75
μέγιστος ἔργου παντός ἐστ' ἐπιστάτης.

ΗΛΕΚΤΡΑ

ἰώ μοί μοι δύστηνος.
Πα. καὶ μὴν θυρῶν ἔδοξα προσπόλων τινὸς
ὑποστενούσης ἔνδον αἰσθέσθαι, τέκνον.
Ορ. ἆρ' ἐστὶν ἡ δύστηνος Ἠλέκτρα; θέλεις   80
μείνωμεν αὐτοῦ κἀπακούσωμεν γόων;
Πα. ἥκιστα. μηδὲν πρόσθεν ἢ τὰ Λοξίου
πειρώμεθ' ἔρδειν κἀπὸ τῶνδ' ἀρχηγετεῖν,
πατρὸς χέοντες λουτρά· ταῦτα γὰρ φέρειν
νίκην τέ φημι καὶ κράτος τῶν δρωμένων.   85

Ηλ. ὦ φάος ἁγνὸν καὐγῆς ἰσόμοιρ' ἀήρ, ὥς μοι
πολλὰς μὲν θρήνων ᾠδάς,
πολλὰς δ' ἀντήρεις ᾔσθου
στέρνων πληγὰς αἱμασσομένων,   90
ὁπόταν δνοφερὰ νὺξ ὑπολειφθῇ·
τὰ δὲ παννυχίδων κήδη στυγεραὶ
ξυνίσασ' εὐναὶ μογερῶν οἴκων,
ὅσα τὸν δύστηνον ἐμὸν θρηνῶ
πατέρ', ὃν κατὰ μὲν βάρβαρον αἶαν   95
φοίνιος Ἄρης οὐκ ἐξένισεν,

77 δύστηνος] del. Dindorf   81 κἀπακούσωμεν Nauck (ἐπακούσωμεν Lᵗˢ):
κἀνακούσωμεν vel κἂν ἀκ– codd.: κἀξακούσωμεν Blaydes   83 ἔρδειν
LKCOV: ἒ– cett.   84 χέοντες] χέσοντες L: χεύσοντες Lˢ: χέαντες Wecklein   84–5 φέρειν νίκην τέ φημι Tournier: φέρει νικὴν τ' ἐφ' ἡμῖν codd.
87 καὐγῆς Hussey et Russell: καὶ γῆς codd. et Suidas iv. 698.13   ἰσόμοιρ'
WaWbWc, coni. Porson: ἰσόμοιρος cett. (etiam Λ et Suidas), sed –ος sup.
lin. habent DZrCOPVZc   90 πληγὰς V et Suidas: πλαγὰς cett.   91
ὑπολειφθῇ] ἀπο– RT   92 παννυχίδων] –ίων Blaydes   κήδη Fröhlich:
ἤδη codd.   στυγεραὶ] –ὰ GᵗʸᴾN et Gnom.   93 οἴκων aCHNOPt:
οἰκιῶν lrFVZc: οἴκτων Blaydes   94 τὸν δύστηνον] inverso ordine
Fraenkel   96 ἐξένισε(ν) LˣΛrZrFHNOPV et Suidas iii. 493.1: ἐξείνισε(ν)
LˣADXrXsZcZfZgT: ἐξέναρεν West (ἐνάριξεν iam van Gent)

μήτηρ δ' ἡμὴ χὠ κοινολεχὴς
Αἴγισθος ὅπως δρῦν ὑλοτόμοι
σχίζουσι κάρα φονίῳ πελέκει.
κοὐδεὶς τούτων οἶκτος ἀπ' ἄλλης   100
ἢ 'μοῦ φέρεται, σοῦ, πάτερ, οὕτως
ἀκῶς οἰκτρῶς τε θανόντος.
ἀλλ' οὐ μὲν δὴ λήξω θρήνων στυγερῶν τε γόων,
ἔστ' ἂν παμφεγγεῖς ἄστρων   105
ῥιπάς, λεύσσω δὲ τόδ' ἦμαρ,
μὴ οὐ τεκνολέτειρ' ὥς τις ἀηδὼν
ἐπὶ κωκυτῷ τῶνδε πατρῴων
πρὸ θυρῶν ἠχὼ πᾶσι προφωνεῖν.
ὦ δῶμ' Ἀίδου καὶ Περσεφόνης,   110
ὦ χθόνι' Ἑρμῆ καὶ πότνι' Ἀρά,
σεμναί τε θεῶν παῖδες Ἐρινύες,
αἳ τοὺς ἀδίκως θνήσκοντας ὁρᾶθ',
αἳ τοὺς εὐνὰς ὑποκλεπτομένους,
ἔλθετ', ἀρήξατε, τείσασθε πατρὸς   115
<UU – UU – > φόνον ἡμετέρου,
καί μοι τὸν ἐμὸν πέμψατ' ἀδελφόν.
μούνη γὰρ ἄγειν οὐκέτι σωκῶ
λύπης ἀντίρροπον ἄχθος.   120

99 φονίῳ ADXrZrNOPT: φοιν–**lr**XsCFHVZc   100 ἄλλης] –ων Blaydes
102 ἀκῶς scripsi: αἰκ–Blomfield post Brunck: ἀεικ– Σ et Suidas i. 62.15: ἀδίκως
codd.   105 ἂν Reisig: ἂν λεύσ(σ)ω codd. et Suidas iv. 295.14–15: ἄστρων
delere malunt Elmsley et Dobree   106 δὲ τόδ'] τόδε τ' Blaydes   108
κωκυτῷ] –ῶν L^{ac}F^{ac} et Suidae iv. 295.16 codd. AV (cum δὲ pro τῶνδε): –οῖς
Suidae codd. cett.   τῶνδε] τήνδε Musgrave   109 ἠχὼ] ἠχὴν Nauck
προφωνεῖν] προφαίνειν J (verum J^s)   111 πότνι' Ἀρά] ποινία ἀρά L^{γρ}K^{γρ}
112 θεῶν παῖδες] om. Suidas iv. 115.11–12   Ἐρινύες LKGF: –νν– cett.
113–14 ὁρᾶθ', αἳ Dobree: ὁρᾶτε codd. et Suidas iv. 115.12   114 τοὺς codd.
plerique et Suidae cod. V: τούς τ' XrFN et Suidae codd. GM: τοὺς τὰς T: τὰς
Zf et Suidae cod. A   115 τείσασθε Nauck: τίσ– codd.: om. Suidas iv. 115.13
116 lacunam ante φόνον statuit Diggle: ante ὑποκλεπτομένους Hermann, ante
τείσασθε Monk, ante ἔλθετ' Enger   119 ἄγειν] om. Suidas iv. 405.33

ΧΟΡΟΣ

ὦ παῖ παῖ δυστανοτάτας   [str. 1
Ἠλέκτρα ματρός, τίν' ἀεὶ
    τάκεις ὧδ' ἀκόρεστον οἰμωγὰν
τὸν πάλαι ἐκ δολερᾶς ἀθεώτατα
ματρὸς ἁλόντ' ἀπάταις Ἀγαμέμνονα   125
κακᾷ τε χειρὶ πρόδοτον; ὡς ὁ τάδε πορὼν
ὄλοιτ', εἴ μοι θέμις τάδ' αὐδᾶν.

Ηλ. ὦ γένεθλα γενναίων,
ἥκετ' ἐμῶν καμάτων παραμύθιον·   130
οἶδά τε καὶ ξυνίημι τάδ', οὔ τί με
φυγγάνει, οὐδὲ θέλω προλιπεῖν τόδε,
μὴ οὐ τὸν ἐμὸν στενάχειν πατέρ' ἄθλιον.
ἀλλ' ὦ παντοίας φιλότατος ἀμειβόμεναι χάριν,
ἐᾶτέ μ' ὧδ' ἀλύειν,   135
αἰαῖ, ἱκνοῦμαι.

Χο. ἀλλ' οὔτοι τόν γ' ἐξ Ἀίδα   [ant. 1
παγκοίνου λίμνας πατέρ' ἀν –
    στάσεις οὔτε γόοισιν, οὔτ' †λιταῖσιν†·
ἀλλ' ἀπὸ τῶν μετρίων ἐπ' ἀμήχανον   140
ἄλγος ἀεὶ στενάχουσα διόλλυσαι,

121 ὦ t: ἰὼ cett. et Suidas ii. 153.20   παῖ παῖ] παῖ semel rZrCHNOPV
et Suidas   123 τάκεις codd. plerique (Kˣˢ habet ς): τάκεαι Pˡˢ: τείνεις
West: κλαίεις Fröhlich   ἀκόρεστον οἰμωγὰν] ἀκόρεστος οἰμωγᾶν voluit P²ˢ
124 ἀθεώτατα Erfurdt et Porson: –ας codd. plerique: ἀθλιωτάτας Zr   126
ὡς LᵃᶜKCFOP: ὢς cett.   129 γένεθλα codd. plerique (etiam Lᵃᶜ): γενέθλα
LᵖᶜK   post γενναίων habent πατέρων lraFNᵍˡ, τοκέων CHNOPVZcJt:
del. Monk   130 παραμύθιον] –ιοι Blaydes   131 ξυνίημι] συν– Suidae
iv. 772.1 codd. FV   132 οὐδὲ θέλω XrXst: οὐδ' ἐθέλω ADZr: οὐδ'
αὖ θέλω lrpZc   133 στενάχειν Elmsley: στεναχεῖν KFNOPV, fort. Lˡˢ:
στοναχεῖν cett.   134 φιλότατος Elmsley: φιλότητος codd.   137 τόν γ'
lrXrXsNPVZc: τόνδ' ADZrCFᵖᶜHO   138 πατέρ'] om. Suidas iv. 1.22
138–9 ἀνστάσεις] ἀνα– XrZrFᵖᶜO et Suidae cod. Sᵖᶜ   139 γόοισιν Vʳˢ,
Livineius: γόοις cett. (etiam Λ)   οὔτε lrapZc et Suidas iv. 1.22: οὐ t
λιταῖσι(ν) lrCⁱᵖᶜFHZc et Suidas iv. 1.22: –ῆσιν NPV: –αις at: εὐχαῖς Erfurdt:
ἄνταις Hermann

ἐν οἷς ἀνάλυσίς ἐστιν οὐδεμία κακῶν.
τί μοι τῶν δυσφόρων ἐφίη;
Ηλ. νήπιος, ὃς ὧν οἰκτρῶς   145
οἰχομένων γονέων ἐπιλάθεται.
ἀλλ᾽ ἐμέ γ᾽ ἁ στονόεσσ᾽ ἄραρεν φρένας,
ἃ Ἴτυν αἰὲν Ἴτυν ὀλοφύρεται,
ὄρνις ἀτυζομένα, Διὸς ἄγγελος.
ἰὼ παντλάμων Νιόβα, σὲ δ᾽ ἔγωγε νέμω θεόν,   150
ἅτ᾽ ἐν τάφῳ πετραίῳ,
αἰαῖ, δακρύεις.

Χο. οὔτοι σοὶ μούνᾳ,   [str. 2
τέκνον, ἄχος ἐφάνη βροτῶν,
πρὸς ὅ τι σὺ τῶν ἔνδον εἶ περισσά,   155
οἷς ὁμόθεν εἶ καὶ γονᾷ ξύναιμος,
οἷα Χρυσόθεμις ζώει καὶ Ἰφιάνασσα,
κρυπτᾷ τ᾽ ἀχέων ἐν ἥβᾳ
ὄλβιος, ὃν ἁ κλεινὰ   160
γᾶ ποτε Μυκηναίων
δέξεται εὐπατρίδαν, Διὸς εὔφρονι
βήματι μολόντα τάνδε γᾶν Ὀρέσταν.
Ηλ. ὃν γ᾽ ἐγὼ ἀκάματα προσμένουσ᾽ ἄτεκνος,
τάλαιν᾽ ἀνύμφευτος αἰὲν οἰχνῶ,   165
δάκρυσι μυδαλέα, τὸν ἀνήνυτον
οἶτον ἔχουσα κακῶν· ὃ δὲ λάθεται
ὧν τ᾽ ἔπαθ᾽ ὧν τ᾽ ἐδάη. τί γὰρ οὐκ ἐμοὶ

142 κακῶν] –οῦ Zc   145 ὅς] ὅστις t   ὧν Stinton: ων Lᵃᶜ: τῶν L¹ᵖᶜ
et cett. (etiam Suidas i. 408.30, iv. 620.10)   147 ἐμέ γ᾽ codd. (nisi quod
fort. Kˢ ἐμοῦ) et Suidas i. 63.28: ἐμὲ Suidas i. 409.1   148 αἰὲν codd.
et Suidas i. 63.28, 409.1: αἰαῖ Velke   ὀλοφύρεται] γ᾽ ὀλοφύρεται t
150 παντλάμων LADXsZrFHOVt: παντλᾶμον rXrCPZc, fort. Nᵃᶜ   152
αἰαῖ] αἰὲν V: ἀεὶ Zc: αἰεὶ Zg, coni. Reiske   156 οἷς] αἷς G   157 οἷα AZct:
οἷα cett.   160–3 choro tribuit Tyrwhitt: Electrae codd.   160 ὄλβιος]
–ον Hᵃᶜ, coni. Brunck   163 βήματι] νεύματι Fröhlich   164 ὃν γ᾽ ἐγὼ
Hermann: ὃν ἔγωγ᾽ codd. (etiam Λ) et Suidas i. 75.16   166 δάκρυσι
μυδαλέα] inverso ordine Suidas iii. 422.17   167 ὃ vel ὅ KrHNOZc: ὁ
aCFPVt: ὥδ᾽ Lᵃᶜ   δὲ λάθεται KaCPVt: δ᾽ ἐλάθετο KˢrFHNOZcJ: ἐλάθε-
ται Lᵃᶜ   168 ἔπαθ᾽ ΛADXrZrt: ἔπαθεν cett.

33

ἔρχεται ἀγγελίας ἀπατώμενον;   170
ἀεὶ μὲν γὰρ ποθεῖ,
ποθῶν δ᾽ οὐκ ἀξιοῖ φανῆναι.

Χο. θάρσει μοι, θάρσει,   [ant. 2
τέκνον. ἔτι μέγας οὐρανῷ
Ζεύς, ὃς ἐφορᾷ πάντα καὶ κρατύνει·   175
ᾧ τὸν ὑπεραλγῆ χόλον νέμουσα
μήθ᾽ οἷς ἐχθαίρεις ὑπεράχθεο μήτ᾽ ἐπιλάθου·
χρόνος γὰρ εὐμαρὴς θεός.
οὔτε γὰρ ὁ τὰν Κρίσᾳ   180
βούνομον ἔχων ἀκτὰν
παῖς Ἀγαμεμνονίδας ἀπερίτροπος
οὔθ᾽ ὁ παρὰ τὸν Ἀχέροντα θεὸς ἀνάσσων.

Ηλ. ἀλλ᾽ ἐμὲ μὲν ὁ πολὺς ἀπολέλοιπεν ἤδη   185
βίοτος ἀνέλπιστος, οὐδ᾽ ἔτ᾽ ἀρκῶ·
ἅτις ἄνευ τεκέων κατατάκομαι,
ἇς φίλος οὔτις ἀνὴρ ὑπερίσταται,
ἀλλ᾽ ἀπερεί τις ἔποικος ἀναξία
οἰκονομῶ θαλάμους πατρός, ὧδε μὲν   190
ἀεικεῖ σὺν στολᾷ,
κεναῖς δ᾽ ἀμφίσταμαι τραπέζαις.

Χο. οἰκτρὰ μὲν νόστοις αὐδά,   [str. 3
οἰκτρὰ δ᾽ ἐν κοίταις πατρῴαις,
ὅτε οἱ παγχάλκων ἀνταία   195

171 ἀεὶ XsZrPZc^{ac}t: αἰεὶ Zc^{pc} et cett.   173–4 θάρσει, τέκνον] inverso ordine Σ 823   174 ἔτι L^{ac}: ἔστι(ν) cett.   μέγας Livineius: μέγας ἐν codd.: μέγας ἔτ᾽ ἐν Hermann   180 Κρίσᾳ Musgrave: Κρίσσα P: Κρίσ(σ)αν cett.: Κρίσας Nauck: Κρῖσαν Hermann   181 βούνομον L^{ac}: βουνόμον L^{pc}Ga F^{ac}NPV: βούνόμαν RCF^{pc}HOZc^{1pc}t: βουνόμενον K   186 ἀνέλπιστος codd. et Suidas iv. 619.2, 656.1: –ον Nauck e Σ   187 τεκέων WaWc, coni. Meineke: τοκέων cett. et Suidas iv. 619.3, 656.2   189 ἀπερεί vel ἄπερ εἴ vel ἄπερ εἴ LKRADXsZrPt: ὡσπερεί fere GXrC^{pc}F^{pc}HNOVZc: ὥπερ fort. C^{ac}F^{ac}   192 ἀμφίσταμαι KNOPVZg^{ac} et Eustathius 1692.57: ἀφ– L^{ac}Λ: ὑφ– C: ἐφ– cett.   195 οἱ Hermann: σοι codd. et Suidas i. 516.25

γενύων ὠρμάθη πλαγά.
δόλος ἦν ὁ φράσας, ἔρος ὁ κτείνας,
δεινὰν δεινῶς προφυτεύσαντες
μορφάν, εἴτ᾽ οὖν θεὸς εἴτε βροτῶν
ἦν ὁ ταῦτα πράσσων.   200

Ηλ. ὦ πασᾶν κείνα πλέον ἁμέρα
ἐλθοῦσ᾽ ἐχθίστα δή μοι·
ὦ νύξ, ὦ δείπνων ἀρρήτων
ἔκπαγλ᾽ ἄχθη·
τοῖς ἐμὸς ἴδε πατὴρ   205
θανάτους ᾀκεῖς διδύμαιν χειροῖν,
αἳ τὸν ἐμὸν εἷλον βίον
πρόδοτον, αἵ μ᾽ ἀπώλεσαν·
οἷς θεὸς ὁ μέγας Ὀλύμπιος
ποίνιμα πάθεα παθεῖν πόροι,   210
μηδέ ποτ᾽ ἀγλαΐας ἀποναίατο
τοιάδ᾽ ἀνύσαντες ἔργα.

Χο. φράζου μὴ πόρσω φωνεῖν.   [ant. 3
οὐ γνώμαν ἴσχεις ἐξ οἵων
τὰ παρόντ᾽; οἰκείας εἰς ἄτας   215
ἐμπίπτεις οὕτως ᾀκῶς;
πολὺ γάρ τι κακῶν ὑπερεκτήσω,
σᾷ δυσθύμῳ τίκτουσ᾽ αἰεὶ

197 δόλος . . . ἔρος hoc ordine codd. et Suidas iv. 759.18–19: inverso
Wakefield   ἔρος L^{pc}**at**: ἔρως L^{ac} et cett.   198 προφυτεύσαντες
ΛΚΑΧrXs^{1pc}ZrFHNOVt: προφη– L^{ac}**r**DXs^{ac}C^{ac}PZc   199 μορφάν]
μομφάν Wakefield   204 ἄχθη codd. plerique (etiam Λ): πάθη L^{γρ}K^{γρ}G^{γρ}
et lemma ΣR   205 τοῖς Johnson: τοὺς codd.: τούς τ᾽ Paley: ὅτ᾽ Fröhlich
ἴδε Brunck: οἶδε G: εἶδε cett.   206 ᾀκεῖς scripsi: αἰκ– Seidler: ἄϊκ–
L, coni. Brunck: ἀεικ– cett.   χειροῖν Livineius: χερ– codd. (etiam Λ)
211 ἀποναίατο] ὀναίατο Suidas iii. 537.17   212 ἀνύσαντες Groeneboom: ἀν– codd.   213 πόρσω LK^{γρ}**r**ADXrZrS^{γρ}**t**: πρόσω KG^{γρ}Xs**p**Zc
φωνεῖν] φώνει Morstadt   216 ἐμπίπτεις] ἐπι– **t**: ἐμπίπτους᾽ Seyffert
ᾀκῶς scripsi: ἄϊκ– Brunck: ἀεικ– codd. et Suidas i. 62.9   218 αἰεὶ
ADXrXs**t**: ἀεὶ LK**r**Zr**p**Zc

ψυχᾷ πολέμους· τάδε—τοῖς δυνατοῖς
οὐκ ἐριστά—τλᾶθι.   220

Ηλ. δείν᾽ ἐν δεινοῖς ἠναγκάσθην·
      ἔξοιδ᾽, οὐ λάθει μ᾽ ὀργά.
      ἀλλ᾽ ἐν γὰρ δεινοῖς οὐ σχήσω
      ταύτας ἀχάς,
      ὄφρα με βίος ἔχῃ.   225
      τίνι γάρ ποτ᾽ ἄν, ὦ φιλία γενέθλα,
      πρόσφορον ἀκούσαιμ᾽ ἔπος,
      τίνι φρονοῦντι καίρια;
      ἄνετέ μ᾽ ἄνετε παράγοροι.
      τάδε γὰρ ἄλυτα κεκλήσεται·   230
      οὐδέ ποτ᾽ ἐκ καμάτων ἀποπαύσομαι
      ἀνάριθμος ὧδε θρήνων.

Χο. ἀλλ᾽ οὖν εὐνοίᾳ γ᾽ αὐδῶ,   [ερ.
      μάτηρ ὡσεί τις πιστά,
      μὴ τίκτειν σ᾽ ἄταν ἄταις.   235
Ηλ. καὶ τί μέτρον κακότατος ἔφυ; φέρε,
      πῶς ἐπὶ τοῖς φθιμένοις ἀμελεῖν καλόν;
      ἐν τίνι τοῦτ᾽ ἔβλαστ᾽ ἀνθρώπων;
      μήτ᾽ εἴην ἔντιμος τούτοις
      μήτ᾽, εἴ τῳ πρόσκειμαι χρηστῷ,   240

219–20 sic interpunxit Jackson   219 τάδε DHO: τὰ δὲ cett. et Suidas iv.
138.19–20   τοῖς δυνατοῖς codd. et Suidas: τῶν δυνατῶν Dawe   220
τλᾶθι Wakefield: τλάθειν Zc¹ˢ: πλαθεῖν codd. cett. et Suidas   221 δείν᾽
ἐν δεινοῖς ἠναγκάσθην Pearson: ἐν δεινοῖς ἠναγκάσθην ἐν δεινοῖς codd.
(nisi quod ἐ. δ. ἠ. δή Τ): δεινοῖς ἠναγκάσθην, δεινοῖς Brunck   224 ἀχάς
Blaydes: ἄτας codd.   225 με βίος ἔχῃ] με βίος ἔχει ΛΝ: μ᾽ ἔχῃ βίοτος t   226 ἄν] om. ΛΛZcSᵃᶜ et Suidas iii. 84.13   φιλία LᵖᶜKᵃᶜaCHP
et Suidae codd. plerique: φίλια LᵃᶜKᵖᶜrFNV: φίλα Ot et Suidae cod. A:
φιλίᾳ Zc   γενέθλα LᵖᶜADXrXs: γένεθλα LᵃᶜKrZrp: γενέθλᾳ Zc: γέν-
νεθλαΤ   230 κεκλήσεται] κεκλύσεται RZc: κεκλαύσεται Fröhlich   231
ἐκ καμάτων] ἀκαμάτων Reiske   233 εὐνοίᾳ γ᾽ codd. plerique et Suidas
i. 403.6: εὔνοιαν Lᵃᶜ et fort. Vᵃᶜ   234 πιστά] πικτή Suidas   236
κακότατος LKᵃᶜrZrNPVZc: –ητος KᵖᶜADXrXsCFOt   238 ἐν τίνι] εἴ
τισι Reiske, puncto interrogationis deleto   ἔβλαστ᾽ AXrXsPZct: ἔβλασ-
τεν LKrDZrCFHᵖᶜNOV

36

ξυνναίοιμ᾽ εὔκηλος, γονέων
ἐκτίμους ἴσχουσα πτέρυγας
ὀξυτόνων γόων.
εἰ γὰρ ὁ μὲν θανὼν γᾶ τε καὶ οὐδὲν ὢν   245
κείσεται τάλας,
οἱ δὲ μὴ πάλιν
δώσουσ᾽ ἀντιφόνους δίκας,
ἔρροι τἂν Αἰδὼς
ἁπάντων τ᾽ Εὐσέβεια θνατῶν.   250

Χο. ἐγὼ μέν, ὦ παῖ, καὶ τὸ σὸν σπεύδουσ᾽ ἅμα
     καὶ τοὐμὸν αὐτῆς ἦλθον· εἰ δὲ μὴ καλῶς
     λέγω, σὺ νίκα· σοὶ γὰρ ἑψόμεσθ᾽ ἅμα.
Ηλ. αἰσχύνομαι μέν, ὦ γυναῖκες, εἰ δοκῶ
     πολλοῖσι θρήνοις δυσφορεῖν ὑμῖν ἄγαν.   255
     ἀλλ᾽, ἡ βία γὰρ ταῦτ᾽ ἀναγκάζει με δρᾶν,
     σύγγνωτε. πῶς γάρ, ἥτις εὐγενὴς γυνή,
     πατρῷ᾽ ὁρῶσα πήματ᾽, οὐ δρῴη τάδ᾽ ἄν,
     ἁγὼ κατ᾽ ἦμαρ καὶ κατ᾽ εὐφρόνην ἀεὶ
     θάλλοντα μᾶλλον ἢ καταφθίνονθ᾽ ὁρῶ;   260
     ᾗ πρῶτα μὲν τὰ μητρός, ἥ μ᾽ ἐγείνατο,
     ἔχθιστα συμβέβηκεν· εἶτα δώμασιν
     ἐν τοῖς ἐμαυτῆς τοῖς φονεῦσι τοῦ πατρὸς
     ξύνειμι, κἀκ τῶνδ᾽ ἄρχομαι κἀκ τῶνδέ μοι
     λαβεῖν θ᾽ ὁμοίως καὶ τὸ τητᾶσθαι πέλει.   265
     ἔπειτα ποίας ἡμέρας δοκεῖς μ᾽ ἄγειν,
     ὅταν θρόνοις Αἴγισθον ἐνθακοῦντ᾽ ἴδω
     τοῖσιν πατρῴοις, εἰσίδω δ᾽ ἐσθήματα
     φοροῦντ᾽ ἐκείνῳ ταὐτά, καὶ παρεστίους
     σπένδοντα λοιβὰς ἔνθ᾽ ἐκεῖνον ὤλεσεν,   270
     ἴδω δὲ τούτων τὴν τελευταίαν ὕβριν,

---

249 τἂν Martin: τ᾽ ἂν codd.   253 ἅμα] ὁμοῦ ΣD: ἀεί Morstadt   256
ἀλλ᾽ ἡ βία με ταῦτ᾽ ἀναγκάζει ποιεῖν Arist. Met. 1015ᵃ31   257 ἥτις
LKGʳˢADCFᵃᶜNPZct: εἴ τις rXɪXsZrFᵖᶜHV   271 τούτων] τοῦτον rZcˡˢ:
πάντων Schenkl

τὸν αὐτοφόντην ἧμιν ἐν κοίτῃ πατρὸς
ξὺν τῇ ταλαίνῃ μητρί, μητέρ᾽ εἰ χρεὼν
ταύτην προσαυδᾶν τῷδε συγκοιμωμένην·
ἣ δ᾽ ὧδε τλήμων ὥστε τῷ μιάστορι   275
ξύνεστ᾽, Ἐρινὺν οὔτιν᾽ ἐκφοβουμένη·
ἀλλ᾽, ὥσπερ ἐγγελῶσα τοῖς ποιουμένοις,
†εὑροῦσ᾽† ἐκείνην ἡμέραν, ἐν ᾗ τότε
πατέρα τὸν ἀμὸν ἐκ δόλου κατέκτανεν,
ταύτῃ χορούς ἵστησι καὶ μηλοσφαγεῖ   280
θεοῖσιν ἔμμην᾽ ἱερὰ τοῖς σωτηρίοις.
ἐγὼ δ᾽ ὁρῶσα δύσμορος κατὰ στέγας
κλαίω, τέτηκα, κἀπικωκύω πατρὸς
τὴν δυστάλαιναν δαῖτ᾽ ἐπωνομασμένην
αὐτὴ πρὸς αὑτήν· οὐδὲ γὰρ κλαῦσαι πάρα   285
τοσόνδ᾽ ὅσον μοι θυμὸς ἡδονὴν φέρει.
αὕτη γὰρ ἡ λόγοισι γενναία γυνὴ
φωνοῦσα τοιάδ᾽ ἐξονειδίζει κακά,
"ὦ δύσθεον μίσημα, σοὶ μόνῃ πατὴρ
τέθνηκεν; ἄλλος δ᾽ οὔτις ἐν πένθει βροτῶν;   290
κακῶς ὄλοιο, μηδέ σ᾽ ἐκ γόων ποτὲ
τῶν νῦν ἀπαλλάξειαν οἱ κάτω θεοί."
τάδ᾽ ἐξυβρίζει, πλὴν ὅταν κλύῃ τινὸς
ἥξοντ᾽ Ὀρέστην· τηνικαῦτα δ᾽ ἐμμανὴς
βοᾷ παραστᾶσ᾽, "οὐ σύ μοι τῶνδ᾽ αἰτία;   295
οὐ σὸν τόδ᾽ ἐστὶ τοὔργον, ἥτις ἐκ χερῶν
κλέψασ᾽ Ὀρέστην τῶν ἐμῶν ὑπεξέθου;
ἀλλ᾽ ἴσθι τοι τείσουσά γ᾽ ἀξίαν δίκην."

272 αὐτοφόντην codd. (etiam Λ): αὐτοέντην LᵞᵖKᵞᵖSᵞᵖ   275 ἣ δ᾽ scripsi:
ἡ δ᾽ Schaefer: ἥδ᾽ codd.   276 Ἐρινὺν Dindorf: Ἐρινῦν LᵃᶜKrFOᵃᶜPV:
Ἐρινῦν vel –ὺν aCFˡˢHNOᴵᵖᶜZct et Suidas iv. 565.15   277 ὥσπερ
ἐγγελῶσα] ὥσπερεὶ γελῶσα (vel χλιδῶσα) Schmidt: ὥσπερεὶ χλίουσα vel
ὥσπερ ἐγχλίουσα Groeneboom   278 εὑροῦσ᾽] ἱεροῦσ᾽ Seyffert: τηροῦσ᾽
Reiske: φρουροῦσ᾽ Nauck: αἱροῦσ᾽ Fröhlich   279 πατέρα] τὸν πατέρα S,
coni. Blaydes   ἀμὸν XsZf: ἁμὸν LᵖᶜADZrt: ἐμὸν LᵃᶜKrXrp   ἐκ δόλου]
ἐν δόλῳ Fᵖᶜ, coni. Blaydes   282 ὁρῶσα fort. Aᵃᶜ: ὁρῶσ᾽ ἡ cett. (etiam Zf)
285 αὐτὴν LKrCHNOVZc: αὐτ– aFPt   286 φέρει] ἔχει Nauck   298
τείσουσά γ᾽ Nauck: τίσουσά γ᾽ codd.: τείσουσ᾽ ἔτ᾽ Blaydes

τοιαῦθ᾽ ὑλακτεῖ, σὺν δ᾽ ἐποτρύνει πέλας
ὁ κλεινὸς αὐτῇ ταὐτὰ νυμφίος παρών,   300
ὁ πάντ᾽ ἄναλκις οὗτος, ἡ πᾶσα βλάβη,
ὁ σὺν γυναιξὶ τὰς μάχας ποιούμενος.
ἐγὼ δ᾽ Ὀρέστην τῶνδε προσμένουσ᾽ ἀεὶ
παυστῆρ᾽ ἐφήξειν ἡ τάλαιν᾽ ἀπόλλυμαι.
μέλλων γὰρ ἀεὶ δρᾶν τι τὰς οὔσας τέ μου   305
καὶ τὰς ἀπούσας ἐλπίδας διέφθορεν.
ἐν οὖν τοιούτοις οὔτε σωφρονεῖν, φίλαι,
οὔτ᾽ εὐσεβεῖν πάρεστιν· ἀλλ᾽ ἔν τοι κακοῖς
πολλή 'στ᾽ ἀνάγκη κἀπιτηδεύειν κακά.
Χο. φέρ᾽ εἰπέ, πότερον ὄντος Αἰγίσθου πέλας   310
λέγεις τάδ᾽ ἡμῖν, ἢ βεβῶτος ἐκ δόμων;
Ηλ. καὶ κάρτα. μὴ δόκει μ᾽ ἄν, εἴπερ ἦν πέλας,
θυραῖον οἰχνεῖν· νῦν δ᾽ ἀγροῖσι τυγχάνει.
Χο. ἦ δὴ ἂν ἐγὼ θαρσοῦσα μᾶλλον ἐς λόγους
τοὺς σοὺς ἱκοίμην, εἴπερ ὧδε ταῦτ᾽ ἔχει.   315
Ηλ. ὡς νῦν ἀπόντος ἱστόρει· τί σοι φίλον;
Χο. καὶ δή σ᾽ ἐρωτῶ, τοῦ κασιγνήτου τί φής,
ἥξοντος, ἢ μέλλοντος; εἰδέναι θέλω.
Ηλ. φησίν γε· φάσκων δ᾽ οὐδὲν ὧν λέγει ποεῖ.
Χο. φιλεῖ γὰρ ὀκνεῖν πρᾶγμ᾽ ἀνὴρ πράσσων μέγα.   320
Ηλ. καὶ μὴν ἔγωγ᾽ ἔσωσ᾽ ἐκεῖνον οὐκ ὄκνῳ.
Χο. θάρσει· πέφυκεν ἐσθλός, ὥστ᾽ ἀρκεῖν φίλοις.

300 versum om. Suidas iv. 638.11–13 dum 299 et 301 citat   ταὐτὰ
Blomfield: ταῦτα codd.   301 πάντ᾽ ἄναλκις codd. et Suidas i. 174.19:
πάντα κλεινὸς Suidas iv. 638.12   303 τῶνδε προσμένουσ᾽ ἀεὶ] προσμέ-
νουσ᾽ ἀεί ποτε LʳʸP   305 ἀεὶ **lr**DᵃᶜZ**rp**Z**c**t: αἰεὶ LᵖᶜADᵗᵖᶜXrXs   μου
codd. plerique, Suidas iii. 357.8, Eustathius 191.29: μοι ΔWaWb, Thomas
Magister 88.11 Ritschl   306 διέφθορεν] –ας Eustathius 191.29   308
εὐσεβεῖν] εὐστομεῖν Morstadt   τοι Hermann: τοῖς codd.   309 πολ-
λῆστ᾽ L: πολλή γ᾽ NOPVJZfZg et Gnom.: πολλή τ᾽ **Kra**FHZcT: πολλή δ᾽ C
312 καὶ Meineke: ἢ codd.   313 θυραῖον] –αίαν vel –αῖαν Kˢ**r**CFHNOˣ
314 ἦ δὴ ἂν Hermann: ἢ δ᾽ ἂν (vel ἦδ᾽, ἦδ᾽) **Krp**Zc et forte Lᵖᶜ: ἢ κἂν **at** et
forte Lᵃᶜ: ἦ τἂν Blomfield   316 νῦν] νυν Monk   τί] ὅ NOˣ: τό Matthiae
319 φησίν LKAOVZg: φησί cett. (nisi quod φασί P)   ποεῖ Lᵖᶜ**r**: ποιεῖ Lᵃᶜ
et cett.   320 πρᾶγμ᾽] πᾶς Suidas iii. 515.8   321 ἔγωγ᾽ ἔσωσ᾽] inverso
ordine HP

Ηλ. πέποιθ', ἐπεί τἁν οὐ μακρὰν ἔζων ἐγώ.
Χο. μὴ νῦν ἔτ' εἴπῃς μηδέν· ὡς δόμων ὁρῶ
τὴν σὴν ὅμαιμον, ἐκ πατρὸς ταὐτοῦ φύσιν,   325
Χρυσόθεμιν, ἔκ τε μητρός, ἐντάφια χεροῖν
φέρουσαν, οἷα τοῖς κάτω νομίζεται.

ΧΡΥΣΟΘΕΜΙΣ

τίν' αὖ σὺ τήνδε πρὸς θυρῶνος ἐξόδοις
ἐλθοῦσα φωνεῖς, ὦ κασιγνήτη, φάτιν,
κοὐδ' ἐν χρόνῳ μακρῷ διδαχθῆναι θέλεις   330
θυμῷ ματαίῳ μὴ χαρίζεσθαι κενά;
καίτοι τοσοῦτόν γ' οἶδα κἀμαυτήν, ὅτι
ἀλγῶ 'πὶ τοῖς παροῦσιν· ὥστ' ἄν, εἰ σθένος
λάβοιμι, δηλώσαιμ' ἂν οἷ' αὐτοῖς φρονῶ.
νῦν δ' ἐν κακοῖς μοι πλεῖν ὑφειμένη δοκεῖ,   335
καὶ μὴ δοκεῖν μὲν δρᾶν τι, πημαίνειν δὲ μή.
τοιαῦτα δ' ἄλλα καὶ σὲ βούλομαι ποεῖν.
καίτοι τὸ μὲν δίκαιον οὐχ ᾗ 'γὼ λέγω,
ἀλλ' ᾗ σὺ κρίνεις. εἰ δ' ἐλευθέραν με δεῖ
ζῆν, τῶν κρατούντων ἐστὶ πάντ' ἀκουστέα.   340
Ηλ. δεινόν γέ σ' οὖσαν πατρὸς οὗ σὺ παῖς ἔφυς
κείνου λελῆσθαι, τῆς δὲ τικτούσης μέλειν.
ἅπαντα γάρ σοι τἀμὰ νουθετήματα
κείνης διδακτά, κοὐδὲν ἐκ σαυτῆς λέγεις.
†ἔπειθ' ἑλοῦ γε† θάτερ', ἢ φρονεῖν κακῶς,   345
ἢ τῶν φίλων φρονοῦσα μὴ μνήμην ἔχειν·
ἥτις λέγεις μὲν ἀρτίως, ὡς εἰ λάβοις

324 νῦν] νυν Monk   325 φύσιν LKᵖᶜADXsZrt: φύσαν vel φῦσαν rXгpZc (unde φῦσαν ἐκ ταὐτοῦ πατρός Fröhlich)   328 ἐξόδοις] –ους Blaydes   329 ἐλθοῦσα] ἀλγοῦσα Seebeck: ἔλκουσα Dawe   331 θυμῷ ματαίῳ] ψυχῇ ματαίᾳ LᵞᵖDᵍˡSʸᵖ: ψυχῇ gl. in nonnullis (etiam K)   332 γ'] om. COZfZgt   336 μὲν] om. XsCOV   337 δ'ἄλλα Dindorf: δ'ἀλλὰ codd.: τἀμ', ἃ Schneidewin   ποεῖν LrD¹ᵖᶜHZc, fort. Nᵃᶜ: ποιεῖν aCFOPVT   341 γέ σ'] σέ γ' Blomfield et Monk   οὗ σὺ] καὶ σὺ O: οὗ γὰρ R: οὗ καὶ Dawe   344 κείνης] –η r   διδακτά] δίδαγμα Page   345 ἔπειθ' ἑλοῦ γε] ἐπεί γ' Page, ἑλοῦ σύ Blaydes   θάτερ'] θάτερον PZcT

σθένος, τὸ τούτων μῖσος ἐκδείξειας ἄν·
ἐμοῦ δὲ πατρὶ πάντα τιμωρουμένης
οὔτε ξυνέρδεις τήν τε δρῶσαν ἐκτρέπεις.   350
οὐ ταῦτα πρὸς κακοῖσι δειλίαν ἔχει;
ἐπεὶ δίδαξον, ἢ μάθ᾽ ἐξ ἐμοῦ, τί μοι
κέρδος γένοιτ᾽ ἂν τῶνδε ληξάσῃ γόων.
οὐ ζῶ; κακῶς μέν, οἶδ᾽, ἐπαρκούντως δ᾽ ἐμοί.
λυπῶ δὲ τούτους, ὥστε τῷ τεθνηκότι   355
τιμὰς προσάπτειν, εἴ τις ἔστ᾽ ἐκεῖ χάρις.
σὺ δ᾽ ἡμὶν ἡ μισοῦσα μισεῖς μὲν λόγῳ,
ἔργῳ δὲ τοῖς φονεῦσι τοῦ πατρὸς ξύνει.
ἐγὼ μὲν οὖν οὐκ ἄν ποτ᾽, οὐδ᾽ εἴ μοι τὰ σὰ
μέλλοι τις οἴσειν δῶρ᾽, ἐφ᾽ οἷς σὺ νῦν χλιδᾷς,   360
τούτοις ὑπεικάθοιμι· σοὶ δὲ πλουσία
τράπεζα κείσθω καὶ περιρρείτω βίος.
ἐμοὶ γὰρ ἔστω τούς με χρὴ λυπεῖν μόνον
βόσκημα· τῆς σῆς δ᾽ οὐκ ἐρῶ τιμῆς λαχεῖν,
οὐδ᾽ ἂν σύ, σώφρων γ᾽ οὖσα. νῦν δ᾽ ἐξὸν πατρὸς   365
πάντων ἀρίστου παῖδα κεκλῆσθαι, καλοῦ
τῆς μητρός. οὕτω γὰρ φανῇ πλείστοις κακή,
θανόντα πατέρα καὶ φίλους προδοῦσα σούς.

Χο.   μηδὲν πρὸς ὀργὴν πρὸς θεῶν· ὡς τοῖς λόγοις
      ἔνεστιν ἀμφοῖν κέρδος, εἰ σὺ μὲν μάθοις   370
      τοῖς τῆσδε χρῆσθαι, τοῖς δὲ σοῖς αὕτη πάλιν.

Χρ.   ἐγὼ μέν, ὦ γυναῖκες, ἠθάς εἰμί πως
      τῶν τῆσδε μύθων· οὐδ᾽ ἂν ἐμνήσθην ποτέ,

348 ἐκδείξειας] ἐν– OV   354 ἐπαρκούντως] ἀπ– Thomas Magister 24.16
Ritschl   δ᾽ ἐμοί FV, coni. Brunck (ἐμοί Thomas): δέ μοι cett.   359
οὖν] om. LPZc   360 μέλλοι LAXrXsFNOVZc: μέλλει rDZrCHPt   οἷς
σὺ Jg, coni. Blomfield: οἶσι cett.   363 τούς με χρὴ λυπεῖν μόνον
Tournier: τοὐμὲ μὴ λυπουμενον Π²: τοὐμὲ μὴ λυπεῖν μόνον codd.: τὸ
μὴ λυπεῖν τὸν πατέρα Lʳˢ: pro λυπεῖν malunt λιπεῖν Canter, λυποῦν
Erfurdt: τοῦπ᾽ ἔμ᾽ ἡ λύπη μόνον Jaya-Suriya: τοὐμέ νιν λυπεῖν μόνον Brunck
364 λαχεῖν LʳˢXrʸᵖFHNOPVˣWb et Gnom.: τυχεῖν Π²LKraCVˣZctWbʳˢ
367 πλείστοις] –ον Nauck   370 ἀμφοῖν κέρδος] inverso ordine KCN
371 αὕτη CNOPVZct: αὐτὴ LKraFH   373 οὐδ᾽] κοὐκ t

41

ΣΟΦΟΚΛΕΟΥΣ ΗΛΕΚΤΡΑ

εἰ μὴ κακὸν μέγιστον εἰς αὐτὴν ἰὸν
ἤκουσ᾽, ὃ ταύτην τῶν μακρῶν σχήσει γόων. 375
Ηλ. φέρ᾽ εἰπὲ δὴ τὸ δεινόν. εἰ γὰρ τῶνδέ μοι
μεῖζόν τι λέξεις, οὐκ ἂν ἀντείποιμ᾽ ἔτι.
Χρ. ἀλλ᾽ ἐξερῶ σοι πᾶν ὅσον κάτοιδ᾽ ἐγώ.
μέλλουσι γάρ σ᾽, εἰ τῶνδε μὴ λήξεις γόων,
ἐνταῦθα πέμψειν ἔνθα μήποθ᾽ ἡλίου 380
φέγγος προσόψει, ζῶσα δ᾽ ἐν κατηρεφεῖ
στέγῃ χθονὸς τῆσδ᾽ ἐκτὸς ὑμνήσεις κακά.
πρὸς ταῦτα φράζου, καί με μήποθ᾽ ὕστερον
παθοῦσα μέμψῃ. νῦν γὰρ ἐν καλῷ φρονεῖν.
Ηλ. ἦ ταῦτα δή με καὶ βεβούλευνται ποεῖν; 385
Χρ. μάλισθ᾽· ὅταν περ οἴκαδ᾽ Αἴγισθος μόλῃ.
Ηλ. ἀλλ᾽ ἐξίκοιτο τοῦδέ γ᾽ οὕνεκ᾽ ἐν τάχει.
Χρ. τίν᾽, ὦ τάλαινα, τόνδ᾽ ἐπηράσω λόγον;
Ηλ. ἐλθεῖν ἐκεῖνον, εἴ τι τῶνδε δρᾶν νοεῖ.
Χρ. ὅπως πάθῃς τί χρῆμα; ποῦ ποτ᾽ εἶ φρενῶν; 390
Ηλ. ὅπως ἀφ᾽ ὑμῶν ὡς προσώτατ᾽ ἐκφύγω.
Χρ. βίου δὲ τοῦ παρόντος οὐ μνείαν ἔχεις;
Ηλ. καλὸς γὰρ οὑμὸς βίοτος ὥστε θαυμάσαι.
Χρ. ἀλλ᾽ ἦν ἄν, εἰ σύ γ᾽ εὖ φρονεῖν ἠπίστασο.
Ηλ. μή μ᾽ ἐκδίδασκε τοῖς φίλοις εἶναι κακήν. 395
Χρ. ἀλλ᾽ οὐ διδάσκω· τοῖς κρατοῦσι δ᾽ εἰκαθεῖν.
Ηλ. σὺ ταῦτα θώπευ᾽· οὐκ ἐμοὺς τρόπους λέγεις.
Χρ. καλόν γε μέντοι μὴ ᾿ξ ἀβουλίας πεσεῖν.

374 εἰς αὐτὴν] εἰσάντην Platt   375 ταύτην] τούτων Blaydes   376
γάρ] δὲ Elmsley   378 σοι LKCFHNOZc^gl: τοι L^sraPVt   379 λήξεις L^pcraHZct: –ης vel –ης L^acKCFNOPV   γόων] λόγων L^γρ   380
μήποθ᾽ codd. et Eustathius 1839.61: μηκέθ᾽ Nauck   381 προσόψει] κατ-
Eustathius: καθορῇ Ammonius 170 (p. 43.8 Nickau) (nisi quod προσόψει
cod. N)   382 στέγῃ codd. plerique et Suidas iii. 76.20: –ει RXrHN
ἐκτὸς codd. et Suidas iv. 640.14 (om. iii. 76.20): ἐντὸς Schenkl   383 καί
με] κἀμὲ Brunck: κοῦ με Blaydes   385 δή LKraFHNZc: γάρ COVt: γε P
με LKraFZc: μοι CHNOPVt   βεβούλευνται] –ευται G^acZrH   ποεῖν
LKrD^pcFZc et Eustathius 1326.58: ποιεῖν aCHNOPV et Eustathius 694.26
387 οὕνεκ᾽] εἵνεκ᾽ Κ: ἕνεκ᾽ P   390 πάθῃς] μάθῃς V^ac: πάθοις CNP   396
εἰκαθεῖν Elmsley: εἰκάθειν codd.

42

Ηλ. πεσούμεθ', εἰ χρή, πατρὶ τιμωρούμενοι.
Χρ. πατὴρ δὲ τούτων, οἶδα, συγγνώμην ἔχει.   400
Ηλ. ταῦτ' ἐστὶ τἄπη πρὸς κακῶν ἐπαινέσαι.
Χρ. σὺ δ' οὐχὶ πείσῃ καὶ συναινέσεις ἐμοί;
Ηλ. οὐ δῆτα. μή πω νοῦ τοσόνδ' εἴην κενή.
Χρ. χωρήσομαί τἄρ' οἷπερ ἐστάλην ὁδοῦ.
Ηλ. ποῖ δ' ἐμπορεύῃ; τῷ φέρεις τάδ' ἔμπυρα;   405
Χρ. μήτηρ με πέμπει πατρὶ τυμβεῦσαι χοάς.
Ηλ. πῶς εἶπας; ἦ τῷ δυσμενεστάτῳ βροτῶν;
Χρ. ὃν ἔκταν' αὐτή· τοῦτο γὰρ λέξαι θέλεις.
Ηλ. ἐκ τοῦ φίλων πεισθεῖσα; τῷ τοῦτ' ἤρεσεν;
Χρ. ἐκ δείματός του νυκτέρου, δοκεῖν ἐμοί.   410
Ηλ. ὦ θεοὶ πατρῷοι, συγγένεσθέ γ' ἀλλὰ νῦν.
Χρ. ἔχεις τι θάρσος τοῦδε τοῦ τάρβους πέρι;
Ηλ. εἴ μοι λέγοις τὴν ὄψιν, εἴποιμ' ἂν τότε.
Χρ. ἀλλ' οὐ κάτοιδα πλὴν ἐπὶ σμικρὸν φράσαι.
Ηλ. λέγ' ἀλλὰ τοῦτο. πολλά τοι σμικροὶ λόγοι   415
       ἔσφηλαν ἤδη καὶ κατώρθωσαν βροτούς.
Χρ. λόγος τις αὐτήν ἐστιν εἰσιδεῖν πατρὸς
       τοῦ σοῦ τε κἀμοῦ δευτέραν ὁμιλίαν
       ἐλθόντος ἐς φῶς· εἶτα τόνδ' ἐφέστιον
       πῆξαι λαβόντα σκῆπτρον οὑφόρει ποτὲ   420
       αὐτός, τανῦν δ' Αἴγισθος· ἔκ τε τοῦδ' ἄνω
       βλαστεῖν βρύοντα θαλλόν, ᾧ κατάσκιον
       πᾶσαν γενέσθαι τὴν Μυκηναίων χθόνα.
       τοιαῦτά του παρόντος, ἡνίχ' Ἡλίῳ

---

399 τιμωρούμενοι] –μεναι G et fort. F^ac   403 μή πω] μὴ 'γὼ Blaydes
405 ποῖ LKaFZct: ποῦ rCHNOPV   τῷ G^rgl D^yp CHNO^1pc PWbt: ποῖ
LKRAXrZrFZc: ποῦ GV: πῇ DXs   408 ὃν <γ'> Monk   409 τῷ]
πῶς Herwerden   411 συγγένεσθέ γ' codd. plerique et Suidas iv. 449.14:
συγγένεσθ' PV et Suidas i. 98.1 et iv. 449.14 cod. V: συγγένεσθέ τε Priscian iii.
196.20 Keil   413 λέγοις Turnebus: λέγεις codd.   414 ἐπὶ] ἔπος Fröhlich
σμικρὸν codd. plerique (etiam L^pc Xs^1pc): –ῶν L^spc Xs^ac: –ῶ(ι) KAFZct: L^ac
non legitur   415 πολλά τοι codd. plerique et Suidas iv. 156.16: πολλά τοι
καὶ Xr: πολλάκις K^s CH^gl NP^1pc: πολλὰ χοῖ Dawe   419 ἐς] εἰς RCHNPZf
421 τε] δὲ r   422 ᾧ] τῷ(ι) LK^ac rFHOPZc   424 του L^pc KaCFNVZc:
τοῦ L^ac rHOPt

δείκνυσι τοὔναρ, ἔκλυον ἐξηγουμένου. 425
πλείω δὲ τούτων οὐ κάτοιδα, πλὴν ὅτι
πέμπει μ᾽ ἐκείνη τοῦδε τοῦ φόβου χάριν.
[πρός νυν θεῶν σε λίσσομαι τῶν ἐγγενῶν
ἐμοὶ πιθέσθαι μηδ᾽ ἀβουλίᾳ πεσεῖν·
εἰ γάρ μ᾽ ἀπώσῃ, σὺν κακῷ μέτει πάλιν.] 430

Ηλ. ἀλλ᾽, ὦ φίλη, τούτων μὲν ὧν ἔχεις χεροῖν
τύμβῳ προσάψῃς μηδέν· οὐ γάρ σοι θέμις
οὐδ᾽ ὅσιον ἐχθρᾶς <—> γυναικὸς ἱστάναι
κτερίσματ᾽ οὐδὲ λουτρὰ προσφέρειν πατρί·
ἀλλ᾽ ἢ πνοαῖσιν ἢ βαθυσκαφεῖ κόνει 435
κρύψον νιν, ἔνθα μήποτ᾽ εἰς εὐνὴν πατρὸς
τούτων πρόσεισι μηδέν· ἀλλ᾽ ὅταν θάνῃ,
κειμήλι᾽ αὐτῇ ταῦτα σῳζέσθω κάτω.
ἀρχὴν δ᾽ ἄν, εἰ μὴ τλημονεστάτη γυνὴ
πασῶν ἔβλαστε, τάσδε δυσμενεῖς χοὰς 440
οὐκ ἄν ποθ᾽ ὅν γ᾽ ἔκτεινε τῷδ᾽ ἐπέστεφε.
σκέψαι γὰρ εἴ σοι προσφιλῶς αὐτῇ δοκεῖ
γέρα τάδ᾽ οὖν τάφοισι δέξασθαι νέκυς
ὑφ᾽ ἧς θανὼν ἄτιμος ὥστε δυσμενὴς
ἐμασχαλίσθη κἀπὶ λουτροῖσιν κάρᾳ 445
κηλῖδας ἐξέμαξεν. ἆρα μὴ δοκεῖς
λυτήρι᾽ αὐτῇ ταῦτα τοῦ φόνου φέρειν;
οὐκ ἔστιν. ἀλλὰ ταῦτα μὲν μέθες· σὺ δὲ
τεμοῦσα κρατὸς βοστρύχων ἄκρας φόβας

425 δείκνυσι] δείκνυε Σ OC 477 (p. 29.21 De Marco) ἐξηγουμένου
LKGᶜaCHPᶦˢVˣZct: —ης LᶦKˢrPNᵃᶜ, fort. O 427 φόβου] τάρβους J:
τάφου N 428–30 del. Morstadt 428 ante hunc versum (et non ante
431) personae notam ΗΛ. habent omnes codd. praeter rZgt 430 εἰ]
ἦν Blaydes 433 ἐχθρᾶς LKrpZc: ἐχθρᾶς ἀπὸ aNᵍˡVᵍˡZcᵍˡt: post ἐχθρᾶς
inseruit ἐκ Meineke, παρὰ Dawe, πρὸς Dindorf 435 πνοαῖσιν] πνοῆσιν
P: πυρᾷ δὸς vel ῥοαῖσιν Reiske 436 κρύψον] ῥῖψον Todt ἔνθα] ἔνθεν t,
coni. Meineke 439 δ᾽ ἄν] γάρ LᶦˢXrZrHOPt 440 δυσμενεῖς] δυσσεβεῖς Nauck 443 δέξασθαι codd. et Suidas iii. 336.4: δέξεται Vˢ: δέξεσθαι
Heath 445 κάρᾳ Cᵃᶜ et Eustathius 1857.7: κάρα Cᵖᶜ et cett. (etiam Suidas
iii. 336.5) 449 φόβας LKaCHNᶦˢOPZct, Suidas iv. 746.25: κόμας LᶦˢrF

44

ΣΟΦΟΚΛΕΟΥΣ ΗΛΕΚΤΡΑ

κἀμοῦ ταλαίνης, σμικρὰ μὲν τάδ᾽, ἀλλ᾽ ὅμως 450
ἄχω, δὸς αὐτῷ, τήνδε τ᾽ ἀλιπαρῆ τρίχα
καὶ ζῶμα τοὐμὸν οὐ χλιδαῖς ἠσκημένον.
αἰτοῦ δὲ προσπίτνουσα γῆθεν εὐμενῆ
ἡμῖν ἀρωγὸν αὐτὸν εἰς ἐχθροὺς μολεῖν,
καὶ παῖδ᾽ Ὀρέστην ἐξ ὑπερτέρας χερὸς 455
ἐχθροῖσιν αὐτοῦ ζῶντ᾽ ἐπεμβῆναι ποδί,
ὅπως τὸ λοιπὸν αὐτὸν ἀφνεωτέραις
χερσὶ στέφωμεν ἢ τανῦν δωρούμεθα.
οἶμαι μὲν οὖν, οἶμαί τι κἀκείνῳ μέλειν
πέμψαι τάδ᾽ αὐτῇ δυσπρόσοπτ᾽ ὀνείρατα· 460
ὅμως δ᾽, ἀδελφή, σοί θ᾽ ὑπούργησον τάδε
ἐμοί τ᾽ ἀρωγά, τῷ τε φιλτάτῳ βροτῶν
πάντων, ἐν Ἅιδου κειμένῳ κοινῷ πατρί.
Χο. πρὸς εὐσέβειαν ἡ κόρη λέγει· σὺ δέ,
εἰ σωφρονήσεις, ὦ φίλη, δράσεις τάδε. 465
Χρ. δράσω· τὸ γὰρ δίκαιον οὐκ ἔχει λόγον
δυοῖν ἐρίζειν, ἀλλ᾽ ἐπισπεύδειν τὸ δρᾶν.
πειρωμένη δὲ τῶνδε τῶν ἔργων ἐμοὶ
σιγῇ παρ᾽ ὑμῶν πρὸς θεῶν ἔστω, φίλαι·
ὡς εἰ τάδ᾽ ἡ τεκοῦσα πεύσεται, πικρὰν 470
δοκῶ με πεῖραν τήνδε τολμήσειν ἔτι.

Χο. εἰ μὴ ᾽γὼ παράφρων μάντις ἔφυν [str.
καὶ γνώμας λειπομένα σοφᾶς,
εἶσιν ἁ πρόμαντις 475
Δίκα, δίκαια φερομένα χεροῖν κράτη·
μέτεισιν, ὦ τέκνον, οὐ μακροῦ χρόνου.

451 τήνδε τ᾽ ἀλιπαρῆ Fröhlich (γ᾽ pro τ᾽ Erfurdt): τήνδ᾽ ἀλιπαρῆ codd., Suidas ii. 512.20, Eustathius 787.50: τήνδε λιπαρῆ novit ex commentario Σ: τήνδε γ᾽ ἀλίπαρον Hartung 459 κἀκείνῳ] –ου P μέλειν Blaydes: –ον codd. 460 δυσπρόσοπτ᾽] δυσπρόσωπ᾽ CNO 461 ὅμως] ὁμῶς Dawe 463 Ἅιδου] –η r 466 post δίκαιον interpungunt XrCt οὐκ] οὐδ᾽ Eggert 467 ἐπισπεύδειν] –ει Stob. Ecl. 3.11.6 471 δοκῶ] δόκει Meineke 472 ἔφυν] ἐξέφυν r 475 πρόμαντις] πρόφαντος Herwerden

ὕπεστί μοι θάρσος
ἁδυπνόων κλύουσαν 480
ἀρτίως ὀνειράτων.
οὐ γάρ ποτ᾿ ἀμναστεῖ γ᾿ ὁ φύ –
σας σ᾿ Ἑλλάνων ἄναξ,
οὐδ᾿ ἁ παλαιὰ χαλκόπλη –
κτος ἀμφήκης γένυς, 485
ἅ νιν κατέπεφνεν αἰσχίσταις ἐν ᾀκείαις.

ἥξει καὶ πολύπους καὶ πολύχειρ [ant.
ἁ δεινοῖς κρυπτομένα λόχοις 490
χαλκόπους Ἐρινύς.
ἄλεκτρ᾿ ἄνυμφα γὰρ ἐπέβα μιαιφόνων
γάμων ἁμιλλήμαθ᾿ οἷσιν οὐ θέμις.
πρὸ τῶνδέ τοι θάρσος 495
μήποτε μήποθ᾿ ἡμῖν
ἀψεγὲς πελᾶν τέρας
τοῖς δρῶσι καὶ συνδρῶσιν. ἦ –
τοι μαντεῖαι βροτῶν
οὐκ εἰσὶν ἐν δεινοῖς ὀνεί –
ροις οὐδ᾿ ἐν θεσφάτοις, 500
εἰ μὴ τόδε φάσμα νυκτὸς εὖ κατασχήσει.

ὦ Πέλοπος ἁ πρόσθεν [ep.
πολύπονος ἱππεία, 505

478 θάρσος   L^pc**ra**CFHOPVZc^pc: θράσος   L^ac**KNt**   480 κλύουσαν   LDXrXsZrOPVZct: –α(ι)   **Kr**A: –η   CHN   482 ἀμναστεῖ
KADXrXsCNOPVt: –ηστεῖ **Lr**ZrFHZc et Suidas i. 143.9   γ᾿] σ᾿
Wakefield   483 σ᾿ Wa, coni. Fröhlich: om. cett. et Suidas i. 143.11
484–5 χαλκόπληκτος] –πλακτος J: –πηκτος Wakefield   487 αἰσχίσταις
ἐν] –αισιν XsH   ᾀκείαις scripsi: αἰκείαις Porson: αἰκίαις codd.   489
πολύπους] πολύπαις ex commentario novit ΣL: πολύφρων West   491
Ἐρινύς **rF**, coni. Dindorf: Ἐρινῦς L^ac**KN**^acPV: Ἐρινῦς (vel –ύς) **a**CHN^1pcOZc**t**
492 ἐπέβα] ἐπέβαν RZg, coni. Blaydes   494 ἁμιλλήμαθ᾿] ὁμιλήμαθ᾿ Musgrave   495 θάρσος Wunder: μ᾿ ἔχει θάρσος **r**P: μ᾿ ἔχει **la**C^1pcHNOVZc**t**
(sed ἐλπὶς vel θάρσος gl. in nonnullis)   496 μήποτε μήποθ᾿ **apt**: μήποθ᾿
lrZc   ἡμῖν] ὑμῖν CN^pcZc**t**, coni. Reiske   497 ἀψεγὲς] ἀψευδές C
(verum C^18): ἀψεφὲς Bergk   τέρας] πέρας K^ac   498 συνδρῶσιν] μὴ
δρῶσιν P

ὡς ἔμολες αἰανὴς
τᾷδε γᾷ.
εὖτε γὰρ ὁ ποντισθεὶς
Μυρτίλος ἐκοιμάθη,
παγχρύσων δίφρων   510
δυστάνοις ᾀκείαις
πρόρριζος ἐκριφθείς,
οὔ τί πω
ἔλιπεν ἐκ τοῦδ' οἴκου
πολύπονος ᾀκεία.   515

ΚΛΥΤΑΙΜΗΣΤΡΑ

ἀνειμένη μέν, ὡς ἔοικας, αὖ στρέφῃ.
οὐ γὰρ πάρεστ' Αἴγισθος, ὅς σ' ἐπεῖχ' ἀεὶ
μή τοι θυραίαν γ' οὖσαν αἰσχύνειν φίλους·
νῦν δ' ὡς ἄπεστ' ἐκεῖνος, οὐδὲν ἐντρέπῃ
ἐμοῦ γε· καίτοι πολλὰ πρὸς πολλούς με δὴ   520
ἐξεῖπας ὡς θρασεῖα καὶ πέρα δίκης
ἄρχω, καθυβρίζουσα καὶ σὲ καὶ τὰ σά.
ἐγὼ δ' ὕβριν μὲν οὐκ ἔχω, κακῶς δέ σε
λέγω κακῶς κλύουσα πρὸς σέθεν θαμά.
πατὴρ γάρ, οὐδὲν ἄλλο, σοὶ πρόσχημ' ἀεί,   525
ὡς ἐξ ἐμοῦ τέθνηκεν. ἐξ ἐμοῦ· καλῶς

506 αἰανὴς LᵃᶜKᵖᶜ: -ὴ vel -ῇ LᵖᶜKᵃᶜ et cett.   510 παγχρύσων] -έων Hermann   511 δυστάνοις] -οισιν T   ᾀκείαις scripsi: αἰκείαις Kaibel: αἰκίαις codd.   512 ἐκριφθείς LˡˢrAXrZrCHNZc: ἐκριφείς LKDᵖᶜXsOPVt et Suidas iv. 219.8: ἐκτριφθείς Reiske   513 τί R, coni. Hermann: τις cett.   514 ἔλιπεν rDᵍˡCHOP: διέλιπεν ΣL: ἔλειπεν LKaNVZct   οἴκου] οἴκους LᵃᶜROˣVᵃᶜt (verum Tˢ), fort. GᵃᶜCᵃᶜ   515 πολύπονος] πολυπά-μονας Bergk (πολυπήμονας iam Bothe) e ΣL (τοὺς πολυκτήμονας δόμους) ᾀκεία scripsi: αἰκεία Kaibel: αἰκία codd.   516 στρέφῃ] τρέφη(ι) LΛOᵖᶜPᵃᶜ, Eustathius 168.37, Suidae i. 213.15 cod. Mᵃᶜ: ἐκτρέφῃ Suidae codd. cett. (om. αὖ Suidae codd. AF)   517 σ'] om. LᵃᶜPVᵃᶜ   ἐπεῖχ' ἀεὶ] ἐπεῖχεν ἂν Nauck   518 θυραίαν] -αῖον fort. Xsᵃᶜ, coni. Blomfield   521 θρασεῖα] τραχεῖα Morstadt   522 punctum post ἄρχω om. Brunck   525 σοὶ] τοι Lᵃᶜ (verum Lˡᵖᶜ)

ἔξοιδα· τῶνδ᾽ ἄρνησις οὐκ ἔνεστί μοι.
ἡ γὰρ Δίκη νιν εἷλεν, οὐκ ἐγὼ μόνη,
ᾗ χρῆν σ᾽ ἀρήγειν, εἰ φρονοῦσ᾽ ἐτύγχανες.
ἐπεὶ πατὴρ οὗτος σός, ὃν θρηνεῖς ἀεί,   530
τὴν σὴν ὅμαιμον μοῦνος Ἑλλήνων ἔτλη
θῦσαι θεοῖσιν, οὐκ ἴσον καμὼν ἐμοὶ
λύπης, ὅτ᾽ ἔσπειρ᾽, ὥσπερ ἡ τίκτουσ᾽ ἐγώ.
εἶέν· δίδαξον δή με <τοῦτο>· τοῦ χάριν
ἔθυσεν αὐτήν; πότερον Ἀργείων ἐρεῖς;   535
ἀλλ᾽ οὐ μετῆν αὐτοῖσι τήν γ᾽ ἐμὴν κτανεῖν.
ἀλλ᾽ ἀντ᾽ ἀδελφοῦ δῆτα Μενέλεω κτανὼν
τἄμ᾽ οὐκ ἔμελλε τῶνδέ μοι δώσειν δίκην;
πότερον ἐκείνῳ παῖδες οὐκ ἦσαν διπλοῖ,
οὓς τῆσδε μᾶλλον εἰκὸς ἦν θνήσκειν, πατρὸς   540
καὶ μητρὸς ὄντας, ἧς ὁ πλοῦς ὅδ᾽ ἦν χάριν;
ἢ τῶν ἐμῶν Ἅιδης τιν᾽ ἵμερον τέκνων
ἢ τῶν ἐκείνης ἔσχε δαίσασθαι πλέον;
ἢ τῷ πανώλει πατρὶ τῶν μὲν ἐξ ἐμοῦ
παίδων πόθος παρεῖτο, Μενέλεω δ᾽ ἐνῆν;   545
οὐ ταῦτ᾽ ἀβούλου καὶ κακοῦ γνώμην πατρός;
δοκῶ μέν, εἰ καὶ σῆς δίχα γνώμης λέγω.
φαίη δ᾽ ἂν ἡ θανοῦσά γ᾽, εἰ φωνὴν λάβοι.
ἐγὼ μὲν οὖν οὐκ εἰμὶ τοῖς πεπραγμένοις
δύσθυμος· εἰ δὲ σοὶ δοκῶ φρονεῖν κακῶς,   550
γνώμην δικαίαν σχοῦσα τοὺς πέλας ψέγε.
Ηλ.   ἐρεῖς μὲν οὐχὶ νῦν γέ μ᾽ ὡς ἄρξασά τι
λυπηρὸν εἶτα σοῦ τάδ᾽ ἐξήκουσ᾽ ὕπο·

---

528 ante hunc versum lacunam statuit West   ἡ γὰρ] ἀλλ᾽ ἡ Schenkl:
τί γάρ; Schmidt   εἷλεν οὐκ L^{ac}**a**: εἷλε κοὐκ cett.   530 οὗτος σός]
inverso ordine Erfurdt   531 Ἑλλήνων] Ἀργείων P   533 τίκτουσ᾽]
τεκοῦσ᾽ Zct   534 εἶέν fort. L: εἶεν cett.   δή **a**Zct: δέ **lr**CNPV, fort.
O   τοῦτο· τοῦ χάριν Schmalfeld: τοῦ χάριν τίνος L^s (partim erasum),
L^{pc}**Kra**H^{gl}V^x: τοῦ χάριν τίνων L^{ac}D^mCNOPV^xZct   536 post μετῆν add.
γ᾽ **r**   540 πατρὸς] πάρος Nauck, versu 541 deleto   541 ἧς] οἷν Herw-
erden   542 ἢ] ἦ Brunck   Ἅιδης τιν᾽ ἵμερον] Ἅιδην τις ἵμερος Blaydes
543 δαίσασθαι] λήσασθαι Schmidt   548 δ᾽] τ᾽ Morstadt

ἀλλ᾿ ἦν ἐφῇς μοι, τοῦ τεθνηκότος θ᾿ ὕπερ
λέξαιμ᾿ ἂν ὀρθῶς τῆς κασιγνήτης θ᾿ ὁμοῦ.   555
Κλ.   καὶ μὴν ἐφίημ᾿· εἰ δέ μ᾿ ὧδ᾿ ἀεὶ λόγους
ἐξῆρχες, οὐκ ἂν ἦσθα λυπηρὰ κλύειν.
Ηλ.   καὶ δὴ λέγω σοι. πατέρα φῂς κτεῖναι. τίς ἂν
τούτου λόγος γένοιτ᾿ ἂν αἰσχίων ἔτι,
εἴτ᾿ οὖν δικαίως εἴτε μή; λέξω δέ σοι,   560
ὡς οὐ δίκῃ γ᾿ ἔκτεινας, ἀλλά σ᾿ ἔσπασεν
πειθὼ κακοῦ πρὸς ἀνδρός, ᾧ τανῦν ξύνει.
ἐροῦ δὲ τὴν κυναγὸν Ἄρτεμιν τίνος
ποινὰς τὰ πολλὰ πνεύματ᾿ ἔσχ᾿ ἐν Αὐλίδι·
ἢ ᾿γὼ φράσω· κείνης γὰρ οὐ θέμις μαθεῖν.   565
πατήρ ποθ᾿ οὑμός, ὡς ἐγὼ κλύω, θεᾶς
παίζων κατ᾿ ἄλσος ἐξεκίνησεν ποδοῖν
στικτὸν κεράστην ἔλαφον, οὗ κατὰ σφαγὰς
ἐκκομπάσας ἔπος τι τυγχάνει βαλών.
κἀκ τοῦδε μηνίσασα Λητῴα κόρη   570
κατεῖχ᾿ Ἀχαιούς, ἕως πατὴρ ἀντίσταθμον
τοῦ θηρὸς ἐκθύσειε τὴν αὑτοῦ κόρην.
ὧδ᾿ ἦν τὰ κείνης θύματ᾿· οὐ γὰρ ἦν λύσις
ἄλλη στρατῷ πρὸς οἶκον οὐδ᾿ εἰς Ἴλιον.
ἀνθ᾿ ὧν βιασθεὶς πολλά τ᾿ ἀντιβὰς μόλις   575
ἔθυσεν αὐτήν, οὐχὶ Μενέλεω χάριν.
εἰ δ᾿ οὖν, ἐρῶ γὰρ καὶ τὸ σόν, κεῖνον θέλων
ἐπωφελῆσαι ταῦτ᾿ ἔδρα, τούτου θανεῖν
χρῆν αὐτὸν οὕνεκ᾿ ἐκ σέθεν; ποίῳ νόμῳ;
ὅρα τιθεῖσα τόνδε τὸν νόμον βροτοῖς   580
μὴ πῆμα σαυτῇ καὶ μετάγνοιαν τιθῇς.

554 θ᾿ XrZrSZgt: γ᾿ ADXsJZf: om. lrpZc   555 κασιγνήτης] –ου XsCHVˣ
556 λόγους LᵃᶜΛ: –οις cett.   560 λέξῳ] δείξω Morstadt   561 γ᾿] σφ᾿
Blaydes   ἔσπασεν LADXsZr: –σε rXrpZct   564 ποινὰς LᵃᶜKR, coni.
Musgrave: –ᾶς GCNOPVZc: –ῆς LᵖᶜaHt   πολλὰ πνεύματ᾿] πλοῖα πνεύ-
ματ᾿ Housman: πλοῖ᾿ ἀπνεύματ᾿ Fröhlich   ἐν] ἐπ᾿ Wolff   567 ποδοῖν
codd. et Suidas ii. 305.6: ποδὶ O, coni. Herwerden   569 τι] om.
LGADOVZcᵃᶜ   571 ἕως Fröhlich: ὡς codd.   572 αὑτοῦ XsH¹ᵖᶜPˣ:
αὐτ– cett. (etiam Hᵃᶜ)   575 τ᾿ ἀντιβὰς Walter: κἀντιβὰς codd.   581
τίθη(ι)ς vel τιθῇ(ι)ς codd. et Suidas iii. 534.25: κτίσῃς Dawe

49

εἰ γὰρ κτενοῦμεν ἄλλον ἀντ' ἄλλου, σύ τοι
πρώτη θάνοις ἄν, εἰ δίκης γε τυγχάνοις.
ἀλλ' εἰσόρα μὴ σκῆψιν οὐκ οὖσαν τίθης.
εἰ γὰρ θέλεις, δίδαξον ἀνθ' ὅτου τανῦν   585
αἴσχιστα πάντων ἔργα δρῶσα τυγχάνεις,
ἥτις ξυνεύδεις τῷ παλαμναίῳ, μεθ' οὗ
πατέρα τὸν ἀμὸν πρόσθεν ἐξαπώλεσας,
καὶ παιδοποιεῖς, τοὺς δὲ πρόσθεν εὐσεβεῖς
κἀξ εὐσεβῶν βλαστόντας ἐκβαλοῦσ' ἔχεις.   590
πῶς ταῦτ' ἐπαινέσαιμ' ἄν; ἢ καὶ ταῦτ' ἐρεῖς
ὡς τῆς θυγατρὸς ἀντίποινα λαμβάνεις;
αἰσχρῶς δ', ἐάν περ καὶ λέγῃς. οὐ γὰρ καλὸν
ἐχθροῖς γαμεῖσθαι τῆς θυγατρὸς οὕνεκα.
ἀλλ' οὐ γὰρ οὐδὲ νουθετεῖν ἔξεστί σε,   595
ἢ πᾶσαν ἵης γλῶσσαν ὡς τὴν μητέρα
κακοστομοῦμεν. καί σ' ἔγωγε δεσπότιν
ἢ μητέρ' οὐκ ἔλασσον εἰς ἡμᾶς νέμω,
ἢ ζῶ βίον μοχθηρόν, ἔκ τε σοῦ κακοῖς
πολλοῖς ἀεὶ ξυνοῦσα τοῦ τε συννόμου.   600
ὁ δ' ἄλλος ἔξω, χεῖρα σὴν μόλις φυγών,
τλήμων Ὀρέστης δυστυχῆ τρίβει βίον·
ὃν πολλὰ δή μέ σοι τρέφειν μιάστορα
ἐπῃτιάσω· καὶ τόδ', εἴπερ ἔσθενον,
ἔδρων ἄν, εὖ τοῦτ' ἴσθι. τοῦδέ γ' οὕνεκα   605
κήρυσσέ μ' εἰς ἅπαντας, εἴτε χρῇς κακὴν
εἴτε στόμαργον εἴτ' ἀναιδείας πλέαν.

583 τυγχάνοις Xs, coni. Turnebus: –εις cett. (etiam Λ), nisi quod –ης
R   584–6 om. LᵃᶜΛ: add. Lʳ   588 ἀμὸν XsZft: ἀμὸν ADXrZrZg: ἐμὸν
lrXrˢpZc   590 βλαστόντας aN: βλαστῶντας lrCHOPVZct   591
ἐπαινέσαιμ' ἄν codd. (etiam Λ): –έσωμεν Lʸᵖ   ἢ] ἦ Brunck   ταῦτ' ἐρεῖς
Seager: τοῦτ' ἐρεῖς codd.   592 λαμβάνεις aHOPVZct: λαμβάνει Lʳ supra
rasuram: τυγχάνει KrCN: τυγχάνει vel λαγχάνει Λ: L in lin. non legitur   593–4 del. Blaydes   593 δ] γ' C, coni. Hartung: om. G   οὐ]
ποῦ . . . ; Dobree   594 οὕνεκα] εἵνεκα Zr: ἕνεκα OPV, fort. Aᵃᶜ   595
σε GADᵖᶜXsZrT¹ˢ: σοι LᵃᶜKRXrpZct   596 ἵης XrOVt: ἵεις lraCHNPZc
601 ἄλλος] ἀμὸς Wex   606 χρῇς Wunder: χρὴ codd.

εἰ γὰρ πέφυκα τῶνδε τῶν ἔργων ἴδρις,
σχεδόν τι τὴν σὴν οὐ καταισχύνω φύσιν.

Χο. ὁρῶ μένος πνέουσαν· εἰ δὲ σὺν δίκῃ   610
ξύνεστι, τοῦδε φροντίδ᾽ οὐκέτ᾽ εἰσορῶ.

Κλ. ποίας δ᾽ ἐμοὶ δεῖ πρός γε τήνδε φροντίδος,
ἥτις τοιαῦτα τὴν τεκοῦσαν ὕβρισεν,
καὶ ταῦτα τηλικοῦτος; ἆρά σοι δοκεῖ
χωρεῖν ἂν ἐς πᾶν ἔργον αἰσχύνης ἄτερ;   615

Ηλ. εὖ νυν ἐπίστω τῶνδέ μ᾽ αἰσχύνην ἔχειν,
κεἰ μὴ δοκῶ σοι· μανθάνω δ᾽ ὁθούνεκα
ἔξωρα πράσσω κοὐκ ἐμοὶ προσεικότα.
ἀλλ᾽ ἡ γὰρ ἐκ σοῦ δυσμένεια καὶ τὰ σὰ
ἔργ᾽ ἐξαναγκάζει με ταῦτα δρᾶν βίᾳ·   620
αἰσχροῖς γὰρ αἰσχρὰ πράγματ᾽ ἐκδιδάσκεται.

Κλ. ὦ θρέμμ᾽ ἀναιδές, ἦ σ᾽ ἐγὼ καὶ τἄμ᾽ ἔπη
καὶ τἄργα τἀμὰ πόλλ᾽ ἄγαν λέγειν ποεῖ.

Ηλ. σύ τοι λέγεις νιν, οὐκ ἐγώ. σὺ γὰρ ποεῖς
τοὔργον· τὰ δ᾽ ἔργα τοὺς λόγους εὑρίσκεται.   625

Κλ. ἀλλ᾽ οὐ μὰ τὴν δέσποιναν Ἄρτεμιν θράσους
τοῦδ᾽ οὐκ ἀλύξεις, εὖτ᾽ ἂν Αἴγισθος μόλῃ.

Ηλ. ὁρᾷς; πρὸς ὀργὴν ἐκφέρῃ, παρεῖσά μοι
λέγειν ἃ χρῄζοιμ᾽, οὐδ᾽ ἐπίστασαι κλύειν.

Κλ. οὔκουν ἐάσεις οὐδ᾽ ὑπ᾽ εὐφήμου βοῆς   630
θῦσαί μ᾽, ἐπειδὴ σοί γ᾽ ἐφῆκα πᾶν λέγειν;

Ηλ. ἐῶ, κελεύω, θῦε, μηδ᾽ ἐπαιτιῶ
τοὐμὸν στόμ᾽· ὡς οὐκ ἂν πέρα λέξαιμ᾽ ἔτι.

Κλ. ἔπαιρε δὴ σὺ θύμαθ᾽ ἡ παροῦσά μοι
πάγκαρπ᾽, ἄνακτι τῷδ᾽ ὅπως λυτηρίους   635

608 ἔργων] κακῶν C¹ᵖᶜOPVS et Eustathius 1969.18: λόγων Suidas ii.
611.17   610 ante hunc versum lacunam statuit Lloyd-Jones   611 τοῦδε
φροντίδ᾽] τῆσδε φροντίς Dawe   612 δ᾽ ἐμοὶ Nauck post Monk: δέ μοι
codd.   614 ἆρα lCNOPVᵃᶜZc: ἆρ᾽ οὐ LᵖᶜraFᵖᶜHVᵖᶜt   618 προσεικότα DᵖᶜXrXsZrCHNVt: –ηκότα lrFᵖᶜOPZc et Suidae ii. 321.16 codd.
plerique: –ήκοντα AFᵃᶜ, Suidae cod. G, Gnom.   623 ποεῖ LᵖᶜKᵖᶜrDᵖᶜFᵖᶜ,
fort. Zcᵃᶜ: ποιεῖ LᵃᶜKᵃᶜZc¹ᵖᶜ et cett.   624 ποεῖς LKRDᵖᶜHVZcᵃᶜ: ποιεῖς
Zc¹ᵖᶜ et cett.   628 παρεῖσά μοι H: μεθεῖσά μοι cett.: μεθεῖσά με Lloyd-Jones
630 ὑπ᾽] ἐπ᾽ AN

εὐχὰς ἀνάσχω δειμάτων, ἃ νῦν ἔχω.
κλύοις ἂν ἤδη, Φοῖβε προστατήριε,
κεκρυμμένην μου βάξιν. οὐ γὰρ ἐν φίλοις
ὁ μῦθος, οὐδὲ πᾶν ἀναπτύξαι πρέπει
πρὸς φῶς παρούσης τῆσδε πλησίας ἐμοί,   640
μὴ σὺν φθόνῳ τε καὶ πολυγλώσσῳ βοῇ
σπείρῃ ματαίαν βάξιν εἰς πᾶσαν πόλιν.
ἀλλ' ὧδ' ἄκουε· τῇδε γὰρ κἀγὼ φράσω.
ἃ γὰρ προσεῖδον νυκτὶ τῇδε φάσματα
δισσῶν ὀνείρων, ταῦτά μοι, Λύκει' ἄναξ,   645
εἰ μὲν πέφηνεν ἐσθλά, δὸς τελεσφόρα,
εἰ δ' ἐχθρά, τοῖς ἐχθροῖσιν ἔμπαλιν μέθες·
καὶ μή με πλούτου τοῦ παρόντος εἴ τινες
δόλοισι βουλεύουσιν ἐκβαλεῖν, ἐφῇς,
ἀλλ' ὧδέ μ' αἰεὶ ζῶσαν ἀβλαβεῖ βίῳ   650
δόμους Ἀτρειδῶν σκῆπτρά τ' ἀμφέπειν τάδε,
φίλοισί τε ξυνοῦσαν οἷς ξύνειμι νῦν,
εὐημεροῦσαν καὶ τέκνοις ὅσων ἐμοὶ
δύσνοια μὴ πρόσεστιν ἢ λύπη πικρά.
ταῦτ', ὦ Λύκει' Ἄπολλον, ἵλεως κλυὼν   655
δὸς πᾶσιν ἡμῖν ὥσπερ ἐξαιτούμεθα.
τὰ δ' ἄλλα πάντα καὶ σιωπώσης ἐμοῦ
ἐπαξιῶ σε δαίμον' ὄντ' ἐξειδέναι·
τοὺς ἐκ Διὸς γὰρ εἰκός ἐστι πάνθ' ὁρᾶν.

Πα.   ξέναι γυναῖκες, πῶς ἂν εἰδείην σαφῶς   660
      εἰ τοῦ τυράννου δώματ' Αἰγίσθου τάδε;
Χο.   τάδ' ἐστίν, ὦ ξέν'· αὐτὸς ἤκασας καλῶς.

636 ἃ   LKD^gl Xr^gl **pt**: ὧν **ra**Zc^gl   642 εἰς   LKrDCFNZc: ἐς
AXrXsZrHOPVt   644 νυκτὶ τῇδε] inverso ordine ZrHOPV: τῇ νυκτὶ D
646–7 εἰ . . . εἴ] ἦ . . . ἦ Wecklein   646 πέφηνεν] πέφυκεν CZc, ΣLO
647 ἐχθρά] αἰσχρά CN   649 post ἐκβαλεῖν add. μ' OVZg   650
ἀβλαβεῖ βίῳ] –ῇ –ον Arnold   653 εὐημεροῦσαν] –σα H, coni. Erfurdt:
–σιν L^s   τέκνοις Xr^rs, coni. Fröhlich: τέκνων cett.   ὅσων] ὅσοις Xr^rs
655 κλυὼν West: κλύων codd.   656 πᾶσιν codd. et Suidas ii. 448.24:
πρᾶξιν Herwerden: αἶσι' Mähly   659 del. Jahn   πάνθ'] πάνθ' L^ac KV,
unde πᾶν Wecklein   662 ἤκασας Brunck: εἴκασας codd.

Πα. ἦ καὶ δάμαρτα τήνδ᾽ ἐπεικάζων κυρῶ
κείνου; πρέπει γὰρ ὡς τύραννος εἰσορᾶν.
Χο. μάλιστα πάντων· ἥδε σοι κείνη πάρα.   665
Πα. ὦ χαῖρ᾽, ἄνασσα. σοὶ φέρων ἥκω λόγους
ἡδεῖς φίλου παρ᾽ ἀνδρὸς Αἰγίσθῳ θ᾽ ὁμοῦ.
Κλ. ἐδεξάμην τὸ ῥηθέν· εἰδέναι δέ σου
πρώτιστα χρῄζω τίς σ᾽ ἀπέστειλεν βροτῶν.
Πα. Φανοτεὺς ὁ Φωκεύς, πρᾶγμα πορσύνων μέγα.   670
Κλ. τὸ ποῖον, ὦ ξέν᾽; εἰπέ. παρὰ φίλου γὰρ ὢν
ἀνδρός, σάφ᾽ οἶδα, προσφιλεῖς λέξεις λόγους.
Πα. τέθνηκ᾽ Ὀρέστης· ἐν βραχεῖ ξυνθεὶς λέγω.
Ηλ. οἲ ᾽γὼ τάλαιν᾽, ὄλωλα τῇδ᾽ ἐν ἡμέρᾳ.
Κλ. τί φῇς, τί φῇς, ὦ ξεῖνε; μὴ ταύτης κλύε.   675
Πα. θανόντ᾽ Ὀρέστην νῦν τε καὶ πάλαι λέγω.
Ηλ. ἀπωλόμην δύστηνος, οὐδέν εἰμ᾽ ἔτι.
Κλ. σὺ μὲν τὰ σαυτῆς πρᾶσσ᾽, ἐμοὶ δὲ σύ, ξένε,
τἀληθὲς εἰπέ, τῷ τρόπῳ διόλλυται;
Πα. κἀπεμπόμην πρὸς ταῦτα καὶ τὸ πᾶν φράσω.   680
κεῖνος γὰρ ἐλθὼν ἐς τὸ κλεινὸν Ἑλλάδος
πρόσχημ᾽ ἀγῶνος Δελφικῶν ἄθλων χάριν,
ὅτ᾽ ᾔσθετ᾽ ἀνδρὸς ὀρθίῳ κηρύγματι
δρόμον προκηρύξαντος, οὗ πρώτη κρίσις,
εἰσῆλθε λαμπρός, πᾶσι τοῖς ἐκεῖ σέβας·   685
δρόμου δ᾽ ἰσώσας τῇ φύσει τὰ τέρματα
νίκης ἔχων ἐξῆλθε πάντιμον γέρας.

669 ἀπέστειλεν L^{ac}KO: -λε L^{pc} et cett.   670 πορσύνων] –ειν Reiske
671 τὸ ποῖον] ποῖον HV: ὁποῖον DXs   ξέν᾽] ξεῖν᾽ CNZf   673
λέγω LG^sADXrCFNV^xZct: λόγῳ K^{ac}rXsZrHOPV^x   676 πάλαι λέγω
LrFHNVt: πάλιν λέγω KC^{is}OP: τότ᾽ ἐννέπω L^{yp}aZcT^{yp}   679
διόλλυται] διώλλυτο N^{1pc}   681 κλεινὸν] κοινὸν Thomas Magister
286.4 Ritschl   683 ὀρθίῳ κηρύγματι Earle: ὀρθίων κηρυγμάτων codd.:
ὀρθίων γηρυμάτων Herwerden   684 δρόμου rXrCFHN^{ac}PZct: –ου
LKADXsZrOV   προκηρύξαντος] –ύσσοντος Blaydes   685 λαμπρός]
–όν r, fort. Zc^{ac}   686 δρόμου] –ῳ Suidas ii. 141.24   τέρματα codd. et
Suidae codd. AF: πράγματα Suidae codd. cett.   δρόμον . . . τά τ᾽ ἔργματα
Pearson (τότ᾽ ἔργματα iam Wolff)

χὤπως μὲν ἐν παυροῖσι πολλά σοι λέγω,
οὐκ οἶδα τοιοῦδ᾿ ἀνδρὸς ἔργα καὶ κράτη·
ἓν δ᾿ ἴσθ᾿· ὅσων γὰρ εἰσεκήρυξαν βραβῆς,   690
[δρόμων διαύλων πένταθλ᾿ ἃ νομίζεται,]
τούτων ἐνεγκὼν πάντα τἀπινίκια
ὠλβίζετ᾿, Ἀργεῖος μὲν ἀνακαλούμενος,
ὄνομα δ᾿ Ὀρέστης, τοῦ τὸ κλεινὸν Ἑλλάδος
Ἀγαμέμνονος στράτευμ᾿ ἀγείραντός ποτε.   695
καὶ ταῦτα μὲν τοιαῦθ᾿· ὅταν δέ τις θεῶν
βλάπτῃ, δύναιτ᾿ ἂν οὐδ᾿ ἂν ἰσχύων φυγεῖν.
κεῖνος γὰρ ἄλλης ἡμέρας, ὅθ᾿ ἱππικῶν
ἦν ἡλίου τέλλοντος ὠκύπους ἀγών,
εἰσῆλθε πολλῶν ἁρματηλατῶν μέτα.   700
εἷς ἦν Ἀχαιός, εἷς ἀπὸ Σπάρτης, δύο
Λίβυες ζυγωτῶν ἁρμάτων ἐπιστάται·
κἀκεῖνος ἐν τούτοισι Θεσσαλὰς ἔχων
ἵππους, ὁ πέμπτος· ἕκτος ἐξ Αἰτωλίας
ξανθαῖσι πώλοις· ἕβδομος Μάγνης ἀνήρ·   705
ὁ δ᾿ ὄγδοος λεύκιππος, Αἰνιὰν γένος·
ἔνατος Ἀθηνῶν τῶν θεοδμήτων ἄπο·
Βοιωτὸς ἄλλος, δέκατον ἐκπληρῶν ὄχον.
στάντες δ᾿ ὅθ᾿ αὐτοὺς οἱ τεταγμένοι βραβῆς

688 παύροισι πολλά Bergk et Nauck: πολλοῖσι παῦρα codd.   689
τοιοῦδ᾿] τοιάδ᾿ Zr   ἔργα καὶ] ἔργ᾿ οὐδὲ ZrT^{υρ}   690 ὅσων] ὅσον K^{ac}
ut vid. et Suidas i. 492.10   βραβῆς LZc^{1s}: –εῖς cett. et Suidas   691 del.
Lachmann (διαύλων . . . τούτων del. Nauck): habent codd. et Suidas i. 492.11
πένταθλ᾿] πεντάεθλ᾿ A^{pc}DXrZrt   692 τούτων] ἄθλων Tournier post Hermann   694 κλεινὸν] κοινὸν Schneidewin   697 δύναιτ᾿ codd. et Suidas
ii. 675.8, 699.11: δύναι᾿ Meineke   ἰσχύων] ὁ σθένων Heimsoeth   698
ἱππικῶν] –ὸς Blaydes   703 ἐν] ἦν Herwerden: ἐπὶ Nauck   ἔχων]
ἄγων ZrHt^{s}   705 ξανθαῖσι] –ῆσι Zc: –έσι GOV   706 λεύκιππος]
tamquam nomen proprium praebent rDXrXs, ΣL   Αἰνιὰν P et
Eustathius 83.3, 335.20, 524.31: –ειὰν vel –ειᾶν cett. (nisi quod –ειῶν O)
707 post ἔνατος add. δ᾿ HOVZgT   709 ὅθ᾿ αὐτοὺς L^{pc}aCHNOZcT:
ὅτ᾿ αὐτοὺς L^{ac}KrFPV: ὅθεν αὐτοὺς Wc, unde ὅθεν σφιν Diggle:
ἵν᾿ αὐτοὺς Nauck: ὅθι σφᾶς Kuiper post Wecklein   βραβῆς LZc^{s}: –εῖς cett.
et Eustathius 419.3

κλήροις ἔπηλαν καὶ κατέστησαν δίφρους,   710
χαλκῆς ὑπαὶ σάλπιγγος ᾖξαν· οἳ δ᾽ ἅμα
ἵπποις ὁμοκλήσαντες ἡνίας χεροῖν
ἔσεισαν· ἐν δὲ πᾶς ἐμεστώθη δρόμος
κτύπου κροτητῶν ἁρμάτων· κόνις δ᾽ ἄνω
φορεῖθ᾽· ὁμοῦ δὲ πάντες ἀναμεμειγμένοι   715
φείδοντο κέντρων οὐδέν, ὡς ὑπερβάλοι
χνόας τις ἄλλων καὶ φρυάγμαθ᾽ ἱππικά.
ὁμοῦ γὰρ ἀμφὶ νῶτα καὶ τροχῶν βάσεις
ἤφριζον, εἰσέβαλλον ἱππικαὶ πνοαί.
κεῖνος δ᾽ ὑπ᾽ αὐτὴν ἐσχάτην στήλην ἔχων   720
ἔχριμπτ᾽ ἀεὶ σύριγγα, δεξιὸν δ᾽ ἀνεὶς
σειραῖον ἵππον εἶργε τὸν προσκείμενον.
καὶ πρὶν μὲν ὀρθοὶ πάντες ἔστασαν δίφροις·
ἔπειτα δ᾽ Αἰνιᾶνος ἀνδρὸς ἄστομοι
πῶλοι βίᾳ φέρουσιν, ἐκ δ᾽ ὑποστροφῆς   725
τελοῦντος ἕκτον ἕβδομόν τ᾽ ἤδη δρόμον
μέτωπα συμπαίουσι Βαρκαίοις ὄχοις·
κἀντεῦθεν ἄλλος ἄλλον ἐξ ἑνὸς κακοῦ
ἔθραυε κἀνέπιπτε, πᾶν δ᾽ ἐπίμπλατο
ναυαγίων Κρισαῖον ἱππικῶν πέδον.   730
γνοὺς δ᾽ οὑξ Ἀθηνῶν δεινὸς ἡνιοστρόφος
ἔξω παρασπᾷ κἀνοκωχεύει παρεὶς

710 κλήροις codd. plerique et Eustathius: –ους C (verum C¹ˢ), coni.
Wunder   711 οἳ vel οἱ codd.: οἳ scripsi   713 ἐν LKrACFNOPVZcT: ἐκ
GˢDXrXsZrH   715 ἀναμεμειγμένοι Kaibel: ἀναμεμιγμένοι codd.   717
ἄλλων Musgrave: αὐτῶν codd.: αὐτὸς Blaydes: ἰτύων Dawe   718–22 post
740 traiecit Dawe (720–2 iam Piccolomini)   718 γὰρ] δ᾽ ἄρ᾽ F   720
ἐσχάτην codd. et Suidas iv. 432.4, 479.15: ἔσχατος Dobree   ἔχων codd.
et Suidas: ὄχων Fröhlich   721 ἔχριμπτ᾽ L¹ˢKADVZcT, Suidae iv. 479.15
codd. plerique: ἔχριπτ᾽ LGHP: alii alia   δ᾽] om. LᵃᶜCP: τ᾽ T   722
προσκείμενον LKRDXsZrCHNZcT: προκ– GAXrFOPV   723 δίφροις
KCᵖᶜHPV: –οι LraCᵃᶜNOT: –ῳ Kaibel   724 Αἰνιᾶνος P, v.l. ap. Plut.
Mor. 521 c, Eustathius 335.20: –ειᾶνος cett. (nisi quod –ειώνος O)   725
φέρουσιν] φοροῦσιν Plut. loc. cit.: ᾽κφέρουσιν Herwerden   726 τελοῦντος
Musgrave: –τες codd.   730 Κρισαῖον PS: –σσ– cett.   732 παρασπᾷ]
περισπᾷ Suidas ii. 31.10–11   κἀνοκωχεύει Cobet: κἀνα– codd. et Suidas

55

κλύδων' ἔφιππον ἐν μέσῳ κυκώμενον.
ἤλαυνε δ' ἔσχατος μέν, ὑστέρας ἔχων
πώλους, Ὀρέστης, τῷ τέλει πίστιν φέρων·   735
ὃ δ' ὡς ὁρᾷ μόνον νιν ἐλλελειμμένον,
ὀξὺν δι' ὤτων κέλαδον ἐνσείσας θοαῖς
πώλοις διώκει, κἀξισώσαντε ζυγὰ
ἠλαυνέτην, τότ' ἄλλος, ἄλλοθ' ἅτερος
κάρα προβάλλων ἱππικῶν ὀχημάτων.   740
καὶ τοὺς μὲν ἄλλους πάντας ἀσφαλὴς δρόμους
ὠρθοῦθ' ὁ τλήμων ὀρθὸς ἐξ ὀρθῶν δίφρων·
ἔπειτα τανύων ἡνίαν ἀριστερὰν
κάμπτοντος ἵππου λανθάνει στήλην ἄκραν
παίσας· ἔθραυσε δ' ἄξονος μέσας χνόας,   745
κἀξ ἀντύγων ὤλισθε· σὺν δ' ἑλίσσεται
τμητοῖς ἱμᾶσι· τοῦ δὲ πίπτοντος πέδοι
πῶλοι διεσπάρησαν ἐς μέσον δρόμον.
στρατὸς δ' ὅπως ὁρᾷ νιν ἐκπεπτωκότα
δίφρων, ἀνωτότυξε τὸν νεανίαν,   750
οἷ' ἔργα δράσας οἷα λαγχάνει κακά,
φορούμενος πρὸς οὖδας, ἄλλοτ' οὐρανῷ
σκέλη προφαίνων, ἔστε νιν διφρηλάται,
μόλις κατασχεθόντες ἱππικὸν δρόμον,
ἔλυσαν αἱματηρόν, ὥστε μηδένα   755
γνῶναι φίλων ἰδόντ' ἂν ἄθλιον δέμας.
καί νιν πυρᾷ κέαντες εὐθὺς ἐν βραχεῖ

734 post ὑστέρας add. δ' L^{pc}GaHPZfT   736 ὃ (vel ὁ) δ' ὡς
L^{pc}K^{pc}**ap**Zc^{1pc}T: ὅπως δ' L^{ac}K^{ac}**r**   ἐλλελειμμένον] ἐκλ– **r**XsC: ἐνλ–
LKF   738 κἀξισώσαντε LKCF^{ac}P: –ες fere cett. (etiam K^{1s}C^{1s}F^{pc})
739 τότ' ἄλλος] τόθ' ἄλλος Blaydes: τότ' αὐτός Nauck   741 ἀσφαλὴς
Reiske: –εῖς codd.: –ῶς Blaydes   743 τανύων Toepfer: λύων codd.: δ'
ἕλκων Fröhlich: ἀνέλκων Arndt   746 ὤλισθε] –εν LKHOV, quo recepto ἐν
pro σὺν coni. Nauck   747 πέδοι Dindorf: πέδῳ codd.   750 ἀνωτότυξε
Herwerden: ἀνωλόλυξε codd. et Eustathius 643.32   751 λαγχάνει codd.
plerique (etiam Λ): τυγχάνει L^{ryp}KD^{gl}Xs^{gl}C   754 κατασχεθόντες N^{ac},
coni. Elmsley: –έθεντες **r**HZf: –έθοντες fere cett.   ἱππικὸν δρόμον] –ῶν
–ων **t**, C^{1gl}   755 μηδένα] μηδέν' ἂν Tournier   757 κέαντες Brunck:
καί– OV: κεί– PT: κη(ι)– cett. (nisi quod κήοντες G)

ΣΟΦΟΚΛΕΟΥΣ ΗΛΕΚΤΡΑ

χαλκῷ μέγιστον σῶμα δειλαίας σποδοῦ
φέρουσιν ἄνδρες Φωκέων τεταγμένοι,
ὅπως πατρῴας τύμβον ἐκλάχοι χθονός.   760
τοιαῦτά σοι ταῦτ᾽ ἐστίν, ὡς μὲν ἐν λόγοις
ἀλγεινά, τοῖς δ᾽ ἰδοῦσιν, οἵπερ εἴδομεν,
μέγιστα πάντων ὧν ὄπωπ᾽ ἐγὼ κακῶν.
Χο. φεῦ φεῦ· τὸ πᾶν δὴ δεσπόταισι τοῖς πάλαι
πρόρριζον, ὡς ἔοικεν, ἔφθαρται γένος.   765
Κλ. ὦ Ζεῦ, τί ταῦτα, πότερον εὐτυχῆ λέγω,
ἢ δεινὰ μέν, κέρδη δέ; λυπηρῶς δ᾽ ἔχει,
εἰ τοῖς ἐμαυτῆς τὸν βίον σῴζω κακοῖς.
Πα. τί δ᾽ ὧδ᾽ ἀθυμεῖς, ὦ γύναι, τῷ νῦν λόγῳ;
Κλ. δεινὸν τὸ τίκτειν ἐστίν· οὐδὲ γὰρ κακῶς   770
πάσχοντι μῖσος ὧν τέκῃ προσγίγνεται.
Πα. μάτην ἄρ᾽ ἡμεῖς, ὡς ἔοικεν, ἥκομεν.
Κλ. οὔτοι μάτην γε. πῶς γὰρ ἂν μάτην λέγοις;
εἴ μοι θανόντος πίστ᾽ ἔχων τεκμήρια
προσῆλθες, ὅστις τῆς ἐμῆς ψυχῆς γεγώς,   775
μαστῶν ἀποστὰς καὶ τροφῆς ἐμῆς, φυγὰς
ἀπεξενοῦτο· καί μ᾽, ἐπεὶ τῆσδε χθονὸς
ἐξῆλθεν, οὐκέτ᾽ εἶδεν· ἐγκαλῶν δέ μοι
φόνους πατρῴους δείν᾽ ἐπηπείλει τελεῖν·
ὥστ᾽ οὔτε νυκτὸς ὕπνον οὔτ᾽ ἐξ ἡμέρας   780
ἐμὲ στεγάζειν ἡδύν, ἀλλ᾽ ὁ προστατῶν
χρόνος διῆγέ μ᾽ αἰὲν ὡς θανουμένην.
νῦν δ᾽ – ἡμέρᾳ γὰρ τῇδ᾽ ἀπηλλάγην φόβου
πρὸς τῆσδ᾽ ἐκείνου θ᾽· ἥδε γὰρ μείζων βλάβη

758 μέγιστον σῶμα] –ου –ατος LˢCˢNPˢ: quo recepto δειλὴν σποδὸν Wecklein, βαιὰν σποδὸν Nauck   δειλαίας σποδοῦ] –αν –ὸν NʳˢP²ˢ, coni. Neue:
Lˢ non legitur   760 ἐκλάχοι codd. plerique (etiam Λ): –ῃ JS, coni. Musgrave
761 λόγοις L¹ˢΛˢKRaCFNOPVZct: λόγῳ LrH   762 οἵπερ] ὥσπερ Δ,
coni. Hartung   767 δ] γ᾽ Fröhlich   768 τοῖς codd. et Suidas iii.
606.20: τῶν Seidler   769 τῷ νῦν lraCFHNZct: ποίῳ OPV   771 τέκῃ
aCFHOPV, Stob. Ecl. 4.24.20: τέκει lrZc: τέκοι Nt   781 προσ<σ>τατῶν
Meineke   783 ἀπηλλάγην KrN et Suidas iv. 233.20, fere C: –αγμαι
LADXrXsFHOPVZc: ἀνήλλαγμαι Λ

ξύνοικος ἦν μοι, τοὐμὸν ἐκπίνουσ᾽ ἀεὶ   785
ψυχῆς ἄκρατον αἷμα – νῦν δ᾽ ἔκηλά που
τῶν τῆσδ᾽ ἀπειλῶν οὕνεχ᾽ ἡμερεύσομεν.

Ηλ. οἴμοι τάλαινα· νῦν γὰρ οἰμῶξαι πάρα,
Ὀρέστα, τὴν σὴν ξυμφοράν, ὅθ᾽ ὧδ᾽ ἔχων
πρὸς τῆσδ᾽ ὑβρίζῃ μητρός. ἆρ᾽ ἔχει καλῶς;   790

Κλ. οὔτοι σύ· κεῖνος δ᾽ ὡς ἔχει καλῶς ἔχει.

Ηλ. ἄκουε, Νέμεσι τοῦ θανόντος ἀρτίως.

Κλ. ἤκουσεν ὧν δεῖ κἀπεκύρωσεν καλῶς.

Ηλ. ὕβριζε· νῦν γὰρ εὐτυχοῦσα τυγχάνεις.

Κλ. οὔκουν Ὀρέστης καὶ σὺ παύσετον τάδε;   795

Ηλ. πεπαύμεθ᾽ ἡμεῖς, οὐχ ὅπως σὲ παύσομεν.

Κλ. πολλῶν ἂν ἥκοις, ὦ ξέν᾽, ἄξιος τυχεῖν,
εἰ τήνδ᾽ ἔπαυσας τῆς πολυγλώσσου βοῆς.

Πα. οὐκοῦν ἀποστείχοιμ᾽ ἄν, εἰ τάδ᾽ εὖ κυρεῖ.

Κλ. ἥκιστ᾽· ἐπείπερ οὔτ᾽ ἐμοῦ κατάξι᾽ ἂν   800
πράξειας οὔτε τοῦ πορεύσαντος ξένου.
ἀλλ᾽ εἴσιθ᾽ εἴσω· τήνδε δ᾽ ἔκτοθεν βοᾶν
ἔα τά θ᾽ αὑτῆς καὶ τὰ τῶν φίλων κακά.

Ηλ. ἆρ᾽ ὕμιν ὡς ἀλγοῦσα κὠδυνωμένη
δεινῶς δακρῦσαι κἀπικωκῦσαι δοκεῖ   805
τὸν υἱὸν ἡ δύστηνος ὧδ᾽ ὀλωλότα;
ἀλλ᾽ ἐγγελῶσα φροῦδος. ὦ τάλαιν᾽ ἐγώ·
Ὀρέστα φίλταθ᾽, ὥς μ᾽ ἀπώλεσας θανών.
ἀποσπάσας γὰρ τῆς ἐμῆς οἴχῃ φρενὸς

785 ἦν μοι] ἡμίν Naber   790 ἔχει] ἔχεις Müller: ἔχω Schmidt   791 οὔτοι σύ] οὐ σοί γε Reiske   792 Νέμεσι LᵖᶜADXsPᵃᶜV: –σσι* Lᵃᶜ: –σσι KZf: –σις rXrZrCFHNOZct   795 οὔκουν LRCHNOPV: οὐκοῦν Gat: utroque accentu KZc   punctum interrogationis posuit Fröhlich   796 σὲ Blaydes: σε KraCFHNPZct: om. Lᵃᶜ ut vid., OV   797 ἂν ἥκοις] ἂν ἥκεις GZcT, fort. Cᵃᶜ: ἆρ᾽ ἥκεις Morstadt   τυχεῖν KRapt: φίλος G: φιλεῖν LᵃᶜΛ 799 οὐκοῦν] οὔκουν Dindorf   punctum interrogationis posuit Elmsley 800 κατάξι᾽ ἂν Bothe: κατ᾽ ἀξίαν vel καταξίαν CHOVZg: καταξίως LKrADXsZrFPt   802 τήνδε δ᾽ LᵖᶜKrAXrZrCFNOVt: τήνδε θ᾽ LᵃᶜΛ: τήνδ᾽ DXsHPZc   ἔκτοθεν LKrCᵃᶜFNOV: –σθε(ν) ADXrXsC¹ᵖᶜHZct 809 οἴχῃ φρενὸς LᵖᶜaSt: inverso ordine lrpZc

αἴ μοι μόναι παρῆσαν ἐλπίδων ἔτι,　　　　810
σὲ πατρὸς ἥξειν ζῶντα τιμωρόν ποτε
κἀμοῦ ταλαίνης. νῦν δὲ ποῖ με χρὴ μολεῖν;
μόνη γάρ εἰμι, σοῦ τ᾽ ἀπεστερημένη
καὶ πατρός. ἤδη δεῖ με δουλεύειν πάλιν
ἐν τοῖσιν ἐχθίστοισιν ἀνθρώπων ἐμοί,　　　815
φονεῦσι πατρός. ἆρά μοι καλῶς ἔχει;
ἀλλ᾽ οὔ τι μὴν ἔγωγε τοῦ λοιποῦ χρόνου
ἔσομαι ξύνοικος, ἀλλὰ τῇδε πρὸς πύλῃ
παρεῖσ᾽ ἐμαυτὴν ἄφιλος αὐανῶ βίον.
πρὸς ταῦτα καινέτω τις, εἰ βαρύνεται,　　　820
τῶν ἔνδον ὄντων· ὡς χάρις μέν, ἢν κτάνῃ,
λύπη δ᾽, ἐὰν ζῶ· τοῦ βίου δ᾽ οὐδεὶς πόθος.

Χο.　ποῦ ποτε κεραυνοὶ Διός, ἢ ποῦ　　　　[str. 1
　　　φαέθων Ἅλιος, εἰ ταῦτ᾽ ἐφορῶντες
　　　κρύπτουσιν ἔκηλοι;　　　　825
Ηλ.　ἒ ἔ, αἰαῖ.
Χο.　ὦ παῖ, τί δακρύεις;
Ηλ.　φεῦ. Χο. μηδὲν μέγ᾽ αὔσῃς. Ηλ. ἀπολεῖς. Χο. πῶς;　830
Ηλ.　εἰ τῶν φανερῶς οἰχομένων
　　　εἰς Ἀίδαν ἐλπίδ᾽ ὑποίσεις, κατ᾽ ἐμοῦ　　835
　　　τακομένας μᾶλλον ἐπεμβάσῃ.

Χο.　οἶδα γὰρ ἄνακτ᾽ Ἀμφιάρεων χρυ—　　　[ant. 1
　　　σοδέτοις ἕρκεσι κρυφθέντα γυναικῶν
　　　καὶ νῦν ὑπὸ γαίας —

812 ποῖ codd. plerique (etiam Λ): πῆ AXs　813 τ᾽] δ᾽ G: γ᾽ Dawe　815 τοῖσιν] τοῖσί γ᾽ Monk　816 om. R, del. Morstadt　818 ἔσομαι ξύνοικος Dawes: ξύνοικος ἔσ(σ)ομ᾽ codd. (etiam Λ): ξύνοικος εἴσειμ᾽ Hermann　819 ἄφιλος] –ον Wc, coni. Monk　αὐανῶ Blaydes: αὐ– codd.　821 κτάνῃ] θάνω Σ 975　824 ἅλιος ADXsZrt: ἄλιος N: ἀέλ(λ)ιος IXrCFHOPVZc: ἥλιος Suidae iv. 691.27 codd. plerique　ἐφορῶντες] ἀφ– r　post ἐφορῶντες lacunam statuit Musgrave: <νέμεσιν> inseruit Schubert　830 αὔσῃς] εἴπῃς r　832 εἰς rZrCNt: ἐς LKADXrXsFHOPVZc　836 ἐπεμβάσῃ] –ᾶσα Kaibel　838 γυναικῶν Brunck (γυναικὸς mavult Fröhlich): ἀπάταισιν Triclinius e coniectura: γυναικῶν ἀπάτῃ fort. K: γυναικῶν ἀπάταις cett.

Ηλ.　ἒ ἔ, ἰώ.　840

Χο.　πάμψυχος ἀνάσσει.

Ηλ.　φεῦ. Χο. φεῦ δῆτ'· ὀλοὰ δ' οὖν – Ηλ. ἐδάμη. Χο. ναί. 845

Ηλ.　οἶδ' οἶδ'· ἐφάνη γὰρ μελέτωρ
　　　　ἀμφὶ τὸν ἐν πένθει· ἐμοὶ δ' οὔτις ἔτ' ἔσθ'· ὃς γὰρ ἔτ'
　　　　ἦν, φροῦδος ἀναρπασθείς.

Χο.　δειλαία δειλαίων κυρεῖς.　　　　　　　　　　[str. 2

Ηλ.　κἀγὼ τοῦδ' ἴστωρ, ὑπερίστωρ,　850
　　　　πανσύρτῳ παμμήνῳ πολλῶν
　　　　δεινῶν στυγνῶν τ' αἰῶνι.

Χο.　ἰδομένᾳ θροεῖς.

Ηλ.　μή μέ νυν μηκέτι
　　　　παραγάγῃς, ἵν' οὐ – Χο. τί φής;　855

Ηλ.　πάρεισιν ἐλπίδων ἔτι κοινοτόκων
　　　　εὐπατριδᾶν ἀρωγαί.

Χο.　πᾶσι θνατοῖς ἔφυ μόρος.　　　　　　　　　[ant. 2 860

Ηλ.　ἦ καὶ χαλάργοις ἐν ἁμίλλαις
　　　　οὕτως, ὡς κείνῳ δυστάνῳ,
　　　　τμητοῖς ὁλκοῖς ἐγκῦρσαι;

845 δ' οὖν West: γὰρ codd. (nisi quod γοῦν t): τ' ἄρ' Wolff: μὰν Wecklein: γ' ἄρ' Lloyd-Jones et Wilson　846 οἶδ' bis codd. plerique: semel rZr, fort. F　848 ἔτ' ἔσθ'] ἔσθ' KrZrHOV　850 ἴστωρ] ῐ– LGHOPVZc　851 πανσύρτῳ codd. et Suidas ii. 673.20: –ων testatur se invenisse Triclinius ἕν τινι τῶν παλαιῶν βιβλίων: πανδύρτῳ Bergk et Nauck　852 αἰῶνι Hermann: ἀχέων codd. plerique et Suidas: ἀχαιῶν t (ex eodem vetustissimo codice): ἀχαίων A: ἀχέ*ων Lᵃᶜ: ἀρχαίων Triclinius e coniectura: ἄχθει olim Hermann (τε post δεινῶν addito)　853 ἰδομένᾳ θροεῖς Diggle: εἴδομεν ἃ θροεῖς codd.: εἴδομεν ἀθρήνεις Dindorf (ἃ θρηνεῖς iam Erfurdt)　855 τί φής; Triclinius e coniectura: τί φής; αὐδᾷς δὲ ποῖον; codd.　857 εὐπατριδᾶν codd. plerique et Suidae iv. 29.12 cod. G: –ιδῶν ZrC: εὐπατρίδων Suidae codd. cett., coni. Neue　τ' ante ἀρωγαί testes praeter Suidam et V　ἀρωγαί rWaˢΣL: –οί cett. et Suidas (nisi quod –ή Suidae cod. G)　860 πᾶσι] πᾶσιν LK　861 χαλάργοις Dindorf: χαλαργοῖς codd.　ἐν] γ' ἐν O　863 ἐγκῦρσαι r: ἐγκύρσαι fere cett.

Χο. ἄσκοπος ἀ λώβα.
Ηλ. πῶς γὰρ οὔκ; εἰ ξένος   865
    ἄτερ ἐμᾶν χερῶν – Χο. παπαῖ.
Ηλ. κέκευθεν, οὔτε του τάφου ἀντιάσας
    οὔτε γόων παρ' ἡμῶν.   870

Χρ. ὑφ' ἡδονῆς τοι, φιλτάτη, διώκομαι
    τὸ κόσμιον μεθεῖσα σὺν τάχει μολεῖν.
    φέρω γὰρ ἡδονάς τε κἀνάπαυλαν ὧν
    πάροιθεν εἶχες καὶ κατέστενες κακῶν.
Ηλ. πόθεν δ' ἂν εὕροις τῶν ἐμῶν σὺ πημάτων   875
    ἄρηξιν, οἷς ἴασις οὐκ ἔνεστ' ἔτι;
Χρ. πάρεστ' Ὀρέστης ἧμιν, ἴσθι τοῦτ' ἐμοῦ
    κλύουσ', ἐναργῶς, ὥσπερ εἰσορᾷς ἐμέ.
Ηλ. ἀλλ' ἦ μέμηνας, ὦ τάλαινα, κἀπὶ τοῖς
    σαυτῆς κακοῖσι κἀπὶ τοῖς ἐμοῖς γελᾷς;   880
Χρ. μὰ τὴν πατρῴαν ἑστίαν, ἀλλ' οὐχ ὕβρει
    λέγω τάδ', ἀλλ' ἐκεῖνον ὡς παρόντα νῷν.
Ηλ. οἴμοι τάλαινα· καὶ τίνος βροτῶν λόγον
    τόνδ' εἰσακούσασ' ὧδε πιστεύεις ἄγαν;
Χρ. ἐγὼ μὲν ἐξ ἐμοῦ τε κοὐκ ἄλλου σαφῆ   885
    σημεῖ' ἰδοῦσα τῷδε πιστεύω λόγῳ.
Ηλ. τίν', ὦ τάλαιν', ἰδοῦσα πίστιν; ἐς τί μοι
    βλέψασα θάλπη τῷδ' ἀνηκέστῳ πυρί;

866 χερῶν LKADXsZrFHOVZc: –οῖν XrPt: χειρῶν rC^xN   867 του
L^{pc}KADXrXsFZc: τοῦ L^{ac}ZrCHNOP: om. rZg   871 τοι] σοι Brunck
876 οἷς] ὧν Blaydes   ἴασις L^{s}KZrHOPV et Suidae ii. 605.2 codd. plerique:
–ιν LK^{s}rADXrXsCFNZc et Suidae codd. IT   οὐκ ἔνεστ'] οὐκ ἔνεστιν
Suidas, fere Zc: οὐκέτ' ἔστιν CN: οὐκέτ' ἔστ' Thiersch   ἔτι L^{s}HOPV: ἰδεῖν
KraCFH^{gl}NZct et Suidas   οὐκέτ' ἔστι δή Blaydes   878 ἐναργῶς] –ής
Wecklein   881 ὕβρει] –ιν L^{ac}KZr, fort. Zc^{ac} 882 νῷν] νόει RG^{γρ}N^{γρ}:
νῦν P   884 εἰσακούσασ'] ἐξ– Blaydes   885 ἄλλου] –ης LGCO (verum
G^{1s}), fort. K^{ac} 887 ἰδοῦσα] ἔχουσα Meineke   888 ἀνηκέστῳ codd.,
Suidas i. 215.8, Eustathius 651.59: ἀνηφαίστῳ Bergk et Nauck: ἀνεικάστῳ
Meineke

Χρ. πρός νυν θεῶν ἄκουσον, ὡς μαθοῦσά μου
     τὸ λοιπὸν ἢ φρονοῦσαν ἢ μώραν λέγῃς.   890
Ηλ. σὺ δ᾽ οὖν λέγ᾽, εἴ σοι τῷ λόγῳ τις ἡδονή.
Χρ. καὶ δὴ λέγω σοι πᾶν ὅσον κατειδόμην.
     ἐπεὶ γὰρ ἦλθον πατρὸς ἀρχαῖον τάφον,
     ὁρῶ κολώνης ἐξ ἄκρας νεορρύτους
     πηγὰς γάλακτος καὶ περιστεφῆ κύκλῳ   895
     πάντων ὅσ᾽ ἔστιν ἀνθέων θήκην πατρός.
     ἰδοῦσα δ᾽ ἔσχον θαῦμα, καὶ περισκοπῶ
     μή πού τις ἡμῖν ἐγγὺς ἐγχρίμπτει βροτῶν.
     ὡς δ᾽ ἐν γαλήνῃ πάντ᾽ ἐδερκόμην τόπον,
     τύμβου προσεῖρπον ἆσσον· ἐσχάτης δ᾽ ὁρῶ   900
     πυρᾶς νεώρη βόστρυχον τετμημένον·
     κεὐθὺς τάλαιν᾽ ὡς εἶδον, ἐμπαίει τί μοι
     ψυχῇ σύνηθες ὄμμα, φιλτάτου βροτῶν
     πάντων Ὀρέστου τοῦθ᾽ ὁρᾶν τεκμήριον·
     καὶ χερσὶ βαστάσασα δυσφημῶ μὲν οὔ,   905
     χαρᾷ δὲ πίμπλημ᾽ εὐθὺς ὄμμα δακρύων.
     καὶ νῦν θ᾽ ὁμοίως καὶ τότ᾽ ἐξεπίσταμαι
     μή του τόδ᾽ ἀγλάϊσμα πλὴν κείνου μολεῖν.
     τῷ γὰρ προσήκει πλήν γ᾽ ἐμοῦ καὶ σοῦ τόδε;
     κἀγὼ μὲν οὐκ ἔδρασα, τοῦτ᾽ ἐπίσταμαι,   910
     οὐδ᾽ αὖ σύ· πῶς γάρ; ᾗ γε μηδὲ πρὸς θεοὺς
     ἔξεστ᾽ ἀκλαύτῳ τῆσδ᾽ ἀποστῆναι στέγης.
     ἀλλ᾽ οὐδὲ μὲν δὴ μητρὸς οὔθ᾽ ὁ νοῦς φιλεῖ
     τοιαῦτα πράσσειν οὔτε δρῶσ᾽ ἐλάνθαν᾽ ἄν·

889 νυν **t**: νῦν cett.   μου] ἐμὲ Fröhlich   890 λοιπὸν XsᵖᶜZrᵖᶜ**St**: λοιπόν μ᾽ fere LK**r**DXrXsᵃᶜZrᵃᶜ**pz**c: τὰ λοιπά μ᾽ Blaydes   λέγῃς LʳˢADXrXs: –οις LKˢRFNOVZcT: –εις KGZrCHPTa   891 τῷ λόγῳ] τῶν λόγων Reiske   892 κατειδόμην] κατείδομεν Nauck   896 ἔστιν] εἰσιν Lˢ   898 ἐγχρίμπτει Nauck: –ίμπτῃ KJZf: –ίπτῃ vel –ίπτει fere cett. 900–1 ἐσχάτης . . . πυρᾶς] –η . . . –ᾷ Schaefer (ἐσχάτη Nᵃᶜ)   901 νεώρη Dindorf: νεωρῆ codd.   902 μοι] μου L (verum Lˢ)   903 ψυχῇ] ψυχῆς LᵃᶜK**r**CᵃᶜHˢ   ὄμμα] φάσμα Nauck   904 del. Paley   912 ἀκλαύτῳ Dindorf: –στῳ codd.   914 ἐλάνθαν᾽ ἄν Heath: –ανεν codd. (L non legitur)

　　　ἀλλ᾿ ἔστ᾿ Ὀρέστου ταῦτα τἀπιτίμια.　　　　915
　　　ἀλλ᾿, ὦ φίλη, θάρσυνε. τοῖς αὐτοῖσί τοι
　　　οὐχ αὑτὸς αἰεὶ δαιμόνων παραστατεῖ.
　　　νῷν δ᾿ ἦν τὰ πρόσθε στυγνός· ἡ δὲ νῦν ἴσως
　　　πολλῶν ὑπάρξει κῦρος ἡμέρα καλῶν.
Ηλ.　φεῦ τῆς ἀνοίας, ὥς σ᾿ ἐποικτίρω πάλαι.　　920
Χρ.　τί δ᾿ ἔστιν; οὐ πρὸς ἡδονὴν λέγω τάδε;
Ηλ.　οὐκ οἶσθ᾿ ὅποι γῆς οὐδ᾿ ὅποι γνώμης φέρῃ.
Χρ.　πῶς δ᾿ οὐκ ἐγὼ κάτοιδ᾿ ἅ γ᾿ εἶδον ἐμφανῶς;
Ηλ.　τέθνηκεν, ὦ τάλαινα· τἀκ κείνου δέ σοι
　　　σωτήρι᾿ ἔρρει· μηδὲν ἐς κεῖνόν γ᾿ ὅρα.　　925
Χρ.　οἴμοι τάλαινα· τοῦ τάδ᾿ ἤκουσας βροτῶν;
Ηλ.　τοῦ πλησίον παρόντος, ἡνίκ᾿ ὤλλυτο.
Χρ.　καὶ ποῦ 'στιν οὗτος; θαῦμά τοί μ᾿ ὑπέρχεται.
Ηλ.　κατ᾿ οἶκον, ἡδὺς οὐδὲ μητρὶ δυσχερής.
Χρ.　οἴμοι τάλαινα· τοῦ γὰρ ἀνθρώπων ποτ᾿ ἦν　930
　　　τὰ πολλὰ πατρὸς πρὸς τάφον κτερίσματα;
Ηλ.　οἶμαι μάλιστ᾿ ἔγωγε τοῦ τεθνηκότος
　　　μνημεῖ᾿ Ὀρέστου ταῦτα προσθεῖναί τινα.
Χρ.　ὦ δυστυχής· ἐγὼ δὲ σὺν χαρᾷ λόγους
　　　τοιούσδ᾿ ἔχουσ᾿ ἔσπευδον, οὐκ εἰδυῖ᾿ ἄρα　935
　　　ἵν᾿ ἦμεν ἄτης· ἀλλὰ νῦν, ὅθ᾿ ἱκόμην,
　　　τά τ᾿ ὄντα πρόσθεν ἄλλα θ᾿ εὑρίσκω κακά.
Ηλ.　οὕτως ἔχει σοι ταῦτ᾿· ἐὰν δ᾿ ἐμοὶ πίθῃ,
　　　τῆς νῦν παρούσης πημονῆς λύσεις βάρος.
Χρ.　ἦ τοὺς θανόντας ἐξαναστήσω ποτέ;　　　940
Ηλ.　οὐ τοῦτό γ᾿ εἶπον· οὐ γὰρ ὧδ᾿ ἄφρων ἔφυν.

915 τἀπιτίμια codd. et Suidas ii. 388.26: τἀπιτύμβια Dindorf　917 οὐχ αὑτὸς Brunck: οὐκ αὑτὸς codd.　αἰεὶ] ἀεὶ rXsF　918 δ᾿] om. LCF　τά] ὁ Lloyd-Jones　πρόσθε LKrNt: –εν aCFHOPZc　920 ἐποικτίρω Nauck: –τείρ– codd.　922 φέρῃ] φόρῃ fort. L^{ac} (verum L^{pc}): ἔφυς L^{γρ}K^{γρ}　924 τἀκ κείνου Canter: τἀκείνου codd.　δέ] γε Blaydes　925 μηδὲν] μηκέτ᾿ Nauck　929 δυσχερής codd. et Eustathius 645.16: –μενής L^{γρ}　931 τάφον] –ῳ Blaydes　938 δ᾿ ἐμοὶ Brunck: δέ μοι codd.　941 οὐ τοῦτό γ᾿ Blaydes: οὐκ ἔσθ᾿ ὅ γ᾿ L^{s}K^{s}RaNPZc: οὐκ ἔσθ᾿ ὅδ᾿ vel sim. LKGOZg: οὐκ ἐς τόδ᾿ CHV, coni. Haupt

Χρ. τί γὰρ κελεύεις ὧν ἐγὼ φερέγγυος;
Ηλ. τλῆναί σε δρῶσαν ἂν ἐγὼ παραινέσω.
Χρ. ἀλλ᾽ εἴ τις ὠφέλειά γ᾽, οὐκ ἀπώσομαι.
Ηλ. ὅρα, πόνου τοι χωρὶς οὐδὲν εὐτυχεῖ.   945
Χρ. ὁρῶ. ξυνοίσω πᾶν ὅσονπερ ἂν σθένω.
Ηλ. ἄκουε δή νυν ᾗ βεβούλευμαι τελεῖν.
      παρουσίαν μὲν οἶσθα καὶ σύ που φίλων
      ὡς οὔτις ἡμῖν ἐστιν, ἀλλ᾽ Ἅιδης λαβὼν
      ἀπεστέρηκε καὶ μόνα λελείμμεθον.   950
      ἐγὼ δ᾽ ἕως μὲν τὸν κασίγνητον βίῳ
      θάλλοντ᾽ ἔτ᾽ εἰσήκουον, εἶχον ἐλπίδας
      φόνου ποτ᾽ αὐτὸν πράκτορ᾽ ἵξεσθαι πατρός·
      νῦν δ᾽ ἡνίκ᾽ οὐκέτ᾽ ἔστιν, ἐς σὲ δὴ βλέπω,
      ὅπως τὸν αὐτόχειρα πατρῴου φόνου   955
      ξὺν τῇδ᾽ ἀδελφῇ μὴ κατοκνήσεις κτανεῖν
      Αἴγισθον· οὐδὲν γάρ σε δεῖ κρύπτειν μ᾽ ἔτι.
      ποῖ γὰρ μένεις ῥάθυμος, ἐς τίν᾽ ἐλπίδων
      βλέψασ᾽ ἔτ᾽ ὀρθήν; ᾗ πάρεστι μὲν στένειν
      πλούτου πατρῴου κτῆσιν ἐστερημένη,   960
      πάρεστι δ᾽ ἀλγεῖν ἐς τοσόνδε τοῦ χρόνου
      ἄλεκτρα γηράσκουσαν ἀνυμέναιά τε.
      καὶ τῶνδε μέντοι μηκέτ᾽ ἐλπίσῃς ὅπως
      τεύξῃ ποτ᾽· οὐ γὰρ ὧδ᾽ ἄβουλός ἐστ᾽ ἀνὴρ
      Αἴγισθος ὥστε σόν ποτ᾽ ἢ κἀμὸν γένος   965
      βλαστεῖν ἐᾶσαι, πημονὴν αὑτῷ σαφῆ.
      ἀλλ᾽ ἢν ἐπίσπῃ τοῖς ἐμοῖς βουλεύμασιν,
      πρῶτον μὲν εὐσέβειαν ἐκ πατρὸς κάτω

942 ὧν <γ᾽> Kaibel   945 τοι] γε Gnom.   947 νυν Blomfield: νῦν
codd.   τελεῖν KaCHNOPVt: πο(ι)εῖν LrDᵍˡXsᵍˡFZc   948 καὶ σύ που
Kᵖᶜrapt: καὶ πού (ποῦ) σοι LKᵃᶜAᵞᵖXsʳᵞᵖS   950 μόνα] –αι HNˣOV
λελείμμεθον] –θα rH, coni. Elmsley (verum Gᴵᵖᶜ)   952 θάλλοντ᾽ ἔτ᾽
Reiske: θάλλοντά τ᾽codd. (nisi quod θάλλοντ᾽ Zr)   956 κατοκνήσεις ADC:
–η(ι)ς fere cett.   957 del. Wunder   σε] με CNO   μ᾽] σ᾽ CN   960
ἐστερημένη] –ην Oᴵᵖᶜ, coni. Elmsley   961 πάρεστι δ᾽] πάρεστιν LᵃᶜKCN
(verum Lᵖᶜ)   967 βουλεύμασιν LᵃᶜGXsZrPt: –σι Lᵖᶜ et cett.

θανόντος οἴσῃ τοῦ κασιγνήτου θ' ἅμα·
ἔπειτα δ', ὥσπερ ἐξέφυς, ἐλευθέρα   970
καλῇ τὸ λοιπὸν καὶ γάμων ἐπαξίων
τεύξῃ· φιλεῖ γὰρ πρὸς τὰ χρηστὰ πᾶς ὁρᾶν.
λόγων γε μὴν εὔκλειαν οὐχ ὁρᾷς ὅσην
σαυτῇ τε κἀμοὶ προσβαλεῖς πεισθεῖσ' ἐμοί;
τίς γάρ ποτ' ἀστῶν ἢ ξένων ἡμᾶς ἰδὼν   975
τοιοῖσδ' ἐπαίνοις οὐχὶ δεξιώσεται,
"ἴδεσθε τώδε τὼ κασιγνήτω, φίλοι,
ὢ τὸν πατρῷον οἶκον ἐξεσωσάτην,
ὢ τοῖσιν ἐχθροῖς εὖ βεβηκόσιν ποτὲ
ψυχῆς ἀφειδήσαντε προὐστήτην φόνου.   980
τούτω φιλεῖν χρή, τώδε χρὴ πάντας σέβειν·
τώδ' ἔν τ' ἑορταῖς ἔν τε πανδήμῳ πόλει
τιμᾶν ἅπαντας οὕνεκ' ἀνδρείας χρεών."
τοιαῦτά τοι νὼ πᾶς τις ἐξερεῖ βροτῶν,
ζώσαιν θανούσαιν θ' ὥστε μὴ 'κλιπεῖν κλέος.   985
ἀλλ', ὦ φίλη, πείσθητι, συμπόνει πατρί,
σύγκαμν' ἀδελφῷ, παῦσον ἐκ κακῶν ἐμέ,
παῦσον δὲ σαυτήν, τοῦτο γιγνώσκουσ', ὅτι
ζῆν αἰσχρὸν αἰσχρῶς τοῖς καλῶς πεφυκόσιν.
Χο. ἐν τοῖς τοιούτοις ἐστὶν ἡ προμηθία   990
    καὶ τῷ λέγοντι καὶ κλύοντι σύμμαχος.
Χρ. καὶ πρίν γε φωνεῖν, ὦ γυναῖκες, εἰ φρενῶν
    ἐτύγχαν' αὕτη μὴ κακῶν, ἐσῴζετ' ἂν
    τὴν εὐλάβειαν, ὥσπερ οὐχὶ σῴζεται.
    ποῖ γάρ ποτε βλέψασα τοιοῦτον θράσος   995
    αὑτή θ' ὁπλίζῃ κἄμ' ὑπηρετεῖν καλεῖς;

---

973 λόγων Bothe: –ω codd.   974 πεισθεῖσ' ἐμοί] πεισθεῖσά μοι
fere CHOPV   985 ζώσαιν θανούσαιν] –ντοιν –ντοιν Papageorgius
'κλιπεῖν **lrp**Z**c**t: λιπεῖν **a**   987 ἀδελφῷ] –ῆ OPV, coni. Nauck
990 τοῖς] τοι Blaydes   προμηθία] προθυμία GZc   991 κλύοντι
ΛDXrXsFHOV**t**: τῷ κλύοντι LK**r**AZrCNPZc   995 ποτε βλέψασα Π³Zr
et Monac. gr. 334, coni. Doederlein: ποτ' ἐκβλέψασα fort. K: ποτ' ἐμβλέψασα
cett. (etiam ΛKˢ)

οὐκ εἰσορᾷς; γυνὴ μὲν οὐδ᾽ ἀνὴρ ἔφυς,
σθένεις δ᾽ ἔλασσον τῶν ἐναντίων χερί.
δαίμων δὲ τοῖς μὲν εὐτυχὴς καθ᾽ ἡμέραν,
ἡμῖν δ᾽ ἀπορρεῖ κἀπὶ μηδὲν ἔρχεται.   1000
τίς οὖν τοιοῦτον ἄνδρα βουλεύων ἑλεῖν
ἄλυπος ἄτης ἐξαπαλλαχθήσεται;
ὅρα κακῶς πράσσοντε μὴ μείζω κακὰ
κτησώμεθ᾽, εἴ τις τούσδ᾽ ἀκούσεται λόγους.
λύει γὰρ ἡμᾶς οὐδὲν οὐδ᾽ ἐπωφελεῖ   1005
βάξιν καλὴν λαβόντε δυσκλεῶς θανεῖν.
[οὐ γὰρ θανεῖν ἔχθιστον, ἀλλ᾽ ὅταν θανεῖν
χρῄζων τις εἶτα μηδὲ τοῦτ᾽ ἔχῃ λαβεῖν.]
ἀλλ᾽ ἀντιάζω, πρὶν πανωλέθρους τὸ πᾶν
ἡμᾶς τ᾽ ὀλέσθαι κἀξερημῶσαι γένος,   1010
κατάσχες ὀργήν. καὶ τὰ μὲν λελεγμένα
ἄρρητ᾽ ἐγώ σοι κἀτελῆ φυλάξομαι,
αὐτὴ δὲ νοῦν σχὲς ἀλλὰ τῷ χρόνῳ ποτέ,
σθένουσα μηδὲν τοῖς κρατοῦσιν εἰκαθεῖν.

Χο. πείθου. προνοίας οὐδὲν ἀνθρώποις ἔφυ   1015
κέρδος λαβεῖν ἄμεινον οὐδὲ νοῦ σοφοῦ.

Ηλ. ἀπροσδόκητον οὐδὲν εἴρηκας· καλῶς δ᾽
ἤδη σ᾽ ἀπορρίψουσαν ἀπηγγελλόμην.
ἀλλ᾽ αὐτόχειρί μοι μόνη τε δραστέον
τοὔργον τόδ᾽· οὐ γὰρ δὴ κενόν γ᾽ ἀφήσομεν.   1020

997 οὐδ᾽] οὐκ GZrt (verum Tˢ)   998 ἔλασσον Π³, coni. Brunck:
ἔλαττον codd.   χερί] χεροῖν Zcˡˢt   999 εὐτυχὴς LraNˡᵖᶜPTˡˢ: –εῖ
LKCFHNᵃᶜOᵖᶜVZcT   1005 ἡμᾶς Π³ et codd.: ἡμῖν Elmsley   1007–
8 del. Nauck (1007 om. LᵃᶜKᵃᶜRᵃᶜ: add. LʳKʳRʳ): habet Π³ et codd.
cett.   1007 οὐ γὰρ] οὐχ ὡς Λ: οὐδ᾽ αὖ Michaelis   1008 χρῄζων
LˡˢaCFHNOPZct: χρῄζῃ Kr, fort. Lᵃᶜ   1010 τ᾽ ὀλέσθαι] τ᾽ ὀλέσαι
O: ὀλέσθαι Wecklein: τ᾽ ἀπολέσαι West   1011 ὀργήν] ὁρμήν O
1014 εἰκαθεῖν Elmsley: –άθειν codd.   1015 πείθου lraCFHNOPaVZct:
πιθοῦ XrʳʸᵖOˡˢPWbʳʸᵖ   1018 ἤδη Brunck: ἤδη Thomas Magister 143.7
Ritschl: ᾔδειν codd.   ἀπηγγε(λ)λόμην] ἃ ᾽πηγγειλάμην Thomas Magister
1019 αὐτόχειρι codd. (etiam Λ): οὐδὲν ἧσσον Lʳʸᵖ   1020 ἀφήσομεν] –ομαι
RNOᵖᶜ

ΣΟΦΟΚΛΕΟΥΣ ΗΛΕΚΤΡΑ

Χρ. φεῦ·
     εἴθ᾽ ὤφελες τοιάδε τὴν γνώμην πατρὸς
     θνήσκοντος εἶναι· πᾶν γὰρ ἂν κατηργάσω.
Ηλ. ἀλλ᾽ ἦ φύσιν γε, τὸν δὲ νοῦν ἥσσων τότε.
Χρ. ἄσκει τοιαύτη νοῦν δι᾽ αἰῶνος μένειν.
Ηλ. ὡς οὐχὶ συνδράσουσα νουθετεῖς τάδε.   1025
Χρ. εἰκὸς γὰρ ἐγχειροῦντα καὶ πράσσειν κακῶς.
Ηλ. ζηλῶ σε τοῦ νοῦ, τῆς δὲ δειλίας στυγῶ.
Χρ. ἀνέξομαι κλύουσα χὤταν εὖ λέγῃς.
Ηλ. ἀλλ᾽ οὔ ποτ᾽ ἐξ ἐμοῦ γε μὴ πάθῃς τόδε.
Χρ. μακρὸς τὸ κρῖναι ταῦτα χὠ λοιπὸς χρόνος.   1030
Ηλ. ἄπελθε· σοὶ γὰρ ὠφέλησις οὐκ ἔνι.
Χρ. ἔνεστιν· ἀλλὰ σοὶ μάθησις οὐ πάρα.
Ηλ. ἐλθοῦσα μητρὶ ταῦτα πάντ᾽ ἔξειπε σῇ.
Χρ. οὐδ᾽ αὖ τοσοῦτον ἔχθος ἐχθαίρω σ᾽ ἐγώ.
Ηλ. ἀλλ᾽ οὖν ἐπίστω γ᾽ οἷ μ᾽ ἀτιμίας ἄγεις.   1035
Χρ. ἀτιμίας μὲν οὔ, προμηθίας δὲ σοῦ.
Ηλ. τῷ σῷ δικαίῳ δῆτ᾽ ἐπισπέσθαι με δεῖ;
Χρ. ὅταν γὰρ εὖ φρονῇς, τόθ᾽ ἡγήσῃ σὺ νῶν.
Ηλ. ἦ δεινὸν εὖ λέγουσαν ἐξαμαρτάνειν.
Χρ. εἴρηκας ὀρθῶς ᾧ σὺ πρόσκεισαι κακῷ.   1040
Ηλ. τί δ᾽; οὐ δοκῶ σοι ταῦτα σὺν δίκῃ λέγειν;
Χρ. ἀλλ᾽ ἔστιν ἔνθα χἠ δίκη βλάβην φέρει.
Ηλ. τούτοις ἐγὼ ζῆν τοῖς νόμοις οὐ βούλομαι.
Χρ. ἀλλ᾽ εἰ ποήσεις ταῦτ᾽, ἐπαινέσεις ἐμέ.
Ηλ. καὶ μὴν ποήσω γ᾽ οὐδὲν ἐκπλαγεῖσά σε.   1045
Χρ. καὶ τοῦτ᾽ ἀληθές, οὐδὲ βουλεύσῃ πάλιν;

1021–2 πατρὸς θνήσκοντος] πατρὶ θνήσκοντί γ᾽ F   1022 πᾶν Dawes:
πάντα codd. (etiam Λ)   γὰρ ἂν L^{ac}KXsCNZc: ἂν γὰρ H: γὰρ
L^{pc}rADXrZrFOPPaVT: γ᾽ ἂν Musgrave: τᾶν Arnold   κατηργάσω
Groeneboom: κατει– codd.   1023 ἦ Elmsley: ἦν codd.   1026
γάρ] κάκ᾽ Wakefield   πράσσειν LKaCFNPZcT et Suidas ii. 525.7:
πράττειν HOPaVT^{is}: πάσχειν K^{gl}O^{gl}S   1029 πάθῃς ADXrXsPZc:
μάθῃς LKrZrCFHN^{1pc}OPaVTZc^{is}   1036 προμηθίας LaCFN: –είας
KRHOPPaVZcT: προθυμίας G   1038 ὅταν] εὖτ᾽ ἂν G   1043 post
1047 citat Suidas ii. 495.9   1045 ποήσω XrZc^{pc}: ποιήσω cett.

67

Ηλ. βουλῆς γὰρ οὐδέν ἐστιν ἔχθιον κακῆς.

Χρ. φρονεῖν ἔοικας οὐδὲν ὧν ἐγὼ λέγω.

Ηλ. πάλαι δέδοκται ταῦτα κοὐ νεωστί μοι.

[Χρ. ἄπειμι τοίνυν· οὔτε γὰρ σὺ τἄμ᾽ ἔπη 1050
τολμᾷς ἐπαινεῖν οὔτ᾽ ἐγὼ τοὺς σοὺς τρόπους.

Ηλ. ἀλλ᾽ εἴσιθ᾽. οὔ σοι μὴ μεθέψομαί ποτε,
οὐδ᾽ ἢν σφόδρ᾽ ἱμείρουσα τυγχάνῃς· ἐπεὶ
πολλῆς ἀνοίας καὶ τὸ θηρᾶσθαι κενά.]

Χρ. ἀλλ᾽ εἰ σεαυτῇ τυγχάνεις δοκοῦσά τι 1055
φρονεῖν, φρόνει τοιαῦθ᾽· ὅταν γὰρ ἐν κακοῖς
ἤδη βεβήκῃς, τἄμ᾽ ἐπαινέσεις ἔπη.

Χο. τί τοὺς ἄνωθεν φρονιμωτάτους οἰωνοὺς [str. 1
ἐσορώμενοι τροφᾶς κη—
δομένους ἀφ᾽ ὧν τε βλάστω— 1060
σιν ἀφ᾽ ὧν τ᾽ ὄνησιν εὕρω—
σι, τάδ᾽ οὐκ ἐπ᾽ ἴσας τελοῦμεν;
ἀλλ᾽ οὐ τὰν Διὸς ἀστραπὰν
καὶ τὰν οὐρανίαν Θέμιν
δαρὸν οὐκ ἀπόνητοι. 1065
ὦ χθονία βροτοῖσι Φάμα,
κατά μοι βόασον οἰκτρὰν
ὄπα τοῖς ἔνερθ᾽ Ἀτρείδαις,
ἀχόρευτα φέρουσ᾽ ὀνείδη.

ὅτι σφὶν ἤδη τὰ μὲν ἐκ δόμων †νοσεῖ†, [ant. 1 1070

1047 οὐδέν ἐστιν hoc ordine codd. et Suidas ii. 495.8: inverso Par. gr.
2820 1050–4 del. Lloyd-Jones et Wilson (1052–7 del. Morstadt): 1050–
1 Sophoclis Phaedrae tribuit Stob. Ecl. 3.2.28–9: post 1052 lacunam
statuit Dawe 1053 ἢν LKADXsZrNPZc: εἰ **r**XrHPa**Vt** τυγχάνῃς
LKADXsC¹ᵖᶜFNPZc: –εις L¹ˢ**r**XrCᵃᶜHOPa**Vt**, fort. Zrᵃᶜ 1060–1 βλάστ-
ωσιν Schaefer: βλαστῶσιν codd. 1061 ὄνησιν codd. et Suidas i. 230.5:
ὄνασιν Brunck 1062 ἐπ᾽ ἴσας LᵖᶜK: ἐπίσης CHPaT et Suidas: ἐπίσας
cett. 1063 οὐ Triclinius e coniectura: οὐ μὰ codd. 1065 δαρόν <γ᾽>
Fröhlich 1066 βροτοῖσι] φθιτοῖσι Blaydes Φάμα] φήμα K¹ˢ: φήμη
DᵃᶜOᵃᶜ 1070 σφὶν Schaefer: σφίσιν fere LK**r**ADXr**Xsp**Zc: σφίσι γ᾽ Zr:
σφίσ᾽ **t** νοσεῖ] νοσεῖται Par. gr. 2794: νοσοῦσι Pᵍˡ: νοσεῖ δή **t**: νοσώδη
Erfurdt

68

τὰ δὲ πρὸς τέκνων διπλῆ φύ–
λοπις οὐκέτ᾽ ἐξισοῦται
φιλοτασίῳ διαίτᾳ.

πρόδοτος δὲ μόνα σαλεύει
ἁ παῖς, οἶτον ἀεὶ πατρὸς   1075
δειλαία στενάχουσ᾽ ὅπως
ἁ πάνδυρτος ἀηδών,
οὔτε τι τοῦ θανεῖν προμηθὴς
τό τε μὴ βλέπειν ἑτοίμα,
διδύμαν ἑλοῦσ᾽ Ἐρινύν.   1080
τίς ἂν εὔπατρις ὧδε βλάστοι;

οὐδεὶς τῶν ἀγαθῶν < – >   [str. 2
ζῶν κακῶς εὔκλειαν αἰσχῦναι θέλει
νώνυμος, ὦ παῖ παῖ·
ὡς καὶ σὺ πάγκλαυτον αἰ–   1085
    ῶνα †κοινὸν† εἵλου,
τὸ μὴ† καλὸν καθοπλίσα–
    σα δύο φέρειν <ἐν> ἑνὶ λόγῳ,
σοφά τ᾽ ἀρίστα τε παῖς κεκλῆσθαι.

ζώης μοι καθύπερθεν   [ant. 2 1090
χειρὶ καὶ πλούτῳ τεῶν ἐχθρῶν ὅσον
νῦν ὑπόχειρ ναίεις·

1075 ἁ παῖς Schneidewin, οἶτον Mudge: Ἠλέκτρα τὸν codd.: Ἠλέκτρα θάνα-
τον Fröhlich, ἀεὶ deleto   1077 πάνδυρτος Porson et Erfurdt: πανόδυρτος
fere codd.   1080 Ἐρινύν LPV: –ιννύν vel –ιννῦν cett.   1081 ἂν Triclinius
e coniectura: ἂν οὖν LKaFHOPPaVZc: οὖν C: οὖν ἂν N: ἄρ᾽ οὖν R:
τἄρ᾽ οὖν G   βλάστοι N²ᵖᶜ, coni. Schaefer: βλαστοῖ cett.   1082 post
ἀγαθῶν add. γὰρ Hermann, ἂν Schneidewin, τοι Lange   1083 θέλει] –οι
Schneidewin   1084 νώνυμος] –ον Dᵃᶜ et Gnom.: –υμνος Lᵃᶜ (verum Lᵖᶜ)
1085 πάγκλαυτον Lt: –αυστον cett.   1086 κοινὸν] κλεινὸν Sirks: κεῖνον
Fröhlich   1087 τὸ μὴ] τομῇ Most: ἄκος Lloyd-Jones   καθοπλίσασα]
ὑπεροπλίσασα Heimsoeth: καθιππάσασα Hermann   1088 <ἐν> add.
Brunck   1090 καθύπερθεν DZrH et Eustathius 1083.18: –θε cett.   1091
χειρὶ SV et Eustathius: χερὶ cett.: χεροῖν Dawe   καὶ πλούτῳ codd. plerique
et Eustathius: πλούτῳ τε t   τεῶν Hermann: τῶν codd.   1092 ὑπόχειρ
Musgrave: ὑπὸ χεῖρα codd. et Eustathius

ἐπεί σ᾿ ἐφηύρηκα μοί–
ρᾳ μὲν οὐκ ἐν ἐσθλᾷ
βεβῶσαν, ἃ δὲ μέγιστ᾿ ἔβλα–   1095
στε νόμιμα, τῶνδε φερομέναν
ἄριστα τᾷ Ζηνὸς εὐσεβείᾳ.

Ορ. ἆρ᾿, ὦ γυναῖκες, ὀρθά τ᾿ εἰσηκούσαμεν
      ὀρθῶς θ᾿ ὁδοιποροῦμεν ἔνθα χρήζομεν;
Χο. τί δ᾿ ἐξερευνᾷς καὶ τί βουληθεὶς πάρει;   1100
Ορ. Αἴγισθον ἔνθ᾿ ᾤκηκεν ἱστορῶ πάλαι.
Χο. ἀλλ᾿ εὖ θ᾿ ἱκάνεις χὠ φράσας ἀζήμιος.
Ορ. τίς οὖν ἂν ὑμῶν τοῖς ἔσω φράσειεν ἂν
      ἡμῶν ποθεινὴν κοινόπουν παρουσίαν;
Χο. ἥδ᾿, εἰ τὸν ἄγχιστόν γε κηρύσσειν χρεών.   1105
Ορ. ἴθ᾿, ὦ γύναι, δήλωσον εἰσελθοῦσ᾿ ὅτι
      Φωκῆς ματεύουσ᾿ ἄνδρες Αἴγισθόν τινες.
Ηλ. οἴμοι τάλαιν᾿, οὐ δή ποθ᾿ ἧς ἠκούσαμεν
      φήμης φέροντες ἐμφανῆ τεκμήρια;
Ορ. οὐκ οἶδα τὴν σὴν κληδόν᾿· ἀλλά μοι γέρων   1110
      ἐφεῖτ᾿ Ὀρέστου Στροφίος ἀγγεῖλαι πέρι.
Ηλ. τί δ᾿ ἔστιν, ὦ ξέν᾿; ὥς μ᾿ ὑπέρχεται φόβος.
Ορ. φέροντες αὐτοῦ σμικρὰ λείψαν᾿ ἐν βραχεῖ
      τεύχει θανόντος, ὡς ὁρᾷς, κομίζομεν.
Ηλ. οἲ ᾿γὼ τάλαινα, τοῦτ᾿ ἐκεῖν᾿, ἤδη σαφές·   1115
      πρόχειρον ἄχθος, ὡς ἔοικε, δέρκομαι.
Ορ. εἴπερ τι κλαίεις τῶν Ὀρεστείων κακῶν,
      τόδ᾿ ἄγγος ἴσθι σῶμα τοὐκείνου στέγον.

1093 ἐφηύρηκα Dindorf: ἐφεύρηκα codd.   1094 ἐν ADXrXsCNZc¹ᵖᶜ: ἐπ᾿
KXrʳʸᵖOPPaVt: om. LrZrFHZcᵃᶜ   1095 ἔβλαστε LKrADXrCFNPaVZc:
–εν XsZrHOPt   1096 τῶνδε] τῶν Erfurdt   1097 ἄριστα] ἐριστά
novit ΣL   Ζηνὸς Lʳʸᵖt: Διὸς cett.   1099 θ᾿ Kt: om. Lᵃᶜ: δ᾿ Lᵖᶜ
et cett.   1100 τί δ᾿] τίν᾿ Dawe   1101 Αἴγισθον] –ος novit ΣZc
ἱστορῶ] μαστεύω LʳʸᵖSʸᵖ   1102 ἀλλ᾿ εὖ θ᾿] ὀρθῶς KOPPa   θ᾿]
γ᾿ Turnebus   1107 Φωκῆς L: –εῖς cett.   ματεύουσ᾿ aPaˣt: μαστ– fere
cett.   1108 οὐ] ἦ LˢCFᵖᶜH   1111 Στροφίος LK: Στρό– cett.   1113
σμικρὰ LFt: μικρὰ cett.   1115–16 alii aliter interpungunt

ΣΟΦΟΚΛΕΟΥΣ ΗΛΕΚΤΡΑ

Ηλ. ὦ ξεῖνε, δός νυν πρὸς θεῶν, εἴπερ τόδε
κέκευθεν αὐτὸν τεῦχος, ἐς χεῖρας λαβεῖν,   1120
ὅπως ἐμαυτὴν καὶ γένος τὸ πᾶν ὁμοῦ
ξὺν τῇδε κλαύσω κἀποδύρωμαι σποδῷ.

Ορ. δόθ᾽, ἥτις ἐστί, προσφέροντες· οὐ γὰρ ὡς
ἐν δυσμενείᾳ γ᾽ οὖσ᾽ ἐπαιτεῖται τόδε,
ἀλλ᾽ ἢ φίλων τις, ἢ πρὸς αἵματος φύσιν.   1125

Ηλ. ὦ φιλτάτου μνημεῖον ἀνθρώπων ἐμοὶ
ψυχῆς Ὀρέστου λοιπόν, ὡς <σ᾽> ἀπ᾽ ἐλπίδων
ὑφ᾽ ὧνπερ ἐξέπεμπον εἰσεδεξάμην.
νῦν μὲν γὰρ οὐδὲν ὄντα βαστάζω χεροῖν,
δόμων δέ σ᾽, ὦ παῖ, λαμπρὸν ἐξέπεμψ᾽ ἐγώ.   1130
ὡς ὤφελον πάροιθεν ἐκλιπεῖν βίον,
πρὶν ἐς ξένην σε γαῖαν ἐκπέμψαι χεροῖν
κλέψασα ταῖνδε κἀνασώσασθαι φόνου,
ὅπως θανὼν ἔκεισο τῇ τόθ᾽ ἡμέρᾳ,
τύμβου πατρῴου κοινὸν εἰληχὼς μέρος.   1135
νῦν δ᾽ ἐκτὸς οἴκων κἀπὶ γῆς ἄλλης φυγὰς
κακῶς ἀπώλου, σῆς κασιγνήτης δίχα·
κοὔτ᾽ ἐν φίλαισι χερσὶν ἡ τάλαιν᾽ ἐγὼ
λουτροῖς σ᾽ ἐκόσμησ᾽ οὔτε παμφλέκτου πυρὸς
ἀνειλόμην, ὡς εἰκός, ἄθλιον βάρος,   1140
ἀλλ᾽ ἐν ξένησι χερσὶ κηδευθεὶς τάλας
σμικρὸς προσήκεις ὄγκος ἐν σμικρῷ κύτει.
οἴμοι τάλαινα τῆς ἐμῆς πάλαι τροφῆς

1119 ξεῖνε LAXrXsZrCFNZct: ξένε KrDHOPPaV   νυν t: νῦν cett.
1124 ἐπαιτεῖται KaHPPaVt: ἐπαιτεῖ LrCFNO: ἀπαιτεῖται Zc   τόδε
LrZrCFHNOPaVt: τάδε   KADXrXsPZc   1125 del. Jahn   τίς
<ἐστιν> Fröhlich, deleto φύσιν   1127 σ᾽ N^gl, add. Brunck: om. cett.
1128 ὑφ᾽ ὧνπερ Wecklein: οὐχ ὥνπερ codd. plerique: οὐχ ὄνπερ Bb, coni.
Fröhlich: οὐχ ὥσπερ HOPa   1129 σ᾽ post οὐδὲν H, add. Dawe   1131
ὤφελον L^pcGAXrXs^1pcCFNVZcT: ὤφελες L^acXr^1sHN^1sOJ, coni. Porson:
ὄφελον ZrP: ὄφελες R   1135 εἰληχὼς codd. plerique (etiam Λ): εἰληφὼς
ZcZg   1137 κασιγνήτης] –του RXsZr^pcCHNO   1139 σ᾽ PV, coni.
Schaefer: om. cett.   πυρὸς] πυρᾶς Wecklein   1141 ξένησι LKrpT:
–αισι ADXrZc   1142 σμικρὸς] μικρὸς Zr et Suidas iii. 506.19   σμικρῷ
LrCFNt: μικρῷ KaHOPPaVZc et Suidas

71

ἀνωφελήτου, τὴν ἐγὼ θάμ' ἀμφὶ σοὶ
πόνῳ γλυκεῖ παρέσχον. οὔτε γάρ ποτε   1145
μητρὸς σύ γ' ἦσθα μᾶλλον ἢ κἀμοῦ φίλος,
οὔθ' οἱ κατ' οἶκον ἦσαν ἀλλ' ἐγὼ τροφός,
ἐγὼ δ' ἀδελφὴ σοὶ προσηυδώμην ἀεί.
νῦν δ' ἐκλέλοιπε ταῦτ' ἐν ἡμέρᾳ μιᾷ
θανόντα σὺν σοί. πάντα γὰρ συναρπάσας,   1150
θύελλ' ὅπως, βέβηκας. οἴχεται πατήρ·
τέθνηκ' ἐγὼ σοί· φροῦδος αὐτὸς εἶ θανών·
γελῶσι δ' ἐχθροί· μαίνεται δ' ὑφ' ἡδονῆς
μήτηρ ἀμήτωρ, ἧς ἐμοὶ σὺ πολλάκις
φήμας λάθρᾳ προὔπεμπες ὡς φανούμενος   1155
τιμωρὸς αὐτός. ἀλλὰ ταῦθ' ὁ δυστυχὴς
δαίμων ὁ σός τε κἀμὸς ἐξαφείλετο,
ὅς σ' ὧδέ μοι προὔπεμψεν ἀντὶ φιλτάτης
μορφῆς σποδόν τε καὶ σκιὰν ἀνωφελῆ.
οἴμοι μοι.   1160
ὢ δέμας οἰκτρόν. φεῦ φεῦ.
ὢ δεινοτάτας, οἴμοι μοι,
πεμφθεὶς κελεύθους, φίλταθ', ὥς μ' ἀπώλεσας,
ἀπώλεσας δῆτ', ὢ κασίγνητον κάρα.
τοιγὰρ σὺ δέξαι μ' ἐς τὸ σὸν τόδε στέγος,   1165
τὴν μηδὲν ἐς τὸ μηδέν, ὡς σὺν σοὶ κάτω
ναίω τὸ λοιπόν. καὶ γὰρ ἡνίκ' ἦσθ' ἄνω,
ξὺν σοὶ μετεῖχον τῶν ἴσων· καὶ νῦν ποθῶ

1145 παρέσχον codd. et Suidas iv. 732.15: παρεῖχον Nauck   1146 φίλος
codd. et Suidas: τέκος Dindorf: θάλος Arnold   1148 del. Herwerden: post
hunc versum lacunam indicavit Dawe   ἐγὼ δὲ μήτηρ σὴ προσηυδώμην,
κάσι Nauck   σοὶ **Lra**CN: σὴ L^rsKFHOPPaVZc**t**   προσηυδώμην
L^acK^acAXrZrPaZc**t**: –όμην L^pcK^pc**r**XsCFHNOPV   1149 ταῦτ'] πάντ'
Blaydes   1150 θανόντα **r**C^1pcF^pcHNVZc**t**: –όντι LKR^s**a**F^acOPPa
1152 ἐγὼ σοί Jebb: ἐγώ σοι codd.: ἐγώ· σὺ Erfurdt: ἐγὼ 'ν σοί Groeneboom
1155 προὔπεμπες] προὔπεμψας P   1160 μοι] οἴμοι T   1162 μοι] οἴμοι
F   1163 κελεύθους L^pcDXrXsZrF^pcP^1pcT^s: –ου **lr**ACF^acHN^acOP^acPaVZc**t**
1168 μετεῖχον] κατ– Λ, fort. L^ac

τοῦ σοῦ θανοῦσα μὴ ἀπολείπεσθαι τάφου.
τοὺς γὰρ θανόντας οὐχ ὁρῶ λυπουμένους. 1170
Χο. θνητοῦ πέφυκας πατρός, Ἠλέκτρα, φρόνει·
θνητὸς δ' Ὀρέστης· ὥστε μὴ λίαν στένε·
πᾶσιν γὰρ ἡμῖν τοῦτ' ὀφείλεται παθεῖν.
Ορ. φεῦ φεῦ, τί λέξω; ποῖ λόγων ἀμηχάνων
ἔλθω; κρατεῖν γὰρ οὐκέτι γλώσσης σθένω. 1175
Ηλ. τί δ' ἔσχες ἄλγος; πρὸς τί τοῦτ' εἰπὼν κυρεῖς;
Ορ. ἦ σὸν τὸ κλεινὸν εἶδος Ἠλέκτρας τόδε;
Ηλ. τόδ' ἔστ' ἐκεῖνο, καὶ μάλ' ἀθλίως ἔχον.
Ορ. οἴμοι ταλαίνης ἄρα τῆσδε συμφορᾶς.
Ηλ. οὐ δή ποτ', ὦ ξέν', ἀμφ' ἐμοὶ στένεις τάδε; 1180
Ορ. ὦ σῶμ' ἀτίμως κἀθέως ἐφθαρμένον.
Ηλ. οὔτοι ποτ' ἄλλην ἢ 'μὲ δυσφημεῖς, ξένε.
Ορ. φεῦ τῆς ἀνύμφου δυσμόρου τε σῆς τροφῆς.
Ηλ. τί δή ποτ', ὦ ξέν', ὧδ' ἐπισκοπῶν στένεις;
Ορ. ὡς οὐκ ἄρ' ᾔδη τῶν ἐμῶν οὐδὲν κακῶν. 1185
Ηλ. ἐν τῷ διέγνως τοῦτο τῶν εἰρημένων;
Ορ. ὁρῶν σε πολλοῖς ἐμπρέπουσαν ἄλγεσιν.
Ηλ. καὶ μὴν ὁρᾷς γε παῦρα τῶν ἐμῶν κακῶν.
Ορ. καὶ πῶς γένοιτ' ἂν τῶνδ' ἔτ' ἐχθίω βλέπειν;
Ηλ. ὁθούνεκ' εἰμὶ τοῖς φονεῦσι σύντροφος. 1190
Ορ. τοῖς τοῦ; πόθεν τοῦτ' ἐξεσήμηνας κακόν;
Ηλ. τοῖς πατρός. εἶτα τοῖσδε δουλεύω βίᾳ.

1169 μὴ ἀπολείπεσθαι LᵃᶜFNOZc: μὴ 'πο– Lᵖᶜ**a**Paᵖᶜ**t**: μὴ ξαπο– KHPPaᵃᶜV: μὴ ἐκ– **r** 1170 del. Zippmann 1173 ex Aristophanis Polyido citat Stob. Ecl. 4.51.15: del. Bergk 1174 ἀμηχάνων codd. (etiam Λ): –ανῶν Heath post Johnson 1175 γλώσσης L¹ᵖᶜΛaFˢHOPaZcWb**t**: γνώμης Lˡˢ**Kr**FPVWbʳʸᵖ: γνώσσης Lᵃᶜ 1176 ἔσχες] ἔσχε σ' Bergk 1177 Ἠλέκτρας] –α L(verum Lˢ), **r**ZrCᵃᶜFᵃᶜNᵃᶜ 1180 οὐLʳˢ et ut vid. novit ΣL: τί codd. 1184 δή ποτ' L¹ᵖᶜ**Kra**FHOPPaVZc: μοί ποτ' LᵃᶜCN**t** et Suidas ii. 378.28: δῆτά μ' Lloyd-Jones et Wilson 1185 ὡς] ὅσ' Plüss ᾔδη Heath: ᾔδειν codd. οὐδὲν] ἐγώ L (partim erasum) 1190 Electrae sententiam interrumpi credit Eitrem: aut hoc aut τοι pro τοῖς scribendum credit West 1191 ἐξεσήμηνας ADᵖᶜXrXsZrFᵖᶜHPPaVZc**t**: –ανας KRDᵃᶜO: –ανες C: –ηνες N, fort. Fᵃᶜ: L non legitur: [ ]ες Λ

73

Ορ. τίς γάρ σ᾽ ἀνάγκη τῇδε προτρέπει βροτῶν;
Ηλ. μήτηρ καλεῖται· μητρὶ δ᾽ οὐδὲν ἐξισοῖ.
Ορ. τί δρῶσα; πότερα χερσίν, ἢ λύμῃ βίου;   1195
Ηλ. καὶ χερσὶ καὶ λύμαισι καὶ πᾶσιν κακοῖς.
Ορ. οὐδ᾽ οὑπαρήξων οὔθ᾽ ὁ κωλύσων πάρα;
Ηλ. οὐ δῆθ᾽· ὃς ἦν γάρ μοι σὺ προὔθηκας σποδόν.
Ορ. ὦ δύσποτμ᾽, ὡς ὁρῶν σ᾽ ἐποικτίρω πάλαι.
Ηλ. μόνος βροτῶν νυν ἴσθ᾽ ἐποικτίρας ποτέ.   1200
Ορ. μόνος γὰρ ἥκω τοῖσι σοῖς ἀλγῶν κακοῖς.
Ηλ. οὐ δή ποθ᾽ ἡμῖν ξυγγενὴς ἥκεις ποθέν;
Ορ. ἐγὼ φράσαιμ᾽ ἄν, εἰ τὸ τῶνδ᾽ εὔνουν πάρα.
Ηλ. ἀλλ᾽ ἐστὶν εὔνουν, ὥστε πρὸς πιστὰς ἐρεῖς.
Ορ. μέθες τόδ᾽ ἄγγος νυν, ὅπως τὸ πᾶν μάθῃς.   1205
Ηλ. μὴ δῆτα πρὸς θεῶν τοῦτό μ᾽ ἐργάσῃ, ξένε.
Ορ. πιθοῦ λέγοντι κοὐχ ἁμαρτήσῃ ποτέ.
Ηλ. μὴ πρὸς γενείου, μὴ ᾽ξέλῃ τὰ φίλτατα.
Ορ. οὔ φημ᾽ ἐάσειν. Ηλ. ὦ τάλαιν᾽ ἐγὼ σέθεν,
    Ὀρέστα, τῆς σῆς εἰ στερήσομαι ταφῆς.   1210
Ορ. εὔφημα φώνει· πρὸς δίκης γὰρ οὐ στένεις.
Ηλ. πῶς τὸν θανόντ᾽ ἀδελφὸν οὐ δίκῃ στένω;
Ορ. οὔ σοι προσήκει τήνδε προσφωνεῖν φάτιν.
Ηλ. οὕτως ἄτιμός εἰμι τοῦ τεθνηκότος;
Ορ. ἄτιμος οὐδενὸς σύ· τοῦτο δ᾽ οὐχὶ σόν.   1215
Ηλ. εἴπερ γ᾽ Ὀρέστου σῶμα βαστάζω τόδε.
Ορ. ἀλλ᾽ οὐκ Ὀρέστου, πλὴν λόγῳ γ᾽ ἠσκημένον.
Ηλ. ποῦ δ᾽ ἔστ᾽ ἐκείνου τοῦ ταλαιπώρου τάφος;
Ορ. οὐκ ἔστι· τοῦ γὰρ ζῶντος οὐκ ἔστιν τάφος.

1193 σ᾽] om. L^{ac}rCV   ἀνάγκη K^{pc}ADT: –η LK^{ac}rXrXsZrpZcTa
προτρέπει] προστρέπει Reiske: προστρίβει Wilson   1197 οὔθ᾽ ὁ
LΛrAXrXsCFNZc: οὐδ᾽ ὁ KDZrHOPPaVt   1199 ἐποικτίρω Nauck:
–είρω codd.   1200 νυν t: νῦν codd.   νυν <μ᾽> Papageorgius ἐποικτίρας Nauck: –είρας codd.   ποτέ] με σύ Xr: ἐμέ ZrZg, coni. Herwerden   1201 τοῖσι σοῖς] τοῖς ἴσοις LΛP   1205 ἄγγος] ἄλγος r (verum
G^{γρ})   1207 πιθοῦ KXr^{18}F^{pc}H^{pc}OPPa: πείθου LraCF^{ac}NVZct   1208
μὴ ᾽ξέλῃ codd. et Eustathius 129.16: μ᾽ ἐξέλῃ Elmsley   1212 πῶς] πῶς·
LKZcZg: πῶς; Dawe   1213 φάτιν] ταφήν Fröhlich (φάτην Xs)   1217
γ᾽ ἠσκημένον] γε, σῶμ᾽ ἔνι Fröhlich

74

Ηλ. πῶς εἶπας, ὦ παῖ; Ορ. ψεῦδος οὐδὲν ὧν λέγω.   1220
Ηλ. ἦ ζῇ γὰρ ἀνήρ; Ορ. εἴπερ ἔμψυχός γ᾽ ἐγώ.
Ηλ. ἦ γὰρ σὺ κεῖνος; Ορ. τήνδε προσβλέψασά μου
     σφραγῖδα πατρὸς ἔκμαθ᾽ εἰ σαφῆ λέγω.
Ηλ. ὦ φίλτατον φῶς. Ορ. φίλτατον, συμμαρτυρῶ.
Ηλ. ὦ φθέγγμ᾽, ἀφίκου; Ορ. μηκέτ᾽ ἄλλοθεν πύθῃ.   1225
Ηλ. ἔχω σε χερσίν; Ορ. ὡς τὰ λοίπ᾽ ἔχοις ἀεί.
Ηλ. ὦ φίλταται γυναῖκες, ὦ πολίτιδες,
     ὁρᾶτ᾽ Ὀρέστην τόνδε, μηχαναῖσι μὲν
     θανόντα, νῦν δὲ μηχαναῖς σεσωμένον.
Χο. ὁρῶμεν, ὦ παῖ, κἀπὶ συμφοραῖσί μοι   1230
     γεγηθὸς ἕρπει δάκρυον ὀμμάτων ἄπο.

Ηλ. ἰὼ γοναί,   [str.
     ἰὼ σωμάτων ἐμοὶ φιλτάτων,
     ἐμόλετ᾽ ἀρτίως,
     ἐφηύρετ᾽, εἴδετ᾽, <ἐλάβεθ᾽> οὓς ἐχρῄζετε.   1235
Ορ. πάρεσμεν· ἀλλὰ σῖγ᾽ ἔχουσα πρόσμενε.
Ηλ. τί δ᾽ ἔστιν;
Ορ. σιγᾶν ἄμεινον, μή τις ἔνδοθεν κλύῃ.
Ηλ. ἀλλ᾽ οὐ τὰν θεὰν τὰν ἀεὶ ἀδμήταν,
     τόδε μὲν οὔποτ᾽ ἀξιώσω τρέσαι,   1240
     περισσὸν ἄχθος ἔνδον
     γυναικῶν ὂν αἰεί.
Ορ. ὅρα γε μὲν δὴ κἂν γυναιξὶν ὡς Ἄρης
     ἔνεστιν· εὖ δ᾽ ἔξοισθα πειραθεῖσά που.

1222 μου] μοι Morstadt   1224 συμμαρτυρῶ] ξυμ– rCN   1226
χερσί(ν) aZct: χεροῖν LKrp, unde χειροῖν Neue   1229 σεσωμένον Wecklein: –σμένον codd.   1232–3 γοναί, ἰὼ Nauck: γοναὶ LrZrCFHNZc:
γοναί, γοναὶ KADXrXsOPPaVt   1235 ἐφηύρετ᾽ Dindorf: ἐφεύρετ᾽ codd.
εἴδετ᾽, <ἐλάβεθ᾽> supplevi post Heimsoeth, qui <εἴλεθ᾽> mavult: εἴδεθ᾽
OPaWc: ἦλθετ᾽, εἴδεθ᾽ cett.   1239 ἀλλ᾽ οὐ LrAXs^{ac}FNP^{ac}VZcT: ἀλλ᾽ οὐ
μὰ KDXrXs^{1pc}ZrHOPa: μὰ Hartung: οὐ Seidler   θεὰν Steinhart (θεὸν
mavult West): Ἄρτεμιν codd.   ἀεὶ S, coni. Arndt: αἰὲν cett.   1242 ὂν
αἰεί KRCFNOVZct: ὂν ἀεί LGaHPPa: ὃ ναίει Viketos   1244 om. t

75

Ηλ.   ὀττοτοῖ < ∪ – ∪ – >,   1245
      ἀνέφελον ἐνέβαλες οὔποτε καταλύσιμον,
      οὐδέ ποτε λησόμενον ἀμέτερον
      οἷον ἔφυ κακόν.   1250
Ορ.   ἔξοιδα καὶ ταῦτ'· ἀλλ' ὅταν παρουσία
      φράζῃ, τότ' ἔργων τῶνδε μεμνῆσθαι χρεών.

Ηλ.   ὁ πᾶς ἐμοί,   [ant.
      ὁ πᾶς ἂν πρέποι παρὼν ἐννέπειν
      τάδε δίκᾳ χρόνος.   1255
      μόλις γὰρ ἔσχον νῦν ἐλεύθερον στόμα.
Ορ.   ξύμφημι κἀγώ· τοιγαροῦν σῴζου τόδε.
Ηλ.   τί δρῶσα;
Ορ.   οὗ μή 'στι καιρὸς μὴ μακρὰν βούλου λέγειν.
Ηλ.   τίς †οὖν† ἀξίαν σοῦ γε πεφηνότος   1260
      μεταβάλοιτ' ἂν ὧδε σιγὰν λόγων;
      ἐπεί σε νῦν ἀφράστως
      ἀέλπτως τ' ἐσεῖδον.
Ορ.   τότ' εἶδες, ὅτε θεοί μ' ἐπώτρυναν μολεῖν
      <× – ∪ –   × – ∪ –   × – ∪ – >
Ηλ.   ἔφρασας ὑπερτέραν   1265
      τᾶς πάρος ἔτι χάριτος, εἴ σε θεὸς ἐπόρισεν
      ἀμέτερα πρὸς μέλαθρα· δαιμόνιον
      αὐτὸ τίθημ' ἐγώ.   1270
Ορ.   τὰ μέν σ' ὀκνῶ χαίρουσαν εἰργαθεῖν, τὰ δὲ
      δέδοικα λίαν ἡδονῇ νικωμένην.

1245 ὀττοτοῖ vel –οῖ codd. plerique: ὀτοττοῖ L: ὀτοτοττοῖ P: ὀττο<τοτοῖ ὄττο>τοῖ West: ὀτοτοτοῖ τοτοῖ Dindorf et Hermann: ὀττοτοῖ <ὀττοτοῖ> Bergk   1246 ἐνέβαλες ΣL: ὑπ– Vat. gr. 40: ἐπ– cett.   1251 παρουσία] παρρησία Monac. gr. 507: παρρησίαν J: unde παρρησία Pearson   1255 δίκᾳ Lᵞᵖt (ἔν τινι τῶν παλαιῶν βιβλίων ΣΤ): δίκαια cett., sed α alterum supra lin. habent COPPaZcZg   1260 οὖν ἀξίαν LrZrFP: οὖν ἂν ἀξίαν KADXrH: οὖν ἀναξίαν CNᵃᶜZc: ἂν οὖν ἀξίαν XsPaᵃᶜV: ἂν ἀναξίαν O: ἀνταξίαν Arndt: an ἆρ' ἀξίαν?   σοῦ γε Seidler: γε σοῦ codd. 1261 μεταβάλοιτ'] μεταλάβοιτ' Wecklein   1264 ὅτε] ὅταν D: εὖτε Jebb ἐπώτρυναν Reiske: ὤτρυναν codd.   post hunc versum lacunam indicavit Heath, ante ὤτρυναν Michaelis   1266 ἐπόρισεν Dindorf: ἐπόρσεν Lᵃᶜ: ἐπῶρσεν Lᵖᶜ et cett.   1271 εἰργαθεῖν Elmsley: –άθειν codd.

Ηλ.   ἰὼ χρόνῳ   [ep.
      μακρῷ φιλτάταν ὁδὸν ἐπαξιώ–
      σας ὧδέ μοι φανῆναι,
      μή τί με, πολύπονον ὧδ' ἰδών–   1275
Ορ.   τί μὴ ποήσω; Ηλ. μή μ' ἀποστερήσῃς
      τῶν σῶν προσώπων ἡδονὰν μεθέσθαι.
Ορ.   ἦ κάρτα κἂν ἄλλοισι θυμοίμην ἰδών.
Ηλ.   ξυναινεῖς; Ορ. τί μὴν οὔ;   1280
Ηλ.   ὦ φίλαι, ἔκλυον ἂν ἐγὼ οὐδ' ἂν ἤλπισ' αὐδάν.
      $< - \cup - \times >$ ἔσχον ὀργὰν ἄναυδον
      οὐδὲ σὺν βοᾷ κλύουσ' ἁ τάλαινα.
      νῦν δ' ἔχω σε· προὐφάνης δὲ   1285
      φιλτάταν ἔχων πρόσοψιν,
      ἇς ἐγὼ οὐδ' ἂν ἐν κακοῖς λαθοίμαν.

Ορ.   τὰ μὲν περισσεύοντα τῶν λόγων ἄφες,
      καὶ μήτε μήτηρ ὡς κακὴ δίδασκέ με
      μήθ' ὡς πατρῷαν κτῆσιν Αἴγισθος δόμων   1290
      ἀντλεῖ, τὰ δ' ἐκχεῖ, τὰ δὲ διασπείρει μάτην·
      χρόνου γὰρ ἄν σοι καιρὸν ἐξείργοι λόγος.
      ἃ δ' ἁρμόσει μοι τῷ παρόντι νῦν χρόνῳ
      σήμαιν', ὅπου φανέντες ἢ κεκρυμμένοι
      γελῶντας ἐχθροὺς παύσομεν τῇ νῦν ὁδῷ.   1295
      $< \times - \cup - \quad \times - \cup - \quad \times - \cup - >$

1275 πολύπονον J: πολύστονον cett.   1277 ἡδονὰν] ἁδονᾶν Porson:
ἁδονὰν Dindorf   1278 κἂν] τᾶν Monk   1280 μὴν Seidler: μὴ codd.
1281 φίλαι] φίλε C¹ᵖᶜ: φίλ' Wunder   1283 alii aliter suppleverunt: <πρὶν
μὲν οὖν ἐπ–> Dawe: <ἀλλ' ὅμως ἐπ–> Lloyd-Jones et Wilson   ὀργὰν]
ὁρμὰν Blomfield   1284 κλύουσ' ἁ Hartung post Hermann: κλύουσα codd.
1287 λαθοίμαν LDXrXsZrF¹ˢZct: –μην AF: –μ' ἂν rCHNOPPaV, fort. K
1288 ἄφες] μέθες r   1289–92 del. Ahrens   1292 χρόνου codd. et Suidas
iv. 107.28: ἔργου Reiske   ἐξείργοι codd. et Suidae iv. 107.28: ἐξείργει
FHOV: ἐξήργει Suidae iv. 828.3 codd. SM: ἐξαίρη Suidae codd. GF: ἐξαιροῖ
Hartung   1294 ὅπου] ὅπῃ Oᵖᶜ, coni. Vauvilliers: ὅπως Xs   1295 post
hunc versum lacunam statuit Dawe: <μέμνησο μέντοι τήνδε κρύψασθαι
χαρὰν> ex. gr. supplevi

οὕτως, ὅπως μήτηρ σε μὴ 'πιγνώσεται
φαιδρῷ προσώπῳ νῷν ἐπελθόντοιν δόμους·
ἀλλ᾽ ὡς ἐπ᾽ ἄτῃ τῇ μάτην λελεγμένῃ
στέναζ᾽· ὅταν γὰρ εὐτυχήσωμεν, τότε
χαίρειν παρέσται καὶ γελᾶν ἐλευθέρως.   1300

Ηλ. ἀλλ᾽, ὦ κασίγνηθ᾽, ὧδ᾽ ὅπως καὶ σοὶ φίλον
καὶ τοὐμὸν ἔσται τῇδ᾽· ἐπεὶ τὰς ἡδονὰς
πρὸς σοῦ λαβοῦσα κοὐκ ἐμὰς ἐκτησάμην.
κοὐδ᾽ ἄν σε λυπήσασα δεξαίμην βραχὺ
αὐτὴ μέγ᾽ εὑρεῖν κέρδος· οὐ γὰρ ἂν καλῶς   1305
ὑπηρετοίην τῷ παρόντι δαίμονι.
ἀλλ᾽ οἶσθα μὲν τἀνθένδε, πῶς γὰρ οὔ; κλύων
ὁθούνεκ᾽ Αἴγισθος μὲν οὐ κατὰ στέγας,
μήτηρ δ᾽ ἐν οἴκοις· ἣν σὺ μὴ δείσῃς ποθ᾽ ὡς
γέλωτι τοὐμὸν φαιδρὸν ὄψεται κάρα.   1310
μῖσός τε γὰρ παλαιὸν ἐντέτηκέ μοι,
κἀπεί σ᾽ ἐσεῖδον, οὔ ποτ᾽ ἐκλήξω χαρᾷ
δακρυρροοῦσα. πῶς γὰρ ἂν λήξαιμ᾽ ἐγώ,
ἥτις μιᾷ σε τῇδ᾽ ὁδῷ θανόντα τε
καὶ ζῶντ᾽ ἐσεῖδον; εἴργασαι δέ μ᾽ ἄσκοπα·   1315
ὥστ᾽, εἰ πατήρ μοι ζῶν ἵκοιτο, μηκέτ᾽ ἂν
τέρας νομίζειν αὐτό, πιστεύειν δ᾽ ὁρᾶν.
ὅτ᾽ οὖν τοιαύτην ἧμιν ἐξήκεις ὁδόν,
ἄρχ᾽ αὐτὸς ὥς σοι θυμός. ὡς ἐγὼ μόνη
οὐκ ἂν δυοῖν ἥμαρτον· ἢ γὰρ ἂν καλῶς   1320
ἔσωσ᾽ ἐμαυτήν, ἢ καλῶς ἀπωλόμην.

1296 οὕτως scripsi: οὕτως δ᾽ codd. plerique: οὕτω δ᾽ Ht: ὅρα δ᾽ Schmidt:
φράζου δ᾽ olim Dawe   1297 ἐπελθόντοιν L^{pc}KG^{γρ}RaNO^{pc}PPaVZct:
–ων L^{ac}GCFHO^{ac}: ἐσελθόντοιν Nauck   δόμους] –οις OV   1298 ἀλλ᾽]
σὺ δ᾽ Gnom.   τῇ] μὴ Reiske   λελεγμένη] δεδεγμένη LF^{ac} (verum
L^s)   1302 τῇδ᾽] τάσδ᾽ Morstadt   1304 δεξαίμην F^{ac}O^{s}PZg: λεξαίμην L:
βουλοίμην fere cett.   1306 ὑπηρετοίην Musgrave: –οίμην codd.   1307
κλύων] κλυών Lloyd-Jones et Wilson   1310 τοὐμὸν φαιδρὸν LrCHNPZc:
φαιδρὸν τοὐμὸν KAXrXsZrFOPa: φαιδρῷ τοὐμὸν DVt   1312 χαρᾷ
Schaefer: –ᾶς codd.   1319 ὥς] ὧν Dawe

ΣΟΦΟΚΛΕΟΥΣ ΗΛΕΚΤΡΑ

Ορ. σιγᾶν ἐπήνεσ᾿· ὡς ἐπ᾿ ἐξόδῳ κλύω
τῶν ἔνδοθεν χωροῦντος. Ηλ. εἴσιτ᾿, ὦ ξένοι,
ἄλλως τε καὶ φέροντες οἷ᾿ ἂν οὔτε τις
δόμων ἀπώσαιτ᾿ οὔτ᾿ ἂν ἡσθείη λαβών.   1325

Πα. ὦ πλεῖστα μῶροι καὶ φρενῶν τητώμενοι,
πότερα παρ᾿ οὐδὲν τοῦ βίου κήδεσθ᾿ ἔτι,
ἢ νοῦς ἔνεστιν οὔτις ὑμὶν ἐγγενής,
ὅτ᾿ οὐ παρ᾿ ἀκροῖς ἀλλ᾿ ἐν αὐτοῖσιν κακοῖς
τοῖσιν μεγίστοις ὄντες οὐ γιγνώσκετε;   1330
ἀλλ᾿ εἰ σταθμοῖσι τοῖσδε μὴ ᾿κύρουν ἐγὼ
πάλαι φυλάσσων, ἦν ἂν ἡμῖν ἐν δόμοις
τὰ δρώμεν᾿ ὑμῶν πρόσθεν ἢ τὰ σώματα·
νῦν δ᾿ εὐλάβειαν τῶνδε προὐθέμην ἐγώ.
καὶ νῦν ἀπαλλαχθέντε τῶν μακρῶν λόγων   1335
καὶ τῆς ἀπλήστου τῆσδε σὺν χαρᾷ βοῆς
εἴσω παρέλθεθ᾿· ὡς τὸ μὲν μέλλειν κακὸν
ἐν τοῖς τοιούτοις ἔστ᾿, ἀπηλλάχθαι δ᾿ ἀκμή.

Ορ. πῶς οὖν ἔχει τἀντεῦθεν εἰσιόντι μοι;
Πα. καλῶς· ὑπάρχει γάρ σε μὴ γνῶναί τινα.   1340
Ορ. ἤγγειλας, ὡς ἔοικεν, ὡς τεθνηκότα.
Πα. εἷς τῶν ἐν Ἅιδου μάνθαν᾿ ἐνθάδ᾿ ὢν ἀνήρ.
Ορ. χαίρουσιν οὖν τούτοισιν; ἢ τίνες λόγοι;
Πα. τελουμένων εἴποιμ᾿ ἄν· ὡς δὲ νῦν ἔχει,
καλῶς τὰ κείνων πάντα, καὶ τὰ μὴ καλῶς.   1345
Ηλ. τίς οὗτός ἐστ᾿, ἀδελφέ; πρὸς θεῶν φράσον.
Ορ. οὐχὶ ξυνίης; Ηλ. οὐδέ γ᾿ †ἐς θυμὸν φέρω†.

1322–3 usque ad χωροῦντος choro tribuit Fröhlich (1322–5 Dawe)   1322
post κλύω habet τινὸς Zgˢ: τινὸς pro κλύω Fröhlich   1324 οἷ᾿ ἂν aZct: οἵαν
vel οἵαν LᵃᶜKrXrᵞᵖp   1328 ἐγγενής] ἐκγ– LKGᵞᵖZg: εὐγ– r   1329
παρ᾿ ἄκροις Dawe et Diggle: παρ᾿ αὐτοῖς codd.: παραυτίκ᾿ Meineke (cum
ἤδη pro τοῖσιν)   1332 ἡμῖν] ἡμῖν KHO, fort. Dᵃᶜ: ὑμὶν vel ὑμῖν fere cett.:
ἡμὶν Blaydes   1333 ὑμῶν] ὑμὶν V, coni. Morstadt: ἡμῶν R: οἶμαι Nauck
1334 del. Ahrens   1337–8 κακὸν . . . δ᾿ del. Nauck, cum μὴ pro μὲν
1341 ἔοικεν] ἔοικέ, μ᾿ Fröhlich   1343 οὖν KaHOPaVZct: ἐν LΛrCFNP
1347 ξυνίης RXrFᵖᶜHOPaVZcˡˢt: –ίεις LGADXrˡˢXsZrCFᵃᶜNPᵃᶜZc   ἐς
θυμὸν φέρω] ἠσθόμην σφέ πω Wilson

79

ΣΟΦΟΚΛΕΟΥΣ ΗΛΕΚΤΡΑ

Ορ. οὐκ οἶσθ' ὅτῳ μ' ἔδωκας ἐς χεῖράς ποτε;
Ηλ. ποίῳ; τί φωνεῖς; Ορ. οὗ τὸ Φωκέων πέδον
　　 ὑπεξεπέμφθην σῇ προμηθίᾳ χεροῖν.　　　　　　　1350
Ηλ. ἦ κεῖνος οὗτος ὅν ποτ' ἐκ πολλῶν ἐγὼ
　　 μόνον προσηῦρον πιστὸν ἐν πατρὸς φόνῳ;
Ορ. ὅδ' ἐστί. μή μ' ἔλεγχε πλείοσιν λόγοις.
Ηλ. ὦ φίλτατον φῶς, ὦ μόνος σωτὴρ δόμων
　　 Ἀγαμέμνονος, πῶς ἦλθες; ἦ σὺ κεῖνος εἶ,　　　1355
　　 ὃς τόνδε κἄμ' ἔσωσας ἐκ πολλῶν πόνων;
　　 ὦ φίλταται μὲν χεῖρες, ἥδιστον δ' ἔχων
　　 ποδῶν ὑπηρέτημα, πῶς οὕτω πάλαι
　　 ξυνών μ' ἔληθες οὐδ' ἔσαινες, ἀλλά με
　　 λόγοις ἀπώλλυς, ἔργ' ἔχων ἥδιστ' ἐμοί;　　　1360
　　 χαῖρ', ὦ πάτερ· πατέρα γὰρ εἰσορᾶν δοκῶ·
　　 χαῖρ'· ἴσθι δ' ὡς μάλιστά σ' ἀνθρώπων ἐγὼ
　　 ἤχθηρα κἀφίλησ' ἐν ἡμέρᾳ μιᾷ.
Πα. ἀρκεῖν δοκεῖ μοι· τοὺς γὰρ ἐν μέσῳ λόγους,
　　 πολλαὶ κυκλοῦνται νύκτες ἡμέραι τ' ἴσαι,　　　1365
　　 αἳ ταῦτά σοι δείξουσιν, Ἠλέκτρα, σαφῆ.
　　 σφῷν δ' ἐννέπω γε τοῖν παρεστώτοιν ὅτι
　　 νῦν καιρὸς ἔρδειν· νῦν Κλυταιμήστρα μόνη·
　　 νῦν οὔτις ἀνδρῶν ἔνδον· εἰ δ' ἐφέξετον,
　　 φροντίζεθ' ὡς τούτοις τε καὶ σοφωτέροις　　　1370
　　 ἄλλοισι τούτων πλείοσιν μαχούμενοι.
Ορ. οὐκ ἂν μακρῶν ἔθ' ἡμῖν οὐδὲν ἂν λόγων,
　　 Πυλάδη, τόδ' εἴη τοὔργον, ἀλλ' ὅσον τάχος

1348 χεῖρας KraCHOPaVT: χερ– LFNPZc　　1350 προμηθίᾳ LrFHᵖᶜ:
-εία(ι) LˢKaCHᵃᶜNPaVZct: προθυμία P　　1351 ποτ'] τότ' Meineke
1352 προσηῦρον Dindorf: -εῦρον codd.　　1353 πλείοσιν LAXrZrt:
-σι KrDXspZc　　1354 ὦ φίλτατον] ὦ φίλτατον Lloyd-Jones et Wilson
1357 φιλτάται . . . χεῖρες] –ας . . . –ας Bothe　　δ' ἔχων] δὲ
νῷν Emperius　　1359 ἔσαινες Lloyd-Jones et Wilson: ἔφαινες codd.
1362 σ'] om. LᵃᶜrNOPZc　　1365 κυκλοῦνται LᵃᶜKˢrCFNPt: –οῦσι(ν)
KaHOPaVZc　　1367 γε] om. K: 'γὼ Hermann　　1368 Κλυταιμήστρα
L: –μνήστρα cett.　　1370-1 ἄλλοισι καὶ σοφωτέροις τούτων παλαισταῖς
Nauck　　1372 οὐκ ἂν] οὐ τἂν Dawe　　οὐδὲν ἂν] ἐνδεὲς vel ἐνδέον Fröhlich

80

ΣΟΦΟΚΛΕΟΥΣ ΗΛΕΚΤΡΑ

χωρεῖν ἔσω, πατρῷα προσκύνανθ᾽ ἔδη
θεῶν, ὅσοιπερ πρόπυλα ναίουσιν τάδε.   1375
Ηλ. ἄναξ Ἄπολλον, ἵλεως αὐτοῖν κλύε,
ἐμοῦ τε πρὸς τούτοισιν, ἥ σε πολλὰ δὴ
ἀφ᾽ ὧν ἔχοιμι λιπαρεῖ προὔστην χερί.
νῦν δ᾽, ὦ Λύκει᾽ Ἄπολλον, ἐξ οἵων ἔχω
αἰτῶ, προπίτνω, λίσσομαι, γενοῦ πρόφρων   1380
ἡμῖν ἀρωγὸς τῶνδε τῶν βουλευμάτων
καὶ δεῖξον ἀνθρώποισι τἀπιτίμια
τῆς δυσσεβείας οἷα δωροῦνται θεοί.

Χο. ἴδεθ᾽ ὅπου προνέμεται   [str.
ὁ δυσέριστον αἷμα φυσῶν Ἄρης.   1385
βεβᾶσιν ἄρτι δωμάτων ὑπόστεγοι
μετάδρομοι κακῶν πανουργημάτων
ἄφυκτοι κύνες,
ὥστ᾽ οὐ μακρὰν ἔτ᾽ ἀμμενεῖ
τοὐμὸν φρενῶν ὄνειρον αἰωρούμενον.   1390

παράγεται γὰρ ἐνέρων   [ant.
δολιόπους ἀρωγὸς εἴσω στέγας,
ἀρχαιόπλουτα πατρὸς εἰς ἐδώλια,
νεακόνητον αἷμα χειροῖν ἔχων·
ὁ Μαίας δὲ παῖς   1395
Ἑρμῆς σφ᾽ ἄγει δόλον σκότῳ
κρύψας πρὸς αὐτὸ τέρμα κοὐκέτ᾽ ἀμμένει.

1375 ὅσοιπερ KDXrXsCHNOPPa^{ac}V: ὅσοι LrAZrFPa^{pc}Zct   πρόπυλα]
–λαι H: –λαια OPaVt   1379 Λύκει᾽] Λυκί᾽ XrFH et Suidas ii. 322.22
(verum iii. 274.13)   1380 προπίτνω A: προπιτνῶ L^{pc}KXrXs^{ac}ZrC^{pc}t
et Suidae iii. 274.14 codd. plerique: προσπιτνῶ L^{ac}rDXr^{1s}Xs^{1pc}pZc et
Suidas ii. 322.22 (et iii. 274.14 cod. A): προπίπτω Jebb   1384 ὅπου]
ὅποι Schneidewin: ὅπῃ Fröhlich   1385 ὁ Blaydes: τὸ codd.   1386
βεβᾶσιν] –σι δ᾽ VZgt   1389 post μακρὰν add. γ᾽ t   ἀμμενεῖ Wunder
ex Σ: –ένει LKaCFPPaVt: ἐμμένει rNO   1390 τοὐμὸν LK^{ac}G^{m}aFHVt:
τοὐμῶν K^{pc}rCF^{s}NOPPa   1393 ἐδώλια LrXr^{γρ}pt: ἐδράσματα L^{γρ}aZc,
GCV^{gl}   1394 χειροῖν L^{ac}: χειρῶν t: χεροῖν cett.   1396 σφ᾽] om. La
ἄγει KrHOPaV^{ac}Zct: ἐπάγει L^{ac} ut vid., CFNPa

81

Ηλ.   ὦ φίλταται γυναῖκες, ἄνδρες αὐτίκα   [str.
      τελοῦσι τοὔργον· ἀλλὰ σῖγα πρόσμενε.

Χο.   πῶς δή; τί νῦν πράσσουσιν; Ηλ. ἡ μὲν ἐς τάφον   1400
      λέβητα κοσμεῖ, τὼ δ' ἐφέστατον πέλας.

Χο.   σὺ δ' ἐκτὸς ᾖξας πρὸς τί; Ηλ. φρουρήσουσ' ὅπως
      Αἴγισθος <ἡμᾶς> μὴ λάθῃ μολὼν ἔσω.

Κλ.   αἰαῖ. ἰὼ στέγαι
      φίλων ἐρῆμοι, τῶν δ' ἀπολλύντων πλέαι.   1405

Ηλ.   βοᾷ τις ἔνδον. οὐκ ἀκούετ', ὦ φίλαι;

Χο.   ἤκουσ' ἀνήκουστα δύστανος, ὥστε φρῖξαι.

Κλ.   οἴμοι τάλαιν'. Αἴγισθε, ποῦ ποτ' ὢν κυρεῖς;

Ηλ.   ἰδοὺ μάλ' αὖ θροεῖ τις. Κλ. ὦ τέκνον τέκνον,   1410
      οἴκτιρε τὴν τεκοῦσαν. Ηλ. ἀλλ' οὐκ ἐκ σέθεν
      ᾠκτίρεθ' οὗτος οὔθ' ὁ γεννήσας πατήρ.

Χο.   ὦ πόλις, ὦ γενεὰ τάλαινα, νῦν σοι
      μοῖρα καθημερία φθίνει φθίνει.

Κλ.   ὤμοι πέπληγμαι. Ηλ. παῖσον, εἰ σθένεις, διπλῆν.   1415

Κλ.   ὤμοι μάλ' αὖθις. Ηλ. εἰ γὰρ Αἰγίσθῳ γ' ὁμοῦ.

Χο.   τελοῦσ' ἀραί· ζῶσιν οἱ
      γᾶς ὑπαὶ κείμενοι.
      παλίρρυτον γὰρ αἷμ' ὑπεξαιροῦσι τῶν κτανόντων   1420
      οἱ πάλαι θανόντες.

      καὶ μὴν πάρεισιν οἵδε· φοινία δὲ χεὶρ   [ant.
      στάζει θυηλαῖς Ἄρεος, οὐδ' ἔχω ψέγειν.

1402 φρουρήσουσ'] –σασ' KZrH   1403 <ἡμᾶς> J^gl, coni. Reiske: αὐτὸς
t: pro Αἴγισθος ponit ὁ θεοῖσιν ἐχθρὸς Jackson   1404 αἶ seu αἲ bis
LZrCFNP, ter HZc, quater KrADXrXsVT, octiens Pa   1409 ποῦ] ποῖ
LFNPZc   1410 ὦ τέκνον τέκνον ZrHOVt: ὦ τέκνον bis cett.   1411 οἴκτιρε
Nauck: οἴκτειρε codd.   οὐκ] οὔτ' Bellermann   1412 ᾠκτίρεθ' Nauck:
ᾠκτείρεθ' codd.   οὔθ' LKraCFNPPaV^{τpc}Zct: οὐδ' HOV^{ac}   οὔθ' ὁ γεννήσας πατήρ del. Wilamowitz   1413 σοι Hermann: σε codd.   1414
καθημερία] καθα– **t**   φθίνει bis LKrpZct: semel **a**   1416 γ' Hermann:
δ' GHO: θ' LKRaCFNPPaVZct   1417 τελοῦσ' **t**: –σιν cett.   1418 ὑπαὶ
κείμενοι Brunck: ὑποκείμενοι codd.   1420 παλίρρυτον Bothe: πολύρρυτον fere codd.   1422–3 coryphaeo tribuit Hermann, Electrae fere codd.
1423 θυηλαῖς Bergk: –ῆς codd.   Ἄρεος LKaFHOVZct: –ως rCNPPa
ψέγειν Erfurdt: λέγειν codd.

Ηλ.   Ὀρέστα, πῶς κυρεῖτε; Ορ. τὰν δόμοισι μὲν
      καλῶς, Ἀπόλλων εἰ καλῶς ἐθέσπισεν.   1425

Ηλ.   τέθνηκεν ἡ τάλαινα; Ορ. μηκέτ᾽ ἐκφοβοῦ
      μητρῷον ὥς σε λῆμ᾽ ἀτιμάσει ποτέ.

Ηλ. $< - \cup\cup - \cup -$
      $\times - \cup - \quad \times - \cup - \quad \times - \cup -$

Ορ. $\times - \cup - \quad \times - \cup - \quad \times - \cup - >$

Χο.   παύσασθε, λεύσσω γὰρ Αἴγισθον ἐκ προδήλου.

Ορ. $<\times - \cup - \quad \times - \cup - \quad \times - \cup - >$

Ηλ.   ὦ παῖδες, οὐκ ἄψορρον; Ορ. εἰσορᾶτε ποῦ   1430
      τὸν ἄνδρ᾽ <ἰόντ᾽> ἐφ᾽ ἡμῖν; Ηλ. $< - \times - \cup - >$
      χωρεῖ γεγηθὼς οὗτος ἐκ προαστίου.

Χο.   βᾶτε κατ᾽ ἀντιθύρων ὅσον τάχιστα,
      νῦν πάλιν εὖ θέμενοι τάδ᾽, ὡς τὰ πρίν.

Ορ.   θάρσει· τελοῦμεν. Ηλ. ἦ νοεῖς ἔπειγε νῦν.   1435

Ορ.   καὶ δὴ βέβηκα. Ηλ. τἀνθάδ᾽ ἂν μέλοιτ᾽ ἐμοί.

Χο.   δι᾽ ὠτὸς ἂν παῦρά γ᾽ ὡς
      ἠπίως ἐννέπειν
      πρὸς ἄνδρα τόνδε συμφέροι, λαθραῖον ὡς ὀρούσῃ   1440
      πρὸς Δίκας ἀγῶνα.

ΑΙΓΙΣΘΟΣ

      τίς οἶδεν ὑμῶν ποῦ ποθ᾽ οἱ Φωκῆς ξένοι,
      οὕς φασ᾽ Ὀρέστην ἡμῖν ἀγγεῖλαι βίον

1424 κυρεῖτε Reisig et Elmsley: κυρεῖ LKra FHNPaVZcT: κυρεῖς COP
τὰν] γε; τὰν PaZcT: δέ; τὰν Hermann: τάδ᾽; ἐν Kolster   1426 τέθνηκεν
ἡ τάλαινα Electrae tribuit Erfurdt, Oresti codd.   μηκέτ᾽] μηδὲν CNPPa
1427 post hunc versum lacunam indicavit Erfurdt, post 1429 Seidler   1430
ποῦ Hermann: που codd.   1431 <ἰόντ᾽> Martin   1432 hoc ordine
CNPPa: οὗτος ἐκ προαστίου ante χωρεῖ γεγηθὼς cett. et Suidas iv. 198.12
προαστίου LA¹ˢNPPa et Suidas iv. 198.11: -είου cett.   1433 ἀντιθύρων]
ἀμφιθύρων Musgrave   1434 πάλιν . . . τὰ πρίν Musgrave: τὰ πρὶν . . .
πάλιν codd.   1435 ἦ νοεῖς Electrae tribuit Erfurdt, Oresti codd.   νῦν]
νυν Turnebus   1436 μέλοιτ᾽] μέλοι γ᾽ t   1437–41 choro tribuit t, Electrae
codd.   1437 γ᾽ ὡς] πως Fröhlich   1438 ἠπίως] νηπίῳ cum ον sup.
lin. Lᵞᵖ: ἤπιον Triclinius e coniectura   1442 Φωκῆς LˢPaᵃᶜ, fort. Nᵃᶜ: -εῖς
cett.

λελοιπόθ᾽ ἱππικοῖσιν ἐν ναυαγίοις;
σέ τοι, σὲ κρίνω, ναὶ σέ, τὴν ἐν τῷ πάρος   1445
χρόνῳ θρασεῖαν· ὡς μάλιστα σοὶ μέλειν
οἶμαι, μάλιστα δ᾽ ἂν κατειδυῖαν φράσαι.

Ηλ. ἔξοιδα· πῶς γὰρ οὐχί; συμφορᾶς γὰρ ἂν
ἔξωθεν εἴην τῶν ἐμῶν γε φιλτάτων.

Αι. ποῦ δῆτ᾽ ἂν εἶεν οἱ ξένοι; δίδασκέ με.   1450

Ηλ. ἔνδον· φίλης γὰρ προξένου καθήνυσαν.

Αι. ἦ καὶ θανόντ᾽ ἤγγειλαν ὡς ἐτητύμως;

Ηλ. οὔκ, ἀλλὰ κἀπέδειξαν, οὐ λόγῳ μόνον.

Αι. πάρεστ᾽ ἄρ᾽ ἡμῖν ὥστε κἀμφανῆ μαθεῖν;

Ηλ. πάρεστι δῆτα, καὶ μάλ᾽ ἄζηλος θέα.   1455

Αι. ἦ πολλὰ χαίρειν μ᾽ εἶπας οὐκ εἰωθότως.

Ηλ. χαίροις ἄν, εἴ σοι χαρτὰ τυγχάνει τάδε.

Αι. σιγᾶν ἄνωγα κἀναδεικνύναι πύλας
πᾶσιν Μυκηναίοισιν Ἀργείοις θ᾽ ὁρᾶν,
ὡς εἴ τις αὐτῶν ἐλπίσιν κεναῖς πάρος   1460
ἐξῇρετ᾽ ἀνδρὸς τοῦδε, νῦν ὁρῶν νεκρὸν
στόμια δέχηται τἀμά, μηδὲ πρὸς βίαν
ἐμοῦ κολαστοῦ προστυχὼν φύσῃ φρένας.

Ηλ. καὶ δὴ τελεῖται τἀπ᾽ ἐμοῦ· τῷ γὰρ χρόνῳ
νοῦν ἔσχον, ὥστε συμφέρειν τοῖς κρείσσοσιν.   1465

Αι. ὦ Ζεῦ, δέδορκα φάσμ᾽ ἄνευ φθόνου μὲν οὐ
πεπτωκός· εἰ δ᾽ ἔπεστι νέμεσις οὐ λέγω.

1445 ναὶ Reiske: καὶ codd.   1446 σοὶ Blaydes et Fritzsche: σοι codd.
1449 ἐμῶν] ἐμοί F, coni. Vauvilliers   γε φιλτάτων FOPa¹ᵖᶜ: τε φιλτάτων
LKRXrCZc: φιλτάτων HPaᵃᶜ: τῶν φιλτάτων GʸᵖNP: τῆς φιλτάτης
LˢGADXsZrVt   φιλτάτης γε τῶν ἐμῶν Blaydes   1450 δίδασκέ με]
μήνυέ μοι LʸᵖΛᵐ   1451 καθήνυσαν Dobree: κατ– codd. et Eustathius
405.17   1453 μόνον] –ω(ι) KrCNP   1456 μ᾽ codd. plerique (etiam Λ):
om. a   1457 τυγχάνει] –οι LAFˢZc   1458 σιγᾶν] οἴγειν Wecklein
κἀναδεικνύναι] καὶ διοιγνῦναι Fröhlich   πύλας] πέλας XsV, coni. Reiske
οἴγειν πύλας ἄνωγα κἀναδεικνύναι Wilamowitz   1460 αὐτῶν] ἀστῶν
Benedict   πάρος] μάτην r   1461 ἐξῇρετ᾽] ἐπ– Blaydes   1465 κρείσσοσιν LFHNOPVZct: –ττ– raCPa   1467 λέγω] ψέγω Dawe

84

χαλᾶτε πᾶν κάλυμμ᾽ ἀπ᾽ ὀφθαλμῶν, ὅπως
τὸ συγγενές γε κἀπ᾽ ἐμοῦ θρήνων τύχῃ.
Ορ. αὐτὸς σὺ βάσταζ᾽. οὐκ ἐμὸν τόδ᾽, ἀλλὰ σόν,   1470
τὸ ταῦθ᾽ ὁρᾶν τε καὶ προσηγορεῖν φίλως.
Αι. ἀλλ᾽ εὖ παραινεῖς, κἀπιπείσομαι· σὺ δέ,
εἴ που κατ᾽ οἶκόν μοι Κλυταιμήστρα, κάλει.
Ορ. αὕτη πέλας σοῦ· μηκέτ᾽ ἄλλοσε σκόπει.
Αι. οἴμοι, τί λεύσσω; Ορ. τίνα φοβῇ; τίν᾽ ἀγνοεῖς;   1475
Αι. τίνων ποτ᾽ ἀνδρῶν ἐν μέσοις ἀρκυστάτοις
πέπτωχ᾽ ὁ τλήμων; Ορ. οὐ γὰρ αἰσθάνῃ πάλαι
ζῶν τοῖς θανοῦσιν οὕνεκ᾽ ἀνταυδᾷς ἴσα;
Αι. οἴμοι, ξυνῆκα τοὔπος· οὐ γὰρ ἔσθ᾽ ὅπως
ὅδ᾽ οὐκ Ὀρέστης ἔσθ᾽ ὁ προσφωνῶν ἐμέ.   1480
Ορ. καὶ μάντις ὢν ἄριστος ἐσφάλλου πάλαι;
Αι. ὄλωλα δὴ δείλαιος. ἀλλά μοι πάρες
κἂν σμικρὸν εἰπεῖν. Ηλ. μὴ πέρα λέγειν ἔα,
πρὸς θεῶν, ἀδελφέ, μηδὲ μηκύνειν λόγους.
[τί γὰρ βροτῶν ἂν σὺν κακοῖς μεμειγμένων   1485
θνήσκειν ὁ μέλλων τοῦ χρόνου κέρδος φέροι;]
ἀλλ᾽ ὡς τάχιστα κτεῖνε καὶ κτανὼν πρόθες
ταφεῦσιν ὧν τόνδ᾽ εἰκός ἐστι τυγχάνειν,
ἄποπτον ἡμῶν. ὡς ἐμοὶ τόδ᾽ ἂν κακῶν
μόνον γένοιτο τῶν πάλαι λυτήριον.   1490
Ορ. χωροῖς ἂν εἴσω σὺν τάχει· λόγων γὰρ οὐ
νῦν ἐστιν ἀγών, ἀλλὰ σῆς ψυχῆς πέρι.

1469 γε Turnebus: τε LKrA¹ᵖᶜXsᵃᶜCFᵃᶜHNOPPaVᵖᶜZct: τοι DXsᵗᵖᶜXrZr: τι
Blaydes   1471 φίλως LᵃᶜKGˢXsᵗᵖᶜCDᵍˡFNOPVt: –ος LᵖᶜrADXrZrHTᵞᵖ:
–ους Pa, coni. Purgold   1473 μοι LKap: μου Zc: ἡ t: om. r
Κλυταιμήστρα L¹ᵖᶜ: –μνήστρα fere cett. (etiam Lᵃᶜ)   1475 τίν᾽]
μῶν Nauck   1478 ζῶν τοῖς] ζῶντας Tyrwhitt   1481 ἐσφάλλου
ADXs¹ᵖᶜPaVt: –άλου LᵃᶜKrXrZrCFHNOPZc, Tzetzes Epist. 30.13
Leone, Chil. 7.242 (p. 264 Leone)   1483 σμικρὸν ADXrXsHOPaV: ἐπὶ
σμικρὸν RZrC: ἐπὶ μικρὸν lGFNPZc   1485–6 om. LᵃᶜKᵃᶜWb (prae-
bet Λ, K¹ᵐ): del. Dindorf   1485 τί GaCFVZct: τίς KRHNᵃᶜOPPaᵃᶜ
κακοῖς raFHPaVZct: –ῶ CNOP   μεμειγμένων Kaibel: μεμιγμένων
ADXrXs: –μένον fere cett.   1487 πρόθες LᵖᶜAXrXsZrᵖᶜFHᵖᶜVt: πρόσθες
LᵃᶜKrDZrᵃᶜCNOPPaZc   1488 τόνδ᾽] τῶδ᾽ C, coni. Reiske (i.e. τώδ᾽)
1492 ἀγών Heath: ἀ– codd.

Αι. τί δ' ἐς δόμους ἄγεις με; πῶς, τόδ' εἰ καλὸν
     τοὔργον, σκότου δεῖ, κοὐ πρόχειρος εἶ κτανεῖν;
Ορ. μὴ τάσσε· χώρει δ' ἔνθαπερ κατέκτανες   1495
     πατέρα τὸν ἀμόν, ὡς ἂν ἐν ταὐτῷ θάνῃς.
Αι. ἦ πᾶσ' ἀνάγκη τήνδε τὴν στέγην ἰδεῖν
     τά τ' ὄντα καὶ μέλλοντα Πελοπιδῶν κακά;
Ορ. τὰ γοῦν σ'· ἐγώ σοι μάντις εἰμὶ τῶνδ' ἄκρος.
Αι. ἀλλ' οὐ πατρῴαν τὴν τέχνην ἐκόμπασας.   1500
Ορ. πόλλ' ἀντιφωνεῖς, ἡ δ' ὁδὸς βραδύνεται.
     ἀλλ' ἔρφ'. Αι. ὑφηγοῦ. Ορ. σοὶ βαδιστέον πάρος.
Αι. ἦ μὴ φύγω σε; Ορ. μὴ μὲν οὖν καθ' ἡδονὴν
     θάνῃς· φυλάξαι δεῖ με τοῦτό σοι πικρόν.
     [χρῆν δ' εὐθὺς εἶναι τήνδε τοῖς πᾶσιν δίκην,   1505
     ὅστις πέρα πράσσειν γε τῶν νόμων θέλοι,
     κτείνειν· τὸ γὰρ πανοῦργον οὐκ ἂν ἦν πολύ.

Χο. ὦ σπέρμ' Ἀτρέως, ὡς πολλὰ παθὸν
     δι' ἐλευθερίας μόλις ἐξῆλθες
     τῇ νῦν ὁρμῇ τελεωθέν.]   1510

1496 ἀμόν XrT: ἀμόν cett.   ἄν] om. LKraF   1497 πᾶσ'] πάντ'
West   1505–7 del. Dindorf   1506 ὅστις πέρα τι τῶν νόμων πράσσειν θέλει Nicephorus Progymn. 6: eadem praeterquam πέραν et θέλοι
Gnom.   γε] τι Wunder   νόμων] ἄλλων r   θέλοι LKrCFHNᵃᶜPZc:
–ει aOPaVt   1507 πανοῦργον] κακοῦργον Nicephorus   1508–10 del.
Ritter   1508 παθὸν] –ὼν KˣAZrHZcZg   1509 ἐλευθερίας] –ίαν Viketos   1510 τελεωθέν LraPPaV et Eustathius 881.34: τελει– KCHᵃᶜNOZcᵃᶜT

86

COMMENTARY

COMMENTARY

PROLOGUE (1–85)

1–85 *Electra* is one of the six surviving Sophoclean tragedies whose prologue takes the form of a dialogue. Like *Philoctetes* and *OC*, it opens with the entrance of two characters via an eisodos. One character acts as a guide to the other, either because the guide already knows the area (*El.*, *Phil.*), or because the guide's companion is blind (*OC*). The guide describes the physical characteristics of their new surroundings (2–10n.). The *Electra* prologue shows further similarities with that of *Philoctetes*. In each the guiding character, who speaks first, stands *in loco parentis* to his companion, a young and inexperienced man whose father is dead. The new arrivals have a plan to carry out, which involves hostile action against an inhabitant of this new land. And this plan is to be based not on open force, but on trickery and deception.

δόλος in *Philoctetes* is always presented as an ethically disreputable act. Neoptolemus eventually finds himself unable to go through with his companion's strategy, so great is the moral revulsion which he has come to feel towards it. In the end the play reaches its dénouement through the intervention of the god Heracles, not through the lies and deceit which have by then been discredited. Some scholars have argued that similar attitudes towards δόλος can be found in *Electra*. Orestes' use of deceit, they claim, is a mark of moral depravity (doxography in MacLeod (2001) 30 n. 21). This view, however, fails to take account of the different presentations of δόλος in these dramas. Most important, in *Electra* no less an authority than Apollo has commanded Orestes to use δόλος to obtain justice for his father (35–7). Divine backing for δόλος is absent from *Philoctetes*. Furthermore, the moral issues surrounding δόλος in *Philoctetes* are programmatically highlighted by the debate between Odysseus and Neoptolemus in that play's prologue. The audience's attention is thus drawn towards this question from the beginning. In *Electra*, by contrast, the Paedagogus and Orestes are at one over the correct way to proceed; nor is there any subsequent objection to the ethical basis of their strategy.

A further, positive reason justifies Orestes' use of δόλος. As we shall soon be reminded, Agamemnon was himself killed through δόλος (cf. 124–5, 197): and it was a common and accepted characteristic of avengers that they effected their punishments in a manner which recalled the features of the original crime (cf. Hirzel (1907–10) 433–4; Segal (1966) 511 with n. 43 has missed this point). Philoctetes, on the other hand, has committed no crime, least of all one involving δόλος, and hence the plan directed against him is altogether more dubious. An alleged hesitation by Orestes over the morality of δόλος turns out, on proper inspection, to be no such thing (59–66n.).

The emphasis on the strategy of δόλος, together with Apollo's authorisation for it, can also be found in Aeschylus: cf. *Cho.* 555–9 αἰνῶ δὲ κρύπτειν τάσδε συνθήκας ἐμάς, | ὡς ἂν δόλῳ κτείναντες ἄνδρα τίμιον | δόλῳ γε καὶ ληφθῶσιν, ἐν ταὐτῷ βρόχῳ | θανόντες, ᾗ καὶ Λοξίας ἐφήμισεν, | ἄναξ Ἀπόλλων, μάντις ἀψευδὴς τὸ πρίν. No moral opprobrium is attached to δόλος in that play either. A Homeric allusion points in the same direction. The *Electra* prologue looks back to the encounter between Odysseus and Athena in *Odyssey* 13 (cf. Davidson (1988) 56–8). There Athena points out the sights of Ithaca to the newly arrived Odysseus: a harbour, an olive tree, a cave of the Naiads, a wooded mountain (13.344–51). Like Odysseus, Orestes has returned to his homeland after many years. During that time his home has been usurped; he has now returned to take his vengeance, and will do this through guile. Like Odysseus, he is urged by his guide to plan for action (16n.), and subsequently makes a prayer to the protecting deities of the locality (67–72n.). And just as Odysseus' use of δόλος is a source not of shame but of legitimate pride to the hero (cf. especially 9.19–20), and a strategy supported by his patron Athena (she disguises him), so too Orestes' use of δόλος lacks any negative colouring.

Together with the Aeschylean parallel, this Odyssean link reinforces the positive presentation of δόλος in our play. This presentation accords with the atmosphere of the prologue as a whole, which is bright and confident: at long last the decisive moment for action has arrived. The juxtaposition with the following laments of Electra will thus be especially moving.

The scene is set at Mycenae, as in Homer. Aeschylus set it at Argos; Stesichorus (fr. 216 *PMGF*), Simonides (fr. 549 *PMG*) and Pindar (*P.* 11.16, 11.32; cf. *N.* 11.34, Paus. 3.19.6, J. M. Hall (1997) 92 n. 124) at Lacedaemon (cf. Hdt. 7.159, West (1985) 132).

[1] Σ Eur. *Phoen.* 1–2 (= i. 245.1–4 Schwartz) παλαιά τις φέρεται δόξα ὡς Σοφοκλῆς μὲν ἐπιτιμήσειεν Εὐριπίδῃ ὅτι μὴ προέταξε τούτους τοὺς δύο στίχους, ὁ δὲ Εὐριπίδης ὅτι μὴ προέταξεν ἐν Ἠλέκτρᾳ ὁ Σοφοκλῆς τὸ 'ὦ τοῦ στρατηγήσαντος ἐν Τροίᾳ ποτέ' indicates that the authenticity of Eur. *Phoen.* 1–2 and S. *El.* 1 was doubted in antiquity. Papyrus evidence confirms the doubts over the Euripidean lines (cf. Haslam (1975a) 161–5, (1975b) 149–66). A second-century papyrus hypothesis, P.Oxy. 2455 fr. 17 col. xx.289–90 (a better text at Haslam (1975b) 151 and van Rossum-Steenbeek (1998) 225), cites line 3 as the play's incipit. The hypothesis may not go back to Dicaearchus, as Haslam argues (see Mastronarde's edition, p. 140 n. 1): Diggle (2005) argues on the basis of clausulae that the collection of hypotheses dates to the first century BC–first century AD. Two other papyri, P.Oxy. 3321 (late 2nd/early 3rd) and 3322 (late 1st/early 2nd), both give line 3 as the beginning of the drama. The indirect tradition adds a third strand to the case: for while line 3 is strongly represented there, lines 1–2 do not feature until the fourth century AD at the earliest. In particular, Theodectas 72 F 10 *TrGF* and Accius 581–4 Ribbeck both imitate the opening of the play without referring to lines 1–2 (cf. also Habicht (1990)). Since the opening lines of a play are especially susceptible to such citation, the absence of *Phoen.* 1–2 is all the more telling. The cumulative effect of this evidence is strong, and recent attempts to counter it (e.g. van der Valk (1982), Erbse (1984) 224–7, Carrara (1992)) all involve a good deal of special pleading.

Since it is probably correct in the Euripidean passage, the scholium must be taken seriously in the case of the Sophoclean line too. There are no relevant papyri here, but there is material from the indirect tradition which tells against the authenticity of the line. At Plut. *Quaest. conv.* 737ab and Machon 226–30 Gow *El.* 2 is used as a witty conclusion to a pair of anecdotes. Opening lines tend to be more memorable, and thus can be especially suited to parody. The anecdote from Plutarch involves an actor named Theodorus, who insisted on being given the opening part of a play (Arist. *Pol.* 1336b27–31). Hence for his wife to use the opening line of a play back at him would make the joke especially amusing. Ll-J/W (*Second Thoughts*) object that *El.* 1 is irrelevant to the purpose of the anecdotes, and thus the failure to quote it has no bearing on its authenticity. But this ignores the point about the actor's fondness for first lines. It also seems unlikely that the second line of a piece could obtain so much celebrity independently of its first line. So although the indirect evidence is slighter than for the *Phoenissae* opening, it nevertheless suggests inauthenticity.

Questions of style are more subjective, but still appear to support deletion. Of S.'s six other surviving plays, five contain a vocative early in the first speech (*Aj., Ant., OR, Phil., OC*). The addresses *Aj.* 1 ὦ παῖ Λαρτίου and *OC* 1 τέκνον τυφλοῦ γέροντος Ἀντιγόνη are brief and simple. So too is *OR* 1 ὦ τέκνα, but the following appositional phrase Κάδμου τοῦ πάλαι νέα τροφή gives it more weight. This leaves *Ant.* 1 ὦ κοινὸν αὐτάδελφον Ἰσμήνης κάρα and *Phil.* 3–4 ὦ κρατίστου πατρὸς Ἑλλήνων τραφείς | Ἀχιλλέως παῖ Νεοπτόλεμε as elaborate addresses which are possible parallels for the Paedagogus' address in *El.* 1–2. But in both of these plays the elaboration serves a purpose. Antigone stresses her kin-relationship with her sister to make her more receptive to her plan; while the glorification of Achilles prepares us for a play in which Neoptolemus is constantly measured against his father.

Does *El.* 1 serve any such purpose? According to Kaibel, 'Troia bedeutet Agam.s glänzendste und glücklichste Zeit, Or. wird als Sohn des siegreichen Vaters bezeichnet, das ist für ihn gute Vorbedeutung' (p. 67). This could apply to 694–5 ὄνομα δ᾽ Ὀρέστης, τοῦ τὸ κλεινὸν Ἑλλάδος | Ἀγαμέμνονος στράτευμ᾽ ἀγείραντός ποτε or Eur. *El.* 880–1 ὦ καλλίνικε, πατρὸς ἐκ νικηφόρου | γεγώς, Ὀρέστα, τῆς ὑπ᾽ Ἰλίῳ μάχης, where the victory of Orestes elicits a mention of the victory of his father. But at *El.* 1–2 victory is not at issue. The Paedagogus points out the sights of the Argolid to his charge, and encourages him to plan his next move: we must wait for Orestes' own speech to hear of the glory which he is to win (65–72). Moreover, the glorification of Agamemnon alleged by Kaibel is surprisingly weak. There is no reference to his victory (contrast Eur. *El.* 880 πατρὸς ἐκ νικηφόρου), or to his famous army (contrast S. *El.* 694–5 κλεινὸν . . . στράτευμα): merely the bare fact that he was a general at Troy (στρατηγήσαντος). If S. did set out to glorify Agamemnon here, he has been unusually unsuccessful in doing so.

Haslam (1975) 166 may go too far in calling *El.* 1 'a wretchedly feeble verse', but it does lack the force of other Sophoclean openings. With its removal, we get a simple vocative opening as in *Ajax* and *OC*: we can then proceed to the sights of the Argolid without the purposeless reference to Agamemnon's command at Troy. When we combine this with the case already made against the line on independent, external evidence, the case for deletion is strong enough for the line to be ejected. West (1978b) 241 approves, and Dawe has bracketed the verse in his second and third editions.

For ὦ introducing an interpolation cf. Eur. *Med.* 1121, *Tro.* 634–5, *Or.* 71, 852 [ὦ τλῆμον, ὦ δύστηνε τοῦ στρατηλάτου] | Ἀγαμεμνονος παῖ . . ., *Phoen.* 291–2 (om. Π), Haslam (1979) 99–100. The fact that 'apostrophes were evidently liable to prefatory expansion' (Haslam (1976) 10) strengthens Haslam's case.

στρατηγήσαντος: the variant τυραννήσαντος is probably a conjecture, perhaps motivated by the weakness of the transmitted text. For Agamemnon as στρατηγός cf. *Aj.* 1116, Eur. *IT* 17–18, Pl. *Resp.* 522d1, Liban. *Decl.* 6.2.18 ὁ στρατηγήσας ἐν Τροίᾳ.

ποτέ: can have a 'nostalgic' sense 'to denote a former happy state' (Renehan (1976) 41–2; cf. 420, 695, Headlam on Herodas 6.54); it is found in victory inscriptions without reference to whether the victory in question took place long in the past (cf. D. C. Young (1983) 36–42). But for ποτέ used at the end of a line in interpolations (often merely to pad out the verse) cf. *Aj.* 314, 1106, Eur. *Her.* 1291, *Hel.* 292, *Phoen.* 520.

2–10 The Paedagogus describes the topography of the Argolid to Orestes. Dramatic prologues often contain brief references to the setting of the play (cf. Nestle (1930) 44–5, Katsouris (1997) 85–101); late Sophoclean prologues have a description of a new locality from one figure acting as a guide to another (*Phil.* 1–2, 16–21, *OC* 14–18). Enn. *Med. Ex.* 239–40 Jocelyn *asta atque Athenas, anticum opulentum oppidum,* | *contempla et templum Cereris ad laevam aspice* perhaps looks back to a similar Greek precedent. The emphasis on place is typically Sophoclean: cf. e.g. *Aj.* 859–63 (Ajax's dying address to Salamis and Troy), *Phil.* 1452–68 (Philoctetes' valediction to Lemnos), *OC* 668–719 (ode to Colonus). But the poetic value of these lines is not accompanied by a concern for the realities of Argive topography. Neither the Heraeum nor the temple of Lycian Apollo would be visible from Mycenae (cf. Pöhlmann (2001) 36–8, with maps).

The Paedagogus' words also look back to two Homeric passages: Athena's description of the sights of Ithaca to Odysseus at *Od.* 13.344–51 (ἀλλ᾽ ἄγε τοι δείξω Ἰθάκης ἕδος, ὄφρα πεποίθῃς κτλ.; cf. 1–85n.), and Achilles' words to the dead Patroclus at *Il.* 19.331–3, when he tells him how he had envisaged ὡς ἄν μοι τὸν παῖδα θοῇ ἐνὶ νηὶ μελαίνῃ | Σκυρόθεν ἐξαγάγοις καί οἱ δείξειας ἕκαστα, | κτῆσιν ἐμήν, δμῶάς τε καὶ ὑψερεφὲς μέγα δῶμα. These parallels suggest the Paedagogus' importance and his authority over Orestes. More generally, they lend an epic grandeur to this crucial moment in Orestes' history.

Beginning with the plain of Argos and the two most important temples within it, we move first to Mycenae, and finally to the house of the Pelopids: for a similar geographical *priamel* cf. Ov. *Trist.* 3.1.27–36, where a description of the buildings of Rome culminates in the house of Augustus. In each case this stresses the political centrality of the ruler's residence: yet elsewhere in our play this wider political view will only rarely come to the fore.

2 Enter Orestes, Pylades and the Paedagogus from eisodos A, probably with attendants. We do not know how S. designated the Paedagogus. Kaibel (p. 1) thought that the term παιδαγωγός (which never occurs in the play) may have been suggested by the word at Eur. *El.* 287: but there the reference is to the Paedagogus of Agamemnon, not Orestes.

ἐκεῖν᾽ '= *illa*, of what is well-known, often referred to' (Moorhouse 158, comparing 278 and *OR* 1454; cf. Diggle (1978) 162 = (1994) 180). This demonstrative may also be used because the sights are 'presented from Orestes' point of view during the past' (Ruijgh (2006) 155).

3 παρόντι λεύσσειν: for the expression cf. Diggle (1973) 262 n. 60 = (1994) 81 n. 60.

ὧν πρόθυμος ἦσθ᾽ ἀεί: cf. Hom. *Od.* 23.5–6 ἔγρεο, Πηνελόπεια, φίλον τέκος, ὄφρα ἴδηαι | ὀφθαλμοῖσι τεοῖσι τά τ᾽ ἔλδεαι ἥματα πάντα, Aesch. *Cho.* 215 εἰς ὄψιν ἥκεις ὧνπερ ἐξηύχου πάλαι, Eur. *Phoen.* 194–5 ἐπεὶ πόθου | ἐς τέρψιν ἦλθες ὧν ἔχρῃζες εἰσιδεῖν, Theocr. 10.17, Sall. *Cat.* 20.14 *en illa, illa quam saepe optastis libertas, praeterea divitiae decus gloria in oculis sita sunt.* Exile can make the sights of one's homeland take on a particular intensity (4 οὐπόθεις): cf. Hom. *Od.* 1.41 ὁππότ᾽ ἂν ἡβήσῃ τε καὶ ἧς ἱμείρεται αἴης, Alcaeus fr. 130.16–20 *PLF* = 130b.1–5 Voigt ὁ τάλαις ἔγω | ζώω μοῖραν ἔχων ἀγροϊωτίκαν | ἰμέρρων ἀγόρας ἄκουσαι | καρυ[ζο]μένας Ὠγεσιλαΐδα | καὶ β[ό]λλας, Ov. *Trist.* 3.2.21, 3.4.57–8 (= 3.4b.11–12), *Epist. Pont.* 1.2.47–8, 1.8.33–8. For Sophocles' 'Kühnheit im Wortgebrauch' in taking πρόθυμος with a genitive see Haupt *ap.* Belger (1979) 220. For the spelling of ἀεί see Threatte i. 275: between *c.* 450–350 both this form and αἰεί were regularly used in inscriptions. L's practice is detailed in Jebb's apparatus on *Ant.* 76.

93

4 τὸ . . . παλαιὸν Ἄργος: i.e. the plain of the Argolid, not the city of Argos itself, as the following line makes clear. This sense is first found in Homer (cf. *LfgrE* s.v. τὸ Ἄργος B II 1, *pace* Strab. 8.6.9 = ii. 494.39–40 Radt), and subsequently in poetry (cf. Eur. fr. 228.6 *TrGF* ἐλθὼν ἐς Ἄργος ᾤκισ᾽ Ἰνάχου πόλιν, *IT* 508–10) and prose (e.g. Thuc. 4.133.2, 5.63.1, 6.105.1). ἄργος could denote 'plain' in general, but this usage is not found before Callimachus (fr. 299.2 Pfeiffer = 116.2 Hollis, with H.'s n.): the only possible instance before him, Eur. *El.* 1 (also with παλαιόν), is rightly obelised by Diggle (*contra* Denniston *ad loc.*). It could have developed as a more generalised sense out of the specific use to denote the Argive plain. Alternatively, the frequency of 'Argos' as a place-name suggests that the word for plain came first and was reapplied to the city in each case (cf. J. M. Hall (1995) 580). For a map of the Argolid see Tomlinson (1972) 9.

For the alleged antiquity of the Argives cf. Ael. Arist. 1.357 = 126.12–13 Lenz and Behr Ἀργεῖοι παλαιότατοι τῶν Ἑλλήνων ἀξιοῦσιν εἶναι. At Aesch. *Suppl.* 250–1 the King of Argos is the γηγενοῦς . . . Παλαίχθονος | ἶνις.

5 τῆς οἰστροπλῆγος . . . Ἰνάχου κόρης: that is, Io: cf. [Aesch.] *PV* 681–2 (Io speaking) οἰστροπλὴξ δ᾽ ἐγὼ | . . . ἐλαύνομαι, 589–90, Aesch. *Suppl.* 16, 573. For the gadfly as the bane of the cow cf. Jeremiah 46.20 with West (1997) 445–6. Latin authors substituted a grander pest for the gadfly (e.g. Ov. *Met.* 1.725 (an Erinys); cf. Eitrem (1916) 1736.35–45). The river-god Inachus is usually the father of Io (cf. Eitrem (1916) 1732.36–43), although a variant tradition held that her father was one Peiren (cf. [Hes.] fr. 124 M–W, Acusilaus *FGrHist* 2 F 26 = fr. 26 *EGM*, West (1985) 76–7); a later account gave the father as Iasus (cf. J. M. Hall (1995) 609–10). On these genealogies see further J. M. Hall (1997) 77–89; for the myth of Io more generally see Forbes Irving (1990) 69–71, 211–16.

ἄλσος: cf. Σ Pind. *O.* 3.31b (= i. 113.18–20 Drachmann) ἔλεγον γὰρ πᾶν χωρίον ἀφιερωμένον θεῷ, κἂν ψιλὸν φυτῶν ᾖ, ἄλσος, S. *Ant.* 844–5 Θήβας . . . εὐαρμάτου ἄλσος, Hom. *Il.* 2.506. At [Apollod.] *Bibl.* 2.1.3 Io is tethered by Argus to an olive tree ἐν τῷ Μυκηναίων . . . ἄλσει. For the Argolid as an ἄλσος cf. the Ἀργεῖον . . . τέμενος of Pind. *N.* 10.19.

6–7 τοῦ λυκοκτόνου θεοῦ | ἀγορὰ Λύκειος: the temple of Apollo Lycius in Argos was τῶν ἐν τῇ πόλει τὸ ἐπιφανέστατον . . . ἱερόν (Paus. 2.19.3). It stood in the agora (Thuc. 5.47.11), probably on its north-west side (cf. Marchetti (1994) 158–9, Courbin (1998) 261), although archaeologists have yet to discover it. Euripides' *Telephus* may have been set in front of this temple (see p. 24 of Cropp's edition). See further Tomlinson (1972) 204–5, Graf (1985) 222–4, Courbin (1998). On the cult of Apollo Lycius more generally see Graf (1985) 221–6, Gershenson (1991) 13 n. 60.

The epithet λύκειος was probably associated by the Argives with the word
λύκος. Paus. 2.19.3–4 derives the name of the temple from the killing of an
ox by a wolf shortly before its foundation by Danaus (cf. Gershenson (1991)
9). Argive coinage shows a wolf on the obverse from its beginnings in the first
quarter of the fifth century (cf. Kraay (1976) 96, Gershenson (1991) 8). Apollo
was also identified with wolves in other contexts (cf. Aesch. *Sept.* 146–7 καὶ
σὺ Λύκει᾿ ἄναξ, Λύκειος γενοῦ | στρατῷ δαΐῳ, Servius on Virg. *Aen.* 4.377 =
i. 531.24–5 Thilo and Hagen). But for S. Ἀπόλλων λύκειος is not λύκος but
rather λυκοκτόνος. For this Apolline epithet cf. Phaedimus *A.P.* 13.22.3 = 2913
HE, Plut. *De sollert. anim.* 966a, Porph. *De abst.* 1.22 (p. 101.5 Nauck), *EG* 821.8
(Lerna, 2nd–3rd c. AD), Gershenson (1991) 10; for its use to explain λύκειος cf. Σ
Ar. *Av.* 369c (p. 65 Holwerda), Σ Dem. 24.231 (= ii. 354.32–355.6 Dilts). Apollo
the wolf-killer is related to Apollo νόμιος, the protector of flocks (for which cf.
OR 1102 τῷ (sc. Ἀπόλλωνι) πλάκες ἀγρόνομοι πᾶσαι φίλαι, [Hes.] fr. 216 M–
W, Williams on Call. *Hym.* 2.47, Diod. Sic. 4.81.2, Gershenson (1991) 10). This
connexion was made by Aristarchus in his note on our passage (*ap.* Hesych.
λ 1390 = ii. 613.1–2 Latte):[1] cf. Cornutus *Theol. Graec.* 32 (p. 69.8–9 Lang =
p. 284.9–10 Ramelli) νόμιον καὶ λύκιον καὶ λυκοκτόνον προσαγορεύοντες,
Servius on Virg. *Aen.* 4.377 (= i. 532.2–3 Thilo and Hagen) *quod pastoralis deus
lupos interemit.* The killing of wolves served as an *aition* for the name of the temple
of Apollo Lycius at Sicyon (Paus. 2.9.7).

The actual origin of the epithet remains unclear. A popular derivation in
modern times involves the god's supposed Lycian ancestry: on this Burkert
(1977) 227 ≈ (1985) 144 pronounces *non liquet.* See further Bruchmann (1893)
27, Kruse (1927b) 2268–9, Friis Johansen and Whittle on Aesch. *Suppl.* 686,
Graf (1985) 220–1, Gershenson (1991) 15–23. It is found elsewhere in this play
at 645, 655 and 1379.

The transmitted form Λύκειος is the same as that found in Argive inscriptions: cf. *IG* iv. 557.8, 559.13.

7–8 οὒξ ἀριστερᾶς δ᾿ ὅδε | Ἥρας ὁ κλεινὸς ναός: parodied by Python *TrGF*
91 F 1.2–3 οὒξ ἀριστερᾶς δ᾿ ὅδε | πόρνης ὁ κλεινὸς ναός. For the word order
article, preposition, (pro)noun, δέ see Diggle (1981a) 79. Looking south from
Mycenae, the Heraeum would indeed be on the viewer's left. Alternatively, the
temple on the left could indicate that the actors entered from the spectators'
right. But this is less likely, as by now they are probably facing the audience
directly, whatever direction they arrived in.

The Heraeum was fifteen stades south-east of Mycenae (Paus. 2.17.1). The
archaic temple was built in the mid-seventh century or perhaps a little earlier
(cf. Kõiv (2003) 54 n. 148). There was a fire there in 423 (Thuc. 4.133.2–3, Paus.

[1] For Aristarchus' work on S. see fr. 70 Schironi (especially p. 530 n. 4).

2.17.7), which may have prompted the rebuilding of the temple at about that date (cf. Tomlinson (1972) 230–45). Many scholars, however, now believe that the rebuilding was already under way at the time of the fire (cf. Hornblower on Thuc. 4.133.2, Hornblower (2004) 126 with n. 146; also Pfaff (2003) 6–7, 191).

For ὁ 'of what is familiar, well known' (Moorhouse 144, noting its frequent association with κλεινός) cf. 9, 160, 300, *OR* 8, *Tr.* 19, *Phil.* 654.

9 φάσκειν: the imperatival infinitive in S. is often markedly solemn: cf. *OR* 461–2 κἂν λάβῃς ἐψευσμένον, | φάσκειν ἔμ' ἤδη μαντικῇ μηδὲν φρονεῖν, 1466, *Phil.* 1411–12 φάσκειν δ' αὐδὴν τὴν Ἡρακλέους | ἀκοῇ τε κλύειν λεύσσειν τ' ὄψιν. But this may be coincidence: Bers (1984) 180–1 cites eight Aristophanic examples of the construction, none of which parodies a high style. See further Goodwin §784, Bruhn §123, Wackernagel (1926–8) i. 267, S–D ii. 380–2, Diggle (1981a) 10–11, Moorhouse 243, Bers (1984) 168–82. For φάσκειν . . . ὁρᾶν cf. *Phil.* 1411–12, Theocr. 22.56 φάθι λεύσσειν.

Μυκήνας: Homer uses the plural only at *Il.* 2.569 and 4.376. Aeschylus sets the *Oresteia* at Argos, and never mentions Mycenae in his extant works. The tragedians were sometimes said in antiquity to identify Argos and Mycenae (cf. Elmsley on Eur. *Hcld.* 188 (our 187)). There is some evidence for this: cf. Eur. fr. 228a.13–14 *TrGF* ὅς τ' Ἄργους πόλιν | εἶχεν Μυκήνας, frr. 228.6, 752h.34 *TrGF*. But in our case Mycenae is distinguished from Argos and the rest of the Argolid (as it is at Eur. *IT* 508–10). See further Saïd (1993).

The classical town of Mycenae was destroyed by Argos in 468 (cf. Diod. Sic. 11.65, Strab. 8.6.19 = ii. 510.22–3 Radt, J. M. Hall (1995) 589 n. 84).

τάς: 7–8n.

πολυχρύσους: the Homeric epithet for Mycenae (*Il.* 7.180, 11.46, *Od.* 3.304): cf. Hor. *C.* 1.7.9, Alpheus *A.P.* 9.101.5–6 = 3564–5 *GP*, Mundus *A.P.* 9.103.1 = 3931 *GP*, Bergson (1956) 105.

10 πολύφθορον: unlike the πολυ- epithet in the previous line, this adjective is not Homeric (it is first found in Pindar and Aeschylus, and occurs elsewhere in S. at *Tr.* 477–8 ἡ πολύφθορος | . . . Οἰχαλία). The homoearcton draws attention to the juxtaposition: the city is rich in gold, while the palace of its rulers is rich only in slaughter. For the 'house of much destruction' cf. Hor. *C.* 1.6.8 *saevam Pelopis domum*, Ov. *Her.* 8.53–4 *Aegisthus . . . | tecta cruentavit, quae pater ante tuus.*

11–14 The rescue of the young Orestes varies in surviving accounts. Homer does not refer to it. In Pindar his nurse Arsinoa is responsible (*P.* 11.17–18 τὸν δὴ φονευομένου πατρὸς Ἀρσινόα Κλυταιμήστρας | χειρῶν ὕπο κρατερᾶν ἐκ δόλου τροφὸς ἄνελε δυσπενθέος). In Pher. Ath. *FGrHist* 3 F 134 = fr. 134

EGM the nurse's name is Laodamia; her son is killed by Aegisthus in the belief that he is Orestes. The nurse in Stesichorus has the same name (fr. 218 *PMGF*): although his fragments make no reference to the rescue, it is difficult to envisage any other circumstances in which she could have been mentioned.

At Aesch. *Ag.* 877–86 Clytemnestra tells Agamemnon that she sent Orestes to Strophius to protect him from potential civil unrest; the same account is implied at *Cho.* 693. At *Cho.* 913 and 915 Orestes attacks her for having sent him away (τεκοῦσα γάρ μ' ἔρριψας ἐς τὸ δυστυχές . . . ἀκῶς ἐπράθην): but Clytemnestra is allowed a come-back on each point, and her real motive remains unclear (cf. Garvie on 914). What is clear is that Orestes was sent out of Argos by Clytemnestra herself: no rescuing was involved. Euripides' account is closest to S.'s, in that Orestes is brought to safety by an old male servant, the former τροφεύς of Agamemnon. He rescues the boy as he is about to perish at the hands of Aegisthus, and gives him to Strophius (*El.* 16–18, 416).

Electra's participation in the rescue (296–7, 321, 1132–3, 1348–52) is S.'s innovation. The motif is found later in Hyg. *Fab.* 117.2, Sen. *Ag.* 918–46 (where Electra gives Orestes to Strophius, who happens to be passing through), [Sen.] *Oct.* 63–4 (*Orestes*) *tua quem pietas hosti rapuit | texitque fides*. The detail prepares for a play where she will be the focus of attention, and stresses her capacity for resourceful action. Electra later suggests that there was a threat to Orestes' life at the time of his rescue (296–7, 601, 1132–3).[2]

According to Herodorus *FGrHist* 31 F 11 = fr. 11 *EGM* Orestes was three years old at the time of his rescue. This is difficult to reconcile with the separation of his parents during the previous ten years.

11 πατρὸς ἐκ φονῶν: φονῶν is Dindorf's interpretation of the paradosis, printed in his fourth edition, and supported by Bayfield (1901) 252, Gagnepain (1959) 78 and Diggle (1994) 156 n. 4. The same word should also be read at *Tr.* 558 Νέσσου φθίνοντος ἐκ φονῶν ἀνειλόμην (note the similar structure and phraseology). φονή is transmitted at *Ant.* 696, 1003, 1314, Aesch. *Ag.* 447, Eur. *El.* 1207, *Hel.* 154, fr. 370.94 *TrGF*, always in the dative plural. φόνος is commoner in tragedy, and is found in both singular and plural. φοναί always refers not just to a killing, but to the actual moment of slaughter (cf. Pind. *P.* 11.37, Hdt. 9.76.1). This latter sense is never found with φόνοι. Cf. Gagnepain (1959) 80: '[φονή] est proprement la scène de carnage . . . il ne s'agit plus d'un délit, mais d'une situation'. φονῶν here conveys Electra's daring and resourcefulness. She does not merely rescue Orestes after her father's murder, but snatches him away even as his father is falling to a gory death (cf. Pind.

---

[2] Compare how in Electra's lament over the urn S. transfers various motifs to her which are associated with the Nurse in Aeschylus (1126–70n.) or the Old Man in Euripides (1143–4n.).

COMMENTARY: 1–85

P. 11.17 φονευομένου πατρός, where the imperfect participle has the same effect). For the poetic plural see Moorhouse 6–7, Bers (1984) 40–2.

12 ὁμαίμου καὶ κασιγνήτης: cf. Hom. *Il.* 12.371 κασίγνητος καὶ ὅπατρος.

13 ἤνεγκα κἀξέσωσα κἀξεθρεψάμην: the tricolon crescendo (cf. Radt (1983) 214 = (2002) 285–6 = Hofmann (1991) 101) and three-word trimeter (ignoring the καί: cf. Marcovich (1984) 59–60, who compares *Ant.* 901–2 ἔλουσα κἀκόσμησα κἀπιτυμβίους | χοὰς ἔδωκα) emphasise the Paedagogus' personal involvement in Orestes' rescue.

ἤνεγκα: for the form see K–B ii. 559.

κἀξεθρεψάμην: as often with the aorist of τρέφω, the middle does not differ semantically from the active (cf. Moussy (1969) 59–61).

14 τοσόνδ᾽ ἐς ἥβης: cf. Hom. *Od.* 1.40–1 ἐκ γὰρ Ὀρέσταο τίσις ἔσσεται Ἀτρεΐδαο | ὁππότ᾽ ἂν ἡβήσῃ τε καὶ ἧς ἱμείρεται αἴης, [Hes.] fr. 23a.29–30 M–W [Ὀρέστης] ὅς ῥα καὶ ἡβήσας ἀπε[τείσατο π]ατροφο[ν]ῆα, | κτεῖνε δὲ μητέρα [ἣν ὑπερήν]ορα νηλέι [χαλκῷ]; Hom. *Il.* 9.485 (Phoenix to Achilles) καί σε τοσοῦτον ἔθηκα. For the genitive with ἐς τοσόνδε cf. 961.

πατρὶ τιμωρὸν φόνου: the ring composition with πατρὸς ἐκ φονῶν in 11 points to how things have now come full circle: the child snatched away for safety at his father's murder has now returned to avenge that murder.

15–16 φίλτατε ξένων | Πυλάδη: unknown to Homer, Pylades is first found in the *Nostoi* (p. 67 *EGF* = p. 95 *PEG* = p. 156 *GEF*), where he and Orestes win τιμωρία for Agamemnon's murder. At Pind. *P.* 11.15–16 he is described as Orestes' ξένος. His father was Strophius of Phocis (cf. Radke (1959) 2077.67–2078.16). The tradition that his mother was a daughter of Atreus appears first at Eur. *IT* 918–19 (cf. *Or.* 1233, Radke (1959) 2078.42–7). There is no reference to it in this play, and the address here rules it out. He is a mute character, as in Euripides' *Electra*: elsewhere he speaks at Aesch. *Cho.* 900–2 and in the *IT* and *Orestes* of Euripides.

16 τί χρὴ δρᾶν ἐν τάχει βουλευτέον: cf. Hom. *Od.* 13.365 αὐτοὶ δὲ φραζώμεθ᾽ ὅπως ὄχ᾽ ἄριστα γένηται (Athena to Odysseus: see above, 2–10n.), Aesch. *Ag.* 847 ὅπως χρονίζον εὖ μενεῖ βουλευτέον. In 21 the Paedagogus follows this up with ξυνάπτετον λόγοισιν. Inevitably, both βουλεύετον (Porson (1815) 221) and ξυναπτέον (Toup (1760–6) i. 87–8) have been conjectured, but the paradosis should probably be retained in each case. The clause τί χρὴ δρᾶν would sound clumsy depending on an imperative βουλεύετον; whereas the direct and urgent imperative is suited to the Paedagogus' appeal at the close of his speech.

98

17–19 These lines have suffered from overinterpretation. For Williams, 'the εὐφρόνη has indeed gone, along with its euphemism, and a dawn has come that can be represented as a new darkness, the moment at which the light of the stars goes out' ((1993) 174 n. 31; cf. C. P. Segal (1966) 491–2). According to Beare (1927), the mention of birdsong would awaken in an ancient audience the expectation of imminent catastrophe. Jebb goes too far in the other direction when he says that 'the sights and sounds of early morning are in unison with the spirit of this play, in which the παννυχίδες of Electra's sorrow are turned to joy, and the god of light prevails' (for similar appreciations cf. Davies (1999a) 119 with n. 9). But these are certainly lines of great beauty, which can only bear the meaning ascribed to them by Williams *et al.* if one reads into the text things which are not there. They vividly suggest the sense of expectation at the beginning of this most significant day.

Dawn commonly marks the beginning of action: cf. Eur. *El.* 102–3 (Orestes to Pylades) νῦν οὖν – ἕω γὰρ λευκὸν ὄμμ᾽ ἀναίρεται – | ἔξω τρίβου τοῦδ᾽ ἴχνος ἀλλαξώμεθα, *IA* 156–60, Hes. *Op.* 579–81 with West's addenda *ad loc.* (p. 383), Diggle's edition of Euripides' *Phaethon* p. 95, Xen. *Oec.* 5.4, Call. fr. 260.65–9 Pfeiffer = 74.24–8 Hollis, Sheppard (1918) 81 n. 3. For the combination of light and birdsong in a description of dawn cf. Virg. *Aen.* 8.455–6 *Evandrum ex humili tecto lux suscitat alma* | *et matutini volucrum sub culmine cantus* (cf. Servius on *Aen.* 11.183 = i. 497.1–13 Thilo and Hagen *Asinius Pollio dicit, ubique Vergilium in diei descriptione sermonem aliquem ponere aptum praesentibus rebus*). For the combination of the λαμπρὸν ἡλίου σέλας with the μέλαινα . . . εὐφρόνη cf. Hom. *Il.* 8.485–6 ἐν δ᾽ ἔπεσ᾽ Ὠκεανῷ λαμπρὸν φάος ἠελίοιο | ἕλκον νύκτα μέλαιναν ἐπὶ ζείδωρον ἄρουραν. The whole picture recalls *Il.* 10.251–2 μάλα γὰρ νὺξ ἄνεται, ἐγγύθι δ᾽ ἠώς, | ἄστρα δὲ δὴ προβέβηκε.

Electra's anapaests will take up the references to day succeeding night and to birdsong (86–120n.).

17 ἥμιν: for the accentuation of the enclitic see Barrett's edition of Euripides' *Hippolytus*, p. 425, K–B i. 339, Kaczko (2002) 295, Probert (2003) 150–1.

18 For κινεῖ with a sound as its object see Diggle on Eur. *Pha.* 72 = fr. 773.28 *TrGF*.

φθέγγματ᾽: for the orthography see West's Teubner Aeschylus, p. lii.

σαφῆ: 'i.e. not a doubtful twitter here and there, but the unanimous warbling which tells that the morning is really come' (Campbell, memorably).

19 ἄστρων . . . εὐφρόνη 'night of stars': for the genitive of quality cf. 758, Eur. *Or.* 225, Barrett on Eur. *Hipp.* 802, Moorhouse 54, K–G i. 264c. For the 'starry night' cf. Eur. *Hipp.* 850–1 νυκτὸς ἀ– | στερωπὸν σέλας, Eur. *El.* 54

99

COMMENTARY: 1-85

ὦ νὺξ μέλαινα, χρυσέων ἄστρων τροφέ, Enn. *Ann.* 348 Skutsch *hinc nox processit stellis ardentibus apta.*

Housman (1888) 244 = (1972) i. 26–7 translates 'the festal gathering of stars', with εὐφρόνη standing for εὐφροσύνη (cf. Hesych. ε 7280 = ii. 239 Latte εὐφρόνη· νὺξ καὶ εὐφροσύνη). For this picture cf. Aesch. *Ag.* 4 ἄστρων . . . ὁμήγυριν, S. *Ant.* 1147 χοράγ' ἄστρων. Kaibel offers the same interpretation ('dunkle Sternenheiterkeit', p. 70), which is also supported by Diggle (1993) 135 = (1994) 417. However, εὐφρόνη is commonly used to mean 'night' (cf. West on Hes. *Op.* 560, Troxler (1964) 13–19, Hor. *C.* 3.6.41–4, Rosati on Ov. *Her.* 19.33 *noctis amicior hora*), and here it would be hard for an audience to understand it as anything else. Its qualification by μέλαινα makes Housman's interpretation especially difficult (so Vahlen (1904) 9–10 = (1907–8) ii. 507–8). Garvie on Aesch. *Cho.* 415–17 refers to other discussions, none of which agrees with Housman's view. J. S. Smith (1785) 31 gives ἄστρων an ablatival sense (night 'withdraws itself from the stars'), but the ensuing picture is difficult to visualise.

20–2 Schenkl (1869) 537 deletes 20–2 (20 *iam* Nauck³ p. 157, emending to ξυνάπτετ' οὖν in 21; 21–2 ἐνταῦθ' . . . | . . . ἀλλ' *del.* Schwerdt *ap.* Nauck, *ib.*). Dihle (1959) repeats the deletion, but his arguments are flimsy.

21 ξυνάπτετον λόγοισιν: cf. Eur. *Phoen.* 702 ἐς λόγους συνῆψα Πολυνείκει, Ar. *Lys.* 468, *Ach.* 686. The dative is modal. On Toup's ξυναπτέον see 16n.

21–2 ὡς ἐνταῦθ' †ἐμὲν† | ἵν' οὐκέτ' ὀκνεῖν καιρός: of the two manuscript variants ἐσμέν is unmetrical, while ἐμέν is morphologically bizarre. Its only other possible occurrence is in Callimachus (fr. 561 Pfeiffer γρῆές ἐμεν †κορεης δ' οὐκ αἴτιος†): but even if he uses the word there, the collector of recondite lexemes provides no evidence for this being an acceptable form in tragedy. The simplest emendation is Dawes's ἵμεν ((1745) 282 = (1800) 230), printed by Campbell and Dawe. Jebb objects that '[the Paedagogus] speaks of the present', but Orestes uses the future at the conclusion of his speech (75 νὼ δ' ἔξιμεν), a conclusion which imitates the Paedagogus' speech in its reference to καιρός (75–6n.), and which could have imitated it with this verb as well. Moreover, the Paedagogus is not advocating instant action, but rather a period of discussion before they get on their way. This is the time for λόγοι: the time for ἔργα is yet to come (cf. Kvíčala (1864) 394).

Could the corruption lie deeper? Some emendations remove the antecedent ἐνταῦθ', such as Schneidewin's ὡς ἱκάνομεν (in his first edition) or Naber's ἔνθ' ἕσταμεν ((1881) 231): see further p. 207 of Jebb's edition. But S. often uses ἐνταῦθα as an antecedent in a figurative sense to ἵνα (so Jebb, comparing *Phil.* 429), ἔνθα (*El.* 380) or ὅπου (*Tr.* 800), and so it should be kept if possible.

Others introduce the particle μέν: e.g. Raper's ἐνταῦθα μέν (*ap.* Dawes (1827) 9) or Monk's ἐνταῦθα μὲν | οὐκ ἔστ᾽ ἔτ᾽ ((1826) 63–4). But Monk's conjecture robs us of the ἵνα which fits with ἐνταῦθ᾽; nor does a μέν *solitarium* (Denniston 380) seem appropriate here (contrast e.g. 1424n.). The particle is also problematic in one of Hermann's conjectures, ὡς ἐνταῦθα δή.

Jebb prefers Hermann's ὡς ἐνταῦθ᾽ ἵνα | οὐκ ἔστ᾽ ἔτ᾽: for ἐνταῦθ᾽ ἵνα at the end of a line cf. Critias *TrGF* 43 F 19.27 = D–K 88 B 25.27 (= ii. 388.5) = p. 178.27 *TrGFS*, and for ἐσμέν understood cf. 1065n. Jebb explains the corruption by saying that ἔστ᾽ dropped out before ἔτ᾽, that ἵνα was then moved to fill the gap in the next line, and that ἐμέν was finally inserted by a scribe who knew the word from the grammarians. But if it was noticed that line 22 was deficient, it would have been easier to insert a word like ἔστ᾽ straight into line 22, rather than transfer a word from the end of 21, and then fill up that gap with such a recondite word. It is difficult to accept that the rare word ἐμέν was deliberately inserted into the text.

For the sentiment cf. Antiph. Soph. D–K 87 B 55 (= ii. 363.4) = fr. 55 Pendrick ὀκνεῖν, ἵνα οὐδὲν ἔργον ὀκνεῖν.

22 καιρός 'right time': cf. 1368, Carm. Pop. frr. 863.2–3, 865.2–3 *PMG* καιρὸς δὲ καλεῖ | μηκέτι μέλλειν, Nauck (1890) 29, Race (1981) 211–12. The word or its derivatives occurs elsewhere at 31, 39, 85, 228, 1368. For its meanings see Barrett on Eur. *Hipp.* 386–7, J. R. Wilson (1980), Race (1981), Trédé (1992).

ἀκμή is often found in contexts of imminent necessity: cf. 1338, *Phil.* 12 ἀκμὴ γὰρ οὐ μακρῶν ἡμῖν λόγων, *Aj.* 811, Aesch. *Pers.* 407 κοὐκέτ᾽ ἦν μέλλειν ἀκμή, *Ag.* 1353 τὸ μὴ μέλλειν δ᾽ ἀκμή, Eur. *El.* 275 οὐ γὰρ νῦν ἀκμή;, 684 στείχειν δ ᾽ ἀκμή, Bruhn §147.1, Trédé (1992) 49–51.

23–4 ὦ φίλτατ᾽ ἀνδρῶν προσπόλων, ὡς μοι σαφῆ | σημεῖα φαίνεις ἐσθλὸς εἰς ἡμᾶς γεγώς: Jebb compares *As You Like It* 2.3.56 'O good old man, how well in thee appears | The constant service of the antique world'. For further praise of the Paedagogus cf. Electra's words at 1354–63.

ὡς: exclamatory, following the vocative: cf. *Ant.* 572, *Aj.* 14–15, Eur. *Hec.* 990, *Tro.* 1167, *Or.* 217.

25–8 The simile is reminiscent of Ibycus fr. 287.5–7 *PMGF* ἦ μὰν τρομέω νιν (sc. Ἔρωτα) ἐπερχόμενον, | ὥστε φερέζυγος ἵππος ἀεθλοφόρος ποτὶ γήρᾳ | ἀέκων σὺν ὄχεσφι θοοῖς ἐς ἅμιλλαν ἔβα. For the weakness of the old horse cf. also Lucian 36.40. In S. the horse has changed from a reluctant charger into an enthusiastic participant in the fray. For the horse which shows its spirit as it prepares for action cf. Aesch. *Sept.* 393–4, Ap. Rh. 3.1259–62, Ov. *Met.* 3.704–5, Job 39.19–25, West (1997) 556. The Paedagogus stands apart from most old men in tragedy, who are usually

COMMENTARY: 1–85

portrayed as weak and ineffective (cf. Schütz (1964) 76–88). Philostratus refers to this passage at *Vit. Soph.* 2.23.4 καὶ εἶδον ἄνδρα παραπλήσιον τῷ Σοφοκλείῳ ἵππῳ, νωθρὸς γὰρ ὑφ' ἡλικίας δοκῶν νεάζουσαν ὁρμὴν ἐν ταῖς σπουδαῖς ἀνεκτᾶτο. For other equine comparisons see Wilamowitz on Eur. *Her.* 119.

25 For εὐγενής of a 'thoroughbred' horse cf. Theogn. 184.

26 ἐν τοῖσι δεινοῖς: cf. Eur. *Suppl.* 727 ἐν . . . τοῖς δεινοῖσίν ἐστιν ἄλκιμος, Xen. *Ages.* 11.10 ἐν τοῖς δεινοῖς εὐθαρσής, Thuc. 1.70.3 ἐν τοῖς δεινοῖς εὐέλπιδες, 1.84.2 τῶν . . . ἐξοτρυνόντων ἡμᾶς ἐπὶ τὰ δεινά.

θυμὸν . . . ἀπώλεσεν: a Homeric expression (cf. *Il.* 8.90 καὶ νύ κεν ἔνθ' ὁ γέρων ἀπὸ θυμὸν ὄλεσσεν), but here in the sense ἄθυμος ἐγένετο.

26–7 ἀπώλεσεν | . . . ἵστησιν: for the gnomic aorist alongside the present in similes cf. Hom. *Il.* 5.902–3 συνέπηξεν | . . . περιτρέφεται, Chantraine (1942–53) ii. 185–6. Blaydes's ἔστησεν (in his 1873 edition) is thus unnecessary.

27 ὀρθὸν οὖς ἵστησιν: pricked ears are a sign of attentiveness, as at Call. *Hym.* 4.230–1 οὔατα δ' αὐτῆς | ὀρθὰ μάλ', αἰὲν ἑτοῖμα θεῆς ὑποδέχθαι ὁμοκλήν, Ap. Rh. 1.513–15 τοὶ δ' ἄμοτον λήξαντος (sc. Ὀρφέως) ἔτι προὔχοντο κάρηνα | πάντες ὁμῶς ὀρθοῖσιν ἐπ' οὔασιν ἠρεμέοντες | κηληθμῷ; cf. Ter. *Andr.* 933 *arrige auris*, Otto (1890) 49, Diogenianus 8.74 = *CPG* i. 320.5–6 ὠσὶν ἑστῶσιν. Elsewhere they can denote a wide range of emotions: joyful recognition of a friend (cf. Hom. *Od.* 17.291 οὔατα . . . ἔσχεν, of Argus), surprise (cf. Hdt. 4.129.3 οἱ ἵπποι . . . ἐν θώματι ἔσκον, ὀρθὰ ἱστάντες τὰ ὦτα), anger (Lucian 25.23 ὄρθιον ἐφιστὰς τὸ οὖς), physical exertion (Quint. Smyrn. *Post.* 4.511 οὔατα δ' ὠρθώσαντο, of horses in a chariot race), or fear (cf. Eur. *Hipp.* 1203–4, Ov. *Met.* 15.516 with Bömer).

ὡσαύτως δέ: for apodotic δέ after a comparative protasis cf. *Ant.* 426, *Tr.* 116 οὕτω δέ, Bruhn §194, Denniston 179 §iii.

28 ἐν πρώτοις ἔπη: cf. Hom. *Il.* 8.337 Ἕκτωρ δ' ἐν πρώτοισι κίε. The minority reading ἔσῃ is probably the result of a simple graphic error; or perhaps a scribe thought that 'following' was inconsistent with being 'among the foremost men'. The variant is introduced in L by the figure δι^χ, which Jebb (following Elmsley on *Aj.* 1225) and Colonna (p. 139 of his edition) take to mean Δίδυμος, with the chi used to draw attention to the name (on the variety of uses to which this letter is put in papyri see Turner (1968) 116–17). But it is easier to take these letters as a compendium for διχῶς, which is commonly used in scholia to introduce variants: cf. Ludwich (1884–5) i. 31–8, De Marco (1937) 39 [= 143].

30 ὀξεῖαν ἀκοήν . . . διδούς: for ὀξύς 'quick in' cf. Hom. *Il.* 17.256 ὀξὺ δ' ἄκουσεν, Chadwick (1996) 217. For the periphrasis cf. 214, 333–4, 735, *Phil.* 234–5 λαβεῖν | πρόσφθεγγμα, Long (1968) 84 n. 70; also Simon. fr. 543.19–20 *PMG* καί κεν ἐμῶν ῥημάτων | λεπτὸν ὑπεῖχες οὖας.

31 εἰ μή τι καιροῦ τυγχάνω: cf. *Phil.* 1279–80 εἰ . . . μή τι πρὸς καιρὸν λέγων | κυρῶ, *Tr.* 586–7, 712–13, Pl. *Leg.* 687a5–6 τοῦ καιροῦ πως ἂν ἔτυχον, Pind. *N.* 8.4 καιροῦ μὴ πλαναθέντα, Race (1981) 204, Trédé (1992) 39 n. 39.

μεθάρμοσον: cf: [Aesch.] *PV* 309–10 γίγνωσκε σαυτὸν καὶ μεθάρμοσαι τρόπους | νέους, Eur. *Alc.* 1157–8 νῦν γὰρ μεθηρμόσμεσθα βελτίω βίον | τοῦ πρόσθεν.

32–7 Sheppard (1927) 2–3 claims that Orestes should have asked Apollo *whether* he should take revenge on his father's murderers. Instead, he asks only *how*: and as a punishment for his presumption, the god gives him deliberately misleading advice. This influential interpretation (doxography at MacLeod (2001) 28 n. 17) relies on Apollo's behaving as the oracles do at Hdt. 1.157–9 (the Cymeans ask whether they should give up a suppliant to the Persians), 6.86 (Glaucus asks whether he can cheat on an oath for personal gain) and Xen. *An.* 3.1.6–7 (Xenophon is rebuked by Socrates for asking an oracle how and not whether he should do something). But nowhere is Apollo said to have provided misleading advice (contrast Eur. *El.* 971, 1245–6). Sheppard's view is also incompatible with ἐνδίκου in 37, which is part of Apollo's response. Furthermore, a desire to punish the killers of one's father would be taken for granted in contemporary Greek thought (cf. Dover (1974) 180–4, Carawan (1999) 198–9). A man needed no oracle to inform him of that duty. It is thus not a reprehensible act. It could conceivably involve reprehensible means, but as it is the means about which Orestes is inquiring this cannot be used to blacken his behaviour. Sheppard's thesis has been rejected by many scholars, including some, such as Winnington-Ingram, who are in other places sympathetic to his general interpretation of the drama (a list at Hester (1981) 19 n. 15).

32 γάρ: often 'after an expression denoting the giving or receiving of information' (Denniston 59): see further 681 n.

33 πατρός: so most manuscripts, Wunder¹, Schneidewin¹, Pearson and Dawe. Many editors print the minority reading πατρί. But with the expression δίκας ἀροίμην we would rather expect a genitive (cf. Eur. *Andr.* 53, *Or.* 531, 1657 (all metrically guaranteed), Hdt. 8.114.1), whereas the dative would normally denote the person from whom reparation is sought. Some editors (e.g. Wunder², Nauck⁴) claim that the expression is equivalent to τιμωρεῖν or τιμωρῆσαι, with which a dative would be normal (cf. 14): but they do not cite parallels.

35 τοιαῦθ᾽ ὁ: for τοιαῦτα introducing reported speech see Führer (1967) 14–15; for the short first syllable cf. 38, 1001, 1024, 1338, West (1982a) 11. Blomfield's τοιαῦτα (*ap.* Monk (1826) 64) now has slight manuscript support, but the definite article is idiomatic with the god's name even when he has not previously been mentioned (cf. 1385n., Moorhouse 147, Eur. *IT* 711, 1128, *Or.* 191, 329).

36 ἄσκευον . . . ἀσπίδων: for the genitive after negative compound adjectives cf. 232, 1002, *OR* 191 ἄχαλκος ἀσπίδων, *OC* 677–8, 1383, *Phil.* 217, Wilamowitz on Eur. *Her.* 114, Bruhn §244.V.2, Moorhouse 54–5 and 68–9.

αὐτόν 'alone' (cf. Diggle on Theophr. *Char.* 22.13): often, as here, accompanied by a further phrase emphasising and defining the solitude (cf. *OC* 1520–1 αὐτὸς . . . | ἄθικτος ἡγητῆρος, *Aj.* 464, *Tr.* 1063, Hom. *Il.* 5.473–4 ἄτερ λαῶν . . . | οἷος, Pind. *N.* 3.34 μόνος ἄνευ στρατιᾶς, *P.* 9.27–8 μούναν . . . | ἄτερ ἐγχέων).

For unseparated τε καί used to join the two elements of an hendiadys Kovacs (1980) 299 n. 27 compares Eur. *Hipp.* 164 and Bacchyl. 11.12.

στρατοῦ: for Meineke's δορός ((1863a) 249) cf. *OC* 1311–12, 1524–5, Ar. *Pax* 356 = *Vesp.* 1081 = Achaeus 20 F 29 *TrGF* and Blaydes[2] *ad loc.*; Meineke takes στρατοῦ as a gloss on δορός. But στρατός conveys the idea of a numerous host better than δορός.

37 δόλοισι: on δόλος see 1–85n.

κλέψαι 'effect by stealth': cf. *Aj.* 1137 πόλλ᾽ ἂν καλῶς λάθρα σὺ κλέψειας κακά, Eur. fr. 289.1–2 *TrGF* νείκη γὰρ ἀνδρῶν φόνια καὶ μάχας χρεὼν (*coni.*) | δόλοισι κλέπτειν, Pind. *N.* 7.23 σοφία . . . κλέπτει παράγοισα μύθοις, Denniston on Eur. *El.* 364.

χειρὸς ἐνδίκου σφαγάς: manuscript ἐνδίκους leaves χειρός bare without an epithet. For the awkwardness of this see Fraenkel on Aesch. *Ag.* 1495–6: *Aj.* 27 is not a parallel, as Fraenkel notes, and the difficulty is only partly overcome by taking χειρός with δόλοισι. Lange's ἐνδίκου,[3] revived by Hutchinson (on Aesch. *Sept.* 698–701) and adopted by Ll-J/W, is an easy improvement.

38–58: Orestes also sets out the plan before its execution in *Choephori* (554–84). His instructions to Electra there are similar, although not as precise: νῦν οὖν σὺ μὲν φύλασσε τἀν οἴκῳ καλῶς, | ὅπως ἂν ἀρτίκολλα συμβαίνῃ τάδε (579–80).

38 ὅτ᾽ οὖν: Orestes tightly links his actions to the message of the oracle.

---

[3] Ll-J/W (*Sophoclea*) say that this conjecture is found in Lange (1860), but I did not find it there.

39 σὺ μέν: corresponding to ἡμεῖς δέ in 51.

καιρός 'opportunity': cf. *Phil.* 466 καιρὸς . . . καλεῖ, 1450–1, Race (1981) 212. For the abstract noun as subject of a personal verb see 1251–2, *Ant.* 95–6, *OR* 681–2, 1024, *Phil.* 900–1.

40 τὸ δρώμενον: for the participle as a substantive cf. 85, 1333, *Tr.* 588 ἀλλ᾽ εἴ τις ἐστὶ πίστις ἐν τοῖς δρωμένοις, Moorhouse 257.

42–3 οὐ γάρ σε μὴ γήρᾳ τε καὶ χρόνῳ μακρῷ | γνῶσ᾽, οὐδ᾽ ὑποπτεύσουσιν ὧδ᾽ ἠνθισμένον: contrast Eur. *El.* 630–1, where Orestes is assured by the Old Man that he will not be recognised. V's ὑποπτεύσωσιν (*coni.* Turnebus) would give us a pair of subjunctives, but for the future in this position cf. *OC* 450–2 οὐ . . . μὴ λάχωσι . . . | οὐδέ . . . | ὄνησις ἥξει, Moorhouse 337–8. Lloyd-Jones's proposal to add a comma after ὑποπτεύσουσιν ((1983b) 172) was anticipated by Kamerbeek. Ll-J/W claim that 'the syntax is easier if the two datives are taken with the participle' (*Sophoclea*): but γνῶναι with a bare dative is regular (cf. Eur. *Her.* 665–6, *IT* 1178, *Ion* 1344; also (ἐπιγνῶναι) S. *El.* 1296–7).

χρόνῳ μακρῷ: the order is reversed in some manuscripts, probably because of *vitium Byzantinum* (cf. Eur. *Hipp.* 1322, S. *Aj.* 764, *OR* 715, 1175, Reynolds and Wilson (1991) 229).

γνῶσ᾽: see Friis Johansen and Whittle on Aesch. *Suppl.* 483 for the first element of a trimeter being occupied by the final word of a clause begun in the previous line(s); cf. 340.

ὧδ᾽ ἠνθισμένον: for the 'flowering' of grey hair cf. *OR* 742 λευκανθὲς κάρα, Ar. *Vesp.* 1064–5 πολιώτεραι δὴ | αἵδ᾽ ἐπανθοῦσιν τρίχες, Erin. fr. 401.46 *SH* πραϋλόγοι πολιαί, ταὶ γήραος ἄνθεα θνατοῖς, and especially Hosea 7.9 καὶ πολιαὶ ἐξήνθησαν αὐτῷ, καὶ αὐτὸς οὐκ ἔγνω with Cyr. Alex. *Comm. in xii Proph. Min.* i. 160.20 Pusey τουτέστι, μακροῦ διαγεγονότος χρόνου. The verb is used metaphorically at Hdt. 1.98.6 ἠνθισμένοι . . . φαρμάκοισι, Philemon fr. 82.6 *PCG* (ἰχθὺν) ἄνωθεν ἐξηνθισμένον, Epicrates fr. 6.4–5 *PCG* δελφάκων . . . κρέα | κάλλιστ᾽ ὄπωπα πυρὸς ἀκμαῖς ἠνθισμένα. The scholia (p. 100.17–21 Papageorgius) complain that a covering of grey hairs would not be enough to disguise the Paedagogus, and take the participle in the sense ἠσκημένον. The objection is pedantic, the alternative meaning semantically impossible.

44 λόγῳ . . . χρῶ τοιῷδ᾽: for this anticipation of the following statement see Fraser (2001) 18 with n. 21.

45 Cf. Aesch. *Cho.* 674 ξένος μέν εἰμι Δαυλιεὺς ἐκ Φωκέων.

Φωκέως παρ᾽ ἀνδρὸς Φανοτέως: Φωκέως is Bentley's conjecture for manuscript Φωκεύς ((1816) 45). A bare ἀνδρός qualifying the proper name Φανοτέως is difficult. There are possible parallels in Homer (*Il.* 11.92 (though note West's punctuation), *Od.* 7.22–3) and Herodotus (8.82.1): but alleged tragic instances of the idiom turn out on closer inspection to be no such thing. So at *Aj.* 817–18 ἀνδρός goes with μισηθέντος and is in apposition to Ἕκτορος, while at *OC* 109–10 οἰκτίρατ' ἀνδρὸς Οἰδίπου τόδ' ἄθλιον | εἴδωλον the point is that Oedipus is the mere shadow of a man. No such special reasons apply in our case, and so Bentley's small change should be welcomed.

Phanoteus was the eponymous hero of the town in Phocis (for which see McInerney (1999) 295–6). He is mentioned in Homer at *Il.* 23.665 as the father of Epeus, while the town is referred to at *Il.* 2.520, 17.307, *Od.* 11.581 and [Hes.] fr. 70.21 M–W (cf. Visser (1997) 384–6). He and Crisus, eponymous hero of Crisa (for which see McInerney (1999) 309–12), were the twin sons of Phocus, son of Aeacus (cf. Asius fr. 5 *EGF* = *PEG* = *GEF*). The pair were said to have quarrelled while still in the womb (cf. [Hes.] fr. 58.7–15 M–W, Hepding (1922) 1893.40–52). Strophius, to whom the infant Orestes was sent for safe-keeping, was the son of Crisus, and consequently a hereditary enemy of his uncle Phanoteus. An alliance between Phanoteus and Aegisthus is therefore mythologically plausible, given that Phanoteus' enemy is looking after the son of Aegisthus' enemy. The alliance may be S.'s invention. The name is always Πανοπεύς in Homer and Hesiod. Φανοτεύς is the later form, found in e.g. Thuc. 4.76.3; cf. Strab. 9.3.14 (= iii. 96.24 Radt) Πανοπεὺς δ' ὁ νῦν Φανοτεύς. For more on Phanoteus see Hanslik (1949) 649.

ὅ: for the accentuation (first restored here by Erfurdt) see West's Teubner Aeschylus, p. xlix.

46 μέγιστος 'greatest, closest', not 'most powerful': cf. *Aj.* 1331, *Phil.* 586.

δορυξένων: denotes the 'establishment of hospitable relations as a result of brotherhood in arms' (Wilamowitz on Aesch. *Cho.* 562, translated by Fraenkel on Aesch. *Ag.* 880). Cf. Ar. Byz. fr. 302 Slater δορύξενοι δὲ οἱ κατὰ πόλεμον ἀλλήλους φιλοποιησάμενοι.

47 ἄγγελλε δ' ὅρκον προστιθείς: ὅρκον is Reiske's conjecture ((1753) 11). Manuscript ὅρκῳ requires a harsh ellipse of either ὅρκον or τὰ ἀγγελλόμενα. The accusative, on the other hand, is paralleled by fr. 472.1–2 *TrGF* ὅρκου δὲ προστεθέντος ἐπιμελεστέρα | ψυχὴ κατέστη; cf. also *Tr.* 255 ὅρκον αὐτῷ προσβαλὼν διώμοσεν. Ar. *Vesp.* 201 τῇ δοκῷ προσθείς may provide a parallel for the corruption: in his edition Sommerstein prints Dobree's emendation τὴν δοκόν. Kells (1977) argues that in each case the προσ– prefix encouraged the change from accusative to dative. Alternatively, the common confusion of iota and nu (683n.) may have been to blame. Zakas (1890–1) ii. 64 and Dawe (1968) 14 prefer ὅρκους, but that corruption is not so easily explained.

The Paedagogus takes no oath when he gives his account, but it would be unwise to adopt Musgrave's ὄγκον on that account. At *Tr.* 377–8 Deianira

COMMENTARY: 1–85

asks ἆρ' ἀνώνυμος | πέφυκεν, ὥσπερ οὐπάγων διώμνυτο even though Lichas had taken no oath (cf. Hirzel (1902) 72–3 n. 3). By the Paedagogus' next entry the minds of the spectators will not be on whether the Paedagogus is following Orestes' instructions to the letter.

Scholars have criticised Orestes because of his cavalier approach to perjury (doxography in MacLeod (2001) 35 n. 33): for recourse to false oaths as a characteristic of the immoral cf. Lucian 41.22. But perjury can be regarded as one aspect of the δόλος which Apollo has enjoined on him. Once we have accepted that δόλος has been divinely sanctioned and is therefore not reprehensible, it is difficult to see what difference is made by the addition of a false oath.

48 τέθνηκ' Ὀρέστης: the Paedagogus uses this phrase at 673 (n.).

For ἐξ used 'of the base of an action, its underlying condition or manner of performance (often equivalent to an adverb of manner)' (Moorhouse 110) cf. 279, 455, 725, 742, *Tr.* 875, *Phil.* 91, Bruhn §68.1, Diggle (1973) 249 = (1994) 67–8, Rijksbaron (1991) 23–4 n. 51.

ἀναγκαίας τύχης: cf. *Aj.* 485, 803, Eur. *IA* 511.

49 ἄθλοισι Πυθικοῖσιν: the Pythian games were not founded until 582 B.C., and the scholia (p. 101.20–1 Papageorgius) consequently note an anachronism. But according to a different tradition the Pythian games were founded by Apollo, with figures such as Heracles and Peleus among the first victors (cf. Easterling (1985) 7–8). Easterling argues that the chronological 'problem' arose as a consequence of Aristotle's compilation of the Delphic victor-lists: so at *Poet.* 1460ᵃ31 ἐν Ἠλέκτρᾳ οἱ τὰ Πύθια ἀπαγγέλλοντες is cited as something ἄλογον. There is thus no reason to postulate an anachronism.

51 ἡμεῖς δέ: answering σὺ μέν in 39.

ὡς ἐφίετο: the imperfect is often used of an oracular response (cf. *OR* 110 ἐν τῆδ' ἔφασκε γῆ, Aesch. *Cho.* 1039 Λοξίας ἐφίετο), as well as with verbs of command (cf. Moorhouse 191; also 68on.). Apollo is the subject, even though he has not been mentioned since 35: for similar ellipses cf. *OR* 106, Ar. *Ran.*182, 319.

52 The offerings are later seen by Chrysothemis (894–901). In Aeschylus' *Choephori* Orestes makes the offerings in the prologue. Euripides' Orestes has already made them by the time he arrives on stage (*El.* 90–2 νυκτὸς δὲ τῆσδε πρὸς τάφον μολὼν πατρὸς | δάκρυά τ' ἔδωκα καὶ κόμης ἀπηρξάμην | πυρᾷ τ' ἐπέσφαξ' αἷμα μηλείου φόνου).

λοιβαῖσι: better attested than the fussy λοιβαῖς τε (cf. the similar divide at *OC* 608). The Suda's λοιβαῖς τό (χ 340 = iv. 810.14 Adler) gives the wrong sense (τὸ πρῶτον = 'in the first place, originally'). λοιβῇσι is also possible

(1141 n.). For the pouring of offerings at the tomb cf. Garland (2001) 113–15, Stengel (1920) 149, Burkert (1977) 123 ≈ (1985) 71–2.

καρατόμοις χλιδαῖς: for χλιδή of the hair cf. Aesch. fr. 313.1 *TrGF* χλιδῶν τε πλόκαμος ὥστε παρθένοις ἁβραῖς, Eur. *Phoen.* 223–4 κόμας ἐμᾶς | . . . παρθένιον χλιδάν; perhaps also S. fr. 659.10 *TrGF* τὴν πάρος χλιδήν (*coni.* Brunck; φόβην codd.). The opulence of the expression mirrors the luxuriousness of the offering: contrast the meagreness of Electra's hair at 449. καρότομος must mean 'cut from the head': elsewhere it has the sense 'beheaded, beheading' (e.g. Eur. *Tro.* 564–5 καρότομος ἐρημία | νεανίδων, [Eur.] *Rhes.* 606 καρατόμους σφαγάς).

'The hair was felt as a detachable, and therefore conveniently dedicable, extension of its owner's personality' (Dodds on Eur. *Ba.* 493–7): cf. 448–9, *Aj.* 1173–5, Hom. *Il.* 23.135–7, 141–53, Arist. fr. 101 Rose, Eitrem (1915) 344–415, Jax (1933) 104 n. 253, Meuli (1946) 205–6 n. 1 = (1975b) ii. 928–9 n. 2, Woodbury (1979) 284–5 n. 39 = (1991) 332 n. 39, Garvie on *Cho.* 6, West (1997) 39 with n. 155, Alexiou (2002) 208 n. 40, Lightfoot's edition of Lucian's *De dea Syria*, pp. 531–3. In each of the tragedians, and also in Stesichorus, Orestes' dedication of his hair is connected with his recognition (cf. 900–1 n., 892–919n.). Offerings of hair were commonly made at various transitional stages in a lifetime, especially puberty (cf. Sommer (1912) 21–34, Diggle on Theophr. *Char.* 21.3). Orestes' offering may thus point to his assumption of manhood as he returns to avenge his father.

53 For στέψαντες of religious offerings cf. 441, 458, 895, *Ant.* 431 χοαῖσι τρισπόνδοισι τὸν νέκυν στέφει, Aesch. *Cho.* 95 with Garvie, Eur. *Phoen.* 1632, S. *Aj.* 93, Σ *OR* 3 (p. 161.10–11 Papageorgius), Eur. *Hec.* 126.

εἶτ' ἄψορρον ἥξομεν πάλιν: cf. *OR* 430–1 οὐχὶ . . . πάλιν | ἄψορρος οἴκων τῶνδ' ἀποστραφεὶς ἄπει;, Hom. *Il.* 3.33 παλίνορσος. For εἶτα or ἔπειτα with a finite verb in coordination with a preceding nominative participle see Olson on Ar. *Ach.* 23–4. In tragedy he compares [Aesch.] *PV* 777, Eur. *El.* 921–2; add S. *El.* [1008].

54 τύπωμα χαλκόπλευρον: τύπωμα denotes anything formed or moulded: its only other occurrence in classical literature is at Eur. *Phoen.* 162 μορφῆς τύπωμα. Other –πλευρος compounds occur at S. fr. 24.3 *TrGF* τὸν ἀντίπλευρον κῆπον, Eur. *El.* 472 περιπλεύρῳ . . . κύτει, Pind. *P.* 4.235 ἐριπλεύρῳ φυᾷ. For the expression cf. fr. 378.2 *TrGF* χαλκηλάτους λέβητας, Aesch. *Cho.* 686 λέβητος χαλκέου πλευρώματα.

55 It is not clear how the urn can already have been hidden near the tomb, since Orestes and the Paedagogus are only now setting off in that direction. The audience will not have lingered over the point, but it remains an inconcinnity.

θάμνοις . . . κεκρυμμένον: cf. Tr. Adesp. P. Köln 245.21 = fr. 672a *TrGF* (vol. v/2, p. 1143.21) κρύψω πέπλ[ο]υς δὲ τοὺς ἐμοὺς θάμνῳ τινί with Parca. που 'no doubt', 'surely', with οἶσθα: cf. 948, 1244, *Phil.* 553, *OC* 1587–8 and Blaydes's n. (in his 1873 edition) on our passage; the alternative rendering 'somewhere in the bushes' (advocated by Dawe (1976) 229) unhelpfully suggests that Orestes is not sure of the precise location. Wunder[2] and Schneidewin[1] prefer the variant μοι, but the sense is problematic: it cannot mark the agent with κεκρυμμένον, as this would require ἐμοί, while an ethic dative would be inappropriate here.

56 λόγῳ κλέπτοντες: cf. Eur. *Phoen.* 992 κλέψας λόγοισιν, ὥσθ᾿ ἃ βούλομαι τυχεῖν, Hom. *Il.* 1.132 κλέπτε νόῳ.

57 φέρωμεν: most manuscripts have φέροιμεν; but G's reading is right, as the verb depends on ἥξομεν, not κεκρυμμένον, ἡρμένοι or ἐφίετο (suggested by Moorhouse 287). For the corruption of subjunctive to optative cf. perhaps 760, *OC* 11.

58 φλογιστὸν ἤδη καὶ κατηνθρακωμένον: cf. Aesch. fr. 281.4 *TrGF* στέγην πυρώσω καὶ κατανθρακώσομαι. There are no other occurrences of φλογιστός in classical Greek (though Aristotle uses the word to mean 'inflammable').

59–66 Orestes spends several lines justifying the decision to have his death falsely reported. For some scholars this signals the fundamental immorality of the plan (e.g. Winnington-Ingram (1980) 236). But the hesitation is not prompted by ethical scruples: rather, Orestes is concerned that his plan, although morally justified and supported by Apollo, nevertheless involves the breaking of a taboo. To speak of oneself as already dead is commonly assumed to be unlucky: according to Plutarch, οὐ . . . ἐνόμιζον (sc. οἱ Ἕλληνες) ἁγνοὺς οὐδὲ κατεμείγνυσαν ἑαυτοῖς οὐδ᾿ εἴων ἱεροῖς πλησιάζειν, οἷς ἐκφορὰ γεγόνει καὶ τάφος ὡς τεθνηκόσι (*Mor.* 264f = *Quaest. Rom.* 5). Cf. Sen. *Tro.* 608–9 *fingit an quisquam hoc parens,* | *nec abominandae mortis auspicium pavet?*, R. C. T. Parker (1983) 61 n. 100; Falstaff's stout defence of a strategy similar to Orestes' at *1 Henry IV* 5.4.120 ('To counterfeit dying, when a man thereby liveth, is to be no counterfeit, but the true and perfect image of life indeed') may betray the same concern. Orestes and Falstaff seek to avert the power of the taboo by challenging it: Orestes does so in particular by citing precedents for the success of this strategy (cf. 62–6n.).

The same idea is found in Euripides' *Helen*, where Helen saves herself and Menelaus by pretending that Menelaus is dead. At 1050 she asks her husband βούλῃ λέγεσθαι μὴ θανὼν λόγῳ θανεῖν;, to which he replies (1051) κακὸς μὲν ὄρνις· εἰ δὲ κερδανῶ, λέγε. Dale on Eur. *Hel.* 1050 ff. (cf. (1969) 228–9) notes how both Orestes and Menelaus use the prospect of κέρδος to justify the plan (cf. 61). Together with Vögler (1967) 100–102, she claims that Menelaus' comment παλαιότης γὰρ τῷ λόγῳ γ' ἔνεστί τις (1056) refers to the plan in S.'s play, which she consequently dates to a little before the *Helen* (412 BC). The line makes sense without an extra-dramatic reference: Menelaus is initially unenthusiastic about his wife's plan, and so he points to a potential weakness in it. But rather than emphasise the danger of the plan or the likelihood of failure, he complains that it lacks originality – a most unusual objection. Dale's hypothesis does at least give an explanation for his choice of complaint.

Even if we accept that an extra-dramatic point is being made, however, we need not take it as a reference to Sophocles' play. As Vögler (1967) 101 points out, both Aeschylus' *Oresteia* (458) and Euripides' *Cresphontes* (*c.* 430–24, according to Harder's edition, pp. 3–4) use the motif of a falsely announced death. Vögler claims that these plays were too distant in time to be the referent here, but (i) this distance could lend piquancy to the charge of παλαιότης, and (ii) the use of Aeschylus' *Oresteia* in the two *Electra* plays indicates the continued popularity of the older work. Sophocles' play itself gestures towards the παλαιότης motif at 62–3 ἤδη γὰρ εἶδον πολλάκις, which also suggests that the strategy is a hoary trick. The *Helen* passage thus does not help us to date our play.

60 ἔργοισι: for the plural cf. 287, Eur. fr. 360.13 *TrGF* = 50.13 Austin λόγῳ πολίτης ἐστί, τοῖς δ' ἔργοισιν οὔ, Denniston on Eur. *El.* 47.

κἀξενέγκωμαι κλέος: cf. *Tr.* 497 ἐκφέρεται νίκας ἀεί. For κλέος used of Orestes' achievement cf. Hom. *Od.* 1.298 ἢ οὐκ ἀΐεις οἷον κλέος ἔλλαβε δῖος Ὀρέστης;, 3.204.

61 Some scholars take this line as a sophism which indicates the immorality of Orestes' plan (cf. 59–66n.). They compare *Phil.* 111 (Odysseus) ὅταν τι δρᾷς ἐς κέρδος, οὐκ ὀκνεῖν πρέπει; cf. also fr. 833 *TrGF* τὸ κέρδος ἡδύ, κἂν ἀπὸ ψευδῶν ἴῃ. In fact, Orestes defends his action because some might regard it not as wicked, but as ill omened and dangerous. He thus states that if this course brings him κέρδος, as he can reasonably expect given the divine support it enjoys, then it cannot also be ill omened or harmful to him (κακόν; cf. *Ant.* 1001, *OC* 1433). *Ant.* 1326 κέρδη παραινεῖς, εἴ τι κέρδος ἐν κακοῖς provides another opposition between κέρδος and κακόν. Here too the chorus does not claim that κέρδος is the antithesis of wickedness: the contrast is rather between personal advantage and personal misfortune. Only when taken out of context can κακόν here mean 'morally wrong'.

δοκῶ μέν: cf. 547, *OC* 995, fr. 85.1 *TrGF* δοκῶ μέν, οὐδείς, *Phil.* 339, Call. fr. 203.33 Pfeiffer, Bruhn §156. Such affirmations do not mark secret doubt: cf. *OC* 1214, *Phil.* 864, Wolf (1910) 39–44.

62–6 The Greeks knew of 'disappearing and reappearing shamans' (Dodds (1951) 141), mysterious figures thought to be able to leave their bodies and return to them. Democritus wrote a treatise on these miracle-workers: τὴν μὲν περὶ τῶν ἀποθανεῖν δοξάντων ἔπειτα ἀναβιούντων ἱστορίαν ἄλλοι τε πολλοὶ τῶν παλαιῶν ἤθροισαν καὶ Δ. ὁ φυσικὸς ἐν τοῖς Περὶ τοῦ Ἅιδου γράμμασιν (D–K 68 B 1 = ii. 130.16–19). Burkert (1962) 123–41 ≈ (1972) 147–61 discusses various instances of the phenomenon. Several fit the pattern of a man who allows others to think that he is dead and who receives honours when discovered alive (e.g. Aristeas (cf. Bolton (1962) 144–5), Salmoxis, Epimenides of Crete, Hermotimus of Clazomenae and Pythagoras; Burkert (1962) 140 ≈ (1972) 160–1 thinks the last identification most likely in our case). Aristeas and Salmoxis have their stories recorded in Herodotus (4.14–15, 4.94–6), which may mean that our passage shows direct Herodotean influence (for which cf. perhaps *Ant.* 904–15, *OC* 337–45, S. R. West (1999)).

Others have seen a reference to figures of heroic myth whose deaths were wrongly reported, such as Heracles, Theseus and Odysseus. The last of these would seem especially relevant given the Odyssean colouring of this prologue (cf. Davidson (1988) 56–8); Odysseus too can plausibly be described as σοφός (cf. e.g. *Phil.* 431–2). But none attempts to spread a false account of his death, which is simply assumed because of the hero's lengthy absence. There is thus no σοφία on the part of the hero (so rightly Burkert (1962) 140 n. 277 ≈ (1972) 161 n. 225).

Another possible candidate is Sisyphus (advocated by Lloyd-Jones (1959) 480), whose escape from the dead (cf. S. *Phil.* 624–5) can be regarded as a supreme instance of cunning (cf. Alcaeus 38a.5–7 *PLF*, Voigt). But he did not spread a report that he was dead – he was dead, and only returned from death by a trick. Nor did he enjoy honours as a result of his escape. His eventual punishment would make him an unfortunate model for Orestes to evoke.

62 ἤδη . . . εἶδον: for this combination introducing an *exemplum* cf. *Aj.* 1142, Theogn. 915, 920, Eur. *Med.* 92, *El.* 369, fr. 295.1 *TrGF*, Fraenkel (1960b) = (1964) i. 505–10, West (1997) 521, Davies (1999c) 431 n. 24. Cf. *vidi ego* in Latin 'per motivare una massima o un insegnamento, chiamando a testimone la propria esperienza di vita' (Fedeli on Prop. 1.13.14).

63 μάτην 'falsely': cf. 1298, *Phil.* 345. At Aesch. *Cho.* 845–6 the paradosis reads λόγοι | . . . θνήσκοντες μάτην: Portus's –οντος would give the same sense as in our passage, but the transmitted text should probably be retained with Page and West (see Garvie).

64 ἐκτετίμηνται: for the 'gnomic perfect' cf. *OC* 1235, Moorhouse 200.

COMMENTARY: 1–85

65 κἄμ᾽ ἐπαυχῶ: accusative for expected nominative with infinitive (cf. K–G ii. 30–2, Bruhn §119, Moorhouse 317). For the verb ('assert confidently') see Fraenkel on Aesch. *Ag.* 1497, Barrett on Eur. *Hipp.* 952–5.

ἄπο 'as a consequence of' (cf. *Ant.* 695 κάκιστ᾽ ἀπ᾽ ἔργων εὐκλεεστάτων φθίνει).

66 δεδορκότ᾽ 'living': cf. Aesch. *Eum.* 322 ἀλαοῖσι καὶ δεδορκόσιν, Hom. *Il.* 1.88 οὔ τις ἐμεῦ ζῶντος καὶ ἐπὶ χθονὶ δερκομένοιο, Davies on *Tr.* 828, West (2004) 5. The minority variant δεδυκότ᾽ shows a corruption to a word more usual in astronomical contexts.

ἄστρον: the epic image conveys the bright splendour of the hero (cf. λάμψειν at Hom. *Il.* 6.295, 19.381, *Od.* 15.108 ἀστὴρ δ᾽ ὣς ἀπέλαμπεν, Theodoridas *A.P.* 6.156.3 = 3514 *HE* ἴσον ἀστέρι λάμπει) and the menace he presents to his enemies (cf. Hom. *Il.* 5.4–8, 11.62–5 (Hector compared to an οὔλιος[4] ἀστήρ), 22.25–32 (Achilles compared to Sirius), 22.317–19, Antonius *A.P.* 9.102.2 = 3585 *GP* πικρὸν Ἰλιάδαις ἀστέρα (of Agamemnon)). On star imagery see further Whitman (1958) 142–4, Gow on Theocr. 25.141.

ἔτι: often in threats and menaces: cf. 471 n., *Tr.* 255–7, *Aj.* 607, [Aesch.] *PV* 168, 907, Eur. *Alc.* 731, *Andr.* 492, *Ba.* 306, 534–6, Fraenkel on Aesch. *Ag.* 1429–30, Olson on Ar. *Ach.* 1156–8.

67–72 The returning traveller in tragedy often invokes the land (cf. Wagener (1931) 86, Fraenkel on Aesch. *Ag.* 503) and local gods (cf. Diggle (1982c) 128). Cf. *Phil.* 1040 ἀλλ᾽, ὦ πατρῷα γῆ θεοί τ᾽ ἐπόψιοι, Ov. *Fast.* 1.509–14; also West's supplement at Aesch. *Suppl.* 22a (cf. West (1990) 126–7). A prayer can conclude a scene of plotting: cf. Eur. *El.* 671–82, Matthiessen (1964) 42 n. 2.

67 For ἀλλά beginning a prayer see Ausfeld (1903) 537, Davies on *Tr.* 119 ff.

θεοί τ᾽ ἐγχώριοι: for the gods of the locality in tragedy cf. *Tr.* 183, *Ant.* 199, Aesch. *Suppl.* 482, 520, 704–6, *Sept.* 14, *Ag.* 810, 1645.

68 For δέξασθε with the speaker of the prayer as its object cf. *OC* 44 ἀλλ᾽ ἵλεῳ μὲν τὸν ἱκέτην δεξαίατο, Aesch. *Suppl.* 28, Ausfeld (1903) 537. εὐτυχοῦντα is proleptic, as at 162 δέξεται εὐπατρίδαν.

ταῖσδε ταῖς ὁδοῖς: cf. 1295 τῇ νῦν ὁδῷ, *OC* 553–4 τανῦν θ᾽ ὁδοῖς | ἐν τᾷσδε λεύσσων μᾶλλον ἐξεπίσταμαι.

69 σύ τ᾽, ὦ πατρῷον δῶμα: for the address to the house by a returning traveller cf. Eur. *Her.* 523, *Or.* 356, Leo (1908) 30.

---

[4] West prints Αὔλιος: cf. (2001) 211.

112

COMMENTARY: 1–85

70 καθαρτής: for the killer as purifier cf. Aesch. *Cho.* 967–8 ὅταν ἀφ' ἑστίας μύσος <ἅ> παν ἐλάσῃ | καθαρμοῖσ <ιν> ἀτᾶν ἐλατηρίοις, *Julius Caesar* 2.1.180 'We shall be called purgers, not murderers'. For the house in need of purification cf. *OR* 1227–8, Aesch. *Eum.* 63 δωμάτων καθάρσιος (of Apollo). S. uses the noun elsewhere at fr. 34 *TrGF* στρατοῦ καθαρτὴς κἀπομαγμάτων ἴδρις.

πρὸς θεῶν ὡρμημένος: cf. Aesch. *Cho.* 940–1 ὁ πυθόχρηστος φυγὰς | θεόθεν εὖ φραδαῖσιν ὡρμημένος, Eur. *El.* 590–1 θεὸς αὖ θεὸς ἁμετέραν τις ἄγει | νίκαν.

71 ἄτιμον 'without τιμή' (cf. 64), but also 'without achieving my aims': cf. *OR* 788–9 ὁ Φοῖβος ὢν μὲν ἱκόμην | ἄτιμον ἐξέπεμψεν.

72 For the ellipse of a positive imperative cf. 648–51, K–G ii. 566–7 k, Bruhn §199, Fraenkel on Aesch. *Ag.* 398.

ἀρχέπλουτον: the prefix ἀρχι– is not found before Aeschylus (except in the name Ἀρχίλοχος, first attested in Pindar). ἀρχε– is an older form (cf. Chantraine (1999) s.v. ἄρχω B 2a). In compounds it means either 'beginner of' (e.g. Hom. *Il.* 5.63 ἀρχεκάκους, Eur. *Tro.* 151 ποδὸς ἀρχεχόρου) or 'master of' (Pind. *P.* 9.54 ἀρχέπολιν, Aesch. *Pers.* 297 ἀρχελείων). The latter sense at first seems the more appropriate: Orestes seeks to restore the fortunes of his house, not to create them from nothing. But given that καταστάτην must mean something like 'establisher' (cf. LSJ⁹ s.v. καθίστημι A II 2b), the former meaning also seems to be present. Orestes' intervention in the fortunes of his house is such that he can be reckoned a second founder (cf. 83n.).

Aeschylus' Orestes also wishes to recover his family's possessions: cf. *Cho.* 301 καὶ πρὸς πιέζει χρημάτων ἀχηνία, 135–6 ἐκ δὲ χρημάτων | φεύγων Ὀρέστης ἐστίν, *Eum.* 757–8 Ἀργεῖος ἀνὴρ αὖθις, ἔν τε χρήμασιν | οἰκεῖ πατρῴοις. The motif is not as prominent in Euripides, but cf. *El.* 810, where Orestes prays that he may λαβεῖν πατρῷα δώματ'. In our play the wealth of the house is mentioned twice elsewhere (1290–1, 1393). 'To modern taste [this theme] . . . may seem excessively materialistic . . . But for a Greek Orestes' status is bound up with his inheritance . . . Without it he is ἄτιμος indeed' (Garvie on Aesch. *Cho.* 299–304); cf. Jones (1962) 109–10).

73 εἴρηκα μέν νυν ταῦτα: similar concluding formulae at *Aj.* 480 πάντ' ἀκήκοας λόγον, *Ant.* 402. For εἴρηκα = *dixi* cf. *Tr.* 374, Eur. *Or.* 678.

νυν: according to ancient grammarians, νυν always took a circumflex accent when its vowel was long, whether inferential or temporal (cf. Ruijgh (1957) 64–7). I retain the traditional accentuation to provide a visual distinction between the senses.

73–4 σοὶ δ' ἤδη, γέρον, | τὸ σὸν μελέσθω βάντι φρουρῆσαι χρέος: either τὸ σὸν . . . χρέος is the subject of μελέσθω with φρουρῆσαι an epexegetic

113

infinitive, or else μελέσθω is impersonal with τὸ σὸν . . . φρουρῆσαι χρέος as subject. As often in S., the meaning is clear, while the precise construction eludes us. For the expression cf. *Phil.* 150–1 μέλον πάλαι μέλημά μοι λέγεις, ἄναξ, | φρουρεῖν ὄμμ' ἐπὶ σῷ μάλιστα καιρῷ.

75–6 Orestes concludes with καιρός, just as the Paedagogus did. The similarity in their endings stresses the unity of their purpose. The enjambment of the final *gnome* is common in S. (cf. Griffith on *Ant.* 67–8). For praise of καιρός cf. *Phil.* 837–8 καιρός τοι πάντων γνώμαν ἴσχων | <πολύ τι> πολὺ παρὰ πόδα κράτος ἄρνυται, Pind. *P.* 9.78–9, West on Hes. *Op.* 694, Trédé (1992) 15. For καιρός as the μέγιστος ἐπιστάτης Bissinger (1966) 49 compares *Aj.* 933, where χρόνος is a μέγας . . . ἄρχων; for personification of καιρός more generally cf. Ion of Chios fr. 742 *PMG*, Paus. 5.14.9, Palladas *A. P.* 10.52.1, Denniston (1952) 32.

77–85 At Aesch. *Cho.* 10–21 Orestes sees a procession of women entering from the *skene*, among whom he identifies his sister. Rather than depart, he and Pylades take cover and observe the new arrivals unseen. Eur. *El.* 107–11 shows the same pattern, though with a variant: Orestes hides himself from someone whom he takes to be a slave-girl, but who turns out to be his sister. In our play too Orestes proposes that his party should stay to listen to Electra's laments, a proposal which implies concealment. He is immediately overruled, however, by the Paedagogus, and the two depart before the entry of Electra. In the prologue of *OC* S. is happy to employ the concealment motif (cf. 111–16). Here, by contrast, he draws attention to its rejection.

The interchange stresses the urgency, and looks forward to the Paedagogus' subsequent castigation of the dilatory Orestes (1326–38). It also shows another side to Orestes' character: he shows a genuine concern for his sister, and only leaves her because of the pressing need to fulfil the god's instructions. But the full significance of the exchange only emerges when it is compared with its Aeschylean predecessor. By raising the possibility that Orestes will observe Electra from a hiding-place, only to have this possibility emphatically dismissed, S. programmatically distances himself from Aeschylus' handling of the myth. As Fraenkel put it, 'es ist als wenn Sophokles sagte, "ich habe die Choephoren nicht vergessen, aber ich mache es anders"' ((1962) 22 n. 1): cf. Kaibel's comment cited below (82n.), Davies (1998) 398, Handley (1993) 114 n. 22.

77 Electra delivers a catalectic anapaestic dimeter from within the *skene*. Like the anapaests which are to follow (86–120), it is spoken, not sung (cf. δύστηνος rather than δύστανος), although the contraction of the last biceps is typical of lyric anapaests. The contrast in metrical form between her words and those of her brother reinforces the contrast in content. Euripides' Medea has a whole series of exclamations in anapaests before she comes on stage (beginning 96 ἰώ, δύστανος ἐγὼ μελέα τε πόνων etc.).

δύστηνος: deleted by Dindorf (1836) 141, but cf. *Ant.* 850, *OR* 1307, *OC* 876 for adjectives in lamentatory exclamations.

78 For καὶ μήν 'calling attention to something just seen or heard' cf. 1422, Denniston 356 §7.

θυρῶν: could be a genitive of place, denoting the place from which the sound had issued (so Moorhouse 59; cf. 900–1 n.); or else it could be dependent on ἔνδον in 79, even given the large gap between the words (cf. 541, 578–9, 1349–50, *OR* 857–8, Aesch. *Pers.* 337, *Suppl.* 1006–7, *Ag.* 1056–7 (reading πάρος), Eur. *Med.* 1367, *Hec.* 25, fr. 142.4 *TrGF*, Diggle (1996b) 104). Campbell's note gives a happy compromise: 'the harshness of the unusual genitive, θυρῶν = "e regione ostii," is softened by the addition of ἔνδον, with which θυρῶν is to be resumed'.

79 ὑποστενούσης: ὑπο– denotes 'softly' (cf. *Aj.* 321–2 ἀψόφητος ὀξέων κωκυμάτων | ὑπεστέναζε ταῦρος ὡς βρυχώμενος, Moorhouse 131). Electra's lament takes the form of a low wailing, not a high-pitched cry.

τέκνον is more of a kinship term than ὦ παῖ (Dickey (1996) 66–8); the speaker is almost always either a parent or (as here) someone *in loco parentis*. The chorus uses it of Electra (154 etc.).

80–5 Nauck[8] gave 80–1 to the Paedagogus and 82–5 to Orestes. Sandbach (1977) revived this proposal, and Dawe[2–3] put it in his text. Sandbach argued as follows. (i) With the transmitted attribution Orestes 'here for the only time in the play submit[s] the determination of his action to the wishes of another'. (ii) It is inappropriate for the Paedagogus to refer to Agamemnon as πατρός. (iii) πειρώμεθ' implies that the speaker is going off to pour libations to Agamemnon, which is not the Paedagogus' task (39–41). None of these points is valid. (i) is false, as 1326–38 makes clear. In any case, at 29–31 Orestes encourages the Paedagogus to advise and admonish him when required, and this is exactly what he does in these two situations. (ii) The context indicates that πατρός refers to Orestes' father. (iii) The plural verb need only imply the Paedagogus' participation in the plan.

The transition between 78–9 and 80–1 also tells against Nauck's proposal. In 78–9 the speaker thinks that the sound came from a slave-girl, in 80–1 that it came from Electra. If all these lines were spoken by a single person, we require an 'or' at the start of 80. Nauck, though not Sandbach, must have observed this difficulty, as he also suggested προσμολὼν πέλας in 78 and τινός for τέκνον in 79. The need for these further changes does nothing to commend his attribution.

80 ἆρ' ἐστὶν ἡ δύστηνος Ἠλέκτρα; 'Could the wretched woman be *Electra*?' The name Electra is predicative, and ἡ δύστηνος picks up the δύστηνος of 77. Other translations, such as 'can it be the hapless Electra?' (Jebb) or 'is it the unfortunate Electra?' (Lloyd-Jones), must be wrong: Orestes has not foreseen the wretched state of his sister (cf. 1098–1125n.).

80–1 θέλεις | μείνωμεν: for βούλομαι and (ἐ)θέλω followed by a bare subjunctive cf. *OR* 651, *Phil*. 761, Goodwin §287, Stevens (1976) 60–1, Waś (1983) 94–6. Here 'the "poetic" form θέλειν would perhaps modify the colloquial character of this idiom' (Stevens).

81 κἀπακούσωμεν: transmitted κἀνα- could represent ἀνακούω (not found elsewhere) or ἐνακούω (in the classical period only in some Hippocratic treatises, used to mean 'be sensitive, amenable', and rare thereafter). Nauck's change of a single letter (in his fourth edition) gives a verb S. uses frequently elsewhere (*OR* 708, 794, *Phil*. 1417, *OC* 694), and which is given as a gloss in the scholia (p. 104.7 Papageorgius). ἐπακούσωμεν is found above the line in L, written in by the scholiast, perhaps as a gloss. The verb often means 'overhear' (cf. Dodds on Pl. *Gorg*. 487c5), which is exactly the sense we require.

82 'Das energische ἥκιστα . . . bezeichnet deutlich die bewusste Abweichung von Aischylos, der Zuschauer weiss jetzt, dass er ein ganz andres Drama sehen wird' (Kaibel, p. 81). The word may be colloquial (cf. Stevens (1976) 14, Thesleff (1955) 93).

Λοξίου: often used of Apollo the prophet: cf. *OR* 410, Aesch. *Eum*. 19, Bruchmann (1893) 26–7, Kruse (1927a).

83 ἀρχηγετεῖν: the verb is a *hapax*, and is a solemn word for 'begin'. ἀρχηγέτης denotes the god or hero who founds a new settlement (cf. Pind. *O*. 7.78, *P*. 5.60, LSJ⁹ s.v. 1), and is frequently connected with Apollo (cf. Pasquali (1913) 27–31 = (1986) i. 178–82, Hornblower (2004) 116–17). This sense fits Orestes' words above, which suggest that he has come as a second founder of his house (72n.).

84 πατρός: for the genitive cf. Aesch. *Pers*. 619, Eur. *Alc*. 613, *Suppl*. 974b, *IT* 160, *Or*. 123.

λουτρά: 'libations to the corpse after burial could be spoken of as χέρνιψ or λουτρόν, as though the process of purification continued' (R. C. T. Parker (1983) 35 n. 11): cf. 434 and Hesych. χ 440 (= iv. 285 Schmidt) χθόνια λουτρά· τὰ τοῖς νεκροῖς ἐπιφερόμενα· ἐκόμιζον γὰρ ἐπὶ τοὺς τάφους λουτρά.

In connexion with the dead the word usually refers to the washing of the corpse (on which see 1139n.).

84–5 φέρειν | νίκην τέ φημι: so Tournier[1] for transmitted φέρει | νίκην τ᾽ ἐφ᾽ ἡμῖν. This simple change requiring the transposition of a single letter has been adopted by Nauck (in his sixth edition, p. 171), Kaibel, Pearson, Dawe and Ll-J/W. For φέρειν . . . φημί introducing a strong assertion cf. *OR* 362, 366–7, *Ant.* 443, *Phil.* 1389: Broadhead (1961) 51 is thus wrong to claim that it lacks vigour. The paradosis would have to mean 'brings victory in our power' (Moorhouse 112): but while ἐφ᾽ ἡμῖν can mean 'in our power' (cf. *Phil.* 1003 μὴ 'πὶ τῷδ᾽ ἔστω τάδε, *OC* 66), the preposition does not take this sense elsewhere with a verb of motion (so rightly Ll-J/W, *Sophoclea*). Scholars have tried to show that it can, without success. Vahlen (1904) 7–8 = (1907–8) ii. 505–6 points to Hom. *Od.* 16.375 λαοὶ δ᾽ οὐκέτι πάμπαν ἐφ᾽ ἡμῖν ἦρα φέρουσιν, but there tmesis complicates the issue. LSJ[9] s.v. ἐπί B I 2b translates Hom. *Il.* 2.89 πέτονται ἐπ᾽ ἄνθεσιν as 'fly *on to* the flowers *and settle there*' (their italics), but 'fly to the flowers' gives as good sense without requiring an odd meaning from the preposition. Aesch. *Ag.* 1448–51 τίς ἂν . . . | . . . | μόλοι τὸν αἰεὶ φέρουσ᾽ ἐν ἡμῖν | μοῖρ᾽ ἀτέλευτον ὕπνον probably does show a pregnant construction (cf. Conington *ap.* Fraenkel on 1450: 'ἐν ἡμῖν must be taken with φέρουσα, which has thus the force of φέρουσα εἰς ἡμᾶς καὶ τιθεῖσα ἐν ἡμῖν'): but ἐν is not ἐπί.

85 νίκην . . . κράτος: for the combination cf. *Tr.* 186 σὺν κράτει νικηφόρῳ, Tyrt. fr. 4.9–10 *IEG* δήμου τε πλήθει νίκην καὶ κάρτος ἕπεσθαι | Φοῖβος γὰρ περὶ τῶν ὧδ᾽ ἀνέφηνε πόλει, Hes. *Theog.* 647, [Simon.] *A.P.* 6.50.1 = 736 *FGE*, Aesch. *Suppl.* 951, *Ag.* 942–3, *Cho.* 478–80, 499, Tr. Adesp. fr. 97 *TrGF*, Pl. *Leg.* 962a1–2, Dem. 19.[130], Polyb. 21.37.6, Plut. *De Pyth. or.* 403b, *De def. or.* 412b, *Aem. Paul.* 10.4, Oppian *Hal.* 4.105; also Livy 8.9.7, Tac. *Hist.* 3.20.3 *vim victoriamque*.

τῶν δρωμένων: cf. *OC* 115–16 ἐν γὰρ τῷ μαθεῖν | ἔνεστιν ηὐλάβεια τῶν ποιουμένων (also in a *sententia* at the end of a prologue).

Following this 'feierliche Schlussformel, durch welche Apollons prophetischer Spruch selbst hindurchklingt' (Schneidewin[1]), Orestes, Pylades and the Paedagogus, with attendants if there are any, leave via eisodos B. Leaving the stage in response to the arrival of another is a common feature of ancient prologues: cf. Eur. *Hipp.* 51–3, *Hec.* 52–4, Leo (1908) 68, Fraenkel (1962) 22–6, J. R. Wilson (1967) 206, Taplin (1977a) 334–5.

THRENOS APO SKENES (86–120)

86–120 Electra delivers an anapaestic lament from the *skene*. Tragic anapaests may be either chanted with music ('recitative', sometimes known as 'marching anapaests', though they are often delivered by stationary characters) or sung with music ('lyric'). West (1982a) 121 sets out the distinctions between the two types. Most of Electra's anapaests fail to meet the criteria for sung anapaests, and so must be recitative. They lack (criterion (i) on West's list) a Doric dialect colouring (πλαγάς at 90 is the one possible exception: see n.), (ii) dimeters without word-division between the metra (94 forms a single exception, but there word-division occurs one short syllable into the second metron, which is an acceptable licence in recitative (cf. L. P. E. Parker (1958) 82)), (iii) frequent contraction of bicipitia, (v) acatalectic dimeters in final place, (vi) sequences of four shorts, and (vii) admixtures of non-anapaestic cola.

However, some catalectic anapaests do show lyric features. Four of these are found in sequence (at 88, 89, 105, 106), a phenomenon which would be unusual in recitative anapaests (West (iv)). These four lines all have contracted bicipitia throughout (West (iii)), and lack word-division between the metra, with the overlap in three of the four cases consisting of a full long syllable (88, 89, 105; West (ii)). The catalectic dimeters at 102 and 120 which conclude the two halves of the piece also show this overlap, in 120 by two short syllables: but these dimeters do not show any other potentially lyric features, and are best taken as recitative.

We thus have a system of recitative anapaests which at 88–89 and 105–6 moves towards lyric, probably as a mark of Electra's intense emotion. Lyric anapaests are often associated with lamentation (cf. Parker (1997) 57). This shift would presumably have been accompanied by some change in the manner of delivery. Alternations between the two anapaestic styles are not rare (cf. West (1982a) 122).

Although mainly recitative, the piece as a whole shares many structural similarities with some of the monodies delivered by actors in Euripides. Such monodies almost always express powerful negative emotions (cf. Beverley (1997) 18–19), and usually emphasise the isolation, physical or mental, of the singing character (*ib.* 3). The passage is especially close to those monodies which occur immediately before the parodos (Eur. *Andr.* 103–16, *Hec.* 59–89, *El.* 112–66, *Tro.* 98–152). All of these except the *Andromache* passage follow a prologue in which the monodist played no part: in each case there is a broad divide between the two sections, such that 'the [prologue] speech sets up the plot, the monody the lyric tenor of the play' (Beverley (1997) 10). In each case (again excepting *Andromache*) the prologue gives the audience some information which the monodist lacks (Beverley (1997) 10): this information may be to the monodist's advantage (the return of Orestes in the *Electra* plays, the future wreck of the Greek fleet in the *Troades*) or disadvantage (the death of Polydorus in the *Hecuba*). All these monodies are followed by the entrance of a female chorus which has come to sympathise with the monodist's predicament, and which begins by addressing her (Beverley (1997) 11). Two of the Euripidean examples (*Electra* and *Troades*) resemble our play in having a parodos in the form of a lyric dialogue, meaning that the monodist continues to sing. There is also considerable continuity in metrical shape between monody and parodos. Beverley (1997) 37 thinks that our play does not conform to this tendency: but while the dominant metre of the parodos is dactylic, anapaests are also important in the third strophic pair and in the epode.

No other passage in S. stands as close to this particular tragic form, which elsewhere is so characteristic of Euripides. All the other Sophoclean examples of actors' monody as cited by Beverley (1997) 36 (*Aj.* 394–427, *Tr.* 983–1043, *Ant.* 806–82, *Phil.* 1081–1162, *OC* 237–53) form part of a wider lyric system, often with spoken interventions from the chorus or other characters. The stricter use of the monodic form here fits with the tendency of this play to engage with formal structures (such as the *agon*, the messenger speech, the recognition scene, the formal lament, the off-stage homicide scene) more than any other Sophoclean tragedy. But the sharper structure does not mean that these anapaests make up a thoughtless imitation of Euripides. In particular, the choice of recitative rather than lyric anapaests constitutes an important distinction between this piece and its Euripidean parallels. The reason for this choice is probably the exceptional length of the sung section which follows the anapaests. A further thirty-five lines of song added to the hundred and thirty of the parodos would have given us a lyric section of Aeschylean proportions. The use of recitative anapaests, on the other hand, allowed the change from the less emotional world of the prologue to be marked in metrical terms, while also leaving room for a further change in the mode of delivery at the entrance of the chorus. The effect of the whole is thus more varied than if Euripidean practice had been followed more exactly. As with many of these other typical scenes, S. here 'seems to be deliberately adapting a Euripidean pattern to his own ends' (Beverley (1997) 42).[5]

These anapaests are traditionally set out in accordance with the colometry transmitted in the mediaeval manuscripts, which presents them in series of dimeters with an occasional monometer. However, manuscript colometry cannot be earlier than the third century BC, and is of no value for determining S.'s own practice (cf. L. P. E. Parker (2001)). West (1977) 89–94 makes a good case for regarding the anapaestic trimeter as a unit of metrical composition of which the tragedians could avail themselves. In this text 86–7 and 103–4 have each been printed as a single anapaestic trimeter, since in each case this gives an articulation more sympathetic to the

---

[5] On tragic monody see further E. M. Hall (1999b).

rhetorical shape of the Greek than the usual presentation as monometer and dimeter.[6]

The monody falls into two halves (86–102, 103–120), marked off by a catalectic dimeter and strong sense pause at 102. In the first half Electra proclaims how she laments day and night (86–93), describes the murder of her father (94–9), and points to the solitary nature of her lamentation (100–2). Then in the second half she declares that she will not stop lamenting day or night (103–9), calls for vengeance on her father's murderers (110–16), and asks her brother to relieve her from her solitary lamentation (117–20). The first half contains one more anapaestic metron than the second. Recited anapaests need not show correspondence, even when found in association with a corresponding lyric section: cf. Fraenkel's edition of Aeschylus' *Agamemnon*, vol. iii. p. 716 n. 3 and e.g. *OC* 138–48 and 170–5. But in those passages there is no trace of any symmetry: here, however, the structural similarity between the two halves is so marked, and the metrical correspondence between the two halves so close, that it makes sense to assume that a metron has indeed dropped out, especially given that lacunae are a common vice of anapaestic systems (see Fraenkel, *ib.* p. 717). Each of lines 110–14 falls naturally into a dimeter, so a lacuna ought to occur somewhere in 115–20. Monk (1826) 67–8 (followed by Dawe) placed one after ἀρήξατε in 115, but this interrupts the powerful ascending tricolon. Better is Diggle's preference (*per litteras*) for a gap after πατρός: he supplements <τοῦ καπφθιμένου> *exempli gratia*. This gives exact correspondence without impeding the rhetorical force of the passage.

The prologue of Aeschylus' *Choephori* is followed by the entrance of Electra and the chorus through the *skene* door. In the parodos which follows (22–83) the slave women sing of their grief and describe the recent events in the palace which have led Clytemnestra to send an offering to Agamemnon's tomb. Electra takes no part in the lyric, nor does the chorus refer to her. In S. too the prologue is followed by the entry of Electra from the *skene*, but there the similarities end. His Electra, unlike Aeschylus', is unaccompanied by the chorus. Only here and at *Aj.* 815–65 does a Sophoclean character appear alone on stage (cf. Leo (1908) 12–13; *Tr.* 1–48 is the only other possible instance, but see Davies on 52). In each case this physical loneliness corresponds to an intense emotional isolation (cf. Medda (1983) 67 with n. 135). The motivation for the entry is also different in S.'s play. The new arrivals in the *Choephori* have come to fulfil a task laid on them by Clytemnestra. S.'s Electra, by contrast, leaves the palace to defy her mother and proclaim the wickedness of her actions. Her

---

[6] Zwierlein (1983), 182–202 argues for greater use of the anapaestic trimeter in the lyrics of Seneca's tragedies. In that case, however, manuscript colometry does carry some authority, as by the time of the composition of those tragedies it had become standard practice to set anapaests out in dimeters. Recent editors, including Zwierlein himself in his OCT, have tended to retain the transmitted colometry.

unceasing lamentation is emphasised throughout, again in contrast with the Aeschylean scene. In the latter we see a one-off response to recent developments in a specific situation, in the former a single instance taken from a lifetime of woe.

Electra's lament also contrasts with the opening scene of the play. The optimism which characterised the Paedagogus' speech and the careful, detailed plans set out by Orestes now yield to the dark tones and fraught grief of Electra's deep emotion. The unified purpose of three men intent on the task confronting them yields to the desperate solitude of a lonely woman. For Orestes and the Paedagogus this is the crucial day which will change everything: for Electra it is merely the latest in the long series of days since her father's death. We can see similar reversals on the level of individual details taken up from the opening scene and given a negative colouring, as in Electra's opening appeal to light (86n.), or in her concluding prayer (110–20n.). There is also a greater concentration on the event which began this suffering, the killing of Agamemnon: only briefly alluded to in the previous scene (11), here it is recounted in all its vividness (95–9). The move from spoken trimeters to the more emotional recitative anapaests reinforces this change of atmosphere.

The lament ends with Electra's wish for the return of her brother (117–20). The dramatic irony is obvious. Just as striking, however, is the admission of personal weakness which the request involves. Up till now Electra has seemed a woman ready to champion her father's cause, whatever the pain and suffering that this might cause her. And so she is: but now she concedes that she may no longer have the strength to continue this solitary defiance. This awareness of her own limitations, and her readiness to seek help rather than revel in her isolation, is an attractive characteristic and will recur (cf. e.g. 254–309n., 616–21n.). Here it suggests that though this woman begins the drama in a more isolated condition than any other extant Sophoclean hero, this is nevertheless not her natural state. Her character thus seems all the more rounded, and the pathos of her predicament all the more intense.

The opening scene of the pseudo-Senecan drama *Octavia* shows signs of being influenced by this speech: see Lader (1909) and Ferri's commentary.

86 Enter Electra from the *skene*. Her clothing befits a slave rather than a princess (cf. 190–1). Her mask may have the hair cut short: for this as a characteristic of women in mourning in the later theatre see Pollux 4.141 (= i. 243.3–4 Bethe) with Pickard-Cambridge (1988) 181.

For the entrance of a new character singing a monody see Barner (1971) 304 (1). Pickard-Cambridge (1988) 242 claims that the chorus enters during Electra's anapaests. But even if there were a parallel for such a silent entrance by the chorus, we would not want to lose the dramatic effect of Electra's initial solitude (86–120n.).

COMMENTARY: 86–120

'Often in tragedy a character under stress of some strong emotion calls on the elements and declares that emotion to them, or calls them to witness what is happening' (Barrett on Eur. *Hipp.* 601). These elements may include earth and heaven (Eur. *Med.* 57, Philemon fr. 82.1–2 *PCG*), earth and light / sun (Eur. *Med.* 148, *Hipp.* 601, 672), aether (Eur. *Andr.* 93, *IT* 43, *Ion* 1445), or a whole series ([Aesch.] *PV* 88–92, Eur. *Hec.* 68–72, *El.* 866–7, Plaut. *Merc.* 4–5). This usually stresses the solitude of the speaking character. Laments may also be directed at the character's local surroundings rather than the elements, with similar effect (cf. *Phil.* 936–9 ὦ λιμένες, ὦ προβλῆτες, . . . | . . . | ὑμῖν τάδ᾿, οὐ γὰρ ἄλλον οἶδ᾿ ὅτῳ λέγω, | ἀνακλαίομαι παροῦσι τοῖς εἰωθόσιν, Virg. *Ecl.* 2.1–5, Prop. 1.18.1–4). Ajax's final words combine both techniques (859–63).

ὦ φάος ἁγνόν: probably a reference to the sun, whose light is hallowed (cf. Eur. fr. 443.1 *TrGF* ὦ λαμπρὸς αἰθὴρ ἡμέρας θ᾿ ἁγνὸν φάος, *Med.* 746 ἡλίου θ᾿ ἁγνὸν σέβας (v.l.: see Diggle (1983) 356–7 = (1994) 270–1), Williger (1922) 56–7; also (ἱερός) S. fr. 535.1 *TrGF*, *Ant.* 879–80, *OR* 1424–8, Eur. *IT* 193–4), just as earth (cf. *Aj.* 859 γῆς ἱερὸν οἰκείας πέδον) and water (cf. *OR* 1428 ὄμβρος ἱερός) are holy. Electra's invocation of light (cf. Wagener (1931) 82) contrasts with her Euripidean counterpart's invocation of darkness in her opening words (*El.* 54 ὦ νὺξ μέλαινα, χρυσέων ἄστρων τροφέ). It is still dark at this point in Euripides' play (cf. 78, 102), whereas in S. dawn has already broken (cf. 17–19). But while the arrival of light is often associated with release from troubles and a joyful new beginning (e.g. *Ant.* 100–109, *Phil.* 867–8, Aesch. *Ag.* 22–3, Fraenkel on *Ag.* 1577), there is no such optimism here. The contrast with the world of the prologue (especially 17–19) is marked: 'the dawn that calls Orestes to action rouses Electra to fresh grief' (Sheppard (1918) 82).

87 καὐγῆς ἰσόμοιρ᾿ ἀήρ: is a conjecture suggested to me during the summer of 2004, first by Edward Hussey and then independently by Donald Russell. With this text αὐγῆς ἰσόμοιρ᾿ is a predicate applying both to φάος ἁγνόν and to ἀήρ, and so the phrase as a whole means 'o holy sun and air, which have an equal share in light.' The light which Electra sees is generated by the sun (for singular αὐγή of sunlight in tragedy cf. e.g. fr. 1131.5 *TrGF*, Tr. Adesp. fr. 452 *TrGF*) and travels through the air: both elements are thus involved in it. The change of upsilon for iota is palaeographically insignificant: in addition, the postulated crasis would have been a source of confusion to scribes (cf. Fraenkel (1967) 85, supplemented in Davies's *Trachiniae* commentary, p. 237 n. 41).

The transmitted text καὶ γῆς ἰσόμοιρ᾿ ἀήρ has been explained in various ways. They involve either taking the genitive γῆς as a dative, or seeing φάος ἁγνόν as a reference to aether: yet each of these interpretations is unsatisfactory. The Hussey–Russell conjecture allows the genitive to take its natural sense and eliminates the untragic distinction between air and aether by allowing φάος ἁγνόν to take its natural referent (namely the sun). In addition, the simplicity of the picture it presents is a decided advantage over the cosmological analyses required by interpreters of the paradosis, analyses which some may feel are truer to the world of Euripides' plays than those of Sophocles.[7] The presence of a word for 'light' is also appropriate in the context of a speech the beginning of which is 'built around the antithesis of day and night' (Hussey). Invocations to the elements may contain references to earth, but need not do so (86n.): one would in any case look for an apostrophe of γῆ rather than the indirect reference found in the paradosis.

Interpretations of the transmitted text are as follows. (i) ἀὴρ ἰσόμοιρος τῇ γῇ, 'air that has a μοῖρα equal to that of earth', and thus 'air coextensive with earth' (so Σ p. 104.19–26 Papageorgius, Porson (1815) 221, Jebb, LS[8] s.v. ἰσόμοιρος 2, Moorhouse 54 and 60). For this picture cf. Hes. *Theog.* 126–7 (cited by the scholia) Γαῖα δέ τοι πρῶτον μὲν ἐγείνατο ἶσον ἑωυτῇ | Οὐρανὸν ἀστερόενθ', ἵνα μιν περὶ πάντα καλύπτοι. If heaven is 'equal' to earth, it is only a short step to say that air, as a substance which takes up at least some of the space between earth and heaven, must be 'equal' to earth too. More generally, the equality of the main components of the universe is an important element in Greek cosmological thinking: cf. Anaxag. D–K 59 B 6 (= ii. 35.13–14), Anon. Pyth. D–K 58 B 1a (= i. 449.9–11), Vlastos (1947) 169 = (1995) i. 76–7. For μοῖρα of a part of the universe cf. Pher. Syr. D–K 7 B 5 (= i. 49.23–4) = fr. 83 Schibli κείνης δὲ τῆς μοίρας (Hades?) ἔνερθέν ἐστιν ἡ ταρταρίη μοῖρα, Aesch. *Cho.* 319–20 σκότῳ φάος ἀντίμοιρον (ἰσοτίμοιρον M). The same picture is probably implied in claims that air and aether (κατ)έχειν the earth: cf. Ar. *Nub.* 264 ὦ δέσποτ' ἄναξ, ἀμέτρητ' Ἀήρ, ὃς ἔχεις τὴν γῆν μετέωρον, Eur. fr. 919 *TrGF* κορυφὴ δὲ θεῶν ὁ περὶ χθόν' ἔχων | φαεννὸς αἰθήρ, *Ba.* 292–3 τοῦ χθόν' ἐγκυκλουμένου | αἰθέρος, Anaxag. D–K 59 B 1 (= ii. 32.14–15) πάντα γὰρ ἀήρ τε καὶ αἰθὴρ κατεῖχεν, ἀμφότερα ἄπειρα ἐόντα, perhaps also Eur. *Tro.* 884 ὦ γῆς ὄχημα κἀπὶ γῆς ἔχων ἕδραν (spoken of Zeus).

The cosmology can be defended: but does the grammar work? Elsewhere with ἰσόμοιρος a genitive denotes the thing shared: cf. Xen. *Cyr.* 2.1.31 τοὺς . . . ὑπηρέτας ἰσομοίρους πάντων ἀεὶ ἐποίει, Isaeus 6.25, 7.19. When it refers to the person or thing with which something is shared, as Jebb would have it do in our case, it should take a dative. So too with the associated noun and verb, the genitive denotes the object shared, the dative the person with whom it is shared: cf. Solon fr. 34.7–9 *IEG* οὐδέ μοι . . . | ἁνδάνει . . . πιεί[ρ]ης χθονὸς | πατρίδος κακοῖσιν ἐσθλοὺς ἰσομοιρίην ἔχειν, Isaeus 1.35 ἐθέλοντες ἡμῖν ἰσομοιρῆσαι τῆς

---

[7] As Hussey writes, 'We needn't suppose that there is any specific theory of light intended. Electra would simply be invoking whatever it is that causes or composes what she experiences as daylight, and, as often in invocations, she is mentioning all the beings or powers she takes to be relevant'.

οὐσίας. Jebb's only parallel for the genitive in his sense with an ἰσο– compound is at [Arist.] *De Mund.* 399ᵃ8 ἥλιος . . . καὶ οἱ τούτου ἰσόδρομοι: but (i) the change from τούτῳ to τούτου would be an easy corruption and (ii) this text is late, probably dating from after the death of Posidonius, and therefore not a helpful parallel. Jebb's other supposed instances of dative for genitive in related expressions do not stand up to scrutiny.[8] More examples with the ἰσόμοιρ– root can be found in Helly (1990) 96–101 ≈ (1991) 327–32, though his treatment of individual passages, including our own, is superficial.

(ii) ἀὴρ ἰσόμοιρος γῆς καὶ φάους, 'air that has an equal share in earth and aether' (so Schneidewin¹). Here ἀήρ stands between γῆ and αἰθήρ (denoted here by φάος) and partakes equally of both these elements. This view makes sense of the genitive, but creates three further difficulties of its own. (a) While φάος and αἰθήρ are often associated (cf. Eur. fr. 443.1 *TrGF, Phoen.* 809 φέρεν αἰθέρος εἰς ἄβατον φῶς, [Aesch.] *PV* 1091–2, Plut. *De E ap. Delph.* 390a τὸν . . . οὐρανόν, οἱ δὲ φῶς οἱ δ᾽ αἰθέρα καλοῦσιν, Σ Ar. *Nub.* 265a.1–2 (p. 67.1–2 Holwerda) τὸ τοῦ ἡλίου φῶς αἰθὴρ καλεῖται ἀπὸ τοῦ αἴθειν), this does not mean that a bare reference to φῶς or φάος can be taken to mean αἰθήρ in the absence of other indications. (b) We are forced to understand φάους from the earlier nominative φάος. For the ellipse of φάους Schneidewin cites Ar. *Av.* 187 ἐν μέσῳ δήπουθεν ἀήρ ἐστι γῆς (sc. καὶ οὐρανοῦ): but there οὐρανοῦ is omitted because it is the closer of the two extremes from the point of view of the speaker, as is regular in such ellipses (cf. Dunbar *ad loc.*, Olson on Ar. *Ach.* 434, Mastronarde on Eur. *Phoen.* 583). In our passage it is the more distant extreme from Electra's perspective which is omitted from the expression. (c) Although Pl. *Phaed.* 111a8–9 implies that a distinction between the lower ἀήρ and the upper αἰθήρ could be made in the classical period, elsewhere in tragedy ἀήρ is either indistinguishable from αἰθήρ, or has the nuance of air in motion (cf. West (1982b) 5).

(iii) ἀὴρ ἰσόμοιρος τῷ φάει τῆς γῆς, 'air that shares earth equally with aether' (Kaibel p. 83, Bruhn, LSJ⁹ s.v. ἰσόμοιρος 1). For air and aether as partners sharing earth between them cf. Anaxag. D–K 59 B 1 (= ii. 32.14–15) (cited above, this n.). It is just as difficult to understand a dative φάει from the preceding vocative φάος as it was to understand a genitive under Schneidewin's interpretation (cf. (ii) (b)). This difficulty can be surmounted, however, if (as with the conjecture, above) we take γῆς ἰσόμοιρ᾽ as a predicate applying both to φάος ἁγνόν and to ἀήρ, giving 'air and aether which share earth equally'.

---

[8] At Eur. *Her.* 131–3 ἴδετε πατέρος ὡς γορ– | γῶπες αἵδε προσφερεῖς | ὀμμάτων αὐγαί Bond *ad loc.* claims that πατέρος is compendious for τῶν τοῦ πατρὸς ὀμμάτων: but the word could more easily stand for τοῖς τοῦ πατρὸς ὄμμασι. Jebb's other allegedly erratic genitive is at Pind. *O.* 8.70–1 μένος | γήραος ἀντίπαλον, but while ἀντίπαλον with the genitive is unparalleled, the bare prefix ἀντί (unlike ἴσος) is regularly found with this case, and hence the 'abuse' is not comparable.

But serious problems still remain: the difficulties (a) and (c) associated with (ii) also apply to this interpretation.

ἰσόμοιρ᾽ is Porson's conjecture, now found in Wa and Wc. But the correct reading is probably supposed in other manuscripts by ἰσόμοιρος with –ος *supra lineam*. The elision is necessary because ἀήρ almost always has a long α (LSJ⁹ s.v. *fin.* cites Arist. fr. 642 Rose and Ps.-Phocyl. 108 Young for ἀήρ with a short vowel, but both these sources are much later than S.).

The expression in this line was parodied by Pherecrates in his *Persae* (fr. 141 *PCG*): we do not know how.

88–9 For the combination of laments and self-beating cf. *Aj.* 630–3 ὀξυτόνους μὲν ὠδὰς | θρηνήσει, χερόπληκτοι δ᾽ | ἐν στέρνοισι πεσοῦνται | δοῦποι, *OC* 1608–9 οὐδ᾽ ἀνίεσαν | στέρνων ἀραγμοὺς οὐδὲ παμμήκεις γόους, Aesch. *Pers.* 1054, *Cho.* 423–8, Eur. *Or.* 960–4, Lucian 40.12, Alexiou (2002) 207 n. 27.

πολλὰς μὲν . . . | πολλὰς δ᾽: the parallelism in these adjacent clauses, along with that in 110–11, 113–14 and 193–4, is a typical feature of ancient laments (cf. Reiner (1938) 27–8 n. 5, Schauer (2002) 207).

88 θρήνων ὠδάς: for the generic noun qualified by a more specific noun in the genitive cf. Eur. *Tro.* 609 θρήνων . . . ὀδυρμοί, Renehan (1985) 148. For the combination cf. *Aj.* 630–1 (cited above, this n.), *Ant.* 883 ἀοιδὰς καὶ γόους.

89 ἀντήρεις: adjectives formed with –ήρης usually keep the same sense as that of their stem: cf. Wilamowitz on Eur. *Her.* 243, Wackernagel (1889) 41 = (1953–79) ii. 937. The scholia see a metaphor from rowing: ὅταν κατ᾽ ἴσον ἐρέσσωσιν καὶ μὴ εἰς θάτερον περιωθῆται ἡ ναῦς (p. 105.18–20 Papageorgius). Rowing metaphors are found in tragedy in the context of lamentation (cf. Aesch. *Pers.* 1046, *Sept.* 855, Barrett on Eur. *Hipp.* 1464), but it is difficult to see how this adjective could trigger such a meaning. It does not have a metaphorical sense elsewhere, and the regular sense 'against' fits perfectly here. Blanc (1992) argues for a derivation of the adjective from ἀντ–αείρω, with ἀντ–αϝέρης giving ἀντήρης by regular sound change. According to him, 'Electre fait allusion aux coups *qui s'élèvent* (et donc *s'abattent*) nombreux sur sa poitrine ensanglantée' (p. 253, his italics). But even with this justification, 'lifting' is less appropriate than 'against'. It is certainly the latter which is found at 195–6 ἀνταία | . . . πλαγά.

90 στέρνων πληγὰς αἱμασσομένων: for the beating of the breast in lamentation cf. *Aj.* 630–4, *OC* 1608–9 (both cited above, 88–9n.), Aesch. *Pers.* 1054 στέρν᾽ ἄρασσε, Eur. *Suppl.* 87 στέρνων κτύπον, *Tro.* 794. For the language used here cf. Aesch. *Cho.* 467–8 παράμουσος Ἄτας | αἱματόεσσα πλαγά.

πληγάς: so V and the Suda φ 88 (= iv. 698.14 Adler). If the majority reading πλαγάς is correct, this would be the only attested occurrence of the Doric alpha in 86–120. Electra's anapaests display some lyric characteristics (86–120n.): but elsewhere these are limited to the catalectic dimeters 88–9 and 105–6. The majority reading is thus probably the result of an easy corruption: for Doric forms imported into non-lyric anapaests see Diggle (1991) 122, (1995–6) 102. The reverse corruption has happened with this word in M *in linea* at Aesch. *Cho.* 468; cf. also the variant readings at Eur. *Andr.* 844, *Tro.* 151.

91 For δνοφερά as an epithet of night cf. Hom. *Od.* 13.269, 15.50, Hes. *Theog.* 107, Bergson (1956) 76.

ὑπολειφθῇ 'fails' (cf. 19).

92–3 'And my hateful bed in the miserable house knows of the sorrows of my sleepless nights' (Lloyd-Jones).

τὰ . . . παννυχίδων κήδη: κήδη *coni*. Fröhlich; ἤδη codd. ἤδη is itself not objectionable (for Jebb's "ere now" cf. 62), while τὰ . . . παννυχίδων could stand for τὰς παννυχίδας (cf. 261 n.), though admittedly this has a prosaic ring. παννυχίς denotes a joyful festival lasting through the hours of darkness (cf. Call. fr. 227 Pfeiffer, Dover on Ar. *Ran.* 371, Bravo (1997), R. C. T. Parker (2005) 166); here it ironically refers to Electra's sleepness nights of lamentation (cf. Posid. 53.1–2 A–B κλαίουσιν . . . | . . . λυπρὴν τὴν τότε παννυχίδα). But in the bare phrase τὰ . . . παννυχίδων the irony is abrupt: contrast λυπρήν in the Posidippus passage just cited, or Aesch. *Ag.* 645 παιῶνα τόνδ' Ἐρινύων, where the addition of an adjective or phrase marks the reversal of a usually positive term. Fröhlich's conjecture provides just such a qualification in our case. It also provides a better antecedent to ὅσα in 94.

The conclusion to the *kommos* of the *Choephori* may provide further support for Fröhlich's conjecture. As seen above, line 90 of our play is strikingly paralleled by Aesch. *Cho.* 468. The following line in Aeschylus runs ὦ δύστον' ἄφερτα κήδη: so if S. were imitating the previous passage, he might well have chosen to use the strong word κῆδος, rare in tragedy, soon after line 90. The lyric in Aeschylus concludes with a prayer to the chthonic powers to send assistance (477 πέμπετ' ἀρωγήν), which provides a further parallel with our passage.

Dawe prefers παννυχίων . . . | . . . οἴκτων (*coni*. Blaydes', p. 277, perhaps anticipated by Bentley (1816) 246). This also attempts to deal with the problem of the bare phrase τὰ . . . παννυχίδων, albeit at greater palaeographical cost. For the corruption of οἴκτων to οἴκων cf. *Ant.* 859, Aesch. *Ag.* 134, Eur. *Hel.* 164; perhaps also *Tr.* 1274, though see Davies's n. But the removal of οἴκων is not an attractive change, as it masks the opposition between Electra's daily laments, which are proclaimed to the elements, and her nightly sorrows, which

126

are confined to the house. The new phrase τὰ παννυχίων μογερῶν οἴκτων is also clumsy.

For laments at night cf. *Aj*. 928–32 (πάννυχα), *Tr*. 29–30, 103–111, Eur. *El*. 141–2, 181.

οἴκων: for Blaydes's οἴκτων see previous n.

94–5 τὸν δύστηνον ἐμὸν θρηνῶ | πατέρ': 'Die Beklagung . . . noch verstärkt dadurch, daßman ausdr¨ucklich sagt, man beklage den Verstorbenen' (Reiner (1938) 22 with n. 2). Fraenkel reverses the order of τόν and δυστηνόν to give a regular caesura ((1917–18) 185 n. 1 = (1964) i. 189–90 n. 2), but word-division occurring one short syllable into the second metron is an acceptable licence in recitative anapaests (cf. L. P. E. Parker (1958) 82).

96 φοίνιος Ἄρης: for the combination cf. Eur. *Phoen*. 1006, *IA* 775, Bruchmann (1893) 42–3; also 1385n.

οὐκ ἐξένισεν: ἀντὶ τοῦ οὐκ ἀπέκτεινεν· ξένια γὰρ Ἄρεως τραύματα καὶ φόνοι (Σ p. 106.15–16 Papageorgius). Words from the ξέν– stem often have an ironical sense: cf. Hom. *Od*. 9.370 τὸ δέ τοι ξεινήϊον ἔσται (of being eaten last), Archil. fr. 6 *IEG* ξείνια δυσμενέσιν λυγρὰ χαριζόμενοι, Eur. *Hel*. 480 θάνατος ξένιά σοι γενήσεται, *Cycl*. 342, 551, Mnasalces *A.P.* 6.9.3–4 = 2609–10 *HE*, Corrêa (1998) 256–9, also Plaut. *Amph*. 161–4, 296. Translate 'did not make his guest' (Lloyd-Jones). West (*per litteras*) conjectures ἐξέναρεν (ἐνάριξεν *iam* van Gent (1858) 222), comparing fr. 724.1–2 *TrGF* and Eur. *Andr*. 1182. The above parallels should make this unnecessary, however.

For the paradox that Agamemnon survived great dangers abroad only to be murdered by his wife at home cf. *Od*. 11.406–12 (Agamemnon speaking) οὔτ᾽ ἐμέ γ᾽ ἐν νήεσσι Ποσειδάων ἐδάμασσεν | . . . | οὔτε μ᾽ ἀνάρσιοι ἄνδρες ἐδηλήσαντ᾽ ἐπὶ χέρσου, | ἀλλά μοι Αἴγισθος τεύξας θάνατόν τε μόρον τε | ἔκτα σὺν οὐλομένῃ ἀλόχῳ, οἶκόνδε καλέσσας, | δειπνίσσας, ὥς τίς τε κατέκτανε βοῦν ἐπὶ φάτνῃ. | ὣς θάνον οἰκτίστῳ θανάτῳ, 11.383–4, 24.30–4, Aesch. *Cho*. 345–53 εἰ γὰρ ὑπ᾽ Ἰλίῳ | πρός τινος Λυκίων πάτερ | δορίτμητος κατηναρίσθης κτλ. with Garvie, *Eum*. 625–37, Liban. *Decl*. 6.18. Cf. also S. *Tr*. 1048–63, [Sen.] *Oct*. 43–4 (Claudius) *inter . . . gentes barbaras tutus fuit* | . . . *coniugis scelere occidit* with Ferri on 43.

97 κοινολεχής: a *hapax*, defined by the Suda κ 2555 (= iii. 201.16 Adler) as ὁ μοιχός: but this reflects the present instance, where the man designated κοινολεχής happens also to be a μοιχός, rather than a pejorative sense intrinsic to the word itself. The same is probably true for κοινόλεκτρος at Aesch. *Ag*. 1441 (used by Clytemnestra to designate Cassandra), as in its only other occurrence ([Aesch.] *PV* 560) the term is neutral; neutral also are similar words for 'spouse' elsewhere in tragedy (Eur. *Or.* 508 ὁμόλεκτρος, *Her.* 1268 σύλλεκτρος). The –λεχής element occurs elsewhere at Lyr. Adesp. fr. 1037.29 *PMG* ὁμολεχής (context uncertain). In all these cases, however, the term is used of a woman who shares the bed of a man. By designating Aegisthus it stresses his subordination to Clytemnestra.[9]

98 ὅπως δρῦν ὑλοτόμοι: the comparison has a Homeric precedent at *Il.* 13.389–91 = 16.482–4 ἤριπε δ᾽, ὡς ὅτε τις δρῦς ἤριπεν ἢ ἀχερωὶς | ἠὲ πίτυς βλωθρή, τήν τ᾽ οὔρεσι τέκτονες ἄνδρες | ἐξέταμον πελέκεσσι νεήκεσι νήϊον εἶναι; cf. also 4.482–7, 13.178–80, Simon. eleg. fr. 11.2–3 *IEG*. A simile describing the killing of a warrior in combat is reapplied to the treacherous murder of a king in his house. A different comparison is used at *Od.* 4.535 = 11.411, where Agamemnon is despatched ὡς τίς τε κατέκτανε βοῦν ἐπὶ φάτνῃ.

99 σχίζουσι: cf. Aesch. *Cho.* 396 κάρανα δαΐξας. Moorhouse 186 points to 'the change to the present for the violent action [cf. *Tr.* 565, *OR* 113], as also for the positive statement'; see further 725n., Bruhn §103.

κάρα: an accusative of respect: ὅν in 95 is the direct object of σχίζουσι. Cf. *Phil.* 1301 μέθες με, πρὸς θεῶν, χεῖρα, Wilamowitz on Eur. *Her.* 162; also Lesbonax fr. 12 Blank (for the figure involved, the σχῆμα Ἰωνικόν, also known as the the καθ᾽ ὅλον καὶ μέρος construction), Diggle (1990) 102 n. 4 = (1994) 365 n. 4, (1996c) 195. Alternatively, it could be a direct object, with the slight anacoluthon sometimes found in a clause appended to a relative clause (see Jebb's edition of the *OC*, pp. 278–9). The snake representing Agamemnon which appears to Clytemnestra at Stes. fr. 219.1 *PMGF* is κάρα βεβροτωμένος ἄκρον. At Eur. *Or.* 496–7 Tyndareus describes how ἐξέπνευσεν Ἀγαμέμνων βίον, | κάρα θυγατρὸς τῆς ἐμῆς πληγεὶς ὕπο (*coni.*). The head is the likeliest location for wounds dealt by an axe.

πελέκει: Agamemnon is also said to have been killed by an axe at Eur. *Hec.* 1279, *El.* 160 (with Denniston on 164), 279, 1160, *Tro.* 361: on each occasion the word πέλεκυς is used. The snake representing Agamemnon at Stes. fr. 219.1 *PMGF* has a wound in the head, which suggests a blow from an axe (see previous n.). At Hom. *Od.* 11.424 a φάσγανον is used, and it is almost certain that the same weapon was used in Aeschylus' *Oresteia* (see Fraenkel's edition of the *Agamemnon*, vol. iii. pp. 806–9). Davies (1987) reasserts the case for an axe in Aeschylus, but he has been refuted by Sommerstein (1989) and Prag (1991). The weapon is referred to again in our play at 484–5. Davidson (1990a) claims that S.'s decision to use the axe as the murder weapon may have been influenced by the occurrence of an axe in the Homeric simile employed in the

---

[9] *OR* 1364 would be an exception to this tendency if Dawe is right to accept Meineke's ὁμολεχής for transmitted ὁμογενής. Ll-J/W print the paradosis.

present passage (98n.): but it is more likely that he first chose the axe before reaching for the simile.

100 ἄλλης: the feminine replaces the expected masculine by attraction to the gender of Electra; contrast 885, where ἄλλου is probably to be read (n.).

101 πάτερ: for the address to the dead man in a lament see Reiner (1938) 15–16 n. 6.

102 ἀκῶς: ἀεικῶς Σ p. 107.9–10 Papageorgius and Suda α 627 (= i. 62.15 Adler), ἀϊκῶς Brunck (in his 1779 edition), αἰκῶς Blomfield *ap.* Monk (1826) 72 (cf. 206). ἀ̆– is best of all because ἀει– contracts to form a long diphthong (cf. West's Teubner Aeschylus, p. xlv). The αἰκ– stem is often associated with the killings of the house: cf. 206, 216, 486, 511, 515. Most subsequent editors adopt the change, but Lanza and Fort (1991) 30–1 advocate ἀδίκως, comparing Dio Cass. 52.18.2 εἰ γὰρ ἐκεῖνοι μήτ᾽ ἀδίκως μήτ᾽ οἰκτρῶς οὕτως αὐτὸν ἀπεκτόνεσαν. However, even supposing that there is an allusion to this passage (and there is no good reason to think this), that still leaves a good deal of time between S. and Dio for the corruption to occur. ἀδίκως is weak, and could have been inserted as an anticipation of 113.

For οἰκτρῶς of Agamemnon's death cf. Hom. *Od.* 11.412 (cited above, 96n.).

103 ἀλλ᾽ . . . μὲν δή: adversative, giving '(I alone pity you). Yet for all that . . .' (Denniston 394).

104 λήξω θρήνων στυγερῶν τε γόων: for γόοι with θρῆνοι cf. Hom. *Il.* 24.722–3, Aesch. *Pers.* 686–7, Eur. *Med.* 1211, *Andr.* 92, *Hel.* 165–6. λήγειν γόων recurs at 353, 379; cf. Aesch. *Pers.* 705, Bion *Epit. Ad.* 97.

105–6 The transmitted text will not form either anapaestic dimeters or paroemiacs. The deletion of a disyllable will give us a pair of the latter, which is a desirable outcome given the two paroemiacs in the same place in the first half of these anapaests. Elmsley (in Bodley MS. Clar. Press d. 46 fol. 169, corrigenda written shortly after his edition of 1805, and thus anticipating Monk (1826) 66–7 (first published 1813)) and Dobree (1833–43) ii. 49 removed ἄστρων, but this word is needed to effect the contrast with ἦμαρ. Better with Reisig ((1816) 268) and then Hermann to delete the first λεύσσω, which is clumsy, and could have been interpolated through failure to understand the ἀπὸ κοινοῦ construction, or just written above the line as a gloss (cf. Kiefner (1964) 72–3). For the verb in the second only of two clauses cf. *Ant.* 1105–6 μόλις μέν, καρδίας δ᾽ ἐξίσταμαι | τὸ δρᾶν, *OR* 1163 ἐμὸν μὲν οὐκ ἔγωγ᾽, ἐδεξάμην δέ του, Diggle (1973) 244 n. 15 = (1994) 62 n. 15, Nisbet and Hubbard on Hor.

C. 1.30.6. Blaydes's λεύσσω τόδε <τ'> ἦμαρ (in his first edition) enfeebles the style.

παμφεγγεῖς ἄστρων | ῥιπάς: cf. Lyr. Adesp. fr. 927.3 *PMG* ἀστερομαρμαροφεγγής. The use of ῥιπαί to denote the light of the stars is striking.

107 Electra compares herself to Procne, who killed her son Itys to avenge the rape of her sister Philomela by her husband Tereus. Procne was subsequently turned into a nightingale, whose cry was thought to reflect her perpetual lamentation for her dead son. Electra makes this comparison here and at 147–9 because both she and Procne perpetually lament a dead relative. In Electra's case this is a father, not a son; and she, unlike Procne, bears no responsibility for the death which she mourns. But the comparison also suggests Electra's potential for violent action against her kin (cf. 604–5, 947–89). See further 145–52n.

For the Procne myth see further Cazzaniga (1950–1), Tarrant on Sen. *Ag.* 670 ff., Friis Johansen and Whittle on Aesch. *Suppl.* 58–67, Dunbar on Ar. *Av.* 15, Forbes Irving (1990) 99–107, 248–9. The story was treated by S. in his *Tereus* (frr. 581–95b *TrGF*), on which see Fitzpatrick (2001). For the nightingale in tragedy see further Kannicht on Eur. *Hel.* 1107–12, Diggle on Eur. *Pha.* 70 = fr. 773.26 *TrGF* (with (1996c) 194), Rehm (1994) 174 n. 22, Barker (2004) 189–91. For a bird as a more general comparandum to a human in mourning cf. *Ant.* 423–4 ἡ παῖς ὁρᾶται κἀνακωκύει πικρῶς | ὄρνιθος ὀξὺν φθόγγον, *Tr.* 105, Schauer (2002) 225–6.

μὴ οὐ: for (τὸ) μὴ οὐ after a verb of denial, refusal etc. that is itself negated see Moorhouse 328–30, Moorhouse (1940) 73.

τεκνολέτειρ᾽: a *hapax*, but cf. [Eur.] *Rhes.* 547–50 ὑμνεῖ ... | ... παιδολέτωρ | μελοποιὸν ἀηδονὶς μέριμναν (this noun elsewhere at Aesch. *Sept.* 726, Eur. *Med.* 1393) and παιδολέτειραν at Eur. *Med.* 849.

For τις in comparisons cf. 234, Rappold (1876) 16–17, Vahlen (1895–6) 4–5 = (1907–8) ii. 181–2. It does not preclude a specific reference: cf. Aesch. *Ag.* 55 ἤ τις Ἀπόλλων ἢ Πὰν ἢ Ζεύς.

108 ἐπὶ κωκυτῷ 'to the accompaniment of wailing': for ἐπί + dative denoting attendant circumstances see Moorhouse 113, K–G i. 502, Eur. *El.* 132–4, *IA* 1175–6. In this case κωκυτός and ἠχώ are not differentiated (cf. Eur. *Tro.* 315–17).

108–9 τῶνδε πατρῴων | πρὸ θυρῶν: hence Clytemnestra's complaints at 517–18 (n.). Musgrave's τήνδε qualifies an otherwise bare ἠχώ, and may be right.

109 ἠχώ: often with reference to a *loud* sound: cf. LSJ⁹ s.v. 2.

COMMENTARY: 86–120

πᾶσι προφωνεῖν: for πάντες as the addressees of a public proclamation see Diggle (1996a) 111.

110–20 As Orestes did only a moment ago, Electra prays for the assistance of various deities. But while Orestes had apostrophised his ancestral δῶμα, Electra calls upon the house of Hades; and instead of the γῆ invoked by her brother she rather appeals to a succession of chthonic deities. This quick succession of vocatives addressed to gods of the underworld, together with the tight formal patterning which pervades the piece (anaphora in ὦ . . . καὶ . . . | ὦ . . . καὶ . . ., αἳ τοὺς . . . | αἳ τοὺς (cf. 88–9n.); tricolon crescendo in ἔλθετ', ἀρήξατε, τείσασθε), convey a primal emotion quite different from the tone of Orestes' prayer. The Greeks were in general reluctant to name the powers of the underworld (cf. Rohde (1925a) 206–8 ≈ (1925b) 159–60, Harder on Eur. fr. 448a.56–7 *TrGF* = 66.56–7 Austin, Henrichs (1991) 163 n. 5 and *passim*): here Electra shows no hesitation in naming a whole series of them. All these deities are named elsewhere in tragedy (nn.): what is remarkable here is their sheer concentration. Electra needs the attention of these figures, and so she calls on them directly without fear of the consequences. This refusal to be bound by conventions of speech and action will continue to characterise her.

110 ὦ δῶμ' Ἅιδου: for the reluctance to name Hades cf. 184, Farnell (1896–1909) iii. 281–2: Pluto was the euphemistic alternative (cf. Henrichs (1991) 194 with n. 73, 196 n. 78). Electra invokes Hades on behalf of Agamemnon just as at Eur. fr. 448a.56 *TrGF* (*Cresphontes*) ὦ νερτέρα χθὼν . . [ ] . . ἄπο | Ἅιδη θ' ὃς ἄρχει[ς] . . [ ] . κάτω the hero calls upon him as he returns to avenge his dead father. For the combination of Hades and Persephone cf. Hom. *Il.* 9.569, *Od.* 10.534, Hes. fr. 280.19–20 M–W, [Hes.] fr. 185.4 M–W.

Περσεφόνης: Electra invokes Persephone by name at Aesch. *Cho.* 490 ὦ Φερσέφασσα, δὸς δέ γ' εὔμορφον κράτος (for the orthography of the name there see West's Teubner Aeschylus, p. lii). The chorus also uses her name in the vocative at Eur. *Phoen.* 684, but not in a chthonic context. Her name occurs elsewhere in tragedy at *Ant.* 894, [Aesch.] fr. 451s70.9 *TrGF*, Eur. *Hec.* 136, *Suppl.* 1022 and *Hel.* 175 (*Or.* 964 is corrupt, probably interpolated). But for Persephone as the ἄρρητος κόρη whose name is mentioned only with reluctance cf. Kannicht on Eur. *Hel.* 1306–7, Meleager *A.P.* 7.352.1–2 = 4742–3 *HE*, Henrichs (1991) 178–9 n. 36.

111 χθόνι' Ἑρμῆ: for Hermes' chthonic aspect, evident in his function as *psychopomp*, cf. *Aj.* 831–2, Aesch. fr. 273a.8 *TrGF* (*Psychagogoi*) χθόνιόν θ' Ἑρμῆν πομπὸν φθιμένων, *Cho.* 1 with Garvie, *IG* ix.2 638.7 = *EG* 505.6 (Larisa, 3rd BC) (and other Thessalian inscriptions, with Waś (1983) 16–17), Bruchmann

(1893) 111, Garvie (1970), Henrichs (1991) 183 n. 46. Hermes will again be mentioned as the avengers move on Clytemnestra (1395–6n.).

πότνι' Ἀρά must refer to a curse uttered by the dying Agamemnon, as probably also at Aesch. *Cho.* 406 ἴδετε πολυκρατεῖς Ἀραὶ †φθειμένων†. Kaibel (pp. 87–8) compares Aesch. *Cho.* 327–8 ὀτοτύζεται δ' ὁ θνῄσκων, | ἀναφαίνεται δ' ὁ βλάπτων, but there ὀτοτύζεται is passive, not middle, and refers to the lamentation over the dead man (cf. Schadewaldt (1932) 319–23 = (1970) i. 254–8, Fraenkel (1933) 242 n. 9). The invocation of the curse precedes the invocation of the Erinyes: for this association cf. Aesch. *Sept.* 70 Ἀρά τ' Ἐρινὺς πατρὸς ἡ μεγασθενής, 787–91, *Eum.* 417 (spoken by the Erinyes) Ἀραὶ δ' ἐν οἴκοις γῆς ὑπαὶ κεκλήμεθα, S. *OC* 1389–91, Watson on Hor. *Ia.* 5.91–6, Wüst (1956) 86–7, Corlu (1966) 274–6, Geisser (2002) 242–52. The curse is the last resort of the weak and desperate against the powerful (cf. Watson (1991) 6–7), and thus an appropriate weapon for both Agamemnon and Electra.

πότνι': though not elsewhere found qualifying ἀρά, the epithet has strong chthonic connotations (cf. Usener (1896) 225–6, Wackernagel (1897) 39 = (1953–79) i. 800, Garvie on Aesch. *Cho.* 722) and strong associations with the Erinyes (cf. *OC* 84 ὦ πότνιαι δεινῶπες, Aesch. *Eum.* 951 μέγα γὰρ δύναται πότνι' Ἐρινύς, Wüst (1956) 91).

112 σεμναί: a cult title of the Erinyes (cf. Wüst (1956) 91, Henrichs (1991) 170 n. 18), and commonly applied to them in literature (cf. *Aj.* 837, *OC* 89–90 θεῶν | σεμνῶν ἕδραν, Aesch. *Eum.* 383, 833, 1041).

θεῶν παῖδες: various accounts of the lineage of the Erinyes are extant (cf. Wüst (1956) 84–5). According to Hes. *Theog.* 183–5 they were born from an Earth impregnated by the drops of blood shed from the castration of Uranus. Epimenides of Crete made them the children of Cronus and sisters of Aphrodite and the Moirai (D–K 3 B 19 = i. 36.3–4). At Aesch. *Eum.* 416 they are the Νυκτὸς αἰανῆ τέκνα (cf. 844 = 876), at S. *OC* 40 the Γῆς τε καὶ Σκότου κόραι. For the description adopted here cf. e.g. *Ant.* 1075 Ἅιδου καὶ θεῶν Ἐρινύες; also West on Hes. *Theog.* 240.

Ἐρινύες: the reluctance to name these beings is manifest at *OC* 129 ἃς τρέμομεν λέγειν, Eur. *Or.* 37–8, 409–10; cf. 110–20n.

113 αἳ τοὺς ἀδίκως θνῄσκοντας ὁρᾶθ': in tragedy the Erinyes are usually said to punish killings within the family rather than unjust killings at large. On occasions, however, they moved 'from being champions of the rights of relatives [to become more generally] champions of justice' (Lloyd-Jones (1990c) 204 = (2005) 91–2): cf. Aesch. *Eum.* 421 βροτοκτονοῦντας ἐκ δόμων ἐλαύνομεν, 316–20. They have in any case an old association with δίκη, arising from their concern with the preservation of the natural order: cf. Heracl. D–K 22 B 94 (= i. 172.9) Δίκης ἐπίκουροι with Kirk's edition, p. 287.

ὁρᾶθ᾽: the Erinyes are sometimes said to see the crimes which they punish: cf. *Aj.* 836 ἀεὶ θ᾽ ὁρώσας πάντα τὰν βροτοῖς πάθη, *OC* 42 τὰς πάνθ᾽ ὁρώσας Εὐμενίδας.

113–14 αἵ . . . | αἵ: the anaphora 'stresses [not so much] the Erinyes' double task as the double crime committed by the perpetrators towards Agamemnon' (Kamerbeek). For the 'inceptive asyndeton . . . [coinciding] with asyndetic anaphora of the rel. pron.' cf. 207–8, 978–9, Friis Johansen and Whittle on Aesch. *Suppl.* 23.

114 αἵ τοὺς εὐνὰς ὑποκλεπτομένους: this is the only unambiguous statement from antiquity that the Erinyes punish adultery. Quint. Smyrn. *Post.* 12.547 (cited by Wüst (1956) 117.41), where the Erinyes rush through Troy ἄκρα γάμου κεχολωμέναι αἰνοῦ, presupposes a similar attitude. In Wüst's other parallel, Ov. *Her.* 2.117–18, the Erinyes are present at the union of Phyllis and Demophon. But nothing suggests that they are there to punish Demophon for the breach of faith which he will later commit against Phyllis: they rather point to the doomed nature of the partnership ('si tratta . . . solo di simboli infausti, intesi astrattamente': Barchiesi *ad loc.*, p. 163).

Two passages in Aeschylus provide material that is more relevant. At *Ag.* 744–9 a νυμφόκλαυτος Ἐρινύς presides over the marriage of Paris and Helen (cf. Lloyd-Jones (1969a) 104 = (1990a) 317), which in this context emphasises the adulterous character of this union and the punishment which will spring from it. And at *Ag.* 1192–3 (compared with our passage by Jones (1962) 149) (αἱ Ἐρινύες) ἐν μέρει δ᾽ ἀπέπτυσαν | εὐνὰς ἀδελφοῦ τῷ πατοῦντι δυσμενεῖς the point of the image seems to be the revulsion felt by the Erinyes for the adultery of Atreus' wife Aerope with his brother Thyestes. This adultery constitutes the πρώταρχος ἄτη to which the later evils of the house can be traced (see Fraenkel on 1193), and hence is associated with the Erinyes. So even without a formal statement that these creatures punish adultery, 'Aeschylus . . . goes some way towards the doctrine which Sophocles makes explicit' (Winnington-Ingram (1980) 232 n. 52). For Clytemnestra's adultery cf. 271–3, 275n., 492–3, 585–94.

For ὑποκλεπτομένους in the context of adultery cf. [Liban.] *Decl.* 40.43 τίς γὰρ ἂν εὐνὴν ἑτέρου κακῶς ὑποκλέπτειν ἔτι τολμήσειεν;, also Tib. 3.19.1 *nulla tuum nobis subducet femina lectum*, Prop. 1.8.45 *nec mihi rivalis certos subducit amores*.

115 ἔλθετ᾽, ἀρήξατε, τείσασθε: for the threefold imperative cf. e.g. fr. 314.207 *TrGF*, Eur. *Or.* 1302 with West. The asyndeton lends it great force, as at Aesch. *Sept.* 31–2, where Hutchinson *ad loc.* compares *Eum.* 133, Dem. 8.74; add *Mahabharata* 7.136.9 'slay, strike fearlessly, pierce, cut to pieces', 9.11.46, 9.17.26. For other tricola in asyndeton see Dunbar on Ar. *Av.* 851–2; for the ascending tricolon see Bond on Eur. *Her.* 494. For imperatives in asyndeton in the context of a curse cf. *Aj.* 844 (addressed to the Erinyes) and *Phil.* 1041.

τείσασθε restored by Nauck[9] for manuscript τίσ–: there are only a handful of examples of the spelling ι for inherited ει before 400 (Threatte i. 190).

116 For the lacuna see 86–120n.

116–17 ἡμετέρου | . . . ἐμόν for the shift from plural to singular cf. *Ant.* 734, Ferri on [Sen.] *Oct.* 21–2.

117 Electra's closing wish for the return of her brother is introduced by καί: by breaking the asyndeton, this ensures that this particular request stands out. On the significance of the request see further 86–120n.

πέμψατ᾽: chthonic powers are often said to *send* good or bad things to the world of the living (cf. 460n.): here the motif refers to Electra's brother.

119 μούνη: on the isolation of the Sophoclean hero cf. 812, 950, 1019, 1074, Knox (1964) 32–3.

119–20 ἄγειν . . . | λύπης ἀντίρροπον ἄχθος 'to balance the counterpoising weight of sorrow' (LSJ[9] s.v. ἀντίρροπος 1; cf. *DGE* s.v. I 1). At Aesch. *Ag.* 574 νικᾷ τὸ κέρδος, πῆμα δ᾽ οὐκ ἀντιρρέπει the κέρδος and πῆμα are imagined to hang in opposing sides of the balance: in our case the λύπης ἄχθος is counterpoised by Electra herself, which makes her personal weakness more vivid. The image of the human life 'in the balance' is familiar from Homer, where κῆρες representing human lives are weighed in a golden scale (cf. *Il.* 8.69–72, 22.209–13, though there the loser's κήρ is heavier). Aeschylus used a similar motif in his *Psychostasia* (*TrGF* vol. iii. pp. 374–5): see also West (1997) 393–4. For ἄγειν = 'weigh' cf. Alexis fr. 2.6 *PCG*, Philippid. frr. 9.4, 9.7, 33 *PCG*, Hipparch. fr. 3.2 *PCG*, LSJ[9] A VI. For the metaphorical sense of ἀντίρροπον cf. *IG* i³ 1179.12–13 = *CEG* i. §10.12–13 (for the Athenians killed at Potidaea in 432) φσυχὰς δ᾽ ἀντίρρο[π]α θέντες | ἐ[λλ]άχσαντ᾽ ἀρετὲν καὶ πατρ[ίδ] εὐκλ[έ]ϊσαν ('laying their souls in the balance'). The 'weight of griefs' is also a common metaphor: cf. Eur. *Hel.* 380 ἄχθεα λύπας, *Hec.* 105 ἀγγελίας βάρος ἀραμένη, *IT* 710 ὦ πόλλ᾽ ἐνεγκὼν τῶν ἐμῶν ἄχθη κακῶν, Virg. *Aen.* 4.548–9 *tu prima furentem* | *his, germana, malis oneras,* [Sen.] *Oct.* 5.

G¹ʸᵖR have ἄχος: for the reverse corruption see *OR* 1355.

σωκῶ: the verb elsewhere only at Aesch. *Eum.* 36, where it denotes physical weakness on the part of the Prophetess; the adjective σῶκος is used of Hermes at *Il.* 20.72, and as a name at 11.427. Here presumably 'I am strong enough to' (cf. Apoll. Soph. *Lex. Hom.* 148.21–2 Bekker οὐκέτι σωκῶ . . . ἀντὶ τοῦ οὐκέτι ἰσχύω, referring to our passage).

PARODOS (121–250)

FIRST STROPHIC PAIR (121–52)

121	137	– – – ˈ – – U U – ˈ	cho dim
		– – – ˈ – – ˈ U U –	cho dim
		– – ˈ – U U – U ˈ – – – ‖	glyc ∧ia∧
	140	– U U – U U – ˈ U U – U U ˈ	4da
125		– U U – ˈ U U – U U – U U ˈ	4da
		U – U ‾UU‾ U ˈ ‾UU‾ U ˈ – U ⌢U ˈ U – ˈ	3ia
		U – ˈ – – U – ˈ U – – ‖	ia∧ ∧ia ia∧ [= ia∧ ith]
	145	:: – ⌢UU U – – – ˈ	ia ∧ia∧
130		– U U – ˈ U U – ˈ U U – U U ˈ	4da
		– U U ˈ – U U – U U – U U ˈ	4da
		– U U ˈ – U U – ˈ U U – U U ˈ	4da
		– U U – U U – ˈ U U – U U ˈ	4da
	150	– – – – – ˈ U U – U ˈ U – U U	6da
		– ˈ U U	
135		U̲ – U – ˈ U – – ‖	ia ia∧
		– – ˈ U – – ‖‖	∧ia∧ ∧ia

SECOND STROPHIC PAIR (153–92)

153	173	– – – ˈ – – ˈ	?
		⌢U ˈ U ⌢U U – U – ˈ	lec
155	175	U̲ ⌢U U – – U ˈ – U – – ‖	ia ∧ia ia∧ [= ia ith]
		– ⌢U U – – U – ˈ U – ʊ ‖	ia ∧ia ia∧ [= ia ith]
		– – – U̲U̲ – ˈ ‾UU‾ – ‾UU‾ – U U	6da
		– U̲ ‖	
		‾U‾ – U – U – – ‖	ia ia∧
160	180	– ⌢U ˈ U – – – ˈ	ia ∧ia∧
		– ⌢U ˈ U – – – ˈ	ia ∧ia∧
		– U U – U U – ˈ U U – U U ˈ	4da
		– ⌢U U ‾UU‾ U – U ‾UU‾ ˈ U – – ‖	2ia ia∧
	185	:: – ⌢U U U ⌢U U ˈ ‾UU‾ U – U – – ˈ	2ia ia∧
165		U ‾UU‾ U – – U – U – – ‖	ia ∧ia ia∧ [= ia ith]
		– U U – U U – ˈ U U – U U ˈ	4da
		– U U – U U – ˈ U U – U U ˈ	4da
		– U U – U U – U U – U U ˈ	4da
170	190	– U U – U U – ˈ U U – U U ˈ	4da
		U – – – U – ˈ	ia∧ ∧ia
		U – ˈ – – U – ˈ U – – ‖‖	ia∧ ∧ia ia∧

The first strophic pair opens with two choriambic dimeters (121–2 ∼ 137–8): for this colon in S. see Itsumi (1982) 70. They resemble a pair of paroemiacs (only final ∪ ∪ − instead of − − prevents this analysis), and so allow a smooth transition from the preceding recited anapaests (cf. Ruijgh (1989) 317 n. 19 = (1991–6) ii. 761 n. 19). The following glyc ∧ia∧ at 123 ∼ 139 is a frequent combination, usually (as here) followed by a strong sense pause: Itsumi (1984) 79 suggests that it marks period end, and I have printed accordingly. Dale (1968) 38 and (1971–83) iii. 272 offers a different analysis, preferring to divide after τάκεις to give an aeolo-choriambic decasyllable followed by a dragged choriambic dimeter. But these strangely-shaped cola have nothing to recommend them.

After this choriambic opening, the first two strophic pairs are made up exclusively of dactyls and iambics. S. often employs dactylic runs 'in contexts of passionate despair or urgent pleading or vehement rejection' (Dale (1964) 35 = (1969) 208), especially in his later plays (cf. *Phil.* 1196–1201, 1203–7, *OC* 229–35, 241–52, Dale (1964) 34–6 = (1969) 207–9, L. P. E. Parker (1997) 51). Electra's dactyls go on for longer than do those of the chorus, which reflects the greater intensity of her emotion.

The iambics in the ode tend to act as clausulae to the dactyls (cf. Parker (1997) 32). Their syncopation (including syncopated trimeters, for which see Diggle *ap.* Willink (1989) 53 n. 38) highlights by contrast the rapid sweep of the largely uncontracted dactyls. In several places we move from an acatalectic dactylic length to a colon which does not start on a princeps (126 ∼ 142, 135 ∼ 151, 163 ∼ 183, 171 ∼ 191; also 212 ∼ 232). This is a typically Sophoclean mannerism, though it is also found in other authors, including Euripides (cf. West (1982a) 129–30, Parker (1997) 53–4). We also find many iambics which begin with long anceps and resolved first longum, thus giving as it were a dactylic opening to the colon (128 ∼ 145, 175, 156 ∼ 176, 160–1 ∼ 180–1, 163–4 ∼ 183–5; cf. Raven (1965) 230–1, West (1982a) 130 with n. 129). These techniques ensure a tight relationship between the dactyls and iambics of the lyric.

On the metrical interpretations of 128 ∼ 145 and 153 ∼ 173 see 128n. and 153n. respectively.

THIRD STROPHIC PAIR (193–232)

193	213	⏓ − ⏓ ⏓ − ⏓ | − − ‖	an an∧
		⏓ − ⏓ ⏓ − ⏓ | − ⏓ ⏓ |	2an
195	215	∪ ∪ − | ⏓ ⏓ − ⏓ | − ⏓ ⏓ − |	2an
		<u>∪∪</u> − ⏓ ⏓ − ⏓ | − − ‖	an an∧
		∪ ∪ − ∪ ∪ − | ∪ ∪ − ⏓ ⏓ − |	2an
		⏓ ⏓ − ⏓ ⏓ − | <u>∪∪</u> − ⏓ ⏓ − |	2an
		⏓ ⏓ − | ∪∪ − | ∪ ∪ − ∪ ∪ − |	2an

200	220	– ∪ – ∪ ‧ – ∪ ‖	∧ia ia∧ (= ith)
		:: ⁙ – ⁙ – ⁙ ∪∪ ⁙ ∪∪ ‧	2an
		⁙ – ‧ ⁙ – ⁙ – – ‖	an an∧
		⁙ – ⁙ – ⁙ ‧ – ⁙ – ‧	2an
		⁙ – ‧ ⁙ – ‧	an
205	225	⏗ ⏗ ⏗ ∪ – ‧	δ
		∪∪ – ⏗ – ∪∪ – ‧ ⏗ – ‖	2an
		– ⏗∪ – – ‧ ∪ – ‧	ia ∧ia
		⏗∪ – ∪ – ∪∪ ‖	∧ia ia (= lec)
		⏗ ⏗ ‧ ∪ ⏗ ‧ ∪ – ∪ –	2ia
210	230	⏗ ⏗ ‧ ∪ ⏗ ‧ ∪ – ∪ – ‖	2ia
		– ∪∪ ‧ – ∪∪ – ‧ ∪∪ – ∪∪ ‧	4da
		⏗ ⏗∪ – ∪ ‧ – ∪ ‖‖	ia ia∧

The chorus suddenly abandons dactylic and iambic, and turns to anapaests. This change of metre reflects the change of subject matter, from attempted consolation to a description of the scene of Agamemnon's death (cf. 193–200n., Kraus (1957) 150–1). Anapaests are especially appropriate for this topic, given Electra's use of recited anapaests at 86–120 for a similar purpose. The chorus ends the anapaests with an ithyphallic clausula: Dale (1968) 53 compares the dochmiac clausula after the anapaests in 244.

Electra also begins to sing in anapaests (201–4 ∼ 221–4). 205 ∼ 225 must be a dochmiac metron (cf. Dale (1968) 54): there are no other dochmiacs in the vicinity, but dochmiacs are found sporadically in anapaestic contexts (cf. Parker (1997) 57–8). The combination looks forward to the epode, where a longer series of dochmiacs follows a group of anapaests. From 207 ∼ 227 onwards the metre is iambic, except for the dactylic tetrameter in 211 ∼ 231: for this variation of rhythm in the penultimate colon cf. 856 ∼ 867, West (1982a) 100. Many of these iambics share characteristics with those in the first two strophic pairs, especially 'dactylic' openings (207 ∼ 227, 209–10, 212; cf. also 205 ∼ 225) and anceps after acatalectic dactyl (212 ∼ 232). Electra's song thus follows on from the chorus in the first section of this strophic pair, while also preserving many metrical features found earlier in the lyric.

EPODE (233–50)

233	⁙ – ⁙ – ⁙ – – ‧	an an∧
	⁙ – ⁙ – ⁙ – – ‧	an an∧
235	⁙ – ⁙ – ⁙ – – ‖	an an∧
	:: – ∪∪ – ∪∪ – ∪∪ – ∪∪ ‧	4da
	– ∪∪ – ∪∪ – ∪∪ – ∪∪ ‧	4da
	– ∪∪ – ⁙ – ⁙ – ⁙ ‖	4da
	⁙ – ⁙ – ⁙ – ⁙ – ‧	2an

240   ‥ — ‥ —   ‥ — ‥ — [|]   2an
        ‥ — ‥ —   ‥ — ∪ ∪ — [|]   2an
        ‥ — ‥ —   ‥ — ∪ ∪ ∪ ‖   2an
        — ∪⏜∪ — ∪ — [|]   δ
245   — ∪⏜∪ — ∪ — [|] — ∪⏜∪ — ∪ — [|]   2δ
        — ∪ — ∪ ∪ ‖   hδ
        — ∪ — ∪ — [|]   hδ
        — — — ∪ ∪ — ∪ — [|]   glyc
        — — — — — [|]   δ
250   ∪ — —   — ∪ —   ∪ — — ‖‖   ia∧ ∧ia ia∧ [= ia∧ ith]

The chorus continues with the anapaests which had dominated its contribution to the third strophic pair, though here with completely contracted
bicipitia and an anapaestic close rather than an iambic one. Whereas before
Electra had begun her response with anapaests, here she starts off with uncontracted dactyls: her brisk double-short movement contrasts with the chorus's
successive long syllables. Her move back to anapaests at 239–42 is assisted at
238 by an ambiguous dactylic colon, which could be an anapaestic dimeter:
it lacks a medial diaeresis, but then again so do the anapaests which follow.
There is a similarly transitional colon at Ar. *Av.* 254, for which see L. P. E.
Parker (1997) 57, 303. Parker compares Eur. *Phoen.* 826–31 and *IA* 1319–32
for the exploitation of the rhythmic ambiguity between anapaests and dactyls;
cf. also West (1982a) 120 with n. 105. On the possibility that 'transitions into
anapaests . . . signal a more positive and resolute frame of mind, without . . .
any diminution of passion' see Parker (1997) 224.

The succeeding shifts which close the epode are also carefully handled.
Electra's anapaests begin with contracted bicipitia, but two of the last three
contain a double short (241–2). This change of rhythm leads into the dochmiacs
of 244–5, a metre which suggests a new intensity of emotion at this climactic
moment in the lyric (cf. West (1982a) 108, Parker (1997) 67). For the association
of anapaests and dochmiacs more generally cf. 205 ~ 225, 853 ~ 64, Parker
(1997) 57–8, Tibaldi (1999). The hypodochmiacs of 246–7 with their single-
short rhythm allow a smoother move to the iambics, at the end (on the metre
of 249 see *ad loc.*); before these iambics, a single glyconic recalls the — ∪ ∪ —
∪ — rhythm of the earlier dochmiacs. The variety of names on the metrical
scheme can thus obscure the careful patterning and delicate transitions which
characterise this piece.

121–250 A female chorus enters in response to the sufferings of a wretched
woman: the same pattern occurs in Euripides' *Medea*, *Hippolytus*, *Andromache*,
Helen and *Orestes*. But the closest parallel to this parodos is found in S.'s *Trachiniae*

(94–140). In both plays the chorus stresses that the heroine's laments are unceasing (*El.* 122, 141, 218; *Tr.* 104 ἀεί, 106 οὔποτ', 110 τρύχεσθαι). It encourages the heroine not to give way to her laments (*El. passim*, *Tr.* 124–35): but despite its criticisms it remains well disposed towards her (*El.* 121–2, 233–4; *Tr.* 122–3 ὧν ἐπιμεμφομένας ἀ– | δεῖα μέν, ἀντία δ' οἴσω). The following scene has a similar form in both plays, with the heroine recounting her sufferings to the chorus (254–309n.).

The great difference between the two parodoi lies in their scale. At 130 lines, the *Electra* parodos is longer than any lyric in S. or Euripides, with the exception of the parodos to *OC* (137 lines): the *Trachiniae* parodos is less than half its size, at 47 lines. This greater length arises from the greater intensity with which the motif of attempted consolation is handled. In *Trachiniae* the chorus contents itself with a brief description of the mutability of human affairs, framed by references to Zeus (126–140). Our chorus moves through a succession of consolatory *topoi*: the uselessness of tears (137–44), the presence of companions in her grief (153–7), the prospect of help from her brother (158–63), the power of Zeus and Time to annul suffering (173–84). After turning from this course to describe the death which Electra is lamenting (193–200), the chorus returns to it at the end with greater urgency. It reminds Electra of the power wielded by hostile authority (213–20), and concludes with a last appeal not to continue creating misery for herself (233–5). Each of these attempts is rebuffed by Electra.

The greater elaboration with which the theme of consolation is handled in this play reflects the special intensity and immoderate length of Electra's mourning as opposed to Deianira's. The successive, but unsuccessful, attempts by a group of friends to persuade a great figure to give up an ungovernable passion against the authorities have various literary parallels (e.g. the book of Job). The most relevant of these is the Embassy scene in *Iliad* 9, where Achilles resists the different arguments put forward by Odysseus, Phoenix and Ajax. Achilles is conscious of his χόλος (cf. 9.646), just as Electra is of her ὀργά, and this self-reflective aspect to their character is something that sets them apart. Yet Achilles is at least partly swayed by the pleas of his companions, while Electra never retreats from her position. Her cause for grief is after all more intense than Achilles': the confiscation of a concubine weighs lightly against the murder of a father. And unlike Agamemnon in the *Iliad*, Electra's opponents are not offering any restitution or apology for their crimes.

Such comparisons bring out the particular intensity of Electra's grief and its causes. Yet despite her rejection of the chorus's consolation, she maintains a friendly attitude towards it, addressing it with all politeness and acknowledging its good motives (cf. 130n., 226). Electra's lack of contempt for her advisors separates her from other Sophoclean heroes (most notably Antigone). Moreover, her recognition of the unpleasant aspects of her behaviour reveals a self-awareness absent from many of S.'s protagonists. There is more to her than monolithic defiance.

Does the parodos have a darker side? According to Winnington-Ingram, 'along with the expression of poignant emotion, there is a deployment of ideas, and of ideas closely related to the thought of Aeschylus, which must at least raise questions, however they are to be answered, about the quality of the act of matricide to come' ((1980) 338–9). But many of his judgments on the lyric are so arbitrary (e.g. 149n., 157n.) that it often seems that he knew what he would find before he looked for it. His belief that the matricide is important for our understanding of the parodos cannot be justified from the text. S. in fact distances his handling of the myth from that of Aeschylus, especially in the description of the death of Agamemnon (193–200n.). The concept of a defiant Electra departs from the Aeschylean account (86–120n.). So too does the emphasis on the need for justice for the killing of Agamemnon, rather than on the seemingly unbreakable chain of killings which forms an important theme in the *Oresteia*. As often in this play, a comparison with Aeschylus reveals not S.'s dependence, but his distinctive handling of his material.

121 Enter the chorus from eisodos A. We learn almost immediately that it is made up of women older than Electra (cf. the vocatives in 121, 254n.), that these women are also noble by birth (129; cf. 1227), and that they hate the rule of Aegisthus (126–7). See further Burton (1980) 186 (though his idea that 'if married they may well be the wives of citizens who form a party in opposition' shows a lapse into the 'documentary fallacy' (cf. Diggle (1982d) 13); the term was coined by Waldock (1951) 11–24). For the entrance of the chorus immediately after an actor's monody see Barner (1971) 305 (5).

ὦ παῖ παῖ: marking the age difference between Electra and the chorus (cf. Kovacs (1994) 163 with n. 1, Dickey (1996) 68). The repeated vocative may denote the chorus's sympathy for Electra (cf. *Ant.* 949). For the address at the start of the parodos cf. *Aj.* 134–5, Eur. *Hec.* 98. ὦ is only found in Triclinius, with ἰώ elsewhere: for the corruption see Diggle *ap.* Willink's commentary on Euripides' *Orestes*, p. 362 (addenda to 1465).

122 τίν' 'what' in the sense 'what sort of', 'what does it amount to' (cf. 328, *OR* 2).

123 τάκεις ὧδ' ἀκόρεστον οἰμωγάν: οἰμωγάν is a verbal noun which governs τὸν . . . Ἀγαμέμνονα in 124–5. For this construction cf. 556, Schwyzer (1940) 13 = (1983) 453, Fraenkel on Aesch. *Ag* 1090, Renehan (1976) 50–4, Davies on *Tr.* 208–9, Diggle (1996c) 193–4. οἰμωγάν is also the object of τάκεις, in a periphrasis which can be translated 'you waste away while lamenting'. Alleged parallels for this construction do not always satisfy. At *Aj.* 55 ἔκειρε πολύκερων φόνον 'he killed the cattle by hacking them', or at *Ant.* 972–3 ἕλκος | τυφλωθέν, implying 'he inflicted a wound by blinding them', both the verbal and nominal element of the phrase involve a transitive sense. In τάκεις . . . οἰμωγάν the periphrasis is more difficult, because only οἰμωγάν, and not τάκεις, refers to an action of Electra's directed at Agamemnon. But a similar construction can still be found. At Aesch. *Sept.* 289–90 μέριμναι ζωπυροῦσι τάρβος | τὸν ἀμφιτειχῆ λεών 'my cares kindle fear of the host which surrounds the walls', the noun τάρβος governs λεών, while ζωπυροῦσι τάρβος makes up another metaphorical expression analogous to τάκεις οἰμωγάν. But ζωπυροῦσι itself does not refer to an action directed against the λεών. If we translate 'my cares are inflamed with fear of the host', then the parallel with our instance 'why do you waste away with lamentation for Agamemnon?' becomes yet clearer. See further Hutchinson *ad loc.*: he supports the retention of the paradosis in our case. For other (less striking) periphrases which go on to govern another noun in this way cf. *OC* 1120, Moorhouse 37–8, Diggle (1981 a) 58, (1996c) 193–4.

Ll-J/W adopt F. I. Schwerdt's λάσκεις (*ap.* Nauck[3] p. 158; λακεῖς *iam* Reiske (1753) 12) instead of τάκεις. But although the verb can denote the noise made by lamentation (cf. Eur. *Hel.* 185), this is a rare sense. Willink (2003) 75 prefers γ' ἀχεῖς, though the γε is unsatisfactory. But τήκω is exactly the right word for Electra's drawn-out process of mourning (cf. 283, 835 etc.), and should be preserved if at all possible. In *Second Thoughts* Ll-J/W withdraw their support for λάσκεις, and instead point to Kvíčala's conjecture τίς . . . | τάκει σ' . . . ἀκόρεστος (or –ον) οἰμωγά ((1864) 397–9). Lloyd-Jones prints this in the revised edition of his Loeb, following Blaydes'. For τήκει with a non-personal subject and personal object cf. Eur. *IA* 398 ἐμὲ δὲ συντήξουσι νύκτες ἡμέραι τε δακρύοις. Ll-J/W believe that the *Septem* passage cited above favours this conjecture. But there, as we have seen, τάρβος governs only λεών. With Kvíčala's text οἰμωγά must govern both σε (via the verb τάκει) and τὸν Ἀγαμέμνονα (in its capacity as a verbal noun), and this two-fold function is significantly more awkward. As Ll-J/W themselves point out in *Sophoclea*, the conjecture 'renders the following accusative even more difficult'. The *Septem* passage they cite in fact provides support for the paradosis, as explained above. If a conjecture is required, West's τείνεις (*per litteras*) for τάκεις is better than any yet offered.

For the idea that lamentation should have a limit cf. Hom. *Il.* 23.157 γόοιο μὲν ἔστι καὶ ἆσαι. Contrast the nightingale at Aesch. *Ag.* 1143 which is ἀκόρετος βοᾶς.

124 δολερᾶς: for Clytemnestra's δόλος cf. Hom. *Od.* 11.422 Κλυταιμήστρη δολόμητις, 4.92 δόλῳ οὐλομένης ἀλόχοιο, Aesch. *Ag.* 155, 886, 1636 τὸ γὰρ δολῶσαι πρὸς γυναικὸς ἦν σαφῶς, *Cho.* 888. It forms a defining characteristic of the killing of Agamemnon: cf. 197, 279, Αἴγισθος δολόμητις at Hom. *Od.* 3.198, 4.525 etc., Pind. *P.* 11.18, Aesch. *Ag.* 1129, 1495 = 1519, *Cho.* 556, 1003,

Ar. *Ran*. 1141–3 ὁ πατὴρ ἀπώλετο | αὑτοῦ βιαίως ἐκ γυναικείας χερὸς | δόλοις λαθραίοις (the last part of this is printed by West as Aesch. *Cho*. 3bc; cf. West (1990) 230–1).

ἀθεώτατα: so Erfurdt and Porson (1815) 221 for unmetrical –ας. For the word cf. 1181, *Tr*. 1036 σὰ μάτηρ ἄθεος, Aesch. *Cho*. 46 δύσθεος γυνά, Fahr (1969) 15–17.

126–7 ὡς ὁ τάδε πορὼν | ὄλοιτ᾽: a generalising masculine. Dawe and Ll-J/W print ὅς, but for ὡς with a wish see Barrett on Eur. *Hipp*. 407–9. Ll-J/W point to Hom. *Il*. 14.142, but there and at 18.107 West rightly prefers ὡς.

127 εἴ μοι θέμις τάδ᾽ αὐδᾶν: the 'combination of such a ferocious sentiment with the cautionary εἰ θέμις . . . is a nice piece of character-drawing' (Hollis on Call. fr. 49.15 = 368 Pfeiffer = 287(b).25 *SH*). For the reluctance to curse or criticise those in authority cf. *Ant*. 1259–60 (of Creon) εἰ θέμις εἰπεῖν . . . | . . . αὐτὸς ἁμαρτών, *OR* 530, Eur. *Med*. 83 ὄλοιτο μὲν μή· δεσπότης γάρ ἐστ᾽ ἐμός, *El*. 1245–6; also S. *Tr*. 809 εἰ θέμις δ᾽, ἐπεύχομαι (Hyllus speaking to Deianira).

128 ὦ γένεθλα γενναίων: advocated by Stinton (1977a) 129–30 = (1990) 274–6, who also prints ὦν instead of the majority reading τῶν in 145. Most editors print γενέθλα (and τῶν): this gives − ∪ ∪ − − − −, which is metrically troubling. The most likely interpretation would be dactylic: but as Stinton notes, the dactyls elsewhere in this lyric have almost exclusively uncontracted bicipitia. Dale's contracted hemiepes pendant ((1968) 38, (1971–83) iii. 272) involves the same difficulty. Ll-J/W (*Sophoclea*) follow Kraus (1957) 149 in taking it as an iambo-choriambic dimeter: but neither Ll-J/W nor Kraus provide parallels for such a form of this metre. Parallels are also hard to find for Dawe's 'chor. + anc. + sp.'. By printing ὦν in 145, Stinton obtains an iambic dimeter with double syncopation in the second metron, a metrical form which occurs at 160–1 ∼ 180–1 and several times elsewhere in S. (see the metrical introduction to the first stasimon). Syncopated iambics also occur at the end of Electra's words at 135–6 ∼ 151–2. Stinton's change would be the best course even given a unanimous manuscript tradition favouring τῶν. It is nevertheless welcome to discover that L^{ac} reads ων, and has a tau written above the omega. The cross-bar of the tau indicates that it was not written as a correction by the scribe, and may thus be the result of cross-collation with another manuscript.[10]

Possessive ὅς is an epic usage (Hom. *Il*. 1.404 etc.), but is found in tragedy too. It is more often accompanied by the definite article (*Tr*. 266, 525, *Aj*. 442, *OR* 1248, Aesch. *Sept*. 641), but can, as here, occur without it (cf. *OC* 1639,

---

[10] Papathomopoulos (1993) 87 claims that L^{ac} may read ὃς ἑῶν, but I do not see evidence for this in the facsimile.

Aesch. *Suppl.* 101 (v.l.), *Eum.* 365–6, Eur. *Med.* 955). The comparative rarity of the construction would facilitate the corruption to the definite article. γενέθλα is found at 226 (metrically secure), but elsewhere in tragedy γένεθλον is the norm (including lyric: e.g. *OR* 180, *Ant.* 1149). Stinton's choice of readings thus replaces a metrical anomaly with a typically Sophoclean metrical phrase, gives vocabulary more in accordance with tragic usage, and involves a corruption which is easily explained.

The manuscripts follow this address with πατέρων or τοκέων, neither of which corresponds to anything in the antistrophe. The former has the better authority, and is supported by Kaibel (p. 91), Wilamowitz (1921) 511 n. 1, Fraenkel (1917–18) 185 n. 1 = (1964) i. 189–90 n. 2. These scholars consequently posit a lacuna after οἰκτρῶς in 145 (so e.g. ἀϊκῶς τ' Porson (1815) 221; Blumenthal (1934) 454 tries νήπιος, ὃς τῶν <ὦν> οἰκτρ<οτάτ>ως), though the sense there is not incomplete, and the ensuing metre is problematic. Monk's deletion ((1826) 69) is rather to be preferred. A scholion on this passage γενναίων· πατέρων shows how the word could be used as a gloss (so Stinton (1977a) 129–30 = (1990) 274–6). Alternatively, πατέρων was added to clarify the sense and give a combination of words found elsewhere in tragedy (Eur. *Cycl.* 41, *Hyps.* fr. 753c.17 *TrGF*, *Ion* 262–3). So also at Eur. *El.* 115 the phrase ἐγενόμαν Ἀγαμέμνονος has the unmetrical κούρα attached to it in L (see Denniston on 115–19).

130 Electra acknowledges the good intentions which have motivated the entry of the chorus: cf. Eur. *Or.* 132–3 αἵδ' αὖ πάρεισι τοῖς ἐμοῖς θρηνήμασιν | φίλαι ξυνῳδοί, Ferri on [Sen.] *Oct.* 76.

παραμύθιον: 'an internal accusative (of the kind often called "in apposition to the sentence"), specifying that in which the action of a verb consists or results' (Barrett on Eur. *Hipp.* 752–7): see further 564, Moorhouse 45–6, Diggle (1978) 171 = (1994) 191–2, (1982a) 59–60 = (1994) 223–4.

131–2 οἶδά τε καὶ ξυνίημι τάδ', οὔ τί με | φυγγάνει: for the combination of a statement with the negation of its opposite cf. 885, 929, 1049, Bruhn §208; it occurs in a formula of admission at e.g. 222, *Ant.* 443.

ξυνίημι: the first iota is short, as in dramatic lyric elsewhere at Aesch. *Pers.* 941 and Pl. Com. fr. 168.4 *PCG* (cited by Dunbar on Ar. *Av.* 853–4). The phenomenon is probably also found in dialogue (cf. Maas (1913) 357 n. 1 = (1973) 55 n. 5, Dunbar on Ar. *Av.* 946).

132 φυγγάνει: the verb is found elsewhere at [Aesch.] *PV* 513, [Hippocr.] *Int. aff.* 12; cf. also Alc. fr. 421 *PLF*, Voigt πεφύγγων. Its compounds are more widespread, especially in the Hippocratic corpus. For other such nasal presents, usually based on the aorist stem, alongside alternative present stems cf. Kujoṛe (1973) 196–8, S–D i. 699–700; also Page on Eur. *Med.* 800. S. also has κλαγγάνω at frr. 314.315 and 959.4 *TrGF*, a verb found elsewhere only at Xen. *Cyn.* 4.5, 6.23 and Aesch. *Eum.* 131 κλαγγαίνεις (codd.; –άνεις Wakefield).

For οὐδέ '[setting] a negative idea in the scale against a preceding positive idea' (Denniston 191 (i)) cf. *OC* 481, Fraenkel on Aesch. *Ag.* 263. θέλω is the usual tragic form of this verb (cf. Arnott (2002) 197 n. 14; contrast Diggle on Theophr. *Char.* 24.6). The majority reading οὐδ' αὖ θέλω is unmetrical: for intrusive αὖ see Dawe, *STS* i. 155 (on *Aj.* 871).

133 For μὴ οὐ after a verb negated by οὐ see 107n.

στενάχειν: so Elmsley (on *OR* 181 (our 185)). Most manuscripts have στοναχεῖν, the minority στεναχεῖν. On the verbs στενάχω (< στένω) and στοναχέω, στοναχίζω (< στοναχή) see West's Teubner *Iliad* vol. i. p. xxxv. Elsewhere in tragedy only στενάχειν is transmitted (141, 1076, [Aesch.] *PV* 99, Eur. *Tro.* 106, *Phoen.* 1551 (corrupt), fr. 263 *TrGF*), so it makes sense to print the same here.

134 ὦ . . . ἀμειβόμεναι: for ὦ with a vocative participle taking the place of a substantive see Moorhouse 27, 30.

φιλότατος: Elmsley rightly restores the Doric alpha (in his edition; so also Willink (2003) 76): cf. 236 κακότατος.

135 For ἐᾶτε in the mouth of Sophoclean heroes see Knox (1964) 17–18.

ὧδ' ἀλύειν: with reference to her unconventional behaviour. Hutchinson (1999) 53–4 n. 11 compares Virg. *Aen.* 12.680 *hunc, oro, sine me furere ante furorem*, where Turnus may be taking the viewpoint of his interlocutor rather than making an admission of madness (for the same technique cf. Solon fr. 10.1 *IEG* δείξει δὴ μανίην μὲν ἐμὴν βαιὸς χρόνος ἀστοῖς). However, ἀλύω need not have the pejorative connotations of *furere* (cf. *Phil.* 174, where the tone is one of pity).

137–9 The uselessness of grief is a common consolatory motif: cf. Hom. *Il.* 24.550–1 οὐ γάρ τι πρήξεις ἀκαχήμενος υἷος ἑοῖο, | οὐδέ μιν ἀναστήσεις, S. fr. 557 *TrGF*, Eur. *El.* 193–5, Hor. *C.* 1.24.11–18, Kassel (1958) 70, Arnould (1990) 108–13.

137 τόν γ' ἐξ Ἀίδα: the construction reflects the view of an outsider (Moorhouse 108–9): cf. 1070, *Phil.* 1076 τά τ' ἐκ νεώς, Fraenkel on Aesch. *Ag.* 538, K–G i. 546. The verb ἀναστάσεις will also have influenced it. The γ' should be taken with the whole noun phrase, giving οὔτοι τόν γ' ἐν Ἅιδου ὄντα πατέρα ἐξ Ἅιδου ἀναστήσεις (so Kaibel, p. 93). Denniston 140–1 (i) prefers to class the particle among examples of limitative γε where the extension of application is not excluded. He thus glosses our text 'whether or not prayer is likely to be successful in other cases': but the dry irony is not in place here. The variant reading τόνδ' gives a similarly unwelcome effect.

138 παγκοίνου: cf. *Aj.* 1193 τὸν πολύκοινον Ἅιδαν, *Ant.* 810–11 παγ– | κοίτας (codd; *coni.* πάγκοινος), Aesch. *Sept.* 860.
λίμνας: for Hades as a marsh or lake cf. fr. 523.2 *TrGF*, Aesch. fr. 273, 273a.2 *TrGF* φοβερᾶς λίμνας, Eur. *Alc.* 443 λίμναν Ἀχεροντίαν, Hermesianax fr. 7.5–6 *CA*, Virg. *Aen.* 6.107 *tenebrosa palus Acheronte refuso*, Lucian 34.24, 38.10, Radermacher (1949) 308, Tib. 1.10.38 with Murgatroyd, Henrichs (1989) 16 n. 44, Davies (1988a) 280–1 n. 22 (on water at the entrance to the underworld).

139 –στάσεις οὔτε γόοισιν, οὔτ᾽ †λιταῖσιν†:   the transmitted –στάσεις οὔτε γόοις οὔτε λιταῖσ(ιν) has the metrical form − − − ∪ ∪ − − ∪ ∪ − – (−): this does not correspond to the − − − ∪ ∪ − ∪ − − − of the strophe. The simple change γόοισιν (V⁸, *coni.* Livineius) instead of transmitted γόοις will give us a short seventh element as we require. οὔτε must then be followed by a two-syllable word beginning with a vowel which parallels γόοισιν. Erfurdt's εὐχαῖς (approved by Wilamowitz (1921) 511 n. 1) is the most likely suggestion. εὐχή is the general, all-purpose Greek word for prayer (cf. Pulleyn (1997) 63–4). Its appearance might have led to a gloss λιταῖς aimed at making it clear what sort of prayers were meant. This gloss could then displace εὐχαῖς from the text. For λιταί used as a gloss cf. Hesych. ι 520 (= ii. 359 Latte) ἱλασμοῖς· λιταῖς. See 797–8n. for a common word displaced by a gloss aimed at clarifying its sense. Willink (1997) 300–1 prefers ἄταις, but we need a word meaning 'prayers', 'laments' or 'tears'. Hermann conjectured ἄνταις 'by prayers', a word he takes from Hesych. α 5372 (= i. 185 Latte) ἀντήσει· λιτανείαις. ἀντήσεσιν, where he interprets the transmitted lemma as ἄντησι. Dain and Colonna both adopt this text. But for all its palaeographical simplicity, a conjecture which depends on the reinterpretation of a single lemma in Hesychius is unlikely to win many converts.

Adopting a different approach, Stinton (1977a) 128–9 = (1990) 273–4 advocates στάσεις οὔτε γόοισιν, οὐ λιταῖς (− − − ∪ ∪ − ∪ − ∪ −), which has some slight manuscript support (οὐ only in Triclinius). This is supported by Diggle (1994) 259 n. 33 and printed by Ll-J/W. But while the existence of 'glyc − −' is not in doubt (Itsumi (1984) 78–9 counts 23 examples; Willink lists some at (1997) 300 n. 12), the alleged colon 'glyc ∪ −' is less certain. Stinton himself cites two supposed instances of 'glyc ∪ −', in each case corresponding with 'glyc − −'. Of these, *Phil.* 209 ~ 219 is textually insecure, and neither Dawe nor Ll-J/W adopt a text which supports Stinton's argument. The other, Eur. *Med.* 159 ~ 183, does display the phenomenon desired by Stinton if and only if we keep the majority reading εὐνέταν at 159, which corresponds to ὁρμᾶται in 183. Diggle retains the paradosis (cf. (1983) 346–8 = (1994) 258–60), but

Murray, Page and Mastronarde all adopt Tyrwhitt's εὐνάταν (which has some slight manuscript support). The conjecture is probably right, as it removes a metrical anomaly at trivial palaeographical cost. Diggle now accepts it (cf. Willink (1997) 300 n. 15).

Evidence for 'glyc ∪ —' is thus unreliable at best, and probably non-existent. Stinton's text involves a further difficulty, in that it leaves us with the combination οὔτε ... οὐ, which is unusual when the negatives are separated by only one word (cf. Denniston 510–11). This combination of problems would render suspect even a unanimous manuscript tradition. They certainly rule out this particular conjecture.

140 ἀλλ': the repetition of ἀλλά so soon after its appearance in 137 is not troubling: cf. Jebb on *Phil.* 524–5, Denniston lxii–lxiv, Davies on *Tr.* 88 ff.

ἀπὸ τῶν μετρίων: for immoderation as a characteristic of the Sophoclean hero see Knox (1964) 24.

141 στενάχουσα: for the orthography see 133n.

142 ἀνάλυσις ... κακῶν: cf. Aesch. *Sept.* 135 ἐπίλυσιν φόβων, Pind. *N.* 10.76–7 λύσις | ... πενθέων.

143 δυσφόρων 'may carry a suggestion of mental sickness', according to Winnington-Ingram (1980) 335. Mental sickness is indeed δύσφορος: but so are many other things, and hence the word cannot in itself carry the resonance which Winnington-Ingram suspects.[11]

145–52 Electra stresses the immorality of forgetting a dead parent, a proposition which commands ready assent. But instead of applying this *gnome* to her own situation, her words at 147 ἀλλ' ἐμέ γε rather mark a strong break with what precedes. The *gnome*, it turns out, is unsatisfactory as a description of Electra's actions. She does not merely remember her dead father, as an ordinary person might: she has devoted her existence to a constant process of keeping alive the memory of his suffering. An appeal to a generalised human norm is thus not enough: she rather turns to two great heroines of mythology, Procne (107n.) and Niobe (150n.), to exemplify her conduct. S. handles this pair with some variety: rather than simply stating 'I am like ...' (cf. *Ant.* 832–3), Electra first declares that she is fixated (147 ἄραρεν) with Procne (not named), and then invokes Niobe, by name, as a deity. The two mythological paradeigmata are thus cited without heavy-handedness or artificiality.

---

[11] Cf. Austin and Olson on Ar. *Thesm.* 72–3: 'the fact that [δυσφορεῖν] *can* bear a technical medical meaning is no reason for assigning it that meaning wherever it occurs'.

Each of these comparisons goes back to Homer. Penelope compares herself to Ἀηδών, who was turned into a nightingale and perpetually mourned the child whom she had killed (*Od.* 19.518–24);[12] while at *Il.* 24.601–19 Achilles persuades Priam to eat by using Niobe as an *exemplum*. Each of these figures is most famous for her perpetual lamentation, which turned the one into a nightingale, the other into a rock on Mount Sipylus. This perpetual lamentation connects them with Electra. The comparison becomes more involved when we remember that both Procne and Niobe lament the loss of a child or children. The nightingale in particular often features as a comparison for a woman who has lost her child(ren): cf. Gow and Page on Philip *A.P.* 9.262.5–6 = 2831–2 *GP*. Electra's loss, however, is of a father, not a child: and unlike Procne and Niobe, she bears no responsibility for the death which she laments.

145 νήπιος, ὅς: an epic expression not elsewhere in tragedy: cf. Hom. *Od.* 11.449, [Hes.] fr. 61 M–W, *Cypria* fr. 25 *EGF* = 33 *PEG* = 31 *GEF*, Theogn. 439.

ὧν: L^{ac} has ων *in linea*; for the majority reading τῶν see 128n.

146 γονέων: the poetic plural seems odd, given that Electra has such a different attitude towards her two parents: cf. however 241–2n., Aesch. *Cho.* 681–2, *Eum.* 152 (where the chorus describe Orestes as τοκεῦσι πικρόν).

147 ἁ στονόεσσ': for στένω used of the nightingale cf. 1076, Aesch. *Ag.* 1144.

ἄραρεν appears at first to be a transitive aorist like the Homeric ἤραρεν (short alpha), with the (rare) omission of the temporal augment (cf. Austin and Reeve (1970) 4, Diggle (1989) 201 = (1994) 347). But the regular senses 'join, fit, furnish' are all inappropriate. According to LSJ^9 s.v. ἀραρίσκω A III 2 it means 'please' or 'gratify', but this is an unexpected and unexampled sense for the verb (Pind. *N.* 5.44, cited by LSJ, is certainly not a parallel).

K–B ii. 372 takes it instead as an intransitive perfect ('is fixed'), comparing Hom. *Od.* 4.777 πᾶσιν ἐνὶ φρεσὶν ἤραρεν ἡμῖν for the unexpected short alpha; cf. also Cic. *Att.* 9.10.3 *mihi autem haeserunt illa*, cited by Hutchinson (1999) 53–4

---

[12] The Homeric scholia (= ii. 683.19–27 Dindorf = Pher. Ath. *FGrHist* 3 F 124 = fr. 124 *EGM*) claim that this Aedon was the wife of Zethus; in jealousy at the number of children belonging to her sister-in-law Niobe she attempted to kill one of them and mistakenly killed her own son. The relationship of this version of the myth to the more familiar Procne account is unclear, though several details are shared between them. Despite the subsequent reference to Niobe, it is improbable that Electra is here referring to Aedon rather than Procne. The audience will have recognised the figure mentioned as Procne by the end of 148, and there is nothing in the mention of Niobe to change this identification. The reference to Itys rather than the Homeric Itylus also supports this view.

n. 11. The sense is just what we need: the example of Procne 'is fixed' in Electra's mind, since she provides the perfect parallel for her perpetual remembrance of her father. The contrast with the preceding condemnation of people forgetful of dead parents is thus brought out. The two accusatives ἐμέ and φρένας can be justified by the σχῆμα Ἰωνικόν (cf. 99n., especially Diggle's n. there cited).

148 Ἴτυν . . . Ἴτυν: 'the combination of the onomatopoeic (and hence readily repeated) name with a verb of complaining or lamenting became a favourite element of the nightingale motif' (Fraenkel on Aesch. *Ag.* 1144–5, with examples; cf. also Wills (1996) 55). The upsilon of Ἴτυς is usually short, but is long at Ar. *Av.* 212. For the different scansions of Ἴτυν in the same line see Fehling (1969) 178–9, Hopkinson (1982).

The child killed by the nightingale is named Itylus in Homer (*Od.* 19.522), Pherecydes of Athens (*FGrHist* 3 F 124 = fr. 124 *EGM*) and Catullus (65.14). Elsewhere the name Itys is used (cf. Fitzpatrick (2001) 90 with n. 5).

αἰέν: Dawe adopts G. Velke's αἰαῖ in his third edition, having independently conjectured the same at *STS* i. 177. He compares the interjection φεῦ at Aesch. *Ag.* 1143 in the description of the nightingale, and suggests that αἰέν and αἰαῖ in 148 and 152 have changed places. But given the significance of the motif of perpetual weeping (cf. also 1075), it is important that a word for 'always' appears prominently in the first mythological exemplum (cf. also Hom. *Od.* 19.521 θαμά). Nor is the Aeschylean parallel so close as to justify intervention, as the exclamation there does not occur between the repeated accusatives Ἴτυν Ἴτυν. On the text of 152 see *ad loc.*

149 ὄρνις: the short iota occurs elsewhere in tragedy at *Ant.* 1021, frr. 581.3, 654 *TrGF*, Eur. *Her.* 72, fr. 636.5 *TrGF* (all from spoken iambic trimeters). The only possible comic instance is at Philemon fr. 82.10 *PCG*, although a simple transposition by Meineke would remove it. Ar. *Av.* 168 is not an example: see Dunbar *ad loc.* Both the alleged epic examples cited in *LfE* (Hom. *Il.* 12.218, 24.219) can be emended away: West does so in his edition. If he is right, then the prosody was an innovation in Attic tragedy which could be imitated on occasion by later poets (e.g. Rhianus fr. 76.3 *CA*). But as the evidence from comedy suggests that the short iota was not a feature of contemporary Attic, it remains possible that the tragedians were taking up a feature which they had found in two Homeric passages.

Διὸς ἄγγελος: the nightingale is sometimes the harbinger of spring (cf. Hom. *Od.* 19.518–19, Sappho fr. 136 *PLF*, Voigt ἦρος ἄγγελος ἱμερόφωνος ἀήδων), though that season is more usually associated with the swallow (cf. West on Hes. *Op.* 569, Nünlist (1998) 42–3). As the seasons came from Zeus (cf. Hom. *Od.* 24.344 Διὸς ὧραι, Lucian 24.26 (Ζεὺς) προσέταττεν . . . ταῖς

COMMENTARY: 121–250

ὥραις ἃ δεῖ ποιεῖν), this could be the reason for this description. According to Winnington-Ingram (1980) 336 there is a reference to vengeance, but it is difficult to see this in the text.

150 For the differing accounts of the Niobe myth see Forbes Irving (1990) 293–7. The fragments of S.'s *Niobe* are edited by Barrett in Carden (1974) 171–235 and by Radt, frs. 441a–451.

For ἰώ with a long first syllable cf. *Tr.* 1031 (a near-certain emendation, also at the start of a dactylic hexameter), Ll-J/W, *Second Thoughts* p. 49.

παντλάμων: the παν– element lends the word a force similar to that of a superlative, which is idiomatic in the context of a paradigm: cf. 841 πάμψυχος, Davies (1985), especially p. 249 (citing e.g. Hom. *Il.* 1.266–7, Sappho fr. 16.6–8 *PLF*, Voigt, *Ant.* 823 etc.). For the nominative of exclamation see Diggle on Eur. *Pha.* 240 ≈ fr. 781.27 *TrGF*: Willink (2003) 76 prefers the variant –ον. The adjective adds to the paradox in the following phrase.

σὲ . . . ἔγωγε νέμω θεόν: the only other reference to Niobe as a divinity is at *Ant.* 834, where the chorus stresses the difference between Antigone and Niobe with the words ἀλλὰ θεός τοι καὶ θεογεννής (cf. 837 τοῖς ἰσοθέοις). There the chorus must be pointing to her descent from Zeus via her father Tantalus. But Electra is not referring to Niobe's genealogy, which would not be relevant here: rather, she excitedly hails her by using a typical form of the μακαρισμός, for which cf. Sappho fr. 31.1 *PLF*, Voigt φαίνεταί μοι κῆνος ἴσος θέοισιν. Niobe is an unlikely target for such acclamation: her intense and unending grief sets her apart from the gods, who proverbially are free from care and trouble (cf. Hom. *Il.* 24.526). Contrast e.g. *Ant.* 823, where the heroine introduces the story of Niobe with the words ἤκουσα δὴ λυγροτάταν ὀλέσθαι. Electra's statement becomes even more unusual when we remember that Niobe's lamentation was caused by her foolish boasting that she surpassed a divinity in the number of her children. The emphatic ἔγωγε emphasises that Electra's judgment is unconventional.

For δ' delayed by a vocative cf. *OR* 1096 Φοῖβε, σοὶ δέ: the phenomenon is 'mainly confined to serious poetry' (Denniston 189).

151 ἅτ': for ὅστε in tragedy cf. Fraenkel on Aesch. *Ag.* 1122, Ruijgh (1971) 1002–4, Diggle (1987) 172 = (1994) 325. The phrase beginning with a relative pronoun coming so soon after an invocation and an attribution of godhead may remind listeners of similar relative phrases used prominently in prayers (cf. Norden (1913) 168–76 = (2002) 287–96).

ἐν τάφῳ πετραίῳ: cf. Hom. *Il.* 24.614 νῦν δέ που ἐν πέτρῃσιν, ἐν οὔρεσιν οἰοπόλοισιν. But the phrase 'rocky tomb' has a more claustrophobic aspect than is usual in accounts of the Niobe story: this fits well with Electra's own confinement (310–13, 516–20 etc.). It also looks forward to the plan to imprison

149

Electra in a place where, like Niobe, she may lament as much as she wishes (379–84). For other proleptic uses of myth cf. Davies (1989b).

152 αἰαῖ: the fundamental point of comparison between Electra and Niobe is their perpetual weeping. The paradosis does not ascribe such a quality to Niobe, and so some editors (Nauck[7], Dawe[2–3]) have adopted V's αἰέν (cf. ἀεί Zc; αἰεί Zg, *coni.* Reiske (1753) 12). However, tragic lyric tends to repeat words and ideas in the same position from strophe to antistrophe (cf. Easterling (1978) 154, Diggle (1996c) 197), especially in clausulae (cf. Dale (1936) 193–4 = (1969) 12–13). Hence αἰαῖ in 136 supports the exclamation here. There may be no word for 'always' in the description of Niobe, but that does not mean that the notion of perpetuity is not strongly felt. The prominent use of αἰέν in 148 ensures that its force continues into the second mythological exemplum. So too the reference to the rocky tomb points allusively to the same motif, since Niobe's petrifaction is regularly associated with insatiable lamentation (cf. Theodoridas *A.Pl.* 132.5–6 = 3584–5 *HE*, Ov. *Met.* 6.309–10 *saxum est.* | *flet tamen*, Sen. *Ag.* 378 (= 395 Tarrant) *flebile saxum*, Hygin. *Fab.* 9.3 *flendo lapidea facta est*).[13] Homer may have suppressed this element because Niobe must stop lamenting to serve as a paradigm (cf. *Il.* 24.613 ἐπεὶ κάμε δάκρυ χέουσα: a trace may nevertheless remain at 617 ἔνθα λίθος περ ἐοῦσα θεῶν ἐκ κήδεα πέσσει).

Other accounts of Niobe imply rather than mention her perpetual weeping (cf. *Ant.* 831–2, Call. *Hym.* 2.22–4, Prop. 2.20.7–8, 3.10.8, Sen. *HF* 391). Leon. Alex. 7.549.3 = 1904 *FGE* λήξει δ' οὐδ' αἰῶνι γόου is an exception.

153–5 'Not to you alone has come the sorrow, with regard to which you are excessive [in your laments] in comparison with those within.'

οὔτοι σοὶ μούνᾳ: for this common consolation cf. 289–90, *Ant.* 944–87, Eur. *Alc.* 417–18, 892–3, Theocr. *ap.* Stob. *Ecl.* 4.56.34 (= v. 1132.2–3 Wachsmuth and Hense) θάρρει, βέλτιστε, οὐ σοὶ μόνῳ ταῦτα γέγονεν, Cic. *Tusc.* 3.79. See further Otto (1890) 328, Kassel (1958) 63, Harder on Eur. fr. 454.1 *TrGF* = 72.1 Austin, Ferri on [Sen.] *Oct.* 201.

The metre of 153 ~ 173 is unclear. Wilamowitz (1921) 512 takes it as a fully dragged dochmiac, but there are no dochmiacs in the vicinity to support this. Dochmiacs also imply emotional excitement, which is inappropriate here. Dale (1971–83) iii. 273 calls it a fully contracted hemiepes, but such a double contraction in a dactylic phrase does not fit with the almost exclusively uncontracted dactyls elsewhere in this lyric. It might be related to anapaestic metra

---

[13] A later tradition ascribed the petrifaction to Niobe's permanent silence brought about by her grief: cf. Philemon fr. 102.3–6 *PCG*, Cic. *Tusc.* 3.63, perhaps Lucian 45.41 ἡ ἐπὶ τῷ πένθει σιγή.

(cf. Diggle (1974) 25 = (1994) 121), but there are no anapaests in the vicinity. Ll-J/W's proposal (*Sophoclea*) to take it as a molossus followed by a spondee smacks of desperation.

154 The analysis of 154 ~ 174 ∪∪|∪∪|∪∪−∪− is disputed. The split resolution rules out 'ia cr', as the split would be emphasised by a rhetorical pause after the second element in both strophe and antistrophe (cf. L. P. E. Parker (1968) 243–4). The alternative 'cr ia' analysis (so Wilamowitz and Schroeder) is accepted by Parker (*ib.*), who compares Aesch. *Sept.* 235 ~ 241. Willink (2003) 77 n. 12 objects that there is no other resolution in the *Septem* passage and hence it is not properly comparable. He suggests instead moving ἄχος to give τέκνον, ἐφάνη βροτῶν ἄχος, and in 174 reads τέκνον. ἔτι μέγας ἐν οὐρανῷ. But this still involves split resolution together with another resolution in the antistrophe: and in the strophe ἄχος is uncomfortably placed at the end of the sense unit, where βροτῶν has its natural place. Older analyses (e.g. Brunck, Hermann) placed both instances of τέκνον at the end of the preceding line, but the ensuing pattern (a colon of seven long syllables followed by a dochmiac kaibelianus) is not appropriate in this metrical context.

τέκνον: on the form of address see 79n. Here it strikes the necessary note of reassurance (see Davies on *Tr.* 61). The warmth and intimacy of the address will contrast with the aggressive manner of Electra's real mother (516n.).

155 τῶν ἔνδον: in contrast to Electra's transgressive status outside the house (cf. 312–13n.).

περισσά: for this adjective used of the Sophoclean hero see Knox (1964) 24–5.

156 οἷς ὁμόθεν εἶ καὶ γονᾷ ξύναιμος: for the expansiveness cf. *Hom. Hym.* 5.135 σοῖς τε κασιγνήτοις, οἵ τοι ὁμόθεν γεγάασιν.

157 Χρυσόθεμις . . . καὶ Ἰφιάνασσα are two of the daughters of Agamemnon mentioned at Hom. *Il.* 9.144–5 = 9.286–7. There is no reference to Laodice, the remaining member of Homer's trio, but a post-Homeric tradition identified her with Electra (962n.), so she was an obvious candidate for omission if the playwright wanted only two names to make a contrast with Electra. A scholium on our passage (p. 110.22–4 Papageorgius) is our source for the *Cypria*'s version, in which Agamemnon had four daughters (fr. 17 *EGF* = 24 *PEG* = 20 *GEF*): S. follows this account. The number of daughters varies in early epic: three in Homer (where Iphigenia and Electra are never mentioned), two in [Hes.] fr. 23a.13–30 M–W (Iphimede (sacrificed at Aulis) and Electra). At Eur. *Or.* 23 the three daughters are Chrysothemis, Iphigenia and Electra.

According to Winnington-Ingram (1954–5) 24 n. 1 ≈ (1980) 336 (cf. (1980) 224 n. 26), the reference to Iphianassa is meant to remind the audience of Iphigenia. He does not say whether he believes in a similar allusion at Hom. *Il.* 9.145 = 9.287, but it would be inconsistent to accept one and not the other.

Hiatus in tragedy is elsewhere only found with exclamations, imperatives and the like (cf. West (1982a) 15 with n. 24). Here it arises from an epicising retention of the digamma, a phenomenon which occurs elsewhere in tragedy only with οἷ (195n.). The phrase καὶ Ἰφιάνασσα, complete with effective digamma, is taken unchanged from Hom. *Il.* 9.145 = 9.287; the allusion is yet stronger for its occurrence in a dactylic hexameter.

158–60 κρυπτᾷ τ' ἀχέων ἐν ἥβᾳ | ὄλβιος, ὄν: ἀχέων is a genitive dependent on the adjective κρυπτᾷ : cf. Eur. *Hipp.* 154 κρυπτᾷ κοίτᾳ λεχέων σῶν, Aesch. *Suppl.* 296. Hermann thus translated *semotus a doloribus in iuventa felix*, and he has been followed by Campbell, Kaibel (p. 96), Kamerbeek, Moorhouse 68 and Lloyd-Jones ('he who is happy in his youth concealed from painful things'). While not wrong, this translation obscures how ὄλβιος looks forward rather than backward: as Jebb rightly notes, 'the respect in which he is "happy" is defined by the following clause, according to a frequent poetical idiom' (cf. de Heer (1969) 69). For ὄλβιος, ὅς cf. Hes. *Theog.* 96, 954, Alcman fr. 1.37 *PMGF*, Theogn. 1013–14, Emped. D–K 31 B 132 (= i. 365.5), Virg. *Georg.* 2.490, Hor. *Ia.* 2.1 *beatus ille, qui*, Norden (1913) 100 n. 1 ≈ (2002) 221 n. 100. The same phraseology is found in the language of mystery cults: cf. S. fr. 837 *TrGF*, Richardson on Hom. *Hym.* 2.480.

Jebb also takes ἀχέων as a participle, on the grounds that a reference to Orestes' sorrow is more appropriate in the context. Here he is mistaken, however, as the oxymoron ἀχέων . . . ὄλβιος makes this impossible; nor is ἀχέω found elsewhere in tragedy. For Orestes *semotus a doloribus* cf. Aesch. *Cho.* 696–7 Ὀρέστης, ἦν γὰρ εὐβούλως ἔχων, | ἔξω κομίζων ὀλεθρίου πηλοῦ πόδα.

161 γᾶ is taken up by γᾶν in 163. For near-immediate repetition in tragic lyric see p. 430 of Hutchinson's edition of Greek lyric poetry.

162 δέξεται εὐπατρίδαν: cf. 68 δέξασθέ μ' εὐτυχοῦντα.

162–3 Διὸς . . . | βήματι: the latter word here uniquely possesses a causal sense, as does βαίνω in its forms βήσω and ἔβησα. Haupt's ποδός instead of Διός ((1865a) 11–12 = (1875–6) ii. 296; supported by Kaibel p. 96) aims to remove this unusual meaning: but we do not need to be told that Orestes returned to Mycenae *on foot*. The corruption would also be hard to explain: the name can hardly be a gloss. For Zeus's rôle in preserving Orestes cf. Aesch. *Eum.* 759–61.

εὔφρονι: Fraenkel on Aesch. *Ag.* 806 discusses the meanings of εὔφρων: here 'with a friendly disposition', and hence 'kindly' (Jebb, Lloyd-Jones) makes the best sense, with the adjective transferred from Zeus himself.

163 Ὀρέσταν: the name is delayed for emphasis (cf. 957n., Fraenkel on Aesch. *Ag.* 681 ff., Bruhn §174), and is drawn into the case of the preceding relative pronoun (cf. Aesch. *Sept.* 553, Eur. *Hipp.* 101 with Barrett, K–G ii. 419–20).

164–72, 185–92 After her invocation of the great mythological lamenters in the previous antistrophe, Electra's replies in this strophic pair now focus on the distressing details of her personal privations. She first mentions her status as a woman without children or husband in the strophe (164–5 ἄτε-κνος | . . . ἀνύμφευτος), then at greater length in the antistrophe (187–8). Even her brother, the one man who should look after her, never makes good his promises to return (167–72). As a result her condition in the house is equivalent to that of a slave (189–92). These topics will be taken up again: first in Electra's speech immediately after the parodos (254–309), but also in her appeal to Chrysothemis for aid against Aegisthus (958–66, especially 961–2). Here they remind us of the personal hardships which Electra endures.

164 ὅν γ᾿ ἐγώ: Hermann's movement of a single letter restores exact responsion with 185 and rids us of the false emphasis which the paradosis gives to ἐγώ. After ὅν the γε gives precisely the sense we need: it 'carries on a sentence which is already complete in itself, . . . giving a new and malicious turn to the thought' (Denniston 137 (viii) b). Cf. Eur. *Suppl.* 818 (Αδ.) ἔχεις ἔχεις (sc. τὰ τέκνα) (Χο.) πημάτων γ᾿ ἅλις βάρος.

ἀκάματα: elsewhere of a host of men (e.g. Aesch. *Pers.* 901), monsters (e.g. Hes. *Theog.* 519, 824) or great natural or cosmic phenomena (e.g. Hom. *Il.* 5.4, Aesch. fr. 204b.3 *TrGF* (fire), Emped. D–K 31 B 111.3 (= i. 353.11) (winds), S. *Ant.* 339 (earth), 607–8 (months)). Its use to qualify a single human conveys Electra's extraordinary endurance. The initial alpha is long in epic and Bacchylides (5.25, where see Maehler).

164–5 ἄτεκνος | . . . ἀνύμφευτος: for similar combinations cf. 962 ἄλεκτρα . . . ἀνυμέναιά τε with n. For the repetition of alpha-privative adjectives in general see Griffin on Hom. *Il.* 9.63, Friis Johansen and Whittle on Aesch. *Suppl.* 143 = 153, Fehling (1969) 238–9.

166 δάκρυσι μυδαλέα: cf. [Hes.] *Scut.* 270 (κόνις) δάκρυσι μυδαλέη, Aesch. *Pers.* 539–40 διαμυδαλέους δάκρυσι κόλπους | τέγγουσ᾿, Hesych. μ 1776 (= ii. 681 Latte), Suda μ 1373 (= iii. 422.17–20 Adler).

153

166–7 τὸν ἀνήνυτον | οἶτον ἔχουσα κακῶν 'having that fate in which there is no ἄνυσις of my κακά'. This interpretation, in which the alpha-privative ἀνήνυτον goes with κακῶν (cf. K–G i. 401–2 Anm. 6), is preferable to taking κακῶν with the whole phrase (as in e.g. Jebb's 'bearing that endless doom of woe'). οἶτος always denotes an evil fate, so qualifying it with κακῶν is weak: whereas with the preferred translation we acquire a useful emphasis on Electra's perpetual woe. τόν is demonstrative: cf. 176, *Aj.* 1187–8 τὰν ἄπαυστον . . . ἄταν ἐπάγων, 1149. For οἶτον ἔχουσα cf. Hom. *Il.* 9.563 ἀλκυόνος πολυπενθέος οἶτον ἔχουσα.

167 ὃ δὲ λάθεται: the hiatus caused by the v.l. δ' ἐλάθετο would require period-end, which is impossible owing to the corruption at the end of 188. The verb is pointed after 146. For the accentuation of ὅ see 45n.

168 ὧν τ' ἔπαθ' ὧν τ' ἐδάη: Jebb sees a reference to (i) the wrongs done to Orestes by Clytemnestra and Aegisthus and (ii) the messages sent by Electra to Orestes during his exile. But there is no mention of messages passing from Electra to her brother here or elsewhere (contrast Eur. *Or.* 615–21), and this is too oblique a manner of referring to them. The parallel clauses also make better rhetoric if they denote roughly similar actions. Schneidewin's 'Or. vergisst was ich ihm geleistet in That und Wort', with the two verbs corresponding as in ἔργον and ἔπος, should thus probably be preferred. The Leistungen in question would be Electra's original rescue of the infant Orestes, as well as her continuing struggle against their mutual enemies in the palace.

168–70 τί γὰρ οὐκ ἐμοὶ | ἔρχεται ἀγγελίας ἀπατώμενον; For the messages sent by Orestes to Electra cf. 319, 778–82, 1154–6. For the partitive genitive ἀγγελίας cf. *Ant.* 1229, *Aj.* [314], *Phil.* 174–5, K–G i. 278–9, Moorhouse 57–8.

171–2 ποθεῖ, | ποθῶν δ': contemptuous, as at 319 φησίν γε· φάσκων δ'.

172 φανῆναι: often of the emergence of an avenger: cf. 846, Stes. fr. 219.2 *PMGF* (cited below, 417–27n.), Aesch. *Cho.* 143 φανῆναι . . . τιμάορον, *Eum.* 320 πράκτορες αἵματος αὐτῷ τελέως ἐφάνημεν; also *Tr.* 860–1 ἁ δ' ἀμφίπολος Κύπρις . . . | τῶνδ' ἐφάνη πράκτωρ.

173–84 The chorus's consolation takes on a cosmic aspect: it points to Zeus at the beginning of its song and Hades at its end, with the mighty Orestes standing between them. Electra's response breaks away from this larger vision and insistently returns to reality.

174 τέκνον: 154n.

ἔτι: so Lᵃᶜ. For the metre see 154n.; the majority reading ἔστι is unmetrical. For ἔτι of the permanence of divine power cf. *OC* 623 εἰ Ζεὺς ἔτι Ζεύς, Hom. *Od.* 24.351 Ζεῦ πάτερ, ἦ ῥα ἔτ᾽ ἐστὲ θεοὶ κατὰ μακρὸν Ὄλυμπον. For μέγας predicated of Zeus cf. 209, Bissinger (1966) 67–71.

οὐρανῷ: cf. Pl. *Phaedr.* 246e4 ὁ . . . μέγας ἡγέμων ἐν οὐρανῷ Ζεύς; for the dative without ἐν cf. Pind. *N.* 10.58 οἰκεῖν . . . οὐρανῷ, Hom. *Il.* 4.166 = Hes. *Op.* 18 αἰθέρι ναίων, Moorhouse 86–7, Bruhn §50.1. The unmetrical ἐν of the manuscripts probably represents the normalising of a poetic usage (cf. D. C. C. Young (1965) 255 = Calder and Stern (1970) 105): Willink's attempt to retain it by altering the strophe is unattractive on other grounds (154n.). Hermann's μέγας ἔτ᾽ ἐν affects the metre by making the second syllable of τέκνον long (he puts τέκνον at the end of the preceding colon, for which see 154n.).

175 Ζεύς: 'the reference to Zeus' power is idiomatic in the consolatory context' (Davies on *Tr.* 127, comparing fr. 684 *TrGF*, Hom. *Od.* 4.236–7, 6.188–9).

ὃς ἐφορᾷ πάντα: for Zeus as all-seeing cf. *OC* 1085–6 ἰὼ θεῶν πάνταρχε παντ– | ὄπτα Ζεῦ, Hes. *Op.* 267, Aesch. *Suppl.* 137, *Eum.* 1045, Tr. Adesp. frr. 43, 167a.4, 421, 480, 485, 491, 499.4 *TrGF*. For the all-seeing god see 659n. The verb ἐφοράω denotes 'not just witnessing but supervising or taking an active interest in what one sees' (West (1990) 262): cf. 824, Garvie (1970) 89 n. 8.

176 ᾧ τὸν ὑπεραλγῆ χόλον νέμουσα 'make over to him (sc. Zeus) your grievous anger' (Lloyd-Jones). The chorus advises Electra that the anger which she feels towards her father's killers should be transferred to Zeus, so that he feels it instead. LSJ⁹ s.v. νέμω A I 1 list this instance of the verb alongside others meaning 'deal out, dispense'; but in all these alleged parallels the verb is used to denote the giving of a reward, offering or punishment to someone, which does not apply here. The sense is closer to instances of the verb meaning 'confer, assign, devote' (Chadwick (1996) 204–5) or 'attribuer ce qui est dû' (Laroche (1949) 25): 'wrath against evil-doers is an attribute and a prerogative of Zeus, to whom the injured should leave the task of inflicting retribution' (Jebb).

τόν: demonstrative (166–7n.).

177 The chorus encourages Electra to remember her father, but without the intense pain caused by her constant laments.

ὑπεράχθεο: instead of the regular contracted imperative ὑπεράχθου: cf. *OC* 182 ἕπεο, 227 ὑπέσχεο, Eur. *Andr.* 1225 ὄψεαι (cited by K–B ii. 68 Anm. 3). Absence of contraction in tragedy is especially common in dactylic verse (cf. Lobeck on *Aj.* 421).

COMMENTARY: 121–250

178 χρόνος . . . εὐμαρὴς θεός: for time as a soother of grief cf. fr. 954 *TrGF* χρόνος δ' ἀμαυροῖ πάντα κεῖς λήθην ἄγει, *OC* 7, 437. But as the following lines indicate, there is also a sense that in time Orestes will return to her. Such an appeal seems doomed to failure, however, since 'time and its imperatives of change are in fact precisely what the Sophoclean hero defies' (Knox (1964) 27). The usual sense of εὐμαρής is 'easy to do' (cf. Fraenkel on Aesch. *Ag.* 1326); for the meaning 'easy, gentle' cf. Eur. *Her.* 17–18 συμφορὰς δὲ τὰς ἐμὰς | ἐξευμαρίζων, as well as *facilis* at e.g. Ov. *Fast.* 2.451, *TLL* vi/1 62.28–79.

178–80 γάρ . . . | . . . γάρ: 'γάρ in 178 gives the reason for moderation in grief; γάρ in 180 gives the reason for confidence that vengeance will come' (Russell, *per litteras*); this is preferable to Denniston's view (64 (6)) that 'the healing effect of time, and the possibility of future retribution, are both urged as reasons for calmness'.

180–1 ὁ . . . | . . . ἔχων: this form of predicate describing location appears more appropriate to a description of a deity, and is paralleled by a similar expression denoting Hades in 184. This reinforces the link between Orestes and Hades already conveyed by οὔτε . . . οὔτε: the chorus suggests the power of the brother in whom Electra has placed her trust.

Κρίσα: so Musgrave, followed by Dawe. Ll-J/W follow Hermann in keeping the paradosis,[14] but the ensuing apposition is awkward. For the simple dative of a place name used to denote location see Diggle (1981a) 47. The corruption to the accusative was almost inevitable given the surrounding accusatives; and the confusion of –αι and –αν is common in any case (cf. Meurig Davies (1949); also 683n.). Nauck's Κρίσας (in his third edition, p. 158) is another possibility. For Orestes' stay with Strophius at Crisa see 11–14n., 45n.; Crisa will also be the site of Orestes' 'death' in the chariot race (730). The land was not given over to agricultural use (hence 181 βούνομον . . . ἀκτάν).

182 παῖς Ἀγαμεμνονίδας: cf. Eur. *Or.* 838 Ἀγαμεμνόνιος παῖς, Moorhouse 164.

ἀπερίτροπος 'heedless': cf. Suda α 3046 s.v. (= i. 273.18–19 Adler), where Orestes ἔχει ἐπιστροφὴν καὶ ἐπιμέλειαν ποιεῖται. Jebb compares ἐντρέπομαι, μετατρέπομαι = 'have regard for'.

184 ὁ παρὰ τὸν Ἀχέροντα θεὸς ἀνάσσων: that is, Hades, whose aid Electra has already invoked (110): the chorus's reluctance to name the god contrasts

---

[14] They print Κρῖσαν, probably rightly despite the manuscripts (which have Κρίσαν): cf. Herodian ii. 12.12–14 Lentz, Nonn. *Dion.* 13.128. Hermann refers to Draco Stratonicensis 21.4 (his edition), but this is a 16th century forgery.

156

with Electra's willingness to invoke a whole series of chthonic deities (110–20n.). J. S. Smith (1785) 184 and Campbell see a reference to Agamemnon, but he cannot be described as a θεός.

παρὰ τὸν Ἀχέροντα: 'παρά with accusative is correct in reference to a river, the notion being that his abode extends along its banks' (Jebb on *Ant.* 1123–4); cf. Aesch. *Cho.* 366 παρὰ Σκαμάνδρου πόρον τεθάφθαι, Eur. *Her.* 390 with Wilamowitz.

185 ἐμὲ μέν: after the chorus's proud description of Orestes, Electra emphatically returns to her own miserable state.

For ὁ πολύς with a noun cf. 564, 931, *OC* 87, Aesch. *Ag.* 1456.

186 ἀνέλπιστος: Kaibel and Ll-J/W print –ον (*coni.* Nauck⁴ᵃ). The scholia paraphrase ὁ πλείων με, φησί, βίος ἀπολέλοιπεν μηδέποτε ἐν ἀγαθῇ ἐλπίδι γενομένην (p. 112.20–1 Papageorgius), and this has been taken to support Nauck's conjecture. But since ἀνέλπιστος, if right, could look like a transferred epithet, it would not be surprising if the paraphrase of a scholiast interpreted the word as if it qualified Electra. The scholium thus does not help to determine the text. Most editors retain the paradosis, and rightly: the active sense 'leaving no hope' is unremarkable in an adjective of this sort, and nothing is gained by changing it to the accusative (cf. also Williger (1928) 37). For the form see Fraenkel on Aesch. *Ag.* 649, Harder on Eur. fr. 240.2 *TrGF* = 14.2 Austin.

οὐδ' ἔτ' ἀρκῶ: cf. 119–20.

187 ἄνευ τεκέων: so WaWc, *coni.* Meineke (1863a) 252–3; for the corruption cf. Eur. *Hec.* 475, *Tro.* 201. The reference to childlessness balances ἄτεκνος at 164, just as 188 will balance ἀνύμφευτος in 165. Campbell defends the majority reading τοκέων, claiming that 'her father is dead, and her mother is worse than lost to her', but Dawe (*STS* i. 177) well asks whether Electra would describe both Agamemnon and Clytemnestra with the same word τοκέων. Finkelberg (2003) argues at length for τοκέων, saying Electra laments her lack of parents because without such guardians she suffers a lack of status in the community. But it is difficult to understand κυρίων from τοκέων. Electra might use τοκέων to mean just Agamemnon (cf. 241), but the responsion of theme in the strophe at 164 makes τεκέων by far the likelier alternative.

κατατάκομαι: for τήκω, τήκομαι of strong emotion see Finkelberg (2003) 371–2.

188 ὑπερίσταται: a rarer and stronger alternative to προΐσταμαι, with the ὑπέρ having a similar force to that found in ὑπερμάχεσθαι etc. (so Kaibel, p. 100). It also contains a more literal sense of standing over, as in the idioms whereby a god holds a hand over a city (cf. Hom. *Il.* 4.249, 9.419–20, Solon fr. 4.4 *IEG*, Theogn. 757–8) or else stands over it (cf. Hom. *Il.* 1.37) as a sign of protection.

189 ἔποικος ἀναξία 'a worthless stranger': for ἀναξία Monk (1826) 72 prefers the translation 'undeserving of such treatment', but for the complaint cf. Achilles' ὡς εἴ τιν' ἀτίμητον μετανάστην (Hom. *Il.* 9.648 = 16.59). At Pl. *Leg.* 742a4–5 ἔποικοι are associated with δοῦλοι and μισθωτοί: see further Casevitz (1985) 157. For the absolute use of ἀνάξιος cf. *Phil.* 439.

190 οἰκονομῶ θαλάμους: cf. 262–5, 814–15, 1192, Aesch. *Cho.* 135 κἀγὼ μὲν ἀντίδουλος, Eur. *El.* 1004–5 δούλη . . . ἐκβεβλημένη | δόμων πατρῴων δυστυχεῖς οἰκῶ δόμους, 1008 (to Clytemnestra) αἰχμάλωτόν τοί μ' ἀπῴκισας δόμων. For compound verbs made up of a nominal and verbal stem treated as a simple transitive verb cf. 280, *Tr.* 760–1, Bruhn §52, Diggle (1968) 2, Moorhouse 38. The verb effectively means 'dwell in', and does not in itself convey anything of Electra's misery (cf. Descat (1988) 106). Seaford (1990) 78 claims that θάλαμοι also denotes Electra's bridal chamber and Agamemnon's tomb, but this is far-fetched: Electra is singing about her position in the house (cf. the variant δόμους at Suda οι 72, 73, ν 300 = iv. 619.4, 619.11, 656.3 Adler). For θάλαμοι denoting a house cf. Hutchinson on Pind. *O.* 6.1.

ὧδε: perhaps accompanied by appropriate pointing by the actor (cf. the τάδ' of Eur. *El.* 185, quoted 191 n.).

190–2 μὲν | . . . | . . . δ': for the change from a prepositional phrase to an independent construction in a μὲν . . . δέ clause see Denniston 369 n. 1.

191 ἀεικεῖ σὺν στολᾷ: for Electra's wretched appearance cf. 452, 1177, 1181, Eur. *El.* 184–5 σκέψαι . . . | . . . τρύχη τάδ' ἐμῶν πέπλων. For the disgrace attached to wearing tattered clothes cf. Aesch. *Pers.* 846–8. They are more commonly associated with Euripidean characters (especially in comedy: see Olson on Ar. *Ach.* 412–13), but Philoctetes provides a Sophoclean parallel.

192 κεναῖς δ' ἀμφίσταμαι τραπέζαις: cf. Pind. *O.* 1.50 τραπέζαισι . . . ἀμφί. Most manuscripts have ἀφ' or ἐφ' instead of ἀμφ': for the corruption Dawe, *STS* i. 177–8 compares [Aesch.] *PV* 702 (see Page's apparatus). For this aspect of Electra's privations cf. 265: contrast Chrysothemis' πλουσία | τράπεζα at 361–2. For tables in contexts of poverty cf. Hom. *Od.* 20.259 ὀλίγην τε τράπεζαν (set out for the beggar Odysseus), Eur. *Alc.* 2 θῆσσαν τράπεζαν; also Eur. fr. 670.1–2 *TrGF* βίος δὲ πορφυροῦς θαλάσσιος | οὐκ εὐτράπεζος. One's place at table denotes one's social status: cf. *OR* 1462–4 (Oedipus' daughters were always at table with him), Hom. *Il.* 22.492–8.

193–200 Turning away from its attempts at consolation, the chorus describes the scene of Agamemnon's death. The description is brief and impressionistic. Instead of a connected narrative, vivid details suddenly flash out in the midst of an ominous, troubling atmosphere: the cry at Agamemnon's killing, the dreadful axe which struck the blow. This vagueness makes the picture all the more menacing. Such a description seems far removed from the chorus's earlier moves to encourage and console the heroine: having previously urged her to overcome her grief, it now lingers over a grim account of the event which gave rise to her suffering. But a purpose can be identified in this change of focus. The chorus acknowledges the horror of Agamemnon's death just as much as Electra herself does, and thus establishes its credentials as a friend: its attempted consolation (which returns in the antistrophe) is therefore all the more convincing.

The death of Agamemnon in the *Odyssey* is described on several occasions, with varying degrees of emphasis placed on different aspects of the story according to the poet's purpose in each situation (see Prag (1985) 68–84 for a useful summary). He is killed at a feast (4.531, 4.534–5 ≈ 11.410–11) in a μέγαρον (11.420) alongside his companions (11.388–9, 412–13). The location of this feast is once said to be the house of Aegisthus (11.389). The same is implied at 4.532, where Aegisthus invites (καλέων: cf. 10.231, 17.382, LSJ⁹ s.v. καλέω I 2) Agamemnon to a feast: one does not invite people to dinner at a house other than one's own. But at 3.234 Agamemnon is killed ἐφέστιος, which can only refer to death at his own hearth. This is likely to reflect a trace of an older tradition which the poet has elsewhere altered for his own purposes.

The death of Agamemnon is rarely depicted in archaic and classical art: the surviving examples are collected in Prag (1985) 1–5. Of these only the so-called *Nostoi* bowl (*Nostoi* T2 *EGF* = fr. 10 *PEG* = fr. 10 *GEF*) suggests that Agamemnon was killed at a feast: this may reflect the account from the *Nostoi* in the Epic Cycle (cf. March (1987) 86 n. 35).

S.'s decision to have Agamemnon killed at a feast (cf. 194, 203) thus has good epic precedent. We later learn, with greater precision, that the murder took place in Agamemnon's palace, at the hearth (269–70): although not in accordance with the main tradition in Homer, this too does have a Homeric resonance (cf. *Od.* 3.234). By keeping to the *Odyssey*'s account S. diverges from that of the *Oresteia*, where Clytemnestra kills Agamemnon in his bath (cf. *Ag.* 1108–9, *Cho.* 491, *Eum.* 633, Seaford (1984) 248 n. 12). This version could be an Aeschylean innovation.[15] It is then taken up by Euripides, whose references

---

[15] Seaford (1984) 248 n. 11 claims that the bath is probably not an Aeschylean innovation, since the fatal bath occurs in other myths. But these other myths might just as easily have provided Aeschylus with his inspiration. The Boston crater (324–40n.) was once thought to provide evidence that the death in the bath preceded Aeschylus, but current scholarship is more sceptical: see Prag (1985) 4 and 108 with n. 34.

to it (*El.* 157–8 and *Or.* 367) are brief enough to suggest that it had become the usual account, at least in tragedy. S.'s avoidance of it here reminds us of the distance which separates his treatment of the Orestes myth from that of his tragic predecessor (cf. 77–85n.). For Agamemnon's death at a feast in later authors cf. Tarrant on Sen. *Ag.* 875 ff., Seaford (1984) 247 n. 4.

193–4 οἰκτρά . . . | οἰκτρά: anaphora is a typical feature of laments (88–9n.): cf. especially the repetition at Eur. *El.* 159–62 (also from a description of the death of Agamemnon in the parodos) ἰώ μοι <ἰώ> μοι | πικρᾶς μὲν πελέκεως τομᾶς | σᾶς, πάτερ, πικρᾶς δ᾽ †ἐκ | Τροίας ὁδοῦ βουλᾶς†. The two οἰκτρὰ μὲν . . . | οἰκτρὰ δ᾽ clauses both refer to Agamemnon's death cry (so Schneidewin[1], Kells and (tentatively) March). Jebb (p. 208) claims that the phrasing μὲν . . . | . . . δ᾽ denotes two separate occasions. But as Denniston 370 makes clear, the antithesis conveyed by μὲν . . . δέ need not be so strong, 'particularly . . . when the same word is repeated before μὲν and δέ'. The two clauses can refer to the same action (cf. Hom. *Il.* 1.288 πάντων μὲν κρατέειν ἐθέλει, πάντεσσι δ᾽ ἀνάσσειν), or represent the same action as considered from two different perspectives (cf. *Tr.* 229 ἀλλ᾽ εὖ μὲν ἵγμεθ᾽, εὖ δὲ προσφωνούμεθα). The latter pattern fits our case. The clauses emphasise two horrific aspects of Agamemnon's death: he was murdered (i) as he returned home (193) and (ii) at a feast.

Homeric parallels support this interpretation. Agamemnon is frequently said to be killed at his νόστος: cf. *Od.* 1.36 τὸν δ᾽ ἔκτανε νοστήσαντα, 11.384 ἐν νόστῳ δ᾽ ἀπόλοντο κακῆς ἰότητι γυναικός, 24.96 ἐν νόστῳ γάρ μοι Ζεὺς μήσατο λυγρὸν ὄλεθρον. An audience hearing of a pitiful cry at a νόστος in this context would thus think of Agamemnon's death cry. Sense and syntax thus both point in the direction of this interpretation.

Jebb took the first clause to denote the moment of Agamemnon's return, with the following clause (194–6) referring to the killing which follows during the feast that evening (cf. J. S. Smith (1785) 193–4, Burton (1980) 192, Davidson (1988) 52). But then the meaning of οἰκτρὰ . . . αὐδά is not immediately apparent. A defeated monarch may be welcomed home with lamentation (cf. e.g. Aesch. *Pers.* 935–40), but Agamemnon returns after not a defeat, but a glorious victory. The cry can only look forward to his coming destruction. It must therefore be uttered by someone who is aware that his death is imminent (which rules out Agamemnon and Electra), and who has no motive to keep that information secret (which rules out Aegisthus and Clytemnestra). The only candidate, as Jebb saw, is Cassandra. Her lengthy cries and laments at Aesch. *Ag.* 1072–1330 take place before we hear the king's death-cries, and could well be described as an οἰκτρὰ . . . αὐδά.

There is, however, no mention of Cassandra in the text, here or elsewhere (584–94n.). A reference to her here thus depends on an allusion to Aeschylus'

Agamemnon generated by the three words οἰκτρά ... νόστοις αὐδά. No linguistic similarity assists the allusion. At Hom. *Od.* 11.421–2 οἰκτροτάτην δ' ἤκουσα ὄπα Πριάμοιο θυγατρός, | Κασσάνδρης (cited by Jebb) Cassandra's pitiable cry takes place as she is killed alongside Agamemnon, not before his murder. This could only make the Aeschylean allusion still more difficult to grasp, especially as in the other details of Agamemnon's killing S. stands closer to Homer than to Aeschylus.

It could be objected that an oblique reference to Cassandra fits with the obscure language of the parodos. The piece is indeed impressionistic, with vivid details taking the place of connected narrative (193–200n.). But nowhere else are we in doubt as to what is being described. Under Jebb's interpretation, we are faced with a phrase more baffling than mysterious.

νόστοις: a temporal dative denoting the occasion, on the analogy of νυκτί, νουμηνίᾳ etc. (cf. K–G i. 445): ἐν in the following parallel clause helps the construction (cf. Kiefner (1964) 74–5).

194 ἐν κοίταις πατρῴαις: κοίτη can denote either the state or the place of lying (cf. Barrett on Eur. *Hipp.* 131–4). Here either 'at your father's couch' or 'as your father lay there' (Lloyd-Jones) would be possible. The latter provides a neater parallel with νόστοις in the preceding line. The word does not seem to be used elsewhere for reclining at dinner, but this must be its sense here. Campbell understands the phrase to mean 'where he lay in death' (cf. Aesch. *Ag.* 1494 = 1518). But Agamemnon cannot cry out if he is already dead; and the axe blow described in 195–6 must be the stroke which kills him, not an additional stroke directed at a corpse. At Eur. *El.* 158 Agamemnon is killed κοίτᾳ ἐν οἰκτροτάτᾳ θανάτου, though there the reference is to a bath rather than a feast.

195 ὅτε οἱ: so Hermann for transmitted ὅτε σοι. For the hiatus cf. *Tr.* 650 ἃ δέ οἱ, Wackernagel (1916b) 109, Maas (1929) 29 = (1962) 82. Campbell supports the paradosis on the grounds that it 'marks that Electra was the chief sufferer from all that happened'. The motif whereby the mourner endures physical torment similar to that of the actual sufferer is not unknown to ancient literature (cf. Luke 2.35). But in a description of the last moments of Agamemnon such a reference would be confusing and inept.

196 For γενύων denoting the blade of an axe cf. 485, *Phil.* 1205, Gronewald (1975) 113, Seaford on Eur. *Cycl.* 395.

197 δόλος ἦν ὁ φράσας, ἔρος ὁ κτείνας: both δόλος and ἔρος are frequently associated with the murder of Agamemnon, the former from Homer onwards (124n.), the latter first in Pindar (562n.). Wakefield's transposition ((1789–95)

161

ii. 118–19) must be taken seriously, and is in fact adopted by Nauck⁴ᵃ and Wecklein¹: after all, ἔρος provided the motive for the crime (cf. φράσας, Ov. *Met.* 8.90 *suasit amor facinus*), whereas δόλος was employed in its performance (cf. κτείνας). Kaibel defends the paradosis on the grounds that 'die Liebe eine ἀφραδία ist, die nicht überlegt sondern leidenschaftlich handelt' (p. 102): though as calculation is denoted not by φράζω but by φράζεσθαι this point has little force. Nevertheless, the paradosis is probably right. ἔρος goes naturally with κτείνας, since Greek thought commonly associated erotic passion with violence (cf. 561 n.). So here ἔρος was the root cause of the act and hence can be said to have performed the killing (compare Clytemnestra's claim at 528). By providing the means δόλος 'pointed the way' to how this killing could be achieved.

ἔρος is metrically guaranteed at Hom. *Il.* 14.315 and in the formula ἐξ ἔρον ἕντο (*Il.* 1.469 etc.). ἔρως occurs twice in the manuscript tradition (3.442, 14.294), but on each occasion ἔρος would also fit the metre. Hesiod has guaranteed ἔρος or ἔρον five times: in fr. 298 M–W ἔρως is transmitted, but here too ἔρος would be metrically acceptable. ἔρος is also the usual form in the *Hymns* (but 4.449 has guaranteed ἔρωτα). Both ἔρος and ἔρως are found in the lyric and elegiac poets. ἔρος is not found elsewhere in S. (or in Aeschylus, though Euripides has it): here it probably forms another of the epic features which characterise this section of the lyric.

See Diggle on Eur. *Pha.* 99 = fr. 773.56 *TrGF* (augmented at (1996c) 195) for the solemn effect created by 'the . . . metrical correspondence of the two asyndetic cola, fortified by internal and concluding rhyme'. Antithetical cola are often found in ritual laments: cf. Thomson (1953) 82–3, Alexiou (2002) 234 n. 50.

198 δεινὰν δεινῶς: for the repetition cf. *Phil.* 166, 1369, Thesleff (1954) 195, Gygli-Wyss (1966) 39–40. Reiske's proposal –ἀν –ῶν ((1753) 13; attributed by Dawe³ to Diggle) is possible, but no improvement.

προφυτεύσαντες: for φυτεύω in the sense 'give rise to (something unpleasant)' cf. *Aj.* 953 φυτεύει πῆμα, *OR* 873 ὕβρις φυτεύει τύραννον, Hom. *Il.* 15.134 κακὸν μέγα πᾶσι φυτεῦσαι, *Od.* 2.165 (≈ 17.82) φόνον καὶ κῆρα φυτεύει, LSJ⁹ s.v. I 3. A temporal sense would not be appropriate here for the προ– prefix, which probably means something like the English 'bringing *forth*': cf. *Othello* 1.3 *ad fin.*'Hell and Night | Must bring this monstrous birth to the world's light'.

199 μορφάν: 'the scene of the murder, visualized as a picture' (Russell, *per litteras*); cf. LSJ⁹ s.v. μορφή 2 'appearance, form, fashion'. For Jebb, the phrase denotes 'the act of murder, embodied in the image of a supernatural ἀλάστωρ', for Kaibel, 'das Schreckengespenst des Mordes selbst, die Erinys' (p. 102). However, there is no parallel for (δεινή) μορφή denoting an Alastor, Erinys or other supernatural being: contrast the monstrous connotations often applied to the word φάσμα (see Davies's *Trachiniae*, p. 142 n. 17). Others more prosaically see a reference to Agamemnon's corpse (so Schneidewin[1]): but προφυτεύσαντες can hardly denote the changing of a living body into a dead one. No other emendation commends itself: Wakefield's μομφάν (1789–95) iii. 119 would be weak.

εἴτ' οὖν θεὸς εἴτε βροτῶν: 'the chorus [is] . . . doubting whether so horrible a crime could be merely of human contrivance' (March). θεός does not imply that the deed enjoyed divine support: cf. *Aj.* 243–4 κακὰ δεννάζων ῥήμαθ', ἃ δαίμων | κοὐδεὶς ἀνδρῶν ἐδίδαξεν, where the κακότης of Ajax's words is stressed rather than annulled by their allegedly divine origin. Cf. also Aesch. *Ag.* 1500–3 (Clytemnestra speaking) φανταζόμενος δὲ γυναικὶ νεκροῦ | τοῦδ' ὁ παλαιὸς δριμὺς ἀλάστωρ | Ἀτρέως χαλεποῦ θοινατῆρος | τόνδ' ἀπέτεισεν with Fraenkel on 1501: 'she is not making excuses for herself . . . The deed now appears to her so frightful that, at least at this moment, she is convinced that only the spirit of vengeance, Alastor, can have done it.' For the polar expression 'divinity or mortal' Kemmer (1903) 199 compares *OR* 42–3, Aesch. *Cho.* 119.

For οὖν in the first member of an εἴτε . . . εἴτε expression cf. 560, *OR* 1049, K–G ii. 159, Denniston 418–19, Fraenkel on Aesch. *Ag.* 491. According to K–G οὖν is emphatic, but Denniston rightly prefers Bäumlein's view that it denotes indifference ('whether, in point of fact, . . .'). The partitive genitive denoting the second of two alternatives is paralleled at *Aj.* 243–4 (cited above), *OR* 1258–9 δαιμόνων δείκνυσί τις· | οὐδεὶς γὰρ ἀνδρῶν κτλ., Diggle (1969) 45 n. 2 ≈ (1994) 17 n. 13 (though in each case, apart from our passage, there is a τις or οὐδείς to make the construction smoother).

200 ὁ ταῦτα πράσσων: for the 'timeless' present participle see Garvie on Aesch. *Cho.* 327.

201–12 The chorus's words cause Electra's succession of exclamations: its description of her father's death has caused her great pain (cf. 1246–7n.). She recalls her opening words (86–93) by invoking day before then describing the sorrows brought by night. But whereas there she was describing the continual process of suffering which she endures every day and night, her reference now is to that single day and night which brought death to Agamemnon, and which signalled the beginning of her own grief. For sensitive remarks on the 'perfective' and 'imperfective' aspects of this section and the lyric as a whole see Hutchinson (1999) 52–3.

201–2 ὦ πασᾶν κείνα πλέον ἀμέρα | ἐλθοῦσ' ἐχθίστα δή μοι: the construction begins as a comparative intensified by πασᾶν (cf. Thesleff (1954) 129–30). But instead of the expected positive form of the adjective to follow πλέον, we instead meet with a superlative. For the intensification Thesleff (1954) 171–2 compares *Phil.* 631, Eur. *Alc.* 790, *Med.* 1323. But each of these instances involves a superlative qualified by another superlative (e.g. πλεῖστον ἐχθίστης): the unusual pattern here may be still more emphatic.

203 ὦ νύξ: for addresses to night see Wagener (1931) 96 with n. 69. For other references to disastrous nights in tragedy see Ferri on [Sen.] *Oct.* 18–20.

δείπνων: for the plural see Braswell on Pind. *P.* 4.31(a); for Agamemnon's death at dinner see 193–200n. Kaibel (p. 103) sees a reference to the Thyestean banquet: but this is not mentioned elsewhere, and would disrupt the progression of thought.

204 ἔκπαγλ' ἄχθη: the variant ἔκπαγλα πάθη shows the substitution of the more familiar word. The variant is also metrically unappealing, as it breaks the exact responsion which characterises most of the anapaests of this lyric, and introduces an uncontracted biceps into a sequence of metra which otherwise avoids them.

205 τοῖς: *coni.* Johnson (his edition, p. 223). Some editors defend transmitted τούς as a relative (cf. Moorhouse 267–9) referring to ἄχθη but drawn into the case of θανάτους, which stands in apposition to ἄχθη. Johnson's simple change replaces this awkward construction with a local dative referring to δεῖπνα in 203. θανάτους in 206 facilitated the corruption.

ἴδε: for the omission of the augment see 147n.

206 θανάτους ἀκεῖς: is probably a poetic plural for singular: cf. 779, Denniston on Eur. *El.* 484, Bers (1984) 41–2, Diggle (1977a) 113 = (1994) 156. There may also be a reference to the killing of Agamemnon's followers at the banquet, as in the *Odyssey* (cf. 193–200n.). For the adjective used of Agamemnon's death and for its spelling see 102n.

διδύμαιν χειροῖν 'attempts on his life by two pairs of hands' (Diggle (1977a) 113 = (1994) 156): cf. Pind. *P.* 2.9 χερὶ διδύμᾳ. For the feminine dual ending see 977n.

207–8 αἳ τὸν ἐμὸν εἷλον βίον | πρόδοτον, αἳ μ' ἀπώλεσαν: Electra speaks of herself as 'betrayed' and 'destroyed' by Aegisthus and Clytemnestra, thus marking her self-association with her father's suffering. This is common in lamentation for the dead (cf. 847n.). For the asyndeton with repetition of the relative pronoun see 113–14n.

208 αἳ μ' ἀπώλεσαν: related to the motif 'you have killed me by your death', for which see 808n.

209 οἷς: i.e. the persons represented by the 'hands' in 206. For μέγας applied to Zeus see 174n.

210 For the π alliteration cf. 504-5, 544-5, 639-42, 729, 1463, *Phil.* 927 ὦ πῦρ σὺ καὶ πᾶν δεῖμα καὶ πανουργίας, Heracl. D–K 22 B 53 (= i. 162.7-9), Pind. *P.* 1.23-4, Fraenkel on Aesch. *Ag.* 268. Here the alliteration and *figura etymologica* πάθεα παθεῖν heighten the rhetoric (cf. Slings (1993) 28).

211–12 μηδέ ποτ' ἀγλαΐας ἀποναίατο | τοιάδ' ἀνύσαντες ἔργα: cf. Hom. *Od.* 17.244-5 (Odysseus to Melanthius, speaking of himself) τῷ κέ τοι ἀγλαΐας γε διασκεδάσειεν ἁπάσας, | τὰς νῦν ὑβρίζων φορέεις.

211 ἀποναίατο: Lautensach (1916) 114-15 counts twenty-nine instances of the 3rd plural in –ατο in tragedy and comedy. Wackernagel (1916a) 251-3 = (1916b) 91-3 argues that these are likely to have been the original Attic forms, with –ντο being generalised from other historic 3rd plural endings during the fifth century.

212 ἀνύσαντες: so Groeneboom[1] for manuscript ἀνύσαντες: on the orthography see West's Teubner Aeschylus, p. xxx.

213–20 The chorus rebukes Electra here and at 233-5 not because of ethical objections to her lamentation, but because of its concern that her behaviour will lead her into trouble with the authorities (cf. MacLeod (2001) 47-8, with doxography).

213 φράζου μὴ πόρσω φωνεῖν 'be advised to say no more' (Jebb). For admonitory φράζου cf. 383, Hom. *Il.* 5.440 φράζεο, Τυδεΐδη, καὶ χάζεο, West on Hes. *Op.* 367 (adding *ib.* 448, fr. 283.2 M–W). Morstadt's conjecture φώνει ((1864) 15) has some attractions. A subordinate clause after the imperative of φράζομαι usually takes ὅπως with the future (cf. *Aj.* 1040-1) or (when that clause is negative) μή with the subjunctive (cf. Hom. *Il.* 16.446, Theocr. 6.13). But verbs of precaution can take an infinitive, with or without μή (cf. LSJ[9] s.v. φυλάσσω C II 3, also Hom. *Il.* 19.401 φράζεσθε σαωσέμεν), so the change is not necessary. Furthermore, two imperatives in asyndeton would be too blunt (as in Lloyd-Jones's translation 'take care, speak no more!'). By subordinating the request that Electra keep quiet, the command appears more polite, which would suit the attitude of this chorus.

πόρσω is the majority reading. πρόσω would not satisfy the metre, whereas πόρρω is limited to prose and comedy. πόρσω is corrupted to πρόσω or πόρρω in at least some manuscripts in all its appearances in tragedy (*OC* 178, 181, 226, Eur. *Alc.* 911, *Her.* 752, *Tro.* 189, *Ion* 796, *Ba.* 392, [Eur.] *Rhes.* 482, and also Pind. *O.* 10.55, Aratus 298): see further Diggle on Eur. *Pha.* 7 = fr. 772.2 *TrGF.*

214–16 This punctuation, found in LZc and the **a** group (*teste* Kopff (1993) 157), and first adopted by Bergk, gives two powerful questions instead of the rambling sentiment offered by the unpunctuated text. The first means 'do you not understand in whose power the present lies?': Lloyd-Jones renders 'do you not understand from what beginnings the present came?', but the suggestion of hostile authority fits with the preceding warning to avoid excess of speech, and is taken up in 219–20. Pearson understands οἰκείας . . . | . . . ᾳκῶς as a statement, but this is less forceful.

214 γνώμαν ἴσχεις: periphrasis for γιγνώσκεις: cf. *Phil.* 837, 853, 30n.

216 ᾳκῶς: for the orthography see 102n.

217 For τι as an intensifier cf. *Tr.* 497 with Davies, Dem. 18.159, Plut. *Cim.* 1.2, LSJ⁹ s.v. τις A II 8; perhaps *Phil.* 838 (*suppl.*).

218 τίκτουσ᾿: often followed by an abstract (cf. 235, fr. 663 *TrGF* τίκτουσι γάρ τοι καὶ νόσους δυσθυμίαι, Eur. fr. 1071 *TrGF*); for its occurrence with πόλεμους cf. Eur. fr. 340.3 *TrGF* (Κύπρις) τίκτει πόλεμον, Pl. *Resp.* 547a4 (ἀνομοιότης) ἀεὶ τίκτει πόλεμον καὶ ἔχθραν.

219–20 τάδε—τοῖς δυνατοῖς | οὐκ ἐριστά—τλᾶθι: so Jackson (1955) 138, adopting τάδε from DHO and τλᾶθι from Wakefield (1789–95) iii. 35–6; τὰ δέ and πλάθειν are the majority forms. τλάθειν in Zc⁸ may reflect the truth. The syntax of the paradosis is clumsy, as Jebb's translation brings out ('but those things cannot be waged with the powerful, so that one should come into conflict with them').¹⁶ Contrast the clarity of Hom. *Od.* 18.38–9 ἐρίζετον ἀλλήλοιϊν | χερσὶ μαχέσσασθαι: contrast also Pind. *N.* 10.72 χαλεπὰ δ᾿ ἔρις ἀνθρώποις ὁμιλεῖν κρεσσόνων, where the infinitive follows χαλεπά more naturally than it would ἐριστά. Dawe's τῶν δυνατῶν (in his first edition) is an improvement on the paradosis, and may be right: the corruption could easily have arisen from a desire to provide a dative with ἐρίζειν. But the Wakefield – Jackson conjecture is recommended by its greater simplicity. Isolated as it was by a parenthesis, τλᾶθι was especially vulnerable to corruption (cf. Diggle (1981 a) 115–16, (1994) 429 n. 40); for π / τ confusion see Friis Johansen and Whittle on Aesch. *Suppl.*

---

¹⁶ Jackson's additional criticism of the alleged weakness of πλάθειν is unwarranted: cf. Hdt. 9.74.1 ὅκως πελάσειε . . . τοῖσι πολεμίοισι, S. *Tr.* 1093 λέοντ᾿, ἄπλατον θρέμμα, Pind. *P.* 1.21 ἀπλάτου πυρός, fr. 93.1–2 S–M ἄπλατον . . . | Τυφῶνα, Bacchyl. 5.62 ἀπλάτοι᾿ Ἐχίδνας, 13.51–2.

100–1. Hor. *Ser.* 1.9.42–3 *ego, ut contendere durum est* | *cum victore, sequor*, cited by Wakefield, provides a close parallel in sense and style. For the impersonal predicative use of the neuter plural adjective ἐριστά see Moorhouse 12. For the idea that one should not struggle against the powerful cf. 340, 396, 1014, 1465, Hom. *Il.* 7.111 μηδ᾽ ἔθελ᾽ ἐξ ἔριδος σε᾽ (*coni.*) ἀμείνονι φωτὶ μάχεσθαι.

221 δείν᾽ ἐν δεινοῖς ἠναγκάσθην: so Pearson. The paradosis ἐν δεινοῖς ἠναγκάσθην ἐν δεινοῖς is scarcely sense; it also needs to lose two long syllables for the responsion. Pearson's text solves these difficulties while giving an idiomatic juxtaposition δειν– δειν–; it also conveniently places ἠναγκάσθην in a single anapaestic metron. The word δείν᾽ could easily have dropped off at the beginning of the colon. For these reasons Pearson's text is superior to δείν᾽ ἠναγκάσθην ἐν δεινοῖς, conjectured by Wolff¹. Kaibel's ἐν δεινοῖς δείν᾽ ἠναγκάσθην (his commentary, p. 105; printed by Ll-J/W) has similar advantages to Pearson's conjecture, but the postulated corruption is not quite as easy to explain.

Other solutions are less satisfactory. Brunck's δεινοῖς ἠναγκάσθην, δεινοῖς (in his 1786 edition) is appealingly neat, and is printed by Schneidewin¹, Jebb and Dawe. But it throws all the emphasis onto the external compulsion applied to Electra, whereas the context (especially 222) requires a reference to the terrible acts to which she is driven (so rightly Willink (2003) 78). Triclinius's ἐν δεινοῖς ἠναγκάσθην δή shows the Byzantine scholar resorting to one of his favourite particles.

The term ἀνάγκη 'is applicable to any physical, legal or moral force to which resistance is shameful, painful, perilous or for any other reason difficult' (Dover (1973) 65 = (1987a) 145); it is 'much more the compulsion imposed on men in concrete circumstances than predestined rigid necessity' (Wilamowitz (1899–1906) ii. 26, translated by Fraenkel on Aesch. *Ag.* 218).

222 ἔξοιδ᾽: the ἐκ- verbal prefix is rather a mannerism of S. (Wilamowitz on Eur. *Her.* 155); for this verb see Tsitsoni (1963) 33.

ὀργά: intense suffering is often accompanied by anger directed against its cause: cf. Eur. *Med.* 176 etc., [Sen.] *Oct.* 47–8 *nec graves luctus valet* | *ira coacta tegere*. Chrysothemis later encourages Electra to restrain her ὀργά (1011).

223 ἀλλ᾽ . . . γάρ: for this combination 'marking the contrast between what is irrelevant or subsidiary and what is vital, primary or decisive' cf. 595, 619, Denniston 101–2.

223–4 οὐ σχήσω | ταύτας ἀχάς: so Blaydes¹: ἄτας codd. ἄτη can denote either the state of infatuation, or the ruin that arises from that infatuation. The latter sense is appropriate at 215 and 235: neither is appropriate here.

Lloyd-Jones translates the paradosis 'I shall not hold back from this ruinous action', but the word cannot have this meaning. We rather need Electra to say 'I will not stop my lamentation' (cf. Jebb's 'I will never curb these frenzied plaints', although he prints the paradosis), a sense which Blaydes's conjecture provides at the cost of changing a single letter. The presence of ἄτη nearby in 215 and 235 (bis) encouraged the corruption.

225 ὄφρα . . . ἔχῃ: for the omission of ἄν cf. Aj. 555, Phil. 764–5, K–G ii. 449–50 Anm. 4. ὄφρα occurs elsewhere in tragedy only at Aesch. Cho. 360, Eum. 339: in both of these cases the initial syllable must be short.

226 τίνι 'in whose eyes', 'in the judgment of what person' (Jebb): for the dative cf. Ant. 904 καίτοι σ' ἐγὼ 'τίμησα τοῖς φρονοῦσιν εὖ, K–G i. 421–2, Wilamowitz on Eur. Her. 1413. Moorhouse 82 follows Kaibel (p. 105) in preferring 'from whom could I hear a suitable word', comparing Hom. Il. 16.515–16 δύνασαι δὲ σὺ πάντοσ' ἀκούειν | ἀνέρι κηδομένῳ: but there the dative is associated with that found with verbs of obeying (cf. Chantraine (1942–53) ii. 70).

228 τίνι φρονοῦντι καίρια; ea sentiens quae res ipsa postulat (Dawe, adapted): cf. Race (1981) 208–9. For the appeal to an intelligent observer cf. Simon. fr. 581.1 PMG τίς κεν αἰνήσειε νόῳ πίσυνος . . .;

229 ἄνετε 'is more than ἐᾶτε [135], since it implies relaxing a strain' (Jebb, comparing 721 and Ant. 1101).

230 ἄλυτα: cf. the verb λύω in similar contexts (939n.).
κεκλήσεται: 'they must be permanently accounted such' (Jebb). Ruijgh (1976) = (1991–6) i. 701–63 describes the 'valeur permansive' possessed by the perfect passive of καλέω (cf. especially (1976) 376–83 = (1991–6) i. 744–51): cf. 366, 1089, Phil. 85. For the confident future cf. Aesch. Eum. 174 τὸν οὐκ ἐκλύσεται.

231 ἐκ καμάτων ἀποπαύσομαι: for ἐκ cf. 291, 987, Eur. Med. 46 ἐκ τροχῶν πεπαυμένοι, El. 1108, fr. 105.2 TrGF, Ar. Ran.1531, Hermesianax fr. 7.46 CA ἐκ παντὸς παυσάμενος καμάτου. Reiske's ἀκαμάτων ((1753) 13–14; cf. 164) leaves ἀποπαύσομαι uncomfortably isolated.

232 ἀνάριθμος . . . θρήνων: for the syntax cf. Tr. 247 ἡμερῶν ἀνήριθμον, OR 179; 36n.

233–50 The intensity of Electra's refusals to give way leads the chorus to reassert its fundamental goodwill (233–4), as if anxious that the argument should not become a fully-fledged confrontation. These remarks look forward to the beginning of the next episode, where the chorus yields to Electra's defiance and offers to go along with her wishes. Electra reacts to the chorus here with typical energy: three rhetorical questions (236–8) and two negative wishes (239–44) follow each other in quick succession as she distances herself from the suggestion that she might moderate her lamentation. The lyric ends with a powerful closing statement (245–50) which sums up her position and the values for which she stands.

233 ἀλλ' οὖν follows the rejection of a suggestion, usually introducing a more moderate proposal: here 'well, if you cannot heal your sorrows, at least forbear from making them worse' (Denniston 443). Cf. 1035, *Ant.* 84 ἀλλ' οὖν προμη-νύσῃς γε τοῦτο μηδενί (following Antigone's rejection of Ismene's advice to abandon the plan), Bruhn §146.II.

εὐνοίᾳ γ': the giver of advice often emphasises his good intentions: cf. Head-lam on Herod. 1.66, West on Hes. *Op.* 286.

234 μάτηρ ὡσεί τις πιστά: maternal similes usually emphasise the tenderness and care of the *comparandum*: cf. e.g. Hom. *Il.* 4.130–1, Simon. fr. 519.92 col. i. 6–7 *PMG*, Lyr. Adesp. fr. 929(g).3 *PMG*, Ap. Rh. 1.268–9.[17] For the parental mantle assumed by the giver of advice cf. Theogn. 1049–50 σοὶ δ' ἐγὼ οἷά τε παιδὶ πατὴρ ὑποθήσομαι αὐτός | ἐσθλά, Heliod. 4.5.7 οὐχὶ πατήρ εἰμί σοι τὴν ἡλικίαν, καὶ πλέον τὴν εὔνοιαν; In this case the comparison has special force, since Electra's own mother is the last person who would offer her consolation or advice. The adjective πιστά, not elsewhere found as an epithet for μήτηρ, brings out this implicit contrast between the chorus and Clytemnestra.

For redundant τις in comparisons see 107n. For ὡσεί in tragedy see Rappold (1876) 33.

235 μὴ τίκτειν σ' ἄταν ἄταις 'I dissuade thee from adding misery to miseries' (Jebb). For the polyptoton cf. Aesch. *Cho.* 403–4 ἄτην ἑτέραν ἐπάγουσαν ἐπ' ἄτῃ with Garvie, Kannicht on Eur. *Hel.* 366, K–G i. 444 Anm. 4, Schwyzer (1940) 14 = (1983) 454, Gygli-Wyss (1966) 75 with n. 4. ἄταις is a 'dative of what is affected, or added to' (Moorhouse 85). Kaibel (p. 107) takes it to be instrumental (cf. Lloyd-Jones's translation 'telling you not to create misery by means of misery'): but the *Choephori* parallel cited above, among others, tells against this. For the verb see 218n. For the advice 'don't make your troubles worse' see Medda (1983) 87 with n. 194.

[17] S. *Tr.* 526 ἐγὼ δὲ μάτηρ μὲν οἷα φράζω is sometimes compared with this passage: but it is hopelessly corrupt, and not in a paraenetic context.

236 For καί in an indignant question cf. 883, *Aj.* 462–3, Denniston 311 (ii)a.

κακότατος: i.e. the wickedness of the murder of Agamemnon. The word is usually taken to refer to Electra's own wretchedness (so e.g. Σ p. 116.4 Papageorgius, Jebb, Lloyd-Jones). But in countering the chorus's requests for moderation Electra must cite the reason for this immoderation. Her own physical torments are a consequence, not a cause, of her perpetual lamentation. This interpretation also fits better with the two succeeding rhetorical questions, which stress the importance of remembering her father, not the extent of her own sufferings. For the thought Campbell compares *Antony and Cleopatra*, 4.15.4 'But comforts we despise; our size of sorrow, | Proportional to our cause, must be as great | As that which makes it.'

ἔφυ = ἔστι: cf. 1250, Bruhn §231.I.

238 ἐν τίνι τοῦτ᾽ ἔβλαστ᾽ ἀνθρώπων; 'Who among men has such an instinct?' (Lloyd-Jones).

239 μήτ᾽ εἴην ἔντιμος τούτοις: for the sense cf. Hdt. 9.79.2 ἐγὼ δὲ . . . μήτε Αἰγινήτῃσι ἄδοιμι μήτε τοῖσι ταῦτα ἀρέσκεται, ἀποχρᾷ δέ μοι Σπαρτιήτῃσι ἀρεσκόμενον ὅσια . . . ποιέειν; also *Ant.* 373–5 μήτ᾽ ἐμοὶ παρέστιος | γένοιτο μήτ᾽ ἴσον φρονῶν | ὃς τάδ᾽ ἔρδοι.

240–1 μήτ᾽, εἴ τῳ πρόσκειμαι χρηστῷ, | ξυνναίοιμ᾽ εὔκηλος 'never may I live contentedly with any good thing I may have' (Lloyd-Jones).

For πρόσκειμαι in the sense 'be bound up with, involved in' cf. 1040, Eur. fr. 418.2 *TrGF* κακοῖς γὰρ οὐ σὺ πρόσκεισαι μόνη; also Theogn. 320 τολμᾷ δ᾽ ἔν τε κακοῖς κείμενος ἔν τ᾽ ἀγαθοῖς.

ξυνναίοιμ᾽: ξυν– because the sense is ξὺν ἐκείνῳ τῷ χρηστῷ: for 'dwelling with' a good thing as a possessive idiom cf. Pl. *Resp.* 587c2–3 ἡδοναῖς συνοικεῖ, *Phileb.* 63d3; also 599–600n.

εὔκηλος: De Marco (1937) 73 [= 177] recovered εὔζηλος from the scholia: he rendered the text with this 'sehr beachtenswerte Variante' (Maas (1938) 200) as *neque ego in honore apud hos sim, nec si quid boni mihi est hoc fruar a ceteris ob praeclaram rem invidiata.* Hesych. ε 6812 (= ii. 224 Latte) εὔζηλος· ἐπὶ καλῷ ζηλουμένη provides a little support for the reading, as the nominative singular of this adjective is not found elsewhere, and the feminine gloss suits. Nevertheless, the reading of the manuscripts should probably stand, though on grounds of sense rather than authority. εὔζηλος would denote the objective fact of being envied. εὔκηλος, on the other hand, can have a bitter and reproachful tone, which makes it the more appropriate here (cf. Hom. *Od.* 3.263; also 825n. on ἔκηλος): Electra scornfully rejects the ignoble ease into which the chorus would lead her. This adjective occurs elsewhere in tragedy at Aesch. *Sept.* 238, 590 (metrically guaranteed over ἔκηλος), Eur. *IA* 644.

241–2 γονέων | ἐκτίμους: proleptic: 'so as to dishonour my father'. An individual's concern with τιμή did not end with his life (cf. 355–6, Aesch. *Cho.* 356–7, 484–5). The ἐκ here has the function of an alpha-privative: for negative compounds taking a genitive see 36n.

Lloyd-Jones prints Morstadt's conjecture γονέως ((1864) 16) in his Loeb. In *Second Thoughts* Ll-J/W note the difficulty of the transmitted plural for singular given that 'Electra's relations with her two parents are so diverse'. But there are parallels for plural words for 'parent' being used to describe only one of Agamemnon or Clytemnestra, so no change is necessary (cf. 146n.).

242–3 πτέρυγας | ὀξυτόνων γόων: for the image cf. the Homeric ἔπεα πτερόεντα (*Il.* 1.201 etc.); also Theogn. 237–8, Pind. *I.* 5.63 πτερόεντα . . . ὕμνον. For the winged lament cf. 'va pensiero, sull' ali dorate' from Act 3 of Verdi's *Nabucco*.

245–50 For the sentiment cf. *OR* 895–6 εἰ γὰρ αἱ τοιαίδε πράξεις τίμιαι, | τί δεῖ με χορεύειν;

245 γᾶ τε καὶ οὐδὲν ὤν: cf. Eur. fr. 532 *TrGF* κατθανὼν δὲ πᾶς ἀνὴρ | γῆ καὶ σκιά, fr. 839.8–9 *TrGF* χωρεῖ δ' ὀπίσω | τὰ μὲν ἐκ γαίας φύντ' εἰς γαῖαν, *Suppl.* 531–6, Hom. *Il.* 24.54, 7.99, Theogn. 878, Müller (1965) 167–73. The two expressions, tightly bound together as they are, must be synonymous: this rules out Moorhouse's translation of οὐδὲν ὤν as 'being of no account, worthless' ((1965) 35). For the metaphorical use of that phrase see 677n.

οὐδὲν ὤν is found in the protasis because the phrase is an attribute, not a predicate, and in such cases the negative used is regularly οὐ (cf. Moorhouse (1948), (1965) 135 n. 1). The following part of the protasis, by contrast, contains the expected negative μή, because it does negate δώσουσι, whereas οὐδέν did not negate κείσεται (cf. Moorhouse 321–2). For the neuter used for a person in such expressions cf. 1129, 1166.

247 πάλιν: often found in association with retributory justice: cf. 1420, *OR* 100–1 φόνῳ φόνον πάλιν | λύοντας, Hom. *Od.* 1.379 παλίντιτα ἔργα.

248 ἀντιφόνους: for the ἀντι- prefix in contexts of retribution cf. Archil. fr. 126.2 *IEG*, Aesch. *Sept.* [1049], *Cho.* 121, 144, 274, 310–13, *Eum.* 464, 982, S. *Phil.* 1156.

249–50 ἔρροι τὰν Αἰδὼς | ἁπάντων τ' Εὐσέβεια θνατῶν: the departure of Aidos from the earth is sometimes represented as an act which has already occurred (cf. Eur. *Med.* 439–40 βέβακε δ' ὅρκων χάρις, οὐδ' ἔτ' αἰδὼς | Ἑλλάδι τᾷ μεγάλᾳ μένει, αἰθερία δ' ἀνέπτα, Theogn. 291–2 αἰδὼς μὲν γὰρ ὄλωλεν, ἀναιδείη δὲ καὶ ὕβρις | νικήσασα δίκην γῆν κατὰ πᾶσαν ἔχει, 647–8). But at Hes. *Op.* 197–201 the departure of Aidos and Nemesis in response to human wickedness lies in the future, just as in this lyric Electra implies that Aidos can still be found on the earth, although it is threatened by the injustice done to Agamemnon. Our passage has other similarities with the Hesiodic account. Aidos departs in both (ἔρροι τᾶν, *Op.* 199 ἀθανάτων μετὰ φῦλον ἴτον προλιπόντ᾽ ἀνθρώπους), though Electra uses a stronger verb to denote that departure in accordance with her greater emotion. In both this departure is the result of a neglect of δίκη (248, *Op.* 174–96; cf. Cairns (1993) 152). In both Aidos is the first of a pair of abstract qualities which human injustice is driving away. And in both the speaker is passionately concerned with winning the justice which (s)he has so far been denied. This Hesiodic allusion raises the magnitude of Electra's sufferings to a cosmic level: in a play which can often seem narrowly focussed on the house of Atreus, we are reminded that the failure to punish such a crime has implications for the values of society. It may also justify printing Αἰδώς and Εὐσέβεια with capital initials.

τᾶν (i.e. crasis of τοι ἄν) is F. Martin's reinterpretation of the paradosis τ᾽ ἄν (*ap.* Nauck³ p. 158), also accepted by Dawe. The resulting dochmiac with double drag is supported by the dochmiacs in 243–7. τ᾽ ἄν, on the other hand, gives a rarer metrical shape (∧ia∧ ∧ia, or − − ∪ − −). The word order with τε (effectively ἔρρει τ᾽ αἰδὼς εὐσέβειά τε) is also unparalleled: Jebb cites *OR* 258, but syntactic complications prevent that sentence from being truly comparable. See Denniston 538 for τοι in lyric dialogue in tragedy: it is especially appropriate here, as Electra pushes home the force of her argument.

αἰδώς and εὐσέβεια are not connected elsewhere: but for other σέβ– root words associated with or replacing αἰδώς cf. Aesch. *Eum.* 545–9, Cairns (1993) 137–8, 206–14. For the verb cf. Tr. Adesp. fr. 556.1 *TrGF* αἰδὼς ἀπώλεσ᾽ αὐτόν, ἐρρέτω, κακή, Ap. Rh. 3.785–6 ἐρρέτω αἰδώς, | ἐρρέτω ἀγλαΐη, Aristaen. 2.5.42–3 ἐρρέτω αἰδώς, ἐρρέτω σωφροσύνη.

FIRST EPISODE (251–471)

251–3 The chorus suddenly gives way to Electra, having argued against her throughout the parodos. This change partly arises from Electra's intransigence, partly from the eloquence of her self-defence in 236–50. Compare *OC* 254–7, where the chorus takes on a more sympathetic tone after Antigone's impassioned appeal in the epode to the parodos.

This shift might have taken place at the end of Electra's *rhesis* rather than at its beginning. Such a pattern is familiar from Aristophanes, where a hostile chorus is persuaded to come round to the protagonist's point of view in *Acharnians*, *Wasps* and *Birds*. But this would have affected the tone of the *rhesis*, leaving it more directly confrontational and argumentative (cf. *OC* 258–91): and we shall have more than enough confrontation later in the scene. As it is, a sympathetic chorus provides a suitable audience for the moving description of Electra's sufferings (cf. Reinhardt (1979) 141 ≈ (1947) 152).

251 ὦ παῖ: 121 n.

251–2 καὶ τὸ σὸν σπεύδουσ' ἅμα | καὶ τοὐμὸν αὐτῆς 'in zeal for thy welfare no less than for mine own' (Jebb). But how is the chorus's welfare at issue? The phrase might be a polar expression, in which καὶ τοὐμὸν αὐτῆς emphasises τὸ σόν without carrying independent meaning of its own (cf. 305–6n.). It is better taken, however, as a sign of the chorus's deep concern for Electra: it claims that its welfare is inextricably bound up with hers. Cf. the closeness implied by μάτηρ ὡσεί τις πιστά in 234.

For σπεύδω in this sense cf. Eur. *IT* 579–80 ὑμῖν τ' ὄνησιν, ὦ ξένοι, σπεύδουσ' ἅμα | κἀμοί, *Hec.* 120; for τὸ σόν and τὸ ἐμόν cf. *Aj.* 1313 πρὸς ταῦθ' ὅρα μὴ τοὐμόν, ἀλλὰ καὶ τὸ σόν, Mastronarde on Eur. *Phoen.* 473–4. The combination of possessive genitive with possessive adjective is unremarkable: cf. *OR* 415–16 ἐχθρὸς ὢν | τοῖς σοῖσιν αὐτοῦ, Moorhouse 164, S–D ii. 177.

253 σὺ νίκα: the language of victory and defeat is common in tragic arguments (cf. *Aj.* 1353, Aesch. *Ag.* 941–2 τὸ νικᾶσθαι, νίκην, Eur. *Alc.* 1108 νίκα νυν, *Suppl.* 947). The chorus's concession marks the change to a less agonistic mood.

For ἅμα with ἕπεσθαι cf. *Aj.* 814, *OR* 471, Hom. *Il.* 9.512, Eur. *Med.* 1143, Pl. *Leg.* 631 c5. Its repetition from 251, there too in final position, is suspicious to modern taste: ἀεί (Morstadt (1864) 16) and δή (Nauck⁵ p. 162), along with ὁμοῦ in the scholia to D, are possible replacements.[18] But such repetition is common in tragedy (335–6n.). Of the three tragedians, S. is the fondest of repetition over a short interval (cf. Pickering (2000) 89, 99), and ἅμα is itself often so repeated (Bruhn §214). Nor is it remarkable that the word occurs each time at the end of a line (cf. Di Benedetto on Eur. *Or.* 1128–9).

254–309 Electra's first *rhesis* describes her predicament to the chorus. Similar speeches occur elsewhere in S. at *Tr.* 141–77 (Deianira) and *Phil.* 254–316 (Philoctetes): all three are moving statements of prolonged suffering and torment, interspersed with hopes of rescue that always come to nothing. In our case Electra has already described her wretchedness in the parodos. Such repetition of content in lyrics and *rheseis*, in song and speech, is common in tragedy (cf. Schadewaldt (1926) 14 n. 1 and 143–4, Greenwood (1953) 131–40, Matthiessen (1964) 20–2, Garvie's edition of Aeschylus' *Choephori*, p. 174,

---

[18] ἄρα (suggested by Ll-J/W, *Sophoclea*) is impossible: with the future this is normally found in questions (Denniston 37 (3)). Ll-J/W compare Eur. *Phoen.* 1658, but the meaning there must be 'well then' or 'in that case', which is inappropriate here.

Buxton (1995) 14), and is often accompanied by an alternation of tone: iambic trimeters encourage a more reflective style, after the plangent lyric passage.

This change of tone marks not a lessening in emotional intensity, but a change to a different sort of emotion. In the former the emotion is conveyed primarily through excited exclamations, images and invocations, in the latter through description, reflection and analysis. For the pattern cf. the *rheseis* at *Tr.* 1046–1111, *Ant.* 891–928, *Aj.* 430–80, *OR* 1369–1415, Aesch. *Ag.* 1178–97, Eur. *Alc.* 280–325, *Med.* 214–66, *Hel.* 255–305, *Ba.* 1202–15, Fauner (1912). The examples from *Medea* and *Helen*, both of which follow straight on from a parodos, stand particularly close to our passage.

The general style of this *rhesis* has been well brought out by Gould, who uses its formal similarity with the *Medea* passage to point to the peculiar qualities which each possesses. For Gould, the *rhesis* in *Medea* is dominated by a 'pervasive intellectualism', a '[constant] reaching out after general propositions in an attempt . . . to seize and stabilize the quality of things, in the abstract' ((1978) 53 = (2001) 96); Electra, on the other hand, 'focuses sharply upon the physical feel and texture of her daily experience, on Aegisthus' humiliating . . . possession of Agamemnon's throne, his clothes, his hearth, his bed, and on Klytaimestra's vindictive festival . . . and her ferocious verbal outbursts against Electra herself' ((1978) 52 = (2001) 95). Traditionally it is Euripides, not S., who is associated with οἰκεῖα πράγματ' εἰσάγων, οἷς χρώμεθ', οἷς ξύνεσμεν (Ar. *Ran.* 959). But the author of *Philoctetes* was not averse to including vivid and down-to-earth details in his plays; more generally, his frequent descriptions of place show a similar ability to evoke a real and palpable setting alongside the emotional qualities associated with it.

This interest in Electra's daily life and experience is familiar from Euripides' play, especially 304–13. But Euripides' heroine focuses more on her personal privations, such as her participation in household tasks and the emptiness of her social calendar; the audience knows that some of these injuries are ostentatiously self-inflicted (e.g. 57–8). But S.'s Electra gives us only a brief description of her humiliating treatment (262–5). Her focus is more on the humiliation meted out to her father, and her own distress at seeing it happen (258n.). We hear of Clytemnestra's adultery, the details of her celebration of Agamemnon's death, and the actual words of abuse which she directs against her daughter. In Euripides Clytemnestra is the focus of attention for a mere five lines (314–18), which mention only her enjoyment of the luxuries brought back by Agamemnon from Troy. And while in both speeches Aegisthus' appropria-tion of Agamemnon's trappings is described in bitter tones, S. makes the details of his usurpation more personal and hurtful (261–74n.).[19] Nor does Euripides'

---

[19] Cf. Wuhrmann (1940) 21: 'die Schändlichkeiten der Mutter und ihres Buhlen wer-den nicht als objektive Tatsachen hingestellt, wie an der entsprechenden Stelle bei Euripides . . . jede einzelne ist eine persönliche Beleidigung auch Elektra gegenüber'.

Electra show the appalled self-awareness so characteristic of her Sophoclean counterpart. In comparison to his contemporary, S. has gone to great lengths to stress the pathos and horror of his heroine's situation. The bitterness of her plight is conveyed without a hint of self-indulgence.

Electra's admissions of wrongdoing at 254–7 and 307–9, which enclose the *rhesis* in ring-composition, have been the focus of particular critical scrutiny. Her first word, αἰσχύνομαι, is synonymous with αἰδέομαι (cf. *OR* 1424–6, Cairns (1993) 138–9, 205 n. 102, 299 n. 121). At first sight it is inconsistent with her claims at 245–50: as Cairns puts it (*ib.* 248), 'Electra's statement that she is acting to safeguard *aidos* is immediately qualified by a statement that this very conduct causes her to act in ways which *aidos* (or *aischune*) should preclude'. There seems an equally flagrant contradiction at the end of the speech (307–8). Electra declares that her condition will not allow her to be εὐσεβής or σώφρων, yet at the end of the parodos εὐσέβεια was one of the standards which she championed. Hence, according to Cairns, 'the pursuit of *eusebeia* . . . necessitates its negation' (*ib.* 249). And as αἰδώς is often associated with σωφροσύνη (cf. *IG* ii/iii² 6859 = *CEG* i. §102.1 (*c.* 400 BC) Πότνια Σωφροσύνη, θύγατερ μεγαλόφρονος Αἰδοῦς, Thuc. 1.84.3, Pl. *Phaedr.* 253d6), by disclaiming σωφροσύνη and fighting for αἰδώς Electra seems to involve herself in a further contradiction. Cairns concludes that there is a fundamental moral ambivalence at the heart of Electra's conduct: she transgresses the norms of αἰδώς as much as she upholds them. Burton goes further, but his talk of 'a psychological "split" . . . [indicating] that the mind is obsessed and the judgement confused' ((1980) 195) will not win many adherents today.

But Cairns assumes that all aspects of αἰδώς, σωφροσύνη and εὐσέβεια are on the same level of moral seriousness. MacLeod (2001) 56–60 is right to emphasise that they are not. Electra knowingly violates one form of εὐσέβεια (piety towards her mother), and one form of αἰδώς/σωφροσύνη (restrained and circumspect behaviour in public); she does so, however, to remain loyal to another, more important aspect of these virtues, namely loyalty to her dead father. This distinction between different aspects of an abstract quality is paralleled by Antigone's τὴν δυσσέβειαν εὐσεβοῦσ' ἐκτησάμην (*Ant.* 924). Antigone acknowledges that her act of εὐσέβεια can be regarded as a sort of δυσσέβεια (cf. the chorus's σέβειν μὲν εὐσέβειά τις at 872). But she does not see her act as morally ambivalent; and in the event, the gods, via Tiresias, endorse it.

Electra's passionate commitment to her dead relative matches that of Antigone. She has, however, a keener awareness of the ἀπρέπεια that her behaviour involves, even if this does not outweigh the overwhelming moral imperative in obedience to which she leads her life. This ability to distinguish a hierarchy of values, to appreciate that her actions are open to objections, and consequently to ask for forgiveness, all justify Knox's description of her as 'the most self-analytical of all the Sophoclean heroes' ((1964) 38). Cairns claims that 'it is part of her tragedy that she is compelled to act in ways which she perceives, with more or less clarity, to be discreditable' ((1993) 248): but 'discreditable' should not be used as a synonym for 'immoral', nor does this perception alienate the audience from Electra or encourage us to condemn her. Rather, it secures our sympathy for the depth of her moral vision and her capacity to communicate it. The chorus shares in this reaction, when at 464–5 it attributes to Electra the two virtues which she had earlier disclaimed. This self-awareness was already evident in the parodos (cf. 221); Electra will demonstrate it again after the *agon* with Clytemnestra, in language strongly reminiscent of this speech. But there Electra's apology is delivered not to a friendly chorus, but to her greatest enemy; and this difference makes her words take on a new intensity (616–21 n.).

254 γυναῖκες: the chorus is always so addressed by Electra (1227, 1398) and Chrysothemis (372, 992): this indicates that it is composed of women rather older than the sisters (cf. 121, 234, Burton (1980) 186).

εἰ: regularly found after verbs expressing emotion where we might expect ὅτι (K–G ii. 369–70).

255 δυσφορεῖν 'may denote being swept along by sinister or painful feelings . . . by madness, grief, or rage' (Hutchinson on Aesch. *Sept.* 780); cf. 144 τί μοι τῶν δυσφόρων ἐφίη;

256 ἀλλὰ . . . γάρ: both particles fulfil their normal functions independently (cf. *Phil.* 81, Denniston 98–9).

ἡ βία . . . ταῦτ' ἀναγκάζει με δρᾶν: for ἀνάγκη see 221n. The variant ἀλλ' ἡ βία με ταῦτ' ἀναγκάζει ποιεῖν (*ap.* Arist. *Met.* 1015ᵃ31) is not textually significant. As often in the secondary tradition, the original has become a self-contained unit suitable for quoting in isolation.

257 σύγγνωτε: requests for forgiveness are not often found in the mouths of Sophoclean protagonists. For a parallel we must look to *Ant.* 65–6 ἐγὼ μὲν οὖν αἰτοῦσα τοὺς ὑπὸ χθονὸς | ξύγγνοιαν ἴσχειν, ὡς βιάζομαι τάδε, spoken by the timid Ismene. On the implications of this request see 254–309n.

εὐγενής: Electra justifies her actions by the principle of *noblesse oblige* (cf. *Aj.* 479–80, Knox (1964) 28, Barrett on Eur. *Hipp.* 26, Dover (1974) 94–5). Her nobility is inherited from the father whom she is championing. She will later attack Chrysothemis for not living up to her paternity (341–2), and sees Clytemnestra's nobility of birth as belied by her abusive conduct (287n.). At 1081 the chorus will hail her as εὔπατρις.

258 ὁρῶσα: emphasis falls on what Electra *sees* (260, 267, 268, 271, 282): cf. the focus on painful details (254–309n.) and on Electra's powerlessness. The only thing she can do is watch.

259 ἁγώ: the ἅ looks back to πήματα, not τάδε.

κατ' ἦμαρ καὶ κατ' εὐφρόνην: for the combination cf. Kemmer (1903) 149–50, 161. Night followed by day is the more usual order (cf. West on Hes. *Th.* 124), but there are many exceptions (cf. Gerber on Pind. *O.* 1.6). The division between day and night, already prominent in Electra's opening anapaests (86–93) and in the parodos (201–4), will be maintained in the coming account of Electra's sufferings (266–70, 271–4); cf. Eur. *El.* 181–2.

260 θάλλοντα . . . καταφθίνονθ': for the combination cf. [Hippocr.] *De loc. in Hom.* 24.1 ὅ τε σπλὴν θάλλει καὶ τὸ σῶμα φθίνει; also *Tr.* 547–8 ὁρῶ . . . ἥβην τὴν μὲν ἕρπουσαν πρόσω, | τὴν δὲ φθίνουσαν. For the metaphor cf. *Phil.* 258–9 νόσος | ἀεὶ τέθηλε, Bacchyl. 15.57–9 ἀφροσύναις | . . . θάλλουσ'. . . | Ὕβρις, Aesch. *Suppl.* 104–10.

261–74 The three elements πρῶτα μὲν (261), εἶτα (262) and ἔπειτα (266) introduce progressively longer grievances. The final ἔπειτα begins a nine-line sentence which is itself split into three sections, introduced by ἴδω (267), εἰσίδω (268) and ἴδω (271), and successively increasing in length. For such τάξις in S. cf. 968–72, *OC* 632–5; it was a characteristic of contemporary oratory (cf. Antiph. 5.10–11 etc., Lausberg (1998) §443). But the tricola do not make the speech appear excessively schematic, as the introductory elements are placed in different parts of their trimeters. Contrast the more straightforward πρῶτον μὲν . . . | ἔπειτα (both at the beginning of a line) of Eur. *Hel.* 270–3, in Helen's speech describing her sorrows. This accords with a 'clearly perceptible tendency' in S. 'for one structural member to run into, or fuse with, another, for lines of structural division to be blurred or half-denied' (Gould (1978) 51 = (2001) 92–3).

The three sections in 261–74 increase in emotional intensity as well as in length: from Aegisthus' usurpation of political authority, to the more intimate detail involved in his wearing Agamemnon's royal clothes, to his adultery with his victim's wife. As Jones (1962) 148–9 notes, 'we are observing [S.] sharpen and narrow the subversion of the *oikos* into a theme of personal usurpation'; cf. also Gould (cited above, 254–309n.). In the comparable passage from Euripides' *Electra* (319–22 ὃς δ' ἐκεῖνον ἔκτανεν | ἐς ταὐτὰ βαίνων ἅρματ' ἐκφοιτᾷ πατρί, | καὶ σκῆπτρ' ἐν οἷς Ἕλλησιν ἐστρατηλάτει | μιαιφόνοισι χερσὶ γαυροῦται λαβών), only political and military aspects are mentioned. The totality of the usurpation in S. explains the intensity of Electra's emotional response, spurred on as she is by constant reminders of her father's dishonour: cf. Pl.

Leg. 865e2–3 where the dead man is in turmoil ὁρῶν . . . τὸν ἑαυτοῦ φονέα ἐν τοῖς ἤθεσι τοῖς τῆς ἑαυτοῦ συνηθείας ἀναστρεφόμενον. These emotionally-charged references to Agamemnon are all emphatically held back until the end of each phrase (τοῖσιν πατρῴοις, ἐκείνῳ ταὐτά, ἔνθ' ἐκεῖνον ὤλεσεν, ἐν κοίτῃ πατρός).

261 ἥ: causal relative; as at *OC* 632–4 ὅτῳ πρῶτον μέν . . . ἔπειτα δ' it influences the syntax of only the first clause.

τὰ μητρός 'my relations with my mother' (similarly *OC* 268 τὰ μητρὸς καὶ πατρός); contrast e.g. Eur. *Or.* 580–1 εἰ δὲ δὴ τὰ μητέρος | σιγῶν ἐπήνουν ('my mother's actions'). Often this construction adds nothing to the meaning of the basic noun: cf. 1203, 1345, *OR* 977 τὰ τῆς τύχης (= ἡ τύχη).

ἥ μ' ἐγείνατο: cf. *Aj.* 1172, fr. 187.2 *TrGF*, Aesch. fr. 175.2 *TrGF*, Eur. *El.* 964, *Or.* 29, Bruhn §210. The phrase sharpens the paradox of the following ἔχθιστα (cf. 775, 1412 (nn.), Eur. *Or.* 29–30, Battezzato (2003) 18 n. 4).

262 ἔχθιστα συμβέβηκεν: for συμβαίνω with a bare adjective cf. *Tr.* 1174 ταῦτ' οὖν ἐπειδὴ λαμπρὰ συμβαίνει, Eur. *Hel.* 622–3 ξυμβεβᾶσί μοι (Willink; –ιν οἱ L) λόγοι | οἱ τῆσδ' ἀληθεῖς.

262–4 εἶτα δώμασιν | ἐν τοῖς ἐμαυτῆς τοῖς φονεῦσι τοῦ πατρὸς | ξύνειμι: 'numerous texts speak of voluntary association with a kinsman's killer as the worst of crimes, compulsory association as the bitterest of degradations' (R. C. T. Parker (1983) 122). The *locus classicus* is Antiph. 5.11 ἅπαντα τὰ δικαστήρια ἐν ὑπαίθρῳ δικάζει τὰς δίκας τοῦ φόνου . . . ὁ διώκων τὴν δίκην τοῦ φόνου ἵνα μὴ ὁμωρόφιος γίγνηται τῷ αὐθέντῃ (cf. [Arist.] *Ath. Pol.* 57.4); cf. Eur. *Andr.* 657–8 καὶ τῇδέ γ' εἰσέρχῃ σὺ ταὐτὸν ἐς στέγος | καὶ ξυντράπεζον ἀξιοῖς ἔχειν βίον (Menelaus is amazed that Peleus can live with a relative of his son's killer), *Tro.* 660 δουλεύσω δ' ἐν αὐθεντῶν δόμοις (Andromache). The same motif is found at S. *Tr.* 1236–7 κρεῖσσον κἀμέ γ', ὦ πάτερ, θανεῖν, | ἢ τοῖσιν ἐχθίστοισι συνναίειν ὁμοῦ: Hyllus is appalled by the prospect of living with the woman who has caused his father's death.

Electra makes the same complaint to Orestes at 1188–92; living freely with Agamemnon's killers forms one of the accusations she makes first against Chrysothemis (358), and then Clytemnestra (587–8). It is only during Aegisthus' absence that she has a chance to leave the house she so loathes (86, 312–13n., 516–18, 911–12). She regards life alone in an underground cave as a preferable alternative (378–84n.), and after hearing of Orestes' death she declares that she will never return inside (817–19). The house was the scene of her father's killing (269–70), and is now the location for his daughter's suffering. It will also be the place where Aegisthus meets his end (1495–1506). Contrast the complaint of Euripides' Electra, who has been turned out of the ancestral home (*El.* 60–1); for all the pain associated with exile, the grief which this evokes in her is not on the same scale as that of her Sophoclean counterpart.

263–9 The scholia are alive to the emotional impact of these lines; cf. ἀνιαρὸν λίαν (263 = p. 117.7 Papageorgius), ἔτι δὲ τοῦτο χαλεπώτερον (264 = 117.10), πάνυ γὰρ τοῦτο περιπαθές (269 = 117.18), ζηλοτυπίας μεστὸν τὸ πρᾶγμα, κινητικὸν δὲ πρὸς οἶκτον (271 = 117.23–4).

264 κἀκ τῶνδ' . . . κἀκ τῶνδε: for the bitter repetition cf. Hom. *Il.* 1.287–8; for Electra's unwillingness to be controlled see Knox (1964) 40–1. For ἐκ used 'of the agent from whom power, authority etc. proceeds' (Gow on Theocr. *Id.* 1.140) cf. *Ant.* 63 ἀρχόμεσθ' ἐκ κρεισσόνων, *OC* 67, Moorhouse 109. Here ἐκ with ἄρχομαι allows a smoother transition to λαβεῖν, which could not take ὑπό; for more on expressions of agency in S. cf. George (2005) 204–12.

265 λαβεῖν . . . τὸ τητᾶσθαι: the tenses distinguish the act of receiving from the state of privation (cf. *Phil.* 95 with Jebb). For the passive of τητάω used absolutely to mean 'suffer deprivation' cf. Hes. *Op.* 408. Blomfield's κἀποτητᾶσθαι (*ap.* Monk (1826) 73) is unnecessary, as the presence of the definite article with only one of the verbs is not unusual (cf. Kiefner (1964) 41–2). For articles attached to only one member of a pair see 991, 1023, 1405, 1498, Bruhn §171.VII, Fraenkel on Aesch. *Ag.* 926 (vol. ii. pp. 419–20).

266 ποίας ἡμέρας δοκεῖς μ' ἄγειν: form and tone are mirrored by *Phil.* 276–7 ποίαν μ' ἀνάστασιν δοκεῖς | αὐτῶν βεβώτων ἐξ ὕπνου στῆναι τότε;, Eur. *IA* 1173–6 τίν' ἐν δόμοις με καρδίαν ἕξειν δοκεῖς; | ὅταν θρόνους τῆσδ' εἰσίδω πάντας κενούς, | κενοὺς δὲ παρθενῶνας, ἐπὶ δὲ δακρύοις | μόνη κάθωμαι, τήνδε θρηνῳδοῦσ' ἀεί, *Hcld.* 832–3. For 'the physical feel and texture of [Electra's] daily experience' cf. Gould, cited above, 254–309n.

ἡμέρας: for the aspirate (established after *c.* 450) see Threatte i. 500.

267–71 For the variation ὅταν . . . ἴδω . . . εἰσίδω . . . ἴδω cf. *Ant.* 898–9 φίλη . . . προσφιλὴς . . . φίλη, *Phil.* 530–2 φίλτατον . . . φίλοι . . . προσφιλῆ, Bruhn §218.III. For the repeated verbs of seeing cf. 258n.

267–8 ὅταν θρόνοις Αἴγισθον ἐνθακοῦντ' ἴδω | τοῖσιν πατρῴοις: artistic representations of the death of Aegisthus regularly show him on a chair or throne (cf. Prag (1985) 10–34, M. I. Davies (1969) 232–3); this tradition has left a trace at Aesch. *Cho.* 572. March thinks that the audience would recognise an allusion to this part of the story and consequently have its spirits lifted. It would be better to see the transference of a motif from a happy to a pathetic

179

context: Orestes slays the usurper in his father's chair, whereas all Electra can do is watch him sit there.

269 For ἐκείνῳ used as if πατρός not πατρῴοις had preceded see Diggle's commentary on Eur. *Pha.* 113–14 = fr. 774.70–1 *TrGF*, supplemented at (1996c) 195.

269–70 παρεστίους | σπένδοντα λοιβάς: libations to Hestia precede and follow a feast: cf. S. fr. 726 *TrGF* ὦ πρῷρα λοιβῆς Ἑστία, *Hom. Hymn* 29.4–6, Pind. *N.* 11.6, Sophron fr. 41 *PCG*, Hordern with H.'s n., Lloyd-Jones (1960) 78–9 = (1990a) 307. The hearth was located in the centre of the house (cf. *Hom. Hymn* 5.29–30, Aesch. *Ag.* 1056), and was a focus of familial and political authority (Gernet (1951) = (1968) 382–402 ≈ (1981) 322–39, Vernant (1963) 19–24 = (1985) 164–9 ≈ (1983) 134–8, Gaster (1969) 479–80). At *Ant.* 372–5 the chorus says of the wicked man μήτ' ἐμοὶ παρέστιος γένοιτο . . . ὃς τάδ' ἔρδοι (cf. [*OR*] 249–51); here the guilty man is not only παρέστιος but is pouring παρέστιοι λοιβαί as head of the household. This marks his usurpation, just as 'in ascribing to Aegisthus the αἴθειν πῦρ ἐφ' ἑστίας ἐμῆς Clytemnestra assigns to him the position of the legitimate lord of the house' (Fraenkel on Aesch. *Ag.* 1435). In turn, Aegisthus' deposition will be signalled by a dream involving the hearth (417–23), while at 881 the hearth is invoked by Chrysothemis in her solemn assertion that Orestes has returned.

270 ἔνθ' ἐκεῖνον ὤλεσεν: at Hom. *Od.* 3.234–5 Agamemnon is killed at his own hearth (ἐφέστιος); elsewhere in the poem he is always murdered at a banquet at Aegisthus' house (cf. 193–200n.). At Liban. *Decl.* 6.57 Agamemnon is killed παρὰ τὴν πατρῴαν ἑστίαν. As the most sacred place in a Greek house, the hearth had its own taboos (cf. Hes. *Op.* 733–4 with West), and afforded potent protection to suppliants (cf. Gould (1973) 97–8 = (2001) 62–4, Hom. *Od.* 7.153, 248, 14.159, Thuc. 1.136.3, Ap. Rh. 4.693–4, Plut. *Them.* 24.4). Murder at the hearth thus constituted desecration on a spectacular scale; consequently tragedians use it as a location for unpleasant killings (cf. *Tr.* 262, Eur. *Med.* 1334 (with S. fr. 343 *TrGF*); also Eur. *El.* 784–5). Orestes will later insist that Aegisthus be killed there (1495–6).

For the unsettling juxtaposition of libations with murder cf. Aesch. *Ag.* 245–7, 1385–7, Tac. *Ann.* 15.64, 16.35. For the related association between blood and wine cf. Hordern on Timoth. fr. 780.4 *PMG* (adding Sall. *Cat.* 22.1–2). Here the connexion fits with the murderers' perversion of ritual activity (cf. 280n.).

271–3 On Clytemnestra's adultery see Jones (1962) 149–53, who notes the absence of a corresponding emphasis in Aeschylus' *Oresteia*; also C. P. Segal

(1966) 493–4, Winnington-Ingram (1980) 231. At Eur. *El.* 211–12 Electra concludes her catalogue of sufferings with μάτηρ δ' ἐν λέκτροις φονίοις | ἄλλῳ σύγγαμος οἰκεῖ. Hermione similarly (but with less justice) condemns Andromache for sleeping with the son of her husband's killer at Eur. *Andr.* 170–3 (δύστηνε σύ, | ἣ παιδὶ πατρὸς ὃς σὸν ὤλεσεν πόσιν | τολμᾷς ξυνεύδειν καὶ τέκν' αὐθεντῶν πάρα | τίκτειν); cf. also S. *Tr.* 1236–7 (cited above, 262–4n.).

271 τούτων: probably neuter rather than feminine (sc. τῶν ὕβρεων) or masculine (sc. Αἰγίσθου καὶ Κλυταιμήστρας).

τὴν τελευταίαν ὕβριν: the internal accusative (130n., 564) emphatically delays the climactic description of Clytemnestra's adultery. Fisher (1992) 1 defines ὕβρις as an act inflicting dishonour, whose motive is the pleasure involved in expressing a sense of superiority over another; see also Cairns (1994). For ὕβρις in the play see Fisher (1992) 298–302. Electra uses words built on its stem to characterise Clytemnestra's behaviour at 293, 790 and 794; Clytemnestra denies the charge at 522, and uses the same term to accuse Electra at 613.

272 αὐτοφόντην: elsewhere only at Eur. *Med.* 1269 and Lycophr. 438, and then in scholia and Byzantine writers. L and K contain a γράφεται-variant αὐτοέντην; cf. also Phryn. *Praep. soph.* s.v. αὐθέντης (p. 24.7–9 de Borries = *Anec. Gr.* i. 15.11–13 Bekker): Σοφοκλῆς δὲ λύσας τοὔνομα αὐτοέντης εἶπεν. ἔστι δὲ πολιτικώτερον τὸ αὐθέντης. In the classical period αὐτοέντης appears only at *OR* 107; the alternative αὐθέντης is commoner (the etymology, and hence the relative age of the two forms, is unclear: cf. Bond on Eur. *Her.* 1359, Chantraine (1999) s.v., Shipp (1979) 115). There is no reason to prefer αὐτοέντην to the better attested αὐτοφόντην. The γράφεται-variants could have been introduced through collation with *OR* 107 (so Dawe, *STS* i. 178). Phrynichus' testimony need only refer to the *OR* passage, and is thus no value for recovering the text.

For αὐτο– compounds denoting the killing of self or kin see Fraenkel on Aesch. *Ag.* 1091 ff., R. C. T. Parker (1983) 350. For αὐτοφόντης with μιάστωρ cf. Eur. *Andr.* 614–15 αὐθέντην δέ σε | μιάστορ' ὥς τιν' ἐσδέδορκ' Ἀχιλλέως.

ἥμιν: αὐθέντης regularly takes a dative of the person whose relative has been murdered (a sort of dative of disadvantage): cf. Hdt. 1.117.3 μήτε θυγατρὶ τῇ σῇ μήτε αὐτῷ σοὶ εἴην αὐθέντης, R. C. T. Parker (1983) 122 n. 69. Whichever word we read at the start of the line, a similar construction can be assumed.

273 ταλαίνη: for this and 275 τλήμων (both <IE* *telh₂* 'bear') in a derogatory rather than a consolatory sense cf. 1426, *Tr.* 792, Aesch. *Ag.* 222–3, 1107, *Cho.* 384–5, Eur. *Hec.* 1063. Just as τλάω can mean both 'to endure suffering' and

COMMENTARY: 251–471

'to steel one's heart to crime', so too the adjectives from this root can mean either 'suffering' or 'relentless' (Denniston on Eur. *El.* 1171, developed by J. R. Wilson (1971)). Chadwick's attempt ((1996) 262–6) to show that the word only ever has a mild derogatory sense fails to account for his own examples.

273–4 μητέρ᾽ εἰ χρεών | ταύτην προσαυδᾶν τῷδε συγκοιμωμένην: for the *topos* cf. 597–8, 1154, 1194, *Tr.* 817–18, Aesch. *Cho.* 190–1 ἐμή γε μήτηρ, οὐδαμῶς ἐπώνυμον | φρόνημα παισὶ δύσθεον πεπαμένη, Hom. *Od.* 23.97, Griffith (1978), especially 86 n. 12. The juxtaposition with πατρός (272) emphasises the polarisation of Electra's relations with her parents. For the form cf. Cic. *Mil.* 33 *leges, si leges nominandae sunt.* For συγκοιμάομαι used of transgressive sexual relations cf. Aesch. *Ag.* 1258–9 αὕτη δίπους λέαινα, συγκοιμωμένη | λύκῳ λέοντος εὐγενοῦς ἀπουσίᾳ, Eur. *Phoen.* 54 ἡ τεκοῦσα παιδὶ συγκοιμωμένη; perhaps also Hdt. 3.69.2. Despite this, the verb does not in itself carry a negative colouring: it is used in the Hippocratic corpus as a neutral term to denote sexual relations, while at Eur. *Andr.* 1273 Peleus addresses Thetis ὦ γενναῖα συγκοιμήματα.

275 μιάστορι 'polluted killer' (603n.). Aegisthus is polluted because he is sleeping with his victim's wife (cf. Winnington-Ingram (1980) 231–2). So Oedipus at *OR* 821–2 declares λέχη δὲ τοῦ θανόντος ἐν χεροῖν ἐμαῖν | χραίνω, δι᾽ ὧνπερ ὤλετο: now he thinks that he may be Laius' killer, and so his union with Laius' wife may be polluted. Alternatively, it is the mere fact of adultery which is designated a pollution (cf. R. C. T. Parker (1983) 94–7, especially 95 n. 84, Fisher (1992) 79; also 114n.), but this is less powerful.

276 Ἐρινύν: the mention of the Erinys is prompted by the reference to pollution in the previous line. The chorus will see the Erinys as the punisher of Clytemnestra's adultery (489–93).

οὔτιν᾽ ἐκφοβουμένη: but later a fearful dream will cause Clytemnestra to send offerings to Agamemnon (410). For emphatic οὔτις cf. Aesch. *Ag.* 186 μάντιν οὔτινα ψέγων with Fraenkel, 1099.

277 ὥσπερ ἐγγελῶσα τοῖς ποιουμένοις: the participle refers to Agamemnon's murder, which Clytemnestra mocks: *pace* Jebb and Moorhouse 107 it cannot mean 'exulting in'. For the tense of the participle cf. the active present participle of δράω at e.g. *Aj.* 1280, *Ant.* 319, 325: 'in such cases the present tense has its source in the continuing result of the action' (Moorhouse 257). Nauck's πεπραγμένοις is possible (in his third edition, p. 158; cf. 549): cf. τοῖς δεδεγμένοις versus τῶν ποιουμένων in *OC* 92, 116.

Sophocles' heroes cannot bear mockery, and 'even if the hero does not experience this face to face he imagines it in his moments of brooding despair'

182

(Knox (1964) 30). Cf. 807, 879–80, 1153, 1295, *Ant.* 838–41, Dem. 54.9 (mockery as the culminating ὕβρεως . . . σημεῖον καὶ τεκμήριον), Arnould (1990) 36–42, Halliwell (1991) 286, Wright (2005) 180 n. 37. Mocking the dead is especially reprehensible: cf. Hom. *Od.* 22.412, Archil. fr. 134 *IEG*, Crat. fr. 102 *PCG*, Eur. *El.* 900–5, Plut. *Solon* 21.1, Halliwell (1991) 286 n. 22.

Inscriptions suggest that forms of ποιέω whose endings begin with an omicron were always preceded by ποι–, not πο– (Threatte i. 329): I have printed accordingly here and in 302. Elsewhere in the play all forms of the verb have endings begining with ε or η which are preceded by a short syllable (319, 337, 385, 623, 624, 1044, 1045, 1276). I have printed these with πο– rather than ποι–, but whether or not a glide was heard in their pronunciation is impossible to tell. See further Arnott (2001a) 44 n. 5.

278 †εὑροῦσ᾽ †: the verb can denote results reached by investigation (cf. Gow on Theocr. *Id.* 30.27, Davies on *Tr.* 1177–8), but the resulting sense 'finding the day' is inept here: as Dawe (1976) 230 notes, 'women who murder their husbands do not have to institute inquiries to find out what day they did it on'. Despite his defence of the paradosis in *Sophoclea*, Lloyd-Jones translates 'she observes the day' in the first printing of his Loeb translation: not so much a mistranslation, perhaps, as a great scholar's subconscious recognition that the text before him is faulty.[20] Dawe adopts Seyffert's ἱεροῦσ᾽ ((1868) 19); this rare verb (found in tragedy, in compounds, at Aesch. *Eum.* 304, 451) could easily have been altered into εὑρίσκω, while its religious resonance prepares for the paradox of a sacred celebration commemorating a murder (cf. 270n.). Nauck's φρουροῦσ᾽ (in his fourth edition, p. 159) and Reiske's τηροῦσ᾽ ((1753) 14) suggest Clytemnestra's eager anticipation of the anniversary (Nauck compares Eur. *Alc.* 27, where Thanatos is described as φρουρῶν τόδ᾽ ἦμαρ ᾧ θανεῖν αὐτὴν (sc. Alcestis) χρεών).

ἐκείνην ἡμέραν: according to Σ p. 118.5–7 Papageorgius οἱ Ἀργολικοὶ συγγραφεῖς, including Deinias (late third century bc; *FGrHist* 306.2), put the death of Agamemnon on 13th Gamelion. For ἐκείνην of what is well-known cf. 2n.

τότε: denotes a past occasion previously brought to our attention (cf. *Aj.* 650, *Ant.* 391, Eur. *Hel.* 1081, *Or.* 99, Diggle (1994) 491–2).

279 ἀμόν 'my', as always in S. and Euripides (cf. 588, 1496, *Phil.* 1314, Friis Johansen and Whittle on Aesch. *Suppl.* 106–7, Garvie on *Cho.* 428). Only Xs and Zf have the correct *spiritus asper* (for which see West's Teubner Aeschylus, p. xxx); at 588 they share the truth with T and Ta.

ἐκ δόλου: the secrecy of the killing contrasts with the openness of its celebration: cf. 124n., 197. For ἐκ cf. 48n.

---

[20] The mistake is corrected in the 1997 printing.

280 χορούς ἵστησι καὶ μηλοσφαγεῖ: for dancing and sacrifice in a celebration cf. Bacchyl. 11.111–12 χραῖνόν τέ μιν (sc. βωμὸν) αἵματι μήλων | καὶ χορούς ἵσταν γυναικῶν. For ἵστημι with χοροί cf. Aesch. *Ag.* 23 χορῶν κατάστασις, Eur. *Alc.* 1155, *El.* 178, *IA* 676, Ar. *Av.* 219 with Dunbar, Henrichs (1994–5) 95 n. 36. Contrast the celebrations which Electra envisages after the killing of Aegisthus (982–3): though they are for the assassination of a tyrant rather than the murder of a husband. For μηλοσφαγεῖ as a transitive verb cf. 190n.

281 θεοῖσιν . . . τοῖς σωτηρίοις: cf. Clytemnestra's later prayer to Φοῖβε προστατήριε (637). The adjective is ironical: the gods who betrayed Agamemnon have preserved Clytemnestra.

ἔμμην' ἱερά: for monthly festivals cf. Hdt. 8.41.2, Dem. 25.99, Pl. *Leg.* 828c2, Mikalson (1975) 13–24. Some evidence suggests that rites took place on the thirtieth day after death in the classical period, and that a funerary meal was shared by relatives 'on the thirtieth day' (Seaford (1985) 317 nn. 23–4; cf. Garland (2001) 39–40). Clytemnestra's feast takes place not one month after the burial, but every month; and 'so far from contributing to the restoration of normality, it renews every month the insult to Agamemnon, and thereby contributes to the dual impossibility of incorporating Elektra back into the world of the living on the one hand and her angry, suffering father into the world of the dead on the other' (Seaford (1985) 317). Elsewhere Seaford connects this perversion of ritual activity on Clytemnestra's part with a similar perversion on Electra's: the former 'transgresses the temporal limit set to the commemoration of the dead and reverses the mood of mourning', as a response to which the latter 'transgresses the temporal limit by her perpetual lamentation, which is moreover a means of causing pain to her mother and Aigisthos [cf. 355]' ((1994) 376). But the two characters have different motives for this trangression: Clytemnestra humiliates the husband whom she has murdered, Electra commemorates the father whom she has lost.

282 Electra remains inside while others have gone to the festival. Cf. Aesch. *Cho.* 445–50 (especially 449 χέουσα πολύδακρυν γόον κεκρυμμένα), Hom. *Od.* 1 (Telemachus is separated from the suitors who feast on his father's substance), *Hamlet* 1.4 (the prince, in mourning for his dead father, remains isolated outside while the murderer and his court celebrate within).[21]

ὁρῶσα: unlike ὁρῶσ' ἡ this gives a caesura in the second metron (omitted elsewhere in tragedy only at Aesch. *Pers.* 501: cf. West (1982a) 83 with n. 21). For δύσμορος without the article cf. *Tr.* 1005.

283 Note the ascending tricolon (13n.).

---

[21] For more connexions between the play and *Hamlet* see Harvey (1977) 261–3.

κλαίω, τέτηκα: for the combination cf. *Ant.* 977–80 κατὰ δὲ τακόμενοι μέλεοι μελέαν πάθαν | κλαῖον, Eur. *Or.* 860 ἐξετηκόμην γόοις, Hom. *Il.* 3.176 τὸ καὶ κλαίουσα τέτηκα, *Od.* 19.204 τῆς δ' ἄρ' ἀκουούσης ῥέε δάκρυα, τήκετο δὲ χρώς, Arnould (1986); for solitary weeping see Arnould (1990) 57–9.

283–4 πατρὸς | τὴν δυστάλαιναν δαῖτ' ἐπωνομασμένην: 'the usurpers even named their celebratory feasts after Agamemnon, like a hero cult' (Seaford (1985) 317). The analogy should not be pressed, however, as χοροί (cf. 280) did not have a place in hero cult (they are not mentioned in Ekroth (2002)). Agamemnon's death at a banquet (193–200n.) gives particular sharpness to τὴν δυστάλαιναν. For the feast which follows a sacrifice see Diggle on Theophr. *Char.* 9.3. For ἐπονομάζομαι + genitive = 'I am named after x' cf. K–G i. 375 Anm. 4, Eur. *Or.* 1008 τά . . . ἐπώνυμα δεῖπνα Θυέστου.

285 αὐτὴ πρὸς αὐτήν: in such phrases (examples at Bruhn §78) the second αὐτ- element should probably be unaspirated (cf. Fraenkel on Aesch. *Ag.* 836, Garvie on *Cho.* 221). The enjambment followed by a pause at the end of a long sentence gives great emphasis to the phrase denoting Electra's isolation. Lamentation is usually communal, so Electra's solitude is a kind of ritual transgression.

286 θυμὸς ἡδονὴν φέρει: cf. Pherecr. fr. 155.2 *PCG* ἐμοί τε λέξαι θυμὸς ἡδονὴν ἔχει. For the idea that desire for lamentation needs to be satisfied cf. Hom. *Od.* 10.499 αὐτὰρ ἐπεὶ κλαίων . . . ἐκορέσθην; for the pleasure or relief afforded by lamentation cf. Hom. *Od.* 4.102 γόῳ φρένα τέρπομαι, Aesch. fr. 385 *TrGF* οἵ τοι στεναγμοὶ τῶν πόνων ἐρείσματα, [Aesch.] *PV* 637–9, Eur. *El.* 125–6, *Tro.* 608–9, frr. 563, 573 *TrGF*, Ov. *Trist.* 4.3.37–8, Heliod. 2.15.1 ἀνέπνευσε στεναγμῷ τὸ πάθος ἐπικουφίσας, *Ecclesiastes* 7.3, Arnould (1990) 96–7, Wright (2005) 182 with n. 42.

287 λόγοισι γενναία 'supposedly noble': though γενναῖος by birth (cf. Aesch. *Ag.* 614), Clytemnestra fails to live up to this (contrast 257n.): cf. *Aj.* 1095–6 (I shan't ever now be surprised at the bad actions of a low-born man) ὅθ' οἱ δοκοῦντες εὐγενεῖς πεφυκέναι | τοιαῦθ' ἁμαρτάνουσιν ἐν λόγοις ἔπη. Neither 'noble in her professions' or 'spoken of by others as noble' makes sense as a description of Clytemnestra. For the plural λόγοισι cf. 60n.

288 φωνοῦσα: the emphasis moves from the visual to the aural; again the murderers take the initiative, while Electra remains passive.

289–92 The incorporated *oratio recta* (cf. Bers (1997) 45–62) provides an accurate insight into Clytemnestra's character before her arrival (cf. *Aj.* 288–94,

767–9, 774–5, *Tr.* 797–802): contrast Euripides' *Electra*, where our preconceptions of Clytemnestra and Aegisthus are frustrated. Clytemnestra's abuse of her children is also put into direct speech at Liban. *Decl.* 6.17. The structure is similar to 295–8. Both begin with two rhetorical questions followed by a threat; both are then followed by a two word phrase equivalent to 'such were her words'.

289 Aristophanes parodied this line in his *Gerytades* (fr. 175 *PCG*); we do not know how.

δύσθεον: 'hated by the gods' rather than 'god-hating' fits better with 291–2. μίσημα: cf. *Phil.* 991 ὦ μῖσος, *Ant.* 760, Aesch. *Eum.* 73 μισήματ' ἀνδρῶν καὶ θεῶν Ὀλυμπίων. For –μα substantives denoting persons cf. 622, K–G i. 10–11, Bruhn §236; such forms are 'particularly associated with personal invective both in colloquial and exalted speech' (Long (1968) 41).

289–90 σοὶ μόνη πατὴρ | τέθνηκεν; οὐκ ἀνηρέθη φησίν, ἀλλὰ τέθνηκεν, τῷ προσχήματι τῆς λέξεως παραλογιζομένη τὴν παρανομίαν (Σ p. 118.18–20 Papageorgius). This consolation (cf. 153n.) is singularly inappropriate in the mouth of the dead man's killer. Cf. *Hamlet* 1.1.84–5 'But you must know, your father lost a father; | That father lost, lost his' (spoken by Claudius), 1.2.72 'Thou know'st, 'tis common; all that live must die' (Gertrude).

290 ἐν πένθει: cf. 847, Pl. *Resp.* 605d1 ἐν πένθει ὄντα.

291 κακῶς ὄλοιο: for the blunt curse cf. *Phil.* 961, 1019.

ἐκ γόων: cf. 231 ἐκ καμάτων. At first sight there is a paradox: as a punishment for her excessive lamentation, Clytemnestra wishes that Electra should never cease lamenting. But this is over-literal (cf. 375n.).

292 οἱ κάτω θεοί: the gods of the underworld are invoked by Electra at 110–11 (n.) and assist the revenge at 1391–7. Anthropologists characterise mourning as 'participation in the transitional state of the recently dead' (Seaford (1985) 315): because of Electra's permanent state of lamentation, Clytemnestra can say that she is in the grip of the gods of the dead, who are reluctant to release their victims (cf. Aesch. *Pers.* 689–90 οἱ κατὰ χθονὸς θεοὶ | λαβεῖν ἀμείνους εἰσὶν ἢ μεθιέναι).

293 πλήν at first suggests that Clytemnestra occasionally relents from her aggressive behaviour: what we see is an intensification of it (so Kaibel, p. 114). Ll-J/W punctuate before this word with a colon; but while πλήν can introduce a main clause (e.g. *OC* 1643–4, S–D ii. 543), it is not doing so here.

τινός: cf. 778–9, where Orestes himself threatens Clytemnestra with his return.

293–4 ὅταν … | … τηνικαῦτα: for the coordination cf. Diggle on Theophr. *Char.* 30.6.

294 Ὀρέστην: Orestes' name is insistently repeated over a short passage (297, 303).

295 μοι: regular dative of disadvantage with αἴτιος (e.g. Hom. *Il.* 1.153).

296–7 ἐκ χερῶν | κλέψασ' Ὀρέστην τῶν ἐμῶν ὑπεξέθου: Clytemnestra's ferocity (cf. βοᾷ παραστᾶσα) suggests that she wanted to kill the young Orestes: cf. 601, 1132–3. That is certainly Aegisthus' intention at Eur. *El.* 16–18, where it is Clytemnestra who does the saving. For Electra's involvement in his rescue cf. 11–14n.

297 ὑπεξέθου: the ὑπο– prefix conveys secrecy: cf. 1350 ὑπεξεπέμφθην, Eur. *Hec.* 6, Thuc. 1.89.3.

298 ἀλλ' ἴσθι τοι: 'the unusual combination . . . seems to display a loud and overbearing attempt at authority' (Hutchinson on Anacr. fr. 417.3 *PMG*); cf. *Ant.* 473–4 ἀλλ' ἴσθι τοι τὰ σκλήρ' ἄγαν φρονήματα | πίπτειν μάλιστα, Denniston 549, Coray (1993) 7 (on ἴσθι).

τείσουσα: for the spelling (restored by Nauck[8] p. 168) see 115n.

299 For ὑλακτεῖ of wild, reckless speech cf. Aesch. *Ag.* 1631, 1672 ὑλάγματα, Pind. *N.* 7.105 μαψυλάκας, also Latin *latrare* at Cic. *Brut.* 58, *TLL* vii/2 1014.10–20; for the metaphorical use of the verb more generally cf. Hom. *Od.* 20.13 κραδίη δέ οἱ ἔνδον ὑλάκτει, Eur. *Alc.* 760 ἄμουσ' ὑλακτῶν, Eupolis fr. 220.3 *PCG*.

σύν: possibly in tmesis (so LSJ[9] s.v. συνεποτρύνω; cf. Ellendt s.v. σύν p. 705 col. ii, Kannicht on Eur. *Hel.* 106), but better taken as an adverb (Bruhn §64.3, *Ant.* 85, *Aj.* 959), as συνεποτρύνω does not exist elsewhere. Along with πέλας, the word emphasises Aegisthus' subordinate status.

300–2 'A chantlike diatribe, the sound and rhythm of which make present the monotony and intensity of her hatred' (Kitzinger (1991) 307). For the piling-up of terms of abuse, along with repetition of the article, cf. Aesch. *Sept.* 571–5, [Aesch.] *PV* 944–6, Ar. *Thesm.* 392–4, S. *Aj.* 364–5, Fraenkel (1963a), Davies on *Tr.* 541–2.

300 ὁ κλεινὸς . . . νυμφίος: calling Aegisthus 'the bridegroom' so long after his marriage emphasises that his relationship with Clytemnestra is his only source of authority: cf. Eur. *El.* 326–7 τῆς ἐμῆς μητρὸς πόσις | ὁ κλεινός, 803 μητρὸς εὐνέτης σέθεν; also 931 ὁ τῆς γυναικός, οὐχὶ τἀνδρὸς ἡ γυνή and S. *Ant.* 761 (probably an insult). For sarcastic κλεινός cf. Eur. *Tro.* 358, *El.* 326–7 (perhaps also *El.* 776 and *Her.* 38, though Diggle there emends to καινός).

ταὐτά: governs αὐτῇ; Blomfield's reinterpretation of the paradosis (*ap.* Monk (1826) 73) is likely because ἐποτρύνω elsewhere does not take a dative if not followed by an infinitive. It also improves the sense: Aegisthus lacks the wit to invent insults different from Clytemnestra's.

For παρών used 'um der lebendigen Anteilnahme des Subjekts, der Person an der Handlung eine Nuance zu geben' see Von der Mühll (1962) = (1976) 286–8. It often conveys support and assistance: cf. *Phil.* 373 ἐγὼ γὰρ αὐτ' ἔσωσα κἀκεῖνον παρών, Eur. *Hipp.* 1242.

301 ὁ πάντ' ἄναλκις οὗτος: for the weakness of Aegisthus cf. Hom. *Od.* 3.310 ἀνάλκιδος Αἰγίσθοιο, Aesch. *Ag.* 1224 λέοντ' ἄναλκιν; for his cowardice in not going to Troy cf. Eur. *El.* 916–17, Ov. *Rem.* 161–2 *Aegisthus . . .* | *. . . desidiosus.* Elsewhere in the play Aegisthus is more menacing (310–23n.).

For πάντα strengthening adjectives cf. 349, *Aj.* 911 ὁ πάντα κωφός, ὁ πάντ' ἄιδρις, Davies's *Trachiniae*, p. 173.

ἡ πᾶσα βλάβη: for βλάβη personified or predicated of an individual cf. 784, *Phil.* 622, *Ant.* 1103–4, Bruhn §234; for πᾶς intensifying an insult cf. *Phil.* 927 πᾶν δεῖμα, fr. 269a.24 *TrGF* τὸ πᾶν μύσος. The phrase may be a colloquialism: cf. Fraenkel (1977) 61, Ar. *Ach.* 909 ἅπαν κακόν.

302 ὁ σὺν γυναιξὶ τὰς μάχας ποιούμενος: the reference is not to Aegisthus' verbal assaults on Electra, but to his killing of Agamemnon (cf. Aesch. *Ag.* 1644 οὐκ αὐτὸς ἠνάριζες, ἀλλὰ σὺν γυνή, Hom. *Od.* 24.97): σύν means 'with the aid of', not 'against'. Aegisthus' effeminacy is an important theme in Aeschylus and Euripides (cf. Aesch. *Ag.* 1625 with Fraenkel (vol. iii. pp. 769–70), *Cho.* 304–5, Eur. *El.* 947–9).

303 τῶνδε προσμένουσ' ἀεί: the variant προσμένουσ' ἀεί ποτε is unattractive: ποτε is feeble, and παυστῆρ' difficult without τῶνδε.

304 παυστῆρ' with τῶνδε (neuter), as in *Phil.* 1438 παυστήρ . . . νόσου. For the παυ– root cf. 795–8, 987–8, 1295, Hutchinson (1999) 52–7.

ἐφήξειν: Jahn's ἔθ' ἥξειν could be right (cf. 811 ἥξειν in a similar context). But the transmitted compound, while rare in classical Greek, is used by S. twice elsewhere (*Aj.* 34, *Ant.* 1257), and should perhaps be kept as a word distinctively Sophoclean.

ἡ τάλαιν᾽ ἀπόλλυμαι: cf. *Phil.* 311–13 ἀπόλλυμαι τάλας | ἔτος τόδ᾽ ἤδη δέκατον ἐν λιμῷ τε καὶ | κακοῖσι, Eur. *Hipp.* 39 ἡ τάλαιν᾽ ἀπόλλυται.

305–6 For Electra's complaint cf. 164–72 (especially 171–2); also *Phil.* 300–13 (Philoctetes' hopes of rescue are perpetually frustrated).

δρᾶν τι: for τι = 'something of value' cf. 336, *Tr.* 160 ἀλλ᾽ ὥς τι δράσων εἷρπε, Stevens (1945) 100 §8.

τὰς οὔσας τέ μου | καὶ τὰς ἀπούσας ἐλπίδας: for the polar expression cf. Hom. *Il.* 10.249, S. *Ant.* 1108–9 ἴτ᾽ ἴτ᾽ ὀπάονες, | οἵ τ᾽ ὄντες οἵ τ᾽ ἀπόντες, Eur. *El.* 564, Vahlen (1879) 3–4 = (1907–8) i. 77–8, Wilamowitz on Eur. *Her.* 1106, Kemmer (1903), Barrett on Eur. *Hipp.* 441–2, West on Hes. *Op.* 529, G. E. R. Lloyd (1966) 90–4, Fehling (1969) 274–6, West (2004) 7. Often only one of the terms (usually the first) is relevant (cf. Hooker (1979) 214 = (1996) 612 (on Alcm. fr. 1.43–4 *PMGF*)). Here the sense is emphatically 'all my hopes' (Kemmer (1903) 59). It would be strained to see a distinction between Electra's hopes in herself and her hopes in the distant Orestes; nevertheless, it is possible that 'the hopes placed in an absent person have . . . influenced the expression here, however illogically' (Pelling, *per litteras*). There may be another polar expression at 780–1, where Clytemnestra complains that sleep did not cover her at night or during the day. Again, the polar expression conveys the totality of Clytemnestra's insomnia. 251–2 might also be an example, but see *ad loc.*

μου: for the genitive cf. 638. The minority variant μοι (supported by Porson (1812) 208) can be rejected as 'the kind of change easily made by scribes familiar with Attic idiom' (N. G. Wilson (1976) 174). For the confusion cf. 902, *Aj.* 515, *OC* 1137. As well as μοι here, Thomas Magister also supplies us with readings of note at 354, 681 and 1018. They appear intelligent conjectures rather than isolated preservations of the truth.

306 ἐλπίδας: Electra's hopes sustain her in her isolation (323). The news of Orestes' death destroys them (809–10), and she resists the efforts of the chorus to inspire her with new ones (830–6, 854–7). She then uses the hopelessness of their plight as a means of urging her sister to action (952, 958, 963). She last refers to her hopes at 1127–8; Aegisthus will later dismiss them with disdain (1460–1).

307–9 Through ring composition we return first to Electra's sorrow, and then to her admission of wrongdoing. The address to the chorus also balances that of 254.

307–8 ἐν οὖν τοιούτοις οὔτε σωφρονεῖν, φίλαι, | οὔτ᾽ εὐσεβεῖν πάρεστιν: contrast Electra's timid prayer at Aesch. *Cho.* 140–1 αὐτῇ τέ μοι δὸς σωφρονεστέραν πολύ | μητρὸς γενέσθαι χεῖρά τ᾽ εὐσεβεστέραν. For the connexion between σωφροσύνη and εὐσέβεια cf. Theogn. 1137–41 ᾤχετο δ᾽ ἀνδρῶν | Σωφροσύνη . . . εὐσεβέων δ᾽ ἀνδρῶν γένος ἔφθιτο, Critias eleg. fr. 6.21 *IEG* τὴν Εὐσεβίης γείτονα Σωφροσύνην. On the apparent contradiction of Electra's sentiments as stated at the end of the parodos see 254–309n. For Electra's 'proverbial' σωφροσύνη and εὐσέβεια see Garvie on Aesch. *Cho.* 140–1.

οὖν: marks the ring composition, formally subordinating the rest of the speech to 307–9, which is itself a recapitulation of 254–7.

308 ἀλλ᾽ ἔν τοι κακοῖς: Hermann's conjecture is more forceful than transmitted τοῖς, and few corruptions could be easier (cf. *Aj.* 776, Ar. *Av.* 1438). There are dozens of examples of ἐν κακοῖς in tragedy (in this play at 335, 1056, 1287); I have found only three of ἐν τοῖς κακοῖς (Eur. *Hec.* 1226, *Or.* 666, fr. 175.12 *TrGF*). For ἀλλά . . . τοι see Denniston 549; for τοι between preposition and substantive see Denniston 548 (3). For the meaning of the phrase ('in the midst of evils', 'in misfortune') see Fraenkel on Aesch. *Ag.* 1612.

309 πολλή ᾽στ᾽ ἀνάγκη: the phrase recurs at *OC* 293 and *Tr.* 295: there too it confuses the manuscripts.[22] For prodelided ἐστί in S. see Friis Johansen and Whittle on Aesch. *Suppl.* 718.

310–23 Electra's description of her step-father had been characterised by scorn rather than fear (300–2): but the chorus's elaborate attempts to check that he is away betray its apprehension. Even Electra is intimidated by this figure (312–13), whose return is a threatening prospect throughout (386, 517, 627, 1402–3). The *nostoi* of Aegisthus and Orestes frame the drama: the former occurs at its end, the latter at its beginning. Aegisthus' absence is temporary and left unexplained; Orestes' has lasted almost all his life and is only too well motivated. The former's return promises to Electra an increase of misery, the latter's release from it: but in the event Aegisthus returns only to fall neatly into a trap, whereas, in the short term, Orestes' return brings Electra to a new intensity of suffering. For the *nostos* motif elsewhere in S. cf. *Tr.*, *OR*, *Phil.*, *OC*, Taplin (1977a) 124–5.

---

[22] Dawe claims that L's πολλή᾽στ᾽ is the result of a later correction, with πολλῆς τ᾽ being the reading of L^{ac}; Ll-J/W agree with him on the first point and are silent on the second. πολλή᾽στ᾽ certainly is L's reading: but from the facsimile I see no evidence of a correction, and not a trace of a circumflex. The diacritics are written on with greater brio than usual, it is true, but that need not reflect a different hand: for the word occurs at the top of a page, and a similar exuberance is shown at e.g. the top of page 19a (l. 164). πολλή᾽στ᾽ is also the reading of L at *OC* 293 (where Ll-J/W mislead) and *Tr.* 295.

Orestes' likely movements have been discussed at 164–72 and 303–6. Compare *Tr.* 232–3, where Deianira asks Lichas whether Heracles is still alive, despite having just been told by the first messenger that he is; for the dramatic, rather than psychological, motivation for this see Davies's commentary, p. 105. So too at *Ant.* 211–22 (stichomythia between a post-parodos rhesis and the entrance of a new character) the short exchange does not advance the plot, but gives important insights into the character of Creon, the chorus, and their relationship.

310 φέρ' εἰπέ: marks a slight break with what has preceded (cf. *OR* 390, *Phil.* 433). In S. φέρε usually occurs with the imperative (always εἰπέ) rather than with the subjunctive (cf. *Phil.* 300, 1452); in Euripides and comedy the latter is more common. φέρε + imperative is probably the higher in register (cf. Stevens (1976) 42). See further Waś (1983) 220–7.

312–13 For the lack of freedom of movement accorded to women in tragedy cf. Aesch. *Sept.* 232, Eur. *Hcld.* 43–4, 476–7, *Andr.* 595–601, *El.* 341–4, *Tro.* 647–50, *Phoen.* 89–91, 1274–6, *IA* 1028–30, Dover (1974) 98, Golden (1990) 122 with 218 n. 25; also Sen. *Ag.* 954 *quo more coetus publicos virgo petis?* This may reflect an aspect of contemporary Athenian society, although the extent to which women were confined to their houses is debatable (cf. Mendelsohn (2002) 40–1 n. 79). Electra's presence outside is a transgressive act, as is Antigone's location ἐκτὸς αὐλείων πυλῶν at the start of *Ant.* (18–19): but 'the house is in so perverted a state that she is entitled to question her obligation to obey its rules' (Easterling (1987) 20). For Electra's fear of her stepfather catching her outside cf. Men. *Dysc.* 204–6 (a young girl speaking) ἆρ' ὁ πάππας ἔρχεται; | ἔπειτα πληγὰς λήψομ' ἄν με καταλάβῃ | ἔξω. Clytemnestra later associates her presence outside with the absence of Aegisthus (516–18); cf. also Chrysothemis' description of the restrictions she endures (911–12).

312 καὶ κάρτα: *coni.* Meineke (1863a) 255. Transmitted ἦ κάρτα never occurs as an independent affirmative; for the corruption (caused by the similarity of a minuscule compendium for καί to an eta) cf. Bast (1811) 815, Wyse on Isaeus 5.5.2, Diggle (1981a) 27. Neither phrase can strengthen a prohibition (cf. West (1978b) 240), so the punctuation after κάρτα is necessary.[23]

'Yes indeed' may not seem a helpful answer to an alternative question. Here Electra agrees with the second of the chorus's suggestions, while in 319 she uses a similarly vague affirmative to agree with the first. In each case her subsequent words make her meaning clear.

---

[23] *puncto post* κάρτα *addito* in the OCT apparatus suggests that Meineke added this punctuation mark. According to the facsimile the mark is found in L.

313 θυραῖον: two-termination, as at *Tr.* 533, Eur. *Alc.* 805 (metrically guaranteed in each case). For an adjective instead of an adverbial expression cf. 419, K–G i. 273–5, especially 274a, S–D ii. 178–9, Bruhn §8.
ἀγροῖσι: locative dative (174n.).

314 ἦ δὴ ἄν: ADXsXrZrTTa have ἦ κἄν; other manuscripts have some articulation or other of ηδαν. Both a delta and a kappa can be found in L, but it is difficult to tell which is original. Dawe claims that κἄν is the result of the correction, though I am inclined to think the opposite: in either case, Ll-J/W's bare claim that L reads ἦ δ' ἄν is misleading. Jebb reads ἦ κἄν on the grounds that ἦ καί can express a certain eagerness on the part of a questioner (cf. 663, 1452, *OR* 368, 757). But the presence of θαρσοῦσα μᾶλλον and the final εἴπερ clause make a question awkward. A statement is most easily obtained by interpreting the majority reading ἦ δ' ἄν as ἦ δᾶν (i.e. crasis of ἦ δὴ ἄν; cf. Hermann (1827–77) iv. 382–3). Dawe, *STS* i. 178 objects that this crasis is unexampled, and the collocation of particles unknown to Denniston: cf. however ἐπειδάν, Pl. *Symp.* 199b4 δᾶν, Call. fr. 195.22 Pfeiffer, Usener (1878) 66–7 = (1912–14) i. 242–6. ἦ δᾶν is also a possible interpretation of ΗΔ᾿ ΑΝ at fr. 555b.19 *TrGF* (so Pfeiffer (1933) 12 = (1960) 94–5; *pace* Carden (1974) 105).

316 For an imperative accompanied by a genitive absolute with ὡς see Fraenkel on Aesch. *Ag.* 1421–4. The single line amid a group of double lines is not odd enough to require a lacuna, as Jahn would have: for the reverse phenomenon cf. *Aj.* 105–6, *OR* 936–7, J. G. A. Gross (1905) 32–3.
τί σοι φίλον; Before the Hellenistic period, τίς is used instead of ὅστις only with indirect questions (as in 317), not in relative clauses. A few exceptions had emerged by our period: cf. Eur. *Pha.* 46 Diggle = fr. 773.2 *TrGF* αἰτοῦ τί χρήζεις ἕν with D.'s n., S. *OC* 48 πρίν γ᾿ ἄν ἐνδείξω τί δρᾷς (Zo, δρῶ *vel* δρᾶν *cett.*) with Moorhouse 266–7. K–G ii. 517–18 and Moorhouse 266–7 take the present instance as another exception. But the punctuated text gives unremarkable sense and syntax; nor does the addition of punctuation constitute interference with the paradosis.

317 For καὶ δή 'in response to a definite command, often with a word of the command echoed' see Denniston 251; the answer is usually in the present tense (cf. 558, 892, 1436, 1464). The chorus delays its request for a further half-line, again marking its anxiety (310–23n.).
τοῦ κασιγνήτου τί φής: for the plain genitive without περί cf. *Phil.* 439 ἀναξίου μὲν φωτὸς ἐξερήσομαι, *Aj.* 1236 ποίου κέκραγας ἀνδρός, Hom. *Od.* 11.174 εἰπὲ δέ μοι πατρός τε καὶ υἱέος, Bruhn §37, S–D ii. 132β, Lightfoot on Lucian 44.33; perhaps 1154. According to K–G i. 363c (cf. Denniston on Eur. *El.* 228) this genitive is only used with an accusative or subordinate clause which

takes the place of the object. But such an accusative or subordinate clause is not always present with such a genitive (cf. *Phil.* 441, *OC* 307), and even when it is, there is no reason to assume that the genitive must be dependent on it (so Moorhouse 72–4).

The orthography of the verb was disputed in antiquity. Apollonius Dyscolus preferred φής, while Herodian read φῇς with iota subscript (ii. 419.11–13 Lentz), as had Aristarchus before him (fr. 23 Schironi, with her commentary *ad loc.* (pp. 205–11)). The form with iota is probably the older. IE *$b^h eh_2$-si should give Greek *$p^h a$: *hi* > $p^h ai$:, which is extant in Alcaeus fr. 340 *PLF*, Voigt φαι: Lobel and Page obelise the word, but Voigt rightly keeps it, referring to Schwyzer (1930) 242–3 = (1983) 756–7. After this a sigma would be added on the analogy of other 2nd singular endings. Ionic φής then becomes φῇς on the analogy of forms like τίθης. I print the older form (found in L), although the last change may have already occurred by the end of the fifth century. See further Stolz (1903) 15–20; for the accent see Wackernagel (1877) 461–6 = (1953–79) ii. 1062–7, Schironi's edition of Aristarchus, p. 208 n. 11.

318 εἰδέναι θέλω: for the phrase used to fill out a line see Garvie on Aesch. *Cho.* 175.

319 φησίν γε: a brief and contemptuous reply to a roundabout question.

φησίν . . . φάσκων . . . λέγει: the verb alters, but the sense does not: cf. *Tr.* 346–7 ἀνὴρ ὅδ᾿ οὐδὲν ὧν ἔλεξεν ἀρτίως | φωνεῖ δίκης ἐς ὀρθόν, *OR* 54 ὡς εἴπερ ἄρχεις τῆσδε γῆς, ὥσπερ κρατεῖς.

320 The dramatic irony is strong: time and again in the prologue the need for immediate action was stressed (cf. 21–2, 75–6).

321 A further powerful retort to the chorus's bland generalisation. On Electra's rescue of the infant Orestes cf. 11–14n.

καὶ μήν: adversative (cf. 1188, Denniston 357–8); for more on this combination see 556–7n.

322 πέφυκεν: stresses Orestes' nobility in terms of his lineage. The chorus soon refers to Chrysothemis' φύσις (325); Electra will attack her failure to live up to this (341–2). For φύσις-terms in S. cf. Hajistephanou (1975) 9–54.

323 For Electra's hopes see 306n.

ἐπεί: for the omission of a phrase meaning 'otherwise' cf. 1448–9, Headlam on Herodas 2.72, K–G ii. 483–4, Bruhn §114, Denniston 62–3.

For adverbial μακράν see Wilamowitz on Eur. *Her.* 681, Fraenkel on Aesch. *Ag.* 916. It is used temporally at e.g. 1389, *OR* 220–1. Continued yearning for her brother has made the time seem long: cf. Theocr. 12.2 οἱ δὲ ποθεῦντες ἐν ἤματι γηράσκουσιν, Dioscor. *A.P.* 12.171.3–4 = 1517–18 *HE*. Electra believes the chorus not through faith in her brother, but because she must simply to keep alive (cf. Tib. 2.6.19–20, Sen. *HF* 312–14).

324–40 Chrysothemis acts as a foil to her sister: her willingness to cooperate with her father's killers highlights Electra's intransigence. On the one vase where she appears as a named character she performs a similar function. A red-figure pelike ascribed to the Berlin Painter (510–500 BC; Vienna 3725; *ARV²* 204.109, 1633, *Para.* 342, *Addenda²* 193) depicts a terrified young woman inscribed ΚΡΥΣΟΘΕΜΙΣ standing to the left of Orestes as he kills a seated Aegisthus. Prag says of her 'this is not Electra, who appears in many fifth century renderings as an active participant, but a much weaker character, used by the painter to symbolise fear and irresolution as a foil to the charged and energetic figures on either side of her' ((1985) 16). Compare the contrasting female figures in the scene of the death of Agamemnon from a red-figure calyx crater attributed to the Dokimasia Painter (*c.* 470; Boston 63.1246; *ARV²* 1654, *Para.* 373.34, *Addenda²* 234). One stands to the right of the stricken king, facing Aegisthus who has just stabbed him; another, of similar build and appearance, is running away on the other side. The former has been plausibly identified with Electra, the latter with Chrysothemis. Whether these identifications are correct or not, S. was evidently not the first to decide to highlight the boldness of one of Agamemnon's daughters by contrasting her with a less courageous counterpart of the same age and sex.

She forms an obvious pair with Ismene (cf. Σ *El.* 328 = p. 120.1–4 Papageorgius): yet there are significant differences between the two figures (cf. Easterling (1977) 124 = E. Segal (1983) 141 = McAuslan and Walcot (1993) 61). Most important, Chrysothemis lacks the pained sense of concern for her sister which Ismene always displays (cf. Winnington-Ingram (1980) 241 n. 80, Blundell (1989) 158 n. 38). The latter's grief-stricken description of the family's woes at *Ant.* 49–60, or her impassioned exclamations at 82 or 98–9, show genuine feeling: contrast Chrysothemis' offhand, prosy excuses at 332–4, her trite naval metaphor in 335, or the frigid paradox of 339–40.

324 Chrysothemis enters from the skene. She will have been noticeably better dressed than her sister. She is carrying the grave-offerings herself (cf. 431), and hence is probably not accompanied by attendants. This sharpens the focus on the confrontation of one sister against another.

μὴ νῦν ἔτ' εἴπῃς μηδέν: Chrysothemis is apparently not to be trusted. The stichomythia ends as it began, with the chorus afraid to speak openly owing to fear of the authorities (310–23n.).

δόμων: for the bare genitive used to denote motion from see S–D ii. 91, Moorhouse 66.

325–6 The emphasis on the shared heredity of the sisters (cf. *Ant.* 513 ὅμαιμος ἐκ μιᾶς τε καὶ ταὐτοῦ πατρός) makes their subsequent arguments the more striking. Compare how Antigone's effusive description of her kinship with Ismene at *Ant.* 1 soon gives way to insults. In particular, ἐκ πατρὸς . . . | . . . ἔκ τε μητρός turns out to be no mere neutral introduction: Chrysothemis must decide with which of her parents her loyalty lies (341–2, 365–7).

326 ἐντάφια: both libations and burnt offerings (cf. 405–6, 434). They are not mentioned again before 405; the reference to them stirs the audience's curiosity. Someone else, for whatever reason, is showing concern for the dead Agamemnon.

327 οἷα τοῖς κάτω νομίζεται: the usual phrase for 'to pay funeral rites' was τὰ νομιζόμενα ποιεῖν/φέρειν: cf. Aeschin. 1.14, Dem. 18.243, also Eur. *Alc.* 99, 609, Fahr (1969) 18 n. 2. For visiting graves to leave offerings see Garland (2001) 104–20.

328–9 τίν' . . . τήνδε . . . | . . . φωνεῖς . . . φάτιν: for the wide separation of the interrogative adjective from its noun see Fraenkel on Aesch. *Ag.* 1448 ff.: he sees the usage not as specifically poetic, but rather characteristic of 'everyday speech . . . where it is coloured by emotion'. For τίν' = 'what sort of remarks . . .' cf. 122n. For τίς ὅδε cf. 388, Diggle (1981a) 42.

328 αὖ: Chrysothemis has heard it all before (372–3): cf. 516, fr. 314.124 *TrGF* τίν' αὖ τέχνην σὺ τήν[δ' ἄρ' ἐξ]ηῦρες, τίν' αὖ; For questions 'used to rebuke, browbeat, or admonish another person' cf. Mastronarde (1979) 13–14, *Aj.* 288–91.

πρὸς . . . ἐξόδοις: a reproach (cf. 312–13n.).

θυρῶνος 'vestibule', or the part of the house immediately inside the main door: cf. *OR* 1242, Plut. *Quaest. Rom.* 290c, Orlandos and Traglos (1986) 132.

329 ἐλθοῦσα: Dawe[3] prints his own conjecture ἕλκουσα, which stresses the notion of a repeated excuse (LSJ[9] s.v. ἕλκω A II 6 cites Ar. *Lys.* 726–7, Hdt. 6.86.1): but it is uncomfortable to have two words next to each other governing φάτιν when one is metaphorical and the other is not. If emendation is called for ἀλγοῦσα is preferable (so Seebeck (1865) *fin.*), but the transmitted text, though unexciting, is not obviously faulty.

330 This line is divided into two halves by its caesura, one of fifteen such lines in Sophocles (excluding those with elision over the join): cf. Schein (1979) 38, Stephan (1981).

ἐν χρόνῳ μακρῷ: 178n.

διδαχθῆναι: thrown back at Chrysothemis in 343-4: her warnings to Electra to 'learn' are themselves 'learnt' from Clytemnestra. On such criticisms see Knox (1964) 25-6.

331 θυμῷ ματαίῳ ... χαρίζεσθαι κενά: similar language is often used to denote self-indulgent emotion: cf. Theogn. 1223-4 οὐδὲν Κύρν' ὀργῆς ἀδικώτερον, ἣ τὸν ἔχοντα | πημαίνει θυμῷ δειλά χαριζομένη, Simon. fr. 20.12 IEG, Bacchyl. 20B.20, Eur. fr. 31 TrGF, Antiph. 4.3.2, Antiph. Soph. D-K 87 B 58 (= ii. 364.9) = 58.14-15 Pendrick, Xen. An. 7.1.25, Pl. Leg. 935a3-4, Plut. Sert. 18.11; also S. OC 855. θυμῷ is better than the minority variant ψυχῇ, as it conveys notions of anger and passion (cf. Kaibel p. 122).

332 καίτοι τοσοῦτόν γ' οἶδα: same phrase at OR 1455; cf. Aj. 441 καίτοι τοσοῦτόν γ' ἐξεπίστασθαι δοκῶ. καίτοι often has 'a certain combative tone' (Denniston 556): its occurrence twice over a short section (cf. 338) accentuates the quarrelsome mood of Chrysothemis' speech.

κἀμαυτήν, ὅτι: the subject of the indirect statement precedes it in the accusative (cf. 520-1, Fraser (2001) 27 with n. 44).

333 ἀλγῶ 'πὶ τοῖς παροῦσιν: very bland; τὰ παρόντα sounds trite after Electra's eloquent description of her sorrows.

333-4 ἄν ... | ... ἄν: the unstressed particle gravitates to second position in sentence (or colon) in accordance with Wackernagel's Law (Wackernagel (1892) = (1953-79) i. 1-104), but as ἄν is a modal particle it also tends to move to the verb (ib. 393 = i. 61). The repetition of the particle (for which cf. 439-41, 697, K-G i. 246-8, Bruhn §116, Wackernagel (1892) 399-402 = (1953-79) i. 67-70) reflects a compromise between the two tendencies (ib. 399 = 67), and may also be associated with pragmatic factors, such as the level of complication of the sentence (cf. Slings (1992) 102-4).

εἰ σθένος | λάβοιμι: for the periphrasis see 30n. For the sense cf. Hom. Il. 22.20 = Od. 2.62 εἴ μοι δύναμίς γε παρείη.

334 δηλώσαιμ' ἂν οἷ' αὐτοῖς φρονῶ 'I would show them what are my feelings towards them' (Lloyd-Jones); cf. Isaeus 1.32 προσηπείλησεν ὅτι δηλώσειέ ποτ' ἂν τούτῳ ὡς διάκειται πρὸς αὐτόν. For φρονῶ with the dative cf. Eur. Telephus fr. 707 TrGF = 13 Preiser Τηλέφῳ δ', ἀγὼ φρονῶ (ap. Ar. Ach. 446), Pax 661.

335 ἐν κακοῖς: 308n.

ὑφειμένη: for middle ὑφίεμαι 'lower one's sails' (sc. in the face of danger) cf. Eur. *Or.* 607 ἐπεὶ θρασύνῃ κοὐχ ὑποστέλλῃ λόγῳ, Ar. *Ran.* 1220–1 ὑφέσθαι μοι δοκεῖ· | τὸ ληκύθιον γὰρ τοῦτο πνευσεῖται πολύ, Plut. *Lucullus* 3.3 ὑφειμένοις πλέων τοῖς ἱστίοις καὶ ταπεινοῖς, van Nes (1963) 135; for the same idea cf. *Ant.* 715–17, Ar. *Ran.* 997–1002, Eur. *Med.* 522–5.

335–6 δοκεῖ | . . . δοκεῖν: for ancient poetry's 'blissful ignorance of the deplorable modern convention . . . that it is illiterate to say the right thing twice, if you employ the same word on each occasion' cf. Jackson (1955) 17, 220–2, Diggle on Eur. *Pha.* 56 = fr. 773.12 *TrGF*, Sier's *Choephori*, p. 122 n. 12, Pickering (2000), (2002).

336 Chrysothemis' criticism of Electra does not do justice to the pain which the latter's laments cause Clytemnestra (cf. 287–98, 355, 783–7). The first μή goes with both clauses: cf. Dem. 18.179 οὐκ εἶπον μὲν ταῦτα, οὐκ ἔγραψα δέ, S. *OC* 277–8 καὶ μὴ θεοὺς τιμῶντες εἶτα τοὺς θεοὺς | ποιεῖσθ' ἀμαυροὺς μηδαμῶς.

δρᾶν τι: 305–6n.

337 τοιαῦτα δ᾿ ἄλλα: so Dindorf[1] for manuscript ἀλλά, supported by Vahlen (1876) 8–9 = (1907–8) i. 18. For τοιαῦτα ἄλλα as a formula of assent cf. Gow on Theocr. 14.1, Lloyd-Jones (1964b) 96–7. Schneidewin's τοιαῦτα τἄμ᾿, ἃ καί κτλ. (in his first edition) is approved by Dawe (2002–3) 6; the corruption is an easy uncial error, for which cf. *Ant.* 436, *OC* 1266. Schneidewin compares *Ant.* 207 τοιόνδ᾿ ἐμὸν φρόνημα, but there the noun makes a difference. τοιαῦτα τἀμά at Theodorus Prodromus *Rhodanthe et Doricles* 7.145 (p. 115 Marcovich; cited by Dawe) is too late to be relevant.

338 καίτοι 332n.

338–9 λέγω | . . . κρίνεις: 'the contrast is between the pronouns rather than between the verbs' (Jebb). Chrysothemis ironically pretends to defer to Electra's judgment.

339 εἰ . . . με δεῖ: not just εἰ μέλλω: through this and ἀκουστέα in 340 Chrysothemis 'is represented as justifying her obedience by attributing it to some external necessity' (Schein (1998) 299).

339–40 εἰ δ᾿ ἐλευθέραν με δεῖ | ζῆν, τῶν κρατούντων ἐστὶ πάντ᾿ ἀκουστέα: contrast the heroic sentiment at fr. 940 *TrGF* εἰ σῶμα δοῦλον, ἀλλ᾿ ὁ νοῦς ἐλεύθερος (with Pearson, Kannicht on Eur. *Hel.* 726–33); contrast also

Electra's life as a slave (cf. 190n.). The apodosis makes clear the limitations of Chrysothemis' ἐλευθερία.

For the pause after ζῆν cf. 42–3n. For the idea 'one must obey the powerful' cf. 219–20, 396, 1014, *Ant.* 63 ἀρχόμεσθ' ἐκ κρεισσόνων, *Aj.* 668 ἄρχοντές εἰσιν, ὥσθ' ὑπεικτέον. τί μήν;, Eur. *Hec.* 404 τοῖς κρατοῦσι μὴ μάχου, *Append. Prov.* 1.100 = *CPG* i. 394.1 δοῦλε δεσποτῶν ἄκουε καὶ δίκαια κἄδικα, West (1984) 184, Garvie on Aesch. *Cho.* 78–81. Contrast the hero's refusal to listen to others (cf. Knox (1964) 18–19). See further Schein, cited above, 339n. For the plural ἀκουστέα see Diggle (1994) 507, adding Ar. *Ran.* 1180.

341–68 Electra rejects her sister's recommendations in a speech which becomes more forceful as it progresses. Its first ten lines are made up of five couplets, each a single sense-unit. At 351 there is an acceleration, with the first of a series of rhetorical questions. Interruptions to the flow of the verse are now frequent, through strong sense-pauses in different parts of the line (e.g. 352, 354, 359–60, 365–7). From 357 there is a rapid alternation of personal pronouns, as Electra opposes her own actions against her sister's (357 σὺ δ'... 359 ἐγὼ μέν... τὰ σά... 360 σύ (v.l.)... 361 σοὶ δέ... 363 ἐμοὶ γάρ... 364 τῆς σῆς... 365 οὐδ' ἂν σύ): these pronouns are put in different parts of their respective trimeters, which prevents the section from seeming schematic (see Gould, cited above, 261–74n.). The speech ends with a recapitulation of the opening couplet, this time with supporting superlatives and a dramatic enjambment (366–7n.).

Electra's speech has an Achillean resonance. Both Electra and Achilles remove themselves from their community out of strong emotion. Both endure the attempts of others to persuade them to reintegrate themselves into that community (cf. Hom. *Il.* 9). Both reject the perceived hypocrisy of their counsellor (cf. *Il.* 9.312–13). Neither values the physical and material comfort which they could obtain by giving way. In Achilles' case, this takes the form of the rejection of the gifts offered by Agamemnon (cf. *Il.* 9.378–87). In our play there is no prospect of 'gifts' being 'brought' to Electra if she relents; and δῶρα is not quite the right word for the luxuries enjoyed by Chrysothemis. So it is striking to hear Electra reject her sister's choices in language more appropriate to Achilles' situation than her own: 'I will not yield οὐδ' εἴ μοι τὰ σά | μέλλοι τις οἴσειν δῶρ'' (359–60). Immediately after this Electra declares that she has no need for Chrysothemis' lavish diet; she is nourished by causing pain to her enemies (363–4n.). This too is Achillean in its resonance: in *Il.* 19 Achilles demonstrates the depth of his desire to avenge his friend by refusing to consider the need for food (cf. Griffin (1980) 14–17, Davies (1997) 98 with n. 7). It would be crude to say that Electra is being compared to Achilles: there are major differences in their situations, and the links between them are in no way as clear as, say, between Ajax and Eurysaces in *Aj.* 530–82 and Hector and Astyanax in *Il.* 6.466–84. Rather, S. is tapping into a heroic idiom best exemplified by the greatest of the Homeric heroes, which elevates Electra and brings out the magnitude of her passions.[24]

341 δεινόν γε: 'a common preface to an indignant reflection' (Diggle on Eur. *Pha.* 164 = fr. 776.1 *TrGF*); cf. *Phil.* 1225 δεινόν γε φωνεῖς, Denniston 127. Blomfield and Monk (*ap.* Monk (1826) 73–4) transpose γε and σε: this lays an inappropriate emphasis on the latter.

341–2 ἔφυς | . . . τικτούσης: the distinction is between Electra's father and her mother, not between the two verbs of begetting (cf. the lack of a distinction between λέγω and κρίνεις in 338–9): contrast Eur. *Or.* 552–3 πατὴρ μὲν ἐφύτευσέν με, σὴ δ' ἔτικτε παῖς, | τὸ σπέρμ' ἄρουρα παραλαβοῦσ' ἄλλου πάρα, where the senses of the verbs are different; contrast also Aesch. *Eum.* 658–66.

342 λελῆσθαι: a vice deplored by Electra (145–6, 167–8, 237); contrast her later stress on remembrance (482–7).

τῆς . . . τικτούσης: the present denotes a continuing relationship: cf. 533, *OR* 437 τίς δέ μ' ἐκφύει βροτῶν;, S–D ii. 272, Barrett on Eur. *Hipp.* 419–21, Rijksbaron (1991) 1–4, Mastronarde on Eur. *Phoen.* 289.

μέλειν: used personally: cf. *Aj.* 689, Aesch. *Ag.* 370, Eur. *Her.* 772, LSJ⁹ s.v. μέλω B I 1.

343 τἀμὰ νουθετήματα: the expected objective genitive is replaced by a possessive adjective (cf. *OR* 969 τὠμῷ πόθῳ, *OC* 332, 419, Bruhn §30.3).

344 κείνης: not a genitive of agent, for which the tragic evidence is weak (Moorhouse 75–6), but perhaps formed through analogy with μανθάνω + genitive = 'I learn from' (cf. S–D ii. 119δ, Dawe, *STS* i. 179).

κοὐδὲν . . . λέγεις: cf. 885–6, *Tr.* 320 εἶπ', ὦ τάλαιν', ἀλλ' ἡμὶν ἐκ σαυτῆς.

345–6 'Then take thy choice, – to be imprudent; or prudent, but forgetful of thy friends' (Jebb).

345 †ἔπειθ' ἑλοῦ γε† The paradosis contains two serious difficulties. (i) The force of ἔπειτα is obscure. The word occasionally has an inferential sense in Homer (LSJ⁹ s.v. II 1; e.g. *Il.* 5.812, 10.243), but never in Attic. (ii) The

---

[24] Cf. Wuhrmann (1940) 24: 'nicht die klagende Elektra braucht hier der Dichter wie im Kommos und der nachfolgenden Rechtfertigungsrede, sondern eine Heldin, welche das Gefühl ihres Rechtes mit Stolz und absoluter Überlegenheit zur Schau trägt'.

force of γε is obscure. According to Jebb it emphasises the verb, 'opposing a definite *choice* to a compromise' (his italics), but this is strained. No emendation is satisfactory. Blaydes's ἐπεὶ 'ξελοῦ γε (in his 1873 edition) does not work because ἐξαιρέομαι never means simply 'choose'; nor does it deal with the problem of the γε. Lloyd-Jones's ἐπεί γ' ἑλοῦ σύ ((1978) 219; ἐπεί γ' *iam* Page *ap.* Dawe¹, ἑλοῦ σύ *iam* Blaydes¹ p. 289) and Diggle's (tentative) ἐπεί γε θάτερ', ἢ φρονεῖν κακῶς, ἑλοῦ ((1981a) 22) both have an imperative introduced by ἐπεί γε, which is unparalleled. Renehan (1992) 353–4 compares how ἐπειδή, although interchangeable with ἐπεί in a variety of contexts, is never found before an imperative.

347–8 The protasis repeats Chrysothemis' own from 333–4, again with enjambment, although τὸ τούτων μῖσος is precisely the sort of passionate language which Chrysothemis avoided.

349 πατρὶ ... τιμωρουμένης: the middle of τιμωρέω normally means 'punish' (+ accusative of the person punished, + dative of the person avenged); here it takes only a dative and means 'avenge' (cf. 399, Eur. *El.* 1095).
πάντα: an intensifier (cf. 301 n.).

351 πρὸς κακοῖσι: cf. *Tr.* 330–1 μηδὲ πρὸς κακοῖς | τοῖς οὖσιν ἄλλην πρός γ' ἐμοῦ λύπην λάβῃ, Eur. *Hcld.* 17.
δειλίαν: cf. Electra's later stress on ἀνδρεία (983).

352 ἐπεὶ δίδαξον: cf. Eur. *Hec.* 1208 ἐπεὶ δίδαξον τοῦτο, S. *OC* 969–71 ἐπεὶ δίδαξον ... | πῶς ἂν δικαίως τοῦτ' ὀνειδίζοις ἐμοί, *OR* 390 ἐπεὶ φέρ' εἰπέ, ποῦ σὺ μάντις εἶ σαφής; In each case ἐπεί 'introduces a fact which proves the correctness of what has been said (and which was not previously known to, or adequately recognized by, the person addressed)' (Moorhouse 304). The fact is expressed as a rhetorical question, rather than as a statement such as normally follows ἐπεί.

354 The broken rhythm reflects the angry sarcasm: note the two elisions, punchy opening monosyllables, an unusually strong pause in second position, and parenthetic οἶδ' in the middle with sense breaks either side.
ἐπαρκούντως 'sufficiently'; for ἐπαρκέω (normally 'ward off, assist') = 'to suffice' cf. Solon fr. 5.1 *IEG* δήμῳ μὲν γὰρ ἔδωκα τόσον γέρας ὅσσον ἐπαρκεῖν (Brunck, -εῖ Plut., ἀπαρκεῖ [Arist.]), S. *Ant.* 612–13 καὶ τὸ πρὶν ἐπαρκέσει | νόμος ὅδ'. Thomas Magister's ἀπαρκούντως (*Ecloge* 24.16 Ritschl) is probably an intelligent conjecture (see 305n.).
δ' ἐμοί: Brunck (in his 1779 edition) rightly preferred the stressed form of the pronoun: the emphasis is important for the argument (as at 363).

355–6 τῷ τεθνηκότι | τιμὰς προσάπτειν: for τιμή owed to the dead see 241–2n. For προσάπτω in this context cf. Hom. *Il.* 24.110 (with κῦδος), Pind. *N.* 8.36–7 (κλέος), Pl. *Soph.* 231a3 (γέρας), Eur. *Med.* 1382 (ἑορτὴ καὶ τέλη), Livingstone on Isocr. 11.5.

356 εἴ τις ἔστ᾽ ἐκεῖ χάρις: 'a doubt whether the dead perceive what is done and said in the world of the living was often expressed by the Greeks, even in circumstances in which we might have expected a more positive affirmation of faith' (Dover (1974) 243); cf. (in addition to D.'s examples) Eur. *Or.* 1231–2, 1241–2, Ant. Sid. *A.P.* 7.23.6 = 251 *HE* εἰ δή τις φθιμένοις χρίμπτεται εὐφροσύνα, Meleager *A.P.* 7.476.6 = 4287 *HE*, Virg. *Aen.* 6.213 *ingrato cineri* with Norden, Ov. *Epist. Pont.* 2.2.97–8. Electra devotes her existence to honouring a dead man, when she cannot be sure that such devotion brings him any joy. For χάρις of the relationship between the living and the dead cf. Aesch. *Cho.* 320–1 χάριτες δ᾽ ὁμοίως | κέκληνται γόος εὐκλεὴς | προσθοδόμοις Ἀτρείδαις, Pind. *O.* 8.79–80, Leon. Tar. *A.P.* 7.657.11–12 = 2072–3 *HE*, Ant. Sid. *A.P.* 7.423.7–8 = 368–9 *HE*, [Simon.] *A.P.* 7.300.3–4 = 1000–1 *FGE, A.P.* 7.77.2 = 1029 *FGE*, R. C. T. Parker (1998) 112 n. 25; for the chthonic aspect of χάρις cf. MacLachlan (1993) 46. For ἐκεῖ of Hades cf. *Ant.* 76, *Aj.* 855, 1372, Eur. *Med.* 1073, *Hcld.* 594, Ar. *Ran.* 82.

357 ἡ μισοῦσα = ἡ μισεῖν φάσκουσα; cf. 171 ἀεὶ . . . ποθεῖ = ἀεὶ φησὶ ποθεῖν. The abbreviation adds to the irony: the phrase is, as it were, in inverted commas.

358 ξύνει '*ab eorum partibus stas*' (Nauck⁶). Electra objects not to Chrysothemis' living with her father's killers (so does she), but to her living with them willingly and without demur: contrast 262–4n.

359 τὰ σά: contemptuous, as at 364 τῆς σῆς, Eur. *Hec.* 1206–7 ὁ χρυσὸς . . . | ἔκτεινε τὸν ἐμὸν παῖδα καὶ κέρδη τὰ σά; cf. also 1037, *Phil* 1251.

360 οἷς σύ: so Jg (*teste* Damiralis (1888)), *coni.* Blomfield *ap.* Monk (1826) 74; οἷσι *cett.* σύ fits effectively into the quick-fire succession of personal pronouns (341–68n.).

361 ὑπεικάθοιμι: conduct advocated by Chrysothemis at 396, 1014; cf. Knox (1964) 16–17.

361–2 πλουσία | τράπεζα: τράπεζα and its compounds frequently mean little more than 'food' (cf. Wilamowitz on Eur. *Her.* 382). Hence a rich table signals gastronomic abundance (cf. Eur. *Hipp.* 109–10, Chaucer *General Prologue* 353–4), while a poor or empty table represents poverty (cf. 192). The rejection of luxury is consequently often figured as the rejection of loaded tables: cf. Eur. *Suppl.* 864–5 φεύγων τραπέζαις ὅστις ἐξογκοῖτ' ἄγαν | τἀρκοῦντ' ἀτίζων, *Hel.* 294–6, fr. 1052 *TrGF*.

362 Note the chiasmus.

περιρρείτω: implies luxurious abundance: cf. Plut. *Per.* 16.5 οὐδενὸς οἷον ἐν οἰκίᾳ μεγάλῃ καὶ πράγμασιν ἀφθόνοις περιρρέοντος, Dion. Hal. *Dem.* 18 [λέξις] περιρρέουσα τοῖς νοήμασιν.

βίος 'livelihood', a sense not found in Homer but common from Hesiod onwards (*Op.* 31 etc.).

363–4 ἐμοὶ γὰρ ἔστω τούς με χρὴ λυπεῖν μόνον | βόσκημα: so Tournier (1882) 120–1; τοὐμὲ μὴ λυπεῖν codd. The transmitted text means 'for me, let it be food enough that I do not pain myself (by a base compliance with the murderers)' (Jebb; cf. Kaibel, p. 127). This cannot be right. Throughout the play Electra's championing of her dead father causes λύπη both to herself (cf. 120, 822, 1170) and to her opponents (cf. 355, 553, 557, 654). To recommend this course on the grounds that it involves an absence of λύπη is thus blatantly and unnecessarily inconsistent (so rightly Dawe (1976) 231). Tournier's conjecture (printed by Dawe) gives us sense at the price of a small alteration: it also neatly picks up λυπῶ δὲ τούτους κτλ. from 355. Arnold (1866) 40–1 objects that in a speech which is built around antitheses, we should expect a reference to Electra's wretched state and its contrast with the τιμή enjoyed by Chrysothemis (364). But the real contrast is between the πλουσία τράπεζα of Chrysothemis and the βόσκημα of Electra, representing the fruits of the former's collaboration and the latter's defiance respectively.

Some conjectures remove λυπεῖν (e.g. λιπεῖν Canter (in his edition, p. 430), Wakefield (1789–95) iii. 143–4, λλιπεῖν Doederlein), but the λύπ-stem is so often connected with Electra that it should be preserved if possible. Erfurdt suggested λυποῦν, which he rendered *mihi tantum fit, quod me non excruciet, pabulum* or *mihi enim id tantum fit pro pabulo, quod mihi dolorem non afferat* (his edition, p. 426; cf. Σ p. 121.7–9 Papageorgius); it is printed by Campbell and misprinted in the apparatus to the first impression of the OCT. But this runs into the same objection as the paradosis.

Better is Jaya-Suriya's τοὖπ' ἔμ' ἡ λύπη ((1966) 147; later conjectured by Diggle), which means 'so far as I am concerned, let grief be my only food'. The conjecture contrasts the easy luxury of Chrysothemis' life and the λυπηρόν but ethically superior alternative which Electra prefers. The following passages support it (mostly owed to Diggle): (i) for grief as a nourishment cf. Aesch. *Cho.* 26 δι' αἰῶνος δ' ἰυγμοῖσι βόσκεται κέαρ, Psalm 42.3 'my tears have been my meat day and night', 80.5 'thou feedest them with the bread of tears', *Coriolanus* 4.2.50 'anger's my meat'; (ii) for the construction τοὖπ' ἔμ' cf. *Ant.* 889, Eur. *Alc.*

666, *Hec.* 514, *Or.* 1345, *IA* 1557, [Eur.] *Rhes.* 397; (iii) for the pleonasm ἐμοὶ . . . τοὖπ' ἔμ' cf. *Her.* 170–1 τῷ τοῦ Διὸς μὲν Ζεὺς ἀμυνέτω μέρει | παιδός· τὸ δ' εἰς ἔμ', Ἡράκλεις, ἐμοὶ μέλει κτλ. However, in this last passage the phrase τὸ δ' εἰς ἔμ' does not mean 'as far as I'm concerned', as would be the case at *El.* 363. Rather, we must understand μέρος from the previous line, giving 'as regards Zeus's part in his son, let Zeus himself defend it. As for my own part [lit. 'as for that part which falls to me'], Heracles, my care is to show . . .' (Kovacs). This strong phrase is then followed by the weaker ἐμοί to give a construction with μέλει. There is thus no pleonasm. At *El.* 363 we would have to translate 'but for me, as far as I'm concerned, let grief be my only nourishment', which is decidedly awkward.

Conradt's substitution of δή for μή ((1894) 578 n. 1) gives a similar sense to that of Jaya-Suriya's conjecture, without the awkward pleonasm: but δή gives a false emphasis to τοὐμέ. For further conjectures see Jebb's appendix (his edition, p. 210). The use of ἐμέ for ἐμαυτήν is unremarkable (cf. 65). βόσκημα and βόσκω are often used metaphorically in tragedy (cf. Seaford on Eur. *Cycl.* 165, S. *Ant.* 1246, frr. 591.4–5, 948 *TrGF*, LSJ⁹ s.v. βόσκω II 2; also John 4.34 ἐμὸν βρῶμά ἐστιν ἵνα ποιήσω τὸ θέλημα τοῦ πέμψαντός με).

364 τῆς σῆς . . . τιμῆς: cf. Achilles' similar rejection οὔ τί με ταύτης | χρεὼ τιμῆς at Hom. *Il.* 9.607–8. For the tone of the possessive adjective see 359n.

λαχεῖν should perhaps be preferred over the variant τυχεῖν as the less ordinary verb; cf. also *Ant.* 699 οὐχ ἥδε χρυσῆς ἀξία τιμῆς λαχεῖν; For the corruption cf. 592n. The ends of lines can often seem especially vulnerable to corruption (see Fraenkel on Aesch. *Ag.* 1216), perhaps final disyllables most of all (e.g. 379, 797, 876, Aesch. *Ag.* 1041, 1672–3).

The author of the reading λαχεῖν in Lˢ is disputed. The OCT apparatus suggests that it may be a *manus recentior*, whereas according to Dawe, *STS* ii. 62 it is the work of the original scribe or scholiast. From the facsimile, the second of Dawe's alternatives seems most likely.

365 οὐδ' ἂν σύ: for the ellipse after ἂν cf. *Tr.* 462, *Phil.* 115, K–G ii. 572–3.

365–7 ἐξὸν πατρὸς | πάντων ἀρίστου παῖδα κεκλῆσθαι, καλοῦ | τῆς μητρός: for the opposition cf. fr. 564.3 *TrGF* γαστρὸς (παρὰ προσδοκίαν for μητρός) καλεῖσθαι παῖδα, τοῦ πατρὸς παρόν, Eur. *El.* 933–5 κἀκείνους στυγῶ | τοὺς παῖδας, ὅστις τοῦ μὲν ἄρσενος πατρὸς | οὐκ ὠνόμασται, τῆς δὲ μητρὸς ἐν πόλει, 1103–4 οἱ μέν εἰσιν ἀρσένων, | οἱ δ' αὖ φιλοῦσι μητέρας μᾶλλον πατρός. The phrase restates the opposition at 341–2. The conflict between the values represented by a father and a mother is also prominent in *Trachiniae*, where Heracles urges his son to forget his mother and honour him alone (1064–5). So in *Philoctetes* Neoptolemus is encouraged to substitute a different, baser set of values for those which he has inherited from his father (88–9). *Pace* Kaibel (p. 128) there is no evidence that illegitimate children in Athens were known by their matronymic.

366 πάντων ἀρίστου: honorific descriptions of Agamemnon recur at 462–3 and 694–5.

κεκλῆσθαι: for the 'valeur permansive' of the perfect passive of καλέω see 230n.

367 τῆς μητρός: for the bare genitive cf. Bond on Eur. *Her.* 31, K–G i. 374–5. The enjambment and lack of an adjective lends a certain bluntness to the end of the sentence.

πλείστοις: Electra is not so isolated that she has no concern for the opinions of others (254–309n.). Here she envisages near-universal contempt for Chrysothemis' actions, just as later she predicts the universal acclaim which the pair of them will win (975–6, 984–5).

368 The form is paralleled by Eur. *Med.* 483 αὐτὴ δὲ πατέρα καὶ δόμους προδοῦσ' ἐμούς.

369–71 The studiously non-committal air of such choral interventions often contrasts with the greater emotional involvement of the characters. It is hard to see what compromise is possible between the sisters – and as we have just seen, compromise is not Electra's strongest suit.

369 πρὸς ὀργήν: for πρός with the accusative denoting manner cf. 464, 921, 1462, *Phil.* 90, 594, Ar. *Ran.* 856, Bruhn §72.II.

For the omission of a verb in prohibitions cf. *Ant.* 577 μὴ τριβὰς ἔτ', K–G ii. 571–2, Diggle (1996d) 8.

371 τῆσδε . . . αὕτη: both pronouns refer to the same sister: this is probably Chrysothemis, since in such interventions the chorus normally addresses the character who has just finished speaking. For the pairing of these two pronouns cf. 981, *Phil.* 841, 1434–5, Eur. *Ion* 1411, frr. 670.4, 941.3 *TrGF*, K–G i. 644–5, Bruhn §218.I, Diggle (1981a) 86, Ruijgh (2006) 156–61.

πάλιν 'in turn': cf. *OR* 618–19, Call. *Hymn* 3.87, *A.P.* 7.728.1 = 1255 *HE* = 40.1 Pfeiffer.

372–5 Chrysothemis addresses her answer not to her sister, but to the chorus – both an indication of her inability to reply to Electra's charges, and a snub. For this technique cf. 612, 788, *Ant.* 473–96, *OC* 1348–53, Mastronarde (1979) 78.

372 ἐγὼ μέν: with a suppressed 'others may think differently' (cf. Bruhn §156.II).

γυναῖκες: 254n.

ἠθάς: wearily, Chrysothemis notes how all this has happened before (328n., 408n.). For ἠθάς + genitive = 'accustomed to' cf. ἐθάς + genitive at Thuc. 2.44.2.

For πως 'used sometimes in speaking of one's own character or feelings' (Dover on Ar. *Ran.* 414) cf. Eur. *Cycl.* 583–4.

374 κακὸν μέγιστον εἰς αὐτὴν ἰόν: for the verb of motion cf. *Ant.* 9–10 ἤ σε λανθάνει | πρὸς τοὺς φίλους στείχοντα τῶν ἐχθρῶν κακά, *Aj.* 1255–6, *OC* 1770–2, Eur. *Alc.* 173–4, *Her.* 544, Bruhn §254.

374–5 αὐτὴν . . . | . . . ταύτην: the repetition emphasises that this is a problem which Electra and no-one else will face. If an emendation is needed Platt's εἰσάντην for εἰς αὐτήν ((1899) 147) is best; the word is attested at Bacchyl. 5.110 (cf. εἰσάντα at Hom. *Od.* 5.217 and [Hes.] fr. 193.3 M–W). Blaydes's τούτων (in his 1873 edition) is less attractive, as it creates an ugly accumulation of genitive plurals.

375 ὃ ταύτην τῶν μακρῶν σχήσει γόων: Electra's removal underground can be imagined either as putting a stop to her laments (because no-one can hear them) or as allowing her to lament to her heart's content. The definite article 'refers to what has been mentioned already, or is widely known' (Moorhouse 143; cf. K–G i. 598). The tone is caught by the English 'these laments of hers'; ταύτην and μακρῶν also have a scornful edge.

376 Electra does not hesitate to address her sister (contrast 372–5n.).

φέρ᾽ εἰπὲ δή: elsewhere only at *Ant.* 534, where Creon is roughly addressing Ismene. On φέρε with an imperative see 310n. δή rarely accompanies an imperative in tragedy: though not foreign to the grand style, it was mainly colloquial in the fifth and fourth centuries (Denniston 216 (iii)).

τὸ δεινόν: for the sarcasm cf. *Ant.* 95–6 ἀλλ᾽ ἔα με καὶ τὴν ἐξ ἐμοῦ δυσβουλίαν | παθεῖν τὸ δεινὸν τοῦτο, Eur. *Ba.* 492 εἴφ᾽ ὅτι παθεῖν δεῖ· τί με τὸ δεινὸν ἐργάσῃ;

εἰ γὰρ τῶνδέ μοι: on a strict interpretation this counts as a breach of Porson's bridge: but postpositives can sometimes be treated as independent monosyllables (cf. Eur. *Andr.* 230 τῶν κακῶν γὰρ μητέρων, perhaps also S. *OC* 115 ἐν γὰρ τῷ μαθεῖν; West (1982a) 85, Diggle (1994) 457), so Elmsley's δέ ((1811) 79), though possible (for the corruption cf. *Ant.* 672, Headlam (1891) 119–20, Arnott on Alexis fr. 91.1 *PCG*), is probably unnecessary.

378–84 The plan to imprison Electra is not referred to elsewhere; even in this scene it is soon displaced as the focus of attention.[25] Yet its dramatic significance is considerable. It confirms the violent and brutal image of Aegisthus and Clytemnestra in Electra's *rhesis*. It heightens the urgency of the situation, and indicates the consequences for Electra of any delay in Orestes' plan. It indicates the impact which Electra's perpetual mourning is having on the murderers: 'this new threat is proof of her efficacy as an interim avenger, for its aim is to deprive her of that function' (Blundell ((1989) 180). And Electra's reaction to this threat conveys her defiance, as well as her wretchedness. So great is her misery that she welcomes a life alone in an underground cave with passionate eagerness.

Seaford (1990) 79 compares the use of this motif in our play and in *Antigone*. Both Antigone and Electra suffer through devotion to a dead blood-relative. Both are imprisoned alive in an overhanging cave; both refer to how Niobe was encased in a rocky tomb, and draw a connexion between that figure and themselves (150–2, *Ant.* 823–33). Imprisonment is often associated with the frustration, negation or perversion of female sexuality, especially through the agency of the girl's own kin (Seaford (1990) 80–4). But while in *Antigone* this is a prominent motif, no trace of it appears in *Electra*.

Aegisthus threatens Electra with imprisonment at Pacuvius, *Dulorestes* 158–9 Ribbeck (*nam te in tenebrica saepe lacerabo fame* | *clausam* (Jahn; *clausum* codd.) *et fatigans artus torto distraham*), and at Sen. *Ag.* 988–993 (*abstrusa caeco carcere et saxo exigat* | *aevum . . .* | *aethere negato sero succumbet malis*); see Tarrant's n. on the latter.

378 ἀλλ' ἐξερῶ: see Denniston 17 (i) for 'assentient' ἀλλά followed by future indicative.

For πᾶν introducing a speech cf. 680, 892, *Aj.* 284, *Tr.* 749, Eur. *Hcld.* 799, *IA* 1540; also [Aesch.] *PV* 641–2.

379 γάρ: 681 n.

εἰ . . . μὴ λήξεις: for the future tense in the protasis cf. 1044, *Aj.* 1155 εἰ γὰρ ποήσεις, ἴσθι πημανούμενος, Moorhouse 277–8.

γόων: also in word-final position at 375, but for such a repetition cf. 253n.; the variant λόγων is weak.

380 ἐνταῦθα: regularly used for motion towards in prose and verse (K–G i. 444).

---

[25] Compare how in the third episode a second plan is brought up which is barely mentioned elsewhere (947–1057).

380–1 ἔνθα μήποθ' ἡλίου | φέγγος προσόψει: cf. 436–7, *OR* 796–7, 1412 ἐκρίψατ', ἔνθα μήποτ' εἰσόψεσθ' ἔτι, *Tr.* 799–800 καὶ μάλιστα μέν με θὲς | ἐνταῦθ' ὅπου με μή τις ὄψεται βροτῶν, *Aj.* 658–9. The use of μήποτε in similar circumstances at 436, *OR* 796 and 1412 tells against μηκέθ' (*coni.* Nauck[6]).

The deprival of light is often mentioned in descriptions of imprisonment: to the passages cited at 378–84n. add *Ant.* 944–5 ἔτλα καὶ Δανάας οὐράνιον φῶς | ἀλλάξαι δέμας, Eur. fr. 472e.48–9 *TrGF* ≈ 7.48–9 Cozzoli (*Cretans*) ἄγο]ντες αὐτὰς εἴρ[ξατ' ἐς κρυπτ]ήριον, | [ὡς μ]ηκέτ' εἰσίδ[ωσιν ἡλίου κ]ύκλον, Aesch. *Ag.* 1641–2, Sall. *Jug.* 14.15, Sen. *Med.* 464 (*paelicem*) *clausam . . . saxo noctis aeternae obruat.*

The manuscripts read προσόψει, and regularly have –ει as the 2nd singular middle ending in this verb and βούλει (e.g. *Tr.* 199). In other verbs they read –ῃ. Since inscriptions provide no evidence for the correct spelling (Threatte ii. 451–2), Dawe rightly keeps to the paradosis in each case (his edition[3], p. xii; cf. Dain's edition of Sophocles, vol. i. p. lvii). Ll-J/W print ὄψῃ and βούλῃ throughout, but do not explain why, or acknowledge that a change is being made in their apparatus. See further Arnott (2001 b) (especially p. 37).

381 ζῶσα conveys the paradox that Electra will be underground and deprived of the light of the sun, two states more often associated with a corpse, and yet be alive. Cf. *Ant.* 774 κρύψω πετρώδει ζῶσαν ἐν κατώρυχι, 887–8 εἴτε χρῆ θανεῖν | εἴτ' ἐν τοιαύτῃ ζῶσα τυμβεύειν στέγῃ, 920 ζῶσ' ἐς θανόντων ἔρχομαι κατασκαφάς.

κατηρεφεῖ 'roofed-over', as at *Ant.* 885, *Phil.* 272.

382 χθονὸς τῆσδ' ἐκτός: Schenkl's ἐντός ((1869) 538) postulates a case of polar corruption, whereby a word is erroneously replaced by its exact opposite (cf. Ll-J/W in *Second Thoughts, OR* 566, Davies on *Tr.* 677, Timpanaro (1974) 127–32 ≈ (1976) 147–52). But the justification adduced for it, that burying Electra outside the Argolid would allow Orestes to rescue her, is too literal-minded: the dramatist can ignore such issues when it suits him. Malcolm Davies (*per litteras*) suggests a better defence of the conjecture (though without endorsing it): pointing to the theme of Electra's restriction within the palace (262–4n.), he argues that 'imprisonment within the χθών would be a claustrophobic intensification of the preexisting torment'. Though this sense is attractive, the phrase χθονὸς τῆσδ' ἐντός remains curious. Seaford (1990) 79–80 argues that it refers to the earth in which Electra will be encased; he compares *OC* 1546 μοῖρ' ἀνδρὶ τῷδε τῇδε κρυφθῆναι χθονί. But there the demonstrative means 'in this land, Attica, as opposed to that land, Thebes': here there are no such alternatives, and τῆσδ' is therefore difficult. By contrast, the transmitted reading stresses the marginality of the Sophoclean hero even in death, a point which Electra herself takes up at 391. Compare Antigone's burial place in an ἔρημος . . . βροτῶν στίβος (773), or Ajax's death away from the camp on the seashore; compare also the location of Euripides' Electra on the edge of Argive territory (96 etc.).

ὑμνήσεις κακά: cf. *Ant.* 658 πρὸς ταῦτ᾽ ἐφυμνείτω Δία | ξύναιμον (spoken by Creon as he orders Antigone's imprisonment). The verb may convey the notion of a performance often repeated (cf. *Aj.* 292, *OR* 1275). Compare Clytemnestra's wish at 291–2.

383 πρὸς ταῦτα: 'often joined to the imperative in warning or menace' (Jebb, citing 820, *OR* 426, *OC* 455, *Ant.* 658, *Aj.* 971, 1066, 1115; add *Aj.* 1313, Eur. *Hec.* 861 πρὸς ταῦτα φρόντιζ᾽, Mastronarde on Eur. *Phoen.* 521).

φράζου: 213n.

383–4 καί με μήποθ᾽ ὕστερον | παθοῦσα μέμψῃ: for the thought cf. *Tr.* 470–1 πιθοῦ (*coni.*) λεγούσῃ χρηστά, κοὐ μέμψῃ χρόνῳ | γυναικὶ τῇδε; also the proverbial παθὼν / ῥεχθὲν δέ τε νήπιος ἔγνω (Hom. *Il.* 17.32, Hes. *Op.* 218 with West).

384 ἐν καλῷ: 'virtually equivalent to καλόν' (Wilkins on Eur. *Hcld.* 971); cf. *Phil.* 1155, *OR* 78, K–G i. 463–4, Stevens (1937) 189, Gow on Theocr. 15.73.

φρονεῖν: a favourite word of Chrysothemis' in her admonitions of her sister: cf. 394, 890, 992, 1038, 1048, 1056, Knox (1964) 13.

385–404 In this stichomythia Electra frequently picks up her sister's words with contempt: cf. 390–1 (ὅπως), 392–3 (βίου, βίοτος), 398–9 (πεσεῖν, πεσούμεθ᾽), Pfeiffer-Petersen (1996) 101–2. For this technique elsewhere cf. 1031–2, *OR* 547–52, J. G. A. Gross (1905) 84–6, Hancock (1917) 34–5.

385 Electra is not disconcerted by Chrysothemis' news (so rightly Pfeiffer-Petersen (1996) 100 n. 8, against Kaibel, p. 131).

ἦ ταῦτα δή: οὗτος and δή together have a scornful tone: cf. *Phil.* 565–6 ἦ ταῦτα δὴ Φοίνιξ τε χοἰ ξυνναυβάται | . . . δρῶσιν . . .;, Denniston 208 (viii). The minority variant ἦ . . . γάρ usually asks whether an inference is correct (cf. Denniston 284–5), whereas 'here the question is virtually no more than an astonished comment' (so Jebb). γάρ also displaces the true reading in 439 (n.).

For καί marking surprise or indignation cf. *Aj.* 44 ἦ καὶ τὸ βούλευμ᾽ ὡς ἐπ᾽ Ἀργείοις τόδ᾽ ἦν;, *Ant.* 726, 770, Bruhn §153.II.3, Denniston 316.

βεβούλευνται: the perfect marks the finality of the plan, as at Pl. *Crito* 46a4–5 ἀλλὰ βουλεύου – μᾶλλον δὲ οὐδὲ βουλεύεσθαι ἔτι ὥρα ἀλλὰ βεβουλεῦσθαι; cf. also 947, 1049.

386 μάλισθ': for this in a reply cf. 665, Thesleff (1955) 80–1. It is probably not colloquial (so Waś (1983) 139–40).

ὅταν περ οἴκαδ' Αἴγισθος μόλῃ: 310–23n.

387 Before Electra was afraid of the prospect of Aegisthus' return (312–13); now she wants him to return as quickly as possible. This comes as a surprise to Chrysothemis, who has only just been describing how familiar she is with her sister's sentiments (372–3). Cf. Antigone's οἴμοι, καταύδα (*Ant.* 86–7, also to a weaker sister; also 461–2, 497–9).

ἀλλ' ἐξίκοιτο: when ἀλλά is followed by a wish or prayer, 'there is no strong break-off . . . (it) merely marks a gentle transition from the known present to the unknown and desired future' (Denniston 15 (5)); cf. 437, *OC* 44 ἀλλ' ἵλεῳ μὲν τὸν ἱκέτην δεξαίατο.

τοῦδέ γ' οὕνεκ' 'so far as that's concerned': cf. 605, 787, *OC* 22, *Phil.* 774, Bruhn §70, Kannicht on Eur. *Hel.* 885–6.

388 'What is this imprecation that you have uttered against yourself?' (Lloyd-Jones); cf. *Tr.* 184 τίν' εἶπας, ὦ γεραιέ, τόνδε μοι λόγον;

ὦ τάλαινα: 'the word can express not only pity for suffering or execration of vice, but [also] contempt, without hatred, for folly' (Hutchinson on Aesch. *Sept.* 262); cf. 273n., 879n.

ἐπηράσω: for this verb cf. Dem. 18.142 τί οὖν ταῦτ' ἐπήραμαι καὶ διετεινάμην οὑτωσὶ σφοδρῶς; (following a passage in which the orator has called on the gods to punish him if he is lying). ἐπαράομαι is frequent 'in der Selbstwünschungsformel' (Wankel *ad loc.*); cf. Corlu (1966) 280–1. For the aorist see 668n.

389 Cf. Aesch. *Ag.* 1059 σὺ δ' εἴ τι δράσεις τῶνδε, μὴ σχολὴν τίθει; for the τι see 305–6n.

390–1 ὅπως πάθῃς . . . | ὅπως . . . ἐκφύγω: according to Moorhouse 196, these are the only Sophoclean instances of final clauses with the subjunctive after a verb in historic sequence (ἐπηράσω). But there is no need to take the subjunctives as dependent on this verb, and not on an understood 'I desire this' or similar.

390 ποῦ ποτ' εἶ φρενῶν; This partitive genitive is found with nouns both abstract (922, 1035, *Tr.* 375, *Ant.* 42, *OR* 413) and concrete (404, 922, *Phil.* 1179–80): cf. Moorhouse 58, K–G i. 340–1, Bruhn §32.1, Diggle (1981a) 35.

391 ἀφ' ὑμῶν: 'bitterly identifying her sister with her foes, whom she has hitherto called "them" (348, 355, 361)' (Jebb); πάνυ θυμικῶς καὶ τὴν ἀδελφὴν αὐτοῖς συγκαταλέγει ὡς τὰ αὐτῶν αἱρουμένην (Σ p. 121.25–6 Papageorgius). Antigone's Κρέοντ᾽ ἐρώτα· τοῦδε γὰρ σὺ κηδεμών (549) makes the same point explicitly.

ὡς προσώτατ᾽: again, the stress is on Electra as a marginal figure (382n.).

392 βίου . . . τοῦ παρόντος: i.e. as opposed to life in the cave.

μνείαν ἔχεις: 'abstract nouns which are used in periphrasis as the subject of a copula or object of an auxiliary verb often close the fifth foot of the iambic trimeter' (Long (1968) 59).

393 For ironical καλός see Friis Johansen and Whittle on Aesch. *Suppl.* 459.

For γάρ in sarcastic retort see Jebb on *Aj.* 1320, Ar. *Ach.* 71 (on which see Denniston 76). Similar (though less aggressive) irony at *OC* 144–5.

θαυμάσαι: for the 'active' infinitive see Hutchinson on Aesch. *Sept.* 322.

394 φρονεῖν: 384n.

395 μή μ᾽ ἐκδίδασκε: 330n.

396 τοῖς κρατοῦσι δ᾽ εἰκαθεῖν: cf. 219–20, 361 n. εἰκαθεῖν is Elmsley's correction for manuscript εἰκάθειν (in his n. on Eur. *Med.* 186 (our 189), p. 113 n. y (= pp. 285–6 n. q of the second edition)).

398 For γε μέντοι introducing an objection in dialogue cf. *OR* 442, Aesch. *Ag.* 938, Denniston 412.

'ξ ἀβουλίας πεσεῖν: cf. Aesch. *Ag.* 268 πέφευγε τοὔπος ἐξ ἀπιστίας.

399 εἰ χρή: cf. *OC* 1441 εἰ χρή, θανοῦμαι, Wakker (1994) 262–3.

τιμωρούμενοι: when a woman speaks of herself in the plural, she always uses the masculine (cf. *Ant.* 926, *Tr.* 492, Eur. *Med.* 314–15, *Hec.* 237, K–G i. 83, Wackernagel (1926–8) i. 99–100, Friis Johansen and Whittle on Aesch. *Suppl.* 204). The feminine plural, on the other hand, would mean 'we women' (Barrett on Eur. *Hipp.* 670–1).

400 The capacity of the dead to perceive the world of the living is often doubted in Greek literature (356n.). However, 'these doubts do not preclude strong affirmations when emotion or need prompt it' (Dover (1974) 243); cf. *OC* 998–9 οὐδὲ τὴν πατρὸς | ψυχὴν ἂν οἶμαι ζῶσαν ἀντειπεῖν ἐμοί. Ismene's words at *Ant.* 65–6 ἐγὼ μὲν οὖν αἰτοῦσα τοὺς ὑπὸ χθονὸς | ξύγγνοιαν ἴσχειν, though formally similar, are different in a crucial respect: she begs for the forgiveness of the dead, while Chrysothemis claims to have it already (cf. οἶδα).

210

δέ: sometimes a strong adversative, 'particularly in Sophocles, who not infrequently uses δέ in answers, to introduce a protest or objection' (Denniston 166). For parenthetic οἶδα cf. Eur. *El.* 684 πάντ', οἶδ', ἀκούει τάδε πατήρ (also of the dead Agamemnon).

401 = πρὸς κακῶν ἔστι ταῦτα τὰ ἔπη ἐπαινέσαι; cf. Aesch. *Sept.* 717 οὐκ ἄνδρ' ὁπλίτην τοῦτο χρὴ στέργειν ἔπος.
πρός + genitive = 'in the nature of' (first in Aeschylus' *Oresteia*, e.g. *Ag.* 592); cf. Bruhn §72.I.

402 Chrysothemis remains calm in the face of her sister's aggressive irony, though the jingle in ἐπαινέσαι . . . συναινέσεις may show some irritation. There is no 'herber Spott' in her words (*pace* Kaibel, p. 132).
σὺ δ' οὐχὶ πείσῃ: cf. *Aj.* 592 (same phrase). For σὺ δέ introducing an interrogative see Fraenkel on Aesch. *Ag.* 1614.

403 For the sentiment cf. Eur. *Hec.* 1278 μήπω μανείη Τυνδαρὶς τοσόνδε παῖς.
οὐ δῆτα: often in 'a negative answer to a question which . . . recognizes with reluctance or surprise that a negative answer may be given' (cf. 1198, Denniston 275 (vi)).
μή πω 'never': cf. *OR* 105 ἔξοιδ' ἀκούων· οὐ γὰρ εἰσεῖδόν γέ πω with Kamerbeek, Dawe (1964) 122–3.
νοῦ . . . κενή: cf. *OC* 931 τοῦ νοῦ κενόν, *Ant.* 754 φρενῶν . . . κενός, fr. 929.2 *TrGF*. Chrysothemis has often urged φρόνησις on her sister (384n.); Electra now returns the criticism.

404 Up to now Chrysothemis' entry has not been motivated; the only indication of her purpose has been the reference to the ἐντάφια which she is carrying (326–7). We now receive this information piecemeal; this maintains suspense, and lets us see Electra's responses to each new piece of news.
τἄρ' (= τοι + ἄρα; cf. Denniston 555) marks the change of topic ('well then', or the like); as at *OC* 1442 and *Phil.* 1253, it follows on from an interlocutor's refusal to obey the speaker. See further J. C. B. Lowe (1973) 57.
οἷπερ . . . ὁδοῦ: for the partitive genitive see 390–1 n.

405 The movement of the stichomythia is reversed: Electra takes the rôle of questioner from her sister (cf. J. G. A. Gross (1905) 69–70).
τῷ: the variant ποῖ has stronger manuscript support, but τῷ leads better into Chrysothemis' reply and gives a pleasing *variatio*. ποῖ at the beginning of the line means that the *utrum in alterum* argument also favours τῷ.
The combination of ἔμπυρα with χοάς in 406 has caused concern, as libations have nothing to do with fire. Jackson consequently emended to τῷ φέρεις

δὲ τἄπυρα ((1955) 50–1). But the terms do not need to match precisely. In each case, a reference to a part of the offerings is used to denote the offerings as a whole. For the combination of burnt gifts with libations in offerings to the dead cf. Lucian 26.22, Casabona (1966) 206, Garvie on Aesch. *Cho.* 483–5; also Eur. *IA* [59–60] δι' ἐμπύρων | σπονδὰς καθεῖναι, Suda ε 1092 (= ii. 267.6–7 Adler) (cf. Hesych. ε 2586 = ii. 85 Latte) ἐναγίζειν· . . . τὸ χοὰς φέρειν . . . ἢ τὸ διὰ πυρὸς δαπανᾶν.

ἔμπυρον can refer to 'an utensil or vas (*sic*) or small altar keeping materials that are on fire' (Sokolowski (1979) 66, citing epigraphic evidence); Ll-J/W are persuaded that this is the sense here. But if Chrysothemis is holding such containers, she must also have something to burn with the fire they contain. Hence it is hard to see what is wrong with taking ἔμπυρα in its commoner sense of 'burnt offerings' (so Jebb and Kaibel, p. 133; cf. *Ant.* 1005).

406 πέμπει: present for aorist: the relationship continues until the mission is completed (cf. 427). Cf. 680 ἐπεμπόμην.

τυμβεῦσαι 'to present as offerings at a tomb' (cf. *Ant.* 901–2 ἐπιτυμβίους | χοὰς ἔδωκα); elsewhere 'bury' (cf. *Aj.* 1063, Eur. *Hel.* 1245, Ar. *Thesm.* 885) or 'dwell underground' (*Ant.* 888). Denominative verbs in –εύω often have a wide semantic range (cf. S–D i. 732γ, Ernst Fraenkel (1906) 190). For the final-consecutive infinitive after a verb of motion cf. 871–2, Bruhn §126.1, Diggle on Eur. *Pha.* 97 = fr. 773.53 *TrGF* (supplemented by (1996c) 195), Diggle's commentary on Theophrastus' *Characters*, p. 360.

407 τῷ δυσμενεστάτῳ: the dead man does not relent in his anger against his killers (439–48n.).

βροτῶν: refers to all mortals whether dead or alive: cf. 462, Aesch. *Pers.* 632 μόνος . . . θνητῶν (i.e. Darius). Commentators also cite Aesch. *Cho.* 129 κἀγὼ χέουσα τάσδε χέρνιβας βροτοῖς, but this is probably corrupt (see Garvie *ad loc.*).

408 ὃν ἔκταν' αὐτή: Monk's γ' after ὅν ((1826) 75) should be rejected, despite the frequency of this particle in replies to questions (Denniston 130–8): '*non enim ipsa his verbis respondet Chrysothemis, sed quid Electra in mente habeat, dicit*' (Hermann *ad loc.*).

τοῦτο γὰρ λέξαι θέλεις: through long experience Chrysothemis can antic-ipate Electra's likely outburst (cf. 372n.).

409 ἐκ: approximates to ὑπό, as at 264 (n.). Here it allows a better connexion with 410.

τῷ τοῦτ' ἤρεσεν; There is no difficulty with Porson's bridge, since τῷ and τοῦτ' are not felt to belong to the same word-group. Elmsley's τόδ' for τοῦτ'

((1811) 79) is thus unnecessary. πῶς instead of τῷ (coni. Herwerden (1872) 14) gives the second question a different emphasis from that of the first: but the stress on the originator of the action does have a point, with Electra caustically assuming that Clytemnestra could not be acting on her own initiative.

410 Aeschylus' Clytemnestra was also driven by a nightmare to send offerings to her husband's tomb: cf. *Cho.* 523–5 ἔκ τ᾽ ὀνειράτων | καὶ νυκτιπλάγκτων δειμάτων πεπαλμένη | χοὰς ἔπεμψε τάσδε δύσθεος γυνή. Davies (1979) ii. 972–3 argues for a similar motivation in Stesichorus' *Oresteia*, though the evidence is thin. For sacrifice as a response to a dream cf. Aesch. *Pers.* 200–4, Xen. *Symp.* 4.33, Men. *Dysc.* 407–9, van Lieshout (1980) 201–3, [Sen.] *Oct.* 756–9 with Ferri.

δείματος: bad dreams generate fear: cf. 412 τάρβους, 427 φόβου, Aesch. *Cho.* 523–5 (cited above), Eur. *Hec.* 69–70, *Hel.* 1190–1, Tr. Adesp. fr. 375 *TrGF*, fr. 626.9 *TrGF* δ]εῖμα νύκτερον with Stephanopoulos (1988a) 242, fr. 626.37 *TrGF* φό]βος τις αὐτὴν δεῖμά τ᾽ ἔννυχον πλανᾷ, Lycophr. 225, Gaster (1969) 770, 813, Dumortier (1975) 34, Ferri on [Sen.] *Oct.* 760–1.

νυκτέρου: for dreams seen in the night cf. 501, Aesch. *Pers.* 518 ὦ νυκτὸς ὄψις ἐμφανὴς ἐνυπνίων, [Aesch.] *PV* 645 ὄψεις ἔννυχοι, Eur. *IT* 1261–2 νύχια | . . . | . . . φάσματ᾽ ὀ<νείρων>, West (1997) 549.

δοκεῖν ἐμοί 'as it seems to me', expressing Chrysothemis' hesitation and uncertainty (cf. 414, 417, 426–7). Contrast Electra's sudden confidence in 411 and her 'calm and assured' instructions beginning at 431 (Ll-J/W, *Sophoclea*). For the bare infinitive, more normally found with ὡς, cf. *OR* 82 ἀλλ᾽ εἰκάσαι μὲν, ἡδύς, 1220–1, fr. 479.1–2 *TrGF* σὺν θεῷ | εἰπεῖν.

411 Electra's immediate confidence contrasts with her sister's confusion and ignorance. Similarly, at *OC* 44–5 new information gives Oedipus a sudden resolution which his interlocutor finds hard to comprehend. The content of the dream is now revealed in an atmosphere of excitement, optimism and expectancy.

ὦ θεοί: 'as commonly in strong emotion, on suddenly learning (or realizing, or suspecting) something that affects one deeply' (Barrett on Eur. *Hipp.* 1169–70, comparing *Alc.* 1123, *El.* 771, *IT* 780). For the synizesis of θεός see Battezzato (2000).

πατρῷοι: cf. 67, *OC* 756 πρὸς θεῶν πατρῴων, Sier on Aesch. *Cho.* 800–1. In the mouth of Electra this epithet has a special resonance.

συγγένεσθε: cf. Aesch. *Cho.* 456 (Orestes to Agamemnon) σέ τοι λέγω, ξυγγενοῦ πάτερ φίλοις. For **γ᾽** with an imperative see Diggle (1981a) 22.

ἀλλὰ νῦν 'now at least', 'now at any rate'. There is an implied protasis, giving the sense '(even if you have not helped me before), now, however, lend me aid'. For this use of ἀλλά cf. 415, 1013, *Ant.* 779 ἢ γνώσεται γοῦν ἀλλὰ τηνικαῦθ᾿, 552, *Tr.* 201, *Phil.* 1041, Bruhn §146.I, Denniston 13. Electra implies that the gods have not been her allies up till now: for this hint of bitterness in a prayer cf. Hom. *Od.* 6.325–6 νῦν δή πέρ μευ ἄκουσον, ἐπεὶ πάρος οὔ ποτ᾿ ἄκουσας / ῥαιομένου, ὅτε μ᾿ ἔρραιε κλυτὸς ἐννοσίγαιος. For the motif 'though favourable, yet slow' see Tarrant on Sen. *Ag.* 403a, Nisbet and Hubbard on Hor. *C.* 1.15.19.

412 θάρσος τοῦδε τοῦ τάρβους πέρι: for the combination cf. Hom. *Il.* 24.171 θάρσει, Δαρδανίδη Πρίαμε, φρεσί, μηδέ τι τάρβει, *Od.* 7.50–1, 18.330–1, Aesch. *Sept.* 34–5. The chorus will likewise claim θάρσος as a consequence of the dream (479–81); cf. Plut. *Mul. virt.* 253a διὰ τὴν ὄψιν εὐθαρσὴς γεγενημένος. For dreams and fear cf. 410n.

413 For ὄψιν of a dream cf. Kessels (1973) 135–7.
εἴποιμ᾿ ἂν τότε: for the word division see Diggle (1974) 16 n. 5 ≈ (1994) 109 n. 61.

414 ἐπὶ σμικρόν 'to a small extent': cf. Hdt. 4.129.3 (ἐπὶ σμικρόν τι), Pl. *Theaet.* 174e7, *Leg.* 922e2 (with an accompanying genitive), Arist. *Eth. Nic.* 1167b10, *Met.* 1078b19, Dover (1969) 124–5 ≈ (1988) 37; also *Aj.* 1268 οὐδ᾿ ἐπὶ σμικρὸν λόγον (Reiske; –ῶν –ων codd.), *OC* 620 ἐκ σμικροῦ λόγου (v.l.).
φράσαι: almost redundant, as at *OC* 35, 50, 1582.

415–16 The stichomythia which had begun in hostility and anger ends on a note of support and encouragement. For the two-line ending to a passage of single-line stichomythia cf. J. G. A. Gross (1905) 19–21.

415 ἀλλά: 411n.
τοι: Dawe condemns this particle as 'a little sententious and condescending' (*STS* i. 179), and proposes χοἰ in its place (cf. *Aj.* 649, *Ant.* 1045–6, *Phil.* 431–2): but τοι often occurs in generalisations without the negative resonances that Dawe claims for it (cf. *Tr.* 327–8, Denniston 542 n. 1).
σμικροὶ λόγοι: 'speaking about small things' (Lloyd-Jones, adapted) is better than Jebb's 'few' or March's 'trivial'.

416 ἔσφηλαν . . . καὶ κατώρθωσαν: for parallelism of σφάλλεσθαι and κατορθοῦν cf. Ar. *Ran.* 735–6, *Plut.* 350–1, Xen. *Hell.* 7.1.9, Kemmer (1903) 232–3.

417–27 Clytemnestra's dream has two literary precedents. It is first found in Stesichorus, where the only surviving part is the frustratingly ambiguous τᾷ δὲ δράκων ἐδόκησε μολεῖν κάρα βεβροτωμένος ἄκρον | ἐκ δ' ἄρα τοῦ βασιλεὺς Πλεισθενίδας ἐφάνη (fr. 219 *PMGF*; cf. Davies (1979) ii. 952–74). In Aeschylus Clytemnestra dreams that she gave birth to a snake, put it in swaddling clothes, and offered it her breast; the snake bites the breast and draws forth a gout of blood (*Cho.* 527–33). Orestes identifies himself with the snake, and interprets the dream to mean that he will kill his mother (*ib.* 540–50). There is no snake in *Electra*. The emphasis has shifted from murder and revenge towards the divinely-guaranteed perpetuity of Agamemnon's line (cf. Bowman (1997)).[26]

417 λόγος τις: with this phrase 'there is no implication that the speaker regards the tradition as disputed' (Friis Johansen and Whittle on Aesch. *Suppl.* 295); it 'simply marks an affirmation as being beyond the speaker's direct knowledge' (*id.* on *ib.* 230 ὡς λόγος). See further Kannicht on Eur. *Hel.* 18.

εἰσιδεῖν: a common Greek expression for 'to have a dream' was ὄναρ ἰδεῖν: cf. Alcm. fr. 47 *PMGF*, Eur. *IT* 518, Ar. *Eq.* 1090, Hdt. 3.124.1–4, Xen. *Anab.* 6.1.22, Pl. *Crito* 44a6–7, Theophr. *Char.* 3.2, Alexis fr. 274.1 *PCG* with Arnott, Björck (1946) 311–12, Kessels (1973) 140–1. Here and at 644 a compound is used instead of the simplex verb without a change in meaning: cf. Aesch. *Pers.* 200 εἰσιδεῖν, Eur. *Hec.* 706 ἐσεῖδον, perhaps *IT* 47.

418 τοῦ σοῦ τε κἀμοῦ: we have not heard such a stress on the common origin of the sisters since the chorus's introductory remarks at 325–6. This reflects the drop in tension between the pair, noticeable since the first mention of the dream (410–11).

δευτέραν ὁμιλίαν: the object of εἰσιδεῖν. Kaibel (p. 136) takes it as an internal accusative with ἐλθόντος, but this gives unnatural syntax by leaving εἰσιδεῖν hanging uncomfortably. *Tr.* 394 δίδαξον, ὡς ἕρποντος, εἰσορᾷς, ἐμοῦ is not a parallel, as ὡς there complicates the picture.

Attempts have been made to show that ὁμιλίαν has a sexual sense (brief doxography at Fialho (1992) 169 n. 18). The case is best set out by W. Ferrari (1938) 34–7 who compares Hdt. 1.182.2, Eur. *Hel.* 1400, and ὁμιλέω at *OR* 367 and 1185 (add Aesch. fr. 136 *TrGF*). He also makes much of the second clause '*then* he placed his sceptre': εἶτα, he claims, must imply that Agamemnon *did* something before planting his sceptre. But Agamemnon's rising from the dead is itself an act of great significance. More important, in the examples he cites the sexual sense is always unmissable: here such a meaning would be impossibly allusive. A third objection arises from the choice of verb: to say that

[26] Euripides does not seem to use the dream in his accounts of the legend. At *Or.* 618 ὀνείρατ' ἀγγέλλουσα τἀγαμέμνονος Diggle rightly accepts the emendation ὄνειδος, for which Willink argues *ad loc.*

215

somebody 'sees' an ὁμιλία is a strange way of saying that they took part in the union which the noun is supposed to denote. In the main body of his article, Ferrari claims that Agamemnon and Clytemnestra had sexual intercourse in the Stesichorean dream: this does not stand up to scrutiny (see Davies (1979) ii. 971–2; Davies also doubts Ferrari's interpretation of our passage). See also 421–2n.

Any hint of sexual relations between Agamemnon and Clytemnestra would jar with the coming narration, where Agamemnon produces a plant representing Orestes entirely through his own efforts: Clytemnestra plays no part in the generative process. This symbolises Orestes' special status as κάρτα τοῦ πατρός. A similar point might be present in Stes. fr. 219.2 *PMGF* (cited above, 417–27n.): if the βασιλεὺς Πλεισθενίδας refers to Orestes, he is born from the snake representing his father with no female assistance. Not enough of the passage survives, however, to tell us whether Orestes or Agamemnon is meant (cf. Davies (1979) ii. 965–9).

419 ἐλθόντος ἐς φῶς: 'similar language is regularly used of escapes from the Underworld' (Olson on Ar. *Pax* 306–8; to his examples add Aesch. *Pers.* 630, Bacchyl. 5.61, Tr. Adesp. fr. 680.18 *TrGF*, Lucian 26.1). The verb of coming is also idiomatic for the 'approach' of the dream, or the subject of the dream, to the dreamer: to the examples cited by Dodds at (1951) 122 n. 16 add Hom. *Od.* 4.802, 14.495, Stes. fr. 219.1 *PMGF* (cited above, 417–27n.), Pind. *P.* 4.163, Aesch. *Pers.* 183. For the appearance of a deceased person to the dreamer cf. Hom. *Il.* 23.65–107 (Patroclus to Achilles), West (1997) 186–7.

εἶτα: perhaps a suggestion of the naïve narrative style sometimes found in ancient dream narratives: cf. Ar. *Vesp.* 34–49 κἄπειτα . . . εἶτα . . . εἶτα . . . εἶτα, Enn. *Ann.* 43 Skutsch *exim*, Plaut. *Rud.* 600 *postibi*, Accius *Brutus* (pp. 283–4 Ribbeck) *inde . . . deinde . . . exim*, Sen. *Tro.* 451 *tum*, Lucian 22.12 εἶτα; perhaps also ἐκ . . . τοῦ in Stes. fr. 217.1 *PMGF*. The naïve style of αἶνοι shows a similar tendency (cf. Fraenkel (1920) = (1964) i. 235–9), as does that of comic narrative (cf. Dover (1981) 24 = (1987a) 28–9, (1997) 76–7, Fraenkel (1962) 126–7); cf. Davies (1989a) 26 n. 63.

419–20 ἐφέστιον | πῆξαι: the hearth was the centre of familial and political power (269–70n.), and had been the scene of Agamemnon's own death, an act of the gravest defilement (270n.). It is thus a charged location for the reassertion of Agamemnon's authority. At Pind. *O.* 1.11–12 the sceptre and the hearth are juxtaposed in a context which glorifies the power of the monarch. According to Artemidorus 2.37 (p. 173.11–12 Pack) the appearance of Hestia in a ruler's dream represents ἡ τῆς ἀρχῆς δύναμις. For the adjective cf. *OR* 1411–12 θαλάσσιον | ἐκρίψατ᾽, 313n.

420–1 λαβόντα σκῆπτρον οὐφόρει ποτὲ | αὐτός, τανῦν δ' Αἴγισθος: by carrying Agamemnon's σκῆπτρον Aegisthus marks his usurpation (cf. Eur. *El.* 320–1, cited above, 261–74n.). By recovering it, Agamemnon demonstrates how he will wrest power back from the usurper through his son. Cf. Moses' dream in Ezekiel, *Exagoge* (*TrGF* i. §128) 68–89, in which a figure representing God gives Moses a sceptre and crown as a sign of authority (cf. Jacobson (1983) 90–1). For the sceptre as a symbol of royal authority cf. 651, Hom. *Il.* 2.100–8, Braswell on Pind. *P.* 4.152(c), Garvie on Aesch. *Cho.* 360–2, Easterling (1989), West (1997) 17, 134–5, 563. Agamemnon's sceptre was worshipped at Chaeronea in later antiquity; Pausanias speculates that it was brought there by Electra (9.40.11–12).

The symbolic power of Agamemnon's sceptre is like that of his spear in the two earliest artistic depictions of his killing. On a late seventh-century terracotta pinax from Gortyn (Heraklion Mus. 11152, Prag (1985) plate 1, M. I. Davies (1969) 228), Aegisthus is gripping the spear to prevent the seated Agamemnon from using it, thus demonstrating the latter's powerlessness; while on a shield band from Olympia (Olympia Mus. B1654, 575–550 BC, Prag (1985) plate 2a) the spear is propped up on the edge of the picture. As Prag comments, 'the symbol of Agamemnon's authority . . . [is] now pointedly set to one side and separated from the king by the usurper' ((1985) 2); cf. M. I. Davies (1969) 230 n. 4.

οὐφόρει: φορέω is 'the normal word for anything one has constantly about one' (Barrett on Eur. *Hipp.* 316; cf. also Ll-J/W on *OC* 1262 (*Sophoclea*)). It is commonly corrupted into φέρω (hence V's οὐφέρει; cf. 922, Most (2002) 263 n. 39).

ποτέ: [1]n.

421–2 ἐκ . . . τοῦδ' ἄνω | βλαστεῖν βρύοντα θαλλόν: the woman who dreams of a tree or plant which undergoes miraculous growth is a common motif in folk tale. The dream typically indicates the future greatness of the woman's child (cf. Hdt. 1.108.1–2, Ov. *Fast.* 3.27–38, Loomis (1948) 19). For plant imagery suggesting the potent fertility of Agamemnon's line cf. Aesch. *Cho.* 204 σμικροῦ γένοιτ' ἂν σπέρματος μέγας πυθμήν; also Eur. *IT* 170–1 (of Orestes) Ἀγαμεμνόνιον θάλος.

The growth of Orestes from the hearth is a further mark of his royal status. Compare the Roman myths of the royal infants Caeculus and Servius Tullius (on which see the Verona scholia (p. 116.21–3 Bascbera) and Servius (ii. 181.3–17 Thilo and Hagen) on Virg. *Aen.* 2.678–81, Ov. *Fast.* 6.629–36, Bremmer and Horsfall (1987) 49–53, Thomsen (1980) 57–64). The former is either found as an infant at the hearth or impregnated in a woman by means of a spark flying from the hearth, while the latter is the product of a union between a slave-girl and a male member that grows from the royal hearth. We cannot tell whether similar stories were known to S. If they were, then just as Livy sanitised the myth of the birth of Servius Tullius (1.39.1, with Ogilvie), so too S. has replaced the crudity of a male member with the more dignified picture of a royal staff. A trace of the former may nevertheless remain in the undeniably phallic nature of the sceptre thrust into the hearth.

The image of the sceptre bursting into foliage may have been suggested by Hom. *Il.* 1.234–7, where this event features as an *adynaton*. The motif occurs elsewhere at Ov. *Met.* 15.561–4 (Romulus' staff), and is also common in folk tale: cf. S. Thompson (1955–8) ii. 156 (D 1254), iii. 252 (F 971.1). In mediaeval Christian hagiography, for example, several saints thrust their staffs into the ground and thereby cause them to flower (Loomis (1948) 94, Gaster (1969) 301; cf. Aaron's staff at Numbers 17.11). The flowering of the Pope's staff is a famous element in the *Tannhäuser* legend (cf. Moser (1977)): in one of the versions which Moser cites the Pope thrusts the staff into the ground immediately before it blossoms (Moser p. 96, citing a ballad published in the early nineteenth century which probably incorporates earlier accounts). For further material see de Waele (1927) 200–3. The flowering of the staff shows Agamemnon's status as the true king. The staff of office can act in miraculous ways, now it has been returned to its rightful owner.

τε: GR have δέ, a common confusion (cf. Diggle (1981a) 59).

422–3 ᾧ κατάσκιον | πᾶσαν γενέσθαι τὴν Μυκηναίων χθόνα: at Hdt. 1.108.1–2 and 7.19.1 the spreading of foliage over an expanse of territory represents the future conquest of that area by the dreamer or the dreamer's descendants. At Daniel 4 a great tree represents the king and his dominion (cf. Pelling (1996) 69 n. 8). The reference to shade is also significant. At Ov. *Met.* 15.561–4 the foliage growing from Romulus' spear provides shade for the onlookers (cf. 564 *non expectatas dabat admirantibus umbras*). At Hdt. 1.209.1 Cyrus dreams that the future king Darius sprouts a pair of wings with which he overshadows (ἐπισκιάζειν) both Europe and Asia. A king may be a protective shade to his people: cf. Aesch. *Ag.* 966–7 ῥίζης γὰρ οὔσης φυλλὰς ἵκετ' ἐς δόμους | σκιὰν ὑπερτείνασα Σειρίου Κυνός (Clytemnestra speaking of the return of Agamemnon), Gaster (1969) 827–8, West (1997) 572. In formal laments 'a good man might be compared with a full grown tree, whose foliage affords welcome shade from the heat of summer' (Alexiou (2002) 198).

For the infinitive in a relative clause in oratio obliqua cf. K–G ii. 550–2.

424 For τοιαῦτα at the end of a narrative see Pfeiffer (1958) 26 = Diller (1967) 483–4, Fraenkel on Aesch. *Ag.* 613–14; also 761n.

του: we need the indefinite, as at Eur. *Med.* 67 ἤκουσά του λέγοντος, οὐ δοκῶν κλύειν. τοῦ would imply that the presence of a single person, and no more than one, was to be expected on such an occasion (though see below on ἐξηγουμένου). The enclitic form of τις is in its expected position (cf. Diggle (1998) 42 = López Férez (1999) 136–7).

The scholia explain τοῖς γὰρ παλαιοῖς ἔθος ἦν ἀποτροπιαζομένους ('by way of expiation') τῷ ἡλίῳ διηγεῖσθαι τὰ ὀνείρατα (p. 122.15–16 Papageorgius). This may merely be an inference from the present passage, but cf. Σ *OC* 477 (pp. 29.18–30.4 De Marco), Eur. *IT* 42–3, Val. Fl. 5.329–32. For other apotropaic actions performed in response to a dream see R. C. T. Parker (1983) 220 n. 71, van Lieshout (1980) 201–4, Ferri on [Sen.] *Oct.* 756–9.

Ἡλίῳ: Babylonian and Assyrian prayers aimed at nullifying the power of bad dreams are normally directed to the sun-god Shamash (cf. West (1997) 54, 548).

425 δείκνυσι: for the historic present in a temporal clause followed by an aorist in the main clause cf. Bruhn §104.II.4.

ἐξηγουμένου: according to van Lieshout (1980) 171–2, this indicates that Chrysothemis heard the news from an exegete, a religious official charged with giving advice on matters of religious ceremonial (cf. Jacoby (1949) 8–51, Garvie on Aesch. *Cho.* 118); he thus reads the definite τοῦ in 424. For such figures elsewhere in tragedy cf. Aesch. *Ag.* 409, *Cho.* 38 (and ἐξηγοῦ in 552), Eur. *Hec.* 87–9. But as Dodds points out (in a letter cited by van Lieshout, *ib.*), the verb refers to the narration of this third party to Chrysothemis, and nothing in the text suggests that this individual was anything more than a chance bystander.

Ll-J/W incorrectly claim that L^ac reads ἐξηγουμένης, and that the truth is the result of a correction. In fact, L has the correct form *in linea*, as Papathomopoulos (1993) 87 points out. Two letters written above the –ου have been mostly erased, but the traces in the facsimile are consistent with –ης (so correctly Dawe, *STS* ii. 63–4).

427 πέμπει: on the tense see 406n.; note the ring composition.

μ' ἐκείνη: whether this or με κείνη should be printed 'is a question which is perhaps unreal (did the pronunciation differ?) and in any case irresoluble' (Barrett on Eur. *Hipp.* 319–21). The normal Attic form ἐκείνη is the commoner manuscript reading when the preceding word ends in an elidible vowel other than ε (with ε manuscript evidence is valueless). Hence with Barrett we may as well print it in cases such as this.

φόβου: J's τάρβους probably arose from a reminiscence of 412 (both instances are preceded by τοῦδε τοῦ); or else it may be an attempt to introduce a poetic word (so N. G. Wilson (1987) 11). This manuscript presents us with readings of note at 760, 1251, 1275 and 1403. They may reflect either isolated preservations of the truth or, more likely, some sort of emendation. For the association of fear and dreams see 410n.

[428–30] These lines are attributed to Chrysothemis in GRZgTTa and to Electra in the other manuscripts. Such attributions carry no authority (cf. West (1973) 55 with nn. 6–7). This impassioned address is unsuitable as an opening to Electra's calm and confident instructions (*pace* Heubner (1961)). Mastronarde (1979) 82 argues that the lines should be spoken by Chrysothemis: Electra then ignores them, in a figure which he identifies as 'a self-willed maintenance of one's own topic'. But the lines do not suit Chrysothemis, either. The dream has left her confused and bewildered (410n.; cf. 426–7): she is not in a position to encourage Electra to follow her lead, even if it were clear what act of obedience ἐμοὶ πιθέσθαι denotes. The force of νυν is also difficult to gauge. Given these difficulties, the near-exact repetition of μὴ 'ξ ἀβουλίας πεσεῖν from 398 may indicate that the passage originated as a reworking and amplification of that line. Ll-J/W rightly adopt Morstadt's deletion ((1864) iv).

[428] θεῶν . . . τῶν ἐγγενῶν: cf. *Ant.* 199 θεοὺς τοὺς ἐγγενεῖς, 938 θεοὶ προγενεῖς; contrast the commoner formulation θεοὶ πατρῷοι (411 n.).

431–63 Electra tells her sister to abandon the offerings (431–8). She then explains the futility of these gifts and Clytemnestra's audacity in sending them (439–48). Finally, she instructs her to make a different offering in their place, and sends her on her way with encouraging words (448–63). Her tone is very different from that of her previous *rheseis*. Gone is the bitter anguish and passionate anger which had characterised her former utterances (254–309, 341–68). In their place, we see a confidence and self-assurance which demonstrates both the change in her situation and the extent of her capacity for emotional expression. This shift in tone was first identifiable at 411, but only briefly and without explanation. Now it receives a full and satisfying exposition.

In *Choephori* Orestes follows the account of the dream by interpreting its contents (540–50); the chorus then acknowledges his success as a τερασκόπον (551–2). Here Electra does not explicitly state the significance of the vision. Instead, she seizes the opportunity to persuade her sister. She addresses her as φίλη and ἀδελφή for the first time, but the speech is not an exercise in flattery: the persuasiveness of her case comes rather from the exhilarating directness with which it is presented, and the strength of the resolution from which it originates. Note her firm imperatives, confident rhetoric, and what Reinhardt calls 'the rich use of figures of speech which penetrate through [*hinüberdringenden*] so as to involve the other person' ((1979) 260 n. 11 ≈ (1947) 275, citing σκέψαι γάρ (442), ἆρα μὴ δοκεῖς (446), οὐκ ἔστιν (448)).

Does Chrysothemis abandon the offerings on stage, and if so, when? She might carry them away with her, leaving the audience to assume that she disposes of them before reaching the grave. But the act of abandonment would be of such symbolic importance that it ought to take place on stage. She should put them down, or perhaps even throw them away (cf. 435–6, 448), during her words at 466–71, since this is the moment when she complies with her sister's request. An earlier abandonment would risk bathos: Electra's appeal would be directed at someone who had already demonstrated her obedience. The objects are probably small enough not to be in the way during the remainder of the play; if that is not the case, extras could remove them during the following choral song.

431 ἀλλ᾽: according to Denniston 14, this 'introduces an objection in the form of a command'; after 427, Electra tells her sister 'all the same, don't do as she says'.

ὦ φίλη: expresses Electra's change of tone (cf. 461 n.).

ὧν ἔχεις χεροῖν: probably an indication that Chrysothemis does not have any handmaids (324n.). So too at Eur. *Or.* 111 Helen sends Hermione to make offerings at Clytemnestra's tomb on her own.

432–4 For the distrust of an enemy's gift cf. *Aj.* 665 ἐχθρῶν ἄδωρα δῶρα κοὐκ ὀνήσιμα, Virg. *Aen.* 2.49 *timeo Danaos et dona ferentis*. Electra implies that the dead remain implacably hostile towards their killers; this is made explicit at 442–8. Compare *Aj.* 1393–5, where Teucer is afraid to let Odysseus take part in Ajax's burial, lest the involvement of his enemy be τῷ θανόντι . . . δυσχερές: the signal services which Odysseus has just rendered Ajax do not change the matter.

432–3 οὐ . . . θέμις | οὐδ᾽ ὅσιον: for the combination cf. *Phil.* 662 ὅσιά τε φωνεῖς ἔστι τ᾽, ὦ τέκνον, θέμις, fr. 742 *TrGF* ἀθέμιστα καὶ ἀνόσια δρᾶν; also Sall. *Cat.* 15.1 *contra ius fasque*, Cic. *Att.* 1.16.6, Mynors on Virg. *Georg.* 1.269, Oakley on Livy 8.5.8. For οὐ θέμις see further Burkert (1966) 117 n. 70 = (2001) 35 n. 70.

433 Most manuscripts have nothing between ἐχθρᾶς and γυναικός. The minority reading ἀπό (found in only one manuscript group) is probably no more than an attempt to fill the gap. A resolved princeps made up of a single disyllabic word is rare in S. (cf. West (1982a) 87). Müller (1866) 91 also points out that ἀπό would give us two resolutions in the same line, something paralleled in this play only at 326, where one of the resolutions is the result of a proper name. Note, however, Diggle (2007) n. 52 for a few other examples of this licence in S.

Possibilities include πρός (attributed by editors to Dindorf), ἐκ (Meineke (1863a) 257) and παρά (cf. Dawe, *STS* i. 179–80). Nauck³ prefers to re-arrange, giving οὐδ᾽ ὅσιον ἐχθρᾶς ἱστάναι κτερίσματα | γυναικὸς κτλ. (cf. (1862) 179):

the separation of ἐχθρᾶς from γυναικός thus achieved throws an attractive emphasis onto the former.

434 κτερίσματ᾽ and λουτρά are here distinguished; cf. 931, *OC* 1410, Eur. *Suppl.* 309, *Tro.* 1249, *Hel.* 1391, where the former is used of funeral rites or offerings in general, like the Homeric κτέρεα. The difference owes more to rhetoric than sense, the denial being more emphatic if it comprises two objects. The two nouns also balance the two prospective fates for the offerings described in the next line, as well as the twofold οὐ . . . θέμις | οὐδ᾽ ὅσιον in 432–3. For λουτρά of libations to the corpse see 84n.

435–6 For unwanted items thrown to the winds cf. Eur. *Tro.* 418–19, 454, *Ba.* 350, Ap. Rh. 1.1334–5, Gow on Theocr. 22.167–8, Virg. *Aen.* 11.795, Nisbet and Hubbard on Hor. *C.* 1.26.2, Tib. 1.5.35–6, Ov. *Trist.* 1.2.15. The figure is also common as a metaphor (e.g. *Tr.* 467–8, Aesch. *Sept.* 690). Burial in the dust is not as common a method of disposal (though cf. *Aj.* 658–9): here it leads into the grim humour of 437–8. The two different methods of destruction heighten the rhetoric: cf. Hor. *C.* 1.16.2–4 *quem criminosis cumque voles modum | pones iambis, sive flamma, | sive mari libet Hadriano,* Tib. 1.9.49–50; also S. *Aj.* 1192–3 ὄφελε πρότερον αἰθέρα δῦ- | ναι μέγαν ἢ τὸν πολύκοινον Ἀίδαν.

436 κρύψον: the verb is strictly applicable only to the second of the alternatives in 435. For this zeugma cf. [Aesch.] *PV* 21–2 ἵν᾽ οὔτε φωνὴν οὔτε του μορφὴν βροτῶν | ὄψει with Griffith, Bruhn §198.II, Fraenkel on Aesch. *Ag.* 797–8.

νιν = αὐτά, a purely tragic usage (cf. 624, Friis Johansen and Whittle on Aesch. *Suppl.* 729).

ἔνθα: ἔνθεν (Meineke (1863a) 257 and TTa) is over-literal. ἔνθα μήποτε is something of a Sophoclean formula, compare 380, *OT* 796, 1412, and similar expressions in 1436, *Aj.* 659, *Tr.* 800. ἔνθεν has a pedantic look, and is likely to be an improvement by Triclinius᾽ (West (1978a) 107).

For εὐνήν of a final resting-place cf. Aesch. *Cho.* 318 ἔνθα σ᾽ ἔχουσιν εὐναί, *Sept.* 1004 πῆμα πατρὶ πάρευνον, *IG* v/2.176.2 = *GVI* 2080.3 (Tegea, 2nd cent. BC), *EG* 431.3 = *GVI* 704.3 = *SGO* iv. 20/03/05.3 (Syrian Antioch, 1st cent. AD) κεῖμαι ἐς αὐχμηροὺς καὶ ἀλαμπέας Ἀίδος εὐνάς, Seaford (1984) 251 n. 31.

437–8 ἀλλ᾽ ὅταν θάνῃ, | κειμήλι᾽ αὐτῇ ταῦτα σῳζέσθω κάτω: sentiment and form are paralleled by *Aj.* 660 ἀλλ᾽ αὐτὸ νὺξ Ἅιδης τε σῳζόντων κάτω. Electra's tone is ironical, especially with the predicative κειμήλια: the sense combines 'little good will they do her then' and 'no-one else is likely to bring her offerings'. For ἀλλ᾽ see 387n. κειμήλια is regularly used of objects laid up or stored away (see Diggle on Eur. *Pha.* 56 = fr. 773.12

COMMENTARY: 251–471

TrGF). For the imperative cf. Hom. *Il.* 23.618 σοὶ τοῦτο . . . κειμήλιον ἔστω.

439–48 Cf. Aesch. *Cho.* 514–22, where Orestes wonders why Clytemnestra should have sent offerings to his father. The act seems futile for two reasons. First, the dead man will not relent in his anger against his killers (517–18 θανόντι δ' οὐ φρονοῦντι δειλαία χάρις | ἐπέμπετ'); cf. *Cho.* 40–1 μέμφεσθαι τοὺς γᾶς νέρθεν περιθύμως | τοῖς κτανοῦσί τ' ἐγκοτεῖν, *Aj.* 1394–5, Sier on Aesch. *Cho.* 326, Macleod on Hom. *Il.* 24.592–4, Braswell on Pind. *P.* 4.159a. Second, the guilt of murder cannot be washed away with libations (520 τὰ πάντα γάρ τις ἐκχέας ἀνθ' αἵματος | ἑνός, μάτην ὁ μόχθος); cf. *Cho.* 48, *Eum.* 647–8. In Aeschylus Orestes' questions follow the *kommos*, and serve as a transition to news of the dream. S. has transferred all this to an explicitly deliberative context: Electra uses these points as arguments to persuade her sister. There is a consequent intensification in the rhetoric. 442–8 is particularly striking: a long sentence full of emotionally-charged and unpleasant details (νέκυς, θανὼν ἄτιμος, ἐμασχαλίσθη, κηλῖδας ἐξέμαξεν) leads into a confident rhetorical question, which is itself answered with the curt οὐκ ἔστιν (448n.). A similar pattern (long sentence, short rhetorical question, even shorter denial) occurs at *Ant.* 284–9.

439 ἀρχήν: *omnino*, as at *Ant.* 92 and *Phil.* 1239 (there also preceding a negative).
δ' ἄν: the alternative γάρ feels like a *lectio facilior*. γάρ also displaces the true reading in some manuscripts at 385 (n.), and in all manuscripts at 845 (n.).

439–40 τλημονεστάτη γύνη | πασῶν: for the superlative with the genitive plural of πᾶς see Hutchinson on Aesch. *Sept.* 927.

440 ἔβλαστε: the light first syllable is unusual: cf. West (1982a) 16–17.
δυσμενεῖς: the hostility of the woman is transferred to the offerings she sends. Nauck's δυσσεβεῖς (in his sixth edition, p. 174; for the reverse corruption cf. R's reading at *Ant.* 516) takes away this force from the word.

441 ὅν . . . τῷδ': for ὅδε after a relative cf. *Ant.* [666], *OC* 1332.
ἐπέστεφε: often of honouring the dead with offerings (53n.). Its proximity to ἔκτεινε stresses the paradox.

442–3 δοκεῖ | . . . δέξασθαι: many editors adopt B. Heath's δέξεσθαι ((1762) 17), perhaps rightly. Opinions relating to future events are normally expressed by δοκέω with the future infinitive. But there are exceptions: cf. *Aj.* 1081–3 ὅπου δ' ὑβρίζειν . . . παρῇ, | ταύτην νόμιζε τὴν πόλιν χρόνῳ ποτὲ | . . . ἐς βυθὸν πεσεῖν, Aesch. *Sept.* 428–9 οὐδὲ τὴν Διὸς | ἔριν πέδοι σκήψασαν

223

ἐμποδὼν σχεθεῖν with Hutchinson, K–G i. 195–7, S–D ii. 296. S fr. 339 *TrGF* ἦ φὴς ὑπομνὺς ἀνθυπουργῆσαι χάριν; is particularly relevant, as it counters Dawe's objection that all these exceptions involve a strong aorist infinitive (*STS* i. 180). In our instance the alteration would be of only one letter, and Willink claims that in general 'routine corrections of –σαι to –σειν and of –σασθαι to –σεσθαι should not be resisted' (on Eur. *Or.* 1527; cf. also Kovacs (1987) 257–8). But given that there are several metrically-guaranteed instances of this idiom, and given that the manuscripts (and Suda, μ 274 = iii. 336.4 Adler) are unanimous, the transmitted text should probably be retained. V's δέξεται *supra lineam* is probably a gloss rather than a trace of original δέξεσθαι (so Dawe, *STS* i. 180).

444 θανὼν ἄτιμος: at Aesch. *Cho.* 345–54 Orestes laments that his father was denied an honourable death in battle; at *Eum.* 625–39 Apollo describes Agamemnon's unheroic end to excite indignation.

445 ἐμασχαλίσθη: the verb occurs elsewhere only at Aesch. *Cho.* 439 ἐμασχαλίσθη δέ γ', ὡς τόδ' εἰδῇς. The noun μασχαλισμός is scarcely more common: in the classical period it is found only at S. fr. 623 *TrGF* πλήρη μασχαλισμάτων and Tr. Adesp. fr. 593a *TrGF*. The practice which it denotes is described in the lexica (see Slater on Ar. Byz. fr. 412, which is probably their source): the dead man's extremities were removed, strung together and tied under his neck and armpits (μασχάλαι). There are two likely explanations, both mentioned in the scholia (pp. 123.4–124.6 Papageorgius). It may have been an attempted expiation of the pollution accruing from the murder, like wiping the sword on the head (445–6n.), or spitting out the dead man's blood (cf. Aesch. fr. 186a *TrGF*). So at Ap. Rh. 4.477–9 Jason cuts off the dead man's ἐξάργματα and spits out his blood; the poet then comments on Jason's propitiatory aim (see Livrea). But it may also have been aimed at disabling the dead man and rendering him incapable of vengeance (see Garvie and (especially) Sier on Aesch. *Cho.* 439). Here Clytemnestra's motivation is not at issue: Electra mentions it to incite her sister against his killer.

The same terminology is also used to denote a religious practice. According to Ar. Byz. fr. 412 Slater, σημαίνει ... ἡ λέξις καὶ τὰ τοῖς μηροῖς ἐπιτιθέμενα ἀπὸ τῶν ὤμων [ὠμῶν Rohde] κρέα ἐν ταῖς τῶν θεῶν θυσίαις, while μασχαλίσματα are mentioned on an Attic *lex sacra*, perhaps of the third century BC (Vanderpool (1970) 48, lines 16–17). It is not clear, however, whether the practice originated with sacrificial or murder victims (R. C. T. Parker (1984)).

445–6 κἀπὶ λουτροῖσιν κάρα | κηλῖδας ἐξέμαξεν: an attempt to remove the pollution caused by the murder and put it back on the dead man (cf. Σ p. 123.6 Papageorgius ὥσπερ ἀποτροπιαζόμενοι τὸ μύσος τὸ ἐν τῷ φόνῳ,

Eust. 1852.7, Suda μ 274 (= iii. 335.23–4 Adler). Russo on Hom. *Od.* 19.92 ἔρδουσα μέγα ἔργον, ὃ σῇ κεφαλῇ ἀναμάξεις suggests that the expression alludes to 'a ritual custom by which wiping blood from a sacrificial knife on to the victim was a means of transferring the guilt to the victim . . . Such a custom would form part of the *Unschuldskomödie*, the "comedy of innocence", performed in ritual slaughter as a device for warding off the guilt-feelings that must inevitably attach to the "murderer".' Consequently, this may be a perversion of a ritual practice associated with sacrifice (as could also be the case with the μασχαλισμός described above).

For guilt on the head more generally cf. Aesch. *Eum.* 176–7, Hdt. 1.155.3, Olson on Ar. *Pax* 1063, Wankel on Dem. 18.290; for curses directed at the head cf. Murgatroyd on Tib. 1.2.11–12, Gibson on Ov. *Ars* 3.241–2. For 'wiping off' as a means of removing pollution see Burkert (1984) 62 = (1992) 61–2.

445 ἐπὶ λουτροῖσιν 'in place of the ceremonial washing', which relatives gave to the corpse (1138–9). Agamemnon is washed not in water, but in his own blood; not as a mark of honour and respect, but to humiliate him and transfer the guilt of his killing on to himself. Such abuse of funerary convention makes Clytemnestra's offerings seem all the more hypocritical.

κάρᾳ: only in C^{ac} and Eust. 1857.7, a pair who also coincide at *Aj.* 579 (see Dawe, *STS* i. 103); *coni.* Wakefield (1789–95) i. 105. Other manuscripts have κάρα; however, the iotas of dative endings often disappear from the paradosis, and were not always written in antiquity. For the form of the dative see K–B i. 460. For Eustathius's importance as a source for the text see Miller (1946).

446 ἐξέμαξεν: the subject suddenly shifts to Clytemnestra. For other such abrupt changes of subject in a relative clause cf. *Aj.* 457–8 ὅστις ἐμφανῶς θεοῖς | ἐχθαίρομαι, μισεῖ δέ μ' Ἑλλήνων στρατός, *Ant.* 531–2, Bruhn §191.

ἆρα μή rarely opens a question in classical Greek. Its nuance is not 'surely . . . not', but 'can it be that . . .?': it 'does not necessarily imply the expectation of a negative reply, but merely that the suggestion made is difficult of acceptance' (Denniston 47–8). The other Sophoclean instance is at *Ant.* 632–3 ἆρα μὴ . . . | . . . πατρὶ λυσσαίνων πάρει; Either of the interpretations mentioned by Denniston would fit these passages (so Moorhouse 320); but without a certain example of ἆρα μή = 'surely . . . not', we should adopt the sense which Denniston prefers. The same meaning is found with questions introduced with μή: cf. *Tr.* 316, Fraenkel on Aesch. *Ag.* 683, Diggle (1977a) 117 = (1994) 160.

447 λυτήρι': on the word and its formation see Hutchinson on Stes. fr. 222(b).226 *PMGF*.

448 οὐκ ἔστιν: Electra sums up with potent brevity; compare *Tr.* 449, *Aj.* 470 οὐκ ἔστι ταῦτα, Virg. *Aen.* 2.583 *non ita*.

ἀλλά: marks 'a transition from arguments for action to a statement of the action required . . . [it] usually occurs near the end of a speech, as a clinching and final appeal' (Denniston 14; cf. 1009).

ταῦτα μὲν μέθες: returns by ring composition to the opening of the speech.

σὺ δέ 'marks an antithesis, not of persons, but of clauses' (Jebb): cf. 711, 1472n., Hom. *Il.* 6.46 ζώγρει, Ἀτρέος υἱέ, σὺ δ' ἄξια δέξαι ἄποινα, Fraenkel on Aesch. *Ag.* 1061.

449–50 For the dedication of hair to the dead cf. 52n. Both sisters will contribute. Electra emphasises the meagreness of her offering of hair, which is already cut short in mourning (cf. Eur. *Phoen.* 322–3, Diggle (1981a) 25). Contrast the delight taken in their hair by women in Eur. *IT* 1149, *Phoen.* 222–4, Alcm. frr. 1.51–4, 3.71–2 *PMGF*, Aesch. fr. 313.1 *TrGF*. Electra's offering makes for a pathetic contrast with the luxuriant foliatory tribute offered earlier by her brother (52; cf. C. P. Segal (1981) 274). There is also a touch of the 'widow's mite' motif: small but sincere offerings are worth more than rich gifts presented by hypocrites such as Clytemnestra (cf. Ov. *Fast.* 2.535–6 *parva petunt manes: pietas pro divite grata est | munere; non avidos Styx habet ima deos*, Epist. Pont. 3.4.79–82, 4.8.31–42, Wehrli (1931) 46–60, R. C. T. Parker (1998) 119 with n. 48).

In artistic depictions postdating Aeschylus' *Choephori* Electra is regularly depicted with short hair and poor clothing. A terracotta relief of 445–430 BC (Berlin, Staatliche Museen TI 6803) shows Electra in mourning at Agamemnon's tomb with a plain, open peplos, her hair cut short, and no jewellery, hairband or footwear. A scyphos ascribed to the Penelope Painter (*ARV²* 1301.5; Copenhagen, National Museum inv. 597; *c.* 440 BC) depicts her with hair cut short and no jewellery. This contrasts with the Electra of earlier art, where she appears at the killing of Aegisthus in the dress of a princess.

450–1 σμικρὰ μὲν τάδ', ἀλλ' ὅμως | ἄχω: for the phrase 'small, but my own' cf. Achilles' γέρας . . . ὀλίγον τε φίλον τε (Hom. *Il.* 1.167). Contrast Eur. *Or.* 128–9, where Electra attacks Helen for making such an offering when she was capable of more: ἴδετε γὰρ ἄκρας ὡς ἀπέθρισεν τρίχας, | σῴζουσα κάλλος· ἔστι δ' ἡ πάλαι γυνή.

451 ἀλιπαρῆ can be interpreted as follows. (i) The negation of λιπαρής ('suited for supplication' (cf. 1378)); hence Hermann's *comam non accommodatam supplicationi*. But while Electra emphasises the poverty of her offerings, she cannot describe them as 'unsuitable for supplication' without obscuring a vital contrast. Her gifts are a suitable tribute to her father, while her mother's are not. (ii) The negation of λιπαρός ('oily'). This gives attractive sense: it balances οὐ χλιδαῖς ἠσκημένον in the following line, while the stress on Electra's unkempt and dirty hair is appropriate in the context (cf. Σ p. 124.13 Papageorgius ἀντὶ τοῦ αὐχμηράν, Hesych. α 3029 = i. 107 Latte, Suda α 1239 = i. 113.12 Adler, Eur. *El.* 184 σκέψαι μου πιναρὰν κόμαν, Renehan (1992) 354). However, this reading involves the following difficulties. (a) λιπαρός has a short iota, and hence we would expect ἀλιπαρής to have one too. For the line to scan, we thus need to insert a τ' (Fröhlich) or a γ' (Erfurdt, in his edition, p. 434). (b) Alpha-privatives from adjectives ending in –ρος are very rare. Ll-J/W make much of this in *Sophoclea* and *Second Thoughts*: but Renehan, in his defence of this reading ((1992) 354–6), cites not just ἀνελεύθερος and ἀνίερος (both first attested in Aeschylus) but ἄπικρος (in pseudo-Aristotle) and ἄγλισχρος (Hippocrates, Theophrastus). (c) An alpha-privative from an adjective in –ρος should itself end in –ρος, not –ρής. But –ος adjectives do sometimes develop alternative forms in –ης (cf. Meissner (1995) 238–9). Renehan cites four alpha-privatives in –ής which stand alongside commoner alternatives in –ος. Of these, the instances of ἀεναής, ἀεργής and ἀνηλιφής are too late to be relevant. This leaves us with ἀνωμαλής, which is found in Theophrastus. A further pair not mentioned by Renehan is ἄπηρος and ἀπηρής: the former is found at Hdt. 1.32.6, the latter at Ap. Rh. 1.556, 1.888. However, there is no instance of *ἀλίπαρος beside which a putative ἀλιπαρής could stand: with Renehan's examples we are always dealing with pairs of words. (d) The word ἀλιπαρής itself may not occur elsewhere until St Cyril of Alexandria (*Glaphyra in Genesin* 3.82). It twice occurs as a v.l. in Lucian, however (see Renehan); Ll-J/W in *Second Thoughts* argue against putting it in the text in both these places. They prefer the variant τὸ λιπαρές; but while this may well be right in one of the passages, τὸ ἀλιπαρές is more likely in the other.[27] (iii) Ll-J/W prefer λιπαρῆ, giving the sense 'suppliant hair' (for which

---

[27] In each case the disputed phrase forms part of a list. At Lucian 70.24 (= iv. 36.4 Macleod) it is followed by καὶ τὸ μὴ ἐνδοῦναι μηδὲ μαλακισθῆναι πολλοῖς τοῖς δυσχερέσιν, and this reference to perseverance naturally takes τὸ λιπαρές as its accompaniment. At 41.9 (= ii. 321.20 Macleod) an expert is giving advice to a tyro on how to become an expert rhetorician. The text runs πόνον δὲ καὶ ἀγρυπνίαν καὶ ὑδατοποσίαν καὶ τὸ (ἀ)λιπαρὲς ἀναγκαῖα ταῦτα καὶ ἀπαραίτητα φήσει. ἀδύνατον γὰρ εἶναι ἄνευ τούτων διανύσαι τὴν ὁδόν. ὃ δὲ πάντων ἀνιαρότατον, ὅτι σοὶ καὶ τὸν χρόνον πάμπολυν ὑπογράψει τῆς ὁδοιπορίας κτλ. Ll-J/W (*Second Thoughts*) follow Macleod in preferring the variant τὸ λιπαρές on the grounds that (i) 'the idea of pertinacity is stressed in the words that follow the list of requirements for the aspirant', and (ii) '"fatless food" or "Spartan fare" [Renehan's translations of τὸ ἀλιπαρές] consort somewhat oddly with the *abstract* nouns that figure in the lists'. Neither reason stands up to scrutiny. In (i) Ll-J/W do not take account of the strong break which intervenes

cf. *Aj.* 1174–5 κόμας ἐμὰς . . . | ἱκτήριον θησαυρόν, *OR* 3 ἱκτηρίοις κλάδοισιν, *OR* 143 ἱκτῆρας κλάδους). This reading is found in a scholium, according to which ἐν δὲ τῷ ὑπομνήματι λιπαρῇ, ὅ ἐστιν ἐξ ἧς αὐτὸν λιπαρήσομεν, ὡς εἰ ἔλεγεν ἱκέτιν τρίχα (p. 124.13–15 Papageorgius); the corruption into the manuscript reading is only of a single letter.

The rhetoric of the passage strongly favours the meaning 'unkempt', which gives a parallel with the following clause οὐ χλιδαῖς ἠσκημένον. On grounds of sense ἀλιπαρῆ is preferable to λιπαρῆ; nor does the scholiast's evidence afford much support for the latter, since such an uncommon word was almost bound to be corrupted into the more usual adjective. But has Renehan demonstrated that such a word is possible? Problems (a) and (b) are not troubling; (d) too is not a difficulty. The word is probably found in Lucian, and certainly in St Cyril; and even if it were not, *hapaxes* in Sophocles are hardly unknown. It is (c) which goes to the heart of the matter. Could –ος adjectives have alpha-privatives in –ής in S.'s day? And could such alpha-privatives exist without an alpha-privative in –ος to stand beside them? In considering this question we must remember that the number of these words is small indeed. Without the Herodotean example of ἄπηρος, for example, we should not know that this word existed in the classical period. Given the amount of Greek that we have lost, it is possible that ἀλίπαρος *did* exist, but was so infrequent that we have no surviving evidence for it. We should therefore keep ἀλιπαρῆ, and consequently must add a τε to heal the metre. Rhetoric demands it, and philology probably does not prevent it.

452 For ζῶμα of a woman's girdle (more usually ζώνη) cf. Alcaeus fr. 42.10 *PLF*, Voigt, Aesch. *Suppl.* 462.

Here, as the scholia suggest (p. 124.20–1 Papageorgius), Electra's girdle is probably intended as a makeshift ταινία, such as were commonly wound around grave stelae. Kurtz (1975) contains contemporary illustrations of the practice, which is also depicted on the Copenhagen scyphos (cited above, 449–50n.). See also Garland (2001) 116 and 170–1. For clothes in general offered to the dead cf. Eur. *Or.* 1436, Thuc. 3.58.4.

between the list and the mention of perseverance. The sentence beginning ἀδύνατον looks back to the list; but then ὃ δὲ πάντων ἀνιαρότατον, far from 'following the list of requirements', must signal the introduction of a fresh idea, not one which has just been mentioned as one term among many in a list. In (ii) Ll-J/W focus on Renehan's suggested translations for τὸ ἀλιπαρές rather than on the Greek. τὸ ἀλιπαρές is no less abstract a means of expression than, say, τὸ κάλλος or τὸ δίκαιον. Far from 'consorting oddly' with the other items on the list, τὸ ἀλιπαρές makes a better connexion than the text preferred by Macleod and Ll-J/W. Toil, lack of sleep, drinking (only) water (i.e. not drinking wine) – all these are physical privations, which the would-be orator must undergo. A 'Spartan diet' fits naturally alongside these, especially next to ὑδατοποσίαν: both liquid and solid nourishment must be curtailed.

COMMENTARY: 251–471

οὐ χλιδαῖς ἠσκημένον: on the poverty of Electra's attire cf. 449–50n. ἀσκέω here = 'adorn' (LSJ⁹ s.v. I.2); cf. [Eur.] fr. 1132.2 *TrGF* οὐκ ἐν πολυχρύσοισιν ἤσκηται χλιδαῖς.

453–4 The aid of the dead Agamemnon is often invoked by his offspring in tragedy: cf. Aesch. *Cho.* 459 ἄκουσον ἐς φάος μολών, | ξὺν δὲ γενοῦ πρὸς ἐχθρούς, 489 ὦ Γαῖ, ἄνες μοι πατέρ' ἐποπτεῦσαι μάχην, Eur. *El.* 677–80 σύ τ' ὦ κάτω γῆς ἀνοσίως οἰκῶν πάτηρ | . . . | ἄμυν' ἄμυνε τοῖσδε φιλτάτοις τέκνοις. | νῦν πάντα νεκρὸν ἐλθὲ σύμμαχον λαβών, *Or.* 1225–6 ὦ δῶμα ναίων Νυκτὸς ὀρφναίας πάτερ, | καλῶ σ' Ὀρέστης παῖς σὸς ἐπίκουρον μολεῖν; also Aesch. *Eum.* 598 ἀρωγὰς δ' ἐκ τάφου πέμπει πατήρ. Cf. also the prayer at [Sen.] *Oct.* 134–5 *emergere umbris* [Heinsius; *undis* codd.] *et fer auxilium tuae* | *natae invocanti, genitor.*

In *Choephori* Agamemnon is invoked during a monumental *kommos* (306–478). Euripides in his *Electra* reduces it to a shorter section (677–84). In S. it does not occur on stage. The younger dramatists preferred to concentrate their efforts in areas of the story relatively neglected by Aeschylus. More generally, great static scenes were not favoured by S. and Euripides, whereas they were quite a favourite device of Aeschylus' (cf. the central shield scene in *Septem*).

453 προσπίτνουσα γῆθεν: an effective juxtaposition: Chrysothemis is to fall to the ground, to urge her father to rise up from the ground.

For εὐμενῆ as a standard epithet for chthonic powers when viewed under their beneficial aspect cf. Henrichs (1991) 163 n. 6.

454 For ἀρωγόν of an avenger cf. *OR* 126–7 Λαΐου δ' ὀλωλότος | οὐδεὶς ἀρωγὸς . . . ἐγίγνετο, Aesch. *Cho.* 376, 477, 725.

αὐτὸν εἰς ἐχθροὺς μολεῖν: 'prayers for assistance usually ask the god or hero to come in person, as if he could not act from a distance' (West on Eur. *Or.* 1226, referring to his note on Hes. *Op.* 2). For αὐτός used to denote Agamemnon in a similar context cf. Aesch. *Cho.* 454.

455–6 Similar is Electra's prayer at Aesch. *Cho.* 138–9: ἐλθεῖν δ' Ὀρέστην δεῦρο σὺν τύχῃ τινὶ | κατεύχομαί σοι, καὶ σὺ κλῦθί μου πάτερ.

455 ἐξ ὑπερτέρας χερός 'with superior strength'; cf. 1090–1 καθύπερθεν | χερί. For ἐξ see 48n.

456 αὐτοῦ 'here': Electra's concern is, as ever, with the absence of her brother (cf. δεῦρο at Aesch. *Cho.* 138, cited previous n.). Taken as genitive singular with ἐχθροῖσιν or παῖδ' the word would be intolerably weak: it is already clear whose child and whose enemies are being referred to.

229

ζῶντ': accusative, as the 3rd declension dative singular does not elide in tragedy (cf. West (1982a) 10 with n. 13. The few seeming exceptions in K–B i. 235–6 can easily be emended away). There is a contrast between the aid afforded by the dead Agamemnon and the living Orestes; but Jebb sees the real thrust of the phrase when he comments 'the thought is, "may he live to do it"'. So too at 811 the sense is 'I hoped that you would live to avenge our father.'

ἐπεμβῆναι ποδί: for the verb used in similar contexts cf. 836, *Aj.* 1348 οὐ γὰρ θανόντι καὶ προσεμβῆναί σε χρή; with Jebb, Eur. *Hipp.* 668. For feet causing pain or dishonour cf. Aesch. *Pers.* 515–16 ὦ δυσπόνητε δαῖμον, ὡς ἄγαν βαρὺς | ποδοῖν ἐνήλω παντὶ Περσικῶι γένει, Casali on Ov. *Her.* 9.11–12; also λάξ at e.g. *Cho.* 643, *Eum.* 110, 540–2. Compare the chorus's later prayer that Electra will be καθύπερθεν | . . . ἐχθρῶν (1090–1).

457–8 Worshippers regularly hold out the prospect of richer offerings to the power to which they are appealing: cf. Aesch. *Cho.* 255–7 (to Zeus) καὶ τοῦ θυτῆρος καὶ σὲ τιμῶντος μέγα | πατρὸς νεοσσοὺς τούσδ'ἀποφθείρας πόθεν | ἕξεις ὁμοίας χειρὸς εὔθοινον γέρας;, 483–5 (to Agamemnon) οὕτω γὰρ ἄν σοι δαῖτες ἔννομοι βροτῶν | κτιζοίατ᾿· εἰ δὲ μή, παρ' εὐδείπνοις ἔσηι| ἄτιμος ἐμπύροισι κνισωτοῖς χθονός, also *Sept.* 76–7, Theogn. 775–9, Agis *A.P.* 6.152.3–4 = 12–13 *HE*, Apollonides *A.P.* 6.238.5–6 = 1135–6 *GP*, Ausfeld (1903) 528–9, West (1997) 574–5, R. C. T. Parker (1998) 108 n. 11, 111 n. 23. There is also a suggestion of the future prosperity of the house (cf. 72).

458 στέφωμεν: 53n.

459 οἶμαι . . . οἶμαι: the repetition conveys Electra's excitement: cf. 495–6n., Ar. *Plut.* 114 οἶμαι γάρ, οἶμαι, S. fr. 846 *TrGF*, Eur. *Phoen.* 584 with Mastronarde, *Or.* 1143, Dem. 21.46 οὐ γὰρ ἔστιν, οὐκ ἔστιν etc. For anadiplosis at the start of the trimeter cf. Diggle (1996c) 196–7; some of his examples have the repeated words separated by a particle.

μὲν οὖν: each particle retains its separate force.

τι κἀκείνῳ: 'she means that, though the *gods* below are the primary authors of the vision, the spirit of the dead was also in some measure active' (Jebb). However, the dream need not have been sent by the gods below, as the Olympians were also involved in the sending of dreams: cf. Hom. *Il.* 1.63 καὶ γάρ τ᾿ ὄναρ ἐκ Διός ἐστιν.

μέλειν (*coni.* Blaydes') for manuscript μέλον is inevitable, as οἶμαι does not elsewhere take a participial construction. We cannot make οἶμαι parenthetic, and then either understand ἦν with μέλον (cf. *OC* 653 ἀλλὰ τοῖσδ' ἔσται μέλον) or emend it to 'μελεν (Kamerbeek (1972) 32): a word which begins a sentence can hardly be parenthetic (cf. Ll-J/W, *Sophoclea*).

460 πέμψαι: powers beneath the earth often 'send' things up from below: the verb used is normally ἀνίημι (cf. Henrichs (1991) 199 n. 83), but for πέμπω cf. 117, Aesch. *Pers.* 630, *Cho.* 147 ἡμῖν δὲ πομπὸς ἴσθι τῶν ἐσθλῶν ἄνω, 477, Eur. *Hel.* 569 ὦ φωσφόρ᾽ Ἑκάτη, πέμπε φάσματ᾽ εὐμενῆ.

δυσπρόσοπτ᾽ is the majority reading; CNO have δυσπρόσοπτ᾽. At *OC* 286 the manuscripts are also split between –οπτον and –ωπον. Apart from Tr. Adesp. fr. 339a *TrGF* δυσπρόσωπα ὄμματα, neither word is found elsewhere before Plutarch. As their meanings are difficult to distinguish, we may as well adopt the better attested variant.

461 ὅμως δ᾽: i.e. 'Agamemnon is indeed already helping us, but nevertheless go and ask for his help at his tomb'. Cf. Aesch. *Eum.* 64–74 (Apollo to Orestes) (I won't betray you, and have put the Erinyes to sleep); ὅμως δὲ φεῦγε, μηδὲ μαλθακὸς γένη.

ἀδελφή: only now does Electra address Chrysothemis as 'sister'. Familial titles have a special significance for Electra (cf. 273–4, 597–8, 1148): the term marks the warmth she feels towards Chrysothemis for the news she has brought, as well as an attempt to secure her compliance through her friendliness. ἀδελφή is an extremely rare form of address (Dickey (1996) 227); ἀδελφέ is not common either, though more evidence for it exists. Dickey suggests that ἀδελφέ marks an especially close emotional bond ((1996) 88, 226–7; its only Sophoclean instances are in this play, at 1346 and 1484): the same is likely to be true of ἀδελφή.

The technique is found in reverse in the prologue to *Antigone*: Antigone begins by addressing Ismene in terms elaborately expressive of family ties (1), but soon abandons them when it is clear that she will not assist her. Cf. ὦ φίλη in the peroration to Electra's subsequent appeal to Chrysothemis (986).

461–2 σοί θ᾽ . . . | ἐμοί τ᾽: the syntax reflects the move from confrontation to conciliation: contrast Electra's previous use of oppositional δέ to express the sisters' relationship (349, 357, 364).

462 ἀρωγά: internal accusative with ὑπούργησον; cf. *Phil.* 1326 νοσεῖς τόδ᾽ ἄλγος.

462–3 βροτῶν | πάντων, ἐν Ἅιδου κειμένῳ κοινῷ: bracketed by West (1978a) 118 as an example of *Binneninterpolation*, but the words should stay. Electra is keen on the superlative when describing members of her own family (cf. 366, 407, 439–40, 1126). And 'in the solemn appeal of one sister to another, stress on Agamemnon's dearness to both and on his common fatherhood is not surprising' (Ll-J/W, *Sophoclea*).

463 For κειμένῳ predicated of the dead cf. 1418, *Ant.* 1174, *OC* 401, Bagordo (2003) 123 with n. 343.

κοινῷ 'whom we have in common'; cf. 417–18 πατρὸς | τοῦ σοῦ τε κἀμοῦ.

464–5 The chorus attributes to Electra the two virtues which she had disclaimed at 307–8; contrast also the parodos, where the chorus implicitly charges Electra with a lack of σωφροσύνη. On the issues this raises see 254–309n.

464 πρὸς εὐσέβειαν: cf. 1097 τᾷ Ζηνὸς εὐσεβείᾳ; for the preposition see 369n.

465 εἰ σωφρονήσεις: cf. Ar. *Lys.* 1093, Wakker (1994) 260.

ὦ φίλη: mirroring Electra's own form of address (431–63n.); Chrysothemis reciprocates at 469.

466–71 Chrysothemis gives way to her sister's appeal. She acknowledges the justice of Electra's cause, without the sarcasm of her earlier concession (338–9), and concludes with a request for silence from the chorus (469n.). This caution contrasts with Electra's confidence: she had made no reference to the dangers involved in her plan. Chrysothemis' remarks thus remind us of the menacing atmosphere of the early part of the episode, which the news of the dream had gone some way to dispel. The fear which Chrysothemis displays towards her mother confirms the picture of Clytemnestra which we have already gained from Electra. Her remarks are still fresh in our mind when Clytemnestra enters at the beginning of the next episode.

466 δράσω: the omission of expected τάδε (cf. Fraenkel (1962) 81–2) may distance the register of Chrysothemis' response from everyday language.

466–7 τὸ γὰρ δίκαιον οὐκ ἔχει λόγον | δυοῖν ἐρίζειν, ἀλλ' ἐπισπεύδειν τὸ δρᾶν 'for as far as justice is concerned, it is not fitting for two people to argue about it – rather, one should strive to carry it out'. With this interpretation, which Jebb prefers, τὸ δίκαιον is an anticipatory accusative of respect, while οὐκ ἔχει λόγον is an impersonal construction. The former gives an idiom characteristic of Sophocles, who 'sometimes . . . project[s] to the head of the sentence an accusative whose construction only later emerges' (Stinton (1977a) 132 = (1990) 278): cf. 1364–5, K–G i. 330–1 Anm., Diggle (1996d) 13–14. The sense is paralleled by the Homeric ὦ φίλοι, οὐκ ἂν δή τις ἐπὶ ῥηθέντι δικαίῳ | ἀντιβίοις ἐπέεσσι καθαπτόμενος χαλεπαίνοι (*Od.* 18.414–15 = 20.322–3); cf. also Eur. fr. 362.9–10 *TrGF* = 53.9–10 Austin δυοῖν παρόντοιν πραγμάτοιν πρὸς θάτερον | γνώμην προσάπτων τὴν ἐναντίαν μέθες.

Other interpretations are less satisfactory. One could take τὸ δίκαιον as subject of οὐκ ἔχει λόγον, rendering 'that which is right does not afford any ground . . .' But there is no parallel for ἔχει λόγον in this sense. Punctuation after δίκαιον would leave τό demonstrative, as at *Phil.* 154–5 τὸ γάρ μοι | μαθεῖν οὐκ ἀποκαίριον. This interpretation was once supported by Dawe, who followed it through by emending οὐκ to οὐδ' ((1968) 14; he was anticipated in this by Eggert (1868) 16–17). But the beginning of Chrysothemis' utterance then becomes jerky, and her final sentiment banal: for 'it is not any action, but *just* action, that one should get on with and not dispute about' (Stinton; his italics). Stinton himself followed Wunder[3] in seeing a διὰ μέσου construction, by which δίκαιον was the object of δρᾶν: this is over-complicated and artificial.

Chrysothemis' reference to justice looks forward to the prominence of Δίκη in the coming stasimon.

467 δυοῖν denotes Electra and Chrysothemis. According to Hermann, Chrysothemis says that she will not argue against Electra and the chorus; but this raises the unhelpful possibility that she is merely giving way to superior numbers. Nor should the chorus be represented as a partner in the argument alongside Electra, given that its contribution to the debate has been limited to a single couplet.

ἐπισπεύδειν: we must understand ἔχει λόγον with the second clause: cf. *OR* 817–19 ὃν μὴ ξένων ἔξεστι μηδ' ἀστῶν τινι | δόμοις δέχεσθαι, μηδὲ προσφωνεῖν τινα, | ὠθεῖν δ' ἀπ' οἴκων, 236–41, *OC* 1400–4. Ll-J/W print ἐπισπεύδει from Stob. *Ecl.* 3.11.6 (= iii. 430.11–12 Wachsmuth and Hense). The corruption they assume would have been easy, given the ending –ειν only two words before. On the other hand, the above parallels suggest that the infinitive is good idiom.

469 σιγῇ παρ' ὑμῶν πρὸς θεῶν ἔστω, φίλαι: 'no intrigue in Greek tragedy can take place without the complicity of the Chorus; consequently it is a commonplace that a character should pledge them to secrecy' (Barrett on Eur. *Hipp.* 710–12): cf. Aesch. *Cho.* 555, 581–2, Eur. *Med.* 259–67, Lee on *Ion* 666–7, *IT* 1056–77, *Hel.* 1387–9, *IA* 542, also *El.* 272–3, *Or.* 1103–4, Hose (1990–1) i. 299–307, Arnott (1982) 37–8.

παρ' ὑμῶν 'on your part'; cf. *Tr.* 596 μόνον παρ' ὑμῶν εὖ στεγοίμεθ'.

φίλαι: more friendly an address than the ὦ γυναῖκες of 372: the atmosphere is more relaxed, and Chrysothemis is making a polite request.

470 πεύσεται: εἰ with the future in the protasis often expresses a threat or warning (Moorhouse 277, Goodwin §447): cf. *Ant.* 229–30 κεῖ τάδ' εἴσεται Κρέων | ἄλλου παρ' ἀνδρός, πῶς σὺ δῆτ' οὐκ ἀλγυνῇ;

πικράν: predicative: cf. *Aj.* 1239, Eur. *Ba.* 356–7 ὡς ἂν λευσίμου δίκης τυχὼν | θάνῃ, πικρὰν βάκχευσιν ἐν Θήβαις ἰδών. For emphatic πικρός in tragedy see Fraenkel on Aesch. *Ag.* 606, Barrett on Eur. *Hipp.* 725–7.

471 με: for infinitive with accusative when we would expect nominative cf. 65.

πεῖραν: internal accusative, as at *Aj.* 2. The word (emphasised through πειρωμένη in 468) suggests a dangerous venture: cf. *Aj.* 470, 1057, *Tr.* 591.

ἔτι: often in threats (cf. 66n.) or fears for the future: cf. *Aj.* 607–8 κακὰν ἐλπίδ᾿ ἔχων | ἔτι μέ ποθ᾿ ἀνύσειν τὸν ἀπότροπον ἀΐδηλον Ἀΐδαν.

Exit Chrysothemis via eisodos B.

FIRST STASIMON (472–515)

STROPHIC PAIR (472–501)

472	489	– – – ∪∪ – – ∪∪ –	asclep
	490	– – – – ∪∪ – ∪ –	mol dodr
475		– ∪ – ∪ – Ū ‖	∧ia ia∧(= ith)
		∪ – ∪ – ∪‿∪∪ – ∪ – ∪ – ᐟ	3ia
		∪ – ∪ – – ∪ – ∪ – ∪ – ‖	ia ∧ia ia
	495	∪ – ∪ – – ∪ ‖	ia ∧ia∧
480		– ∪∪ – ∪ – ∪ ‖	cho ia∧
		– ∪ – ∪ – ∪ – ᐟ	∧ia ia (= lec)
		– – ∪ – – – ∪ –	2ia
		– ᐟ – – – ∪ – ᐟ	mol ∧ia
		– – ∪ – – – ∪ –	2ia
485	500	∪ – – – ∪∪ ‖	ia∧ ∧ia
		– – ∪∪ – ∪ – Ū – ∪ – – – ‖	tel ia ∧ia∧

The strophic pair consists mainly of iambics, with a few aeolic rhythms at either end. The metre of 472–3 ~ 489–90 is printed according to Dale's analysis ((1971–83) iii. 214, (1968) 140–1), which gives an asclepiadic-type colon (in effect a lesser asclepiad without final ∪ –). Such lengths are common in S. (cf. Dale (1968) 155, West (1982a) 118), and this instance is nicely paralleled by *Ant.* 950 ~ 960 – – – ∪∪ – – ∪∪ – – ∪∪ – (cf. Dale (1968) 144). The analysis 'mol dodr' of 473 ~ 490 is not so easy to parallel, but there are molossi later in this stasimon (483 ~ 498, 511, 514) which lend it support. Instead of this analysis, Pearson, Dawe and Ll-J/W all prefer colon end before γνώμας ~ δεινοῖς in 473 ~ 490, which gives – – – ∪∪ – – ∪∪ – – | – – – ∪∪ – ∪ –. The prepositive at the end of the first colon (καί | ἀ) gives us an instance of 'dovetailing' (to use West's term), which does occur in blunt aeolic cola (cf. West (1982a) 117, Kaimio (1970) 232 n. 1), but is questionable following pendant (or catalectic) cola (cf. L. P. E. Parker (1976) 23). Wilamowitz (1921) 512 interprets the beginning of the ode as three ionics followed by a glyconic, but ionics are out of place in this context.

In 485 ~ 500 a molossus corresponds to a bacchiac at the start of the line: for this phenomenon see Diggle (1981b) 86 = (1994) 201. The bacchiac in 485 is unusually neither preceded nor followed by word-end (cf. Parker (1976) 20 with n. 17); apart from this bacchiac, 482–5 ~ 498–500 consist of the repetition of the same metrical pattern. As transmitted, 495–6 do not correspond with the strophe; see 495–6n. for a possible solution.

Stinton (1977b) 41–2 = (1990) 329 compares the final colon of the strophic pair to *OR* 1096–7 ~ 1108–9 and 885–6 ~ 900–901. He interprets it as 'a standard enoplian compound, similar to the archilochian' (cf. Willink (2001) 77 n. 51; also Itsumi (1991–3) 253–4). But the analysis above is more straightforward, as well as more appropriate to the metrical context.

EPODE (504–15)

504	– ⏝UU – – – |	ia ∧ia∧
505	U ⏝UU – – – ‖	ia ∧ia∧
	– ⏝UU – – – |	ia ∧ia∧
	– U – ‖	∧ia
	– ⏝UU – – – |	ia ∧ia∧
	– ⏝UU – – – |	ia ∧ia∧
510	– – – U – |	∧ia∧ ∧ia
	– – – – – – |	2mol
	– – U – – – |	ia ∧ia∧
	– U – ‖	cr
	⏝UU – – – – |	cr mol
515	U ⏝UU – – – ‖‖	ia ∧ia∧

The epode is mainly made up of iambic dimeters with double contraction in the second metron, all except 512 with resolution in the first longum of the first metron. Similar metra are found elsewhere in S. (Dale (1968) 84–5, L. P. E. Parker (1968) 258–60; cf. 128 ~ 145, 160–1 ~ 180–1, *Aj.* 193, *Tr.* 828–9 ~ 838–9, *OC* 1076), but usually in isolation. The striking concentration of the rhythm here lends the epode a monotony quite different from the more varied pattern of the strophic pair. We should not overemphasise the break in metrical form between the two sections, however: similar dimeters (though without resolution) have already been found in the body of the strophic pair (478 ~ 495) and at its conclusion (486 ~ 501). The metre of the epode represents not a shift to a new theme, but an idiosyncratic development of an idea already present in the strophic pair, creating a different metrical texture and mood.

West (1982a) 102 suggests that 510–11 consist of a fully dragged dochmiac followed by a fully dragged dochmius kaibelianus. However, the absence of dochmiacs elsewhere in the stasimon makes this interpretation unattractive. West's only parallel for the fully dragged kaibelianus is the colon of six longs at Aesch. *Eum.* 925 ~ 947 ((1982a) 100), which could be almost anything: in his edition of Aeschylus (p. 503) he calls it a hemiepes pendant with double contraction. Hermann's easy change παγχρυσέων would give a regular dochmius kaibelianus in 510 (the first syllable of δίφρων can be scanned long or short); but there seems no way of rescuing a dochmiac analysis for 511. Emendation to δύστανος is not possible, as ἀκείαις demands an epithet (so Wilamowitz (1921) 513); this also tells against emending πολύπονος in 515.

511 is better interpreted as a molossic dimeter. The molossus is not a common length in any of the tragedians; Griffith (1977) 264 claims it for a characteristic of S., but none of his examples outside this ode is convincing. Nevertheless, it does occur, and occasionally in groups of more than one metron (cf. *Phil.* 837 for what seems to be a molossic trimeter, L. P. E. Parker (1997) 356 (on Ar. *Av.* 1722)). Perhaps the appearance of molossi here is facilitated by the other unusual syncopated iambic lengths, some of which might be analysed as resolved cretic plus molossus; cf. also the molossus at 483 ~ 498. So too there are molossi in the vicinity of *Phil.* 837 (831, 833, 834). This interpretation does not absolutely rule out a dochmiac analysis of 510 (accepting Hermann's emendation παγχρυσέων): for a molossus following a dochmiac see Diggle (1990) 108 with n. 35, 120 = (1994) 375 with n. 35, 394 and Medda (1993) 185–9. But more suitable in the context is the iambic interpretation printed above. 514 too is better rendered 'cr mol' than kaibelianus with double drag. If, however, we read imperfect ἔλειπεν (see *ad loc.*), we get an iambic metron instead of the cretic.

472–515 The patterning of the two stanzas of the strophic pair is notably tight. Each begins with a mighty figure of myth advancing to wreak vengeance on Clytemnestra and Aegisthus. Each contains an evocative description of their crimes, murder in the first stanza, adultery in the second: we have already encountered this parallelism in Electra's monody (113–14). This is accompanied by confident claims that the dream will have a favourable issue, as well as by assertions that the prophetic status of the chorus, and then the power of mortal prophecy in general, depend on the result of the vision. These themes are in ring composition – the sequence prophecy, confidence in the dream, description of the crime in the strophe is reversed in the antistrophe. Many of these motifs have already occurred in the previous episode (cf. e.g. *Phil.* 676–728 with Davies (2001) 55). The chorus's confidence recalls Electra's own sudden boldness at the news of the dream (387). Electra has already suggested that Agamemnon remembers his killing (442–6) and sent the dream as a result

(459–60); she has also emphasised her mother's adultery, and twice associated its punishment with the Erinyes (112–14, 276). This is not mere recapitulation (cf. Kranz (1933) 212): rather, the chorus's echoing of Electra's feelings and ideas expresses the change in its attitude since the parodos, and how firmly it is now on her side. It also prepares us for the ironic 'reversal' of the next episode, where (it seems) the chorus's confidence comes to nothing.

In the epode the chorus's optimism is replaced by a grim meditation on the past sufferings of the house. The swiftness of the shift of mood has attracted critical attention: Goward (1999) 109–10 claims that 'there is a great narrative disjunction at this point, unmediated by any link'. Compare *OR* 463–511 (the first stasimon), where at 483 the chorus moves from confident predictions of the capture of Laius' killer to expressions of dread prompted by the words of Tiresias. In our case, the shift has seemed so sudden that scholars have invoked stage action to explain it. Errandonea (1955) 379–80 suggests that Clytemnestra enters at the end of the antistrophe, thereby forcing the chorus to change the subject quickly: cf. *Phil.* 718–28, where the deceit practised by the chorus seems to make little sense unless Philoctetes has by then returned on stage.[28] But while the strophic pair would indeed be unsuitable for Clytemnestra's ears, the epode is scarcely less so. If one were searching for a subject which would not offend the murderer of the son of Atreus and the adulterous lover of the son of Thyestes, the woes of the house of Pelops would hardly be the first topic that sprang to mind. Clytemnestra's entry at 515 is also preferable for dramatic reasons: the abruptness of her opening words would be more effective if they followed on from a sudden entrance.

However, the break between antistrophe and epode is not in fact as total as Goward claims. There is a degree of metrical continuity from the strophic pair into the epode. So too the Erinys which begins the antistrophe links the uncomplicated figure of Dike in the strophe with the foreboding world of the epode. The theme of motion (475n.) is picked up by ἔμολες in 506. And the αἰσχίσταις . . . ἀκείαις (486) in which Agamemnon met his end recur with the δυστάνοις ἀκείαις of the death of Myrtilus: the link is made more explicit by the statement that πολύπονος ἀκεία has never yet left the house. While there is undeniably a change of tone between the two sections, these links suggest that the epode is intimately connected with the rest of the lyric, not a mere add-on prompted by the entrance of another character.

The tone of the epode leads us into the second episode, an altogether darker scene than the first. It also gives us a glimpse into the history of this troubled family. According to Burton, S. here 'reveals himself as an adherent of the traditional doctrine of inherited sin arising from a single act and potent throughout

---

[28] The parodos of Aeschylus' *Agamemnon* is not a parallel, as Clytemnestra does not enter during the chorus's anapaests: cf. Fraenkel on 83 ff., Taplin (1977a) 280–5, Mastronarde (1979) 101–3.

each generation' ((1980) 202). Inherited guilt is certainly a concept of great importance in Aeschylus' *Oresteia*, where the killings of Iphigenia, Agamemnon and Clytemnestra form part of a chain of suffering which began with the adultery of Atreus' wife and the banquet of Thyestes (cf. Fraenkel on Aesch. *Ag.* 1193, 1468–9). So too in Eur. *Or.* 982–1012 Electra goes through each incident in her family's history to plot its woes back to Tantalus and Pelops. And in our play there are also references to a theme of suffering within the family, and at significant moments through the drama. The troubles of the house of Pelops are elsewhere referred to by implication at line 10 (the πολύφθορον . . . δῶμα Πελοπιδῶν), and directly by Aegisthus at 1498 (τά τ' ὄντα καὶ μέλλοντα Πελοπιδῶν κακά); while the chorus will later see in the 'death' of Orestes (also in a chariot accident) the final rooting-out of the ancient γένος (764–5).

Is this a sign, then, that the theological backdrop to the play is equivalent to that of the *Oresteia*? Stinton (1986) 79 = (1990) 471 is right to stress the differences between this ode and Aeschylus' trilogy: the tracing of the woes back to Pelops, the absence of Atreus and Thyestes, the failure to mention the curse.[29] And as R. C. T. Parker (1999) 18, notes, 'the kind of weaving of the particular action of the play into a long pattern of divine purpose so characteristic of Aeschylean choruses is far less common in Sophocles, and where it does occur far less insistent'; on our passage he comments 'emphasis lies not on the idea of crime and punishment but simply on the continuity of trouble since that time'.[30] Inherited guilt and curses are not in fact helpful notions for our understanding of the drama. There is a pattern to the suffering in the house of Pelops, but this pattern cannot be reduced to a hereditary affliction. S. leaves the matter obscure, and thus all the more ominous. The structure of the ode may act as a metaphor for this. The present (represented by the strophic pair) and the past (epode) are, in one sense, divided off from each other by the break in tone between the two sections of the lyric. On the other hand, the links between the two parts, metrical, verbal and thematic, emphasise that there is some connexion between the vengeance on Clytemnestra and the killing of Myrtilus. Such a connexion is a paradox: the death of Myrtilus involved the killing of a benefactor, whereas the death of Clytemnestra will constitute the just punishment of a murderer and adulteress. Yet as the following *agon* will indicate, there is never an easy distinction between killings.

[29] For S.'s general reluctance to put curses and so forth in the foreground see West (1999). For the curse uttered by Myrtilus cf. Watson (1991) 15 n. 69.

[30] Compare the same scholar's remarks on the second stasimon of *Antigone*: '[the ode] portray[s] the Labdacid house as one in which not so much guilt as suffering is endemic over the generations' ((1997) 154).

472–3 εἰ μὴ 'γὼ παράφρων μάντις ἔφυν | καὶ γνώμας λειπομένα σοφᾶς: the opening recalls *OR* 1086–7 εἴπερ ἐγὼ μάντις εἰ– | μὶ καὶ κατὰ γνώμαν ἴδρις (opening of the third stasimon), where the chorus's confidence turns out to be disastrously misplaced. The 'joy before disaster' ode was quite a characteristic of S.'s (cf. *Aj.* 693–718, *Tr.* 633–62, *Ant.* 1115–52, Henrichs (1994–5) 101 n. 76), and connoisseurs in the audience may well have taken these words as a sign of impending catastrophe. Here we see a variation on this theme: Electra and the chorus will soon think that their optimism was misplaced, whereas we in the audience will know better.[31] For the preface 'if I am a true prophet' cf. Fraenkel (1957) 358 with n. 3, Nisbet and Rudd on Hor. *C.* 3.17.12–13 (adding Lucian 65.1).

472 μάντις: taken up by πρόμαντις in 475; for such repetition in Sophoclean lyric cf. εἴσιν . . . μέτεισιν (475–7), δρῶσι . . . συνδρῶσιν (498), *Ant.* 586–8 ἁλός . . . ὕφαλον, 1147–51 νυχίων . . . πάννυχοι (cited by Easterling (1978) 144).

473 γνώμας λειπομένα: cf. *Phil.* 910 εἰ μὴ 'γὼ κακὸς γνώμην ἔφυν, *Ant.* 1250 γνώμης . . . οὐκ ἄπειρος; for λείπομαι = 'be lacking in' cf. LSJ[9] s.v. λείπω B II 4, *Tr.* 936–7 ὁ παῖς . . . ὀδυρμάτων | ἐλείπετ' οὐδέν.

475 εἴσιν: for a verb of motion predicated of Δίκη cf. Aesch. *Cho.* 935, Eur. *Ba.* 992–3 = 1011–12 ἴτω Δίκα φανερός, ἴτω | ξιφηφόρος, *Suppl.* 1145, *El.* 42, 771, *Her.* 738–9 (*coni.*). The verb is taken up by ἥξει at the start of the antistrophe; also by μέτεισιν in 477 (for the addition of a prefix to the second instance cf. 472n.). Long (1968) 136 stresses the 'mood of speed and violence' and the 'theme of inexorable motion': cf. the verbs denoting movement (477, 489, 497, 501, 506), as well as the intense energy suggested by 492–3. This is picked up by ἔμολες in the epode, which strikingly attributes motion to the abstract ἱππεία; at the end of the ode, it is the absence of motion which is to the fore.

πρόμαντις 'that has predicted the outcome' (Lloyd-Jones); Justice sent the dream, which the chorus takes as a prediction of the triumph of Agamemnon and his family. Cf. the description of Clytemnestra's dream in Aeschylus as a τορὸς . . . ὀρθόθριξ δόμων | ὀνειρόμαντις (*Cho.* 32–3).

---

[31] Joyful odes in S. are not always followed by catastrophe; nor even is the prediction of the future always a hazardous undertaking for the Sophoclean chorus. In *OC* 1044–95 the chorus is remarkably assured about the coming battle; its confidence culminates in the declaration μάντις εἰμ' ἐσθλῶν ἀγώνων (1080), which according to the usual view of Sophoclean irony should almost guarantee imminent disaster. Yet no evil results, and the chorus later refers explicitly to its success as a prophet (1096–7).

476 Δίκα: personified elsewhere in S. at 528 (n.), *Ant.* 854 and *OC* 1381–2, perhaps also *El.* 1441; cf. Hes. *Theog.* 902, *Op.* 256–62, Aesch. fr. 281a *TrGF*, Eur. fr. 223.86–7 *TrGF* ≈ 48.57–8 Kambitsis (cited below, 477n.). For the combination of Δίκα with κράτος cf. Solon fr. 36.15–17 *IEG* ταῦτα μὲν κράτει | ὁμοῦ βίην τε καὶ δίκην ξυναρμόσας | ἔρεξα, Aesch. *Cho.* 244–5 Κράτος τε καὶ Δίκη . . . | . . . συγγένοιτό μοι; also Aesch. fr. 381 *TrGF* ὅπου γὰρ ἰσχὺς συζυγοῦσι καὶ δίκη, | ποία ξυνωρὶς τῶνδε καρτερώτερα;, Hom. *Il.* 16.542 δίκῃσί τε καὶ σθένεϊ ᾧ. The prominent position of Δίκα soon after the beginning of the strophe will be taken up in the similarly emphatic location of the Ἐρινύς in the antistrophe: these figures are associated at e.g. *Tr.* 808–9 ὧν σε ποίνιμος Δίκη | τείσαιτ᾽ Ἐρινύς τ᾽, *Aj.* 1390 μνήμων τ᾽ Ἐρινὺς καὶ τελεσφόρος Δίκη, Aesch. *Ag.* 1432–3 μὰ τὴν τέλειον τῆς ἐμῆς παιδὸς Δίκην | Ἄτην Ἐρινύν θ᾽, *Cho.* 646–52.

δίκαια . . . κράτη: cf. Aesch. *Suppl.* 437 δίκαια Διόθεν κράτη, 951 εἴη δὲ νίκη καὶ κράτος (Nauck; –η M) τοῖς ἄρσεσιν. For the repetition δίκη δίκαια cf. Hes. *Op.* 217 κρείσσων ἐς τὰ δίκαια· δίκη δ᾽ ὑπὲρ ὕβριος ἴσχει.

φερομένα: for the middle cf. Hom. *Il.* 13.486 αἶψά κεν ἠὲ φέροιτο μέγα κράτος ἠὲ φεροίμην, LSJ⁹ s.v. φέρω A VI 3; *Tr.* 497 ἐκφέρεται νίκας.

χεροῖν: 'bearing away just triumphs of prowess' or 'carrying just victory in her hands': either of Jebb's alternatives could be right. With the latter there may be a nod to Homer's description of Eris as πολέμοιο τέρας μετὰ χερσὶν ἔχουσαν (*Il.* 11.4), but here the picture is not as precise.

477 μέτεισιν: often used of vengeful pursuit: cf. Aesch. *Cho.* 273 εἰ μὴ μέτειμι τοῦ πατρὸς τοὺς αἰτίους, *Ag.* 1666, Eur. *Andr.* 260; LSJ⁹ s.v. μέτειμι II 2 c.

ὦ τέκνον: 79n., 154n.

οὐ μακροῦ χρόνου: for the genitive used to refer to time (past, present or future) or place with reference to a point within a larger unit cf. 501, 698, 780, 817, *OC* 397 ἥξοντα βαιοῦ κοὐχὶ μυρίου χρόνου, Bruhn §44.I, Moorhouse 58–9. At the moment of the revenge in Euripides' *Antiope* the chorus sings Δίκα τοι Δίκα χρόνιος ἀλλ᾽ ὅμως | ἐπιπεσοῦσ᾽ ἔλαθεν ἔλαβεν, ὅταν ἴ[δ]ῃι| τιν᾽ ἀσεβῆ βροτῶν (fr. 223.86–7 *TrGF* ≈ 48.57–8 Kambitsis). For the delay of Justice see Harder on Eur. fr. 255.5 *TrGF* = 29.5 Austin, Garvie on Aesch. *Cho.* 61–5.

478–80 μοι . . . | . . . κλύουσαν: for accusative predicates and appositional phrases qualifying datives in impersonal expressions cf. 959–62, K–G ii. 112, Bruhn §121.II, Ros (1938) 248–50, Diggle (1981a) 44, Rijksbaron (1991) 131–2, Arnott on Alexis fr. 264.3–4 *PCG*. The variants with (or implying) the dative singular can be rejected as *lectiones faciliores*.

θάρσος: there is no semantic distinction between θάρσος and θράσος in the fifth century (cf. Wilamowitz on Eur. *Her.* 624, Fraenkel on Aesch. *Ag.* 803–4).

θάρσος must be chosen on metrical grounds: it yields a double syncopated iambic metron such as dominates the epode, whereas θράσος gives us an odd-looking iambic tripody. For the combination with ὕπεστι cf. Aesch. *Cho.* 91 πάρεστι θάρσος.

480–1 ἀδυπνόων ... | ... ὀνειράτων: cf. *Phil.* 827–8 Ὕπν'... | εὐαὴς ἡμῖν ἔλθοις, Prop. 1.3.7 *mollem spirare quietem*; at Sappho fr. 63.3 *PLF*, Voigt γλύκυς θ[έ]ος, ἦ δεῖν' ὀνίας μ[, the reference is probably to the Ὄνοιρε addressed in the first line. For πνέω in the context of a dream cf. S. fr. 65 *TrGF* θάρσει, γύναι· τὰ πολλὰ τῶν δεινῶν, ὄναρ | πνεύσαντα νυκτός, ἡμέρας μαλάσσεται, Aesch. *Cho.* 33 ἐξ ὕπνου κότον πνέων. Sweetness is also predicated of a divine message at *OR* 151 ὦ Διὸς ἀδυεπὲς φάτι. The dream was not sweet for the person who experienced it; cf. the *Philoctetes* passage cited above, where the sleep invoked by the chorus would have turned out to be painful in the long run for Philoctetes himself.

482–3 οὐ ... ποτ' ἀμναστεῖ γ' ὁ ... | ... Ἑλλάνων ἄναξ: Agamemnon remembers his death, and hence is active against his killers (cf. 459–60, 1417–21). The memory of a crime is often associated with a desire for its punishment: cf. Aesch. *Cho.* 491 μέμνησο (Orestes and Electra to the dead Agamemnon), *Ag.* 155 μνάμων Μῆνις τεκνόποινος. In our play too, Electra has declared that she will never forget her dead father (145–6). The act of remembering is also commonly predicated of the Erinyes (cf. *Aj.* 1390 (cited above, 476n.), Aesch. *Eum.* 382–3, [Aesch.] *PV* 516 μνήμονες ... Ἐρινύες, Simondon (1982) 223–7); this assists the transition to the antistrophe. For more on 'remembering evils' see Diggle (1995) 42, Simondon (1982) 215–22, Loraux (1988) ≈ (1997) 146–72 ≈ (1998) 84–109 ≈ (2002) 145–69; for the importance of memory in revenge tragedy more generally see Kerrigan (1996) 170–92.

The verb is found elsewhere in tragedy at Eur. fr. 727b.13 *TrGF* [ἀ]μνηστεῖν; the more usual form is ἀμνημονέω. The honorific periphrasis for Agamemnon is in part a way of consoling Electra for his loss; it also suggests that the power and authority he enjoyed while alive have stayed with him after death (cf. the chorus's description of Amphiaraus at 837–41).

482 γ': for Wakefield's σ' see next n.

483 σ' Wa; *coni.* Fröhlich. The disappearance of the sigma elsewhere in the tradition is owed to haplography. For the word order cf. *OC* 994 πατήρ σ' ὁ καίνων. Wakefield's emendation of γ' to σ' ((1789–95) iii. 93–4) is less attractive. The σ' would then go ἀπὸ κοινοῦ with ἀμναστεῖ and φύσας, but we lose the mighty vagueness of 'Agamemnon does not forget'; the replacement, 'Agamemnon does not forget you', is less imposing.

COMMENTARY: 472–515

484–5 οὐδ᾿ ἁ παλαιὰ . . . | . . . γένυς: the theme of memory is extended from the dead Agamemnon to the lifeless axe. For the attribution of feeling to an inanimate instrument Campbell compares Philoctetes' address to his bow (1130–9 ἦ που ἐλεινὸν ὁρᾷς, φρένας εἴ τινας | ἔχεις κτλ.); there, however, the personification is softened by the εἰ clause. A weapon can be called to witness the killing which it was used to commit (cf. Aesch. *Cho.* 1010–11 μαρτυρεῖ δέ μοι | φᾶρος τόδ᾿, ὡς ἔβαψεν Αἰγίσθου ξίφος, *Eum.* 460–1); but that is altogether less remarkable than the long period of brooding attributed to this axe. It is as if the awful act which it was made to perform has left it charged with a dreadful power; it certainly suggests the lasting potential in the house for violent killing. So at Eur. *El.* 279 Electra says she will kill her father's killers ταὐτῷ γε πελέκει τῷ πατὴρ ἀπώλετο.

For the personification of the murder-weapon cf. the Buphonia rite at the Athenian Dipoleia festival: according to Pausanias (1.24.4), the axe used in the sacrifice was put on trial for the killing, after which it 'would presumably have been kept elsewhere, in the shrine, as a primordial symbol of consecrated violence' (Burkert (1983) 140 ≈ (1997) 158–9). At Eur. *Suppl.* 1205–9 Athena orders that the knife used to kill sacrificial animals for the peace treaty between Athens and Argos should be buried in the ground, as it too will acquire a mysterious potency: φόβον γὰρ αὐτοῖς, ἤν ποτ᾿ ἔλθωσιν πόλιν, | δειχθεῖσα θήσει καὶ κακὸν νόστον πάλιν (1208–9). The personification of a weapon, along with its longing for action, is transferred to a humorous context at Plaut. *Mil. glor.* 5–8 nam ego hanc machaeram mihi consolari volo, | ne lamentetur neve animum despondeat | . . . | quae misera gestit fartem facere ex hostibus.

χαλκόπλη– | κτος: not found elsewhere (except Hesych. χ 113 = iv. 272 Schmidt χαλκοτύπους· χαλκοπλήκτους). Such adjectives can be either active ('striking with its brazen edge') or passive ('made of beaten bronze'); here both senses are probably felt (cf. 714n.). The use of bronze in the murder weapon was specified at 195. Editors claim that Vat. gr. 45 shares J's reading χαλκόπλακτος, but according to Kopff (1993) 157 it has the majority reading.

485 ἀμφήκης: for the two-headed axe cf. Hom. *Od.* 5.235 ἀμφοτέρωθεν ἀκαχμένον, Gronewald (1975) 113. Some editors claim that ἀμφάκης is found in Hesychius. The manuscript reading is ἀμφακλῆς· ἀξίνη (α 3893 = i. 135 Latte); Latte emends the lemma to ἀμφακές on the basis of Sophron fr. 4.7 PCG, Hordern. Whether he is right or not, there is no reason to suppose that this is relevant here. ἀμφή- should be retained, in any case: see Björck (1950) 237.

γένυς is delayed: as with Ἐρινύς in the next stanza, the crucial word is held back until the end (491 n.). For γένυς = '(blade of an) axe' cf. 196n.

486 ἐν denotes situation or circumstance generally (Moorhouse 106).

242

ᾳκείαις: frequently used in the context of Agamemnon's death (cf. 102, 206, 216); the word is then taken up in the epode (511, 515). For the ᾳ see 102n.; for the –ει– see K–B ii. 277 Anm. 2.

489–91 The monstrous picture of the Erinys balances that of Δίκα in the strophe; it also looks forward to the grimmer world of the epode. Its attributes do not build up into a single consistent picture. S. is combining the characteristics of various mythological beasts to evoke the creature's strange, demonic power.

489 ἥξει: cf. εἶσιν in 475 (n.).

πολύπους καὶ πολύχειρ: the emphatic repetition of word-initial πολυ– has 'an intensive force, without having an exactly defined significance' (Campbell, comparing 798 πολυγλώσσου); cf. Fehling (1969) 247, Mastronarde on Eur. *Phoen.* 1022, Hom. *Il.* 5.613, 9.154, [Hes.] fr. 70.6 M–W, *Hom. Hymn* 2.31, Aesch. *Pers.* 83 πολύχειρ καὶ πολυναύτας, Theocr. 10.42, Call. *Hymn* 4.266. Winnington-Ingram claims that the phrase is used because '[the Erinys] will work through a plurality of human agents' ((1954–5) 22 = (1980) 219 = E. Segal (1983) 212): this is impossibly obscure.

For references to the feet of the Erinyes cf. *Ant.* 1104 ποδώκεις . . . Βλάβαι, *Aj.* 837 σεμνὰς Ἐρινῦς τανύποδας, Aesch. *Sept.* 791 καμψίπους Ἐρινύς, *Eum.* 374 καταφέρω ποδὸς ἀκμάν, Geisser (2002) 210–11. At Aesch. *Ag.* 1660 δαίμονος χηλῇ βαρείᾳ δυστυχῶς πεπληγμένοι and *Pers.* 515–16 (cited above, 456n.) the offensive capacity of the demon's foot is emphasised. Multiple hands were the defining attribute of the Hekatoncheirs, not the Erinyes (cf. Hes. *Theog.* 150–2). There may, however, be a parallel in Pind. fr. 52i(A).19–21 S–M (*Pae.* 8a) ἔδοξ[ε γὰρ] | τεκεῖν πυρφόρον ἐρι[ ] | ἑκατόγχειρα, if the supplement Ἐρι[νύν] of Grenfell and Hunt is correct (*contra* Rutherford (2001) 235–6; see however Finglass (2005b)).

For the mention of foot and hand to suggest untiring effort in the quest for vengeance cf. Aeschin. 2.115 τιμωρήσειν καὶ χειρὶ καὶ ποδὶ καὶ φωνῇ καὶ πάσῃ δυνάμει, 3.109, 3.120, Hdt. 6.86γ.2 ἀλλ' Ὅρκου παῖς ἐστὶν ἀνώνυμος, οὐδ' ἔπι χεῖρες | οὐδὲ πόδες· κραιπνὸς δὲ μετέρχεται, εἰς ὅ κε πᾶσαν | συμμάρψας ὀλέσῃ γενεὴν καὶ οἶκον ἅπαντα; also the emphasis on the hands and feet of the monstrous Typhon in Hes. *Theog.* 823–4.

West replaces πολύπους with πολύφρων ((1979) 104), and the scholia (p. 125.27 Papageorgius) record the variant πολύπαις from a ὑπόμνημα; but the repetition πολύπους . . . χαλκόπους presents no difficulty (cf. F. Ferrari (1983) 31–3). Repetition occurs in almost exactly the same parts of the strophe (μάντις . . . πρόμαντις); for this phenomenon cf. 1232–3~1253–4, *Aj.* 879~925, *Ant.* 360~70, 1306~28, *Tr.* 947–8~950–1, Diggle (1996c) 197.

490 κρυπτομένα: an appropriate word, given that the punishment for Agamemnon's death will be effected by δόλος (cf. 1–85n., 1396–7). Cf. also [Sen.] *Oct.* 36 *latentis . . . Fortunae impetu* with Ferri's n.

λόχοις: cf. *Ant.* 1074–5 τούτων σε λωβητῆρες ὑστεροφθόροι | λοχῶσιν Ἅιδου καὶ θεῶν Ἐρινύες.

491 χαλκόπους: predicated of various fantastic monsters: divine horses (Hom. *Il.* 8.41, 13.23), Aeetes' fire-breathing bulls (Pher. Ath. *FGrHist* 3 F 112 = fr. 112 *EGM*, Ap. Rh. 3.230, 410, 496, Ov. *Met.* 7.105 *aeripedes tauri*), Hecate (Tzetzes on Lycophr. 1030 = ii. 319.2–3 Scheer), the Empusa (Ar. *Ran.* 294, a σκέλος χαλκοῦν). For the chthonic connotations of bronze see Dieterich (1891) 42–4 = (1911) 101–2. Here it suggests the creature's relentless and untiring power; the Suda (χ 53 = iv. 783.25–6 Adler) defines the phrase ἡ στερεὰ καὶ ἀκοπίατος ἐν τῷ ἐπιέναι κατὰ τῶν φονέων. For the form of the compound cf. *OR* 418 δεινόπους ἀρά.

Ἐρινύς: 'the periphrastic descriptions are at last clarified and completed by the terrible name, falling with all the more weight for having been held back' (Lloyd-Jones (1969a) 102 = (1990a) 314). He refers to Aesch. *Sept.* 723, where the periphrases are admittedly more elaborate, but the atmosphere of mysterious anticipation is the same (cf. Aesch. *Ag.* 59, 749, *Cho.* 652 with Sier; also 484–5n., Fraenkel on Aesch. *Ag.* 681 ff.).

492–3 'For the drive to a polluting marriage, that brought an accursed bed, an accursed bridal, came upon those for whom it was forbidden' (Lloyd-Jones). These lines '[create] a terrifying atmosphere by weighty compound adjectives and vivid personifications' (Long (1968) 137); the language becomes twisted and obscure, as the chorus searches for expressions capable of evoking the horror of the crime. For the emphasis on adultery cf. 114, 197, 271–4.

492 ἄλεκτρ᾿ ἄνυμφα: predicative, with ἀμιλλήμαθ᾿; in translating, however, these adjectives should be taken with γάμων. Such enallage is relatively common in tragic lyric (cf. 1390, *Ant.* 793–4 νεῖκος ἀνδρῶν | ξύναιμον, *Phil.* 952 σχῆμα πέτρας δίπυλον), and can sometimes be found in trimeters (cf. 1290). This case is distinctive, however, as two epithets are transferred: Aesch. *Sept.* 348–50 βλαχαὶ δ᾿ αἱματόεσσαι |τῶν ἐπιμαστιδίων | ἀρτιτρεφεῖς βρέμονται provides the only parallel (cf. Diggle (1993) 136 = (1994) 418–19). There is a paradox in designating a γάμος as ἄλεκτρος and ἄνυμφος. For the repetition of alpha-privative adjectives see 164–5n. For this particular combination see 962n.

ἐπέβα: often with an unpleasant abstract noun as subject: cf. *Phil.* 193–4 τὰ παθήματα κεῖνα πρὸς αὐτὸν | τῆς ὠμόφρονος Χρύσης ἐπέβη, *OR* 1299–1300 τίς σ', ὦ τλῆμον, | προσέβη μανία;, *Tr.* 298, *Aj.* 137–8. Here the subject is ἁμιλλήμαθ', the object an implied τούτοις which acts as antecedent to οἷς. The theme of motion continues to be stressed (475n.).

493 γάμων: probably a genitive of aim after ἁμιλλήμαθ', as in Lloyd-Jones's translation above; however, it and ἁμιλλήμαθ' may also make up a single unit, giving 'strivings, struggles which took the form of intercourse', as in the *Ion* passage cited below (so Pelling, *per litteras*).

ἁμιλλήμαθ': 'ἅμιλλα, like "race", may imply simply rapid movement, without any suggestion of "racing" in the competitive sense' (Lloyd-Jones (1972b) 270 = (1990a) 396, citing e.g. Eur. *Or.* 456). Here this vigorous word suggests the perverted enthusiasm of the pair for their union. For ἅμιλλα as subject of a verb cf. Eur. *Hipp.* 1140–1 νυμφιδία δ' ἀπόλωλε φυγᾷ σᾷ | λέκτρων ἅμιλλα κούραις; for terms for 'contest' applied to sexual union cf. Eur. *Ion* 939 ἐνταῦθ' ἀγῶνα δεινὸν ἠγωνίσμεθα. The term leads into the epode, which shows the disastrous aftermath of a competition.

495–8 'Therefore I am confident that we shall never see the portent draw near to the murderess and her accomplice without giving them cause to complain of it' (Jebb). τέρας is ambiguous (497n.).

495 πρό: denotes the reason for action (K–G i. 455). Moorhouse 121–2 compares *Tr.* 504 πρὸ γάμων, where 'to win her as bride' should be preferred over the weak 'before the marriage'; cf. also Hom. *Il.* 17.666–7 περὶ γὰρ δίε μή μιν Ἀχαιοὶ | ἀργαλέου πρὸ φόβοιο ἕλωρ δήιοισι λίποιεν, correctly translated by Jebb as *prae timore*.

495–6 θάρσος | μήποτε μήποθ' ἡμῖν: most manuscripts have μ' ἔχει | μήποτε μήποθ' ἡμῖν; LKΛZc omit μήποτε. Neither of these versions makes sense; the resulting scansion of 495 (∪ − ∪ − ∪ −) is also problematic (cf. 478–80n.). GR have μ' ἔχει | θάρσος μήποθ' ἡμῖν; P the same with μήποτε repeated. θάρσος is likely to be genuine (so rightly Wunder²): not only does it occur in the same place of the strophe, but the scholion paraphrasing this passage (cited below, 497n.) begins with θαρρῶ. θάρσος at the end of 495 also gives us correspondence with 479 (∪ − ∪ − − −). μ' ἔχει, however, is suspicious: for while there are parallels for abstract nouns with ἔχω governing an accusative (225, 897), such expressions do not seem to go on to govern an accusative + infinitive construction. Perhaps the μ' ἔχει was added (on the analogy of phrases like *Phil.* 686 θαῦμά μ' ἔχει) because a bare θάρσος was felt to be syntactically defective; the gloss then either replaced θάρσος or pushed it into replacing μήποτε. Wilamowitz (1921) 512–13 employs similar reasoning. For the choice of θάρσος over θράσος see 478–80n.

The gemination of μήποτε suits the excited mood of the chorus (cf. 459n., *Phil.* 687, *OR* 830, 1211, [Aesch.] *PV* 688, 894, Eur. *Phoen.* 190, *Andr.* 943, Vahlen (1895) 7 = (1907–8) ii. 162). The use of 'never' rather than simply 'not' may suggest the repeated assaults of the Erinyes: the chorus imagines a drawn-out, imperfective process of suffering rather than a single act of violence.

496 ἡμῖν 'in our judgment', a dative of reference, not to be taken with the participles in 498. The poorly-attested variant ὑμῖν (*coni.* Reiske (1753) 15) may have originated from a belief that the datives were meant to be taken together; but an address to the murderers here would be surprising.

497 ἀψεγές: θαρρῶ ὅτι τοῖς δρῶσι ταῦτα τὰ ἄδικα καὶ συνδρῶσιν αὐτοῖς οὐκ ἔσται ἄψεκτος ὁ ὄνειρος (Σ p. 126.21–3 Papageorgius); cf. Pl. *Leg.* 716b4 ὑποσχὼν τιμωρίαν οὐ μεμπτήν, Vahlen (1895) 7 = (1907–8) ii. 162–3. Bergk printed ἀψεφές (ἀφρόντιστον. Σοφοκλῆς Φαίδρα: Hesych. s.v. (α 8952 = i. 302 Latte = S. fr. 692 *TrGF*)): this weakens the sense.

πελᾶν: from πελάω, the Attic future of πελάζω; cf. *OC* 1060, perhaps *Phil.* 1150, [Aesch.] *PV* 281. This is preferable to seeing it as the present infinitive of the verb πελάω found at *Hom. Hymn* 7.44.

τέρας: is taken by Stein (1909) 56 to refer to the portent seen by Clytemnestra. For this sense in the context of a dream he compares Nonn. *Dion.* 40.504: cf. now also Pind. fr. 52i(A).24 S–M (= *Pae.* 8a). The phrase τόδε φάσμα in 501 does indeed suggest that the dream is currently the subject of discourse. But τέρας can also mean 'monster' (cf. Stein (1909) 17–25, Calame on Alcman fr. 146 *PMGF*(his fr. 106); also Pizzani (2000) 537), and this meaning fits better with the future tense verb: for while the dream has already reached Clytemnestra, the Erinys is yet to come. For the connexion of this stem with Erinyes cf. Lucian 34.5 ἀλλά με ὥσπερ αἱ Ἐρινύες ἐξήλασαν πολλὰ τεράστια καὶ ἀλλόκοτα διεξιόντες. Both senses are probably present, and the ambiguity stresses the connexion between the two. For a comparable ambiguity cf. Aesch. *Cho.* 548–51, where τέρας in 548 must refer to the monstrous snake, while the chorus's τερασκόπον in 551 is most naturally taken as 'interpreter of the portent'.

498 τοῖς δρῶσι καὶ συνδρῶσιν: for the repetition of the simplex form with a preposition added cf. 472n. The first term must refer to Clytemnestra, the second to her accomplice Aegisthus, ὁ σὺν γυναιξὶ τὰς μάχας ποιούμενος (302).

ἤ– | τοι: disjunctive, marking the unthinkable alternative (cf. J. C. B. Lowe (1973) 53 n. 23, Denniston 554).

498–501 For the thought that the failure of one particular prophecy condemns prophecy as a whole cf. *OR* 708–9 ἐμοῦ 'πάκουσον καὶ μάθ' οὕνεκ' ἔστι σοι |

βρότειον οὐδὲν μαντικῆς ἔχον τέχνης, 897–910 (especially 902–3 εἰ μὴ τάδε χειρόδεικτα | πᾶσιν ἁρμόσει βροτοῖς).

501 νυκτός 'seen in the night', a genitive of time within which (477n.); Moorhouse's 'pertinentive genitive' (52) is not a helpful term. For dreams seen in the night cf. 410n.

εὖ κατασχήσει: for this seafaring term (cf. *Phil.* 221, 270) used in a metaphorical sense cf. Eur. *Cycl.* 348–9 ἐς ἀνδρὸς ἀνοσίου | ὠμὴν κατέσχον ἀλίμενόν τε καρδίαν; also cf. Hdt. 1.120.4 (I am confident) ἐξήκειν . . . τὸν ὄνειρον, *Aj.* 684 ἀμφὶ μὲν τούτοισιν εὖ σχήσει. Another seafaring term in an oracular context is found at *Tr.* 827–8 καὶ τάδ᾽ ὀρθῶς | ἔμπεδα κατουρίζει. There is a contrast with δεινοῖς in 499: what is a dreadful dream for Clytemnestra will have beneficial effects for Electra and the chorus if it comes true.

504–15 Oenomaus, king of Elis, had decreed that only the man who defeated him in a chariot-race could marry his daughter Hippodamia. His charioteer Myrtilus helped Pelops to win her by replacing the ἔμβολον of Oenomaus' chariot with a wax imitation (or in Pher. Ath. *FGrHist* 3 F 37a = fr. 37a *EGM*, simply by removing it). In some accounts Hippodamia persuaded him to do this, having fallen in love with Pelops (Pher. Ath. *ib.*, [Apollod.] *Epit.* 2.6); in others it was Pelops himself (Nicolaus of Damascus *FGrH* 90 F 10, Dio. Sic. 4.73.5, Hyg. *Fab.* 84.4). Pelops afterwards killed Myrtilus by throwing him into the sea. This is first recounted in Pher. *FGrHist* 3 F 37b = fr. 37b *EGM*, cited by a scholium on this passage (p. 127.6–11 Papageorgius): Πέλοψ νικήσας τὸν ἀγῶνα καὶ λαβὼν τὴν Ἱπποδάμειαν ὑπέστρεφεν ἐπὶ τὴν Πελοπόννησον μετὰ τῶν ὑποπτέρων ἵππων καὶ τοῦ Μυρτίλου· καθ᾽ ὁδὸν δὲ καταλαβὼν αὐτὸν προϊόντα πρὸς τὸ φιλῆσαι αὐτὴν ἔρριψεν εἰς θάλασσαν. In tragedy his death is recounted at Eur. *Or.* 991–7 Πέλοψ . . . ἐπὶ πελάγεσι διε– | δίφρευσε Μυρτίλου φόνον | δικὼν ἐς οἶδμα πόντου, | λευκοκύμοσιν πρὸς Γεραιστίαις | ποντίων σάλων | ἀϊόσιν ἁρματεύσας· | ὅθεν δόμοισι τοῖς ἐμοῖς | ἦλθ᾽ ἀρὰ πολύστονος, 1547–8 ἔπεσ᾽ ἔπεσε μέλαθρα τάδε δι᾽ αἱμάτων | διὰ τὸ Μυρτίλου πέσημ᾽ ἐκ δίφρου (he is not mentioned in the other brief reference to Pelops' race at Eur. *Hel.* 386–7).

Pelops' motive for killing his helper varies from one account to another. In Pherecydes and [Apollod.] *Epit.* 2.8 Myrtilus attempts to force himself on Hippodamia and Pelops reacts accordingly. In Nicolaus, Pelops has already agreed to let Myrtilus marry Hippodamia; in Servius on Virg. *Georg.* 3.7 (iii. 273.10–11 Thilo and Hagen) Pelops is to be the bridegroom, but Myrtilus will enjoy the *ius primae noctis*. The deal is different again in Hyginus: there Myrtilus' reward is to be half of Oenomaus' kingdom. In each case Pelops thinks better of his bargain when Oenomaus has been dispatched. The traditional location of the immersion was at Geraestus in Euboea (cf. Tzetzes on Lycophr.

157 = ii. 74.9–10 Scheer; hence, for some, the name of the Μυρτῷον πέλαγος south of Euboea). This is contested by Paus. 8.14.10–12, who locates his grave at Pheneos in Arcadia. Pindar does not mention Myrtilus in his account of Pelops' victory in *O.* 1, since his hero hardly emerges with credit from this episode. It is disputed whether he was present on the east pediment of the mid-fifth-century temple of Zeus at Olympia, which depicted Pelops and Hippodamia (cf. Gerber on Pind. *O.* 1.87). For the differing literary accounts of this part of the Pelops myth see further W. Hansen (2000) 23–4, Davidson (2003).

An aryballus from the second half of the fourth century (Berlin Staatl. Mus. F3072 = *LIMC* VI/2 413 §25; cf. Triantis (1992) 695) depicts Myrtilus falling from Pelops' chariot; above the scene flies an Erinys. For iconographical representations of Pelops see Lacroix (1976). For the folk-tale associations of the story see W. Hansen (2002) 58–62.

504–6 ὢ … | … ἱππεία, | ὡς ἔμολες: for the pathetic apostrophe cf. Eur. *El.* 432, *Phoen.* 1019, *IA* 573, Kranz (1933) 239. These apostrophes were common enough in Euripidean choral odes to be satirised by Aristophanes at *Ran.* 1309–28 (where see Dover); the placing of such apostrophes at the start of a section of the ode, not just at the beginning of the ode itself, is also typically Euripidean (cf. Kranz (1933) 192). The language is ornate: it is not Pelops, but Pelops' ἱππεία which arrives in the land.

505 πολύπονος ἱππεία: picked up by πολύπονος ἀκεία at the end of the epode; the ring composition emphasises the continuance of woe in the house from that day to this.

506 ἔμολες: a further instance of the theme of motion (475n.), which connects the epode to the rest of the song. But whereas most of the previous verbs of motion had been in the future tense (475, 477, 489, 497, 501), this one is in the past (cf. 492). Suffering arrived in the house of Pelops long ago, and remains with it: justice and punishment are yet to come.

αἰανής: only L^{ac}K^{pc}, *coni.* Blomfield on Aesch. *Pers.* 935 (our 941; in his first edition); αἰανή *cett.* For the corruption see West (1981) 77 n. 19. At *Aj.* 672 L alone has the correct accentuation αἰανὴς (αἰανῆς *cett.*). The word can mean either 'grim' or 'long-lasting' (cf. Braswell on Pind. *P.* 4.236(a)), and both senses are appropriate here.

508 εὖτε 'from the time when' (514n.).

ποντισθείς: the verb ποντίζω is found twice elsewhere before the imperial period, both times in Aeschylus (*Ag.* 1013, fr. 47a.780 *TrGF*); Euripides has the noun ποντίσματα (*Hel.* 1548). Compounds with κατα– are more common.

509 ἐκοιμάθη: Sleep and Death are brothers in Homer and Hesiod (cf. West on Hes. *Op.* 116), and are often associated in the visual arts (cf. Wöhrle (1995) 24–35). Sleep is often used as a euphemism for death (cf. *Aj.* 831–2 καλῶ δ' ἅμα | πομπαῖον Ἑρμῆν χθόνιον εὖ με κοιμίσαι, *OC* 621 οὑμὸς εὕδων καὶ κεκρυμμένος νέκυς); this later becomes a favourite consolatory *topos* (cf. Kassel (1958) 76–9, Nisbet and Hubbard on Hor. *C.* 1.24.5). But in a description of the actual moment of a violent death the word is startling. It recalls the grim understatements of Hom. *Il.* 11.241 ὡς ὁ μὲν αὖθι πεσὼν κοιμήσατο χάλκεον ὕπνον and 14.482–3 φράζεσθ' ὡς ὑμῖν Πρόμαχος δεδμημένος εὕδει | ἔγχει ἐμῷ, which are anything but consolatory; cf. Posid. 33.7 A–B τὸν δὲ θεοῖς ἐρίσαντα μέλας κατεκοίμισεν Ἄρης.

510 παγχρύσων: 'objects belonging to the gods are often called golden from Homer on' (Lloyd-Jones (1963) 85 = (1990b) 173): cf. Dodds on Eur. *Ba.* 553–5, Bömer on Ov. *Met.* 8.15–16, West (1997) 112. At Pind. *O.* 1.87 Poseidon gives Pelops a golden chariot. The beauty of the chariot contrasts with the description of violence and death which surrounds it.

511 ἀκείαις: 102n.

512 πρόρριζος ἐκριφθείς: we need a word denoting how Myrtilus was flung out of the chariot, and ῥίπτω fulfils that need: hence Reiske's ἐκτριφθείς ((1753) 15) should be rejected, despite Hdt. 6.86δ ἐκτέτριπται . . . πρόρριζος, Eur. *Hipp.* 684 πρόρριζον ἐκτρίψειεν, Headlam on Herod. 6.27. The orthographic variant ἐκριφείς is well-attested but metrically undesirable.

πρόρριζος is found in tragedy only here and at 765, Eur. *Hipp.* 684, Aesch. *Pers.* 812 (and possibly fr. 154a.13 *TrGF*; see Radt's apparatus). In its two epic occurrences (Hom. *Il.* 11.157 and 14.415) it retains its literal meaning 'by the roots'; by the end of the fifth century it generally means little more than 'utterly' (e.g. Ar. *Ran.* 587, Andoc. 1.146). Here translate e.g. 'to his destruction'.

513–15 ὁ νοῦς τοιοῦτός ἐστιν, ἀφ' οὗ ὁ Μυρτίλος ἀπέθανεν οὐ διέλιπεν αἰκία τοὺς πολυκτήμονας δόμους (Σ p. 127.19–21 Papageorgius); this led Bergk to read οἴκους and instead of πολύπονος to conjecture πολυπάμονας after Bothe ('wealthy'; found elsewhere only at Hom. *Il.* 4.433, excluding grammarians, lexicographers and the Sibyl). But it is the suffering, not the wealth, of the house that is the point here; and as in 511, ἀκεία demands an epithet. For the sentiment cf. Accius 657–9 Ribbeck *quinam Tantalidarum internecioni modus | paretur? aut quaenam umquam ob mortem Myrtili | poenis luendis dabitur satias supplici?*

514 ἔλιπεν: for intransitive λείπω or its compounds in similar contexts cf. Eur. *Or.* 816–18 ὅθεν (i.e. from the time of the golden lamb) πόνῳ πόνος ἐξαμεί– | βων δι' αἵματος οὐ προλεί– | πει δισσοῖσιν Ἀτρείδαις, *Her.* 133 τὸ δὲ κακοτυχὲς οὐ λέλοιπεν ἐκ τέκνων, *Hel.* 1155–6 οὔποτ' ἔρις | λείψει κατ' ἀνθρώπων πόλεις, S. *Ant.* 584–5 οἷς γὰρ ἂν σεισθῇ θεόθεν δόμος, ἄτας | οὐδὲν ἐλλείπει γενεᾶς ἐπὶ πλῆθος ἕρπον, LSJ⁹ s.v. λείπω A II 2. Both the imperfect and aorist forms are attested, although confusions of ει and ι are so common that the conflicting manuscript readings tell us almost nothing. Ll-J/W and West (1982a) 102 n. 71 are probably right in preferring the aorist, since leaving is a punctual action; nevertheless, the possibility remains that the imperfect is correct ('has never looked like leaving' – Dawe (1976) 232). Willink (2003) 78–9 suggests λείπει 'κ, which gives us a line of five long syllables such as may occur at 510: but in the context cretic plus molossus makes better metrical sense. The stress on motion in the ode is now put into reverse: the suffering of the house has so far proved unmoveable.

ἐκ τοῦδ' οἴκου: οἴκους also has good manuscript authority. The *utrum in alterum* argument cuts both ways: the accusative could have turned into a genitive under the influence of the preceding τοῦδ', or the reverse could have been effected to create an object for the verb. But the meaning strongly favours the genitive. The deictic 'from this house' makes excellent sense for a chorus standing before the πολύφθορον δῶμα of the house of Atreus (cf. 10, Aesch. *Ag.* 1186 τὴν γὰρ στέγην τήνδ' οὔποτ' ἐκλείπει χορός (sc. Ἐρινύων)), and might be accompanied by an appropriate gesture. The accusative, on the other hand, is bare, even bland, without anything to qualify it, as would be Dobree's οἶκον ((1833–43) ii. 50), or the dative οἴκοις conjectured by Willink (2003) 79. For λείπω with ἐκ cf. Ritchie (1964) 182. Nor is there a difficulty with the εὖτε in 508, since 'in Tragedy εὖτε with the aorist indicative, where the meaning is temporal and not causal, normally means "from the time when"' (Fraenkel on Aesch. *Ag.* 306–8, citing Aesch. *Ag.* 986 and *Sept.* 745): it therefore does not need to be picked up by a following ἐκ τοῦδ'. The causal sense is also felt here: for this LSJ⁹ s.v. II cites S. *Aj.* 716 (lyr.), *Phil.* 1097 (lyr.), *OC* 84.

515 πολύπονος: 505n.
ἀκεία: 102n.

SECOND EPISODE (516–822)

516–633 The episode begins with a tragic *agon*. In its most formal guise, this consists of a pair of long speeches followed by hostile stichomythia; the whole is bracketed by an entrance and exit, or other clear break. This is the norm in Euripides, but in S. it occurs only three times (here, *Aj.* 1047–1162, 1226–1315). S. prefers passages which contain *agon*-like features, but lack the sharp structural definition outlined above (cf. *Ant.* 441–525, *OR* 513–677, *OC* 720–1104, M. A. Lloyd (1992) 11–13). This difference is usually associated with a general distinction between the two playwrights: S. tends to blur structural elements, while Euripides draws attention to them (261–74n.). Euripides too is capable of using *agon*-elements in the construction of other scenes, a point obscured by Lloyd's strict definition of what does and does not constitute an *agon* (cf. Mossman (1994)). It is also possible that S.'s surviving work is unrepresentative, and that formal *agones* were more common in the lost plays. Nevertheless, the extant dramas do provide many opportunities for this form, opportunities which S. does not take up. The confrontations between Antigone and Creon, Philoctetes and Odysseus, and Oedipus and Creon (in *OR* and *OC*) are all vividly depicted without recourse to the formal *agon*. It would be unduly sceptical to deny that this is a difference between the two playwrights.

So why a formal *agon* here? One answer may lie in the position of this scene. For the third time a newly arrived character reproaches Electra for her perpetual lamentation. The vehemence of these criticisms has progressively increased, in a kind of ascending tricolon: the chorus is gentle and consoling, Chrysothemis is ironical but not unfriendly, while Clytemnestra is abrupt and aggressive.[32] These changes in tone are mirrored and reinforced by changes in form. The parodos is an amoebaean exchange between Electra and her interlocutors; the participants disagree, but without the hostility which arises from two massive speeches in confrontation. The scene with Chrysothemis takes a step towards the formal *agon*: it contains two opposing speeches (though Chrysothemis' is short and weak), and, after a gap, some opposing stichomythia. In Clytemnestra, however, Electra encounters a truly formidable opponent with a case that needs answering. The especially bitter hostility between them is conveyed through the cold formality of a fully-fledged *agon*. The tragic form which most marks hostility and antagonism is a worthy vessel for this most confrontational pair.

This *agon* is also important for our understanding of the moral dilemmas and paradoxes raised by the play.[33] The issue at stake is whether Clytemnestra's killing of Agamemnon was a just act or not, a subject which also dominates the *kommos* at Aesch. *Ag.* 1407–1576 and the *agon* of Eur. *El.* 998–1122. In Aeschylus the chorus begins by unreservedly condemning Clytemnestra's action, but later comes to appreciate that the killing may have formed part of a broader divine plan (*Ag.* 1485–9); while in Euripides Clytemnestra makes powerful arguments in her defence which are never contradicted. In each case the killing of Agamemnon is not simply an immoral act; the justifications adduced in its favour are as powerful and unanswerable as the criticisms made

---

[32] Cf. N. Lowe (2000) 71: 'A well-paced plot will be phased into a series of episodes of *rising affective intensity*, with the strongest discharge of energy at the end and the other main punches spaced out in roughly ascending order through the text' (his italics).

[33] Cairns's claim that 'there is no need to get involved in the rights and wrongs of this exchange' ((1993) 243; cf. Goward (1999) 112) is the exact opposite of the truth.

of it. S. handles the matter differently. Here Clytemnestra's sole justification for Agamemnon's death is his sacrifice of Iphigenia; his adultery with Cassandra, a major part of her case in Aeschylus and Euripides (584–94n.), goes unmentioned. Electra convincingly rebuts her mother's argument (566–76n.), and shows that her real motivation lay in adulterous passion for Aegisthus. This contrasts with Electra's response in Euripides (*El.* 1060–99), where she points out flaws and inconsistencies in her mother's case, but barely addresses, let alone refutes, either of her main charges. In S. it is Clytemnestra who fails to respond adequately to the accusations laid against her (612–33n.).

The view we take of Clytemnestra's arguments is reinforced by the presentation of her character. She is abrupt and aggressive throughout, entirely in accordance with the picture of her we received earlier from Electra (287–98); the contrast with her Euripidean counterpart is again clear (612–33n.). This is especially apparent in the most important section of her speech, where she deals with the sacrifice of her daughter. Her insistent stress on the first-person pronoun forfeits our sympathy (532 ἐμοί . . . 533 ἐγώ . . . 536 τήν γ᾿ ἐμήν . . . 538 τἀμά . . . μοι . . . 542 τῶν ἐμῶν . . . 544 τῶν ἐξ ἐμοῦ). True, she does have legitimate rights and claims in Iphigenia's case: but this incessant emphasis suggests that her grievance consists not in the death of her daughter *per se* as in the slight thereby done to herself. Contrast the maternal tenderness shown even by Aeschylus' Clytemnestra (*Ag.* 1417–18, 1525–6); contrast too the brief, yet intensely moving, details of the sacrifice given by the Clytemnestras of the other tragedians (*Ag.* 1415–17 (cf. 228–47), Eur. *El.* 1020–3). In our play anything that could mollify our view of her character is carefully avoided. Rhetorical theorists would later place great emphasis on the importance of assuming the correct ἦθος in a speech; Aristotle calls it the κυριωτάτη of the πίστεις ἔντεχνοι (*Rhet.* 1356ᵃ13; cf. Russell (1990), Lausberg (1998) §355). Here the repulsiveness of Clytemnestra's ἦθος strongly disposes the audience against her.

Some scholars have tried to show that Electra's character, as displayed in the *agon*, is equally unpleasant. Yet her request for permission to speak is made with studied politeness (552–7n.), while her exposition of the deficiencies of her mother's case is set out with calmness and clarity. This calmness does not last throughout her speech, however. Its final section, where she repeats many of the charges made against her mother, is angry and impassioned; even the usually sympathetic chorus comments unfavourably (610–11n.). But Winnington-Ingram's implication that the *agon* depicts violence and aggression on both sides in equal measure ((1954–5) 22–3 = (1980) 222–3 = E. Segal (1983) 213) is a grotesque misinterpretation of the text. Clytemnestra goes out of her way to humiliate and torment her daughter for her continued championing of her father's cause; Electra's anger, however bitter and violent, is a response to this attack. The heavy moral censure Electra receives from some critics owes much to anachronistic Stoic or Christian notions of the appropriate manner to respond to insults; we may wonder how many members of a late fifth-century audience would have been urging Electra to turn the other cheek. And even if an audience were receiving negative impressions of her character in the closing section of her speech, these will be countered by Electra's later daring admission of remorse (616–21 n.).

Yet despite the defeat of Clytemnestra's argument, and despite the wide differences in character between the two women, this *agon* does raise more troubling issues. Electra is not content merely to counter Clytemnestra's case as it stands: twice she makes a hypothetical point, aimed at showing that even under circumstances more favourable to Clytemnestra, her mother would still be wrong. This is a familiar rhetorical technique, aimed at demonstrating the weakness of one's opponent's case: one can concede all this, and still be right. But Electra's concessions have unfortunate implications for the killing in which she will later be involved. First she admits that a killing that is δίκαιον may also be αἰσχρόν (558–60n.). Second and more seriously, she claims that even if Agamemnon's killing of Iphigenia had been unjust, and hence even if Clytemnestra's killing of Agamemnon had been just, Clytemnestra would still be subject to death as a punishment in her turn (577–83). Electra thus concedes that even a just killer may be legitimately killed in his or her turn, and this concession has unfortunate implications for her own situation. S. has been at pains to show that the killing of Agamemnon was an act motivated not by justice but by lust; the punishment of his killers will be an act of a different moral status. Yet we are forced to consider that even this most just of killings will still be a killing, and still be shameful; and the distinction between δίκη–killing and *talio*–killing, though not abolished, is decidedly blurred (577–83n.).

The confrontation between mother and daughter at Sen. *Ag.* 953–80 shows signs of being influenced by this passage (see Tarrant on 953 ff.).

516 Clytemnestra enters from the *skene*. She is dressed more elaborately than Chrysothemis had been, in a manner that befits a queen consort (cf. 664), and is accompanied by at least one attendant (cf. 634), again in contrast to Chrysothemis, who had confronted Electra on her own. The visual contrast with Electra's miserable attire and lonely state is thus even more striking.[34] She intends to pray to Apollo before his statue (635n.) as a consequence of her dream, though we do not learn this until 630–1; the offerings carried by her attendant(s) may give the audience a hint, however. Diverted from her purpose by the sight of Electra, she reproaches her for her presence outside the house.

---

[34] For this contrast in appearance between two participants in an *agon* cf. Eur. *Andr.* 147–272, *El.* 998–1122, *Tro.* 914–1059.

The similarities with Chrysothemis' entry encourage us to use the previous scene in our interpretation of this encounter (cf. 516–633n.).

Clytemnestra's entry is not announced by the chorus. This is not in itself remarkable: in tragedy only a minority of entrances from the *skene* are so introduced (cf. Mastronarde (1979) 26–7, Hamilton (1978) 69–70). But it does convey the suddenness of Clytemnestra's attack. Such an abrupt opening to an *agon* is paralleled only at Eur. *Andr.* 147, where Hermione's outburst against Andromache takes place immediately after a choral ode, again without a choral introduction. Contrast the opening to the *agon* of Euripides' *Electra*, where Clytemnestra begins speaking only after considerable provocation from her daughter (1004–6, 1008–10).

In *agones* the character whose rôle approximates to that of prosecutor usually speaks first, followed by the speaker whom he is attacking. This order is reversed in our play, as well as in Eur. *El.* 998–1122 and *Tro.* 914–1059, since in these cases 'the natural defendants have already been so much criticized . . . that a further prosecution speech would be superfluous' (Lloyd (1992) 17). But given that so much of each speech is concerned with the rights and wrongs of Agamemnon's actions, Clytemnestra's speech does in that sense correspond to a prosecution speech, and Electra's to a defence.

See Schein (1979) 46–50 for a detailed metrical analysis of the opening of Clytemnestra's speech.

ἀνειμένη 'on the loose'; cf. *Ant.* 578–9 ἐκ δὲ τοῦδε χρὴ | γυναῖκας εἶναι τάσδε μηδ' ἀνειμένας, Eur. *Andr.* 727–8. Again the issue of Electra's freedom of movement is raised (312–13n.); we know how deeply this rankles with Clytemnestra and Aegisthus (378–84n.).

μέν: speeches in drama frequently open with μέν *solitarium* (Denniston 382–3; cf. *OR* 1369, *Aj.* 815).

αὖ: used also by Chrysothemis at 328; cf. the chorus's ἀεί at 122. Clytemnestra continually refers to the repetitive nature of Electra's laments (cf. 520 πολλὰ πρὸς πολλούς, 524 θαμά, 525 ἀεί, 530 ἀεί; also Electra's πολλὰ δή at 603). This emphasis is typical of quarrels (cf. Macleod on Hom. *Il.* 24.62–3, 72–3), though here the accusation is hardly an exaggeration.

στρέφῃ: normally implying busy, energetic movement (cf. *Tr.* 907, Hom. *Il.* 5.40, Solon frr. 4.23, 36.27 *IEG*), but here a pejorative substitute for εἶ. Electra is unlikely to be moving about at this point, as that would distract from the dancing of the chorus.

517 Again the absence of Aegisthus; again the suggestion that he is the real menace (310–23n.).

ἐπεῖχ' ἀεί: having declared that her daughter is out *again*, Clytemnestra now tells Electra that Aegisthus *always* used to keep her inside: this formal contradiction led Nauck[4a] to conjecture ἐπεῖχεν ἄν. But there is no real difficulty with the paradosis, as ἀεί can easily stand for 'whenever Aegisthus was at home'.

518 On the freedom of movement accorded to women in tragedy see 312–13n.
μή τοι . . . γ᾽: each particle functions independently (cf. *OC* 1407, *Aj.* 472, Denniston 546–7). Campbell (*PS*) claims that 'the emphatic γε seems to imply that the offence indoors was hardly less', but this is over-subtle. Emphasis is always put on the transgressive nature of Electra's presence outside the house; nowhere is she attacked for her behaviour inside. The force is rather 'disgrace your kin, *as you do* by roaming outside' (Diggle, *per litteras*), with the γ᾽ emphasising the participial phrase.

θυραίαν: θυραῖον *coni.* Blomfield (on Aesch. *Ag.* 1022 (our 1055)): but while this adjective can be two-termination (313n.), it need not be (cf. e.g. Eur. *Hipp.* 395, *Phoen.* 848).

αἰσχύνειν φίλους: deeply ironic. Electra has gone outside precisely to honour her closest φίλος; nor would she use this term to designate most of the current occupants of the house.

520 καίτοι: 'you disregard my authority, *and yet* complain of it as oppressive' (Jebb; cf. Denniston 556). The particle can also be continuative, meaning 'and further' (Denniston 559–61; this is rare in verse, however). With this sense Clytemnestra would be exemplifying her previous statement οὐδὲν ἐντρέπῃ | ἐμοῦ γε. But 'and yet' is more forceful. Clytemnestra points out what she sees as the inconsistency of Electra's position: her treatment, she suggests, is not as bad as Electra maintains. For more on καίτοι see Jacquinod (1997).

δή: goes equally well with πολλά or πολλούς, and so should probably be taken with both.

521 θρασεῖα καὶ πέρα δίκης: against Morstadt's τραχεῖα ((1864) 20) cf. Pl. *Leg.* 630b6 θρασεῖς καὶ ἄδικοι καὶ ὑβρισταί, Eur. *IT* 275 ἀνομίᾳ θρασύς; also 1506.

522 ἄρχω: taken by Brunck (his 1786 edition, ii. 203) with the participle to mean ἄρχω ὕβρεως (cf. Hom. *Il.* 2.378 ἐγὼ δ᾽ ἦρχον χαλεπαίνων, Hdt. 4.119.4 ἄρξῃ . . . ἀδικέων). The question of who begins insulting whom is important (cf. 523–4, 552–3): nevertheless, the essence of Electra's complaint must be Clytemnestra's violent behaviour, not her tendency to assume priority in their confrontations.

καθυβρίζουσα: with accusative as at Eur. *El.* 698 (with genitive at *OC* 960, *Phil.* 1364). For ὕβρις see 271 n.

καὶ σὲ καὶ τὰ σά: for the tone cf. *Aj.* 1147 καὶ σὲ καὶ τὸ σὸν λάβρον στόμα, *Ant.* 573 καὶ σὺ καὶ τὸ σὸν λέχος. τὰ σά is here almost equivalent to σέ; its addition stresses Clytemnestra's contempt.

523 ὕβριν . . . ἔχω: cf. Hom. *Od.* 1.368 ὑπέρβιον ὕβριν ἔχοντες, S. *Ant.* 300 πανουργίας . . . ἔχειν, Lloyd-Jones (1992) 55 = (2005) 106.

523–4 κακῶς δέ σε | λέγω κακῶς κλύουσα πρὸς σέθεν θαμά: Clytemnestra's claim would be more convincing if she had not just begun abusing Electra so abruptly (516n.). For the sentiment cf. *Aj.* 1322–3 ἐγὼ γὰρ ἀνδρὶ συγγνώμην ἔχω | κλυόντι φλαῦρα συμβαλεῖν ἔπη κακά, Hes. *Op.* 721, Alcaeus fr. 341 *PLF*, Voigt, Juv. 1.1–2.

525 οὐδὲν ἄλλο: in apposition to πατήρ, and hence followed by a comma; if it is taken as the predicate of πρόσχημα, the following ὡς ἐξ ἐμοῦ τέθνηκεν is left hanging uncomfortably. The phrase is a reproach to Electra for failing to vary the subject of her complaints; under the circumstances, we may well wonder what other excuse she should offer for her behaviour.

σοί: the accented form should probably be preferred because the word carries some rhetorical emphasis; σοι is possible, however, since the enclitic pronoun can go with the words which follow it even when preceded by a pause (cf. Diggle's apparatus on Eur. *Andr.* 551, *Hel.* 78).

πρόσχημα: 'pretext' is better in this context than 'what you are always putting forward'. Clytemnestra implies that Electra's true motive is different; the audience is aware that this is not the case.

ἀεί: 516n.

526 ἐξ ἐμοῦ . . . ἐξ ἐμοῦ: the repetition of the first person pronoun conveys indignation (cf. *Ant.* 32 κἀμοί, λέγω γὰρ κἀμέ), as do the asyndeton and short, staccato sense-units. 528 then comes as a climax.

527 ἔξοιδα: for the prefix see 222n.

τῶνδ' ἄρνησις οὐκ ἔνεστί μοι: most editors take the phrase to mean 'I do not deny it'. West (1978a) 119 points out that it must rather mean 'I cannot deny it', and that this does not fit with the γάρ of 528. He discusses various emendations (τί γάρ; F. W. Schmidt ((1886–7) i. 123–4, printed by Dawe³), ἀτάρ Polle, σὺν δ' ἡ Hense, ἀλλ' ἡ Schenkl ((1869) 538; he also deletes 527)), and he himself suggests a short lacuna before 528 containing e.g. ἀλλ' οὐκ ἐγὼ γὰρ αἰτία φόνου κυρῶ. Ll-J/W (*Sophoclea*) agree that there is a problem, but claim that it can be resolved by interpreting εἷλεν in 528 as 'convicted' rather than 'killed' (as Kaibel suggests, p. 156). But even if true (see *ad loc.*), this does not solve our problem. We rather should pay greater attention to the meaning of γάρ. The connexion it introduces is not always logically watertight, and we often need to suppose a brief ellipse to make sense of the particle (cf. Denniston 61–2, *OR* 317, *Phil.* 1167). So here Clytemnestra's thought must be along the lines of 'I can't deny it [, and I won't], for it was Justice that killed him, not I alone'.

For the expression cf. *OR* 578 ἄρνησις οὐκ ἔνεστιν ὧν ἀνιστορεῖς. Asyndeton is common when a claim or admission is followed by a phrase meaning 'I don't / can't deny it': cf. Aesch. *Pers.* 738, *Eum.* 463 ἔκτεινα τὴν τεκοῦσαν, οὐκ ἀρνήσομαι, 588 ἔκτεινα· τούτου γ' (Nauck; δ' codd.) οὔτις ἄρνησις πέλει, Eur. *Hel.* 579.

528 ἡ . . . Δίκη νιν εἷλεν: Clytemnestra invokes Justice, and Justice alone, as her ally: she sees Agamemnon's death not as a further casualty in a long series of *talio* killings, but as a merited punishment for the unjust killing of his daughter. Aeschylus' Clytemnestra is also concerned with justice (cf. *Ag.* 1432–3 μὰ τὴν τέλειον τῆς ἐμῆς παιδὸς Δίκην | Ἄτην Ἐρινύν θ', ἦσι τόνδ' ἔσφαξ' ἐγώ, Garvie on *Cho.* 461), though she also sees her act in more transcendent terms: at *Ag.* 1501–2 she attributes Agamemnon's death to ὁ παλαιὸς δριμὺς ἀλάστωρ | Ἀτρέως χαλεποῦ θοινατῆρος, while at *Cho.* 910 she pleads in extenuation ἡ Μοῖρα τούτων, ὦ τέκνον, παραιτία. She sees herself as the embodiment or agent of the fatal curse which had lain upon the house since the banquet of Thyestes.

For personifications of Δίκη in this context cf. 475–6, Eur. *Hcld.* 941 εἷλέ σ' ἡ Δίκη χρόνῳ, Aelian fr. 89.24–5 Domingo-Forasté ἀπέκτεινε δὲ αὐτὸν πρῶτον μὲν ἡ Δίκη, εἷτα ἡ χεὶρ ἡ Χιόνιδος (Χίωνος Chalcondyles), Hamdorf (1964) 51–2. Similar figures are found in oratory: cf. Lys. 1.26 οὐκ ἐγώ σε ἀποκτενῶ, ἀλλ' ὁ τῆς πόλεως νόμος, [Dem.] 59.115.

εἷλεν: taken by Kaibel (p. 156) and Ll-J/W (*Sophoclea*) to mean 'convicted'. Clytemnestra is indeed emphasising the judicial character of her act; nevertheless, it seems perverse in this context to take the verb to mean anything other than 'killed'.

οὐκ ἐγὼ μόνη: Clytemnestra's claim that she shares responsibility with a deity is not impious (cf. Fraenkel on Aesch. *Ag.* 811). The following relative clause runs more easily with οὐκ than with the majority reading κοὐκ (so Dawe, *STS* i. 181).

529 εἰ φρονοῦσ' ἐτύγχανες: Chrysothemis had frequently urged φρόνησις on her sister (384n.), meaning a willingness to tolerate the rule of the stronger. More surprising is Clytemnestra's claim that active support for the killing of Agamemnon would deserve this designation.

530–3 Clytemnestra adduces Iphigenia's death as a reason for Agamemnon's killing at Aesch. *Ag.* 1414–20, 1525–9, 1551–9 and Eur. *El.* 1018–29. On its strength as an argument in this play see 516–633n.

Iphigenia is not mentioned in Homer: τὸ γὰρ Ἰφιγενείας ὄνομα οὐδὲ οἶδεν ὁ ποιητής (Σ T Hom. *Il.* 1.106b = i. 40.27–8 Erbse). Agamemnon's outburst against Calchas at *Il.* 1.106 μάντι κακῶν, οὔ πώ ποτέ μοι τὸ κρήγυον εἶπας is sometimes cited as evidence to the contrary: but 'the hyperbole is fully explicable in terms of the rhetoric of argument and invective' (Davies, in his *Trachiniae* commentary, p. xxi). This does not mean that the legend itself was not in circulation at that time. Homer frequently suppresses details of myths which do not suit his poetic purpose; in particular, the uses to which the Orestes story are put in the *Odyssey* positively demand that any such act on Agamemnon's part be quietly expunged. For the post-Homeric tradition see March (1987) 86–91. In the *Cypria* Calchas orders Iphigenia's sacrifice at Aulis; she is summoned from home by the news that she is to marry Achilles (cf. Eur. *IA*). Artemis rescues her before she can be sacrificed, and substitutes instead a deer at the altar (p. 32 lines 58–63 *EGF* = p. 41 lines 45–9 *PEG* = p. 74 *GEF*). [Hes.] fr. 23a.17–18 M–W describes how the Greeks sacrificed Agamemnon's daughter Iphimede to secure their passage to Troy; Artemis saves the girl and makes her immortal. A similar account seems to have occurred in Stesichorus' *Oresteia* (fr. 215 *PMGF*). Pind. *P.* 11.22–3 is the first known text to associate Clytemnestra's killing of Agamemnon with the sacrifice of Iphigenia.[35] See further Lloyd-Jones (1983a) 95 = (1990b) 318–19.

530 πατὴρ οὗτος σός: the combination of οὗτος and σός is probably contemptuous ('that father of yours', Lloyd-Jones, similarly Jebb); the late placing of σός may have a similar effect, though at e.g. Eur. *Hipp.* 899 καὶ μὴν ὅδ' αὐτὸς παῖς σὸς ἐς καιρὸν πάρα there is no such force.

ἀεί: 516n.

531 τὴν σὴν ὅμαιμον: balancing πατὴρ οὗτος σός in the previous line, as if to stress that Electra's concern for one family member is leading her to forget another.

μοῦνος Ἑλλήνων: perhaps a twist of a praise motif, as at Lys. 3.45: cf. Hdt. 6.121.2, Isocr. 5.108, Eur. *Ba.* 962.

---

[35] March (1987) 92 argues that the speed with which Pindar suggests this link means that the idea must have already been familiar to his audience; she speculates (92–8) that it may have occurred in an *Oresteia* by Simonides. But (i) poets do not always feel the need to labour the introduction of new details into a myth (cf. Pind. *I.* 4.53, where the striking claim that Heracles was slight in stature is made with equivalent speed); (ii) there is no good evidence for an *Oresteia* by Simonides (fr. 549 *PMG*, the only possible reference to one, might be from any number of poems).

The scholia to Pindar's *Eleventh Pythian* give two possible dates for the poem, 474 and 454. The former is much the more likely: see the introduction to my forthcoming edition of the poem (Cambridge 2007/8).

531–2 ἔτλη | θῦσαι θεοῖσιν: cf. Aesch. *Ag.* 223–5 ἔτλα δ᾽ οὖν | θυτὴρ γενέσθαι | θυγατρός, 1417–18 ἔθυσεν αὐτοῦ παῖδα, φιλτάτην ἐμοὶ | ὠδῖν᾽, Eur. *IT* 784, Casabona (1966) 78–80, Henrichs (2000) 183 with n. 39. Distinguish this from the metaphorical use of sacrificial terminology to describe deaths in tragedy (e.g. Aesch. *Ag.* 1118, 1503, Eur. *El.* 1222–3, *Or.* 562). For τλάω in this context cf. also Eur. *IT* 862 ᾤμωξα κἀγὼ τόλμαν ἣν ἔτλη πατήρ, *IA* 98, 887; for the sense 'steel one's heart to crime' see 273n.

532–3 οὐκ ἴσον καμὼν ἐμοὶ | λύπης, ὅτ᾽ ἔσπειρ᾽, ὥσπερ ἡ τίκτουσ᾽ ἐγώ: Clytemnestra contrasts the pain of bringing up a child (cf. Aesch. *Cho.* 749–62), especially childbirth (cf. Eur. *Med.* 250–1, Aesch. *Ag.* 1417–18, Ar. *Lys.* 589), with the pleasure a man takes in begetting one (bitterly conveyed by sarcastic understatement).

532 ἴσον (cognate accusative) must be taken with the dative ἐμοί and the ὥσπερ clause. For the latter construction cf. Eur. *Her.* 667 (ἴσον ἅτε), *Ion* 1363 (ἴσον ὡς).

533 ὅτ᾽ ἔσπειρ᾽: for 'human reproductive processes . . . compared to the ploughing and planting of a field' see Braswell on Pind. *P.* 4.255(b), Bond on Eur. *Hyps.* fr. 1 iii. 25–6 = 752g.25–6 *TrGF*, and cf. *Tr.* 31–3 κἀφύσαμεν δὴ παῖδας, οὓς κεῖνός ποτε | . . . | σπείρων μόνον προσεῖδε κἀξαμῶν ἅπαξ. Contrast Clytemnestra's brusque tone with Electra's moving evocation of the labour involved in bringing up a child (1143–5).

ἡ τίκτουσ᾽: for the present aspect see 342n.

534–46 Clytemnestra's attempt to prove her assertion in 528 is based on the rhetorical technique of *hypophora* (Latin *subiectio*). With this device, the speaker sets out a problem or question, and suggests various solutions to it, typically in the form of rhetorical questions. Each solution is dismissed in turn, often by means of a further rhetorical question (cf. [Cic.] *Rhet. Her.* 4.33, Quint. *Inst.* 9.2.15, Carey on Lys. 31.24–33, G. L. Cooper (1971) 10–31, Lausberg (1998) §771–5). The technique is common in tragedy, both in *agones* and elsewhere (cf. *Aj.* 457–70, *OR* 1375–86, Eur. *Her.* 1281–90 with Bond, M. A. Lloyd (1992) 29 n. 40). It is normally deliberative in character, referring to the impossibility of a proposed action (cf. Eur. *Alc.* 1049–61 ('Where shall I put a new wife?'), *Andr.* 344–51 ('What excuse will you give for Hermione's divorce when you try to marry her off again?'), etc.). Here the *hypophora* is forensic: it is employed to show the illegitimacy of a act which has already occurred. Among the instances cited by Lloyd, the only parallel is Eur. *Hec.* 258–64; there Hecuba, like Clytemnestra in our case, is asking why the Greeks sacrificed her daughter. Forensic *hypophora* comes close to a method of argumentation developed by the

Eleatics and subsequently by Gorgias. A thesis is broken down into a number of subtheses, which are each rejected in turn; when each of these has been successively disproved, the main thesis can itself be rejected (M. A. Lloyd (1992) 30). In our case the two subtheses (namely, that Agamemnon killed Iphigenia for the sake of the Argives, or for the sake of Menelaus) are not fundamentally different from each other. Their similarity of content, however, is masked by the difference of form used to express them: the first question is given a brisk answer, whereas with the second point the hypophoric question and answer are telescoped into a single rhetorical question. After this the *hypophora* proper rather breaks down. Clytemnestra began by suggesting real arguments which a supporter of Agamemnon might have used, and to which she feels capable of giving an answer. But her final questions involve ridiculous motives: merely to state them makes their inapplicability clear. Secure that she has preempted any attempt at defending her husband's action, she descends into mere mockery, sarcasm and abuse; this culminates in the alliterative outburst of 544–5.

Budelmann (1999) 66–71 takes a different view of the passage. He claims that these questions represent a genuine inquiry on Clytemnestra's part into Agamemnon's motivation, a motivation which remains mysteriously unknown to us. His approach is vitiated, however, by his failure to consider the rhetorical form. He thus does not explain whether he thinks that all occurrences of *hypophora* conform to this theory, or else what makes this instance so decidedly different from the others.

534 For εἶέν 'introducing a transition to a fresh point by a backward glance at what has been established: "So far so good, (and now . . .)"' see Stevens (1976) 34, Waś (1983) 112–14. It begins a flurry of hypophoric questions at Eur. *Med.* 386, *Suppl.* 1094, *Phoen.* 1615, *IA* 1185 (cf. Fowler (1987) 8 n. 6). For the formation see S–D ii. 557–8.

<τοῦτο·> τοῦ χάριν: so Schmalfeld (1868) 22 n. 15. Most manuscripts read τοῦ χάριν τίνος. Punctuating after χάριν gives us 'for the sake of what, or what', which is inept. Hermann punctuates τοῦ, χάριν τίνος, translating *pro qua re, cuius gratia*; but this seems forced, even confusing. τίνων is found in some manuscripts instead of τίνος. Taken as a part of τίς, this leads into the following phrase πότερον Ἀργείων ἐρεῖς; Here too, however, the double question causes problems. Other instances of repeated questions (cf. 409, 958–9, *Tr.* 707–8, *Phil.* 1029 καὶ νῦν τί μ' ἄγετε; τί μ' ἀπάγεσθε; τοῦ χάριν;, Eur. *Andr.* 548 τί ταῦτα, πῶς ταῦτ'; (v.l.), *Or.* 732) never approach the extraordinary brevity of 'for the sake of what, or whom?' Nor could this elliptical mode of questioning be meant to convey Clytemnestra's impatience: such verbal idiosyncrasies are foreign to Greek tragedy. Campbell (*PS*) takes τίνων to be a part of τίνω: for the short iota cf. *OC* 635, [Aesch.] *PV* 112. This would require the emendation of τοῦ to τῷ, however (so Mähly

(1889) 37) and we would then be hard pressed to explain the construction of Ἀργείων in 535. The best solution is Schmalfeld's conjecture, adopted by Dawe and Ll-J/W, which postulates corruption arising from a simple *saut du même au même*, followed by the insertion of a τίνος or τίνων to heal the metre. Schmalfeld compares Eur. *Hec.* 1208 ἐπεὶ δίδαξον τοῦτο· πῶς κτλ. The staccato phrasing which the line obtains as a consequence recalls that of 526–7. Clytemnestra offers a similar question at Eur. *IA* 1166 τίνος ἕκατί νιν κτενεῖς.

536 ἀλλ᾿ ... γ᾿: also used in an answer to a hypophoric question at *Aj.* 469.
For the force of μετῆν cf. *Ant.* 48 ἀλλ᾿ οὐδὲν αὐτῷ τῶν ἐμῶν <μ᾿> εἴργειν μέτα, Borecky (1965) 64.

537 ἀλλ᾿: commonly introduces questions in *hypophora* (Denniston 10–11). For a question beginning ἀλλά following one beginning with πότερον cf. *Aj.* 460–9 (where, as here, the ἀλλά is strengthened with δῆτα), Aesch. *Ag.* 274–6 with Fraenkel on 276. 'When it is convenient to use the same particle two or three times at short intervals, the same particle is used two or three times (though when undergraduates write Greek prose, they will cut themselves with knives rather than do this)' (Denniston lxii): cf. 881–2, 915–16.
ἀντ᾿ 'because of' (cf. 575, 585, Moorhouse 99). Jebb prefers 'in his stead' (i.e. 'to prevent him from killing his own child'), but Clytemnestra has not yet begun to argue that Menelaus should offer up one of his own children.

538 τἄμ᾿: for the neuter used for persons cf. 972, 1208, Moorhouse 14–15, Bruhn §4. The usage is not in itself contemptuous (cf. *Ant.* 48 (cited above, 536n.), *Phil.* 434).

539 παῖδες ... διπλοῖ: in Homer, Menelaus and Helen have only one child, Hermione; Menelaus' son Megapenthes is the offspring of a slave-girl (*Od.* 4.10–14; cf. also *Il.* 3.175). But the scholia on our line (p. 128.14–15 Papageorgius) cite [Hes.] fr. 175 M–W ἢ τέκεθ᾿ Ἑρμιόνην δουρικλειτῷ Μενελάῳ· | ὁπλότατον δ᾿ ἔτεκεν Νικόστρατον, ὄζον Ἄρηος, which supplies a precedent for S.'s account; cf. also *Cypria* fr. 10 *EGF* = 12 *PEG*, where Helen has a son Pleisthenes (presumably by Menelaus). As the scholia go on to note (p. 128.20–2 Papageorgius), the Hesiodic version favours Clytemnestra's argument. Menelaus would have a legitimate child remaining after sacrificing the other to Artemis.
A man's daughter is killed to recapture his brother's wife: the imbalance involved is exploited three times elsewhere in tragedy. Clytemnestra makes the same argument in Eur. *IA* 1201–2 as she does in our play. At Eur. *Or.* 658–9 Orestes sarcastically tells his uncle ἃ δ᾿ Αὐλὶς ἔλαβε σφάγι᾿ ἐμῆς ὁμοσπόρου, | ἐῶ σ᾿ ἔχειν ταῦθ᾿· Ἑρμιόνην μὴ κτεῖνε σύ. More complicated is Clytemnestra's

argument at Eur. *El.* 1041–5. She changes the sex of the participants to effect a spectacularly hypothetical variant: if Menelaus had been seized, she asks, would she have been justified in sacrificing Orestes to effect his return? This does not provide evidence for the priority of S.'s play (*pace* Denniston on 1030–48); Euripides is often fond of daringly artificial argumentation, regardless of whether he is trying to distance himself from a predecessor.

540 τῆσδε: ὅδε 'may be applied to an absent person who is present *to the speaker's thoughts*' (Lloyd-Jones (1965) 242 = (1990a) 397 (his italics), comparing Eur. *Alc.* 881); cf. 1192, K–G i. 644, S–D ii. 209, Moorhouse 155, Stockert on Eur. *IA* 71–2.

πατρός: see next n.

541 On the grounds that the feminine singular ἧς sits uneasily with the preceding πατρὸς | καὶ μητρὸς ὄντας Nauck⁴ᵃ (cf. *id.* (1874) 100–1) deleted 541 and altered πατρός in 540 to πάρος (same confusion at Eur. *Her.* 930; for the pleonastic use of πάρος cf. *OC* 418). Housman (1892) 37–8 = (1972) i. 218–19 adopted the latter change and altered καί in 541 to ἐκ (again, not a difficult alteration: cf. *OC* 792). But with either of these changes, we get a series of lines with the main sense breaks only at line ends (536–44): this is contrary to Sophocles' usual practice (cf. Schein (1979) 45, Allen (1973) 120–1), and would impede the rhetorical force of the passage. ἐκείνης in 543 is also difficult if 541 is removed with its reference to Helen (so rightly Heimsoeth (1872b) xviii). Nor is the inconcinnity as great as has been claimed, given the proximity of μητρός to the following relative.

Helen is regularly cited as the cause of the Trojan war: cf. Hom. *Il.* 9.338–9, 19.325, *Od.* 11.438, Hes. *Op.* 165, [Hes.] fr. 200.11 M–W, Semon. fr. 7.117–18 *IEG*, Aesch. *Ag.* 62, 448–9, 799–800, Aeschin. 1.149 = Hom. *Il.* 23.[81a], Davies (1986a) 260 n. 15, Pallantza (2005) 265–75. Herwerden's οἷν ((1899) 382) should be avoided for that reason.

542–3 Ἅιδης τιν' ἵμερον . . . | . . . ἔσχε: cf. *Ant.* 519 ὅμως ὅ γ' Ἅιδης τοὺς νόμους τούτους ποθεῖ.

543 δαίσασθαι: the dead could be described as food for scavengers (cf. Aesch. *Suppl.* 800–1 with Friis Johansen and Whittle), but the gods of the underworld usually take liquid, not solid, refreshment from their victims (cf. Hom. *Od.* 11.96, Eur. *Alc.* 844–5, *Hec.* 536–7; but note Psalm 49.14 'death shall feed on them'). The eating of children, however, was an especially horrific feature of some myths, including the banquet of Thyestes (though there is no specific reference to that event here, which is not a part of the mythical world of this play). The perversion of this 'feast' may also remind us of the gruesome meal instituted by Clytemnestra to celebrate the murder of her husband (277-81). For the epexegetic infinitive after a genitive see Bruhn §127.II.

544-5 Alliteration of π conveys Clytemnestra's anger (cf. 210n.).

546 ἀβούλου: for this word used to describe a father's attitude to a child cf. *Tr.* 139-40 τίς ὧδε | τέκνοισι Ζῆν' ἄβουλον εἶδεν; This along with κακοῦ γνώμην ensures that the speech closes with the emphasis still firmly on Agamemnon's intentions. The closing word πατρός is also significant: Clytemnestra claims that Agamemnon failed in his duty as a father.

548 At Aesch. *Ag.* 1555-9 Clytemnestra makes a vivid and wounding appeal to Iphigenia's likely thoughts about her sacrifice, by sarcastically claiming that she will greet her father with a kiss when he arrives in Hades. Here the mention of Iphigenia is brief and colourless. We may also wonder whether Iphigenia would have endorsed her mother's arguments, given the latter's continual focus on the offence done to herself. For appeals to the opinion of the dead cf. Lucian 40.13 ὁ νεκρὸς αὐτὸς ἀποκρίναιτ' ἄν, εἰ λάβοι φωνήν, Nauck (1880) 663 n. 61; also 400n. Similar phraseology is found in appeals to other silent sources: cf. Aesch. *Ag.* 37-8 οἶκος δ' αὐτός, εἰ φθογγὴν λάβοι, | σαφέστατ' ἂν λέξειεν with Fraenkel on 37, adding to his examples Eur. *Hipp.* 1074 ὦ δώματ', εἴθε φθέγγμα γηρύσαισθέ μοι.

γ': Dawe (1976) 232 brings out the force of the particle: 'as for the dead Iphigeneia, there is no doubt what *her* opinion would be' (his italics).

549-50 Clytemnestra ends with a defiant *je ne regrette rien*: contrast the contrition shown by Euripides' Clytemnestra at *El.* 1105-6 (καὶ γὰρ οὐχ οὕτως ἄγαν | χαίρω τι, τέκνον, τοῖς δεδραμένοις ἐμοί). This lack of self-awareness and self-criticism in S.'s Clytemnestra distinguishes her not just from her Euripidean counterpart, but also from her daughter (cf. 254-309n., 616-21n.).

550-1 For a similar riposte at the end of a speech of self-justification cf. *Ant.* 469-70 σοὶ δ' εἰ δοκεῖ νῦν μῶρα δρῶσα τυγχάνειν, | σχεδόν τι μώρῳ μωρίαν ὀφλισκάνω.

500 φρονεῖν κακῶς: wickedness, not incapacity in argument: cf. γνώμην δικαίαν σχοῦσα in the following line.

551 For τοὺς πέλας used to denote people in general see Wilamowitz on Eur. *Her.* 192.

ψέγε: R's λέγε shows a common corruption: cf. 1423, *OC* 594, Garvie on Aesch. *Cho.* 989, Friis Johansen and Whittle on Aesch. *Suppl.* 168–9.

552–7 Electra's response is measured and polite (note the optative in 555), and surprises even her mother. The contrast with Clytemnestra's violence and abruptness is remarkable; so is the contrast with the corresponding passage in Euripides (*El.* 1055–9), where Electra sharply reminds her mother of her right to speak. This restraint directs our sympathies towards Electra before her speech begins; for a similar effect caused by a juxtaposition of tones cf. 616–21 n. It also illustrates the power relationship between the two women: cf. Eur. *Andr.* 186–7 and M. A. Lloyd (1992) 27 for participants in an *agon* having to establish their right to speak in the face of hostile authority.

552–3 For the sentiment cf. Hes. *Op.* 721 εἰ δὲ κακὸν εἴπῃς, τάχα κ᾽ αὐτὸς μεῖζον ἀκούσαις, Pearson on S. fr. 929.4.

552 ἐρεῖς . . . οὐχί: cf. *Ant.* 223 ἐρῶ . . . οὐχ. Electra refers to her mother's words at 523–4 (n.).

554 τοῦ τεθνηκότος θ᾽: metre and meaning demand θ᾽: the sense of the alternative reading γ᾽ is less appropriate, whether limitative or emphatic. Nauck[3] p. 160 prefers to transpose τοῦ τεθνηκότος with τῆς κασιγνήτης in the next line, but the omission of the first θ᾽ is awkward: moreover, Electra must put Agamemnon first, not Iphigenia (so Arnold (1866) 24).

556–7 Clytemnestra's reply echoes the phrasing of Electra's request (ἐφίημι~ ἐφῇς; ἐξῆρχες~ ἄρξασα; λυπηρά~ λυπηρόν).

καὶ μήν: see Denniston 353 (3) for this collocation 'with an echoed word, in substantiating a required condition'; cf. 1045. According to Wakker (1997), μήν usually indicates that the speaker actively vouches for the assertion. She argues (*ib.* 215–18) that καὶ μήν expresses assent when the addressee is unlikely to expect it, whereas in καὶ δή there is no such connotation. This element of unexpectedness means that καὶ μήν can be used in a contradiction, whereas καὶ δή cannot.

λόγους | ἐξῆρχες: a periphrastic expression equivalent to a transitive verb: cf. 123n.

558–609 Electra's speech falls into the following sections: (i) introduction (558–62), (ii) the real reason for the sacrifice of Iphigenia (563–76), (iii) a claim that even on its own terms, Clytemnestra's argument is unsatisfactory (577–83), (iv) the real reason for the killing of Agamemnon (584–94), (v) an attack on Clytemnestra for her treatment of her children (595–609).

558 καὶ δή: 317n.

πατέρα φῇς κτεῖναι: brevity and asyndeton mark out the opening phrase; πατέρα is prominently positioned. The early emphasis on the magnitude of the matter in hand is a common rhetorical technique (cf. [Cic.] *Rhet. Her.* 1.7, Lausberg (1998) §270). For the orthography of φῇς see 317n.

558–60 τίς ἂν | τούτου λόγος γένοιτ' ἂν αἰσχίων ἔτι, | εἴτ' οὖν δικαίως εἴτε μή; For the idea 'just but shameful' cf. Eur. *El.* 1051 δίκαι' ἔλεξας, ἡ δίκη δ' αἰσχρῶς ἔχει. According to Adkins (1960) 156 (cf. (1966) 84), 'to say that an action is *aischron* is to play the ace of trumps: to justify performing it, one cannot press the claim that it is *dikaion*, for this is of less importance, but must maintain that it is in fact not *aischron* after all'. This misunderstands the force of the rhetoric. Electra will in fact spend the greater part of her speech exploring the justice (or otherwise) of Agamemnon's death; but before beginning this investigation, she opens with the clearer point that his killing was αἰσχρόν. That charge is so self-evident precisely because it is independent of whether the act was just or not. As Stinton points out, 'αἰσχρός . . . does not simply outrank δίκαιος as a moral "ace of trumps" . . .: it belongs to a different scale of values . . . though I grant that to predicate both of them of the same action is a paradox' ((1986) 78 = (1990) 469). Adkins's argument is refuted in Dover (1983) 41 = (1987a) 86.

Electra's words have implications beyond the argument in hand. She concedes that the same act might be both δίκαιον and αἰσχρόν, a point which will be picked up later (1042), and which will be of great significance for our view of the matricide. For if the killing of a spouse must be αἰσχρόν, even if it is also δίκαιον, then the same must also be true of the killing of a mother. S. did not need to give Electra this line of argument: she might easily have kept to the subject of δίκη, where the contrast between the killings of Agamemnon and Clytemnestra is at its clearest. Electra goes beyond what is necessary to win her case; but in doing so she points to criteria by which her own actions will later be found wanting (cf. further 577–83n.).

560 εἴτ' οὖν δικαίως εἴτε μή; Cf. Aesch. *Eum.* 468 σὺ δ' εἰ δικαίως εἴτε μή κρῖνον δίκην, 612. For the οὖν see 199n.

λέξω δέ σοι: speakers in tragedy sometimes say 'I am telling you' or the like part of the way through a speech (cf. Fraenkel on Aesch. *Ag.* 1421; all his examples are in the present, but note λέξω at *Phil.* 1324, 1418, Eur. *El.* 1013). Morstadt's δείξω ((1864) 21), printed by Dawe, avoids the repetition λέγω . . . λόγος . . . λέξω, and is palaeographically elegant (Λ for Δ is a common uncial error; on the particular corruption postulated here see Diggle (1982b) 322 = (1994) 237). Repetition of this sort is not a problem, however (335–6n.).

561–2 Electra sets out the two aims of her speech at the beginning, a good example of rhetorical *taxis* (cf. Bond on Eur. *Her.* 172, Lausberg (1998) §443). But the structure is not as explicitly formal as that of many Euripidean *agon*-speeches (cf. M. A. Lloyd (1992) 34–5).

561 ἔσπασεν: cf. *Ant.* 791–2 σὺ καὶ δικαίων ἀδίκους | φρένας παρασπᾷς ἐπὶ λώβᾳ, Pl. *Leg.* 644ε1–3 ταῦτα τὰ πάθη … οἷον νεῦρα … σπῶσί τε ἡμᾶς καὶ ἀλλήλαις ἀνθέλκουσιν ἐναντίαι οὖσαι ἐπ' ἐναντίας πράξεις, Lucian 37.23 εἰς δάκρυα κατεσπῶντο οἱ ἀκούοντες. For violent action attributed to πειθώ cf. Aesch. *Ag.* 385 βιᾶται δ' ἁ τάλαινα Πειθώ, Gorgias *Helen* D–K 82 B 11(8) (= ii. 290.15–20) (though in our passage, as in Aeschylus, there is no suggestion that πειθώ removes the guilt from the culprit).

562 πειθὼ κακοῦ πρὸς ἀνδρός: Clytemnestra's lust for Aegisthus is implied at Hom. *Od.* 3.263–72 (e.g. 264 πόλλ' Ἀγαμεμνονέην ἄλοχον θέλγεσκεν ἔπεσσιν) and Stes. fr. 223 *PMGF*. It is first mentioned explicitly at [Hes.] fr. 176.5–6 M–W, and first suggested as a motivation for Agamemnon's murder at Pind. *P.* 11.24–5 ἦ ἑτέρῳ λέχεϊ δαμαζομέναν | ἔννυχοι πάραγον κοῖται; For the erotic connotations of πειθώ cf. Aesch. *Ag.* 385–6, West on Hes. *Op.* 73, Buxton (1982) index s.v. eros, N. P. Gross (1985). For the construction with πρός see Diggle (1981 a) 69.

ᾧ τανῦν ξύνει: this point is developed in full at 585–94.

563 κυναγόν: always with an alpha in tragedy (Björck (1950) 137–8, Chantraine (1956) 87); the Attic equivalent is κυνηγέτης. Artemis is addressed as ὦ κυναγὲ παρσένε at Ar. *Lys.* 1272; at *OC* 1092–3 she is described as the πυκνοστίκτων ὀπαδὸν | ὠκυπόδων ἐλάφων.

564 ποινάς: not in apposition to τὰ πολλὰ πνεύματ', but an internal accusative to be taken with the whole of the sentence (cf. 130n.). The punishment consisted not of the winds, but of the holding back of the winds.

For τὰ πολλά with a noun cf. 185n. Housman (1887) 240 = (1972) i. 10 reads πλοῖα, noting that the Greek fleet was normally held at Aulis by adverse winds (cf. *Cypria* p. 32 lines 57–8 *EGF* = p. 41 lines 44–5 *PEG* = p. 74 *GEF*, Aesch. *Ag.* 147–50, 192–8), and that in any case a calm sea would not have impeded a fleet of oared ships. But at Eur. *IT* 15 Agamemnon is held at Aulis δεινῇ δ' ἀπλοίᾳ [Madvig; –ῆς –ας L] πνευμάτων τ' οὐ τυγχάνων, and Housman's attempt to emend this parallel away does not convince: cf. also Eur. *IA* [9–11], 88–9, 352, Call. *Hymn* 3.228–32, Σ Eur. *Or.* 658 (= i. 165.7 Schwartz), Ov. *Met.* 13.183–4, Sen. *Ag.* 160–1, Bury (1946) 5. His suggestion that Agamemnon should have rowed to Troy lies firmly ἐκτὸς τοῦ δράματος. See further Diggle (2007).

565 Deleted by Jahn. Several lines in tragedy which begin with ἤ are likely to be interpolations: cf. Wilamowitz (1875) 205–7, Bond on Eur. *Her.* 452, Davies on *Tr.* 84. Bond rejects our line as 'pedantic', and may be right: perhaps a scribe felt that the appeal to Artemis to give an explanation in 563–4 was inconsistent with Electra's delivery of the account in 566–76. However, ἤ᾽γὼ φράσω is nicely paralleled by 352 ἤ μάθ᾽ ἐξ ἐμοῦ, which performs a similar function but cannot be deleted. The case for excision is too subjective to be secure. For ἤ 'or rather' see K–G ii. 297 §538.3.

κείνης: for the simple genitive after a verb meaning 'to learn' cf. 668, *Phil.* 370.

οὐ θέμις: for this with the infinitive cf. Aesch. *Eum.* 471–2, Long (1968) 66 with n. 17.

566–76 Electra argues that her father was not to blame for Iphigenia's sacrifice because Artemis left him no choice. There are two ways of countering this defence: by claiming that Electra's account is false, or that it supplies an inadequate excuse. The former approach has been more popular: Winnington-Ingram speaks for many scholars when he asserts 'Electra's account of Aulis, admittedly second-hand . . ., is the story she would like us to believe, and we can hardly suppose that Sophocles wishes us to take it too seriously as an explanation of events' ((1980) 220; cf. Sheppard (1927) 7, Long (1968) 69 n. 26, Kells on 566 ff. and 573). These scholars point to the phrase ὡς ἐγὼ κλύω, which, they claim, indicates that Electra's narrative is based on hearsay. But this phrase and others like it are never used with this meaning. Far from marking unreliability, they convey that one speaker is better informed than another, and highlight the truth and authority of his words. It is not the κλύω, but the ἐγώ, that is stressed (cf. *Tr.* 72, Eur. *Ba.* 770–2, Gow on Theocr. 15.107, van Erp Taalman Kip (1996) 517–21, Hutchinson on Sappho fr. 16.3 *PLF*, Voigt).

Moreover, this is a drama, not a detective novel: if Electra's narrative is false, we would expect this to be made clear to us somewhere. But no-one ever contradicts Electra, although Clytemnestra has every opportunity to do so (612–33n.). Electra does not cite evidence for her claim; neither, however, does Lichas when he claims knowledge of divine motivation at *Tr.* 274–9, and there is no suggestion that this part of his account is to be disbelieved. Were an audience to wonder about the origin of this information, it would in both cases conclude that it came from a prophet (so correctly R. C. T. Parker (1999) 17). Since gods did not often appear on the tragic stage, different conventions were developed by which their actions and opinions could be communicated. As N. Lowe (2000) 171 remarks (without mentioning the present passage), 'the divine control level . . . [is often removed] . . . to the domain of *secondary* narrative . . . Such messages still, by generic convention, carry complete authority' (his italics).

So the account is true. But does it supply an adequate excuse for the sacrifice? S. has adapted the traditional story to ensure that it does. In Aeschylus and Euripides Artemis prevents the Greeks from going to Troy, but the possibility of a return home remains. Agamemnon thus has a real decision to make: he can either kill his daughter or have the expedition aborted, and the tragic potentialities of this choice are exploited by both poets (573-4n.). In S. the Greek fleet can neither go to Troy nor return home: a great dilemma is thereby reduced to an awful necessity. In addition, S.'s Artemis wills the sacrifice of Iphigenia (571-2), again in contrast to the usual version. 'Sophocles' Electra ... says that Artemis produces the calm ... *so that* [reading ὡς; see *ad loc.*] he would have to kill Iphigeneia: this puts a straightforward divine purpose in place of the more complex and obscure forces emphasised by Aeschylus, in which Artemis plays one part in a long history' (Williams (1993) 135, cited by Ll-J/W, *Second Thoughts*; Williams's italics). Agamemnon no longer has a choice, and thus cannot be held responsible for the sacrifice.[36]

Admittedly, this situation has come about because of culpable behaviour on Agamemnon's part. His boast is not recounted, but Artemis' reaction will have led an audience to assume that it was similar to his famous boast in the *Cypria* (569n.). Nevertheless, the lack of emphasis is striking. It is merely an ἔπος τι, the result of a sudden, unexpected encounter with a stag, not the premeditated act of a *contemptor divom* (cf. also 567n.). Electra will hardly use language which accentuates her father's guilt; but if Agamemnon's boast is the factor which determines the justice of his killing, we could reasonably expect more emphasis to be put on it. As it is, his action appears a chance error, enough to anger a goddess into exacting a terrible punishment, but not enough to justify his death at the hands of his wife. In any case, the punishment for the boast has already been supplied by Artemis, and supplied in abundance: the offence has nothing to do with Clytemnestra, and cannot be represented as a justification for Agamemnon's death. The single justification she had offered was Agamemnon's sacrifice of his daughter: and that has been adequately rebutted by Electra.

566 ποθ': for ποτέ beginning a narrative see Fraenkel on Aesch. *Ag.* 1040, Braswell on Pind. *N.* 9.18.

566-7 θεᾶς | ... κατ' ἄλσος: the same offence is mentioned by Dictys *FGrHist* 49 F 5, in which Artemis is angered διὰ τὸ φονεῦσαι αὐτὸν τὴν ἱερὰν αἶγα τὴν

---

[36] So also Zieliński (1925) 267: 'ut ... ad minimum reducat Agamemnonis culpam, inextricabili nodo eum constrictum fuisse ait'. Compare Dodds's remarks on Agamemnon's dilemma in Aeschylus: 'had the sacrifice of Iphigeneia been a punishment for boasting ... or for killing a sacred deer ... then Agamemnon would really have had no choice' ((1960) 28 = (1973) 58).

τρεφομένην ἐν τῷ ἄλσει αὐτῆς καὶ πρὸς τούτῳ καυχησάμενον εἰπεῖν ὅτι οὐδὲ ἡ Ἄρτεμις οὕτως ἂν ἐτόξευσε. Artemis' grove at Aulis is elsewhere mentioned at Eur. *IA* 185–6, 1544. ἄλσεα . . . σκιόεντα are dear to Artemis at *Hom. Hymn* 5.20; cf. Nisbet and Hubbard on Hor. *C.* 1.21.5, adding Theocr. 2.67. ἄλσος in tragedy often denotes a flat open space, such as would be suitable for hunting (cf. *Ant.* 844–5, Aesch. *Suppl.* 508, Sommerstein (1995–6)). Sacred ἄλση were protected by various taboos: cf. 567n., *OC* 36–40 with Elliger (1975) 232–4, Barrett on Eur. *Hipp.* 73–6, Sokolowski (1962–9) i. §116 (a Chian law, fourth century).

567 παίζων: for this verb associated with hunting cf. Hom. *Od.* 6.104–6, Plut. *Alex.* 23.4; also Eur. *Ba.* 866–7 ὡς νεβρὸς χλοεραῖς ἐμπαί– | ζουσα λείμακος ἡδοναῖς, Ar. *Ran.* 442–3 ἀνθοφόρον ἀν' ἄλσος | παίζοντες.

ἐξεκίνησεν: for κινέω used in descriptions of hunting to denote the expulsion of an animal from its home cf. Xen. *Cyr.* 2.4.25, van de Wijnpersse (1929) 16.

ποδοῖν 'by his footfall' (Lloyd-Jones). Agamemnon is on foot because riding in a sacred grove was forbidden (cf. Sokolowski (1960), Shackleton Bailey (1989) = (1997) 275). This detail stresses his piety; it also suggests that he did not enter the grove with the intention of hunting (cf. παίζων), and so confirms our impression that his act was unpremeditated (566–76n.). His success in hunting down the stag on foot suggests Heraclean valour (cf. Pind. *N.* 3.51–2, van de Wijnpersse (1929) 17–19).

568 στικτόν 'dappled' (cf. *Phil.* 184, *OC* 1092–3, Eur. *Ba.* 111, 835, *EG* 1082.4 στικτὴν ἔλαφον).

κεράστην ἔλαφον: cf. fr. 89.1–2 *TrGF* κερούσσ' . . . | . . . ἔλαφος, Eur. *IA* fr. i. 1–2 Diggle (vol. iii., p. 422), Hom. *Il.* 3.24, 11.475, 15.271, 16.158 ἔλαφον κεραόν.

κατά 'concerning' or 'on the occasion of' (the slaughter of which).

569 ἐκκομπάσας ἔπος τι τυγχάνει: Agamemnon's boast is mentioned in Proclus' summary of the *Cypria* (p. 32 lines 55–7 *EGF* = p. 41 lines 42–4 *PEG* = p. 74 *GEF*): Ἀγαμέμνων ἐπὶ θηρῶν βαλὼν ἔλαφον ὑπερβάλλειν ἔφησε καὶ τὴν Ἄρτεμιν. Compare Dictys (cited above, 566–7n.), Hyg. *Fab.* 98.1 *superbius . . . in Dianam est locutus*, Σ Eur. *Or.* 658 (= i. 165.9–11 Schwartz); also Call. *Hym.* 3.263 οὐδὲ γὰρ Ἀτρεΐδης ὀλίγῳ ἐπὶ κόμπασε μισθῷ (in the context of a list of sinners against Artemis). At Eur. *Ba.* 337–40 Actaeon is torn apart by his own dogs κρείσσον' ἐν κυναγίαις | Ἀρτέμιδος εἶναι κομπάσαντ' (not the usual account: see Dodds *ad loc.*, Davies (1989b) 10–11). On the folk-tale element to this story see W. Hansen (2002) 54–6.

τυγχάνει must be taken with what precedes, as with βαλών it would imply that the boast preceded the hit; nor can ἔπος go with βαλών, as that would strain the word order.

570 For ἐκ τοῦδε stressing the causal connexion see Fraenkel on Aesch. *Ag.* 1223.

μηνίσασα: cf. *Cypria* p. 32 line 57 *EGF* = p. 41 line 44 *PEG* = p. 74 *GEF* μηνίσασα δὲ ἡ θεὸς ἔπεσχεν αὐτούς. For the anger of Artemis cf. Hom. *Il.* 9.538, Bacchyl. 5.99, Timoth. fr. 778(b) *PMG*, Hordern λυσσάδα, Call. fr. 96 Pfeiffer θεοὶ πάντες κομποῖς νεμεσήμονες, ἐκ δέ τε πάντων | Ἄρτεμις, Ov. *Her.* 20.99–100, Aristaenetus 1.10.65–6, Cole (1998) 30–2.

571 ἕως: Dawe and Ll-J/W adopt Fröhlich's conjecture for manuscript ὡς. This fits better with the imperfect κατεῖχ᾿ : the goddess holds back the winds right up till Agamemnon is made to yield. In this way 'the divine purpose is no less evident, and the stress on Agamemnon's reluctance . . . is brought out even more clearly' (Ll-J/W, *Second Thoughts*). For the corruption cf. *Aj.* 1117, *Phil.* 1330, *OC* 1361; in the first two instances ἕως has kept a foothold in the transmission. In later Greek ὡς itself takes over the meaning of ἕως (cf. LSJ⁹ s.v. ὡς Ad 2), which would have made the corruption still easier. The synizesis is unremarkable (cf. Diggle (1981a) 93, 120). For the importance of this clause for the argument cf. Williams, cited above, 566–76n. (his translation implies ὡς, but Fröhlich's emendation does not affect his argument).

571–2 ἀντίσταθμον | τοῦ θηρός: the genitive is dependent on the prepositional part of the adjective (cf. *Phil.* 401 λεόντων ἔφεδρε, Moorhouse 54).

572 ἐκθύσειε: used in the middle to mean 'expiate' or 'propitiate', but in the active merely a strengthened θύειν; see further Gibert (2003) 167–72.

τὴν αὑτοῦ κόρην: the possessive pronoun stresses that Agamemnon too had a share in Iphigenia (though Clytemnestra's language earlier had scarcely allowed this), and that Agamemnon's offence has led to the sacrifice of Agamemnon's daughter.

573 ὧδ᾿ ἦν: for εἰμί with an adverb cf. Fraenkel on Aesch. *Ag.* 1396, Diggle (1973) 245 = (1994) 63.

θύματ᾿: on this word see Casabona (1966) 146–53.

573–4 οὐ γὰρ ἦν λύσις | ἄλλη στρατῷ πρὸς οἶκον οὐδ᾿ εἰς Ἴλιον: the absence of the possibility of retreat is crucial for the justification of Agamemnon's action (566–76n.). Contrast Aesch. *Ag.* 212–13, where return home is shameful, but nevertheless possible; and Eur. *IA* 94–6, where it is ordered.

575 ἀνθ᾿ ὧν 'for which reason' (cf. *OR* 1021, Eur. *Hipp.* 764, *Hec.* 1136; also 585). Not 'in requital for which': the mention of Agamemnon's offence in the grove is too distant for it to be the antecedent here.

βιασθεὶς πολλά τ' ἀντιβὰς μόλις: three successive phrases reinforce the point that Agamemnon sacrificed Iphigenia only through inevitable compulsion. Contrast Aesch. *Ag.* 218–23, where the emphasis is on Agamemnon's own participation in the sacrifice (cf. ἀνάγκης ἔδυ λέπαδνον, and hence τὸ παντότολμον φρονεῖν μετέγνω).

πολλά: intensificatory (cf. *Phil.* 254 ὦ πόλλ' ἐγὼ μοχθηρός, Hom. *Il.* 11.557 πόλλ' ἀέκων, Virg. *Georg.* 4.301 *multa reluctanti*).

τ': so Walter (1877) for manuscript καί: this allows πολλά to go with ἀντιβάς, which is bare without it.

ἀντιβάς 'resisting': cf. Hdt. 3.72.5, 6.73.2, 8.3.1, Eur. *IA* 1016.

577–83 According to Kells, these lines form '*the crux of the whole ethical situation*' (on 582–3, his italics): Electra's argument against reciprocal killing will apply to her and Orestes as well as to her mother, and thus reveals the fundamental moral equivalence between the two sides (cf. Friis Johansen (1964) 19, Newiger (1969) 148, Winnington-Ingram (1954–5) 22 = (1980) 221 = E. Segal (1983) 212). This interpretation has been challenged by recent scholarship, however, which tends to argue along the following lines. Clytemnestra's claim that Agamemnon's death was a just punishment has been demolished. Electra now points out that Clytemnestra's only other defence is the *ius talionis*, the principle of blood for blood without regard for motive or circumstance. But this new defence would be problematic for Clytemnestra. A just homicide is not subject to punishment; but a homicide based on the *ius talionis* is itself punishable under that same law. Scholars who take this view note that Electra herself never appeals to the *ius talionis* to defend her own actions. Her aim is not blood for blood revenge, but the just punishment of an unjust killing. Hence the point she makes here is inapplicable to her own case, and does not have anything to do with the morality of the matricide. Such in essentials is the position of Swart (1984) 26, Stinton (1986) 76–7 = (1990) 468, Burnett (1998) 137 with n. 57, MacLeod (2001) 87–9.

Electra has indeed demonstrated that Clytemnestra's killing of Agamemnon was unjust. She does not, however, then tell her mother 'since your act was unjust, you must take refuge in the principle of the *talio*, which has unfortunate consequences for you'. She does not follow on from her previous argument at all. Rather, she returns to Clytemnestra's original case, and accepts her reasoning for the sake of argument (that is the force of εἰ δ' οὖν, ἐρῶ γὰρ καὶ τὸ σόν), in order to attack her mother's position from a further angle. Electra now claims that even if Agamemnon had been motivated by a desire to help his brother – that is, even if Agamemnon's killing of Iphigenia was unjust – Clytemnestra should still not have killed him, and having killed him she is open to a killing in her turn. She explicitly raises the point implicit in her opening remarks (558–60n.): that there are other standards apart from justice by which actions can be judged. These standards do not replace justice; but they do mean that an act can still be just, and yet shameful or otherwise ethically deficient. As Chrysothemis will put it later, ἀλλ' ἔστιν ἔνθα χἠ δίκη βλάβην φέρει (1042).

A second difficulty with the line of Swart et al. is the strict distinction it draws between killings based on the *talio* and killings aimed at justly punishing another for a crime. For the *talio* itself is a form of justice, however primitive or bloody. At Aesch. *Cho.* 310–13 the chorus put the classic statement of retributive justice into the mouth of Δίκη, while at Eur. *El.* 1093–6 Electra tells her mother εἰ δ' ἀμείψεται | φόνον δικάζων φόνος, ἀποκτενῶ σ' ἐγώ | καὶ παῖς Ὀρέστης πατρὶ τιμωρούμενοι. | εἰ γὰρ δίκαι' ἐκεῖνα, καὶ τάδ' ἔνδικα. In our play, Electra tells her mother that if one death is to follow another (that is, if the *talio* were in general operation), she would herself die, εἰ δίκης γε τυγχάνοις (582–3). It seems that any killing, however just, partakes in some way of the mentality of the *talio*, and is subject to its implications.

Electra's argument can thus be turned back against the matricide. Unlike the killing of Agamemnon, this will be a just action, motivated not by lust, nor by a desire for *talio*-justice (*pace* Winnington-Ingram (1954–5) 22 = (1980) 221 = E. Segal (1983) 212), but by a wish to punish one person for her murder of another. The people who effect it have been the focus of the audience's sympathy throughout the play, whereas the victim could hardly have been painted in blacker terms. It is wrong to claim that the killing cannot be morally distinguished from Clytemnestra's action (this is where I differ from Kells's approach). But it is the paradox of this play, a paradox to which these lines draw our attention, that this distinction is not absolute, and that even the most just of killings cannot be separated from a murder motivated by lust and revenge.[37]

577 εἰ δ' οὖν: is used 'when a speaker hypothetically grants a supposition which he denies, doubts, or reprobates' (Denniston 465): cf. *OR* 851, Aesch. *Ag.* 1042.

ἐρῶ γὰρ καὶ τὸ σόν 'I will state your version also' (Lloyd-Jones); cf. *Tr.* 479 δεῖ γὰρ καὶ τὸ πρὸς κείνου λέγειν.

578–9 τούτου θανεῖν | χρῆν αὐτὸν οὕνεκ' ἐκ σέθεν; It is not clear whether emphasis falls on θανεῖν or ἐκ σέθεν: in other words, was it wrong that Agamemnon *was killed*, or that he was killed *by Clytemnestra*? The latter seems attractive,

37 M. Heath argues that 'an audience used to the conventions of tragic rhetoric would receive [Electra's words] as making a case against Clytaemnestra, but would not be inclined to explore their implications beyond this limited context' ((1987) 137); he is supported by March on 580–3. Such an *a priori* assumption about tragic rhetoric is not supported by any evidence, internal or external to the plays.

since the phrase is prominently placed at the end of its sentence (cf. the prominent positioning of ἐξ ἐμοῦ in 526); cf. Plato's *Euthyphro*, which turns on the strangeness of a son prosecuting a father, even though this is done out of justice. But in her subsequent remarks Electra condemns not merely killings within the family, but any killing intended as a requital of another: hence it is likely that θανεῖν is the operative word. The argument in 577–83n. is not affected either way.

For the large gap between τούτου and οὕνεκ' see 78n.

580 τιθεῖσα . . . νόμον: 'the fact that the Greeks could think of νόμος as having had a beginning in time leads easily into its use in connection with an act by which a precedent might be or actually is established' (Ostwald (1969) 52; he compares e.g. *OC* 907–8 νῦν δ' οὕσπερ αὐτὸς τοὺς νόμους εἰσῆλθ' ἔχων | τούτοισι κοὐκ ἄλλοισιν ἁρμοσθήσεται, Eur. *Suppl.* 541 οὗτος ἦν τεθῇ νόμος, Thuc. 1.40.4–6). For τίθημι cf. Eur. *Alc.* 57 πρὸς τῶν ἐχόντων, Φοῖβε, τὸν νόμον τίθης, S. *Ant.* 8 κήρυγμα θεῖναι, K–G i. 106–7.

581 πῆμα . . . μετάγνοιαν: '"trouble" and "regret" give a deceptively mild forecast of the later action' (Long (1968) 54). Contrast the explicit threat uttered by Electra at 604–5. μετάγνοια is a *hapax* for the more familiar μετάνοια: cf. ξύγγνοια at *Ant.* 66 for the usual συγγνώμη.

τιθῇς: Dawe's κτίσῃς ((1968) 14) is unnecessary as the repetition of this verb in 580–4 is not a problem (335–6n., Diggle (1981a) 66–7). The subjunctive should be preferred over the indicative because the πῆμα and μετάγνοια are still in the future (cf. 1003–4). But at 584 the excuse is being cited now, so the indicative is used (cf. Men. *Sam.* 530 μή με βουκολεῖς ὅρα, Goodwin §369, K–G ii. 394–5).

582–3 εἰ γὰρ κτενοῦμεν . . . | . . . εἰ δίκης γε τυγχάνοις: for two protases, the second subordinate to the first, cf. *Aj.* 782–3 εἰ δ' ἀπεστερήμεθα, | οὐκ ἔστιν ἀνὴρ κεῖνος, εἰ Κάλχας σοφός, *OR* 883–91, Eur. *Suppl.* 1084–6, Bruhn §141.

ἄλλον ἀντ' ἄλλου: for polyptoton in accounts of *talio* justice cf. Aesch. *Cho.* 310–13, Eur. *El.* 1094 (cited above, 577–83n.).

584–94 The final part of Electra's speech is itself loosely divided into three sections (584–94, 595–602, 603–9). Electra begins by attacking Clytemnestra for her adultery, fulfilling an earlier promise to show that lust, not justice, was her true motivation (cf. 560–2; also 197). This subject wounds Electra deeply; earlier she described it as the τελευταία ὕβρις of the pair's crimes (271), while here it constitutes αἴσχιστα πάντων ἔργα (586). The fertility of this union is also a source of pain to her (589–90), and contrasts with her own conspicuously unwedded state (cf. 187–8, 961–2).

The effectiveness of this charge is strengthened by the omission of Cassandra (stressed by van Erp Taalman Kip (1993) 5–6). In Aeschylus and Euripides Clytemnestra cites Agamemnon's adultery to justify her own (*Ag.* 1438–47, *Cho.* 918 ἀλλ' εἶφ' ὁμοίως καὶ πατρὸς τοῦ σοῦ μάτας, *El.* 1035–40; cf. also *Tro.* 356–60, 404–5, 460–1). Euripides' Clytemnestra even says that she would not have killed Agamemnon but for his return with Cassandra (*El.* 1030–4). Here there is no mitigatory plea to counter Electra's accusation.

584 σκῆψιν: cf. Eur. *El.* 1067–8 (you killed Agamemnon) σκῆψιν προτείνουσ' ὡς ὑπὲρ τέκνου πόσιν | ἔκτεινας. For the meaning ('grounds for excuse') see Fraenkel on Aesch. *Ag.* 886: as with πρόσχημα in 525, the sense is probably 'false excuse' or 'pretence'.
οὐκ οὖσαν 'false' (cf. Ar. *Ran.* 1052–3, Thuc. 6.16.5).
τίθης: for the mood see 581 n.

585 εἰ . . . θέλεις: for the 'ironical courtesy' (Jebb) cf. Hom. *Il.* 9.359 ὄψεαι, ἢν ἐθέλησθα καὶ αἴ κέν τοι τὰ μεμήλῃ.

587 παλαμναίῳ: found elsewhere at *Tr.* 1207 φονέα γενέσθαι καὶ παλαμναῖον σέθεν, Aesch. *Eum.* 448, Eur. *IT* 1218, and then fewer than half a dozen instances before the imperial period. It can be used of the polluted killer, the demons that attack him, and the demonic pollution that radiates from him (cf. R. C. T. Parker (1983) 108, Geisser (2002) 162–3).

588 ἁμόν: for the breathing see 279n.

589–90 Euripides' Electra makes the same complaint (60–3): ἡ γὰρ πανώλης Τυνδαρίς, μήτηρ ἐμή, | ἐξέβαλέ μ' οἴκων, χάριτα τιθεμένη πόσει· | τεκοῦσα δ' ἄλλους παῖδας Αἰγίσθῳ πάρα | πάρεργ' Ὀρέστην κἀμὲ ποιεῖται δόμων. Cf. also Eur. fr. 338 *TrGF* ὄντων δὲ παίδων καὶ πεφυκότος γένους | καινοὺς φυτεῦσαι παῖδας ἐν δόμοις θέλεις, | ἔχθραν μεγίστην σοῖσι συμβάλλων τέκνοις. According to Tzetzes on Lycophr. 1374 (= ii. 379.11–13 Scheer), Erigone, daughter of Aegisthus and Clytemnestra, was Orestes' prosecutor in his trial before the Areopagus; in the cyclic poet Cinaethon she is the daughter of Aegisthus and the mother of Orestes' illegitimate son Penthilus (fr. 4 *EGF*, *PEG*, *GEF*). S. wrote an *Erigone*, as did others: cf. *TrGF* iv. 233. Hyg. *Fab.* 122 tells of Aegisthus' son Aletes (his mother is not named) and his attempt to obtain the throne of Mycenae from Orestes. Stobaeus cites fragments under the lemma Σοφοκλέους Ἀλείτης, but *TrGF* lists them among the *adespota* (vol. ii. F 1 b) on stylistic grounds.
παιδοποιεῖς: the middle is commoner (cf. LSJ⁹ s.v. παιδοποιέω II), but cf. Eur. *Hcld.* 524 and Ar. *Eccl.* 615.

τούς . . . πρόσθεν: sc. παῖδας, supplied from the preceding verb (cf. Davies on *Tr.* 259–60).

εὐσεβεῖς | κἀξ εὐσεβῶν: cf. *OR* 1397 κακὸς . . . κἀκ κακῶν, *Phil.* 874 εὐγενής . . . κἀξ εὐγενῶν, *Aj.* 1304, Bruhn §263, Gygli-Wyss (1966) 93 n. 1. For Electra's εὐσέβεια see 307–8n., 464.

ἐκβαλοῦσ᾽ ἔχεις: cf. Liban. *Decl.* 6.17 οἱ δὲ παῖδες (sc. τοῦ Ἀγαμέμνονος) ἀπερριμμένοι. For aorist or perfect participles with ἔχω see K–G ii. 61–2, Bruhn §111, Moorhouse 206. Here it is equivalent to a transitive perfect, emphasising that the results of Clytemnestra's action still endure (cf. Aerts (1965) 130–48). Paradoxically, this 'throwing out' of the legitimate children involves (in Electra's case) their attempted confinement.

591 πῶς ταῦτ᾽ ἐπαινέσαιμ᾽ ἄν; Cf. *Phil.* 451 ποῦ χρὴ τίθεσθαι ταῦτα, ποῦ δ᾽ αἰνεῖν . . .; L^{γρ}'s ἐπαινέσωμεν might be right: for the deliberative subjunctive after πῶς cf. e.g. *Aj.* 214, Aesch. *Ag.* 212–13, Wunder (1838) 37.

ἦ καὶ ταῦτ᾽ ἐρεῖς: Electra pretends to anticipate her mother's response; as with Clytemnestra's earlier rhetorical questions (542–5), the implication is that the adversary must now take refuge in absurdities. For the point that the sacrifice of Iphigenia does not justify Clytemnestra's adultery cf. Liban. *Decl.* 6.31 δι᾽ ἐκείνην (sc. Iphigenia) οὐκ ἐσωφρόνει (sc. Clytemnestra). ἆρ᾽ οὖν ἀχθομένης ταῦτα καὶ ζητούσης τὴν παῖδα;

Manuscript τοῦτ᾽ requires a pause after ἐρεῖς, giving 'or will you say this – that you . . .' More powerful is Seager's ταῦτ᾽ ((1813) 247, mis-spelled Saeger by van Paassen and Dawe³; attributed to Dobree ((1833–43) ii. 50) in previous editions), which leaves us with 'or will you say that you take *this* as recompense for your daughter?'. The cutting reference to Clytemnestra's defence greatly improves the paradosis.

592 λαμβάνεις: the majority reading. KGRCN have τυγχάνει, while Λ may have λαγχάνει (both Dawe and Ll-J/W express caution). L^{ac}'s reading has been erased, and over the erasure the scholiast has written in λαμβάνεις; the length of the erasure is consistent with τυγχάνεις or λαγχάνεις. The two minority variants lack the final sigma, and thus in the first instance seem less trustworthy than the majority reading. τυγχάνει(ς) is the least likely of the three – the same verb occurs at the end of 583 and 586, and thus could easily have displaced the original verb here. The rarer λαγχάνει(ς) is more attractive; for the confusion of this verb with λαμβάνω cf. *Aj.* 825 (where each form has good manuscript authority). λαγχάνω can also be confused with τυγχάνω (cf. 364, 751 (where the latter occurs as a gloss on the former)), and so it is just possible that the τυγχάνει in some manuscripts here represents not a corruption arising from 583 and 586, but an intrusive gloss based on an original λαγχάνει. The meaning also seems more forceful – Clytemnestra has not just 'taken' all this as her reward, but she 'has it as her allotted portion'. On the other hand, it is not even certain that the verb occurs in any surviving text – Λ's reading is obscure, while L^ac's is unobtainable. λαμβάνεις should thus be preferred.

593–4 Blaydes's deletion (in his 1st edition) is approved by Wilamowitz (1883) 219 n. 1 = (1935–72) vi. 166 n. 1 and Reeve (1973) 162: but the lines effectively emphasise Clytemnestra's hypocrisy.

οὐ γὰρ καλὸν | ἐχθροῖς γαμεῖσθαι τῆς θυγατρὸς οὕνεκα: cf. Hyllus' refusal at *Tr.* 1230–7 to marry Iole, since he regards her as responsible for his parents' destruction (especially 1236–7 κρεῖσσον κἀμέ γ', ὦ πάτερ, θανεῖν | ἢ τοῖσιν ἐχθίστοισι συνναίειν ὁμοῦ).

594 The plural ἐχθροῖς helps the generalisation, even though Electra has one person particularly in mind (Bruhn §259); cf. 940 and the plurals in Clytemnestra's coming prayer. The word balances θυγατρός later in the line, stressing the contrast.

οὕνεκα: found in tragedy almost to the exclusion of ἕνεκα, from which it is derived (see Barrett on Eur. *Hipp.* 453–6, Olson on Ar. *Pax* 210). For its use in inscriptions see Threatte ii. 668–9.

595–602 The focus moves to Clytemnestra's treatment of her children. Many of the details are recapitulated from Electra's earlier speeches (597–8~273–4; 599~354; 599–600~262–4; 601–2~303–4): having previously described her wretchedness to others, she now confronts Clytemnestra with it directly. Despite her anger Electra does not descend into mere abuse: she rather keeps to the actual wrongs and injuries that she and her brother have suffered. None of these charges is mentioned, let alone answered, by Clytemnestra in her response.

595 ἀλλ'. . . γάρ: 223n.

596 πᾶσαν ἵης γλῶσσαν: cf. fr. 929.3 *TrGF* πολλὴν γλῶσσαν ἐγχέας μάτην, *Tr.* 323, Theogn. 94, Pind. *O.* 2.87–8, Eur. *Hec.* 337–8, Pl. *Euthyd.* 293a1, *Leg.* 890d3–4. πᾶσαν may have a negative resonance (615n.).

597 κακοστομοῦμεν: a *hapax*; compare however εὐστομέω at *OC* 18, Eur. *IA* 1001 λέσχας . . . κακοστόμους, Archil. fr. 23.15 *IEG* κακο[στομέειν] (*suppl.* Lobel) and, for –στομεῖν compounds in tragedy more generally, Friis Johansen and Whittle on Aesch. *Suppl.* 502. Clytemnestra makes this accusation against Electra at 520–4.

καί: probably 'and indeed' rather than 'and yet': it 'refer[s] to the instance of harshness already given' (Jebb; cf. Blomqvist (1979) 49).

597–8 καί σ᾽ ἔγωγε δεσπότιν | ἢ μητέρ᾽ οὐκ ἔλασσον εἰς ἡμᾶς νέμω: for the *topos* cf. 273–4n. For the swift change from first person plural to singular see Bruhn §187.

599 ζῶ βίον: for the combination (in fact a *figura etymologica*, though one which would not have been apparent in S.'s time) cf. Philetaer. fr. 7.2 *PCG*, Schwyzer (1940) 10 = (1983) 450, S–D ii. 75–6.

599–600 κακοῖς | . . . ξυνοῦσα: for 'dwelling with' an unpleasant abstract cf. *Aj.* 611, *OR* 303 νόσῳ σύνεστιν, 1205–6, *Phil.* 1168, *OC* 514 ἀλγηδόνος ᾇ ξυνέστας, 1134, Eur. *Hcld.* 996, Bruhn §257, Dover (1972) 47–8.

601 ὁ . . . ἄλλος: i.e. 'the other member of our family' (so rightly Jebb).
χεῖρα σὴν μόλις φυγών: an indication that Clytemnestra had tried to kill the infant Orestes (cf. 296–7n.).

602 τλήμων Ὀρέστης: a recurring epithet of Orestes (cf. 742 and Willink on Eur. *Or.* 35); the name is delayed for emphasis.
δυστυχῆ τρίβει βίον: 'τρίβειν βίον (much the same as *aetatem terere*, etc.) as a rule does not indicate a way of living in the neutral sense, but is disparagingly used of a dragging life which is wearisome, miserable, purposeless, etc.' (Fraenkel on Aesch. *Ag.* 465); cf. *OR* [248], Eur. *Hcld.* 84, Ar. *Pax* 589 with Olson, *Plut.* 526, Jane Austen, *Sense and Sensibility* ch. 44 'I must rub through the world as well as I can.' For the miseries of exile cf. *OC* 444 φυγάς σφιν ἔξω πτωχὸς ἠλώμην ἀεί, Eur. *Hipp.* 1048–9, *Phoen.* 388–407, Braswell on Pind. *N.* 9.14.

603–9 Electra concludes by directly threatening her mother and claiming that whatever bad qualities she has, she has inherited them from her. Electra's critics put great stress on her closing two lines. Winnington-Ingram (1980) 246 asks 'Is not Sophocles here – and perhaps in the whole of the scene – bringing out a dreadful similarity between mother and daughter? Could it not be that the violence and extremism of Electra are part of her inheritance in the female line?' (cf. Pacuvius *Dulorestes* 139 Ribbeck *utinam nunc matrescam ingenio, ut meum patrem ulcisci queam*). Cairns (1993) 246 claims that 'the real irony is that the similarity in *phusis* between the two is genuine'. But there is an important difference between a woman who kills her husband out of lust for a usurper and a girl who hates her mother for having killed her father and attempted to kill her brother. The idea of moral equivalence between the two is a fantasy. Nevertheless, these lines display a disturbing intensity of violent emotion. S. could have made Electra angry with her mother without having her explicitly advocate her killing, as she does here; he could have finished her speech with quiet contempt, or even resignation, and not the fierce defiance of these closing lines. This passage stresses the degradation which Electra has undergone, degradation of which she is aware (616–21n.). Yet 'paradoxically, Elektra's willingness to acknowledge the nature she shares with her mother marks the difference between the two women' (Kitzinger (1991) 316).

603 For δή after πολύς cf. 1377, Denniston 205.

μιάστορα 'avenger' (cf. Eur. *Med.* 1371, Aesch. *Eum.* 177, Geisser (2002) 160–2); at 275 (n.) the word means 'polluted killer' (cf. Hesych. μ 1317 = ii. 665 Latte μιάστωρ· μυσαρός, λυμεών, Geisser (2002) 159–60). Multiplicity of meaning is typical in words denoting pollution (cf. R. C. T. Parker (1983) 109 n. 15; also 587n. on παλαμναίῳ). Are the two senses both felt here? They are not in the *Medea* passage, where Jason predicates the word of his dead children. On the other hand, the double-edged quality of Electra's arguments above (558–60n., 577–83n.) may have made the audience receptive to such a double meaning. The killing of Clytemnestra is not completely different from the murder of Agamemnon, and the same, conspicuous, word denoting people responsible for these two actions may reinforce that point. Winnington-Ingram is thus probably right to see an ambiguity ((1980) 245 n. 93).

604–5 καὶ τόδ', εἴπερ ἔσθενον, | ἔδρων ἄν: formally similar to Chrysothemis' words at 333–4, but here with passionate sincerity and aggression. The referent of τόδε is usually taken as the nurturing of Orestes into an avenger; but this does not fit with the protasis εἴπερ ἔσθενον. Rather, Electra must be telling Clytemnestra that she would have already dispatched her, if only she were strong enough to do it (so correctly Sommerstein (1997) 204–6). On the implications cf. 603–9n.

605 εὖ τοῦτ᾽ ἴσθι: 'molto duro' (Fraenkel (1977) 37 (on *Aj.* 1308)). He compares the minatory use of this and similar expressions at e.g. *Ant.* 305, 1064, *Tr.* 1107, Hdt. 7.14, 7.39.1. They may also simply introduce a passionate asseveration (as at 616, *OR* 658, Aesch. *Pers.* 435).

605–7 For Electra's contempt for criticism cf. Eur. *Hcld.* 978–80 πρὸς ταῦτα τὴν θρασεῖαν ὅστις ἂν θέλῃ | καὶ τὴν φρονοῦσαν μεῖζον ἢ γυναῖκα χρὴ | λέξει.

605 τοῦδέ γ᾽ οὕνεκα: cf. 387n.

606 κήρυσσέ μ᾽ εἰς ἅπαντας: disregard for the opinion of others is a characteristic of Sophoclean heroes, most notably Antigone (cf. *Ant.* 86–7 οἴμοι, καταύδα· πολλὸν ἐχθίων ἔσῃ | σιγῶσ᾽, ἐὰν μὴ πᾶσι κηρύξῃς τάδε). Here it marks the extent of Electra's passion: elsewhere she is sensitive to the opinions of others (254–309n., 616–21 n.). For κηρύσσω 'to contrast clear, loud, open or widespread disclosure with suppression or secrecy' see Dover (1976) 49–50 = (1987a) 186–7.

606–7 εἴτε . . . | εἴτε . . . εἴτ᾽: for the contemptuous dismissal of a number of possibilities cf. Hom. *Il.* 12.238–40 τῶν οὔ τι μετατρέπομ᾽ οὐδ᾽ ἀλεγίζω, | εἴ τ᾽ ἐπὶ δεξί᾽ ἴωσι πρὸς ἠῶ τ᾽ ἠέλιόν τε, | εἴ τ᾽ ἐπ᾽ ἀριστερὰ τοί γε ποτὶ ζόφον ἠερόεντα; for εἴτε repeated twice cf. Eur. fr. 129a *TrGF* (*Andromeda*) = 20.2–3 Bubel, [Eur.] *Rhes.* 485–7.

606 χρῆς: Wunder's conjecture ((1841) 16–17, and then in his third edition) for transmitted χρή must be right: cf. Eur. *Med.* 1358 πρὸς ταῦτα καὶ λέαιναν, εἰ βούλει, κάλει. Hesych. χ 721 (= iv. 296 Schmidt) glosses the word θέλεις, χρήζεις; it is found at Eur. fr. 918.1 *TrGF*, Cratinus fr. 134.2 *PCG*, and Dindorf restored it at *Aj.* 1373 and *Ant.* 887 (where the scholia (p. 259.3 Papageorgius) presuppose it). Its rarity, especially compared with χρή, assisted its corruption.

607 στόμαργον 'furious, aggressive in speech', derived from στόμα + ἀργός 'swift'; cf. Eur. *Med.* 524–5 ὑπεκδραμεῖν | τὴν σὴν στόμαργον, ὦ γύναι, γλωσσαλγίαν, Aesch. *Sept.* 447, Chantraine (1970) 92–3. Blanc (1991) objects that 'swift' does not mean 'furious': but it is not hard to see how the latter meaning might develop from the former, while Blanc's preferred derivation from στόμα + μαργός is improbable. The word is found in Mycenaean, where it occurs as a name (or epithet?) for bulls (*to-ma-ko*: KN Ch 897, 898, 1015), and must mean 'white-mouth'.

ἀναιδείας πλέαν: cf. Eur. *Alc.* 727 ἀναιδείας πλέων, S. *Aj.* 1150 μωρίας πλέων.

608 ἔργων: Dawe, *STS* i. 182 argues for the minority variant κακῶν, the other readings being glosses. He could be right: aside from its attestation in C^{1pc}OPV and Eustathius, κακῶν may also be implied by Σ 607 (p. 130.20–1 Papageorgius) εἰ γέγονα τούτοις τοῖς κακοῖς ἔνοχος. But the word may rather be a reminiscence of Eur. *Med.* 285 κακῶν πολλῶν ἴδρις (so Nauck[3] p. 160), while the Suda's λόγων may be a polar error for original ἔργων rather than a gloss for κακῶν.

609 σχεδόν τι: for the pointed understatement at the end of a speech cf. *Ant.* 470 σχεδόν τι μώρῳ μωρίαν ὀφλισκάνω.

τὴν σὴν οὐ καταισχύνω φύσιν: particularly bitter, since this form of expression is more usually found in compliments or exhortations (cf. Alcaeus fr. 6.13–14 *PLF*, Voigt καὶ μὴ καταισχύνωμεν [ ] | ἔσλοις τόκηας γᾶς ὕπα κε[ιμένοις], Eur. *Ion* 735–7, *Hel.* 941–3, *IA* 504–5 γενναῖ᾽ ἔλεξας . . . | . . . προγόνους

279

οὐ καταισχύνεις σέθεν, Hom. *Od.* 24.508). For the notion that an aggressive character can be inherited cf. especially *Ant.* 471–2 τὸ γέννημ᾽ ὠμὸν ἐξ ὠμοῦ πατρὸς | τῆς παιδός, Aesch. *Cho.* 421–2. Tarrant on Sen. *Ag.* 956 compares Juv. 6.239–40 *scilicet expectas ut tradat mater honestos | atque alios mores quam quos habet?*

610–11 Who speaks these lines, and to whom do they refer (doxography in Booth (1977))? The manuscript attribution, itself of no authority, has been challenged, with Fitton Brown (1956) 38 assigning the lines to Electra, Lilley (1975) to Clytemnestra. But their tone is different from the characters' rancour; and ὁρῶ . . . εἰσορῶ emphasises passive observation rather than participation in an argument. The Coryphaeus speaks the lines, then; but to whom does he refer? Some have argued that he moves from one woman to another, with ὁρῶ . . . πνέουσαν referring to Electra and the rest to Clytemnestra (Σ pp. 130.27–131.6 Papageorgius), or else the reverse (Wecklein); the change from one woman to the other might also take place after ξύνεστι, with that and πνέουσαν referring to one woman and the φροντίς belonging to the other. But such distinctions could only have been conveyed through gesture, as nothing in the Greek indicates that different people are meant. And while at Ar. *Ran.* 1413 τὸν μὲν ἡγοῦμαι σοφόν, τῷ δ᾽ ἥδομαι gesture may indicate which adjectives refer to which people (though there the ambiguity may be deliberate: see Dover's edition, p. 19), this is not found elsewhere in tragedy, and is hardly to be postulated here when other solutions are available.

Hence either Electra or Clytemnestra is being described. Musgrave, Jebb, Booth (1977) and C. P. Segal (1982) support the former, Campbell, Kaibel (pp. 168–9), Gregor (1950), Kells and Kamerbeek argue for the latter. Most of the available criteria are indecisive. The chorus's generally sympathetic attitude to Electra does not decide the issue. It was not slow to reproach Electra in the parodos, and it took a studiedly neutral line in its intervention after the debate with Chrysothemis (369–71): there is no reason why it should not criticise Electra here, given the vehemence of her closing comments. Nor are we helped by Clytemnestra's taking up of the word φροντίς from 611 when she begins her speech. She may be picking up a word addressed to herself or to Electra (requiring ἐμοί in 612). The question of δίκη also fails to resolve the matter. Segal is wrong to say that to Clytemnestra 'justice has never been a dominant issue' ((1982) 135): both women have taken strong positions on the justice of Agamemnon's killing. The reference to μένος is indecisive: Segal is right to refer to Electra's final words as a 'closing tirade', but Clytemnestra too has shown anger in this scene, rather more than Electra has, in fact, and this is about to break out again. The only real evidence is the tendency of such choral comments to refer to the character who has just finished speaking. Even this is not an absolute rule: at Eur. *Andr.* 232–3 and *Tro.* 966–8 (both in *agones*) the Coryphaeus addresses the character who has just been silent. But in both these instances the opening vocative makes clear the identity of the addressee, as if to signal that a convention is being broken. In our case no such indication is present, and hence Electra must be meant. Lloyd-Jones (1978) 219 suggests a lacuna before 610, in which the chorus made it clear that it was referring to Clytemnestra; this is adopted by the OCT and warmly commended by Günther (1996) 43. Ll-J/W (*Sophoclea*) are offended by the asyndeton and the bare participle in 610, but neither is remarkable: for the former cf. 464, and for the latter see Diggle (1969) 53 = (1994) 25. The two-line choral comment is also the norm in such cases (though not invariably so: cf. *Aj.* 784–6, *OR* 404–7, 1416–18).

The chorus is shocked by the impropriety of a daughter threatening her mother. Its criticism is all the more forceful for coming from a friendly source. In addition, by reproaching Electra's μένος it encourages us to expect a yet more intense conflict between mother and daughter. Yet this expectation is not fulfilled; and the choral comment here, far from presaging renewed violence on Electra's part, throws into relief her daring acknowledgement of shame (cf. 612–33n.).

μένος πνέουσαν: cf. Hom. *Il.* 3.8 μένεα πνείοντες Ἀχαιοί, Aesch. *Cho.* 33 κότον πνέων, 952, *Eum.* 840–1 = 873–4 πνέω τοι μένος | ἅπαντά τε κότον, van der Valk (1967) 131–43; also 1385 αἷμα φυσῶν (n.).

σὺν δίκῃ | ξύνεστι: cf. *Phil.* 1251 ξὺν τῷ δικαίῳ ('with justice on my side'). The repetition of preposition and preverb is not suspicious: cf. *OC* 115–16 ἐν γὰρ τῷ μαθεῖν | ἔνεστιν ηὐλάβεια, *Phil.* 1056 πάρεστι . . . | Τεῦκρος παρ' ἡμῖν, Aesch. *Pers.* 531. The subject of the verb must be the referent of the whole of 610–11, not μένος, which could hardly be σὺν δίκῃ.

611 οὐκέτ': not 'no longer', but 'not the further, and perhaps expected, step' (Dawe on *OR* 115); here Dawe translates 'this is a further point that I cannot make out' (cf. 963, 1316, 1474, West on Hes. *Op.* 174, J. R. Wilson (1987)).

612–33 The chorus eventually gave in to Electra (251–3), while Chrysothemis was outargued and then persuaded to disobey her mother. But although Electra convincingly wins the argument against Clytemnestra, her victory does not lead to an improvement in her miserable condition (Swart (1984) 27): for it is a typical feature of *agones* that victory in the debate does not lead to concrete results (M. A. Lloyd (1992) 15, W. Allan (2000) 129 with n. 54). The contrast with preceding scenes is again brought out by this particular dramatic form.

The *agon* has ended on a note of rage; by convention, we now expect a section of aggressive stichomythia. Clytemnestra certainly rises to the occasion: she contemptuously addresses her opening remarks not to Electra, but to the chorus (cf. 372–5n.), and follows this up with a tirade of empty insults and threats (614–15, 626–7), which sometimes verge dramatically on the colloquial (626n., 630n.). Electra, however, begins by admitting her remorse (616–21n.) and refuses to react to her mother's attacks. Instead she points to her mother's passion, and gives way immediately when asked for silence (632–3). Once more Electra has surprised us; once more she has gained our sympathy. Through the stichomythia S. has kept the structure of the typical *agon*; but this only highlights the atypical content. For similar structural dexterity cf. *Ant.* 639–765, where an *agon* begins with two polite and courteous speeches; only in the stichomythia does hostility emerge.

The contrast with the corresponding section of Euripides' *Electra* is instructive. There, in the aftermath of Electra's speech, Clytemnestra poignantly confesses her unhappiness at the results of her actions (1102–10). She receives no sympathy from her daughter, however, who uses this admission to press home her attack with renewed viciousness; it is Clytemnestra who tries to avoid such passion, even exclaiming at one point ὁρᾷς; ἀν' αὖ σὺ ζωπυρεῖς νείκη νέα (1121; cf. S. *El.* 628). Clytemnestra thus becomes the target of the audience's sympathy; in S.'s play exactly the reverse occurs.

Clytemnestra's aggression displays her ugly character, and also points to the defeat of her case. Falling back on mere abuse, she makes no attempt to deal with her daughter's arguments. Yet there are occasions in *agones* where the first speaker is given the right of reply: most notably at Eur. *Med.* 585–7, where Medea strikes a brief but crushing blow against Jason's case. If Electra's account of her mother's behaviour, or of the events at Aulis, is meant to be misleading or otherwise unsatisfactory, now was the moment for this to be indicated.

612 ποίας ... φροντίδος: for 'the repetition of a single word in an indignant or incredulous question ... often [with] an indignant ποῖος' see Diggle (1981a) 50–1, Vahlen (1902) 7–12 = (1907–8) ii. 437–42. For the sentiment cf. Ar. *Nub.* 1034 δεινῶν δέ σοι βουλευμάτων ἔοικε δεῖν πρὸς αὐτόν.

δ' ἐμοί or δέ μοι? With the former (proposed by Nauck[7]; ἐμοί *iam* Monk (1826) 78), Electra must be the referent of 610–11: after a mention of Electra's φροντίς, Clytemnestra rejoins 'and what sort of φροντίς should *I* have . . .' (cf. 790–1 for an emphatic pronoun indicating a change of referent). The unstressed pronoun, by contrast, would show that Clytemnestra is already the topic of discourse. Unfortunately, there is no way of determining the correct reading here, independently of the controversy over 610–11. Manuscript evidence is of no value in matters of word-division. If we could say confidently that ποίας, being a question word, must form its own *Kurzkolon* (cf. Fraenkel (1964) i. 136–7), we would have to read ἐμοί, as the unstressed μοι would not be able to begin a colon. But question words do not always form *Kurzkola*, and hence can be followed by unstressed particles (e.g. *Aj.* 1215 τίς μοι, τίς ἔτ᾽ οὖν τέρψις ἐπέσται;).

613 τὴν τεκοῦσαν ὕβρισεν: for ὕβρις cf. 271 n.

614 καὶ ταῦτα: for this adverbial phrase linked with an appositional phrase cf. *OR* 37, *Ant.* 322; the latter is aggressive, like the present instance.

τηλικοῦτος: (two-termination only here and *OC* 751) probably not 'Electra is old enough to know better', but 'someone so young should not speak disrespectfully to an older person'. Clytemnestra is not appealing to Electra's good sense and maturity: she would hardly pay her daughter even so backhanded a compliment. Cf. *Ant.* 726–7 (Creon to Haemon) οἱ τηλικοίδε καὶ διδαξόμεσθα δὴ | φρονεῖν πρὸς ἀνδρὸς τηλικοῦδε τὴν φύσιν;, also Pacuvius, *Dulorestes* 126 Ribbeck (probably Clytemnestra to Electra) *ni turpassis vanitudine aetatem tuam.* Calculations of Electra's likely age are irrelevant: this is an insult, not a dispassionate assessment of how old she is.

ἆρα: commonly begins a question expecting the answer 'yes'; the usage 'ostensibly leaves the issue open to the person addressed, and the appeal for confirmation is the more confident because less obviously stressed' (Denniston 46; cf. *OR* 822, *Aj.* 1282, *OC* 753). The question sits uneasily in the mouth of an adulteress and murderer.

615 χωρεῖν . . . ἐς πᾶν ἔργον: such phrases with πᾶν usually have a negative connotation: cf. 631, *Phil.* 633–4, *OC* 761–2, Bruhn §247.23, as well as πανοῦργος etc.

616–21 Cf. 254–7 (especially αἰσχύνομαι . . . εἰ δοκῶ | . . . δυσφορεῖν ὑμῖν . . . | ἀλλ᾽ ἡ βία γὰρ ταῦτ᾽ ἀναγκάζει με δρᾶν); 621 also recalls 308–9. Linguistic similarities are accompanied by similarities in tone. But whereas before Electra admitted her shame before an anonymous, friendly group, she now does so before her greatest enemy, and in a dramatic form, the *agon*, which sets a premium on anger and insult rather than regret and remorse (612–33 n.).

616 νυν for νῦν is owed to Monk (1826) 78.

αἰσχύνην: picking up a word from the last line of the preceding speech, just as Clytemnestra had done at 612–33 (n.); Electra does so, however, not in anger, but to acknowledge the truth in her adversary's accusation.

618 ἔξωρα 'unfitting' (cf. Hesych. ο 1689 = ii. 791 Latte οὐκ ἔξωροι· οὐκ ἄκαιροι, Suda ε 1850 = ii. 321.20 Adler ἔξωρος· ὁ γεγηρακώς, ἢ ἄκαιρος). In its only other classical occurrence (Aeschines 1.95) the word means 'past one's prime'.

COMMENTARY: 516–822

κοὐκ ἐμοὶ προσεικότα: cf. *Phil.* 902–3 ἅπαντα δυσχέρεια, τὴν αὐτοῦ φύσιν | ὅταν λιπών τις δρᾷ τὰ μὴ προσεικότα.

619 ἀλλ᾽. . . γάρ: 223n.
ἡ . . . ἐκ σοῦ δυσμένεια: cf. *Ant.* 95 τὴν ἐξ ἐμοῦ δυσβουλίαν, *Tr.* 631 τὸν πόθον τὸν ἐξ ἐμοῦ.

620 ἐξαναγκάζει: on ἀνάγκη see 221n.
βίᾳ: for the redundancy cf. *Phil.* 998, *Aj.* 498, Aesch. *Sept.* 47.

622–5 Clytemnestra's deeds are contrasted with Electra's words. This opposition emphasises the daughter's weakness: she has only words with which to respond to her mother's actions (cf. *OC* 873 (Oedipus to Creon) ἔργοις πεπονθὼς ῥήμασίν σ᾽ ἀμύνομαι). On the other hand, by keeping alive Agamemnon's memory and causing pain to his murderers her words do have a real power (cf. Markantonatos (2002) on the power of words in the *OC*). Ironically, it will be a further λόγος which puts an end to the power of Electra's speech over her mother (797–8).

622 ὦ θρέμμ᾽ ἀναιδές: cf. Ar. *Lys.* 369 οὐδὲν γὰρ ὧδε θρέμμ᾽ ἀναιδές ἐστιν ὡς γυναῖκες. θρέμμα is not always derogatory (cf. *Phil.* 243), but often is (cf. Aesch. *Sept.* 182 θρέμματ᾽ οὐκ ἀνασχετά, Eur. *Andr.* 261). For –μα nouns in hostile periphrasis see 289n.

624 σύ τοι λέγεις νιν, οὐκ ἐγώ: cf. Eur. *Hipp.* 352 (Τρ.) Ἱππόλυτον αὐδᾷς; (Φα.) σοῦ τάδ᾽, οὐκ ἐμοῦ, κλύεις, Aesch. *Cho.* 923 σύ τοι σεαυτήν, οὐκ ἐγώ, κατακτενεῖς.
τοι: forcefully draws attention to one's interlocutor (cf. J. C. B. Lowe (1973) 43–4).
νιν = αὐτά (436n.), referring to the whole of Clytemnestra's statement.

626 οὐ μὰ τὴν δέσποιναν Ἄρτεμιν: oaths in tragedy are rarer and more elaborate than their comic counterparts: they are distanced from the simpler oaths of everyday life through a reference to more than one divinity or through some other form of amplification (Dover (1985) 328 = (1987a) 48; cf. *id.* (1997) 62–3). Here the only elaboration is the single epithet δέσποιναν; thus it may have seemed unusually close to everyday language, and served to mark the speaker's passion (cf. Hermione's μὰ τὴν ἄνασσαν at Eur. *Andr.* 934, cited by Dover as an exception, where the lack of ornamentation conveys Hermione's rage).
Artemis is invoked elsewhere in tragedy only by unmarried girls (e.g. by Electra at 1239) and Hippolytus (a special case); this exclusivity is not shared

284

by comedy. Clytemnestra's invocation throws back in Electra's face the goddess whose motivation she had earlier seemed so confident in expounding; it could be a reproach for unmaidenly conduct, and perhaps also a jibe at her unmarried state. Compare 881 for another carefully-chosen oath.

626–7 οὐ . . . | . . . οὐκ: for the repeated negative in an oath cf. Hom. *Il.* 1.86–90, 23.43–4, Ar. *Ran.* 1043.

δέσποιναν: used of Artemis at fr. 442.10 *TrGF*, Eur. *Hipp.* 74, Anacr. fr. 348.3 *PMG*, [Sappho] *A.P.* 6.269.5 = 676 *FGE*; cf. Henrichs (1976) 260 n. 18.

θράσους | τοῦδ' οὐκ ἀλύξεις: the genitive normally denotes the penalty for the offence, not the offence itself (cf. *Ant.* 488–9 οὐκ ἀλύξετον | μόρου κακίστου); here the usage is compressed, as at *OR* 354–5 οὕτως ἀναιδῶς ἐξεκίνησας τόδε | τὸ ῥῆμα; καὶ ποῦ τοῦτο φεύξεσθαι δοκεῖς; (cf. Bruhn §203.II). Moorhouse 68 prefers to see a causal genitive, but this is awkward.

627 εὖτ' ἂν Αἴγισθος μόλῃ: on the return of Aegisthus see 310–23n.

628 ὁρᾷς; Used in quarrels elsewhere at *Ant.* 735, Eur. *El.* 1121 (cited above, 612–33n.); cf. 997, Diggle (1981a) 12. Its lively effect may also be colloquial (cf. Waś (1983) 49, 158–60, Austin and Olson on Ar. *Thesm.* 490).

πρὸς ὀργὴν ἐκφέρῃ: cf. Thuc. [3.84.1] ἀπαιδευσίᾳ ὀργῆς πλεῖστον ἐκφερόμενοι; LSJ⁹ s.v. ἐκφέρω III.

παρεῖσά μοι: so H; Ll-J/W prefer the majority reading μεθεῖσα, and change μοι to με (first proposed by Lloyd-Jones (1978) 219). The latter verb, however, means 'release' or 'let go' rather than 'allow' (cf. *Ant.* 653, *OC* 906, Dawe, *STS* i. 182). Ll-J/W consider this 'most expressive' (*Sophoclea*), and cite as parallels Eur. *Ion* 233–4 μεθεῖσαν δεσπόται | με θεοῦ γύαλα τάδ' εἰσιδεῖν and *Hec.* 1128 μέθες μ' ἐφεῖναι τῆδε μαργῶσαν χέρα. But in both those passages movement or lack of movement is the point at issue. It is irrelevant in our passage, which rather demands a word meaning 'allow' such as H's reading. It may well be an accident or conjecture, but the interchange of prepositions in this verb is not uncommon (so Dawe, *ib.*; cf. the confusions μέθες / ἄφες at 1288 and ἀφῆκ' / μεθῆκ' at *OC* 906). So if an emendation, it is not a wild one.

629 χρήζοιμ': optative because dependent on παρεῖσα in 628.

630–1 Clytemnestra appeals for εὐφημία before beginning her prayer (cf. Ar. *Pax* 96–7, *Av.* 959, Austin and Olson on Ar. *Thesm.* 39–40). The word 'does not denote silence, but merely abstention from certain forms of (ill omened) speech' (Pulleyn (1997) 184); cf. Aesch. *Ag.* 595–6, *Cho.* 581–2. For ways in which the appeal may be made see Wilamowitz on Eur. *Her.* 1185.

630 οὔκουν ἐάσεις: see Denniston 431 for οὔκουν with 2nd person future indicatives in 'impatient questions at the start of a speech'. The usage is probably colloquial: cf. *OR* 676 οὔκουν μ' ἐάσεις κἀκτὸς εἶ;, Anacr. fr. 412 *PMG*, Ar. *Eq.* 336, 338, fr. 628 *PCG*, Fraenkel (1969) 158, (1977) 69. Contrast Electra's request for permission to speak (552–7n.).

ὑπ' εὐφήμου βοῆς: for ὑπό denoting accompaniment or attendant circumstances cf. Blaydes¹ *ad loc.*, 711n., Ion *TrGF* i. 19 F 29 ὑπὸ δὲ τῆς εὐφημίας | κατέπινε καὶ τὰ κᾶλα καὶ τοὺς ἄνθρακας, Bruhn §74.II, K–G i. 523–4, LSJ⁹ s.v. A II 4–5. The strong word βοή is striking: cf. *Tr.* 783 ἅπας δ' ἀνηυφήμη-σεν οἰμωγῇ λεώς, *OC* 489 ἄπυστα φωνῶν μηδὲ μηκύνων βοήν. It may look forward to Clytemnestra's words at 641–2 (n.).

631 γ': Denniston 142 implies that this emphasises the whole clause; but the sense is better if it is taken with σοί ('won't you allow me, since I allowed *you*').

ἐφῆκα πᾶν λέγειν: referring to 556–7; yet as we have only just seen (626–9), Clytemnestra has failed to keep to her agreement. On the connotations of πᾶν see 615n.

632 ἐῶ, κελεύω, θῦε: the imperative is contemptuous: cf. [Aesch.] *PV* 937 σέβου, προσεύχου, θῶπτε τὸν κρατοῦντ' ἀεί.

κελεύω 'exhort, beg', not 'order': cf. [Xen.] *Ath. Pol.* 2.18.2 κωμῳδεῖν δ' αὖ καὶ κακῶς λέγειν τὸν μὲν δῆμον οὐκ ἐῶσιν, ἵνα μὴ αὐτοὶ ἀκούωσι κακῶς, ἰδίᾳ δὲ κελεύουσι, *IG* i³ 78.32–3 (Eleusis, *c.* 422?) ἐκέ[νοις] δὲ μὲ ἐπιτάττοντας, κελεύοντας δὲ ἀπάρχεσθαι.

632–3 μηδ' ἐπαιτιῶ | τοὐμὸν στόμ': the noun is frequently used with extended application in S. (cf. 607 στόμαργον, *OR* 426–7 καὶ Κρέοντα καὶ τοὐμὸν στόμα | προπηλάκιζε).

633 οὐκ ἂν πέρα λέξαιμ' ἔτι: cf. *OR* 343 οὐκ ἂν πέρα φράσαιμι.

Electra may now withdraw to one side of the stage, probably towards eisodos A (66on.), as her mother takes up her position in front of the statue of Apollo (635n.) for her prayer.

634 θύμαθ': cf. Jocasta's στέφη . . . κἀπιθυμιάματα at *OR* 913; also 573n.

ἡ παροῦσα: 'the articular use of the nominative of a noun in address generally occurs in speech to inferiors' (Moorhouse 25); cf. Ar. *Ran.* 521 ὁ παῖς ἀκολούθει δεῦρο, Pl. *Symp.* 218b5–7. Attendants and menials are always unnamed in tragedy, except at Aesch. *Cho.* 732.

635 πάγκαρπ': cf. fr. 398.3 *TrGF* ἐνῆν δὲ παγκάρπεια συμμιγὴς ὀλαῖς, Eur. fr. 912.3–5 *TrGF* (spoken to Zeus) σὺ δέ μοι | θυσίαν ἄπυρον παγκαρπείας | δέξαι πλήρη προχυταίαν (*coni.*).

ἄνακτι τῷδ᾽: just as a representation of Apollo *Agyieus* could often be found outside Greek houses, so too many scenes in classical drama presuppose an image of Apollo (e.g. *OR* 919–20, Aesch. *Ag.* 1080–9, Eur. *Phoen.* 631, Ar. *Vesp.* 875 with Blaydes, Men. *Dysc.* 659 with Gomme and Sandbach, Diggle (1981a) 34, Poe (1989) 131 n. 67). The image will have stood just in front of the entrance to the *skene* (cf. Ar. *Vesp.* 875, Poe (1989) 132). The nature of the representation is disputed. It must have included an altar: one is required here and at *OR* 911–23 for the sacrifice. Pollux too tells us that ἐπὶ . . . τῆς σκηνῆς . . . ἀγυιεὺς ἔκειτο βωμὸς πρὸ τῶν θυρῶν (4.123 = i. 237.10–11 Bethe), while S. fr. 370.1 *TrGF* refers to an ἀγυιεὺς βωμός. But archaeological evidence (cf. Di Filippo Balestrazzi (1984)) suggests that it did not simply consist of a conventional rectangular altar. The earliest altars to Apollo *Agyieus* (first half of the fourth century) consist of a pillar with a broad, flat base suitable for sacrifices (Poe (1989) 132 n. 73, 136); cf. the colossal statue of Apollo at Amyclae (*c.* 600), which had its body in the form of a pillar with head and arms, and rested on a broad base described by Pausanias as a βωμοῦ σχῆμα (3.19.3). This fits Hesychius' reference to ὁ πρὸ τῶν θυρῶν ἑστὼς βωμὸς ἐν σχήματι κίονος (α 856 = i. 33 Latte); it also accounts for the confusion in some lexicographers as to whether the stage representation took the form of an altar or a κίων ἐς ὀξὺ λήγων (Harpocr. α 22 = p. 4 Keaney, Fehrentz (1993) 133 n. 106). Mastronarde on Eur. *Phoen.* 631 speculates that in tragedy some more life-like representation than a pillar depicted the god's features. See further R. C. T. Parker (2005) 18.

λυτηρίους: cf. Eur. *Alc.* 224 (prayer to Apollo) λυτήριος ἐκ θανάτου γενοῦ; also Jocasta's wish for a λύσιν . . . εὐαγῆ at *OR* 921. Its combination with δειμάτων in 636 may be paralleled by Aesch. *Cho.* 820, if Ahrens's δειμάτων for M's δωμάτων is right. See 447n. for the formation.

636 εὐχὰς ἀνάσχω: offerings or hands were regularly raised during prayer (cf. 634, [Arist.] *De mundo* 400a16–17 πάντες ἄνθρωποι ἀνατείνομεν τὰς χεῖρας εἰς τὸν οὐρανὸν εὐχὰς ποιούμενοι, Hom. *Il.* 3.318, Eur. *Hel.* 1095, Pulleyn (1997) 188–95, West (1997) 42–3); it is a short step to the notion that prayers too are 'raised' to the gods (cf. Eur. *El.* 592–3 ἄνεχε χέρας, ἄνεχε λόγον, ἵει λιτὰς | ἐς θεούς, Psalm 141.2).

δειμάτων: cf. 410, 427.

ἅ: the manuscripts are split between this and ὧν; given the ending of the preceding word the *utrum in alterum* argument favours ἅ.

637–59 Clytemnestra audaciously prays for the preservation of the wealth and power which she has usurped through murder and adultery. And that is only the open part of her prayer: in the section she conceals, we are probably meant to suppose that she wishes for the death of her son (638n.). Yet beneath the audacity are ironies of which Clytemnestra is unaware. She prays to

Apollo:[38] but Apollo has already declared his support for her son (35–7), and is aiding him even now to recapture what she is praying to retain. The immediate entry of the Paedagogus will seem like the god's answer to her prayer: indeed he has been sent on his way by the god, but to bring Clytemnestra destruction. This he effects through a speech which, like Clytemnestra's prayer, has its meaning concealed. But while in her case this meant hiding her wishes for Orestes' death, his speech does not reveal that Orestes is still alive and aiming for vengeance. Just before the avengers enter to punish her, Electra will utter a prayer before the same altar of Apollo, a prayer which this time will indeed be answered (1376–83; cf. Aubriot (1994) 16–17). Compare the simpler irony of Aegisthus' prayer to the Nymphs in Euripides' *Electra*, reported by a messenger at 805–8, where he hopes that Clytemnestra and he may prosper while his enemies do the opposite; he is not aware that one of these enemies, who is about to kill him, is in his presence even as he speaks.

The situation recalls *OR* 911–23. The queen consort, disturbed by events which forebode ill for the royal house, prays to Apollo for security. A messenger immediately arrives (660–79n.), telling of a death which seems to answer that prayer. The queen is delighted, but subsequent events prove that her joy was misplaced, and she dies as a result. Apollo is responsible for this turn in events (1425, *OR* 1329–30). Although the structure is the same in each play, the prayer in *Electra* forms more of a set-piece than it had in *OR*; it is correspondingly more important in displaying Clytemnestra's character and playing with the various ironies described above.

Prayers have an important structural rôle in tragedy, often coming at the end of a scene or other unit (cf. 1376–83, *Phil.* 133–4, Ar. *Ach.* 816–17, Plaut. *Rud.* 257–8, Leo (1908) 29, Schadewaldt (1926) 101–4). Here the prayer marks the end of the first half of a long episode.

637 κλύοις ἄν: second person opt. + ἄν is sometimes described as a 'mild' or 'polite' command; so it is here, but that is not always the tone (cf. 1491, *Ant.* 444, Bruhn §113, Garvie on Aesch. *Cho.* 788–9). For appeals to the god to listen at the start of a prayer cf. 1376, Ausfeld (1903) 516. For κλυεῖν as 'the *vox propria* for the hearing of a prayer' see Garvie on Aesch. *Cho.* 5.

Φοῖβε προστατήριε: cf. *Tr.* 208–9 ἴτω κλαγγὰ τὸν εὐφαρέτραν | Ἀπόλλω προστάταν, *OR* 882 θεὸν οὐ λήξω ποτὲ προστάταν ἴσχων, Aesch. *Sept.* 449–50 προστατηρίας | Ἀρτέμιδος εὐνοίασι, J. K. Davies (1997) 61 n. 48. As at Aesch. *Ag.* 976, 'we perceive a local meaning but at the same time something more (*patrona*)' (Fraenkel *ad loc.*): Apollo is invoked as defender of the house

---

[38] Apollo was sometimes identified with Helios, to whom she had earlier related the contents of her dream (see Diggle's edition of Euripides' *Phaethon*, p. 147).

(cf. Σ p. 132.8 Papageorgius ὅτι πρὸ τῶν θυρῶν ἵδρυται) and protector from evil (cf. Ar. *Vesp.* 161, *Av.* 61). For other deities connected with the outside of houses and temples see Hutchinson on Aesch. *Sept.* 449.

638 κεκρυμμένην μου βάξιν: 'hidden' because Clytemnestra refuses to speak aloud part of her prayer. It is not an aside, since it contains nothing which Clytemnestra needs to hide from Electra (Bain (1977) 77–8). It is certainly not 'muttered' (*recte* Musgrave, *pace* Pulleyn (1997) 187). But what does Clytemnestra not wish to speak aloud? Whatever it is, it must be something that Electra in particular may not hear. The only plausible solution is that Clytemnestra is praying for the death of Orestes. We know that she regards him as a particular menace (293–8, 603–5), and may have tried to kill him as a child (296–7). A prayer for his death would fit with what we know of her character, with her fears for her own safety, and with the need to keep it secret from Electra. The construction of the scene clinches the argument: an audience will naturally assume that the news of Orestes' death, following on from Clytemnestra's prayer, is meant to be a (false) fulfilment of it (cf. Mikalson (1989) 90). Jebb argues that she is concealing the details of her dream and the names of the people to whom she refers in 644–54. But the dark and mysterious emphasis that Clytemnestra puts on her concealment (638–43, 657–9) is too strong for this alone to be meant; while the contrast in 655–7 between ταῦτα and τὰ ἄλλα πάντα must mean that she is hiding something quite separate from any concealment in 644–54.

For other prayers in tragedy whose speakers conceal the full import of their words to deceive another character on stage cf. Eur. *IT* 1230–3, *Ion* 410–12, *Hel.* 1405–6, Langholf (1971) 95–6. Silent prayer was a target of criticism throughout antiquity: for references see Mayor on Juv. 10.289–90, Kißel on Persius 2.6–7, van der Horst (1994) 1–9, Pulleyn (1997) 184–8. It was not regarded as an intrinsically evil act: it could be necessitated by circumstance, or even required by cult practice (cf. *OC* 488–9), and was only reprehensible when motivated by a wish to conceal immoral desires.

For this verb in this context cf. Theogn. 681 ταῦτά μοι ἠνίχθω κεκρυμμένα τοῖς ἀγαθοῖσιν (after a brief allegory whose moral he declines to draw explicitly).

638–9 οὐ . . . ἐν φίλοις | ὁ μῦθος: contrast Ar. *Ach.* 513 φίλοι . . . οἱ παρόντες ἐν λόγῳ. The phrase is paradoxical, given that Clytemnestra is standing outside her own house next to her own daughter.

639–42 The strong labial alliteration suggests Clytemnestra's anger and contempt for her daughter (210n.).

639 πρέπει: Clytemnestra realises that the revelation of her desires would be ἄπρεπες, but not that her having them at all is far more culpable.

640 πρὸς φῶς: cf. *Phil.* 580–1 δεῖ δ' αὐτὸν λέγειν | ἐς φῶς ὃ λέξει.

641 πολυγλώσσῳ βοῇ: same phrase at 798. Hesych. π 170 (= p. 10 Hansen) reads παλι<γ>γλώσσῳ· βλασφήμῳ, and this encouraged Meineke to emend to παλιγλώσσῳ here ((1857) 602–3); cf. 1420, Dawe (1964) 86 n. But there is no reason to think that the lemma is taken from our passage. The sense is also unattractive: the emphasis has been too firmly on the volume and frequency of Electra's complaints (cf. 109, 255, 520, 623).

642 σπείρῃ: cf. fr. 653 *TrGF* μὴ σπεῖρε πολλοῖς τὸν παρόντα δαίμονα· | σιγώμενος γάρ ἐστι θρηνεῖσθαι πρέπων, Aesch. fr. 78a.65 *TrGF* σπείρεις δὲ μῦθον τ[ό]νδε, Eur. fr. 846.1 *TrGF*, Ov. *Met.* 8.267 *sparserat Argolicas nomen vaga fama per urbes.*

ματαίαν βάξιν 'vain rumours' (Lloyd-Jones), rather than 'false': cf. Eur. *Hipp.* 119 μάταια βάζει, Aesch. *Ag.* 1672. Clytemnestra is not afraid that Electra would distort her words were she to hear them: her actual wishes for Orestes could hardly be blackened further. Her fear is rather that she will have the audacity to go and reveal them to the city.

εἰς πᾶσαν πόλιν: indicates that Clytemnestra has in mind a βοή, an appeal to the citizenry for aid at a moment of need: cf. *OC* 887, Hom. *Od.* 22.77 (≈133) ἔλθωμεν δ' ἀνὰ ἄστυ, βοὴ δ' ὤκιστα γένοιτο, Aesch. *Ag.* 1349 πρὸς δῶμα δεῦρ' ἀστοῖσι κηρύσσειν βοήν, Schulze (1918) 481–511 = (1934) 160–89, Wilkins on Eur. *Hcld.* 69 ff., Diggle (1994) 480 n. 178. Previously Clytemnestra's concern was that Electra's shouts would disturb the sacrifice (630–1): now she alludes to the wider political danger that they may cause.

643 ὧδ' 'hear my prayer in this covert form, for I on my part (κἀγώ) can use no other' (Jebb).

ἄκουε: the aorist imperative is far commoner in Greek prayers than the present: the ratio for S. is 31 to 5, according to Moorhouse 218. Moorhouse follows the analysis of W. F. Bakker (1966), according to which a speaker uses the present imperative when he sees his request as being connected in some way to the existing situation, and the aorist when he does not see such a connexion. Hence here, as at 792 and 1376, the request 'listen' would be in the present because it is essential that the god listens *now*. The other requests can be put in the aorist, perhaps because it is not so important that they are accomplished that moment. But the criterion of being 'connected to the existing situation' is too vague to be useful (cf. Pulleyn (1997) 221–6, especially 225–6). Perhaps the present is used for the request for the god's attention because the listening is conceived as being a durative process, during which discrete petitions are made, requiring the aorist. But the factors governing the choice of aspect in imperatives and infinitives remain quite mysterious (see Pulleyn (*ib.*) for further bibliography).

644 γάρ: 681n.

προσεῖδον: 417n.

645 δισσῶν 'ambiguous'; cf. Hesych. δ 1975 (= i. 464 Latte) δισσός· δύο τρόπους ἔχων, διπλοῦς, Fraenkel on Aesch. *Ag.* 122–3, Page on Gaetulicus *A.P.* 7.244.1 = 203 *FGE*, Lucian 42.10 διττούς τινας καὶ ἀμφιβόλους καὶ λοξοὺς χρησμοὺς συγγράφων.

Λύκει': Ἀpollo is often invoked in tragedy as Λύκειος to be a protective friend to one's friends and a dangerous enemy to one's foes' (Most (1985) 116 n. 98; cf. 655, 1379). For this epithet of Apollo more generally see 6–7n.

ἄναξ: for this address in prayers cf. 1376, Ausfeld (1903) 521.

646–7 εἰ μέν . . . | εἰ δ': cf. Aesch. *Pers.* 217–19 εἴ τι φλαῦρον εἶδες, αἰτοῦ τῶνδ' ἀποτροπὴν τελεῖν | τὰ δ' ἀγάθ' ἐκτελῆ γενέσθαι σοί τε καὶ τέκνοις σέθεν | καὶ πόλῃ φίλοις τε πᾶσι, West (1997) 548; also Xen. *An.* 3.1.12 τὸ ὄναρ τῇ μὲν ἔκρινεν ἀγαθὸν . . . τῇ δὲ καὶ ἐφοβεῖτο. Clytemnestra's doubt contrasts with her daughter's confidence (411n., 431–63n.).

646 δὸς τελεσφόρα: cf. Eur. *Phoen.* 641–2 τελεσφόρον διδοῦσα | χρησμόν, Aesch. *Cho.* 540–1 ἀλλ' εὔχομαι Γῇ τῇδε καὶ πατρὸς τάφῳ | τοὔνειρον εἶναι τοῦτ' ἐμοὶ τελεσφόρον, Waanders (1983) 191–2.

647 τοῖς ἐχθροῖσιν ἔμπαλιν μέθες: for the ἀποπομπή, the wish that a prospective evil should be diverted on to one's enemies cf. Weinreich (1929) 169–94, Fraenkel on Aesch. *Ag.* 1573, *id.* (1957) 410–11, Nisbet and Hubbard on Hor. *C.* 1.21.13, Henrichs (1991) 178 n. 35, Ov. *Ars* 3.247 *hostibus eveniat*, Ferri on [Sen.] *Oct.* 756–9.

τοῖς ἐχθροῖσιν: cf. Eur. *El.* 807–8, where Aegisthus' prayer finishes with the words τοὺς δ' ἐμοὺς ἐχθροὺς κακῶς; the messenger then adds λέγων Ὀρέστην καὶ σέ. So too here, even though a wish that one's enemies may suffer need have no specific application, Clytemnestra may be referring specifically to Orestes: the following two lines make this especially likely.

ἔμπαλιν 'away', 'in the other direction'; cf. *Ag.* 1424 ἐὰν δὲ τοὔμπαλιν κραίνῃ θεός.

648–9 Clytemnestra is aware that Orestes wants to depose her (293–4, 603–4, 778–84); the vague τινες is thus better taken as a concealed reference to him than as a more general wish (cf. 652n., 653n.). The irony is obvious to the spectator: this, and more, is exactly what Orestes is doing.

648 πλούτου τοῦ παρόντος: it would be wrong to censure Clytemnestra for excessive materialism (cf. 72n.): on the other hand, this wealth is not something that properly belongs to her. Contrast Aesch. *Ag.* 1567–76, especially 1575, where Clytemnestra would be happy with only a κτεάνων . . . μέρος βαιόν. Her wealth will have been visually apparent in the contrast between her dress and Electra's (cf. 664).

650–1 ἡ τῶν ὄντων νῦν ἀγαθῶν ὄνησις was a frequent, legitimate and usually commendable component of a prayer (cf. Fraenkel (1957) 138–9 with n. 4): but its use here is immoral, as the ἀγαθά in question were unjustly acquired.

650 ἀλλ' ὧδε: for the omission of a second imperative cf. 72n.

ἀεὶ ζῶσαν: Clytemnestra's wish that her present life may last for ever contrasts with Electra's desperate desire that her own life may change for the better. In the event, she will not be ζῶσαν at all.

ἀβλαβεῖ βίῳ: we might have expected a cognate accusative, as conjectured by Arnold ((1864) 456, (1866) 46–7; cf. 599n.), but cf. *Tr.* 168 τὸ λοιπὸν ἤδη ζῆν ἀλυπήτῳ βίῳ, S–D ii. 166 §3, Moorhouse 91.

651 δόμους Ἀτρειδῶν: cf. Aesch. *Ag.* 1672–3 <ἐγὼ> | καὶ σὺ θήσομεν κρατοῦντε τῶνδε δωμάτων <καλῶς>. Clytemnestra admits that the palace belongs to the Atridae even as she prays that her usurpation of it may continue.

σκῆπτρα: the symbol of royal authority, reclaimed by Agamemnon in her dream (420–1 n.).

ἀμφέπειν: cf. Pind. *O.* 1.12 θεμιστεῖον ὃς ἀμφέπει σκᾶπτον.

652 φίλοισι: although formally general in application, this must refer primarily to Aegisthus: no other φίλος of Clytemnestra is mentioned elsewhere. Cf. Aesch. *Cho.* 716–17.

653 εὐημεροῦσαν: ἑκάστη ἡμέρᾳ εὖ διάγουσαν (Σ p. 133.13 Papageorgius).

τέκνοις: *coni.* Fröhlich (later by Benedict (1820) 37–8). The manuscripts have –ων, although Xr has –οις written above both the genitive endings in this line. The paradosis, if correct, shows an original dative attracted into the case of the relative:[39] but the attraction is problematic. Elsewhere in S. words

---

[39] Jebb suggests that τέκνων is a partitive, ὅσων an abl. genitive ('with those of my children from whom'); but it is awkward to have adjacent genitives in such different senses.

so attracted fall into one of two categories: they either precede the clause which determines their 'proper' case, normally by some distance (cf. *Tr.* 283–5 τάσδε δ' ἅσπερ εἰσορᾷς | . . . | χωροῦσι πρὸς σέ, *OR* 449–51 τὸν ἄνδρα τοῦτον, ὃν πάλαι | ζητεῖς . . . | . . . οὗτός ἐστιν ἐνθάδε, K–G ii. 413–14, Diggle (2002) 84), or else they are incorporated into the relative clause (e.g. *OC* 56–7 ὃν δ' ἐπιστείβεις τόπον | χθονὸς καλεῖται τῆσδε χαλκόπους ὁδός, K–G ii. 416–20, Diggle (2002) 85). Here neither of these applies: it is as if we had *ἐνθάδε ἐστὶν τὸν ἄνδρα ὃν ζητεῖς or *οὕτως καλεῖται τὸν τόπον ὃν ἐπιστείβεις. One possible parallel, Eur. *Med.* 11–13, is not textually secure (cf. Diggle (1984a) 50–2 = (1994) 273–6); *Tr.* 151–2 τότ' ἄν τις εἰσίδοιτο . . . | . . . κακοῖσιν οἷς ἐγὼ βαρύνομαι may provide some support, but this may be an indirect question with inversion of οἷς κακοῖσιν rather than case attraction. Attraction out of the dative is also unusual, whereas corruptions to the case of the following word are common (cf. Diggle (1984a) 50–1 = (1994) 274).

There may nevertheless be a Sophoclean parallel for this curious attraction. At *OC* 1226–7 the chorus sings that the second-best thing in life is βῆναι κεῖθεν ὅθεν περ ἥ– | κει πολὺ δεύτερον ὡς τάχιστα. There the word κεῖθεν gives us precisely the opposite sense from that which we require. Yet it is not obviously corrupt, and Ll-J/W (*Sophoclea*) rightly keep it in their text: it seems to be the result of an attraction to the following ὅθεν. This suggests that an attraction turning *τέκνοις into τέκνων in our passage might be correct, and perhaps even distinctively Sophoclean. On the other hand, few corruptions could be easier, and in the absence of a parallel from iambic trimeters emendation is probably the better course.

The reference is probably to the children of 589, and perhaps to Chrysothemis as well. The Iphianassa of 157 is long forgotten.

654 δύσνοια . . . πρόσεστιν ἢ λύπη πικρά: cf. *Tr.* 453 ὡς ἐλευθέρῳ | ψευδεῖ καλεῖσθαι κὴρ πρόσεστιν οὐ καλή.

655 ταῦτ': often found in summing-up formulae in prayers: cf. Ausfeld (1903) 537.

ὦ Λύκει' Ἄπολλον: the same phrase is used by Jocasta to invoke Apollo at *OR* 919. See further 6–7n., 645n.

For ἵλεως in prayers see Ausfeld (1903) 538, Davies on *Tr.* 660.

κλυών: West (1984) 175 restores the aorist.

656 For the closing request to the god in a prayer see Willi (2003) 45–6.

πᾶσιν ἡμῖν: thereby including Aegisthus and Chrysothemis among the beneficiaries of her prayer; again she refuses to name names.

657–8 Compare Eur. *IT* 1232–3 τἆλλα δ' οὐ λέγουσ' ὅμως | τοῖς τὰ πλείον' εἰδόσιν θεοῖς σοί τε σημαίνω, θεά, at the end of Iphigenia's short prayer to Artemis. She prays for the success of the escape plan, but does not reveal its contents because Thoas, the object of the deception, is standing nearby. Here the atmosphere is more mysterious, and we must work out the contents of the prayer for ourselves. The Watchman's dark and ominous words at Aesch. *Ag.* 36–9 provide a better parallel for the tone. On attitudes to silent prayer in antiquity see 638n.

657 τὰ δ' ἄλλα πάντα: on this summing-up formula see Fraenkel on Aesch. *Ag.* 899–902 (ii. 406–7), Ll-J/W, *Second Thoughts* p. 72.

659 τοὺς ἐκ Διὸς γὰρ εἰκός ἐστι πάνθ' ὁρᾶν: cf. Cic. *Div.* 1.129 *homines, etiam cum taciti optent quid aut voveant, non dubitent quin di illud exaudiant.* Reeve (1973) 162–3 revives Jahn's deletion, arguing 'logic demands not πάνθ' ὁρᾶν but πάντ' εἰδέναι..., and though all δαίμονες are expected πάντ' εἰδέναι, not all δαίμονες are ἐκ Διός'. The first point is untenable, as the distinction between seeing and knowing is not a sharp one in Greek (cf. Pettazzoni (1955) 23 ≈ (1956) 12, cited by West on Hes. *Op.* 267). Zeus is described as all-seeing and hence all-knowing (cf. 175), and Apollo is associated with his father's powers (cf. Aesch. *Eum.* 19 Διὸς προφήτης δ' ἐστὶ Λοξίας πατρός, S. *OC* 623, *OR* 151, Xen. *Hell.* 4.7.2, Ov. *Met.* 1.517–18). Thus Apollo too is all-knowing (cf. Pind. *P.* 9.44–9 (Chiron to Apollo) ἐξερωτᾷς, ὦ ἄνα; κύριον ὃς πάντων τέλος | οἶσθα καὶ πάσας κελεύθους κτλ., Hdt. 1.47.3), and consequently all-seeing. As for Reeve's latter point, it is correct to say that most δαίμονες are not children of Zeus; but in Homer Zeus can be described as πατὴρ ἀνδρῶν τε θεῶν τε (*Il.* 1.544 etc.) even though this is not literally true. Even if τοὺς ἐκ Διός refers only to those individuals descended from Zeus, there is no difficulty. Clytemnestra states first that Apollo, as a δαίμων, should be omniscient; she then adds that this should be especially true of a son of Zeus, perhaps because of Zeus's special character as an all-seeing god, or perhaps because the king of the gods and his sons should show the qualities of the divine to an especially conspicuous degree (this nuance may be present at *OC* 1767 χὠ πάντ' ἀίων Διὸς Ὅρκος).

The closing stress on the gods' omniscience ironically contrasts with Clytemnestra's own ignorance and her imminent deception by the Paedagogus. This quality of deity is particularly stressed in contexts of divine justice (cf. Hes. *Op.* 267–73, S. *Aj.* 835–7, Eur. *El.* 771 Δίκη τε πάνθ' ὁρῶσ', *Antiope* fr. 223.86–7 *TrGF* ≈ 48.57–8 Kambitsis (cited above, 477n.), [Men.] *Monost.* 225, Harder on Eur. fr. 255.3 *TrGF* = 29.3 Austin, Diggle (1996a) 119). Hence 'en déclarant que «les enfants de Zeus voient tout», elle affirme (sans le vouloir) la nécessité de son propre châtiment' (Aubriot (1994) 14). Aubriot well compares the irony of Clytemnestra's prayer Ζεῦ Ζεῦ τέλειε, τὰς ἐμὰς εὐχὰς τέλει· | μέλοι δέ τοί σοι τῶνπερ ἂν μέλλῃς τελεῖν at Aesch. *Ag.* 973–4: Clytemnestra does not realise that not only Agamemnon's death, but also her own, will be effected as Zeus moves the house of Atreus towards its fated τέλος.

For εἰκός in prayers (in a context referring to the god's power) cf. *Aj.* 824, Ar. *Thesm.* 1144.

660–79 The Paedagogus' entry can be seen as a (false) fulfilment of Clytemnestra's prayer (cf. 637–59n., 638n.), just as the arrival of the messenger at *OR* 924 represents a false fulfilment of Jocasta's prayer. Seneca uses the same technique in his *Phaedra*: a prayer in which Phaedra asks that Hippolytus may fall in love with her is followed by the immediate entrance of Hippolytus (423–4). The 'unmotivated' entry of Aegeus at Eur. *Med.* 663, just at the moment that Medea needs him, may also be seen as the result of divine patterning (cf. Kovacs (1993) 58, Mastronarde's commentary, p. 33).

There are close verbal and thematic parallels with the *OR* passage, too. The messenger begins by asking for the house of the local ruler (τοῦ τυράννου δώματ' 661, *OR* 925; cf. *El.* 1098–1101 and Eur. *Andr.* 881–2 ξέναι γυναῖκες, ἦ τάδ' ἔστ' Ἀχιλλέως | παιδὸς μέλαθρα καὶ τυραννικαὶ στέγαι;). In his absence he addresses his wife, who is identified for him by the chorus (665, *OR* 928). He announces that he brings great benefits both for her and for her husband (666–7, *OR* 934); the surprise caused by the news leads the woman to question him again, and he repeats his message (675–6, *OR* 943–4). Both messengers bring a message which the queen understands to mean that a near relative is dead, yet in both cases this impression is wrong: in *OR* the dead man turns out not to be a relative, while in *Electra* the relative turns out not to be dead. In both plays the news is met with considerable happiness: for Oedipus lived in perpetual fear that he would kill his father (from whom he had exiled himself), while Clytemnestra had lived in perpetual fear that she would be killed by her son (who also had been living in exile). Yet while Polybus dies a peaceful death, a luxury in a Greek tragedy, which is described in a single, beautiful line (*OR* 961), Orestes dies in circumstances which could hardly be more painful, and which are narrated in terrifying detail. Polybus' death leaves one woman alive whom Oedipus must still fear, his mother Merope; Orestes' death still leaves his sister alive, but she is rendered powerless by the loss of her brother. Yet in the event Oedipus' downfall will not be effected by Merope, whereas Electra will have an important rôle in the killings which conclude the drama.

Of the two plays *Electra* is more likely to be the later, given the characteristics which it shares with *Philoctetes* and *OC*; on the other hand, the date of *OR* can hardly be determined with any degree of precision (why not the 410s?). Whichever way round they come, it is striking to see a playwright repeating so many of the characteristics of a scene while at the same time creating such different effects.

660 The Paedagogus enters via eisodos B. This suggests that at 633 (n.) Electra moved towards eisodos A, so that here the Paedagogus encounters Clytemnestra first. This ensures that Electra is isolated from the other two characters during the Paedagogus' narration, representing in spatial terms the pathos of her situation.

In Aeschylus it is usual for a newly arrived character to address the chorus before speaking to another character (Taplin (1977a) 86–7); this is not the case in S. or Euripides. Nevertheless, 'there are . . . passages which suggest that it is conventional "etiquette" for a newcomer . . . to deal with a chorus before addressing a female character on stage (especially, but not solely, if the newcomer is a stranger)' (Mastronarde (1979) 21, comparing 1098–1105, 1442–4, *OR* 924–8, Aesch. *Pers.* 249–89, *Ag.* 810–54; at *Ant.* 988–90 and *OC* 728–39 the character on stage is male).

πῶς ἂν εἰδείην: for the potential optative used as a wish cf. *Aj.* 388–91, *Phil.* 531–2, Bruhn §112. A new arrival from an eisodos regularly begins with a question: cf. 1098–9, 1442–4, Poe (1992) 140 n. 53.

662 ὦ ξέν': 'the regular address to one coming from outside the speaker's own setting, whether friend or stranger' (Gow on Theocr. 5.66; cf. Dickey (1996) 146–9).

663 ἐπεικάζων κυρῶ: for κυρῶ with participle meaning 'be right in saying' (more commonly with τυγχάνω) cf. Aesch. *Suppl.* 588–9 καὶ τόδ' ἂν γένος λέγων | ἐξ Ἐπάφου κυρήσαις, Garvie on Aesch. *Cho.* 14–15.

664 πρέπει . . . ὡς τύραννος εἰσορᾶν: people of noble birth can sometimes be recognised from their appearance: cf. Hom. *Od.* 24.252–3 οὐδέ τι τοι δούλειον ἐπιπρέπει εἰσοράασθαι | εἶδος καὶ μέγεθος· βασιλῆι γὰρ ἀνδρὶ ἔοικας, Eur. *Hyps.* fr. 757.854–5 *TrGF* τῷ γὰρ εὐπρεπεῖ σ' ἰδὼν | τοὐλεύθερόν σοι προστίθημι τῇ φύσει, *Ion* 237–8, Hom. *Hymn* 2.213–15. For the form of the expression cf. Aesch. *Suppl.* 719–20 πρέπουσι δ' ἄνδρες νάϊοι . . . | . . . ἰδεῖν, Eur. *Suppl.* 1056 ὡς οὐκ ἐπ' ἀνδρὶ πένθιμος πρέπεις ὁρᾶν, *Ba.* 1188 πρέπει γ' ὥστε θὴρ ἄγραυλος φόβᾳ.

On τύραννος see V. Parker (1998), especially 158–61. In tragedy it is almost always a neutral term for 'ruler'. Exceptions occur at Aesch. *Ag.* 1354–5 (see Fraenkel on 1355), 1364–5 and *OR* 873; the present passage is not one of them. The word is used of a royal woman at Eur. *Med.* 957, 1066, 1125, *Andr.* 204.

665 μάλιστα πάντων: same phrase in a reply at Ar. *Av.* 1531, *Eccl.* 768; cf. Pl. *Phaedr.* 262c8 πάντων γέ που μάλιστα; 386n.

ἥδε σοι κείνη πάρα: for similar phrases cf. *OC* 138, *Ant.* 384, Blaydes on Ar. *Nub.* 1167. For the combination of ὅδε and ἐκεῖνος see Bruhn §83.

666 ὦ χαῖρ', ἄνασσα: for ὦ with the imperative see Moorhouse 28. The usage is not confined to any one register (cf. Fraenkel on Aesch. *Ag.* 22).

φέρων ἥκω: commonly of messengers: cf. *Phil.* 1267, Aesch. *Sept.* 40, *Cho.* 659, Eur. *Or.* 854, 1628, *IA* 1536, Ellendt 761–2.

666–7 λόγους | ἡδεῖς: cf. the ἡδεῖαν φάτιν of 56. The Paedagogus adopts a persona which assumes that his news will be welcome to Clytemnestra, an assumption which turns out to be all too valid, and which suggests a widespread knowledge of the extent of the troubles within the house. Contrast Aesch. *Cho.* 659 φέρω καινοὺς λόγους, S. *OR.* 936–7 (where a mixture of emotions is expected to the news of a death in the family which nevertheless brings benefits with it).

668 ἐδεξάμην τὸ ῥηθέν: the 'immediate' or 'contemporaneous' aorist: cf. 78, 388, 1322, 1479, K–G i. 163–5, Goodwin §60, Bruhn §105, S–D ii. 282, Wackernagel (1926–8) i. 176, Moorhouse 195–6. The speech act is regarded as occurring fractionally after the action it describes, and hence this latter action is described in the aorist. M. A. Lloyd (1999) prefers to see the aorist as a less direct, and thus more polite, alternative to the present, though his examples do not support this explanation.

For parallels for the expression cf. Eur. *El.* 622 προσηκάμην τὸ ῥηθέν, Hdt. 8.115.1 ὁ μὲν δὴ δεξάμενος τὸ ῥηθὲν ἀπαλλάσσετο, 1.63.1. The usage is often associated with the accepting of positive omens: cf. Hdt. 9.91.2 δέκομαι τὸν οἰωνόν, Aesch. *Ag.* 1653 δεχομένοις λέγεις θανεῖν σέ· τὴν τύχην δ' αἱρούμεθα, Xen. *An.* 1.8.17, Plut. *Aem. Paul.* 10.8, Cic. *Div.* 1.103 *accipio . . . omen* (with Pease).

εἰδέναι . . . σου: for the genitive see 565n.

670 Φανοτεὺς ὁ Φωκεύς: 45n.

πορσύνων: Dawe, *STS* i. 183, approves Reiske's πορσύνειν ((1753) 17); for the construction see 406n. But the verb suits Phanoteus better than the Paedagogus: the action is the result of the former's intention, while the latter merely carries it out on his behalf.

671 τὸ ποῖον: cf. *OR* 935 τὰ ποῖα ταῦτα;, 120, Bruhn §84, Stevens (1937) 185–6.

For εἰπέ subjoined to a direct question see Barrett on Eur. *Hipp.* 1171–2.

673 τέθνηκ' Ὀρέστης: 'the climactic release of suspense by means of a blunt revelation' (Henderson on Ar. *Lys.* 715) is a common feature of messenger speeches: cf. 877, *OR* 1234–5, *OC* 1579–80, Friis Johansen and Whittle on Aesch. *Suppl.* 600–24, de Jong (1991) 32 with n. 77, Goward (1999) 184 n. 25, Tarrant on Sen. *Ag.* 925–7. It is first found in Homer, at *Il.* 18.20 κεῖται Πάτροκλος (for the initial verb cf. 16.541, Eur. *Or.* 366); cf. ΣΤ Hom. *Il.* 18.20–1 (= iv. 439.31 Erbse) ἐν βραχεῖ πάντα ἐδήλωσε.[40] Milton imitates the terrible simplicity of this and similar openings at *Samson Agonistes* 1570 'Then take the worst in brief – Samson is dead.' The same expression was used at the start of 48; what there was a matter of simple instructions has become a statement of dramatic emotional impact.

ἐν βραχεῖ ξυνθεὶς λέγω: cf. [Aesch.] *PV* 505 βραχεῖ δὲ μύθῳ πάντα συλ-λήβδην μάθε, Eur. fr. 362.5 *TrGF* βραχεῖ δὲ μύθῳ πολλὰ συλλαβὼν ἐρῶ, *Suppl.* 1126 ἐν . . . ὀλίγῳ τἀμὰ πάντα συνθείς, Diggle (1969) 48 = (1994) 19.

674–9 A brief section of question and answer regularly occurs between the initial announcement and the full messenger speech (cf. Goward (1999) 184 n. 26). The difference between the women's reactions is striking. The differ-ent responses of Oedipus and Jocasta to the messenger in *OR* (compared by Goward (1999) 115) are not a true parallel: there the true polarisation occurs at 1056–85, only after Oedipus has subjected the messenger to extensive ques-tioning. Here the emotional force is more direct and immediate.

The passage forms the most powerful example of a third-party intervention in extant tragedy: other instances, such as Eur. *Hcld.* 99–100 and *Phoen.* 623 (cf. Mastronarde (1979) 95), do not approach its impact. It is all the more effective because Electra has been silent since 633, and because her words are so movingly brief; Clytemnestra's vicious stifling of her daughter's intervention, meanwhile, is perhaps her blackest moment. The technique is then repeated for maximum emphasis.

674 οἳ 'γώ: rarer than οἴμοι, this combination marks intense grief: cf. 1115, Aesch. *Cho.* 691 (Clytemnestra's response to the news of Orestes' death). It is not found outside tragedy.

ὄλωλα: cf. 677, 808, 1152.

τῇδ' ἐν ἡμέρᾳ: the news of Orestes' death puts an end to the hopes which Electra had had in him over many long years. Hutchinson (1999) 54 analyses how this single 'perfective' event brings to an end the 'imperfective' phase

---

[40] Unfairly, the scholium goes on to claim οὐκ ἐζηλώσαν δὲ τοῦτο οἱ τραγικοί, ἀλλὰ τοῖς λυπουμένοις μακρὰς ἐπάγουσι τὰς διηγήσεις τῶν συμφορῶν (= iv. 439.32–440.34 Erbse).

of Electra's perpetual hopes. This theme of the momentous day is, as it were, taken up first by Clytemnestra's triumphalism (783) and then by Chrysothemis' seemingly misplaced hopefulness (918–19). All around this day is regarded as a crucial moment of change (cf. 1149n.). So it is, but quite otherwise from how the characters expect.

675 τί φῄς, τί φῄς: 'τί φῄς . . . is not an enquiry; it expresses surprise, horror or indignation at what has just been said' (Dover (1963) 25 = (1987a) 305); cf. Ar. *Nub.* 1443 τί φῄς, τί φῄς σύ;, *Lys.* 710 τί φῄς; τί φῄς;, S. *Phil.* 1237 τί φῄς, Ἀχιλλέως παῖ; τίν' εἴρηκας λόγον;, Mastronarde (1979) 12–13. The phrase is more emotional than the πῶς εἶπας; of e.g. *OR* 943 and *Phil.* 414 (so rightly Jebb). Clytemnestra's excitement over the news of the death of her child can be contrasted with the similar emotion, again conveyed by repeated questions, shown by the aged Oedipus at the recovery of his children (*OC* 1099 ποῦ ποῦ; τί φῄς; πῶς εἶπας;). For the excited repetition cf. Bruhn §240, Shisler (1942) 283–4. For the orthography see 317n.

μὴ ταύτης κλύε: the pronoun is scornful: cf. *OR* 429 ἦ ταῦτα δῆτ' ἀνεκτὰ πρὸς τούτου κλύειν;

676 For the repetition of the news of a death cf. *Tr.* 877 (Χο.) τέθνηκεν ἡ τάλαινα; (Τρ.) δεύτερον κλύεις.

θανόντ' Ὀρέστην . . . λέγω: for verbs of saying and thinking taking a participle cf. 882, 1341, 1443–4, 1452, *OC* 1580, [Eur.] *Rhes.* 755, K–G ii. 72 Anm. 2, Goodwin §910, Moorhouse 318, Fraenkel on Aesch. *Ag.* 269 ('some of the not very numerous instances give the impression that the participial construction is much more emphatic than the infinitive: thus Homer ψ 2 φίλον πόσιν ἔνδον ἐόντα, "Odysseus is really at home" ').

νῦν and πάλαι are commonly connected: cf. *Ant.* 181 νῦν τε καὶ πάλαι δοκεῖ, *Phil.* 966, Hom. *Il.* 9.105 ἠμὲν πάλαι ἠδ' ἔτι καὶ νῦν, Kemmer (1903) 181; also 1049. πάλαι can be used to denote recent time (cf. 1101, 1477, Dawe, *STS* i. 208 n. 1, Bruhn §247.22); the variant τότ' ἐννέπω (cf. 907, Pearson (1923) 16–17) is probably a conjecture made through ignorance of this meaning (so rightly Dawe, *STS* i. 183).

677 οὐδέν εἰμ' ἔτι: cf. *Phil.* 1217 ἔτ' οὐδέν εἰμι, 951, Eur. *Andr.* 1077 οὐδέν εἰμ᾿ ἀπωλόμην, *Hel.* 1194 ὄλωλα· φροῦδα τἀμὰ κοὐδέν εἰμ᾿ ἔτι, Ar. *Ach.* 1185, Taplin (1971) 39 n. 29, Schauer (2002) 234–5.

678 σὺ μὲν τὰ σαυτῆς πρᾶσσ': interfering in the business of another (πολυπραγμοσύνη) could be regarded as a vice: cf. Hom. *Il.* 6.490 = *Od.* 1.356, 21.350 τὰ σ' αὐτῆς ἔργα κόμιζε, S. *Tr.* 616–17, Critias D–K 88 B 41a (= ii. 395.11), Pl. *Resp.* 433a8–9, Mewaldt (1929) 85–93, Dover (1974) 188–90,

L. B. Carter (1986) 58. Here the remark is cruelly unjustified ('hartherzig, als ob der Tod des Bruders El. nicht anginge' (Schneidewin[1])).

679 τῷ τρόπῳ διόλλυται; Since a messenger typically gives the main point of his news immediately (673n.), his speech is normally concerned not so much with what happened as with how it happened. It is thus often prefaced with a πῶς question from the recipient of the news (cf. *OR* 1236, *OC* 1585, Eur. *Med.* 1134, *Hipp.* 1171–2, *El.* 772–3, de Jong (1991) 33 with n. 81, Bal (1978) 68–9 ≈ (1997) 95, Stokes *ap.* Woodman and Martin on Tac. *Ann.* 3.16.2).

680–763 ὁ δὲ ἱππόδρομος ἔοικε τοῦ Ἀπόλλωνος τάχα μέν που καὶ αὐτὸς τῶν ἱππευόντων τινὰ ἀνιᾶσαι, ἅτε ἀνθρώποις τοῦ δαίμονος ὁμοίως ἐπὶ ἔργῳ παντὶ καὶ ἀμείνω καὶ τὰ χείρω νέμοντος (Paus. 10.37.4).

The Paedagogus' speech is often passed over in critical discussions of the drama: hailed as a virtuoso display of narrative fireworks, it is then largely ignored (brief doxography in MacLeod (2001) 107 n. 1; Marshall (forthcoming) is a notable exception). It is indeed an extraordinary set-piece of remarkable vividness and excitement; but it also forms a vital and integrated part of the drama, and cannot properly be considered in isolation.

S.'s immediate model is Aesch. *Cho.* 674–90, where Orestes announces his own death to his mother; he claims that Strophius asked him to pass the news on as he was leaving Phocis for Argos. In Aeschylus the message is short and functional: we are not prepared for it in advance, and it does not have a wider significance beyond the part it plays in the plan of revenge. We do not even learn how Orestes is meant to have died. S. has taken a motif left undeveloped in his precedessor's play, and worked it into something more prominent (compare how the urn, or indeed Electra herself, is given a new significance in S.'s drama, having played a minor rôle in Aeschylus). The speech is not only more elaborate than in Aeschylus: it has also been anticipated in the prologue (47–50), though the brevity of Orestes' reference to it there, coupled with the Aeschylean precedent, may have added to the audience's surprise at the eventual length of the account. It is in their handling of Electra, however, that the most important difference between the two dramatists emerges. When the news of Orestes' death is given in Aeschylus, Electra has disappeared from the play, not to return (cf. Garvie on Aesch. *Cho.* 691–9). In S. she is present as the Paedagogus tells his tale, and unaware that it is false. Her initial brief cries of despair make clear the impact which the news has on her (674, 677). She does not then speak for over a hundred lines, a silence lasting well beyond the length of the narrative; for once, this most eloquent of characters has nothing to say. As we listen to the Paedagogus' account, we shall consider the effect it is having on Electra and anticipate the intensity of her eventual response. This is, for us, arguably the most profoundly moving aspect of the speech (cf.

Lloyd-Jones (1972a) 224 = (1982) 232 = (1990a) 413). We know Orestes is alive and are thus, to an extent, emotionally insulated from the news of his death; but nothing protects us from the overwhelming pathos of Electra's reaction, or the equally overwhelming tension as we await it. Here it is obvious how the speech's effect is heightened when it is considered in its position within a drama rather than as a freestanding composition.

But why a chariot race? There is some slight evidence that athletic success formed part of the preexisting tradition surrounding Orestes (cf. Linforth (1963) 99, Egan (1983) 196–7, citing Pind. *P.* 11, Sen. *Ag.* 935–9), and this could have included success or failure in a chariot race; there are also metaphorical references to chariot-driving in Aeschylus' *Choephori* (e.g. 1022–3). But even if these references reflect previous tradition, they cannot explain S.'s choice to retain and develop this particular part of the myth rather than any other. Rather than engage in speculative search for origins, we should consider what literary effects, if any, result from the manner of Orestes' death. This must begin by considering the allusive relationships of the speech with other literary models, before moving on to the effect of this narrative in the context of the play as a whole.

The two chief literary influences on the speech are the chariot race of *Iliad* 23 and the genre of epinician poetry. The former provides a model for several chariot races in ancient literature (e.g. Stat. *Theb.* 6.296–549, Quint. Smyrn. *Post.* 4.500–95, Nonn. *Dion.* 37.116–484); here too there are similarities of form and content which bring the Homeric passage to mind (cf. 701–8n., 712n., 714n., 714–15n., 715n., 720–2n.). It is a sign of the success of S.'s narrative that it can recall such an episode without suffering through the comparison. As with the Aeschylean model, it is the difference between the two passages which is most significant. In Homer the race acts as relief from the poem's main action, and sometimes as a parody of it; its tone is never intense, and often humorous. Nor is its outcome revealed to us beforehand; rather, a series of unexpected reverses ensures that we are always expecting something new. But in S. the race marks for Electra the beginning not of relief, but of new anguish. And its fatal outcome is known to its audience from the beginning; it thus overshadows the whole narration, as we wait for the inevitable to occur.

The relation with the second model is less clear-cut. There are, after all, fundamental differences between this speech and the epinician ode: the latter almost always avoids descriptions of the actual equestrian (or athletic) event at issue. So too our speech lacks the mythological comparisons, abrupt transitions, and ornately effusive language so characteristic of epinician. These differences aside, several motifs which feature in the Paedagogus' narrative do also occur in epinician poetry, enough to suggest an attempt to evoke the aura of the latter (681n., 685n., 686n., 688n., 689n., 690n., 694–5n., 696–7n.). And once this atmosphere is suggested, we can begin to see how the speech subverts several important epinician themes. The odes of Pindar and Bacchylides glorify a victorious athlete, who enjoys support from the gods and honour among men. His past successes serve as foil to his present victory, or else as harbingers of greater glory in the future. There may be a mention of the enthusiastic reaction of the spectators, while strong emphasis is often put on his triumphant return home. But here the majestic power of the Paedagogus' language describes not a triumph but a catastrophic failure. The account of Orestes' earlier successes foreshadows this disaster, not the customary crowning victory. The sole mention of the gods is brief and ominous. The crowd cries out not in acclamation but in horror. And at the end, his *nostos* is not in a victorious revel, but a funerary urn. S. recalls a genre aimed at celebrating success and delighting its listeners only to invert this purpose, and emphasise the sorrow and pain which this contest has created.[41]

We have already encountered a chariot race that ends in death, in the first stasimon: comparisons between this and the Paedagogus' speech have often been drawn (cf. MacLeod (2001) 109 n. 10). Stinton is sceptical about the merits of making a connexion, claiming that 'an unconsciously ironic reference to a non-event is a little far-fetched' ((1986) 79 = (1990) 471). But it can hardly be coincidence that two deaths resulting from a chariot-race, both bringing sorrow to the house of Pelops, should be narrated within two hundred lines of each other. Moreover, the foreshadowing of an event by the earlier narration of a myth is common in tragedy (cf. Davies (1989b)). But though we may feel this connexion, it is not easy to identify its nuance. It might indicate that Orestes is under a curse, since his death corresponds to Myrtilus'; hence Thomson's claim that 'as we listen . . . we realise that he (sc. Orestes) is doomed' ((1973) 334, cited approvingly by Winnington-Ingram (1980) 236). Yet since this death is only a fiction, it is more plausible to see an indication of how Orestes has broken free from his family's troubled history, dying only in word as he declared in the prologue; his false death in a chariot race, which will lead to the rescue of the house, reverses the polarity of the original death which began the house's troubles. As well as this, the connexion with the death of Myrtilus may be present because, from a tragic perspective, it is fitting that a Pelopid should die in this fashion. Compare the account in Arist. *Poet.* 1452a4–11, where the murderer of one Mitys is killed by a statue of Mitys falling on him. Such a death, Aristotle claims, is more likely to stir pity and fear in an audience because of its mysterious 'appropriateness': ἔοικε γὰρ τὰ τοιαῦτα οὐκ εἰκῇ γίνεσθαι. Similar reasoning may explain the location of the death at the Pythian games, which were sacred to Apollo. Orestes' death answers the

---

[41] For other instances of sustained epinician influence on tragedy cf. *Tr.* 497–530, where Easterling and Davies have useful remarks *ad loc.*; also Eur. *Her.* 637–700 with Parry (1965).

prayer which Clytemnestra has just been making to this god (637–59n.), and it thus seems 'appropriate' that Orestes meets his end during a festival in honour of this god. Deaths in tragedy do not occur at random; we are generally encouraged to see them in some larger perspective, suggestive of some larger purpose which may or may not be clear to us. This is one of the most 'appropriate' deaths in all tragedy: the irony is that despite this, it is only a fiction.

This speech can be profitably considered from many perspectives, and yet does not lose its moorings as a tragic messenger speech (cf. 680n., 681n., 762n.). One basic convention of this genre, however, it strikingly breaches: for this 'tour de force of a Messenger speech, rivalling the most elaborate efforts of Euripides . . . is devoted to the presentation of a lie' (Winnington-Ingram (1980) 236). The best tragic parallel is the False Merchant scene in *Philoctetes* (542–627); there too an underling narrates a false story according to an arrangement made in the prologue. Menander's *Aspis* is also based around the narration of the 'death' of a returning warrior, with the aim of deceiving and then defeating his enemies.[42] Neither case comes close to this instance, however, in terms of emotional force or dramatic power. This power is important for making the speech convincing: 'the precise details, the pompous setting of the scene, the skilful creation of tension, the splendid array of rhetorical devices [make up] everything that a Greek would have called *peitho*' (Reinhardt (1979) 152 ≈ (1947) 162); cf. Woodard (1965) 204–5). It is the vividness of the Paedagogus' account that leads Clytemnestra to hail it as πιστὰ τεκμήρια of her son's death (774n.), and that leads Electra to refer to her brother as 'clearly' dead (831 φανερῶς). For the power of λόγοι exhibited in this speech cf. 1359–60, Woodard (1964) 187.

But does the deceptive tale have implications for the morality of the matricide? According to C. P. Segal (1981) 282, 'the lie about the Delphic festival . . . is a paradigm for the corrupted ritual and civic order'; so too he sees an opposition between 'the high registers of epic and epinician poetry' and 'the low registers of lie and deception'. This can hardly be got out of the text, however: contrast the importance such concerns have in *Philoctetes*, where the ethical question of whether it is right to use δόλος in a good cause is to the fore from beginning to end (1–85n.). More interesting is the contrast between the world of the narrative with the world of the play as a whole. See especially the summary of Kitzinger (1991) 318: 'the *agon* of the chariot race takes place in a Panhellenic, all-male, emotionally straightforward context where victory brings civic honor, whereas the *agon* to which Apollo has in fact sent Orestes will require his contending in a familial, closed, emotionally charged world where victory cannot be unambiguously honorable.' This ambiguity is, in its fashion,

---

[42] On these and other parallels see de Jong (2004) 266–7.

as important for our assessment of the matricide as were the ambiguities in
Electra's *agon*-speech (558–6on., 577–83n.).[43]

680 Messengers in S. regularly begin their speeches by declaring their intention
to narrate (cf. 892, *Aj.* 284, 719, *Tr.* 180–1, 749, 899, *OR* 1240, *Ant.* 234, 245,
407, 1192–3; related expressions at *Aj.* 748, *OC* 1586). On Euripides' practice
see 681 n.

κἀπεμπόμην: 'certain verbs, especially of *ordering, advising*, take an imperfect instead of an aorist when referring to a past, non-durative occurrence,
apparently because they initiate an action which needs to be carried out by
another: the impf. will then refer to the mere giving of the order etc., leaving
it open whether the order was later carried out' (Moorhouse 191 (his italics),
citing S–D ii. 277). This also applies to verbs of sending: cf. *Ant.* 19, *Phil.* 495,
Braswell on Pind. *P.* 4.114(a) and the present πέμπει at 406, 427. The repeated
καί approximates to ὥσπερ . . . οὕτως (so Schneidewin[1], comparing the τε . . .
καί of *Ant.* 1112 and *Tr.* 626). Denniston 321 claims that the καί emphasises the
verb, but it is not clear why the verb needs such emphasis.

τὸ πᾶν φράσω: cf. 378n.

681–5 A long, flowing sentence begins the narrative by evoking a glorious
and confident atmosphere. The combined emphasis on the aural (the herald's
cries) and the visual (the sight of Orestes) awakens the actual sights and sounds
of the place in the listener's mind. Descriptive scene-setting is typical of the
opening of the messenger speech: cf. *OR* 1241–3, *Ant.* 1196–8, Goward (1999)
170 n. 10.

681 γάρ: often found 'after an expression denoting the giving or receiving
of information' (Denniston 59; cf. 32, 644, 893, Braswell on Pind. *P.* 4.70a).
Sophoclean messenger speeches are typically preceded by such expressions
(68on.); hence they typically begin with this particle (cf. 893, *Aj.* 285, 749, *Tr.*
181, *Ant.* 249, 407, *OR* 1241, *OC* 1587, possibly *Tr.* 900 (but see Davies *ad loc.*), de
Jong (1997), especially 180–1). In Aeschylus this use of γάρ is found at *Sept.* 42,

---

[43] I reserve for a footnote the suggestion that the description of the race is so vivid
that the audience is carried away into thinking that Orestes is dead. This curious
idea was first put forward by Kaibel (on 660, pp. 174–5) and Tycho von Wilamowitz
((1917) 188–93), and has been taken up surprisingly often by later commentators:
even the usually sober Winnington-Ingram does not rule it out ((1980) 236 n. 66).
But Orestes has already appeared on stage, alive and well; it would be a strangely
forgetful audience who could fail to remember this. The notion that an audience
becomes so carried away by the vividness of events on stage that it forgets they are
not real has been rebutted by Bain (1977) 1–7: Kaibel's theory is a variation on this
error. Matthiessen (1964) 116 n. 2, van Erp Taalman Kip (1990) 100–2 and MacLeod
(2001) 108 are properly sceptical.

458, *Ag.* 650 (the last with a greatly extended 'statement of intent to narrate', lasting 14 lines); also at [Aesch.] *PV* 645. Messenger speeches in Euripides, by contrast, usually begin with ἐπεί, referring back to some previously mentioned fact (Rijksbaron (1976)). Preliminary statements are rarer, and hence so is introductory γάρ; where it does occur (*Alc.* 158, *Held.* 800, *IA* 1543; perhaps *Phoen.* 1428 (v.l.; see Finglass (2005a)), a preliminary statement expressing intention to narrate always precedes. The pattern occurs in the tragic adespota at fr. 625.30–1 *TrGF*.

κλεινόν: Thomas Magister (*Ecloge* 286.4 Ritschl) read κοινόν, which is probably a conjecture (305–6n.); for a possible instance of the reverse corruption see 1085–6n. The adjective goes with the whole phrase πρόσχημα ἀγῶνος (cf. 785–6, 1390, Bruhn §10.I). Praise of the site of the games is common in epinician: cf. Simon. fr. 511a.7 *PMG* λιπαρὰ . . . Πυθ[ώ, Pind. *P.* 5.20–1 κλεενᾶς . . . | . . . παρὰ Πυθιάδος, 8.61–3.

681–2 Ἑλλάδος | . . . ἀγῶνος: on double genitives see Wilamowitz on Eur. *Her.* 170; the former is possessive, the latter defining. The singular ἀγών can denote an athletic festival, not just a single contest (LSJ⁹ s.v. II).

682 πρόσχημ' denotes anything 'put forward' to be noticed by others and hence 'ornament', 'showpiece', καλλώπισμα (Thomas Magister, *Eclogue* 286.2 Ritschl). Cf. Hdt. 5.28 ἡ Μίλητος . . . μάλιστα δὴ τότε ἀκμάσασα καὶ δὴ καὶ τῆς Ἰωνίης ἦν πρόσχημα, Ar. *Ran.* 913, Polyb. 3.15.3, Strab. 10.2.3 (= iii. 176.23–4 Radt), Plut. *Alex.*17.1.

Δελφικῶν ἄθλων: on the supposed anachronism see 49n.

683 ὀρθίῳ κηρύγματι: Earle's conjecture ((1903) 209 = (1912) 80–1) for transmitted ὀρθίων κηρυγμάτων, revived by Diggle (1994) 463–4 and printed by Dawe³. Diggle has two objections to the paradosis. First, elsewhere in S. a non-personal object with αἰσθάνομαι is always accusative. Second, while an aorist participle can be coincident in time with a main verb (Goodwin §150, Barrett on Eur. *Hipp.* 289–92, Braswell on Pind. *P.* 4.36–7), here the participle is not directly dependent on ἤσθετο, and hence cannot be treated as coincident with it. This leaves us with the translation 'when he heard the loud proclamations of a man who had proclaimed', which does not make sense. A slight change which rids us of these oddities can thus be readily welcomed. It is also palaeographically plausible. Iota and nu (including non-ephelkystic nu) are often omitted or added erroneously at the end of a word (cf. D. C. C. Young (1964) 92–3), while the corruption of one to the other is a common error (cf. Headlam (1891) 124–5). After such a corruption with ὀρθίῳ, the ending of κηρύγματι would have been altered accordingly: for the dative in this context cf. fr. 314.46 *TrGF* [βοῶ]ντος ὀρθίοισι σὺν κηρύγμασ[ιν], Eur.

IA 94–5 ὀρθίῳ κηρύγματι | Ταλθύβιον εἶπον πάντ᾽ ἀφιέναι στρατόν. Ll-J/W prefer Herwerden's γηρυμάτων ((1868) 12), but ancient tolerance of repetition was greater than our own (see 335–6n.); for this particular figure cf. Aesch. *Eum.* 566 κήρυσσε κῆρυξ, Xen. *Hell.* 1.7.9, Aeschines 3.23, 3.154.

ὀρθίῳ denotes 'loud' rather than 'shrill' (cf. Kaimio (1977) 178–9). For the importance of clarity in a herald cf. Hom. *Il.* 9.10, Lucian 38.7, Crowther (1994b) 141 = (2004) 188–9.

684 οὖ πρώτη κρίσις: the foot race comes first, as in Homer's Phaeacian games (*Od.* 8.120); cf. Pl. *Leg.* 833a7–8. For κρίσις denoting a "trial" of skill or strength in a contest' see Braswell on Pind. *P.* 4.253c, adding Call. fr. 384.13 Pfeiffer.

685 εἰσῆλθε: for this verb used in an athletic context cf. 700, Dem. 18.319 (of an Olympic victor) τῶν εἰσελθόντων πρὸς αὐτὸν ἄριστ᾽ ἐμάχετο, Paus. 6.20.11; also Pind. *P.* 6.51.

λαμπρός: denotes glory or success: cf. *OR* 80–1 εἰ γὰρ ἐν τύχῃ γέ τῳ | σωτῆρι βαίη λαμπρός, Eur. fr. 282.10 *TrGF* (of athletes) λαμπροὶ δ᾽ ἐν ἥβῃ καὶ πόλεως ἀγάλματα, Ar. *Eq.* 556–7 μειρακίων . . . λαμ- | πρυνομένων ἐν ἅρμασιν. The adjective is used of an incoming competitor in the Pythian games at Lucian 31.8. Brightness is often predicated of athletic success in Pindar (cf. *O.* 1.23 with Gerber, *P.* 8.96–7, *I.* 1.22–3, fr. 227.2–3 S–M). Cf. also 66 and the pathetic use of the word by Electra at 1130. The v.l. λαμπρόν (GR, perhaps Zc) may be a misplaced 'correction' by someone who knew that σέβας is neuter.

πᾶσι: the repeated use of πᾶς-words in this section (cf. 687 πάντιμον, 692 πάντα) conveys the extent of Orestes' achievements.

σέβας 'object of veneration', a term normally applied to divinities (cf. fr. 582 *TrGF* (coni.), Aesch. *Ag.* 515, [Aesch.] *PV* 1091). Cf. however Aesch. *Cho.* 157, Eur. *IA* 633 ὦ σέβας ἐμοὶ μέγιστον, Ἀγαμέμνων ἄναξ, Bain *ap.* Taplin (1979) 128 n. 19.

686 δρόμου δ᾽ ἰσώσας τῇ φύσει τὰ τέρματα: Kaibel (p. 177) correctly paraphrases λαμπρὰ μὲν ἡ φύσις ἦν αὐτοῦ, οὐχ ἧττον δὲ λαμπρὸν τὸ τοῦ δρόμου τέλος; so also the scholia (p. 134.17–21 Papageorgius), Fraenkel (on Aesch. *Ag.* 637 (ii. 315–16)) and Ll-J/W (*Sophoclea*). For φύσις meaning 'appearance' see Holwerda (1955) 62–5, Davies on *Tr.* 308; the emphasis on this quality fits with the stress on Orestes' outward form in 685. The sentiment is found in Homer (*Il.* 13.431–2 ἐκέκαστο | κάλλεϊ καὶ ἔργοισιν ἰδὲ φρεσί), but is more common as an epinician *topos* (cf. Pind. *O.* 9.94 ὡραῖος ἐὼν καὶ καλὸς κάλλιστά τε ῥέξαις, 8.19, *N.* 3.19, Race (1990) 187–92). Cf. also Ar. *Thesm.* 165–7 αὐτός τε καλὸς ἦν . . . | διὰ τοῦτ᾽ ἄρ᾽ αὐτοῦ καὶ κάλ᾽ ἦν τὰ δράματα. | ὅμοια γὰρ ποιεῖν ἀνάγκη τῇ φύσει, [Simon.] *A.Plan.* 2.3 = 806 *FGE*, *CIL* i² 6–7.3 *quoius forma uirtutei parisuma fuit* (from the funerary *elogium* of L. Cornelius Scipio Barbatus, cos. 298), Ov. *Met.* 14.324 *par animus formae*, Plut. *Romul.* 7.5.

Musgrave on Eur. *Phoen.* 1121 (our 1100) conjectured τῇ 'φέσει ('starting-place': cf. Paus. 5.15.5, 6.20.9, Suda α 3271 (= i. 293.3–4 Adler). This was taken up by Brunck¹ and Jebb (the latter writing τἀφέσει); a similar corruption (ἀφέσεως to φύσεως) has occurred at Aelius Aristides 50.76 (= 444.26 Keil). But the meaning is unsatisfactory. Of Jebb's translation Campbell curtly commented ' "when he came back to the point from which he started" is intelligible enough, but hardly requires so elaborate a form of expression' (*PS*). Musgrave and Brunck preferred 'having made the end seem simultaneous with the start': cf. Ant. Thess. *A.P.* 9.557.5–6 = 513–14 *GP* ἢ γὰρ ἐφ' ὑσπλήγων ἢ τέρματος εἶδέ τις ἄκρου | ἠΐθεον, μέσσῳ δ' οὔποτ' ἐνὶ σταδίῳ). But this rococo conceit hardly fits the elevated tone of the passage.

687 νίκης . . . γέρας: laurel at the Pythian games (Paus. 10.7.8, Pind. *P.* 10.40). For the form of the expression cf. Bacchyl. 7.8–9 πρεσβύ[τατο]ν . . . γέρας | νίκας; also 11.36 ὑπέρτατον . . . γέρας.

ἐξῆλθε: for this verb in an agonistic context cf. *Tr.* 505–6.

688 χὥπως μὲν ἐν παύροισι πολλά σοι λέγω 'to say much in a few words'; so Bergk (his edition, p. xlvi) and Nauck³ (p. 160) for manuscript πολλοῖσι παῦρα. For the sense cf. Aesch. fr. 99.4 *TrGF* τί οὖν; τὰ πολλὰ κεῖνα διὰ παύρων λέγω, Pind. *O.* 13.98 Ἰσθμοῖ τά τ' ἐν Νεμέᾳ παύρῳ ἔπει θήσω φανέρ' ἀθρό', *P.* 1.81–2, Eur. *Suppl.* 901 Τυδέως δ' ἔπαινον ἐν βραχεῖ θήσω μέγαν, Thuc. 2.45.2 βραχείᾳ παραινέσει ἅπαν σημανῶ. The corruption, a sort of polar metathesis, would be easy. The transmitted text would have to mean 'to speak briefly, when there is much that might be told', an unproblematic sentiment (cf. Thuc. 8.53.1 λόγους ἐποιοῦντο ἐν τῷ δήμῳ κεφαλαιοῦντες ἐκ πολλῶν). But the sense required of ἐν πολλοῖσι is difficult: the line seems rather to mean 'to tell you a little in a long speech', which is hardly appropriate. Pind. *P.* 9.76–8 ἀρεταὶ δ' αἰεὶ μεγάλαι πολύμυθοι· | βαιὰ δ' ἐν μακροῖσι ποικίλλειν | ἀκοὰ [ἀκόνα *coni.* Wilamowitz] σοφοῖς is cited as an epinician parallel for the construction. But the parallel is not a close one. As Carey notes *ad loc.* (without reference to our passage), the issue at hand here is compression, not selection: 'μακροῖσι is not πολλοῖσι'.

689 οὐκ οἶδα τοιοῦδ' ἀνδρὸς ἔργα καὶ κράτη 'I do not know the mighty deeds of such a man', and hence 'I have never seen his equal'. Compare the 'negative superlative' in epinician, where the poet declares that no-one is greater (etc.) than the *laudandus*: cf. Ibyc. fr. S166.23–6 *PMGF* (if epinician), Pind. *O.* 2.92–5, *P.* 2.58–61, *N.* 6.24–6, Bacchyl. 3.63–6, 8.22–5, fr. 20c.21–4 (an encomium),

Eur. fr. 755.3 *PMG*. The use of κράτος to denote victory is also frequent in epinician (see Carey on Pind. *P.* 2.5).

The Paedagogus is sparing with the first person; this makes instances all the more persuasive when they do occur. We do not find another until the end of the speech (762–3); there it is employed to stress the magnitude of Orestes' catastrophe, just as here it vouches for the greatness of his achievements. Elsewhere depersonalised objectivity is the rule. Even implicit focalisation from the Paedagogus' perspective is avoided: the only exception is his designation of Orestes as ὁ τλήμων in 742 (n.).

Zr's τοιάδ᾽ is adopted by Brunck (ed.), but *pace* Ll-J/W was not conjectured by him: as his note *ad loc.* shows (in his first edition), he took it from a manuscript. It leaves ἀνδρός bare, however, and so is best avoided.

690 ἓν δ᾽ ἴσθ᾽: a short, arresting phrase leads into the climactic account of Orestes' success. 'The laudator will not describe all the successes of his favorite, but is confident that by recalling a single outstanding success he will accomplish all that the complete tale could hope to accomplish' (Bundy (1962) 18 = (1986) 18, citing [Dem.] 61.27).

εἰσεκήρυξαν: cf. *Aj.* 1240 ἀγῶνας . . . κηρῦξαι.

βραβῆς: people appointed by the Amphictyonic council to oversee the games; they are occasionally represented on vases (Kefalidou (1996) 44–51). For the ending see Threatte ii. 239–48.

[691] δρόμων διαύλων πένταθλ᾽ ἃ νομίζεται: deleted by Lachmann (1822) 45 and Hermann (1831) 51 = (1827–77) vi. 13. According to Ll-J/W the deletion is owed to Porson, though I have found no evidence for this; at (1815) 211 he proposes the conjecture ἆθλ᾽ ἅπερ νομίζεται. The transmitted line neither scans nor makes sense; the plural διαύλων is also troubling. Nor does the line ring true as poetry: the list of different contests is redolent of the pedantry of an interpolator. Perhaps it began life as a metrical gloss, written by someone with a smattering of knowledge about Greek athletics, but a less than secure grasp of the iambic trimeter. For erroneous prosody as a sign of interpolation see Günther (1996) 99 n. 290. In the text of his third edition Nauck prefers to delete διαύλων . . . | τούτων, which gives us δρόμων instead of τούτων in 692 (cf. Jachmann (1936) 134–5 = (1982) 539–40): but why should Orestes' prowess be limited to the foot-races?

692 ἐνεγκών: in the sense of winning a prize the middle is more common (cf. 969, *Tr.* 497); for the active cf. Hom. *Il.* 18.308, Hes. *Op.* 657, Moorhouse 177.

τἀπινίκια 'prizes' (cf. Dion. Hal. *Ant. Rom.* 3.27.2); the word normally denotes a song or sacrifice in honour of victory (e.g. Aesch. *Ag.* 174).

308

COMMENTARY: 516–822

693 ἀνακαλούμενος: the winner is proclaimed by a herald (cf. Eur. *Her.* 960–1, Ar. *Plut.* 585, Timoth. fr. 802 *PMG*, Hordern, Dem. 18.319, Posid. 71.3, 82.5–6 A–B). The fullest form of this proclamation, as used here, consists of the victor's name, father's name and home city: cf. Pind. *O.* 5.8 νικάσας . . . καὶ ὃν πατέρ᾽ Ἄκρων᾽ ἐκάρυξε καὶ τὰν νέοικον ἕδραν, *P.* 1.32 Πυθιάδος δ᾽ ἐν δρόμῳ κάρυξ ἀνέειπέ νιν (the city of Aetna). So at Philod. *De vitiis* col. xiv lines 27–8 (p. 25 Jensen) an arrogant competitor, when asked for his homeland as he enters a contest, replies τοῦ κήρυκο[ς] . . . ἀκούσει [μ]ικρὸν ὕσ[τερ]ον). For representations on vases of heralds proclaiming athletic victors see Kefalidou (1996) 60–2.

694 ὄνομα δ᾽ Ὀρέστης: cf. Eur. *Andr.* 884–5 Ἀγαμέμνονός τε καὶ Κλυταιμήστρας τόκος, | ὄνομα δ᾽ Ὀρέστης.

694–5 Ἑλλάδος | . . . στράτευμ᾽ ἀγείραντός: cf. Hom. *Il.* 9.338–9 λαὸν . . . ἀγείρας | Ἀτρεΐδης, Thuc. 1.9.1 τὸν στόλον ἀγεῖραι (of Agamemnon), Eur. *Or.* 647–8, *Andr.* 605–6 Ἑλλήνων ὄχλον | τοσόνδ᾽ ἀθροίσας ἤγαγες πρὸς Ἴλιον (of Menelaus). 'Epinician is eager to forge connections between prowess in games and in battle' (Hutchinson on Pind. *O.* 6.10): cf. Pind. *P.* 8.25–7, D. C. Young (1971) 39 with n. 130, Thuc. 4.121.1 with Hornblower, Lucian 37.24. Here Agamemnon's military prowess is balanced by Orestes' sporting triumphs: the son's achievements have not disgraced those of his father. There is a further connexion: both Agamemnon and Orestes (in the story) are killed shortly after their greatest achievement. The emphasis on the Panhellenic scope of their achievements (cf. 681–2, Lucian 37.36 ἀνακηρυττομένους ἐν μέσοις τοῖς Ἕλλησι (of successful athletes)) provides another link: contrast the narrow focus of the rest of the play on a single house and its occupants.

695 Ἀγαμέμνονος: the word order is unusual, with the name placed between definite article and participle; cf. *OR* 1245 καλεῖ τὸν ἤδη Λάιον πάλαι νεκρόν. In each case the hyperbaton lends emphasis to the proper name: cf. Collard on Eur. *Suppl.* 1036–7, Bond on Eur. *Her.* 145. For the bare genitive used to denote origin or parentage see Bruhn §29.

ποτε: the 'nostalgic' use, identified at [1]n.

696 καὶ ταῦτα μὲν τοιαῦθ᾽: cf. Pl. *Theaet.* 173b3 καὶ οὗτοι μὲν δὴ τοιοῦτοι; also *Apol.* 34b7, *Hipp. Maj.* 293c7. The phrase marks the end of this part of the narrative (cf. 761).

696–7 ὅταν δέ τις θεῶν | βλάπτῃ, δύναιτ᾽ ἂν οὐδ᾽ ἂν ἰσχύων φυγεῖν: for the sentiment cf. *Aj.* 455–6 εἰ δέ τις θεῶν | βλάπτοι, φύγοι τἂν χὠ κακὸς τὸν κρείσσονα, *OC* 252–3 οὐ γὰρ ἴδοις ἂν ἀθρῶν βροτὸν ὅστις ἄν, | εἰ θεὸς

309

ἄγοι, | ἐκφυγεῖν δύναιτο, Pind. *P.* 2.49–52, Nisbet and Hubbard on Hor. *C.* 1.34.12, West on Hes. *Op.* 5 ff.

Tragic messengers normally give their accounts without the benefit of hindsight (cf. de Jong (1991) 34, 45–6). This encourages the audience to see the events they describe from the perspective of an onlooker: compare their use of the historic present (725n.). There are exceptions. In five speeches a messenger makes use of *ex eventu* knowledge from the beginning of his account (*Tr.* 749–812, Aesch. *Pers.* 353–432, Eur. *Andr.* 1085–1165, *IT* 1327–1419, *Hel.* 1526–1618); in each case he is describing the revelation of an intrigue, and is revealing the true state of affairs early on 'with the express purpose of indicting another . . . or exculpating [himself]' (de Jong (1991) 56). Closer to our example are instances where *ex eventu* knowledge intrudes into a speech told mainly from an experiencing focalisation (e.g. Eur. *Ion* 1184–6, de Jong (1991) 49–52). But the sudden appearance of this weighty *gnome* is unlike anything in other messenger speeches. Its massive brevity is more typical of choral lyric, and particularly of Pindar, where 'in the midst of the story a general idea is abruptly introduced; the incident singled out as a παράδειγμα is attached to it with (καὶ) γάρ; and the story goes on' (Friis Johansen (1959) 59, citing *O.* 7.24–30, *P.* 9.39–43, *N.* 8.24–7). So too its content recalls ideas prominent in Pindar: the barriers of the divine world which confront even the mightiest of victors (cf. Race (1990) 192–5), and the jealousy of the gods which can afflict the successful (cf. Pind. *P.* 10.19–21). This is appropriate given the preceding description of Orestes' astonishing success.

There is also a significant echo of epic poetry: Hom. *Il.* 16.688 ἀλλ' αἰεί τε Διὸς κρείσσων νόος ἠέ περ ἀνδρός, a one-line[44] *gnome*, provides an exact parallel to our instance (Friis Johansen's claim that this technique is 'totally alien to epic tradition' ((1959) 60) is thus exaggerated). Even as Patroclus enjoys his greatest success, the narrator reminds us of the power of the gods and prepares us for the hero's downfall. But while narrative prolepsis is common in Homer, there is no other epic instance of the narrator's voicing a general truth about the universe in this way (cf. S. Richardson (1990) 144). The content too has a familiar epic feel: Homer's heroes are often reminded of the gulf that separates them from the gods (e.g. *Il.* 5.440–2). These resonances give the *gnome* a weight and power which go far beyond its size. The link with epinician is close: the warning against divine envy with which Pindar admonishes his patrons here takes on a terrifying reality.

Nauck[3] suggests that the *gnome* may also apply to Clytemnestra; the meaning of ἰσχύων ('physically strong') tells against this, however.

---

[44] The following two lines are spurious: see Janko *ad loc.*

697 βλάπτῃ: used of divine agency at e.g. *Aj.* 455–6 (cited previous note), *Ant.* 1103–4, Tr. Adesp. fr. 296.1 *TrGF*; cf. N. J. Richardson on Hom. *Il.* 22.15. At Aesch. *Ag.* 120 βλαβέντα λοισθίων δρόμων it is used of checking a runner's course.

ἄν … ἄν: for the repetition see 333–4n.; for the separation of the particles by a bare negative see Friis Johansen and Whittle on Aesch. *Suppl.* 771.

ἰσχύων: 'in some cases where we feel the absence of τις as subject, there is a participle taking its place' (West on Hes. *Op.* 12): cf. 1323, Hom. *Od.* 5.400, K–G i. 35–6, Vahlen (1904) 11–15 = (1907–8) ii. 511–15, Wackernagel (1926–8) i. 111–12, Fraenkel on Aesch. *Ag.* 71. The omission stresses the gnomic character of the expression (K–G i. 608–9, S–D ii. 245).

698 ἄλλης ἡμέρας 'on another day' (see 477n. for the genitive of time).

698–9 ἱππικῶν | … ὠκύπους ἀγών: cf. *Aj.* 935–6 ἀριστόχειρ | … ὅπλων … ἀγών, Bers (1974) 73; also 861. The epithet ὠκύπους is found in epic, lyric and epinician poetry, almost always with reference to horses (Bergson (1956) 99; [Hes.] *Scut.* 302 is an exception). In tragedy its range of reference is greater (cf. *OC* 1093, Eur. *Hipp.* 1127–8).

699 ἡλίου τέλλοντος: the simplex is used intransitively only here in classical Greek, though ἀνατέλλω is used intransitively at *OC* 1246, Ar. *Nub.* 754 and several times in Herodotus. The sense is probably 'when the sun is reaching its goal', and hence 'rising' (see Braswell on Pind. *P.* 4.257). For the intransitive use of normally transitive verbs in S. cf. 916, 1417, Bruhn §99; *Phil.* 1330–1 ἕως … ἥλιος | … αἴρῃ is particularly close to the present instance. For the principle involved see S–D ii. 224.

Xen. *Hell.* 7.4.29 implies that on a certain day of the Olympic games of 364 the chariot races preceded the pentathlon. If this was a universal practice, the former would indeed have had to be held in the early morning. See further Maehler (2004) on Bacchyl. 5.40.

700 εἰσῆλθε: 685n.

πολλῶν ἁρματηλάτων: nine, it turns out. There are only five contestants in the chariot race in *Iliad* 23; but the crown games in the fifth century probably had rather more participants. Pind. *P.* 5.49–53 says that Carrhotus was one of forty competitors in the Pythian chariot-race (462); Alcibiades entered seven teams at Olympia in 416, which would hardly have been possible if ten were a *numerus clausus*. Archaeology also suggests a larger number of entrants: the Olympic *aphesis*, described in Pausanias 6.20.10–14, may have provided room for between forty-eight and sixty chariots (cf. Crowther (1993b)

46 = (2004) 177). S. could hardly have included a catalogue of sixty charioteers, however.

701–8 In *Iliad* 23 the catalogue of contestants lasts over sixty lines (287–351). This includes Nestor's long speech to Antilochus (306–48); of the other contestants, Menelaus gets 8 lines, Diomedes 3, Eumelus 2 and Meriones 1. The catalogue form is essentially an epic device which marks out the special significance of this contest; Pind. *P.* 4.171–83, however, shows that it could be used in epinician too. *OC* 1313–25 provides another example of a Sophoclean catalogue, this time enumerating the Seven against Thebes. Its entries are a little longer than the ones here: after all, some of the Seven did have personal characteristics which needed to be mentioned. Nevertheless, the overall impression recalls the feel of our passage: short, clipped entries which maintain a sense of urgency.

Many of the places mentioned have strong associations with horse-rearing (see individual nn.). The large proportion of competitors from central or northern Greece may at first seem a little parochial: Delphi was, after all, receiving rich dedications from the Aegean islands, Ionia, Egypt and Magna Graecia from the sixth century (Jacquemin (1999) 69–72), and Pindar's *Pythians* suggest that the contest had an international flavour. But the victor lists at Olympia suggest that Peloponnesian competitors always predominated at that competition, including the equestrian events (Moretti (1957)). The default hypothesis must be that there was a local bias at Delphi too. In any case, a fifth of the competitors do come from overseas: we have no way of knowing whether this proportion was typical.

701 εἷς . . . εἷς: for repeated εἷς in distributing numbers larger than two see Gow on Theocr. 7.71–2.

Ἀχαιός: in Hom. *Il.* 2.682–4 the Achaeans are located in the area round Phthia (cf. Hdt. 7.132.1, 7.173.1, 7.197.1). But the catalogue makes better sense if the word here refers to the Achaea of the classical age, on the south side of the Gulf of Corinth; the ensuing anachronism is not significant or likely to be noticed. This gives us two competitors from the Peloponnese at the start of the list, with Greeks from north of the Isthmus beginning at 703 (including Orestes, despite 693). References to Achaea's cavalry are rare and post-classical (cf. Spence (1993) 8–9).

εἷς ἀπὸ Σπάρτης: Λακεδαιμόνιοι ... μετὰ τὴν ἐπιστρατείαν τοῦ Μήδου διετέθησαν πάντων φιλοτιμότατα Ἑλλήνων πρὸς ἵππων τροφάς (Paus. 6.2.1): cf. Hodkinson (2000) 303–33. A celebratory stele from Sparta, listing the victories of one Damonon and capped with a relief of a *tethrippon*, is testament to a thriving set of such competitions inside Laconia itself (*IG* v/1 213 = *CEG* i. §378 (*c.* 440–435); Moretti (1953) 36–40, Hornblower (2004) 236–7). But while Ibycus probably wrote epinician for Spartan victors (cf. fr. S166

PMGF, Barron (1984), Jenner (1986)), it seems that Pindar and Bacchylides did not. Hodkinson (2000) 317–19 connects this with the status of epinician as an outlet for prestige displays by aristocrats, something frowned upon in fifth-century Sparta: see however Hornblower (2004) 239–43 for a contrary view. In war Sparta's cavalry was of more limited value (Spence (1993) 2–4).

δύο: the catalogue is a line old, and we have already reached the fourth contestant (cf. 701–8n.).

702 Λίβυες: for Libya's association with horsemanship cf. Pind. *P.* 4, 5, Hdt. 4.189.3 τέσσερας ἵππους συζευγνύναι παρὰ Λιβύων οἱ Ἕλληνες μεμαθήκασι, Xen. *Cyr.* 6.1.27, [Lucian] 58.23, Hesych. β 237 = i. 313 Latte = Mnaseas fr. 40 *FHG* = 43 Cappelletto, Moretti (1953) 95–6, Braswell on Pind. *P.* 4.2b, Arnott on Alexis fr. 241.2–3 *PCG*, Pfeiffer on Call. fr. 716.2. One of the Libyans comes from Barca (727).

ἁρμάτων ἐπιστάται: cf. Eur. *Hel.* 1039–40 οἵτινες τετραζύγων | ὄχων ἀνάσσουσ', 1267 ἐρετμῶν ἐπιστάτας, Aesch. *Pers.* 379 ὅπλων ἐπιστάτης. Phrases of the form 'lord of the x' (where x is a weapon, vehicle etc.) are not found in Greek before Aeschylus; West (1997) 545–7 suggests a Semitic origin (cf. the Akkadian *bēl narkabti* = 'lord of the chariot').

703 ἐν 'among', which Nauck[4a] emended to ἐπί ('in addition to'): for the corruption see Arnott on Alexis fr. 187.2 *PCG*. But as Jebb notes, there is no reason to think that the competitors are being listed in their starting order, rather than as a group.

703–4 Θεσσαλὰς . . . | ἵππους: Thessaly was famed for its horses and horsemanship, which it owed to its open plains and horse-rearing oligarchy; cf. Hdt. 7.196, Pl. *Hipp. maj.* 284a4–6, Isocrates 15.298, Theocr. 18.30 with Gow, Posid. 71.4 with Austin and Bastianini, Σ Hom. *Il.* 2.761–5 (= i. 334.60–3 Erbse), Philip *A.P.* 9.543.1 = 2995 *GP*, anon. *A.P.* 9.21.1 = 1326 *FGE*, Lucan 6.397, Moretti (1953) 96, Spence (1993) 23–5. Poseidon ἵππιος was the subject of particular cult there (see Maehler's introduction to Bacchyl. 14).

Here and at 734–5, 737–8 the feminine plural denotes Orestes' horses, even though at 721–2 and 744 one of his horses is denoted by the masculine singular. This is regular for teams of horses in tragedy and lyric, being 'a question not of sex but of gender' (Barrett on Eur. *Hipp.* 231; cf. Σ Eur. *Phoen.* 3 (= i. 246.6–7 Schwartz) ἔθος . . . τοῖς ποιηταῖς θηλυκῶς λέγειν τοὺς ἵππους). McDevitt (1994) argues that the horses are in fact female; in the singular they are denoted by a 'generalising' masculine singular (771n.) because then their sex is not at issue. But this would mean that every team of horses in extant tragedy is made up of mares, which seems odd; nor is it clear why the sex of the horses is relevant in the plural, but not in the singular.

COMMENTARY: 516-822

703 ἔχων: the minority variant ἄγων may have arisen from ἀγών at the end of 699. The same corruption has occurred in V at *Ant.* 1258.

704 Αἰτωλίας: cf. Strab. 8.8.1 (= ii. 540.26–7 Radt) ἡ τῶν Αἰτωλῶν... ἐρημία πρὸς ἱπποτροφίαν εὐφυὴς γέγονεν οὐχ ἧττον τῆς Θετταλίας. Central and northern Greece had strong associations with horse-rearing (cf. Spence (1993) 32).

705 ξανθαῖσι πώλοις: for ξανθός predicated of horses cf. Hom. *Il.* 9.407, S. fr. 475.2 *TrGF*, West (1965) 195 n. 4, Diggle on Eur. *Pha.* 74 = fr. 773.30 *TrGF*. Ξάνθιππος, –η are common Greek names.

Μάγνης ἀνήρ: for the horse-rearing capabilities of the Μάγνητες οἱ ἐπὶ Μαιάνδρῳ cf. Arist. *Pol.* 1289b38–40; but given the North Greek context it is more likely that Magnesia in Thessaly is meant. It is there that Jason asks for the λευκίππων... δόμους πατέρων (Pind. *P.* 4.117).

706 λεύκιππος: a traditional epithet of gods (cf. Pind. *O.* 6.95, Gow on Theocr. 13.11) and heroes (cf. Hom. *Il.* 10.437, Hippon. fr. 72.5–7 *IEG*, Ibyc. fr. 285.1 *PMGF*, Virg. *Aen.* 12.84). See further Braswell on Pind. *P.* 4.117a, Kannicht on *Hel.* 204–9, Hopkinson's edition of Callimachus' sixth *Hymn*, p. 40 with n. 2; also (for such horses as a mark of social status) Plaut. *Asin.* 279, Hor. *Sat.* 1.7.7–8 and (for their place in a Roman triumph) Bömer on Ov. *Fast.* 6.724.

Αἰνιὰν γένος: in Homer the Αἰνιῆνες are located around Mount Dodona (*Il.* 2.749–50), but by the time of Herodotus they are settled in the valley of the river Spercheus (cf. Visser (1997) 722 with n. 71, Stählin (1924) 219–21). There is no evidence for a settlement itself called Αἰνία (cf. Daux (1946)). The Αἰ– spelling in Homer is confirmed by papyri (West (2001) 182).

707 Ἀθηνῶν: προσχαρίζεται Ἀθηναίοις ἐν Ἀθηναίοις λέγων (Σ p. 135.14 Papageorgius): cf. 731 n. For Athens's cavalry see Spence (1993) 9–17.

θεοδμήτων: used of Athens at Eur. *Hipp.* 974, *IT* 1449. Found once in Homer (*Il.* 8.519), it is most common in epinician (cf. Pind. *O.* 6.59, Bacchyl. 11.58, Bergson (1956) 132).

708 Βοιωτός: cf. [Hes.] *Scut.* 24 Βοιωτοὶ πλήξιπποι. At Thuc. 3.62.5 the Thebans claim to be providing ἵππους τε... καὶ παρασκευὴν ὅσην οὐκ ἄλλοι τῶν ξυμμάχων (cf. 2.12.5, 2.22.2, Spence (1993) 19–22).

For ἄλλος used of a further member of a series cf. Aesch. *Sept.* 424 γίγας ὅδ' ἄλλος, *Suppl.* 220, Hdt. 4.54 πέμπτος ποταμὸς ἄλλος, Krüger §50.4.11.

δέκατον ἐκπληρῶν ὄχον: for ἐκπληρόω used of the final group described in a catalogue cf. Hdt. 7.186.2 οὗτοι... ἐκπληροῦσι τὰς ἴσας μυριάδας ἐκείνοισι, 9.30.

314

709 στάντες: cf. Hom. *Il.* 23.358 στὰν δὲ μεταστοιχί, Stat. *Theb.* 6.392 *stant uno margine clausi*, Quint. Smyrn. *Post.* 4.507 ἐπὶ νύσσῃ δ' ἔσταν ἕκαστοι.

ὅθ': elsewhere in tragedy ὅθι occurs only in lyric (*OC* 1044, fr. 730d.6 *TrGF*, and nine times in Euripides), and is never elided (though it is at e.g. Hom. *Il.* 10.520 ὅθ' ἕστασαν ὠκέες ἵπποι). Nauck[3] printed ἵνα, but it is hard to account for the corruption: ἵνα in this sense is common in S., and the rare ὅθι can hardly be a gloss. Some manuscripts have ὅτ', but we need a word meaning 'where', not 'when'. Ll-J/W mention Diggle's ὅθεν σφιν approvingly (*Sophoclea*). Noting Jebb's citation of the reading ὅθεν αὐτούς in Wc, Diggle compares *Tr.* 701–2 ἐκ δὲ γῆς, ὅθεν | προὔκειτ', Eur. *Tro.* 522–3 ἀνὰ δ' ἐβόασεν λεώς | Τρωϊάδος ἀπὸ πέτρας σταθείς and other passages where 'the preposition of motion away from is used in an anticipatory sense, reflecting a subsequent action named or implied in the context' (Mastronarde on Eur. *Phoen.* 1009; cf. Jebb on *Ant.* 411, Wackernagel (1926–8) i. 55). But in all his examples the clause exerting the attraction is close nearby. In our case we must wait more than two lines for the distant ᾖξαν; in the meantime, the proximity of στάντες and ὅθεν would seem curious.

Perhaps ὅθ' should be retained after all: the epicism is not out of place in a passage which already owes much to Homeric style and language. If the elision is offensive, Wecklein's ὅθι σφιν (in his third edition) would get rid of it; better would be the accusative plural σφᾶς (so Kuiper, *teste* van Paassen: also Powell (1905) 230; ὅπου σφᾶς *iam* Wecklein (1869a) 22). But ὅθι is commonly elided in Homer; and as in this passage it can only be defended as an epicism, it would be inconsistent to cavil at something with good epic precedent.

The mechanism used at Olympia to ensure that all the chariots started simultaneously is described at Paus. 6.20.10–13; cf. Harris (1968), Valavanis (1999) 5 n. 26. Attempts have been made on the basis of this passage to show that a similar structure was in use at Delphi (Martin (1898), Lacombrade (1959)). This must be the default hypothesis, but our text does not provide evidence one way or the other.

709–10 αὐτούς . . . | κλήροις ἔπηλαν 'sorted them with lots'. Many editors print αὐτοῖς and κλήρους (so C, *coni.* Wunder[2]). Campbell, however (followed by Ll-J/W), rightly prints the paradosis, citing the close Homeric parallels *Il.* 7.171 κλήρῳ νῦν πεπάλαχθε and *Od.* 9.331 τοὺς ἄλλους κλήρῳ πεπαλάσθαι ἄνωγον; cf. also Aesch. *Sept.* 731 χθόνα ναίειν διαπήλας, where the meaning is 'sort (by the casting of lots)'. κλήροις and ἔπηλαν make up, as it were, a single verbal idea. For this close connexion between the words Ll-J/W (*Sophoclea*) compare Hom. *Hymn* 4.129 κληροπαλεῖς and Stes. fr. 222(b).223 *PMGF* κλαροπαληδόν; add *Ant.* 396 κλῆρος . . . ἐπάλλετο. C's κλήρους is almost certainly not an ancient reading: this manuscript also has ἵππους at 712, and hence its scribe may have found it difficult to distinguish between iota and upsilon in its source (Dawe, *STS* i. 184).

For the allocation of starting-positions by lot cf. Hom. *Il.* 23.352–7, Stat. *Theb.* 6.389–90, Nonn. *Dion.* 37.226–9. According to Paus. 6.20.11, this was the procedure at the chariot race at Olympia.

βραβῆς: 690n.

710 κατέστησαν: cf. Pind. *P.* 9.114–14a ἔστασεν . . . ἅπαντα χορόν (sc. of competitors in a foot-race) | ἐν τέρμασιν αὐτίκ᾽ ἀγῶνος.

711 χαλκῆς ὑπαὶ σάλπιγγος: for the trumpet announcing the beginning of a race cf. Virg. *Aen.* 5.139–40, Ov. *Met.* 10.652–3, Stat. *Theb.* 6.404, Sid. Ap. *Carm.* 23.339; also Aesch. *Sept.* 393–4 (ἵππος) βοὴν σάλπιγγος ὁρμαίνει μένων, which may refer to a race or a battle. An Attic black-figure amphora, name vase of the Conservatori Painter (*c.* 530–20; Rome, Museo dei Conservatori 74; *ABV* 317, *Para.* 138, *Addenda*[2] 86) shows a stationary *tethrippon* from the front; its charioteer has his head turned to one side, as if waiting for the signal. See further Crowther (1994*b*) 142–3, 147 = (2004) 189–90, 193–4, Manakidou (1994) 42; for the ancient trumpet see West (1992) 118–21, Petretto (1995), Hale (2003).

ὑπαί: is found elsewhere in tragedy at 1418 (*coni.* Brunck), *Ant.* 1035, fr. 269c.20 *TrGF*, Aesch. *Ag.* 892, 944, *Eum.* 417, Eur. *El.* 1188. For its use in Homer see N. J. Richardson on Hom. *Hymn* 2.271; see further Schmitt (1967) 228–9. Moorhouse 130 claims the sense is causal, since the start of the race is the result of the sound; he is probably differentiating this meaning rather too sharply from the more common use denoting accompaniment (cf. 630n., Ar. *Ach.* 1001 πίνειν ὑπὸ τῆς σάλπιγγος; perhaps Simon. fr. 7.4 *IEG* ὡς ὑπὸ σάλ[πιγγος]).

ἦξαν: the verb of motion is prominently placed at the end of a long sense-unit, conveying the sudden motion of the horses at the beginning of the race. The following strong pause in an unusual place in the trimeter gives a jolting effect as the horses start; the subsequent lines (711–15) continue this untypical placing of pauses, which suggests the force and movement of the chariots (cf. the unusual placing of pauses in the account of Orestes' accident, where also a particular effect seems to be created (745n.)).

οἱ δ᾽ does not here mark a change of subject (448n.). For the accentuation see 45n.

712–13 ἵπποις ὁμοκλήσαντες ἡνίας χεροῖν | ἔσεισαν: the description is modelled on Hom. *Il.* 23.362–4 οἱ δ᾽ ἅμα πάντες ἐφ᾽ ἵπποιιν μάστιγας ἄειραν, | πέπληγόν θ᾽ ἱμᾶσιν ὁμόκλησάν τ᾽ ἐπέεσσιν | ἐσσυμένως; cf. also (for

316

exhortation coupled with shaking of the reins) Ov. *Met.* 5.403–4 *exhortatur equos, quorum per colla iubasque | excutit obscura tinctas ferrugine habenas.*

712 ἵπποις ὁμοκλήσαντες: for vocal encouragement to horses in a race cf. 737, Hom. *Il.* 23.402–16, 442–5, Stat. *Theb.* 6.460–6.

712–13 ἡνίας χεροῖν | ἔσεισαν: a plausible emendation at Eur. *IA* 151 would give us σεῖε χαλινούς. Note the vigorous verb at the end of a long sentence, emphasised by enjambment and the following pause: cf. Virg. *Georg.* 3.103–4, Ov. *Met.* 10.652–3, Stat. *Theb.* 6.404–5.

713 ἐν is probably adverbial (LSJ⁹ s.v. A V C) rather than in tmesis with ἐμεστώθη. The verb ἐμμεστόω is not found elsewhere; but as one of the two surviving instances of the adjective ἔμμεστος is in S. (fr. 314.289 *TrGF*), the tmesis cannot be ruled out. The same holds for *Ant.* 420–1 ἐν δ' ἐμεστώθη μέγας | αἰθήρ; for other possible examples see Moorhouse 94, Bruhn §63.3.

δρόμος: here 'racecourse', at 726 'lap'; for the various meanings of this word in sporting contexts see Crowther (1993a) = (2004) 241–4.

714 κτύπου κροτητῶν ἁρμάτων: cf. Hom. *Il.* 11.160 ὄχεα κροτάλιζον, 15.453 ὄχεα κροτέοντες, [Hes.] *Scut.* 308–9 τὰ δ' ἐπικροτέοντα πέτοντα | ἅρματα κολλήεντ', *Hom. Hymn* 3.234 ὄχεα κροτέουσιν, Ar. *Eq.* 552 χαλκοκρότων ἵππων κτύπος.

κροτητῶν 'rattling'. Jebb *ad loc.* rightly rejects his former interpretation 'welded'; the context, parallels and alliteration of κ and τ all support a reference to sound (cf. fr. 241.1 *TrGF*). Verbal adjectives in –τός originally had neither an active nor a passive meaning, and in our period can usually have either sense: see Wackernagel (1926–8) i. 136, 288, Fraenkel on Aesch. *Ag.* 12, Barrett on Eur. *Hipp.* 677–9, Moorhouse 171.

714–15 κόνις δ' ἄνω | φορεῖθ': cf. Hom. *Il.* 23.365–6 ὑπὸ δὲ στέρνοισι κονίη | ἵστατ' ἀειρομένη ὥς τε νέφος ἠὲ θύελλα, 372 κονίοντες πεδίοιο, 11.151–2, [Hes.] *Scut.* 62–3 κόνις δέ σφ' ἀμφιδεδήει | κοπτομένη πλεκτοῖσιν ὑφ' ἅρμασι καὶ ποσὶν ἵππων, Simon. fr. 516 *PMG* κονία δὲ παρὰ τροχὸν μεταμώνιος ἤρθη, Eur. *El.* 476–7 τετραβάμονες ἵπποι ἔπαλλον, | κελαινὰ δ' ἀμφὶ νῶθ' ἵετο κόνις, Moretti (1953) 94 = Ebert (1972) 176 = *SGO* i. 06/02/21 ὁ δ' Ἀττάλου ἴσος ἀέλλῃ | δίφρος ἀεὶ προτέραν ποσ[σ]ὶν ἔφαινε κόνιν (Pergamum, *c.* 280–72 BC), Virg. *Georg.* 3.110–11 *at fulvae nimbus harenae | tollitur*, Stat. *Theb.* 6.411–12, Quint. Smyrn. *Post.* 4.518–21, [Lucian] 58.24, Nonn. *Dion.* 37.284–5.

715 φορεῖθ': –αι does not elide in tragedy (Diggle (1984b) 67 = (1994) 313; *pace* Hose (1994)). Hence this must be an augmentless past tense, like φείδοντο

317

in the following line. Outside lyrics, where they are common (Diggle (1981a) 65–6), there are 17 instances of unaugmented past tense verbs in tragedy (listed and discussed by Page on Eur. *Med.* 1141). All occur in messenger speeches. In 12 cases emendation to restore the augment would be metrically impossible. 15 instances are line-initial; one of the others is sentence-initial. In only 4 cases does the word at the end of the preceding line end with a vowel or diphthong, and hence the lack of the augment cannot be put down to aphaeresis (see Kaibel on 714 (p. 182), Bergson (1953) 124–5). Omission of the augment is frequent in Homer, occurring in about half of finite verb forms; the phenomenon is commoner in narrative than in speeches. Page (*ib.*) duly regards the lack of the augment as an epicism, arguing that 'in this least dramatic, most epic, part of his play the poet turns to the language of the epic poets for one or two tricks of style'. Bergson disagrees, on the grounds that such forms are rare in tragic messenger speeches. Noting that nearly all the instances are in initial position, he claims that they are metrically conditioned: 'an anapaest formed by an augmented verb was avoided by the tragic poets in the first foot of the iambic dialogue' ((1953) 126). But first-foot anapaests are not uncommon in the tragic trimeter (West (1982a) 81–2): with Bergson's thesis we gain a slight metrical benefit at the price of a startling morphological irregularity. Furthermore, were Bergson right, we would expect a wider distribution of the phenomenon, even given the frequency of past tenses in messenger speeches (so Dodds, in his edition of Euripides' *Bacchae*, p. 170 n. 2).

ὁμοῦ . . . πάντες: for the intensificatory sense of this combination see Mastronarde on Eur. *Phoen.* 1192.

ἀναμεμειγμένοι: so Kaibel for transmitted ἀναμεμιγμένοι. Inscriptional evidence suggests that μειγ– rather than μιγ– was usual with this verb until at least well into the fourth century, although the present itself is not attested until late (Threatte ii. 623–4).

716 κέντρων: charioteers in tragedy tend to be equipped with goads (Pearson on fr. 129; these have a double point, if we can generalise from *OR* 809). On the other hand, the words κέντρον and μάστιγξ seem to be interchangeable in Homer (cf. *Il.* 23.384, 387, 390), and thus the same might apply here.

ὡς 'in order that', not 'whenever': '[the latter] would imply that no driver used his goad until a rival was about to pass him; whereas we require rather a picture of the eagerness which each man felt to outstrip the rest' (Jebb). For this eagerness cf. Chrysippus *SVF* iii.726 (*ap.* Sen. *Ben.* 2.25.3) *magna illi* (i.e. a competitor at the start of the race) *contentione opus est, magna celeritate, ut consequatur antecedentem* (van Arnim incorrectly transposes *celeritate* and *contentione*).

717 χνόας: the 'nave' or 'hub' of the wheel; cf. Parmenides D–K 28 B 1.6–8 (= i. 229.1–3), Emped. D–K 31 B 46 (= i. 331.12) (*coni.* Panzerbieter), Aesch.

Sept. 153 ἔλακον ἀξόνων βριθομένων χνόαι, 371, fr. 451 m.35.1 *TrGF*, [Eur.] *Rhes.* 118. On the orthography see Pfeiffer on Call. fr. 384.5.

ἄλλων: *coni.* Musgrave. Transmitted αὐτῶν must be taken with either τις (= ἕκαστος τις: cf. LSJ⁹ s.v. τις A II 2) or χνόας . . . καὶ φρυάγμαθ᾽ ἱππικά. The former gives us '(they made every effort) in order that each one of them might overtake the axles and neighing horses', the latter '. . . so that each one might overtake their axles and neighing horses'. In each case αὐτῶν appears unpleasantly otiose, while we are missing a word for 'the others' in the genitive to qualify χνόας . . . καὶ φρυάγμαθ᾽ ἱππικά. Lloyd-Jones felt the need for such a word in his Loeb, where he translates 'each hoping to pass the wheels and the snorting horses *of the others*' (my italics): yet it cannot be recovered from the text which he prints. Musgrave's conjecture neatly solves each of these problems at minimal palaeographical cost; it is thus more convincing than Dawe's ἰτύων (in his third edition; cf. (1998) 121–2).

φρυάγμαθ᾽ ἱππικά: an elevated periphrasis for ἵππους φρυασσομένους, also found at Aesch. *Sept.* 245, 475. S. 'frequently makes abstract nouns and epithet exchange places in lyric or ornate dialogue as a means of embellishing the style' (Long (1968) 77, comparing 1358 and *Aj.* 632–4; add 754).

718–19 On Dawe's transposition of these lines to after 740 see 720–2n.

718 γάρ: how does the breathing of horses on the backs of the charioteers in front (718–19) constitute a reason for the repeated attempts of one charioteer to overtake the other (715–17)? Denniston 61 warns us that 'the connexion of thought [with γάρ] is sometimes lacking in logical precision', though that does not solve the difficulty. Perhaps each charioteer is under pressure to overtake those in front of him because of the constant pressure he is experiencing at his own back: so close are the chariots that each rider must overtake or himself be overtaken.

Radt (1971) 200 n. 1 = (2002) 65 n. 20 claims that the γάρ must mean ὥστε, which would be attractive if it were possible. But his parallels do not convince: *Phil.* 701 usually has its γάρ emended away on metrical grounds, *Ant.* 620 can be interpreted as a regular γάρ ('no-one realises the potentially disastrous consequences of hope, for a man's wits are confused when the gods are leading him to disaster') and *OR* 582 is not comparable (cf. Denniston 244 (4), cited by Radt). This leaves *Phil.* 1053–4 νῦν δὲ σοί γ᾽ ἑκὼν ἐκστήσομαι. | ἄφετε γὰρ αὐτόν, which Denniston 61 puts in a class of its own, saying that the particle provides 'confirmation of what precedes': but the single use of γάρ in this sense to introduce a command cannot be compared with its appearance in a passage of narrative. The difficulty of this γάρ is not an argument in favour of Dawe's transposition (720–2n.): it is no less difficult after 740 than after 717.

τροχῶν βάσεις: periphrasis for τροχοὺς βαίνοντας. Long (1968) 100 n. 130 sees this expression as one of 'a group of ornate expressions containing verbal nouns' in the speech, comparing 681–2, 725 and 740; cf. also the more ornamental language at 698–9, 717, 754. 'Sophocles has permitted himself in this speech of intrigue a kind of diction which as a tragic writer he had probably long abandoned' (Reinhardt (1979) 151 ≈ (1949) 161). These embellishments do not reach the levels of linguistic daring found in lyric (whether tragic or epinician); but in company with the features identified at 680–763n. they give an epinician flavour to the style (cf. expressions such as Pind. *P.* 2.12 σθένος ἵππιον, *O.* 6.22 etc.).

719 ἤφριζον, εἰσέβαλλον: verbal asyndeton is common in tragic lyric (Diggle (1974) 10 = (1994) 99–100) and dialogue (Mastronarde on Eur. *Phoen.* 1193). The second verb almost never has fewer syllables than the first, and usually has more. Cf. 1380, *Aj.* 60, K–G ii. 340–1, Bruhn §158.

ἱππικαὶ πνοαί: cf. Hom. *Il.* 23.380–1 πνοιῇ δ' Εὐμήλοιο μετάφρενον εὕρεε τ' ὤμω | θέρμετ'; also 13.385–6, 17.501–2, Virg. *Georg.* 3.111 *umescunt spumis flatuque sequentum*, Nonn. *Dion.* 37.294–6 Ἐρεχθέος ἵππος ἀγήνωρ | διχθαδίῳ μυκτῆρι παλίμπνοον ἄσθμα τιταίνων | ἀλλοτρίου θέρμαινε μετάφρενον ἡνιοχῆος. Ll-J/W (*Sophoclea*) compare the variants on this motif at Bacchyl. 5.43–5 οὔπω νιν ὑπὸ προτέ[ρω]ν | ἵππων ἐν ἀγῶνι κατέχρανεν κόνις | πρὸς τέλος ὀρνύμενον and Call. fr. 254.8–9 *SH* ἔθρεξαν προ[τέρω]ν†οὗτινες† ἡνιόχων | ἄσθματι χλι[αίνοντες ἐ]πωμίδας (οὗτινας *coni.* Kassel); cf. its transference to an amatory context by Ovid at *Met.* 1.541–2, 5.616–17.

720–2 For Orestes' tactic cf. Hom. *Il.* 23.334 (Nestor advises Antilochus) τῷ [sc. the turning-post] σὺ μάλ' ἐγχρίμψας ἐλάαν σχεδὸν ἅρμα καὶ ἵππους, Xen. *Symp.* 4.6 ἁρματηλατοῦντα δεῖ ἐγγὺς μὲν τῆς στήλης κάμψαι, Posid. 79.3–4 A–B τάχει δ' ἀπελίμπανεν ἵππων | δίφρος ἐπεὶ [κάμψα]ι τὸν πολὺν ἡνίοχον, Theocr. 24.119–20 (Amphitryon teaches the young Heracles) ἵππους δ' ἐξελάσασθαι ὑφ' ἅρματι καὶ περὶ νύσσαν | ἀσφαλέως κάμπτοντα τροχοῦ σύριγγα φυλάξαι, Virg. *Aen.* 5.162–4, Ov. *Ars* 2.426 *interior curru meta terenda meo est* with Janka, Stat. *Theb.* 6.440–2, Nonn. *Dion.* 37.205–6, Apostol. 9.65 = *CPG* ii. 475.10–13 with García Romero (2001) 78–9. Orestes follows to the letter the advice given by Nestor to Antilochus; this ironically leads not to victory, but to death. J. Barrett (2002) 140–9 tries to show that Orestes' strategy, like the one recommended by Nestor, is one based on μῆτις, and that this parallels his preference for δόλος in the attempt to avenge his father. But there is no reference to any μῆτις on Orestes' part in the speech: his tactic is ambitious, but involves no trickery.

COMMENTARY: 516–822

Piccolomini (1877) 756–7 transposed 720–2 after 740;[45] Pearson followed him, as did Dawe, who asks (*STS* i. 185) 'why should Orestes' technique of driving round the end pillar be mentioned before the general accident, in which he was not involved, when it was his failure with this technique which led to the particular accident which caused his death?' There is a good reason why: an early mention of these risky tactics will make an attentive audience suspect that they will cause Orestes' downfall, and through the rest of the narrative this ominous anticipation will persist. A lesser objection to Piccolomini is that with the transposition Orestes is not mentioned in the narrative for a full thirty lines (704–734): rather large a gap in a narrative where he is the only figure of interest.[46]

Dawe (*STS* i. 184–7) in fact goes even further than Piccolomini, transposing 718–19 as well as 720–2; Günther ((1996) 54–8) transposes 718–19 too, while also (bizarrely) deleting 720–2. But 718–19 make better sense when describing the massed group of chariots, rather than the final two competitors (so Ll-J/W, *Sophoclea*); nor do we want this general description slowing down the narrative at its high point. Dawe (p. 185) finds the γάρ difficult to understand in its current location. In fact it is no more and no less difficult than it would be in the new position which he advocates for it.

720 ὑπ' 'up close to': cf. Hom. *Il.* 13.615 ἄκρον ὑπὸ λόφον αὐτόν, Moorhouse 129.

ἐσχάτην 'the post at the end of the course'. The word could also mean 'the edge of the turning-post' (cf. 744, 900–1); but 720–1 already give sufficient emphasis to the closeness of the turning chariot to the post.

στήλην 'turning post' (cf. Xen. *Symp.* 4.6). The epic word is νύσσα, whereas elsewhere in tragedy καμπή is found (Eur. *El.* 659, *IA* 224); καμπτήρ occurs at e.g. Xen. *Cyr.* 7.1.6. Vase paintings suggest that in the early fifth century it took the form of a moderately tall pillar on a broad two-stepped base (e.g. *ABV* 430.21, cited 721–2n.).

ἔχων: sc. τοὺς ἵππους; cf. Hom. *Il.* 23.325 ἀλλ' ἔχει ἀσφαλέως καὶ τὸν προὔχοντα δοκεύει.

721 ἔχριμπτ': used transitively elsewhere at [Aesch.] *PV* 712–13 and (accepting Diggle's conjecture) Eur. *Hcld.* 824; cf. Diggle (1982a) 62 = (1994) 227.

[45] Burges had already transposed 720–2 to after 733 (his edition of Euripides' *Troades*, p. xxii).

[46] Kaibel opposed the transposition on the grounds that κεῖνος δ' would be ambiguous after 740 (p. 184 n.1; cf. Ll-J/W, *Sophoclea*, Günther (1996) 56). But bare κεῖνος describes Orestes at 681, 698 and 703, and it would be no more ambiguous after 740 than after 719 (cf. Dawe, *STS* i. 186).

321

Manuscript omission of the μ with this verb is common (cf. Diggle (*ib.*) and Friis Johansen and Whittle on Aesch. *Suppl.* 790).

σύριγγα 'pipe', and hence any hollow object. Here it denotes the inner part of the wheel through which goes the axle, the 'nave' or 'hub'. In this sense, not found before the fifth century, it is synonymous with χνόη (717n.): cf. Hesych. χ 568 (= iv. 290 Schmidt) χνόαι· αἱ χοινικίδες, αἱ τοῦ ἄξονος σύριγγες. Lexicographers sometimes claim it refers to the opening in the nave, but this is never a necessary sense, and is sometimes impossible. At Aesch. *Suppl.* 181 σύριγγες οὐ σιγῶσιν ἀξονήλατοι (where see Friis Johansen and Whittle) and *Sept.* 205 σύριγγες ἔκλαγξαν ἑλίτροχοι the screeching noises are not being made by a *hole*; nor can the word be so translated at Eur. *Hipp.* 1234 σύριγγές τ' ἄνω | τροχῶν ἐπήδων ('holes do not fly in the air': Barrett *ad loc.*).

721–2 δεξιὸν δ' ἀνεὶς | σειραῖον ἵππον εἶργε τὸν προσκείμενον: at Hom. *Il.* 23.336–7 Nestor advises his son (at the moment of the turn) ἀτὰρ τὸν δεξιὸν ἵππον | κένσαι ὁμοκλήσας, εἶξαί τέ οἱ ἡνία χερσίν; cf. Ov. *Amor.* 3.2.72 *tende, precor, valida lora sinistra manu*, Stat. *Theb.* 6.440–2. This exact manoeuvre is depicted on a Panathenaic black-figure amphora from the Leagros Group (*c.* 520–500; Taranto 4595 (9887); *ABV* 369.113, *Addenda²* 98): the charioteer loosens his hold on the right trace-horse while straining to hold back the left. An Attic black-figure oenochoe of *c.* 500 (Class of Vatican G.47, Athens, National Museum 523, *ABV* 430.21) depicts chariots turning round the στήλη in a similar fashion.

For more on trace-horses see Vigneron (1968) 117–21. Their purpose was to assist at the turn (cf. Eur. *IA* 224 ἀντήρεις καμπαῖσι δρόμων); this need for sudden action from the right-hand horse at a moment of need explains Ares' epithet δεξιόσειρος at *Ant.* 140. But such horses will also have given extra power for running the lengths of the course. An Attic black-figure kylix of *c.* 550 in the manner of the Heidelberg Painter (Athens, National Museum 529; *ABV* 67.1, *Para.* 27) shows several *tethrippa* where the trace-horses are moving more energetically than the central pairs. Aesch. *Ag.* 1640–1 implies that trace-horses were given special rations (see Fraenkel on 1641). There are no such horses in the race in *Iliad* 23; when they are used in Homer, there appears to have been only one of them per chariot (the παρήορος of e.g. Hom. *Il.* 16.470–1, *Od.* 4.590).

722 εἶργε τὸν προσκείμενον 'checked the horse on the inner side'. Ll-J/W, *Sophoclea* incorrectly take this to mean 'blocked off his pursuer'. Rather, 'we need a contrast between his action with the trace-horse and his action with the horse on the near side (προσκείμενον, sc. τῇ στήλῃ) . . . The purpose of giving the right trace-horse its head is to ensure that it runs faster than the inside horse, because it has a greater distance to travel in the same time. Blocking a rival is no part of this technique' (Diggle, *per litteras*). Ll-J/W cite Nestor's advice to Antilochus in *Iliad* 23, but nothing there supports their interpretation.

723 μέν: 'premonitory of the reversal of fortune' (Kamerbeek on 741–2); cf. 741, *Tr.* 763, Eur. *Ion* 1201 καὶ ταῖς μὲν ἄλλαις ἄνοσος ἦν λοιβὴ θεοῦ. It is picked up by ἔπειτα in 724 (cf. 741–3, Denniston 376–7). The Paedagogus prepares us for imminent disaster by stressing that the charioteers had been safe up to this point. This technique is used again, with greater force, at 741–2.

ὀρθοί 'safely' (742n.).

ἕστασαν: the regular Attic and Homeric 3rd plural pluperfect form (S–D i. 665δ, 776–7); cf. Hom. *Il.* 23.369–70 τοὶ δ' ἐλατῆρες | ἕστασαν ἐν δίφροισι.

δίφροις: most manuscripts have δίφροι, but while ὀρθοί could qualify either drivers or chariots (cf. 742), it would be inept to use ἕστασαν of the latter. Kaibel's δίφρῳ (p. 185) is possible, but the Homeric parallel and manuscript support tip the balance in favour of the plural.

The nature of the chariot pile-up is set out by Greene (1907) 137 (after Musgrave): 'the Aenian, who is leading, has got round the post, and is preparing to drive back in the opposite direction to the other competitors . . . Directly after the turn has been made . . . his horses bolt, swerve to the left, and meet the Barcaean team, the second in the race, front to front'. As he notes, μέτωπα συμπαίουσι strongly suggests a head to head collision, as at Lucian 34.1 τὰ μέτωπα συναράττουσιν ὥσπερ οἱ κριοί. Jebb's notion that the Aenian collides with the left side of the Barcaean chariot is therefore untenable. Greene quotes from a letter from Jebb, who acknowledges the advantage of this interpretation over his own.

724 ἄστομοι: a word with a variety of meanings: 'unable to speak' (S. fr. 76 *TrGF*), 'unable to hold with the teeth' (Xen. *Cyn.* 3.3), 'without a mouth' (e.g. Strab. 2.1.9 = i. 174.22 Radt), and possibly 'without speaking' (if restored at fr. 269a.29 *TrGF*). The Suda s.v. στόμις ἵππος (σ 1137 = iv. 437.12 Adler) has ἀπειθὴς καὶ βίαιος, ὄν τινες ἄστομόν φασι (cf. Aeschylus' use of στόμις to mean ὁ ὥσπερ στόματι ἀντερείδων χαλινοῖς at fr. 442 *TrGF*): this must be the sense here. How it means ἀπειθής is another question: perhaps 'without a στόμιον' developed into 'without a mouth to feel or obey the στόμιον' (so Kugler (1905) 4–5; hence perhaps Σ p. 136.10 Papageorgius σκληρόστομοι). Bruhn claims that it represents an intensified form of δύστομος (cf. Leontius Scholasticus *A.Pl.* 16.361.3–4 οὔτε χαλινοῖς | δύστομος ἱππείη σοῖς ἀπίθησε γένυς), but this is less plausible, as there seems to be only a single, late, parallel for δύστομος used in this sense.

725 βίᾳ φέρουσιν sc. τὸ ἅρμα. The same phrase is used of horses bolting at Eur. *Hipp.* 1224; cf. also Aesch. *Cho.* 1023–4 φέρουσι γὰρ νικώμενον | φρένες δύσαρκτοι, where the image of horses careering off course is used figuratively (cf. Dover on Ar. *Ran.* 995).

φέρουσι is the first historic present in the speech. This device lends greater vividness to the narrative, presenting it as if it were happening at the time of speaking (cf. [Longinus] *De subl.* 25 ὅταν γε μὴν τὰ παρεληλυθότα τοῖς χρόνοις εἰσάγῃς ὡς γινόμενα καὶ παρόντα, οὐ διήγησιν ἔτι τὸν λόγον ἀλλ' ἐναγώνιον πρᾶγμα ποιήσεις, S–D ii. 271–2). In tragedy it is especially common in messenger speeches; de Jong sees it as 'in keeping with the messenger's technique of mentally going back in time and recounting the events as he experienced them, . . . of narrating according to his experiencing focalization' ((1991) 45; cf. 696–7n.). In our passage it occurs nine times (725, 727, 732 (twice), 736, 738, 744, 746, 749); in the same section of narrative (724–56) there are eleven past tense indicatives. Although numbers of present and past tense forms are about equal, and although past tenses are used for dramatic occurrences (e.g. 729, 745–6) and present tenses for less arresting ones (e.g. 732), it is nevertheless notable that present forms are used for the initial crash and Orestes' striking of the turning-post, which are arguably the two most crucial events in the narrative. Similar effects are discussed in *Ant.* 407–36, *OR* 794–813, *OC* 1587–1655 by Moorhouse 185–6 and in Aesch. *Ag.* 281–311, 1382–92, *Pers.* 181–99 by Fraenkel on *Ag.* 1383. But de Jong's formulation, that 'historic presents highlight actions which are thereby marked (by the speaker) as important or decisive' ((1991) 41) is too strong. In 425, for example, δείκνυσι is a historic present, but there is no reason for that action to be marked. It seems rather that especially striking actions tend to be put in the historic present, but that it is also used for more ordinary ones to increase the vividness of the narrative as a whole.

Further examples and discussions at 902n., K–G i. 132–4, Bruhn §103–4, Wackernagel (1926–8) i. 162–5, de Jong (1991) 185–7, Sicking and Stork (1997) 137–45, Rijksbaron (2006).

ἐκ δ' ὑποστροφῆς: used to mean 'wheeling right round' in Polybius (e.g. 3.14.5); cf. Hdt. 9.22.3 ἀναχωρήσιός τε γινομένης καὶ ὑποστροφῆς. Since it seems to denote complete reversal of movement, it must here refer simply to the turning round the post, and not to any accompanying swerving (*pace* Campbell, Jebb, Kaibel (p. 185)). For ἐκ cf. 48n.

726 τελοῦντος *coni.* Musgrave; –ντες codd. The sixth and seventh laps of a chariot race cannot be completed simultaneously. Hence the word must mean 'finishing' with ἕκτον and 'entering upon' with ἕβδομον. The alternative, that one chariot has lapped another, is less obvious. Blaydes' suggests that the sense is 'sixth *or* seventh', comparing Hom. *Od.* 2.374 and Thuc. 1.82.2: add the ambiguity of Proverbs 6.16 'these six things doth the Lord hate: yea, seven are an abomination unto him'. But such an ambiguity would not accord with the precision found elsewhere in the speech.

The paradosis reads τελοῦντες, but πῶλοι are usually feminine (cf. 705, 734). The instances cited by Jebb to show that they can be masculine are all in the singular and therefore irrelevant: the same gender distinction also applies to horses (703–4n.). There is no good evidence to suggest that a participle in –ντες may qualify a feminine (see Fraenkel on Aesch. *Ag.* 562), and so emendation is required. Musgrave's alteration neatly solves our difficulty by giving us a participle which qualifies the driver of the horses rather than the horses themselves. The corruption will have arisen out of a belief that the participle should qualify the subject of συμπαίουσι in 727 rather than the relatively more distant Αἰνιᾶνος ἀνδρός of 724.

ἕκτον ἕβδομόν τ': the *tethrippon* at the historical Pythian Games had twelve double laps (cf. Pind. *P.* 5.33), as also at the Olympics (*id. O.* 2.50, 3.33, 6.75); cf. H. M. Lee (1986) 170–3.

δρόμον: 713n.

727 For the founding of Barca (*c.* 600–550 BC) see Hdt. 4.160.1.

728–30 The mass chariot crash is depicted in classical literature with surprising frequency: cf. Aesch. fr. 38.1 *TrGF* ἐφ' ἅρματος γὰρ ἅρμα καὶ νεκρῷ νεκρός (from a description of the chariot-crash where Glaucus is fatally wounded), Pind. *P.* 5.49–51 ἐν τεσσαράκοντα γὰρ | πετόντεσσιν ἀνιόχοις ὅλον | δίφρον κομίξαις ἀταρβεῖ φρενί, Ar. *Pax* 901–4 ἅρματα δ' ἐπ' ἀλλήλοισιν ἀνατετραμμένα | φυσῶντα καὶ πνέοντα προσκινήσεται· | ἕτεροι δὲ κείσονταί γ' ἀπεψωλημένοι | περὶ ταῖσι καμπαῖς ἡνίοχοι πεπτωκότες. According to [Dem.] 61.29, for many people ἐν τοῖς ἱππικοῖς ἀγῶσιν ἡδίστην θέαν παρέχεται τὰ ναυαγοῦντα (!). For more on the dangers of such racing see Crowther (1994a) = (2004) 229–40.

730 ναυαγίων Κρισαῖον ἱππικῶν πέδον: for the interlaced word-order see Diggle (1993) 136–7 = (1994) 419–20. For the metaphor in ναυαγίων cf. 1444, [Dem.] 61.29 (cited above, 728–30n.), Wærn (1951) 56, van Nes (1963) 107–8, C. P. Segal (1981) 267–8. The naval imagery is sustained in 732–3 (κάνοκωχεύει, κλύδων', κυκώμενον). For the reverse image (ships compared to horses or chariots) see Hordern on Timoth. fr. 791.17 *PMG*.

Κρισαῖον . . . πέδον: the Delphic hippodrome was located beneath the sanctuary, in the plain of Crisa (cf. Paus. 10.37.4, *CID* i. 10.35–6 = *IG* ii–iii² 1126.35–6), a fact often alluded to in epinician (e.g. Pind. *P.* 5.34–9, Bacchyl. 4.14).

731 οὐξ Ἀθηνῶν δεινὸς ἡνιοστρόφος: πρὸς εὔνοιαν . . . τῶν ἀκροωμένων ἐπαινεῖ αὐτὸν ὡς Ἀθηναῖον (Σ p. 136.17–18 Papageorgius); cf. Arist. *Rhet.* 1367b8–9 οὐ χαλεπὸν Ἀθηναίους ἐν Ἀθηναίοις ἐπαινεῖν (referring to Pl. *Menex.* 235d), Quint. *Inst.* 3.7.23–4, R. C. T. Parker (1997) 150 n. 27, Fraenkel (in my Appendix 2).

732 κάνοκωχεύει: the transmitted κάνα- is a mistake commonly found when dealing with this verb. The simplex ὀκωχεύειν is defined by Hesychius (o 504 = ii. 749 Latte) as ἔχειν, συνέχειν. It is probably derived from ὄκωχα, an old Ionic perfect of ἔχω restored by Cobet (1856) 188–9 = (1858) 168–9 at Hom. *Il.* 2.218 συνοκωχότε, and so printed by West. S. fr. 327 *TrGF* reads πιστοί με κωχέουσιν ἐν φορᾷ δέμας, but the verb κωχεύω is not found elsewhere and has no obvious origin, and Pearson adopted Schmidt's emendation μ' ὀκωχεύουσιν. The verb ἀνακωχεύω ('hold back', trans. or intrans.) and noun ἀνακωχή ('cessation, armistice') are found in the manuscripts of Herodotus and Thucydides (e.g. Hdt. 6.116, 9.13.1, Thuc. 1.40.4, 4.117.1, 5.32.7), always with α-vocalism. However, at Thuc. 4.38.1 P.Oxy. 16 (1st cent. AD) col. i. 48 has the form with o-vocalism written above the line. Ael. Dion. *Attika Onomata* α 144 (= p. 107.9 Erbse) tells us ἀνοκωχήν διὰ τοῦ ο τὴν ἀνοχὴν λέγουσι· πολὺ δέ ἐστι παρὰ Θουκυδίδη. Hence we should probably restore the o-vocalism in Thucydides. Whether we should do the same in Herodotus and here is open to question. Chantraine (1928) 12–13 accepts the testimony of [Ammon.] *De adf. voc. diff.* 46 (p. 13.10–13 Nickau), which gives different definitions of ἀνακωχή and ἀνοκωχή; Cobet, on the other hand ((1856) 189 = (1858) 169) thunders '*hoc probum et genuinum est, illud ex Graeculorum inscitia profectum et* τοῦ πονηροῦ κόμματος'. In such a situation Occam's Razor is the only guide: it does not seem plausible that in the fifth century there were two sets of forms, with the same meaning, differing only in a single vowel. The remarks of the later grammarians are an attempt to deal with a situation where textual corruption has created the α-vocalism forms alongside the originals (cf. Chantraine (1999) s.v. ἔχω §5: 'l'orthographie ἀνα- s'est répandue par oubli de la forme redoublée originelle').

The scholia note how the word is used μεταφορικῶς of riding out a storm (p. 136.21–6 Papageorgius); cf. 730n.

733 κλύδων: normally 'billow' (e.g. *OR* 197, *OC* 1687); used metaphorically of a surging mass at Pl. *Leg.* 758a5–6 πόλις . . . ἐν κλύδωνι τῶν ἄλλων πόλεων διαγομένη.

κυκώμενον: often used of seething rivers and seas (cf. Hom. *Il.* 21.235, 240, 324, *Od.* 12.241).

734 ἔσχατος μέν: corresponds with ὃ δ' ὡς in 736 ('he was last, but when he saw he was the only one left . . .').

734–5 ὑστέρας ἔχων | πώλους: the adjective probably means 'inferior' rather than 'in last position'. The latter sense would be pointlessly pleonastic with ἔσχατος; while the former nicely parallels Homer's Antilochus, whose horses are βάρδιστοι θείειν (*Il.* 23.310). Nestor's words at 319–23 are especially relevant: ἄλλος μέν θ᾿ ἵπποισι καὶ ἅρμασιν οἷσι πεποιθὼς | ἀφραδέως ἐπὶ πολλὸν ἑλίσσεται ἔνθα καὶ ἔνθα, | ἵπποι δὲ πλανόωνται ἀνὰ δρόμον, οὐδὲ κατίσχει· | ὃς δέ κε κέρδεα εἰδῇ ἐλαύνων ἥσσονας ἵππους, | αἰεὶ τέρμ᾿ ὁρόων στρέφει ἐγγύθεν κτλ.

735 Ὀρέστης: the name is held back for dramatic effect (cf. 602n.).

τῷ τέλει πίστιν φέρων: for Orestes' tactic cf. Nestor's strategy quoted in the previous note; also Cic. *Acad.* 2.94 *ego enim, ut agitator callidus, prius quam ad finem veniam, equos sustinebo,* Lucilius fr. 1305 Marx *sustineas currum, ut bonus saepe agitator equosque,* Liban. *Epist.* 1438.1 σκόπει οὖν ὅπως ἀεὶ τὰ δεύτερα ἔσται βελτίω. τοιοῦτοι γὰρ οἱ τῶν δρομέων ἀγαθοί with García Romero (2001) 15–17. Günther (1996) 57 n. 149 gives a modern parallel. For the periphrasis cf. *OR* 1445; also 30n.

736 ὃ δ᾿ ὡς does not imply a change of subject (448n.); it also gives a livelier start to the sentence in which Orestes accelerates, just as it does at the beginning of the race in 711. The minority variant ὅπως δ᾿ may be an unconscious anticipation of 749, where too the phrase precedes ὁρᾷ. Cf. perhaps also *OR* 1265, where Ll-J/W print Blaydes's ὁ δ᾿ ὡς ὁρᾷ for transmitted ὅπως (δ᾿) ὁρᾷ. For the accentuation see 45n.

737 δι᾿ ὤτων: cf. 1437, Gow on Theocr. 14.27. For the vocal encouragement of horses see 712n.

ἐνσείσας 'sent vibrating' through the ears; for this meaning 'drive in (with force)' cf. *Ant.* 1274 ἐν δ᾿ ἔσεισεν ἀγρίαις ὁδοῖς, LSJ⁹ s.v. ἐνσείω I 1.

739 ἄλλος . . . ἅτερος: for the combination cf. Hom. *Il.* 9.313 ὅς χ᾿ ἕτερον μὲν κεύθῃ ἐνὶ φρεσίν, ἄλλο δὲ εἴπῃ, Hdt. 1.32.8, Theocr. 7.36 (with Gow for the omission of the article with one of the correlatives). For the partitive apposition with ἠλαυνέτην cf. *Ant.* 411–14, Xen. *An.* 7.3.47 οἱ ἱππεῖς οἴχονταί μοι ἄλλος ἄλλῃ διώκων, Pl. *Phaedr.* 248a8–9 [αἱ ψυχαὶ] συμπεριφέρονται . . . ἑτέρα πρὸ τῆς ἑτέρας πειρωμένη γενέσθαι.

740 κάρα προβάλλων ἱππικῶν ὀχημάτων: ἱππικῶν ὀχημάτων goes with κάρα; the latter refers analogically to 'man, car, and steeds, considered as one object' (so Campbell). Jebb prefers to take ἱππ. ὀχ. as governed by the προ of προβάλλων, translating 'showing his head in front of the chariots'. This dynamic image is common on vases (e.g. an Attic black-figure stamnos of *c.* 510

attributed to the Michigan Painter (Würzburg 327; *ABV* 343.5, *Addenda²* 93));
cf. also *pronus* at Virg. *Georg.* 3.107, *Aen.* 5.147, 10.586, Stat. *Theb.* 6.416. But
the presence of the adjective ἱππικῶν with ὀχημάτων suggests that the noun
denotes not just the chariot, but the chariot and horses taken together (for
this usage cf. Diggle on Eur. *Pha.* 173 = fr. 779.6 *TrGF*). Hence the charioteers
cannot be leaning forward in front of them. Furthermore, the point at issue
ought to be the relative position not of the drivers' heads, but of the teams as
a whole. It is that which will determine the result.

741–2 As at 723 (n.), these lines act as foil to the imminent disaster. In repeating
the motif, S. has made it more dramatic: hence the imperfect (implying an
imminent punctual action), the reference to Orestes as ὁ τλήμων (the first
such 'proleptic' remark since the *gnome* of 696–7 (n.)) and the stress on the ὀρθ–
root through polyptoton, all of which build our anticipation of the disaster.

741 μέν: 723n.

ἀσφαλής: Reiske's small conjecture ((1753) 17) for manuscript ἀσφαλεῖς
leads to a clearer sentence, without a cluttering of adjectives qualifying δρόμους.

δρόμους: internal accusative with the following verb.

742 ὠρθοῦθ' 'had a prosperous course' (Jebb), 'dirigeant sa course avec sûreté'
(Machin (1988) 53) is better than 'be set upright' (LSJ⁹ s.v. ὀρθόω). Nauck
conjectured ὠχεῖθ' (his third edition, p. 161), but see below.

ὁ τλήμων: this recurring epithet of Orestes (602n.) is all the more
emphatic because of the surrounding words built on the ὀρθ– root, which
seem rather to stress his safety. Apart from the first-person statements at
the beginning and end of the piece (689, 762–3), this is the only word in
the speech which expresses a subjective value-judgment on the part of the
Paedagogus.

ὀρθὸς ἐξ ὀρθῶν δίφρων: according to Machin (1988) 51 the adjectives
'indique[nt] une progression en ligne droite', but this fits uncomfortably with
a race that involves a good deal of turning. Preferable is Jebb's 'steadfast in his
steadfast car'.

For polyptoton in tragedy see Moorhouse 169–70, Bruhn §223, Denniston
on Eur. *El.* 337, Gygli-Wyss (1966) 123–6, Diggle on Eur. *Pha.* 94 = fr. 773.50
TrGF. In some cases (e.g. Eur. *Ba.* 1073 ὀρθὴ δ' ἐς ὀρθὸν αἰθέρ' ἐστηρίζετο) one
adjective stresses the other; here each retains its full meaning. Three forms
from the same stem in the same line are also found at *Aj.* 866 πόνος πόνῳ
πόνον φέρει (see Lobeck *ad loc.*), Aesch. *Pers.* 1041 κακὰν κακῶν κακοῖς; in each
case, the repetition is strongly emphatic. Nauck's ὠχεῖθ' (in his third edition;
cf. (1859–62) ii. 152–3) is thus unnecessary.

The ἐξ is probably related to the usage discussed at 48n.; English 'with' best conveys the nuance of causality. Hom. *Od.* 21.420 αὐτόθεν ἐκ δίφροιο καθήμενος is an illusory parallel: for the usage there compare the passages cited in support of Diggle's conjecture at 709n.

743–5 The use of word-order is masterly: we hear first of the manoeuvre, then are told that Orestes has missed something (λανθάνει), then are confronted with the climactic παίσας.

743 τανύων 'tightening' (so Toepfer (1831) 24–6); λύων ('slackening') codd. Slackening the reins of the left-hand trace-horse will not cause the chariot to crash against the turning-post. If Orestes slackened them before turning the post, the chariot would simply carry on straight forward. If he did so during or after the turn, the chariot would veer off at a wide angle, but would not make contact with the post (*pace* Campbell, *PS*). Only by tightening the left reins could such a crash take place.

Toepfer's conjecture gives us the sense which we require at little palaeographical cost: ΕΠΕΙΤΑΤΑΝΥⲰΝ became ΕΠΕΙΤΑΝΥⲰΝ by haplography, and the Ν was then 'corrected' to Λ to give what seemed like sense. The ensuing resolution is not a problem, as the ×−∪/∪∪ pattern in the first metron is common in Sophocles (cf. 30, 310, 368, 1195, Müller (1866) 33). The verb is not found elsewhere in tragedy (the one possible exception, Eur. *IA* 792, is from a corrupt lyric passage), but is common in Homer, which makes it more than appropriate in this Homeric passage. Especially noteworthy is its occurrence in Nestor's speech before the chariot race at *Il.* 23, at line 324 ὅπως τὸ πρῶτον τανύσῃ βοέοισιν ἱμᾶσιν ('[the chariot-driver] does not forget how from the start to keep (his horses) taut with the ox-hide reins' – Richardson on 323–5).

Tightening them in the initial stages of the turn would cause the horses to crash, whereas the narrative indicates the chariot makes contact (744–6; also 754). Hence Orestes' error occurs after he has partly travelled round the post.

744 κάμπτοντος: intransitive. Cf. Theocr. 24.119–20, Kannicht on Eur. *Hel.* 1666–9; perhaps also Aesch. fr. 25e.15 *TrGF* ≈ p. 3 *TrGFS* κάμπτο]νθ' ἅπερ τέθριππον (Diggle's text: cf. *id.* (1995–6) 99), Audollent (1904) §187.60 μὴ καλῶς κάμψῃ.

στήλην: for the turning-post as the point of particular danger cf. Hom. *Il.* 23.340–1 λίθου δ' ἀλέασθαι ἐπαυρεῖν, | μή πως ἵππους τε τρώσῃς κατὰ θ' ἅρματα ἄξῃς, Lys. fr. 38.4 Gernet-Bizos ἀλλὰ περὶ τοῦτον τὸν κάπηλον ὡς περὶ στήλην διαφθείρονται. Many curse tablets directed at chariot-drivers express the desire that the target comes to grief at this point in the race (examples at Audollent (1904) 566 s.v. οἱ καμπτῆρες; on these tablets see also Gager (1992) 53–74).

745–7 Cf. Hom. *Il.* 23.465–8 (Idomeneus speaks) οὐδὲ δυνάσθη | εὖ σχεθέειν περὶ τέρμα, καὶ οὐκ ἐτύχησεν ἑλίξας· | ἔνθα μιν ἐκπεσέειν οἴω σύν θ' ἅρματα ἄξαι, | αἱ δ'ἐξηρώησαν, ἐπεὶ μένος ἔλλαβε θυμόν, Eur. *Hipp.* 1234–5 σύμφυρτα δ' ἦν ἅπαντα· σύριγγές τ' ἄνω | τροχῶν ἐπήδων ἀξόνων τ' ἐνήλατα, Ap. Rh. 1.757–8 ἄξονος ἐν πλήμνῃσι παρακλιδὸν ἀγνυμένοιο | πῖπτεν. Aesch. frr. 36–9 *TrGF* contain what seems to be a messenger speech describing Glaucus' fatal chariot crash; cf. fr. 36b.2 col. ii, where the words παίειν (line 8), καμπαισ[(11), καὶ λοισθι[(12) and νίκης αρεσ[(13) suggest that the accident occurred round the turning-post on the last lap. An Attic black-figure pyxis of *c.* 510–500, name-vase of the Painter of Athens 18577 (*Para.* 306.1, *Addenda²* 143–4), depicts a chariot race where one chariot has been overturned and broken up; the driver is on the ground, while the horses are running in the opposite direction.

The strong pauses in these lines convey the jolting of the chariot crash (similarly at Ov. *Met.* 15.524–6, Stat. *Theb.* 6.504–7); cf. 711 n.

745 παίσας: is heavily emphasised by its position at the end of a long sense unit (cf. ἔπαισε at Eur. *El.* 841 and Astydamas II *TrGF* i. 60 F 2a.18). It is followed by the first major interlinear pause since 739, and then by a verb conveying violent action.

μέσας 'across the middle'.

χνόας: 717 n.

746 ἐξ ἀντύγων ὤλισθε: cf. Eur. *Phoen.* 1193 ἔθρῳσκον [Earle; ἔθνῃσκον codd.], ἐξέπιπτον ἀντύγων ἄπο, Hom. *Il.* 23.394 αὐτὸς δ' ἐκ δίφροιο παρὰ τροχὸν ἐξεκυλίσθη. The ἄντυξ was the rail which protected the front and sides of the chariot, made of fig wood at *Il.* 21.37–8. Homer never uses the word to mean simply 'chariot', though that sense is found in tragedy (see Gow on Theocr. 2.166); here the specific sense is probably meant. As he turned, Orestes would have been leaning slightly to one side (cf. Hom. *Il.* 23.335–6); at the moment of the accident he would then veer over the rail.

σὺν δ' ἑλίσσεται: for the tmesis cf. *Ant.* 432–3 σὺν δέ νιν | θηρώμεθ', 713 n. The verb (in its Ionic form) is found elsewhere in tragedy at Eur. *Ion* 1164 σπείραις συνειλίσσοντ' (L; σπείραισιν εἱλίσσοντ' Hermann). Nauck's ἐν for σύν (in his fourth edition, p. 162; cf. Eur. *Hipp.* 1236 ἡνίαισιν ἐμπλακείς) is possible but unnecessary.

747 τμητοῖς ἱμᾶσι: cf. Hom. *Il.* 10.567 ἐϋτμήτοισιν ἱμᾶσιν, Eur. *Hipp.* 1245 τμητῶν ἱμάντων. Campbell suggests that the word also retains an active sense, which conveys the reins' biting in to Orestes' flesh; but the Homeric parallels tell against this. Orestes is entangled in the reins because of the crash, not because he previously tied reins round his body for greater security: the present ἑλίσσεται makes the latter impossible. For the picture cf. [Apollod.] *Epit.* 2.7 ταῖς ἡνίαις συμπλακέντα συρόμενον ἀποθανεῖν (of Oenomaus), Eur. *Hipp.* 1236 ἡνίαισιν ἐμπλακείς, Ον. *Met.* 15.524 (≈ *Fast.* 6.743) *excutior curru, lorisque tenentibus artus* etc., Diod. Sic. 4.62.3, Sen. *Phaedr.* 1085–6 (all of Hippolytus).

πίπτοντος πέδοι: dative of motion towards, or 'final-directive' (Moorhouse 80–1); cf. *Tr.* 789–90 χθονὶ | ῥίπτων ἑαυτόν, Hom. *Il.* 5.82 πεδίῳ πέσεν, Aesch. *Eum.* 479 πέδοι (Dindorf; πέδω codd.) πεσών, Bruhn §51. The manuscripts give πέδῳ, but πέδοι (first made by Dindorf[6]) should probably be preferred (cf. Garvie's edition of Aeschylus' *Choephori*, p. 221). For the verb in this context see Fraenkel on Aesch. *Ag.* 1245.

748 πῶλοι διεσπάρησαν: Jebb renders 'were scattered', claiming that the verb implies that some of the horses came loose from the chariot; but Campbell's 'plunged wildly about the course' may capture the sense better. In any case, it is not the fate of the horses that concerns us.

749 στρατός 'people', 'crowd': cf. *Tr.* 795, Pind. *P.* 2.87, Aesch. fr. 47a.766 *TrGF*, *Eum.* 566, Renehan (1975) 182. A sixth-century dinos by Sophilus vividly depicts the emotional involvement of the spectators of a chariot race (Athens, National Museum 15499; *ABV* 39.16, *Para.* 18, *Addenda*[2] 10); cf. Manakidou (1994) 41 with n. 40.

749–50 ὅπως ὁρᾷ ... | ... ἀνωτότυξε: for the present in a temporal clause with aorist in the main clause see Moorhouse 186, 294, Bruhn §104.II.4, de Jong (1991) 41 with n. 109; often the present verb is one of seeing or hearing (e.g. *Aj.* 307–8, *OR* 807–9).

ἐκπεπτωκότα | δίφρων: cf. 50 δίφρων κυλισθείς.

750 ἀνωτότυξε: *coni.* Herwerden (1878) 269 for manuscript ἀνωλόλυξε. Ll-J/W and Dawe[3] print the conjecture; Diggle (1994) 479–80 also approves, comparing the corruption of Aesch. *Ag.* 1074 ἀνωτότυξας into ἀνωλόλυξας at Σ Eur. *Phoen.* 1028 (= i. 357.22 Schwartz). There are two difficulties with the paradosis. (i) Before the Hellenistic period ὀλολυγή does not denote a cry of grief. Deubner (1941) 8–9 = (1982) 614–15 disagrees, citing [Hom.] *Batr.* 101, Ar. *Av.* 222, and Philemon fr. 82.17 *PCG*. But the first of these texts can hardly be from the classical period; while in the latter two the word should be understood in its regular sense 'cry of joy or excitement' (see Dunbar on the *Birds* passage). This leaves Eur. *Tro.* 999–1000 ποίαν βοὴν | ἀνωλόλυξας: in his edition Diggle retains the paradosis, but at (1994) 480 sets out a cogent case for emending to Wecklein's ἀνωτότυξας. (ii) The ὀλολυγή is typically uttered by women (cf. Pulleyn (1997) 178–81). There are exceptions to this rule in comedy (cf. Ar. *Eq.* 616, 1327, *Pax* 97, *Av.* 222), but not in tragedy outside our passage

331

(Diggle (1994) 479 n. 172). Given these difficulties with the transmitted text, Herwerden's small alteration should be adopted.

For the distress of the crowd at a chariot accident cf. Dio Chrysostom 32.46 νυνὶ δὲ τὸ μὲν τῶν ἡνιόχων τινὰ ἐκπεσεῖν ἐκ τοῦ δίφρου δεινὸν ἡγεῖσθε καὶ συμφορὰν πασῶν μεγίστην (cf. Crowther (1994a) = (2004) 229–40); for a similar reaction by a crowd in a messenger speech cf. *Tr.* 783 ἅπας δ' ἀνηυφήμησεν οἰμωγῇ λεώς. Bacchyl. 3.9–14 depicts the crowd roaring its admiration of a victor (cf. Gerber on Pind. *O.* 9.93); the reaction here underlines the reversal in the narrative of epinician motifs.

751 οἷ' ἔργα δράσας οἷα λαγχάνει κακά: for the repetition cf. Thuc. 7.75.6 ἀπὸ οἵας λαμπρότητος καὶ αὐχήματος τοῦ πρώτου ἐς οἵαν τελευτὴν καὶ ταπεινότητα ἀφῖκτο, S. *Aj.* 557, 923 ὦ δύσμορ' Αἴας, οἷος ὢν οἵως ἔχεις, *Tr.* 994, 1044–5 κλύουσ' ἔφριξα τάσδε συμφοράς, φίλαι, | ἄνακτος, οἵαις οἷος ὢν ἐλαύνεται, *Ant.* 942, Eur. *Alc.* 144, Bruhn §223.I. For the construction cf. Simon. fr. 91.2 *IEG* οἰκτίρω σε . . . οἷ' ἔπαθες; also *Phil.* 169–75 οἰκτίρω νιν ἔγωγ', ὅπως κτλ. For λαγχάνω denoting the 'lot of death' cf. Borecky (1965) 51. The reference to Orestes' previous ἔργα (cf. 689n.) stresses the drastic *peripeteia* that has afflicted him.

752 φορούμενος πρὸς οὖδας: cf. Eur. *Hipp.* 1238 σποδούμενος μὲν πρὸς πέτραις φίλον κάρα, *Suppl.* 689–90 τοὺς ἄνω τε καὶ κάτω φορουμένους | ἱμᾶσιν. Jebb sees a reference to Orestes' original fall, but 'the frequentative form and the continuous tense seem both against this view' (Campbell, *PS*). Given that the coordinate clause refers to Orestes' motion along the ground, it is natural that this one should too. There is no verbal parallel with Hom. *Il.* 22.395–404, where Hector is dragged along the ground behind Achilles' chariot: but the similarity in situation may add pathos to Orestes' final moments. At least Hector was already dead by this point.

ἄλλοτ': for the absence of ἄλλοτε in the first of a set of coordinate clauses cf. *Tr.* 11–12, Eur. *Hec.* 28, Hom. *Il.* 24.511, Pind. *N.* 8.37–8, Bruhn §190.

753–5 Others intervene to release the trapped charioteer at Stat. *Theb.* 6.510–11; in Aesch. fr. 39 *TrGF* the mangled body of Glaucus is carried off the track.

753 σκέλη προφαίνων: damage to the charioteer's legs is specified in curse tablets (cf. 744n.) at Audollent (1904) §§239.46–8, 240.55–60 μετὰ βλάβης τοῦ σώματος καὶ σκελῶν κατάγματος; cf. also Lucian 31.9 τὰ σκέλη καθηματωμένος. The injury may thus have seemed particularly painful and humiliating.

755–6 ὥστε μηδένα | γνῶναι φίλων ἰδόντ' ἂν ἄθλιον δέμας: for the difficulty of recognising the corpse cf. Hom. *Il.* 16.638–40 οὐδ' ἂν ἔτι φράδμων περ ἀνὴρ Σαρπηδόνα δῖον | ἔγνω, ἐπεὶ βελέεσσι καὶ αἵματι καὶ κονίῃσιν | ἐκ κεφαλῆς εἴλυτο διαμπερὲς ἐς πόδας ἄκρους, Eur. *Med.* 1196. The earlier stress on Orestes' glorious appearance (685–6) makes the *topos* more moving. The failure of a φίλος to recognise Orestes will play an important rôle in a later part of the play.

756 ἄθλιον δέμας: used elsewhere of mutilated bodies at *Tr.* 1079, *OR* 1388, *OC* 576, Eur. *Tro.* 777.

757–60 are excised by Günther (1996) 111–12; he argues that the men bringing Orestes to Mycenae would probably not have also been the people who burnt his body, and that Electra's surprise at 1112 means she is unaware that Orestes' body is being returned. The first point is excessively literal. The second point is false: Electra's reaction at 1108–9 and 1112 need not be surprise rather than pain arising from the confirmation of foreboding. Even if Günther were right in claiming that Electra was surprised at this point, no audience would notice the inconsistency. The pathos of these lines also seems distinctively Sophoclean.

At the end of a messenger speech narrating a catastrophe, we are often told that the dead or dying person is to be brought on stage; cf. *Tr.* 805–6, Eur. *El.* 855–7 and Di Gregorio (1967) 18 with n. 70.

757 κέαντες *coni.* Brunck¹ (ii. 205). Homeric ἔκηα (<*ἔκηϝα: see S–D i. 349) undergoes quantitative metathesis (S–D i. 245) to give the old Attic aorist ἐκέα, found in an inventory of 408/7 (Threatte ii. 529); cf. Aesch. *Ag.* 849, Ar. *Pax* 1133. This was easily corrupted owing to its unfamiliarity. If καί– in OV is the result of misspelling of phonetic equivalents (cf. Fraenkel on Aesch. *Ag.* 1653, D. C. C. Young (1965) 251 = Calder and Stern (1970) 100–1, Arnott on Alexis frr. 103.4, 149.2 *PCG*), it may reflect the original κε–, just as at [Eur.] *Rhes.* 97, where ἐκκαίαντες is a v.l. for metrically guaranteed ἐκκέαντες.

ἐν βραχεῖ: 758n.

758 χαλκῷ 'bronze vessel'; cf. 54, Hom. *Il.* 18.349, *Od.* 10.360.

μέγιστον σῶμα δειλαίας σποδοῦ 'a huge frame, reduced to pathetic dust' (Long (1968) 103). σποδοῦ is related to the genitive of definition (cf. 19), denoting what the body now consists of. The phrase is an example of the 'use . . . in which the genitive and the governing noun are co-extensive, and only present different aspects of the same notion. By this means both words receive an emphasis' (Campbell, in his edition, i. 17 §6): cf. *OC* 1029–30 ἐς τοσήνδ' ὕβριν | ἥκοντα τόλμης τῆς παρεστώσης τανῦν.

COMMENTARY: 516–822

For the contrast between the greatness of the living hero and the smallness of his remains after cremation cf. Aesch. *Ag.* 437–44 Ἄρης . . . | . . . | . . . | φίλοισι πέμπει . . . | . . . ἀν– | τήνορος σποδοῦ γεμί– | ζων λέβητας εὐθέτους, Eur. *Suppl.* 1127–30 φέρεις . . . σποδοῦ τε πλῆθος ὀλίγον ἀντὶ σωμάτων | εὐδοκίμων δή ποτ᾽ ἐν Μυκήναις, Posid. 32.5–6 A–B τὸν βαρὺν ἥρω | ἐκ δῆων ὀλίγην ἦλθεν ἄγων σποδιήν, Prop. 2.9A.13–14 *tanti corpus Achilli* | *maximaque in parva sustulit ossa manu,* Ov. *Met.* 12.615–16 *iam cinis est, et de tam magno restat Achille* | *nescioquid parvam quod non bene compleat urnam.* See further 1140n., Patrocles *TrGF* i. 57–8 F 1.1–2, Lattimore (1942) 172–4, Nisbet and Hubbard on Hor. *C.* 1.28.2. Blaydes's φλόγιστον (in his edition; cf. 58; favourably mentioned by Diggle (1993) 136 = (1994) 418) takes away this moving contrast.

μέγιστον: seven cubits long, if we believe the Tegean blacksmith at Hdt. 1.68.3. For the great size of ancient heroes cf. Hainsworth on Hom. *Il.* 12.449, Arist. *Pol.* 1332b16–18, Von der Mühll (1930) 12–13 = (1976) 443–4. μέγας and its derivatives rarely qualify the body as a whole, as opposed to part of the body: Bissinger (1966) 85 compares only *Aj.* 1077.

σποδοῦ: cf. Erinna *A.P.* 7.710.2 = 1782 *HE* = fr. 5.2 Neri τὰν ὀλίγαν σποδιάν (with N.'s n.), *EG* 696.8 = *GVI* 715.8 (Rome, 1st–2nd cent. AD) τὴν ὀλίγην σποδιὴν οὐκ ὀλίγης ὀδύνης.

760 ὅπως πατρῴας τύμβον ἐκλάχοι χθονός: cf. Hegesippus *A.P.* 13.12.7–8 = 1923–4 *HE* προξείνων ὑπὸ χερσὶ λαχὼν πυρὸς ἵκετο πάτρην | Ἄβδηρα κρωσσῷ χαλκέῳ περισταλείς, Ov. *Trist.* 3.3.32 *ut saltem patria contumularer humo.* For the motif whereby a dead man gains the earth in which he is buried as his allotted portion (here used in a pathetic sense) cf. 1135, *OC* 789–90, Eur. *Suppl.* 309, Borecky (1965) 60. There is an ironic echo of Orestes' opening speech: he has indeed returned to reclaim his ancestral land (67–72).

ἐκλάχοι: the expected subjunctive, conjectured by Musgrave, is in J and S (*teste* Kopff (1993) 157). It could be right: for a similar error see 57. But in final clauses in primary sequence our manuscripts occasionally have an optative, which seems to arise from some notion of pastness implied in the main sentence even though the verb on which it is dependent is present (K–G ii. 382–3, S–D ii. 323; Goodwin §322 is brief and sceptical). Of these, ταλαιπωροῖτο at Ar. *Ran.* 24 is metrically guaranteed: this indicates that we are dealing with a real phenomenon, not simply sporadic manuscript corruption. So here Moorhouse 287 (following Campbell and Vahlen (1887) 11 = (1907–8) i. 376–7) claims that 'the opt. . . . relates neatly to the purpose of the *senders,* rather than to that of the *carriers* of the verb' (his italics). This gives good sense, but the possibility of textual corruption cannot be excluded. For more on J's readings see 427n.

761–3 For the idea that autopsy has its own particular pain cf. *Tr.* 896–7 μᾶλλον δ᾽ εἰ παροῦσα πλησία | ἔλευσσες οἷ᾽ ἔδρασε, κάρτ᾽ ἂν ᾤκτισας,

334

Aj. 1000–1 ἀγὼ κλυὼν δύστηνος ἐκποδὼν μὲν ὢν | ὑπεστέναζον, νῦν δ᾽ ὁρῶν ἀπόλλυμαι, *OR* 1237–8 τῶν δὲ πραχθέντων τὰ μὲν | ἄλγιστ᾽ ἄπεστιν· ἡ γὰρ ὄψις οὐ πάρα, Hor. *AP* 180–2 *segnius irritant animos demissa per aurem* | *quam quae sunt oculis subiecta fidelibus et quae* | *ipse sibi tradit spectator.* But such assertions by tragic messengers are often belied by the impact their speeches have, both on their listeners inside the play and on the audience outside it (cf. de Jong (1991) 172–3). This is especially the case here, where Orestes' death has never been witnessed by anyone, and where the intensity of Electra's reaction could not easily be surpassed even if it had been. For the related *topos* of eyes being more trustworthy than ears cf. Apostol. 18.71 = *CPG* ii. 744.2 ὠτίων πιστότεροι ὀφθαλμοί, Heracl. D–K 22 B 101a (= i. 173.15–16), Call. fr. 282 Pfeiffer = 109 Hollis (with H.'s n.), Otto (1890) 251, Walbank on Polyb. 12.27.1, Woodman and Martin on Tac. *Ann.* 3.16.1.

761 τοιαῦτά σοι ταῦτ᾽ ἐστίν: cf. 696, *OC* 62–3 τοιαῦτά σοι ταῦτ᾽ ἐστίν, ὦ ξέν᾽, οὐ λόγοις | τιμῶμεν᾽, ἀλλὰ τῇ ξυνουσίᾳ πλέον. For τοιαῦτα at the end of a messenger speech cf. Eur. *Alc.* 196, *Andr.* 1161; also 424n.

ὡς: limiting, as at *OC* 20, 76, *Ant.* 1161, *Aj.* 395: 'at least as far as words can give the impression' would be an overtranslation.

762 τοῖς δ᾽ ἰδοῦσιν, οἵπερ εἴδομεν: tragic messengers regularly refer to their status as eyewitnesses (instances gathered at de Jong (1991) 9 n. 20 and 183–4).

οἵπερ: Hartung's ὥσπερ is found in Δ and paralleled at 994, *Aj.* 991 and *OR* 54; this could be right, but is no improvement on the majority reading.

763 μέγιστα πάντων: for the emphatic superlative at the conclusion to a tale of disaster cf. Thuc. 7.87.6 πανωλεθρίᾳ δὴ τὸ λεγόμενον.

764–822 The final part of the episode resembles Aesch. *Cho.* 691–718. The news of Orestes' death provokes an emotional outburst from his mother (766–8, *Cho.* 691–9).[47] The messenger is disconcerted by this reaction (769, 772, *Cho.* 700–6); but Clytemnestra quickly recovers and accompanies him inside to show him hospitality (773, 800–3, *Cho.* 707–18). This similarity in form highlights S.'s differences from his predecessor's treatment. Most important among these is the reaction of the two Clytemnestras to the news of Orestes' death. In Aeschylus Clytemnestra laments the death of her son in words of great pathos, and sets it in the wider context of the troubles which have afflicted the house (766–8n.). The response of S.'s Clytemnestra is decidedly cooler. There is no expression of sorrow or grief: she is shocked, not saddened, and her focus remains on her own personal advantage (766–8n.). A further contrast can

---

[47] Clytemnestra, not Electra, speaks these lines: see Garvie *ad loc.*

335

be seen between the women's subsequent reactions. The grief of Aeschylus' Clytemnestra soon subsides, and in her next speech she calmly describes the hospitality she will afford the travellers. But her tone does not approach the delight and exultation displayed by the Clytemnestra of our play (773–787), which soon turns into the ugly triumphalism of the remarks she directs towards her daughter (791, 793 etc.). The presence of Electra forms another significant difference in the two dramatists' treatments. She remains silent for over twenty lines after the Paedagogus has finished speaking, a sign of genuine grief (cf. Aesch. *Pers.* 290–2 σιγῶ πάλαι δύστηνος ἐκπεπληγμένη | κακοῖς κτλ., Ov. *Met.* 6.583–5, Sen. *Phaedr.* 607 *curae leves loquuntur, ingentes stupent*, Schadewaldt (1926) 55–6 n. 3). Her anguish at 788–90 reminds us what a sincere expression of sorrow should look like,[48] while the despairing hopelessness of her words in the stichomythia brings out the cruelty of her mother's taunting. This interaction with the Aeschylean model shapes and intensifies our emotional responses.

The greater elaboration S. gives to this part of the play allows a correspondingly more intricate exploration of the dramatic ironies inherent in it. These ironies are most effectively brought out through the repetition of words or phrases by different speakers (cf. Pfeiffer-Petersen (1996) 112–13; also Hancock (1917) 37), which focuses our attention on their nuances. Three times Clytemnestra picks up a phrase used by the preceding speaker, twice in a coarse and aggressive tone (773 μάτην, 791 καλῶς ἔχει, 793 ἤκουσεν). On each occasion, however, her statement is truer than she realises. Remarks which she intends to be sarcastic are also accurate reflections of what we know is soon to happen. At almost every turn in the stichomythia the audience is aware of the limitations of Clytemnestra's perspective (cf. also 795, 798). Twice Electra picks up her mother's words (788 νῦν, 796 πεπαύμεθ᾽, παύσομεν); again, there are ironies. The focus on νῦν in 783, 786, 788 and 794 reminds us that the decisive moment is indeed at hand, as was emphasised in the prologue (21–2, 75–6; Schwindt (1993) 73–81). But this will be manifested in a fashion which neither woman is now expecting. So too the emphasis given to παύ– words in 795–6 reflects a concept of wider thematic significance (304n.). Contrary to Electra's cry of despair, this day will put a stop to her torment; it will also bring Clytemnestra's anxiety to an end, but again, not in the manner which she expects (cf. Heracles' words at *Tr.* 1164–73). These ironies undermine Clytemnestra's position still further in the minds of the audience. The same words express her vulgar self-congratulation and the

---

[48] Compare and contrast the Nurse's later response to the death of Orestes in *Choephori* (734–65), which is probably more affecting than Clytemnestra's: there, however, we do not have a split between insincere and sincere forms of lament.

inevitability of her punishment; and we are comforted to think that a woman who behaves like this will shortly meet the justice she deserves. Electra's case is more complex. The power of her emotional response is intensely moving. We know that her despair is misplaced, however, and this mitigates the intensity of our own reaction. After all, we are aware that Orestes is alive, and expect this fact to be communicated to Electra before long. But in a different way we are afflicted with a kind of suffering by which Electra is untouched. This is the pain which comes from the sight of needless grief, of a human being experiencing torments which are quite unnecessary, and which could easily be taken away. The case of Laertes in *Odyssey* 24 is similar. This is the emotion which will dominate our experience of the episode following the second stasimon. For now, it forms part of the complex and varied mixture of feelings which this scene creates.

For all that they pick up each other's words, there is little true contact between mother and daughter. Clytemnestra's speech at 773–87 mentions Electra only in the third person, and she leaves the stage before Electra's concluding lament begins at 804. Even during the stichomythia, where it is difficult to avoid contact with one's interlocutor, the pair take some time before directly confronting one another. Electra begins with invocations first of her brother (788–90), and then of Nemesis (792); only then does she deign to address her mother. Both these invocations are striking for their failure to establish contact: yet after each of them Clytemnestra makes contact in the roughest and most offensive manner possible, by picking up one of Electra's words and throwing it back at her. Eventually she breaks off altogether from addressing her daughter, and turns to the Paedagogus to express her triumph (797–8). 'Die Gestaltung der Szene entspricht ingesamt der vollständigen Entfernung der Standpunkte voneinander' (Pfeiffer-Petersen (1996) 113).

764–5 The chorus sets Orestes' death in the wider perspective of the sufferings endured by his family. On the significance of such references see the introduction to the first stasimon. Here the broad view taken by the chorus contrasts with the egotism of Clytemnestra's response (766–8n.). Compare the laments for the house of Tantalus by the chorus at Eur. *Or.* 345–7.

764 δεσπόταισι τοῖς πάλαι: for the dative see Diggle (1974) 14 = (1994) 105.

765 πρόρριζον: on this word see 512n., where it occurs in a similar context. Here it may keep some of its original metaphorical sense 'root and branch': the image of the falling tree is a common feature of Greek laments over the dead (cf. Alexiou (2002) 198–201).

ὡς ἔοικεν: often used in S. to qualify a statement which the speaker would prefer to be untrue (cf. 772, 1116, *Ant.* 576, 740; so too Eur. *Hipp.* 1090, *Hec.* 766). It never conveys doubt or disbelief: but in our case, there is an irony of which only the audience is aware.

766–8 Kells saw Clytemnestra's responses here and at 770–1 as 'the very centre of the play', constituting an 'enormous reversal . . . in the stage-action, with . . . far-reaching significance for the play's total meaning' (his edition, p. 7; cf. *ib.* p. 139 and his comments at (1986) 154). He is not troubled by the brevity of the queen's remarks; indeed, for Winnington-Ingram this 'brings out the tragic character of the situation, when they are stifled by an over-mastering relief from fear' ((1980) 232). But it is not the length, but the content of Clytemnestra's words which makes Kells's interpretation untenable. She wonders whether to call the death of her son 'fortunate' (εὐτυχῆ), or 'terrible, but profitable' (δεινὰ μέν, κέρδη δέ). This is hardly the reaction of a grief-stricken mother. Self-advantage lies at the heart of each alternative: even in these first moments after the news of the death of her son, Clytemnestra's grief is firmly subordinate to considerations of her own interest. In her subsequent comments she makes a single reference to suffering (771). Characteristically, she means her own.[49] This point becomes still clearer when we compare the corresponding passage in Aeschylus (*Cho.* 691–9). There Clytemnestra delivers a substantial and moving lament: she invokes the Ἀρά of the house, describes Orestes as the family's ἐλπίς, and claims that she herself is now friendless and παναθλία. This is powerful and expressive language which suggests great, if temporary, sorrow.[50] There is nothing in S. which can match this.

766 τί ταῦτα: listed by Stevens (1976) 31 as a possible colloquialism; cf. *OC* 543, *Phil.* 201 and the verbal ellipses which he cites at (1945) 101, along with many parallels from Euripides and Aristophanes. But here the phrase may go with λέγω, and hence is not a true ellipse. The alternative, punctuating these two words as a question, is clumsy.

---

[49] Waldock (1951) 183, Gellie (1972) 117, Stevens (1978) 115 and MacLeod (2001) 119 (with the brief doxography in n. 33) are also hostile to Kells's approach. But they all focus on the brevity of Clytemnestra's lament, or else claim that it is insincere. None draws attention to Clytemnestra's revealing choice of alternatives.

[50] 'There is . . . not a word in the speech that need be taken as anything other than the sincere and natural reaction of a mother who has lost her son' (Garvie *ad loc.*). Her tone soon changes, and the Nurse will later attack her insincerity (*Cho.* 737–41); but this does not affect our interpretation of her initial reaction. Nor is her hypocrisy in *Agamemnon* relevant; for in that play it constitutes a strategy for ensnaring her husband, whereas here it would have no obvious purpose. In the absence of strong indications to the contrary, it is good method to accept the sincerity of what is said on stage (cf. 566–76 n.).

769 Tragic messengers are typically rewarded for bringing good news or useful information (cf. *Tr.* 190–1, *OR* 1005–6, *Phil.* 551–2, Wilkins on Eur. *Hcld.* 784–7). The Paedagogus' surprise and subsequent disappointment (772) at Clytemnestra's reaction thus accords with the ἦθος required of him by the deception plot: for similar dismay on the part of a messenger cf. Eur. *Med.* 1008 τάδ' οὐ ξυνῳδὰ τοῖσιν ἐξηγγελμένοις. It also gives us a further indication of the shallowness of Clytemnestra's sorrow: she needs only the briefest of prompts to begin her exultation in the death of her son (cf. MacLeod (2001) 120–1).

γύναι: regularly used to address a queen (cf. *OR* 678, Wackernagel (1912) 25–6 = (1953–79) ii. 992–3).

τῷ νῦν λόγῳ: same phrase at *OR* 90, *OC* 801. The variant ποίῳ is grammatically possible, but 'the ineptness of some one asking ποίωι λόγωι when he has himself just delivered a long speech about a son's death hardly needs stressing' (Dawe, *STS* i. 187).

770–1 Cf. Sen. *Phaedr.* 1114–17 *o nimium potens | quanto parentes sanguinis vinclo tenes | natura! quam te colimus inviti quoque! | occidere volui noxium, amissum fleo* (cf. Tarrant on Sen. *Ag.* 579). Closer in tone are the words of Euripides' Theseus, when he declares μίσει μὲν ἀνδρὸς τοῦ πεπονθότος τάδε | λόγοισιν ἥσθην τοῖσδε· νῦν δ' αἰδούμενος | θεούς τ' ἐκεῖνόν θ', οὕνεκ' ἐστὶν ἐξ ἐμοῦ, | οὔθ' ἥδομαι τοῖσδ' οὔτ' ἐπάχθομαι κακοῖς (*Hipp.* 1257–60, also after the death of an estranged son in a chariot crash); though Clytemnestra here disclaims the μῖσος which Theseus openly acknowledges. Like Clytemnestra, Theseus cites the bond of kinship as a reason for tempering the severity of his response. But in neither instance does the speaker exhibit tenderness or grief at the occurrence.

770 δεινὸν τὸ τίκτειν ἐστίν: the emotional bond arising from kinship, especially motherhood, is a familiar *topos*; δεινός is idiomatic in the context. Cf. (for kinship in general) Aesch. *Sept.* [1031] δεινὸν τὸ κοινὸν σπλάγχνον, [Aesch.] *PV* 39 τὸ συγγενές τοι δεινὸν ἥ θ' ὁμιλία, Eur. *Andr.* 985; (for motherhood) Eur. *Phoen.* 355 δεινὸν γυναιξὶν αἱ δι' ὠδίνων γοναί, *IA* 917 δεινὸν τὸ τίκτειν καὶ φέρει φίλτρον μέγα, fr. 103 *TrGF*, Ar. *Lys.* 884. Cf. also *OC* 1189–91, where Antigone urges on Oedipus a kinder treatment of Polynices on the ground that he is his father. Kells's translation 'it is a queer thing to be a mother' does not quite catch the tone.

770–1 οὐδὲ γὰρ κακῶς | πάσχοντι μῖσος ὧν τέκῃ προσγίγνεται: the φιλία of blood-relations can persist even through personal enmity: cf. Eur. *Phoen.* 1446 (the dying Polynices on Eteocles) φίλος γὰρ ἐχθρὸς ἐγένετ', ἀλλ' ὅμως φίλος, also 'family-φιλία existed even despite the absence of good-will, unself-interested well-doing and the other practical attitudes and actions that in Aristotle's account serve to define φιλία' (J. M. Cooper (1999) 313 n. 3; cf. MacLeod (2001) 121–2).

771 πάσχοντι: the masculine participle is used because the phrase is of general reference; cf. Davies on *Tr.* 151–2, Theocr. 11.75, Bruhn §1. On the significance of this reference to suffering see 766–8n.

ὧν τέκῃ: for the absence of ἄν see Bruhn §144.III, Goodwin §540, K–G ii. 426 Anm. 1, Bers (1984) 155–7.

772 μάτην ἄρ': commonly found in combination. To the examples cited by Elmsley on Eur. *Med.* 1229 (our 1262) add *Phil.* 345 and Eur. frr. 377.1, 494.1 *TrGF*; also Ar. *Av.* 265–6 ἄλλως ἄρ' οὔπω, ὡς ἔοικ', εἰς τὴν λόχμην | ἐμβὰς ἐπόπωζε.

773 For the significant repetition of μάτην see 764–822n.

774 εἰ: the meaning of this word often seems to shade into 'since' (cf. 1425), and this must be the sense in which Clytemnestra is using it. She regards the protasis as a self-evident truth; the audience knows better.

θανόντος: see Moorhouse 258–9 for non-articular substantival participles.

πίστ'. . . τεκμήρια: not the urn, which has not yet arrived (its designation by the phrase ἐμφανῆ τεκμήρια in 1109 is not relevant here). Clytemnestra rather refers to the persuasive account of Orestes' death given by the Paedagogus (so rightly de Jong (1994)). This speech hardly constitutes 'trustworthy evidence' as we understand the term. De Jong compares Clytemnestra's account of the fall of Troy at Aesch. *Ag.* 320–50; this convinces a previously sceptical chorus, which hails it with the phrase which we are discussing (*ib.* 352). There it is the vividness of the account which makes the difference. De Jong cites the conclusion of Fraenkel's discussion (in his commentary, ii. 181–4): '[Clytemnestra's] suggestive imagination lends colour to what before were bare outlines, and adds reality to the sound of words. Under the spell of her speech the Elders feel that all she has said is true to life; it cannot have been otherwise, it must in fact have happened as she says.' So too the chorus of Aeschylus' *Supplices* uses the phrase at 54 to refer to the account of Io which it later gives (291–324): it regards the story itself as 'trustworthy evidence'. That said, Clytemnestra's grounds for belief are rather stronger than in the Aeschylean examples. An independent witness seems to be at hand: a man with excellent credentials (669–70; cf. 927), and who has no obvious reason to deceive her. Her trust in his message is rather more 'humanly intelligible' than the sudden volte-face of the chorus in *Agamemnon*, which moves from scepticism to belief in response to a story from someone whose access to the truth is no greater than its own (in the following stasimon it undergoes the shift in reverse!). Neither playwright's version would satisfy the demands of modern realism: but, as often, it is Aeschylus who lies particularly remote from it (cf. Lloyd-Jones (1964a) 374 = (1990a) 277 = E. Segal (1983) 56).

775 τῆς ἐμῆς ψυχῆς γεγώς: cf. Aesch. *Cho.* 749 τῆς ἐμῆς ψυχῆς τριβήν. There the tender expression forms part of the Nurse's moving lament; here it has a hollow ring, and jars with Clytemnestra's growing excitement at the news of her son's death. Orestes was not literally born from Clytemnestra's 'life', but the metaphor is clear enough: Kaibel (p. 192) deals trenchantly with the proposed emendations. Compare the effect of ἥ μ' ἐγείνατο in 261.

776 μαστῶν ἀποστὰς καὶ τροφῆς ἐμῆς: cf. Eur. *Hyps.* fr. 759a.1615 *TrGF* ἀπομαστίδιόν γ' ἐμῶν στέρνων, *IA* 1151–2 βρέφος . . . τοὐμὸν . . . | μαστῶν βιαίως τῶν ἐμῶν ἀποσπάσας. For the participle see next n.

φυγάς: except at *Ant.* 108, this word in S. always denotes a political exile. In using it, 'Klytaimnestra reveals that she sees [Orestes] more as a political rival and a threat to her power than she does as a son' (MacLeod (2001) 120); she 'describes his absence not as a parent speaking of a child, but as a ruler speaking of a dissident subject: he has "*revolted from* her breasts and nurture" (ἀποστάς, the regular word for civic dissension and political rebellion) and has become an "exile" . . . Here speaks the woman whom her daughter characterizes as "tyrant (δέσποτις) rather than mother" (597–98)' (C. P. Segal (1966) 498, cited at MacLeod (2001) 121; Segal's italics). The strong participle ἀποστάς suggests a deliberate act on the part of Orestes, as if an infant were capable of such a decision. We have already heard that the young child had to be rescued from his mother, probably from an attempt on his life (296–7n.). Harrison (1943) 63 prefers to take φυγάς with what precedes, but that leaves the following verb isolated.

777 ἀπεξενοῦτο 'became estranged': cf. Eur. *Hipp.* 1084–5 οὐκ ἀκούετε | πάλαι ξενοῦσθαι τόνδε προὐννέποντά με;, *Hec.* 1221 πατρῴας γῆς ἀπεξενωμένοις, Aesch. *Cho.* 1042 ἐγὼ δ' ἀλήτης τῆσδε γῆς ἀπόξενος. Compare and contrast Electra and Clytemnestra, who see all too much of each other (785 ξύνοικος, with n.).

779 φόνους: for the poetic plural see 206n.
δείν' ἐπηπείλει τελεῖν: cf. Hom. *Il.* 1.388 ἠπείλησεν μῦθον, ὃ δὴ τετελεσμένος ἐστίν. These threats are mentioned by Electra at 1154–6; cf. also Clytemnestra's reaction to news of Orestes' imminent arrival at 295–8.

341

780–1 ὥστ᾽ οὔτε νυκτὸς ὕπνον οὔτ᾽ ἐξ ἡμέρας | ἐμὲ στεγάζειν ἡδύν: for sleeplessness as a response to fear cf. Hom. *Il.* 10.3–4, 25–6, Aesch. *Ag.* 14–15, 891–4. The reference to it here fits with the earlier account of the dream, which also prevented her from resting. At Eur. *El.* 617 the Old Man tells Orestes that Aegisthus φοβεῖται . . . σε κοὔχ εὕδει σαφῶς.

Sleep is proverbially sweet (cf. Hom. *Il.* 4.131, 23.62, *Od.* 1.363–4, 13.79–80, *Hom. Hymn* 4.241, Eur. *Hec.* 915, *Or.* 211–12, Jeremiah 31.26), as well as a relief from toil and worry (cf. *Phil.* 827 Ὕπν᾽ ὀδύνας ἀδαής, Ὕπνε δ᾽ ἀλγέων, Eur. *Ba.* 282, [Men.] *Monost.* 76); Clytemnestra's anxiety denies her even this comfort. The noun and adjective are split into corresponding clauses, as at *Ant.* 205 ἐᾶν δ᾽ ἄθαπτον καὶ πρὸς οἰωνῶν δέμας (cf. Bruhn §167.II); the effect may be to make the adjective predicative.

780 ὥστ᾽ οὔτε: ὥστε usually takes μή when followed by an infinitive, even when the infinitive refers to something that has occurred (Wackernagel (1926–8) ii. 282). Moorhouse 323 suggests that '[S.] is combining here the ideas of the likely consequence and the actual result, and stressing the latter'; so too Jebb argues that the construction arises from 'the prominence of the negative *fact* in the speaker's mind' (his commentary, p. 218). Cf. Eur. *Hel.* 108 [Troy has been destroyed] ὥστ᾽ οὐδ᾽ ἴχνος γε τειχέων εἶναι σαφές (Moorhouse's other parallel, *Phoen.* 1358, is bracketed by Diggle and Mastronarde). See further Jebb's appendix, Goodwin §598–9, K–G ii. 188–9.

νυκτὸς . . . ἐξ ἡμέρας: another polar expression (305–6n.), which expresses the permanence of Clytemnestra's restlessness. Descriptions of prolonged suffering often combine night and day: cf. *OR* 198–9 εἴ τι νὺξ ἀφῇ, | τοῦτ᾽ ἐπ᾽ ἦμαρ ἔρχεται, Tr. Adesp. fr. 7.2–3 *TrGF* πόνῳ πόνον | ἐκ νυκτὸς ἀλλάσσουσα τὸν καθ᾽ ἡμέραν. See 477n. for the genitive of time. The preposition is found with only the second element of the coordinate expression: cf. Eur. *Ba.* 1008 ἦμαρ ἐς νύκτα τ᾽, Bruhn §171.VI.

781–2 ὁ προστατῶν | χρόνος: προστατέω means 'stand before', either literally or in the metaphorical senses of 'rule' (e.g. Eur. *El.* 932) or 'defend' (e.g. Aesch. *Sept.* 396): cf. Fraenkel's note on Aesch. *Ag.* 976 προστατήριον, cited above, 637n. Meineke (1863b) 719–20 emends to προσσ–, but the transmitted προ- element gives good sense. The primary meaning of the verb is 'time which stands in front of the present, the imminent or coming time' (so Σ p. 137.16 Papageorgius ὁ ἐπιγινόμενος); but the metaphorical sense 'time which controls me' is also present, especially given the degree of personification inherent in making χρόνος the subject, not the object, of διῆγε (cf. 178, *Aj.* 646–7, Hutchinson on Pind. *O.* 6.96–8). Suggestions of control and authority would be appropriate in the context (see next n.).

COMMENTARY: 516–822

782 διῆγε: for the meaning 'make to continue, or keep, in a certain state' cf. Aesch. *Eum.* 994–5 καὶ γῆν καὶ πόλιν ὀρθοδίκαιον | πρέψετε πάντως διάγοντες, Dem. 18.89 ὁ γὰρ τότε ἐνστὰς πόλεμος . . . ἐν πᾶσι τοῖς κατὰ τὸν βίον ἀφθονωτέροις καὶ εὐωνοτέροις διήγαγεν (v.l. διῆγεν) ὑμᾶς τῆς νῦν εἰρήνης, LSJ⁹ s.v. διάγω III. The usual χρόνον διάγω is inverted: Clytemnestra makes herself seem a passive victim (so Campbell, *PS*). Compare 225 and 897 for other such inversions.

ὡς θανουμένην: cf. fr. 381.2 *TrGF*, Huys (1995) 247.

783 νῦν δ' . . . γάρ: for this combination cf. Hom. *Il.* 12.326–8, 24.223–4 (cited by Vahlen (1891) 355 = (1911–23) ii. 358–9 n. 8). The repeated νῦν δ' in 786 marks off the intervening clause more sharply than in these examples, and hence we need to print a dash; see Fraenkel on Aesch. *Ag.* 800 for γάρ in such parentheses. The jerky syntax conveys Clytemnestra's relieved excitement. For the recapitulation of this νῦν δ' in 786 after a substantial gap cf. *OR* 258–63, Aesch. *Cho.* 696–8, Bruhn §192.II.

ἀπηλλάγην: so KGRN and the Suda (π 2810 = iv. 233.20 Adler); cf. also ἀπαλλάγην in C. Λ's ἀνήλλαγμαι may also imply this reading, since ἀλλάσσω does not elsewhere take the prefix ἀνά before the imperial period. In the conclusion to her speech Clytemnestra will stress the state of tranquillity that she will now enjoy (787), and this might seem to favour the perfect ἀπήλλαγμαι found in most manuscripts (so Lanza and Fort (1991) 30–1), which is printed by Jebb and Dawe. But here the focus is on this day as the decisive moment of change from one condition to another (cf. νῦν δ', ἡμέρα . . . τῇδ): hence an instantaneous/contemporaneous aorist (668n.) is exactly what we need. This also balances the imperfects ἐπηπείλει and διῆγε (779, 782): Clytemnestra's imperfective state of torment is brought to an end by the perfective moment when the news was received. For the corruption of aorists to perfects Pearson (1923) 17 cites K–G i. 150 Anm. 3, Jebb's edition of *Antigone*, p. 3.

784 βλάβη: see next n.

785 ξύνοικος . . . ἐκπίνουσ': for this combination cf. *Ant.* 531–2 σὺ δ', ἣ κατ' οἴκους ὡς ἔχιδν' ὑφειμένη | λήθουσά μ' ἐξέπινες and *Tr.* 1054–6 (the robe) πλεύμονός τ' ἀρτηρίας | ῥοφεῖ ξυνοικοῦν· ἐκ δὲ χλωρὸν αἷμά μου | πέπωκεν ἤδη. The suffering caused by having to live with one's enemies has been an important theme (cf. 262–4n.); here it reaches a new level of horror by the mention of blood-sucking. This common metaphor for unpleasant treatment or punishment is frequent in comedy and mime: cf. Headlam on Herodas 5.7, Blaydes on Ar. *Nub.* 712, Ar. fr. 615 *PCG*, Theogn. 349, Eur. fr. 687.1–2 *TrGF* (satyr play), Plaut. *Bacch.* 372 with Fantham (1972) 101–2, Hor. *AP* 476.

343

Clytemnestra expresses the loathing she feels for her daughter through an ugly and colloquial image.

There may be an allusion to the snake of Aesch. *Cho.* 527–33. Clytemnestra attempts to suckle this creature in a dream, but it bites her breast, bringing forth a θρόμβον αἵματος (533); it is later identified with her son (549–50). There is no reference to a snake in S. Nevertheless, in both passages we do find the motif of blood-sucking in connexion with Clytemnestra and one of her children. In Aeschylus the act of blood-sucking stands for the single action of the matricide: this is obvious to Orestes at the time (540–50), and is mentioned by Clytemnestra immediately before her death (928–9). S. uses the motif to describe the long pain which Clytemnestra endured because of Electra's continued championing of her father. This adoption of a perfective image in Aeschylus into an imperfective context marks the changed focus of S.'s play, where the effects of lasting periods of suffering and passion form a major theme.

Winnington-Ingram (1954–5) 26 = (1980) 233 = E. Segal (1983) 216 suggests that Electra is being compared to an Erinys. These creatures are regularly associated with the sucking of blood (cf. Pearson on fr. 743, Garvie on Aesch. *Cho.* 577–8, Sommerstein on Aesch. *Eum.* 132, Padel (1992) 172–6), and at *Ant.* 1104 they are probably designated by the term Βλάβαι. But both the accusation of blood-sucking and the term βλάβη (301 n.) were common forms of abuse, and are not enough to make the identification secure. The failure to mention a snake would also be surprising were Winnington-Ingram's thesis correct, given the ubiquitous association of snake and Erinys (cf. Sansone (1988) 13 n. 68). The comparison of Orestes and Electra to ἄφυκτοι κύνες at 1388, a phrase which does have strong connotations of the Erinyes, is irrelevant here. Such an allusion cannot affect the interpretation of a passage six hundred lines before. Winnington-Ingram's view stems from an erroneous belief that this play is haunted by Erinyes. While they are occasionally mentioned, it is difficult to accept the level of thematic importance with which he credits them.

785–6 τοὐμὸν . . . | ψυχῆς . . . αἷμα: not τῆς ἐμῆς, as ψυχῆς and αἷμα form a single notion: cf. 1390, Bers (1974) 23. For the close association of the blood with the spirit or life see Gaster (1969) 65–6, Ar. *Nub.* 712 τὴν ψυχὴν ἐκπίνουσιν, Timocles fr. 37.1 *PCG* τἀργύριόν ἐστιν αἷμα καὶ ψυχὴ βροτοῖς.

786 ἄκρατον αἷμα: a sign of particular brutality: cf. Aesch. *Cho.* 577–8 φόνου δ' Ἐρινὺς οὐχ ὑπεσπανισμένη | ἄκρατον αἷμα πίεται. The point is not that civilised people always remember to dilute blood before drinking it; rather, the barbaric connotations of drinking wine neat (cf. Pl. *Leg.* 637e2–3, Gow and Page on Call. *A.P.* 7.725.1 = *Epigr.* 61.1 Pfeiffer = 1233 *HE*, E. M. Hall (1989) 133–4 with n. 91) are here transferred to the blood-sucking which

Clytemnestra attributes to Electra. For other connexions between blood and wine see 270n.

που: 'ironically expressing quiet assurance' (Denniston 491; cf. Wackernagel (1895) 22 = (1953-79) i. 701). The same dry confidence can be found at *Ant.* 777-8 κἀκεῖ τὸν Ἅιδην . . . | αἰτουμένη που τεύξεται τὸ μὴ θανεῖν.

787 τῶν τῆσδ᾿ ἀπειλῶν οὕνεχ᾿ 'as far as her threats are concerned' (cf. 387n.). **ἡμερεύσομεν:** cf. 653 εὐημεροῦσαν.

788 οἴμοι . . . οἰμῶξαι: for the picking up of the exclamation by the verb cf. *OC* 820, Jackson (1955) 86.

τάλαινα: on this adjective see 273n.

νῦν: on the significance of this word see 764-822n.

For **γάρ** immediately after an expression of sorrow cf. Eur. *Hel.* 857, Ferri on [Sen.] *Oct.* 9.

οἰμῶξαι πάρα: cf. Aesch. *Pers.* 471 πάρα στένειν.

789 Ὀρέστα: the direct address of the dead man (also at 808) marks the intensity of the speaker's grief (cf. *Aj.* 1269).

789-90 ὅθ᾿ ὧδ᾿ ἔχων | πρὸς τῆσδ᾿ ὑβρίζῃ μητρός: Electra laments first not her brother's death, but her mother's exultation in her brother's death. Compare Aesch. *Ag.* 1399-1400, where the chorus seems more shocked by the defiant tone of Clytemnestra's boasting than by the murder she has just committed. For **ὑβρίζῃ** see 271n.

ἆρ᾿ ἔχει καλῶς; Ll-J/W adopt F. W. Schmidt's ἔχω ((1886-7) i. 137-8), which is also advocated by Broadhead (1968) 117. This cannot be right. In 788-90 Electra is outraged by Clytemnestra's mockery of her dead son. The concluding ἆρ᾿ ἔχει καλῶς; asks whether such treatment is appropriate; the question expects the answer 'no' (as at 804-6 and 816; cf. Denniston 46 II (2)). ἔχω, however, would put the focus on Electra's own state. Yet apart from the opening οἴμοι τάλαινα, Electra's words here are concerned with the insult done to her brother. Unlike Clytemnestra, she does not regard her own condition as of primary importance: an ἔχω in 790 would thus jar with the context. Ll-J/W cite 816 as a parallel: but there the focus has been on Electra's own state since 812, and hence the μοι is entirely appropriate (816 may be an interpolation (n.), but that does not affect the argument). More relevant is the Paedagogus' εἰ τάδ᾿ εὖ κυρεῖ in 799; with ἔχει here, there is a contrast between two utterances close in form, but opposed in emotional content.

A second difficulty with Schmidt's emendation is the transition from 790 to 791; in particular, the emphatic οὔτοι σύ in 791. It makes perfect sense for Clytemnestra to pick up on Electra's 'Is this well?' with an aggressive '*You're* not, I tell you; as for *him*, he's well as he is.' With ἔχω, however, this stressed second person pronoun seems quite out of place: the consequent (Electra) 'Am I well?' (Clytemnestra) '*You're* not' does not quite ring true, even given the following κεῖνος δέ. Ll-J/W's adoption of Schmidt's ἔχω, far from removing a 'slight awkwardness' (*Sophoclea*), seems rather to have introduced one.

791 οὔτοι σύ: not a wish for Electra's death (*pace* Jebb); Pfeiffer-Petersen (1996) III n. 29 rightly sees it as a reference to Electra's miserable condition.

κεῖνος . . . καλῶς ἔχει: Kaibel's 'er hat's gut' (p. 194) catches the tone; cf. Aesch. *Cho.* 892 (Orestes to Clytemnestra) σὲ καὶ ματεύω· τῷδε (sc. Aegisthus) δ' ἀρκούντως ἔχει, with Garvie. Clytemnestra's words recall a formula used elsewhere as a consolatory euphemism for death (as at Eur. *Tro.* 268 ἔχει καλῶς, said by Talthybius of the dead Polyxena); this further marks the sarcasm. For another play with καλός in the context of death cf. Plut. *Ant.* 85.8. For the anticipation of that phrase by ὡς ἔχει see Fraser (2001) 32 with n. 56.

792 ἄκουε: on the aspect see 643n.

Νέμεσι: outrageous statements such as Clytemnestra's in 791 are often met with an invocation of νέμεσις: cf. Eur. *Phoen.* 182–4, Pittacus D–K 10 ε 5 (= i. 64.13–14), Pl. *Leg.* 717d2–3, Call. *Hymn* 6.56, Meleager *A.P.* 12.33.3–4 = 4482–3 *HE*, anon. *A.P.* 12.140.3 = 3714 *HE*, Nonn. *Dion.* 37.422–3. Such invocations reflect the rôle of νέμεσις as 'the counterpart and companion of *aidos*, the angry resentful aspect of *aidos* which comes into operation at the lack of it in another' (MacLeod (2001) 129): for this well-established connexion between νέμεσις and αἰδώς cf. Cairns (1993) 51–4, adding to his examples Hes. *Op.* 200 with West, *Cypria* fr. 7.5–6 *EGF* = 9.5–6 *PEG* = 10.5–6 *GEF*. The address to νέμεσις suggests a degree of personification: for the cult of this goddess see Mastronarde on Eur. *Phoen.* 182.

Contrast the link between νέμεσις and ὕβρις, which is popularly supposed to be fundamental to Greek tragedy. It is in fact rare: outside our passage instances occur at Eur. *Phoen.* 183–5, Paus. 1.33.2 and Mesomedes 3.1–6 Heitsch. Nor are the two connected in classical art: the two surviving depictions of the goddess Nemesis trampling over a figure representing Hybris (*LIMC* s.v. Nemesis §§268, 274; cf. Rausa (1992) 766) are both of late imperial date.

The form of the vocative is metrically guaranteed at Eur. *Phoen.* 182, as is ξύνεσι at Ar. *Ran.* 893.

τοῦ θανόντος: 'the grammatical classification of the genitive case is necessarily a problem in the history of religion' (Dover (1974) 245 n. 5). It may refer either to a general personified νέμεσις (sc. of the gods), which here shows outrage at the insults done to the dead, or else to a specific νέμεσις that belongs to the dead man, functioning as a sort of chthonic power (cf. Fisher (1992) 301). νέμεσις usually refers to a νέμεσις of the gods, and four of its occurrences in tragedy explicitly signal this divine origin. *Phil.* 517–18, 601–2 and Eur. *Or.* 1361–2 all qualify it with θεῶν; while in Aesch. fr. 266.4–5 *TrGF* ἡμῶν γε μέντοι Νέμεσις ἔσθ᾽ ὑπερτέρα | καὶ τοῦ θανόντος ἡ Δίκη πράσσει κότον the speaker is probably the god Hermes. But the need to signal its divine origin by the addition of a genitive implies that other beings can have their own νεμέσεις too: the concept 'well merits its ᾗπερ when a poet is going to describe its functions for us in any given particular context' (Dawe, *STS* iii. 127; cf. anon. *A.P.* 12.160.6 = 3781 *HE*, *A.P.* 6.283.2 = 3819 *HE*).

Positive evidence for a chthonic νέμεσις is generally late: cf. *EG* 119.4 = *GVI* 480.4 (Piraeus, 2nd–3rd cent. AD) φθιμένων ὠκυτάτη Νέμεσις, *EG* 367.9 = *GVI* 675a.9 = *SGO* 16/32/12.9 (Phrygia, 3rd cent. AD; Kaibel's text) ἔστι γὰρ καὶ ἐν φθιμένοις Νέμεσις μέγα, ἔστι ἐπὶ τύμβοις, Timaeus Locrus *De nat. mund.* 104e5 (p. 150 Marg) (Nemesis acts σὺν δαίμοσι παλαμναίοις χθονίοις τε), Dietrich (1965) 165–70. But Dem. 41.11 mentions an Athenian festival called the Νεμέσια, which is described by the scholia and lexicographers as ἡ ἐπὶ τοῖς νεκροῖς γινομένη πανήγυρις, ἐπεὶ ἡ νέμεσις ἐπὶ τῶν νεκρῶν τέτακ-ται (Deubner (1966) 230; see however R. C. T. Parker (1996) 246 n. 101 on the possibility of textual corruption). In art Nemesis is often depicted with a snake, a creature with prominent chthonic associations (cf. *LIMC* s.v. Neme-sis §§154, 162, 230d, 232–8 (VI/2 pp. 440, 445)), and according to Σ Clem. Al. *Protr.* 2.37.2 (p. 308.13 Stählin) Zeus took on that form to woo her. This seems sufficient evidence to establish the existence of a νέμεσις with chthonic connotations, who is associated with the dead. We should not be swayed by Dover's claim that 'even in the fifth century, the ghost's capacity for direct action on its own initiative . . . was regarded as limited; it was rather the gods' interest in the rights of the dead that mattered' ((1974) 254). His exam-ples are taken mainly from oratory; in tragedy the lasting power of the angry dead is a familiar concept. It is especially appropriate in our play, with its emphasis on the continuing animus of the dead Agamemnon against his killers.

ἀρτίως: elsewhere in S. always of recent time in the past (a few hours ago at most); here 'ἀρτίως θανών *Orestes dicitur, quod modo audiverant de eius morte*' (Ellendt s.v.). For the position of the adverb cf. *Aj.* 635 ὁ νοσῶν μάταν, [Aesch.] *PV* 216 τῶν παρεστώτων τότε, Andoc. 1.53 τῶν ἀπολωλότων ἤδη. ἄρτι regularly follows its verb in prose (cf. Diggle on Theophr. *Char.* 12.7).

793 ὧν: probably masculine or feminine plural (referring to Clytemnes-tra) rather than neuter (referring to Clytemnestra's prayer). This makes for a better contrast with the preceding line ('she has listened not to you, but to me').

κἀπεκύρωσεν: found elsewhere in tragedy at Eur. *Or.* 862, where as here it has a judicial tone (also 1013 κατακυρωθείς: cf. Isaeus 7.42, Thuc. 5.45.4). Along with the other aorist ἤκουσεν, the verb carries notions of finality which Clytemnestra will soon find to be mistaken.

καλῶς: continuing the play with this word from 790–1 (nn.).

794 ὕβριζε: on ὕβρις see 271n.

νῦν . . . εὐτυχοῦσα τυγχάνεις: 'der Hörer . . . empfindet . . . in El.s Antwort . . . das νῦν anders als es El. gemeint, als Gegensatz nicht zur Vergangenheit sondern zur nächsten Zukunft' (Kaibel, pp. 194–5); cf. 764–822n. on νῦν. For 'hybris generated by prosperity' (Nisbet and Hubbard on Hor. *C.* 2.3.3) cf. Solon fr. 6.3–4 *IEG*, Theogn. 153–4.

795 'The form of a question is important for the irony, because it allows also the correct answer, yes, to form in the audience's mind' (Kitzinger (1991) 319).

οὔκουν: questions beginning with this word tend to have an emotional or excited edge (cf. Denniston 431–2). For the distinction between this particle and οὐκοῦν cf. Sicking (1997). For the tone cf. *OR* 440 (Tiresias to Oedipus) οὔκουν σὺ ταῦτ' ἄριστος εὑρίσκειν ἔφυς;

παύσετον: the repetition of παυ-words is ironic (cf. 764–822n.). For the 'stopping' motif see 304n.

796 A powerful admission of failure from the indomitable Electra.

οὐχ ὅπως σὲ παύσομεν 'not to speak of stopping you' (cf. LSJ⁹ s.v. ὅπως II 2, Goodwin §707, K–G ii. 257–60). In such expressions the οὐχ ὅπως (or οὐχ ὅτι) normally comes in the first clause, followed by another beginning ἀλλά or ἀλλὰ καί (e.g. Thuc. 1.35.4). Occasionally, however, it comes in the second clause (cf. Goodwin §708, K–G ii. 260 §4a, LSJ⁹ s.v. ὅπως II 2 b). I have not found a verse parallel for this usage, and it may be colloquial (cf. Stevens (1945) 100–1; Waś (1983) 180 is cautious).

σέ: the accented form is justified by the contrast with ἡμεῖς.

797–8 Clytemnestra addresses the Paedagogus in tones of cosy familiarity, in contrast with the contempt she shows her daughter.

797 ἂν ἥκοις 'it would seem that you have come'. For optative plus ἄν 'as rather cautious variants of the present or future indicative' see Rijksbaron (1991) 159–60. Morstadt's ἄρ' ἥκεις ((1864) 26) would give much the same meaning, but the minority variant ἥκεις provides little support for such a reading, since optatives are often corrupted to indicatives.

τυχεῖν: G has φίλος, LᵃᶜΛ φιλεῖν; the remaining manuscripts have τυχεῖν. Dawe's suggestion that the two readings beginning φίλ- originated from a gloss φίλ' on ξέν' accounts for the different variants. Similar glosses occur in L at *Tr.* 263 (Σ p. 295.19 Papageorgius), in FON at *Aj.* 817 (Christodoulou's edition of the scholia, p. 320), and in CFb at Aesch. *Sept.* 727 (Smith's edition of the scholia, ii. fasc. 2 p. 317 line 21). For the construction with τυχεῖν cf. *Aj.* 924 ἄξιος θρήνων τυχεῖν; also *Ant.* 699 ἀξία τιμῆς λαχεῖν.

Lloyd-Jones (1978) 219 suggests that ἄξιος, which commonly takes an infinitive, caused an original φίλος to became φιλεῖν; this was altered to τυχεῖν by a reader who noticed that it did not make sense. φίλος is used by Clytemnestra to designate the messenger in the comparable section of *Choephori* (708, cited below, 800n.), which lends this reading some support; but ἄξιος with bare πολλῶν seems odd. Vahlen (1895) 10–14 = (1907–8) ii. 165–71 prefers φιλεῖν. After noting the common use of ἄξιος with an 'active' infinitive when the meaning required is passive (e.g. Eur. *Or.* 1153–4 ἀξία στυγεῖν ἔφυ | ἡ Τυνδαρὶς παῖς, *El.* 1016 etc.; historically speaking what we call the 'active' infinitive is neither active nor passive), he cites instances where this usage is accompanied by παντός, such as Pl. *Phaedr.* 260b8 παντὸς ἄξιον τὸ θρέμμα οἴκοι τε κεκτῆσθαι καὶ ἐπὶ στρατιᾶς, Ar. *Av.* 797 ἄρ' ὑπόπτερον γενέσθαι παντός ἐστιν ἄξιον; But in these examples παντός functions as an intensifier, and there is no reason to suppose that πολλῶν should be able to take on this function.

798 εἰ τήνδ' ἔπαυσας: for εἰ + aorist indicative of what is known to be true cf. *OC* 974–5 εἰ δ'. . . | ἐς χεῖρας ἦλθον πατρὶ καὶ κατέκτανον, Aesch. *Pers.* 217 εἴ τι φλαῦρον εἶδες. There may nevertheless be a sarcastic 'nuance of disbelief and scepticism' in Clytemnestra's words (so Wakker (1994) 143): she pretends not to be able to believe that Electra has been silenced. Wunder's τήνδε παύσαις ((1843) 1–19, and then in his third edition) ruins this effect by giving us a future remote condition, which is not appropriate here: see Schneidewin (1852).

πολυγλώσσου βοῆς: the same phrase at 641, where Clytemnestra had been afraid Electra would interrupt her prayer. Now her shouting is of no consequence (802–3).

799–802 The Paedagogus offers to leave; Clytemnestra insists that he receives the hospitality owing to him. Cf. Eur. *Hyps.* fr. 752e *TrGF* (with Bond's commentary, p. 11), *Alc.* 538–9 (Ηρ.) ξένων πρὸς ἄλλων ἑστίαν πορεύσομαι. | (Ἀδ.) οὐκ ἔστιν, ὦναξ· μὴ τοσόνδ' ἔλθοι κακόν. Here the niceties of hospitality are juxtaposed with Clytemnestra's savage cruelty towards her daughter.

799 οὐκοῦν: without a question mark, as editors print at Ar. *Eccl.* 853 οὐκοῦν βαδιοῦμαι δῆτα (cf. Denniston 436, S–D ii. 589). An οὔκουν question (795n.), as printed by Dindorf[1] and Ll-J/W, would be too pointed and excited in this context.[51] Hutchinson on Aesch. *Sept.* 248 claims that the following ἥκιστ' 'demands a question' in this line; see however the passage from Euripides' *Hypsipyle* cited in the previous n. for ἥκιστα in response to a similar statement.

εἰ τάδ' εὖ κυρεῖ: the Paedagogus pretends not to have noticed the bitter dispute before him (cf. *OR* 530). His uninvolved, matter-of-fact tone contrasts with the anguish of Electra's ἆρ'ἔχει καλῶς; (790; cf. also 816), and the taunting of Clytemnestra's κἀπεκύρωσεν καλῶς (793).

800 Cf. Aesch. *Cho.* 707–8 οὔτοι κυρήσεις μεῖον' ἀξίας σέθεν, | οὐδ' ἧσσον ἂν γένοιο δώμασιν φίλος.

ἥκιστ': 82n.

ἐπείπερ: for the absence of a protasis meaning 'if you were to leave' see 323n.

κατάξι' ἄν: Hermann and Jebb keep the majority reading καταξίως; the latter claims that ἄν is understood here from the previous line. But in his parallels (*OR* 937 ἥδοιο μέν, πῶς δ'οὐκ ἄν; ἀσχάλλοις δ' ἴσως, Pl. *Lys.* 208b3–4, Xen. *An.* 4.6.13) the gap between the clauses is smaller than here, and they both have the same grammatical construction. In this instance 'it is a bold act to take an ἄν from a potential optative, close in tone to a simple indicative, and to use it again with an optative standing in the apodosis of a conditional sentence with a suppressed protasis' (Dawe, *STS* i. 188). The syntax requires Bothe's κατάξι' ἄν (in his first edition): for this we need not even emend, but rather simply reinterpret the minority variants καταξίαν and κατ' ἀξίαν. The adverbial accusative plural is often glossed by the adverb in –ως (Pearson (1919) 118), which can lead to corruption (e.g. *Aj.* 196, possibly *OC* 911).

802 εἴσιθ' εἴσω: cf. *Aj.* 296 εἴσω δ' ἐσῆλθε, Bruhn §206.

βοᾶν probably 'bawl' rather than 'lament', as with the latter meaning the following accusatives would be unusual (cf. Page on [Anacr.] *A.P.* 7.226.2 = 485 *FGE*).

803 'Our last glimpse of Klytaimnestra as she departs inside the palace gives us not Kells' "horror-stricken mother", but a woman overjoyed and full of relief at the death of an enemy: her son' (MacLeod (2001) 125). Clytemnestra speaks the final lines as she accompanies the Paedagogus inside. This normally indicates that the speaking character has the upper hand (cf. 1504, Taplin (1977a) 310, 343 on Aesch. *Cho.* 718); in our case it provides a final irony.

[51] Elmsley on Eur. *Ba.* 191 had already advocated printing the line as a question, though with οὐκ οὖν rather than οὔκουν.

804–22 Clytemnestra and the Paedagogus leave through the *skene*; Electra moves to a more central position on the stage for the first time since 633. Her lament balances her mother's speech at 773–87; the difference in tone and content need not be laboured. Her focus now moves to the consequences of Orestes' death for her own future. Orestes had always been the source of her hopes (306n.); she lived in the expectation that he would return (ἥξειν 294, 304) alive (ζῶντα 456) to avenge their father (455–6). In 809–12 all these motifs are repeated from earlier on, only to be poignantly dismissed with the following νῦν δέ. She then considers a return to her former mode of existence (812–16): but whereas before the hope of Orestes' return had sustained her in her wretchedness (323), this consolation has now gone. Suddenly at 817 she seizes on a new resolve, to remain outside, to suffer and die (cf. Easterling (1987) 20–1). Even now she retains her capacity to surprise us, to do the unexpected: 'her monologue . . . with its shifting to and fro, contains yet again enough inner movements to make a drama in itself' (Reinhardt (1979) 153 ≈ (1947) 163). The firmness of her purpose looks forward to the following *kommos*, in which she will repeatedly reject the chorus's attempts at consolation.

804–7 Electra is appalled that her mother fails to display any of the usual outward signs of grief. Compare Dido's words to Aeneas (Virg. *Aen.* 4.369–70) *num fletu ingemuit nostro? num lumina flexit? | num lacrimas victus dedit . . . ?*; also Ter. *Andr.* 877–8 *num cogitat quid dicat? num facti piget? | vide num eius color pudori' signum usquam indicat.* She describes her mother's reaction in still stronger terms at 1153–4.

804 ἄρ': 790n.
ἀλγοῦσα κὠδυνωμένη: for the combination cf. Pl. *Gorg.* 525b7 δι' ἀλγηδόνων καὶ ὀδυνῶν.

805 δεινῶς: often of sounds marking emotional agitation: cf. Kaimio (1977) 175–6.
δακρῦσαι κἀπικωκῦσαι: for the combination cf. Hom. *Od.* 19.541 αὐτὰρ ἐγὼ κλαῖον καὶ ἐκώκυον.

806 ἡ δύστηνος: perhaps 'wicked', as at 121 (cf. Ellendt s.v.); but the sense is more forceful if Electra is using the word sarcastically in its usual meaning 'wretched'.
ὧδ' ὀλωλότα: not least among Electra's sorrows is the gruesome manner in which Orestes perished (cf. 861–3; Ov. *Trist.* 1.2.51).

807 ἀλλ' ἐγγελῶσα φροῦδος: the verbless phrase forms a curt climax to a long, emotionally-charged sentence: cf. Eur. *Or.* 720–1 τὰ δ' Ἀγαμέμνονος | φροῦδ'.

For Electra's horror of laughter see 277n. Contrast Aeschylus' Clytemnestra, who at least has the decency to conceal her subsequent delight (*Cho.* 738–9).

808 Ὀρέστα φίλταθ': on the force of the invocation see 789n.

ὥς μ' ἀπώλεσας θανών: a frequent motif in contexts of grief: cf. 208, 1152, 1163–4, *Aj.* 901, 1025–7, Eur. *Hipp.* 810, 839. It is related to the 'dead are killing the living' *topos* (1417–21 n.).

809 ἀποσπάσας: cf. *OR* 1432 ἐλπίδος μ' ἀπέσπασας.

812 ποῖ με χρὴ μολεῖν; A common cry from those reduced to despair: cf. *Aj.* 403, 1006, *OC* 1748–9, Eur. *Med.* 502, Enn. *Med. Ex.* 217 with Jocelyn, Catullus 64.177, Sall. *Jug.* 14.15, Fowler (1987), Schauer (2002) 232–3. The question is often, as here, followed by a statement expressing the desire for death (cf. *Tr.* 705, 719–20, *Aj.* 404, 416–17, Fowler (1987) 17 with n. 28).

813 μόνη . . . εἰμι: at 118–20 Electra prayed for her brother's return because she could no longer bear her suffering alone. With his death, she is permanently on her own: cf. 950, 1019, 1074, Knox (1964) 32–3.

τ': Dawe prints his own conjecture γ', arguing that 'Electra is alone *because* she no longer has her brother or her father . . . rather than because she has lost *both* brother *and* father' (*STS* i. 188). But as he himself points out, the force of τε . . . καί is not as strong as that of the English 'both . . . and'.

814 δουλεύειν: cf. 189–92, 264–5 etc.

815 On Electra's pain in having to live with her father's killers cf. 262–4n.

816 Morstadt's deletion ((1864) 26–7) is worth considering; it is easy to imagine how a scribe might amplify 815 by adding φονεῦσι πατρός, and then fill in the rest of the line with a phrase adapted from 790. On the other hand, the line is not noticeably lower in quality than the verses around it, nor is the appalled question inappropriate in the context.

ἄρά: 790n.

817 For adversative ἀλλ' . . . μήν see Denniston 341–2, Fraenkel on Aesch. *Ag.* 1640; accompanied by ἔγωγε, it marks a strong break (cf. *Phil.* 1273).

τοῦ λοιποῦ χρόνου: for the genitive of time see 477n.

818 ἔσομαι ξύνοικος: manuscript ξύνοικος ἔσ(σ)ομαι is unmetrical; Dawes's transposition ((1745) 281 = (1800) 229) is the simplest and best solution. This is a common corruption (cf. Headlam (1902), Jackson (1955)

228–31). In this case it is just possible that a recollection of 785's line-initial ξύνοικος may have assisted the mistake. Hermann's ξύνοικος εἴσειμ᾽, adopted by Jebb, Pearson and Dawe, may throw too great a stress on the *act* of going inside, given that through the play it has been the *state* of living inside that has so tormented Electra (262–4n.).

819 παρεῖσ᾽ ἐμαυτήν 'allowing myself to sink to the ground' (Jebb); cf. *Tr.* 938 πλευρόθεν | πλευρὰν παρεὶς ἔκειτο, Eur. *Ba.* 683 ηὗδον δὲ πᾶσαι σώμασιν παρειμέναι, Sappho fr. 42 *PLF*, Voigt ταῖσι . . . ψῦχρος μὲν ἔγεντο ὁ θῦμος | πὰρ δ᾽ ἴεισι τὰ πτέρα, Suda (π 601 = iv. 54.2–3 Adler) καὶ παρεὶς ἑαυτὸν ὑπὸ λύπης ἔκειτο, Ov. *Trist.* 1.3.91 –2 *illa dolore amens tenebris narratur obortis* | *semianimis media procubuisse domo*, Isaiah 3.26 'and she being desolate shall sit upon the ground'.

αὐανῶ βίον: cf. *Phil.* 954 ἀλλ᾽ αὐανοῦμαι τῷδ᾽ ἐν αὐλίῳ μόνος, Eur. *El.* 239 ξηρὸν δέμας (of Electra), [Aesch.] *PV* 147. For the aspiration (inserted by Blaydes (1899) 250) see West's Teubner Aeschylus, p. xxx.

821–2 Speeches in S. often end with an antithetical formulation (cf. 1320–1, Reeve (1970) 288–9); for this technique as a closural device in literature more generally see Smith (1968) 168–71. A sentence with an imperative followed by one beginning with ὡς is also common at the end of a speech: cf. *Phil.* 1040–4, 1440–4, *Tr.* 484–9, Fraenkel (1963*b*) 66–7.

821 κτάνῃ: Σ 975 (p. 144.20 Papageorgius) in its quotation of this line replaces this word with θάνω, which is approved by Brunck[1]. But θανεῖν is so much the regular antithesis to ζῆν that such a corruption is not surprising; for this confusion see Diggle (1981 a) 82, adding perhaps Eur. *El.* 685 (θανεῖν L, κτανεῖν Seidler, adopted by Kovacs). Corruption from θανεῖν into the rarer κτάνῃ is less likely.

822 τοῦ βίου δ᾽ οὐδεὶς πόθος: cf. Eur. *Med.* 226–7 βίου | χάριν μεθεῖσα κατθανεῖν χρήζω, φίλαι, Eur. *Her.* 316–17 οὐδὲ τοῦ βίου πόθος | θανεῖν ἐρύκει μ᾽, Sappho fr. 95.10–13 *PLF*, Voigt, Ar. *Lys.* 865; for the form cf. Xen. *Mem.* 1.4.7 πόθον τοῦ ζῆν.

Electra's situation resembles that of Philoctetes after the loss of his bow (*Phil.* 1207–8). Deprived of her one great resource, she can only lament and wait for death.[52] The mother has just entered the house in triumph; the daughter remains outside in despair.

---

[52] 'Each [of these two plays] has a framework of intrigue which carries pain and loneliness to their limits before relief comes' (Reinhardt (1979) 136 ≈ (1947) 146).

KOMMOS (823–70)

FIRST STROPHIC PAIR (823–848)

823	837	– ⏔ ⏑ – – ⏑ ⏑ –	ia 3cho ad
		– ⏑ ⏑ – ˈ – ⏑ ⏑ – – ⏑ ⏑ – – ˈ	
825		– – ⏑ ⏑ – – ‖	reiz
	840	∷ ⏑ ⏑ – – ‖	io
		∷ – – ⏑ ⏑ – – ‖	reiz
830	845	∷ – ∷ – – ⏑ ⏑ – – ∷ ⏑ ⏑ – ∷ – ‖	pher^c
		∷ – – ⏑ ⏑ – – ⏑ ⏑ –	
835		– ⏑ ⏑ – – ⏑ ⏑ – – ⏑ ⏑ –	tel^{6c} (dragged)
		– ⏑ ⏑ – ˈ – ⏑ ⏑ – – – ‖‖‖	

The choriambic analysis printed above is that preferred by Kannicht (1973) 121 = (1996) 163 and Griffith (1974) 213. Dale (1971–83) i. 36–7 offers instead a predominantly ionic analysis for the stanza. The colon ×–U–– (823 ~ 837) begins a series of ionics at e.g. 1058 ~ 1070, Anacr. fr. 412 *PMG*, Aesch. *Sept.* 720, [Aesch.] *PV* 128 and Eur. *Phoen.* 1509, while the catalectic UU––– at 836 ~ 848 may end such a series at *Tr.* 850. Under this analysis 831–6 ~ 846–8 must begin with an acephalous ionic metron, for which there does not seem to be a parallel. But if ionic runs can begin –UU–– (cf. West (1982a) 125–6), there should be no difficulty with one beginning ––UU––. Dale (1968) 122 n. 2 prefers to render this final section as a series of ionics *a maiore* (i.e. ––UU); but there is no good evidence for the existence of this metron, which is probably a fiction of Hephaestion's (cf. L. P. E. Parker (1997) 64).

However, a choriambic analysis should be preferred for the following reasons. First and most important, it harmonises better with the word-division of the piece. In all but four places the end of a metron coincides with the end of a word or word group: hence many words fit snugly into a choriamb (οἰχομένων, Ἀμφιάρεων etc.), as often occurs in this metrical context (cf. West (1982a) 32, 118). Under an ionic analysis, however, metron division fails to coincide with a word break in a full fifteen places. Second, the rest of the stanza has a strong aeolo-choriambic colouring, including some choriambic expansion at 830 ~ 45. The only definite ionic metron is at 826 ~ 840, an exclamation and therefore a special case. Finally, aeolic lengths extended by series of choriambs (the asclepiadic metres) are characteristically Sophoclean (Dale (1968) 155, West (1982a) 118); so too is the introduction of these series by an iambic metron instead of an aeolic base (Parker (1997) 79; e.g. *Aj.* 227 ~ 251). Predominantly ionic stanzas, however, are not common in S. 1058–81 of our play forms one example, though even there we are dealing with anacreontics rather than ionics proper. The only other possible instance, *OR* 483–511, is also susceptible to choriambic analysis (cf. Parker (1997) 64).[53]

SECOND STROPHIC PAIR (849–870)

849	860	– ∪ – – ∪ – ∪ – ‖	cr hδ
850		:: ⏓ – ⏓ – ⏓ ⏜∪ ⏓ – ˈ	2an
		⏓ – ⏓ – ⏓ – ⏓ – ˈ	2an
		⏓ – ⏓ – ⏓ – ∪ ‖	an anᴧ
		:: ∪ ⏜∪ – ∪ – ‖	δ
	865	:: – ∪ – – ∪ ∪ ‖	2cr
855		⏜∪ ∪ – ∪ – :: ∪ – ‖	lec
		:: ∪ – ∪ – ∪ – ∪ ∪ – ∪ ∪ – ˈ	iambel
	870	– ∪ ∪ – ∪ – – ‖‖	cho iaᴧ

The interpretation printed for 849 ~ 860 is supported by Wilamowitz (1921) 371 and (tentatively) Medda (1993) 145. Its chief merit is that it balances the cretics and dochmiac later in the stanza, and thus makes the stanza feel more of a metrical unity. Medda compares *Phil.* 1212 for cretic plus hypodochmiac; while for a dochmiac leading into a sequence of anapaests see West (1982a) 112. For the short αι in the δειλαί– element see Jebb on *Ant.* 1310, West (1982a) 11. Less likely is the analysis 'an ia', which involves reading πᾶσιν in 860 and scanning δειλαία in 849 with a long αι. For the δειλαί– element taking two different scansions in close proximity cf. 148n.

For the responsion of the dochmiacs at 853 ~ 864 see 853n.

The sporadic appearance of dochmiacs in an anapaestic context is not unusual (cf. 233–5, L. P. E. Parker (1997) 57). In theory it would be possible to eliminate the dochmiacs from the metrical scheme, by adopting the 'an ia' analysis cited above for 849 ~ 860 and taking 853 ~ 864 as a dodrans (cf. West (1982a) 117 n. 103). However, there is no other aeolo-choriambic element in the stanza to go with the latter, while the iambic metron would also be isolated. The resulting correspondence of final – – with ∪ –, while not impossible in aeolo-choriambic, makes this option still more unattractive (cf. Itsumi (1984) 75; Diggle (1983) 347 = (1994) 258–9 is too sanguine on this point). Parker's parallels show that it is not unusual to find occasional dochmiacs among anapaests; here they are also supported by the cretics, which

---

[53] The opening of the present stanza might alternatively be analysed ia 4cho pher, but this does not match the word division so well. Korzeniewski (1968) 13 attempts to rid us of the ionic metron at 826 ~ 840 by analysing ia 4cho pher^c: however, the hiatus after 825 ~ 839 renders this impossible.

often accompany dochmiacs elsewhere (West (1982a) 111–12, L. P. E. Parker (1997) 43, 66–7).

The interpretation of 854 ~ 865 is supported by Medda (1993) 131 and Ll-J/W (*Second Thoughts*). Period-end before the lecythion allows *brevis in longo* at the end of the cretic dimeter. Willink (2003) 80 prefers cr δ ia for 854–6 ~ 865–7; but the isolated iambic metron, split in half by change of speaker, would be unusual.

The iambelegus of 856 ~ 867 is a dactylo-epitrite length (∪ e ∪ D) found in a variety of contexts. The change to a different metrical type occurs in the penultimate colon (as at 211 ~ 231; cf. West (1982a) 100). Alternatively, the final two lines might be analysed 2ia ‖ 2cho ia∧, but this is a little less likely, as it involves postulating both *brevis in longo* in 856 (ἔτι) and hiatus in 867.

823-70 The *kommos* has obvious similarities with the parodos. A solo lament from Electra leads into a lyric dialogue, in which the chorus repeatedly fails to console her for losing a member of her family. But in the parodos this loss had taken place long in the past, and Electra's continual lamentation was, in part, a way of keeping the dead man's memory alive. Here her grief is for a death that is all too recent, and for that reason is even more intense. And while before there was at least the prospect of an avenger, which could provide some comfort to Electra, here it is that avenger who has just met his end. Now, it seems, there is no hope. The relationship between Electra and the chorus has also undergone a change. Electra no longer acknowledges the friendly motives of the chorus (contrast 130–1, 134), and her rejections of its assistance are more vehement (cf. 830, 861–3). The staccato exchange, different from the leisurely style of the parodos, conveys the increase in tension.

The lyric is carefully structured. The first strophe and antistrophe both contain a gradual movement from the chorus to Electra: the chorus begins by offering attempts at consolation, while she concludes by showing the futility of that consolation. In the second half of the *kommos* Electra dominates the dialogue, as if to express her 'victory' in its first half; the chorus is limited to short, conventional remarks which by their banality highlight Electra's expressive power. Connexions between the two strophes and the two antistrophes can also be observed. At the end of each of the strophes Electra passionately forbids the chorus from even suggesting that her brother might still be alive; in each case, she is briefly interrupted by a choral question (830, 855). The chorus's tone is more directly consolatory at the start of the antistrophes; but on both occasions Electra strongly rejects the attempted succour, and the chorus is reduced to using the words of grief which it had earlier avoided (845 φεῦ, 866 παπαῖ).

Broken-up dialogue is common in late Sophoclean lyric (cf. *Phil.* 1169–1217, *OC* 176–236, 510–48, 833–43, 876–86).[54] In our play it occurs in the recognition duet and Clytemnestra's death scene. While it is occasionally found in Euripides, it never takes on the clipped, agonistic manner seen here. *Phil.* 1169–1217 provides the closest parallel for the present case: both Philoctetes and Electra have just been deprived of their greatest resource (822n.), and now the depth of this loss is brought out by the failure of the chorus's attempts at consolation. The use of dialogue form keeps the focus on the protagonist and his (or her) emotions. But the form also emphasises (paradoxically) the protagonist's increased isolation, dominated as it is by argument and disagreement rather than mutual support and assistance.

Yet despite this loneliness and vulnerability, through her language in this *kommos* Electra reveals a new strength. The range of her expression is very wide: from inarticulate cries to passionate commands, from angry colloquialism to majestic statements of grief. Even at her lowest point, she remains a compelling figure.

For more on the θρῆνος in tragedy see Broadhead's edition of Aeschylus' *Persae*, pp. 311–13.

823–5 At first sight this seems a condemnation of divine indifference to suffering: cf. Bacchyl. 3.38–9 πο]ῦ θεῶν ἐστι[ν] χάρις; | πο]ῦ δὲ Λατοίδ[ας] ἄναξ; with Hutchinson, Ov. *Her.* 12.119 *numen ubi est? ubi di?* with Bessone. But such an attitude would clash with the chorus's following injunction to Electra to avoid blasphemy (830n.); and Electra's response indicates that she believes that the chorus is offering her consolation, not attacking the gods. The εἰ should rather be taken as a true 'if': the chorus is saying 'if the gods see this and do not punish, they are nowhere, but since they exist, they will punish' (so rightly Kamerbeek); cf. *OR* 895–6 εἰ γὰρ αἱ τοιαίδε πράξεις τίμιαι, | τί δεῖ με χορεύειν;, Hes. *Op.* 270–2 νῦν δὴ ἐγὼ μήτ' αὐτὸς ἐν ἀνθρώποισι δίκαιος | εἴην . . . ἐπεὶ κακὸν ἄνδρα δίκαιον | ἔμμεναι, εἰ μείζω γε δίκην ἀδικώτερος ἕξει.

823 ποῦ ποτε κεραυνοὶ Διός; for 'the thunderbolt as the weapon of divine justice' see Nisbet and Rudd on Hor. *C.* 3.4.44 and cf. e.g. *OR* 200–2. Lucian 25.1 cites ποῦ σοι νῦν ἡ ἐρισμάραγος ἀστραπὴ καὶ ἡ βαρύβρομος βροντή as an example of poetic λῆρος; cf. Sen. *Phaedr.* 673–4 *et quando saeva fulmen emittes manu,* | *si nunc serenum est?*, Ferri on [Sen.] *Oct.* 247, Psalm 144.6, Anon. *The Revenger's Tragedy* 4.2.155, 196–7, Tourneur, *The Atheist's Tragedy* 4.3.162–3 'O patient Heav'n, why dost thou not express | Thy wrath in thunderbolts . . .?'

---

54 On this phenomenon see Taplin (1984–5) 118–19: he notes that it takes the place of a stasimon in S. only in *Electra*, *Philoctetes* and *OC*.

824 φαέθων Ἅλιος: the majority reading ἀέλ(λ)ιος probably arises from the common epic phrase ἠέλιος φαέθων (cf. Bergson (1956) 88, Bruchmann (1893) 149), either through reminiscence or an attempt to introduce a Homeric form. For the corruption see Diggle (1978) 173 = (1994) 194. The epic epithet occurs elsewhere in tragedy only at Eur. *El.* 464; it adds grandeur to this solemn appeal to divine justice. Helios is an appropriate target for such an appeal: the god ὃς πάντ᾽ ἐφορᾷ καὶ πάντ᾽ ἐπακούει (Hom. *Od.* 11.109, 12.323) should be especially ready to notice and punish evil deeds (cf. 175, 659n.). He thus often features in imprecations on evil-doers, both in literature (cf. *OC* 869-70, Garvie on Aesch. *Cho.* 984-6, West (1997) 20, 542) and inscriptions (cf. Cumont (1923), (1933), Jordan (1979)).

ταῦτ᾽: referring to Clytemnestra's exulting over the news of Orestes' death (789-90n.).

ἐφορῶντες: normally this verb denotes 'not just witnessing but supervising or taking an active interest in what one sees' (West, cited above, 175n.). Here the gods watch but do not act; the same irony is found at *Tr.* 1269 τοιαῦτ᾽ ἐφορῶσι πάθη. On the possibility that something has dropped out after this word see 838n.

825 κρύπτουσιν: equivalent to οὐκ ἄγουσιν εἰς φῶς (Σ p. 138.11-12 Papageorgius), and hence 'do *not* brand by exposure and chastisement' (Jebb). The alternative, supplying ἑαυτούς after ἐφορῶντες, is less natural. On the possibility that a word has dropped out here see 838n.

ἔκηλοι: reproachful, as at Hom. *Il.* 5.759-60 (the other gods aid the Trojans) ἐμοὶ δ᾽ ἄχος, οἱ δὲ ἔκηλοι | τέρπονται.

827 ὦ παῖ: 121 n. The tone is one of reassurance (cf. 154n.).

τί δακρύεις; The chorus is only too well aware of the reason for Electra's grief. Its question here is a speech act aimed at comforting the addressee, not a request for information (cf. Hom. *Il.* 1.362-3, with Achilles' reply at 365; Davies's commentary on *Tr.*, index s.v. 'style . . . question as exclamation').

830 μηδὲν μέγ᾽ ἀΰσῃς: a common prohibition, aimed at dissuading the addressee from a blasphemous or arrogant statement (cf. *Aj.* 386 μηδὲν μέγ᾽ εἴπῃς, Hom. *Od.* 22.287-8, Headlam on Herodas 6.34, Virg. *Aen.* 10.547, Murgatroyd on Tib. 2.6.11-12, Bissinger (1966) 225-6).

The scholia suggest that the actor playing Electra should now look up to heaven and raise his arms (p. 138.7-8 Papageorgius). This can be no more than a guess, or at best a reflection of post-Sophoclean dramatic technique (cf. Taplin (1977b)). Perhaps its author felt that the chorus's warning is insufficiently motivated by Electra's φεῦ; but her speech preceding the *kommos* has already made it abundantly clear that she is under extreme tension, such as often precedes outbursts against the gods.

The unmetrical εἴπῃς in GR is probably a reminiscence of *Aj.* 386.

ἀπολεῖς: common in comedy (e.g. Olson on Ar. *Ach.* 470, Alexis fr. 177.15 *PCG*; also Eur. *Cycl.* 558) but rare in tragedy; it probably has a colloquial edge (cf. Latin *enicas* at e.g. Plaut. *Cas.* 233 with Adams (1990) 231). Both its other occurrences in S. refer to actual bodily pain (*Tr.* 1008, *Phil.* 817); Agathon *TrGF* 39 F 13.1 ἀπολεῖς μ' ἐρωτῶν is closer to the present instance. For similar expressions (but in a higher register) used to denote intense mental and emotional pain, caused by an interlocutor's unseasonable allusions, cf. *Phil.* 1172 τί μ' ὤλεσας;, Eur. *Hipp.* 329 with Barrett, 1064 τὸ σεμνὸν ὥς μ' ἀποκτενεῖ τὸ σόν. The pronoun is often omitted (cf. Willink on Eur. *Or.* 158-9).

Electra uses the singular to address the chorus (cf. 835, 855), as tends to occur when a character is reacting to the chorus's preceding words. The plural, on the other hand, is normally used in addresses of a more general kind (Kaimio (1970) 230 with n. 2). Given the swift interchanges in this dialogue, it is not surprising that Electra uses only the singular.

πῶς; Were short lyric utterances delivered by the chorus or the coryphaeus? Scholars often argue for the latter (cf. Kaibel (p. 200), Kaimio (1970) 229, Burton (1980) 206), but there is no evidence either way. Electra's consistent use of the singular to address the chorus is determined on other grounds (see above on ἀπολεῖς).

831–6 Electra's refusals throughout the *kommos* even to countenance the possibility that Orestes might be alive are all the more striking for the absence of such a suggestion from the chorus. Previously Orestes' return had been the one hope which had kept her alive (323 etc.): the reversal of her fortunes is marked by her new-found inability to hear this even suggested. This looks forward to the following scene: it 'makes explicit the psychological barrier against the merest hint that Orestes may be alive, so that when Chrysothemis enters immediately afterwards and states that he is indeed alive, we are prepared for Electra's reception of the news' (Burton (1980) 206).

831 τῶν . . . οἰχομένων: Orestes alone is meant. For the genitive dependent on ἐλπίδ' cf. 1460-1.

φανερῶς: the detail and clarity of the report are what made it so persuasive (774n.); cf. *OC* 1439-40 τίς ἄν σ' ὁρμώμενον | ἐς προῦπτον Ἅιδην οὐ καταστένοι;

835 ἐλπίδ' ὑποίσεις: 'hold out, proffer' (LSJ⁹ s.v. ὑποφέρω IV 2a); ὑποτίθημι is commoner in this context (LSJ⁹ s.v. II 1).

835–6 κατ' ἐμοῦ τακομένας | μᾶλλον ἐπεμβάσῃ: a telling reversal: Electra had hoped that Orestes would return to plant his feet on his enemies (456n.), but now it is she who is trodden down in despair. κατά + genitive replaces the dative which usually goes with this verb (comparable substitutions at *Aj.* [969], *OC* 1339). Kaibel's conjecture ἐπεμβᾶσα (p. 202, printed by Dawe[3]) assumes that Electra's whole utterance must form the protasis to her ἀπολεῖς in 830: but there is no reason why this should be the case. For τάκομαι used of Electra's suffering cf. 123, 187, 283.

837–48 The citation of historical or mythological *exempla* to console a sufferer is as old as Homer (e.g. *Il.* 5.382–404), and is found elsewhere in S. at *Ant.* 944–87; cf. Kassel (1958) 70–1 (who cites Ov. *Met.* 15.493–5, Apul. *Met.* 8.7.3; add Panyassus fr. 16 *EGF* = 3 *PEG* = 3 *GEF*, Ov. *Fast.* 1.487–92), Pattoni (1988). The technique aims to assuage a person's grief by pointing out that even mighty gods, kings and heroes have suffered the same. Here the chorus's intention goes beyond that. By claiming a special status for Amphiaraus in the underworld, it implies that Agamemnon too enjoys a similar fate, and that Electra should accordingly take comfort. The association between the two men is strengthened by the details given of the circumstances of Amphiaraus' death: like Agamemnon, he too was an ἄναξ killed through the treachery of his wife. But this attempted assimilation backfires when Electra points out the crucial difference: Amphiaraus was avenged by his son, whereas Agamemnon's son has been killed.[55] The chorus's attempted consolation now seems inept: the similarities between the two cases are outweighed by this vital difference. Electra then presses home her point with force. Yet for all that the chorus's implied comparison will turn out to be entirely valid: like Alcmeon, Orestes will indeed return to avenge his father. For the moment, only the audience appreciates the full relevance of the comparison: for this as a common characteristic of mythological paradigms in epic see Andersen (1987).

Winnington-Ingram (1980) 226 claims that since Alcmeon was pursued by the Erinyes for avenging his father's death, it is implied that Orestes too will suffer a similar punishment. There is no mention of Erinyes here, though this does not necessarily prove him wrong: *Ant.* 944–87 provides a good example of mythological paradigms which seem to have implications for the characters of the play, beyond their formal use as consolatory material directed towards Antigone (cf. Davies (2001) 53 n. 1). But Winnington-Ingram does not explain why he assumes that this particular section of the myth will be felt by the

---

[55] Orestes and Alcmeon are often paired: cf. *Diss. log.* D–K 90 3.9 (= ii. 410.28–9), [Pl.] *Alc.II* 143c9–10, Anacreont. 9.4–5, Suet. *Ner.* 39.2 and Dio 62.16.2 Νέρων Ὀρέστης Ἀλκμέων μητροκτόνος, Diogenianus fr. 2.25 Gercke, Cic. *Tusc.* 3.11. See further Delcourt (1959).

audience, and not, say, Alcmeon's eventual escape from the Erinyes to the Oeniades islands (cf. Thuc. 2.102.5–6); after all, Orestes too manages to escape from their pursuit.

An account of Amphiaraus in literature and art up to and including Pindar can be found at pp. 27–41 of Braswell's edition of Pindar, *Nemean Nine*. The earliest mention of his death is at Hom. *Od.* 15.247 (Ἀμφιάραος) ὄλετ᾽ ἐν Θήβῃσι γυναίων εἵνεκα δώρων; his wife is named at *Od.* 11.326–7 (στυγερήν τ᾽ Ἐριφύλην, | ἣ χρυσὸν φίλου ἀνδρὸς ἐδέξατο τιμήεντα. His shrine at Thebes was large enough in the mid fifth century to attract the attention of Croesus (cf. Hdt. 1.52), and by the late fifth century he was also the object of cult at Oropus (cf. Hutchinson on Aesch. *Sept.* 568–630, Schachter (1981–94) i. 19–26). The special honour accorded to him is elsewhere reflected in tragedy at Eur. *Suppl.* 925–7 (εὐλογοῦσιν ἐμφανῶς). Paus. 9.8.3 describes the spot supposed to have been the location of his katabasis. His entry into the ground in his chariot occasionally features on black-figure vases (*LIMC* I/2, 560–1).

S. wrote at least one, and perhaps two, *Amphiaraus* plays (frr. 113–21 *TrGF*), as well as an *Eriphyle* (frr. 201a–h *TrGF*) and an *Alcmeon* (fr. 108–10 *TrGF*). He describes Amphiaraus' entrance into the underworld in fr. 958 *TrGF* ἐδέξατο ῥαγεῖσα Θηβαία κόνις | αὐτοῖσιν ὅπλοις καὶ τετρωρίστῳ δίφρῳ, while at *OC* 1313–14 the hero is described as τὰ πρῶτα μὲν | δόρει κρατύνων, πρῶτα δ᾽ οἰωνῶν ὁδοῖς. Euripides wrote two *Alcmeon* plays (frr. 78–87a *TrGF*), and Amphiaraus is a character in his *Hypsipyle*. For other literary accounts of Amphiaraus' descent see Rohde (1925a) 114 n. 1 ≈ (1925b) 103 n. 1. The legends concerning Alcmeon are conveniently accessible in R. C. T. Parker (1983) 377.

For the differing forms of the name Amphiaraus see Heubeck (1971) 9–10.

837 οἶδα: for verbs of knowing used to introduce mythological paradeigmata or other exempla cf. Aesch. *Ag.* 1668 οἶδα (with Fraenkel), *Cho.* 602 ἴστω, Hor. *C.* 3.4.42 *scimus*; also S. *Phil.* 680 ἄλλον δ᾽ οὔτιν᾽ ἔγωγ᾽ οἶδα κλυὼν οὐδ᾽ ἐσιδών. Paradeigmata are more usually introduced with εἶδον (e.g. Aesch. *Eum.* 50), ἤκουσα (*Ant.* 823, *Phil.* 676) or ἔκλυον (Eur. *El.* 452); cf. Zagagi (1980) 37 n. 79 and 40 n. 86.

γάρ: Denniston 80 (7) includes this among instances of γάρ referring to a subordinate clause or individual word in the preceding speech; the sense must be along the lines of 'I can give you at least some hope for Orestes, since . . .'

ἄνακτ᾽: used of the seer Tiresias at Hom. *Od.* 11.151 and S. *OR* 284; cf. Eupolis fr. 231 *PCG* Ἱεροκλέες βέλτιστε χρησμῳδῶν ἄναξ, Cic. *Div.* 1.88 *reges fuerunt, sed iidem augures*, Bremmer (1991) 6–8 ≈ (1993) 154–6 (on political honour and authority wielded by seers). But the term is more naturally applied to Agamemnon: as often in similes, the *illustrans* is assimilated to the *illustrandum* ('vehicle' and 'tenor' in I. A. Richards's terminology ((1936) 96); cf. Silk (1974)). It also looks forward to ἀνάσσει in 841; the repetition conveys the idea that the man who enjoyed authority on earth now also enjoys it in the underworld (cf. West (1997) 165–6).

837–8 χρυσοδέτοις ἕρκεσι: Amphiaraus was bound by prior agreement to accept the ruling of his wife Eriphyle in any dispute between him and his brother-in-law Adrastus (Σ Pind. *N.* 9.30b (= iii. 154.1–5 Drachmann) = *Thebaid* fr. 7* *GEF* (not in *EGF* or *PEG*)). The latter bribed Eriphyle with a golden necklace to ensure that Amphiaraus went on the expedition against Thebes, even though Amphiaraus knew that this would lead to his death (Diod. Sic. 4.65.6–7). The image of her receiving this necklace was popular with fifth-century vase-painters (see *LIMC* III/2, 606–8). At Aesch. *Cho.* 617–18 the phrase χρυσεοδμήτοισιν ὅρ– | μοις denotes the bribe given by Minos to Scylla to persuade her to betray her father Nisus. On the erotic connotations of such necklaces cf. Buxton (1982) 36–7.

A necklace encloses the neck, and thus can be denoted by ἕρκος (cf. *Tr.* 615 σφραγῖδος ἕρκει, used of a ring); while χρυσοδέτοις must mean 'bound / covered with gold' (cf. fr. 244.1 *TrGF* χρυσόδετον κέρας, denoting a lyre). But each part of the phrase can also convey notions of entrapment. For the former, cf. *Aj.* 60 εἰς ἕρκη κακά, frr. 2 (with Pearson), 431 *TrGF*. For the latter, cf. Eur. *Phoen.* 805 χρυσοδέτοις περόναις ἐπίσαμον, where again both meanings are probably present; cf. Diggle (1989) 197–8 = (1994) 343. Kaibel (p. 203) claims that this stress on entanglement further assimilates Amphiaraus' fate to Agamemnon's. But while Agamemnon's entrapment in the net is a prominent motif in the *Oresteia* (e.g. *Ag.* 1382–3, *Cho.* 980–1004, *Eum.* 459–61; also Eur. *El.* 154–5), it is not found in our play.

838 κρυφθέντα '(was) entombed'. The word is often found in descriptions of Amphiaraus' *katabasis*: cf. Pind. *N.* 9.24–5 ὁ δ' Ἀμφιαρεῖ σχίσσεν κεραυνῷ παμβίᾳ | Ζεὺς τὰν βαθύστερνον χθόνα, κρύψεν δ' ἅμ' ἵπποις, [Apollod.] *Bibl.* 3.6.8, Ephorus *FGrHist* 70 F 96.

γυναικῶν: the ἀπάταις found in manuscripts after this word does not correspond to anything in the strophe. Triclinius replaced the two words with ἀπάταισιν (*e coniectura*: cf. Kopff (1993) 158); most modern editors rightly prefer Brunck's solution (in his 1779 edition) of deleting ἀπάταις. Ll-J/W (*Sophoclea*) are sympathetic to the idea that something of the metrical shape UU– has instead dropped out before κρύπτουσιν in 824, which would give us ia 4cho instead of ia 3cho ad. They argue that if χρ. ἕρκ. means just 'the gold-bound necklace' then ἀπ. would be needed to go with γυν. But the phrase carries with it notions of entrapment already (837n.): ἀπάταις reads like an addition

362

COMMENTARY: 823–70

made by someone who felt that the idea of deception was not clear enough. Their suggestion μάκαρες will not do in any case: as Willink (2003) 79 points out, the εἰ–clause needs to have the same subject as the main clause. Willink prefers νέμεσιν (suggested by Schubert[1]) to give the verb an object, but this is a rare concept in tragedy (cf. Dawe, *STS* iii. 126–7), which should not be casually introduced in a supplement.

840 ἒ ἔ, ἰώ: 'the exclamations at 840 . . . are necessary to balance those at 826, but they may serve also to give special emphasis to the triumphant πάμψυχος ἀνάσσει by separating these two words from ὑπὸ γαίας, the associations of which wring a cry from Electra' (Burton (1980) 205; cf. Kaibel p. 203).

841 πάμψυχος ἀνάσσει: the scholia (p. 139.20–3 Papageorgius) offer three interpretations: (i) Amphiaraus rules over all the other souls, who stand in need of his prophecy. (ii) Amphiaraus maintains the power of his whole ψυχή (cf. Dobree's παντελῶς ἔμψυχος ((1833–43) ii. 50)). (iii) Amphiaraus' soul is immortal (cf. Xen. *Cyn.* 1.8 ἔτυχε παρὰ θεῶν ἀείζως (Dindorf; ἀεὶ ζῶν codd.) τιμᾶσθαι). The second explanation is right: it picks up Odysseus' description of Tiresias at Hom. *Od.* 10.493–5, where he says of him τοῦ . . . φρένες ἔμπεδοί εἰσι· | τῷ καὶ τεθνηῶτι νόον πόρε Περσεφόνεια | οἴῳ πεπνῦσθαι· τοὶ δὲ σκιαὶ ἀΐσσουσιν. For the form πάμψυχος Lloyd-Jones (1981) 21 = (1990a) 355–6 compares ἄψυχοι denoting the shades of Aesch. fr. 273a.4 *TrGF (Psychagogoi)*. In the context this must mean something like 'not possessing the capacity of thought or reason', and therefore provides an exact antonym (cf. Henrichs (1991) 188–9 with n. 60). Achilles at Eur. *Tro.* 623 is described as an ἄψυχος νεκρός; cf. also Ar. *Ran.* 1334, Ap. Rhod. 4.1280.

The shades of kings or heroes could attain positions of authority in the underworld: cf. Hom. *Od.* 11.485 μέγα κρατέεις νεκύεσσι, 11.491, Aesch. *Pers.* 691 ἐκείνοις ἐνδυναστεύσας, *Cho.* 355–9 (of Agamemnon) φίλος φίλοισι τοῖς ἐκεῖ καλῶς θανοῦ– | σιν κατὰ χθονὸς ἐμπρέπων, | σεμνότιμος ἀνάκτωρ | πρόπολός τε τῶν μεγίστων | χθονίων ἐκεῖ τυράννων. On a fourth-century BC 'Orphic' gold leaf from Strongoli a shade is told καὶ τότ᾽ ἔπειτ᾽ ἄ[λλοισι μεθ᾽] ἡρώεσσιν ἀνάξει[ς] (Brit. Mus. 3155.11): cf. Zuntz (1971) 358–9, Tsantsanoglou and Parássoglou (1987) 15. In the Sumerian poem which describes the death of Bilgames (the Gilgamesh of other epics), the god Enki declares 'Bilgames, in the form of his ghost, dead in the underworld, | shall be the governor of the Netherworld, chief of the shades!' (George's translation, p. 199). In all these instances a consolatory element is implicit, as explicitly at Ov. *Met.* 5.506–7 (Arethusa consoling Ceres at the loss of her daughter) *illa* (sc. Persephone) *quidem tristis . . . | sed regina tamen, sed opaci maxima mundi.*

For the πάμ– element see 150n.

363

845 φεῦ: 840n.

φεῦ δῆτ' '"alas" indeed': cf. 1454–5, *OC* 536, Eur. *Her.* 898–900, Bruhn §150, Denniston 277, Bond's edition of Euripides' *Hypsipyle*, p. 126. For δῆτα in laments see Hutchinson's edition of Aeschylus' *Septem*, p. 180.

ὀλοά: active (the usual sense: LSJ⁹ s.v. ὀλοός I); metre demands that it is feminine nominative singular rather than accusative plural.

(Χο.) ὀλοὰ δ' οὖν – (Ηλ.) ἐδάμη: δ' οὖν *coni.* West (1991) 300 for manuscript γάρ. If the paradosis were right, γάρ should scan long to secure correspondence with the strophe. As the text stands, this is impossible: nor is there a secure instance in S. where the change of speaker in mid-period leads to the lengthening of an otherwise short syllable.[56] Hence either γάρ or ἐδάμη is suspect.

The paradosis could be interpreted as γ' ἄρ' (Ll-J/W, *Second Thoughts*), a combination sometimes found 'in an exclamatory comment on something said by the previous speaker' (J. C. B. Lowe (1973) 45). But while this combination is frequent in comedy, there is no certain tragic instance (Lowe, *ib.* 58; however, at *OC* 534 Ll-J/W make a strong case for its insertion). Moreover, neither 'So the woman was a destroyer indeed!' or (to complete the presumed choral utterance) 'So the destructive woman was killed!' is an appropriate follow-on to Electra's 'Alas'. This leaves emendation. Altering ἐδάμη is undesirable, as it is so important for the death of Eriphyle to be mentioned. Ll-J/W's conjecture δάμαρ ἦν has been rejected by their reviewers (West (1991) 300, Zimmermann (1993) 106, J. M. Bremer and van Erp Taalman Kip (1994) 241), and is withdrawn by the editors in *Second Thoughts*. As they note there, it makes a nonsense of Electra's γάρ in 846, which 'virtually proves that the death of Eriphyle has already been referred to' (Bremer – van Erp Taalman Kip, *ib.*). Hence suspicion falls on the γάρ. This particle is also suspect on other grounds. It looks back to the preceding φεῦ, and introduces an explanation of why lamentation is an appropriate response to the situation being described: but the death of Eriphyle is not a cause for tears. We rather need a particle marking a break. Of suggested emendations (e.g. γοῦν, τ' ἄρ', μάν, κήρ respectively conjectured by Triclinius, Wolff¹, Wecklein², Willink (2003) 80) only West's δ' οὖν gives such a sense: this combination 'leads us back to the main topic, which has temporarily been lost sight of' (Denniston 463). The corruption to γάρ 'might be due to someone not following the sense and thinking that the reference to a death was the occasion for the φεῦ' (West, *per litteras*). It occurs in

---

[56] The one possible example is at *OC* 180 (Οἰ.) ἔτι; (Χο.) προβίβαζε κούρα, where the second syllable of ἔτι must be long. This may, however, be one of the rare cases where mute plus liquid at the beginning of a word causes a preceding short syllable to lengthen (see metrical introduction on 853). This part of the lyric also appears to have experienced considerable textual corruption. Hence it is hardly a case to be argued from.

tragic lyrics elsewhere at e.g. Aesch. *Ag.* 223, 1568. This is not a palaeographical error, though palaeography might nevertheless have helped it along: ν to ρ and ου to α are common minuscule errors (see West (1977) 97 and Friis Johansen and Whittle on Aesch. *Suppl.* 556, respectively), while γ and δ are also often confused (see Diggle (1981 b) 87–8 = (1994) 202–3).

Kaibel (p. 203) claims that the chorus's words are meant as a complete statement; but whatever reading we adopt, this is impossibly abrupt, and it seems better to take Electra's ἐδάμη as an interruption. But is Electra substituting her own word for what the chorus was going to say (so Kamerbeek), or completing the chorus's words? οἶδ' οἶδ' (846) indicates the latter; 'I know, I know' is a response to a point made not by oneself, but by an interlocutor. Nor is there an indication of what the chorus would have said had it been given the chance. The chorus's response ναί suggests that Electra's interruption almost has the force 'were you going to say ἐδάμη?'

The killing of Eriphyle, specifically mentioned by Aristotle as a mythological given which must not be changed by the tragic poet (*Poet.* 1453b22–6), is rarely represented in art (instances at *LIMC* I/2, 410–11; cf. Braswell on Pind. *N.* 9.16).

846 ἐφάνη: for this used of the emergence of an avenger see 172n.

μελέτωρ: ὁ ἐπιμελούμενος, ὁ τιμωρὸς τοῦ πατρός (Suda μ 480 = iii. 352.22 Adler); cf. 237 πῶς ἐπὶ τοῖς φθιμένοις ἀμελεῖν καλόν; The refusal to name Alcmeon explicitly is typical of the allusive nature of mythological paradigms (cf. Davies (1988b)).

847 τὸν ἐν πένθει: anger, not grief, is usually ascribed to the unavenged dead (cf. Aesch. *Cho.* 40 μέμφεσθαι τοὺς γᾶς νέρθεν περιθύμως; *Eum.* 94–116 shows that anger in action). Electra's description of Amphiaraus in mourning assimilates his situation to Electra's own (cf. 1085–6), and highlights the following contrast between them. The assimilation of the living to the dead is a common characteristic of mourning (cf. Seaford (1985) 316 n. 8, (1994) 86–7). For the expression see 290n.

ἐμοὶ δ': shifts the focus from Amphiaraus to Electra. The same expression is used by Aeschylus' Cassandra (*Ag.* 1146–9) in her rejection of a mythological comparison offered by the chorus: (Procne was turned painlessly into a nightingale), ἐμοὶ δὲ μίμνει σχισμὸς ἀμφήκει δορί. Cf. also Eur. *Hyps.* frr. 752g.18–46, 752h.2–9 *TrGF*, where the chorus cites various mythological precedents to console Hypsipyle. She too rejects the consolation by pointing out the particular sadness of her situation: whereas they had other people to lament them, her sufferings (τὰ δ' ἐμὰ πάθε[α, fr. 752h.5 *TrGF*) will be unlamented. See further Zagagi (1980) 33–46 (especially 33–6), Ov. *Epist. Pont.* 1.3.61–84, [Sen.] *Oct.* 57–71.

ὃς γὰρ ἔτ' ἦν: cf. Eur. *Hel.* 277–9 ἄγκυρα δ' ἥ μου τὰς τύχας ὤχει μόνη, | πόσιν ποθ' ἥξειν καί μ' ἀπαλλάξειν κακῶν, | ἐπεὶ τέθνηκεν οὗτος, οὐκέτ' ἔστι δή.

848 φροῦδος ἀναρπασθείς: cf. Hom. *Od.* 1.241–2 νῦν δέ μιν ἀκλειῶς ἅρπυιαι ἀνηρείψαντο· | οἴχετ' ἄϊστος, ἄπυστος (with Page, *FGE* p. 349), Men. *Asp.* 13 νῦν δὲ σὺ μὲν οἴχει παραλόγως τ' ἀνήρπασαι, Lucian 40.13 τέθνηκας καὶ πρὸ ὥρας ἀνηρπάσθης. For the effective absence of a main verb in this clause cf. 807. The language is movingly simple and direct.

849 Defeated by Electra's argument, the chorus stops offering consolation and simply acknowledges the wretchedness of her situation. There is a similar change of emphasis in the parodos at 193.

δειλαία δειλαίων: cf. Eur. *Hec.* 156 δειλαία δειλαίου γήρως, 203–4, 206–7, Gygli-Wyss (1966) 125 with n. 4, Schauer (2002) 206–7.

850–2 '(I know this) by a life which, through all the months, is a turbid torrent of many things dread and horrible' (Jebb). The focus shifts from the individual tragedy of Orestes' death to the long series of Electra's sorrows. Alliteration of π and homoeoteleuton of ω are strong: for such sound-effects in passages of lamentation see Schauer (2002) 207. Cf. also how 'intensifying παν– prefixes often occur in pairs' (Davies on *Tr.* 505–6, citing Aesch. *Sept.* 296 and Fehling (1969) 247).

850 ἵστωρ: for agent nouns combined with a feminine substantive without alteration see Ernst Fraenkel (1910–12) ii. 49–50; this noun is so used at Eur. *IT* 1431.

ὑπερίστωρ: for the intensified repetition cf. *Tr.* 650–1 with Davies, Fehling (1969) 176; perhaps [Aesch.] *PV* 944 τὸν πικρῶς ὑπέρπικρον, though the precise sense is disputed.

851 πανσύρτῳ: πάντα σύροντι τὰ κακά (Σ p. 141.3 Papageorgius); cf. [Plut.] *De lib. educ.* 5f πόλεμος χειμάρρου δίκην πάντα σύρων, Ar. *Eq.* 527–8, Nisbet and Rudd on Hor. *C.* 3.29.33–4. Bergk and Nauck conjectured πανδύρτῳ (in their 1858 editions, p. xlvi and in the text respectively), which is possible but unnecessary. Adjectives in –τος can have either active or passive meaning, and originally had neither (714n.); for the active meaning here cf. 1077 πάνδυρτος ἀηδών, 1139 παμφλέκτου πυρός.

παμμήνῳ: for months denoting a long period cf. *Ant.* 604–8 ('even the ἀκάματοι θεῶν μῆνες cannot overthrow Zeus's power'), Hom. *Od.* 10.469–70, 11.294–5. The image of the torrent contained in the previous word may be continued, as Jebb notes: true χείμαρροι flow only in winter, but Electra's stream of troubles brooks no seasonal variation.

851–2 πολλῶν | δεινῶν στυγνῶν τ': to be taken with either πανσύρτῳ (for which Jebb compares *Ant.* 1184–5 θεᾶς | . . . προσήγορος = θεὰν προσηγοροῦσα), or else with αἰῶνι (giving 'a life consisting of'). For the genitive of description with this noun cf. Eur. *Med.* 647 τὸν ἀμηχανίας ἔχουσα δυσπέρατον αἰῶν' (see Hutchinson *ad loc.* in his commentary on Greek lyric poetry, pp. 462–3).

852 αἰῶνι: the manuscripts have ἀχέων; Triclinius says that he found ἀχαιῶν in an old manuscript, but this is probably just a different spelling for the same word. The paradosis has two problems: ἀχέων does not correspond to 863, and the dative adjectives in 851 lack a noun to qualify. Hermann's conjecture solves both difficulties. He suggests that ἀχέων crept in as a gloss on the neuter plurals δεινῶν στυγνῶν τ'. For αἰῶνι qualified by two intensified adjectives cf. perhaps Aesch. *Ag.* 715 †παμπρόσθη πολύθρηνον αἰῶν' †. For its association with the image of a torrent cf. Marc. Aurel. 4.43 ῥεῦμα βίαιον ὁ αἰών. Contrast the ἄδακρυν . . . | αἰῶνα of the blessed dead at Pind. *O.* 2.66–7. Degani (1961) does not discuss out passage. For the dative of cause see Moorhouse 89.

853 ἰδομένᾳ θροεῖς: *coni.* Diggle (1976) 45 n. 5 = (1994) 149 n. 5; εἴδομεν ἃ θροεῖς codd. The responsion of the dochmiacs at 853 ~ 864 is problematic. If the text is sound, ἃ θρ– in 853 must scan long, but such lengthening at word boundary before mute and liquid is rare in tragedy (cf. Fraenkel's edition of Aeschylus' *Agamemnon*, vol. iii. pp. 826–7, Barrett on Eur. *Hipp.* 760, Mastronarde on Eur. *Phoen.* 166). Most instances involve the article or a preposition, which were felt to go with the following word (e.g. *Aj.* 1220 ὑπὸ πλάκα, where the second syllable is long). There are a handful of cases outside this category where this prosody seems to hold, and where there is no obvious emendation to hand. Nevertheless, a small change which rids us of this anomaly would be welcome. Jebb supports Dindorf's ἀθρήνεις ((1836) 167, after Erfurdt's θρηνεῖς, citing *Phil.* 209 (likely conjecture); Jebb refers to *Aj.* 582, where θροεῖν is a v.l. for θρηνεῖν). But the imperfect does not fit the context; we would rather expect a present or aorist, referring to Electra's immediately preceding words. Diggle's ἰδομένᾳ θροεῖς involves the smallest of changes: indeed, given manuscript confusion between ει and ι, and over the presence of final iotas in dative singulars, it counts more as a reinterpretation of the paradosis than an emendation proper. Ll-J/W rejected it on the grounds that the resulting responsion, of a double dragged to a dragless dochmiac, is unusual (*Sophoclea*). Diggle (1994) 472 n. 147

offers three Sophoclean parallels for the irregularity (*Ant.* 1310 ∼ 1331, *Phil.* 395 ∼ 510, *OC* 1480 ∼ 1494). Of these, the first is suspect since (as Diggle notes) the irregularity disappears if αἰαῖ in 1310 is scanned ∪ −; the text of 1310 is also doubtful, with αἰαῖ being Erfurdt's conjecture for transmitted (and unmetrical) φεῦ φεῦ. The second example (∪ − − − − responding with − ⌣∪ − ∪ −) is irrelevant, as it does not involve the responsion of a double dragged to a dragless dochmiac. But Diggle's third example (− ⌣∪ − − − responding with ∪ − − ∪ −) is a valid parallel. To this L. P. E. Parker (1997) 66 adds two further parallels (*Ant.* 1320 ∼ 1344, *OC* 1561 ∼ 1572). This kind of responsion is thus established for Sophoclean dochmiacs. The same cannot be said of the prosody which opponents of the conjecture are forced to prefer.

For phrases of the form εἰδότι τοι ἐρέω (Pind. *P.* 4.142), with the participle of οἶδα and a verb of speaking cf. Bruhn §251, Fraenkel on Aesch. *Ag.* 1402–3, Diggle (1976) 45 n. 5 = (1994) 149 n. 5, Friis Johansen and Whittle on Aesch. *Suppl.* 742, Braswell on Pind. *P.* 4.142(a). There is no parallel for the participle of ὁράω in such an expression. However, instances such as *Aj.* 543 ἕρποντι φωνεῖς, Aesch. *Ag.* 1653 and Eur. *Her.* 1185 show how the idiom can be used in tragedy with other verbs. The conjecture thus solves a major problem without causing any of its own. Dawe²⁻³ and Willink (2003) 80 put it in the text, rightly.[57]

855 παραγάγῃς 'divert', 'lead astray' (LSJ⁹ s.v. παράγω A II 1–2; cf. *OR* 974 τῷ φόβῳ παρηγόμην).

ἵν': the word must here denote not the place *to* which, but *from* which, Electra does not want to be led; hence 'I who am (now) in a situation where' etc. S. is fond of this word in a figurative sense (cf. 22).

τί φῄς; is followed in the manuscripts by αὐδᾷς δὲ ποῖον;, which is deleted by Triclinius (*e coniectura*: cf. Kopff (1993) 158). Since the latter phrase does not correspond to anything in the antistrophe, either it is an interpolation, or something has dropped out from 866. But it is so verbose that the latter explanation is most unlikely; nor is it clear what the metrical form of the line would be if the phrase were allowed to stay. It nevertheless remains puzzling. For while verbs of speaking are often interpolated (see Fraenkel's commentary on Aeschylus' *Agamemnon*, iii. 756 n. 1), here we already have such a verb; nor can the phrase be a gloss that has entered the text, since τί φῄς; hardly requires further explanation. For 'additions which prolong, amplify or heighten' cf. Tarrant (1987) 139–50. For the orthography of φῄς see 317n. For Triclinius's deletion of words and phrases for metrical reasons see Aubreton (1949) 172.

857 εὐπατριδᾶν should be preferred over the variants εὐπατριδῶν and εὐπα-τρίδων, as we would expect the Doric form in tragic lyric. τ' after this word

57 Lloyd-Jones (*per litteras*) now believes that Diggle's emendation 'may very well be right'.

should be omitted with V and the Suda. ἀρωγαί goes with the defining genitive ἐλπίδων ('aids consisting in hopes'), with εὐπατριδᾶν (a noun qualified by κοινοτόκων) then denoting the source of hope (cf. 1460–1). The two genitive nouns, each performing a different function, are not problematic (681–2n.). Jebb translates 'sustaining hopes from a princely brother'. If we read τ', κοινοτόκων and εὐπατριδᾶν must both be adjectives qualifying ἐλπίδων, but the twin adjectives are rather awkward.[58]

860–3 The chorus's jejune and inappropriate consolation is met by Electra with bitter sarcasm: the piling up of emotive epithets (δυστάνῳ), forceful particles (ἦ καί, οὕτως) and arresting details recalling the description of the crash (χαλάργοις ἐν ἁμίλλαις, τμητοῖς ὁλκοῖς) all contribute to the effect. The contrast between this brief, intense outburst and the dull conventionality of the chorus's preceding words could hardly be greater.

860 ἔφυ 'with reference to a law of nature or fate' (Jebb); cf. OC 1443–4 ταῦτα δ' ἐν τῷ δαίμονι | καὶ τῇδε φῦναι χἀτέρᾳ.

861 ἦ καί: marks the questioner's eagerness or intensity (Denniston 285 (6) (ii)).

χαλάργοις ἐν ἁμίλλαις: the adjective is a *hapax*, meaning 'swift-hooved' (so Hesych. χ 37 = iv. 268 Schmidt, Suda χ 274 = iv. 803.19–20 Adler; cf. 607 στόμαργον). It may be inspired by the Homeric horse's name πόδαργος (Il. 8.185, 23.295), also in Mycenaean (KN Ch 899, 1029 *po-da-ko*). For the ornate epithet with ἅμιλλα cf. OC 1062–3 ῥιμφαρμάτοις | . . . ἁμίλλαις. Dawe (STS i. 189) accepts C's γ' before ἐν: this is possible though not compelling.

862 κείνῳ δυστάνῳ: for an unarticled adjective with the dative pronoun cf. Ant. 879–80, West (1979) 115.

863 τμητοῖς: 747n.
ὁλκοῖς: elsewhere 'hauling machine' or 'furrow, track'; hence here 'the reins that dragged him'; cf. Gagnepain (1959) 67.
ἐγκῦρσαι 'to meet with' + dative: cf. Nauck (1859–62) ii. 123.

864 ἄσκοπος 'immense' (cf. Tr. 246–7 τὸν ἄσκοπον | χρόνον); 'unexpected' (Σ p. 141.25 Papageorgius ἀπροόρατος) would be comically feeble and irrelevant. For λώβα describing a painful death cf. Tr. 996 οἵαν μ' ἄρ' ἔθου λώβαν.

865–70 For Electra's complaint cf. 1138–42.

---

[58] The first printing of the OCT mistakenly included the τ', which Ll-J/W rightly wish to delete. The mistake is corrected in the second printing.

865 πῶς γὰρ οὔκ; A frequent affirmative in prose, which verges on the colloquial in poetry: cf. 1307, *Aj.*1010, *OR* 567 (all passages of excitement or indignation), Aesch. *Cho.* 754 (used by the Nurse), Stevens (1945) 102–3, Denniston
86. It reflects Electra's angry impatience at the chorus's weak response.

866 ἄτερ ἐμᾶν χερῶν: cf. 1138n.

867 κέκευθεν 'lies buried' (cf. *Ant.* 911, *OR* 968, Aesch. *Sept.* 588).

867–70 οὔτε . . . | οὔτε: the protasis is explanatory, referring to something
which the speaker regards as self-evidently the case, and hence takes οὐ rather
than the usual μή (cf. Moorhouse 321–2).
    του 'any', 'at all': cf. *Aj.* 290–1 οὔτε του κλυὼν | σάλπιγγος, *Ant.* 814–16
οὔτ᾿ ἐπὶ νυμ– | φείοις πώ μέ τις ὕμνος ὕ– |μνησεν.
    τάφου . . . | . . . γόων: for this double deprivation cf. *Ant.* 29 ἄκλαυτον
ἄταφον, Hom. *Il.* 22.386 ἄκλαυτος ἄθαπτος, Garvie on Aesch. *Cho.* 431–3.
    ἀντιάσας: the aorist participle of ἀντιάω, which regularly takes a genitive of
the thing gained or enjoyed, can also on occasions have a short alpha (cf. Hom.
Il. 1.67, *Od.* 21.402). For its use in a funerary context cf. *EG* 514.4 = *GVI* 871.4
(Macedonia, 2nd cent. AD) τῶν ὁσίων ἀντίασεν κτερέων. The sense of the
alternative ἀντιάζω is inappropriate ('encounter', 'approach as a suppliant').

THIRD EPISODE (871–1057)

871–1057 For the second time in some two hundred lines, Electra is confronted
by a new entrant from eisodos B. Like the Paedagogus, Chrysothemis brings
news of Orestes, news which she believes will be welcomed by her addressee
(873–4; cf. 666–7). She announces the substance of her message (877–8; cf.
673), and then tells a narrative to provide evidence for it (892–919; cf. 680–
763). Her narrative fails to comfort Electra (920–5; cf. 788–90, 804–22). Later
she departs through the *skene*, leaving Electra alone outside (1057; cf. 803).
Chrysothemis' encounter with her sister thus acts as a kind of second messenger scene, whose basic form recalls that of the previous episode. Yet the
two messengers go about their tasks in different ways, as befits their different
circumstances and motivations. The Paedagogus abstains almost completely
from commenting on the action he unfolds: he thus ensures that his speech is
as objective as possible (689n.). Chrysothemis, on the other hand, makes no
attempt to disguise her joy at the news she is bringing (871n.). This joy provides
the strongest possible contrast with Electra's despair in the *kommos*: the entry
of the Paedagogus, however, is taken by Clytemnestra as a fulfilment of the
prayer she had only just been uttering (660–79n.). Both the Paedagogus and
Chrysothemis show disappointment when their addressee does not react with

the happiness which they had expected (921; 769, 772); but what in the Paedagogus had been the mere acting-out of a messenger's ἦθος is for Chrysothemis a real and bitter sorrow.

There remains a more fundamental set of differences between the two scenes. The Paedagogus announced the death of Orestes; Chrysothemis proclaims his return from exile. His tale was false, and yet received Electra's unquestioning belief; Chrysothemis' account, though true, is immediately rejected by her sister. The Paedagogus' speech consisted of an eye-witness account of Orestes' death. Chrysothemis' claims rely on uncertain inferences from signs and tokens, which for all the conviction of their advocate cannot match the graphic realism of the earlier narration. Electra's belief in the former message and disbelief in the latter is thus a reasonable and rational response. It is also mistaken, and therein lies the dramatic irony.

A still closer interaction can be observed between this episode and the earlier encounter between the sisters (328–471). Various elements are common to both scenes. In each Chrysothemis attacks her sister's intransigence; in each she tells a narrative associated with the return of Orestes. Both scenes show Electra attempting to persuade her sister to act against their father's killers. Both involve a lengthy section of argument in stichomythia. But while individual sections correspond from one scene to the next, the order in which they recur is significantly different. The final part of the first episode consisted of Chrysothemis' narrative followed by a speech from Electra successfully requesting her sister's help. This part corresponds to the beginning of the second meeting between the pair, which opens with a second narrative from Chrysothemis, followed by a second request from Electra for her assistance. This time, however, Chrysothemis refuses to help her sister. Now the action comes to resemble that of the beginning of the first episode. Chrysothemis encourages Electra not to struggle against the powerful (cf. 328–40), and the sisters then continue their argument in a section of stichomythia (cf. 385–404).

In broad outline the earlier episode moved from a hostile to a conciliatory atmosphere, from recrimination to cooperation. The present scene reverses the pattern, a fact stressed on a structural level by the reuse of elements from the earlier scene in the reverse order. The progress made earlier in the sisters' relationship is thus literally turned back on itself. By the end of the episode we see the return of the rancorous atmosphere which had characterised the opening of their previous meeting. The stage business reinforces the relationship between the two scenes. Before Chrysothemis had entered from the *skene* and left via eisodos B: in the present scene she does the opposite.

These reversals are accompanied by an intensification of the repeated elements, which now take on a decidedly bolder form. So Chrysothemis now has a longer and more elaborate narrative which involves actual eye-witness record

(885–6) rather than a message repeated at third hand (424–5). Far from being mystified by her account (426–7), she follows it up with close argumentation to try to draw out its significance (907–15). Electra's plan is now aimed at the elimination of Aegisthus, an altogether more serious affair than the mere abandonment of offerings meant for her father's tomb. Chrysothemis' attack on her sister's intransigence is longer and more impassioned than in the earlier scene. The stichomythia too fits into this trend. Before it had begun with hostility, but news of the dream allowed it to end on a note of conciliation. Now, however, there is no remedy for the sisters' aggression, and from start to end the language remains ill tempered. In each of these cases the second instance is the more striking: such a pattern makes good rhetorical sense. Sophocles makes ample use elsewhere of events arranged in pairs, with the latter instance marking an intensification of the former. This is the so-called 'Sophoclean doublet' (cf. Hinds (1980)), for which cf. the two burials of Polynices in *Antigone*, the two messengers announcing the return of Heracles in *Trachiniae*, or Teucer's encounter with Menelaus and then Agamemnon in *Ajax*. The current scene is thus an elaborate instance of a characteristically Sophoclean technique. Its use here conveys the increased seriousness and urgency of the situation brought about by the news of the death of Orestes.

Given these reversals and intensifications, the episode gives the audience a chance to observe facets of the two characters which were previously not apparent. Chrysothemis starts the scene as a considerably more sympathetic figure than before. No longer a cynical time-server, happy to acquiesce in the rule of the powerful, she now shows a genuine involvement with her brother's fortunes, good and bad (920–46n.). But the manner of her rejection of Electra's appeal hardly endears her to us, for all the soundness of her arguments (992–1014n.). So too her tone in the concluding stichomythia, while less aggressive than that of her sister, is still often unpleasantly ironical (1015–57n.). The change in Electra is even more marked. She begins the scene paralysed by the news of her brother's death: yet only seventy or so lines later she has conceived a plan far more daring than anything she had previously attempted. All the forces of her rhetoric are devoted to persuading her sister to support her. Yet when this fails, she immediately declares that she will carry out the deed on her own, and the emotional tenor of her appeal is now contrasted with the contempt she shows her sister in the concluding stichomythia. These sudden shifts startle the audience as much as they do Chrysothemis. Electra's character is more impetuous, more resourceful, more determined than we could have imagined. Nevertheless, her foolhardiness and aggression prevent our reaction from being simply admiration or approbation; this is especially the case in the final part of the episode (1015–57n.). The following choral ode then goes some way to re-establishing our sympathies, in preparation for her great lament over the urn.

Important as it is with reference to characterisation, as regards the plot the scene turns out to be a dead end. The vivid account of the offerings at the tomb is rejected and forgotten. The plan set out with such vehemence and elaboration is barely referred to elsewhere, and even then obliquely (1080, 1319–21). Chrysothemis herself leaves for good at the end of the episode and has no further impact on the drama. Yet this futility is expressive, in that it conveys how inescapable Electra's torment appears. Moreover, the episode delays yet further the moment when Electra is released from her sufferings, and allows the audience to appreciate fresh nuances to her character, as she attempts to react to and master a situation beyond even her. 'Once Sophocles has created this delicately balanced situation, he extends, draws out and makes full use of its shifts of weight from one side to the other' (Reinhardt (1979) 155 ≈ (1947) 165).

871–91 The opening of the scene is modelled on Hom. *Od.* 23.1–84, in which Euryclea brings Penelope news of her husband's return. Joyfully (871n.), Euryclea rushes (872n.) to her mistress. After a brief preamble stressing the significance of her message for her addressee (873–4n.), she announces the return of Odysseus (877n.). In disbelief Penelope accuses her first of madness (879n.), then of mockery (879–80n.). Euryclea denies the charge of mockery (881–2n.) and repeats her message: Odysseus really is here (882n.).

From this point the two scenes diverge. Penelope is swayed by Euryclea's claim that the Stranger turned out to be her husband in disguise (23.32–8). Later, however, she returns to her former disbelief (23.59–68): it was a god, she claims, who killed the Suitors, whereas Odysseus himself is now dead. As she goes downstairs she still cannot decide whether the report is true (23.85–7). Penelope's oscillation finds its opposite in Electra's unhesitating and total rejection of Chrysothemis' news. For while Penelope suspects her husband is dead, Electra has received sure and trustworthy testimony of her brother's end. She has only just been lamenting this when Chrysothemis arrives, whereas Euryclea comes to Penelope as she enjoys the sweetest sleep she has had for twenty years (23.16–19). Euryclea has seen Odysseus in person, and is able to urge Penelope to go and see him for herself. Chrysothemis has seen not Orestes, but only a series of signs consistent with the hypothesis that he has returned. The contrast between the two scenes brings out why the announcement of Orestes' return falls so flat. Electra has convincing reasons for rejecting any such announcement, whereas Penelope did not; while Chrysothemis' account is in any case less credible than Euryclea's.

There is a further parallel with accounts of the Resurrection of Christ, though it might be over-bold to posit direct influence. Women on a visit to the tomb to anoint Jesus' body with spices (Mark 16.1, Luke 24.1) are persuaded by what they see there that He is alive. They return to their companions with joy

(871n.) and speed (872n.): cf. Matthew 28.8 καὶ ἀπελθοῦσαι ταχὺ ἀπὸ τοῦ μνημείου μετὰ φόβου καὶ χαρᾶς μεγάλης ἔδραμον ἀπαγγεῖλαι τοῖς μαθηταῖς αὐτοῦ. This news is met with disbelief by their audience (Mark 16.11, Luke 24.11), but is later found to be true.

871 Enter Chrysothemis from eisodos B, at a run. Her hurried excitement suddenly breaks the static mood of lamentation which characterised the preceding *kommos*.

ὑφ' ἡδονῆς: for the happiness of a messenger with good news cf. Hom. *Od.* 23.1 καγχαλόωσα (also 59).

For τοι used in 'revealing the speaker's emotional . . . state' cf. 928, Denniston 541 (6): 'I won't conceal it', as it were.

φιλτάτη: in the first episode Chrysothemis had avoided the φίλ– root when addressing her sister. The use of such a form here, and in the superlative, immediately marks her change of tone (cf. 916).

διώκομαι 'I am impelled (by joy)'. The use of the verb seems unparalleled.

872 τὸ κόσμιον μεθεῖσα: εὐκοσμία could be violated by hurried movement: cf. Pl. *Charm.* 159b2–4 εἶπεν ὅτι οἳ δοκοῖ σωφροσύνη εἶναι τὸ κοσμίως πάντα πράττειν καὶ ἡσυχῇ, ἔν τε ταῖς ὁδοῖς βαδίζειν καὶ διαλέγεσθαι, Arist. *Physiogn.* 807b34 κοσμίου σημεῖα· ἐν ταῖς κινήσεσι βραδύς, *EN* 1125ᵃ12–13, Alexis fr. 265 *PCG* with Arnott, Diggle on Theophr. *Char.* 4.2, Green (2001) 42, Cic. *Off.* 1.131 with Dyck, Ov. *Ars* 3.299 *est et in incessu pars non contempta decoris*, Dant. *Purg.* 3.10–11 'quando li piedi suoi lasciar la fretta | che l'onestade ad ogn'atto dismaga'; perhaps also Eur. *Or.* 729 θᾶσσον ἤ μ' ἐχρῆν προβαίνων ἱκόμην δι' ἄστεως (though see West *ad loc.*), Ov. *Met.* 13.797.

σὺν τάχει: for speed as a characteristic of a messenger with good news cf. Hom. *Od.* 23.3 γούνατα δ' ἐρρώσαντο, πόδες δ' ὑπερικταίνοντο, Lucian 64.3, Plut. *De glor. Athen.* 347c = Heracl. Pont. fr. 156 Wehrli, Matthew 28.8 (cited above, 871–91n.). For the combination of joy and speed see 871–91n.

μολεῖν: for a final-consecutive infinitive dependent on a verb of motion see 406n.

873–4 For the brief preamble before the delivery of the news cf. Hom. *Od.* 23.5–6 ἔγρεο, Πηνελόπεια, φίλον τέκος, ὄφρα ἴδηαι | ὀφθαλμοῖσι τεοῖσι τά τ' ἔλδεαι ἤματα πάντα.

For φέρω predicated of a messenger see 666n.

ἡδονάς τε κἀνάπαυλαν: for the combination cf. Plut. fr. 178.45–6 Sandbach τοῦτ' ἐστὶ τὸ τὴν ἡδονὴν ποιοῦν, ἀπόλυσις καὶ ἀνάπαυλα τῆς ψυχῆς. For the repetition of ἡδονή from 871 cf. Ar. *Plut.* 288–9 ὡς ἥδομαι . . . | ὑφ' ἡδονῆς, 335–6n.

ἀνάπαυλαν . . . | . . . κακῶν: for the phrase cf. Dion. Hal. *Ant. Rom.* 8.83.2, Heliod. 8.11.11; for the commoner παῦλα κακῶν cf. *Tr.* 1255, Stephanopoulos (1988a) 231–2.

ὧν: for the relative at the end of a line cf. *Tr.* 819, *OR* 298, *OC* 14. S. is the freest of the three tragedians in admitting prepositives in this position (cf. West (1982a) 83–4).

For εἶχες with κακά as its object cf. Hom. *Od.* 11.482, Aesch. *Cho.* 277, Eur. *Hec.* 808, Philemon fr. 121.3 *PCG*, Xen. *Ages.* 7.7, Pl. *Leg.* 731c8, LSJ⁹ s.v. ἔχω A I 8.

875 The emphatically late placing of σύ suggests Electra's contempt.

876 οἷς ἴασις οὐκ ἔνεστ᾽ ἔτι: Pearson and Ll-J/W rightly adopt the minority reading. Most editors print the majority οἷς ἴασιν οὐκ ἔνεστ᾽ ἰδεῖν, while Dawe prefers οἷς ἴασις οὐκέτ᾽ ἔστ᾽ ἰδεῖν (οὐκέτ᾽ *coni.* Thiersch (1841) 6, who however printed ἴασιν; cf. Dawe, *STS* i. 189). But in both these cases Electra claims not that there is no remedy for her sufferings, but only that it is not possible to see a way out of them. She thus concedes that a way out may exist, contradicting her position from the preceding *kommos* (cf. 829–36, 854–7). This denial is important both for Electra's characterisation and for the mechanics of the plot, preparing as it does for her imminent rejection of Chrysothemis' evidence. It would be inept for the dramatist to have her retreat from this position now. For ἔτι in a similar context in Sophocles cf. *OC* 1269–70 τῶν γὰρ ἡμαρτημένων | ἄκη μέν ἐστι, προσφορὰ δ᾽ οὐκ ἔστ᾽ ἔτι. For the corruption of ἔνεστ᾽ to ἔστιν in some manuscripts cf. [Men.] *Monost.* 233 ἐν γὰρ γυναιξὶ πίστιν οὐκ ἔνεστ᾽ [v.l. ἐστιν] ἰδεῖν.

The corruption is not easy to explain. Ll-J/W (*Sophoclea*) claim that the common impersonal use of ἔνεστι led to the 'almost inevitable' change of ἴασις to ἴασιν: but this change has not occurred at 527, for instance, where we might have expected to see it if it were indeed almost inevitable. Furthermore, the Suda (ι 48 = ii. 605.1–2 Adler) has ἰδεῖν together with ἴασις, while no manuscript has ἴασιν with ἔτι. This may suggest that the corruption of ἔτι came first, and led to the corruption of ἴασις in most but not all subsequent copies. Given the known vulnerability of final disyllables (364n.), a small word like ἔτι could easily have been misplaced (cf. *OR* 1401, *OC* 1749), and ἰδεῖν would provide a handy substitute to fill the line out. The subsequent corruption of ἴασις into the accusative would follow to provide an accusative for the infinitive.

877 πάρεστ᾽ Ὀρέστης ἡμῖν: for the blunt revelation cf. Hom. *Od.* 23.7 ἦλθ᾽ Ὀδυσεὺς καὶ οἶκον ἱκάνεται, ὀψέ περ ἐλθών, 673n. But unlike Euryclea and the Paedagogus, Chrysothemis is overstating her case.

375

878 ἐναργῶς: for ἐνάργεια in evidence see Manieri (1998) 105–12. Ll-J/W are right to punctuate before this word, as the adverb goes with πάρεστ᾽ Ὀρέστης, not with κλύουσ᾽. The important point is Orestes' manifest appearance, not Chrysothemis' audibility. The unusual word order gives special emphasis to the adverb. Wecklein's ἐναργής ((1869a) 71) is also possible (cf. e.g. *OC* 910, *Tr.* 224).

ὥσπερ εἰσορᾷς ἐμέ: cf. Eur. *Hel.* 117–18 ('Ελ.) εἶδες σὺ τὴν δύστηνον, ἢ κλυὼν λέγεις; | (Τε.) ὥσπερ σέ γ᾽, οὐδὲν ἧσσον, ὀφθαλμοῖς ὁρῶ.

879 ἀλλ᾽ ἦ 'puts an objection in interrogative form, giving lively expression to a feeling of surprise or incredulity' (Denniston 27 (4)). It is especially common in answers which take the form of questions (cf. *Phil.* 414, Aesch. *Cho.* 774).

μέμηνας: cf. Hom. *Od.* 23.11–14 μαῖα φίλη, μάργην σε θεοὶ θέσαν κτλ.

τάλαινα: repeated in 883 and 887, the vocative conveys Electra's pity and contempt for what she regards as her sister's folly (cf. 388n.)

879–80 κἀπὶ τοῖς | σαυτῆς κακοῖσι κἀπὶ τοῖς ἐμοῖς γελᾷς; Cf. Aesch. *Cho.* 222 ἀλλ᾽ ἐν κακοῖσι τοῖς ἐμοῖς γελᾶν θέλεις; (spoken by a disbelieving Electra in response to Orestes' self-revelation), Hom. *Od.* 23.15 τίπτε με λωβεύεις πολυπενθέα θυμὸν ἔχουσαν; On Electra's fear of laughter see 277n. Electra allows that Orestes' death will be a cause of grief to Chrysothemis as well as to herself (cf. σαυτῆς and ἐμοῖς).

τοῖς: for the definite article at the end of a line cf. *Ant.* 409, *Phil.* 263, *OC* 351, also 873–4n.

881–2 For the denial of mockery by the speaker cf. Hom. *Od.* 23.26 οὔ τί σε λωβεύω, τέκνον φίλον.

881 μὰ τὴν πατρῴαν ἑστίαν: 'a fitting asseveration here, since the hearth symbolises the very existence of the family' (Jebb). So too at Hom. *Od.* 14.158–9 ἴστω νῦν Ζεὺς πρῶτα θεῶν ξενίη τε τράπεζα | ἱστίη τ᾽ Ὀδυσῆος ἀμύμονος, ἣν ἀφικάνω the oath asserts the imminent return of a family member on whom the safety of the royal house depends. For the importance of the hearth in the play cf. 269n., 270n. Cf. 626n. for another carefully-chosen oath. For an oath beginning μά followed by a clause with οὐ see Moorhouse (1959) 18.

ἀλλ᾽: normally first in its clause except when an oath or apostrophe precedes (Denniston 22–3). For the repetition of ἀλλά in 881–2 see 537n.

ὕβρει: the minority variant ὕβριν arose from scribal misunderstanding of the construction. Kaibel once supported it ((1884) 254), but changed his mind in his commentary (p. 208). For the meaning of ὕβρις see 271n.

COMMENTARY: 871–1057

882 ἀλλ' ἐκεῖνον ὡς παρόντα νῷν: for the reassertion of the original message cf. Hom. *Od.* 23.26–7 ἀλλ' ἔτυμόν τοι | ἦλθ' Ὀδυσεύς καὶ οἶκον ἱκάνεται, ὡς ἀγορεύω. The force of λέγω carries over into this clause, giving 'I say this not in *hybris* – rather, I declare that he is present'. The minority variant νόει probably arose from confusion over this construction, perhaps aided by a reminiscence of *Phil.* 415 ὡς μηκέτ' ὄντα κεῖνον ἐν φάει νόει. For verbs of saying with a participial construction see 676n.; for such constructions with ὡς cf. 1341, Bruhn §135, Monteil (1963) 339–40.

883 οἴμοι τάλαινα: 879n.
καί: probably a sign of indignation (so Campbell): cf. 236n. Denniston sees it as marking a 'strong degree of surprise' (310 (b)), but surprise is too positive a term to denote Electra's reaction to her sister here (ὧδε πιστεύεις ἄγαν in 884 is especially contemptuous).

883–4 λόγον . . . | . . . εἰσακούσασ': Electra assumes that Chrysothemis' account is only second hand: ironically, however, her contempt for her sister's news itself arises from her own all too quick belief in a story which she has heard.

885 μέν: possibly antithetical ('as far as I am concerned, though I cannot speak for anyone else'), but probably better taken as simply emphatic.
ἐξ ἐμοῦ τε κοὐκ ἄλλου: cf. *Tr.* 746–7 αὐτὸς βαρεῖαν ξυμφορὰν ἐν ὄμμασιν | πατρὸς δεδορκὼς κοὐ κατὰ γλῶσσαν κλυών, Aesch. *Pers.* 266, Eur. *Med.* 654–5, *Suppl.* 684, *IT* 901, *Hel.* 117–18, Plaut. *Bacch.* 469, Diggle (1973) 262 n. 60 ≈ (1994) 81 n. 60. For the reverse cf. *Phil.* 676, [Hes.] fr. 199.3 M–W. For τε καί coupling one notion and the negation of its opposite see *OR* 1275 πολλάκις τε κοὐχ ἅπαξ, *OC* 935, Bruhn §155, 208, Denniston 513.
ἄλλου: better attested than the variant –ης; the latter, while possible (cf. 100), is less likely, since the corruption into the feminine is more easily explicable than would be a corruption into the masculine.

885–6 σαφῆ | σημεῖ': Chrysothemis suggests that she has not set eyes on Orestes. For σημεῖα see 892–919n.

886 ἰδοῦσα: rejecting the implications in Electra's εἰσακούσασ' (cf. 883–4n.).

887 ὦ τάλαιν': 879n.
ἰδοῦσα πίστιν: echoing Chrysothemis' ἰδοῦσα . . . πιστεύω in 886.
πίστιν 'grounds for belief' (cf. LSJ⁹ s.v. πίστις II 1, Hutchinson on Aesch. *Sept.* 54). For the related sense 'pledge' cf. *OR* 1420 τίς μοι φανεῖται πίστις ἔνδικος;, *Phil.* 813, *OC* 1632.

377

888 θάλπη: for θάλπω = 'give false comfort' cf. Ar. *Eq.* 210 αἴ κε μὴ θαλφθῇ λόγοις, Men. *Asp.* 448; also S. *Aj.* 478 ὅστις κεναῖσιν ἐλπίσιν θερμαίνεται. The verb often denotes intense emotion of various sorts (cf. Zink (1962) 50–64, Padel (1992) 117 n. 10).

ἀνηκέστῳ 'irresistible': cf. Thuc. 3.45.4, S. *Aj.* 52 with Ll-J/W, *Second Thoughts*. Electra emphasises the extremity of her sister's passion, and implies that she is not in her right mind (as does Athena of Ajax). This sense is not common; nevertheless, the presence of the same word elsewhere in S. with this meaning protects it here.

Both the Oxford and Teubner texts print an emendation. Ll-J/W choose ἀνηφαίστῳ (*coni.* Bergk p. xlvi and Nauck³), which before the Byzantine period occurs only at Eur. *Or.* 621 ἕως ὑφῆψε δῶμ' ἀνηφαίστῳ πυρί. The change is palaeographically slight: in particular, αι and ε are easily confused (757n.). For 'Hephaestus' denoting fire cf. Wilamowitz (1895) 226–7 = (1935–72) v/2 15–16, Malten (1912) 329.20–67. But we do not need an adjective stressing the metaphorical character of the πῦρ (*pace* Ll-J/W, *Sophoclea*). An attentive audience would be aware that Chrysothemis is not literally on fire; and in any case the metaphorical use of πῦρ is familiar enough not to need explanation.

Dawe prefers Meineke's ἀνεικάστῳ ((1863a) 263–4), but the classical evidence for this is thin. Triclinius read ἀνεικάστου at *Aj.* 52 (*supra lineam*). At Dem. 8.46 τὴν μὲν ὑπερβάλλουσαν καὶ ἀνήκεστον ταύτην ῥαθυμίαν ἀποθέσθαι S and L' read ἀνείκαστον for ἀνήκεστον.[59]

For alpha-privative adjectives in metaphorical descriptions see West on Hes. *Op.* 525; add fr. 595 *TrGF* αἰδοῦς ἀχαλκεύτοισιν ἔζευκται πέδαις, Aesch. *Eum.* 250, fr. 292 *TrGF*, Eur. *Or.* 319–20, Leon. Alex. *A.P.* 6.321.3 = 1866 *FGE*. For negatives in ἀνη– alongside negatives in νη– see Moorhouse (1959) 50–9.

889–90 'Brief delaying comments usually focus attention on the weight of the eventual answer by combining a retarding effect with expression of reluctance or with exhortation addressed to the listener' (Mastronarde (1979) 37).

πρὸς . . . θεῶν: a strong intensification of the following imperative: cf. Men. *Sam.* 520 πάτερ ἄκουσον, πρὸς θεῶν. Chrysothemis makes a last appeal to Electra to take her story seriously before beginning her narration.

ὡς μαθοῦσά μου | τὸ λοιπὸν ἢ φρονοῦσαν ἢ μώραν λέγῃς: cf. *OC* 593 ὅταν μάθῃς μου, νουθέτει, τανῦν δ' ἔα. For the corruption of –ῃς to –εις see Fraenkel on Aesch. *Ag.* 1317. Fröhlich's μαθοῦσ'ἐμέ provides an object pronoun for the verb, but this can easily be supplied from μου. For φρονοῦσαν cf. 384n.

891 With δ' οὖν 'the speaker waives any objection that he has . . . to something being done, or contemplated, by another person . . . The particles are

---

[59] So rightly Butcher. Dilts's claim that S has ἀνείκεστον is incorrect, as the facsimile indicates (Omont (1892–3) vol. i. p. 21 verso, 2nd col., 4 lines from the end).

almost invariably preceded by σύ or ὁ (ἡ, οἱ), and the expression nearly always forms the opening of a speech. The tone is usually defiant or contemptuous' (Denniston 466): cf. *Tr.* 329, Bruhn §149.

εἴ σοι τῷ λόγῳ τις ἡδονή: supremely indifferent; cf. Pl. *Hipp. maj.* 301 d2–4 εἰδότι μὲν ἐρεῖς . . . ὅμως δ' εἴ τι σοὶ ἥδιον, λέγε.

892–919 *indignum facinus esse sine testibus coniecturam et suspicionem firmamenti satis habere* ([Cic.] *Rhet. Her.* 2.11).

In each of the three tragedians a character finds some unexpected offerings at Agamemnon's tomb and infers that Orestes may have returned.[60] The discovery of a lock of hair (*Cho.* 168) and then a set of footprints (205–10) provokes a powerful emotional reaction in Aeschylus' Electra (183–7, 193–4, 211). No-one apart from Orestes would have placed such a gift at the tomb (169–73, 187–94). The lock also resembles her own hair, while the footprints match the size (or proportions: cf. Burkert (1963)) of her feet, which suggests that they originated from a relative (174–8, 205–10). As a consequence, she begins to believe that Orestes must have made the offerings. Immediately Electra has finished these anxious speculations, her brother steps forward to identify himself (212–45).

In Euripides the discovery of the offerings is made by an Old Man, once τροφεύς to Agamemnon, who describes to Electra what he saw at the tomb of his former charge. After crying (*El.* 510) and making offerings of wine and myrtle (511–12), he notices a recently-slaughtered black sheep and some locks of hair on the site of the pyre (513–15). He responds with amazement (516), and wonders who could have made the offerings. As it could not have been an Argive, it might have been Orestes (516–19). He now[61] tries to test this hypothesis by comparing the hair and footprints he discovered at the tomb with Electra's hair and feet. Electra does not cooperate, and points out the limited heuristic value of such comparisons (520–37). The Old Man's hope that Orestes might be recognised through some clothing familiar to Electra is also swiftly dismissed by the heroine (538–46).

The accounts of Sophocles and Euripides stand closer to each other here than either does to that of Aeschylus. In neither does Electra find the offerings herself. Instead, another character relays the news of the discovery to her, although in each case Electra rejects the conclusion that Orestes has returned. The two accounts of the discovery follow the same basic pattern, each using a

---

[60] There is no good study of the relationships between these recognition scenes. The little which Brandão (2001) has to say is unsatisfactory, while Martina (1975) 181–95 is not much more than an excited plot summary.

[61] The authenticity of 520–46 has been suspected, without good cause. For a recent defence which refers to earlier literature see Gallagher (2003).

sequence of events influenced by Aeschylus' account (discovery, amazement, inference by process of elimination). But their overall impact is quite different.

In particular, Chrysothemis' case is more forceful and persuasive than the Old Man's. Her speech as a whole is elegantly structured: *narratio* (893–906), *probatio* (907–15) and *peroratio* (916–19) follow each other in an ordered manner (cf. Lausberg (1998) §261), yet without ever seeming schematic. Her narrative is engaging, both in the vividness of her description and the emphasis on the discovery as a process. So the elaborate account of her first sight of the offerings (894–6) is followed by her anxiously ensuring that she is alone (897–99); only then does she come closer to the mound (900), and finally discover the most significant token, the lock (900–1). At each of these stages we observe Chrysothemis' increasing emotion, as she moves from surprise (897) to suspicion (897–8), then to joy (902–6). Some elements in her speech have a colloquial edge to them (894n., 897n. (*bis*)), which conveys the infectious excitement of the narrator. The stress on her personal autopsy of the events (cf. 892, 894, 897, 899, 900, 902, 904, also 903, 906 ὄμμα; also 878, 923) adds persuasive power to her account (761–3n.). The corresponding passage in Euripides (*El.* 513–15) is short, plain and unexciting.

The argumentation which forms the central part of Chrysothemis' speech is no less lively. She eagerly alternates between rhetorical questions and statements of fact (907–14), until, exuding confidence in her own reasoning, she reaches the assured conclusion that only Orestes could have made the offerings (915). The tentativeness of Euripides' Old Man, by contrast (cf. 518 ἴσως, 522 φιλεῖ γάρ), was not likely to inspire confidence in an audience. And if the manner of Chrysothemis' argument is the more engaging, so too its content is the more convincing. She goes through each of the people who could have left the offerings. One by one she eliminates them, by showing that either their mental attitude or physical circumstances would have prevented them. At last only Orestes is left. The passage recalls Aesch. *Cho.* 169–73 and 187–94, though the case is tighter than in Aeschylus and set out more persuasively. The process of deduction entirely displaces the argument from physical similarity found in Aeschylus (cf. Brandão (2001) 124). The Old Man, on the other hand, makes only the briefest of gestures towards this kind of reasoning (517–18). Instead, Euripides has him concentrate on the less convincing of the two arguments found in Aeschylus, the argument from physical resemblances. Electra does not hesitate to point out how absurd this case is.

The process of elimination on which Chrysothemis bases her argument does not constitute a watertight case, for all the certainty she shows here and elsewhere. In the absence of other evidence, however, it does give a plausible explanation of the sights which Chrysothemis has encountered. Unfortunately for Chrysothemis, other evidence is precisely what Electra already possesses, in the form of the statement of a man who saw Orestes die. Chrysothemis' deductive arguments are opposed to the eye-witness account delivered by the Paedagogus. The latter's evidence constitutes a πίστις ἄτεχνος (Lausberg (1998) §351–4), the statement of a witness (cf. Anaximenes, *Rhet. Alex.* 15.1– 3, [Cic.] *Rhet. Her.* 2.9–12, Quint. *Inst.* 5.7). Chrysothemis' argument forms a πίστις ἔντεχνος (Lausberg (1998) §355–72), a deduction from σημεῖα (*ib.* §358– 60). The conflict between the accounts thus constitutes a clash between two different kinds of proof.

The relative importance of these two types of evidence was a moot point in rhetorical theory and practice (cf. Quint. *Inst.* 5.7.33 *saepe inter testes et argumenta quaesitum est*, [Cic.] *Rhet. Her.* 2.11). There was certainly no fixed view that witnesses provided a more trustworthy basis for judgment. But in these circumstances it is no surprise that Chrysothemis fails to dispel Electra's belief in the Paedagogus' account. He appears to be an unimpeachable witness, with none of the disabilities which could be attacked in such a figure (cf. Caplan's n. on [Cic.] *Rhet. Her.* 2.11): his character appears blameless, his testimony is clear, he has no obvious motive to lie. Chrysothemis, on the other hand, despite her claim to have seen σαφῆ σημεῖα (885–6), has supplied evidence which later rhetorical theorists would classify as *signa non necessaria*. That is, her account suggests certain conclusions, but without providing actual proof that they are true ([Cic.] *Rhet. Her.* 2.6, Quint. *Inst.* 5.9.8–14, Lausberg (1998) §363–5). And while the power of Chrysothemis' narrative is such that it emerges favourably from a comparison with the Old Man's account in Euripides, it comes a poor second when set against the extraordinary effect of the Paedagogus' tale. In isolation it is a *tour de force*, a speech of remarkable argumentative power and rhetorical acumen. In the context of the play it cannot hope to match the even more remarkable and convincing account which precedes it.

892 καὶ δή: 317n.
λέγω . . . πᾶν: 378n.

893 γάρ: 681 n.
πατρὸς ἀρχαῖον τάφον: the emphasis on the antiquity of the tomb of Agamemnon stresses the solemnity of the place. On burial mounds in the archaic and classical periods see Kurtz and Boardman (1971) 79–84, 105–8.

894 ὁρῶ: Chrysothemis' narrative oscillates between past tenses (5) and historic presents (6, excluding ἔστιν in 896 and ἐγχρίμπτει in 898). This switching is often colloquial (cf. Dover (1981) 23 = (1987a) 27, (1997) 67–8). The verb here is picked up by the participle ἰδοῦσα in 897 (n.).

895 πηγὰς γάλακτος: the phrasing suggests the abundance of the offerings (cf. Ant. Sid. *A.P.* 7.23.3 = 248 *HE*, Lucian 61.7). For πηγαί of libations cf. *OC*

479. For milk as an offering to the dead cf. Aesch. *Pers.* 611 βοός τ᾽ ἀφ᾽ ἀγνῆς λευκὸν εὔποτον γάλα, Virg. *Aen.* 5.78, Wyß (1914) 25–32. It is often offered with honey (cf. Hom. *Od.* 10.519 = 11.27 πρῶτα μελικρήτῳ, μετέπειτα δὲ ἡδέϊ οἴνῳ (with Eust. 1668.22 μελίκρατον δὲ οἱ παλαιοὶ μίγμα φασὶ μέλιτος καὶ γάλακτος ἐνταῦθα), Eur. *IT* 163–5, *Or.* 114–15 ἀμφὶ τὸν Κλυταιμήστρας τάφον | μελίκρατ᾽ ἄφες γάλακτος, Alcaeus *A.P.* 7.55.3–4 = 72–3 *HE*, Ov. *Met.* 7.246–7, Eitrem (1915) 103 with n. 4), but can also accompany wine, blood and other offerings (see Bömer on Ov. *Met.* 7.246).

895–6 περιστεφῆ κύκλῳ | πάντων ὅσ᾽ ἔστιν ἀνθέων: the Old Man in Euripides offers myrtle at the tomb (*El.* 512; contrast 323–5). For offering flowers at a tomb cf. Aesch. *Pers.* 618 ἄνθη τε πλεκτά, παμφόρου Γαίας τέκνα, Eur. *Tro.* 1143–4, 1247, Lattimore (1942) 129–31, Garland (2001) 171. For the construction cf. *OR* 83 πολυστεφὴς ... παγκάρπου δάφνης.

896 θήκην: a general term for any tomb or sepulchre (cf. *OC* 1763, Aesch. *Pers.* 405, *Ag.* 453, LSJ⁹ s.v. 2).

897 ἰδοῦσα: the participle picks up the main verb ὁρῶ from 894. This is a feature of 'unsophisticated' or 'unelevated' narrative: cf. Hdt. 1.8.1 οὗτος δὴ ὢν ὁ Κανδαύλης ἠράσθη τῆς ἑωυτοῦ γυναικός, ἐρασθεὶς δέ, Pl. *Prot.* 320d6–7, 7–8 καὶ οὕτω πείσας νέμει. νέμων δέ, Bruhn §230.I, van Otterlo (1944) 21–7. The effect of 900–2 ὁρῶ | ... | ... ὡς εἶδον is similar.

Connective δ᾽ when the sentence begins with a participle or subordinating conjunction (cf. 899 ὡς δ᾽) is not common in comedy, though it is often so found in oratory or historiography (so Dover (1968) 85–6). This should warn us against designating Chrysothemis' narrative style *in toto* as simply 'colloquial'.

ἔσχον θαῦμα: cf. Eur. *El.* 516–17 κάθαυμάσ᾽, ὦ παῖ, τίς ποτ᾽ ἀνθρώπων ἔτλη | πρὸς τύμβον ἐλθεῖν. The expression is an inversion of the normal θαῦμά μ᾽ ἔχει (cf. e.g. *Phil.* 686, Hom. *Od.* 10.326), probably through the analogy of other typically Sophoclean periphrases (30n.): cf. 1176, Ellendt s.v. ἔχω (p. 293, end of col. i), Davies on *Tr.* 673, Mastronarde on Eur. *Phoen.* 330.

καί: repeated use of connecting καί (cf. 902, 905) is often taken as colloquial, though it can be found in various types of vivid narrative (cf. Trenkner (1960) 16–21, Dover (1981) 24 = (1987a) 29, (1997) 70–3).

898 ἐγχρίμπτει: only KJZf have the mu: for the corruption see 721 n. Nauck³ rightly restores the indicative for the subjunctive: on seeing the freshly-made offerings, Chrysothemis is afraid not that their donor may return, but that he may still be at the tomb (581 n.). Manuscript evidence is valueless on such a question, as S. would probably have represented either as –ΕΙ.

899 So in Euripides the Old Man emphasises that the tomb is deserted (*El.* 510 ἐρημίας τυχών).

ὡς δ᾽: for the register see 897n.

ἐν γαλήνῃ: for the metaphor see van Nes (1963) 64–5.

900–1 ἐσχάτης . . . | πυρᾶς: the genitive could denote either space within which (so Jebb, Ll-J/W, *Sophoclea* etc.; cf. Moorhouse 59–60) or the place from which an object strikes the sense (Campbell and Kamerbeek). Schaefer's ἐσχάτῃ . . . | πυρᾷ (his edition, i. 243) is more natural, however, and may be right.

πυρᾶς: refers to the place of burial although the actual pyre has long been extinguished: cf. Eur. *Hec.* 386, *El.* 325, Erucius *A.P.* 7.397.1–2 = 2244–5 *GP*.

901 νεώρη: here equivalent to νεωστί. For the form see Wackernagel (1889) 49 = (1953–79) ii. 945. For the accentuation (corrected by Dindorf³) see [Arcadius'] epitome of Herodian 117, p. 135.9 Schmidt (= Herodian i. 72.4 Lentz).

βόστρυχον τετμημένον: cf. Aesch. *Cho.* 168 ὁρῶ τομαῖον τόνδε βόστρυχον τάφῳ. The use of the lock in the recognition of Orestes goes back to Stesichorus (fr. 217.11–12 *PMGF*). The offering of hair is mentioned by Orestes at 52. The other recognition token found in Aeschylus is omitted. The naïve conceit of a brother and sister with matching footprints would jar in a tragedy by Sophocles, who employed a greater degree of naturalism than his predecessor (cf. 774n.).

902–4 The sight of the lock does not merely prompt Chrysothemis to conclude that Orestes has returned: it causes her to experience an internal vision of her brother. The sudden vividness of this image is quite different from the reactions which the lock provokes in Aeschylus and Euripides.

902 κεὐθύς: Sophoclean narrative often combines καί and εὐθύς: cf. *Phil.* 356, 367, 374 (all from one speech, marking the impetuosity of Neoptolemus), *Tr.* 566, *Ant.* 429; also Eur. *IT* 1409. For the crasis see Diggle (1981a) 70.

ἐμπαίει: the last three verbs of the narrative (902–6 ἐμπαίει, δυσφημῶ, πίμπλημι) are all historic presents, whereas up till now historic presents had alternated fairly evenly with past tenses. This tense may be used here to mark the climax of the narrative (cf. 725n.).

903 ψυχῇ σύνηθες ὄμμα 'an image familiar to my mind'. For this common metaphorical meaning of ὄμμα cf. *Aj.* 1004 ὦ δυσθέατον ὄμμα, Lloyd-Jones (1993a) 301 = (2005) 110–11. On discovering the lock Chrysothemis immediately assumes that it came from Orestes. This thought prompts her to imagine the mental picture of her brother, a picture which she has long cherished (such

is the force of ψυχῇ σύνηθες: cf. Σ p. 143.6–7 Papageorgius ὅραμα ὃ ἀεὶ ἐφαν-
ταζόμην κατὰ ψυχήν,[62] *Tr.* 88, *Phil.* 894). ὁρᾶν is final-consecutive (406n.;
'so that I saw that this was evidence for . . .'). Alternatively, ψυχῇ could be
taken with ἐμπαίει, as Jebb recommends. But the stress on the familiarity of
the sight to Chrysothemis' mind does have a rhetorical point. Chrysothemis
implies that she as well as Electra has been longing for Orestes. Even though
she can have no idea of what he now looks like (cf. Eur. *El.* 283, *Or.* 377–9), she
nevertheless constantly imagines in her mind what his appearance now might
be (cf. how Andromache cherishes the *imago* of the dead Astyanax at Virg. *Aen.*
3.489–91). Given Electra's own devotion to her brother, the statement acts as
a *captatio benevolentiae*. But it remains possible that ψυχῇ is to be felt with both
verb and adjective: its position would facilitate an ἀπὸ κοινοῦ construction.

According to Lloyd-Jones (1993a) 302–3 = (2005) 112–13 ὄμμα means
'source of brightness / comfort'. For this sense cf. *Aj.* 977 ὦ φίλτατ' Αἴας, ὦ
ξύναιμον ὄμμ' ἐμοί, *OR* 987, *Tr.* 203, D. Bremer (1976) 382 n. 161, Dihle (1983)
88, Garvie on Aesch. *Cho.* 238. He also takes ὁρᾶν to be final-consecutive. But
it is strained to talk of a source of comfort bursting upon oneself, especially
when an alternative, simpler explanation is to hand. In the parallels cited by
Lloyd-Jones the sense 'source of comfort' is the only one available, whereas
here the more usual 'sight' is more natural.

903–4 φιλτάτου βροτῶν | πάντων: in her mention of a family member
Chrysothemis employs the extravagant mode of expression formerly associated
with her sister (462–3n.); cf. also Aesch. *Cho.* 193–4 (cited below, 908n.).

904 Deleted by Paley (*locum non inveni*: it is not in either of his editions), for
whom the direct mention of Orestes' name (strictly unnecessary after 903)
presumably betrayed the hand of an interpolator. But the importance of the
term τέκμήριον in Chrysothemis' rhetoric of persuasion (see below) probably
protects the line.

ὁρᾶν: final-consecutive (903n.).

τεκμήριον: Quint. *Inst.* 5.9.3–4 (following Arist. *Rhet.* 1357b1–21) defines
τέκμηρια as ἄλυτα σημεῖα. But as well as this strong sense 'piece of probative
evidence, proof' (LSJ[9] s.v. I), the term can also have the weaker meaning 'piece
of evidence, sign' (LSJ[9] s.v. II); cf. Gagarin on Antiph. 1.10, Thomas (2000)
190–200. The English word 'evidence' can be used for both. Each of these
senses can be found in Aeschylus (*Eum.* 447, 662; *Ag.* 1366, *Cho.* 205), while in
Euripides the usual sense is 'proof' (cf. Thomas (1997) 138 with n. 29).

---

[62] Nauck[6] emended to φάσμα on the basis of this scholium (cf. (1890) 31): but ὅραμα
protects ὄμμα.

The lock at the tomb has convinced Chrysothemis that her brother has returned. It is therefore most natural to take the word here in the stronger sense of 'proof'. Euripides often uses the term with this meaning in recognition scenes (cf. *El.* 575, *IT* 808, 822, *Ion* 329). It certainly has this sense in its other two occurrences in this play (774, 1109); the contrast between the evidence which Electra does accept and that which she does not is heightened if the word has the same meaning in each case. Its other occurrence in S. (*OC* 1510) should probably be taken in this way too.

905 βαστάσασα: 'βαστάζειν means not a desultory touching, grasping or taking hold of an object . . . but the holding and poising of it, e.g. for careful examination' (Fraenkel on Aesch. *Ag.* 35). In general this is true, but the simpler senses 'clasp' (cf. 1216) and 'lift' (cf. 1470) can also be found in this play (cf. Dale on Eur. *Alc.* 19).

δυσφημῶ μὲν οὔ 'I utter no word of ill omen.' The numinous atmosphere created by the discovery of the lock makes Chrysothemis reluctant even to speak. No words could possibly do justice to the occasion. Jebb interprets 'I do not reproach Orestes for his late coming', but this is too oblique. On εὐφημία see 630–1 n.

For **οὔ** at the end of a line cf. *Ant.* 255, *Aj.* 545, *Phil.* 545.

906 χαρᾷ . . . πίμπλημ᾽ εὐθὺς ὄμμα δακρύων: cf. Aesch. *Cho.* 185–7 ἐξ ὀμμάτων δὲ δίψιοι πίπτουσί μοι | σταγόνες ἄφαρκτοι δυσχίμου πλημυρίδος | πλόκαμον ἰδούσῃ τόνδε. For the combination of joy and tears cf. 1312–13, Hom. *Od.* 23.32–3 ἣ δ᾽ ἐχάρη καὶ ἀπὸ λέκτροιο θοροῦσα | γρηΐ περιπλέχθη, βλεφάρων δ᾽ ἀπὸ δάκρυον ἧκε, Aesch. *Ag.* 270 χαρά μ᾽ ὑφέρπει δάκρυον ἐκκαλουμένη, Eur. *IT* 832–3, Xen. *Hell.* 7.2.9, Plut. *Dion* 42.3; also 1231 n.

907–8 Both immediate instinct and leisurely calculation support Chrysothemis' conclusion that Orestes has returned. Her confidence is paralleled in Aeschylus, where Electra declares εὐξύμβολον τόδ᾽ [i.e. the identity of the owner of the lock] ἐστὶ παντὶ δοξάσαι (*Cho.* 170). She later follows this claim up, as in S.'s play, with arguments from elimination. The lock did not come from herself, one of the citizens, or from Clytemnestra: Orestes is the only other candidate (*Cho.* 172–3, 187–94).

νῦν θ᾽ . . . καὶ τότ᾽: for the combination cf. Ar. *Av.* 24, Hdt. 4.160.1, Thuc. 3.40.2, Dem. 18.31, Kemmer (1903) 179–81.

ἐξεπίσταμαι | μή: for μή with verbs of opinion or knowledge see Hutchinson on Aesch. *Sept.* 36–8. For this verb governing an indirect statement with an infinitive cf. *Ant.* 293–4, Bruhn §124.

908 τοῦ . . . κείνου: the ablatival genitive with a verb of motion (cf. 930, Moorhouse 66) is used personally only here in S. Moorhouse consequently suggests that the genitive might be possessive, as as Aesch. *Cho.* 193 (cited next note): but μολεῖν tells against this.

ἀγλάϊσμα: cf. Aesch. *Cho.* 193–4 εἶναι τόδ᾿ ἀγλάϊσμά μοι τοῦ φιλτάτου | βροτῶν Ὀρέστου, Eur. *El.* 325 πυρὰ δὲ χέρσος ἀγλαϊσμάτων (of Agamemnon's tomb). The formation emphasises the verbal derivation more than ἀγλαΐα would have done: Long translates 'something which gives joy' ((1968) 41; cf. Eur. *Hel.* 11, 282). Unlike ἀγλαΐα, the word is not found in prose until late.

909 τόδε: i.e. the cutting of the hair. Cf. Aesch. *Cho.* 172 οὐκ ἔστιν ὅστις πλὴν ἐμοῦ κείραιτό νιν.

911 For πῶς γάρ; confirming a negative statement see Denniston 86. Cf. 865n. on πῶς γὰρ οὔκ;

911–12 ἥ γε μηδὲ πρὸς θεοὺς | ἔξεστ᾿ ἀκλαύτῳ τῆσδ᾿ ἀποστῆναι στέγης: an exceptionally severe instance of the restriction of movement afforded to women (518n.). Euripides' Electra describes herself as ἀνέορτος ἱερῶν καὶ χορῶν τητωμένη (*El.* 310): but this is an ostentatious act of self-deprivation rather than a genuine restriction on her movement, and in any case she lives in the country, not in the palace. The sympathetic comment is rhetorically effective. It also gives the audience an outside comment on Electra's life: a striking detail consistent with what we have seen of her situation, though not simply repeating earlier material. It thus adds depth to her portrayal.

μηδέ: causal (cf. *Phil.* 255, Bruhn §159.III.2).

πρὸς θεούς: i.e. places of worship: cf. [Aesch.] *PV* 529–30 θεοὺς . . . | . . . ποτινισομένα, Diod Sic. 1.43.2 = Hec. Abd. *FGrHist* 264 F25.43.2, Cic. *Leg.* 2.24 *ad deos*.

ἀκλαύτῳ *impune*: cf. *Ant.* 754 κλαίων φρενώσεις, *OR* 401–2, *Phil.* 1259–60. 'κλαίειν is what naughty *slaves* do in Comedy' (Waś (1983) 213, citing Stevens (1976) 15–16): there may thus be a colloquial edge. The form without a sigma before the tau, restored by Dindorf[4], is the older and commoner in the manuscript tradition (see West's Teubner Aeschylus, p. xliii).

913–14 Cf. Aesch. *Cho.* 189–90 ἀλλ᾿ οὐδὲ μήν νιν ἡ κτανοῦσ᾿ ἐκείρατο, | ἐμή γε μήτηρ; also 173 ἐχθροὶ γὰρ οἷς προσῆκε πενθῆσαι τριχί.

913 ἀλλ᾿ οὐδὲ μὲν δή: progressive ('nor again'): cf. Denniston 395, *Tr.* 1128, *Aj.* 877, fr. 162.1 *TrGF*. ἀλλ᾿ is repeated at 915 and 916 (cf. 537n.).

914 ἐλάνθαν' ἄν: B. Heath's conjecture ((1762) 20) for manuscript ἐλάνθανεν restores the expected counterfactual construction with minimal interference with the paradosis. The matter could be left there, had not Elmsley (on Eur. *Med.* 416–17 (our 426–7), note p, page 150 of his first edition = note e, p. 326 of his second edition) claimed that in Attic poetry the third person singular ending was not elided by ἄν ('Elmsley's Law'). Manuscript evidence, however, provides three counterexamples,[63] (Eur. *Ion* 354 σοὶ ταὐτὸν ἥβης, εἴπερ ἦν, εἶχ' ἂν μέτρον, Ar. *Ran.* 946, *Plut.* 1012). Elmsley was aware of the instances from *Wealth* and *Ion* and advocated emendation, but the most recent standard editions (those of Sommerstein and Diggle) keep the paradosis. The value of Elmsley's statistics has also been called into question (see Harrison (1933)).

Diggle's list of eight tragic exceptions to the Law ((1974) 16–17 n. 5 = (1994) 109 n. 61 and (1981a) 120) is of limited value as evidence, since (apart from Ar. *Ran.* 946, which he also cites) they are all conjectural; nor does Diggle discuss the individual merits of any of the conjectures. A more nuanced analysis is provided by Irvine on Eur. *Ion* 354 (his commentary, vol i. pp. 203–6). He argues that in some cases (e.g. Eur. *Hel.* 1658–9) the omission of ἄν can be justified on the grounds that 'the hypothetical apodosis is envisaged by the speaker as so close to reality that the hypothetical particle could be omitted' (i. 204): for this phenomenon cf. Goodwin §38, Wyse on Isaeus 1.44.5. In our case, however, there is no justification for the vividness which this irregular syntax would provide (cf. Fitton Brown (1956)).

Elmsley's δρῶσ' ἂν ἔλαθεν ἄν ((1811) 67 n. *; also mentioned in the note setting out his 'Law', cited above) is an alternative to Heath's conjecture. For the reverse corruption of imperfect to aorist cf. Eur. *Tro.* 397 (ὢν ἐλάνθαν' ἄν Burges, Schaefer; ὢν ἐλάνθανεν PQ, Chr. Pat. 1658, ἔλαθεν ἂν γεγώς ΣV). But this involves a greater change than Heath's emendation, as does Meineke's ἔληθεν ἄν ((1863a) 264).

915 τἀπιτίμια: so the manuscripts and Suda s.v. (ε 2699 = ii. 388.25–6 Adler). The word usually means 'penalty' (cf. 1382); [Ammon.] *De adf. voc. diff.* 183 (p. 46.15–17 Nickau) distinguishes between ἐπιτίμιον = ἡ ζημία and ἐπίτιμον = τὸ τῆς τιμῆς μετέχον. Dindorf's conjecture τἀπιτύμβια ((1836) 169) has consequently been accepted by several editors (including Jebb, Pearson and Ll-J/W); cf. *Ant.* 901–2, Aesch. *Ag.* 1547, *Cho.* 334–5. But at Hdt. 6.39.2 ἐπιτιμέων is used of honouring a dead brother, while at Aesch. *Sept.* [1021] τοὐπιτίμιον is best taken as 'rites of honour' (see Hutchinson *ad loc.*). Given these parallels, the paradosis needs no alteration (so also Kugler (1905)

---

[63] Claims that other examples can be found in manuscripts of Euripides' *Hecuba* are unfounded (cf. Diggle (1975a) 198, (1981a) 100).

37). τἀγλαΐσματα, a γράφεται-variant in L written by the scholiast (p. 143.15 Papageorgius), probably arose from 908 (so Dawe, *STS* i. 189–90).

916 For ἀλλ᾽ 'near the end of a speech, as a clinching and final appeal' cf. 986, 1009, Denniston 14.

ὦ φίλη: 'the word is appropriate in affectionate expostulation' (Nisbet and Hubbard on Hor. *C.* 2.9.5 *amice*); cf. 871 n.

θάρσυνε: intransitive only here, probably on the analogy of verbs such as βραδύνω and ταχύνω which have both a transitive and intransitive sense: cf. 699n.

916–17 τοῖς αὐτοῖσί τοι | οὐχ αὐτὸς αἰεὶ δαιμόνων παραστατεῖ: for the thought cf. *Tr.* 129–31 ἀλλ᾽ ἐπὶ πῆμα καὶ χαρὰν | πᾶσι κυκλοῦσιν οἷον ἄρ– | κτου στροφάδες κέλευθοι, *Aj.* 131–2, 669–83, *Ant.* 1158–9, *OC* 607–15, Jones (1962) 174–7, 184–6, Krause (1976) especially 179–99, Renehan (1985) 147; contrast Men. fr. 500 *PCG*, where the δαίμων which ἀνδρὶ συμπαρίσταται | εὐθὺς γενομένῳ is always good.

916 τοι 'point[s] the applicability of a universal truth to the special matter in hand: it forces the general truth upon the consciousness of the individual addressed' (Denniston 542 (10)).

917 A δαίμων is frequently referred to in the context of Electra's fortunes (cf. 999–1000, 1156–7, 1305–6). By the fifth century the word had lost a good deal of its personal character (see Fraenkel on Aesch. *Ag.* 1341–2); nevertheless, it keeps the sense of *divinely-apportioned* fate. For differing fortunes from differing δαίμονες cf. *OC* 1567 πάλιν σφε δαίμων δίκαιος αὔξοι, fr. 646.4–5 *TrGF* καθεῖλε . . . | πάμπλουτον ὄλβον δαίμονος κακοῦ δόσις, Hom. *Od.* 5.396, 10.64, 19.201, 24.149. For the idea that a god can produce sudden reversals of fortune see West (1997) 528, Harder on Eur. fr. 262 *TrGF* = 36 Austin.

918 τά: Ll-J/W print Lloyd-Jones's conjecture ὁ (made at (1978) 219). This, they argue (*Sophoclea*), fits better with Chrysothemis' previous words, in which she has declared that we are accompanied by different δαίμονες, each of whom may be good or bad, not that we have a single δαίμων who switches between bad and good. But the transmitted text can be taken to mean 'we used to have a στυγνὸς δαίμων', so the emendation is not an improvement. Nor is the postulated corruption easy to account for: one might have thought that the following στυγνός would have protected an original ὁ.

πρόσθε: S. has many metrically guaranteed instances of this word both with and without final nu. As at *Ant.* 434 and *OC* 394, either would fit the metre here. In this case and at *Ant.* 434 the form with nu has the better manuscript

388

authority, not that this counts for much in such a case. But πρόσθεν is so much the commoner word that the *utrum in alterum* argument favours πρόσθε, which tends to be confined to poetry. Moreover, the language does not favour the combination νσ (> (σ)σ).

στυγνός: cf. Aesch. *Pers.* 472 ὦ στυγνὲ δαῖμον, Eur. *Hipp.* 771, S. *Aj.* 1214–15 νῦν δ᾽ οὗτος ἀνεῖται στυγερῷ δαί– | μονι, Hom. *Od.* 5.396 στυγερὸς δέ οἱ ἔχραε δαίμων.

919 πολλῶν ὑπάρξει κῦρος . . . καλῶν 'will be the consummation of much good' (Campbell). For the sentiment cf. Ar. *Pax* 435–6 σπένδοντες εὐχώμεσθα τὴν νῦν ἡμέραν | Ἕλλησιν ἄρξαι πᾶσι πολλῶν κἀγαθῶν; for the opposite cf. Thuc. 2.12.3 ἥδε ἡ ἡμέρα τοῖς Ἕλλησι μεγάλων κακῶν ἄρξει. The verb ὑπάρξει acts as a strengthened ἔσται (cf. *Ant.* 932, *Phil.* 704). For κῦρος in this sense cf. *OC* 1779 πάντως γὰρ ἔχει τάδε κῦρος. Again, a character asserts the significance of this day, this time with the irony that the assertion is true, and yet will be disbelieved by the addressee. See further 764–822n.

920–46 Electra dismisses her sister's lengthy account with crushing brevity. In bleak, staccato utterances she informs her of Orestes' death and the message which proves it. The starkness of the phrasing contrasts with the rhetorical full-ness of the speech we have just heard. Electra does not need to draw inferences or win over her listener with a dramatic narration and moving peroration. She has, as she believes, the facts of the case, facts which neither require elabo-ration nor permit refutation. A similar brevity characterises Chrysothemis' expressions of sorrow (926, 930 οἴμοι τάλαινα, 934 ὦ δυστυχής): in the face of Electra's words she can say no more. At 934–7 she picks up and rejects the words she had used at the opening of the episode (934n.). The ring composi-tion, break in the stichomythia and absence of any forward movement in the plot all suggest that the end of the scene is in sight.

Electra has other ideas. Her revelation at 938 that she has a plan to free the sisters from their grief is completely unexpected. After hearing of the death of Orestes she had said that she would now wait outside the house in despair for the rest of her life (817–19). Nothing she has said since then has suggested that her mind has changed. The mention of the plan without any preparation is thus a moment of great dramatic suddenness. Once more Electra has surprised us: once more we are frustrated in our attempts to understand her motivations. This suggestion of inscrutability encourages us to regard her as a truly rounded character.

Electra delays her description of the plan (938–47; cf. *Ant.* 37–43), instead giving her sister dark hints that the task before them is a bold one (cf. 943 and especially 945). Compare the effect of Pylades' speech at Eur. *Or.* 1085–99, where only at the end does he reveal that he is advocating an attempt on Menelaus' prosperity. Chrysothemis does not reject her sister's offer out of hand, mysterious though it is. She promises to help as much as lies within her power (944, 946), and there is no reason to doubt her sincerity. But even now we may suspect that Electra's plan will go against what is practicable in Chrysothemis' eyes.

920 τῆς ἀνοίας: is this a genitive of cause, with ἐποικτίρω (Moorhouse 70–1; so Elmsley on Eur. *Med.* 1202–3 (our [1233–4])), or a genitive of exclamation (Moorhouse 71–2)? *Ant.* 82 οἴμοι ταλαίνης ὡς ὑπερδέδοικά σου shows the same ambiguity. But in the similar cases at *Aj.* 367 οἴμοι γέλωτος, οἷον ὑβρίσθην ἄρα and *OC* 1399–1400 the genitives must be exclamatory; cf. also Ar. *Nub.* 1476. The default hypothesis must be that they are exclamatory here too. Genitives with verbs of pitying also usually follow the verb (cf. Aesch. *Ag.* 1321, [Aesch.] *PV* 397, Eur. *Hipp.* 1409, S–D ii. 133–4). The two exceptions to this tendency in S–D (1027 of this play and Thuc. 6.36.1) both bring forward the genitive to make a rhetorical contrast with another genitive. At Eur. *Phoen.* 1425 Mastronarde and Diggle print φεῦ φεῦ, κακῶν σῶν, Οἰδίπου, σ' ὅσον στένω, but given the tendency just noted κακῶν should probably be taken with the exclamations.

The accusation of ἄνοια, referring to Chrysothemis' credulity, is cutting. Close argumentation such as Chrysothemis' would more normally attract the opposite designation, as at *OR* 915–16 οὐδ' ὁποῖ' ἀνὴρ | ἔννους τὰ καινὰ τοῖς πάλαι τεκμαίρεται.

ὡς σ' ἐποικτίρω πάλαι: cf. 1199 (n.), *Phil.* 965–6 ἐμοὶ μὲν οἶκτος δεινὸς ἐμπέπτωκέ τις | τοῦδ' ἀνδρὸς οὐ νῦν πρῶτον, ἀλλὰ καὶ πάλαι, 906, 913.

921 For Chrysothemis' dismayed response to the reception of her news cf. 769n. For the double question, the second more specific than the first, cf. *OR* 938, Aesch. *Ag.* 1306, Eur. *Hel.* 600, Mastronarde (1979) 50 n. 57.

πρὸς ἡδονήν: 369n.

922 Assured of her own superior knowledge, Electra adopts a lofty tone: cf. Eur. *Ba.* 506 (Dionysus to Pentheus) οὐκ οἶσθ' †ὅτι ζῆς† οὐδ' ὃ δρᾷς οὐδ' ὅστις εἶ.

οὐκ οἶσθ' ὅποι γῆς . . . φέρῃ: the expression denotes a state of complete ignorance or other psychological deficiency: cf. Pl. *Resp.* 403e5–6, Men. *Dysc.* 635, *Peric.* 793, *Sic.* 369, Dio Chrysostom 3.63, Apostolius 14.57 = *CPG* ii. 619.3; also S. *Phil.* 805 ποῦ ποτ' ὤν, τέκνον, κυρεῖς; More than one scribe found the phrase difficult to understand, as can be seen from the articulation γ' ἧς in N^rpc GR. But given these parallels, emendations (e.g. Wecklein (1869a) 22 ὃ ποιεῖς, Broadhead (1968) 82–3 ὃ γ' εἶπες) are unnecessary. For the genitive see

390n., adding *OR* 1309 ποῖ γᾶς φέρομαι τλάμων;, Men. *Dysc.* 635 ὦ Γοργία, ποῦ γῆς ποτ᾿ εἶ;

ὅποι γνώμης: an exclusively Sophoclean expression: cf. *Tr.* 705 ὥστ᾿ οὐκ ἔχω τάλαινα ποῖ γνώμης πέσω, *Ant.* 42 ποῦ (v.l. ποῖ) γνώμης ποτ᾿ εἶ; also *OC* 310 ποῖ φρενῶν ἔλθω;

φέρῃ: for the verb of motion in such an expression cf. *Tr.* 705, *OC* 310. L^ac may have read φόρῃ; for this confusion see 420–1 n.

923 κάτοιδ᾿ answers the preceding οἶσθα: cf. *Phil.* 249–50, 1336–43, *Ant.* 1063– 4, *OC* 1474–5, *OR* 1038–41, 1128–34, *Tr.* 76–87, Renehan (1976) 25–6.

κάτοιδ᾿ . . . εἶδον: cf. *Phil.* 250 πῶς γὰρ κάτοιδ᾿ ὅν γ᾿ εἶδον οὐδεπώποτε; Seeing and knowing were connected in Greek thought (659n.); the similarity in the form of the words may have assisted that connexion. For the emphasis on what Chrysothemis saw cf. 892–919n.

924–5 The crushing 'fact' of Orestes' demise is communicated in three devastatingly brief sentences: 'the ear is arrested by brief κόμματα, fired off as it were in suppressed passion' (Fraenkel on Aesch. *Ag.* 39). Cf. Xen. *Hell.* 1.1.23 ἔρρει τὰ κᾶλα. Μίνδαρος δ᾿ ἀπεσσύα. πεινῶντι τὥνδρες. ἀπορίομες τί χρὴ δρᾶν (the Spartan message after the battle of Cyzicus). The asyndeton in 925 lends the words further force (cf. 1151–3). The tone is blunt and direct, with the vocative ὦ τάλαινα (cf. 879n.) expressing Electra's contempt for what she sees as her sister's foolishness. Alternatively the vocative may be commiseratory, but the starkness of Electra's language tells against this.

924 τἀκ κείνου: so Canter (1566) 236–7 (bk. 4 ch. 29) for transmitted τἀκείνου. Keeping the paradosis, Ellendt translates *salus illius, vita deperiit*, comparing *Aj.* 778–9 τάχ᾿ ἄν | γενοίμεθ᾿ αὐτοῦ σὺν θεῷ σωτήριοι for the objective genitive. In the context, however, we rather need a reference to Orestes as the source of the sisters' salvation. Canter's text, which has scarcely less authority than that advocated by Ellendt, fulfils that need. For ἐκ with σωτήρια cf. *OC* 724–5 ἐξ ὑμῶν ἐμοὶ | φαίνοιτ᾿ ἄν ἤδη τέρμα τῆς σωτηρίας, Pl. *Resp.* 494a11, Xen. *Hell.* 7.1.6, Dem. 25.32, Plut. *Them.* 13.4. For the word order see 7–8n.

925 μηδέν: 'mit keinem Blick schau nach ihm aus' (Kaibel, p. 215). μηκέτ᾿ (*coni.* Nauck[4a] p. vii; for the corruption cf. 1426) is considerably weaker: cf. Vahlen (1895) 9–10 = (1907–8) ii. 165.

ὅρα 'look to' (for help): cf. 954n.

926 As at 883, a new and emotionally-laden piece of news causes one of the sisters to exclaim οἴμοι τάλαινα and ask for its source. The mirroring effect stresses the reversal in the sisters' rôles: now Electra appears to have superior knowledge. See further Hutchinson (1999) 55 n. 13; also 920–46n.

927 For the emphasis on the actual presence of the witness (note the imperfect participle) cf. 424, *Tr.* 889 ἐπεῖδον, ὡς δὴ πλησία παραστάτις, Eur. *Hel.* 1199 (how do you know this?) κείνη τέ φησιν ὅ τε παρὼν ὅτ᾽ ὤλλυτο. The imperfect ὤλλυτο hints at the painful, drawn-out process through which Orestes is supposed to have been killed (cf. 806n.)

928 καί in questions denotes a request for more information or an emotional reaction; there is often no sharp distinction between the senses (Denniston 309–10; cf. 236n., 883, Eur. *Ba.* 501 καὶ ποῦ 'στιν;).

θαῦμά τοί μ᾽ ὑπέρχεται 'Amazement steals over me': cf. 1112, LSJ⁹ s.v. ὑπέρχομαι II, Padel (1992) 126 n. 46.

929 ἡδὺς οὐδὲ μητρὶ δυσχερής: μητρί goes with both adjectives. For its position cf. Eur. *Ba.* 860–1 θεὸς | δεινότατος, ἀνθρώποισι δ᾽ ἠπιώτατος (where as here the connecting word is δέ: cf. Diggle (1994) 468), S. *OC* 1399 οἴμοι κελεύθου τῆς τ᾽ ἐμῆς δυσπραξίας, *Ant.* 1155 Κάδμου πάροικοι καὶ δόμων Ἀμφίονος, Aesch. *Ag.* 589 φράζων ἅλωσιν Ἰλίου τ᾽ ἀνάστασιν with Fraenkel. ἡδύς here denotes '*acceptus, welcome*, expressing the effect of the person on others rather than any positive quality of his own' (Gow on Theocr. 14.61): cf. *OR* 82. For the figure 'x and not not-x' cf. 885, Bruhn §208, Denniston 513, Denniston on Eur. *El.* 985–7, Schmitt (1967) 266–9.

930 οἴμοι τάλαινα: for exclamations, apostrophes and questions before a γάρ-clause cf. *OR* 1017 πῶς εἶπας; οὐ γὰρ Πόλυβος ἐξέφυσέ με;, *Phil.* 327–8, Denniston 80 (8). See further 920–46n.

τοῦ: ablatival (908n.).

931 τὰ πολλά 'those many': for the noun with this phrase see 564n. For the emphasis on the extent of the offerings cf. 896.

πρὸς τάφον: 'not πρὸς τάφῳ [Blaydes¹], since the thought is, τίς προσήνεγκε ταῦτα;' (Jebb): cf. Eur. *Or.* 1434–5 ἐπὶ τύμβον ἀγάλ– | ματα, Diggle (1981a) 28–9.

κτερίσματα: 434n.

932–3 At Eur. *El.* 545–6 Electra suggests that a ξένος laid the offerings at the tomb out of a sense of pity.

932 μάλιστ᾽: used of the most likely explanation or outcome: cf. *Phil.* 617 οἴοιτο μὲν μάλισθ᾽ ἑκούσιον λαβών, *OC* 1298, Eur. *Or.* 398.

934–5 The similarity to Chrysothemis' opening words in 871–2 (cf. σὺν χαρᾷ – ὑφ' ἡδονῆς; ἔσπευδον – διώκομαι) stresses the reversal in Chrysothemis' position. See further 920–46n.

935 ἄρα: for this with οἶδα cf. 1185, Bruhn §148, Denniston 36 (2).

936 ἵν' ἦμεν ἄτης: cf. *OR* 367 ἵν' εἶ κακοῦ, 1442–3 ἵν' ἔσταμεν | χρείας, Eur. *Tro.* 685 ἔνθα πημάτων κυρῶ, Bruhn §32.1. For the construction see further 390n., 922n.

938–9 The mood of lamentation is displaced by a new conspiratorial atmosphere (920–46n.).

938 οὕτως ἔχει σοι ταῦτ': Antigone uses the same phrase as she turns from describing Creon's edict to requesting the assistance of her sister (*Ant.* 37).

939 πημονῆς . . . βάρος: cf. Eur. *Suppl.* 818 πημάτων . . . βάρος, *Hipp.* 878 βάρος κακῶν, S. *Tr.* 325 συμφορᾶς βάρος.

λύσεις βάρος: cf. *OC* 1615–16 ἀλλ' ἓν γὰρ μόνον | τὰ πάντα λύει ταῦτ' ἔπος μοχθήματα, *Tr.* 1170–1 ἔφασκε μόχθων τῶν ἐφεστώτων ἐμοὶ | λύσιν τελεῖσθαι, Eur. fr. 573.3–4 *TrGF*; also 230.

940 For the impossibility of raising the dead see 137–9n.

τοὺς θανόντας: for the plural see 594n.

ποτέ: is appropriate in an astonished question (see Kaibel, p. 216).

941 οὐ τοῦτό γ': Blaydes's conjecture (in his 1873 edition) gives this required sense: cf. *Phil.* 442 οὐ τοῦτον εἶπον ('I did not mean him'), Aesch. fr. 78a.24 οὐ τοῦτ' ἐρῶ σ', Eur. *IT* 501 οὐ τοῦτ' ἐρωτῶ, *Hel.* 463 οὐ τοῦτ' ἐμέμφθην. ΟΥΤΟΥΤΟΓΕΙΠΟΝ could easily lose its first ΟΥΤ by haplography, and then the change of Τ to Κ and insertion of ΕΣΘ would be simple alterations aimed at completing the sense and the line (so Renehan (1992) 356–7).

Kaibel (p. 216) supports the majority reading οὐκ ἔσθ' ὃ γ', comparing e.g. Pl. *Alc. 1*. 130b6 οὐκ ἂν δὴ τοῦτό γε εἴη ὃ ζητοῦμεν. However, all his examples have a demonstrative pronoun as antecedent to the relative, which is lacking in our case (noted by Ll-J/W, *Sophoclea*). Hence Kaibel's text must be rendered not 'that is not what I said', but 'it is not what I said', which is not the required sense. Dawe, Bruhn and Pearson print Haupt's οὐκ ἐς τόδ' εἶπον ((1865b) 5 = (1875–6) ii. 299), which has been found to have some manuscript support. But parallels for this kind of expression (e.g. *Tr.* 403 σὺ δ' ἐς τί δή με τοῦτ' ἐρωτήσας ἔχεις;, *OR* 78 ἀλλ' ἐς καλὸν σύ . . . εἶπας, *Phil.* 111 ὅταν τι δρᾷς εἰς κέρδος, [Theocr.] 27.55) never involve a demonstrative pronoun. The sense too is problematic ('I did not speak with reference to that').

οὐ γὰρ ὧδ' ἄφρων ἔφυν: for the mocking self-depreciation cf. 135n.

942 γάρ: used in answer-questions when the speaker 'proffers a new suggestion after the elimination of a previous hypothesis' (Denniston 81 VI (1); cf. *OC* 581, 598).

κελεύεις: here probably 'exhort' rather than 'order' (632n.).

ὧν ἐγὼ φερέγγυος: ὧν ἐγὼ εἰς τὸ πράττειν ἀσφαλής εἰμι (Suda φ 208 = iv. 712.26 Adler). Like ἐχέγγυος, this adjective means 'able to give security' and hence 'capable (for a purpose)'. Elsewhere used absolutely (e.g. Aesch. *Sept.* 449), with an infinitive (*ib.* 396, Hdt. 5.30.4), or with a clause (e.g. Thuc. 8.68.3), only here does it take an objective genitive (cf. however Plut. *Public.* 4.4 οὐδένα νομίζων ἐχέγγυον ἀπορρήτων τηλικούτων, Palladas *A.P.* 10.56.11).

943 τλῆναι . . . δρῶσαν: for τλάω with participle see K–G ii. 55.5, Hutchinson on Aesch. *Sept.* 753–5.

944 ἀλλ': conveying agreement 'not as self-evident, but as wrung from the speaker *malgré lui*' (Denniston 16 (6) (b)); cf. 1055, *Ant.* 98, *Tr.* 472, *Phil.* 645, 1278. The restrictive γ' also suggests Chrysothemis' reluctance.

οὐκ ἀπώσομαι: same phrase at *Tr.* 1249.

945 ὅρα: 'an impressive warning that the task about to be mentioned is a great one' (Jebb): cf. *OC* 587 ὅρα γε μήν· οὐ σμικρός, οὐχ, ἀγὼν ὅδε, Aesch. *Cho.* 924; also S. *El.* 580, 1003, 1243 (combined with a general truth, as here).

πόνου τοι χωρὶς οὐδὲν εὐτυχεῖ: cf. fr. 397 *TrGF* οὔτοι ποθ' †ἥξει† τῶν ἄκρων ἄνευ πόνου, Archil. fr. 17 *IEG* πάντα πόνος τεύχει θνητοῖς μελέτη τε βροτείη, Pind. *P.* 12.28–9 εἰ δέ τις ὄλβος ἐν ἀνθρώποισιν, ἄνευ καμάτου | οὐ φαίνεται, Eur. frr. 134, 233, 236, 364, 432, 461, 474 (= *CPG* ii. 768.9–10), 701, 745 *TrGF*. For the form cf. [Men.] *Monost.* 344 θεοῦ γὰρ οὐδεὶς χωρὶς εὐτυχεῖ βροτῶν.

946 ὁρῶ: follows ὅρα, as at *Phil.* 589 ('Εμ) ὅρα τί ποιεῖς, παῖ. (Νε) σκοπῶ κἀγὼ πάλαι (also 30–1), [Aesch.] *PV* 69–70, Pl. *Soph.* 268a10-b1.

947–89 Faced with a desperate situation, Electra proposes to her companion the assassination of one of their enemies. The pattern is found twice elsewhere in tragedy. An Old Slave in Euripides' *Ion* encourages Creusa to kill Ion (978), now that he has been revealed as her husband Xuthus' son from a previous liaison and thus constitutes a threat to the inheritance of the Erectheidae. In Euripides' *Orestes* Pylades proposes to Electra and Orestes the killing of

Helen (1105) as a means of revenging themselves on Menelaus, who has failed to prevent them from being condemned to death by the Argives for killing their mother. In each case a plot lacking in forward momentum suddenly strikes out in a new and exciting direction. In the two Euripidean instances the plan and its consequences dominate the remainder of the drama. Electra's scheme, however, is immediately rejected by her sister and barely referred to elsewhere.

This rejection does not arise from a want of trying on Electra's part. Whereas in *Antigone* the heroine describes her plan and requests her sister's assistance in a short section of tense stichomythia (37–43), Electra's appeal to Chrysothemis lasts over forty lines. A tangential opening (948–50) leads swiftly to the proposal (955–7). Electra then describes the disadvantages of their position caused by Aegisthus (958–66); she balances this with an account of the advantages which his death will bring them, in both private and public spheres (967–85). She concludes the speech with an emotional peroration (986–9). Some of these elements are also found in Pylades' speech at Eur. *Or.* 1131–52, where he gives his reasons for proposing an attempt on the life of Helen (cf. 947n., 985n.). Emphasis naturally falls on what Chrysothemis is suffering, and the rewards which Chrysothemis could gain from joining with her sister. Yet in her frequent use of the dual (950n., 977n.) Electra also attempts to portray Chrysothemis and herself as a natural pair. This theme reaches its climax in the peroration (986–9n.). Only when the sisters work together, goes the subtext, can they succeed in overcoming their enemies.

For all its force, such a speech was not likely to persuade Chrysothemis. The assassination is a considerably graver matter than the act proposed by Electra in the first episode, where she only just persuaded her sister (466–71). The disadvantages with which the sisters are afflicted are ones which Chrysothemis has been happy to put up with until now (339–40). The heroic vision of public acclamation at 973–85 is not a prospect which Chrysothemis would find appealing. Most significantly of all, there is no suggestion of how the plan could be put into practice. The contrast with the Euripidean parallels is telling. In the *Ion* the Old Man proposes two other possible targets before Creusa settles on the killing of the boy (974–8). After making this decision, the pair spend over fifty lines working out the appropriate means and location for the act (978–1038). The details of the plan also receive considerable attention in *Orestes* (1106–30, 1177–1223). Yet although Electra's target is more powerful than a young boy or a weak woman, in our play she does not even begin to set out how they could effect their scheme. Captured by the righteousness of the act and the glory of its consequences, she is not interested in so mundane a matter. But in a speech aimed at persuading a more practical, less heroic figure such as Chrysothemis, such an omission is fatal from a rhetorical point of view.

This failure in deliberative rhetoric balances the failure in forensic rhetoric delivered by Chrysothemis earlier in the scene. It reveals a lack of understanding on Electra's part, an inability to understand another person and make appeals appropriate to their ἦθος. It also reveals as yet unseen aspects of her own ἦθος. Since the death of Agamemnon Electra had limited her transgressions to perpetual lamentation in public. At the news of Orestes' death she vowed to stay outside the house until she died (817–19): a dramatic but still an essentially passive reaction. Given this background, Electra's sudden switch from lamentation to assassination takes us completely by surprise.[64] There is something both exhilarating and disturbing in this mighty foolhardiness.

947 For the introductory line cf. Eur. *Or.* 1131 ἄκουσον δ᾿ ὡς καλῶς βουλεύομαι.

ἄκουε δή νυν: only here in S.; the phrase occurs 13 times in Euripides, in comedy at Ar. *Eq.* 1014, *Av.* 1513 (both paratragic), Men. *Sam.* 305, and nowhere else.

βεβούλευμαι: for the tense cf. 385n.

τελεῖν: 'the emphatic perfect βεβούλευμαι sorts well with a word implying *decisive* action – "to make an end"' (Campbell, *PS*); cf. 1417, 1435, Fischer (1965) 149. The alternative reading ποιεῖν may have arisen from a reminiscence of 385, where it also appears after βεβούλευνται, or else as a gloss (cf. Hesych. τ 450 = iv. 140 Schmidt τελῶμεν· ποιῶμεν, Σ *OC* 13 (p. 6.14 De Marco), Pearson (1919) 120).

948–50 For Electra, the dangers associated with her isolation constitute a reason for action: contrast the reasoning of Ismene at *Ant.* 58–60 (νῦν δ᾿ αὖ μόνα δή νὼ λελειμμένα σκόπει κτλ.).

παρουσίαν: conveying notions of support and assistance, as often with πάρειμι (LSJ⁹ s.v. I 4; 300n.); here 'the periphrasis and bold word-order have a pathetic effect' (Long (1968) 105).

καὶ σύ που: for που see 55n. The v.l. καὶ πού σοι is clumsy because of the following dative ἡμῖν. So too at 55 we have a v.l. with an unwanted dative.

949 For Hades as the cause of death cf. Lattimore (1942) 147.

950 μόνα: until now Electra's isolation has been to the fore (119n.). The dual form of this word is mildly paradoxical, and shows Electra trying to associate Chrysothemis with that suffering.

---

[64] Winnington-Ingram's claim that 'Electra's new decision to act, mad though it may be in the eyes of Chrysothemis and of the world, was the only decision fully consistent with her earlier attitude' ((1954–5) 24 n. 2 = (1980) 240) does not take account of this difference.

λελείμμεθον: the 1st person dual is found only here and at *Phil.* 1079 νὼ μὲν οὖν ὁρμώμεθον and Hom. *Il.* 23.485 ἢ τρίποδος περιδώμεθον ἠὲ λέβητος (S–D i. 672 §4). It also occurs in Athenaeus and grammarians of the Imperial period. According to Wackernagel ((1926–8) i. 81–2; cf. (1916a) 215 = (1916b) 55), the form was created by analogy on the 2nd person dual (-σθε: -σθον; -μεθα: x). This gave rise to the Sophoclean forms, and the form was then inserted into the text of Homer to avoid hiatus (cf. Chantraine (1942–53) i. 478; in his edition West prints the v.l. περιδώμεθα). It is impossible to tell when the analogous form was created, and Elmsley (in his additional n. on Ar. *Ach.* 733 (1st edition, p. 127)) preferred –μεθα (now found in GRH), on the grounds that the dual was invented in the Imperial period. But if it was post-Sophoclean we may wonder why it was inserted into precisely these two (and only these two) places in Sophocles, and nowhere else in tragedy, especially as there is no problem with hiatus in these instances. The default hypothesis must be that S. used the dual forms, and that their rarity led later to the insertion of the plural in some texts. In both its Sophoclean instances the dual has a powerful effect. In the *Philoctetes* its use by Neoptolemus at the end of an episode suggests that he has finally decided to align himself with Odysseus. Here the dual stresses the bond of suffering between the two sisters.

951–2 βίῳ | θάλλοντ᾿ ἔτ᾿: so Reiske (1753) 18. With manuscript θάλλοντά τ᾿ we must take βίῳ to mean ἐν βίῳ ὄντα, which is impossibly compressed, and coordinate βίῳ with θάλλοντα, which is awkward. The double elision probably defeated some of the scribes. For the combination cf. Critias *TrGF* 43 F 19.17 = D–K 88 B 25.17 (= ii. 387.11) = p. 177.17 *TrGFS* ἀφθίτῳ θάλλων βίῳ, Mace(donius) *Paean in Apollinem et Aesculapium* (pp. 138–9 *CA*) 26 = *IG* ii–iii² 4473.19–20 θ]άλλειν ἐν βιοτῇ, [Orph.] *Hymn* 29.18–19 θάλλουσα . . . | . . . βίῳ εὐόλβῳ, Semon. fr. 7.85 *IEG* θάλλει . . . βίος, Aesch. *Pers.* 677–8 τῆς τ᾿ αἰὲν ἐν φύλλοισι θαλλούσης βίον | ξανθῆς ἐλαίας καρπός, Antiph. Soph. D–K 87 B 60 (= ii. 365.7–8) = 60.6–7 Pendrick ζῆ τοῦτο καὶ θάλλει διὰ παντὸς τοῦ βίου. Cf. the related combination at *Tr.* 235 καὶ ζῶντα καὶ θάλλοντα, Eur. *IA* 1225, fr. 898.13 *TrGF*, Pl. *Symp.* 203e2. On the intensification by elaboration in such phrases see Fraenkel on Aesch. *Ag.* 677.

952 ἐλπίδας: 306n.

953 ποτ᾿ 'sooner or later'.

πράκτορ᾿: '= Latin *exactor*, the man who collects payment of a penalty or exacts an atonement' (Fraenkel on Aesch. *Ag.* 111). The πράκτορες in classical Athens were public officials chosen by lot, perhaps ten in number, who kept a register of state debtors. There is no evidence that they had the power to collect debts, though their title suggests that they had (cf. *IG* i³ 59.48, M. H. Hansen

(1980) 160 with n. 23 (= *SEG* 30 (1980) §9), H. Schaefer (1954) 2538–9). In fifth-century Athens many –τωρ nouns were archaisms; it was probably its use in legal language which kept this word alive (cf. Debrunner (1917) 174, Ernst Fraenkel (1910–12) i. 220). S. uses it with a genitive to mean 'accomplisher' at *Tr.* 251, 861; here the same construction is used to mean 'avenger' of something, as at Aesch. *Eum.* 320 πράκτορες αἵματος.

954 ἡνίκ' οὐκέτ' ἔστιν: for ἡνίκα with the present indicative see Diggle on Theophr. *Char.* 30.6.

ἐς σὲ δὴ βλέπω: 'marks the next resource' (Jebb); cf. *Ant.* 173 ἐγὼ κράτη δὴ . . . ἔχω, which follows ὅτ' οὖν ἐκεῖνοι . . . ὤλοντο in 170. For βλέπω ἐς = 'look to someone for assistance' cf. *Aj.* 514–15 ἐμοὶ γὰρ οὐκέτ' ἔστιν εἰς ὅ τι βλέπω | πλὴν σοῦ, Page on Eur. *Med.* 247, Diggle on Theophr. *Char.* 2.2, LSJ⁹ s.v. βλέπω II.2, *DGE* s.v. A II 1 b, 958–9n.

955–6 ὅπως . . . | . . . μὴ κατοκνήσεις: this clause acts as the object of the appeal implied in ἐς σὲ δὴ βλέπω: cf. Ar. *Eq.* 1255–6 καὶ σ' αἰτῶ βραχύ, | ὅπως ἔσομαί σοι Φανός, Amigues (1977) 19. In such cases ὅπως with future indicative is the regular construction (Goodwin §364). The subjunctive has ousted the indicative in most manuscripts, as often after ὅπως (cf. *Aj.* 557, 569). Manuscript readings in this case have little authority, as S. would probably have written ΕΙΣ for both verb endings.

Cf. Electra's rejection of ὄκνος at 321. For the killer's need to eschew hesitation cf. Eur. *Or.* 1235–6.

αὐτόχειρα . . . φόνου: cf. *OR* 266, [Pl.] *Epist.* 7.334a4; also Pl. *Resp.* 615c2–4. For Aegisthus' responsibility for Agamemnon's death cf. Aesch. *Cho.* 134 Αἴγισθον, ὅσπερ σοῦ φόνου μεταίτιος.

957 Wunder's deletion (in his third edition) is printed by Nauck⁴ᵃ. The only worthwhile argument they put forward is the well-known tendency of proper names to be interpolated to clarify the sense (cf. *Phoen.* [428], *Tro.* [862–3], Merkelbach (1967), Barrett on Eur. *Hipp.* 1403, Diggle (1994) 459 n. 79). The meaning would be complete without 957. But the mention of Aegisthus' name does have dramatic force: it comes as a climactic end to a long sense unit, and is followed by a pause. This same technique is used to emphasise Aegisthus' name at Eur. *El.* 761–4 and Aesch. *Ag.* 1434–6 (see Fraenkel on 1436); cf. 163n., 745n., 1507. This emphasis on Aegisthus fits with the menacing aura which surrounds his name elsewhere (310–23n.). These same points also tell against Bergk's transposition of the verse to between 955 and 956.

Electra mentions only Aegisthus as a target. There is no reference to Clytemnestra, here or elsewhere in her speech. This silence has been variously interpreted (doxography in MacLeod (2001) 141 n. 7). According to Kirkwood

(1942) 90, '[Electra] is now deceiving herself, as well as Chrysothemis . . . she refuses to think of the worse part of what lies before her.' Such psychological intricacies find no support in the text. They are in any case inconsistent with Electra's words at 604–5, where she does not shy away from the prospect of matricide. More popular has been the view that Electra intends to kill Clytemnestra along with Aegisthus, but avoids mentioning the matricide to increase her chances of winning over her sister. Aegisthus' killing, it is argued, can be presented as a morally unobjectionable act (cf. Aesch. *Cho.* 989–90 Αἰγίσθου γὰρ οὐ λέγω μόρον· | ἔχει γὰρ αἰσχυντῆρος, ὡς νόμος, δίκην), the performance of which will win the sisters glory. However, to confront Chrysothemis with the prospect of killing her mother would remove any hope of her participation (so e.g. Friis Johansen (1964) 21–2). But it is difficult to see how an audience could be expected to arrive at this interpretation. Nothing in Electra's speech suggests that her mother will also be a target. The plural τοῖσιν ἐχθροῖς εὖ βεβηκόσιν in 979, sometimes cited as evidence for such a view, should rather be taken as plural for singular or (better) a generalising plural denoting the tyrant and his supporters. The logic of the plan does not require Clytemnestra's death: a woman who requires Aegisthus' help even to keep a young woman indoors (517–20) would be no threat to the sisters once her consort had been eliminated. Nor is it obvious that the rhetorical strategy postulated above is the best available. Matricide is indeed an especially grim kind of homicide, but in this case the killing of the male would be the more alarming prospect from a practical point of view. Given Chrysothemis' concern for the limitations of her capability, the killing of Aegisthus might have sounded the less appealing option. The other passage taken by Friis Johansen to support his view is 1080 διδύμαν ἑλοῦσ᾿ Ἐρινύν. This must refer to Aegisthus and Clytemnestra as a pair, and εἷλον can be used to mean 'kill'. But as in the immediately preceding episode matricide did not form part of the plan which the chorus is discussing, an audience would most naturally take the verb to mean 'conquer' or 'overcome' (cf. Owen (1927) 51). Through Electra's plan to encompass Aegisthus' death, the chorus sings, the power of the two usurpers will be broken.

Electra's plan, then, is aimed only at Aegisthus, at defeating the power of her family's enemies. But having Aegisthus as the sole focus suits the dramatist's purpose as well as Electra's own. To raise the actual prospect of matricide at this point would open up all sorts of difficulties which S. does not yet wish to confront. It would risk unbalancing the scene, and causing the audience to focus on it to the exclusion of all else. Restricting the focus to Aegisthus, whose death is ethically less problematic, makes the ensuing conflict between the sisters more interesting. As Blundell puts it, the absence of Clytemnestra from the plan 'deprives [Chrysothemis] of a potentially powerful appeal to the impiety of matricide. The emphasis on Aegisthus thus creates a starker contrast between Electra's foolhardy pursuit of justice and Chrysothemis' sensible though cowardly rejection of the impossible' ((1989) 160; 'cowardly' is too strong, however (992–1014n.)).

οὐδὲν γάρ σε δεῖ κρύπτειν μ' ἔτι: in this protestation of openness some scholars have seen evidence that Electra is indeed hiding something from her sister – namely, that Clytemnestra will also be a target of her plan alongside Aegisthus. Similarly emphatic denials of concealment are often found in oratory (cf. Pl. *Apol.* 24a5–6, Isocr. 15.140, Dem. 19.3; also Lucian 68.10), where an Athenian jury would not take them at face value. *OC* 755 provides a Sophoclean instance of the figure: Creon assures Oedipus οὐ γὰρ ἔστι τὰμφανῆ κρύπτειν even as he delivers a speech full of lies. But Oedipus immediately accuses Creon of lying, and in the event his charge is shown to be correct. So too in a speech in court the jury will have the opposing speaker to raise the accusation of deceit. In our play nothing subsequently comes to light which could suggest that Electra is being disingenuous.

Parallels elsewhere in drama and epic indicate that such statements are typically used to emphasise an accompanying affirmation. The playwright in this way conveys not its falsehood, but its importance. Cf. *Phil.* 915 οὐδέν σε κρύψω, *Tr.* 474 πᾶν σοι φράσω τἀληθὲς οὐδὲ κρύψομαι, Hom. *Od.* 4.350 = 17.141 τῶν οὐδέν τοι ἐγὼ κρύψω ἔπος οὐδ' ἐπικεύσω, Ar. *Plut.* 26 ἀλλ' οὔ σε κρύψω. In our case, the proposal to kill Aegisthus is so serious that Electra's emphatic addendum is justified.

σε . . . μ': the v.l. με . . . σ' is also possible, though less well attested. Blaydes[2] conjectured μ' — σ' ἔτι (*sic*), presumably also reading ἔδει.

958–66 Electra's description of her sister's sufferings differs from the presentation of her sister's life in the first episode. There Chrysothemis enjoys a luxurious life with her father's killers; here she is growing old unmarried. There is no contradiction: rather, the different rhetorical aims of Electra in each case lead to a difference in emphasis. Put together, the two pictures add depth to the portrayal of the house and Chrysothemis' position within it. She is accorded a higher quality of life as a reward for her submission: nevertheless, as Agamemnon's daughter Aegisthus cannot afford to allow her to marry.

958 For the emotional intensification caused by the repetition of the question cf. *Aj.* 1006 ποῖ γὰρ μολεῖν μοι δυνατόν, εἰς ποίους βροτούς . . .;, *Tr.* 707–8 πόθεν γὰρ ἄν ποτ', ἀντὶ τοῦ . . . | ἐμοὶ παρέσχ' εὔνοιαν . . .;, also 534n.

ποῖ: ἀντὶ εἰς τίνα χρόνον; (Σ p. 144.8 Papageorgius): cf. Ar. *Lys.* 526 ποῖ γὰρ καὶ χρῆν ἀναμεῖναι; The alternative, taking ποῖ with βλέψασ', is less natural. For adverbs of place used to denote time, occasion and circumstance cf. *OR* 390 ποῦ σὺ μάντις εἶ σαφής;, Campbell's edition, vol. i. p. 41.

μένεις: the present should be preferred, as Chrysothemis' waiting is a process which has already begun. So too at *Phil.* 836 πρὸς τί μένομεν (Erfurdt; μενοῦμεν codd.) πράσσειν; the present is better on metrical as well as semantic grounds, and is adopted by Pearson, Ll-J/W and Dale (1971–83) iii. 277.

ῥάθυμος: on the orthography see Wackernagel (1907) 26 = (1953–79) ii. 1057.

958–9 ἐς τίν' ἐλπίδων | βλέψασ': cf. *Aj.* 400 βλέπειν τιν' εἰς ὄνησιν ἀνθρώπων, *Ant.* 922 τί χρή με τὴν δύστηνον ἐς θεοὺς ἔτι | βλέπειν;, Eur. *Andr.* 404 τί δῆτά μοι ζῆν ἡδύ; πρὸς τί χρὴ βλέπειν;, 954n. On Electra's hopes see 306n.

959 πάρεστι μὲν στένειν: cf. *Aj.* 432 νῦν γὰρ πάρεστι καὶ δὶς αἰάζειν ἐμοί, Aesch. *Pers.* 471.

959–61 στένειν | . . . | . . . ἀλγεῖν: for the combination cf. *Phil.* 339–40, *OR* 62–4.

960 πλούτου πατρῴου: cf. 72n., 648–9.

κτῆσιν ἐστερημένη: στερέω normally takes a genitive, not an accusative, of the thing taken away; contrast ἀποστερέω, which can take a genitive or accusative. The possible tragic instances of στερέω with the accusative are Eur. *Hel.* 95 πῶς; οὔ τί που σῷ φασγάνῳ βίον (L; βίου Burges) στερείς; and Aesch. *Ag.* 1530–1 φροντίδος στερηθεὶς | εὐπάλαμον μέριμναν (–ον –αν GFT; –άμων –νᾶν Enger). Burges's emendation easily restores Euripides' usual practice with this verb, and is adopted by recent editors (Dale, Kannicht, Diggle); but though Fraenkel prints Enger's conjecture, neither Page nor West adopts it. Neither instance, then, is a secure parallel. In our case the accusative was probably used because another genitive alongside πλούτου πατρῴου would be confusing. The alternative construction, taking κτῆσιν as the object of στένειν, is less likely. One may groan for one's ancestral wealth, as at *OR* 64 one may groan for a city: it is a different matter to groan for *the possession of* one's ancestral wealth. A direct object with στένειν would also ruin the parallelism between that verb and ἀλγεῖν in 961 (so Fraenkel on Aesch. *Ag.* 1531 = vol. iii. p. 725 n. 1).

961 ἐς τοσόνδε: cf. *OR* 1212 φέρειν . . . | σῖγ' ἐδυνάθησαν ἐς τοσόνδε; For the accompanying genitive cf. 14.

962 ἄλεκτρα . . . ἀνυμέναιά τε: for this combination cf. 492, *Ant.* 917 ἄλεκτρον, ἀνυμέναιον; also *El.* 164–5 ἄτεκνος | . . . ἀνύμφευτος, *Ant.* 876–7, Eur. *Hec.* 416 ἄνυμφος ἀνυμέναιος ὢν μ' ἐχρῆν τυχεῖν, *Or.* 206 (of Electra) ἄγαμος . . . †ἄτεκνος†. For the repetition of alpha-privative adjectives see 164–5n. The three-word trimeter (counting τε as part of the preceding word) may add impact to Electra's appeal (cf. Marcovich (1984) 57–8).

According to the lyric poet Xanthus, Electra was originally called Laodice, but after Agamemnon's death ἄλεκτρον οὖσαν καὶ καταγηρῶσαν παρθένον Ἀργεῖοι Ἠλέκτραν ἐκάλεσαν διὰ τὸ ἀμοιρεῖν ἀνδρὸς καὶ μὴ πεπειρᾶσθαι λέκτρου (fr. 700 *PMG, ap.* Aelian *VH* 4.26). Cf. Eur. *Or.* 72 παρθένε μακρὸν δὴ μῆκος Ἠλέκτρα χρόνου, [663], Etym. Magn. 426.5–6 Gaisford; also Garvie on Aesch. *Cho.* 481–2

γηράσκουσαν: for the motif 'growing old unwedded' cf. Eur. *Ion* 618–19 τὴν σὴν ἄλοχον οἰκτίρω, πάτερ, | ἄπαιδα γηράσκουσαν, *Hel.* 283 θυγάτηρ ἄνανδρος πολιὰ παρθενεύεται. Women were traditionally considered nubile for only a brief period: cf. Pl. *Leg.* 785b2–4 γάμου δὲ ὅρον εἶναι κόρῃ μὲν ἀπὸ ἑκκαίδεκα ἐτῶν εἰς εἴκοσι, τὸν μακρότατον χρόνον ἀφωρισμένον, Ar. *Lys.* 596 τῆς δὲ γυναικὸς μικρὸς ὁ καιρός, West on Hes. *Op.* 698.

For the accusative participle after the dative ᾗ in 959 see 478–80n. For its combination with a preceding dative participle (960) cf. Eur. *Med.* 1236–8 δέδοκται . . . μοι | παῖδας κτανούσῃ τῆσδ' ἀφορμᾶσθαι χθονός, | καὶ μὴ σχολὴν ἄγουσαν ἐκδοῦναι τέκνα.

963 καὶ . . . μέντοι: 'almost always progressive in meaning . . . [this combination] sometimes introduces a new point or argument' (Denniston 413).

τῶνδε: referring to what precedes: cf. *Tr.* 260.

963–4 μηκέτ' ἐλπίσῃς ὅπως | τεύξῃ ποτ': for the construction cf. Eur. *Hcld.* 1051–2 μὴ γὰρ ἐλπίσῃς ὅπως | αὖθις πατρῴας ζῶν ἔμ' ἐκβαλεῖς χθονός, Amigues (1977) 17. For the force of μήκετι see 611n.

964–6 οὐ γὰρ ὧδ' ἄβουλός ἐστ' ἀνήρ | Αἴγισθος ὥστε σόν ποτ' ἢ κἀμὸν γένος | βλαστεῖν ἐᾶσαι: so too in Euripides Aegisthus goes to great lengths to deny Electra offspring. He first keeps her shut up in the house (*El.* 22–4); and then unsuccessfully attempts to kill her (25–30). Finally, he marries her to a poor man to ensure that her children, if any, do not grow up to be a threat to him (34–42, 266–9). For Aegisthus' fear of Agamemnon's prospective grandchildren cf. νήπιος, ὃς πατέρα κτείνας παῖδας καταλείπει (*Cypria* fr. 25 *EGF* = 33 *PEG* = 31 *GEF*; context unknown), Eur. *Andr.* 519–22 καὶ γὰρ ἄνοια | μεγάλη λείπειν ἐχθροὺς ἐχθρῶν, | ἐξὸν κτείνειν | καὶ φόβον οἴκων ἀφελέσθαι, *Hcld.* 468–70, 991–1008, *Her.* 165–9, *Tro.* 721–5, 1158–66, *Hec.* 1138–44, Hdt. 1.155.1–2; also Hom. *Od.* 3.196–7, Kassel (1954) 51–3 = (1991) 47–9.

964 ὧδ' ἄβουλος: cf. *Tr.* 139–40 τίς ὧδε | τέκνοισι Ζῆν' ἄβουλον εἶδεν; (also in the context of relationships between parents and children).

965 σὸν . . . κἀμόν: Radt's σοὶ . . . κἀμοί (cited in *Sophoclea*) is possible: for the confusion of iota and nu at the end of a word see 683n. But the sense it gives is no better than that of the paradosis. καί can be translated 'or mine, for that matter': cf. the emphatic *Ant.* 31–2 τοιαῦτά φασι τὸν ἀγαθὸν Κρέοντα σοὶ | κἀμοί, λέγω γὰρ κἀμέ, κηρύξαντ᾽ ἔχειν, Denniston 306 (iii). There may be a suggestion that Electra's offspring would be the greater threat.

966 πημονήν αὐτῷ σαφῆ: in apposition to γένος βλαστεῖν, or just γένος: cf. 130n.

968 πρῶτον μέν: for the ordering of the speech (cf. 970 ἔπειτα δ᾽) cf. 261–74n.

968–9 εὐσέβειαν . . . | . . . οἴσῃ: cf. *Ant.* 924 τὴν δυσσέβειαν εὐσεβοῦσ᾽ ἐκτησάμην, *Tr.* 461–2 κοὔπω τις αὐτῶν ἔκ γ᾽ ἐμοῦ λόγον κακὸν | ἠνέγκατ᾽ οὐδ᾽ ὄνειδος; also Eur. *Med.* 218, *IT* 676, *Ion* 600.

ἐκ πατρὸς κάτω | θανόντος *a patre apud inferos quippe mortuo* (Vahlen (1895) 4 = (1907–8) ii. 158), taking κάτω and θανόντος separately: cf. *Phil.* 1348–9 ὦ στυγνὸς αἰών, τί μ᾽ ἔτι δῆτ᾽ ἔχεις ἄνω | βλέποντα . . .;, Eur. *Or.* 674–5 τὸν κατὰ χθονὸς | θανόντ᾽ ἀκούειν τάδε δόκει, F. W. Schmidt (1864) 3. In the Sophoclean instances the enjambement keeps adverb and participle apart. For κάτω cf. *infra* = 'in the underworld' at Tib. 1.10.35 (apparently a unique usage: cf. *TLL* vii/1 1482.83–4).

970 ὥσπερ ἐξέφυς: cf. *OR* 1084 τοιόσδε δ᾽ ἐκφύς. On the significance of φύσις cf. 322n.

971 καλῇ: the future middle, used as a passive only here (compare *Phil.* 1074 ἀκούσομαι): cf. K–G i. 114–16.

972 πρὸς . . . ὁρᾶν: for 'looking towards' as a sign of admiration cf. Diggle on Theophr. *Char.* 2.2 ἀποβλέπουσι πρὸς σὲ οἱ ἄνθρωποι.

τὰ χρηστά: for the generalising use of the neuter to denote persons cf. *Phil.* 448–50, Bruhn §2.

973–85 For the Pericles of the Thucydidean funeral oration a woman's δόξα was greatest when her κλέος among men was ἐπ᾽ ἐλάχιστον ἀρετῆς πέρι ἢ ψόγου (Thuc. 2.45.2). This was not the final word on the matter (cf. Plut. *Mul. virt.* 242ef), and women in literature could and did win glory from the community for their actions. So Antigone is praised in the πόλις for the virtue she has shown in attempting to bury her brother (*Ant.* 692–700). But the ἐρεμνὴ . . . φάτις which σῖγ᾽ ἐπέρχεται in that passage (*ib.* 700) is far from the emphatically public acclamation here envisaged by Electra. The reference to ἀνδρεία is also strikingly unusual (983n.). The startling manner of the celebration and the quality which it celebrates is reinforced by various literary resonances. Electra uses a rhetorical device through which a character imagines what people will say in the future (cf. J. R. Wilson (1979)). Often employed to convey likely public disapproval (cf. Hom. *Il.* 4.176–82, S. *Aj.* 500–3, Eur. *Alc.* 954–61, *Hcld.* 28–30), it can also be found, as here, in contexts of praise (cf. Hom. *Il.* 6.479–80, 7.89–91, 12.318–21, Aesch. *Eum.* 756–60, Eur. *Alc.* 1000–5; also [Epicharm.] fr. 244.12–14 *PCG*). But her rhetoric is markedly stronger than in other instances of the form. Rather than leave the speech to a singular, unidentified τις, she emphasises the universal character of the acclamation (975n., 984n.). The imagined speech at seven lines lasts longer than almost all other examples of the figure. The only parallel for such a lengthy τις–Rede occurs at Hom. *Od.* 6.276–84, where Nausicaa reacts with maidenly modesty to the prospect of other people seeing her conducting a stranger into the city. Its content could thus scarcely be more different from Electra's use of the figure, which rather recalls those characters in Homer who predict other people celebrating their glory (Hector in *Il.* 7.89–91, Sarpedon in *Il.* 12.318–21).

But the heroes whom Electra's words evoke here are not merely Homeric. A pair of people carry out a brave and desperate scheme to kill the tyrant at whose mercy they had been living. They enjoy the greatest glory as a consequence and are celebrated in festivals both private and public. Such a pattern is similar to that of the assassination of Hipparchus by the Athenian tyrannicides, Harmodius and Aristogeiton. The reference to eternal fame is paralleled in a *scolium* celebrating the pair (985n.), and the Athenian tyrannicides are celebrated in a public cult (cf. [Arist.] *Ath. Pol.* 58.1 with Rhodes, Taylor (1991) 5–6) just as Electra and Chrysothemis receive emphatically public acclaim. Inscriptions provide evidence for the honours meted out to other historical tyrannicides: cf. e.g. Wilhelm (1915) 30–8 = (1974) i. 204–12 on *SIG*[3] §284 = *IGSK* i–ii §503. At *OGIS* i. §218 = *IGSK* iii §25 (Ilium, early 3rd cent. BC), lines 21–8 the slayer of a tyrant, if ἔναχος (= *honorum capax*: Dittenberger), is to be granted a bronze statue among other honours. Different sets of honours are available if a ξένος or δοῦλος kills a tyrant: the prospect that a woman might perform such an act did not occur to the writers of the inscription. Killing a tyrant is also the subject of praise in tragedy at Eur. *Or.* 923–5, 1137–42.

Electra's great vision thus encompasses heroes of literature and real life: but what makes this vision striking is its application to a pair of women. It is difficult to imagine the likely audience response – or a prospect less likely to appeal to Chrysothemis.[65]

---

[65] Juffras (1991) 103–4 suggests that Electra is describing a monument which she imagines to have been constructed in honour of Chrysothemis and herself, just as other tyrannicides were honoured with such a monument (cf. Taylor (1991) 13–21). But ἡμᾶς

973 λόγων . . . εὔκλειαν: λόγων *coni.* Bothe[1] λόγῳ (i.e. λόγῳ codd.). The genitive makes a better connexion with εὔκλειαν than the dative. For confusion between final iota and nu see 683n. For similarly emphatic delays of οὐχ ὁρᾷς, οὐχ ὁρᾶτε cf. fr. 334 *TrGF*, Eur. frr. 217 *TrGF* = 35 Kambitsis (*Antiope*), 152.1–2 *TrGF* = 41.1–2 Bubel (*Andromeda*), Xen. *Mem.* 3.7.5, Sosiphanes *TrGF* 92 F 3.5–6. Electra's reference to εὔκλεια is taken up by the chorus at 1083.

γε μήν marks the progression to a new point (Denniston 349 (3)); cf. *OC* 587, Eur. *Alc.* 516.

974 προσβαλεῖς: for this sense ('assign') cf. Hdt. 7.51.3 οὐδὲν κέρδος μέγα ἡμῖν προσβάλλουσι, LSJ[9] s.v. προσβάλλω I 2a.

975–6 Instead of the usual τις–Rede formula 'someone will say', Electra uses the more vigorous 'who will not say': cf. Ar. *Plut.* 786–7 ἐμὲ γὰρ τίς οὐ προσεῖπε; ποῖος οὐκ ὄχλος | περιεστεφάνωσεν ἐν ἀγορᾷ πρεσβυτικός;

975 For ποτ' in an introduction to a τις–Rede cf. Hom. *Il.* 6.459, 7.87.

ἀστῶν ἢ ξένων: for the polar expression cf. *Tr.* 187, *IG* i³ 1194 *bis* 1 = *CEG* i. §13.1 (Attica, *c.* 575–50?) εἴτε ἀστό]ς τις ἀνὲρ εἴτε χσένος, *IG* vii 2247.1 = *CEG* i. §112.1 (Boeotia, *c.* 500?), *CEG* i. §123.2 (Thessaly, *c.* 450–25?), Pind. *P.* 4.78, Thuc. 6.16.3, Pl. *Gorg.* 515a7, Dem. 57.24, Kemmer (1903) 90–2. The expression emphasises the universal praise which Electra believes the sisters will win. It also stresses that this acclamation will not be limited to the πόλις, despite 982.

ἡμᾶς ἰδών: τις–Reden are often motivated by the sight of the person or thing which forms the subject of the speech: cf. Hom. *Il.* 6.459, Theocr. 28.24, Eratosth. fr. 35.17 *CA*.

976 ἐπαίνοις: for praise as the motivating factor behind a τις–Rede cf. Semon. fr. 7.29 *IEG* ἐπαινέσει μιν ξεῖνος ἐν δόμοις ἰδών (followed by two lines of speech).

δεξιώσεται: properly 'greet with the right hand' and then 'salute, welcome, honour': cf. *Hom. Hym.* 6.15–16 οἳ δ' ἠσπάζοντο ἰδόντες | χερσί τ' ἐδεξιόωντο, Aesch. *Ag.* 852 θεοῖσι πρῶτα δεξιώσομαι, Ar. *Plut.* 752–3 αὐτὸν ἠσπάζοντο καὶ | ἐδεξιοῦνθ' ἅπαντες, Xen. *Hell.* 5.1.3 οὐδεὶς ἐκεῖνον τῶν στρατιωτῶν ὃς οὐκ ἐδεξιώσατο, καὶ ὁ μὲν ἐστεφάνωσεν, ὁ δὲ ἐταινίωσεν, Pl. *Resp.* 468b2–7 τὸν . . . ἀριστεύσαντά τε καὶ εὐδοκιμήσαντα . . . χρῆναι στεφανωθῆναι . . . [καὶ] δεξιωθῆναι; also Hom. *Il.* 10.541–2 τοὶ δὲ χαρέντες | δεξιῇ

ἰδών in 975 is most naturally taken to refer to the sisters themselves, and nothing in the following lines suggests any other identification. Rather, the stress throughout is on the actual presence of the sisters.

ἠσπάζοντο. For the raising of the hand or arm as an honorific signal see Sittl (1890) 50–1. Since the girls are spoken of in the third person, we are to imagine that the speakers are not so close to them as to be able to clasp their hands.

977 ἴδεσθε: for the imperative of εἶδον in a τις–Rede cf. *Aj.* 501, Eur. *Alc.* 955, *Hcld.* 29.

τώδε τὼ κασιγνήτω: Threatte ii. 91–5 sets out the inscriptional evidence for the feminine dual in Attic. Whereas –α and –αῖν are the only endings found for 1st declension nouns, –ω and –οῖν endings are used for the article (with a single exception, a private dedication from *c.* 350), demonstratives and relatives. Thematic adjectives have either –α –αῖν or –ω –οῖν. There is no good evidence for participles. By contrast, the manuscript tradition of many authors, including S., affords many instances of distinctive feminine duals not only in nouns and adjectives, but also in articles, demonstratives and relatives (cf. e.g. 985, *Ant.* 769, *OR* 1462–3, *OC* 445, 1290). In the belief that they were later insertions, many editors (e.g. Pearson's OCT) have emended all such pronominal forms to –ω and –οῖν.

More recently the trend has been towards keeping the attested forms (cf. Dawe, Ll-J/W). G. L. Cooper (1972) strongly advocates such a course, though he is far from proving his case. The τις-Rede here may provide support for this position. According to all available manuscript evidence, the imaginary speaker uses –ω forms throughout, for articles, demonstratives and relatives, even though he is referring to a feminine pair (cf. *Ant.* 561). Yet if there was a period when feminine dual pronominals in –α and –αῖν were systematically inserted into our texts, it is strange that not a single such form surfaced in this passage, given its high concentration of dual pronouns. It would seem that S. had two sets of forms to choose from, and that this choice is reflected in the manuscripts.

Why then did S. decide to use –ω forms so consistently and emphatically in this speech? Perhaps the apparently 'masculine' endings felt especially appropriate in a speech praising two women for ἀνδρεία. But under such an interpretation it is difficult to account for *Ant.* 561, where Creon uses such forms to refer to Antigone and Ismene. We may also wonder why Electra herself uses distinctively feminine forms for the participles in 985 (contrast 980, as well as Chrysothemis' words at 1003, 1006). It may be that the inscriptional evidence holds a clue. If dual pronouns could only take the common gender in formal civic language, that would explain their presence in inscriptions and in this speech. It also accounts for the switch at 985: these are Electra's own words and are not part of the speech of acclamation. But given the limitations of our evidence this can only be an attractive hypothesis.

978–9 ὢ . . . | ὢ the speaker of a τις–Rede, after drawing attention to his subject in some way, will often go on to add a relative clause which tells us what is remarkable about the subject: cf. *Aj.* 502–3, Hom. *Il.* 6.460–1, 7.89–90, Eur. *Alc.* 955–7, *Her.* 1289–90. Ap. Rh. 3.795–7 repeats the relative, as here (ἥτις . . . ἥτις). For the repetition in asyndeton see 113–14n.

979–80 τοῖσιν ἐχθροῖς . . . | . . . προὐστήτην φόνου 'were the avengers / champions of their father's blood against their foes'. For the verb with dative meaning 'stand before, confront' cf. *Aj.* 1133 ἦ σοὶ γὰρ Αἴας πολέμιος προὔστη ποτέ;, LSJ⁹ s.v. προΐστημι B I 3; for the sense 'support, champion' see LSJ⁹ B II 3. προὔστην with the genitive can mean 'administer' (LSJ⁹ B II 2), and so Jebb translated 'became ministers of bloodshed' (cf. Musgrave, Hermann, Campbell): but φόνος is better taken to refer to the murder of a father rather than the killing of a tyrant.

979 εὖ βεβηκόσιν: for the perfect of βαίνω 'used as a stronger equivalent of εἰμί "be", emphasising the stability of the state reached' (Moorhouse 198) cf. 1057, 1095, Bruhn §231.II. It is often found with εὖ: cf. Archil. fr. 130.3–4 *IEG* πολλάκις δ᾽ ἀνατρέπουσι καὶ μάλ᾽ εὖ βεβηκότας | ὑπτίους, Hdt. 7.164.1 τυραννίδα . . . εὖ βεβηκυῖαν, Plut. *Sert.* 27.4, Paus. 3.7.11, Becker (1937) 196–7 with n. 7.

980 ψυχῆς ἀφειδήσαντε: cf. *SEG* 16 (1959) §497.13–14 (Chios, 3rd-2nd cent. BC) οἳ κτάνον ἄνδρα τύρα[ννον . . .] | ψυχὰς παρθέμενο[ι . . .], Tyrt. fr. 10.14 *IEG* θνήσκωμεν ψυχέων μηκέτι φειδόμενοι, *Carm. Pop.* fr. 856.5 *PMG* μὴ φειδόμενοι τᾶς ζωᾶς, Thuc. 2.43.5 ἀφειδοῖεν ἂν τοῦ βίου, Cic. *Nat. deor.* 3.15 *patriae consulerent, vitae non parcerent*, Lucian 37.24 τῶν σωμάτων ἀφειδεῖν; also Eur. *IA* 1385 οὐδέ τοί <τι> λίαν ἐμὲ φιλοψυχεῖν χρεών. On the verb see further Vahlen (1895) 14–19 = (1907–8) ii. 171–9. The common gender dual is metrically guaranteed: cf. 1003, 1006, Hermippus fr. 81 *PCG*, K–G i. 73–4 Anm. 1, Hasse (1891) 15 and West on Hes. *Op.* 198.

981 τούτω . . . τῷδε: for the combination cf. 371n.

982 ἕν τ᾽ ἑορταῖς ἕν τε πανδήμῳ πόλει: cf. *OR* 1489–90 ποίας γὰρ ἀστῶν ἥξετ᾽ εἰς ὁμιλίας, | ποίας δ᾽ ἑορτάς, Lucian 57.1 καὶ ἑορταῖς καὶ πανηγύρεσι τιμῶμεν αὐτούς, Polyaenus *Strat.* 3.9.31 ἔν γε μὴν ταῖς ἑορταῖς καὶ πανηγύρεσιν, ὅσοι ἀνδρειότεροι τῶν ἄλλων, προετίμα προεδρίαις. At *SIG*³ §284.15–17 = *IEK* 503.14–17 the ἀγορανόμοι must ensure that the statue of Philetos στεφανωθήσεται ἀεὶ ταῖς νουμηνίαις καὶ ταῖς ἄλλαις ἑορταῖς. On the aspiration of ἑορτή see Threatte i. 500–1.

983 On οὕνεκ᾽ see 594n.

ἀνδρείας: always a paradoxical quality to ascribe to women. For Herodotus Artemisia was a θῶμα, in that she ὑπὸ λήματός τε καὶ ἀνδρηίης ἐστρατεύετο (7.99.1, his only use of this noun). Aristotle (*Pol.* 1260a21–4, 1277b20–3) says that men and women possess different kinds of ἀνδρεία (cf. Föllinger (1996) 201–2). The Stoic Musonius, in his fourth *Diatribe* (p. 15.4–19 Hense), asserts that ἀνδρεία must be cultivated by women as well as men. But he revealingly goes on to claim that they need it to defend their chastity and their children, and cites the Amazons to show their potential for valour in war. Thus even for him a woman's ἀνδρεία is conceived in terms of traditional gender rôles, or else associated with fabulous mythological figures. Plutarch's *Mulierum virtutes* might seem the most fertile hunting-ground for descriptions of women's ἀνδρεία. Yet he uses the term of a woman only once, to describe the courage of Eryxo, who lured her husband's killer to her bedroom only to have him dispatched there by her brother (261 d). She plays no part in the homicide itself. In our passage, however, the sisters are acclaimed for an ἀνδρεία which is in no sense distinctively feminine.

The word is rare in high poetry before Euripides (see Hutchinson on Aesch. *Sept.* 52), and occurs elsewhere in S. only at fr. 314.154 *TrGF*. It is conventionally spelled ἀνδρεία, as in the manuscripts here, although this form is never metrically guaranteed; at Eur. *Her.* 475 ἀνδρία is required by the metre (see Bond *ad loc.*).

984 For τοιαῦτα in a conclusion to a τις–Rede cf. *Aj.* 504 (also 1017–18), Eur. *Alc.* 959; also 424n.

πᾶς τις ἐξερεῖ βροτῶν: the emphasis on the universality of the sentiment is not common in the conclusion to τις-Reden (Hom. *Od.* 22.31 ἴσκεν ἕκαστος ἀνήρ provides an example); it is slightly more often found at the beginning of such speeches (Theogn. 22 ὧδε δὲ πᾶς τις ἐρεῖ, Ar. *Vesp.* 623, *Ran.* 981). ἐξερεῖ is unique in this context (Homer has ἐρέει (e.g. *Il.* 4.182, 7.91) or ἐρέουσι (*Il.* 22.108, *Od.* 6.285, 21.329)).

985 For the sentiment cf. *Carm. Pop.* fr. 896.1 *PMG* αἰεὶ σφῷν κλέος ἔσσεται κατ᾽ αἶαν (of the tyrannicides), Hom. *Od.* 24.93–4 ὡς σὺ μὲν οὐδὲ θανὼν ὄνομ᾽ ὤλεσας, ἀλλά τοι αἰεὶ | πάντας ἐπ᾽ ἀνθρώπους κλέος ἔσσεται ἐσθλόν with Watkins (1995) 174–5, Theogn. 245, Pind. *I.* 7.29–30 ἀστῶν γενεᾷ μέγιστον κλέος αὔξων | ζώων τ᾽ ἀπὸ καὶ θανών, S. *Ant.* 209–10, Eur. *Held.* 598–9 τιμιωτάτη | καὶ ζῶσ᾽ ὑφ᾽ ἡμῶν καὶ θανοῦσ᾽ ἔσῃ πολύ, Xen. *Ages.* 9.7 ὀνομαστότατος καὶ ζῶν καὶ τελευτήσας, West (2007) ch. 10. Pylades also concludes his appeal for the killing of Helen with a reference to κλέος (Eur. *Or.* 1151–2).

ζώσαιν θανούσαιν θ᾽: the polar expression conveys the permanence of the sisters' fame (305–6n.); cf. Aesch. *Cho.* 1043 ζῶν καὶ τεθνηκώς with Garvie, *SIG³*

§284.9–10 = *IEK* 503.7–9 μνημονεύων ἀεὶ τῶν εὐεργετῶν καὶ ζώντων καὶ τετελευτηκότων, Pind. *I.* 7.29–30, Pl. *Gorg.* 527c5–6 ἐμοὶ οὖν πειθόμενος . . . εὐδαιμονήσεις καὶ ζῶν καὶ τελευτήσας, Kemmer (1903) 178–9.

'κλιπεῖν: v.l. λιπεῖν. Both verbs are used intransitively in S. and elsewhere (19, 514). ἐκλείπω should be preferred as the better attested alternative and the more likely to succumb to corruption, given the prodelision.

κλέος: for future glory as the consequence of a τις–Rede cf. Hom. *Il.* 7.91 ὡς ποτέ τις ἐρέει, τὸ δ᾿ ἐμὸν κλέος οὔ ποτ᾿ ὀλεῖται.

986–9 Electra stresses the need for action with a carefully arranged succession of imperatives (987n.). The structure knits together the different members of the family, with male and female, dead and living, beneficiaries and helpers all complementing one another. The very symmetry of the syntax demands the participation of Chrysothemis. The short imperatival clauses of 986–8 then give way to the powerful closing *sententia* that takes up the final line (989).

Electra's five imperatives begin with an aorist, after which come a pair of presents and then two further aorists. The usual aspectual distinction between present and aorist offers a possible explanation for the difference. The act of agreeing with Electra will be a single, punctual action. So also will the killing of Aegisthus: or rather, it suits Electra's rhetorical purpose to represent it in this way. Working on behalf of their dead brother and father, however, is taken by Electra to be a durative process. Given her experiences over the time since her father's murder, this is hardly surprising. This can only be a tentative analysis, since the reasons which lie behind the choice of aorist or present stem in imperatives and infinitives are often obscure (643n.). In this context note especially that 'present and aorist imperatives may be found in close proximity with no discernible difference of meaning' (Diggle (1981a) 62; cf. Gerber on Pind. *O.* 1.85).

For the form of the closing appeal cf. Eur. *IT* 983–4 ἀλλ᾿, ὦ φιληθεῖσ᾿, ὦ κασίγνητον κάρα, | σῶσον πατρῷον οἶκον, ἔκσωσον δ᾿ ἐμέ.

986 ἀλλ᾿: 916n.

ὦ φίλη: 461n.

πείσθητι: the aorist passive imperative of this verb is much rarer than the middle in classical and Hellenistic Greek: instances occur at *Phil.* 485, Men. *Peric.* 474, fr. 372.6 *PCG*.

986–7 συμπόνει . . . | σύγκαμν᾿: for the proliferation of συν– terms in descriptions of help and assistance cf. *Ant.* 41 εἰ ξυμπονήσεις καὶ ξυνεργάσῃ σκόπει, Eur. *Hel.* 327–9, Xen. *Cyr.* 7.5.55 συμπονεῖν καὶ συγκινδυνεύειν, Lucian 57.20, Pollux 5.85 (= i. 284.23 Bethe) συγκάμνων συνεργῶν συμπονῶν; also *Aj.*

988 ἴθ', ἐγκόνει, σύγκαμνε, 1378–9 θέλω | καὶ ξυμπονεῖν καὶ μηδὲν ἐλλείπειν. Contrast *El.* 350 οὔτε ξυνέρδεις. For the avoidance of repetition through use of a synonym cf. 1308–9, *Aj.* 458–9, *OR* 54, Bruhn §218.1.

987 ἀδελφῷ: three later manuscripts have ἀδελφῇ (*coni.* Nauck[4a]), but 'the sequence 1) father 2) brother 3) me 4) you guarantees ἀδελφῷ' (Dawe, *STS* i. 89). The paradosis is carefully patterned: two συν– imperatives are associated with the names of dead male members of the family, while the two instances of παῦσον each govern one of the two sisters. A reminiscence of ξὺν τῇδ' ἀδελφῇ from 956 may have assisted the error.

παῦσον ἐκ κακῶν ἐμέ: for the construction cf. 231n.

987–8 παῦσον . . . | παῦσον: for the repetition cf. Eur. *Hipp.* 473–4 ἀλλ', ὦ φίλη παῖ, λῆγε μὲν κακῶν φρενῶν, | λῆξον δ' ὑβρίζουσ'. On παύ– words see 304n.

988 τοῦτο γιγνώσκουσ', ὅτι: as at *Ant.* 188, this phrase delays the concluding *gnome* for emphasis (cf. Stephanopoulos (1988b) 8).

989 For the sentiment cf. *Tr.* 721–2 ζῆν γὰρ κακῶς κλύουσαν οὐκ ἀνασχετόν, | ἥτις προτιμᾷ μὴ κακὴ πεφυκέναι, *Aj.* 479–80, Knox (1964) 41. It is taken up by the chorus at 1082–4. For the importance of εὐγένεια as a factor in determining one's behaviour see 257n.

αἰσχρὸν αἰσχρῶς: a common juxtaposition (198n.), though here each word plays a separate syntactic function (αἰσχρόν ἐστι ζῆν αἰσχρῶς).

990–1 For the sentiment cf. Hdt. 3.36.1 ἀγαθόν τοι πρόνοον εἶναι, σοφὸν δὲ ἡ προμηθία. The chorus's support for προμηθία constitutes a criticism, albeit indirect, of Electra's scheme (cf. 1015–16n.). Burton's claim that the chorus is not rebuking Electra, but reminding her that the plan will require considerable foresight if is to be successful ((1980) 207), is far-fetched.

990 προμηθία: cf. the chorus's praise of πρόνοια at 1015–16n. Chrysothemis later claims to show προμηθία for her sister (1036), and the chorus will sing that through her plan Electra is οὔτε τι τοῦ θανεῖν προμηθής (1078). But it was only through Electra's earlier προμηθία that Orestes was saved as a child (1350). προθυμία in GZc does not fit the sense: for the reverse corruption cf. G[yp]RCP at *OR* 48.

991 καὶ τῷ λέγοντι καὶ κλύοντι: for the polar expression cf. Kemmer (1903) 247–8. Forethought is required by both the proposer of such a plan, and the person who has to judge it.

For σύμμαχος predicated of an abstract cf. fr. 407 *TrGF* οὐκ ἔστι τοῖς μὴ δρῶσι σύμμαχος τύχη, fr. 928.2 *TrGF* ἡ γὰρ σιωπὴ τῷ λαλοῦντι (codd.; τὠγκαλοῦντι Cobet) σύμμαχος, Hdt. 5.65.1, Antiph. 5.37, 5.43, 5.86, Joseph. *Ant. Jud.* 4.114 ὁ θεὸς . . . σύμμαχον εἰς ἅπαντα καὶ ἡγεμόνα τὴν ἑαυτοῦ πρόνοιαν ἐπένευσεν.

992–1014 Chrysothemis refuses to take part in her sister's plan, just as at *Ant.* 49–68 Ismene tells Antigone that she will not help to bury their brother's body. Several arguments are common to both refusals (997n., 998n., 1010n., 1013n.). However, the tone of Chrysothemis' speech is colder than that of Ismene's. Chrysothemis does not attempt to understand her sister's motivations or sympathise with her predicament, and so does not become a focus for the audience's sympathy. On the other hand, her criticisms of Electra's dangerous scheme are entirely pertinent. They do not provide evidence of cowardice (*pace* Blundell, cited above, 957n.) or fundamental ill will towards her sister. She had been willing to help in any way that lay within her power (944, 946): but she had never committed herself to as wild a scheme as this. Her criticisms are different from the trite attacks which she made on her sister's perpetual lamentation in the first episode (324–40n.). There she was opposing Electra's attempts to keep the memory of her dead father alive: now she rejects a plan that is ill conceived and futile. Neither sympathetic nor contemptible, she sets out a sensible case which few could either dispute or admire.

992 As at 372–5 (n.), Chrysothemis expresses her distaste for her sister's words by addressing her opening remarks to the chorus; contrast Ismene's use of the vocative ὦ κασιγνήτη at the start of her speech (*Ant.* 49).

καὶ πρίν γε φωνεῖν: perhaps picking up the chorus's preceding τῷ λέγοντι: Chrysothemis says that Electra should have been careful not just in her speaking, but before she ever opened her mouth.

ὦ γυναῖκες: 254n.

992–3 φρενῶν | . . . κακῶν: for the reference to φρόνησις see 384n.

993 μή: on the late position cf. *Phil.* 66–7 εἰ δ᾽ ἐργάσῃ | μὴ ταῦτα, *OC* 1365–6 εἰ δ᾽ ἐξέφυσα τάσδε μὴ 'μαυτῷ τροφοὺς | τὰς παῖδας, Bruhn §169.1.

994 εὐλάβειαν: first mentioned as a virtue at Theogn. 118 and Adesp. Eleg. fr. 23.2 *IEG* (in the form εὐλαβίη), this term occurs in half a dozen other places in drama (listed at Willink (1990) 184–5, adding Trag. Adesp. fr. 712.10 *TrGF*; see also Bond on Eur. *Her.* 166). More usually the verb σῴζει is predicated of εὐλάβεια itself (cf. Eur. *Phoen.* 782–3, Ar. *Av.* 376; also Polyb. 3.105.8). For the implied contrast between εὐλάβεια and θράσος in the following line cf. Dem. 21.10, Aeschin. 1.25, Dion. Hal. *Ant. Rom.* 7.21.1, Plut. *Artax.* 8.6.

ὥσπερ οὐχὶ σῴζεται: 'the relative clause emphasizes the unreal character of the preceding supposition' (Kamerbeek).

995 ποῖ . . . βλέψασα: the majority reading ἐμβλέψασα normally means 'look in the face'. The verb has this sense at its only other probable instance in tragedy, Eur. *Ion* 732 ἐς ὄμματ᾽ εὔνου φωτὸς ἐμβλέψαι γλυκύ (so the secondary tradition; εἰσβλέψαι L). The variant βλέψασα (Zr, Monac. gr. 334 (*teste* N. G. Wilson (1987) 4) and P.Oxy. 693, *coni.* Doederlein (1814) 65) gives the required meaning. Scribal ignorance of the lengthening properties of –βλ may have led to the corruption (so Dawe, *STS* i. 190). Papyrus evidence thus supports a reading found elsewhere only in two manuscripts of the fifteenth century (cf. Grenfell (1919) 20).

For the sense cf. *Aj.* 1290 δύστηνε, ποῖ βλέπων ποτ᾽ αὐτὰ καὶ θροεῖς; Electra had used a similar expression in her appeal to her sister at 958–9: Chrysothemis turns it back on her in contempt.

995–6 θράσος | . . . ὁπλίζῃ: for the metaphorical use of ὁπλίζομαι cf. Rufinus *A.P.* 5.93.1 = 34.1 Page ὥπλισμαι πρὸς Ἔρωτα περὶ στέρνοισι λογισμόν, Anon. *A.P.* 12.115.2 = 3669 *HE* ὥπλισμαι πολλὴν εἰς ὁδὸν ἀφροσύναν, Achilles Tatius 2.10.3 πολλὰ γὰρ ἦν τὰ τότε ὁπλίζοντά με θαρρεῖν, οἶνος, ἔρως, ἐλπίς, ἐρημία. Compare θωρήσσω = 'make drunk' (LSJ⁹ s.v. II). θράσος is opposed to εὐλάβεια in 994 (n.), and is taken up by the chorus at 1087.

997 οὐκ εἰσορᾷς; For ὁρᾷς; in quarrels see 628n.

γυνὴ μὲν οὐδ᾽ ἀνὴρ ἔφυς: cf. *Ant.* 61–2 ἀλλ᾽ ἐννοεῖν χρὴ τοῦτο μὲν γυναῖχ᾽ ὅτι | ἔφυμεν, ὡς πρὸς ἄνδρας οὐ μαχουμένα.

998 Cf. *Ant.* 63 ἀρχόμεσθ᾽ ἐκ κρεισσόνων.

999–1000 Chrysothemis reverses her sentiments from 916–19.

999 δαίμων: 917n.

καθ᾽ ἡμέραν 'from day to day, every day': cf. fr. 356.2–3 *TrGF* ἥδιστον δ᾽ ὅτῳ | πάρεστι λῆψις ὧν ἐρᾷ καθ᾽ ἡμέραν. The alternative translation 'today' is more difficult for three reasons. (i) When the phrase has this meaning elsewhere in S., it is immediately qualified with τὴν νῦν (*Aj.* 801–2, *OC* 3–4). (ii) Since the following line suggests a gradual ebbing of the sisters' fortunes over a period of time, there is a better balance if this line also refers to their enemies' fortunes in a similar manner. (iii) The sense 'today' implies that Clytemnestra and

Aegisthus might be weaker tomorrow, when Chrysothemis needs to emphasise the durability of their power.

1000 ἀπορρεῖ κἀπὶ μηδὲν ἔρχεται: for the phrase cf. fr. 871.8 *TrGF* πάλιν διαρρεῖ κἀπὶ μηδὲν ἔρχεται. For the verb cf. *Aj.* 523 ἀπορρεῖ μνῆστις, Archil. fr. 196a.27–8 *IEG* [ἄν]θος δ᾽ ἀπερρύηκε παρθενήϊον | [κ]αὶ χάρις ἣ πρὶν ἐπῆν, Pl. *Leg.* 776a6, Theocr. 7.121; S. *Aj.* 1267 χάρις διαρρεῖ, Virg. *Aen.* 2.169–70 *ex illo fluere ac retro sublapsa referri* | *spes Danaum*, Manil. 3.528 (Fortuna) *usque adeo permixta fluit nec permanet usquam*, Fowler on Lucr. 2.69, *TLL* vi/1 973.68–80. ῥέω and its derivatives often describe states of prosperity and its opposite: cf. Theogn. 639–40 γίγνεται εὖ ῥεῖν | ἔργ᾽ ἀνδρῶν, Solon fr. 13.34 *IEG* (*coni.*), Aesch. *Pers.* 601 ὅταν δ᾽ ὁ δαίμων εὐροῇ, Zeno of Citium fr. 184 (i. 46.16 von Arnim) εὔροια βίου, Polyb. 3.10.6 εὔροια τῶν πραγμάτων. Cf. also 362n. (on περιρρέω). For the latter part of the phrase cf. *Phil.* 259 κἀπὶ μεῖζον ἔρχεται, Eur. *Hec.* 622 ὡς ἐς τὸ μηδὲν ἥκομεν.

1002 ἄλυπος ἄτης: cf. *OC* 786 κακῶν ἄνατος, 1519 γήρως ἄλυπα, 36n.

ἐξαπαλλαχθήσεται: for the long word cf. *Aj.* 1019 τέλος δ᾽ ἀπωστὸς γῆς ἀπορριφθήσομαι. The three-word trimeter marks a climax in the argument (cf. Marcovich (1984) 58).

1003 πράσσοντε: for the dual cf. 1006, 980n. Editors claim that Σ *OC* 1676 quotes this line with πάσχοντε, but in fact πράσσοντε is the form found there (p. 65.10 De Marco = p. 465.11 Papageorgius). P. Oxy. 663 has πράσσοντε.

1004 κτησώμεθ᾽: for this verb used of getting into trouble cf. 217.

εἴ τις τούσδ᾽ ἀκούσεται λόγους: an oblique reference to Aegisthus and his supporters: unlike her sister (cf. 957), she is unwilling even to name their bitter adversary (cf. 310–23n.). For her concern cf. 468–71.

1005 λύει γὰρ ἡμᾶς οὐδὲν οὐδ᾽ ἐπωφελεῖ: the parallelism of the line requires that the verbs mean roughly the same: λύει is thus equivalent to λυσιτελεῖ. Jebb takes it to mean 'set free', but that ruins the balance of the sentence; he cites *Tr.* 181 ὄκνου σε λύσω, but there the genitive makes all the difference. λύει = λυσιτελεῖ normally takes a dative; P.Oxy. 663, however, and the mediaeval manuscripts all have ἡμᾶς. Elmsley (on Eur. *Med.* 553–4 (our 566–7), in his first edition) consequently emended to ἡμῖν: this could be right, but cf. Eur. fr. 661.28–9 *TrGF* οὐ γάρ με λύει τοῖσδ᾽ ἐφήμενον δόμοις | κακορροθεῖσθαι, where the accusative is metrically secure. λυσιτελεῖ also is occasionally found with an accusative (LSJ⁹ s.v. λυσιτελέω I 2). The construction with ἐπωφελεῖ may also have influenced the choice of the accusative (so Hermann).

413

1006 δυσκλεῶς θανεῖν: see next note.

[1007–8] Nauck's deletion (in the text of his third edition) is rightly adopted by Dawe and Ll-J/W. The connexion between these lines and 1006 is difficult, and could only work if Chrysothemis is here describing exactly what she means by δυσκλεῶς (cf. Vahlen (1895) 4–6 = (1907–8) ii. 159–60, R. Schmitt (1967) 86–7). But the explanation is heavy-handed and far from the point: she is concerned not with the manner of their deaths, but with the fact of dying. For a comparable interpolation see *Aj.* 554, where in the manuscripts and Suda (ζ 61 = ii. 505.12–13 Adler) ἐν τῷ φρονεῖν γὰρ μηδὲν ἥδιστος βίος is followed by τὸ μὴ φρονεῖν γὰρ κάρτ᾽ ἀνώδυνον κακόν.

The omission of 1007 in Lᵃᶜ Kᵃᶜ Rᵃᶜ arises from the homoeoteleuton of 1006 and 1007 and is not relevant to this argument. P.Oxy. 693 certainly has the line, since the second nu of θανεῖν is visible under the lambda of λαβόντε. This means that the interpolation cannot be later than the third century AD, and is probably much earlier: this papyrus offers an exceptionally good text (995n.), and it would take time for an interpolation to establish itself so firmly in the tradition. For the sentiment see Tarrant on Sen. *Ag.* 996, adding Eur. *Tro.* 637.

[1007] For γάρ used to smuggle in an interpolation cf. [1485], *Aj.* 327, *Phil.* 1034, *OC* 954, Eur. *Alc.* 818, *Med.* 38, *Hipp.* 912, 1050, *Hec.* 90, 1185, *Suppl.* 303, *El.* 386, *Her.* 762, *IT* 38, 258, 907, *Hel.* 257, *Ion* 374, 844, *Phoen.* 886, 973, *Or.* 714, 856, 1533, 1556, *Ba.* 673, Wecklein (1869a) 121–3.

[1008] For εἶτα with a finite verb in coordination with a preceding nominative participle see 53n.

1009–10 For destructive anger see Harder on Eur. fr. 257.1 *TrGF* = 31.1 Austin πολλοὺς δ᾽ ὁ θυμὸς ὁ μέγας ὤλεσεν βροτῶν.

For ἀλλ᾽ beginning a closing appeal see 916n.

πρὶν πανωλέθρους τὸ πᾶν | ἡμᾶς τ᾽ ὀλέσθαι κἀξερημῶσαι γένος 'before we are destroyed and our family is annihilated'. West (1979) 104 complains that with this translation the τε is misplaced, and suggests its deletion; he was anticipated by Wecklein (1922) 21. This would not be a serious change, as τε is often interpolated before a καί; but given its tendency to gravitate to second place in its colon, its position is not a problem. Less attractive is the alternative of taking the subject of the second clause to be 'you' (that is, Electra), since the change of subject between the two clauses is awkward. West's emendation τ᾽ ἀπολέσαι (cf. ὀλέσαι in O) is possible: for the resulting sentence cf. *OR* 330–1 ἐννοεῖς | ἡμᾶς προδοῦναι καὶ καταφθεῖραι πόλιν; But it is easier to keep the paradosis and adopt the translation given above.

For the destruction of the γένος in oaths and curses cf. Antiph. 5.11 ἐξώλειαν σαυτῷ καὶ γένει καὶ οἰκίᾳ τῇ σῇ ἐπαρώμενον, M–L §30A.4–5 (Teos) ἀπόλλυσθαι καὶ αὐτὸν καὶ γένος τὸ κένο, R. C. T. Parker (1983) 186 n. 234.

1009 πανωλέθρους cf. Aesch. *Sept.* 71–2 μή μοι πόλιν γε πρυμνόθεν πανώλεθρον | ἐκθαμνίσητε, Hdt. 6.37.2 πανώλεθρος ἐξαπόλλυται, Lucian 53.13 πανωλεθρία παντὸς τοῦ γένους.

τὸ πᾶν intensifies πανωλέθρους; 764–5 may tempt us to take it with γένος in 1010, but the intervening syntax makes the hyperbaton improbable.

1010 Cf. *Ant.* 58–9 νῦν δ᾽ αὖ μόνα δὴ νὼ λελειμμένα σκόπει | ὅσῳ κάκιστ᾽ ὀλούμεθ᾽ (also in response to the recent fraternal death). The Iphianassa of 157 is long forgotten (cf. *Ant.* 941, where even Ismene has fallen into the background).

κἀξερημῶσαι γένος: cf. Eur. *Or.* 664 (Orestes speaking) θανὼν γὰρ οἶκον ὀρφανὸν λείψω πατρός, Dem. 43.73 ἐπιμέλειαν ἐποιησάμην τοῦ οἴκου τοῦ Ἀγνίου, ὅπως μὴ ἐξερημωθήσεται, 43.76 πῶς ἂν μᾶλλον ἐξερημώσαιεν ἄνθρωποι οἶκον . . . ;

1011 κατάσχες ὀργήν: cf. Eur. *Ba.* 555 φονίου δ᾽ ἀνδρὸς ὕβριν κατάσχες, [Sen.] *Oct.* 98 *animi retine verba furentis* with Ferri. For ὀργή see 222n. C reads ὁρμήν, a common corruption (cf. West (1979) 112).

1011–12 τὰ μὲν λελεγμένα | ἄρρητ᾽ ἐγώ σοι κἀτελῆ φυλάξομαι: for the stress on secrecy cf. *Ant.* 84–5 ἀλλ᾽ οὖν προμηνύσῃς γε τοῦτο μηδενὶ | τοὔργον, κρυφῇ δὲ κεῦθε, σὺν δ᾽ αὔτως ἐγώ.

1013–14 These lines are paralleled at 1464–5.

1013 νοῦν σχές: cf. 1465, Eur. *Hipp.* 105, *Andr.* 943–6, Ar. *Ran.* 534, Knox (1964) 22. σχές is only found in tragedy (*OC* 1169 (*coni.*), Eur. *Hipp.* 1353 (*coni.*), *Hec.* 963, *IA* 1466), excepting later grammarians and scholiasts; its compounds (e.g. ἐπίσχες, παράσχες) are commoner. For the concluding reference to νοῦς cf. *Ant.* 67–8 τὸ γὰρ | περισσὰ πράσσειν οὐκ ἔχει νοῦν οὐδένα.

ἀλλὰ τῷ χρόνῳ: cf. 411 n., *Phil.* 1041 τείσασθε τείσασθ᾽ ἀλλὰ τῷ χρόνῳ ποτέ, Eur. *Med.* 912–13 ἔγνως δὲ τὴν νικῶσαν, ἀλλὰ τῷ χρόνῳ, | βουλήν, Diggle on Eur. *Pha.* 52 = fr. 773.8 *TrGF*.

1014 μηδέν: best explained as arising from the inclusion of σθένουσα in the consecutive construction with εἰκαθεῖν (so Moorhouse 332): this is better than saying that it is influenced by the nearby imperative.

εἰκαθεῖν: for the accentuation see 396n.

1015–57 The substantial block of angry stichomythia which closes the episode marks the final degeneration of the sisters' relationship. The aggressive irony which each employs ensures that neither forms a focus for the audience's sympathy. But even in the midst of this rancour one serious point is made, which has consequences beyond its immediate context (1042n.).

1015–16 The chorus urges Electra to accept Chrysothemis' condemnation of the plan. As at 990–1 it expresses itself through a *sententia*; this is made slightly more direct through the imperative πείθου. Burton's argument that these lines 'should not be taken as downright approval of Chrysothemis' attitude' ((1980) 208) is as mistaken as his interpretation of 990–1 (n.). On the alleged inconsistency with the attitude taken by the chorus in the following stasimon see the introduction to the latter. Petropoulou (1979) assigns these lines to Chrysothemis, but 1014 must conclude the latter's speech.

πείθου: manuscript evidence is almost valueless for decisions between πείθου and πιθοῦ. Of 45 instances of the singular middle imperative of πείθω in tragedy, metrical reasons mean that 4 must be present (*OC* 520, Eur. *Andr.* 233, fr. 440.2 *TrGF*, [Eur.] *Rhes.* 993) and 17 aorist (*OR* 649, 1064, *Ant.* 992, *OC* 1181, 1441, fr. 314.140 *TrGF*, Aesch. *Suppl.* 527 (see Friis Johansen and Whittle *ad loc.*), Eur. *Held.* 174, *Hipp.* 508, 892, *Hec.* 402, *Hel.* 323, 451, *Ba.* 309, *IA* 1435, 1460, *Antiope* fr. 188.1 *TrGF* = 10.1 Kambitsis). 24 cases are not metrically determined. These statistics do not allow a presumption in favour of πιθοῦ, however. πιθοῦ can fit in six places in the iambic trimeter, and in three of these positions it will be metrically guaranteed. πείθου has only four possible locations, only one of which could not also be occupied by πιθοῦ. Thus even on the assumption that both forms were used evenly by the three tragedians, we would still expect guaranteed instances of the present to be substantially fewer than those of the aorist. In the plural, there is a single metrically guaranteed instance of πίθεσθε (Aesch. *Eum.* 794), and five which could be present or aorist.

This leaves semantics as the only possible ground on which to make a decision. Here too any conclusions can only be based on the metrically guaranteed instances. The factors which affect the choice of aorist or present stem in the imperative are not fully understood (643n.). The traditional distinction between punctual actions expressed by the aorist and durative processes expressed in the present will not hold for every case: at *OC* 520 and [Eur.] *Rhes.* 993 πείθου does not denote a process (cf. Hutchinson on Aesch. *Sept.* 712). However, the 14 secure instances of πιθοῦ all refer to some definite action, which suggests that a distinction along these lines has something in its favour. Since at the end of her speech Chrysothemis is urging her sister not simply to abandon her plan, but to change her whole attitude, the present may be more appropriate here. So too at Eur. *Andr.* 233 the chorus uses the present to urge on Hermione a change in attitude rather than a specific act. See further Fraenkel on Aesch. *Ag.* 1054, though his defence of πείθου in that instance places too much emphasis on manuscript evidence.

προνοίας οὐδὲν ἀνθρώποις ἔφυ | κέρδος λαβεῖν ἄμεινον οὐδὲ νοῦ σοφοῦ cf. 990–1, fr. 950.3 *TrGF* προμηθία γὰρ κέρδος ἀνθρώποις μέγα, 302 *TrGF* σωτηρίας γὰρ φάρμακ' οὐχὶ πανταχοῦ | βλέψαι πάρεστιν, ἐν δὲ τῇ προμηθίᾳ, Eur. *Andr.* 690 ἐμοὶ δὲ κέρδος ἡ προμηθία. For examples of the expression 'there is nothing better/worse than x' cf. 1047, *Aj.* 485–6, *Ant.* 295–6, 672, *Phil.* 672–3.

1017 Electra's opening statement is contrary to known facts: she has, after all, recently spent the best part of fifty lines attempting to persuade her sister to join with her in her plan, which she would hardly have done had she been sure of a negative response. Her response here thus shows all the pettiness of someone unable to cope with an unexpected setback. She then surprises us yet again. Her efforts to persuade her sister implied that Chrysothemis' participation was essential for the success of the plan. Her sudden decision to carry it out alone is thus an even more extreme example of foolhardiness.

ἀπροσδόκητον οὐδὲν εἴρηκας: cf. *Ant.* 69–70 οὔτ' ἂν κελεύσαιμ' οὔτ' ἄν, εἰ θέλοις ἔτι | πράσσειν, ἐμοῦ γ' ἂν ἡδέως δρῴης μέτα, also in response to a sister's rejection of a passionate appeal.

δ': for the elision at the end of the line see Jebb on *OR* 29, Dawe on *OR* 30. In extant S. only δέ and τε ταῦτ' (once) are so elided, and only between two long syllables (see West (1982a) 84 n. 24; also Bruhn §268.VI).

1018 ἤδη: the correct Attic form, restored here by Brunck (in his 1779 edition): cf. Choeroboscus ii. 86.1 Hilgard ≈ Aristarchus fr. 4.75–97 Schironi. Thom. Mag. *Ecl.* 143.7 Ritschl has ἤδη (*sic*) in LaRa.

ἀπορρίψουσαν: for the sense 'reject with contempt' cf. *Aj.* 1019 (cited above, 1002n.), Aesch. *Eum.* 215 Κύπρις δ' ἄτιμος τῷδ' ἀπέρριπται λόγῳ, Hdt. 1.32.1 ἡ δ' ἡμετέρη εὐδαιμονίη οὕτω τοι ἀπέρριπται ἐς τὸ μηδέν, Pind. *O.* 9.35–6 ἀπό μοι λόγον | τοῦτον, στόμα, ῥῖψον, Xen. *Mem.* 2.1.31, Dem. 25.75 ἡ μὲν πονηρία τιμᾶται, τὰ χρηστὰ δ' ἀπορρίπτηται, [Anon.] *Progymnasmata* 5 = *RG* i. 609.5–6 ἀλήθεια . . . καταπεφρόνηται καὶ ἀπέρριπται.

ἀπηγγελλόμην 'the offer that I made'; cf. Hdt. 6.35.2. S. uses ἀγγέλλομαι in this sense at *Aj.* 1376. Thom. Mag. *Ecl.* 143.7 Ritschl reads ἅ' πηγγειλάμην, but there is no reason to prefer the aorist over the imperfect.

1019 αὐτόχειρί . . . μόνη τε δραστέον: contrast *Tr.* 1194 αὐτόχειρα καὶ ξὺν οἷς χρῄζεις φίλων. For μόνος cf. 119n. The adjective αὐτόχειρι should be preferred to the adverb αὐτοχειρί: see Porson on Eur. *Or.* 1038 (our 1040).

The γράφεται variant οὐδὲν ἧσσον written by the scholiast of L makes the following τε awkward ('another reckless piece of re-writing by [the scholiast] or his source' – Dawe, *STS* i. 191). The phrase ἀλλ' οὐδὲν ἧσσον occurs elsewhere at Eur. *IT* 1364, [Eur.] *Rhes.* 272, Astydamas II *TrGF* 60 F 1 i.13, Thuc. 7.84.5.

1020 οὐ γὰρ δή . . . γε 'clear[s] the ground by ruling out at least one possibility' (Denniston 243 (2)); cf. *Phil.* 246, *OC* 110, 265–6, Hdt. 3.156.3 οὐ γὰρ δὴ ἐμέ γε ὧδε λωβησάμενος καταπροΐξεται, [Aesch.] *PV* 1065, Eur. *Ion* 954, Thuc. 4.87.4.

κενόν: ἀτελές; cf. 331.

ἀφήσομεν: for the corruption involved in the minority reading ἀφήσομαι (here perhaps aided by the middle 1st singular at the end of 1018) see Diggle (1983) 350 = (1994) 263.

1021 φεῦ: 'the following words lend a sarcastic ring to the commiserative exclamation' (Kamerbeek); 'σχετλιαστικόν, nicht θρηνητικόν' (Kaibel, p. 228). For φεῦ spoken in anger breaking up a stichomythia cf. *Ant.* 323, Eur. *Alc.* 719; also *Ion* 1312.

1022 πᾶν γὰρ ἄν: of the two manuscript readings, πάντα γὰρ ἄν is unmetrical, and πάντα γάρ syntactically deficient. πάντα γ' ἄν (Musgrave) and πάντα τἄν (Arnold (1866) 49) are possibilities, but Dawes's πᾶν for πάντα ((1745) 260 = (1800) 212) is the simplest solution. The ἄν dropped out, and πᾶν was extended to fill out the line to twelve syllables; or else πᾶν was replaced by πάντα and ἄν was then omitted to restore the metre. The same corruption has occurred at [Aesch.] *PV* 617.

κατηργάσω: for the orthography (restored by Groeneboom[1]) see West's Teubner Aeschylus, p. xlii.

1023 Ellendt catches the sense: *natura quidem sese ad omnia audenda, etiam cum adolescentula esset, proclivem fuisse, sed nondum satis consilio valuisse dicit* (s.v. νοῦς, p. 472 col. ii); cf. Holwerda (1955) 41–3 (with p. 133).

φύσιν γε, τὸν δὲ νοῦν: the two nouns are found in antithesis at Ar. *Av.* 371 εἰ δὲ τὴν φύσιν μὲν ἐχθροί, τὸν δὲ νοῦν εἰσιν φίλοι, though there with νοῦς = 'intention' rather than 'understanding'. For the presence of the article with only one of the terms see 265n.

ἤ: so Elmsley (his edition of *OR*, p. 10); ἤν codd. Classical inscriptions have EN (Threatte ii. 587–8), but metrical considerations mean that ἤ should be preferred in S. (cf. Barrett on Eur. *Hipp.* 700).

1024 ἀσκεῖ . . . μένειν: for ἀσκέω with the infinitive cf. fr. 963 *TrGF* οἱ γὰρ γύνανδροι καὶ λέγειν ἠσκηκότες, Eur. fr. 1067.2 *TrGF*, LSJ⁹ s.v. II 3.

δι'αἰῶνος 'always' (cf. Degani (1961) 64–5, Harder on Eur. fr. 245.13 *TrGF* = 19.13 Austin).

1025 ὡς οὐχὶ συνδράσουσα νουθετεῖς τάδε: cf. *Tr.* 1232 ὡς ἐργασείων οὐδὲν ὧν λέγω θροεῖς. For νουθετεῖς cf. 343 νουθετήματα.

1026 ἐγχειροῦντα: sc. κακά. Jebb prefers to take the participle absolutely, but this leaves the καί problematic: his translation 'e'en' is rather desperate. Wakefield (1789–95) iii. 85–6 conjectured κάκ' for γάρ, citing Hes. *Op.* 265 οἷ τ' αὐτῷ κακὰ τεύχει ἀνὴρ ἄλλῳ κακὰ τεύχων (where see West), Eur. *Or.* 413; cf. also S. fr. 962 *TrGF* εἰ δείν' ἔδρασας, δεινὰ καὶ παθεῖν σε δεῖ. Though not necessary, it is certainly attractive: the postulated change is small, and may have been helped by a scribe's dislike of asyndeton. For the masculine participle see 771n.

πράσσειν: the minority reading πάσχειν probably arose under the influence of expressions such as fr. 223b *TrGF* τὸν δρῶντα γάρ τι καὶ παθεῖν ὀφείλεται and Pind. *N.* 4.31–2 ἐπεὶ | ῥέζοντά τι καὶ παθεῖν ἔοικεν. Corruption to πράσσειν is harder to explain.

1027 ζηλῶ σε: ironical: cf. Eur. *Med.* 60 with Page's n.

δειλίας: cf. 351.

1028 ἀνέξομαι κλύουσα χὥταν εὖ λέγῃς: i.e. 'I can put up with your insults as readily as your compliments.' ἀνέξομαι κλύουσα suggests that 'it will be a trial of patience – not less than that of being reproached with δειλία – to hear Electra's acknowledgements and regrets when her rash attempt has failed' (Jebb; cf. 1044, 1056–7). Chrysothemis also points to Electra's sudden changes towards her, and caustically suggests that this mood of anger too will pass.

1029 ἐξ ἐμοῦ γε: γε normally follows the preposition, but there are exceptions, especially in poetry (Denniston 149).

πάθῃς: the minority variant (*coni.* Wakefield (1789–95) iii. 85–6) must be right: μάθησις in 1032 may have assisted the corruption to μάθῃς.

1030 τὸ κρῖναι: for the article with an epexegetic infinitive (probably an accusative of respect) cf. 1078–9, *Ant.* 78–9 τὸ δὲ | βίᾳ πολιτῶν δρᾶν ἔφυν ἀμήχανος, Bruhn §129, K–G ii. 43–5, Goodwin §795.

χὠ λοιπὸς χρόνος: 178n.

1031–2 ὠφέλησις . . . | . . . μάθησις: 'the two -sis nouns intensify an antithesis of attitudes, the ineffectiveness of Chrysothemis and the stubbornness of Electra. Their character is presented through each other's words as a failure to act in a certain way' (Long (1968) 65). For the jingle cf. Men. *Epitr.* 319 οὐχ εὕρεσις τοῦτ' ἔστιν, ἀλλ' ἀφαίρεσις, Tr. Adesp. fr. 409 *TrGF* ὕβρις τάδ', οὐχὶ Κύπρις ἐξεργάζεται, Norden (1909) ii. 833 n. 1. For the picking up of a word or phrase in the preceding line of stichomythia cf. 385–404n., 1035–6, 1044–5, *Ant.* 730–1. In addition, ἔνεστι answers ἔνι and σοί answers σοί. Both lines have a strong pause after an opening word of three syllables; in both the abstract noun comes at the end of the second metron. Parallelism of lexicon, morphology and syntax conveys the antithesis of attitude.

1032 μάθησις 'signifie "le fait d'apprendre", μάθημα "l'objet de l'étude, la science". La valeur active de μάθησις est si nette que le substantif arrive à signifier la possibilité d'apprendre' (Chantraine (1933) 286). The word is as old as Alcman (fr. 125 *PMGF* πῆρά τοι μαθήσιος ἀρχά): as it occurs there in a proverbial expression it is probably much older. Cf. also 330.

1033 μητρὶ . . . ἔξειπε σῇ: cf. *Ant.* 549 Κρέοντ' ἐρώτα· τοῦδε γὰρ σὺ κηδεμών. For Chrysothemis' supposed loyalty to her mother cf. 365–7.

1034 According to Blundell, Chrysothemis 'refuses to adopt the role of enemy which Electra thrusts upon her' ((1989) 161). But rather than deny her hatred, she merely qualifies its extent: hardly a gesture calculated to win her sympathy.
τοσοῦτον ἔχθος ἐχθαίρω: cf. *Phil.* 59 ἔχθος ἐχθήρας μέγα, Bruhn §53.I.1.

1035 For ἀλλ' οὖν see 233n.
οἵ . . . ἀτιμίας: for the genitive see 390n. The ἀτιμία consists in the rejection of Electra's solemn appeal.

1036–8 are bisected by their caesurae (cf. also 1044). Only about 1 % of S.'s trimeters are so divided, and most of them have an elision over the divide (here only in 1037). Even though the rhetorical break comes in the middle, all three lines nevertheless have a break in the regular position (cf. Diggle (1994) 473–4 n. 151). See further Bruhn §175, West (1982a) 82–3, Goodell (1906), Stephan (1981). For the form of this line cf. *Phil.* 1009 ἀνάξιον μὲν σοῦ, κατάξιον δ' ἐμοῦ.

1036 ἀτιμίας . . . προμηθίας: the genitives are unusual: however, 'an answer often follows the structure of the preceding speech though another construction would be more logical' (Campbell, his edition, vol. i. p. 60). As in 990 G has προθυμίας, and as there it must be wrong. Chrysothemis' attitude towards Electra at the moment can hardly be described as one of enthusiasm.

1037 τῷ σῷ δικαίῳ 'what is right according to you'. Contrast Eur. *Hel.* 920 τὸ μὲν δίκαιον τοῦ πατρὸς διαφθερεῖς and *IA* 810 τοὐμὸν μὲν οὖν δίκαιον ἐμὲ λέγειν χρέος, where the phrase means 'my plea, the right on which I rely'. The possessive is contemptuous (359n.). Kells (1963) 8 n. 2 discusses different uses of this phrase in the orators (though his semantic distinctions are unreliable).

1038 ὅταν: G's εὖτ' ἂν may well have arisen from the presence of εὖ in the same metron (so Dawe, *STS* i. 191).

εὖ φρονῇς: 384n.

1039 ἢ δεινὸν εὖ λέγουσαν ἐξαμαρτάνειν: cf. *Ant.* 323 ἢ δεινόν, ᾧ δοκεῖ γε, καὶ ψευδῆ δοκεῖν. Electra contrasts Chrysothemis' fluency of speech (εὖ λέγειν) with the intrinsic badness of that case (ἐξαμαρτάνειν). She cannot be referring to her own failure to move Chrysothemis despite the validity of her arguments, as then Chrysothemis' reply is rather banal.

1040 πρόσκεισαι κακῷ: cf. 240–1n.

1041 For τί δ'; in elliptical questions see Waś (1983) 34, 99–101.

1042 ἀλλ' ἔστιν ἔνθα χἠ δίκη βλάβην φέρει: Chrysothemis' words point to an important theme, though without her showing awareness of its significance: namely, that a just act, for all its justice, may still be shameful or otherwise detrimental to its perpetrators. See further 516–633n., 1398–1441n. For the sentiment see Kassel and Austin on Men. fr. 768 *PCG*, Dyck on Cic. *Off.* 1.33, Haffner on Orion *Flor.* 6.8.

1043 Cf. 397.

1044 ἀλλ' εἰ ποήσεις ταῦτ', ἐπαινέσεις ἐμέ: cf. Theogn. 37–8 ταῦτα μαθὼν ἀγαθοῖσιν ὁμίλει, καί ποτε φήσεις | εὖ συμβουλεύειν τοῖσι φίλοισιν ἐμέ. For the bisection of the trimeter see 1036–8n. For the future tense in the protasis cf. 379n.

ἐπαινέσεις ἐμέ: for ἐπαινῶ with the accusative conveying thanks see Quincey (1966) 154.

1045 καὶ μήν: 556–7n.

ἐκπλαγεῖσά σε: for the accusative with a passive verb see Moorhouse 38–9. The participle is felt to be equivalent to φοβουμένη.

1046 καί 'actually' cf. *Phil.* 921 καὶ ταῦτ' ἀληθῆ δρᾶν νοεῖς;, Denniston 311–12.

COMMENTARY: 871–1057

βουλεύσῃ πάλιν: cf. *Phil.* 961–2 εἰ καὶ πάλιν | γνώμην μετοίσεις, 1270 μεταγνῶναι πάλιν, *Tr.* 358 ἔμπαλιν λέγει, Aesch. *Sept.* [1040], Plut. *Ant.* 13.3, Diod. Sic. 11.37.3.

1047 βουλῆς: either Chrysothemis' advice or Electra's resolve altered to be in agreement with it.

1048 φρονεῖν ἔοικας οὐδὲν ὧν ἐγὼ λέγω: cf. [Aesch.] *PV* 984 ἐρεῖν ἔοικας οὐδὲν ὧν χρῄζει πατήρ. In each case the line signals the imminent close of the stichomythia (cf. Kaibel (1884) 250–2). For φρονεῖν see 384n.

1049 πάλαι δέδοκται ταῦτα κοὐ νεωστί μοι: cf. [Aesch.] *PV* 998 ὦπται πάλαι δὴ καὶ βεβούλευται τάδε, Hom. *Il.* 9.527 μέμνημαι τόδε ἔργον ἐγὼ πάλαι, οὔ τι νέον γε; also 676n., 885n. For the resolution and determination of the Sophoclean hero see Knox (1964) 10–11. For the perfect see 385n.

νεωστί: on the differing quantity of final –ί see Jebb on *OC* 1251, S–D i. 623.

[1050–4] Lloyd-Jones and Wilson delete these lines for the following reasons (listed in *Sophoclea*). (i) Stob. *Ecl.* 3.2.28–9 (= iii. 185.1–3 Wachsmuth and Hense) cites 1050–1 as part of S.'s *Phaedra.* (ii) The contrast of Chrysothemis' words and Electra's habits in 1050–1 'seems to have very little point'. (iii) Electra has no reason to tell Chrysothemis that she will never follow her, however much she might want her to; nor are the words appropriate to Chrysothemis. (iv) Neither sister has reason to say that a futile hunt is a mark of folly. (v) 1055–7 'make a far more pointed reply' to 1049 than 1050–4.

(i) is indecisive: as Ll-J/W themselves point out, Stobaeus' attributions are not always reliable. (ii) The opposition, while not intolerable, is certainly inelegant. The repetition of ἔπη | ... ἐπαινεῖν in 1057 ἐπαινέσεις ἔπη forms another ground for suspicion. (iii) 1052 could not have been spoken by Chrysothemis, as it is she, not Electra, who is about to go inside. But it does make sense in Electra's mouth. Such a statement would act as a counterpart to her words at the end of the previous episode, where she stresses her determination to remain outside until death (817–19). In this context it draws attention to how the physical separation of the sisters will match the irreconcilability of their beliefs (cf. Blundell (1989) 161). However, the following οὐδ' ἦν σφόδρ' ἱμείρουσα τυγχάνῃς ('I shall never follow you, not even if you *really, really* want me to') is intolerably weak. (iv) 1053–4 ἐπεὶ | ... κενά could not be spoken by Electra, but could fit Chrysothemis: cf. Ismene's criticisms of her sister ἀλλ' ἀμηχάνων ἐρᾷς (*Ant.* 90), ἀρχὴν δὲ θηρᾶν οὐ πρέπει τἀμήχανα (*Ant.* 92).

Dawe's lacuna after 1052 (*STS* i. 191–2) deals with some of these problems. Electra speaks 1052, Chrysothemis speaks 1053–7. The weakness of 1050–1 and 1053 still remains, but is not in itself enough to damn the lines. This solution does create a new problem, however. Chrysothemis now ends with a speech of at least six lines, which probably has to be balanced by a correspondingly lengthy speech by her sister immediately beforehand. Yet the stichomythia is long even as it stands, and has been showing every appearance of drawing to an imminent close (1048n.). The ἀλλά of 1055 also seems more forceful if it begins a fresh utterance.

Deletion of this section, as advocated by Ll-J/W and supported by Zimmermann (1993) 104, is the only way of dealing with its many problems. It also has a positive benefit, in that the repetition of φρονέω and δοκέω in 1048–9 and 1055–7 is more effective if Chrysothemis' speech follows on from these lines (point (v) above). This is a typical feature of stichomythic exchange: by contrast, the clumsy repetition of the same phrase by the same speaker in 1050–1 and 1057 is quite different (cf. (i) above).

The interpolation may have been motivated by a desire to lengthen the stichomythia by supplying a clear exit-statement for Chrysothemis. Lloyd-Jones prints 1050–4 as a fragment of the *Phaedra* in his Loeb edition. But this places too much weight on Stobaeus' attribution. These weak lines are probably better regarded as an actor's interpolation than the work of Sophocles.

[1050] ἄπειμι τοίνυν: same phrase at *OR* 444, fr. 730d.4 *TrGF*, Plut. *Dem.* 29.2, Lucian 24.34. For the balance with ἀλλ' εἴσιθ' in 1052: cf. *Aj.* 1159–61 ἄπειμι . . . | . . . | ἄφερπέ νυν, Eur. *Alc.* 729–30 ἀπελθέ . . . | ἄπειμι.

[1051] τολμᾷς 'bring yourself' to do it: cf. *OC* 184–6 τόλμα . . . | . . . ὅ τι καὶ πόλις | τέτροφεν ἄφιλον ἀποστυγεῖν, *Aj.* 528, *Phil.* 481.

[1052] οὐ . . . μὴ μεθέψομαι: a strong denial is normally expressed by οὐ μή with the aorist subjunctive; οὐ μή with the future indicative is used in the second person to convey a strong prohibition. But occasionally the latter construction is used with any person to express a strong denial: cf. *OC* 176–7 οὔ τοι μήποτέ σ' . . . ἄκοντά τις ἄξει, 848–9 (v.l.), Eur. *Phoen.* 1590–1, Ar. *Ran.* 508–9, Aeschines 3.177, Goodwin §295, K–G ii. 221–3, Wackernagel (1926–8) ii. 305. Rijksbaron (1991) 173–4 interprets these examples as emphatic variants of the construction μή + future indicative which is found in oaths.

μεθέπω is occasionally found in Homer (e.g. *Il.* 5.329) and Pindar (e.g. *P.* 2.37). The middle is not found elsewhere until the imperial period.

[1054] καί marks a minimum (Denniston 293 II A (2)); cf. *Phil.* 234–5 φεῦ τὸ καὶ λαβεῖν | πρόσφθεγμα, Ar. *Nub.* 528 ἀνδρῶν οὓς ἡδὺ καὶ λέγειν.

τὸ θηρᾶσθαι κενά: cf. *Ant.* 92 ἀρχὴν δὲ θηρᾶν οὐ πρέπει τἀμήχανα, Chantraine (1956) 70–1.

1055 For ἀλλ᾿ expressing reluctant acquiescence see Denniston 19 (iii) (a).

1056 φρόνει τοιαῦθ᾿: Dawe (2002–3) 9 compares *Ant.* 71 ἀλλ᾿ ἴσθ᾿ ὁποῖά σοι δοκεῖ, taking ἴσθι as the imperative of οἶδα. For the verb see 384n.

1056–7 ὅταν γὰρ ἐν κακοῖς | ἤδη βεβήκῃς, τἄμ᾿ ἐπαινέσεις ἔπη cf. 383–4n. ἐν κακοῖς: 308n.

1057 βεβήκῃς: 979n.
τἄμ᾿ ἐπαινέσεις ἔπη: for ἐπαινέω with the accusative of the thing for which one is thanked cf. Isaeus 2.12, Quincey (1966) 155.

Exit Chrysothemis through the *skene*. The expressive stage-movement is reminiscent of *Ant.* 99: one sister returns to the house, while her more defiant sibling remains outside.

SECOND STASIMON (1058–97)

FIRST STROPHIC PAIR (1058–81)

1058	1070	U – U – – ˈ U U – U – U – – ˈ	ia, cho enneas
		U U – U – U – ˈ –	anacr
1060		U U – U – U – –	anacr
		U U – U – U – –	anacr
		U U – U U – U – – ‖	ionic
	1075	– – – U U – U – ˈ	glyc
		– – – U U – U – ˈ	glyc
1065		– U̲ – U U – – ‖	pher
		– U U – U – U – – ˈ	cho enneas
		U U – U – U – – ˈ	anacr
	1080	U U – U – U – – ˈ	anacr
1069		U U – U U – U – – ‖‖	ionic

The first strophic pair is made up of three periods, the second of which (1063–5 ~ 1075–7) consists of glyconics. The first and third sections are more controversial. The ionic interpretation printed above is that preferred by Ll-J/W (cf. also Hermann (1816) 425–6, Dale (1968) 122 n. 2). Dawe, on the other hand, follows Dale ((1936) 197–8 = (1969) 16–17, (1971–83) ii. 42–3) in adopting an iambo-choriambic analysis for both sections, giving an alternation of iambic and choriambic metra in each case before finishing with an alcaic decasyllable in 1061–2 ~ 1073–4 and with a choriambic enneasyllable plus enoplian in 1067–9 ~ 1079–81 (cf. Wilamowitz (1921) 327, Griffith (1977) 30–1). Zuntz (1984) 63 opposes the ionic analysis because it does not fit with the word-division of the piece or the colometry of the mediaeval manuscripts. In fact, the evidence of word-division tends the other way. With an ionic interpretation of 1058–62 ~ 1070–4 and 1066–9 ~ 1078–81 we have a total of four cola in synartesis, whereas Dale's iambo-choriambic analysis yields ten of the same. As for Zuntz's second point, the manuscripts give us evidence only for the colometry preferred by the scholars of Alexandria, and this need not be correct (see L. P. E. Parker (1997) 94–5, (2001)).

Anacr. fr. 346 *PMG* shows similarities to the ionics in this stasimon:

$$- \cup \cup - \cup - \cup - -$$
$$\cup \cup - \cup - \cup - -$$
$$\cup \cup - - \cup \cup - \cup - -$$

This too is susceptible to a purely iambo-choriambic analysis, but again word-end favours ionics. The first colon of Anacreon's poem is found in 1058 ~ 1070 and 1066 ~ 1078; in the former it is headed by an iambic metron. In each case the colon is followed by one or more anacreontics, a metrical shape with which it has obvious similarities. The colon which concludes Anacreon's stanza also concludes the ionic passages in the stasimon at 1062 ~ 1074 and 1069 ~ 1081, though with its opening metron reduced from $\cup \cup - -$ to $\cup \cup -$. The 'apparently choriambic opening to sequences of anacreontics' (Parker (1997) 64) is not confined to these two lyrics. Among the examples cited by Diggle (1994) 505 cf. e.g. Aesch. *Ag.* 447–51 ~ 466–70, where 2ia followed by the $- \cup \cup - \cup - \cup - -$ colon lead into some ionic rhythms. Aesch. *Sept.* 726 ~ 733 provides a close parallel for the closing colon in 1062 ~ 1074 and 1069 ~ 1081: there a series of ionics is brought to an end with the colon $\cup \cup - - \cup \cup - \cup \cup - \cup - -$.

The rhythm of the anacreontic appears catchy and tripping to us, and thus inappropriate for the elevated subject matter. However, this metre can be used in more solemn contexts: cf. Parker (1997) 62 (citing Σ [Aesch.] *PV* 128 = Anacr. fr. 412 *PMG*), Aesch. *Cho.* 327–30 ~ 358–61.

The one difficulty which arises in both of these analyses is the prosody of οἰωνούς in 1058. There are several parallels for such shortening in tragedy, however (cf. West (1982a) 11). While it tends to be limited to certain words such as τοιοῦτος and παλαιός, there is no reason why S. should not on this occasion have extended it to οἰωνός. On the phonetic principle involved (consonantalisation of an intervocalic iota) see S–D i. 236, Allen (1987) 81–3. A way of avoiding this prosody would be to take 1058–62 ~ 1070–4 as predominantly aeolo-choriambic, with an iambic metron instead of the aeolic base for the first glyconic, and an end consisting of ₐia enopl. Twice, however, this gives us a glyconic in synartesis beginning $\cup -$, a rare and therefore unattractive phenomenon (Itsumi (1984) 70–1).

SECOND STROPHIC PAIR (1082–97)

1082	1090	– – – ∪ ∪ – –	pher
		– ∪ – – – ∪ – – – ∪ –	‸ia 2ia
		– ∪ ∪ – – – ‖	dodr
1085		∪̄ – ∪ – – ∪ –	ia ‸ia
		– ∪ – ∪ – –	‸ia ia‸
	1095	∪ – ∪ ∪̄∪̄ ∪ – ∪ –	2ia
		∪ ⌢∪∪ – ∪ ⌢∪∪ –	2ia
		∪ – ∪ – – ∪ – ∪ – – ‖‖	ia ‸ia ia‸

Sophoclean iambic typically involves 'the restrained, but strategic, use of syncopation . . . lavish resolution, and the heavily syncopated clausular trimeter following an unsyncopated sequence' (L. P. E. Parker (1997) 322, citing examples). All these characteristics can be found here. 1082 ∼ 1090 and 1084 ∼ 1092 might also be analysed as a contracted hemiepes pendant and contracted hemiepes respectively, but the above analysis fits better with the aeolo-choriambic colouring of the first strophic pair. Hemiepe with contracted bicipitia are also generally unusual.

For the correspondence of 1082–3 ∼ 1090–1 see *ad locc.*

The responsion of resolved to unresolved iambic metron in 1087 ∼ 1095 is not a cause for concern: Sophoclean parallels can be found at *Tr.* 649 ∼ 657, *Ant.* 974 ∼ 985, *OR* 891 ∼ 905, *OC* 537 ∼ 544, 702 ∼ 715.

1058–97 The first strophic pair deals with the correct forms of filial piety. Beginning at a general level with the commendation of the behaviour of birds, it moves in the antistrophe to the specific situation portrayed in the previous episode. The spatial range of the strophe, extending from the birds above (1058 ἄνωθεν) and the gods in heaven (1064 οὐρανίαν) to Agamemnon below the earth (1067 κατά), yields in the antistrophe to a concentration on the two sisters, particularly on Electra and her support for her father. The rhetorical questions which begin and end this section of the lyric, praising first the birds and then Electra for piety towards parents, give unity to the piece. So does the avian comparison of Electra in 1076–7.

The second strophic pair suffers from a more than usually corrupt text. In particular, one of the problems which it contains has been an especial source of bafflement (1087, discussed *ad loc.*). But the general sense of this half of the stasimon is uncontroversial. Electra is praised in fulsome terms for her piety towards her father, despite the dangers which accompany this course. This theme is taken up from the first antistrophe, and various other elements connect the two strophic pairs. So both strophes begin with a comment of general application before turning to the specific situation. Both emphasise Electra's life of lamentation (1076, 1085–6). And in each there is a play with ideas of above and below: having ranged in the first strophe from the birds of the air to Agamemnon in the underworld, in the second antistrophe the chorus prays that Electra may move figuratively in the opposite direction, so that she may live above her enemies by as much as she is now below them (1090–2). There are also some semantic links through the ode, such as the repetition of βλαστάνω (1060–1, 1081, 1095–6), as well as some links confined to the second strophic pair (e.g. 1088 φέρειν, 1096 φερομέναν; 1089, 1097 ἄριστα: see further Stokes (1979) 135.

For all its internal unity, however, in an important respect the ode is at odds with the previous episode. The chorus takes a positive attitude to Electra, and in doing so implicitly criticises the behaviour of Chrysothemis (cf. e.g. 1074 πρόδοτος). Electra's plan to take revenge on Aegisthus is now regarded as evidence of her piety, and is rewarded with lavish praise in the second strophic pair. Yet just a moment ago, in its only interventions in the previous scene, the chorus had been criticising Electra's stance, and urging her to moderate her course (990–1, 1015–16 with nn.). The dramatic grounds for this are not difficult to see. Electra will shortly deliver her great lament over the urn: and for this to be as emotionally affecting as possible the audience must have a more favourable attitude towards her than would have been possible during the third episode. Praise for her in the intervening choral ode is a way of achieving this shift.

This does not resolve the problem of consistency in the presentation of the chorus, which utters conflicting sentiments within a few lines. Nothing in the interval could motivate this change on realistic grounds. It rather appears that dramatic necessity has taken precedence over consistency of characterisation. Various factors smooth over the disjunction between episode and stasimon. The choral interventions in the preceding episode were brief and colourless, which means that the inconsistency is not as blatant as it might have been had the chorus made an impassioned appeal on the side of Chrysothemis. It may also be significant that this occurs towards the end of the play, since choruses in both tragedy and comedy tend to become less important, and more supportive of the protagonist, as the action moves towards its dénouement. A similar effect can be observed in *Philoctetes*, where at 827–64 the chorus suddenly loses the sympathy for Philoctetes which it had demonstrated earlier (cf. especially 169–90). That shift too is required by the need to accommodate the presentation of a main character. By this stage Neoptolemus has become more sympathetic towards Philoctetes, and as a result the chorus becomes less sympathetic to highlight by contrast the distinctive attitude of Neoptolemus.

1058–62 The bird most often associated with caring for its parents was the stork: cf. Ar. *Av.* 1353–7, fr. 445 *PCG* (Πελαργοί), Pl. *Alc. 1* 135e1–3, Arist. *HA* 615b23–4, Aelian *NA* 3.23, 10.16, Zenob. vulg. i. 94, Suda α 2707

COMMENTARY: 1058-97

(= i. 242.12–18 Adler), D. W. Thompson (1936) 223. But this quality was predicated of other species too: the crested lark (κορύδαλος; cf. Theocr. 7.23, Thompson (1936) 167–8), the hoopoe (ἔποψ; cf. Aelian 10.16, 16.5, Thompson (1936) 99), the bee-eater (μέροψ; cf. Arist. HA 615ᵇ24–7, Thompson (1936) 203), the swan (Eur. El. 151–6, Ba. 1364–5), and the phoenix (cf. Hdt. 2.73.3). For a comparison with birds used to criticise the behaviour of humans cf. Jeremiah 8.7 'Yea, the stork in the heaven knoweth her appointed times; and the turtle and the crane and the swallow observe the time of their coming; but my people know not the judgment of the Lord'.

1058 ἄνωθεν = ἄνω: cf. Phil. 28, Aesch. Suppl. 597, Cho. 834, Eur. Hel. 1014, Bruhn §28. This development from the original ablatival sense probably took place under the influence of forms like ὕπερθεν (cf. 1090n., Lejeune (1939) 328).

φρονιμωτάτους: the chorus picks up a word used twice in Chrysothemis' departing words (1056), only to use it against her. For φρόνιμος applied to an animal cf. Arist. De part. anim. 687a8, Pl. Polit. 263d3–4, LSJ⁹ s.v. III 3 and the title to Plutarch's πότερα τῶν ζώων φρονιμώτερα, τὰ χερσαῖα ἢ τὰ ἔνυδρα (De soll. anim. 959t).

οἰωνούς: for the prosody see the metrical introduction.

1060–2 For the subjunctives without ἄν see 771n.

1060 ἀφ' ὧν: for the ellipse of τούτων cf. OC 223 δέος ἴσχετε μηδὲν ὅσ' αὐδῶ, Bruhn §92.I.

1062 τάδ' οὐκ ἐπ' ἴσας τελοῦμεν; καλῶς ὁ χορὸς καὶ ἑαυτὸν συγκαταλέγει ἵνα μὴ δοκῇ φορτικὸς εἶναι τούτοις καθ' ὧν τὸν λόγον πεποίηται (Σ p. 148.5–7 Papageorgius); for the first person plural used to suggest a polite tone cf. Wackernagel (1926–8) i. 43, M. A. Lloyd (2006) 227 n. 4.

ἐπ' ἴσας: sc. μοίρας, as at Hdt. 1.74.2, Plut. Fab. 10.6; for the feminine see 1415–16n.

1063 ἀλλ' οὐ: the following μά must be deleted to produce responsion with 1075; for interpolation of μά cf. 1239, OR 660, 1088, Bruhn §159.VII.

Διὸς ἀστραπάν: cf. the mention of the κεραυνοὶ Διός in a punitive context at 823 (n.).

1064 Θέμιν: Zeus's second wife (Hes. Theog. 901–4, Pind. fr. 30.1–5 S–M Θέμιν οὐρανίαν... ἄλοχον Διός, Gerber on O. 9.15–16), Themis was often associated with him, especially in the context of justice: cf. Hom. Od. 2.68 λίσσομαι ἠμὲν Ζηνὸς Ὀλυμπίου ἠδὲ Θέμιστος with S. R. West, [Hes.] fr. 343.16 M–W, Pind.

428

O. 8.21–2 σώτειρα Διὸς ξενίου | πάρεδρος . . . Θέμις, Aesch. *Suppl.* 359–60 with Friis Johansen and Whittle, Eur. *Med.* 168–9, 209, Vos (1956) 47–62.

1065 οὐκ ἀπόνητοι: 'Campbell and Jebb are right in taking the reference to be general, "we" being supplied, as Jebb suggests, from the preceding sentence, though it is the attitude of Chrysothemis that has set the chorus thinking on these lines' (Ll-J/W, *Sophoclea*). We must supply the future first person plural of εἰμί: this is uncommon but not impossible (cf. *Ant.* 634, Denniston on Eur. *El.* 37, Fraenkel (1977) 28 (on *Aj.* 813)), and in our case the preceding verb τελοῦμεν makes the construction possible. Some have seen here a reference to Clytemnestra and Aegisthus, but that would not fit with the preceding lines. Villains they may have been, but a lack of respect for their parents is not one of their faults.

ἀπόνητοι is an alternative form for ἄπονοι. The stem is found elsewhere (before late antiquity) only in Herodotus' ἀπονητότατα (2.14.2, 7.234.3). On such extended forms in tragedy see Wilamowitz on Eur. *Her.* 290, Pearson on S. frr. 249 and 1014, Diggle on Eur. *Pha.* 263 = fr. 781.54 *TrGF.* Alternatively the form might be derived from ἀπονίνημι, giving 'we will not profit in the long run': cf. Hom. *Od.* 11.324, 16.120, 17.293 οὐδ' ἀπόνητο.

1066–9 After the solemn appeal to the lightning of Zeus and Themis who lives in heaven, the chorus pleads for a message to descend into the depths of the earth. The whole universe, above and below, is enlisted in Electra's cause. Cf. the Aeschylean Electra's invocation of Hermes as κῆρυξ μέγιστε τῶν ἄνω τε καὶ κάτω (*Cho.* 165) in the prayer over her libations; also *Cho.* 315–23.

1066 χθονία: τὴν κατὰ γῆς χωρῆσαι δυναμένην (Σ p. 148.11 Papageorgius). For the passing of reports beneath the earth cf. Pind. *O.* 8.81–2 Ἑρμᾷ δὲ θυγατρὸς ἀκούσαις Ἰφίων | Ἀγγελίας, 14.20–1 μελαντειχέα νῦν δόμον | Φερσεφόνας ἔλθ᾽, Ἀχοῖ, πατρὶ κλυτὰν φέροισ᾽ ἀγγελίαν, *P.* 5.101 (βασιλέες ἱεροὶ) ἀκούοντί ποι χθονίᾳ φρενί, C. P. Segal (1985) = (1998) 133–48. Such messages in Pindar allow the dead to participate in the joy of the living (cf. Hom. *Od.* 11.538–40), whereas here the intention is quite otherwise.

βροτοῖσι: a dative of interest, giving 'Rumour who takes a message on behalf of mortals'. The alternative, that the word refers to the dead to whom the message is taken, is more difficult semantically, even given its extended use at 407.

Φάμα: for the personification cf. Hom. *Il.* 2.93–4 μετὰ δέ σφισιν Ὄσσα δεδήειν | ὀτρύνουσ᾽ ἰέναι, Διὸς ἄγγελος, *Od.* 24.413, West on Hes. *Op.* 764, Maehler on Bacchyl. 2.1, Pease on Virg. *Aen.*4.173, S. *OR* 157 ἄμβροτε Φάμα.

1067 κατά μοι βόασον: for tmesis with κατά cf. *OR* 1198, *Ant.* 977, Bruhn §63.4. For the ethic dative ('for me', and hence 'please') cf. 144, 1473.

1068 Ἀτρείδαις: referring to the house of Atreus in general, and Agamemnon in particular, as 1071 τέκνων indicates; cf. Aesch. *Cho.* 322.

1069 ἀχόρευτα φέρουσ' ὄνειδη: cf. Telestes fr. 805b *PMG* ἀλλὰ μάταν ἀχόρευτος ἅδε ματαιολόγων | φάμα προσέπταθ' Ἑλλάδα μουσοπόλων | σοφᾶς ἐπίφθονον βροτοῖς τέχνας ὄνειδος.

ἀχόρευτα: often in unpleasant or inauspicious contexts, especially death: cf. *OC* 1222, Aesch. *Suppl.* 681 (with Friis Johansen and Whittle), Eur. *Tro.* 121, West (1992) 13–14.

ὄνειδη: Jebb rightly prefers the interpretation 'the dishonours of the house'. Alternatively, the word could denote a reproach to the dead Agamemnon for his failure to intervene (see Garvie on Aesch. *Cho.* 495–6, West (1990) 244 for this usage): but the former makes better sense in the context, especially with ἀχόρευτα.

1070 σφίν: so Schaefer for the unmetrical σφίσιν, which shows the intrusion of the commoner word.

ἤδη: 'Hier gehört ἤδη der Stellung nach zu beiden Sätzen, bedeutet also "nun ist es dahin gekommen, dass"' (Kaibel, p. 236).

τὰ . . . ἐκ δόμων 'the fortunes of his house': for the construction see 137n.

†νοσεῖ†: the transmitted text is a syllable short. Erfurdt's νοσώδη is the best conjecture: νοσεῖ could have begun life as a gloss designed to explicate the verbless clause, as it does at Σ *Aj.* 334d (p. 96 Christodoulou). Coulon (1939) 2–4 supports νοσεῖται in Par. gr. 2794 (also printed by Ll-J/W and approved by R. J. Allan (2006) 115): for the corruption into νοσεῖ cf. 1124 (cited by Dawe, *STS* i. 192), Strab. 1.1.16 (= i. 20.13 Radt) μαρτυρεῖ<ται>. But the middle is improbable with this verb. Friis Johansen (1962) 210 also adopts νοσεῖται, but takes the verb as an impersonal passive, with τὰ . . . ἐκ δόμων as an accusative of respect. This is impossible, as Greek lacks an impersonal passive construction like the Latin *itur*. Triclinius's δή is awkward after ἤδη ('a clumsy makeshift': Kamerbeek (1972) 36).

1071 τὰ . . . πρὸς τέκνων: i.e. τὰ τέκνα, an accusative of respect; cf. *OR* 667, where τὰ πρὸς σφῷν = τὰ ὑμέτερα.

1071–2 διπλῆ φύ– | λοπις 'twofold strife' and hence 'the warring pair of sisters'. 'Es war eine Kühnheit das homerische Wort vom Wortstreit zweier Mädchen zu gebrauchen' (Kaibel, p. 237; cf. Σ Hom. *Il.* 6.1 c = ii. 129.11 Erbse).

1072–3 οὐκέτ' ἐξισοῦται | φιλοτασίῳ διαίτᾳ 'the strife between their children is no longer levelled out in loving life together' (Lloyd-Jones); 'is no longer equalised; i.e., cannot be resolved into harmony . . . in a friendly home-life'

430

(Jebb); cf. *DGE* s.v. δίαιτα I 1 'amorosa convivencia'. Alternative renderings are not as satisfactory. LSJ⁹ take διαίτᾳ (s.v. III 1) to mean 'by arbitration' (instrumental rather than a modal dative), but there is no prospect of an arbiter intervening in the sisters' quarrel; φιλοτασίῳ also becomes difficult to understand. Stokes (1979) 135 n. 6 tentatively suggests rendering ἐξισοῦται as 'is no longer equal (to a loving mode of life)': this is possible, but the sentiment is ponderous, and Jebb rightly rejects it as the less natural alternative.

1074 πρόδοτος: Electra has been betrayed by Chrysothemis, who did not fall in with her plan: a remarkably strong reading of the previous scene, which emphasises how much the chorus is now behind Electra.

μόνα: 119n.

σαλεύει: for the metaphor cf. *OR* 22–3 πόλις . . . | ἤδη σαλεύει, *Phil.* 271–2, Pl. *Leg.* 923b2–3 ἐν νόσοις ἢ γήρᾳ σαλεύοντας.

1075 ἁ παῖς, οἶτον: defences of the paradosis Ἡλέκτρα τόν have taken two forms. (i) στεναγμόν has been understood as the cognate object of στενάχουσ', with πατρός dependent on it (so Haupt (1865b) 6–7 = (1875–6) ii. 301, Wilamowitz on Eur. *Her.* 681, Kaibel (p. 237), Bruhn). But the alleged parallels for the ellipse are not convincing: in εἰ μὴ νεναυμάχηκε τὴν περὶ τῶν κρεῶν (Ar. *Ran.*191), or τὸν περὶ ψυχῆς τρέχειν (Liban. *Decl.* 43 part 2 ch. 43), 'nouns like μάχην and δρόμον come to mind far more readily than any noun would come here' (Ll-J/W, *Sophoclea*). For further examples, none comparable to the ellipse postulated here, see K–G ii. 558–9. (ii) πατρὸς . . . στενάχουσ' has been taken to mean 'mourning for her father' (cf. Σ p. 149.1 Papageorgius λείπει ἡ περί), with τὸν ἀεί equivalent to τὸν ἀεὶ χρόνον. The former would be an unusual, though possible, construction (cf. Eur. *IA* 370 Ἑλλάδος μάλιστ' ἔγωγε τῆς ταλαιπώρου στένω, S–D ii. 133 4aα); the latter, however, is not possible Greek.

Emendation is thus required. Pearson conjectured Ἡλέκτρα, τό γ' ἀεὶ πάρος; but while this involves only a small change, it gives appallingly weak sense. Our suspicions should rather be directed at Ἡλέκτρα: after all, proper names are often interpolated (957n.). ἁ παῖς, οἶ(τον), though not certain, solves our difficulties. It provides us with the alternative designation for Electra which we require, and nicely supplies an accusative noun to follow στενάχουσ' without forcing us to emend the article. οἶτος is a common epic word, but rare in tragedy: it occurs elsewhere at 167, *Ant.* 859 πατρὸς τριπολίστου οἶτον (Kᵖᶜ; corrupted to οἶκτον in most manuscripts), Eur. *IT* 1091. It is certainly preferable to Günther's recent attempt ἅδε κῆρά τ' ἀεὶ κτλ. ((1996) 114), where the τ' is ungrammatical.

The conjecture is regularly ascribed to B. Heath, yet it does not appear in his note on this passage ((1762) 21). He rather reports and commends the emendation of his friend the Rev. Zachariah Mudge (1694–1769), prebendary of Exeter and vicar of St. Andrew's church, Plymouth, who conjectured Ἠλέκτρ' οἶτον ἀεὶ πατρός (which involves an impossible elision). Schneidewin conjectured ἁ παῖς in his first edition.[66]

1076 στενάχουσ': for the e-vocalism and accent see 133n.; for this verb in connexion with the nightingale see 147n.

1077 πάνδυρτος: so Erfurdt and Porson (1812) 211 for paradosis πανόδ–: the same mistake occurs in the transmission in the other occurrences of the word (Aesch. *Pers.* 941, 944, Eur. *Hec.* 212). πανόδ– first occurs in Meleager (*A.P.* 7.476.9 = 4290 *HE*, where see Gow and Page). Compare the substitution of ὀδυρομένα for δυρομένα at Eur. *Med.* 158, where the latter is metrically guaranteed (see Page on 159).

ἀηδών: cf. 107n., 147–9.

1078–9 For the repetition of one idea and the negation of its opposite see 131–2n.

1078 προμηθής: 990n.

1079 τό . . . μὴ βλέπειν ἑτοίμα: for the motif 'when I have gained my object let me die content' see Garvie and Sier on Aesch. *Cho.* 438. In this instance the sense is more pointed, as Electra's death is indeed a likely outcome of her plan.

βλέπειν: for this verb used as an antithesis to θνῄσκω cf. *Aj.* 1067–8, Eur. fr. 370.20 *TrGF* = 65.20 Austin; for the article see 1030n. For sight as a metaphor for life see 66n.

1080 διδύμαν ἑλοῦσ' Ἐρινύν: meaning Aegisthus and Clytemnestra, just as 206 διδύμαιν χειροῖν suggests the twin assassins. For human agents designated as Erinyes cf. Aesch. *Ag.* 749 νυμφόκλαυτος Ἐρινύς, Eur. *Med.* 1259–60, *Tro.* 457 (where Cassandra designates herself as 'one of the three Erinyes', the other two being Aegisthus and Clytemnestra: cf. Diggle (1981a) 62), Enn. *Alaxander* 49 Jocelyn *quo iudicio Lacedaemonia mulier Furiarum una adveniet*, perhaps going back to a Euripidean original (see Jocelyn on 45–6), Virg. *Aen.* 2.[573] (Helen); also Aesch. *Ag.* 1500–3, where Clytemnestra claims an association with the παλαιὸς δριμὺς ἀλάστωρ of the house. For the participle ('overcome') see 957n.

---

[66] Some related errors of attribution can be found in recent editions. In Heath's note on *Phil.* 29 ((1762) 82) there is no reference to a conjecture 'στ' by Mudge. Again, at *Ant.* 613 the ἕρπειν usually attributed to Heath is not found in his note *ad loc.* ((1762) 48); it should instead be transferred to Reiske ((1753) 27).

1081 ἄν: Triclinius correctly deleted the following οὖν to restore responsion (cf. 855n.).

εὐπατρις: now that Orestes is thought dead, Electra as it were receives her brother's epithet (162, 858): cf. Winnington-Ingram (1980) 245 n. 91, Burton (1980) 210–11.

1082–4 For the sentiment see 989n.

1082 <—>: the metrical gap could be filled by any number of words. γάρ (Hermann, adopted by Jebb) is a possibility, though its position would be unexpectedly late; so too is Lange's τοι (⟨1859⟩ 19). Ll-J/W prefer Schneidewin's ἄν (printed in his first edition), but this necessitates the further change of θέλει to θέλοι in 1083. Ll-J/W claim that Orion *Flor.* 7.11 (a mistake for 7.12, = p. 105.8–9 Haffner) reads θέλοι, but in fact the manuscript is ambiguous between –ει and –οι (see Haffner's edition, p. 217). Pearson and Dawe do not print a lacuna here, preferring instead to emend in the antistrophe: however, their interference in the text there is rather greater than the simple interventions by other editors here (1091 n.).

1083 θέλει: see previous n.

1084 ὦ παῖ παῖ: consolatory and encouraging, as at *Ant.* 948.

1085–6 πάγκλαυτον αἰ– | ῶνα †κοινόν εἵλου†: the first two words of this phrase denote the life of lamentation which Electra has chosen in response to the killing of her father (so Lange (1859) 21–2, Most (1994) 137–8, Ll-J/W, *Second Thoughts*). Erfurdt (his edition, p. 468), Hermann, Jebb and Kells believe that it refers to Electra's death, which will inevitably result from her plan to kill Aegisthus. Electra is indeed ready to die in effecting her plan (1079–80), but that is different from choosing death. πάγκλαυτος is also an odd adjective to choose to qualify αἰών if the latter means 'death'. Contrast Eur. *Phoen.* 1484 σκοτίαν αἰῶνα and *IA* 1507–8 ἕτερον αἰ– | ῶνα καὶ μοῖραν οἰκήσομεν, where the adjectives make it clear that αἰών has this unusual sense.

κοινόν presents more serious problems. Lamentation and grief are often said to be shared (cf. *Aj.* 267 κοινὸς ἐν κοινοῖσι λυπεῖσθαι ξυνών, Seaford (1985) 316 n. 12), but in our case there is no indication of who shares Electra's suffering. It can hardly be Chrysothemis (*pace* Stokes (1979) 140, Most (1994) 138): she has not been conspicuous in standing up for her dead father, as she herself has tacitly admitted and as the chorus has noted in this ode. Nor are Jebb and Seaford right to see a reference to the dead Agamemnon: for while αἰών can refer to existence in the world of the living or of the dead, it is harsh for it to refer to both at once. Besides this semantic difficulty, the emphasis on Electra's *shared* grief jars with the stress on the loneliness of her stance in 1074. We rather need an adjective which commends the choice of αἰών which Electra has made. Lange suggests ἄοικον ((1859) 23–4), and West ἀμείνον᾽ ((1979) 104–5), but Sirks's κλεινόν ((1861) 129) gives better sense while giving an easier corruption. Wecklein posited the same corruption at *Ant*. 1, and Elmsley at *OC* 379, while Thomas Magister read κοινόν for κλεινόν at 681 (n.).

But the problem of this phrase does not end there. αἰῶνα must refer to Electra's previous life of lamentation, and so εἵλου in this context can only refer to Electra's decision to adopt such a life after the killing of her father, now some years ago. Yet the chorus has not been praising Electra for that decision, but rather for her new bold initiative against her father's killer. So too the text immediately after this phrase, for all its difficulties, must refer to Electra's recent decision to take action against Aegisthus. There we have an aorist participle in coordination with the verb εἵλου, which means that the verb ought to denote some action either contemporary with or subsequent to the participle. This is not possible if it refers to Electra's original choice of a life of mourning. Hence we have a difficulty every bit as urgent as that involving τὸ μή in the following line, yet one which scholars have tended to neglect in favour of the latter: Winnington-Ingram (1979) 9–10 and Most (1994) 137–8 are notable exceptions. Most suggests that instead of εἵλου we need a verb meaning 'reject', such as ἀρνῇ: Electra's decision to take action against Aegisthus thus implies the rejection of her former state of mourning. This fits with her description of the celebrations which will be consequent on its completion (977–83). This would give good sense, but the corruption cannot be explained, and Most does well to obelise εἵλου rather than admit a conjecture to the text. I extend the obeli to include κοινόν, where Most is too sanguine in claiming that the reference is to grief shared with Chrysothemis.

Only LTTa have πάγκλαυτον without the sigma (on which see West's Teubner Aeschylus, p. xliii).

1087–8 †τὸ μή† καλὸν καθοπλίσα– | σα: the problems of this phrase and the attempts to solve them have been set out with exemplary clarity and acumen by Most (1994). The phrase appears to mean 'having armed, equipped what is not noble'. The only conceivable referent for 'what is not noble' is the matricide, and the phrase is so interpreted by Hermann, Stinton (1986) 83 = (1990) 478 and MacLeod (2001) 150–2. But μή rather than οὐ as the negative makes this difficult: 'the phrase is too abstract and general for a precise reference to a single deed' (Most (1994) 131 n. 13). Contrast *Ant*. 370–1 ἄπολις ὅτῳ τὸ μὴ καλὸν | ξύνεστι τόλμας χάριν, where the same phrase is used with the expected non-specific reference.

Various contextual difficulties accompany this linguistic problem. The chorus's attitude to Electra elsewhere in this ode is unreservedly positive. She is warmly commended for her daring plan, which indicates the extent of her piety towards her father; Chrysothemis, by contrast, is implicitly condemned for failing to go along with the scheme. It would thus make no sense for the chorus here to criticise the plan as something 'not noble'. Furthermore, those who take the words in this sense assume that the chorus is describing the matricide rather than the killing of Aegisthus. Yet as we have seen, matricide does not form a part of Electra's plan (957n.). A reference to it here would thus be completely unexpected.

These problems have led scholars to reconsider the meaning of καθο-πλίσασα, or else to emend it away. This approach begins in the scholia, where the phrase is taken to mean καταπολεμήσασα τὸ αἰσχρὸν καὶ νικήσασα (p. 149.23 Papageorgius). Stinton (1965) 146 n. 1 = (1990) 15 n. 10 mentions a proposal of D. S. Colman's to take the verb in the sense 'trampling on', as if it were derived from ὁπλή rather than ὅπλον. But elsewhere the verb means 'arm' or 'equip' (cf. the metaphorical uses at Aesch. *Suppl.* 682, 702), never 'conquer'; the sense advocated by Colman would require the emendation καθο-πλάσασα, a verb elsewhere unattested. We may reasonably suspect that the scholiast is supplying a meaning which he feels that the sense demands, rather than an accurate interpretation of the verb based on independent evidence. ὑπεροπλίσασα (*coni.* Heimsoeth (1865) 359–60, (1872a) iii) does not offer a different meaning from that of the transmitted verb. Others have changed the verb to something meaning 'reject' or 'spurn'. But it is not clear how καθοπλίσασα then got into the text: there is no obvious palaeographical explanation, and it is hardly a glossator's word. Chrysothemis' metaphorical use of the verb ὁπλίζομαι at 996 should rather protect the participle here (so Stokes (1979) 142).

τὸ μή has also been the subject of scrutiny. Kells emended to τὸ μὴ καλόν to τὰ μὴ κάλ᾽ οὐ: but the double negative is ugly, and Lloyd-Jones (1975) 11 rightly dismissed it as flat. Lloyd-Jones (1954) 95 = (1990a) i. 366–7 himself proposes ἄκος, claiming that τομήν was written in as a gloss, given the common notion of the ἄκος τομαῖον (Aesch. *Cho.* 539; cf. *Suppl.* 268, *Ag.* 17, S. *Aj.* 581–2, Eur. *Andr.* 121). This subsequently ousted ἄκος and was reinterpreted as τὸ μή. But τομήν is an odd word to find as a gloss on ἄκος, despite the familiarity of the idea of the ἄκος τομαῖον. Nor is it clear that a bare ἄκος could mean 'cutting remedy' as Lloyd-Jones requires: for 'in none of the parallels cited in support of this conjecture is a word for cutting missing from the text' (Most (1994) 134; see further his discussion).

Most's preferred solution is not to emend at all, but to reinterpret the paradosis as τομῇ, the accusative of the noun τομεύς (with –έα: contracting to give –ῇ: cf. K–B i. 449 Anm. 4), denoting not the person, but the thing which performs the action of cutting. There are similar problems in the tradition at Aesch. *Cho.* 230, where Turnebus's τομῇ must be printed instead of the –το μή found in the manuscript. This too is unsatisfactory. The physical 'chopper' jars with the surrounding context, which is dominated by abstract and intangible nouns. It also removes the metaphorical force from καθοπλίσασα.

Despite the lack of success of their own ingenious conjectures, Most and Ll-J/W are right against Jebb and Dawe in locating the problem in τὸ μή, not in καθοπλίσασα. We need a word denoting Electra's plan, or her state of mind in conceiving this plan. But the actual word which was lost, or why it was replaced by τὸ μή, remains unclear. The difficulties with κοινόν and εἵλου as described above mean that a full six consecutive syllables are probably corrupt. Our chances of recovering the original text without fresh evidence are therefore slight.[67]

1088–9 δύο φέρειν <ἐν> ἑνὶ λόγῳ, | σοφά τ᾿ ἀρίστα τε παῖς κεκλῆσθαι: cf. *Phil.* 117–19 ὡς τοῦτό γ᾿ ἔρξας δύο φέρῃ δωρήματα | . . . | σοφός τ᾿ ἂν αὐτὸς κἀγαθὸς κεκλῇ᾿ ἅμα. For the substantival use of δύο see Lloyd-Jones on Semon. fr. 7.27 *IEG.* φέρειν is final; for the active see 692n.

1088 <ἐν> ἑνὶ λόγῳ: Brunck's supplement (in his 1779 edition) restores the metre: fewer corruptions could be easier (either through haplography or the misreading of ἑνί as ἐνί). For the sense cf. *OC* 1655 ἐν ταὐτῷ λόγῳ (where Ll-J/W unnecessarily adopt Blaydes's χρόνῳ).

1089 κεκλῆσθαι: 230n.

1090–2 On the form of the expression cf. Hom. *Il.* 16.722 αἴθ᾿, ὅσον ἥσσων εἰμί, τόσον σέο φέρτερος εἴην; also 286.

1090 καθύπερθεν: for the figurative sense cf. Theogn. 679 κακοὶ δ᾿ ἀγαθῶν καθύπερθεν, Pind. *P.* 9.31 a μόχθου καθύπερθε. The original ablatival sense of this word has almost entirely disappeared in surviving Greek (cf. Lejeune (1939) 342–3).

1091 As transmitted 1082–3 and 1090–1 do not correspond. Changing τῶν to τεῶν, along with adding a syllable after ἀγαθῶν in 1082, is the easiest solution. τεός is not common in tragedy, occurring only at *Ant.* 604, Aesch. *Sept.* 105 and [Aesch.] *PV* 163 (all lyric); there are no secure Euripidean instances (cf. Page on Eur. *Med.* 1255). Given its rarity, τεῶν before ἐχθρῶν was almost bound to be corrupted into the definite article. Pearson and Dawe prefer to keep 1082–3 and τῶν as transmitted, changing instead the beginning of 1091 to give the

---

[67] The above discussion does not attempt to discuss or even to mention every proposal made on these lines: those seeking fuller information should consult Most's article.

metre ∪ – – – ∪ – – – ∪ –. Pearson prints χερὶ πλούτῳ τε, but the long syllable –ί πλ– is prosodically doubtful (853n.); Dawe's conjecture χεροῖν overcomes this difficulty. However, the only manuscript support for τε here instead of καί comes in Triclinius, and so that is better treated as a conjecture than as independent evidence. The printed text involves less serious changes, and should therefore be preferred.

Ll-J/W (*Sophoclea*) express concern over the combination of χε(ι)ρί with πλούτῳ, which they say 'has the effect of a somewhat harsh zeugma'. However, *Aj.* 129–30 μηδ' ὄγκον ἄρῃ μηδέν', εἴ τινος πλέον | ἢ χειρὶ βρίθεις ἢ μακροῦ πλούτου βάθει provides a parallel close enough to protect the paradosis. The stress on material prosperity is idiomatic in the context (cf. 72n.).

1093 ἐφηύρηκα: with accusative participle, as at Hom. *Od.* 2.109, Eur. *Tro.* 957–8, S–D ii. 394 §6. Dindorf⁴ restored the long diphthong (cf. 1235, 1352): forms in ευ– in related verbs only begin to appear in inscriptions at the end of the fourth century (cf. Lautensach (1899) 47–9, Threatte i. 385, ii. 482–3).

1093–4 μοί– | ρᾳ . . . ἐν ἐσθλᾷ βεβῶσαν: for the participle cf. 979n., *OC* 1358–9 ὅτ' ἐν πόνῳ | ταὐτῷ βεβηκὼς τυγχάνεις κακῶν ἐμοί. ἐν is corrupted to ἐπ' in some manuscripts (cf. 1246).

1095–6 ἃ . . . μέγιστ' ἔβλα– | στε νόμιμα: cf. *Ant.* 454–5 ἄγραπτα κἀσφαλῆ θεῶν | νόμιμα, *OR* 865–6 νόμοι . . . | ὑψίποδες, Arist. *Rhet.* 1373b1–18, Pl. *Leg.* 7.793a-d, Xen. *Mem.* 4.4.19–20. Contrast the νόμοι of Chrysothemis by which Electra does not want to live (1043).

1096 τῶνδε: causal, referring to the νόμιμα ('winning the greatest praise because of them').

1097 τᾷ Ζηνὸς εὐσεβείᾳ: piety towards the gods is elsewhere associated with piety towards one's parents: cf. Eur. fr. 853.2 *TrGF* θεούς τε τιμᾶν τούς τε φύσαντας γονῆς, Pl. *Leg.* 931 de. For Zeus's association with εὐσέβεια cf. *Phil.* 1441–3; for the objective genitive cf. *OR* 239 θεῶν εὐχαῖσι. Only LʸᵖTTa have the form of the genitive that fits the metre. The corruption into the more common Διός is a frequent error: cf. *Tr.* 956, perhaps *Ant.* 1149, perhaps Hom. *Il.* 14.173 (cf. West (2001) 227, West (1984) 183, Diggle (1991) 62).

FOURTH EPISODE, PART ONE (1098–1231)

1098–1125 After the giddy but unsustainable excitement of Chrysothemis' entry, this new arrival seems to take us back to the world of the second episode and the Paedagogus. A character known to the audience, but unrecognised

437

by either the chorus or Electra, enters from eisodos B. He asks the chorus if he has come to the house of Aegisthus (1098–9, 1101; cf. 660–1). After a further question (1103–4; cf. 663–4), he begins to speak to a female character on the stage (1106–7; cf. 666–7). It becomes clear that he is on a mission from Phocis connected with the recent death of Orestes (1110–11 etc.; cf. 673 etc.). But despite these correspondences, this episode will end not by confirming the Paedagogus' message, but by overturning it. What begins as a replay turns out to be a reversal. Since the audience recognises Orestes from his appearance in the prologue, this development does not come as a surprise. The dramatic effect rather arises from our tense anticipation of when and how the good news will eventually be broken to the heroine.

Orestes does not recognise Electra until after her speech of lamentation. Jebb (on 1106) claims that he does, pointing to his recognition of Electra's voice in the prologue (80–1), as well as to line 1125. But if Orestes guessed that a distressed female voice coming from inside the palace might be that of his sister, it does not follow that he will recognise her in person. As his later reaction makes clear, he could never have imagined that his sister had been reduced to loitering outside her home in a state of such physical squalor (cf. 1174–5 etc., Solmsen (1967) 54–5 = (1968–82) iii. 55–6, Ov. *Epist. Pont.* 1.4.5–6). Nor does 1125 hint at an early recognition. Electra's grief at the death of Orestes is so marked that he begins to speculate that she must be connected to him, perhaps by blood. Electra herself speculates in the same way at 1202, as she searches for an explanation for the surprising intensity of the stranger's grief. In each case the irony is felt by the audience, though missed by the speaker. The prolonged encounter between two characters neither of whom recognises the other, despite the closeness of their relationship, is a common technique in Euripidean recognition-plots (cf. *IT* 467–768, *Ion* 1261–1319, *Hel.* 546–64). Its transfer to the Orestes–Electra recognition seems to be S.'s innovation, as it is not found in Aeschylus' or Euripides' accounts. The suspense and irony to which it gives rise are as uncomplicated as they are affecting. Or as Bain puts it, 'what we have is something much simpler and grander than the elaborate pretence envisaged by Jebb' ((1977) 79).

The sight of the urn brings Electra to a new low of grief (1108–9, 1112, 1115–16). Orestes, meanwhile, avoids all signs of emotional involvement in order to imitate the expected ἦθος of a messenger. His behaviour recalls that of his Aeschylean counterpart when he brings news of his own death to Clytemnestra (*Cho.* 668–718). But there Orestes is well aware of the identity of his addressee and the threat which she poses to him. In our play he does not know the woman before him: and while his course is the only safe one in the situation, its sole effect is to prolong the pain of his sister.

Illustrations on a Lucanian bell-crater attributed to the Sydney painter (*LCS* 128.650; Vienna Kunsthistorisches Museum IV 689; 360–40 BC) and a Lucanian hydria attributed to the Brooklyn-Budapest painter (*LCS* Suppl. iii. 70.43; London BM F92; 400–380 BC) may show the influence of this scene in West Greek art (cf. Kossatz-Deissmann (1978) 95). It may also occur on a Tarentine grave relief (The Hague 1589; cf. Klumbach (1937) 15.63).

1098 Enter Orestes and at least two attendants from eisodos B. One of the attendants is carrying an urn. Their arrival was anticipated by the Paedagogus in his speech (757–60). For the opening question to the chorus cf. 66on. For Orestes' politeness in his opening utterances see M. A. Lloyd (2006) 236–8.
ὦ γυναῖκες: 254n.

1098–9 ὀρθὰ . . . | ὀρθῶς: for the combination cf. Pl. *Leg.* 897b2.

1099 θ᾽: so Triclinius for transmitted δ᾽. According to Denniston 513, the combination τε . . . δέ is found when 'the idea of contrast is added to the original idea of addition' (cf. also Pearson (1930) 162). Here there is no such contrast which could justify the retention of the paradosis. The corruption is common (cf. 421–2n.). For corresponsive τε . . . τε with anaphora (ὀρθὰ . . . | ὀρθῶς) see Friis Johansen and Whittle on Aesch. *Suppl.* 219.

1100 τί δ᾽: Dawe's τίν᾽ (*STS* i. 193) gives a slightly better connexion with the naming of Aegisthus in Orestes' response, and at the cost of a trivial emendation. But the change makes the connexion with the preceding lines correspondingly worse, as up to now Orestes has only said that he is looking for a place, not a person. The paradosis should stand.

1101 ᾤκηκεν '"has fixed his abode" – a light touch of dramatic irony, since his tenure of it is so nearly at an end' (Jebb, comparing Pl. *Leg.* 666e2, where those ἐν ἄστεσι κατῳκηκότων are opposed to nomads). The perfect of οἰκέω is rare, but there is some support for the sense of fixity implied in Jebb's note. At *OC* 1258–9 ὁ δυσφιλὴς | γέρων γέροντι συγκατῴκηκεν πίνος (Scaliger; πόνος codd.) such a meaning would add to the pathos; cf. perhaps also Eur. fr. 955h.1 *TrGF*, Dem. 29.3. Orestes may also use such phrasing because 'he does not want to imply that the house belongs to Aegisthus' (M. A. Lloyd (2006) 238).
ἱστορῶ: the variant μαστεύω may have come about through anticipation of 1107, or else by the elevation of a gloss (cf. Hesych. ι 654, μ 396, 403 = ii. 364, 633, 633 Latte).
For πάλαι of recent time see 676n.

1102 For the choral confirmation cf. 662. Given the true identity of the new arrival and the man who guided him to the house, the chorus's remark is truer than it realises.

ἀλλ' εὖ θ' ἱκάνεις: cf. *Tr.* 229 ἀλλ' εὖ μὲν ἵγμεθ'. For assentient ἀλλά see Denniston 18 II (b).

1103–4 For Orestes' request cf. *OC* 70 ἆρ' ἄν τις αὐτῷ πομπὸς ἐξ ὑμῶν μόλοι;

1103 ἄν . . . ἄν: 333–4n.

1104 ποθεινήν 'desired' by Clytemnestra and Aegisthus. Orestes adopts the ἦθος of a messenger by stressing that he brings good news (cf. 666–7 λόγους | ἡδεῖς), despite his having been sent by an enemy of the usurpers (45n.). For ποθεινός of a new arrival cf. Eur. *IT* 515 καὶ μὴν ποθεινός γ' ἦλθες ἐξ Ἄργους μολών, *Hel.* [540] ὡς ποθεινὸς ἄν μόλοις. Campbell argues that the word has an active sense, but this is rarer (cf. Mastronarde on Eur. *Phoen.* 1737) and not natural here.

κοινόπουν παρουσίαν: P's κοινόπλουν is probably a reminiscence of *Aj.* 872 κοινόπλουν ὁμιλίαν. On such periphrases see Bruhn §244.V.3.

1105 τὸν ἄγχιστον 'nearest of kin' to Aegisthus and Clytemnestra: cf. *Ant.* 174 γένους κατ' ἀγχιστεῖα τῶν ὀλωλότων, Eur. *Tro.* 48 τὸν γένει . . . ἄγχιστον πατρός, Hesych. α 908 (= i. 34 Latte) ἄγχιστον· ἔγγιστον γένους. Again, the chorus speaks more truly than it realises: Electra is also ἀγχίστη to the man it is addressing. The alternative, 'nearest of those on stage to the *skene*', is banal. The masculine is used because of the general principle involved (771n.).

γε: emphasising the preceding τὸν ἄγχιστον: see Wakker (1994) 309.

1106 For ἴθ' in entreaties cf. *OR* 46–7, *Phil.* 480.

ὦ γύναι: the regular, neutral form of address for an unknown woman: cf. Dickey (1996) 86–8.

1107 Φωκῆς: Proto-Greek *-e:w-es* > –ῆες (Homer) > ῆς (Attic). From the earliest texts in the Ionian alphabet (late fifth century) to *c.* 350 –ΗΣ predominates in Attic inscriptions (cf. Threatte ii. 239–41). After that the usual form is –ΕΙΣ. Before 403/2 –ΕΣ in the old Attic alphabet could represent either –εῖς or –ῆς. This evidence strongly suggests that –ῆς should be printed here. Only L has the correct spelling: cf. e.g. Aesch. *Pers.* 24, 44, *Ag.* 230.

ματεύουσ': in addition to the basic sense 'look for', the verb also has connotations of hunting and pursuit which are appropriate in the context: cf. Aesch. *Cho.* 892 σὲ καὶ ματεύω (Orestes to Clytemnestra), *Ag.* 1094, *Eum.* 247, S. fr. 314.19 *TrGF*, van de Wijnpersse (1929) 81. The asigmatic form is metrically guaranteed (cf. *OR* 1052, 1061), though it is not always so in tragedy (cf. Fraenkel on Aesch. *Ag.* 1099, Garvie on Aesch. *Cho.* 219, Mastronarde on Eur. *Phoen.* 36).

1108 οὐ δή ποθ': οὐ δή followed by που or ποτε introduces a surprised or incredulous question which anticipates the likely answer ('you don't mean...?'): cf. 1180, 1202, *Tr.* 876 οὐ δή ποθ' ὡς θανοῦσα;, Denniston 223 (ii) (though he is wrong to confine the usage to Sophocles: Kamerbeek (1972) 37 adds Hdt. 9.111.5, where Rosén, though not Hude, rightly retains the paradosis). The minority variant ἦ δή ποθ' is not found elsewhere.

1109 φήμης: often interchangeable with κληδών (1110): cf. Hdt. 5.72.2–4, 9.101.2–3, Philochorus *FGrHist* 328 F 192, Plut. *Camil.* 30.4, Lucian 24.26, Σ Aesch. *Cho.* 505a (= i. 28.14 Smith), Hesych. ε 1027 (= ii. 33 Latte), Suda κ 1770 (= iii. 132.17 Adler).

ἐμφανῆ τεκμήρια: echoing Clytemnestra's description of the Paedagogus as πίστ' ἔχων τεκμήρια (774). On τεκμήριον see 904n.

1110–11 For Strophius see 45n. At Aesch. *Cho.* 677–87 the disguised Orestes describes how Strophius met him by chance as he was on his way to Argos, and told him to announce the death of Orestes there. Here Orestes presents himself as carrying out actual orders from Strophius (cf. 1111 ἐφεῖτο).

1110 οὐκ οἶδα τὴν σὴν κληδόν' 'the report of which you speak': cf. *Aj.* 792 οὐκ οἶδα τὴν σὴν πρᾶξιν, fr. 165.1 *TrGF, Ant.* 573 (with Davies (1986b) 21–2), *Phil.* 1251, [Eur.] *Rhes.* 866, Eur. *Hipp.* 113, Bruhn §80. Orestes' feigned ignorance of the Paedagogus' story means that 'the evidence appears to flow through two channels, which are independent of each other' (Campbell) and hence is all the more credible. For κληδών see 1109n.

1111 Στροφίος: for the accentuation see Fraenkel on Aesch. *Ag.* 881.

1112 ὦ ξέν': 662n.

ὥς μ' ὑπέρχεται φόβος: cf. *Phil.* 1231 ὥς μ' ὑπῆλθέ τις φόβος, 928n.

1113–14 Cf. Aesch. *Ag.* 434–6 ἀντὶ δὲ φωτῶν | τεύχη καὶ σποδὸς εἰς ἑκάσ– | του δόμους ἀφικνεῖται. For the *topos* 'small remains in a small container' cf. 1142, Thallus *A.P.* 7.373.3–4 = 3430–1 *GP* λείψανα δ' αἰαῖ | ἔδρακες ἐν βαιῇ κάλπιδι κευθόμενα. Contrast the *topos* of 758 (n.).

1113 σμικρά: μικρός does not appear in Attic inscriptions until near the end of the fifth century and becomes the commoner form in the fourth (Threatte i. 507–10). There are metrically guaranteed instances of each in

Sophocles and Euripides, though they appear to prefer the sigmatic form (cf. Wecklein (1869b) 54–5, Diggle (1975b) 289–90 = (1994) 145–6).

1114 ὡς ὁρᾷς, κομίζομεν: cf. Eur. *Ba.* 1238–9 φέρω δ᾽ ἐν ὠλέναισιν, ὡς ὁρᾷς, τάδε | λαβοῦσα τὰριστεῖα.

1115 οἲ γώ: 674n.

τοῦτ᾽ ἐκεῖν᾽, ἤδη σαφές· So Kamerbeek and Ll-J/W. τοῦτ᾽ ἐκεῖν᾽ as an independent sense-unit is a colloquialism (cf. Dover (1970) 22–3 ≈ (1987a) 235–6 ≈ Newiger (1975) 141–3, Stevens (1976) 31–2, Willink on Eur. *Or.* 804); here it conveys Electra's sorrow as she sees the urn containing her brother's ashes (cf. Waś (1983) 216). Arist. *Poet.* 1448b 17 cites οὗτος ἐκεῖνος as a formula of recognition. For ἤδη σαφές as a sense-unit cf. δῆλον in fr. 585.1 *TrGF* ἀλγεινά, Πρόκνη, δῆλον, *Aj.* 906, probably *OC* 321. The staccato phrasing followed by asyndeton in 1116 is also expressive of powerful emotion (cf. 924–5, 1151–3).

Printing no punctuation, Jebb takes σαφές as adverbial with δέρκομαι. But the consequent hyperbaton is confusing: by contrast in *Tr.* 223–4, cited as a parallel by Jebb, the syntax is clear. His translation of τοῦτ᾽ as 'there' is also dubious. Punctuating after ἐκεῖν᾽ alone is more plausible: however, it removes the expressive power of the phrasing mentioned above.

For certainty about an impending evil cf. *OR* 1182, Aesch. *Sept.* 848, Eur. *Suppl.* 792–3 νῦν δ᾽ ὁρῶ σαφέστατον | κακόν, Schauer (2002) 229.

1116 πρόχειρον: *quod praesens adest, quasi in manus sumendum* (Ellendt s.v.) is probably better than 'held in the hand' (Campbell); however, Prop. 4.11.14 *en sum quod digitis quinque legatur onus* may support the latter. On the formation see Fraenkel on Aesch. *Ag.* 1651.

ὡς ἔοικε: not a mark of scepticism: cf. 765n.

1117 εἴπερ τι κλαίεις: the audience will appreciate the understatement, marked by the τι.

τῶν Ὀρεστείων κακῶν: the adjectival form instead of a genitive is used in a variety of contexts in tragedy: cf. *OR* 450–1 φόνον | τὸν Λάϊειον, Moorhouse 164, Wackernagel (1926–8) ii. 68–75, Bühler's edition of Zenobius, vol. iv. p. 94. In this case it is possible that a contrast is felt between this essentially poetic usage and the colloquial language of Electra's preceding words. If the latter conveys Electra's emotional reaction to the sight of the urn (1115n.), the former might express the absence of such a reaction in Orestes.

1118 ἄγγος: common in Ionic prose and poetry, but restricted to tragedy in Attic (cf. Rutherford's ed. of Phrynichus, p. 23).

COMMENTARY: 1098–1231

1119 ὦ ξεῖνε: 662n.

εἴπερ: as at 774 (n.), marking what the speaker regards as a self-evident truth, although the audience knows it is not the case.

1120 κέκευθεν: for the perfect of κεύθω used in a transitive sense cf. Aesch. *Cho.* 686–7 λέβητος χαλκέου πλευρώματα | σποδὸν κέκευθεν ἀνδρὸς εὖ κεκλαυμένου, Hom. *Il.* 22.118, *Od.* 3.18, 9.348, [Simon.] *ap.* Thuc. 6.59.2 = 787 *FGE* with Page, Eur. *Hec.* 880, *IA* 112.

1122 κλαύσω κἀποδύρωμαι: for the combination cf. [Aesch.] *PV* 637 ὡς τἀποκλαῦσαι κἀποδύρασθαι τύχας, Plut. *De cohib. ira* 455c, Suda o 206 (= iii. 520.22 Adler) ὀλοφύρεται· ἀποδύρεται, κλαίει; also Hom. *Il.* 24.48, *Od.* 8.577, Aesch. *Sept.* 656, Hdt. 3.119.3, Pl. *Resp.* 388b3.

1123 ἥτις ἐστί 'whoever she is'. ὅστις can have as its antecedent a definite, unnamed individual (cf. Moorhouse 264). But in none of the examples cited by Moorhouse is the individual referred to on stage at the time. This distancing accentuates the pathos (cf. Σ p. 150.18–19 Papageorgius). For the omission of the dative after δόθ' cf. *Ant.* 35–6, Ar. *Pax* 371, Bruhn §92.II, Monteil (1963) 131–3.

1123–4 οὐ γὰρ ὡς | ἐν δυσμενείᾳ γ' οὖσ' ἐπαιτεῖται τόδε: 'friends of Strophius might have reason to suppose those about Aegisthus of being unfriendly to Orestes' (Campbell). Orestes acts every detail of the ἦθος which he has assumed.

1124 ἐν δυσμενείᾳ γ' οὖσ': i.e. δυσμενής: cf. Moorhouse 106.
ἐπαιτεῖται: apart from Heracl. D–K 22 B 58 (= i. 163.12) the middle is not found elsewhere.

1125 πρὸς αἵματος: cf. *Aj.* 1305 τοὺς πρὸς αἵματος, Tr. Adesp. fr. 384 *TrGF*.

1126–70 In the second episode the news of Orestes' death reduced Electra to a mournful and bitter silence. Here it provokes her to one of the most memorable statements of sorrow in extant Greek literature, taken by later rhetorical theorists as a model of speech creating ἔλεος (cf. Griffin (1999b) 81 n. 30). But at a time when Euripides was making increased use of actor's monody to convey intense grief on the part of his female characters (cf. Beverley (1997)), S. here reminds his audience of the emotional potential of a lament in plain iambic trimeters. The speech shows its closest correspondences with another great spoken lament, that of the Nurse at Aesch. *Cho.* 734–65. The Nurse has been asked to take the news of Orestes' death to Aegisthus (*Cho.*

443

734–7, 764–5; cf. 1106–7). Unaware that the news is false, she laments his death in a moving speech. She recalls how she had looked after him as a baby (*Cho.* 749–62; cf. 1143–8): all the hard work that this involved (*Cho.* 752–3; cf. 1145) has been to no avail (*Cho.* 752; cf. 1144). His death has come as the crowning sorrow to a long-suffering house (*Cho.* 744–7; cf. 1151–2), but is a cause of joy to Clytemnestra (*Cho.* 738; cf. 1153–4). In the stichomythia which follows the lament she learns from the chorus that Orestes might be alive after all (*Cho.* 770–82; cf. 1216–19).

This extended allusion stresses the closeness of the bond between Electra and her brother. Up to now Orestes has been presented in grand and heroic terms: the splendid, though ill-fated, competitor in the games, the future avenger of the dead Agamemnon, the coming saviour of Electra herself. This aspect of his character is not forgotten here (cf. 1154–6). Yet the focus is now more on Orestes the helpless baby, who was nurtured by his sister and then rescued by the same. So too Electra is presented in a fresh light. The wild conspirator of the previous episode yields to the tender τροφός of a young boy, now overcome by the frustration of her labour. Yet while evoking the tender intimacy of the Nurse's speech, Electra's lament takes this quality to a still more moving level. For the grief of a household domestic, deep and sincere though it be, cannot compete with the mourning of a sister. Cilissa was Orestes' τροφός (*Cho.* 731), but Electra was both τροφός and ἀδελφή (1147–8). The greater profundity of Electra's speech springs from this vital difference.

The monumental *kommos* at *Cho.* 306–478 provides a second significant Aeschylean parallel. Both pieces are extraordinarily powerful acts of formal lamentation; both take place over the remains of a dead member of the house of Atreus; both will be followed by a scene of plotting for the deaths of the usurpers. But in each case the lament is revealingly different. In Aeschylus communal sorrow gradually turns into a desire for revenge against Agamemnon's killers. The participants' solidarity in grief leads naturally into their solidarity in action. There is no such movement in S.'s lament, where the focus remains fixed throughout on the solitary grief of a single character. The respective invocations of the dead make for a related contrast. Aeschylus' Electra joins with Orestes and the chorus to urge Agamemnon to rise up from his tomb and support them (*Cho.* 456–60). Her Sophoclean counterpart prays for the reverse: that she may join Orestes, dead in his urn (1165). The Electra who barely a hundred lines ago (1017–20) was prepared to take on Aegisthus single-handed seems a distant figure.

Alongside this striking fixity of tone is a thematic emphasis on the idea of sending and receiving. Three times in the first seven lines the verb ἐκπέμπω refers to Electra's sending out of the infant Orestes to Strophius in Phocis (1128, 1130, 1132). During his exile Orestes attempted to reciprocate, sending (1155 προὔπεμπες) secret messages to tell his sister that he would return to avenge his father's death. But in the end, far from returning, Orestes is himself sent back by an ill fated δαίμων (1158 προὔπεμψεν, 1163 πεμφθείς). Sent out alive as the last hope of the house, he is sent back in death to remove all such hopes. The dead Orestes is received (1128 εἰσεδεξάμην) back by his sister Electra: but this relationship too is inverted, with Electra finally begging her dead brother to receive (1165 δέξαι) her into his urn.[68] Having sent him away from her in a failed attempt to secure his life, she now desires to be united with him in the togetherness of death. These malignant reversals contrast the hopeful past with the hopeless present. They also have a powerful closural effect. Orestes has completed his life's journey, out of Argos and now back again. Now, it seems, it only remains for Electra to join him at his final destination.[69]

The central part of the lament juxtaposes the care for the dead body of Orestes, which Electra was denied (1136–42), with the nurture lavished by Electra on Orestes as a child (1143–8). The former is particularly painful for Electra: all that her rescue of the child has achieved is to ensure that Orestes did not receive funerary rites at her hands. In that other Sophoclean lament for a dead brother, Antigone had at least the satisfaction and consolation of having performed these rites for Polynices (*Ant.* 891–928, especially 900–3). The unusual degree of care which the baby Orestes received at his sister's hands (1143–8n.) makes for a poignant contrast with the lack of such attention from her at the close of his life.

Electra's closing wish is to be taken into the urn which holds her brother (1165–7). Lamentation can in general be characterised as the temporary participation of the mourner in the state of the dead (292n.). But Electra here seems to push this *topos* to its limits: it is by no means clear that she is only speaking metaphorically. This self-devotion to the urn is a final evocation of the depth of her sorrow. It also looks forward to the intensity of the moment when her brother will ask her to abandon the object which she now most treasures (1205).

Few laments in ancient literature are as moving as this speech. But just as earlier the Paedagogus' narrative constituted a *tour de force* of a messenger speech, and yet broke the most basic convention of its genre by describing an event which never took place, so too this most affecting of lamentations is based on an entirely false premise. The irony of a character mourning the death of another who is alive, well and near by is first exploited in book 19 of the *Odyssey*, where Penelope weeps for her 'dead' husband, who is even now sitting beside her (209 κλαιούσης ἑὸν ἄνδρα παρήμενον). Virgil hints at it at *Aen.* 1.544–9, and the theme gives rise to a memorable episode in Twain's *Tom Sawyer* (ch. 17). But in none of these cases is the lament for the dead extended

---

[68] Ring composition involving the same verb also occurs in the Nurse's speech at Aesch. *Cho.* 750, 762: cf. van Otterlo (1944) 5. West prints an emendation at 762, but see Garvie *ad loc.* for a defence of M's reading.

[69] Hutchinson (1999) 55–6 has sensitively analysed the different tenses of these verbs.

into a set-piece of such poignancy. This does not take away the power of the speech to move an audience. It rather creates in us a subtle blend of emotions, as we experience the bitter sorrow of Electra while also anticipating that her final release from that sorrow into joy is now closer than ever. Yet even so, our focus is not on Electra alone. For just as in the second episode the audience will have been imagining the crushing effect of the Paedagogus' speech on Electra, so here our attention will also fall on what Orestes feels as he listens. The intensity of this reaction will be made clear in the following part of the scene.

The opening of Menander's *Aspis* (1–18) may be influenced by this passage. There the slave Davus is mourning the death of his master. His state is different now from what he had hoped for when he was setting out (1127–8n.). The death of the great man has snatched everything away with him (1150–1). All that remains is his shield, which the slave is carrying as he utters his laments. Yet we shall later see that his master is not dead at all.

According to Aulus Gellius 6.5 the famous actor Polus once performed this speech while carrying the urn containing the ashes of his dead son: see further Holford-Strevens (1999) 238, (2003) 235.

1126 φιλτάτου . . . ἀνθρώπων: for the superlative cf. 462–3n.

For μνημεῖον and μνῆμα in a funerary context see Henrichs (1993) 172 n. 24.

1127–8 ὡς <σ᾽> ἀπ᾽ ἐλπίδων | ὑφ᾽ ὧνπερ ἐξέπεμπον εἰσεδεξάμην: ὑφ᾽ Wecklein; οὐχ codd. ἀπό means 'far from (my hopes, expectation)': cf. Ap. Rh. 2.863 μάλα πολλὸν ἀπ᾽ ἐλπίδος ἔπλετο νόστος, S. *Tr.* 667 ἀπ᾽ ἐλπίδος καλῆς with Davies, Hom. *Il.* 10.324 ἀπὸ δόξης, K–G i. 456 ('fern von'), LSJ⁹ s.v. A I 3, *DGE* s.v. B V 2. Elsewhere the preposition can denote the means or resource (1378n.), but this cannot be the sense here. As in parallel passages (cf. Men. *Asp.* 2–3 οὐδὲ διαλογίζομαι | παραπλήσι᾽ ὡς τό[τ᾽ ἤλ]πισ᾽ ἐξορμώμεν[ος], Eur. *Her.* 460–1 ἦ πολύ γε δόξης ἐξέπεσον εὐέλπιδος (*coni.*), | ἣν πατρὸς ὑμῶν ἐκ λόγων ποτ᾽ ἤλπισα, here there is a contrast between previous hopes and the present situation. To introduce a new set of hopes, felt by Electra as she now receives her brother's ashes, would complicate that simple opposition. Nor is it clear what hopes these could be, given that Orestes' death has often been said to have removed all of Electra's hopes (306n.). Schaefer's ὑπ᾽ ἐλπίδων ((1808) 124) is problematic for the same reason.

More difficult is the transmitted phrase οὐχ ὧνπερ ἐξέπεμπον. Many editors take ὧνπερ as standing for αἷσπερ, by attraction to ἐλπίδων. So Jebb's note translates 'in a manner how contrary to my hopes – not with those hopes wherewith I sent you forth – have I received you back'. It is as if S. had combined the two sentences ὡς σ᾽ ἐδεξάμην ἀπ᾽ ἐλπίδων ἃς εἶχον ἡνίκ᾽ ἐξέπεμπόν σε and ὡς σ᾽ ἐδεξάμην οὐ ταῖς αὐταῖς ἐλπίσιν ἃς εἶχον ἡνίκ᾽ ἐξέπεμπόν σε. But the combination is clumsy, as the awkwardness of Jebb's rendering indicates. Translations which avoid the desperation of dashes silently omit the οὐχ (e.g. Jebb in his facing translation, Lloyd-Jones, March), which hardly inspires confidence in the transmitted text.

Attempted remedies have tended to focus on ὥνπερ, where ὅνπερ (Bb), supported by Monteil (1963) 169) and ὥσπερ (HOPa) are both possibilities. For the corruptions involved cf. Ar. *Ach.* 441 (variants ὅσπερ, ὥσπερ), 1025 (variants ὥπερ, ὥσπερ, ὅπερ), *Pax* 676 (οὕπερ Bentley, accepted by Olson; ὥσπερ Triclinius, ὅπερ codd.); also S. *Tr.* 715, where editors accept Wakefield's χὥνπερ for manuscript χὥσπερ or χὥσαπερ. With ὅνπερ the sense is 'how I have received you contrary to my hopes, you who are not as you were when I sent you out', while ὥσπερ gives 'how I have received you contrary to my hopes, in a manner different from that when I sent you out'. Both of these are more convincing as Greek than the paradosis. But both are still clumsy, and should not be adopted if another suggestion could commend itself. The difference between the hopeful past and the hopeless present is set out with moving directness at 1129–30. We may wonder why S. could not have achieved a similar effect here too.

Suspicion is better directed at the offending οὐχ. Wecklein's ὑφ' solves our difficulty at a trivial cost. With this emendation the passage can be translated 'how I have received you contrary to the hopes with which I sent you forth'. Such moving simplicity cannot be obtained from the paradosis except by wilful mistranslation. Corruption to οὐχ may have come about through the erroneous belief that ἀπό denoted the means or resource (the commoner sense, as at 1378 (n.)), and that a negative was therefore required to point out the difference between her present hopes and her past ones. For this use of ὑπό cf. Plut. *Arist.* 15.4 μαχεῖται . . . οὐχ ὑπ' ἐλπίδος χρηστῆς οὐδὲ θάρσους, 630n.

1128 ἐξέπεμπον εἰσεδεξάμην: for the antithesis cf. Aesch. *Suppl.* 219 ἀλλ' εὖ τ' ἔπεμψεν εὖ τε δεξάσθω χθονί. For the thought compare Hom. *Il.* 18.438–41 τὸν μὲν ἐγὼ θρέψασα . . . | νηυσὶν ἐπιπροέηκα κορωνίσιν Ἴλιον εἴσω | Τρωσὶ μαχησόμενον, τὸν δ' οὐκ ὑποδέξομαι αὖτις | οἴκαδε νοστήσαντα. For ἐκπέμπω used of sending away a young child cf. Eur. *Hec.* 768, Lys. 16.4, Men. *Sic.* 281.

1129 νῦν μέν: the contrast between the past and the present is idiomatic in the lamentatory context, and is often signalled by repeated use of a word for 'now': cf. 1136, 1149, Hom. *Il.* 19.288–9 ζωὸν μέν σε ἔλειπον ἐγὼ κλισίηθεν ἰοῦσα, | νῦν δέ σε τεθνηῶτα κιχάνομαι, Reiner (1938) 11 n. 7, Alexiou (2002) 165–71.

οὐδὲν ὄντα: for the neuter cf. 245n.

βαστάζω: for the sense see 905n.

1130 For λαμπρόν of the young cf. Thuc. 6.54.2 ὥρᾳ ἡλικίας λαμπροῦ, Eur. *Ion* 476; cf. the frequent comparison of the young to stars (*FGE* p. 161). References to light are common in ritual laments (Alexiou (2002) 187–9). The moving effect here contrasts with its earlier appearances in descriptions of Orestes, where it rather denoted his heroic and glorious status (66, 685). Cf. λάμπω used of young children at [Pl.] *A.P.* 7.670.1 = 586 *FGE*, Theodoridas *A.P.* 6.156.3 = 3514 *HE*.

1131 ὡς: common in wishes in Homer (Goodwin §737), but in Attic εἴθε is more usual (cf. 1021, Goodwin §734). Cf. however Eur. *Ion* 286, Ar. *Ran.* 955. Hom. *Il.* 3.428 ὡς ὤφελες αὐτόθ᾽ ὀλέσθαι may have influenced S.'s choice of word here.

ὤφελον: the minority variant ὤφελες (*coni.* Porson (1815) 222) is attractive, as ritual laments often contain a wish that the death had occurred in some other way: cf. Aesch. *Cho.* 345–54, Eur. *Tro.* 1167–72, Alexiou (2002) 178–80, Schauer (2002) 247–8. But 1132–3 suggest that Electra is meant. 1134 also makes more sense if Orestes' death as a child has not been mentioned before.

1132 For Electra's rescue of the young Orestes see 11–14n.

1133 κλέψασα . . . κἀνασώσασθαι: for the combination cf. Eur. *El.* 556–7, *Diss. log.* D–K 90 3.5 (= ii. 410.21) κλέψαι καὶ σῶσαι τὸν πατέρα, Plut. *Praec. ger. reip.* 819d.

ταῖνδε: for the form of the dual see 977n.

φόνου: that is, Clytemnestra's attempted murder of the infant (cf. 296–7n.)

1134 ὅπως . . . ἔκεισο: secondary tenses of the indicative are found in purpose clauses when the clause is dependent on an unfulfilled condition: cf. [Aesch.] *PV* 747–50, K–G ii. 388–9.7, Goodwin §333, Bruhn §137, Amigues (1977) 208–9.

1135 τύμβου πατρῴου . . . μέρος: for the μέρος θανάτου cf. *Ant.* 147, Eur. *Hcld.* 621, Ar. *Thesm.* 1071–2, Simon. fr. 520.5–6 *PMG*, Bagordo (2003) 146–7.

1136 For the bitterness of death away from home cf. Lattimore (1942) 199–202, Griffin (1980) 106–12, Harder on Eur. fr. 263.2 *TrGF* = 37.2–3 Austin.

νῦν: 1129n.

φυγάς: for the miseries of exile see 602n.

1137 κασιγνήτης: for the v.l. –ου cf. Eur. *Ba.* 1289, 1373. The error is unusual, especially as it occurs in three manuscript groups: preceding σῆς ought to have protected the true form.

1138–40 At *Ant.* 900–3 Antigone proudly lists the ritual observances which she has performed for her dead brother. It is a paradoxical and moving act to list the observances which one did *not* pay to a dead relative: cf. 865–70, Aesch. *Cho.* 8–9 οὐ γὰρ παρὼν ᾤμωξα σὸν πάτερ μόρον | οὐδ᾽ ἐξέτεινα χεῖρ᾽ ἐπ᾽ ἐκφορᾷ νεκροῦ, Hom. *Od.* 24.292–6, 1.236–41, Archil. fr. 9 *IEG*, Ov. *Her.* 11.115–17, *Trist.* 3.3.39–46.

1138 κοὔτ᾽ ἐν φίλαισι χερσίν: the handling of the body is an important part of Greek funerary ritual (cf. *Aj.* 1410, Eur. *Med.* 1034, Seaford (1984) 249 with n. 18). ἐν denotes the means (Moorhouse 106–7). For φίλαισι qualifying χερσίν see Benveniste (1969) i. 350 ≈ (1973) 286, Robinson (1990) 108; here it is opposed to ξένησι in 1141 (n.). φίλῃσι is also a possibility here (cf. *ib.*).

1139 λουτροῖς σ᾽ ἐκόσμησ᾽: for the washing of the corpse cf. *Ant.* 900–1 ἐπεὶ θανόντας αὐτόχειρ ὑμᾶς ἐγώ | ἔλουσα κἀκόσμησα, *OC* 1602–3 λουτροῖς τέ νιν | ἐσθῆτί τ᾽ ἐξήσκησαν, *Aj.* 1404–6, Eur. *Phoen.* 1667, Enn. *Ann.* 147 Skutsch, Virg. *Aen.* 6.219, Lucian 40.11, Mauduit (1994) 135–7. The task is often performed by female relatives (cf. Seaford (1984) 248 n. 14, Alexiou (2002) 39–42). Citing the first two parallels, Jebb translates 'washed and dressed' rather than 'honoured with washings'. This is possible, though not necessary, as the washing is itself an act of honour to the corpse. For κόσμος 'used of the ordered beauty of death ritual' (Seaford (1994) 376 n. 36) cf. 1401, *Ant.* 395–6 τάφον | κοσμοῦσα, 901, Eur. *Tro.* 1147, Hdt. 3.24.2, Isaeus 8.22, Plut. *Eum.* 2.10. Most manuscripts omit the σ᾽, which was conjectured by Schaefer (1808) 132.

1139–40 πυρὸς | ἀνειλόμην: cf. Hom. *Il.* 24.793 ὀστέα λευκὰ λέγοντο κασίγνητοί θ᾽ ἕταροί τε (after Hector's funeral pyre has been put out), 23.239, 252–3 etc.

1140 ἄθλιον βάρος: cf. Aesch. *Ag.* 441–2 βαρὺ | ψῆγμα, Eur. *Suppl.* 1123–5 φέρω | . . . ἐκ πυρᾶς πατρὸς μέλη, | βάρος μὲν οὐκ ἀβριθὲς ἀλγέων ὕπο. The *topos*, related to that of 758 (n.), is followed by an opposite commonplace in 1142 stressing the smallness of the remains (cf. Eur. *Suppl.* 1129–30).

1141 ἐν ξένῃσι χερσὶ κηδευθείς: cf. Demades fr. 87.9 (p. 63.8–9 de Falco) χιλίων Ἀθηναίων ταφῇ μαρτυρεῖ μοι κηδευθεῖσα ταῖς τῶν ἐναντίων χερσίν, Archias *A.P.* 7.278.4 = 3653 *GP* ξείνων χερσὶν ἔκυρσα τάφου, Liban. *Or.* 14.67 ἐπιστρέψει . . . αὐτὸν οὐδέν, . . . οὐκ εἰ τὴν ψυχὴν ἐν ξένων ἀφήσει χερσίν.

ξένῃσι: until *c.* 420 BC –ῃσι regularly occurred in Attic inscriptions, written –ΕΣΙ, or –ΑΣΙ after iota. –ΕΙΣΙ and –ΑΙΣΙ were occasional variants (so Threatte ii. 96–101). Thereafter –αις was the usual form. The orthographic conservatism of inscriptions along with the suddenness of the shift means that –αις is likely to have displaced –ησι somewhat before 420 in everyday speech. The language of tragedy, on the other hand, will probably have kept the older forms for longer. –ησι is better attested here: the v.l. –αις is found in a single manuscript group. The *utrum in alterum* argument also favours –ησι. The evidence suggests that Ll-J/W are right against Barrett (on Eur. *Hipp.* 101) in keeping the form, even in a late play of Sophocles. See further Hutchinson on Aesch. *Sept.* 460 (arguing that Aeschylus may have used both endings), West's Teubner Aeschylus, p. xxxvi (preferring –ησι, –ασι in Aeschylus).

1142 σμικρὸς προσήκεις ὄγκος ἐν σμικρῷ κύτει: for the *topos* see 1113–14.

σμικρὸς . . . σμικρῷ: cf. *Ant.* 1266 νέος νέῳ ξὺν μόρῳ, Hes. *Op.* 361, Bruhn §223.I.

προσήκεις 'you have come', but also perhaps with a shade of 'you belong to me'.

1143–4 τῆς ἐμῆς . . . τροφῆς | ἀνωφελήτου: cf. Aesch. *Cho.* 752–3 (Nurse) καὶ πολλὰ καὶ μοχθήρ'ἀνωφέλητ'ἐμοὶ | τλάσῃ, Eur. *El.* 506–7 (Old Man) ὃν ποτ' ἐν χεροῖν ἔχων | ἀνόνητ'ἔθρεψας, *Tro.* 758–9 διὰ κενῆς ἄρα | ἐν σπαργάνοις σε μαστὸς ἐξέθρεψ'ὅδε, 1187–8 οἴμοι, τὰ πόλλ'ἀσπάσμαθ'αἵ τ'ἐμαὶ τροφαὶ | ὕπνοι τ'ἐκεῖνοι φροῦδά μοι, *Suppl.* 918–24, Collard on 1135–8, Schauer (2002) 227. The tragic examples will all be indebted to Hom. *Il.* 18.434–41 (Thetis on her futile nurture of Achilles; partially quoted above, 1128n.); perhaps also to the play of which Aesch. fr. 350 *TrGF* is the sole remaining piece.

For the care shown by a sister for her brother cf. Eur. *Held.* 574–80, *IA* 1450, Golden (1990) 128–9. The references to τροφή and τροφός (1147) do not imply that Electra was Orestes' wet-nurse: nor could she have been, not having had a pregnancy.

1145 πόνῳ γλυκεῖ: sweetness and pleasure would more normally be opposed to labour (cf. Pind. *I.* 8.8 γλυκύ τι δαμωσόμεθα καὶ μετὰ πόνον, Liban. *Or.* 35.26). For the paradox cf. fr. 374 *TrGF*, Eur. *Ba.* 66–7, 1053, Asclep. *A.P.* 7.11.1 = 942 *HE*, Opp. *Cyn.* 1.62, Nonn. *Dion.* 42.344, *Macbeth* 2.3.56 'the labour we delight in physics pain'. For πόνος used to denote the labour involved in bringing up a child cf. Fraenkel on Aesch. *Ag.* 53–4. The references of Aeschylus' Nurse to urination and so forth (*Cho.* 755–60) do not find a place in Electra's speech, where they would jar with the grander style.

παρέσχον: Nauck's minor change παρεῖχον (in his fifth edition, p. 168) has its attractions, in that Electra's efforts at looking after her brother did not lead to a successful conclusion. The imperfect προσηυδώμην in 1148 might also support the same tense here too. However, the aorist can be used to denote action of even long duration when the emphasis is on its termination (cf. *Aj.* 502 Αἴαντος, ὃς μέγιστον ἴσχυσε στρατοῦ, Thuc. 6.92.4 ἐπολιτεύθην).

According to Ll-J/W, the aorist here refers to an action considered as a single act repeated over a period of time (*Sophoclea*, citing Thuc. 3.37.1 πολλάκις . . . ἔγνων). θάμ' lends this view some support. But the former explanation is still preferable: the sense of finality, of 'looking back on a closed chapter of her life' (Jebb) is more important here than the discrete quality of Electra's acts of care.

1145–6 οὔτε γάρ ποτε | μητρὸς σύ γ᾽ ἦσθα μᾶλλον ἢ κἀμοῦ φίλος: when ἢ καί follows a negative 'two ideas are combined: (i) A is not more true than B; (ii) B is true as well as A' (Denniston 299 (5)). According to Kaibel (p. 249), φίλος with the dative denotes a specific situation which may recur or change, while with the genitive it expresses a relationship which is regularly true. So here 'El. will nicht sagen "du warst der Mutter nicht so lieb wie mir", sondern "du warst nicht so sehr, was das natürliche gewesen wäre, ein geliebtes Kind der Mutter wie du mein eigner Liebling warst".'

For καί in comparisons cf. 1301–2, *Ant.* 927–8, Bruhn §153.II.1.

1147 οἱ κατ᾽ οἶκον: the domestic servants, as at *Tr.* 934 τῶν κατ᾽ οἶκον.

1148 ἀδελφή: a fitting climax after τροφός, as it denotes the relationship which Electra bears to Orestes (so Ll-J/W, *Sophoclea*): cf. Hom. *Il.* 6.429–30 Ἕκτορ, ἀτὰρ σύ μοί ἐσσι πατὴρ καὶ πότνια μήτηρ | ἠδὲ κασίγνητος, σὺ δέ μοι θαλερὸς παρακοίτης, Aesch. *Cho.* 239–43 (Electra to Orestes) προσαυδᾶν δ᾽ ἔστ᾽ ἀναγκαίως ἔχον | πατέρα σε (Schütz; τε M), καὶ τὸ μητρὸς εἰς σέ μοι ῥέπει | στέργηθρον . . . | καὶ τῆς τυθείσης νηλεῶς ὁμοσπόρου· | πιστός τ᾽ ἀδελφὸς ἦσθ᾽, ἐμοὶ σέβας φέρων. Similar uses of this motif can be found at Eur. fr. 866 *TrGF* ἥδε μοι τροφός, | μήτηρ, ἀδελφή, δμωίς, ἄγκυρα στέγης, *Alc.* 645–7, *Hec.* 281, Ar. *Av.* 716. But even without the allusion, ἀδελφή may be a stronger and more unusual form of address than some have allowed (461 n.). Dawe's objections to it (*STS* i. 194) may be discounted.

σοί: 'a slight emphasis on the pronoun better marks the reciprocity of affection' (Jebb).

1149 νῦν: 1129n.

ταῦτ᾽: Blaydes's πάντ᾽ ((1902) 107) is possible: for the corruption see Fraenkel on Aesch. *Ag.* 551 and Diggle (1994) 494. Dawe posits a lacuna between 1148 and 1149, arguing that as the text stands ταῦτ᾽ (or πάντ᾽) has little to refer back to (*STS* i. 194). But as Ll-J/W note (*Sophoclea*), 'to Electra and the poet what is described in 1143–8 amounts to a good deal'.

ἐν ἡμέρᾳ μιᾷ: for the single crucial day cf. 783, 918–19, 1363, Garvie on *Aj.* 131–2. For the motif 'one day destroys everything' cf. Pind. *I.* 4.16–17, Aesch. *Pers.* 431–2, Eur. *Hec.* 285, *Her.* 509–10, Harder on fr. 245.15 *TrGF* = 19.15 Austin, Lucr. 5.95 *una dies dabit exitio*; also *Aj.* 131–2, *OR* 438.

1150 θανόντα: cf. Eur. *Her.* 69 καὶ νῦν ἐκεῖνα μὲν θανόντ᾽ ἀνέπτατο, fr. 734.2–3 *TrGF* κακοῖσι δὲ | ἅπαντα φροῦδα συνθανόνθ᾽ ὑπὸ χθονός; for the motif 'these things died with him' cf. Gorgias D–K 82 B 6 (= ii. 286.15–16), Ar. *Ran.* 868–9. The other manuscript reading, –όντι, is also possible, and has been preferred by most editors (though not Dawe), probably out of a prejudice for L's reading. According to Jebb the dative gives a 'simple pathos' to the σοί: we might rather say that the word is otiose with σοί, but gives a powerful metaphorical sense with ταῦτα, one moreover which is supported by good parallels. The word order is also more natural with the nominative.

1150–1 πάντα γὰρ συναρπάσας | . . . βέβηκας: cf. *OR* 971–2 τὰ δ᾽ οὖν παρόντα συλλαβὼν θεσπίσματα | κεῖται παρ᾽ Ἅιδῃ Πόλυβος ἄξι᾽ οὐδενός. For the perfect of βαίνω used to mean 'be dead' cf. LSJ⁹ s.v. A I 3.

1151 θύελλ᾽ ὅπως: the evocation of speed or (more usually) violence through comparison to a whirlwind is common enough: cf. Aesch. *Ag.* 819 Ἄτης θύελλαι ζῶσι, Hom. *Il.* 13.39 φλογὶ ἴσοι ἀολλέες ἠὲ θυέλλῃ, *Od.* 12.67–8, [Hes.] *Scut.* 345, Lyr. Adesp. fr. 940.2 *PMG* θυέλλης δίκην (interpreted as a tragic fragment at Tr. Adesp. fr. 13a *TrGF*), Cic. *Dom.* 137, Jeremiah 30.23. To speak of a dead man in these terms is more daring.

1151–3 For the expressively short sense-units and asyndeton see 924–5n. See Denniston 164 for the 'connexion . . . varied with asyndeton' ('an astonishingly fine effect').

1152 τέθνηκ᾽ ἐγὼ σοί 'I have been killed by you' (so rightly Ll-J/W, *Sophoclea*). As Fraenkel notes, 'the context leaves no doubt as to the sense; Jebb's "I am dead in relation to thee" is not adequate' (his edition of Aeschylus' *Agamemnon*, vol. iii. p. 629 n. 2). At *Phil.* 1030 τέθνηχ᾽ ὑμῖν πάλαι, cited as a parallel by Jebb, the thought is 'your treatment of me over the last ten years is such that, as far as you are concerned, I am dead', which is not the same. Cf. rather *Aj.* 970 θεοῖς τέθνηκεν οὗτος, οὐ κείνοισιν, οὔ, 1128 τῷδε δ᾽ οἴχομαι, Eur. *Andr.* 334 τέθνηκα τῇ σῇ θυγατρὶ καί μ᾽ ἀπώλεσεν. For the motif 'you have killed me by your death' see 808n.

1153 γελῶσι δ᾽ ἐχθροί: 277n.
μαίνεται δ᾽ ὑφ᾽ ἡδονῆς: for the verb used to denote wild pleasure cf. Plut. *Pomp.* 36.8 ὑφ᾽ ἡδονῆς μαινόμενος, Ar. *Ran.* 103, 751 μᾶλλά πλεῖν ἢ μαίνομαι.

1154 μήτηρ ἀμήτωρ: for the form of expression cf. *Aj.* 665 ἄδωρα δῶρα, *OR* 1214, Aesch. *Pers.* 680, *Ag.* 1545, *Cho.* 44, *Eum.* 457, 1034, Bruhn §222,

Moorhouse (1959) 66–8, Fehling (1968), (1969) 287–9 (its pejorative sense), Wills (1996) 455–7. For the 'mother who is no mother' *topos* see 273–4n.

ἧς: take with either λάθρᾳ or φήμας . . . προὔπεμπες. The latter (denoting the subject of Orestes' messages) gives a rarer construction (317n.), though it makes better sense of the word order. A connexion with τιμωρός is less likely, as a genitive with this word should denote either the person or action to be avenged, not the person who is to suffer vengeance.

1155 φήμας . . . προὔπεμπες: cf. 169–70, 319, 778–82.

1156 αὐτός: for the sense cf. Meleager *A.P.* 5.182.7–8 = 4368–9 *HE* καίτοι τί σε, Δορκάς, | ἐκπέμπω, σύν σοι καὐτὸς ἰδοὺ προάγων;, Ov. *Her.* 1.2 *nil mihi rescribas attinet: ipse veni,* 8.24.

1157 δαίμων: 917n.

1158–9 ἀντὶ φιλτάτης | μορφῆς: cf. Aesch. 434–6 *Ag.* ἀντὶ δὲ φωτῶν | τεύχη καὶ σποδὸς εἰς ἑκάσ– | του δόμους ἀφικνεῖται (also 441–4), Ant. Sid. *A.P.* 7.467.7–8 = 538–9 *HE* ἀντὶ δὲ σεῖο | στάλα καὶ κωφὰ λείπεται ἄμμι κόνις, [Simon.] *A.P.* 7.443.3–4 = 884–5 *FGE*.

1159 σποδόν τε καὶ σκιάν: cf. Hor. *C.* 4.7.16 *pulvis et umbra sumus,* [Sen.] *Oct.* 169–70 *nunc levis tantum cinis | et tristis umbra* with Ferri; also Phaedimus *A.P.* 7.739.3 = 2923 *HE* δεξαμένη σποδιήν τε καὶ ὀστέα, Bühler's edition of Zenobius, vol. iv. p. 186. For σκιά of something insubstantial cf. *Aj.* 125–6 ὁρῶ γὰρ ἡμᾶς οὐδὲν ὄντας ἄλλο πλὴν | . . . κούφην σκιάν, Pind. *P.* 8.95–6 σκιᾶς ὄναρ | ἄνθρωπος, Ar. *Vesp.* 191 περὶ ὄνου σκιᾶς with MacDowell, Greg. Cypr. 3.87 = *CPG* i. 375.6.

ἀνωφελῆ: rounding off this section of the speech by ring composition (cf. 1144); cf. Ov. *Fast.* 5.656 *pulvis inanis*.

1160–2 For the sudden appearance of truncated anapaests in a tragic *rhesis* cf. *Tr.* 1081–2, 1085–6 (with West (1982a) 123 n. 110).

1161 δέμας οἰκτρόν: Orestes' mangled body (cf. 756 ἄθλιον δέμας).

1162–3 δεινοτάτας . . . | . . . κελεύθους: accusative of extent (Moorhouse 44). Despite the previous line, the reference is not to the chariot race: κελεύθους is not the right word for the laps of a hippodrome, and πεμφθείς under this interpretation is obscure. Electra's focus has rather shifted to Orestes' last journey from Crisa to Mycenae. The 'journey of death' motif may also be felt: for this cf. *Tr.* 874–5 βέβηκε Δηάνειρα τὴν πανυστάτην | ὁδῶν ἁπασῶν

COMMENTARY: 1098–1231

ἐξ ἀκινήτου ποδός with Davies, *Ant.* 807–8 τὰν νεάταν ὁδὸν | στείχουσαν, Pind. *O.* 9.34–5, Philetas fr. 6 *CA* = 3 Spanoudakis (with S.'s n.) = 2 Sbardella, Alexiou (2002) 189–93.

1163 ὡς μ᾽ ἀπώλεσας: for the causal connexion between Orestes' death and Electra's cf. 808n., 1152n. The phrase is immediately picked up by ἀπώλε-σας δῆτ᾽ in the following line, and so should be followed by a comma rather than a colon, as in the other examples collected at Denniston 277 (so rightly Hutchinson, in his edition of Aeschylus' *Septem*, p. 180).

1164 δῆτ᾽: 845n.
ὦ κασίγνητον κάρα marks an appeal of special intensity: cf. *Ant.* 915 (also 1), Eur. *IT* 983, *Or.* 237, possibly 294. For further instances see Davidson (1991).

1165–7 For the wish for death see Ambühl (2002) 12–13.

1165 δέξαι: cf. Ov. *Ars* 3.21 *accipe me, Capaneu: cineres miscebimur, CIL* vi.4.1.30115.1 = *ILCV* i. §205.1 *suscipe me sociam tumulis, dulciss[ime coniux]* (Aventine).
τὸ σὸν τόδε στέγος: on the position of τόδε see Theocr. 2.116 ἐς τὸ τεὸν καλέσασα τόδε στέγος, K–G i. 628 Anm. 5.

1166 τὴν μηδέν: μηδείς is used despite the reference to a specific individual: cf. *Tr.* 1107, *Aj.* 1231, 1275. On that ground Moorhouse (1965) 35–40 argues for the semantic equivalence of οὐδεὶς εἶναι and μηδεὶς εἶναι in tragedy. The spread of the latter may result, he thinks, from a desire to avoid hiatus. Like Heracles at *Tr.* 1107 and Creon at *Ant.* 1325, Electra here speaks of herself as already dead. For the neuter cf. 245n.
τὸ μηδέν 'thy nothingness' (Jebb), referring to the urn. The neuter could refer to a person (cf. Eur. fr. 532.2 *TrGF*, S. *Tr.* 1107, *Ant.* 1325), and a slight emendation to τόν would make this still clearer: but the rhetoric of the passage demands that this phrase corresponds to τὸ . . . στέγος in 1165, just as τὴν μηδέν corresponds to μ᾽.

1166–7 ὡς σὺν σοὶ κάτω | ναίω τὸ λοιπόν: for a brother and sister resting together in death cf. *Ant.* 73, 897–9, Eur. *Hec.* 894–7, Golden (1990) 219 n. 43. For the motif in connexion with friends, relatives or lovers cf. *Ant.* 1240, Hom. *Il.* 23.91 ὡς δὲ καὶ ὀστέα νῶιν ὁμὴ σορὸς ἀμφικαλύπτοι, *Od.* 24.76–7, Eur. *Alc.* 363, *Suppl.* 1019–20, *Hel.* 985–6, Aesch. *Cho.* 894–5, 906–7, Propertius 4.7.94 with Fedeli, Ov. *Ars* 3.21–2 with Gibson, *Met.* 4.166 *una requiescit in urna* with Bömer, Apollonides *A.P.* 7.378.3–4 = 1151–2 *GP* ἄμφω δ᾽ ὡς ἅμ᾽ ἔναιον (Tyrwhitt; ὑμέναιον codd.) ὑπὸ πλακὶ τυμβεύονται | ξυνὸν ἀγαλλόμενοι καὶ

454

τάφον ὡς θάλαμον, anon. *A.P.* 7.323 = 1276–7 *FGE*, Lattimore (1942) 247–50, Paduano (1968) 84–90. For the urn or tomb as a home cf. Lattimore (1942) 165–7.

1168 ξὺν σοὶ μετεῖχον τῶν ἴσων: for μετέχω expressing 'participation with somebody in fate, happiness or misfortune' cf. Eur. *El.* 607, Borecky (1965) 62.

1169 ἀπολείπεσθαι: *privari*, not *deserere* (Elmsley on Eur. *Med.* 35): cf. Willink on Eur. *Or.* 80, LSJ⁹ s.v. ἀπολείπω C II 1.

1170 τοὺς γὰρ θανόντας οὐχ ὁρῶ λυπουμένους: Zippmann (1864) 1–4 deletes, claiming that the line loses sight of Electra's particular reason to desire death, namely to be with Orestes: but 1169 would be abrupt as a conclusion. In his third edition Dawe complains 'non placet οὐχ hoc loco positum', but cf. 973, fr. 334 *TrGF*. For the *topos* cf. *Tr.* 1173 τοῖς γὰρ θανοῦσι μόχθος οὐ προσγίγνεται, fr. 698 *TrGF*, *OC* [955], Aesch. *Suppl.* 802–3 τὸ γὰρ θανεῖν ἐλευθεροῦ– | ται φιλαιάκτων κακῶν (with Friis Johansen and Whittle), fr. 255 *TrGF*, Eur. *Alc.* 937, *Suppl.* 86, *Tro.* 606, Call. fr. 263 Pfeiffer = 88.1–2 Hollis.

1171–1231 The recognition of Orestes by Electra does not receive much emphasis in either Aeschylus or Euripides. In *Choephori* Orestes approaches his sister at 212 and identifies himself seven lines later; disbelieving at first, she is quickly persuaded by the various tokens which he presents. Euripides' Orestes is passively recognised by the Old Man (*El.* 558–76), who has identified a childhood scar on his brow. Electra is persuaded by this mark and embraces her brother; there is then a short section of *antilabe* between the pair (577–81). By contrast, in many ways this scene forms the climactic point of S.'s play. The length of time devoted to it is striking. Aeschylus' Nurse has barely finished lamenting the death of Orestes before she is put right by the chorus (*Cho.* 770–82). But though Orestes is now aware that the woman before him is his sister, he does not reveal his own identity for a full fifty lines. Such a delay is unusual in comparable scenes in tragedy, where the recognition of one figure by another is swiftly followed by the self-revelation of the recognising character (cf. Eur. *Ion* 1395–1401, *IT* 772–93, *Hel.* 564–6). For one last time the playwright holds back the recognition of Orestes by his sister, so that when it does come its emotional force is overwhelming (cf. Porph. *Quaest. Hom. Od.* π 188 = 122.19–21 Schrader ὑπερτίθεται δὲ τὰς πρὸς οὓς ἥκιστα ἐχρῆν, τήν τε πρὸς τὴν γυναῖκα καὶ τὸν πατέρα, διώκων τὸ παράδοξον καὶ ἵνα ἐκπληκτικαὶ γένωνται, on the climactic recognitions of Homer's *Odyssey*).

But this desire for a dramatic finale never leads to the delay seeming contrived or artificial. It rather seems to arise as a natural consequence of Orestes' reactions to his sister's speech. His shock at realising the identity of the woman standing before him is so strong that at first he can barely speak to her (1179n.), let alone take the thought to identify himself. Electra's subsequent remark that he can only see a small proportion of her troubles (1188) leads to a further delay as he asks her to describe them. In this long stichomythia we see that Electra's feelings of closeness to her brother are not unreciprocated. Despite the danger of the situation, Orestes is too much affected by grief to concern himself with his plan or the revelation of his identity. This is an important element in establishing our sympathy for him. Contrast the scene between Odysseus and Laertes in book 24 of the *Odyssey* or the conclusion to Euripides' *Alcestis* (both compared with our scene by N. J. Richardson (1984) 229). The temporary refusals of Odysseus and Heracles to make the identifications which would alleviate such great pain on the part of their interlocutors come out of conscious decisions. In particular, Odysseus' delay in identifying himself to his father has struck more than one modern reader as unnecessarily and pointlessly cruel. No motivation is given for his decision (cf. 24.239–40), nor is one apparent from the context. The reason for Orestes' delay, by contrast, is clear: the profound emotion which he experiences at the sight of Electra.

But even after recovering from this emotion, Orestes does not identify himself to his sister straight away. Rather, he delays still further by insisting that Electra relinquish the urn. The visual symbolism is undeniably potent: Electra's abandonment of the object will represent the abandonment of her belief in Orestes' death.[70] But for all the power of this dramatic effect, we must still ask why Orestes delays at this point, now that he is no longer in a state of shock at his sister's appearance. For without sufficient motivation, his actions are likely to be taken by the audience as characterised by the same sort of unnecessary cruelty as has troubled some readers of the recognition scene in *Odyssey* 24.

An answer may lie in other scenes in tragedy where important news is delivered only gradually to its recipient, such as Eur. *Ba.* 1264–80 and *Her.* 1109–45. There Cadmus and Amphitryon lead Agaue and Heracles piecemeal towards the recognition of their terrible actions, on each occasion using stichomythia. The information is so horrible that it must be broken gently in each case: in our case, perhaps, the intensely joyful news must be imparted without suddenness. This idea can be paralleled at ΣQ Hom. *Od.* 24.240 (= ii. 730.6–7 Dindorf), according to which Odysseus does not reveal himself immediately to Laertes ἵνα μὴ τῇ αἰφνιδίῳ χαρᾷ ἀποψύξει ὁ γέρων, ὥσπερ καὶ ὁ κύων ἀπώλετο.[71] This does not accurately reflect what goes on in *Odyssey* 24, where there is no gradual self-revelation on Odysseus' part (cf. S. West (1989) 125–6).

---

[70] For another memorable abandonment of a significant object in S. cf. *Phil.* 1291–2.

[71] Perhaps Aristotelian: cf. Arist. fr. 177 Rose and N. J. Richardson (1984) 228–9.

It seems more applicable to our own passage, and raises the possibility that a fifth-century audience could think in such terms. Orestes' behaviour here, far from indicating cruelty or heartlessness towards his sister, might rather have been taken as a sign of consideration and precaution.

The precise moment when Orestes persuades Electra to abandon the urn is unclear. Electra is still holding it at 1216 (βαστάζω τόδε); by 1226 the abandonment must have taken place (ἔχω σε χερσίν;). Between these two points we cannot pinpoint when she puts it down. She most likely does so between 1220, where she shows the first signs of believing that her brother is alive, and 1224, where she has accepted this as the truth.

After all this delay the actual moment of recognition is handled with breathless speed. In other recognition scenes the descriptions of tokens and other proofs of identity can take many lines, as one character struggles to overcome the doubt or disbelief of the other (cf. *IT* 808–26, *Ion* 1412–36). The only proof which Orestes produces here is his ring, on which barely two lines are spent (1222–3), and which Electra immediately takes as absolute confirmation of Orestes' return (1224). Having spent so long reaching this climactic moment, the dramatist knows that any further delay would be inept. This combination of extreme delay and extreme brevity gives this recognition scene its special quality.

1171–3 The distant response of the chorus to Electra's speech is juxtaposed with the emotional involvement of Orestes' reaction. For choral interventions of more than the usual two lines cf. 369–71, *OR* 1073–5.

1173 πᾶσιν γὰρ ἡμῖν τοῦτ' ὀφείλεται παθεῖν: deleted by Bergk (1835) 961. Stob. *Ecl.* 4.51.15 (= v. 1069.8 Wachsmuth and Hense) cites this line as coming from Aristophanes' *Polyidus* (fr. 468.2 *PCG*), where it follows τὸ γὰρ φοβεῖσθαι τὸν θάνατον λῆρος πολύς. But even if this attribution is correct, this need not tell against its authenticity here. Such a commonplace could easily be used by more than one poet, while a comic poet is quite capable of borrowing a line from tragedy. For the *topos* cf. Eur. *Alc.* 419 ὡς πᾶσιν ἡμῖν κατθανεῖν ὀφείλεται, 782, *Andr.* 1271–2 πᾶσιν γὰρ ἀνθρώποισιν ἥδε πρὸς θεῶν | ψῆφος κέκρανται κατθανεῖν τ' ὀφείλεται, fr. 733 *TrGF*, Psalm 89.48 'what man is he that liveth, and shall not see death?', Lattimore (1942) 250–6, Wankel (1983), especially 148.

1174 τί λέξω; Cf. Eur. *Hcld.* 535 (same phrase), S. *OC* 310 ὦ Ζεῦ, τί λέξω; ποῖ φρενῶν ἔλθω, πάτερ; 'Das Suchen nach Worten ist stehendes Motiv im Anagnorismos und im Amoibaion der Wiedersehensfreude' (Rau (1967) 62, citing Eur. *Hel.* 548–9, 564, 630–1, 656, *IT* 777, 839–40, *Ion* 1446, Ar. *Thesm.* 904).

ἀμηχάνων: the participle –ανῶν (*coni*. Heath (1762) 21, citing Johnson's *ubi sermonum perplexus feror*) is also possible, and is printed by Jebb, Pearson, Dawe and Ll-J/W. However, the close parallel *Phil.* 897 οὐκ οἶδ' ὅπη χρὴ τἄπορον τρέπειν ἔπος tips the balance in favour of the adjective (cf. Campbell, Becker (1937) 199–200 n. 15). Ll-J/W put the –άνων of the manuscripts down to *vitium Byzantinum* (42–3n.). More likely, –άνων is the interpretation which would most naturally occur to whoever first put the accent on, given the preceding λόγων. In any case, this is not relevant to the decision of what to print here. In the matter of accents manuscripts enjoy no authority, *vitia* or not.

1175 κρατεῖν... γλώσσης: cf. [Pythag.] D–K 58 C 6 (= i. 466.20–1) γλώσσης πρὸ τῶν ἄλλων κράτει θεοῖς ἑπόμενος, Apostol. 5.53a.1 = *CPG* ii. 347.17, [Men.] *Monost.* 136, Eur. *Hel.* 1388 κρατεῖν... στόματος, Diggle on Theophr. *Char.* 7.1. Some manuscripts have γνώμης for γλώσσης. The two nouns, often found in combination (cf. Eur. *IA* 1542, fr. 913.6–7 *TrGF*, [Aesch.] *PV* 888–9, Pind. *I.* 6.71–2, Hippocr. *Coac.* 228), are so similar in shape that the error is unsurprising (cf. West (1969)).[72]

1176 ἔσχες ἄλγος: for the instantaneous aorist cf. 1256, 1465, 668n. Bergk reinterprets the paradosis as ἔσχε σ' ἄλγος (his edition, p. xlvi); but for ἄλγος as the object rather than the subject of ἔχει cf. *Aj.* 259, Eur. *Alc.* 197–8, Philip *A.P.* 9.274.4 = 2948 *GP*, also 897n.

1177 ἦ σὸν τὸ κλεινὸν εἶδος Ἠλέκτρας τόδε; Electra's physical appearance is now anything but κλεινόν: cf. *Phil.* 575 ὅδ' ἔσθ' ὁ κλεινός σοι Φιλοκτήτης, ξένε, also *OC* 109–10 οἰκτίρατ' ἀνδρὸς Οἰδίπου τόδ' ἄθλιον | εἴδωλον· οὐ γὰρ δὴ τό γ' ἀρχαῖον δέμας. For Electra's beauty cf. [Hes.] fr. 23a.16 M–W Ἠλέκτρην θ', ἣ εἶδος ἐρήριστ' ἀ[θανά]τῃσιν. For εἶδος in descriptions of feminine beauty see Jax (1933) 95 n. 179.

1178 τόδ' ἔστ' ἐκεῖνο, καὶ μάλ' ἀθλίως ἔχον: by her use of the third person Electra as it were contemplates her own keenly-felt misery from the distant perspective of a bystander. Cf. *OC* 109–10 (cited previous n.).

καί: not 'and' (so Jebb), which would be intolerably flat, but intensificatory with μάλα (cf. 1455, Denniston 317 (1)).

1179 Beginning with this line, Orestes does not address Electra for four successive utterances. The self-absorption which this implies marks the strength of

---

[72] Dawe, *STS* ii. 87 cites L correctly; Ll-J/W mislead. The scribe first wrote γνώσσης (*sic*), and then fashioned a lambda out of the nu. Subsequently (perhaps also by the scribe) ν and μ were written above the λ and σσ.

his emotion: cf. Aesch. *Sept.* 251–6, Eur. *Med.* 328–32, *Hipp.* 337–41, Hancock (1917) 42, Mastronarde (1979) 38–9.

οἴμοι . . . ἄρα: cf. *Aj.* 980 ὤμοι βαρείας ἄρα τῆς ἐμῆς τύχης, *Phil.* 978, Ar. *Nub.* 1476; also 935n. ἄρα is a substitute for ἆρα (cf. Denniston 44–5).

ταλαίνης: qualifies συμφορᾶς: cf. Ar. *Ach.* 1204 ὦ συμφορὰ τάλαινα, Aesch. *Cho.* 1069 μόχθοι τάλανες, S. *Tr.* 1084 ἡ τάλαινα διάβορος νόσος and Headlam on Herodas 3.14 for 'epithets of commiseration or abuse . . . applied not only to persons but to things'. To take the adjective to qualify Electra, with συμφορᾶς a genitive of cause, would strain the syntax.

1180 For οὐ δή ποτ᾽ see 1108n. The v.l. τί is unattractive, and probably arose from the beginning of 1184. Electra is so amazed by the intensity of the stranger's reaction that she asks whether he is really referring to her. Once she has established this (1182), she asks him why he is lamenting her misfortunes (1184). Reading τί here would disturb this subtle progression of thought.

ὦ ξέν᾽: Electra repeats this form of address in 1182 and 1184, emphasising her surprise that a stranger should be moved by her sorrows: cf. Eur. fr. 16 Bubel (*Andromeda*) σὺ δ᾽ εἶ τίς, ὅστις τοὐμὸν ᾤκτιρας πάθος; (possibly spurious: see *TrGF* vol. v|i p. 248). See further 662n.

ἀμφ᾽ ἐμοί: cf. *Aj.* 340, Bruhn §65.

1181 ὦ σῶμ᾽ ἀτίμως κἀθέως ἐφθαρμένον: for the form cf. *OR* 254 γῆς ὧδ᾽ ἀκάρπως κἀθέως ἐφθαρμένης.

ἀτίμως: 189n.

κἀθέως: 124n.

1182 ξένε: 1180n.

1183 ἀνύμφου: 962n.

τροφῆς 'condition', 'way of life': cf. *Aj.* 499 δουλίαν ἕξειν τροφήν, *OC* 1614, Moussy (1969) 87–8.

1184 τί δή ποτ᾽: could have replaced an original τί μοί ποτ᾽ under the influence of οὐ δή ποτ᾽ in 1180 (so West (1978b) 240): but the former is a common means of opening a question, whereas the latter never seems to have this function. The μοι might have arisen out of a mistaken attempt to provide an object for ἐπισκοπῶν. Ll-J/W suggest τί δῆτά μ᾽ (*Sophoclea*): but δῆτα in a question normally has a strong logical connective force with what precedes, and such a force is absent here. The absence of a direct object for ἐπισκοπῶν is unusual, though hardly problematic (cf. 1200n.).

ὦ ξέν᾽: 1180n.

459

1185 ὡς οὐκ ἄρ' ἤδη τῶν ἐμῶν οὐδὲν κακῶν: Dain and Ll-J/W print ὅσ' for ὡς (*coni.* Plüss (1891) 55 n. 4) and L^ac's ἐγώ for οὐδέν. But since Orestes' emotion is so intense the better attested reading gives the more appropriate meaning. In the face of his sister's suffering, Orestes' own troubles as an exile are forgotten. Cf. also Dawe, *STS* i. 194–5.

ἄρ': 935n.

For Heath's ἤδη ((1762) 21) instead of ἤδειν cf. 1018n.

1186 ἐν τῷ διέγνως τοῦτο τῶν εἰρημένων; 'In which of my utterances did you discern the evidence for that?': this is simpler than Jebb's 'by means of what . . .?'

1187 ὁρῶν: Electra had assumed that Orestes was moved by the contents of her speech: his reply indicates that it is rather her appearance which most distresses him.

σε: Jebb prefers σέ, but the emphatic pronoun is out of place here.

πολλοῖς ἐμπρέπουσαν ἄλγεσιν: (ἐμ)πρέπω denotes the state of being conspicuous, whether in a positive or (as here) a negative sense: cf. Aesch. *Cho.* 11–12 φάρεσιν μελαγχίμοις | πρέπουσα, 17–18 πένθει λυγρῷ | πρέπουσαν, *Suppl.* 115, Eur. *Suppl.* 1056, Fraenkel on Aesch. *Ag.* 242.

1188 καὶ μὴν ὁρᾷς γε παῦρα τῶν ἐμῶν κακῶν: cf. Eur. *El.* 354–5 (Ηλ.) σκοποὺς ἔπεμψε τούσδε τῶν ἐμῶν κακῶν· | (Αὐ.) οὔκουν τὰ μὲν λεύσσουσι, τὰ δὲ σύ που λέγεις;

καὶ μήν: adversative: cf. 321n.

1189 For καί in an astonished question cf. 385n.

1190 τοῖς φονεῦσι σύντροφος: West (1979) 105 finds τοῖς too specific, given the absence of a previous reference to the murderers in the dialogue (contrast e.g. 263–4 τοῖς φονεῦσι τοῦ πατρὸς | ξύνειμι). He urges either emending to τοι or indicating by means of three dots that Electra's statement is interrupted by Orestes in the next line: Eitrem (1917) 161–2 had already suggested the latter. But as Ll-J/W point out (*Sophoclea*), 'Electra has spoken of "the murderers", assuming that her interlocutor will know what persons are meant'. A *TLG* search for τοι with ὁθούνεκα also revealed no results. Ll-J/W are wrong, however, in claiming that Orestes responds as he does because he is 'so bent on playing the part of the ignorant foreigner that he demands clarification' (*ib.*). By this stage Orestes has abandoned any attempt at imitating the ἦθος of a messenger. The intensity of his response to his recognition of Electra has made this impossible. An audience would more naturally assume that this state of emotion was the cause of his initial failure to understand Electra's reference, if indeed it needed any explanation for what is to some degree a necessary feature of stichometric exchange.

For Electra's horror of living with her father's killers see 262–4n.

1192 δουλεύω: 190n.

1193 ἀνάγκη: the dative is essential. With the nominative we would have to take τίς ἀνάγκη βροτῶν as equivalent to τίς βροτῶν ἀναγκάζει, which is scarcely possible.

προτρέπει: the paradosis, though difficult, should probably be retained. The prosody (long first syllable) is odd, but for parallels see Barrett on Eur. *Hipp.* 760, Mastronarde on Eur. *Phoen.* 586–7. For the sense Jebb compares Hom. *Il.* 6.336 ἔθελον δ᾽ ἄχεϊ προτραπέσθαι ('to yield to grief'). In his view, the intransitive middle in Homer corresponds to a transitive active in our passage (cf. Wackernagel (1916a) 290–3 = (1916b) 130–3, S–D ii. 233–4), which thus means 'causes you to yield to this necessity'. Pind. *N.* 4.54–6 Παλίου δὲ πὰρ ποδὶ λατρίαν Ἰαολκὸν | πολεμίᾳ χερὶ †προστραπὼν† | Πηλεὺς παρέδωκεν Αἱμόνεσσιν might provide a parallel for this sense of the active. προστραπὼν ('having supplicated') does not fit the context, and Henry *ad loc.* supports Heyne's προτραπών (for the corruption cf. *OR* 1446, Eur. *Hipp.* 715, Diggle on Theophr. *Char.* 2.8). The dative πολεμίᾳ χερί then plays exactly the same function as ἀνάγκη τῇδε does in our passage.

Reiske (1753) 18 (supported by Pearson (1929) 88) emended our verb to προστρέπει, but the sense here is as inappropriate as in the Pindaric passage. Ll-J/W (*Sophoclea*) suggest προστρίβει ('crushes': printed by Lloyd-Jones as Wilson's conjecture in his Loeb edition), but this is too violent a word for Orestes' question, as opposed to Electra's answer (cf. Fraenkel on Aesch. *Ag.* 395).

1194 μητρὶ δ᾽ οὐδὲν ἐξισοῖ: οὐκ ἴσα πράσσει τῷ τῆς μητρὸς ὀνόματι (Σ p. 152.12 Papageorgius, Suda ε 1775 (= ii. 316.11 Adler)); for the *topos* see 273–4n. Elsewhere in S. the verb is always transitive (cf. 738, *OR* 1507 μηδ᾽ ἐξισώσῃς τάσδε τοῖς ἐμοῖς κακοῖς); but for the intransitive use cf. Thuc. 6.87.5 ἐξισώσαντες τοῖς ἄλλοις, 5.71.3.

1195 λύμη βίου: cf. *Tr.* 793 λυμαντὴν βίου, Hermarchus fr. 34.11.4 Longo Auricchio λυμαίνοιτ᾽ ἂν τὸν βίον ἡμῶν, [Men.] *Monost.* 845.

1196 λύμαισι: perhaps λύμῃσι (cf. 1141 n.).

1197 οὐδ᾽ οὑπαρήξων οὔθ᾽ ὁ κωλύσων πάρα: Cf. *Ant.* 261 οὐδ᾽ ὁ κωλύσων παρῆν, *OR* 297 ἀλλ᾽ οὑξελέγξων νιν πάρεστιν, *Phil.* 1242 τίς ἔσται μ᾽ οὑπικωλύσων τάδε;, [Aesch.] *PV* 27 ὁ λωφήσων γὰρ οὐ πέφυκέ πω.

οὐδ᾽ . . . οὔθ᾽: οὔθ᾽ is usually emended into οὐδ᾽, as in many other places in tragedy, but Denniston 509–10 is sceptical of the merits of doing this. For οὐδὲ . . . οὔτε, with the δέ in the former marking the connexion (as at e.g. Eur. *Hel.* 746–7, left unemended by Kannicht) see Denniston 510. The οὐδ᾽ found in some manuscripts here will have arisen under the influence of the preceding οὐδ᾽.

1198 For the absence of an avenger cf. 846–7.

οὐ δῆθ᾽: 403n.

προὔθηκας: a word with appropriately funereal associations, used of laying out of the corpse (cf. LSJ⁹ s.v. προτίθημι II 1, Garland (2001) 23–31).

1199 ὁρῶν σ᾽ ἐποικτίρω πάλαι: cf. Eur. fr. 127 *TrGF* = 13 Bubel (*Andromeda*) ὦ παρθέν᾽, οἰκτίρω σε κρεμαμένην ὁρῶν, 920n. For the orthography of ἐποικτίρω (restored by Nauck[8]) see Threatte ii. 648.

1200 μόνος βροτῶν νυν ἴσθ᾽ ἐποικτίρας ποτέ: cf. Call. fr. 51 Pfeiffer = 60 Massimilla οὕνεκεν οἰκτείρειν οἶδε μόνη πολίων with Pfeiffer.

ποτέ: the v.ll. με σύ and ἐμέ (*coni.* Herwerden (1862) 128) will have arisen from a desire to include a pronoun, for the omission of which cf. 1184, 1341, *Aj.* 496, *OR* 461, *Phil.* 801, 1368.

1201 τοῖσι σοῖς: Dawe prefers to divide τοῖς ἴσοις (*STS* i. 195; cf. Ar. *Vesp.* 747), but then there would be no reason for Electra to ask whether he was a συγγενής (so Jebb, Ll-J/W (*Sophoclea*)).

1202 οὐ δή ποθ᾽: 1108n.

1203 ἐγὼ φράσαιμ᾽ ἄν, εἰ τὸ τῶνδ᾽ εὔνουν πάρα: for the concern for the attitude of the chorus see 469n. Here it emphasises the importance of the coming disclosure and reminds us of the risks inherent in the current situation. But as at Eur. *El.* 272–3 and *Or.* 1103–4 this assurance is kept as short as possible, for obvious dramatic reasons.

τὸ τῶνδ᾽: virtually equivalent to αἵδε: cf. Eur. *IA* 1403 τὸ τῆς τύχης δὲ καὶ τὸ τῆς θεοῦ νοσεῖ, Pl. *Leg.* 657d1–2 οἱ μὲν νέοι . . . τὸ δὲ τῶν πρεσβυτέρων, also 261n.

1204 ἀλλ᾽ 'introduces the substantiation by the second speaker of an hypothesis . . . expressed by the first' (Denniston 20).

1205–10 Dawe proposed rearranging these lines into the order 1205, 1208, lacuna of one line, 1206, 1207, 1209 ((1973) 45–6), with Electra speaking all of 1209–10. His chief objection to the transmitted order is that Electra should speak οὔ φημ' ἐάσειν. But this can mean 'I will not allow (you to keep it)' (cf. *Aj.* 1326 οὔ φησ' ἐάσειν, Ar. *Nub.* 1044, Lys. 23.10, Erbse (1981) 40), rather than 'I will not let it go'. The reassignment is also unattractive given that Electra's utterances in 1206, 1208 and 1209–10 are all essentially plaintive: she begs Orestes not to take the urn away, she cries out that she will be deprived of her brother's ashes. The resolute οὔ φημ' ἐάσειν does not fit here: rather, it belongs in the mouth of her calmer, yet still forceful interlocutor. The *antilabe* in 1209 is also attractive on stylistic grounds (n.).

1205 On Orestes' insistence that Electra abandon the urn see 1171–1231 n.
ἄγγος: 1118n.
τὸ πᾶν: 378n.

1206 ξένε: only four lines ago Electra had suggested that Orestes might be a ξυγγενής: his attempt to recover the urn leads her to revert to this more distant title (662n.; cf. 1112, 1180, 1182, 1184). For a similar distancing cf. *Phil.* 923 (versus 889 etc.).

1207 πιθοῦ λέγοντι: cf. *Tr.* 470 πείθου λεγούσῃ, [Lucian] 74.49. The aorist imperative is probably better than the present here, as the reference is to a definite action (cf. 1205 μέθες, 1015–16n.).

1208 μὴ . . . μή: for the repetition cf. *Aj.* 190, *OC* 210.
πρὸς γενείου: for supplication by touching the chin cf. Hom. *Il.* 1.501–2, Eur. *Med.* 709, *Andr.* 573–4, *Hec.* 344, *Her.* 1206, *IA* 1247, Gould (1973) 76 n. 14 = (2001) 26 n. 14. The expression is figurative, not literal: Electra will hardly remove one of her hands from the precious urn at this critical moment (cf. Kaimio (1988) 55–6).
For τὰ φίλτατα used of persons cf. *OR* 1474, Xen. *Cyr.* 4.3.2, Page on Eur. *Med.* 16, Harder on Eur. fr. 458.2 *TrGF* = 76.2 Austin; also 538n.

1209 For *antilabe* marking emotional agitation cf. 1323, *OR* 626–9, 1173–6, Eur. *Hipp.* 310, *IT* 780, Köhler (1912) 20. Cf. especially Eur. *IA* 310, where stichomythia is similarly interrupted when Menelaus attempts to take the tablet from the Old Man; also 1220n.
οὔ φημ' ἐάσειν: cf. 1205–10n.
ὦ τάλαιν' ἐγὼ σέθεν: cf. *Tr.* 971 οἴμοι ἐγὼ σοῦ, πάτερ, ὦ μέλεος, Ar. *Ach.* 1210 τάλας ἐγὼ ξυμβολῆς βαρείας (*coni.*), Krüger ii. §47.3 Anm. 2.

1210 εἰ στερήσομαι: for εἰ with the future indicative to denote 'a matter of grief or indignation' (Jebb), like the English 'if I am going to be . . .'. cf. *Phil.*

988 εἴ μ' οὗτος ἐκ τῶν σῶν ἀπάξεται βίᾳ, Ar. *Ach.* 315–16, Moorhouse 277–8, Wakker (1994) 286–94.

ταφῆς: 'act of burial': having been unable to perform the other customary rites (1138–42), Electra is now afraid that even this will be denied her. The alternative translation 'burial-place' cannot easily refer to the urn.

1211 εὔφημα φώνει: it is ill-omened to speak of the living as if they were dead (59–66n.).

πρὸς δίκης γὰρ οὐ στένεις: cf. *OR* 1014 πρὸς δίκης οὐδὲν τρέμων.

1212 πῶς: Dawe (1968) 14–15 suggests punctuating after this with a question. Such decisions are subjective, but the line probably works better as a single utterance. πῶς . . . οὐ δίκη στένω; then picks up πρὸς δίκης . . . οὐ στένεις in the previous line.

1213 προσφωνεῖν φάτιν: cf. 329.

1214 ἄτιμος . . . τοῦ τεθνηκότος 'debarred from all rights in': cf. Thuc. 3.58.5 ἀτίμους γερῶν, S. *OR* 788–9 καί μ' ὁ Φοῖβος ὢν μὲν ἱκόμην | ἄτιμον ἐξέπεμψεν, LSJ⁹ s.v. ἄτιμος I 2, Bruhn §23.I (p. 16), Jackson (1955) 203; also 71, *Ant.* 21–2. Jebb and Moorhouse 55 prefer 'dishonoured (by)' (cf. *Aj.* 440 ἄτιμος Ἀργείοισι, *OC* 51 ἄτιμος ἔκ γ' ἐμοῦ φανῇ), but the issue at hand is whether Electra will retain the urn, not whether her dead brother still holds her in honour.

1215 τοῦτο: i.e. the urn. According to Jebb the reference is to τὸ στένειν: this is linguistically possible (cf. 1470–1, Aesch. *Sept.* 232 σὸν δ' αὖ τὸ σιγᾶν καὶ μένειν εἴσω δόμων), but hardly fits with Electra's reply. As the stage action makes clear, the urn is at the centre of things, and the audience would most naturally take it as the referent.

1216 εἴπερ γ': 'the second most overwhelming use of this particle in tragedy' (Buxton (1995) 9, the first being Eur. *Ba.* 1278 λέοντος, ὥς γ' ἔφασκον αἱ θηρώμεναι). For an equally moving instance from historiography cf. Thuc. 3.113.4 ἔ ἴπερ γε ὑμεῖς ἐν Ἰδομενῇ χθὲς ἐμάχεσθε ἀλλ' ἡμεῖς γε οὐδενὶ ἐμαχόμεθα χθές . . .', where the response parallels ἀλλ' οὐκ Ὀρέστου in our passage. The combination is frequent in a response to another's words, where it qualifies the acceptance or correction of those words as precisely as possible (Wakker (1994) 324).

1217 πλὴν . . . γ': cf. *Phil.* 441 ποίου δὲ τούτου πλήν γ' Ὀδυσσέως ἐρεῖς;, Ar. *Vesp.* 857, *Lys.* 5.

λόγῳ . . . ἠσκημένον: 'tricked out with words' (LSJ⁹ s.v. ἀσκέω I 2, taking the word as a metaphor from (personal) adornment).

1219 τοῦ γὰρ ζῶντος οὐκ ἔστιν τάφος: cf. Luke 24.5–6 τί ζητεῖτε τὸν ζῶντα μετὰ τῶν νεκρῶν; οὐκ ἔστιν ὧδε, ἀλλὰ ἠγέρθη.

1220 For antilabai in recognition scenes (a mark of excitement) cf. 1347, 1349, Eur. El. 579–81, J. G. A. Gross (1905) 55–8, Köhler (1913) 6–10, Shisler (1942) 284–5; also 1209n.

πῶς εἶπας: for the astonished question before an anagnorisis cf. Eur. El. 556, 570, 575, IT 808, Rau (1967) 61.

ὦ παῖ: when unqualified by a genitive this vocative is used by unrelated speakers to address children, youths and (occasionally) young men (cf. Phil. 201, 315, 589), by related speakers other than parents to address people under about 20 (cf. OC 1420, 1431, though Polynices' age is not clear), and by parents to refer to their children until they are of middle age (so Dickey (1996) 68). Thus in itself the vocative does not show that Electra has now accepted that the man before her is her brother. But given Electra's previous use of ξένε (1112, 1180, 1182, 1184, 1206), the address here will seem more intimate: 'the change . . . to this less formal mode of address marks her first flash of hope' (Jebb).

1221 εἴπερ ἔμψυχός γ᾽ ἐγώ: an 'obviously realized conditional' (Wakker (1994) 233–4, comparing e.g. Xen. An. 6.1.26 ἥδομαι . . . τιμώμενος, εἴπερ ἄνθρωπός εἰμι; cf. Wakker (1994) 327 with n. 56).

1222 ἦ γὰρ σὺ κεῖνος; Cf. Eur. El. 581 ἐκεῖνος εἶ σύ;, Hom. Od. 24.321 κεῖνος μέν τοι ὅδ᾽ αὐτὸς ἐγώ.

1223 σφραγῖδα πατρός: for recognition by means of a ring cf. Men. Epitr. 386–418, Plaut. Curc. 653–7, Ter. Hec. 574, 811–12, S. Thompson (1955–8) iii. 383 (H 94), Hähnle (1929) 143, van der Lee (1957) 62–3 n. 5. At Eur. El. 573–4 Orestes' identity is proved by a scar, while in Cedrenus i. 236.16–18 Bekker Orestes reveals himself to Iphigenia, ἡ δὲ οὐκ ἐγνώρισεν αὐτόν, ἕως τὸ Πελόπειον τοῦ γένους σήμαντρον τὴν ἐλαίαν εἶδεν ἔχοντα ἐν τῷ ὤμῳ δεξιῷ. For the brevity of the reference to the token see 1171–1231n. Parmentier (1919) 70 follows Morstadt (1864) 36 in giving these words to Electra to avoid a break in the antilabe (Nauck³ p. 162 similarly reassigns this phrase, though he gives Orestes the half-lines ἔκμαθ᾽ εἰ σαφῆ λέγω and τήνδε προσβλέψασ᾽ ἄθρει), but for just such a break see Aj. 984, OC 1440, Köhler (1913) 34–5. Compare Eur. El. 573–4, where immediately before the anagnorisis the

Old Man is given two lines in a section otherwise composed of single-line stichomythia.

1224 ὦ φίλτατον φῶς: although φῶς often denotes the newly recognised character in scenes of *anagnorisis* (e.g. 1354, Eur. *Ion* 1439 ὦ τέκνον, ὦ φῶς μητρὶ κρεῖσσον ἡλίου, *Her.* 531 (Με.) ὦ φίλτατ' ἀνδρῶν (Αμ.) ὦ φάος μολὼν πατρί, also *Hyps.* fr. 759a.1583 *TrGF*), here the noun must denote 'day', as Orestes' reply indicates (so rightly Ciani (1974) 43–4). For the invocation of the day in a similar context cf. *Phil.* 530 ὦ φίλτατον μὲν ἦμαρ, ἥδιστος δ' ἀνήρ, Wright (2005) 188 with n. 58. In our passage φῶς still possesses the 'undertone of rescue from danger' (Wilamowitz on Eur. *Her.* 563, translated by Fraenkel on Aesch. *Ag.* 522) which makes it especially common in recognition scenes (cf. Garvie on Aesch. *Cho.* 130–1, Lossau (1994)).

The superlative φίλτατος is standard in recognition scenes, particularly (as here) in the moments immediately after the recognition has taken place: cf. 1233, 1273, 1286, Aesch. *Cho.* 235, Eur. *Alc.* 1133, *El.* 567, 576, *IT* 795, 815, 828, *Ion* 521, 525, 1437, *Hel.* 625, 636, Men. *Perik.* 824, *Epitr.* 860 with Martina, 865, Gregor (1957) 15.

1225 ὦ φθέγγμ': for the reference to the voice in a recognition scene cf. Eur. *Ion* 561 φίλον γε φθέγγμ' ἐδεξάμην τόδε. For 'voice' in the vocative cf. *Phil.* 234–5 ὦ φίλτατον φώνημα· φεῦ τὸ καὶ λαβεῖν | πρόσφθεγμα τοιοῦδ' ἀνδρὸς ἐν χρόνῳ μακρῷ (though here the speaker has long been deprived of the sound of Greek), *Aj.* 14 ὦ φθέγγμ' Ἀθάνας (though here the addressee is perhaps invisible), *OC* 324–5, 863 ὦ φθέγγμ' ἀναιδές, Song of Solomon 2.8 'The voice of my beloved! Behold, he cometh . . .' See further Long (1968) 123–4. For the orthography see 18n.

ἀφίκου: for a word meaning 'arrive' or 'come' at an *anagnorisis* cf. Eur. *Hel.* 566 (parodied at Ar. *Thesm.* 912), Rau (1967) 146; also Hom. *Od.* 16.23 = 17.41 ἦλθες, Τηλέμαχε, γλυκερὸν φάος, Alcaeus fr. 350.1 *PLF*, Voigt ἦλθες.

μηκέτ' ἄλλοθεν πύθῃ: cf. *OC* 1266 τἀμὰ μὴ ξ ἄλλων πύθῃ. On μηκέτ' see 611n.: the sense here is 'make no further enquiries from anyone else'.

1226 ἔχω σε χερσίν; Recognitions in ancient literature are typically followed by a swift embrace: cf. 1285, Hom. *Od.* 16.214, 21.223, 24.347, Eur. *Alc.* 1134, *El.* 579, *IT* 796, 798–9, 802, 829, 903, *Ion* 1440 ἐν χεροῖν σ' ἔχω, 1443, *Hel.* 628, 634–5, 652 ἔχεις, ἔχω τε σ', 657–8, Ar. *Thesm.* 913, *Ran.* 1322 (both paratragic), Men. *Asp.* 508 ἔχω σε (also in the context of anagnorisis), *Misum.* 214 ἔχω σε, τέκνον (a family reunion), Plaut. *Menaech.* 1124, *Rud.* 1172, 1175, Ov. *Trist.* 4.4.80 *complexus*, Kaimio (1988) 35–9.

ὡς τὰ λοίπ᾽ ἔχοις ἀεί: cf. Eur. *IT* 841 τὸ λοιπὸν εὐτυχοῖμεν ἀλλήλων μέτα, *Ion* 1456–7 ἀλλὰ τἀπίλοιπα τῆς τύχης | εὐδαιμονοῖμεν, *Hel.* 698–9. ὡς here = *utinam*.

1227 ὦ πολίτιδες: *politês* in broad Greek usage suggests a political, public context while the *astos* suggests a domestic, communal one' (Patterson (1981) 160; cf. Mossé (1985) 79). This distinctive form of address allows Electra to put a special emphasis on the chorus's status as members of the community of Mycenae, and thus imply that Orestes' return will have momentous implications for that community. For the difference between the rare πολῖτις and the commoner ἀστή cf. [Dem.] 59.107 with Kapparis.

1228–9 Paradoxes playing with the ideas of life and death are common in recognition scenes, since one of the parties is so often believed to have perished: cf. Eur. *Ion* 1443–4 ἐν χεροῖν σέθεν | ὁ κατθανών τε κοὐ θανὼν φαντάζομαι, *IT* 772 κατθανοῦσ᾽ ἥκει πάλιν;, 831. In Euripides' *Alcestis* the title character has died and been resurrected by the time she is recognised by Admetus. Cf. also Luke 15.32 ὁ ἀδελφός σου οὗτος νεκρὸς ἦν καὶ ἔζησεν, καὶ ἀπολωλὼς καὶ εὑρέθη.

1229 μηχαναῖς σεσωμένον: cf. Eur. *Hyps.* fr. 759a.1627 *TrGF* (Υψ.) ἦ γὰ[ρ] σέσ[ω]τ[α]ι; (Ευν.) Βα[κ]χ[ίου] γε μηχαναῖς. The participle means 'saved': the alternative is 'brought safely home', but when used in this sense this verb is normally accompanied by a term denoting the destination (e.g. *Phil.* 311 σῶσαί μ᾽ ἐς οἴκους, *Tr.* 610–11 ἐς δόμους | . . . σωθέντ᾽, LSJ⁹ s.v. σῴζω II 2). This form (conjectured by Wecklein[1]) should be preferred over transmitted σεσωσμένον (cf. West's Teubner Aeschylus, p. xliv).

1230 ὁρῶμεν . . . μοι: for the combination of singular and plural in connexion with the chorus see Bruhn §186.

συμφοραῖσι: for unqualified συμφορά in a favourable sense cf. Aesch. *Ag.* 24, Simon. fr. 512 *PMG* (*ap.* Ar. *Eq.* 406) πῖνε πῖν᾽ ἐπὶ συμφοραῖς, LSJ⁹ s.v. II 3. Perhaps –ρᾶσι (1141 n.).

1231 γεγηθὸς . . . δάκρυον: for the *hypallage* cf. *Ant.* 527 φιλάδελφα κάτω δάκρυ᾽ εἰβομένη, Eur. *Phoen.* [1071] πενθίμων . . . δακρύων, Campbell (his edition, vol. i. p. 80). For tears at an *anagnorisis* cf. 906, 1312–13, Eur. *IT* 832–3, *Hel.* 633, 654–5, Hom. *Od.* 16.191, 16.214–20, 19.471–2, 21.223, 21.226, Pind. *P.* 4.121–3, Meuli (1975a) 383 n. 3. At Aesch. *Cho.* 236 Electra calls Orestes the δακρυτὸς ἐλπὶς σπέρματος σωτηρίου. For tears of joy in general see Arnould (1990) 94–5.

RECOGNITION DUET (1232–87)

STROPHIC PAIR (1232–72)

1232	1253	∪ – ∪ – ‖	ia
		∪ – – ∪ – ¹ ∪ – – ∪ – ¹	2δ
	1255	∪ ◡◡ – ∪ – ¹	δ
1235		∪ – ∪ – ∪ – ∪ – ∪ – ∪ – ‖	3ia
		∷ ∪ – ∪ – ∪ – ∪ – ∪ – ∪ – ‖	3ia
		∷ ∪ – – ‖	ia∧
		∷ – – ∪ – – – ∪ – ∪ – ∪ – ‖	3ia
	1260	∷ ∪̄ – – ∪ – ¹ – ∪∪ – ∪̄ – ¹	2δ
1240		∪ ◡◡ – ∪ ¹ – ∪ – – ∪ – ¹	2δ
		∪ – ∪ – ∪ – – ¹	ia ia∧
		∪ – – ¹ ∪ – – ‖	ia∧ ia∧
		∷ ∪ – ∪ ∪̄∪̄ ∪̄ – ∪ – ∪ – ∪ –	3ia
		∪ – ∪ – – – ∪ – – – ∪ – ‖	3ia
1245	1265	∷ – ∪ ◡◡ – ∪ – ‖	2cr
		∪ ◡◡ ◡◡ ∪ ◡◡ ¹ – ◡◡ ◡◡ ∪ ◡◡ ¹	2δ
		– ∪ ◡◡ ¹ – ∪ ◡◡ ¹ – ∪ ◡◡ ¹	3cr
1250	1270	– ◡◡ – ∪ – ‖	δ
		∷ ∪̄ – ∪ – – – ∪ – ∪ – ∪ ∪	3ia
		∪̄ – ∪ – – – ∪ – – – ∪ – ‖‖	3ia

The strophic pair is made up of iambics, cretics and dochmiacs, a group of rhythms commonly found in association (cf. 1384–97, Griffith (1977) 49, West (1982a) 111–12, L. P. E. Parker (1997) 43, 66–7), and from which the other tragic amoebaea which follow recognition scenes are constituted (see further below). In late tragic lyric dochmiacs often accompany lyrics of intense joy (cf. Parker (1997) 206). Interspersed among the lyrics are regular iambic trimeters (cf. Dale (1968) 86). These are all spoken by Orestes, while Electra's part is sung.

At 1232 ∼ 1253 an iambic metron introduces a passage of dochmiacs: cf. 1273, *OR* 1313, *OC* 876, Eur. *Tro.* 241, *Hyps.* fr. 759a.1593 *TrGF*, Aesch. *Ag.* 1100, Diggle (1990) 107–8 = (1994) 374. For Willink's preferred colometry see 1232–3n.

1239 ∼ 1260 present difficulties of responsion: see 1239n.

For the split resolution in the dochmiacs at 1240, 1246, 1255, 1266 see L. P. E. Parker (1968) 264–9.

The analysis of 1245 ∼ 1265 is justified at 1245n.

Resolved cretics (paeons) appear among dochmiacs at 1247 ∼ 1267: for this phenomenon cf. Wilamowitz (1921) 332, Dale (1968) 99, 109–10. The paeonic trimeter may be paralleled by Eur. *Hec.* 1100, where a single paeonic tetrameter

468

is followed by a passage probably containing some dochmiacs. Such resolution is regular in cola consisting entirely of cretics (cf. Diggle (1981 a) 119). In tragedy, however, resolution of cretics more often takes the form ⏔ U −, rather than the − U ⏔ which we have here (cf. Parker (1997) 43–4).

EPODE (1273–87)

1273	U − U − |	ia
	U − − U − | U ⏝U − U −	2δ
	− − U − U − − |	ia ia∧
1275	− U ⏝U U ⏝U − U − ‖	cr δ
	:: U − U − − :: − U − U − −	2ia ia∧
	− − U − − − U − U − − ‖	2ia ia∧
	:: − − U − − − U − − − U − ‖	3ia
1280	:: U − − :: U − − ‖	2ia∧
	:: − U U − U U − U − U − U − − ‖	D U ith
	< − U − U > − U − − U − U |	
	− U − U − U − | − U − U |	
1285	− U − U | − U − U |	tr tr∧ 2tr tr∧ 6tr ith
	− U − U − U − U |	
	− U − U | − U − U − − ‖	

Like the strophic pair, the beginning of the epode is made up of iambics, cretics and dochmiacs. There is a change of pace in 1281, and the lyric finishes with a burst of trochaic exuberance at 1282–7. The divide between speech from Orestes and song from Electra now begins to break down somewhat. At 1276 Orestes begins a syncopated, and therefore lyric, iambic trimeter (though without delivering the syncopated part), while in 1280 he has a bacchiac. This coincides with the moment when he concedes to Electra the right to express her joy uninterrupted, and thus would probably suggest to an audience a new sense of concord between the pair. Menelaus in Euripides' *Helen* also has a small amount of lyric in the recognition duet (642–3, 659, 680–1, 685), and other non-singing actors can be given occasional lyric cola (e.g. [Aesch.] *PV* 114–15, 117).

Willink (2003) 83–4 analyses 1273–4 as 2hδ 2ia ia∧, emending ἰώ in 1273 to ὤ. But as the strophe begins with ἰώ and an iambic metron, it makes little sense to emend away a similar opening here.

At 1275 Hermann's πολύπονον is likely for metrical reasons (n.). An iambic analysis − ⏔ U ⏔ U − U − is also possible, but elsewhere in the ode iambic metra are not resolved (with one exception), whereas the resolved cretic and dochmiac in the analysis above have obvious parallels from within the lyric.

For the catalectic iambic trimeters in 1276–7 see Diggle *ap.* Willink (1989) 53 n. 38.

The bacchiac dimeter in 1280 is divided between two speakers: cf. *Tr.* 892, Aesch. *Sept.* 965, Eur. *Or.* 173 ∼ 194, Willink (1989) 54.

The text and colometry of 1281 is justified *ad loc.* I have marked period-end as there must be metrical discontinuity between − ∪ − ∪ − − and the trochees.

The run of trochees is characteristic of late Euripides, and can also be found in the *OC* and at [Aesch.] *PV* 415–17 ∼ 420–2: see West (1982a) 103 n. 74. The anceps is here invariably short, a common feature of trochaics in tragedy which marks them off from the trochaic runs of comedy (cf. Dale (1968) 92). For the ithyphallic as clausula to a trochaic run (1287) cf. *OC* 1223 ∼ 1238, Eur. *Phoen.* 1042 ∼ 1066, 1736, 1757.

1232–87 Tragic recognition-scenes are commonly followed by a lyric interchange or amoebaeum between the participants (cf. Eur. *IT* 827–99, *Ion* 1439–1509, *Hel.* 625–97, *Hyps.* fr. 759a.1579–1632 *TrGF*). In each of these cases a woman sings lyrics whose predominant rhythm is dochmiac (cf. Eur. *El.* 585–95, a short choral passage after a recognition), while a man responds by speaking iambic trimeters. This division probably reflects a belief that a woman in this situation would be less able to control her feelings than a man, dochmiacs being associated with intense emotion. Various *topoi* which recur in the Euripidean dialogues are also found in this amoebaeum (cf. 1235n., 1246–7n., 1263n., 1273–4n., 1277n., 1281n., 1285n.). For the amoebaeum in tragedy more generally see Kannicht (1957), Kannicht's edition of Euripides' *Helen*, ii. 175–6, Matthiessen (1964) 134–8.

But while S.'s handling of the exchange contains much that can be paralleled in Euripides, he has also made some significant innovations. The most obvious of these is the strophic form of the dialogue, in contrast to the ἀπολελυμένα of the Euripidean passages. The tone of the dialogue is also atypical. Euripides' duets begin in a joyous mood, but subsequently move towards brooding over the past and uncertainty for the future. In the *IT* Iphigenia and Orestes both lament how close they had both come to being sacrificed at the hands of a relative (850–72), and Iphigenia is afraid that they will not be able to escape (873–99). The joyful duet of the *Ion* is barely ten lines old when Creusa exclaims ἔτι φόβῳ τρέμω (1452): most of what remains is taken up with the painful details of her seduction by Apollo (1468–1509). Happiness lasts longest in the *Helen*, but there too we experience a shift to a new atmosphere as Menelaus presses Helen for the story of her departure from Sparta (658–60), thus triggering a painful recitation of suffering. The duet from the *Hypsipyle* is missing most of its opening, though enough survives to indicate that we have a switch from joy (fr. 759a.1579–83 *TrGF*) to gloomy reflections on the past *(ib.* 1593–1632). As in these Euripidean instances, S.'s duet does not omit the recollection of the troubles of the past. But its mention of them is brief and imprecise (1244–52), quite unlike the detailed narration of past sufferings which we find in Euripides. Rather than cloud the joyful mood, they highlight it by contrast.

The behaviour of Orestes forms a further distinctive feature of S.'s amoebaeum. In Euripides the male partner in the duet, while mostly avoiding the intense emotion of song, nevertheless does not hesitate to express his delight at the recent recognition. S.'s Orestes, far from echoing his sister's joy, repeatedly commands her to restrain her excitement. Some critics have seen in this a 'callous cruelty' on his part (Schein (1982) 77). But parallels from other recognition scenes suggest a different interpretation. At Hom. *Od.* 19.479–90 and 500–2 Odysseus enjoins upon Euryclea the need for silence, since her emotional reaction to the *anagnorisis* has put the success of his plan in danger (cf. 21.226–9). At Aesch. *Cho.* 233–4 Orestes urges his sister ἔνδον γενοῦ, χαρᾷ δὲ μὴ 'κπλαγῇς φρένας· | τοὺς φιλτάτους γὰρ οἶδα νῷν ὄντας πικρούς (cf. also the chorus's words at 264–8). So too in our play Orestes' words reflect the real and present peril of the situation in which the siblings find themselves. His warnings are given greater emphasis than in Homer or Aeschylus, just as the danger is more imminent than in either of those two cases. After all, Orestes is standing in front of the house of his enemies, and risks disaster if they should learn of his presence. This sense of urgency will soon be reinforced by the Paedagogus' remarks at 1336–8. But despite this stress on the danger of the situation, Orestes is not insensitive to his sister's demands. At the end of the antistrophe he expresses his reluctance to curb his sister's joy (1271), while in the epode he allows her to declare her happiness uninhibited (1281–7). There is nothing unpleasant in Orestes' treatment of his sister.

Differences in style reflect the differences in attitude. Electra's words are full of eager repetition (e.g. 1232–3, 1253–4) and lyrical abundance (e.g. 1246–7). Orestes prefers curt and direct expressions, often effectively juxtaposed with his sister's words (e.g. 1236 πάρεσμεν, 1251 ἔξοιδα καὶ ταῦτ', 1257 ξύμφημι κἀγώ). The metrical separation of the pair reinforces this difference. But if, as seems likely, Orestes sings 1276 and 1280 (see metrical introduction), then the concession he makes in the epode to his sister's happiness is echoed in the harmony of their methods of delivery.

1232–3 ἰὼ γοναί, | ἰώ: so Nauck³, p. 163; Willink (2003) 83 makes the same conjecture. The manuscripts have ἰὼ γοναί or ἰὼ γοναί γοναί. Given that there is only one γοναί in the greater part of the manuscript tradition (including L), the repeated γοναί should probably be taken not as part of the paradosis, but as an example of dittography (cf. Eur. *Ba.* 1182 γένεθλα (B. Heath; γένεθλα γένεθλα cod.), Diggle (1990) 112 = (1994) 381, (1994) 460 n. 83). The ensuing metrical gap is most plausibly filled by Nauck's ἰώ. The loss of such an exclamation is easy, especially so soon after the ἰώ in 1232 (cf. 1245, Eur. *El.* 159, *Tro.* 1327, *Ion* 912, 1454, 1501, Aesch. *Ag.* 1490 = 1513). It also provides a closer match with the pattern of repetition at the start of the antistrophe (ἰὼ γόναι, ἰώ ~ ὁ πᾶς ἐμοί, ὁ πᾶς: cf. 489n.). By contrast, parallels for ἰὼ γοναί, γοναί κτλ. are harder to find. At e.g. Aesch. *Ag.* 1156 ἰὼ γάμοι γάμοι, 1167 ἰὼ πόνοι πόνοι, 1490 = 1513, 1537 there is a pause after the third word of the phrase, not the second, which makes all the difference. The passage thus presents a pleasing instance of the *error Wattianus*, in which the manuscripts repeat the wrong word (cf. Watt (2004)).

Willink also adopts the metrical analysis δ cret δ, comparing Eur. *Ion* 676–7 ~ 695–6. But this analysis is doubtful, as despite his parallel the single cretic between dochmiacs remains unusual. The loss of the opening iambic metron would also be a pity (see metrical introduction), especially as the epode also begins with one.

γοναὶ | . . . σωμάτων ἐμοὶ φιλτάτων: 'son of the father whom I so loved' (Jebb) makes better sense of the Greek than Kaibel's 'liebste Person von allen die je geboren sind' (p. 264). The language is highly ornate, even for tragic lyric. σῶμα denotes a person at *OR* 643, *OC* 355, Ar. *Thesm.* 895 (cited by Bruhn §233), but never in the plural. Possible parallels for this include 1235 οὕς and *OR* 1184–5, but these relative pronouns are less conspicuous than the plural nouns γοναί and σωμάτων. There cannnot be a reference to Pylades and Strophius alongside Orestes and Agamemnon: Electra could hardly put the former on a par with the latter.

1233 φιλτάτων: 1224n.

1235 ἐφηύρετ᾽, εἴδετ᾽, <ἐλάβεθ᾽>: most manuscripts have ἐφεύρετ᾽, ἦλθετ᾽, εἴδεθ᾽. The rhetoric demands that the three verbs are taken together: but ἦλθετ᾽ resists connexions with its neighbours (cf. Heimsoeth (1869) v). Whereas ἐφηύρετ᾽ and εἴδεθ᾽ both take οὕς as their direct object, ἦλθετ᾽ is intransitive. It also occupies the wrong place in the sequence: Orestes' arrival should come not second but first, followed by his discovery and recognition of Electra (contrast the verbs in asyndeton cited below, which in each case come in strict temporal order). The doubts raised by this pair of difficulties are supported by the omission of the offending verb in OPaWc.

We thus need a verb to complete the tricolon, preferably one denoting that final stage of tragic *anagnorisis*, the embrace (1226n.). Heimsoeth's supplement <εἴλεθ᾽> could be right, as given its similarity to εἴδεθ᾽ it might easily have dropped out through haplography. However, there is no parallel for αἱρέω with this sense in other recognition scenes. Better is <ἐλάβεθ᾽>, for which cf. Eur. *Hel.* 627 ἔλαβον ἀσμένα πόσιν ἐμόν, *IT* 903 χειρῶν περιβολὰς . . .

λαβεῖν, Ar. *Thesm.* 913 λαβέ με λαβέ με πόσι (paratragic). For the ensuing resolved iambic metron corresponding with an unresolved metron cf. 1243 ~ 1264.

The three verbs in asyndeton suggest high emotion (cf. 115n., 1380). Like Terence's *imus venimus | videmu'* (*Phormio* 103–4), Julius Caesar's *veni vidi vici* (*ap.* Suet. *Div. Iul.* 37) or Democritus' ἦλθες εἶδες ἀπῆλθες (D–K 68 B 115 = ii. 165.7–8), alliteration and homoeoteleuton bind the elements together (cf. Wölfflin (1881) 16 = (1933) 234).

ἐφηύρετ᾿: for the reference to finding in a recognition scene cf. Eur. *Ion* 521, 523, 571, 1441, 1518, Men. *Epitr.* 869, Plaut. *Menaech.* 1133–4, *Rud.* 1191–2. For the long diphthong (restored by Dindorf⁴) see 1093n.

εἶδετ᾿: for the stress on sight in an *anagnorisis* cf. Eur. *Ion* 1437, Men. *Epitr.* 869–70; contrast *OR* 1274 οὓς δ᾿ ἔχρῃζεν οὐ γνωσοίατο. In the prologue the Paedagogus had pointed out to Orestes the sights of the Argolid which he had long desired (3 ὧν πρόθυμος ἦν ἀεί). This motif is reapplied to Electra herself, with new significance.

1236 σῖγ᾿ ἔχουσα: cf. *Phil.* 258 σῖγ᾿ ἔχοντες, Schwyzer (1923) 27–8 = (1983) 483–4. For πρόσμενε cf. 1399 σῖγα πρόσμενε, *OR* 620 εἰ δ᾿ ἡσυχάζων προσμενῶ. For the command for silence at an *anagnorisis* cf. Hom. *Od.* 19.486 (cited below, 1238n.), 502 ἀλλ᾿ ἔχε σιγῇ μῦθον.

1238 σιγᾶν ἄμεινον: same phrase at Eur. *Tro.* [384], *Or.* 789, [Men.] *Monost.* 710.

μή τις ἔνδοθεν κλύῃ: Hom. *Od.* 14.493 σίγα νῦν, μή τίς σευ Ἀχαιῶν ἄλλος ἀκούσῃ, 19.486 σίγα, μή τίς τ᾿ ἄλλος ἐνὶ μεγάροισι πύθηται.

1239 ἀλλ᾿ οὐ τὰν θεὰν τὰν ἀεὶ ἀδμήταν: the transmitted text ἀλλ᾿ οὐ (μὰ) τὰν Ἄρτεμιν τὰν αἰὲν ἀδμήταν does not correspond with 1260 τίς οὖν (ἂν) ἀξίαν γε σοῦ πεφηνότος. Two small changes, Seidler's transposition σοῦ γε ((1811–12) i. 100) and Arndt's ἀεί ((1844) 3–4; now found in S, *teste* Kopff (1993) 156) for αἰέν leave corresponding dochmiacs in the second half of each line. Seidler's text also improves the sense: emphasis should fall on σοῦ, not ἀξίαν. The ensuing correption of ἀεί is not a difficulty: 'there are enough certain instances [of correption in dochmiacs] in Sophocles . . . to justify ready acceptance of others created by easy conjecture' (Willink (2002) 55 n. 18, with examples: cf. *Aj.* 349, *OR* 686, *Phil.* 854, Conomis (1964) 40–2).

A dochmiac can be restored in the first part of the line through Steinhart's ἀλλ᾿ οὐ τὰν θεάν (resurrected by West (1978b) 240, (1979) 105, (1991) 301, who prefers θεόν). Ἄρτεμιν will then be an intrusive gloss that has replaced the true reading, as often occurs with proper names (cf. 957n.). Dale (1968) 116, (1971–83) iii. 36 and Dawe both favour οὐ τὰν Ἄρτεμιν, but although ἀλλά is sometimes interpolated (cf. *Phil.* 1203, Jackson (1955) 103) this is less likely than the interpolation of the proper name. Pearson printed ἀλλ᾽ οὐ τὰν Ἄρτεμιν (with τίς οὖν ἀντάξι᾽ ἄν), giving 'mol cr' ~ 'ia∧ cr'; but in this context a dochmiac solution would be preferable. Hartung's μὰ τὰν Ἄρτεμιν is unlikely given the frequent interpolation of μά in such asseverations (cf. 1063n.). Brunck (1779 ed.) and Jebb took 1260 as an iambic trimeter, and rearranged 1239 to give ἀλλ᾽ οὐ μὰ τὴν ἄδμητον αἰὲν Ἄρτεμιν (τάν γ᾽ Brunck, 1779 ed.). This has the advantage of giving us a pair of trimeters, as at 1235–6, 1243–4 and 1251–2. But the postulated changes of word order are not easy to account for.

In 1260 οὖν is difficult to understand: the sense we require is adversative, not inferential or continuative. Aesch. *Sept.* [1065] does not provide a parallel, *pace* Hutchinson *ad loc.* Ll-J/W adopt Arndt's ἀνταξίαν ((1844) 4), a word not found elsewhere in tragedy. The extra ἄν found in some manuscripts provides little evidence for such a reading, as this particle is often erroneously interpolated near an optative. Moreover, ἀντάξιος means 'of equal value' (e.g. Hom. *Il.* 11.514, Hdt. 7.103.2, Pl. *Leg.* 728a4–5, Lightfoot on Lucian 44.20 (p. 407)), whereas the sense required here is 'worthy'. A better option might be ἄρ᾽, which regularly follows an interrogative pronoun to add liveliness to a question in poetry (cf. Denniston 45–6). There are not many other options, as neither τίς nor ἀξίαν is obviously corrupt.

For the invocation of Artemis see 626n.

ἄδμηταν: for this adjective in an appeal to Artemis cf. Aesch. *Suppl.* 149–50; also Hor. *C.* 3.4.70–1 *integrae | . . . Dianae.*

1240 μέν: *solitarium*, or possibly implying that while Aegisthus might present a threat, the women indoors certainly do not.

οὔποτ᾽ ἀξιώσω τρέσαι: the negative is attracted by the main verb, but makes better sense with the subordinate infinitive (cf. K–G ii. 180–1 Anm. 3): so not 'I shall never deign to fear' (March, similarly Lloyd-Jones), but 'I shall think it right never to fear' (so correctly Slater (2001) 365).

1241 περισσὸν ἄχθος: cf. Hom. *Il.* 18.104 ἐτώσιον ἄχθος ἀρούρης, *Od.* 20.378–9, S. fr. 945.3 *TrGF* βάρος περισσὸν γῆς ἀναστρωφώμενοι, Pl. *Theaet.* 176d4 οὐ λῆροί εἰσι, γῆς ἄλλως ἄχθη, ἀλλ᾽ ἄνδρες, Men. *Dis exapaton* fr. 6 *PCG* περιττὸν ἄχθος ὄντα γῆς, ὡς εἶπέ τις.

1242 ὃν ἀεί: Dawe²⁻³ and Ll-J/W adopt Viketos's ὃ ναίει ((1975) 256): cf. Eur. *Hipp.* 623–4 ἐν δὲ δώμασιν | ναίειν, *Or.* 928, S. *OC* 343. Given the variant αἰεί this counts as a redivision of the paradosis rather than an emendation. But the resulting sense is flat. By contrast, by printing ἀεί (better attested here than αἰεί, for what that is worth) we obtain the 'always' which so often figures in tragic invective (516n.), and thus allow Electra to finish on a note of contempt. The reproach is pointed in Electra's mouth. She defies the authorities by leaving the palace whenever she can, whereas the other women in the palace remain continuously indoors in accordance with conventional female behaviour, marking their weakness (cf. Pl. *Resp.* 451 d6–7, Schütz (1964) 110 n. 1). Ll-J/W claim (*Sophoclea*) that we would expect ὄν to occur next to ἔνδον, but by the standards of tragic lyric the hyperbaton is hardly exceptional.

1243 γε μὲν δή: adversative (cf. *Tr.* 484, Denniston 395, Fraenkel on Aesch. *Ag.* 887).

1243–4 κἄν γυναιξὶν ὡς Ἄρης | ἔνεστιν: a reversal of the usual sentiment, thus expressing Orestes' caution: contrast Aesch. *Suppl.* 749 γυνὴ μονωθεῖσ᾽ οὐδέν· οὐκ ἔνεστ᾽ Ἄρης, Plut. *Amat.* 761 e Ἄρεος γάρ οὐ πάνυ μέτεστι γυναικί. For the form of the expression cf. [Men.] *Monost.* 232 ἔνεισι καὶ γυναιξὶ σώφρονες τρόποι, Ant. Thess. *A.P.* 9.302.6 = 458 *GP* κἀκείναις (sc. μελίσσαις) πικρὸν ἔνεστι βέλος (Jacobs; μέλι codd.).

1244 Triclinius deleted this line to effect responsion with the antistrophe (1264, a single iambic trimeter, which is capable of standing on its own); he is supported by Haslam (1979) 97. But Heath's lacuna after 1264 ((1762) 22) achieves responsion more easily. As Jebb notes, we need a reference by Orestes to Electra's past sufferings to motivate her flood of grief at 1245–50, and 1243 alone will not suffice to provide this. At Eur. *IT* 850–1 a similarly brief allusion from the male character leads to a sudden and permanent darkening of the atmosphere; cf. also *Hyps.* fr. 759a.1591–2 *TrGF*. The same effect occurs through a question at *Hel.* 658–60, *Ion* 1468–9. Here Electra's reaction suggests that the same pattern will be followed here too (1245–50). In the event, however, the mood of happiness soon reasserts itself at the beginning of the antistrophe.

που: goes with οἶσθα: cf. 55n.

1245 At 1245 ~ 1265 manuscripts have – ∪ × corresponding to × ∪ ∪ ∪ – ∪ –: the short lacuna in the strophe compounds the difficulty in identifying the colon. The cretic analysis adopted above is based on a proposal by Diggle (1981a) 19. With this scheme in 1245–50 ~ 1265–70 we obtain a move from cretic to dochmiac to cretic back to dochmiac. The split resolution in 1265 (– ∪ ∪ ∣ ∪ – ∪ –) is not problematic (cf. L. P. E. Parker (1968) 241–52, (1997) 44–5), nor is the resolution before syncopation (cf. Diggle (1977b) 6, (1981a) 19; if these are 'true' cretics and not syncopated iambics (cf. Parker (1997) 41–2) then this last point does not arise).

The lacuna in 1245 may be filled by restoring ὀττοτοῖ with Bergk, which could easily have dropped out by haplography and is printed by most editors.

The resulting hiatus without period-end is permissible between exclamations (cf. West (1982a) 15 n. 24). But the prevalence of cretics with a resolved second longum in this part of the strophic pair makes it desirable for the restored 1245 to have one too. This is especially the case since exact responsion is the rule for all the other iambics and cretics of the lyric. Hermann and Dindorf (in his 1825 edition) print ὀτοτοτοτοῖ τοτοῖ, but τοτοῖ occurs elsewhere only at Aesch. *Pers.* 551 and 561, and the great freedom with strange exclamations in that play makes its evidence of little value here. ὀττοτοῖ <ὀτοττοτοῖ> (without hiatus) is another possibility. The form ὀτοττοτοῖ is unattested: but a scholion on this passage (Σ p. 153.9 Papageorgius) includes the only extant example of the word ὀτοττοῖ, which is similar, though this may simply be a misspelling of transmitted ὀττοτοῖ rather than a trace of an original ὀτοτ-τοτοῖ. Another possibility would be that ὀττοτοῖ has been simplified from ὀττοτοτοτοττοτοῖ (*coni.* Hermann in his edition of Euripides' *Hecuba*, pp. 71-2; cf. Eur. *Andr.* 1197, 1200 ὀττοτοτοτοῖ). Such cries usually have a double tau at the end of the first syllable, and single taus thereafter. But this need not have been followed in every instance: the author of παππαπαππαπαῖ (*Phil.* 754) hardly lacked boldness in coining exclamations. Still better, however, would be ὀττο<τοτοῖ ὀττο>τοῖ (West, *per litteras*), which gives the required scansion but without recourse to unparalleled forms. One of the forms suggested or another metrically equivalent to them is more likely on metrical grounds to have stood in the lacuna than the ὀττοτοῖ which is generally supplied.

Neither of the remaining possibilities is attractive. (i) 1265 could be a dochmiac ⏑⏑⏑⏑–⏑–, with double short instead of the first anceps. This is a rarer form than is apparent from West (1982a) 111, as many of the supposed instances listed there are suspect: see Barrett's commentary on Euripides' *Hippolytus*, p. 434, Diggle (1984b) 68 = (1994) 315. While not unparalleled (cf. *Aj.* 403 ὀλέθριον αἰκίζει, Parker (1997) 66), such an analysis should not be preferred when another is available. (ii) We could have an instance of a colon × ⏑⏑⏑–× – which some have tried to identify as typically Sophoclean (cf. Diggle (1981a) 19). But most of the supposed examples of this are better analysed ia ₍ia₎ (i.e. × ⏑⏑⏑– – – –; see the introduction to the epode of the first stasimon), which makes it doubtful whether such a colon has a separate existence.

1246-7 For an emotional response to an oblique reference to past suffering cf. 201-4, *Ant.* 857-62 ἔψαυσας ἄλγει- | νοτάτας ἐμοὶ μερίμνας κτλ., *Phil.* 1169-72 πάλιν πάλιν παλαιὸν ἄλ- | γημ' ὑπέμνασας ... | ... | τί τοῦτ' ἔλεξας; τί μ' εἴργασαι;, Eur. *IT* 850-99, *Hel.* 658-97, *Hyps.* fr. 759a.1593-1609 *TrGF*. For the lyric *abundantia* cf. *OR* 1314-15 (also dochmiacs) νέφος ἐμὸν ἀπότροπον, ἐπιπλόμενον ἄφατον, | ἀδάματόν τε καὶ δυσούριστον <ὄν>.

ἀνέφελον . . . | οὐδέ ποτε λησόμενον: metaphorical clouds usually denote pain or sorrow (cf. *Ant.* 528, LSJ⁹ s.v. νέφος I 2, s.v. νεφέλη I 2), but for the association of clouds and forgetting cf. Pind. *O.* 7.45 λάθας . . . νέφος, perhaps Isaiah 44.22 'I have blotted out, as a thick cloud, thy transgressions.'

1246 ἐνέβαλες: we need a word meaning 'mentioned'. The majority reading ἐπέβαλες cannot mean this, while rendering it 'you have laid the burden of the woe upon me' is too artificial (so rightly Jebb). ὑπέβαλες is found in one manuscript, but the sense ('suggest') is too weak, and the form is probably just a corruption from transmitted ἐπέβαλες (for the error see Diggle (1981a) 40). ἐνέβαλες is known to the scholia (p. 153.11 Papageorgius) and paralleled by Pl. *Resp.* 344d6–7 οἷον ἐμβαλὼν λόγον ἐν νῷ ἔχεις ἀπιέναι: cf. Radt (1972) 139 = (2002) 96.

οὔποτε καταλύσιμον: cf. 230 τάδε . . . ἄλυτα κεκλήσεται.

1247 λησόμενον: although this verb does not have a passive elsewhere, we require the sense 'that never can be forgotten'. For the middle used as a passive see 971n. Jebb takes the verb as a middle, and renders it 'that never its own burden can forget', but whether the personified evil can forget itself is not relevant to the context.

1250 ἔφυ: for ἦν: cf. 236, Bruhn §231.I.

1251 For ἔξοιδα see 527n.

καί: 'Orestes is trying to make his sister observe a cautious silence: he has repressed her cries of *joy*; she has now cried aloud concerning her past *sorrows*; and so he says, "I know these things *also*"' (so Jebb, in his edition of *Philoctetes*, p. 233).

1251–2 ἀλλ' ὅταν παρουσία | φράζῃ, τότ' ἔργων τῶνδε μεμνῆσθαι χρεών 'but when their presence prompts us, that will be the moment to recall these deeds' (Lloyd-Jones). This follows Long's analysis ((1964a) ≈ (1968) 141–2), in which 'their' stands for Aegisthus and Clytemnestra. For the absence of a genitive with παρουσία he compares *Phil.* 129 μορφὴν δολώσας, ὡς ἂν ἀγνοίᾳ προσῇ. Then μεμνῆσθαι will mean not 'recall and speak about' but 'recall to oneself': for memory as a spur to retaliatory action see 482–3n. For an abstract noun as subject of a personal verb cf. 39n. φράζῃ is difficult, however ('gives the signal': Long (1968) 143), and the possibility cannot be excluded that it has ousted some other verb such as προσῇ: but no plausible corruption is at hand.

Other interpretations are less satisfactory. Despite the remarks of the scholia (p. 153.17 Papageorgius), παρουσία cannot stand for καιρός, nor can we understand χρόνου with it (cf. Kells (1966) 255–7). The weakly-attested v.ll. παρρησία and –αν led Pearson to conjecture παρρησίᾳ ((1929) 88–9; cf. Eur. *Ba.* 668–9 παρρησίᾳ | φράσω): this probably requires the further alteration φράζῃς. But the resulting sense is trite. Forms of παρρησία have ousted forms of παρουσία in some manuscripts at 1104 and *Aj.* 540 (noted by Dawe, *STS* i. 195).

1253–4 ὁ πᾶς . . . | ὁ πᾶς: for the repetition cf. 1232–3n.

1254–5 ὁ πᾶς . . . | . . . χρόνος 'all time to come': cf. Tr. Adesp. fr. 109a *TrGF* ἐμοὶ μὲν οὐδ' ὁ πᾶς ἂν ἀρκέσαι χρόνος, Pind. *P.* 1.46, Melissus D–K 30 B 7(2) (= i. 271.2) ὀλεῖται πᾶν ἐν τῷ παντὶ χρόνῳ, Pl. *Apol.* 40e3, Isocr. 1.11.

1256 μόλις γὰρ ἔσχον νῦν ἐλεύθερον στόμα: 'i.e. having waited so long for freedom of utterance, she should not now be required to keep silence' (Jebb). Cf. Eur. *Hel.* 625–6 ὁ μὲν χρόνος | παλαιός, ἡ δὲ τέρψις ἀρτίως πάρα.

1257 τοιγαροῦν: first at *Aj.* 490; see further Denniston 567.
σῴζου τόδε: 'guard your freedom' (Dodds on Eur. *Ba.* 792–3).

1259 For καιρός associated with brevity cf. Eur. *IA* 829, Race (1981) 202–3, Trédé (1992) 43 n. 67.
μὴ μακρὰν βούλου λέγειν: cf. *Aj.* 1040 μὴ τεῖνε μακράν, Ar. *Thesm.* 382 μακρὰν ἔοικε λέξειν, Aesch. *Ag.* 916 μακρὰν γὰρ ἐξέτεινας with Fraenkel.

1260 On the text of this line see 1239n.

1261 μεταβάλοιτ' 'take (accusative) in exchange for (gen.)'. But Wecklein's μεταλάβοιτ' ((1922) 41) is also possible: for the corruption cf. *Phil.* 282.
ὧδε: better refers to Orestes' commands for silence (so Paley, Jebb), rather than the general circumstances in which Electra finds herself (so Wecklein).

1263 ἀέλπτως 'belongs to the stock vocabulary expressing joy after the ἀναγνώρισις' (Huys (1986) 34, on Eur. fr. 62 *TrGF* = 13 Snell (*Alexandros*)). Cf. Eur. *Alc.* 1123, 1134, *El.* 570, 579, 580, *Hel.* 656, 783, *Ion* 1395, 1441, 1511, *Phoen.* 310–11, *Hyps.* fr. 761 *TrGF*, Men. *Sic.* 287; also Plaut. *Menaech.* 1132, *Rud.* 1175 (*insperate*).

1264 θεοί μ' ἐπώτρυναν μολεῖν: cf. 70 πρὸς θεῶν ὡρμημένος. For the lacuna see 1244n.

1265–70 Orestes' reference to divine assistance spurs Electra on to another burst of joy.

1265 ὑπερτέραν: understand χάριν from the following χάριτος: cf. Lobeck on *Aj*. 277.

1266 εἰ: not a marker of doubt (1425n.).

Dindorf's ἐπόρισεν (in his 1825 edition; editors wrongly attribute the change to Fröhlich) for transmitted ἐπῶρσεν or ἐπόρσεν restores the required dochmiac. The unusual meaning ('bring, convey') is paralleled by *OC* 1458 δεῦρο Θησέα πόροι.[73]

1270 For otiose αὐτό with no specific referent see Diggle on Eur. *Pha*. 52 = fr. 773.8 *TrGF*.

For τίθημ' in this sense see LSJ⁹ s. v. B II 1.

1271–2 For the first time Orestes shows reluctance to restrain his sister's happiness (cf. ὀκνῶ; λίαν 'too much' also implies that a level of joy exists which he would be prepared to accept). This prepares us for the greater harmony of the pair in the epode.

1271 τὰ μὲν . . . τὰ δέ: adverbial: no noun needs to be understood in either case (cf. Fraenkel (1977) 4 (on *Aj*. 32–3), *Tr*. 534–5).

εἰργαθεῖν: was so accented by Elmsley on the same principle as for εἰκαθεῖν, for which see 396n.

1273–4 The epode, like the antistrophe, begins with time, also the subject of the opening of the antistrophe. For the sense cf. Eur. *El*. 578 ὦ χρόνῳ φανείς, 579, 585, *Hel*. 625–6 (cited above, 1256n.), 644–5, *Hyps*. fr. 759a.1582–3 *TrGF*, Ar. *Thesm*. 912 (paratragic).

1274 φιλτάταν: 1224n.

ὁδόν . . . φανῆναι: for the accusative cf. 1318, *Phil*. 1416, Bruhn §23.III, Moorhouse 39.

1275 πολύπονον: so Hermann. Transmitted πολύστονον cannot stand, as split resolution cannot be followed by long anceps (L. P. E. Parker (1968) 252); Medda's defence of the paradosis ((1993) 112–13) fails to take account of this.

[73] Dawe, *STS* ii. 90 claims that Lᵃᶜ has ἐπόρσεν and Lᵖᶜ ἐπῶρσεν; Ll-J/W agree with him on the first point and are silent on the second. The facsimile suggests that the omega was original, and was corrected into an omicron.

J's πολύπονον postulates an easy copying error (cf. Aesch. *Sept.* 1000, Eur. *Or.* 175, 1011) and removes the metrical anomaly.[74] It is adopted by most editors, including Jebb, Pearson and Ll-J/W.[75] Moreover, πολύπονον is probably more appropriate to the context here than πολύστονον (although that too is a Sophoclean word). After all, the effects of the πόνοι which she has endured are still visible, and Orestes has not yet eliminated their instigators. Her sighs and laments, however, have already been dispelled by the arrival of her brother.

The resulting text is best analysed as 'cr δ', which retains the split resolution (for which cf. Parker (1997) 44-5), though without the offending long anceps immediately afterwards. Of the alternatives, δ cr would require period end after the dochmiac, which is virtually impossible: for assuming that the speaker change at 1275 is accompanied by period end, the final cretic of 1276 must then be assigned its own period. Dale (1971-83) iii. 37 advocates the analysis 2ia, which gives us an iambic metron with two resolutions. While not impossible, this is not attractive in a lyric where there is extensive resolution in cretics and dochmiacs, but none in iambics.

1276 τί μὴ ποήσω; Cf. *Aj.* 77 τί μὴ γένηται;

1276–7 μή μ᾽ ἀποστερήσῃς | τῶν σῶν προσώπων ἡδονὰν μεθέσθαι: fear that the newly rediscovered relative may suddenly disappear occurs in a recognition scene at Eur. *IT* 843–4 δέδοικα δ᾽ ἐκ χερῶν με μὴ πρὸς αἰθέρα | ἀμπτάμενος φύγῃ.

1277 ἡδονάν: for references to pleasure in the recognition scene cf. Eur. *Ion* 1461, 1469, *IT* 794, 842, *El.* 596, *Hel.* 634, 700, Plaut. *Rud.* 1176 (*volup*), 1183. Dindorf (1836) 178 conjectured ἀδονάν (ἀδονᾶν *vel* ἀδονᾶς *iam* Porson (on Eur. *Med.* 734 (our 736) and Ar. *Vesp.* 401 ((1820) 130) respectively)), but the ἡδ- stem should be retained (cf. Björck (1950) 174, 237).

1278 Orestes says that he would be angry if he saw another person leaving someone who loved him, and thus implies that he will not separate himself from Electra.

ἦ κάρτα: strongly emphatic: see Fraenkel on Aesch. *Ag.* 1252.

1280 τί μὴν οὔ; Seidler's μὴν for manuscript μή ((1811–12) i. 136) must be right: for the corruption see Fraenkel on Aesch. *Ag.* 672. τί μὴν οὔ; occurs in

---

[74] The reading is usually described as a conjecture of Hermann's, but J's readings were published (in Leipzig) 23 years before Hermann's edition. Hermann's note (on his 1267) makes it clear that he is taking the reading from a manuscript.

[75] The corrected reprint of Lloyd-Jones's Loeb reverts to reading πολύστονον, which is translated 'strickened (*sic*) by my sorrows'. πολύπονον is relegated to the apparatus.

response to a question at [Eur.] *Rhes.* 706; cf. Garvie (1969) 54 with n. 7. The corruption may have been assisted by Orestes' τί μή at 1276.

1281 φίλαι: Pearson, Dale (1968) 92 and Ll-J/W print φίλ' (*coni.* Wunder²; C¹ᵖᶜ reads φίλε, with the epsilon made out of an alpha (*teste* Dawe, *STS* ii. 90)). This yields attractive metre (a trochaic system from 1281 to 1287), and the corruption would be easy to explain (φίλ' written φίλε by *scriptio plena*; changed to φίλαι through phonetic equivalence (757n.)). But the form is unlikely on other grounds. In recognition scenes the vocative of φίλος used to address the other participant in the duet is regularly in the superlative (1224n.). This is not an unbreakable rule: but of the two exceptions *IT* 830 has φίλτατε preceding (828), while *Ion* 1443 supports the simple vocative with a phrase (ὦ φίλη μοι μῆτερ). A bare address ὦ φίλε, by contrast, would be too weak here. Reading ὦ φίλαι we retain a vocative by which the chorus is often addressed in recognition duets, always by the female character (cf. Eur. *IT* 842, *Hel.* 627, 648). σε in 1285 must refer to Orestes, and this has been taken to support a reference to him at 1281 too. But at Eur. *Hel.* 627 the address to the chorus φίλαι follows soon after a second person address to Menelaus (625), without any loss of clarity. So also in our case there is no danger of confusion.⁷⁶

The analysis suggested in the metrical scheme above gives a pattern common in the tragedians: hemiepes followed by anceps and ithyphallic (cf. *OR* 1094–5 ~ 1106–7, *OC* 1082 ~ 1093, Dale (1968) 180–1, L. P. E. Parker (1997) 88–9). There is no dactylo-epitrite in the vicinity, but with this metre that is only a weak objection. For as Parker notes, 'occasional phrases of dactylo-epitrite type (especially − ∪ ∪ − ∪ ∪ −) are found in a wide variety of metrical contexts' ((1997) 88), a point apparent to anyone examining the first fascicle of Dale (1971–83): and in recognition duets we regularly find 'occasional phrases with dactylo-epitrite affinities, like the hemiepe[s]' (Parker (1997) 206). Eur. *Tro.* 551–67 provides a close parallel: there we find an entirely iambic stanza finishing with D ∪ ith. There is thus no metrical objection to φίλαι, as well as a number of arguments in its favour based on the typology of recognition scenes.

Alternative metrical analyses are less convincing. Dawe takes the passage as 3da ith: but while the ithyphallic often follows on from dactyls (cf. Diggle (1978) 173 = (1994) 194 and (1990) 115 = (1994) 386), we never find one directly after dactyls ending in a double short (cf. Diggle (1990) 121 n. 107 = (1994) 395 n. 107). 3da is also an unusual length for a colon (cf. Parker (1997) 50). Reading ia 2tr (as Griffith (1977) 38 prefers, though he reads φίλ') is also improbable, as the absence of period end at the juncture of iamb and trochee would be

---

⁷⁶ After writing this note I was pleased to find that I had been anticipated in some of these arguments by Matthiessen (1964) 137 n. 3.

irregular (cf. Parker (1990) 337–48). The double resolution is also unattractive given that there is no resolution in the trochees which follow. The colon − ∪ − ∪ − − frequently acts as a clausula to an enoplian period (cf. Itsumi (1991–3) 245, 252), but despite appearances the colon − ∪∪ − ∪∪ − × does not normally show affinities to enoplian (cf. Itsumi (1991–3) 254–5), so this analysis too would seem to be ruled out.

1282 αὐδάν: i.e. the news of Orestes' death given by the Paedagogus (so Kaibel (p. 268), Campbell (*PS*), Kamerbeek, Ll-J/W (*Sophoclea*)). For αὐδή meaning 'report' cf. *OC* 240, Eur. *Hipp.* 567, *Suppl.* 600. For ἐλπίζω used to denote the suspecting of evil cf. *Tr.* 110–11 κακὰν δύστανον ἐλπίζουσαν αἶσαν, Eur. *Suppl.* 790, Ar. *Av.* 956, Matthiae (1832) 76–8, West on Hes. *Op.* 96. Electra's immediate reaction to the announcement had been limited to a bare two trimeters (674, 677). Even after the tale has been told she does not speak for over twenty lines; and even then, her *rhesis* of lamentation (804–22) is further delayed for almost twenty lines more. Such a reaction matches the description here.

According to Jebb the reference is to the voice of the newly returned Orestes (cf. 1225 ὦ φθέγγμ'). This does not fit with the following lines, however. Electra can hardly be said to have repressed her emotion (1283–4) since learning of her brother's return; while the strong antithesis inherent in νῦν δ' ἔχω σε (1285) demands a contrast with what has gone before. Wilamowitz (1921) 514 prefers to take the word to mean Orestes' consent to Electra's request in 1279–80: but again, it is impossible to see what 1283–5 could then mean.

1283 The asyndeton is harsh, and it is likely that something has dropped out. The supplements of Dawe and Ll-J/W give us a trochaic trimeter with syncopation in the second metron, complementing that of 1284.

ὀργάν: Jebb adopts Blomfield's ὁρμάν (*ap.* Monk (1826) 214). But ὁρμάν tends to gloss ὀργάν, not the other way round (1011n.).

ἄναυδον: proleptic: cf. Aesch. *Ag.* 1247 εὔφημον . . . κοίμησον στόμα, *Aj.* 516–17. Wilamowitz's –ος ((1921) 514) is thus no improvement.

1285 νῦν δ': for this phrase at an *anagnorisis* marking the difference between past woe and present felicity cf. Eur. *Ion* 1460, Men. *Epitr.* 869.

ἔχω σε: 1226n.

1286 φιλτάταν: 1224n.

πρόσοψιν: 'expression' or 'face' would work equally well (cf. Long (1964b) 230).

1287 ἐν κακοῖς: 308n.

FOURTH EPISODE, PART TWO
(1288–1383)

1288–1383 This short scene, in which Orestes and Electra ready themselves for their task, culminates with the entry of the avengers into the *skene*. At a structural level it corresponds to Eur. *El.* 967–87, where we see the reactions of the siblings to the arrival of Clytemnestra: that scene too ends with Orestes' departure through the stage door as part of the revenge plan. In Euripides the interchange between Electra and Orestes is not happy. While Electra does not hesitate in her eagerness for the killing (cf. 965, 968 etc.), Orestes' attitude towards it is characterised by sudden revulsion and horror. He dwells on the dreadful nature of matricide (967, 969 etc.), and even doubts the ethical basis of Apollo's prophecy (971, 973, 979, 981). These concerns are not adequately addressed by his sister in her attempted defence of the action. Indeed, her obvious relishing of the imminent killing is as a further disquieting element in the scene. Even before the matricide takes place, the audience is encouraged to view it in strongly negative terms: and that encouragement largely comes from the man whose duty it is to carry it out.

The presentation of the Sophoclean scene could hardly be more different. Here there is no disharmony between the siblings. There is no reference to the matricide or to the killing of Aegisthus; nor is there any suggestion that Orestes' actions are open to ethical objections. Instead of the dark tones of Euripides' episode, S.'s version is dominated by a joyful atmosphere: a rare phenomenon indeed, this late in a Greek tragedy. This comes across at first in Electra's happy acceptance of her brother's commands (1312–17 etc.). It reaches its climax in the subsequent recognition of the Paedagogus by Electra, which forms a less intense, but still deeply affecting, version of the earlier recognition of Orestes (1339–63n.). As Jenkyns reminds us, 'to sustain a mood of pure jubilation or serenity without becoming insipid is a most rare achievement' ((1982) 98): but this scene is as good a candidate as any for a successful instance of such an atmosphere.

Accompanying this joyful tone are constant reminders of the urgency of the situation. Orestes' initial words recommending haste take up a theme prominent in the preceding lyric interchange. When we hear the sudden noise after 1321 it seems that his fears were all too accurate: and though the intruder turns out to be only the Paedagogus, his strongly-worded warnings ensure that the tension is maintained. The scene then concludes on a note of serious piety, as Electra makes a prayer to Apollo which contrasts at every turn with her mother's blasphemous prayer to the same god (1376–83n.). The audience thus swiftly moves from vicarious joy in Electra's new-found happiness, to anxiety at the seemingly imminent danger of the situation, to respect for the reverence in which Electra and the avengers behave towards the gods. There is no room in all this for ethical doubts as to the righteousness of the course in which the characters are engaged.

Thus although the scene formally acts as the prelude to a matricide, S. has so constructed it that the moral implications of this action do not impinge on the audience. While Euripides brings such considerations to the fore, S. is careful to avoid them, and ensures that the focus of the scene lies quite elsewhere. This does not mean that the play as a whole avoids such questions. Rather, the disquieting presentation of the killings which we shall later see will be all the more surprising and dramatically effective for its not having been anticipated here.

1288 'Insistence on returning to the matter in hand is almost formulaic after a recognition' (Cropp on Eur. *El.* 596–7, comparing *IT* 902–6, Hom. *Od.* 21.222–8).

τά . . . περισσεύοντα τῶν λόγων: cf. *Phil.* 24 τἀπίλοιπα τῶν λόγων.

1290 πατρῴαν κτῆσιν . . . δόμων: for the combination of house and its possessions cf. Hom. *Il.* 9.382 ὅθι πλεῖστα δόμοις ἐν κτήματα κεῖται, 19.333, *Od.* 4.79, Theodoridas *A.P.* 6.155.6 = 3511 *HE* οἴκου καὶ κτεάνων. The stress on the ancestral wealth of the house is idiomatic in the context (72n.); at Aesch. *Cho.* 943 the chorus celebrates ἀναφυγᾷ κακῶν καὶ κτεάνων τριβᾶς. For the transferred epithet cf. 1374–5.

1291 ἀντλεῖ: a common metaphorical usage: cf. van Nes (1963) 143–5. For the combination with ἐκχεῖ cf. [Lucian] *A.P.* 9.120.2 = 85.8.2 Macleod.

For τὰ δ' without preceding τὰ μέν cf. *OR* 1228–9 ὅσα | κεύθει, τὰ δ' αὐτίκ' ἐς τὸ φῶς φανεῖ κακά, *Ant.* 201–2, Meisterhans 250 with n. 1955, Wilamowitz on Eur. *Her.* 635, Denniston 166. The omission of τὰ μέν with ἀντλεῖ turns the line into an ascending tricolon.

For ἐκχεῖ: of 'the pouring out of property' (Garvie on Aesch. *Cho.* 520–1) cf. Lucian *A.P.* 9.367.1–2 = 85.9.1–2 Macleod τὸν πατρικὸν πλοῦτον . . . | αἰσχρῶς εἰς ἀκρατεῖς ἐξέχεεν δαπάνας, Aesch. *Pers.* 826 ὄλβον ἐκχέῃ μέγαν.

1292 χρόνου γὰρ ἄν σοι καιρὸν ἐξείργοι λόγος: χρόνου . . . καιρόν stands for τὸ καίριον τοῦ χρόνου (so Hermann; cf. J. R. Wilson (1980) 190). For the sense cf. [Dem.] 61.27 ἅπαντας μὲν οὖν εἰ διεξιοίην τοὺς ἀγῶνας, ἴσως ἂν ἄκαιρον μῆκος ἡμῖν ἐπιγένοιτο τῷ λόγῳ (compared by Race (1981) 203), S. *OC* 1115–16 καί μοι τὰ πραχθέντ' εἴπαθ' ὡς βράχιστ', ἐπεὶ | ταῖς τηλικαῖσδε σμικρὸς ἐξαρκεῖ λόγος, Isocr. 9.34 εἰ μὲν οὖν πρὸς ἕκαστον αὐτῶν τὰς πράξεις τὰς Εὐαγόρου παραβάλλοιμεν, οὔτ' ἂν ὁ λόγος ἴσως τοῖς καιροῖς ἁρμόσειεν οὔτ' ἂν ὁ χρόνος τοῖς λεγομένοις ἀρκέσειεν. Jebb translates καιρός as 'due limit' or 'measure': but under this interpretation ἐξείργοι would have to mean 'cross' or 'surpass', which is not possible. Nor does καιρός mean this elsewhere in S.

1294 ὅπου: Dawe[3] prints O's ὅπῃ (*coni.* Vauvilliers). But the question 'where?' is at least as appropriate to the situation as the question 'how?'
φανέντες ἢ κεκρυμμένοι: for the polar expression cf. Kemmer (1903) 65.

1295 γελῶντας ἐχθροὺς παύσομεν: on laughter see 277n.; on stopping see 304n.

1296–7 'Although the conventional masks would make such displays of emotion invisible to an audience, ancient stage-drama does allude to tears, blushes, threatening eyebrows, etc.' (Tarrant on Sen. *Ag.* 128, comparing e.g. *OC* 319–20, Eur. *Phoen.* 1485–7).

1296 οὕτως: a lacuna is required before this word. Attempts to defend the transmitted text are all unsatisfactory. According to Amigues (1977) 66–7 n. 1 'οὕτω résume la situation: "ainsi", "cela étant"', but there is no parallel for such a sense. Jebb understands σκόπει with the adverb, and compares Ar. *Ran.* 905–6 οὕτω δ᾽ ὅπως ἐρεῖτον, | ἀστεῖα καὶ μήτ᾽ εἰκόνας μήθ᾽ οἷ᾽ ἂν ἄλλος εἴποι (cf. S–D ii. 670). But in that passage οὕτω does not require us to understand a verb. Rather, it anticipates the description of the manner of speaking recommended by the chorus, which we are given in the following line. The punctuation adopted by Dover and Sommerstein (as printed above) makes this clear. Kaibel (p. 270) believes that the οὕτω in our passage is also anticipatory, and looks forward to στέναζ᾽ in 1299: the distance between the words, however, makes this impossible. The phrase φαιδρῷ προσώπῳ in 1297 is closer to οὕτω, but its anticipation by the adverb seems too artificial to be plausible.

It is also peculiar that the paradosis reads οὕτως and not οὕτω although it is followed by a consonant (cf. Friis Johansen and Whittle on Aesch. *Suppl.* 338). Corruption from οὕτω to οὕτως before a consonant is found in L at *Ant.* 220 and in AUY at *Phil.* 888 (though there the following consonant is itself a sigma): but the near-universal testimony for οὕτως in our case is something quite different. The variant οὕτω found in H (as well as in Triclinius) shows a reversion to the expected form before a consonant, and thus is unlikely to reflect any ancient tradition except by chance.

Ll-J/W emend οὕτως to τούτῳ: but it is strange to have the demonstrative fronted with such prominence, as if it were a matter of serious ambiguity which particular face Electra should choose to display to her mother. More plausible are emendations which replace οὕτω with an imperative: so ὅρα (F. W. Schmidt (1886–7) i. 153) or φράζου (Dawe, *STS* i. 197; cf. *Tr.* 604 φράζ᾽ ὅπως). Less likely is that a word qualifying μήτηρ (e.g. κακή) or σε (e.g. λαμπρόν) might have stood at the start (for the resulting word order cf. *OR* 1518 γῆς μ' ὅπως πέμψεις ἄποικον, *Phil.* 1069). But none of these possibilities can be explained on palaeographical lines. Nor is there any obvious reason why οὕτως should have replaced any of them.

Better is the lacuna posited by Dawe between 1295 and 1296, which may have lasted more than one line. The missing text will have finished with an injunction to Electra to behave in a certain manner (e.g. μέμνησο μέντοι τήνδε κρύψασθαι χαράν), and will have ended at οὕτως, which consequently should have a comma after it. For the anticipation of an ὅπως–clause cf. Ar. *Ach.* 929–31 ἔνδησον, ὦ βέλτιστε, τῷ ξένῳ καλῶς τὴν ἐμπολὴν οὕτως ὅπως ἂν μὴ φέρων κατάξῃ; also S. *Phil.* 77–8 ἀλλ' αὐτὸ τοῦτο δεῖ σοφισθῆναι, κλοπεὺς | ὅπως γενήσῃ τῶν ἀνικήτων ὅπλων. For οὕτως and ὅπως together at the start of a line cf. *Tr.* 329–30 πορευέσθω στέγας | οὕτως ὅπως ἥδιστα. The presence of the δ' in our manuscripts is no argument against this idea: in fact, it provides important evidence in its favour. After the text between 1295 and 1296 was lost, it seemed that a new sentence began at 1296. But this new sentence was in asyndeton, and a δ' was added as a result. This change was not followed through, however, and οὕτως was retained even though it was now followed by a consonant and was therefore an anomalous form. Thus Dawe's lacuna not only explicates the syntax: it also accounts for the strange occurrence of οὕτως before a consonant in the paradosis. Conceived as a solution to one problem, it unexpectedly provides a solution to another. It is therefore likely to be right.

1297 φαιδρῷ προσώπῳ: a characteristic expected of those welcoming a long-expected member of the household: cf. Aesch. *Ag.* 520–1 φαιδροῖσι τοισίδ' ὄμμασιν | δέξασθε κόσμῳ βασιλέα πολλῷ χρόνῳ, *Cho.* 565 (Orestes speaking) καὶ δὴ θυρωρῶν οὔ τις ἂν φαιδρᾷ φρενὶ | δέξαιτ', ἐπειδὴ δαιμονᾷ δόμος κακοῖς, Lobon fr. 522.3 *SH.*

1298–9 Electra's perpetual lamentation continues to give pain to her enemies: but while before it was merely a source of annoyance (285–92, 355–6, 379–82), now it will contribute to their destruction. For the phenomenon of 'affect-masking', in which 'one attempts to conceal one's feelings by assuming an opposite facial expression', see Cairns (2003) 45 with nn. 139–40.

1298 ἀλλ': the variant reading σὺ δ' in Gnom. Vat. 36 has also displaced the truth in many manuscripts at *Aj.* 1141.

ἄτη: i.e. the 'disaster' of Orestes' supposed death.

μάτην: 'falsely' (63n.).

COMMENTARY: 1288–1383

λελεγμένη: L (and F^{ac}, *teste* Dawe, on which Ll-J/W are silent) reads δεδεγ-μένη by a common uncial error (560n.). The reverse error occurs in L at 1304 (n.).

1300 χαίρειν . . . καὶ γελᾶν: for the combination cf. Pind. *P.* 10.36, Ar. *Pax* 338–9, Theocr. 24.57–8, Archias *A.P.* 9.91 = 3748–9 *GP*, Hesych. κ 34 (= ii. 387 Latte); note also the corruption at Call. *A.P.* 7.318.2 = *Epigr.* 3.2 Pfeiffer = 1272 *HE*. The success of Orestes and Electra will be marked by their appropriation of the state elsewhere associated solely with their enemies (1295).

1301 ἀλλ᾽: assentient (cf. Denniston 16–17).

ὅπως καὶ σοὶ φίλον: cf. *OC* 1205 ἔστω δ᾽ οὖν ὅπως ὑμῖν φίλον, Pl. *Phaed.* 116a1 οὕτως ὅπως ἄν σοι φίλον ᾖ, Hom. *Od.* 13.145 ἔρξον ὅπως ἐθέλεις καί τοι φίλον ἔπλετο θυμῷ.

1301–2 καὶ . . . | καί: for the repetition cf. *OR* 165–6 εἴ ποτε καὶ προτέρας ἄτας ὕπερ ὀρνυμένας πόλει | ἠνύσατ᾽ ἐκτοπίαν φλόγα πήματος, ἔλθετε καὶ νῦν, Denniston 324 (2) (i).

1302 τοὐμόν: 'my conduct' (cf. *Tr.* 53, *Aj.* 1313).

τῇδ᾽: often found with ὧδε, as at 643, *OC* 1547 τῇδ᾽, ὧδε, τῇδε βᾶτε, Pl. *Tim.* 89e3 τῇδε σκοπῶν ὧδε τῷ λόγῳ διαπεράναιτ᾽ ἄν, Polyb. 3.108.3 ὧδε γὰρ καὶ τῇδέ που συνέβαινε διατετράφθαι; cf. also Hesych. τ 739 (= iv. 151 Schmidt), Suda τ 467 (= iv. 537.11 Adler), Σ *Phil.* 204 (p. 358.3 Papageorgius, where the adverb is glossed by ὧδε). Here it is formally pleonastic, and in consequence Broadhead (1968) 83 advocates Morstadt's τάσδ᾽ ((1864) 37), which is printed by Ll-J/W; they wrongly attribute the conjecture to Brunck. ὧδ᾽ in 1301 might have influenced an absent-minded scribe to change an original τάσδ᾽ to τῇδ᾽ in the following line, given that ὧδε and τῇδε are frequently connected. But the deictic sense is unwanted here, and the resulting word order is unusual. There is no tragic parallel for delayed ἐπεί 'sandwiched' between demonstrative and article: it rarely occurs even between adjective and noun (instances at Eur. *IA* 835–6 τὴν ἐμὴν ἐπεὶ γαμεῖς | παῖδ᾽ and *Tro.* 543). This hardly increases the persuasiveness of the emendation, especially since the grounds for supposing that τῇδ᾽ is corrupt in the first place are insubstantial. Pleonasm alone is not a good enough reason: *OR* 1336 ἦν τᾷδ᾽ ὅπωσπερ καὶ σὺ φής (where τᾷδ᾽ is Nauck's convincing reinterpretation of the paradosis τάδ᾽) provides a parallel for it in our case. As Electra is putting special emphasis on the ὁμόνοια between her brother and herself, the repetition ὧδ᾽ . . . τῇδ᾽ makes a contribution to that effect.

487

1302–3 ἐπεὶ τὰς ἡδονὰς | πρὸς σοῦ λαβοῦσα κοὐκ ἐμὰς ἐκτησάμην: 'he has a right to restrict the joys which he has bestowed' (Jebb).

1304 δεξαίμην: the majority reading βουλοίμην must be a banalisation. L's λεξαίμην is a common uncial error (Λ for Δ: cf. 1298n., 560n.). For δέχομαι + infinitive accompanied by a conditional participle Jebb compares Andoc. 1.5, Aeschin. 3.217. For δέχομαι used to express a similar sentiment cf. Men. *Sam.* 422–3 οὐδ' ἂν ἐπὶ πολλῷ γενέσθαι τὸ γεγονός, μὰ τοὺς θεούς | πρᾶγμ' ἐδεξάμην.

1305 μέγ' εὑρεῖν κέρδος: cf. Adesp. iamb. fr. 35.13 *IEG* μέγ' εὗρε κέρδος.

1305–6 οὐ γὰρ ἂν καλῶς | ὑπηρετοίην τῷ παρόντι δαίμονι: cf. *Phil.* 149 πειρῶ τὸ παρὸν θεραπεύειν.

1306 ὑπηρετοίην: *coni.* Musgrave; ὑπηρετοίμην codd. The active is the form favoured by classical usage; the middle barely occurs in classical or Hellenistic Greek (instances at Hdt. 1.108.5, Xen. *Hell.* 5.2.34), whereas it becomes common in the imperial and Byzantine periods. S. sometimes employs the middle when we would have expected the active (cf. R. J. Allan (2006)): but in this case the frequency of the word in later Greek, coupled with the smallness of the alteration, makes the change attractive. Such mistakes could occur even when the middle forms were not common in the later periods. Campbell compares *OR* 840, where E has ἐκπεφευγοίμην instead of the majority's ἐκπεφευγοίην; see further Elmsley on Eur. *Hcld.* 1017.

τῷ παρόντι δαίμονι: 'our present fortune', an expression found only in tragedy: cf. fr. 653.1 *TrGF* μὴ σπεῖρε πολλοῖς τὸν παρόντα δαίμονα, Aesch. *Pers.* 825, Eur. *Alc.* 561, *Andr.* 974. On δαίμων 'fortune' see 917n.

1307 τἀνθένδε: 'what must be done next' (cf. 1339, *Phil.* 895 τί δῆτ' ἂν δρῷμ' ἐγὼ τοὐνθένδε γε;, *OR* 1267, *OC* 476, Eur. *Suppl.* 560). Jebb claims that τἀνθένδε is here equivalent to τὰ ἐνθάδε, comparing Eur. *Ba.* 48–9 εἰς δ' ἄλλην χθόνα, | τἀνθένδε θέμενος εὖ, μεταστήσω πόδα. But there a putative ἐνθάδε has probably been replaced by ἐνθένδε under the influence of the idea of 'motion from' contained in the phrase ἐς δ' ἄλλην χθόνα (see Dodds *ad loc.*). No such attraction is possible in our passage. Moreover, although Electra does indeed go on to describe the present situation, her purpose in doing so is to illustrate the circumstances under which Orestes must now act.

πῶς γὰρ οὔ; 865n.

κλύων: according to the plan set out in the prologue, the Paedagogus was to discover the state of affairs within the house and then report back to his master

(40–1). He fulfils this task in 1339–45 and 1367–71. With the aorist participle κλυών (printed by Ll-J/W), Electra implies that Orestes has already received a specific report on the situation in the palace, when we know that this has not yet occurred. We should rather read the present participle, which is found in such expressions when 'the reference is not to one particular communication but to things said more than once or at unspecified times' (West (1984) 177).[77]

1308–9 On Aegisthus' absence see 310–23n.

κατὰ στέγας | . . . ἐν οἴκοις: for the *variatio* cf. *OR* 637 οὐκ εἶ σύ τ᾽ οἴκους σύ τε, Κρέον, κατὰ στέγας.

1309–10 ἦν σὺ μὴ δείσῃς ποθ᾽ ὡς | γέλωτι τοὐμὸν φαιδρὸν ὄψεται κάρα: cf. Electra's words at Eur. *Or.* 1319–20 κἀγὼ (i.e. in addition to the chorus, whom she has just instructed to keep their expressions calm) σκυθρωπούς ὀμμάτων ἔξω κόρας, | ὡς δῆθεν οὐκ εἰδυῖα τἀξειργασμένα, where also she adopts a grim expression to deceive an enemy, despite the recent success of her plan. Some scholars see an apology here for the fact that Electra cannot change her mask (Pickard-Cambridge (1988) 172–3, Winnington-Ingram (1969) 130), but such an extra-dramatic reference is neither necessary nor plausible.

For σὺ μή followed by an imperative or equivalent see Diggle on Theophr. *Char.* 7.3. For ὡς or ὅπως after a verb of fearing cf. 1426–7, Eur. *Hcld.* 248–9, Ar. *Eq.* 112, Goodwin §371, Bruhn §138, Monteil (1963) 347. For the light pause before the final ὡς see West (1982a) 84 n. 26.

1311 The brief but powerful reference to Electra's continuing animosity reminds us that her joy has not cancelled out her hatred. She herself points out how both these emotions are acting in unison to determine her behaviour. These two aspects of her character are not easily separated: and while joy is to the fore here, the final scenes of the play will see the other emotion predominate.

μῖσος . . . παλαιόν: cf. Timoth. fr. 791.79–80 *PMG*, Hordern παλαιομίσημα, Plut. *Eum.* 7.11, Paus. 10.2.1.

ἐντέτηκε: cf. Pl. *Menex.* 245d4–6 οὐ μειξοβάρβαροι οἰκοῦμεν, ὅθεν καθαρὸν τὸ μῖσος ἐντέτηκε τῇ πόλει τῆς ἀλλοτρίας φύσεως, Dion. Hal. *Ant. Rom.* 7.46.5 οἷς ἐντέτηκε τὸ πρὸς τοὺς δημοτικοὺς μῖσος ἀδιάλλακτον, S. fr. 941.7–8 *TrGF* ≈ p. 77.7–8 *TrGFS* (Κύπρις) ἐντήκεται γὰρ †πλευμόνων ὅσοις ἔνι | ψυχῆ† with Pearson *ad loc.* and Pattoni (2003) 237 with n. 45, *Tr.* 462–3 ἥδε τ᾽ οὐδ᾽ ἂν εἰ | κάρτ᾽ ἐντακείη τῷ φιλεῖν, Lucian 55.22 τοσοῦτος ἔρως τῆς δόξης ἐντέτηκεν αὐτῷ.

---

[77] Zimmermann (1993) 104 n. 13 wrongly claims that West advocates the aorist here.

1312–13 οὔ ποτ᾿ ἐκλήξω . . . | δακρυρροοῦσα: 'her declaration . . . movingly and pointedly reverses her earlier οὐ μὲν δὴ | λήξω θρήνων (102–3) and the whole theme of ceasing to lament' (Hutchinson (1999) 57): cf. 150–2, 231–2, 285–6, 379.

1312 χαρᾷ: so Schaefer (1808) 113. With manuscript χαρᾶς Electra declares that weeping for show will not deprive her of her joy; with χαρᾷ that she will not stop weeping for joy (*prae gaudio*). The context demands the latter. In 1309–10 Electra says that she will not adopt a cheerful expression. 1311 supplies one reason for this; and since 1312–13 begins with a καί, it must be supplying a further reason. Only with the dative do we obtain such a reason. Corruption to χαρᾶς may have been encouraged by the proximity of ἐκλήξω, since λήγω is regularly followed by a genitive.

1314–15 ἥτις μιᾷ σε τῇδ᾿ ὁδῷ θανόντα τε | καὶ ζῶντ᾿ ἐσεῖδον: cf. Eur. *IA* [1611–12] ἦμαρ γὰρ τόδε | θανοῦσαν εἶδε καὶ βλέπουσαν παῖδα σήν.

1314 μιᾷ . . . ὁδῷ: for the phrase cf. Eur. *Hel.* 765, Diggle on Theophr. *Char.* 4.13.

1315 ἄσκοπα: not 'unexpected' but 'beyond belief' (so Ellendt s.v.; similarly Jebb).

1316–17 This looks forward to her later words to the Paedagogus (1361 n.).

1316 μηκέτ᾿: 611 n.

1317 For τέρας in the sense *res vel facta aliqua de causa insignia et memorabilia* (Stein (1909) 25–9) cf. *Tr.* 1131, Theocr. 1.56, Pl. *Theaet.* 163d6.

1319–21 On her own, Electra tells her brother, she would have gained glory whether she succeeded or failed. It is thus incumbent on her brother to begin an enterprise in which he too will find renown (so Heubner (1963) 379–80, supported by Dawe, *STS* i. 197–8). Ll-J/W prefer to interpret the phrase 'if [Electra] had had to tackle Aegisthus on her own she might have succeeded but might also have failed, whereas she has complete confidence in her brother's ability to overcome him' (*Sophoclea*). But this does not do justice to the force of Electra's rhetoric. The antithesis in the conclusion stresses not the possibility of failure, but the guaranteed prospect of glory (as the repetition of καλῶς makes clear). Heubner (1963) summarises and refutes other opinions. Cf. Eur. *Or.* 1151–2 ἑνὸς γὰρ οὐ σφαλέντες ἕξομεν κλέος, | καλῶς θανόντες ἢ καλῶς

490

σεσωμένοι, *Aj.* 479–80 ἀλλ᾽ ἢ καλῶς ζῆν ἢ καλῶς τεθνηκέναι | τὸν εὐγενῆ χρή.

1319 ὥς σοι: better than ὡς σοί: Orestes has already been emphasised through αὐτός earlier in the line. Dawe's emendation of ὡς to ὤν (*STS* i. 198) makes no difference to the sense.

1320 οὐκ ἂν δυοῖν ἥμαρτον: 'I would not have missed both', and hence 'I would have gained one or the other': cf. Andoc. 1.20 δυοῖν . . . οὐκ ἦν αὐτῷ ἁμαρτεῖν· ἢ . . . ἀποθανεῖν . . . ἢ . . . ἐμὲ ἀποκτεῖναι, Dem. 19.151–2, Lucian 37.17 δυοῖν γὰρ θατέρου πάντως οὐκ ἂν ἁμάρτοιμεν, ἢ . . . ἢ . . . For the closing antithesis see 821–2n.

1322–5 Hermann, supported by Bain (1977) 80 n. 3, gives σιγᾶν . . . | . . . χωροῦντος to the chorus. Dawe (*STS* i. 198) gives it the whole of 1322–5. A scholium reveals that they were not the first to suspect that the chorus spoke some or all of these lines. Hermann's attribution is possible: but since Orestes, not the chorus, has been continually urging restraint on Electra, it is reasonable to assume that he is doing so now too. Dettori (1992) 24 n. 7, 118 n. 1, 173 claims that injunctions to silence and announcements of new characters are regularly made by the Coryphaeus. There are, however, exceptions to this tendency, as listed by Ll-J/W in *Second Thoughts* (e.g. *OC* 111–12). Furthermore, *antilabe* is rare between the chorus and another character (so Jebb; note however *OC* 829–32).

Dawe supports his attribution as follows (*STS* i. 198). (i) Electra could not address Orestes and Pylades with the phrase ὦ ξένοι. (ii) 'The tutor's chastening words . . . are much less effective if the recipients of his advice have already decided for themselves to begin the action'. (iii) The phraseology of 1324–5 is especially characteristic of a chorus. But (i) Electra chooses a more distant form of address because she believes that she is being overheard by an enemy. To risk revealing Orestes' identity by a more intimate form of address could be disastrous. (ii) *Phil.* 539, where the False Merchant enters to speed up proceedings just as Philoctetes and Neoptolemus are about to leave of their own accord, provides a Sophoclean parallel for the situation Dawe dislikes. (iii) The delicate ambiguity of these lines makes them suitable not for the chorus, but for Electra, who now 'begins to speak in the ambiguous, ironical vein which she continues when Aegisthus comes (1448–57)' (Campbell *ad loc.*).

For other instances where characters on stage hear another entering from the *skene* cf. Eur. *Ion* 515–16 ὡς δ᾽ ἐπ᾽ ἐξόδοισιν ὄντος, τῶνδ᾽ ἀκούομεν πυλῶν | δοῦπον, ἐξιόντα τ᾽ ἤδη δεσπότην ὁρᾶν πάρα, *IT* 723–4, *Hel.* 858–60 ἐκβαίνει δόμων | ἡ θεσπιῳδὸς Θεονόη· κτυπεῖ δόμος | κλήθρων λυθέντων, Fraenkel (1912) 60–3.

1322 σιγᾶν ἐπήνεσ': calls for silence are common when an unexpected entrance from the *skene* is imminent: cf. Eur. *Or.* 1311–12, [1366–8], Fraenkel (1912) 63. On the aorist see 668n.

1323 For *antilabe* marking an increase in tension see 1209n.

χωροῦντος: for the omission of τις see 697n.

ὦ ξένοι: Electra so addresses Orestes and Pylades so as not to disclose her relationship to them in the face of a potentially hostile intruder. The same motivation lies behind the chorus's designation of Orestes as ὁ ξένος at Aesch. *Cho.* 730, just as the nurse Cilissa is making her entrance: ξένον τὸν Ὀρέστην καλεῖ, ἵνα δόξωσιν ἀγνοεῖν τὸ σκευώρημα (Σ 730a = i. 35 Smith). Men. *Sam.* 255–9, Ter. *Eun.* 941–6 (cited by Bain (1977) 81 nn. 1–2) provide parallels for a character giving misinformation while affecting to be unaware of another's presence. See further Mastronarde (1979) 28 for instances when a character newly arrived from the *skene* indicates that he has heard the final part of the dialogue spoken before he had entered (e.g. *Ant.* 386–7).

1324–5 οἷ' ἂν οὔτε τις | δόμων ἀπώσαιτ' οὔτ' ἂν ἡσθείη λαβών: 'ostensibly, the relics of a kinsman; in her secret meaning, retribution' (Jebb).

1326–38 As requested at 31, the Paedagogus points out to Orestes his failure to observe due καιρός. Nowhere else in tragedy does a slave castigate his master, or address him with such vehemence: but this is no ordinary slave. The effect of the interruption here is to increase the urgency still further, and reminds us that Orestes was right in the previous lyric duet to encourage his sister to master her joy.

1327 παρ' οὐδὲν . . . κήδεσθ': cf. *Ant.* 465–6 οὕτως ἔμοιγε τοῦδε τοῦ μόρου τυχεῖν | παρ' οὐδὲν ἄλγος.

1328 ἦ νοῦς ἔνεστιν οὔτις ὕμιν ἐγγενής: Jebb's 'was there no wit born in you' catches the sense. A gloss in L renders ἐγγενής as ἄξιος τοῦ γένους (p. 155.9 Papageorgius), but this cannot be right: the family that produced Tantalus, Thyestes and Agamemnon could hardly be said to have been characterised by foresight and intelligence. The v.l. εὐγενής can be ruled out: it is the effectiveness, not the nobility, of the siblings' minds that is in question.

1329 ἄκροις: conjectured independently by Dawe and Diggle (cf. Dawe (1976) 233) for manuscript αὐτοῖς; Dawe prints it in his second and third editions. The repetition αὐτοῖς . . . αὐτοῖσιν in the same line is clumsy: more important, as Dawe points out (*ib.*), '"actual" belongs only in the second half of this phrase'. The sense is 'you are not on the edge of catastrophe, but in its very midst'. For

ἄκρος in a rejected possibility cf. Theophr. *HP* 1.13.4 οὐ μὴν . . . ἐπ᾽ ἄκροις . . .
ἀλλ᾽ ἐν τοῖς ἀνὰ μέσον, Philo *De Vit. Cont.* 31 ἥτις οὐκ ἄκροις ὠσὶν ἐφιζάνει,
ἀλλὰ δι᾽ ἀκοῆς ἐπὶ ψυχὴν ἔρχεται καὶ βεβαίως ἐπιμένει. For ἄκρος with κακός
cf. Eur. fr. 169 *TrGF* ἐπ᾽ ἄκραν ἥκομεν γραμμὴν κακῶν. The corruption from
ἄκροις to αὐτοῖς occurred through a simple anticipatory error (for which cf.
Diggle (1984a) 60 = (1994) 288, (1994) 469–70): the visual similarity of the two
words will have assisted the change.

Ll-J/W (*Sophoclea*) reject the Cambridge conjecture by referring to Kaibel's
note (pp. 275–6): he was however anticipated by Heimsoeth (1873) xii. According to Heimsoeth, the essential contrast in the sentence is between παρά and
ἐν: but since in Greek one cannot say οὐ παρὰ ἀλλὰ ἐν αὐτοῖς κακοῖς, the first
αὐτοῖς is added as a filler. But neither he nor Kaibel provides a parallel for
redundant αὐτοῖς contrasting two prepositions. The parallel from Theophrastus cited above shows how a meaningful change in prepositions (ἐπί to ἐν) need
not exclude the presence of ἄκροις with the first preposition. For the intensifying use of αὐτά with the second preposition cf. Antisthenes 15.8 (p. 27 Caizzi)
ἐγὼ δὲ ἄοπλος οὐ πρὸς τὰ τείχη τῶν πολεμίων ἀλλ᾽ εἰς αὐτὰ εἰσέρχομαι τὰ
τείχη.

See Moorhouse 119 on locative παρά with the dative. On ἐν κακοῖς see
308n.

1331 σταθμοῖσι τοῖσδε . . . ᾽κύρουν ἐγώ: a suitable place for keeping watch
(cf. Hom. *Od.* 22.181 τὼ δ᾽ ἔσταν ἑκάτερθε παρὰ σταθμοῖσι μένοντε). For
σταθμός = 'upright member of a structure' and hence 'doorway, entrance' see
Chadwick (1996) 257–8; also Gagnepain (1959) 87.

1332 ἦμιν: Dawe prints the majority reading ὑμίν, but ethic dative of the
first person pronoun gives a more appropriate tone, well conveyed by Ll-
J/W's 'we should have had [news of] your doings in the house before your
persons' (*Sophoclea*). Corruption to the second person was probably caused by
anticipation of ὑμῶν in the following line.

1333 τὰ δρῶμεν᾽ . . . τὰ σώματα: the partial rhyme sharpens the antithesis:
cf. *OR* 110–11 τὸ δὲ ζητούμενον | ἁλωτόν, ἐκφεύγει δὲ τἀμελούμενον, Bruhn
§243.

ὑμῶν: a possessive genitive with a participle is unusual except when the
participle in question is regularly used as a noun (cf. Eur. *Alc.* 167 αὐτῶν ἡ
τεκοῦσ᾽, K–G i. 334 Anm. 1). Here 'the union with τὰ δρ. is made easier by τὰ
σώματα following, with which ὑμῶν also goes' (Moorhouse 52; see also p. 76).

1334–5 νῦν δ᾽ . . . | καὶ νῦν: νῦν is repeated in successive lines in different
senses: cf. *Tr.* 1075–6 νῦν δ᾽ ἐκ τοιούτου θῆλυς ηὕρημαι τάλας. | καὶ νῦν

493

προσελθὼν στῆθι πλησίον πατρός with Stinton (1985) 38 = (1990) 435–6, Davies on *Tr.* 88 ff.

1334 εὐλάβειαν . . . προὐθέμην: 'set myself as a task' (cf. Pl. *Phaedr.* 259e1 ὅπερ νῦν προυθέμεθα σκέψασθαι, *Ant.* 216, 1249, *Tr.* 1049). The alternative rendering 'I displayed' (cf. Hdt. 6.21.1 πένθος μέγα προεθήκαντο (v.l.), Thuc. 2.42.3) would be inappropriate: display is the last thing that the Paedagogus wants.

1335 For μακροί applied disapprovingly to λόγοι see Diggle on Theophr. *Char.* 3.1.

1336 τῆς ἀπλήστου . . . σὺν χαρᾷ βοῆς: cf. Eur. *Suppl.* 79–80 ἄπληστος ἅδε μ' ἐξάγει χάρις γόων | πολύπονος, *El.* 879 ἴτω ξύναυλος βοὰ χαρᾷ.

1337 A point, not a comma, before ὡς makes the phrasing clearer (as at 21–2).

1338 ἀπηλλάχθαι δ' ἀκμή: the perfect implies immediacy: cf. 64, *OR* 1050 σημήναθ', ὡς ὁ καιρὸς ηὑρῆσθαι τάδε. As in 22, the Paedagogus' speech ends with the urgent ἀκμή.

1339–63 After the Paedagogus' outburst there follows a brief recapitulation of the situation in stichomythia. At 1344–5 the Paedagogus refuses to answer Orestes' question immediately, and speaks two lines instead of one. This has a strong closural effect, and we now expect Orestes to make his way, at last, into the house. In fact, almost forty lines elapse before he does so. For Electra now interrupts to ask the identity of the man who has just come in from the *skene*. The subsequent interchange between her and Orestes lasts a full eight lines (1346–53), after which she expresses her joy in a short but moving speech (1354–63). This relaxed tempo is all the more notable for the pace of the previous part of the scene. This part of the episode could easily have been shorter (cf. Eur. *El.* 553–7), or omitted altogether. It was hardly necessary that Electra should be reacquainted with an old friend from many years ago; and we have only just experienced the recognition scene to end all recognition scenes. By including this section, S. again keeps our attention away from the grim business of killing which lies ahead, and directs it instead on the joyful πάθη of the heroine. While lacking the intensity of the earlier *anagnorisis*, the scene nevertheless makes up a moving recapitulation of the recognition motif, and marks the final stage of Electra's emotional journey which had begun with the deceitful speech of the Paedagogus.

1339 τἀντεῦθεν: 1307n.

1340 Orestes had earlier implied that he would be recognised if he returned to the house (42–3); the story of his death has removed that problem.

ὑπάρχει: 'it is secured, it is the case that'; for this verb with the infinitive cf. Aesch. *Ag.* 961–2 οἴκοις (Porson; οἶκος codd., ἄκος West) δ᾽ ὑπάρχει τῶνδε σὺν θεοῖς, ἄναξ, | ἔχειν, Eur. *Hcld.* 181–2.

1341 ἤγγειλας . . . ὡς τεθνηκότα: for verbs of saying with a participial construction and ὡς see 882n. For the omission of με see 1200n.

1342 'Know that here thou art numbered with the shades' (Jebb). This motif is picked up by Orestes in 1477–8. Campbell translates 'I would have you know that you are the only dead man who is in the light of day': but as Jebb notes, the context demands that ἐνθάδε refer to the house.

εἷς τῶν ἐν Ἅιδου . . . ἀνήρ: for the construction (as opposed to εἷς τῶν ἐν Ἅιδου ἀνδρῶν) see Kuhlmann (1997–8) 80 n. 15.

1343 χαίρουσιν οὖν τούτοισιν: οὖν gives the required inferential sense. The v.l. ἐν was an easy corruption, given the frequency of the phrase ἐν τούτοις. The verb χαίρω does not take ἐν + dative (see Jebb on *Tr.* 1118–19); thus here it would mean 'rejoice under these circumstances', which is inept.

1344–5 The Paedagogus puts off Orestes' questions, and will later do the same with Electra (1364–6). This urgency 'both displays [the Paedagogus'] own character and saves the playwright from covering in detail topics that need no further development' (Mastronarde (1979) 83, comparing e.g. Eur. *Ion* 1453–7).

1344 τελουμένων εἴποιμ᾽ ἄν: for the genitive absol. without expressed subject cf. Aesch. *Sept.* 274 εὖ ξυντυχόντων, K–G ii. 81 Anm. 2, Diggle (1982a) 57 = (1994) 221. For the present tense where we might have expected perfect or aorist cf. Eur. *Andr.* 997–8 (μηχανὴ) ἣν πάρος μὲν οὐκ ἐρῶ | τελουμένων δὲ Δελφὶς εἴσεται πέτρα, Hdt. 1.206.1 οὐ γὰρ ἂν εἰδείης εἴ τοι ἐς καιρὸν ἔσται ταῦτα τελεόμενα, Headlam on Herodas 2.85. The vague, timeless participle suggests a menacing 'tone of mystery and reserve' (Jebb), both here and in the *Andromache* passage. Words from the IE *telh₂*- root occur frequently in the final section of the play, mostly to denote the plan to kill Aegisthus and Clytemnestra: cf. 1399, 1417, 1435, Fischer (1965) 148, Goldhill (1984) (on similar uses of the root in Aeschylus' *Oresteia*).

1345 'All the conditions on their part (that of Clyt. and Aeg.) are good (for us), . . . even those which are not morally good, – viz., Clytaemnestra's joy at the death of her son, and those insults which expressed her new sense of security (773–803)' (Jebb). The obscurity of the expression continues the mysterious tone.

For καλῶ suggesting the imminent success of an impending intrigue cf. Eur. *Hec.* 875, *El.* 648, 965, *IT* 1051, 1055, *Alex.* fr. 62d.24 *TrGF* = 43 col. II.3 Snell, Huys (1986) 24 with n. 49.

τὰ κείνων: 261 n.

1346 ἀδελφέ: 461 n.

1347 οὐδέ γ᾿: 'not even' (Denniston 156 (2)).

†ἐς θυμὸν φέρω†: a frustrating phrase. The sense we require is an action or state of the mind preparatory to ξυνίης (which here must mean 'recognise', as at *Ant.* 1218). Hence Blaydes' translated 'nor do I bring him to mind'. But similar Greek expressions elsewhere mean rather 'take to heart' (cf. *OR* 975 μή νυν ἔτ᾿ αὐτῶν μηδὲν ἐς θυμὸν βάλῃς, [Aesch.] *PV* 705–6 τοὺς ἐμοὺς λόγους | θυμῷ βάλ). There is no parallel for the idiom advocated by Blaydes, which is condemned by Ll-J/W (*Sophocles*) as 'less Greek than English'. N. G. Wilson's ᾐσθόμην σφέ πω is printed by Lloyd-Jones in his Loeb, while Russell (*per litteras*) suggests ἐσθ᾿ ᾧ (or ὃ) συμβαλῶ. These give good sense, and might be right: but the corruption postulated in each case is too extreme for us to admit the conjecture to the text.

1348 For Electra's rescue of the infant Orestes see 11–14n.

1349–50 οὔ . . . | . . . χεροῖν: for the long gap cf. 78n.

1350 ὑπεξεπέμφθην: cf. 297 ὑπεξέθου.
σῇ προμηθίᾳ: cf. 12, 1132–3.

1351 ἦ κεῖνος οὗτος ὅν: expressing amazement: cf. Eur. *El.* 581 ἐκεῖνος εἶ σύ;, Virg. *Aen.* 1.617 *tune ille Aeneas . . .?* For the 'question as exclamation' see Davies's commentary on *Tr.*, index s.v. style, under that lemma.

1352 προσηῦρον: for the long diphthong (restored by Dindorf†) see 1093n.
πιστόν: for this adjective applied to servants in S. see Roisman (1984) 143–7.

1353 ὅδ᾿ ἐστί. μή μ᾿ ἔλεγχε πλείοσιν λόγοις: cf. Aesch. *Cho.* 219 ὅδ᾿ εἰμί· μὴ μάστευ᾿ ἐμοῦ μᾶλλον φίλον (with Garvie *ad loc.* on ὅδ᾿ εἰμί).

1354–6 The accumulation of questions marks emotional agitation: cf. Mastronarde (1979) 39 (comparing *OR* 532–42, Eur. *Andr.* 387–405).

1354 ὦ φίλτατον φῶς: for the metaphorical use of φῶς in intense emotional addresses cf. 1224n., Eur. *Ba.* 608 ὦ φάος μέγιστον ἡμῖν, Shisler (1942) 282. Ll-J/W (*Second Thoughts*) take the word to denote the day, and accordingly Lloyd-Jones prints ὦ φίλτατον φῶς· in the revised 1997 edition of his Loeb. Such a sense is found in a similar context at 1224: but there Orestes' reply indicates that φῶς must mean 'day'. In this case there is no such indication: and given that φῶς is commonly metaphorical, and given that the surrounding text refers exclusively to the Paedagogus, it is most natural to take this as referring to him too. The Loeb punctuation makes an awkward distinction between ὦ and ὢ in close proximity.

1354–5 ὦ μόνος σωτὴρ δόμων | Ἀγαμέμνονος: cf. Aesch. *Cho.* 264 ὦ παῖδες, ὦ σωτῆρες ἑστίας πατρός. For the nominative used in exclamations see Moorhouse 22–3. For μόνος in a praise-*topos* cf. 531 n. It does not imply that Orestes has been downgraded.

1355 πῶς ἦλθες; The question conveys amazement rather than a genuine desire for information (cf. Ar. *Pax* 193).

1355–6 ἦ σὺ κεῖνος εἶ, | ὅς . . . ἔσωσας . . .; cf. Eur. *Hcld.* 945–7 ἐκεῖνος εἶ σύ . . . | ὅς . . . | . . . ἀξιώσας . . .;

1357–8 ὦ φίλταται μὲν χεῖρες, ἥδιστον δ᾽ ἔχων | ποδῶν ὑπηρέτημα: for the straightforward expression followed by a periphrasis with an abstract noun in –μα cf. *Phil.* 867–8 ὦ φέγγος ὕπνου διάδοχον, τό τ᾽ ἐλπίδων | ἄπιστον οἰκούρημα τῶνδε τῶν ξένων. 'Sophocles has probably used ὑπηρέτημα because it is not the feet as such which deserve praise but the services performed by them. While this is equally true of "hands", feet are perhaps an inappropriate object of apostrophe for the tragic poet' (Long (1968) 100). *Phil.* 1188–9 is presumably the exception which proves the rule. φιλτάτας . . . χείρας (Bothe¹) is possible: a scribe could easily have failed to understand the construction with ἔχων and so turned the phrase into an independent vocative.

1359 ἔσαινες: *coni.* Ll-J/W; ἔφαινες codd. Except occasionally in epic (e.g. Hom. *Il.* 11.64), φαίνω cannot mean 'appear'. The sense 'shine forth' would be paralleled only at Eur. *El.* 1234 φαίνουσι, where Diggle (1981 a) 41–2 makes a good case for Hartung's βαίνουσι. J. M. Bremer and van Erp Taalman Kip (1994) 242 follow Kamerbeek's suggestion that we understand συνόντα σε, but this is too compressed. Nauck's deletion, accompanied by insertion of μ᾽ after λόγοις in 1360 (in his third edition, p. 164), is too drastic a remedy. Sense is restored by the change of a single letter in Ll-J/W's ἔσαινες (approved by West (1991) 300). This verb 'is properly "fawn" of a dog showing fondness or gladness; it is then used (chiefly in tragedy) of a person or thing which attempts to rouse, or which in fact rouses, a person's favourable emotion' (Barrett on Eur. *Hipp.* 862–3); it is used 'of a sight or a sound which *appeals for recognition* by vividly striking our senses' (Jebb on *Ant.* 1213–14; his italics). Cf. [Aesch.] *PV* 835, Eur. *Ion* 685.

1359–60 με | . . . ἐμοί: for the occurrence of the stressed pronoun so soon after the unstressed cf. *OC* 811–12 μηδέ με | φύλασσ' ἐφορμῶν ἔνθα χρὴ ναίειν ἐμέ, Diggle (1972) 348.

1360 ἔργ' ἔχων: 'engaged in a course of action' (cf. *Ant.* 300 πανουργίας . . . ἔχειν).

1361 χαῖρ': for this word (and Latin *salve*) in recognition scenes see Gomme and Sandbach on Men. *Perik.* 824–5, adding to their examples Pacuvius 20 Ribbeck (*Antiope*).

ὦ πάτερ: πάτερ as a term of address can be used by any young person to an old man whom he or she respects (Dickey (1996) 78–80). In this context, however, the address is more poignant (cf. Fraenkel (1922) 125 with n. 4 ≈ (1960a) 118–19 with 119 n. 2). The son was rescued through the Paedagogus' action, and this is in some sense equivalent to allowing the father to live again: cf. Aesch. *Cho.* 503–4 καὶ μὴ 'ξαλείψης σπέρμα Πελοπιδῶν τόδε· | οὕτω γὰρ οὐ τέθνηκας οὐδέ περ θανών, Horsley (1980). Minucius' address of Fabius as πάτερ, as described at Plut. *Fab. Max.* 13.8, has a similar significance (cited by Dickey (1996) 79).

1362–3 ἴσθι δ' ὡς μάλιστά σ' ἀνθρώπων ἐγώ | ἤχθηρα κἀφίλησ' ἐν ἡμέρα μιᾷ: for the sentiment cf. Apollonides *A.P.* 9.243.1–2 = 1203–4 *GP* γήθησαν περὶ παιδὸς Ἀριστίπποιο τοκῆες | καὶ κλαῦσαν· μοίρης δ' ἦμαρ ἐν ἀμφοτέρης.

1363 ἐν ἡμέρα μιᾷ: again the stress on the crucial day (cf. 783, 918–19, 1149), but this time in a positive sense.

1364 ἀρκεῖν δοκεῖ μοι: for ἀρκεῖ conveying qualified gratitude before moving on to a new point cf. *Tr.* 1216, Quincey (1966) 141. While not blunt, the expression suggests the lack of subservience which characterises the ἦθος of the Paedagogus.

τοὺς . . . ἐν μέσῳ λόγους: expressions with ἐν μέσῳ may refer to a period of time (i) between the present and some point in the future (cf. *OC* 583–4,

Eur. *Med.* 819, *Hel.* 630–1, *Her.* 94), (ii) between the present and a moment in the past (cf. Eur. *Ion* 1393–4) or (iii) between two past events (cf. Eur. *Or.* 16). In this instance (iii) is impossible. (i) at first seems attractive. Under this interpretation, the Paedagogus is issuing his familiar warning against further λόγοι which would stand between the present moment and the moment of action. But then 1365–6 becomes difficult to understand: for why would Electra need to have such λόγοι 'made clear' to her? Thus (ii) must be right. Electra will later have plenty of time to hear about Orestes' experiences since he left Mycenae as a child (so Jebb).

τοὺς . . . λόγους is picked up by ταῦτα in 1366. The construction can only be explained if we assume an anacoluthon after this line, with τοὺς . . . λόγους forming a loosely prefixed accusative of reference (466–7n.) after which the syntax takes off in a new direction.

1365 πολλαὶ . . . νύκτες ἡμέραι τ': foil to the coming stress on the critical moment (1368–9). For the order 'night and day' 259n.

κυκλοῦνται: the minority reading –οῦσι may be an anticipation of the same ending in 1366. The active with intransitive sense is found elsewhere in classical Greek only at *Tr.* 130 (see Davies on 129 ff.).

1367 δ' . . . γε: the combination often stresses a pronoun ('as for you': cf. *Aj.* 1409, Hutchinson on Aesch. *Sept.* 281–2). Here, by emphasising σφῷν, it marks the Paedagogus' move from Electra to Orestes and Pylades. See further Denniston 155 (4) (i), though he goes too far in claiming that the combination is 'strongly adversative'. Hermann's γώ, printed by Ll-J/W, is no improvement. Jebb, Pearson and Dawe rightly keep the paradosis.

1368–9 νῦν . . . νῦν . . . | νῦν: the anaphora and asyndeton of these three tight verbless phrases convey great force. Cf. Aesch. *Cho.* 725 νῦν ἐπάκουσον, νῦν ἐπάρηξον· | νῦν γὰρ ἀκμάζει, S. *OR* 596–7, Hor. *C.* 1.37.1–2.

1368 On καιρός see 75–6n.

Κλυταιμήστρα only L has the correct spelling (for which see Fraenkel on Aesch. *Ag.* 84).

1369 ἀνδρῶν: referring, it turns out, to the οἰκέται (see next n.).

1370–1 The Paedagogus specifies two sets of potential enemies: (i) 'these people' (τούτοις) and (ii) 'others' (ἄλλοισι) who are σοφώτεροι and πλείονες than the group denoted by τούτοις. The choice of demonstrative pronoun shows that there must already have been a reference to (i). The only plausible referent is the ἀνδρῶν of 1369. The contrast between (i) and (ii) can then only

499

make sense if (i) refers to the men of the household, while (ii) denotes Aegisthus and his bodyguard. The passage is remarkably allusive, particularly since we cannot work out the full sense of ἀνδρῶν in 1369 until a further couple of lines have passed. This ambiguity is deliberate: by avoiding a direct warning to look out for Aegisthus' bodyguard, the Paedagogus creates a more mysterious atmosphere of menace.

1372–3 ἄν . . . | . . . εἴη: statements using ἄν with the optative sometimes seem to have an excited tone, which would be appropriate in this context: cf. 1436, *OR* 1182 τὰ πάντ᾽ ἄν ἐξήκοι σαφῆ, Waś (1983) 74–5.

1373 τόδ᾽ εἴη τοὔργον: governing both λόγων in 1372 and χωρεῖν in 1374. For οὐδὲν ἔργον with the genitive meaning 'there is no need of' see Renehan (1992) 360. For the τόδε cf. Eur. *Andr.* 551–2 οὐ γὰρ ὡς ἔοικέ μοι | σχολῆς τόδ᾽ ἔργον.

1374–5 πατρῷα . . . ἕδη | θεῶν: '*images* of gods, whether sitting or standing; but always with the added notion that they are placed in a temple or holy place as objects of worship' (Jebb on *OR* 886 δαιμόνων ἕδη). For ἕδος in this context cf. Timaeus *Lex. Platon.* ε 5 (p. 93.3 Ruhnkenius) ἕδος· τὸ ἄγαλμα καὶ ὁ τόπος ἐν ᾧ ἵδρυται. Cf. further Aesch. *Ag.* 518–19 ἰὼ μέλαθρα, βασιλέων φίλαι στέγαι, | σεμνοί τε θᾶκοι, δαίμονές τ᾽ ἀντήλιοι, Ar. *Vesp.* 875 ὦ δέσποτ᾽ ἄναξ, γεῖτον Ἀγυιεῦ τοὐμοῦ προθύρου προπύλαιε, Rusten (1983) 291 n. 11. For the transferred epithet cf. 1290.

1374 προσκύνανθ᾽: 'the verb . . . connotes "worship", often with no indication what form the worship takes' (Diggle on Theophr. *Char.* 16.5): here it probably refers to a reverential kiss. The action of Orestes and Pylades here can best be understood as a greeting rather than a formal prayer (cf. Pulleyn (1997) 162).

1375 After a brief gesture of respect towards the statue of Apollo, Orestes, Pylades and the Paedagogus enter the palace. The actor playing the Old Man must move quickly to take up his position at the far end of eisodos A and return as Aegisthus at 1428.

1376–83 The prayer before the statue of Apollo recalls Clytemnestra's earlier prayer to the same deity. Various similarities in the language used encourage the audience to make the comparison between the two (cf. 655–6 ~ 1376, 1379–80, Mikalson (1989) 89 n. 53). This points to the obvious and significant difference: that while Clytemnestra's prayer was a masterpiece of wickedness, Electra's petition is a truly pious one which the god will now bring to a successful end. For more on contrasting prayers see Fraenkel on Aesch. *Ag.* 500.

1376 ἄναξ . . . ἵλεως . . . κλύε: for these three elements in a prayer see 645n., 655n. and 637n. respectively.

αὐτοῖν: the dual is used because the Paedagogus is not thought of as an active participant in this final stage of the plan.

1377–8 For the θυσιῶν ἀνάμνησις see Ausfeld (1903) 526–8, Kannicht on Eur. *Hel.* 969–74, Harder on Eur. fr. 448a.63 *TrGF* = 66.62 Austin, Pulleyn (1997) 31–2, R. C. T. Parker (1998) 106–7.

σε . . . | . . . προῦστην: elsewhere the verb takes a dative (e.g. *Aj.* 1133). Hdt. 1.86.3 ὡς δὲ ἄρα μιν προστῆναι τοῦτο may provide a parallel, if Rosén is right to print the manuscript reading (Hude prefers προσστῆναι). The accusative may be used by analogy with ἱκετεύω (so Moorhouse 38); this may also explain *OR* 31–2 σ᾽. . . ἑζόμεσθ᾽ἐφέστιοι. The text of fr. 660 *TrGF* προστῆναι μέστην | τράπεζαν is too uncertain to be relied on (see Radt *ad loc.*, Kaibel p. 281 n.1).

1377 For temporal πολλά with the aorist cf. θαμά at 1144–5.

1378 ἀφ᾽ ὧν ἔχοιμι: along with ἐξ οἵων ἔχω in 1379, this phrase suggests the poverty of Electra's offerings. Cf. 449–50n., Eur. *Tro.* 1200–2 κομίζετ᾽ ἀθλίῳ κόσμον νεκρῷ | ἐκ τῶν παρόντων. οὐ γὰρ ἐς κάλλος τύχας | δαίμων δίδωσιν· ὧν δ᾽ ἔχω, λήψῃ τάδε, *Hec.* 613–15, fr. 327 *TrGF*, Hes. *Op.* 336 with West *ad loc.*, *IG* i³ 953.4 = *CEG* i. §317.4 θεοῖς ἄφθονος ἐς δύναμιν, Agis *A.P.* 6.152.3 = 12 *HE*, Leon. Tarent. *A.P.* 6.288.8 = 2220 *HE*, Ant. Thess. *A.P.* 9.93.4 = 246 *GP*, Antiphilus *A.P.* 6.199.4 = 880 *GP*, Apollonides *A.P.* 6.238.5 = 1135 *GP*, Zonas *A.P.* 6.98.5 = 3450 *GP*, Gaetulicus *A.P.* 6.190.2 = 182 *FGE*. For ἀπό used to denote the means or resource see LSJ⁹ s.v. III 6, *DGE* s.v. B III 3.

λιπαρεῖ . . . χερί: cf. Aesch. *Pers.* 202–3 ξὺν θυηπόλῳ χερὶ | βωμὸν προσέστην, 451 n.

1379 ὦ Λύκει᾽ Ἄπολλον: 6–7n., 645n.
ἐξ οἵων ἔχω: 1378n.

1380 Note the asyndeton (115n., 1235).

αἰτῶ . . . λίσσομαι: for the two verbs used in combination cf. Hom. *Il.* 5.358; for the latter verb as an intensification of the former cf. Theogn. 1329–30.

προπίτνω: the second syllable is long, as at Aesch. *Pers.* 152 βασίλεια δ᾽ ἐμή· προσπίτνω. Jebb's προπίπτω is thus unnecessary.[78] For confusion between προ– and προσ– see 1193n.

---

[78] L^pc reads προ∗πιτνῶ (so rightly Dawe, *STS* ii. 94); traces of a sigma under the erasure can be observed on the facsimile. Ll-J/W incorrectly claim that L reads προπιτνῶ.

For γενοῦ in a prayer cf. Aesch. *Cho.* 2, 19, Call. *Hec.* fr. 267 Pfeiffer = 75 Hollis.

For πρόφρων in prayers cf. Aesch. *Cho.* 1063, Ausfeld (1903) 538; also ἵλεως at 655 (n.).

1382–3 Prayers often remind the deity of the need to uphold justice and right conduct (cf. Pulleyn (1997) 200–3).

δεῖξον: for this verb used 'to point a moral' cf. *Ant.* 1242–3 δείξας ἐν ἀνθρώποισι τὴν ἀβουλίαν | ὅσῳ μέγιστον ἀνδρὶ πρόσκειται κακόν.

τἀπιτίμια | τῆς δυσσεβείας: cf. Eur. *Hec.* 1086 δράσαντι δ᾽ αἰσχρὰ δεινὰ τἀπιτίμια. The situation is similar to that found in Euripides' *Antiope*: there, immediately before Lycus walks into the trap, Amphion's speech concludes with a prayer and a reminder of the victim's impiety (fr. 223.15–16 *TrGF* ≈ 48.15–16 Kambitsis [. . . . .] πρὸς ἄγραν τ᾽ εὐτυχῶς εἴη μ[ολ]εῖν, | [ὅπως ἕ]λωμεν ἄνδρα δυσσεβέστατον).

1383 οἷα δωροῦνται θεοί: the reference must be to death as a punishment for crime: on this motif in Near Eastern poetry see West (1997) 326. The verb δωρεῖσθαι, normally employed in prayers to denote beneficent giving by the deity (cf. Ausfeld (1903) 531), here refers to the opposite.

Exit Electra into the *skene*. This departure emphasises her solidarity with her brother and her active participation in the plan, and suggests that she may take part in the killing (as at Eur. *Or.* 32, 1235). It also 'marks the removal of the conditions that required her exclusion' from the house (Mantziou (1995) 194): that is, the ending of the tyranny of Clytemnestra and Aegisthus.

THIRD STASIMON (1384–97)

STROPHIC PAIR

1384	1391	⏑̅⏑ ⏑ – ⏑̅⏑ ⏑ – ‖	2cr
1385		⏑ ⏑̅⏑ – ⏑ – ⏑ ¹ – – ⏑ –	2δ
		⏑̠ – ⏑ – ⏑ – ⏑ – ⏑ – ⏑ – ‖	3ia
		⏑ ⏑̅⏑ – ⏑ – ⏑ – – ⏑ –	2δ
	1395	⏑ – – ⏑ – ‖	δ
		– – ⏑ – ⏑ – ⏑ –	2ia
1390		– – ⏑ – ⏑ – ⏑ ¹ – ⏑̅ – ⏑ – ‖‖	3ia

The above analysis agrees with that of Dale (1971–83) i. 38–9. Dochmiacs are common in contexts of emotional excitement (cf. West (1982a) 108, L. P. E. Parker (1997) 67), and often precede a killing off stage (cf. Eur. *Her.* 735–46, *El.* 1147–64, Matthiessen (1964) 152 n. 4, 164 n. 2, 165 n. 1). They are often accompanied by iambics and cretics (West (1982a) 111–12, Parker (1997) 43, 66–7). For a line of cretics in the form $\cup\overline{\cup}\cup -$ (paeons; 1384 ~ 1391) introducing dochmiacs see Seidler (1811–12) i. 125–6, Wilamowitz (1921) 332. In 1385 ~ 1392 and 1387 ~ 1394 the first dochmiac begins with the $\cup\cup\cup -$ rhythm of which the opening cretics in 1384 ~ 1391 are composed. The ode thus provides an example of how 'the manifest resemblance of certain forms of [dochmiacs and cretics] can be exploited' by the tragic poet (Parker (1997) 67; on p. 43 she compares Eur. *Or.* 317–18 ~ 333–4).

1384–97 A roughly similar structure can be observed in each stanza, which gives unity to the stasimon. Both begin with movement (1384 προνέμεται, 1391 παράγεται) into the house (1386, 1392–3) to wreak vengeance on the criminal (1387, 1394), vengeance which will no longer be delayed (1389, 1397). The twin prongs of Orestes' strategy, force and guile, are represented by the two deities, Ares and Hermes, who frame the lyric. Before δόλος has dominated Orestes' approach (1–85n.), and it still has an important part to play. But Ares is now prominent because the time for violent action has arrived. Two gigantomachies show the two gods on either side of a vase (Class of Cabinet des Médailles 390, Geneva Musée d'art et d'histoire 498, *ARV²* 254.7, *Para.* 350; and Havana, Museo Nacional de Bellas Artes 534, Olmos (1993) 105–7): but in general they do not form a pair. However, both gods are found in choruses in Aeschylus' *Choephori* at a similar stage in the action (727, 813, 938). Between the two gods comes the likening of the avengers to ἄφυκτοι κύνες, which implies a reference to the Erinyes (1388n.). Olympians and chthonians are thus marshalled in support of the advancing avengers.

The ode has a number of similarities with the strophic pair in the first stasimon. The chorus expects that the happy events implicitly prophesied by the dream will come to pass (479–81, 498–501; 1389–90). A contrasting pair of deities is at hand to offer assistance (Dike and Erinys, Ares and Hermes); the latter of each pair has a particular association with guile and trickery (490, 1396–7). Verbs expressing the inexorable motion of the avengers are prominently placed near the beginning of all four stanzas (475n., 1384, 1391). But in the first stasimon these verbs were in the future, as the chorus looked forward to the prospect of justice. In the later ode justice is imminent, and the present tense prevails.

Choral interventions at similar points in the action are found in both Aeschylus and Euripides (*Cho.* 719–29, 783–837, 855–67, 935–72, *El.* 1147–64). In each case, the lyric creates suspense by delaying the movement of the plot at a moment of particular tension. Each of the dramatists adopts a different tone for these choral pieces. In Aeschylus only in the final ode (*Cho.* 935–72) is the chorus securely confident of Orestes' success: its three previous interventions are characterised instead by anxious and repeated prayers for divine assistance. The Sophoclean chorus has no such doubts: it confidently proclaims the workings of the gods, who are already bringing Orestes and his companion to victory. In the moments before the killing of Clytemnestra Euripides has his chorus vividly depict the horror of Agamemnon's death, which serves as another reminder of the cycle of violence which has afflicted the house of Tantalus. But that cycle is not a prominent theme in S.'s play. The emphasis in this ode is on the present, not the past: the reasons for Clytemnestra's killing are already clear to us, and the chorus instead focuses on the means through which it will be effected. The happier world of the *anagnorisis* is replaced by a mood of grim and determined resolution, suited to the terrible justice of the coming action.

1384–5 The image of the bloody war god advancing in the context of a kin-killing is paralleled by Aesch. *Ag.* 1509–11 βιάζεται δ' ὁμοσπόροις | ἐπιρροαῖσιν αἱμάτων | μέλας Ἄρης.

1384 ἴδεθ': for the second-person imperative at the beginning of a lyric piece cf. *Tr.* 821 ἴδ' οἷον, ὦ παῖδες. Such imperatives represent instances of self-address on the part of the chorus (cf. Kaimio (1970) 137–43), and are often accompanied by first-person references (cf. Norden (1939) 196–8); so here note τοὐμόν in 1390.

προνέμεται: in the middle only here before late antiquity. The sense is probably similar to that of ἐπινέμοιαι 'go forward in grazing', and hence 'advance with menace' (cf. Thuc. 2.54.5 ἡ νόσος . . . ἐπενείματο . . . Ἀθήνας μὲν μάλιστα, LSJ⁹ s.v. ἐπινέμω II 2 a, Laroche (1949) 44 and 46, Fraenkel on Aesch. *Ag.* 485; Aesch. *Suppl.* 691 πρόνομα . . . βοτά).

1385 ὁ: Blaydes's conjecture for transmitted τό (in his 1873 edition) is adopted by Kaibel.[79] Before the name of a divinity ὁ can retain its old demonstrative sense, with something of the force of Latin *ille* 'the famous, well-known': cf. Aesch. *Cho.* 953–5 ὁ Λοξίας ὁ Παρνασσίας | μέγαν ἔχων μυχὸν | χθονός (where as here the article also introduces a participial phrase), S. *OR* 498 ὁ μὲν οὖν Ζεὺς ὅ τ' Ἀπόλλων (cited by Ll-J/W in *Second Thoughts* on 1473), 35n. With δυσέριστον αἷμα, however, the definite article is unintelligible. The only conceivable sense would be 'his characteristic δυσέριστον αἷμα' (cf. [Simon.] *A.P.* 7.25.3–4 = 3326–7 *HE* = 968–9 *FGE* πνείοντα δ' Ἐρώτων | τὸν γλυκὺν ἐς παίδων ἵμερον), but this is strained. The corruption postulated is slight, and will have been assisted by the proximity of the neuters to the article. Period-end must consequently be posited after 1384 ~ 1391.

---

79 Blaydes also changes δυσέριστον to –ος; Michaelis (*ap.* Jahn²) is the first to suggest the text which I have printed.

COMMENTARY: 1384–97

δυσέριστον: 'against which the guilty will strive in vain' (Jebb).
αἷμα φυσῶν: cf. Eur. *IA* 125 μέγα φυσῶν θυμὸν ἐπαρεῖ, 381 τί δεινὰ φυσᾷς αἱματηρὸν ὄμμ' ἔχων;, *IT* 288 πῦρ πνέουσα καὶ φόνον. Similar metaphors are common with πνέω (LSJ⁹ s.v. V 1, Dover (1987b) 55–6): cf. especially [Eur.] *Rhes.* 322–3 Ἄρης | . . . μέγας πνέων. There may be an echo of the more physical description at Aesch. *Ag.* 1389: cf. also *Aj.* [918], 1412–13.
Ἄρης: apart from here and at 1423, this god is twice elsewhere associated with the vengeance of Orestes. At Pind. *P.* 11.36–7 Orestes χρονίῳ σὺν Ἄρει | πέφνεν τε ματέρα θῆκέ τ' Αἴγισθον ἐν φοναῖς, while at Aesch. *Cho.* 937–8, shortly after Orestes and Pylades have forced Clytemnestra inside the palace, the chorus sings ἔμολε δ' εἰς δόμον τὸν Ἀγαμέμνονος | διπλοῦς λέων, διπλοῦς Ἄρης. March *ad loc.* points to two passages in S. where Ares is invoked as saviour (*Aj.* 706, *Tr.* 653–4); here, however, his violent character is more to the fore.
For the association of Ares with ἔρις cf. Hom. *Il.* 4.439–40, 5.518, 5.891, 7.329–30, Clem. Alex. *Protr.* 10.102.4 (= i. 73.31–2 Stählin). For his association with blood cf. Hom. *Il.* 5.289, 20.78, 22.267 αἵματος ἆσαι Ἄρηα, 7.329–30, Aesch. *Ag.* 1510–11, Hdt. 8.77.2, Meleager *A.P.* 5.180.8 = 4045 *HE*, [Anacr.] *A.P.* 7.226.3 = 486 *FGE* ὁ φιλαίματος Ἄρης, Leon. Alex. *A.P.* 6.324.3–4 = 1874–5 *FGE*, Hor. *C.* 2.14.13 *cruento Marte*, J. E. Carter (1902) 64.

1386 δωμάτων ὑπόστεγοι: here and in the following line the genitives are objective (Moorhouse 52–3). Cf. *Tr.* 376–7 τίν' ἐσδέδεγμαι πημονὴν ὑπόστεγον | λαθραῖον;, *Aj.* 796 σκηνῆς ὕπαυλον.

1387 μετάδρομοι κακῶν πανουργημάτων: Xenophon uses μεταδρομή of the movement of dogs (*Cyn.* 3.7, 6.20, 9.18, 10.21, 10.22), Plutarch of hares (*De Sollert. Anim.* 971d). The word thus forms part of the κύνες metaphor in the following line. The link is all the more effective since hunting terminology is often applied to the Erinyes themselves: cf. Eur. *IT* 941 μεταδρομαῖς Ἐρινύων, Ar. *Ran.* 472 Κωκυτοῦ . . . περίδρομοι κύνες, Sansone (1988) 13 n. 64.

1388 ἄφυκτοι κύνες: the equation of the avengers with dogs only makes sense if we remember that those avengers *par excellence*, the Erinyes, frequently take canine form: cf. Aesch. *Cho.* 924 φύλαξαι μητρὸς ἐγκότους κύνας, 1054, *Eum.* 131–2, 246–7, Eur. *El.* 1342, *Her.* 860 (of the Κῆρες), Ar. *Ran.* 472, Lilja (1976), index s.v. 'Erinyes', Sansone (1988) 11 n. 54, Mossman (1995) 196 n. 71.
There is no further reference to Erinyes. The passage is thus a problem for those who claim that Orestes will be pursued by the Erinyes after the end of the drama, in that here 'the chorus talks [sic] as if Erinyes were with Orestes, not against him' (Padel (1992) 186).

1389 οὐ μακρὰν ἔτ' ἀμμενεῖ: for the force of οὐκέτι see 611n.; for adverbial μακράν see 323n. The adverb μακράν requires the future tense (restored by Wunder²).

1390 τοὐμὸν φρενῶν ὄνειρον: for the genitive with locative sense cf. Aesch. *Ag.* 1308 φρενῶν στύγος.

αἰωρούμενον: not 'hovering in the air' (LSJ⁹ s.v. αἰωρέω II 2a), but 'held in suspense' (cf. *ib.* II 4).

1391 παράγεται: for παράγω meaning 'bring in', with an added notion of secrecy, cf. Hdt. 5.20.3, LSJ⁹ s.v. III 2.

1392 The combination of elements in this line is paralleled by Aesch. *Cho.* 725–6 νῦν ἐπάρηξον· | νῦν γὰρ ἀκμάζει Πειθὼ δολία<ν> ξυγκαταβῆναι, which occurs in a similar context.

δολιόπους: contrast the two other –πους compounds which began the antistrophe of the first stasimon (489, 491). This form is not found elsewhere, but cf. λαθροπόδας at Antiphanes *A.P.* 9.409.4 = 756 *GP*. For the first element cf. Aesch. *Cho.* 947 δολιόφρων ποινά (also in an ode before the killing of Clytemnestra).

ἀρωγός: 454n.

1393 ἀρχαιόπλουτα: 'the adjective is not purely ornamental, but suggests the contrast between the material prosperity of the palace . . . and the sinister presence of . . . the crimes that defile it' (Garvie on Aesch. *Cho.* 800–2, referring to 801 πλουτογαθῆ). On the wealth of the house see 72n. The adjective first occurs at Aesch. *Ag.* 1043, where see Fraenkel.

ἐδώλια: the variant ἐδράσματα (cf. Eur. fr. 305.1 *TrGF*) is likely to have originated as a gloss, since it is so used in the Suda (ε 265 = ii. 207.13 Adler, s.v. ἐδράνων; so Dawe, *STS* i. 199).

1394 νεακόνητον αἷμα χειροῖν ἔχων: 'having keen-edged death in his hands' (Jebb); compare the similarly imprecise δίκαια φερομένα χεροῖν κράτη in 476. Ll-J/W (*Sophoclea*) compare αἷμα = 'a deed of blood' (cf. Eur. *Or.* 285): but the metaphor here is more vivid. Hesych. s.v. αἷμα (α 1936 = i. 70 Latte) has ὁ δὲ Σοφοκλῆς ἐν Ἠλέκτρᾳ τὴν μάχαιραν ἔφη (cf. *Synagoge* B α 526 = p. 565 Cunningham, Photius, *Lexicon* α 597 = i. 68 Theodoridis), though this will not be based on information beyond the present passage.

νεακόνητον: is the alpha long or short? The strophic test is unhelpful, as the second syllable of μετάδρομοι (1387) is anceps. (i) If long, we get a dochmiac kaibelianus ∪ − ∪ − ∪ − surrounded by normal dochmiacs: 'a most uncongenial sequence' (Diggle (1989) 199 = (1994) 345). We would also expect an

506

eta rather than a long alpha (cf. Björck (1950) 173). (ii) A short alpha gives us a regular dochmiac: elsewhere, however, compounds made on the *h₂ek– root always show a long vowel (cf. νεήκης Hom. *Il.* 13.391, Eur. *Phoen.* 372, νεηκονής *Aj.* 820). For the short alpha Jebb compares Nic. *Alex.* 358, 364 νεάλης and Leon. Tar. *A.P.* 7.13.1 = 2563 *HE* νεάοιδος (metrically guaranteed in each). But neither author is early enough to provide evidence for S.'s use, especially given the tendency for the short vowel in compounds to become more prevalent over time (cf. Wackernagel (1889) 63 = (1953–79) ii. 959).

Wackernagel (*ib.* 61–2 = 957–8) lists instances of compounds where we sometimes find a short vowel instead of the expected long. Several arise from the need to supply short syllables for the dactylic hexameter of early Greek epic, and so are not comparable here. But at Eur. *Or.* 147 we find ὑπόροφος instead of the expected ὑπώ– (for which cf. Hom. *Il.* 9.640, Eur. *El.* 1166, *Phoen.* 299), while at Eur. *Her.* 107 transmitted ὑπώροφα must be emended to ὑψόροφα (Musgrave, *prob.* Bond, Diggle) or ὑπόροφα (Elmsley) on metrical grounds (cf. also *Ba.* 38 ἀνόροφος, although in this case the expected ἀνω– is not found until later Greek). These cases indicate that the expected long can sometimes appear as a short, and so suggest that νεακόνητον with a short alpha is acceptable tragic Greek.

For the reference to a whetstone in contexts of killing cf. *Aj.* 820 σιδηροβρῶτι θηγάνη νεηκονής, Aesch. *Ag.* 1535–6, *Sept.* 715.

1395–6 ὁ Μαίας δὲ παῖς | Ἑρμῆς: invoked already (by Electra) at 111, and often called upon in Aeschylus' *Choephori* (1, 727–8, 812–18). Here he is invoked (i) as god of deceit (cf. 1396 δόλον, *Phil.* 133 Ἑρμῆς δ' ὁ πέμπων δόλιος ἡγήσαιτο νῷν, Hom. *Hym.* 4.13–15, 282, 405, Ar. *Thesm.* 1202 with Austin and Olson, Garvie on Aesch. *Cho.* 726–7, Nisbet and Hubbard on Hor. *C.* 1.10.7, Herter (1976) 213) and (ii) as the god who offers guidance and brings enterprises to a successful end (cf. *Phil.* 133, Aesch. *Cho.* 727–8, 812–13 ξυλλάβοι δ' <ἂν> ἐνδίκως | παῖς ὁ Μαίας, Eur. *El.* 461–2 σὺν Ἑρμᾷ, | τῷ Μαίας ἀγροτῆρι κούρῳ, [Eur.] *Rhes.* 216–17 ἀλλ' εὖ σ' ὁ Μαίας παῖς ἐκεῖσε καὶ πάλιν | πέμψειεν Ἑρμῆς). His status as ψυχοπομπός of the recently dead (cf. *Aj.* 831–2, *OC* 1548, Nisbet and Hubbard on Hor. *C.* 1.10.17), despite the context, is not mentioned and therefore not felt.

Proper names often invite the suspicion of the textual critic, and this one is no exception: Neue's ἐπί σφ' ἄγει was printed by Schneidewin¹. But the emendation is unnecessary, as the name 'Hermes' is commonly accompanied by the designation 'son of Maia': cf. Hom. *Od.* 14.435, [Hes.] fr. 217.2 M–W, [Hom.] *Hymn* 4.1 and *passim*, Aesch. fr. 384 *TrGF*, Eur. *El.* 461–2, fr. 223.98 *TrGF* = 48.69 Kambitsis (*Antiope*) (likely supplement), [Eur.] *Rhes.* 216–17, Bruchmann (1893) 110. For the matronymic more generally see Pearson on fr. 564.3, West on Hes. *Theog.* 1002.

1396 σφ': for the vulnerability of this word to omission see Diggle (1981 a) 59.

ἄγει: at Megalopolis Hermes was worshipped under the cult title Ἁγήτωρ (Paus. 8.31.7); cf. *OC* 1547–8, Sier on Aesch. *Cho.* 813–14, Hor. *C.* 1.10.13 *duce te*, Ov. *Fast.* 2.609, 612, Lucian 25.19, Herter (1976) 209, Kahn (1979) 202 with n. 9. On the possibility that Hermes guided Orestes back from exile in a lost version of the myth see Garvie (1970) 87–8.

1396–7 δόλον σκότῳ | κρύψας: for Hermes as a deity 'who works deceitfully in the dark' (Garvie on Aesch. *Cho.* 727–8) cf. Aesch. *Cho.* 817 with Sier on 816–18, *Hom. Hym.* 4.290 μελαίνης νυκτὸς ἑταῖρε, 577–8; for Hermes' association with deceit more generally see 1395–6n.

1397 πρὸς αὐτὸ τέρμα: this, then, is a goal which Orestes will reach in safety, in contrast to his fictive experiences with the στήλη in the Paedagogus' speech.

κοὐκέτ' ἀμμένει: given the length of time that Electra has been waiting for the vengeance, it is probable that οὐκέτι here has its full force of 'no longer' (contrast 611 n.). The verb is repeated from 1389 (there in a different tense).

LYRIC EXCHANGE (1398–1441)

1398	1422	‑ ‑ U ‑ U ‑ U ‑ U ‑ U ‑ ‖	
		U̲ ‑ U̲‑ U̲ U̅U̅ U ‑ U ‑ U ‑ ‖	
1400		:: Ū ‑ U ‑ Ū ‑ U :: ‑ U ‑ U ‑	
	1425	U ‑ U ‑ ‑ ‑ U ‑ U ‑ U ‑	
		:: U ‑ U ‑ Ū ‑ U :: ‑ Ū ‑ U ‑	
		‑ ‑ U ‑ Ū ‑ U ‑ U ‑ U ‑ ‖	
		:: ‑ U͡U ‑ U ‑	δ
1405		U ‑ U ‑ ‑ ‑ U ‑ ‑ ‑ U ‑	
		:: U ‑ U ‑ U ‑ U ‑ U ‑ U ‑ ‖	
		:: ‑ ‑ U ‑ ‑ U ‑ ‑ U ¹‑ U ‑ ‑ ‖	ia 2ᴧia iaᴧ
		:: ‑ ‑ U ‑ ‑ ‑ U ‑ U ‑ U ‑	
1410	1430	:: U̲ ‑ U ‑ U̲ ‑ U :: ‑ U ‑ U ‑ ‖	
		Ū ‑ U ‑ U ‑ U :: ‑ ‑ ‑ U ‑ ‖	
		‑ ‑ U ‑ U̲ ‑ U ‑ Ū ‑ U ‑	
		:: ‑ U U ‑ U U ‑ U ‑ U ‑ Ū ‖	D × e ‑
		‑ U U ‑ U U ‑ U ‑ U ‑ ‖	D × e
1415	1435	:: ‑ ‑ U ‑ Ū :: ‑ U ‑ U ‑ U ‑	
		:: ‑ ‑ U ‑ U :: ‑ U ‑ Ū ‑ U ‑	
		:: U ‑ U ‑ ¹ ‑ U ‑ ‑ U ‑ ¹ ‑ U ‑	ia 3ᴧia
1420	1440	U ‑ U ‑ U ‑ U ‑ Ū ‑ U ‑ U ‑ ‑	3ia iaᴧ
		‑ U ‑ U ‑ Ū ‖‖	ᴧia iaᴧ

In tragic lyric we expect the same character to sing or recite corresponding lines in strophe and antistrophe (cf. Page (1937): the few possible exceptions which he notes (pp. 97–9) can all be reconciled with this principle). Such an arrangement would be difficult in this lyric exchange, given that a speaking character is killed part of the way through the strophe. As a result, lines delivered by Clytemnestra in the latter part of the strophe (1410–21) are matched in the corresponding section of the antistrophe (1430–41) by lines delivered by Orestes. In the same section Electra and the chorus each have parts which correspond as expected. 1407 ∼ 1428 are sung by the chorus. Assuming that Orestes spoke the line which dropped out after 1428 (a safe assumption in the immediate context), we attain response of persons in the whole of 1407–21 ∼ 1428–41, subject to Orestes' taking Clytemnestra's part as described above.

This pattern breaks down in the remainder of the lyric exchange (1398–1406 ∼ 1422–7). Lines sung by Electra in the strophe correspond to lines delivered by Orestes or the chorus in the antistrophe. Electra's part in the antistrophe corresponds to the chorus's and (probably) Clytemnestra's in the strophe. There is no way of restoring full response to the first six lines of the strophic pair. McDevitt (1981) 27 attempts to include 1404–6 and the lines which have dropped out between 1427 and 1428 within the section of complete response. This requires us to assign the first two of these lines to Orestes and the third to Electra. But the forceful brevity of Orestes' words at 1426–7 could only be weakened by an additional two lines from him at this point. We need rather an immediate reaction of happiness to the news from Electra.

Despite this absence of complete response, it would be a mistake to posit a strophic pair consisting of only 1407–21 ∼ 1428–41, as e.g. Brunck does in his 1779 edition. After all, 1398–1406 ∼ 1422–7 do show exact correspondence of speaker changes, which suggests that they form part of a corresponding unit. It seems that while exact response of speakers was the norm, it could be partially ignored if special circumstances applied (cf. McDevitt (1981) 28). In our case, the killing of Clytemnestra meant that correspondence of speaker could not be exact, unless the poor woman's death cries were to span the best part of fifty lines. But Orestes also presented a difficulty. If his part in the antistrophe was limited to lines spoken by Clytemnestra in the strophe, he would have little scope to announce the death of his mother and prepare for the coming of Aegisthus, unless Clytemnestra's part in the strophe were to be extended to an uncomfortable length. S. has thus partially relaxed his own rules of response to cope with the individual dramatic demands of a particular situation.

The metre of the ode is otherwise unexceptional (cf. Dale (1971–83) i. 38–9). The dochmiac is an appropriate metre for Clytemnestra's first cry (cf. West (1982a) 108, L. P. E. Parker (1997) 67). 1430–2 present difficulties of response, for which see *ad loc*. In 1413–14 ∼ 1433–4 we have two dactylo-epitrite cola.

The first was known to ancient metricians as the encomiologicum (cf. West (1982a) 76 n. 107).

The lyric follows straight on from the preceding lyric stasimon, while at the same time also marking the beginning of the final 'act' of the play. As often, S. refuses to delimit his drama into neat, easily-digestible sections (cf. Taplin (1984–5) 119, 261–74n.).

1398–1441 Clytemnestra's death is a high point in the drama, a scene full of unusually fast-paced action after the largely static recognition scenes (cf. Taplin (1977a) 352). Though she is killed off stage, we hear her cries from within the *skene* and observe the consequent reactions of Electra and the chorus. This basic form is used several times in tragedy when a character is killed off stage: cf. Aesch. *Ag.* 1343–71, Eur. *Hec.* 1035–46, *Hipp.* 776–89 (cries off stage from the Nurse discovering Phaedra's body), *El.* 747–60 (noise from down an eisodos), *Or.* 1296–1310, *Antiope* fr. 223.79b–95 *TrGF* ≈ 48.50–66 Kambitsis, Seidensticker (1971) 194 with n. 28, Arnott (1982) 38–43, Hamilton (1987).

In Aeschylus the killing of Clytemnestra takes place silently off stage, while the chorus sings an ode celebrating the return of justice to the house of Agamemnon (*Cho.* 935–71). Euripides' treatment is closer to S.'s, in that we hear the queen's last screams before the deed is accomplished (*El.* 1167). But unlike Euripides, S. does not limit his Clytemnestra to a single line. Instead, she is given five separate cries (1404–16n.), which cover a period of time lasting from her discovery of her enemies (1404–6) to the second blow which finishes her off (1416). These express her isolation (1405n.), her moving appeal to her son (1410–11 n.) and her final screams of pain (1415–16n.). The imminent arrival of Aegisthus provided S. with the perfect opportunity to avoid lingering over the killing of Clytemnestra, if he wished to avoid doing this. He did not. The dramatist who in the previous episode had gone to such lengths to divert our attention from the coming matricide now refuses to spare us the horror of Clytemnestra's final moments.

Still more important in shaping our responses are the reactions of the figures outside the *skene* to the cries. In 1406 and 1410 Electra refers to her mother with the indefinite pronoun τις, an affectation of ignorance which expresses her contempt. The tone is bitter, nasty, jeering: it alienates our sympathies. The chorus pointedly refuses to adopt a similar tone, despite Electra's attempt to associate it with her remarks (cf. 1406 ὦ φίλαι). Its appalled reaction differentiates it not only from Electra's sneers, but from the celebratory response which we regularly encounter from choruses in similar scenes elsewhere (1407n.). There can be little doubt that an audience will find the chorus's response, not Electra's, to be the closer to its own.

Shortly afterwards, at the moment of her mother's death, Electra displays no magnanimity in victory. She rather urges her brother on to further acts of violence, using language of extraordinary ferocity (cf. 1415–16n.). More than at any previous moment, we here see the woman whose character has been profoundly affected by long years of torment. She herself is aware of this process, and in earlier scenes has captured our sympathy by this capacity for self-criticism and self-knowledge (254–309n., 616–21n.). But here this ugly side to her personality, the μῖσος παλαιόν to which she earlier referred (1311), is presented without the self-awareness which might mitigate its harshness. The contrast with the joyful, loving Electra of the previous part of the play accentuates this still further.[80]

For all the terrible impact of Clytemnestra's last moments, we never forget that the killing remains an act of justice. It has the unambiguous support of Apollo (1425n.). The chorus too proclaims its support for Orestes' action, despite its earlier shudders as the deed was performed. Electra reminds us of Clytemnestra's killing of Agamemnon and exultation in the supposed death of her son (1411–12). Orestes recalls the abuse which she was made to suffer at her mother's hands (1426–7), a topic which may have been given further emphasis in the lines lost between 1427 and 1428. The contrast with the comparable section of Euripides' *Electra* is obvious. There the siblings are overcome with remorse (1177–84 etc.), the chorus is appalled rather than supportive (1175–6 etc.), and Apollo is later rebuked by Castor for the foolishness of his oracles (1245–6). References to justice, though not absent (cf. 1189), are overwhelmed by the predominantly negative portrayal of the act. None of this finds an analogue in S.'s play.

This lyric exchange, then, presents the killing of Clytemnestra as a just and proper act. The killer of Agamemnon, the prospective killer of Orestes and the tormentor of Electra meets with the end she deserves. Her dreadful final cries are unlikely to evoke sympathy in an audience which has never seen any redeeming quality in her. But they do bring home the horror of the killing, a horror which is independent of its justice. The *agon* showed us how difficult it is to dissociate just homicides from *talio*-killings: how a just killing may nevertheless be something αἰσχρόν (558–60n.). The second debate between Electra and Chrysothemis had the latter warn her sister how even δίκη can bring about βλάβη. The lyric exchange provides a dramatic depiction of these paradoxes. We see not only the essential horror of the act itself, but also the effect which it has upon Electra, who is less sympathetic here than anywhere else. A woman's passionate desire for justice has had the most terribly deleterious consequences for her own character, of which she has previously shown some awareness, but which we see in their fullest form only now.

---

[80] 'Der Gegensatz von der Elektra der Urnen- und Erkennungsszene und derjenigen des Muttermordes ist . . . furchtbar' (Wuhrmann (1940) 41).

The final section of the lyric is taken up with preparations for the arrival of Aegisthus (1428–41). His return has been represented as a menacing prospect throughout the play (310–23n.): it now comes suddenly after the killing of Clytemnestra. Now, it seems, the play will end with the uncomplicated dispatch of a tyrant and adulterer, thus distracting our attention from the grimmer world of the first half of the lyric exchange, and allowing the play to end with a satisfying, morally uncomplicated conclusion.[81] We shall soon discover that this will not be the case.

The killing of Clytemnestra, as opposed to that of Aegisthus, is rarely represented in art (cf. Prag (1985) 35–43).

1398 Enter Electra from the *skene*. Her swift re-entrance is motivated at 1402–3. As a woman she is excluded from the homicide (cf. the juxtaposition γυναῖκες, ἄνδρες). But she will still be intimately involved at the moment of the killing.

ὦ φίλταται γυναῖκες: 254n.

1398–9 ἄνδρες αὐτίκα | τελοῦσι τοὔργον: cf. Eur. *Or.* 1297 (Electra to chorus) ἄνδρες χεῖρ᾽ ἔχουσιν ἐν φόνῳ, *Antiope* fr. 223.81 *TrGF* ≈ 48.52 Kambitsis καὶ δὴ [πρὸς ἔργῳ]! τῶν νεανιῶν χέρες.

1399 ἀλλὰ σῖγα πρόσμενε: 1236n.

1400 πῶς δή; For the excited question cf. Ar. *Nub.* 664, *Ran.* 1162, Xen. *Symp.* 5.5, Pl. *Theaet.* 164c6.

1400–1 ἡ μὲν . . . | . . . τὼ δ᾽: the opposition both in number (singular versus dual) and gender (masculine against feminine) makes for a menacing sentence. The stress on Clytemnestra's loneliness is taken up in her first two cries (1404–5, 1409).

1401 λέβητα κοσμεῖ: not *the* urn, which was never taken inside. Clytemnestra is preparing a vessel in anticipation of the return of her son's ashes to the house. For λέβης used of a funerary urn see Garvie on Aesch. *Cho.* 686. For κοσμεῖ see 1139n. For the covering of the funeral urn with cloth cf. Kurtz and Boardman (1971) 53, 98–9, N. J. Richardson on Hom. *Il.* 23.254.

According to Kells (on 1400–1), Clytemnestra's tending of the urn here marks the 'horror and ignominy' of the matricide. But the act need not be a sign of newly discovered maternal tenderness. Aeschylus' Clytemnestra is determined to bury the dead Agamemnon (*Ag.* 1551–2), not out of pity, but

---

[81] So Matthiessen (1964) 160: 'eine bloße Handlungstatsache ohne jedes tragische Interesse'.

as a final, gratuitous insult to the man she has murdered. In our case we are given no access to Clytemnestra's state of mind, nor have we seen evidence that her attitude towards Orestes has changed since her departure at 803. Stevens makes a better case when he says that the urn 'point[s] the contrast between [Clytemnestra's] illusion of safety and the presence of the avenger' ((1978) 115). We might also note the parallel with the preceding episode: both Electra and Clytemnestra are forced to relinquish a funerary urn by the newly returned Orestes, but with opposite consequences. To the former he brings new life, to the latter, death. Such interpretations, at least, do not require the invention of psychological states which the dramatist has not revealed to us.

1402–3 S. feels the need to provide some motivation for Electra's return.

1402 σὺ δ᾽ ἐκτὸς ἦξας πρὸς τί; The delay of the interrogative marks the shift of focus to a new person (cf. Thomson (1939) 149).

1403 Αἴγισθος <ἡμᾶς>: Reiske's supplement ((1753) 19, found as a gloss in J) fills the metrical gap. Alternatively, a gloss Αἴγισθος may have forced out a noun phrase (so Jackson (1955) 93; on interpolated personal names see 957n.). Jackson's example ὁ θεοῖσιν ἐχθρός is as good as any (the synizesis is unremarkable, *pace* Diggle (1974) 36 n. 1 = (1994) 136 n. 124: see Battezzato (2000)). Either explanation is plausible, though perhaps the loss of ἡμᾶς is the simpler change. Perhaps ΗΞΑΣ in a similar position in the line above confused a scribe into missing out ΗΜΑΣ in the following line.

On the return of Aegisthus see 310–23n.

1404–16 Clytemnestra is given a full five cries, as opposed to the one or two normally afforded to victims in such scenes. Only the children at Eur. *Med.* 1271–8 are given as many, and they share their allotment.

1404 ἰὼ στέγαι: perhaps an allusion to Cassandra's great cry when confronted with the bloody στέγη of the Atreids at Aesch. *Ag.* 1085–92.

1405 φίλων ἐρῆμοι, τῶν δ᾽ ἀπολλύντων πλέαι: cf. Lycus' lament in Euripides' *Antiope* οἴμοι· θανοῦμαι πρὸς δυοῖν ἀσύμμαχος (fr. 223.88 *TrGF* ≈ 48.59 Kambitsis; *ib.* 223.82 ≈ 48.53); also Tr. Adesp. fr. 347 *TrGF* φίλων ἔρημος, ὦ τάλας, ἀπόλλυμαι with Stephanopoulos (1988a) 226, *Her.* 430 στέγαι δ᾽ ἔρημοι φίλων.

ἀπολλύντων: a pun on the name Apollo (as suggested by March) is wholly implausible. There is no mention of Apollo in the vicinity which could trigger such an etymology: contrast Aesch. *Ag.* 1080–2, where the repeated invocations of the god before the climactic ἀπώλεσας make all the difference (see Fraenkel on 1081, Diggle's edition of Euripides' *Phaethon*, p. 148). For the verb cf. Eur. *Her.* 754 ἀπόλλυμαι δόλῳ (spoken by Lycus as he is killed off stage).

1406 βοᾷ τις ἔνδον. οὐκ ἀκούετ', ὦ φίλαι; In off stage homicide scenes the chorus or a character normally draws attention to the first cry, by asking either 'who is shouting?' (cf. Aesch. *Ag.* 1344, probably S. fr. 815 *TrGF* ἄκουε, σίγα· τίς ποτ' ἐν δόμοις βοή;), or 'did you hear the shout?' (cf. Eur. *Med.* 1273, *Hec.* 1036, *El.* 747, 1166, *Or.* 1297). Sometimes the identity of the victim is explicitly stated (cf. Aesch. *Ag.* 1346, Eur. *Med.* 1273–4, *Or.* 1298). The use of indefinite τις in this context is unparalleled, however. Its tone in 'referring obliquely to a definite person . . . is primarily menacing' (Bond on Eur. *Her.* 747–8, citing e.g. *Ant.* 751, *Aj.* 1138): to his examples add 1410, Ar. *Ran.* 554, 606, 664, Theocr. 5.120, 122, Harder on Eur. fr. 253.2 *TrGF* = 27.2 Austin.

1407 ἤκουσ' ἀνήκουστα δύστανος, ὥστε φρῖξαι: at Eur. *Her.* 751–2 the chorus responds to Lycus' first cry with the joyful τόδε κατάρχεται μέλος ἐμοὶ κλύειν | φίλιον ἐν δόμοις. At a similar point in *Orestes* the chorus prays to Zeus to assist Orestes and Pylades in their task (1299–300); cf. also *Antiope* fr. 223.80–1, 83, 85–7 *TrGF* ≈ 48.51–2, 54, 56–8 Kambitsis. The chorus's shuddering at Clytemnestra's cry is thus generically unexpected. It contributes to the disturbing atmosphere which pervades the strophe. The chorus's response also markedly differs from Electra's (1398–1441 n.). Contrast Eur. *Or.* 1302–1310, where Electra and the chorus, far from being at variance over the homicide within the *skene*, join together to deliver a bloodthirsty commentary as Helen is killed inside.

ἤκουσ' ἀνήκουστα: for the oxymoron cf. Eur. *Hipp.* 362 ἄιες ὦ, | ἔκλυες ὦ, | ἀνήκουστα with Barrett, *Ion* 782–3; also Willink (1989) 62 (where read *OR* 1312 for *OC* 1312).

1408 Αἴγισθε, ποῦ ποτ' ὢν κυρεῖς; Aegisthus' absence had previously made it difficult for Clytemnestra to chastise her daughter (517–20): now it has deadly consequences for Clytemnestra herself. For the sense cf. Eur. *Or.* 1301 (Ἑλ.) Μενέλαε, θνήσκω· σὺ δὲ παρών μ' οὐκ ὠφελεῖς.

1410 For ἰδού in response to a sound cf. *Aj.* 870–1, *OC* 1477–8, C. P. Segal (1977) 93–4. According to Segal 'the combination of sound and sight . . . conveys . . . something of Electra's intense desire to *perceive* as fully and concretely as she can the action which has been the main goal and the driving force of her life, killing her mother' ((1977) 94). But this is far-fetched: Eur. fr. 223.85 *TrGF* = 48.56 Kambitsis (*Antiope*) κλύεις; ὁρᾷ <ς>; is spoken by the chorus in response to Lycus' cries, yet it lacks the distinctive effects which Segal claims to identify in our passage.

μάλ' αὖ: often found in combination (cf. Bruhn §247.16).
τις: 1406n.

1410–11 ὦ τέκνον τέκνον, | οἴκτιρε τὴν τεκοῦσαν: the moving simplicity resembles Eur. *El.* 1165 ὦ τέκνα, πρὸς θεῶν, μὴ κτάνητε μητέρα; Clytemnestra's dying cry is longer at Eur. *Or.* 827–30, as reported by the chorus. In Aeschylus the appeal to Orestes is made on stage. There Clytemnestra appeals to her breast, a motif absent from S.'s treatment (*Cho.* 896–7; cf. Eur. *Or.* 526–8, 567–8, 839–43); note however 922 κτενεῖν ἔοικας ὦ τέκνον τὴν μητέρα, which is closer to this cry. The repetition of the same stem in τέκνον τέκνον . . . τεκοῦσαν adds to the pathos: see further Wills (1996) 138–9 with n. 39. For the orthography of οἴκτιρε (restored by Nauck[8]) see 1199n.

1411–12 ἀλλ' οὐκ ἐκ σέθεν | ᾤκτίρεθ' οὗτος οὔθ' ὁ γεννήσας πατήρ: for the riposte to the victim's cries in an off-stage homicide scene cf. Eur. *Her.* 754–5 (Λύκ.) ἀπόλλυμαι δόλῳ | (Χο.) καὶ γὰρ διώλλυς. In contrast to the comparable part of Aeschylus' version (*Cho.* 900–2), there is no reference to Apollo as yet: the justification offered by Electra omits the divine and concentrates on less elevated motives.

1411 ἐκ: used of the agent: cf. *OC* 51 κοὐκ ἄτιμος ἔκ γ' ἐμοῦ φανῇ, Moorhouse 109–10.

1412 οὔθ': the v.l. οὐδ' has little manuscript authority. Editors elsewhere emend οὔτε (μήτε) to οὐδέ (μηδέ) even when the latter is not transmitted in any manuscript (e.g. *Aj.* 428, *OC* 451, 496), but the grounds for doing this are not good (1197n.). Dawe notes that at 1410 HOV[ac] together with ZrTTa are correct in not having the unmetrical second ὦ found in the rest of the tradition (*STS* i. 199). This is more likely than not to be good fortune, however: cf. rather how at 1416 HO (together with G) read the incorrect δ'.

ὁ γεννήσας πατήρ: 'the fullness of the expression adds to the pathos' (Denniston on Eur. *El.* 964): cf. 261n., Eur. *IT* 360 (same phrase), S. *OR* 793 τοῦ φυτεύσαντος πατρός, *Tr.* 311, *Aj.* 1296 ὁ φιτύσας πατήρ. On Wilamowitz's suggestion that οὔθ' ὁ γεννήσας πατήρ be deleted to ensure responsion with the strophe see 1430–2n.

1413 ὦ πόλις: Schulze (1918) 506 n. 1 = (1934) 184 n. 1 regards the chorus's words as a βοή (642n.), but the strong pause and change of topic after πόλις required by this interpretation forces an unnatural movement on the sentence. The cry must be taken with the following ὦ γενεὰ τάλαινα, and thus serve as an antecedent to σοι (so rightly Ll-J/W (*Sophoclea*)). Hence rather than constituting an appeal to the citizenry, it forms instead a brief gesture towards the wider political contexts of régime change. The brevity of the reference is typical of the play and its focus on οἶκος almost to the exclusion of πόλις.

σοι: φθίνει is not transitive, hence Hermann's emendation. σε could only be kept if we emend the verbs to φθίνειν, φθίνειν, and translate μοῖρα καθημερία as 'it is the doom of this day that'. But the phrase cannot yield this sense: it must rather mean 'the fate which has afflicted this house day by day'. For the sentiment cf. Aesch. *Cho.* 965–6 τάχα δὲ παντελὴς χρόνος[82] ἀμείψεται | πρόθυρα δωμάτων ('soon will (that) time, all-completed, pass out of the front door of the house' (Garvie; similarly Sier)). In both Aeschylus and Sophocles the chorus sings of how a past period of distress and suffering is now coming to an end.

For φθίνω of a waning evil cf. fr. 786 *TrGF* ὕβρις . . . | . . . | . . . ἀνθεῖ τε καὶ πάλιν φθίνει.

1415–16 ὤμοι πέπληγμαι . . . | ὤμοι μάλ' αὖθις: for the intensification of a repeated cry with μάλ' αὖθις cf. Aesch. *Ag.* 1343–5, *Cho.* 875–6, S. *Tr.* 1203–6, *OR* 1316–17, *Phil.* 792–3, Eur. *Med.* 1008–9, *Hec.* 1035–7, *Tro.* 628–9, *Cycl.* 663–5 (ὤμοι μάλ), *Or.* 1018–20, Ar. *Plut.* 934–5. As noted by Boeckh (1808) 244 and Wilamowitz (1883) 236 n. 1 = (1935–72) vi. 182 n. 1, our passage is especially close to the death-cries of Agamemnon at Aesch. *Ag.* 1343–5 ὤμοι πέπληγμαι καιρίαν πληγὴν ἔσω | . . . | ὤμοι μάλ' αὖθις δευτέραν πεπληγμένος (cf. Easterling (2005) 30–1). Hamilton (1987) 594 is sceptical, but the repetition of the verb (not discussed by Hamilton) coupled with the similarity of the situation would have been enough for the audience to feel a connexion. The nuance of the allusion, however, is far from clear. It might cause us to conclude that the two homicides are morally as well as textually close to each other, that Clytemnestra's killing is as evil an act as the killing of Agamemnon. But that is hardly attractive, given that the play has done so much to stress the immorality of Agamemnon's killing and the justice of Clytemnestra's punishment. Alternatively, the allusion could emphasise the complete reversal in the fortunes of the house since the killing of Agamemnon: his killer is now killed in just punishment for her crime, and ironically is made to assume the same language as had characterised the final moments of her own victim. But that may be too optimistic an interpretation, given the dark and troubling atmosphere of this lyric. Perhaps it is better to say that the allusion encourages the audience to compare the two killings, and to confront the similarities and the differences that lie between them. As in the case of the connexion between the deaths of Orestes and Myrtilus (680–763n.), the allusion is difficult to pin down without considering the wider context.

---

[82] West prints πρόμος instead of χρόνος (cf. (1990) 260), but see Lloyd-Jones (1993b) 7–8 = (2005) 174.

1415 παῖσον, εἰ σθένεις, διπλῆν: 'strike twice as hard, if you have the strength' (so rightly Ll-J/W, *Sophoclea*). For the sense of διπλόος cf. LSJ⁹ s.v. II, *DGE* s.v. A V 1. The old translation 'strike a second blow' makes no sense of εἰ σθένεις: as Leofranc Holford-Strevens points out (*ap.* Ll-J/W, *ib.*), 'Orestes must be a feeble specimen if Electra can doubt whether he has a second blow in him.'[83] Both in her edition and at (2004) 42 March ignores Lloyd-Jones's translation and reverts to the old one: surprisingly, she does not explain her decision. Electra's command has an extraordinary power: Jebb's attempt to characterise it as 'an isolated utterance at a moment of extreme tension' is unconvincing.

For the bloodthirsty encouragement to an off stage killer cf. Eur. *Or.* 1302–10. The immediately preceding allusion to Aeschylus' *Agamemnon* is here put to good use: Electra's vigorous shouts of encouragement form the strongest possible contrast with the weak and vacillating debate of the chorus at the comparable moment of that play.

For the ellipse of a word for 'blow' see Gow on Theocr. 14.35. For the feminine see Wilamowitz on Eur. *Her.* 681, Fraenkel on Aesch. *Ag.* 916 (with (1977) 32 (on *Aj.* 1040)), Bruhn §57.

1416 εἰ γὰρ Αἰγίσθῳ γ᾽ ὁμοῦ: Campbell claims that the dative follows the construction of μοι in ὤμοι; but the lament had become such a stereotyped cry that the μοι is unlikely to have been felt as a proper dative. Αἰγίσθῳ is rather dependent on ὁμοῦ, giving 'I wish you were being killed together with Aegisthus': for this cf. Aesch. *Cho.* 894–5 φιλεῖς τὸν ἄνδρα; τοιγὰρ ἐν ταὐτῷ τάφῳ | κείσῃ· θανόντα δ᾽ οὔτι μὴ προδῷς ποτε.

1417–21 The theme of Agamemnon coming back to life (cf. 417–19, 453–4, 1316–17, 1361 n.) now reaches its climax. It is here associated with the *topos* 'the dead are killing the living', for which cf. Aesch. *Cho.* 886 τὸν ζῶντα καίνειν τοὺς τεθνηκότας λέγω, S. *Tr.* 1159–63, *Aj.* 1025–7, *Ant.* 871, Eur. *Hipp.* 810, 839, S. Thompson (1955–8) ii. 421 = E230 ('return from dead to inflict punishment'), ii. 422 = E232 ('return from the dead to slay wicked person'); also ii. 420 = E220 ('dead relative's malevolent return'). Despite its familiarity, the motif here is not unthinking or trite. The regular 'the dead are killing the living' is replaced by the altogether more striking and paradoxical 'the killed are killing the killers'. The method of killing is also out of the ordinary: the dead man drains the blood from the living, an activity characteristic of various monsters (785n.), through which he procures new life for himself (cf. γάρ in 1420). The metaphorical implications of the principle of blood for blood are here pushed to their startling limits.

---

[83] The same objection led F. W. Schmidt to conjecture εἰ θέλεις ((1864) 34).

1417 τελοῦσ᾽: 'are doing their work': so rightly Jebb. The verb can have an intransitive sense (cf. 699n., Aesch. *Pers.* 225, *Sept.* 659, *Cho.* 1021, Bruhn §99, LSJ⁹ s.v. τελέω I 8), which here would give 'are being accomplished'. But its meaning is more powerful if we take it as transitive, with an object (e.g. τὸ ἔργον, as at 1399) understood; it is also paralleled by expressions such as ἀραὶ τελεσφόροι and ἀραί τέλειαι at Aesch. *Sept.* 655, 790, 832, where the curses are accomplishing rather than being accomplished. For choral references to the fulfilment of the deed in off stage homicide scenes cf. Aesch. *Ag.* 1346 τοὔργον εἰργάσθαι δοκεῖ μοι, *Cho.* 872 πράγματος τελουμένου, 874 μάχης . . . κεκύρωται τέλος, Eur. *Hec.* 1038. Words formed from the *telh₂*- root are often associated with curses: cf. *OC* 1407–8, Aesch. *Sept.* 655, 766, 787–91, 832, Corlu (1966) 272.

ἀραί: the curse was first mentioned at 111 n. For the posthumous working of a curse see Watson (1991) 27–30.

ζῶσιν: the plural can only refer to Agamemnon (cf. 146n.).

1418 ὑπαὶ κείμενοι: Brunck's correction of manuscript ὑποκείμενοι (in his 1786 edition) restores responsion; compare the corruption of διαί to διά at Aesch. *Ag.* 448 (with Fraenkel *ad loc.*). On ὑπαί in tragedy see 711n. For κείμενος of the dead see 463n.

1420 παλίρρυτον: *coni.* Bothe¹; πολύρρυτον codd. For the word in this context cf. Eur. *Her.* 738 δίκα καὶ θεῶν παλίρρους πότμος, *El.* 1155 παλίρρους . . . δίκα, and for the idea cf. Eur. *Med.* 410–11. The corruption is easy (641n.). More generally, πάλιν is often found associated with retributory justice (247n.), as well as with the return to life of the dead (cf. Lucian 40.10 πάλιν εἰς τὸν βίον ἀφικνοῦντο). πολύρρυτον, on the other hand, would simply stress the extent of the flow of blood.

αἷμ᾽: blood offerings are a regular feature of hero cult (cf. *OC* 621–2 with Henrichs (1983) 94 n. 29, Eur. *Phoen.* [1574–6], Ekroth (2002) 242–76). Here the dead Agamemnon takes a more active rôle in taking the gifts which are due to him. For the sucking of blood in the context of retributory punishment cf. Aesch. *Eum.* 264–5 ἀλλ᾽ ἀντιδοῦναι δεῖ σ᾽ ἀπὸ ζῶντος ῥοφεῖν | ἐρυθρὸν ἐκ μελέων πελανόν.

ὑπεξαιροῦσι: the ὑπ- prefix denotes both 'from below' (reflecting Agamemnon's position in the underworld) and 'secretly', 'imperceptibly' (cf. 79n.). Cf. Eur. *Hipp.* 633 ὄλβον δωμάτων ὑπεξελών (of a wife wasting her husband's substance). Carawan (1999) 196–7 argues that the verb here also has a meaning of 'bringing guilt to light', comparing *OR* 227 and fr. 757.2 *TrGF*: but it would be difficult to understand this sense alongside its more obvious meaning in this context.

1422–7 The manuscripts assign 1422–3 and 1424 as far as τάδ' to Electra. McDevitt (1981) 25–6 supports Hermann's decision to assign 1422–3 to the chorus. As he notes, πῶς κυρεῖτε as an indirect question (keeping λέγειν in 1423) is 'dull and weak in the extreme, and probably meaningless after the preceding words'. An excited question is also appropriate in the mouth of a sister whose brother has just returned from a testing encounter. If we adopt Erfurdt's conjecture ψέγειν in 1423, then the whole might be assigned to Electra while avoiding the weak indirect question: but that too is unsatisfactory, as the litotes of οὐδ' ἔχω ψέγειν suits a chorus, not a character deeply involved in the action. In 1426 τέθνηκεν ἡ τάλαινα; should also be assigned to Electra (so Erfurdt), again as a question. As a statement from Orestes it would be painfully weak. These reassignments also ensure that changes of speaker occur in the same places in strophe and antistrophe, a strongly desirable outcome. We even obtain matching questions in strophe and antistrophe in 1400 ~ 1424 and 1402 ~ 1426. It is also a common function of the chorus to comment on the entrance of other characters.

1422 Enter Orestes and Pylades from the *skene*. They are carrying their swords unsheathed. For the entry of a character within a lyric strophe cf. *Aj.* 893–5, *OC* 138–9 (Oedipus emerges from his hiding-place), Eur. *Suppl.* 798, *Cycl.* 503 (cited by Taplin (1977a) 174 n. 3).

καὶ μήν: 78n.

1423 στάζει θυηλαῖς Ἄρεος: 'drips with a sacrifice to Ares': so Bergk (his edition, p. xlvii) for manuscript θυηλῆς. The dative gives the expected construction with στάζω (cf. *Aj.* 10 στάζων ἱδρῶτι, LSJ⁹ s.v. I 2). The genitive would have to denote the source of the dripping, as at frr. 534.2 and 687a *TrGF*: Jebb claims that it 'depends on the notion of fulness' (cf. fr. 286 *TrGF* ἀραχνᾶν βρίθει), but parallels for this sense with this verb are lacking. The plural is also the expected form of the noun (cf. Casabona (1966) 122), whose singular is rare (instances at Ap. Rh. 1.420, 4.247, and perhaps also S. fr. 208.6 *TrGF* θυηλη[ ], but the second eta is doubtful: see the plate to P.Oxy. 1175 fr. 3). The combination of unusual case with unusual number makes Bergk's emendation irresistible. For the sacrificial terminology see Burkert (1966) 116 with n. 67 = (2001) 18 with n. 67. For Ares' association with the victorious Orestes see 1385n.

ψέγειν: so Erfurdt (his edition, p. 478). Regarding this as 'intolerably frigid', Campbell in his edition kept the manuscript λέγειν, which he translated 'and I am speechless'. There are no parallels for such an expression with this sense. λέγειν can only be kept if it leads into Ὀρέστα, πῶς κυρεῖτε;, but this is unlikely on other grounds. Erfurdt's conjecture gives the required sense. The corruption it presupposes is common (551 n.). Campbell withdraws his objection to the conjecture in *PS*.

The chorus's approval for the avengers' action is important for shaping our own. Such approval is absent from the reaction of the chorus of Euripides' *Electra* to the returning matricides, which focuses instead exclusively on the bloodiness and wretchedness of the action (1172–6).

1424 πῶς κυρεῖτε; (Ὀρ.) τὰν: manuscript πῶς κυρεῖ; τὰν is a syllable short, and Reisig's conjecture ((1816) 238; also attributed to Elmsley) neatly solves the problem at minimal palaeographical cost. For a 'singular vocative with plural verb' where 'a plurality of persons is appropriately addressed, while the vocative singles out their representative' see Diggle (1994) 506, adding Men. *Sam.* 252, Anaxandrides fr. 1.4 *PCG*. The corruption may have been motivated by a pedantic desire to give a singular verb after the singular vocative. τὰν δόμοισι also gives an attractive tragic idiom (cf. Eur. *Alc.* 807, *Hec.* 1291, *El.* 74, *Her.* 911, *Ion* 622, *Or.* [1368], 1393, *IA* [740]). For the question cf. Aesch. *Cho.* 871 πῶς ἔχει; πῶς κέκρανται δόμοις;, S. *Phil.* 440 τί νῦν κυρεῖ.

Ll-J/W prefer Kolster's πῶς κυρεῖ τάδ᾽; ἐν ((1850) 636). This is palaeo-graphically plausible: ΤΑΔΕΝ could easily have become ΤΑΝ through loss of a syllable, while the elision at the interchange between speakers in *antilabe* is a further source of potential confusion.[84] But the τάδ᾽ is weak, especially when compared to the idiomatic τὰν above. Brunck's πῶς κυρεῖ; τά γ᾽ ἐν (in his 1786 edition) also omits the τὰν, and the γ᾽ is hard to pin down. Triclinius and Hermann read κυρεῖ γέ; and κυρεῖ δέ; respectively (the former is also in Pa and Zc), but neither seems more than a stop-gap.

μέν: 'contrasts the success in the house with the dangers still to come. Orestes is, as always, cautious' (Russell, *per litteras*). Kaibel (p. 290) takes the particle to express an implied contrast between the state of the house and Orestes' own condition. This involves an impossible reading between the lines, or else an impossible interpretation of 1425.

1425 Ἀπόλλων εἰ καλῶς ἐθέσπισεν: 'il senso religioso di un riferimento a un precedente è notevole; εἰ non è ipotetico ed equivale a "proprio come" (Fraenkel (1977) 26 (on *Aj.* 746), comparing *OR* 164, Sappho fr. 1.5 *PLF*, Voigt; add *OC* 623 εἰ Ζεὺς ἔτι Ζεὺς χὠ Διὸς Φοῖβος σαφής, Aesch. *Sept.* 617–18 ἀλλ᾽ οἶδεν ὥς σφε χρὴ τελευτῆσαι μάχῃ | εἰ καρπὸς ἔσται θεσφάτοισι Λοξίου with Hutchinson, Roberts (1984) 57 with n. 46). The statement does not signal doubt

---

[84] In the following list of examples I have starred instances where the phenomenon may have encouraged corruption: *Phil.* 994*, 1182 (lyr.), *OC* 220* (lyr.), 883, Eur. *Cycl.* 261, 672*, *Alc.* 391, *El.* 580, *Her.* 910, 1052 (lyr.), *Tro.* 1310, *Ion* 531, *Phoen.* 606, 623, 1275, *Or.* 791*, 1235, 1239, 1345*, 1525, [1598], 1605, 1607, 1609, 1611, *Ba.* 970, *IA* 1354, 1359, 1465. See further Köhler (1913) 48.

on Orestes' part. Sometimes εἰ can be used by a character to make what he regards as a self-evident statement, but which the audience knows is not true (cf. 773–5, 865–70: van Erp Taalman Kip (1993) 9 unfortunately cites these passages in support of a Fraenkelian view of this line). But for that function of εἰ to be triggered in our case, we the audience would need to be aware of some limitation or fault in Apollo's prophecy, just as at 774 we know that the τεκμήρια are anything but πιστά, and at 865–70 know that Orestes did not die as a ξένος away from his sister. In this case such superior knowledge on the part of the audience is lacking. There has never been any question as to whether the killing of Clytemnestra is sanctioned by Apollo. Nor is it ever suggested that Apollo could give a prophecy that is not καλόν. See further (for a brief doxography) MacLeod (2001) 172 n. 34. Excessive concentration on this εἰ has often blinded scholars to the really disturbing aspect of this lyric exchange – that is, the behaviour of Electra in the strophe.

MacLeod (2001) 173 catches the tone: 'there is no victorious boasting or exultation in the death of his mother, but only a prudent expression that he has acted in accordance with the oracle of Apollo'. Compare the importance given to Apollo's involvement at Liban. *Decl.* 6.2.

1426 ἡ τάλαινα: 273n.; same phrase, with a different tone, at *Tr.* 877.

1427 For ὡς after a verb of fearing see 1309–10n.
ἀτιμάσει: for Electra's ἀτιμία while under her mother's rule see 189n.

1428 παύσασθε, λεύσσω γὰρ Αἴγισθον ἐκ προδήλου: the announcement of Aegisthus' arrival and the reaction this provokes in Orestes, Electra and the chorus are not perceived by Aegisthus himself as he enters along eisodos A. For a similar technique cf. Eur. *El.* 962–87, *Her.* 1153–62, *Or.* 456–69, 1311–20 (cited at Taplin (1977a) 73; cf. *id.* (1971) 41 n. 37 on the two *Electra* plays). For other lengthy entrance announcements for characters arriving from an eisodos see Poe (1992) 125–6 n. 15. Aegisthus would probably have been out of sight of the audience until shortly before he reached the stage (cf. Poe (1992) 127–8).

Aegisthus arrives to be killed in quick succession to his consort, whereas in Euripides there is a considerable interval between the killings. Hamilton (1987) 590–3 discusses tragic scenes where two individuals are killed: our play, he notes, is closest to Aeschylus' *Choephori* in speed and compression.

παύσασθε: once more Electra and Orestes have to be interrupted and told to get on with the task; once more incipient joy is checked by the need for action (cf. 1326–38n.). The situation is paralleled by Eur. *Or.* 1311–20. There the celebrations caused by the apparent death of an enemy inside the *skene* are checked by the arrival of a new character (Hermione) from an eisodos. The chorus urges silence, and Electra turns to the second phase of the plan.

ἐκ προδήλου: 'clearly'; cf. *Tr.* 485 ἐξ ἴσου, *Aj.* 716 ἐξ ἀέλπτων, Moorhouse 110.

1430–2 In 1411, which corresponds to 1431, speaker change occurs after the seventh element. Speaker change elsewhere in this lyric exchange, as far as we can tell, always occurs in corresponding places in strophe and antistrophe. Hence texts such as Ll-J/W's, which posit a change in 1431 in a place other than after the seventh element, should be avoided if at all possible. If we accept the majority transmission, a correctly-positioned change would leave Orestes with the words εἰσορᾶτε ποῦ | τὸν ἄνδρ᾽ ἐφ᾽ ἡμῖν οὗτος, which is nonsense. This difficulty must be taken alongside the lacuna of seven syllables, which we know from the strophic test can be found somewhere in 1430–2.

Transferring οὗτος ἐκ προαστίου from 1431 to after γεγηθώς in 1432 (so Pearson and Dawe) goes some way to solving both problems. This is in fact its location in CNPPa. West (1978a) 119 objects that the phrase is too flat to come at the end of a sentence in this excited exchange (cf. McDevitt (1981) 25). One might rather say that Electra holds back the information sought by her brother, with dramatic effect. In any case, the objection carries little weight in the face of the necessities of responsion. Its removal from 1431 frees the space we need in that line. Pearson gives Orestes εἰσορᾶτέ που | τὸν ἄνδρ᾽ ἐφ᾽ ἡμῖν – ∪, with Electra having the rest of the line for the beginning of her sentence. Pearson's suggestion στάντα as a supplement to Orestes' question is inappropriate given the stress on Aegisthus' movement. βάντα is a possibility (cf. *Ant.* 107, although the text is corrupt); still better might be τὸν ἄνδρ᾽ <ἰόντ᾽> ἐφ᾽ ἡμῖν (so F. Martin *ap.* Nauck³ p. 164). For Electra's words Pearson suggests καὶ γὰρ οὐ μακράν, though with the supplement <ἰόντ᾽> we would need something beginning with a vowel so that ἡμίν can scan –∪. Diggle (*per litteras*) suggests τὸν ἄνδρ᾽ ἐφ᾽ ἡμῖν <ὄντα; (Ηλ.) δορυφόρων γ᾽ ἄτερ>: the reference to an absence of a bodyguard would fit with Aesch. *Cho.* 766–82, where the chorus ensures that Aegisthus will arrive unprotected. Diggle also emends οὗτος to αὐτός 'alone' (36n.) in 1431: cf. Aesch. *Cho.* 771 ἀλλ᾽ αὐτὸν ἐλθεῖν, and 1432n. for a further similarity to this passage.

Rather than posit a lacuna, Wilamowitz (1921) 425 n. 2 preferred to delete οὔθ᾽ ὁ γεννήσας πατήρ in 1412. But this takes away an important phrase and yields unattractive metre (1412–14 ~ 1432–4 as two iambelegi (cf. West (1982a) 196) plus an isolated iambic metron).

1430 ὦ παῖδες: 1220n.

οὐκ ἄψορρον; Cf. *Aj.* 369 οὐκ ἐκτός; οὐκ ἄψορρον ἐκνεμῇ πόδα;, *OR* 430–1 οὐχὶ θᾶσσον αὖ πάλιν | ἄψορρος . . . ἄπει;

ποῦ: not που: 'the chorus have already announced that they see Aegisthus. Orestes will not then ask "do you see him anywhere?" but *"where* do you see him?"' (West (1978a) 119). For the delayed interrogative cf. 1402.

1431 τὸν ἄνδρ᾽: perhaps insulting: cf. Aesch. *Cho.* 894 (Orestes to Clytemnestra) φιλεῖς τὸν ἄνδρα;
 ἐφ᾽ ἡμῖν: 'towards us', not 'in our power' (West (1978a) 119): cf. 84–5n.

1432 γεγηθώς: for joy before disaster in S. see 472–3n. At Aesch. *Cho.* 772 the Nurse is ordered to tell Aegisthus to arrive γαθούσῃ φρενί. Cf. the laughter of the suitors at *Od.* 21.376 at the moment their fate is sealed when Odysseus gains possession of the bow.

1433 κατ᾽ ἀντιθύρων: for the genitive of aim see K–G i. 475–6: unusually, there is here no sense of 'downwards' in the phrase, though no emendation commends itself. The noun ἀντίθυρον ('vestibule', or space immediately inside the front door of the palace) occurs at Hom. *Od.* 16.159 στῇ δέ κατ᾽ ἀντίθυρον κλισίης Ὀδυσῆϊ φανεῖσα and then, except for our passage, not until Lucian (cf. Orlandos and Traglos (1986) 26). Musgrave's ἀμφιθύρων would mean the same (cf. Theocr. 14.42, Orlandos and Traglos (1986) 10–11).

1434 νῦν πάλιν εὖ θέμενοι τάδ᾽, ὡς τὰ πρίν: so Musgrave, transposing τὰ πρίν and πάλιν. The line as transmitted is missing a verb. The strophic test suggests that there is no lacuna: 1414 is complete as it stands. Kaibel (p. 292) follows Hermann in claiming that we can supply εὖ θῆσθε from the participle phrase εὖ θέμενοι, but the syntax is impossibly concise. A main verb may be supplied from a verb in a subordinate clause (cf. Eur. *Or.* 1037 σύ νύν μ᾽, ἀδελφέ, μή τις Ἀργείων κτάνῃ, K–G ii. 574–5), though normally the verb will come at the end of the entire sense unit, thus making it easier for it to be taken with both clauses. *Tr.* 305 μηδ᾽, εἴ τι δράσεις, τῆσδέ γε ζώσης ἔτι provides an instance where the verbless clause occurs at the end of a sentence. But even there we are at least given a finite verb in the subordinate clause, from which the main verb can be supplied. To leave a main clause dangling without a verb, and to supply the verbal element from a preceding participle, is more difficult.

In the OCT the line is broken off by Orestes' words in the following line.[85] But such a break-off would be unusual in tragedy. Moreover, the isolated νῦν at the start of the sentence is clumsy: Lloyd-Jones's translation 'so that you can now, having settled the earlier business, settle this also' nicely brings out the

---

[85] This is indicated by the dash after πάλιν: in *Sophoclea*, however, Ll-J/W claim that they agree with Kaibel's interpretation.

awkwardness of the position of this word. An emendation which restored the syntax would thus be welcome. Musgrave's simple transposition gives sense from nonsense at minimal palaeographical cost. The participle should be taken as coincident with the main verb in the previous line (683n.): by concealing themselves in the house Orestes and Pylades are beginning the process of 'setting things aright' with Aegisthus, having just done the same with Clytemnestra.

For εὖ τίθεμαι cf. Eur. *Ba.* 49 τἀνθένδε θέμενος εὖ, S. *OR* 633, Fraenkel on Aesch. *Ag.* 913, Diggle (1983) 350–1 = (1994) 264–5; for this combination 'used with a euphemism which is so transparent that it is ominous' see Bond on Eur. *Her.* 605.

1435 ἦ νοεῖς ἔπειγε νῦν: all these words must be assigned with Erfurdt to Electra, against the (valueless) manuscript tradition, in which there is a change of speaker after νοεῖς. This maintains responsion with 1415, where there is a change of speaker from Clytemnestra to Electra. The sense too is improved. ἦ νοεῖς needs to denote Orestes' intentions, not the chorus's or Electra's. The καὶ δή at the start of the following line suggests compliance with a preceding imperative. τελοῦμεν is also more powerful on its own.

1436 καὶ δή: 317n.
ἂν μέλοιτ᾽: for the middle cf. 74. For the optative with ἄν cf. 1372–3n.
Exit Orestes and Pylades into the *skene*. The departure of characters at the *end* of a choral ode is rare (Taplin (1971) 41, on *Phil.* 1217). So too, outside prologues, is the departure of a character in response to the imminent entrance of another (Taplin (1977a) 335, comparing Eur. *El.* 962–87, *Pha.* 216–26 Diggle = fr. 781.3–13 *TrGF*).

1437–41 After the hurried action of the greater part of this lyric exchange, the chorus's words prepare us for the leisurely deceit at the start of the exodos.

1437 δι᾽ ὠτός: 737n.
For ὡς with an adverb cf. 1452, LSJ⁹ s.v. Ab III a.

1438 ἠπίως: νηπίῳ and νήπιον are found in Lᵞᵖ (p. 159.6 Papageorgius), and the latter in T; for the reverse corruption cf. Aesch. *Ag.* 1631. However, we need a word to describe the manner in which Electra will effect her trap.

1441 πρὸς Δίκας ἀγῶνα: the personification (476n.) gives better sense ('the contest controlled by Justice' rather than 'the just contest'). For the genitive cf. *Aj.* 1163 ἔσται μεγάλης ἔριδός τις ἀγών.

EXODOS (1442-1510)

1442–1504 The long-awaited Aegisthus does not cut an attractive figure. By turns abrupt (1445–6n.), sarcastic (1456n.) and unctuously hypocritical (1466–7n.), he lacks any positive quality to compensate for these unpleasant characteristics. His behaviour recalls, albeit in a simpler, coarser manner, the brutality of Clytemnestra seen in the second episode. In Euripides' *Electra* we hear of a different Aegisthus: a polite and generous host (cf. 784–9) whose killing in the midst of a sacrifice is a deeply unpleasant act. S.'s figure stands closer to the Aegisthus of Aeschylus' *Oresteia*. His boorish behaviour recalls that of his counterpart at the end of *Agamemnon* (cf. Fraenkel on 1629 ff.), while his eagerness to discover the truth about Orestes' death is exactly paralleled at *Cho.* 838–54. The death of Aeschylus' Aegisthus does not involve moral complications: Orestes later dismisses it with the words Αἰγίσθου γὰρ οὐ λέγω μόρον· ἔχει γὰρ αἰσχυντῆρος, ὡς νόμος, δίκην (*Cho.* 989–90), and after that we hear no more about him. We might thus conclude that the same will hold true for our play; and that since Aegisthus' death has been placed after that of Clytemnestra, the drama will end on a celebratory note untouched by ethical disharmony.

This expectation is destined to be frustrated by the disquieting tone of the final part of the drama – that is, in the moments between the recognition of the corpse by Aegisthus and his entry, followed by Orestes, into the *skene*. Electra's words at 1483–90, her last, stress her passionate need for violent and immediate revenge (n.). She appears to demand mistreatment of Aegisthus' corpse as a means of releasing herself from her sufferings (1487–8n.). Gone is the emphasis on the justice of the killing. The focus is now rather on its speed, and the overall impression is of frenetic haste towards a homicide (1491–2 etc.), irrespective of its moral status. The playwright even allows Aegisthus to suggest that his death will not bring an end to the troubles of the house (1497–8): Orestes' quick response to this question is not especially satisfying. The ending of the play is unfortunately an interpolation: but even if we have lost some lines after 1504, it is hard to see how they could have dispelled the uncomfortable atmosphere which has dominated the last part of the drama.

Such shifts of presentation designed to effect similar shifts in audience sympathy can be found elsewhere in the endings of Greek tragedy (cf. Collard (1975) 64–6 = McAuslan and Walcot (1993) 158–60 = Mossman (2003) 71–3). Two instances are particularly relevant. In *Hecuba* the extremity of the heroine's retaliation against her son's killer may cause an audience to moderate the sympathy in which it has held her for the previous part of the play (cf. Mossman (1995) 164–203). And at the end of *Heraclidae* (928–1055), Alcmene's furious passion for revenge on Eurystheus is so intense that we are left with considerable sympathy for him, although in the rest of the play he had always been portrayed in a negative light (cf. Zuntz (1955) 37). Hence 'the play which all the time . . . moved towards a bright and uplifting finale ends, παρὰ προσδοκίαν, with the spectacle of disgusting cruelty. Like the ambiguous conclusion of a Platonic dialogue, it leaves the spectator with a disquieting question . . .' (Zuntz (1955) 38).

But the closest parallel for the effect of this conclusion comes from outside Greek tragedy. Like our play, Virgil's *Aeneid* ends with the violent death of the hero's main adversary. This killing can be regarded as a just act: it is, after all, a merited punishment for Turnus' many offences, and fulfils the solemn injunctions of Pallas' father Evander, who had charged Aeneas with ending Turnus' life (*Aen.* 11.176–81). But it also has altogether more disturbing implications. It involves the killing of a suppliant, in defiance of the basic precept earlier voiced by Aeneas' father (*Aen.* 6.853), and is committed through passion, not judgment (*Aen.* 12.946–7 *furiis accensus et ira | terribilis*). Furthermore, the placing of the killing at the end of the work means that these difficulties cannot be brought into some kind of harmony, however precarious. As Horsfall puts it, 'for the reasonably acute and sensitive reader, Aeneas remains right, as he always was . . . but there is no general resolution of issues and tensions . . . such as to leave us . . . emotionally at ease or content' ((1995b) 216). Replace 'Aeneas' with 'Orestes' and 'reader' with 'spectator', and the remark applies equally well to S.'s drama.

Why does S. end the play on such a note? For some, the change in atmosphere signifies the imminent arrival of the Erinyes (cf. Roberts (1988) 185–6). Aegisthus' reference to τά τ' ὄντα καὶ μέλλοντα Πελοπιδῶν κακά (1498) supposedly provides especially strong evidence for this view: according to Winnington-Ingram, 'that Aegisthus means by μέλλοντα κακά – and that Sophocles intended to convey – something over and beyond his own death would seem obvious' ((1954–5) 25 = (1980) 227 ≈ E. Segal (1983) 214–15). That latter claim is true: but it does not follow that the 'something' must be the Erinyes. Nowhere has it been suggested that Orestes' actions will entail such a punishment. In this final episode there has not been even a mention of these creatures, in any context. Supporters of the case for Erinyes are forced to argue that the audience would automatically assume a pursuit by the Erinyes because such a pursuit was common in other accounts of the Orestes story. But this fails to take account of the malleability of Greek myth in the hands of Greek poets, and denies S. the possibility of artistic independence. Time and again S. has shaped the story to effect his own poetic purpose, whether by the omission of Cassandra, the reversal of the order of the killings, or the general concentration on the πάθη of Electra. The omission of the Erinyes forms one further such alteration. Their presence in Aeschylus and Euripides does not compel the audience mentally to supply their existence here too. It rather makes their absence here seem all the more deliberate.

The staging of the scene provides a further argument against Erinyes. Orestes, and probably Electra too, ends the play by going inside the *skene*: yet pursuit by the Erinyes would necessitate their leaving via an eisodos. As Taplin notes, 'the stage topography seems purposefully to reject exile' ((1983) 164; cf. also van Erp Taalman Kip (1993) 10). Taplin (*ib.* 163) contrasts the endings of Aeschylus' *Choephori*, where Orestes is chased out of the city via an eisodos, and of Euripides' *Electra*, where the siblings depart into separate exiles via separate exits. The striking internal emphasis of Sophocles' play suggests that something quite different is going on.[86]

But what is Aegisthus hinting at, if not Erinyes? Sommerstein (1997) 214 n. 75 refers to other myths of the travails of the house of Atreus, in particular stories about Aegisthus' son Aletes, and suggests that Aegisthus unintentionally predicts the extinction of his own male line. But again, the play provides no hint of such events. The fact that Roberts and Sommerstein can come up with diametrically opposed interpretations of two simple words of Greek may indicate a basic fault in their approach. It suggests that interpretations based on other accounts of the myth, with no reference to S.'s own presentation of that myth, are bound to end up with arbitrary results.

The play does not provide us with a clear view of a future event which could be denoted by Aegisthus' phrase μέλλοντα κακά.[87] The attempt of various scholars to force on the phrase interpretations for which there is no evidence suggests a reluctance to accept that such indeterminacy could find a place in a great work of literature. Modern scholarship, however, has emphasised the positive aspects of such lack of resolution, and S. has been a notable beneficiary of this approach (cf. Davies (1991) 9–10, D. P. Fowler (1997) 18 = (2000) 302; on *OR* in particular see Fowler (1994) 231–2 = (2000) 6 and (1989) 80–2 = (2000) 244–6). S. hints at future troubles for the house of Pelops. Through careful use of staging he excludes the expectation of Erinyes, but otherwise he refuses to indicate what form these troubles will take. The menace of the impending evil is if anything heightened by this reticence. After all, in the versions of the myth which include the Erinyes, Orestes does manage to evade their pursuit and, in time, die a peaceful death. There is no suggestion here that the μέλλοντα κακά will ever come to a satisfactory τέλος.

As we have seen, the prospect of μέλλοντα κακά is just one of the factors which make this conclusion so uneasy. The whole presentation of the killing, from the shocking blood-lust of Electra to the extraordinary haste of Orestes, will not cause an audience to rejoice in its completion, however much it had

---

[86] Compare the end of *OR*, where the prospect of exile is raised during the course of the play, only to be emphatically denied by the final entrance of Oedipus within the *skene*.

[87] Contrast the clarity of the prophecies uttered by Polymestor at the end of Euripides' *Hecuba* (1259–84), where the deaths of Hecuba, Cassandra and Agamemnon are explicitly described.

been convinced of its justice. From the *agon* onwards there have been hints that even a just killing inevitably possesses a dark and shameful side, however noble the motives of its perpetrators. Those hints were taken up and given a horrible reality in the killing of Clytemnestra during the preceding lyric section (1398–1441 n.). Now for a second time a just homicide is presented in a way which makes the act seem unpleasant: δίκαιον indeed, but also αἰσχρόν (cf. Eur. *Or.* 194). The killing has had consequences for the characters of its perpetrators, particularly Electra, and will have further consequences, though these remain obscure. So the quotation above from Taplin (1983) 164 continues ' . . . but the future of Orestes and Electra *within* this ancestral palace does not look bright either' (his italics). Or as Stinton puts it: 'the irony lies in the tragic situation. Just vengeance is finally accomplished, but at the cost of an ugly act, whose ugliness will not go away; the avengers are cheated of their triumph by the bitterness of success: all is not well within the house' ((1986) 84 = (1990) 479). Each of these scholars well brings out the uneasy atmosphere of the conclusion without being diverted into unwarranted speculation on how its significance will be manifested.

1442 Enter Aegisthus from eisodos A. He is the first character to use this eisodos since Orestes and the Paedagogus at the start of the play. He begins with a question to the chorus, and turns to Electra only in 1445: for this convention see 660n. His opening words resemble Aesch. *Cho.* 839–41 νέαν φάτιν δὲ πεύθομαι λέγειν τινὰς | ξένους μολόντας, οὐδαμῶς ἐφίμερον, | μόρον γ' Ὀρέστου (also near the beginning of his first speech); cf. also Eur. *Antiope* fr. 223.19–22 *TrGF* ≈ 48.19–22 Kambitsis.

Φωκῆς: for the termination see 1107n.

1444 λελοιπόθ': for the participle see 676n.

ἱππικοῖσιν ἐν ναυαγίοις: for the metaphor see 730n.

1445–6 σέ τοι, σὲ κρίνω, ναὶ σέ, τὴν ἐν τῷ πάρος | χρόνῳ θρασεῖαν: Aegisthus roughly addresses Electra, as his consort did at 516. The repeated second person accusative, placed prominently at the beginning of the address, marks his abruptness; while the emphatic particles τοι and ναί suggest the emotive texture. The predicative phrase tagged on to the end, beginning with the definite article, acts as a contemptuous substitute for Electra's name. For other such addresses cf. *Ant.* 441 σὲ δή, σὲ τὴν νεύουσαν ἐς πέδον κάρα, *Aj.* 1228 σέ τοι, τὸν ἐκ τῆς αἰχμαλωτίδος λέγω, Eur. *Hipp.* 1283–4 with Barrett (adding to his examples *Med.* 271, *Phoen.* 1643, *Ba.* 912, [Eur.] *Rhes.* 642, Ar. *Av.* 274). The use of κρίνω for ἀνακρίνω is not found outside S.: its other occurrences (cf. *Aj.* 586, *Ant.* 399, *Tr.* 195, 314, 388) suggest that it may mark 'l'insistenza e l'impazienza di chi interroga' (Longo on *Tr.* 195).

ναί: so Reiske (1753) 19 for manuscript καί. For the corruption cf. Alexis fr. 27.6 *PCG* with Arnott, and possibly Eur. *Or.* 111 (where against other recent editors Diggle adopts Paley's ναί for manuscript καί). Retaining the manuscript reading would leave us with a case of emphatic καί before a pronoun: this is a rare usage (Denniston 320 (5) cites only Pl. *Phileb.* 25b7 and Xen. *An.* 7.7.10, but neither is comparable with our instance).

1446–7 ὡς μάλιστα σοὶ μέλειν | οἶμαι: a deliberately unpleasant understatement. Aegisthus is well aware of Electra's devotion to her brother and the immense suffering the news of his death must have brought her.

1448–57 Electra meets her stepfather's brutish sarcasm with an altogether more deadly irony. At the surface level she answers Aegisthus to his satisfaction, acknowledging his triumph. But as Johnson well notes (his edition, pp. 227–8), each of her utterances can also be understood in a different sense, one which looks forward to the imminent and inevitable doom of her interlocutor. This delicate ambiguity is lost on Aegisthus; the audience, however, will pick it up. The same technique was found at 1323–5 (n.), where the immediate prospect of hostile intruders led Electra to take refuge in similarly riddling language, in words which would convey one meaning to the interlopers and another to Orestes, Pylades and the audience. Before that, the interchange between Electra and Clytemnestra at the end of the second episode was full of hidden meanings appreciated only by the audience, not by any of the characters on stage. But here Electra's use of dramatic irony is deliberate and purposeful: her weaving of linguistic webs around her victim expresses her complete control of the situation, and her active relishing of that control. The exchange builds up the tension as we move towards the dénouement. See further G. Markantonatos (1976).

The sustained use of such 'barbed ambiguity' (Dale (1960) 18) is not common in scenes of entrapment and deception in tragedy; although there are sometimes brief gestures towards the technique (e.g. Eur. *Hec.* 1021–2), only Eur. *El.* 1118–22 and *Hel.* 1412–28 come close to the present instance. The luring of Hermione into the house at Eur. *Or.* 1326–43, a passage which shows certain structural similarities to the present passage, avoids it altogether: there Electra simply lies to achieve her aim.

1448 Cf. *Ant.* 448 ἤδη· τί δ' οὐκ ἔμελλον; ἐμφανῆ γὰρ ἦν.
ἔξοιδα: for the prefix see 222n.

1448–9 For the omission of a word meaning 'otherwise' see 323n.

1449 ἔξωθεν = ἔξω; cf. *Tr.* 601 (ἔσωθεν for ἔσω), 1058n.

ἐμῶν: F's ἐμοί (*coni.* Vauvilliers, p. 41 of the notes to his edition) is stronger than the majority reading and may be right: but for ἐμά with φίλτατα used of persons cf. Eur. *Her.* 514.

γε φιλτάτων: of the four transmitted readings τε φιλτάτων gives impossible sense, while τῶν φιλτάτων is clumsy after the preceding τῶν ἐμῶν. This leaves us with γε φιλτάτων and τῆς φιλτάτης, both of which have good manuscript authority. Jebb prints the latter. Interpreting τῆς φιλτάτης as a possessive genitive with συμφορᾶς, he takes it to denote Clytemnestra in the first instance. In addition, he sees in the whole phrase the hidden meaning 'the most welcome fortune of my kindred': that is, he also takes φιλτάτης to qualify συμφορᾶς directly. This is an ambiguity too far, however, in that it requires us to take the same word simultaneously as noun and adjective. It also requires us to accept that Electra could refer to her mother in the presence of Aegisthus as τῶν ἐμῶν ἡ φιλτάτη. Such language goes way beyond the tone of meek compliance she adopts in this part of the scene: it is one thing for Electra to agree to obey her masters, quite another to describe them in such positive terms. Furthermore, the primary referent of συμφορᾶς in this context should be Orestes' chariot accident, not its impact on Clytemnestra. Jebb's interpretation is thus more baffling than ambiguous.

Hermann prints the same text as Jebb, but translates '*quidni? sortis enim expers essem meorum coniunctissimae*'. This gives a simpler ambiguity, which plays on the two meanings of συμφορά (1230n.): Electra appears to mean the death of her brother, when she really refers to his recent return. But to take συμφορὰ φιλτάτη to mean συμφορὰ τοῦ φιλτάτου puts too great a strain on the Greek. γε φιλτάτων gives the same ambiguity as in Hermann's interpretation, but without the troubling syntax, and is printed by Dawe and Ll-J/W. The manuscript evidence for γε, though not as strong as for τῆς, is nevertheless more powerful than might at first appear. Original γε could easily be changed to the τε found in some manuscripts, and this could then have become τῶν as found in other manuscripts under the influence of the surrounding genitive endings. The corruption of γε φιλτάτων to τῆς φιλτάτης is harder to account for: perhaps it was felt that συμφορᾶς needed an adjective.

1450 Aegisthus' language is blunt and to the point, contrasting with the intricate ironies of his stepdaughter.

δῆτ': commonly after an interrogative in drama (see Denniston 270 (1)).

ἂν εἶεν: for the optative see 797–8n.

δίδασκέ με: a variant μήνυέ μοι is found in L and Λ. Dawe suggests that the noun μηνυτής comes easily to the mind of a glossator (*STS* i. 200, citing Jebb on *OR* 957), and the same is likely with the verb. The less usual sense of δίδασκε ('inform' rather than 'teach') was an obvious target for a gloss.

1451 καθήνυσαν: elsewhere usually takes the accusative (e.g. *OC* 1562–4; also *Aj.* 607, *Ant.* 804–5 (ἀνύω)); for the genitive cf. *OC* 1755 τίνος, ὦ παῖδες, χρείας ἀνύσαι;, Eur. *Hipp.* 364–5 πρὶν σᾶν . . . | καθανύσαι φρενῶν with Barrett. The genitive may be governed by the κατά prefix (Hermann), or else may be parallel to the genitive with verbs of meeting, acquiring and so forth (Moorhouse 62). Electra's ostensible meaning is 'reached, met with'; but the verb is also used in contexts of violence and murder (e.g. Eur. *Or.* 89 ἐξ οὗπερ αἷμα γενέθλιον καθήνυσεν, *El.* 1164), and such a nuance is also felt by the audience. Campbell's 'they have found their way to her' (*PS*) brings out the ambiguity. For the aspiration in the verb (restored here by Porson on Eur. *Phoen.* 463 (our 453) and then Dobree on Ar. *Plut.* 607 (*ap.* Porson (1820) 130)) see West's Teubner Aeschylus, p. xxx.

1452 So too in Aeschylus Aegisthus is keen to learn whether the report of Orestes' death is true or not (*Cho.* 844–7, 851–4).

ἦ καί: expresses a certain eagerness on the part of a questioner (314n.).
θανόντ᾽: for the participle see 676n.
For ὡς with an adverb cf. 1437n.

1453 Cf. *Aj.* 813 χωρεῖν ἑτοῖμος, κοὐ λόγῳ δείξω μόνον.

οὔκ: to Aegisthus the negative refers only to ἤγγειλαν ('they didn't merely *announce* that he was dead, they showed us his remains too'). On another level, the whole of the previous sentence is denied ('they didn't announce with truth that he was dead, but actually showed him to us').

οὐ λόγῳ μόνον: for the phrase cf. Arist. *Met.* 1072a22, Plut. *An sen. resp. ger.* 791 b.

1454 The sight of the dead Orestes would provide the most trustworthy confirmation of the messengers' report (761–3n.).

πάρεστ᾽ . . . ὥστε . . . μαθεῖν: for redundant ὥστε cf. *Phil.* 656 ἆρ᾽ ἔστιν ὥστε κἀγγύθεν θέαν λαβεῖν, Goodwin §588, K–G ii. 8 Anm. 6, 11–12 Anm. 9.
κἀμφανῆ μαθεῖν: cf. *Aj.* 538 ἐμφανῆ τ᾽ ἰδεῖν.

1455 δῆτα: 845n.
καὶ μάλ᾽: 1178n.
ἄζηλος θέα: is more forceful when taken in apposition to the unexpressed subject of πάρεστ᾽ rather than as the subject itself; a comma after δῆτα makes this clearer.

1456 Aegisthus cannot resist a buffoonish jibe at Electra's new-found compliance. His words indicate his true reaction to Orestes' death before the hypocritical display of 1466–9.

πολλά χαίρειν μ' εἴπας: for the idiom cf. *Tr.* 227, Headlam on Aesch. *Ag.* 577. For εἴπας = 'your words mean that' see Garvie on Aesch. *Cho.* 691.

1457 χαίροις ἄν, εἴ σοι χαρτὰ τυγχάνει τάδε: cf. *Tr.* 227–8 χαίρειν . . . τὸν κήρυκα προὐννέπω . . . | . . . χαρτὸν εἴ τι καὶ φέρεις; also Aesch. *Ag.* 1394 χαίροιτ' ἄν, εἰ χαίροιτ'.

εἰ: two meanings are again present, as at 774 (n.). For Aegisthus, the word shades into 'because' and voices a self-evident truth. For Electra it is a true condition, whose protasis will be unfulfilled.

1458 σιγᾶν ἄνωγα κἀναδεικνύναι πύλας: the construction of ἀναδεικνύναι is problematic. Campbell took πύλας as the subject, giving 'I order (everyone) to be silent and the gates to reveal . . .': but the change of subject is unthinkable. Better is the interpretation adopted by Wunder[2], Jebb and Gonda (1929) 66, in which ἀναδεικνύναι πύλας is a compressed phrase meaning 'to open the gates so as to reveal the interior'. Ar. *Nub.* 302–4 ἵνα | μυστοδόκος δόμος | ἐν τελεταῖς ἁγίαις ἀναδείκνυται supports this view. In that passage there can be no question of revealing the *temple*, which is not hidden away. The reference must rather be to the revealing of the temple's *interior*, which is opened up during the Eleusinian Mysteries. Hence the nuance of the verb must be 'open up so as to reveal', which is exactly the sense we require in our case. For δείκνυμι followed by a dative and consecutive infinitive (cf. 1459) cf. Pind. *O.* 9.74–5 ὥστ' ἔμφρονι δεῖξαι | μαθεῖν Πατρόκλου βιατὰν νόον.

πέλας (XsV, *coni.* Reiske (1753) 19, printed by Dawe) is a banalisation, whereas πύλαις (Doederlein (*locum non inveni*) and Dobree (1833–43) ii. 51) is barely grammatical. No change of ἀναδεικνύναι is convincing. Kaibel (p. 295) conjectures that a line such as οἴξασαν οἴκων ἐμφανῆ τεθνηκότα had been lost, but Aegisthus' request then becomes rather wordy. Wilamowitz (*ap.* Kaibel) suggested οἴγειν πύλας ἄνωγα κἀναδεικνύναι, which is printed by Ll-J/W: cf. *OR* 1287–8 βοᾷ διοίγειν κλῇθρα καὶ δηλοῦν τινα | τοῖς πᾶσι Καδμείοισι τὸν πατροκτόνον. This involves more extensive surgery than other possible solutions, though it is not necessarily wrong for that. It does, however, remove Aegisthus' command for silence, which suits what we have seen of his character. Electra has not been especially loquacious, speaking only in answer to her stepfather's questions. Nevertheless, Aegisthus issues a pompous command for silence to solemnise what he believes will be his moment of triumph. Wilamowitz's conjecture, as well as Wecklein's simple substitution of οἴγειν for σιγᾶν ((1869a) 92–3), leave us merely with a flat request for the doors to be opened.

For other commands for the opening of stage doors cf. *Aj.* 344–6, Eur. *Med.* 1314–15, *Hipp.* 808–10, *Her.* 1029–30, *Or.* 1561–2, Taplin (1977a) 443. For the *ekkyklema* see Taplin (1977a) 442–3.

1459–63 Aegisthus gives us a brief glimpse of the wider political significance of Orestes' death. The threat that Orestes poses to Aegisthus' rule is prominent at the end of Aeschylus' *Agamemnon* (1646–8, 1667). In our play this broader perspective is only briefly alluded to, and the play will conclude with its focus on the future of the house, not (as in Aeschylus) of the city.

On the relationship between Mycenae and Argos in tragedy see 9n.; here both names are used to suggest as wide an audience as possible.

1460–1 εἴ τις . . . ἐλπίσιν κεναῖς . . . | ἐξῆρετ' ἀνδρὸς τοῦδε: cf. Aesch. *Ag.* 1668 οἶδ' ἐγὼ φεύγοντας ἄνδρας ἐλπίδας σιτουμένους, spoken by Aegisthus in response to the chorus's mention of Orestes. For 'empty hopes' cf. *Aj.* 478 ὅστις κεναῖσιν ἐλπίσιν θερμαίνεται, Solon. fr. 13.36 *IEG* χάσκοντες κούφαις ἐλπίσι τερπόμεθα, West on Hes. *Op.* 96 (p. 169), Virg. *Aen.* 10.627 *spes pascis inanis*, Bömer on Ov. *Met.* 7.336, *TLL* vii/1 825.83–826.4. For the genitive dependent on ἐλπίς see 831. For Electra's hopes in Orestes see 306n.

1460 πάρος: GR have μάτην, which reads like an attempt to improve the text by inserting a more vigorous word.

1461 ἐξῆρετ': cf. Thuc. 3.45.1 τῇ ἐλπίδι ἐπαιρόμενοι, 1.81.6, LSJ⁹ s.v. ἐξαίρω I 3, III 3.

1462 στόμια δέχηται τἀμά: the mastering of animals is often used as a metaphor for the punishment and disciplining of the intransigent, particularly by tyrants: cf. *Ant.* 477–8 σμικρῷ χαλινῷ δ' οἶδα τοὺς θυμουμένους | ἵππους καταρτυθέντας, *Aj.* 1253–4 μέγας δὲ πλευρὰ βοῦς ὑπὸ σμικρᾶς ὅμως | μάστιγος ὀρθὸς εἰς ὁδὸν πορεύεται, Aesch. *Ag.* 1639–40 τὸν δὲ μὴ πειθάνορα | ζεύξω βαρείαις, also 1624 πρὸς κέντρα μὴ λάκτιζε, μὴ παίσας μογῇς (with Dodds on Eur. *Ba.* 795), Plut. *Comp. Per. et Fab.* 1.4 σπαργῶντι δήμῳ χαλινὸν ἐμβαλεῖν ὕβρεως. Aegisthus throughout has been associated with ideas of control and restraint (310–23n.).

πρὸς βίαν: 369n.

1463 φύσῃ φρένας: cf. *OC* 804–5 οὐδὲ τῷ χρόνῳ φύσας φανῇ | φρένας ποτ', *Ant.* 683 πάτερ, θεοὶ φύουσιν ἀνθρώποις φρένας, LSJ⁹ s.v. φύω A I 4. The alliteration of π and φ may add force to the end of Aegisthus' speech (210n.).

1464 As Electra speaks, she opens the door to the *skene*. Orestes and Pylades enter with the *ekkyklema*, on which lies the veiled body of Clytemnestra. The scene now shifts not to the interior of the house (as 1473 and 1491 make clear), but to the αὐλή or forecourt before the entrance proper (so rightly Taplin (1989) 105). Taplin argues for a similar shift at the end of *Antigone*. An entrant from the *skene* will normally initiate dialogue with those already present; in this instance Orestes is silent because this 'fits the needs of the stratagem' (so Mastronarde (1979) 26–7 n. 33).

καὶ δή: 317n.

τελεῖται τἀπ' ἐμοῦ: cf. *OC* 1628 τἀπὸ σοῦ βραδύνεται, Eur. *Tro.* 74 ἕτοιμ' ἃ βούλῃ τἀπ' ἐμοῦ. The primary reference is to the opening of the door; but the verb may also refer to Orestes' plan (cf. 1344, 1399, 1435). The absence of a specific subject contributes to the mysterious atmosphere (1344).

1464–5 τῷ . . . χρόνῳ | νοῦν ἔσχον: echoing Chrysothemis' advice αὐτὴ δὲ νοῦν σχὲς ἀλλὰ τῷ χρόνῳ ποτέ (1013). The article is idiomatic in such expressions with χρόνος (cf. 1013n.).

1465 συμφέρειν τοῖς κρείσσοσιν: again Electra echoes her sister (340, 396, 1014). The irony lies in the ambiguity in κρείσσοσιν: Aegisthus is meant to see in this word a reference to himself, but we know that power is even now slipping from his hands.

1466–7 Aegisthus loftily refers to mighty abstracts and addresses to the deity. This contrasts with the baseness of his real motive: a desire to make sure that Orestes is dead.

φάσμ': often of a portent: cf. Aesch. *Ag.* 145 and LSJ⁹ s.v. 4.

φθόνου . . . | . . . νέμεσις: Aristotle defines φθόνος as τὸ λυπεῖσθαι ἐπὶ τοῖς κατ' ἀξίαν εὖ πράττουσιν; its opposite is ἐπιχαιρεκακία, which involves τὸ χαίρειν ταῖς παρὰ τὴν ἀξίαν κακοπραγίαις. νέμεσις, he says, is the quality which falls between these two extremes: this he defines as τὸ λυπεῖσθαι μὲν ἐπὶ ταῖς παρὰ τὴν ἀξίαν κακοπραγίαις καὶ εὐπραγίαις, χαίρειν δ' ἐπὶ ταῖς ἀξίαις (*Eth. Eud.* 1233b19–26; cf. *Eth. Nic.* 1108a35–b6). The distinction in S. is more subtle. In *Aj.* 157 πρὸς γὰρ τὸν ἔχονθ' ὁ φθόνος ἕρπει and *OR* 380–2 ὦ πλοῦτε καὶ τυραννὶ . . . | . . . | ὅσος παρ' ὑμῖν ὁ φθόνος φυλάσσεται the term φθόνος denotes envy of good fortune regardless of its moral worth. *Phil.* 776 τὸν φθόνον . . . πρόσκυσον makes this clear: Philoctetes implies that φθόνος may attend the bow's possessor simply because he possesses it. The anger denoted by νέμεσις, however, always involves an ethical dimension: cf. 792n., *Phil.* 601–2 ἦ θεῶν βία | καὶ νέμεσις, αἵπερ ἔργ' ἀμύνουσιν κακά;, *OC* 1753 πενθεῖν οὐ χρή· νέμεσις γάρ. For the practice of the other tragedians see R. C. T. Parker (1997) 151–2 n. 30 (though his brief discussion of S. is unsatisfactory).

Aegisthus ascribes Orestes' death to the workings of φθόνος, with reference to the enormous success at the games which Orestes enjoyed immediately before

COMMENTARY: 1442–1510

his fall (cf. 751). This is the familiar idea that good fortune is often followed by bad. He then raises the possibility that νέμεσις may also be involved: Orestes' death, he suggests with feigned tactfulness, might be a punishment for some unspecified misdeed on his part.

Two alternative interpretations are less plausible. Jebb, following Hermann, asserts that οὐ λέγω is equivalent to *indictum volo*, saying 'Aegisthus corrects himself with hypocritical piety; it is as if he said "but it is not for me to judge my fellow-mortal"' (supported by Opstelten (1945) 203 = (1952) 237). But the articulation of the sentence tells against this: the coordination of μέν and δέ is more natural if both clauses refer to the underlying cause of Orestes' death. Nor is there a good parallel for οὐ λέγω meaning 'may it be unsaid': (Aesch. *Eum.* 866, which Jebb cites, does not provide one; *OR* 711–12 and *Tr.* 500 are also quite different).

Dawe reads ψέγω for λέγω (a common enough corruption: cf. 1423n.), arguing 'if the φθόνος manifested in the death of Orestes was an act of divine punishment, Aegisthus is content. The hypocritical tone is correct for an Aegisthus' (*STS* i. 202). But the hypocrisy is more effective if Aegisthus feigns reluctance to accuse Orestes of being the target of the gods' anger, rather than if he agrees with their anger against him.

For οὐ used prospectively at the end of a line cf. *Ant.* 5, Eur. *Hcld.* 1016, fr. 240.1 *TrGF* = 14.1 Austin.

1467 ἔπεστι νέμεσις: cf. Aesch. *Eum.* 542 ποινὰ γὰρ ἐπέσται, Appian *BC* 1.71.8 αἰδώς τε θεῶν ἢ νέμεσις ἀνδρῶν ἢ φθόνου φόβος οὐδεὶς ἔτι τοῖς γιγνομένοις ἐπῆν; also Hes. *Op.* 754–6 ἔστ' ἐπὶ καὶ τῷ | ποινή . . . | . . . θεός νύ τε καὶ τὰ νεμεσσᾷ.

1468 χαλᾶτε πᾶν κάλυμμ' ἀπ' ὀφθαλμῶν: for the covering of the head of a corpse cf. Eur. *Hipp.* 1458, Seaford (1984) 252 n. 41. For the marital and funereal connotations of the veil in epic and tragedy see Rehm (1994) 40.

1469 Cf. *Aj.* 924 ὡς καὶ παρ' ἐχθροῖς ἄξιος θρήνων τυχεῖν.

τὸ συγγενές: 'das Neutrum ist absichtlich gewählt, weil es τὸν συγγενῆ wie τὴν συγγενῆ bezeichnen kann' (Nauck³, referring to the dramatist's intention, not Aegisthus'); cf. 1471 ταῦθ'.

γε: *coni.* Turnebus. The particle gives exactly the right sense, and could easily have turned into the unintelligible majority reading τε. Orestes was Aegisthus' enemy: nevertheless, insofar as he was his kinsman he will receive proper lamentation. The minority variant τοι, by contrast, gives a purposeless emphasis. Denniston 546 cites *Tr.* 190 for τοι in a final clause, but there Ll-J/W rightly adopt Brunck's σοι (see Davies *ad loc.*).

κἀπ' ἐμοῦ: contrast 432–4 (n.).

535

1470-83 The confrontation between Orestes and Aegisthus leads to the play's third and final recognition scene, which looks back to the earlier recognition of Orestes by Electra (cf. Cave (1988) 225 n. 2, Solmsen (1967) 62 = (1968–82) iii. 63). In each case Orestes in the guise of a messenger tells another character (Electra / Aegisthus) that Orestes is dead. As 'proof' of this he has brought his physical remains back to Mycenae. The other character believes the message without question. To Electra this report brings grief, to Aegisthus joy. Orestes subsequently reveals the truth. In the earlier scene, he forces Electra to give up the urn which she is desperately clutching (1216 βαστάζω), saying that it has no connexion with her (1213 οὔ σοι προσήκει, 1215 τοῦτο δ' οὐχὶ σόν), so that she might hear the truth from him. As she relinquishes it, he reveals his identity. In the later scene he adopts the opposite course: he encourages Aegisthus to touch the body (1470 αὐτὸς σὺ βάσταζ'), saying that this is his duty (1470 οὐκ ἐμὸν τόδ', ἀλλὰ σόν). Orestes does not need to reveal his identity: rather, in a *coup de théâtre* the revelation of the truth occurs simultaneously with the revelation of the body. Aegisthus' dismay is the opposite of Electra's joy: Orestes' return means life to her, but death to him.

1470 βάσταζ': 905n.

οὐκ ἐμὸν τόδ', ἀλλὰ σόν: cf. Pl. *Gorg.* 497b8 πάντως οὐ σὴ αὕτη ἡ τιμή ('it is not for you to estimate their value' – Dodds *ad loc.*), *OC* 197.

1471 ταῦθ': 1469n.

προσηγορεῖν φίλως: cf. *OC* 758-9 τήνδε τὴν πόλιν φίλως | εἰπών. The adverb refers to the sorrowful farewells offered to dead relatives at funerals. The alternative reading φίλος is barely grammatical. Calder (1963) 213–14 = (2005) 151–2 advocates φίλους (Pa, *coni.* Purgold (1802) 147), but 'the word order and position of τε and καί make φίλους impossible in the same sentence as ταῦθ'' (Dawe, *STS* i. 202).

1472 σὺ δέ: editors assume that the words indicate that someone new is addressed, and hence that the command must be given to Electra (cf. Calder (1963) 214 = (2005) 152). But the same phrase is used, in the same part of the line, at 448, without any change in the person addressed. Kaibel (p. 296) is thus at least as likely to be right in saying that the order is given to Orestes.

1473 μοι . . . κάλει: for μοι with κάλει cf. *Tr.* 1147 κάλει τὸ πᾶν μοι σπέρμα σῶν ὁμαιμόνων, and often in the orators (e.g. Dem. 18.137). Ll-J/W follow Triclinius in reading ἥ. They object to the paradosis on the grounds that it involves a medial caesura: in fact we have here not a medial caesura but an enclitic following a normal caesura, which is common enough (cf. West (1982a) 83). Nor is the article appropriate with this proper name (cf. West (1991) 300).

Ll-J/W claim that it denotes a familiar tone of address: 'Aegisthus speaks of his consort in a tone of casual intimacy not calculated to please her children by Agamemnon' (*Second Thoughts*; 'children' is a mistake, as Aegisthus is not yet aware that Orestes is present). But the only evidence they cite in support of this nuance is the article in addresses to slaves (cf. Schulze (1896) 242–3 = (1934) 705). This is a specialised linguistic usage, and there is no reason to suppose that it had been extended to other forms of address.

1474 As Orestes speaks, Aegisthus removes the veil and discovers the body of Clytemnestra. This dramatic moment was consciously employed as a model by Racine in his *Athalie*, where Jonas is suddenly revealed from behind a curtain to Athalie's discomfort: cf. Barnwell (1982) 126–7.[88] At Eur. *Antiope* fr. 223.89–93 *TrGF* = 48.60–4 Kambitsis Lycus is told of his wife Dirce's death by Amphion only when the latter has already begun his assault on him: S.'s presentation is more dramatically satisfying. For the ὀψιμαθής who learns the truth too late see Davies (forthcoming), (forthcoming 2) (as the second article makes clear, Davies and I disagree on the significance of this passage).

μηκέτ᾽ ἄλλοσε σκόπει: cf. Pind. *O*. 1.5–6 μηκέτ᾽ ἀελίου σκόπει | ἄλλο θαλπνότερον . . . ἄστρον, 1225n.; for the force of μηκέτι see 611n.

1475 Αι. οἴμοι, τί λεύσσω; Ορ. τίνα φοβῇ; τίν᾽ ἀγνοεῖς; To what or whom do τί, τίνα and τίν᾽ refer? We might expect the newly unveiled corpse to be the subject of discourse throughout this line and beyond. But as Calder (1963) 215 = (2005) 153–4 points out, there is no reference to it in the following lines (1476–81), where the issue at stake is the identity of Orestes, not Clytemnestra. Calder compares *Tr*. 1141–2, where the reference to Nessus causes Heracles to realise his true peril, and to forget Deianira, whom he never mentions again. In 1475 Orestes' questions might refer ironically to Clytemnestra. On the other hand, the failure of recognition implied by the verb ἀγνοεῖς is more effective if it refers to Aegisthus' previous inability to identify Orestes. But Calder goes too far in claiming that Aegisthus' question τί λεύσσω; also refers to Orestes. The neuter τί more naturally denotes a lifeless corpse than a living man; and while Aegisthus moves quickly from realisation of the body's identity to thoughts of his own safety, that need not exclude an initial cry of horror in response to the unexpected sight. The accompanying stage action is caught by Campbell's note: 'after a glance of horrified recognition at the corpse, Aegisthus looks strangely on Orestes' (though 'strangely' should not be pressed, as Aegisthus is wearing a mask). On the *antilabe* see 1209n.

For the presentation of the moments immediately after the *anagnorisis* cf. Cave (1988) 489: 'an ignorance . . . turns *for the moment* into an implausible

---

[88] For more on Sophocles and Racine see Stone (1964).

and precarious knowledge; the apparently opposite poles of knowledge and ignorance meet in surreptitious complicity' (his italics).

1476–7 ἐν . . . | πέπτωχ': cf. Eur. *Her.* 1091–2 ἐν κλύδωνι καὶ φρενῶν ταράγματι | πέπτωκα δεινῷ, *Or.* 1419 πεσὼν ἐν φόβῳ. For ἐμπίπτω as a hunting term cf. Xen. *Cyn.* 6.10, *Cyr.* 1.6.40, van de Wijnpersse (1929) 28.

1476 ἐν μέσοις ἀρκυστάτοις: the net metaphor is common in scenes where a victim is lured to his death: cf. Eur. *El.* 965 καλῶς ἄρ' ἄρκυν ἐς μέσην πορεύεται, *Her.* 729–30, *Or.* 1315; also Aesch. *Ag.* 1374–6, *Eum.* 112–13 ἐκ μέσων ἀρκυστάτων | ὤρουσεν. An ἄρκυς is 'a staked purse- or tunnel- net, with a running noose, into which the hunted animal is driven' (Garvie on *Cho.* 998–1000). For the capture of the animal in the middle of the net cf. van de Wijnpersse (1929) 37–8.

1477 πέπτωχ' ὁ: Blaydes's πέπτωκα ((1899) 255) is paralleled by *Phil.* 923 ἀπόλωλα τλήμων, *OR* 1175, 1309, Aesch. *Pers.* 912; but for the article cf. Eur. *Ba.* 1360–1 οὐδὲ παύσομαι | κακῶν ὁ τλήμων, *Andr.* 1070 (both metrically guaranteed).

τλήμων: the περιπέτεια is marked by Aegisthus' assumption of an adjective more usually associated with Orestes himself (602n.).

πάλαι: denotes recent time (676n.).

1478 ζῶν τοῖς θανοῦσιν . . . ἀνταυδᾷς ἴσα: Campbell, Dawe and Ll-J/W rightly keep the manuscript reading. Most editors adopt Tyrwhitt's ζῶντας (*ap.* Brunck¹), which Brunck (*ib.* ii. 212) explains as '*non sentis te dudum cum viventibus quasi mortuis confabulari?*', Bruhn as 'Du redest Lebendige gleich Toten an' (for verbs of address taking an accusative for expected dative cf. 556, *Aj.* 764, K–G i. 295–6 Anm. 3), and Jebb as 'thou perversely (ἀντ-) speakest of the living as if they were dead'. Campbell keeps the paradosis and translates 'why, dost thou not perceive that all this while thou, a living man, hast been replying to the dead in tones like theirs?' – that is, 'with a voice that is already close to death'. But all these interpretations fail to note the parallels *OR* 408–9 ἐξισωτέον τὸ γοῦν | ἴσ' ἀντιλέξαι and 543–4 ἀντὶ τῶν εἰρημένων | ἴσ' ἀντάκουσον, which indicate that here ἀνταυδᾷς and ἴσα must be taken together to mean 'speak on equal terms (with)'.

Hence Longman (1954) 193 translated 'thou, a living man, art replying to the dead on equal terms'; Winnington-Ingram's 'are bandying words with' ((1980) 238 n. 69; also preferred by Ll-J/W in *Sophoclea*) catches the meaning more exactly. This gives sharper sense: instead of the banal 'you have been saying that the living are dead', Orestes sarcastically speaks of himself as already dead, mockingly adopting Aegisthus' perspective at the moment that it is shown to be false. So too at Aesch. *Cho.* 886 τὸν ζῶντα καίνειν τοὺς τεθνηκότας λέγω, 'the dead' is effectively a shorthand for 'those whom we had thought dead'. For other such paradoxes involving anomalous relationships between the dead and the living cf. 1417–21 n.

1479 οἴμοι, ξυνῆκα τοὔπος: cf. Aesch. *Cho.* 887 οἲ 'γώ, ξυνῆκα τοὔπος ἐξ αἰνιγμάτων (Clytemnestra, recognising Orestes). For the aorist cf. 668n.

1479–80 οὐ γὰρ ἔσθ' ὅπως | . . . οὐκ: cf. *OC* 97, *OR* 1058–9.

1481 For καί in sarcastic questions see Denniston 311 (ii). Campbell may be right, however, in taking it with μάντις: cf. Pind. *O.* 7.30–1 αἱ δὲ φρενῶν ταραχαὶ | παρέπλαγξαν καὶ σοφόν.

μάντις . . . ἄριστος: Aegisthus' sudden understanding, Orestes ironically implies, shows that he is a great prophet. Prophets in antiquity were expected to know the past and present, as well as the future (cf. Hom. *Il.* 1.70 ὃς ᾔδη τά τ' ἐόντα τά τ' ἐσσόμενα πρό τ' ἐόντα, Fraenkel on Aesch. *Ag.* 1185 with n. 1). For the failure of the μάντις to see his own trouble cf. Lucian 23.20 ἐκεῖνο δέ γε θαυμάζω, ὅπως μάντις ὢν οὐ προεγίγνωσκες ἐπὶ τούτοις κολασθησόμενος. For πάλαι used to denote recent time see 676n.

1482 ὄλωλα δή: 'the emphasis conveyed by δή with verbs is for the most part pathetic in tone, and it is peculiarly at home in the great crises of drama, above all at moments when death or ruin is present or imminent' (Denniston 214 (8)).

1483 κἄν: crasis for καὶ ἐάν, with which πάρῃς or ᾖ must be understood (cf. Ar. *Ach.* 1021 μέτρησον εἰρήνης τί μοι, κἂν πέντ' ἔτη, *Plut.* 126 ἐὰν ἀναβλέψῃς σὺ κἂν μικρὸν χρόνον, K–G i. 244–5 Anm. 2).

1483–90 Electra urges her brother to perform the killing without delay. The contrast with her former behaviour is striking: 'one feels the difference from her lavishly emotional manner at the reunion; now she is as practical and intent on speed as Orestes is, or more. But this intentness is the disquieting expression of fierce desire' (Hutchinson (1999) 57–8). Only the maltreatment of Aegisthus' corpse could constitute λυτήριον for her suffering (1489–90n.). This unpleasant side of Electra's character is presented here with no mitigation or self-awareness on her part (contrast 254–309n., 616–21n.).

Electra's words are formally similar to Pylades' famous speech at Aesch. *Cho.* 900–2. Both characters urge Orestes on to carry out the killing which forms the climax of the drama; both then do not speak again, leaving Orestes and his foe to engage in stichomythia before the latter is forced inside the palace to be finished off. But in Aeschylus Pylades responds to genuine hesitation on

COMMENTARY: 1442–1510

Orestes' part; and he encourages his comrade by reminding him of the significance of Apollo's prophecy. Electra's contribution has no such motivation: she urges haste on her brother although he has shown no sign of delaying. And instead of providing a culminating appeal to the word of Apollo or the justice of the deed, she expresses her own passionate desire for Aegisthus' death in uncompromising terms. Her behaviour recalls that of Alcmena at the end of Euripides' *Heraclidae* (see Zuntz (1955) 37–8, cited above, 1442–1504n.): note especially 1045 τί δῆτα μέλλετ', with its emphasis on immediacy. In each case the intensity of the desire for violent revenge inevitably affects the sympathies of the audience.

A protoattic ovoid krater attributed to the Ram Jug Painter (once Berlin Antiquarium A32) may show Electra urging Orestes on as he leads Aegisthus and Clytemnestra to their deaths (cf. Prag (1985) 7).

1484 ἀδελφέ: 461 n.

μηδὲ μηκύνειν λόγους: cf. Tr. Adesp. fr. 457 *TrGF* × —λαλεῖν δεῖ μηδὲ μηκύνειν λόγον, Pl. *Phileb.* 50d3.

[1485–6] τί γὰρ βροτῶν ἂν σὺν κακοῖς μεμειγμένων | θνῄσκειν ὁ μέλλων τοῦ χρόνου κέρδος φέροι; 'For when mortals are involved in ruin, what does the man whose death is delayed gain by the time?' (Lloyd-Jones). Jebb and Pearson accept the lines, but Dawe and Ll-J/W accept Dindorf's deletion (in his fourth edition). The language presents real difficulties. The gap between τί and κέρδος is longer than we would expect (cf. the similarly long and unacceptable gap between ἐγώ and ἐλεύσσομεν in the interpolation at *Phil.* 1218–21). The word order θνῄσκειν ὁ μέλλων (instead of ὁ μέλλων θνῄσκειν) is odd. And τοῦ χρόνου is hard to explain: whether this is a gain *consisting of* or *taken from* time, the meaning is contorted. The lines are also stylistically ill at ease in Electra's speech: surrounded as they are by urgent imperatives and ferociously direct language, 1485–6 come across as syntactically dense and unappealing. Ejection is thus probably the safest course. Vahlen (1885–6) 11–13 = (1907–8) i. 321–5 prefers to emend to τίς . . . | . . . οὐ χρόνου; but as Ll-J/W note (*Sophoclea*), this makes the definite article in ὁ μέλλων difficult to understand.

According to Ll-J/W, '[Electra] can hardly put forward as a reason for killing Aegisthus at once the fact that a few more moments will not do him any good, since it is clear that she does not wish to do him any good at all' (*Sophoclea*). This is not a satisfactory objection, however, as it ignores the possibility that Electra is speaking ironically: not the deadly, delicate, irony of the first part of the scene (1448–57n.), but an openly bitter sarcasm in which she mockingly pretends that she has Aegisthus' own best interests at heart. For the sentiment cf. *Ant.* 463–4 ὅστις γὰρ ἐν πολλοῖσιν ὡς ἐγὼ κακοῖς | ζῇ, πῶς ὅδ' οὐχὶ κατθανὼν κέρδος φέρει; Contrast Aesch. *Ag.* 1300 ὁ δ' ὕστατός γε τοῦ χρόνου πρεσβεύεται.

540

COMMENTARY: 1442–1510

[1485] For γάρ used to smuggle in an interpolation see 1007n.

βροτῶν . . . σὺν κακοῖς μεμειγμένων: for people mixed with troubles etc. cf. Hom. *Od.* 20.202–3 οὐκ ἐλεαίρεις ἄνδρας . . . | μισγέμεναι κακότητι καὶ ἄλγεσι λευγαλέοισιν, Pind. *I.* 3.3 ἄξιος εὐλογίαις ἀστῶν μεμίχθαι, *Ant.* 1311 δειλαίᾳ δὲ συγκέκραμαι δύᾳ, *Aj.* 895, Ar. *Plut.* 853 οὕτω πολυφόρῳ συγκέκραμαι δαίμονι; also (for trouble mixed with a person) Hdt. 7.203.2 εἶναι δὲ θνητὸν οὐδένα οὐδὲ ἔσεσθαι τῷ κακὸν ἐξ ἀρχῆς γινομένῳ οὐ συνεμίχθη. For the σύν with μείγνυμι cf. Pind. *N.* 3.77–8. μεμειγμένων is Kaibel's emendation (cf. 715n.), though if the interpolation is from after the fourth century then transmitted μεμιγμένων is more likely.

[1486] θνῄσκειν ὁ μέλλων: for the word order see 1485–6n. Both present and future infinitives are common after μέλλω in S. (see Jebb on *OR* 967).

1487 κτεῖνε καὶ κτανών: cf. Eur. *Hec.* 25–7 κτείνει με . . . | . . . καὶ κτανὼν ἐς οἶδμ᾽ ἁλὸς | μεθῆχ᾽, *Her.* 33 with Bond, Bruhn §230.I, Mastronarde on Eur. *Phoen.* 22, Diggle (1996a) 111.

1487–8 πρόθες | ταφεῦσιν . . . τυγχάνειν: the meaning of these words and their likely effect on an ancient audience has been hotly debated (cf. Davies (1999b) 42 n. 14). C. P. Segal (1966) 520–1 argues that Electra's language is so vague that she might be referring to a proper burial (cf. MacLeod (2001) 177 n. 41). But this interpretation makes 1488 extremely weak – if the ταφῆς in question are regular undertakers, why should Electra mention them at all? εἰκός too can only be sarcastic. The phrase must rather be an ironic reference to the dogs and birds which consume the corpses of those who are exposed without burial (cf. *Ant.* 29–30, *Aj.* 830, Eur. *Phoen.* 1634, C. P. Segal (1971) 37, 63 etc., Hordern on Timoth. fr. 791.137–8 *PMG*, Watson on Hor. *Ia.* 5.99–100). Against this interpretation Knox (1968) 157 argues that (i) the only other use of ταφεύς in S. (*OC* 582) is in a solemn context, (ii) the interpretation adopted here makes S.'s Electra worse than Euripides', as in the latter's play Aegisthus does at least attain burial, (iii) had S. wished to present Electra as a malefactor, he would not have done so 'by means of an incidental, ambiguous remark in the closing lines of the play'. But (i) the destruction of the corpse by dogs and birds is often ironically described in terms of burial (cf. [Aesch.] *Sept.* 1020–1 οὕτω πετηνῶν τόνδ᾽ ὑπ᾽ οἰωνῶν δοκεῖ | ταφέντ᾽ ἀτίμως τοὐπιτίμιον λαβεῖν, S. *Ant.* 1081–2 ὅσων σπαράγματ᾽ ἢ κύνες καθήγνισαν | ἢ θῆρες, ἤ τις πτηνὸς οἰωνός, Gorgias D–K 82 B 5a (= ii. 284.21–2) γῦπες ἄψυχοι τάφοι (*ap.* [Longinus] *De subl.* 3.2 with Russell)), (ii) Castor, not Electra, orders the burial in Euripides (1276–7), and (iii) this is not the only place in the exodos where Electra's darker side is prominent.

541

At Hom. *Od.* 3.258–61 Nestor envisages what would have been Aegisthus' fate had Menelaus returned in time: τῶ κέ οἱ οὐδὲ θανόντι χυτὴν ἐπὶ γαῖαν | ἔχευαν, | ἀλλ' ἄρα τόν γε κύνες τε καὶ οἰωνοὶ κατέδαψαν | κείμενον ἐν πεδίῳ | ἑκὰς ἄστεος, οὐδὲ κέ τίς μιν | κλαῦσεν Ἀχαιϊάδων; cf. also Eur. *El.* 896–8 (Orestes to Electra) ὃν εἴτε χρήζεις θηρσὶν ἁρπαγὴν πρόθες, | ἢ σκῦλον οἰωνοῖσιν, αἰθέρος τέκνοις, | πήξασ' ἔρεισον σκόλοπι. A different account is given at Paus. 2.16.7, where Κλυταιμνήστρα . . . ἐτάφη καὶ Αἴγισθος ὀλίγον ἀπωτέρω τοῦ τείχους· ἐντὸς δὲ ἀπηξιώθησαν, ἔνθα Ἀγαμέμνων τε αὐτὸς ἔκειτο καὶ οἱ σὺν ἐκείνῳ φονευθέντες. The use of the verb may be pointed, given that πρόθεσις is a technical term for an aspect of Greek funerary ritual (cf. 1198n.).

1488 τόνδ': Dawe[3] prints τώδ' (τῶδ' C; *coni.* Reiske (1753) 19), but the focus is on Aegisthus' fate alone.

1489–90 ὡς ἐμοὶ τόδ' ἂν κακῶν | μόνον γένοιτο τῶν πάλαι λυτήριον: for the sentiment cf. *Phil.* 1043–4 εἰ δ' ἴδοιμ' ὀλωλότας | τούτους, δοκοῖμ' ἂν τῆς νόσου πεφευγέναι; a more extreme case at Hom. *Il.* 4.34–6 (Zeus to Hera) εἰ δὲ σὺ . . . | ὠμὸν βεβρώθοις Πρίαμον Πριάμοιό τε παῖδας | ἄλλους τε Τρῶας, τότε κεν χόλον ἐξακέσαιο. For the formation of λυτήριον see 447n.

1491 χωροῖς ἂν εἴσω: for the effect of the optative (not politeness) see 637n.

1491–2 λόγων γὰρ οὐ | νῦν ἐστιν ἀγών: cf. Eur. *Phoen.* 588 οὐ λόγων ἔθ' ἁγών, Thuc. 3.44.1 οὐ γὰρ περὶ τῆς ἐκείνων ἀδικίας ἡμῖν ὁ ἀγών, εἰ σωφρονοῦμεν, ἀλλὰ περὶ τῆς ἡμετέρας εὐβουλίας, Diod. Sic. 8.12.9 πρόκειται . . . ἀγὼν οὐ λόγων, ἀλλ' ἔργων.

1492 ἀλλὰ σῆς ψυχῆς πέρι: for the struggle over a ψυχή cf. Hom. *Il.* 22.159–61, Eur. *Or.* [847], Pl. *Phaedr.* 247b5–6, Xen. *Mem.* 3.12.1, Padel (1992) 30 n. 70, Braswell on Pind. *N.* 9.29.

1493–4 πῶς, τόδ' εἰ καλὸν | τοὔργον, σκότου δεῖ . . . ; For bad deeds done in the dark cf. Pl. *Phileb.* 65e10–66a3 τὸ πάντων αἴσχιστον ἑπόμενον ὁρῶντες αὐτοί τε αἰσχυνόμεθα καὶ ἀφανίζοντες κρύπτομεν ὅτι μάλιστα, νυκτὶ πάντα τὰ τοιαῦτα διδόντες, ὡς φῶς οὐ δέον ὁρᾶν αὐτά, John 3.19–20. MacLeod (2001) 183 argues that Orestes kills Aegisthus inside because of his σωφροσύνη, but there is no evidence for this. Aegisthus' accusation pointedly implies that Orestes rejects a principle of retributory justice: cf. Kerrigan (1996) 16–17 'the avenger ['s . . .] killings are distinguished from common murder by the sign, the evidence, of their fittingness. Hence the impulse to display, where the murderer's urge is to conceal'. Aegisthus is killed off stage in Aeschylus; and deaths in tragedy regularly take place out of sight. But if S. had wanted to present the killing indoors as a morally neutral act, it is hard to see why he has Aegisthus score such a hit against his enemy here. Orestes' reply does not deal with the uneasy implications which arise from Aegisthus' words.

1494 πρόχειρος: usually 'at hand' (1116n.); here, 'ready to' (cf. LSJ⁹ s.v. II 1).

1495–6 ἔνθαπερ κατέκτανες | πατέρα τὸν ἀμόν: at the hearth (270n.). Retributive killings are often carried out in the same place as the original crime (Hirzel (1907–10) 442–56). Far from equating the ethical status of the killings of Agamemnon and Aegisthus, Orestes' desire to perform the latter in the same place as the former stresses the causal link between the two. At Aesch. *Cho.* 904–7 Orestes tells Clytemnestra to go inside so he can kill her next to her lover Aegisthus; S. lays greater stress on how the killing constitutes retribution for Agamemnon's death. This goes some way to answering Aegisthus' preceding questions, though the point about the concealment of the act is left hanging.

The death of Aegisthus was common in archaic and classical art: but he is almost always presented as sitting on a throne as Orestes kills him. There is no parallel for his death at the hearth (cf. Prag (1985) 10–32).

On the rough breathing of ἀμόν see 279n.

1497 πᾶσ' ἀνάγκη: cf. *OR* 986, Renehan (1992) 357, Austin and Olson on Ar. *Thesm.* 171. West (1979) 106 conjectures πάντ' for πᾶσ', which gives a better contrast with Orestes' limiting words τὰ γοῦν σ' in 1499. πάντα is found twice elsewhere with the phrase τά τ' ὄντα καὶ μέλλοντα in tragedy (Eur. *Hel.* 13–14 (cited 1498n.), 922–3). But the paradosis is such a standard idiom that we should probably retain it.

1498 On the sense of Aegisthus' remarks here see 1442–1504n. MacLeod (2001) 179–80 n. 51 provides a doxography.

τά τ' ὄντα καὶ μέλλοντα: similar language is often found in descriptions of prophetic knowledge: cf. Eur. *Hel.* 13–14 τὰ θεῖα γὰρ | τά τ' ὄντα καὶ μέλλοντα πάντ' ἠπίστατο, 923, *Ion* 7 τά τ' ὄντα καὶ μέλλοντα θεσπίζων ἀεί, Ov. *Met.* 1.517–18, West on Hes. *Theog.* 32, Yeats, *Sailing to Byzantium, ad fin.* 'of what is past, or passing, or to come'. But *pace* Owen (1927) this does not remove all significance from μέλλοντα in the present instance. ὄντα refers to something, and the audience is consequently left wondering what sense is contained in the other participle.

1499 τὰ γοῦν σ': γοῦν here is limitative (cf. Denniston 450–4), not emphatic (*pace* Stinton (1986) 84 = (1990) 479): after the disturbingly broad scope of the κακά mentioned by Aegisthus in the preceding line, Orestes attempts to narrow the focus to the troubles afflicting Aegisthus. For the elision of accented, emphatic σά cf. *OR* 328–9 ἐγὼ δ' οὐ μή ποτε | τἄμ', ὡς ἂν εἴπω μὴ τὰ σ', ἐκφήνω κακά, *Phil.* 339, Eur. *Hipp.* 323.

ἐγώ σοι μάντις εἰμὶ τῶνδ' ἄκρος: cf. Aesch. *Ag.* 1130–1 οὐ κομπάσαιμ' ἂν θεσφάτων γνώμων ἄκρος | εἶναι, Lucian 27.2 μάντιν ἄκρον βλέπεις; perhaps Eur. *Hcld.* 65 with Herwerden's conjecture (see Diggle's apparatus). Orestes may be taking a dig at Aegisthus' assumption of prophetic language in the preceding lines (1498n.).

1500 ἀλλ' οὐ πατρῷαν τὴν τέχνην ἐκόμπασας: Aegisthus jeers at Agamemnon's failure to foresee his death. For the form of the sentence cf. *Aj.* 1121 οὐ γὰρ βάναυσον τὴν τέχνην ἐκτησάμην.

1501 ἡ δ' ὁδὸς βραδύνεται: cf. *OC* 1628 πάλαι δὴ τἀπὸ σοῦ βραδύνεται.

1502 For the elision in *antilabai* see 1424n. The double break in a single line marks great urgency: cf. *Phil.* 753 (a triple break), 810, 814, 816, *OC* 832, Eur. *Alc.* 391, *Hipp.* 310, Köhler (1913) 42.

βαδιστέον: the verb is rare in tragedy, and perhaps colloquial (cf. Olson on Ar. *Ach.* 393–4): it may thus suggest a rough tone.

1503 ἦ μὴ φύγω σε; '(must I do this) lest . . .' (Jebb (adapted), citing *OR* 1012 ἦ μὴ μίασμα τῶν φυτευσάντων λάβῃς;).

1504 Orestes speaks last because he is the 'dominant' speaker, the one in control of the situation (cf. 803n.).

[1505–7] Dawe accepts Dindorf's deletion (in his fourth edition) on the grounds that (i) S. would not have said that all who act beyond νόμοι should die, (ii) κτείνειν without a subject is odd and (iii) the final expression 'then wickedness would not be much' (not 'so much') is puzzling (*STS* i. 203). With regard to (ii), the construction is loose, but does not constitute a particular difficulty. (iii) is also unproblematic if we translate πολύ as 'widespread' (cf. Pl. *Gorg.* 465d4). (i) is more serious, however. Throughout the play Orestes has been intent on taking vengeance on his father's murderers, and here he fulfils this duty. In the paradosis, he suddenly breaks off from this purpose and enunciates his belief that immediate capital punishment for all lawbreakers would stop the widespread wrongdoing in the world. This moral crusade is not only irrelevant: it also trivialises Orestes' present action. Aegisthus deserves death because of the extremity of his crimes: now we hear that his punishment ought to be the same whether he had killed a king or stolen a drachma. Moreover, Orestes' verbosity in these lines fits ill with the stress on speed in the previous part of the scene, which had only just been marked by the change to single-line utterances (1499, 1500), and then to *antilabe* (1502–3). The γε in 1506 also provides a linguistic difficulty (n.).

Although Ll-J/W keep the lines, their misgivings are strong: in *Second Thoughts* they describe them as 'so trite and so feeble'. They cite Leofranc Holford-Strevens's comparison with Hom. *Od.* 1.47 ὡς ἀπόλοιτο καὶ ἄλλος ὅτις τοιαῦτά γε ῥέζοι, which is spoken by Athena of Aegisthus. But the sentiment voiced by Orestes here is broader and less relevant to the context, as well as considerably more verbose. Newiger (1969) 146, also cited by Ll-J/W, claims that the lines exemplify 'die unnötige Härte' of Orestes' character, but this has been emphasised in the final part of the exodos without recourse to such empty moralising.

Plaut. *Mil. glor.* 1435–7 *iure factum iudico*; | *si sic aliis moechis fiat, minus hic moechorum siet*, | *magi' metuant, minus has res studeant* parallels the sentiment, and also occurs at the end of a play. But even there Pyrgopolynices does not advocate that all lawbreakers should be afflicted with the penalty which he is suffering. Aeschin. 1.196 may provide a parallel for the addition of a moralising conclusion to end of a work stressing the beneficial effects of punishing an offender. The words εἰ οὖν βουλήσεσθε, τὰ δίκαια καὶ τὰ συμφέροντα ὑμῶν ποιησάντων, φιλοτιμότερον ἡμεῖς ἕξομεν τοὺς παρανομοῦντας ἐξετάζειν are absent from one half of the mediaeval manuscript tradition and from a papyrus (P.Oxy. 4034, 2nd–3rd c.). They are retained by the most recent editor, Dilts; so too in his recent commentary Fisher keeps them, although he does not explain his decision. But the weight of manuscript evidence means that there is at least a strong possibility that they are the work of an interpolator. If this is so, however, he has made a better job of fitting his remark into the context than has happened with the interpolation in our play.

[1505] εὐθύς: in retributory killings 'das Ideal ist die momentane Strafe' (Hirzel (1907–10) 456; cf. (1902) 184–5 n. 4): though, naturally enough, the motif is rare, as it is so infrequent that such killings can be carried out instantaneously. The sense here is 'perhaps not so much temporal as logical: one should go straight for this sentence (without argument, automatically)' (West, *per litteras*).

[1505–6] πᾶσιν . . . | ὅστις: cf. *Aj.* 760 (where ὅστις refers to σώματα), *Ant.* 709 (where οὗτοι looks back to ὅστις), K–G i. 56–7, Bruhn §16.II, Diggle (1996c) 197.

[1506] γε: Ll-J/W (*Sophoclea*) defend the awkward position of the particle by noting that its position did not trouble Denniston: but his only parallel (*Aj.* 812, at p. 149 (2) (i)) is rightly deleted by Ll-J/W (following Dindorf) on other grounds. In itself the γε does not indicate that 1505–7 are spurious: when added to the other criticisms, however, it does not help defenders of their authenticity.

Nicephorus Basilaces (12th c.) *Progymn.* 6 = *RG* i. 461.18 = p. 110 Pignani cites this line in the form ὅστις πέρα τι τῶν νόμων πράσσειν θέλει. Although this is more attractive than the text of the manuscripts, it almost certainly does not provide evidence for the paradosis. In a quotation from memory, the curious γε would easily be forgotten; and the unconscious insertion of a τι to fill up the twelve-syllable line would also be a simple change.

[1507] πανοῦργον: Basilaces' κακοῦργον is not a significant variant. It merely reflects the change to a commoner synonym, one frequently used by Basilaces in the rhetorical exercise at the head of which this quotation stands (cf. *RG* i. 461.27, 462.9 etc.).

[1508–10] Dawe deletes the concluding choral anapaests, following Ritter (1861) 430–1. The general sense of the piece is not offensive. It is not profound, but profundity was not required of the conclusions to ancient tragedy (cf. Ll-J/W, *Sophoclea*). Its stress on the conclusion of Orestes' task has an ironic effect which can be paralleled elsewhere in S.: as Roberts (1987) 60 points out, 'two of the most emphatically final codas in tragedy, that of Sophocles' *Electra* and that of his *Oedipus at Colonus* (which refer respectively to fulfilment and to authority), conclude scenes in which it has been subtly suggested that there is more suffering to come' (cf. 1442–1504n.). Where the lines fall is on the level of language. In a small compass they contain three major linguistic anomalies, each of which is more likely to have arisen from a later interpolator's deficient knowledge of tragic Greek than from manuscript corruption of an original Sophoclean text (see nn. on ὦ σπέρμ' Ἀτρέως, παθόν and δι' ἐλευθερίας). There is no reason to suppose that the author of 1508–10 is the same as the author of 1505–7.

Frustratingly, we thus do not know how the original play ended. S. may have written a short choral piece himself as a conclusion, which by some means or other came to be replaced by the present lines. But the final part of this play is so unusually abrupt that we cannot even be sure of that. A playwright who could take the startling decision to leave the climactic death of his drama go unreported might well have made the equally startling decision to end his play abruptly at line 1504.

[1508] ὦ σπέρμ' Ἀτρέως: 'descendant of Atreus' is at first sight an appropriate designation of Orestes, now that he is ridding his ancestral palace of the son of Thyestes. At a linguistic level, however, the expression is troubling. When used metaphorically of a person, σπέρμα is usually found in expressions describing a person's paternity. So all five occurrences of the vocative of σπέρμα in tragedy are accompanied by the name or some other designation of the addressee's father in the genitive (*Aj.* 1393, *Phil.* 364, 582, 1066, *OC* 1275); and twice the word is qualified by the adjectival form of the name of the referent's father ([Aesch.] *PV* 705 Ἰνάχειον σπέρμα, Eur. *IA* 524).

The word can on occasions be given a wider scope. In three cases, apart from the present instance, σπέρμα is qualified by a word or phrase designating a person or persons other than the referent's father (Aesch. *Cho.* 503 σπέρμα Πελοπιδῶν, *Suppl.* 275 σπέρματ' εὐτέκνου βοός, Eur. *IT* 988 Ταντάλειον σπέρμα).[89] But none of these cases parallels our instance, for the following reasons (in decreasing order of significance). (i) σπέρμα in each case refers to a plurality, to the whole group of an ancestor's descendants, not to a single individual as in our play. (ii) The ancestors in question are all people who are often represented as standing at the head of their family's genealogy (Pelops, Tantalus and Io). Atreus, by contrast, is too late in his γένος to be comparable. (iii) None of the three instances is of the form σπέρμα plus genitive of the ancestor's name. Aesch. *Suppl.* 275 has a genitive, but in the form of a periphrasis σπέρματ' εὐτέκνου βοός, which has a quite different effect. In the other two cases, the genitive plural Πελοπιδῶν or the adjectival form Ταντάλειον marks the generality of the phrase.

So although the metaphorical use of σπέρμα is common in tragedy (it is barely found elsewhere), we lack a parallel for its construction in our passage. Ritter (1861) 430 is thus right to say that the phrase can only refer to Agamemnon (though he did not argue his case), which would give nonsense here. No emendation lies to hand. The phrase is most plausibly taken as an unsuccessful attempt by a later writer to imitate a tragic idiom. This writer probably intended to refer to Orestes, not Electra (*pace* Calder (1963) 215–16 = (2005) 155): the audience's attention will be on him, not his sister, as he forces Aegisthus through the stage door.

παθόν: the neuter here and at 1510 τελεωθέν, agreeing with σπέρμα, is unexpected. Since σπέρμα designates a human being, phrases predicated of it should take the masculine gender by the *constructio ad sensum* (so rightly Ritter (1861) 431; cf. Bruhn §16.II). I have not found a parallel for the neuter as transmitted here. It is possible to emend this problem away by reading παθών and τελεωθείς: but the sense-construction elsewhere does not seem to baffle scribes. παθών is weakly attested in five manuscripts, but this will reflect deliberate emendation or carelessness rather than isolated preservation of the

[89] *Ant.* 981–2 ἁ δὲ σπέρμα . . . ἀρχαιογόνων | <ἦν> ἄνασσ' [anon *ap.* Wilamowitz; ἄντασ' codd.] Ἐρεχθεϊδᾶν would constitute another example, if Ll-J/W are right to adopt the emendation which they do. However, Jebb, Pearson and Dawe all keep the paradosis, in which σπέρμα is an accusative of respect, and the genitives are dependent on the verb; Griffith obelises the verb. It is safest to leave this potential instance out of consideration.

truth; τελεωθείς is not found at all. The mistake is better explained as the work of an interpolator who, for whatever reason, was unfamiliar with the usual construction.

[1509] δι' ἐλευθερίας μόλις ἐξῆλθες: the scholia's ἀντὶ τοῦ μετὰ πολλῶν καμάτων μόλις ἠλευθερώθης (p. 160.10–11 Papageorgius) gives the expected sense: cf. the modern translations 'hast thou come forth at last in freedom' (Jebb), 'you have at last emerged in freedom' (Lloyd-Jones), 'you have come at long last to freedom' (March). But δι' ἐλευθερίας cannot denote a final state of freedom, as these translations all imply. Rather, 'in such cases διά seems to signify "in the midst of" rather than "through and out of"' (Denniston on Eur. *El.* 1210): cf. *OR* 773 διὰ τύχης τοιᾶσδ' ἰών ('since I am living through such an experience' – Lloyd-Jones), *Ant.* 742 διὰ δίκης ἰὼν πατρί, Eur. *Alc.* 874 and *El.* 1210 δι' ὀδύνας ἔβας, *Phoen.* 384 διὰ πόθου δ' ἐλήλυθα, Thuc. 6.34.2 ἀεὶ διὰ φόβου εἰσί. In each of these cases the διά phrase 'indicates the route followed . . . and not the end reached' (Moorhouse 103); cf. also Barrett on Eur. *Hipp.* 542–4. So explicitly at Xen. *Mem.* 2.1.11 ὁδός . . . δι' ἐλευθερίας, ἥπερ μάλιστα πρὸς εὐδαιμονίαν ἄγει (the only other classical instance of the phrase), ἐλευθερία is the defining characteristic of the journey, not of the destination.

Moorhouse 103 goes on to argue that the phrase must refer to 'the attitude of independence and resolution which has led Orestes and Electra to their present consummation'. But their behaviour has never been so designated elsewhere. Electra has been constantly associated with words denoting slavery and related concepts (189n.), while Orestes' exile has always been seen in terms of misery rather than independence of spirit (e.g. 601–2). And in the context, it is absurd for ἐλευθερία to denote anything other than the freedom which the siblings are now acquiring through Aegisthus' death.

Emendations are unsatisfactory. Viketos's ἐλευθερίαν ((1987); 'you have emerged on account of freedom') gives still worse sense. If we change the preposition, other possibilities include μετ' ἐλευθερίας (cf. Dem. 18.205 εἰ μὴ μετ' ἐλευθερίας ἐξέσται τοῦτο ποιεῖν, Plut. *Brut.* 29.9 βιώσονται μετ' ἐλευθερίας) or ἐπ' ἐλευθερίαν (cf. Thuc. 8.64.5 ἐχώρησαν ἐπὶ τὴν ἄντικρυς ἐλευθερίαν, Plut. *Arat.* 34.5 ὥρμησαν ἐπὶ τὴν ἐλευθερίαν; this would require παθών in 1508). But a good Sophoclean parallel for these conjectures is lacking, nor is the replacement of either of these prepositions by διά a plausible manuscript error. Again, the problematic phrase is most easily taken as the work of an interpolator who had misunderstood a common tragic idiom and attempted to imitate it without success.

μόλις: 'à grand peine' (Mazon) or 'mit Mühe' (Schadewaldt), rather than Kaibel's 'endlich' (p. 301) or the 'at last' of Jebb, Lloyd-Jones and March (who has 'at long last'): so rightly Calder (1963) 216 = (2005) 155.

[**1510**] ὁρμῇ: 'the enterprise of the avengers against the tyrants' (Jebb).

τελεωθέν: the neuter is problematic and suggests the hand of an interpolator (1508n.). The verb τελεόω is not found elsewhere in tragedy, though τελειόω is found at *OC* 1089 and *Tr.* 1257 (metrically guaranteed in both cases), but that is not significant for authenticity: τέλεος is found in tragedy at e.g. Aesch. *Ag.* 1504, Eur. *Ion* 1419. For the sense cf. *OC* 1088–9 τὸν εὖ– | αγρον τελειῶσαι λόχον ('bring to a successful conclusion') and especially Hdt. 3.86.2 ἐπιγενό-μενα δὲ ταῦτα τῷ Δαρείῳ ἐτελέωσέ μιν ὥσπερ ἐκ συνθέτου τευ γενόμενα with Waanders (1983) 219. 'Consummated', 'perfected', i.e. 'made completely prosperous' (Jebb) best captures the meaning.

B. H. Smith (1968) 172–5 discusses words for 'finish' or 'end' at the conclusion to a work. τέλος or its derivatives come at the end of a play or poem at fr. 590.4 *TrGF* (*Tereus*), *IG* i³ 1163.41 = *CEG* i. §5.8 (Athens, 447–6), *IG* ii–iii² 7227.6 = *CEG* ii. §543 (ii).6 (Piraeus, *c.* 350?), Apollonides *A.P.* 7.742.4 = 1194 *GP*, Bianor *A.P.* 9.423.8 = 1738 *GP*, Archias *A.P.* 7.165.8 = 3665 *GP*, Philip *A.P.* 9.11.6 = 2872 *GP*, Petr. *Satyr.* 132.15. Cf. also Pind. *O.* 13.115 (closing prayer to Zeus τέλειος). The finality implied by this word contrasts with the open-ended, aporetic ending of Aeschylus' *Choephori* (1075–6): ποῖ δῆτα κρανεῖ, ποῖ καταλήξει | μετακοιμισθὲν μένος Ἄτης; This does not make a case for the authenticity of 1508–10, however: many people, including interpolators, would be capable of ending a work with such a word.

Unless the dialogue between the actors continues on past 1504 (which is unlikely), Aegisthus enters the *skene* after that line, followed by Orestes and Pylades (cf. 1502). Electra's movements cannot be recovered with certainty. She could stay on stage while Orestes goes in to set about his task: this view is taken by Mantziou (1995) 194, for whom the play ends with 'the striking visual picture of the heroine standing silent at the palace door'. Better, perhaps, is the idea that she follows the men into the house, thus expressing her active approval of and participation in the death of Aegisthus. Calder (1963) 215 = (2005) 154 argues against this, claiming that 'Electra did not witness the first murder and need not the second': while true, this overlooks how Electra entered the *skene* after 1383, shortly after Orestes and Pylades had done so. If Electra enters now as well, the stage action will reinforce the closing stress on 'inside', as all four actors disappear into the *skene* building. What they will find when they get there is another matter.

Aegisthus' death is not reported. There is no ancient parallel for such extraordinary abruptness.

APPENDIX 1

This appendix contains the location of conjectures which are mentioned in the apparatus but not discussed in the commentary.

5	Blaydes[2]
15	Nauck[8]
43	Bergk (1848) 151
61	Steinhart (1843) 7
77	Dindorf[2] (cf. (1836) 141)
81	Blaydes[2]
84	Wecklein (1922) 41
100	Blaydes (1902) 102
109	Nauck[4] p. 158, (1859–62) ii. 32
113–14	Dobree (1833–43) ii. 49
130	Blaydes[1]
160–3	Tyrwhitt, *ap.* Brunck[1] (cf. ii. 199)
160	Brunck[1]
205	Paley[1]
	Brunck 1779 edn.
206	Seidler (1811–12) ii. 404
	Brunck 1779 edn.
216	Brunck 1779 edn.
238	Reiske (1753) 14
271	Schenkl *ap.* Schubert[1] p. vii
276	Dindorf[1]
277	F. W. Schmidt (1864) 19–21
	Groeneboom (1902) 74–5
279	Blaydes (1902) 103
286	Nauck[3] p. 158
298	Blaydes[1]
308	Morstadt (1864) 17
314	Blomfield *ap.* Monk (1826) i. 73*
316	Monk (1826) 73
	Matthiae (1825–7) ii. 915 (§488.1 Anm.)
324	Monk (1826) 73
328	Blaydes[1] p. 288

---

* The first issue of *Museum Criticum* originally came out in 1813 (cf. Stray (2004) 298–9): hence Blomfield has the priority over Doederlein (1814) 58. There is no identifying 'B.' after the conjecture, but it is printed in the quotation marks which surround Blomfield's other contributions to Monk's article.

341	Dawe[1]
354	Brunck 1779 edn.
363	Brunck 1779 edn.
367	Nauck[4a]
383	Brunck[1]
	Blaydes[1] p. 290
403	Blaydes[2]
430	Blaydes[1]
435	Reiske (1753) 15
436	Todt (1873) 253
461	Dawe[1]
475	Herwerden (1872) 15
487	Porson (1812) 209
492	Blaydes[1]
515	Bothe[2]
530	Erfurdt p. 41
542	Brunck[1]
	Blaydes[2]
543	F. W. Schmidt (1886–7) i. 126–8
548	Morstadt (1864) 9
561	Blaydes[1]
564	Wolff[1]
567	Herwerden, comm. on Eur. *Ion*, p. 256
591	Brunck 1779 edn.
593	Dobree (1833–43) ii. 50
601	Wex (1837) 18
611	Dawe[1]
656	Herwerden (1887) 33
	Mähly (1889) 38
662	Brunck 1779 edn.
684	Blaydes[1]
692	Tournier[1]
694	Schneidewin[1]
697	Meineke (1863a) 261
	Heimsoeth (1866) iv–v
698	Blaydes[1]
703	Herwerden (1899) 382
717	Blaydes[1]
720	Dobree (1833–43) ii. 50
725	Herwerden (1886) 68 n. 1
739	Nauck[4] p. 161
	Blaydes[1]

741	Blaydes¹
754	Elmsley 1805 edn. (his 738)
758	Wecklein (1869a) 77
	Nauck⁵
768	Seidler *ap.* Hermann
785	Naber (1881) 219
790	G. Müller (1978) 8–9
791	Reiske (1753) 17
796	Blaydes¹
815	Monk (1826) 203
819	Monk (1826) 204
852	Hermann *ap.* Erfurdt, p. 63
861	Dindorf⁵
871	Brunck 1779 edn.
876	Blaydes² (bis)
884	Blaydes (1902) 106
887	Meineke (1863a) 263 *tacite*
890	Blaydes¹ p. 312
891	Reiske (1753) 17
892	Nauck⁴ p. 162
917	Brunck 1779 edn.
924	Blaydes¹
938	Brunck 1779 edn.
947	Blomfield (1826) 189
960	Elmsley on Eur. *Med.* 1207 (our 1238; 1st edn.)
985	Papageorgius (1887) 1523
990	Blaydes¹
998	Brunck 1779 edn.
1007	Michaelis *ap.* Jahn²
1061	Brunck¹
1066	Blaydes¹
1070	Schaefer i. 245
	Erfurdt p. 467
1127	Brunck¹
1129	Dawe, *STS* i. 194
1139	Wecklein (1922) 41
1146	Dindorf⁵
	Arnold (1866) 33–4
1148	Herwerden, comm. on *OR*, p. 200
	Nauck⁴ᵃ (cf. (1874) 28–9)
1152	Groeneboom (1898) 137
1200	Papageorgius (1887) 1524

APPENDIX I

1208	Elmsley on *OR* 1522
1222	Morstadt (1864) 36
1245	Dindorf 1825 edn.
1264	Reiske (1753) 18
1278	Monk (1826) 214
1289–92	Ahrens (1859) 8–9
1294	Vauvilliers, p. 38 of his notes
1297	Nauck[3] p. 163
1298	Reiske (1753) 19
1329	Meineke (1863a) 269
1333	Nauck[3] p. 163; Morstadt (1864) 38
1334	Ahrens (1859) 11–12
1337	Nauck[4] p. 164 (cf. (1874) 101–2)
1351	Meineke (1863a) 270
1352	Dindorf[4]
1370–1	Nauck[3]
1372	Dawe[3]
	ἐνδεὲς Fröhlich in edn., ἐνδέον conjectured in 1829 by Fröhlich, *teste* Spengel (1863) 174
1384	Schneidewin[1]
1411	Bellermann *ap.* Wolff[4]
1446	Blaydes[1]
1449	Blaydes[1]
1458	καὶ διοιγνύναι conjectured in 1829 by Fröhlich, *teste* Spengel (1863) 174
1460	Benedict (1820) 55 (cf. *OR* 222)
1461	Blaydes[1]
1469	Blaydes[1]
1475	Nauck[7]
1492	Heath (1762) 23 (ὢ 'γών); cf. *OC* 1148 (H.'s 1210, p. 63)
1506	Wunder[2]

APPENDIX 2

This appendix contains unpublished remarks on the messenger speech of Sophocles' *Electra* written by Eduard Fraenkel (now located in the archive of Corpus Christi College, Oxford, Fraenkel Box 12, Sophokles Heft IV, S. 19–20). It was kindly brought to my attention by Christopher Collard. I am also grateful to Almut Fries for helpful comments on my translation.

Dieser sehr sonderbare breite Botenbericht über den Todessturz des Or<estes>, weit hinausgehend über d<ie> dramat<ische> Notwendigkeit eines Lügenberichts vom Tode des Or<restes>. Was soll das?

Unzureichend Kaibel (zitiert von Tycho 190 n. 1), Tycho 190 ff., Reinhardt[3] 162. Ich vermute Folgendes:

Soph<okles> war sich der gewaltigen Kühnheit bewusst, mit der er den Muttermord als Bagatelle behandelt, alles Interesse von dem, wie diese Tat auf Or<estes> wirken muss (Aesch<ylus>) ablenkt auf das was El<ektra>, bei dem Früheren eine Nebenfigur, empfindet und tut.

Es bestand d<ie> Gefahr, dass d<as> Publikum mit dieser fast unmenschlichen Kühnheit seiner Neuerung nicht mitgehen würden. So erreichet er den Botenbericht zu einer ausgedehnten 'captatio benevolentiae' in ‖ Mitte des Dramas. Er rechnet auf die glühende Teilnahme, die das Publikum gerade auch den tech. Einzelheiten eines solchen Wagenrennens zuwenden mussten.

Und er rechnet auf ihren patriot<ischen> Stolz. Daher das Rühmen des (731) ἐξ Ἀθηνῶν δεινὸς ἡνιοστρόφος. Sehr gut d<as> Schol<ium> zu 731: πρὸς εὔνοιαν δὲ τῶν ἀκροωμένων ἐπαινεῖ αὐτὸν ὡς Ἀθηναῖον 136.17–18 Papageorg). Das lange Prunkstück dieses Berichts in der Mitte des Dramas wird die Zuhörer so warm gestimmt haben, dass sie sich dann auch mit der befremdlichen Behandlung des Muttermords abfanden. Ohne ein solches Wohlwollen (εὔνοια) bestand d<ie> Gefahr, dass das Wagnis des Schlusses abgelehnt wurde.

This very remarkable, far-reaching messenger speech concerning Orestes' fatal fall goes way beyond the dramatic necessity of a false report of Orestes' death. Why is this?

The approaches of Kaibel (cited by T. von Wilamowitz-Moellendorff (1917) 190 n. 1), T. von Wilamowitz-Moellendorff (1917) 190–3 and Reinhardt (1947) 162 ≈ (1979) 151–2 are unsatisfactory.

I suspect the following. Sophocles was aware of his tremendous boldness in treating the matricide as a mere game, and in diverting all interest away from the effect which the deed must have on Orestes (cf. Aeschylus), towards the feelings and actions of Electra, whom the earlier poet had treated as a minor figure.

There was a danger that the audience would respond unfavourably to the almost inhuman boldness of his innovation. He therefore extends the messenger speech into a lengthy *captatio benevolentiae* in the centre of the play. He counts on the keen interest which the audience was particularly likely to show in the technical details of such a chariot race. He also counts on their patriotic pride: hence the praise of the 'cunning charioteer from Athens' (731). The scholium on 731 makes a very good point: 'he praises him to gain the goodwill of the audience, since the man is an Athenian'. The lengthy showpiece of this report in the middle of the play will have had such a positive effect on the audience that it could then also come to terms with the disconcerting treatment of the matricide. Without such goodwill there was a danger that the daring finale would be rejected.

* * *

Fraenkel's approach is thought-provoking and original, but too reductive in taking the speech simply as a means of reconciling the audience to the play's audacious approach to the myth. Other tragedies display similar boldness without the need for anything similar.

BIBLIOGRAPHY

I STANDARD REFERENCE WORKS AND EDITIONS CITED BY AUTHOR'S NAME OR OTHER ABBREVIATION

A–B   C. F. L. Austin and G. Bastianini (eds.) *Posidippi Pellaei quae supersunt omnia* (Biblioteca Classica 3; Milan 2002).

ABV   J. D. Beazley, *Attic Black-Figure Vase-Painters* (Oxford 1956).

Addenda²   T. H. Carpenter *et al.*, *Beazley Addenda²* (Oxford 1989).

ARV²   J. D. Beazley, *Attic Red-Figure Vase-Painters²* (3 vols.; Oxford 1963).

CA   J. U. Powell (ed.) *Collectanea Alexandrina* (Oxford 1925).

CEG   P. A. Hansen (ed.) *Carmina Epigraphica Graeca* (2 vols.; Berlin and New York 1983–9).

CID   G. Rougement *et al.* (eds.) *Corpus des inscriptions de Delphes* (4 vols. to date; Paris 1977–).

CIL   T. Mommsen *et al.* (eds.) *Corpus Inscriptionum Latinarum* (Berlin 1862–).

CPG   E. L. von Leutsch and F. H. Schneidewin (eds.) *Corpus Paroemiographorum Graecorum* (2 vols.; Göttingen 1839–51).

Denniston   J. D. Denniston, *The Greek Particles²* (rev. K. J. Dover; 1st edn. 1934; Oxford 1954).

DGE   F. R. Adrados *et al.* (eds.) *Diccionario Griego-Español* (6 vols. to date; Madrid 1980–).

D–K   H. Diels (ed.) *Die Fragmente der Vorsokratiker⁶* (3 vols.; rev. W. Kranz; Berlin 1951–2).

EG   G. Kaibel (ed.) *Epigrammata Graeca ex lapidibus conlecta* (Berlin 1878).

EGF   M. Davies (ed.) *Epicorum Graecorum Fragmenta* (Göttingen 1988).

EGM   R. L. Fowler (ed.) *Early Greek Mythography* (1 vol. to date; Oxford 2000–).

FGE   D. L. Page (ed.) *Further Greek Epigrams* (revised and prepared for publication by R. D. Dawe and J. Diggle; Cambridge 1981).

FGrHist   F. Jacoby *et al.* (eds.) *Die Fragmente der griechischen Historiker* (1923–).

FHG   K. Müller and T. Müller (eds.) *Fragmenta Historicorum Graecorum* (5 vols.; Paris 1841–72).

GEF   M. L. West (ed.) *Greek Epic Fragments* (London and Cambridge, Mass. 2003).

Goodwin	W. W. Goodwin, *Syntax of the Moods and Tenses of the Greek Verb*[2] (London 1889).
GP	A. S. F. Gow and D. L. Page (eds.) *The Greek Anthology: The Garland of Philip, and Some Contemporary Epigrams* (2 vols.; Cambridge 1968).
GVI	W. Peek (ed.) *Griechische Vers-Inschriften. Grab–Epigramme* (2 vols.; Berlin 1955–7).
HE	A. S. F. Gow and D. L. Page (eds.) *The Greek Anthology: Hellenistic Epigrams* (2 vols.; Cambridge 1965).
IEG	M. L. West (ed.) *Iambi et Elegi Graeci ante Alexandrum cantati*[2] (2 vols.; 1st edn. 1971–2; Oxford 1989–92).
IG i[3]	D. M. Lewis *et al.* (eds.) *Inscriptiones Atticae Euclidis anno anteriores* (3 vols.; Berlin and New York 1981–94).
IG ii–iii[2]	J. Kirchner (ed.) *Inscriptiones Atticae Euclidis anno posteriores* (4 vols.; Berlin 1913–40).
IG iv	M. Fraenkel (ed.) *Inscriptiones Aeginae Pityonesi Cecryphaliae Argolidis* (Berlin 1902).
IG v	G. Kolbe and F. Hiller de Gaertringen (eds.) *Inscriptiones Laconiae Messeniae Arcadiae* (Berlin 1913).
IG vii	W. Dittenberger (ed.) *Inscriptiones Megaridis Oropiae Boeotiae* (Berlin 1892).
IG ix.2	O. Kern (ed.) *Inscriptiones Graeciae Septentrionalis Voluminibus VII et VIII non comprehensae. Pars secunda: Inscriptiones Thessaliae* (Berlin 1908).
IG xii.6	K. Hallof and A. P. Matthaiou (eds.) *Inscriptiones Graecae Insularum Maris Aegaei praeter Delum. Fasciculus VI: Inscriptiones Chii et Sami cum Corassiis Icariaque* (2 vols. to date; Berlin and New York 2000–).
IGSK i–ii	H. Engelmann and R. Merkelbach (eds.) *Inschriften griechischer Städte aus Kleinasien 1–2. Die Inschriften von Erythrae und Klazomenai* (2 vols.; Bonn 1972).
IGSK iii	P. Frisch (ed.) *Inschriften griechischer Städte aus Kleinasien 3. Die Inschriften von Ilion* (Bonn 1975).
ILCV	E. Diehl (ed.) *Inscriptiones Latinae Christianae Veteres* (3 vols.; Berlin 1924–31).
K–B	R. Kühner, *Ausführliche Grammatik der griechischen Sprache. Erster Teil: Elementar- und Formenlehre*[3] (2 vols.; rev. F. Blass; Hannover 1890–2).
K–G	R. Kühner, *Ausführliche Grammatik der griechischen Sprache. Zweiter Teil: Satzlehre*[2] (2 vols.; rev. B. Gerth; Hannover and Leipzig 1898–1904).
Keil	H. Keil, *Grammatici Latini* (7 vols.; Leipzig 1857–80).

Krüger   K. W. Krüger, *Griechische Sprachlehre für Schulen* (Leipzig 1875).

LCS   A. M. Trendall, *The Red-Figured Vases of Lucania, Campania and Sicily* (2 vols.; Oxford 1967).

LCS Suppl. iii.   A. M. Trendall, *The Red-Figured Vases of Lucania, Campania and Sicily. Third Supplement (consolidated)* (BICS Suppl. 41; London 1983).

LfgrE   B. Snell *et al.* (eds.) *Lexikon des frühgriechischen Epos* (20 vols. to date; Göttingen 1955–).

LIMC   *Lexicon Iconographicum Mythologiae Classicae* (8 vols. plus indices; Zürich, Munich and Düsseldorf 1981–1999).

LS⁸   H. G. Liddell and R. Scott, *A Greek-English Lexicon⁸* (Oxford 1897).

LSJ⁹   H. G. Liddell and R. Scott, *A Greek-English Lexicon⁹* (rev. H. Stuart-Jones *et al.*; Oxford 1940).

Meisterhans   K. Meisterhans, *Grammatik der attischen Inschriften³* (rev. E. Schwyzer; 1st edn. 1885; Berlin 1900).

M–L   R. Meiggs and D. L. Lewis (eds.) *A Selection of Greek Historical Inscriptions to the End of the Fifth Century B.C.²* (1st edn. 1969; Oxford 1988).

M–W   R. Merkelbach and M. L. West (eds.) *Fragmenta Hesiodea* (Oxford 1967).

OGIS   W. Dittenberger (ed.) *Orientis Graeci Inscriptiones Selectae* (2 vols.; Leipzig 1903–5).

P. Ant.   C. H. Roberts, J. W. B. Barns, H. Zilliacus (eds.) *The Antinoopolis Papyri* (3 vols.; Graeco-Roman memoirs 28, 37, 47; London 1950–67).

Para.   J. D. Beazley, *Paralipomena: Additions to* Attic Black-Figure Vase-Painters *and* Attic Red-Figure Vase-Painters² (Oxford 1971).

PCG   R. Kassel and C. F. L. Austin (eds.) *Poetae Comici Graeci* (8 vols. to date; Berlin and New York 1983–).

PEG   A. Bernabé (ed.) *Poetae Epici Graeci. Testimonia et Fragmenta: Pars I ²* (Stuttgart and Leipzig 1996).

PLF   E. Lobel and D. L. Page (eds.) *Poetarum Lesbiorum Fragmenta²* (1st edn. 1955; Oxford 1963).

PMG   D. L. Page (ed.) *Poetae Melici Graeci* (Oxford 1962).

PMGF   M. Davies (ed.) *Poetarum Melicorum Graecorum Fragmenta* (1 vol. to date; Oxford 1991–).

P. Oxy.   B. P. Grenfell, A. S. Hunt *et al.* (eds.) *The Oxyrhynchus Papyri* (London 1898–).

RG   C. Walz (ed.) *Rhetores Graeci* (9 vols.; London, Stuttgart, Tübingen, Paris, 1832–6).

S–D   E. Schwyzer, *Griechische Grammatik. Auf der Grundlage von Karl Brugmanns griechischer Grammatik* (4 vols.; rev. A. Debrunner; Munich 1934–71).

SEG   J. J. E. Hondius *et al.* (eds.) *Supplementum Epigraphicum Graecum* (49 vols. to date; Leiden 1923–).

SGO   R. Merkelbach and J. Stauber (eds.) *Steinepigramme aus dem griechischen Osten* (5 vols.; Munich, Stuttgart and Leipzig 1998–2004).

SH   P. H. J. Lloyd-Jones and P. J. Parsons (eds.) *Supplementum Hellenisticum* (Texte und Kommentare 11; Berlin and New York 1983).

SIG³   W. Dittenberger (ed.) *Sylloge Inscriptionarum Graecarum³* (3 vols.; Leipzig 1915).

S–M   B. Snell and H. Maehler (eds.) *Pindari Carmina cum Fragmentis* (2 vols.; Leipzig 1987–9).

SVF   H. F. A. von Arnim (ed.) *Stoicorum Veterum Fragmenta* (4 vols.; Leipzig 1903–24).

Threatte   L. Threatte, *The Grammar of Attic Inscriptions* (2 vols. to date; Berlin and New York 1980–).

TLG   *Thesaurus Linguae Graecae* (available to subscribers online at http://www.tlg.uci.edu).

TLL   *Thesaurus Linguae Latinae* (Leipzig 1900–).

TrGF   *Tragicorum Graecorum Fragmenta*. Vol. 1 *Didascaliae Tragicae, Catalogi Tragicorum et Tragoediarum, Testimonia et Fragmenta Tragicorum Minorum* (ed. B. Snell; Göttingen 1971¹, 1986²); vol. 2 *Fragmenta Adespota* (edd. R. Kannicht and B. Snell; 1981); vol. 3 *Aeschylus* (ed. S. L. Radt; 1977); vol. 4 *Sophocles* (ed. S. L. Radt; 1985¹, 1999²); vol. 5 *Euripides* (ed. R. Kannicht; 2 parts; 2004).

TrGFS   J. Diggle (ed.) *Tragicorum Graecorum Fragmenta Selecta* (Oxford 1998).

2 STANDARD WORKS ON SOPHOCLES CITED BY AUTHOR'S NAME OR OTHER ABBREVIATION

Bruhn   E. Bruhn, *Anhang zu Sophokles* (Berlin 1899).

Campbell, PS   L. Campbell, *Paralipomena Sophoclea: Supplementary Notes on the Text and Interpretation of Sophocles* (London 1907).

Dawe, STS   R. D. Dawe, *Studies on the Text of Sophocles* (3 vols.; Leiden 1973–8).

Ellendt	F. Ellendt, *Lexicon Sophocleum*[2] (rev. H. Genthe; Berlin 1872).
Ll-J/W, *Sophoclea*	P. H. J. Lloyd-Jones and N. G. Wilson, *Sophoclea: Studies on the Text of Sophocles* (Oxford 1990).
Ll-J/W, *Second Thoughts*	P. H. J. Lloyd-Jones and N. G. Wilson, *Sophocles: Second Thoughts* (Hypomnemata 100; Göttingen 1997).
Moorhouse	A. C. Moorhouse, *The Syntax of Sophocles* (Mnem. Suppl. 75; Leiden 1982).
Papageorgius	P. N. Papageorgius, *Scholia in Sophoclis Tragoedias Vetera* (Leipzig 1888).[1]

3 EDITIONS OF SOPHOCLES' *ELECTRA*

Turnebus, A. (Paris 1552).

Canter, W. (Antwerp 1579).

Johnson, T(homas) (Oxford 1705).

Brunck, R. F. P. (Strasbourg 1779, 1786[1], 1786–9[2], 1788[3]).[2]

Capperonnier, J., and Vauvilliers, J.-F. (Paris 1781).

Musgrave, S. (Oxford 1800).[3]

Erfurdt, C. G. A. (Leipzig 1803).

Elmsley, P. (Edinburgh 1805, or shortly afterwards).[4]

Bothe, F. H. (Leipzig and London 1806[1], 1826[2]).

Schaefer, G. H. (Leipzig 1810).

Fröhlich, J. v. G. (Sulzbach 1815).

Hermann, J. G. J. (Leipzig 1825 (revision of Erfurdt); reprinted London 1827 and Leipzig 1864).

Dindorf, K. W. (Leipzig and London 1825, 1830[1], Oxford 1832[2], Oxford 1849[3], Oxford 1860 (i.e. 1859)[4], Leipzig 1868[5], Leipzig 1885[6] (revised by S. Mekler)).

Neue (Nevius) F. (Leipzig 1831).

Wunder, E. (Leipzig 1824[1], Gotha and Erfurdt 1836[2], Gotha 1844[3], Leipzig 1854[4]).

Hartung, J. A. (Leipzig 1850).

Schneidewin, F. H. (Berlin and Leipzig 1853[1], Berlin 1855[2] [non vidi]).

---

[1] For more on the scholia to *Electra* see Scattolin (2003).

[2] The 1779 edition is officially by J. Schweighaeuser, and also includes a text of Euripides' *Andromache*. But as Schweighaeuser points out, the text of the *Electra* which it contains is the work of Brunck, while Musgrave supplied the Euripidean material.

[3] Musgrave died in 1780.

[4] Only one copy is known to survive, in the British Library, shelfmark C.28.i.12. See further Finglass (2007).

4 WORKS CITED BY AUTHOR'S NAME

Bergk, T. (Leipzig 1858).

Nauck, J. A. (revision of Schneidewin; Berlin 1858³, 1862⁴, 1867⁴ᵃ, 1869⁵, 1873⁶, 1877⁷, 1882⁸, 1893⁹).

Jahn, O. (Bonn 1861¹, 1872², 1882³; 2nd and 3rd edns. revised by A. Michaelis).

Wolff, G(ustav) G(eorg) (Leipzig 1863¹, Leipzig 1874² [n.v.], 1880³ (rev. L. Bellermann), 1893⁴, Leipzig and Berlin 1913⁶ [n.v.]).

Tournier, E. (Paris 1867¹, 1877²).

Blaydes, F. H. M. (London 1873¹, Halle 1906²).

Paley, F. A. (London 1880¹, Cambridge 1887²).

Campbell, L. (Oxford 1881).

Schubert, F. (Leipzig 1884¹, 1891²).

Wecklein, N. (Leipzig 1886¹, Munich 1888², 1896³ [n.v.]⁵, 1905⁴).

Jebb, R. C. (London 1867¹ [n.v.], 1870² [n.v.], Cambridge 1894³ [reprinted Bristol 2004]). [References are to the 3rd edn.]

Kaibel, G. (Leipzig 1896).

Groeneboom, P. (Groningen 1903¹, 1935² [n.v.], 1957³).

Bruhn, E. (rev. of Schneidewin-Nauck; Berlin 1912¹⁰).

Pearson, A. C. (Cambridge 1924).

Dain, A. (Paris 1958¹, 1965²).

Kells, J. H. (Cambridge 1973).

Kamerbeek, J. C. (Leiden 1974).

Colonna, A. (Turin 1975).

Dawe, R. D. (Leipzig 1975¹, 1984², Stuttgart 1996³).

Lloyd-Jones, P. H. J., and Wilson, N. G. (Oxford 1990; reprinted with corrections 1992).

Lloyd-Jones, P. H. J. (London and Cambridge, Mass., 1994; reprinted with corrections 1997).

March, J. (Warminster 2001).

4 EDITIONS, COMMENTARIES AND TRANSLATIONS OF OTHER WORKS REFERRED TO BY NAME OF EDITOR OR COMMENTATOR

Adler, A. (1928–38) *Suidae Lexicon* (Lexicographi Graeci 1; 5 vols.; Leipzig).

Arnott, W. G. (1996) *Alexis: the Fragments* (Cambridge Classical Texts and Commentaries 31; Cambridge).

Austin, C. F. L. (1968) *Nova fragmenta Euripidea in papyris reperta* (Kleine Texte für Vorlesungen und Übungen 187; Berlin).

---

⁵ References to Wecklein's third edition are taken from van Paassen's archive.

BIBLIOGRAPHY

Austin, C. F. L., and Olson, S. D. (2004) *Aristophanes*: Thesmophoriazusae (Oxford).

Barchiesi, A. (1992) *P. Ovidii Nasonis Heroidum Epistulae I–III*. (Biblioteca Nazionale serie dei classici greci e latini testi con commento filologico 1; Florence).

Barigazzi, A. (1966) *Favorino di Arelate Opere* (Testi greci e latini con commento filologico 4; Florence).

Barrett, W. S. (1964) *Euripides*: Hippolytos (Oxford).

Baschera, C. (1999) *Gli scolii veronesi a Virgilio* (Verona).

Bekker, I. (1814–21) *Anecdota Graeca* (3 vols.; Berlin).

(1833) *Apollonii Sophistae Lexicon Homericum* (Berlin).

(1838–9) *Georgius Cedrenus* (2 vols.; Bonn).

Bessone, F. (1997) *P. Ovidii Nasonis Heroidum Epistula XII. Medea Iasoni* (Biblioteca Nazionale serie dei classici greci e latini testi con commento filologico 6; Florence).

Bethe, E. (1900–37) *Pollucis Onomasticon* (Lexicographi Graeci 9; 3 vols.; Leipzig).

Blank, D. L. (1988) *Lesbonax Περὶ Σχημάτων*, in Montanari *et al.* (1988) 129–216.

Blaydes, F. H. M. (1890) *Aristophanis Nubes* (Halle).

(1893) *Aristophanis Vespae* (Halle).

Blomfield, C. J. (1814) *Aeschyli Persae* (4th edn. London 1830; Cambridge).

(1818) *Aeschyli Agamemnon* (Cambridge).

Bömer, F. (1957–8) *P. Ovidius Naso Die Fasten* (2 vols.; Heidelberg).

(1969–86) *P. Ovidius Naso Metamorphosen* (7 vols.; Heidelberg).

Bond, G. W. (1963) *Euripides*: Hypsipyle (Oxford).

(1981) *Euripides*: Heracles (Oxford).

Braswell, B. K. (1988) *A Commentary on the* Fourth Pythian Ode *of Pindar* (Texte und Kommentare 14; Berlin and New York).

(1998) *A Commentary on Pindar* Nemean Nine (Texte und Kommentare 19; Berlin and New York).

Broadhead, H. D. (1960) *The* Persae *of Aeschylus* (Cambridge).

Bubel, F. (1991) *Euripides, Andromeda* (Palingenesia 34; Stuttgart).

Bühler, W. (1982–) *Zenobii Athoi proverbia* (3 vols. to date; Göttingen).

Burges, G. (1807) *Euripidis Troades* (Cambridge).

Butcher, S. H. (1903–31) *Demosthenis Orationes* (3 vols.; Oxford).

Caizzi, F. D. (1966) *Antisthenis Fragmenta* (Testi e documenti per lo studio dell' antichità 13; Milan and Varese).

Calame, C. (1983) *Alcman* (Lyricorum Graecorum quae exstant 6; Rome).

Caplan, H. (1964) *Ad C. Herennium Libri IV De Ratione Dicendi* (London and Cambridge, Mass.).

4 WORKS CITED BY AUTHOR'S NAME

Cappelletto, P. (2003) *I frammenti di Mnasea* (Università degli Studi di Milano Pubblicazioni della Facoltà di Lettere e Filosofia 209; Milan).

Carey, C. (1981) *A Commentary on Five Odes of Pindar.* Pythian 2, Pythian 9, Nemean 1, Nemean 7, Isthmian 8 (New York).

(1989) *Lysias: Selected Speeches* (Cambridge).

Casali, S. (1995) *P. Ovidii Nasonis Heroidum Epistula IV. Deianira Herculi* (Biblioteca Nazionale serie dei classici greci e latini testi con commento filologico 3; Florence).

Christodoulou, G. A. (1977) *Τὰ ἀρχαῖα σχόλια εἰς Αἴαντα τοῦ Σοφοκλέους* (Βιβλιοθηκη Σοφιας Ν. Σαριπολου 34; Athens).

Collard, C. (1975) *Euripides*: Supplices (2 vols.; Groningen).

Collard, C., Cropp, M. J., Lee, K. H. (1995) *Euripides*: *Selected Fragmentary Plays Volume 1* (Warminster).

Cozzoli, A.–T. (2001) *Euripide*: *Cretesi* (Testi e commenti, Università di Urbino Istituto di filologia classica 15; Pisa and Rome).

Cropp, M. J. (1988) *Euripides*: Electra (Warminster).

(1995) *Euripides*: Telephus (in Collard *et al.* (1995) (eds.) 17–52).

Cunningham, I. C. (2003) *Synagoge. Συναγωγὴ λέξεων χρησίμων* (Sammlung griechischer und lateinischer Grammatiker 10; Berlin and New York).

Dain, A. (1955–60) *Sophocle* (3 vols.; Paris).

Dale, A. M. (1954) *Euripides*: Alcestis (Oxford).

(1967) *Euripides*: Helen (Oxford).

Davies, M. (1991) *Sophocles*: Trachiniae (Oxford).

Dawe, R. D. (1982) *Sophocles*: Oedipus Rex (Cambridge).

De Borries, J. (1911) *Phrynichi Sophistae Praeparatio Sophistica* (Leipzig).

De Falco, V. (1954) *Demade oratore: testimonianze e frammenti²* (1st edn. 1932; Collana di Studi Greci 25; Naples).

De Marco, V. (1952) *Scholia in Sophoclis Oedipum Coloneum* (Vatican City).

Denniston, J. D. (1939) *Euripides*: Electra (Oxford).

Di Benedetto, V. (1965) *Euripidis Orestes* (Florence).

Diggle, J. (1970) *Euripides*: Phaethon (Cambridge Classical Texts and Commentaries 12; Cambridge).

(1981–94) *Euripides*: Fabulae (3 vols.; Oxford).

(2004) *Theophrastus*: Characters (Cambridge Classical Texts and Commentaries 43; Cambridge).

Dilts, M. R. (1983–6) *Scholia Demosthenica* (2 vols.; Leipzig).

(1997) *Aeschines*: Orationes (Stuttgart and Leipzig).

(2002–) *Demosthenis Orationes* (2 vols. to date; Oxford).

Dindorf, K. W. (1825) *Scholia Graeca in Homeri Odysseam* (2 vols.; Oxford).

Dodds, E. R. (1960) *Euripides*: Bacchae² (1st edn. 1934; Oxford).

BIBLIOGRAPHY

Domingo-Forasté, D. (1994) *Claudii Aeliani Epistulae et Fragmenta* (Stuttgart and Leipzig).

Dover, K. J. (1993) *Aristophanes*: Frogs (Oxford).

Drachmann, A. B. (1903–27) *Scholia vetera in Pindari carmina* (3 vols.; Leipzig).

Dunbar, N. (1995) *Aristophanes*: Birds (Oxford).

Dyck, A. R. (1996) *A Commentary on Cicero*, De Officiis (Ann Arbor).

Easterling, P. E. (1982) *Sophocles*: Trachiniae (Cambridge).

Elmsley, P. (1809) *Aristophanis Comoedia Acharnenses* (Oxford; 2nd edn. 1819).

   (1811) *Sophoclis Oedipus Tyrannus* (Oxford; 2nd edn. 1825).

   (1813) *Euripidis Heraclidae* (Oxford; 2nd edn. 1828).

   (1818) *Euripidis Medea* (Oxford and London; 2nd edn. Oxford 1828).

   (1821) *Euripidis Bacchae* (Oxford).

   (1823) *Sophoclis Oedipus Coloneus* (Oxford).

Erbse, H. (1949) *Untersuchungen zu den attizistischen Lexika* (Abhandlungen der deutschen Akademie der Wissenschaften zu Berlin, phil.-hist. Klasse, n. 2; Berlin).

   (1969–87) *Scholia Graeca in Homeri Iliadem* (7 vols.; Berlin).

Fedeli, P. (1965) *Properzio Elegie Libro IV* (Pubblicazioni della facoltà di lettere e filosofia della università degli studi di Bari 1; Bari).

   (1980) *Sesto Properzio. Il Primo Libro delle Elegie* (Accademia Toscana di Scienze e Lettere La Colombaria Studi 53; Florence).

Ferri, R. (2003) Octavia. *A Play attributed to Seneca* (Cambridge Classical Texts and Commentaries 41; Cambridge).

Fisher, N. R. E. (2001) *Aeschines*: Against Timarchus (Oxford).

Fowler, D. P. (2002) *Lucretius on Atomic Motion. A Commentary on* De Rerum Natura book 2, *lines 1–332* (prepared for publication by P. G. Fowler *et al.*; Oxford).

Fraenkel, E. D. M. (1950) *Aeschylus*: Agamemnon (3 vols.; Oxford).

Friis Johansen, H., and Whittle, E. W. (1980) *Aeschylus*: The Suppliants (3 vols.; Copenhagen).

Gagarin, M. (1997) *Antiphon: the Speeches* (Cambridge).

Gaisford, T. (1848) *Etymologicum Magnum* (Oxford).

Garvie, A. F. (1986) *Aeschylus*: Choephori (Oxford).

   (1998) *Sophocles*: Ajax (Warminster).

George, A. R. (1999) *The Epic of Gilgamesh. The Babylonian Epic Poem and Other Texts in Akkadian and Sumerian* (London).

Gerber, D. E. (1982) *Pindar's* Olympian One: a Commentary (Phoenix Suppl. 15; Toronto, Buffalo, London).

   (2002) *A Commentary on Pindar* Olympian Nine (Hermes Einzelschriften 87; Stuttgart).

Gercke, A. (1885) *Diogeniani Epicurei fragmenta*, Jahrb. für klass. Phil. Suppl. 14: 748–55.

Gernet, L., and Bizos, M. (1955) *Lysias: Discours* (2 vols.; Paris).

Gibson, R. K. (2003) *Ovid*: Ars Amatoria Book 3 (Cambridge Classical Texts and Commentaries 40; Cambridge).

Gomme, A. W., and Sandbach, F. H. (1973) *Menander: a Commentary* (Oxford).

Gow, A. S. F. (1950) *Theocritus* (2 vols.; Cambridge).

(1965) *Machon* (Cambridge Classical Texts and Commentaries 1; Cambridge).

Griffin, J. (1995) *Homer*: Iliad IX (Oxford).

Griffith, M. (1983) *Aeschylus*: Prometheus Bound (Cambridge).

(1999) *Sophocles*: Antigone (Cambridge).

Haffner, M. (2001) *Das Florilegium des Orion* (Palingenesia 75; Stuttgart).

Hainsworth, J. B. (1993) *The* Iliad: *a Commentary. Volume III:* Books 9–12 (Cambridge).

Hansen, P. A. (2005) *Hesychii Alexandrini Lexicon. Volumen III. Π–Σ* (Sammlung griechischer und lateinischer Grammatiker 11/3; Berlin and New York).

Harder, M. A. (1985) *Euripides'* Kresphontes *and* Archelaos (Mnem. Suppl. 87; Leiden).

Headlam, W. G. (1910) *Aeschylus*: Agamemnon (ed. A. C. Pearson; Cambridge).

(1922) *Herodas: the Mimes and Fragments* (ed. A. D. Knox; Cambridge).

Heitsch, E. (1961–4) *Die griechischen Dichterfragmente der römischen Kaiserzeit* (2 vols.; Abhandlungen der Akademie der Wissenschaften in Göttingen, phil.-hist. Klasse 3, Folge 49, 58; Göttingen).

Henderson, J. (1987) *Aristophanes*: Lysistrata (Oxford).

Henry, W. B. (2005) *Pindar's* Nemeans: *A Selection* (Munich and Leipzig).

Hense, O. (1905) *C. Musonii Rufi reliquiae* (Leipzig).

Hermann, J. G. J. (1800) *Euripidis Hecuba* (Leipzig).

(1812) *Draconis Stratonicensis liber de metris poeticis. Ioannis Tzetzae exegesis in Homeri Iliadem* (Leipzig).

Herwerden, H. van (1866) *Sophoclis Oedipus Rex. Accedunt Analecta Tragica et Anecdota Ambrosiana* (Utrecht).

(1875) *Εὐριπίδου Ἴων* (Utrecht).

Hilgard, A. (1889–94) *Georgii Choerobosci scholia in Theodosii Alexandrini canones* (2 vols.; Leipzig).

Hollis, A. S. (1990) *Callimachus*: Hecale (Oxford).

Holwerda, D. (1977) *Scholia in Aristophanem, Pars 1. Prolegomena de comoedia, Scholia in Acharnenses, Equites, Nubes; Fasc. III 1, continens Scholia vetera in Nubes* (Groningen).

(1991) *Scholia in Aristophanem, Pars II. Scholia in Vespas, Pacem, Aves et Lysistratam; Fasc. III, continens Scholia vetera et recentiora in Aristophanis Aves* (Groningen).

Hopkinson, N. (1984) *Callimachus*: Hymn to Demeter (Cambridge Classical Texts and Commentaries 27; Cambridge).

Hordern, J. C. (2002) *The Fragments of Timotheus of Miletus* (Oxford).

(2004) *Sophron's Mimes* (Oxford).

Hornblower, S. (1991–) *A Commentary on Thucydides* (2 vols. to date.; Oxford).

Hude, C. (1908) *Herodoti Historiae* (2 vols.; Oxford).

Hunter, R. L. (1983) *Eubulus: the Fragments* (Cambridge Classical Texts and Commentaries 24; Cambridge).

Hutchinson, G. O. (1985) *Aeschylus*: Septem contra Thebas (Oxford).

(2001) *Greek Lyric Poetry: a Commentary on Selected Larger Pieces* (Oxford).

Irvine, J. A. D. (1995) *Euripides'* Ion. *Commentary, lines 1–568* (2 vols.; diss. Oxford).

Janka, M. (1997) *Ovid: Ars Amatoria, Buch 2* (Heidelberg).

Janko, R. C. M. (1992) *The* Iliad: *a Commentary. Volume IV*: Books 13–16 (Cambridge).

Jebb, R. C. (1896) *Sophocles. The Plays and Fragments. Part VII:* The Ajax (Cambridge).

(1898) *Sophocles. The Plays and Fragments. Part IV:* The Philoctetes² (1st edn. 1890; Cambridge).

(1900) *Sophocles. The Plays and Fragments. Part III:* The Antigone³ (1st edn. 1888; Cambridge).

Jensen, C. (1911) *Philodemi* περὶ κακιῶν *liber decimus* (Leipzig).

Jocelyn, H. D. (1967) *The Tragedies of Ennius* (Cambridge Classical Texts and Commentaries 10; Cambridge).

Kambitsis, J. (1972) *L'Antiope d'Euripide* (Athens).

Kamerbeek, J. C. (1967) *The Plays of Sophocles. Commentaries. Part IV.* The Oedipus Tyrannus (Leiden).

Kannicht, R. (1969) *Euripides: Helena* (2 vols.; Heidelberg).

Kapparis, K. A. (1999) *Apollodorus, Against Neaira [D. 59]* (Untersuchungen zur antiken Literatur und Geschichte 53; Berlin and New York).

Keaney, J. J. (1991) *Harpocration*: Lexeis of the Ten Orators (Amsterdam).

Keil, B. (1898) *Aelii Aristidis Smyrnaei quae supersunt omnia* [17–53 only] (Berlin).

Kirk, G. S. (1954) *Heraclitus: The Cosmic Fragments* (Cambridge).

Kißel, W. (1990) *Persius: Satiren* (Heidelberg).

Kovacs, P. D. (1994–2002) *Euripides* (6 vols.; London and Cambridge, Mass.).

Lang, C. (1881) *Cornuti Theologiae Graecae Compendium* (Leipzig).

Latte, K. (1953–66) *Hesychii Alexandrini Lexicon* [A–O only] (2 vols.; Copenhagen).

Lee, K. H. (1997) *Euripides*: Ion (Warminster).

Lentz, A. (1867–70) *Herodiani Technici Reliquiae* (2 vols.; Leipzig).

Lenz, F. W., and Behr, C. A. (1976–80) *P. Aelii Aristidis Opera quae exstant omnia* [1–16 only] (Leiden).

Leone, P. A. M. (1968) *Ioannis Tzetzae Historiae* (Pubblicazioni dell'Istituto di filologia classica 1; Naples).

(1972) *Ioannes Tzetzes. Epistulae* (Leipzig).

Lightfoot, J. L. (2003) *Lucian*: On the Syrian Goddess (Oxford).

Livingstone, N. (2001) *A Commentary on Isocrates'* Busiris (Mnem. Suppl. 223; Leiden, Boston, Cologne).

Livrea, E. (1973) *Apollonii Rhodii Argonauticon liber quartus* (Florence).

Lloyd-Jones, P. H. J. (1975) *Females of the Species: Semonides on Women* (with M. Quinton; London).

Lobeck, C. A. (1866) *Sophoclis Ajax*[3] (1st edn. Leipzig 1809; Berlin).

Longo, O. (1968) *Commento linguistico alle Trachinie di Sofocle* (Proagones Studi 8; Padua).

Longo Auricchio, F. (1988) *Ermarco: Frammenti* (La scuola di Epicuro 6; Naples).

MacDowell, D. M. (1971) *Aristophanes*: Wasps (Oxford).

Macleod, C. W. (1982) *Homer*: Iliad Book XXIV (Cambridge).

Macleod, M. D. (1972–87) *Luciani Opera* (4 vols.; Oxford).

Maehler, H. (1982–97) *Die Lieder des Bakchylides* (2 vols.; Mnem. Suppl. 62, 167; Leiden, New York, Cologne).

(2004) *Bacchylides. A Selection* (Cambridge).

Marcovich, M. (1992) *Theodori Prodromi De Rhodanthes et Dosiclis Amoribus Libri IX* (Stuttgart and Leipzig).

Marg, W. (1972) *Timaeus Locrus: De Natura Mundi et Animae* (Leiden).

Martina, A. (2000) *Menandro Epitrepontes* (2 vols.; Rome).

Marx, F. (1904–5) *C. Lucilii Carminum Reliquiae* (2 vols.; Leipzig).

Massimilla, G. (1996–) *Callimacho Aitia libri primo e secondo* (1 vol. to date; Biblioteca di Studi Antichi 77; Pisa).

Mastronarde, D. J. (1994) *Euripides*: Phoenissae (Cambridge Classical Texts and Commentaries 29; Cambridge).

(2002) *Euripides.* Medea (Cambridge).

Mayor, J. E. B. (1888–9) *Thirteen Satires of Juvenal* (1st edn. 1878; Cambridge).

Montanari, F., Blank, D. L., and Dyck, A. R. (1988) *I frammenti dei grammatici Agathocles, Hellanikos, Ptolemaios Epithetes. Lesbonax* Περὶ Σχημάτων. *The Fragments of Comanus of Naucratis* (Sammlung griechischer und lateinischer Grammatiker 7; Berlin and New York).

Murgatroyd, P. (1980) *Tibullus 1. A Commentary on the* First Book of the Elegies *of Albius Tibullus* (Pietermaritzburg).

(1994) *Tibullus* Elegies II (Oxford).

Murray, G. G. A. (1902–9) *Euripides: Fabulae* (3 vols.; Oxford).

(1905) (transl.) *The* Electra of *Euripides* (London).

Musgrave, S. (1809) *Euripidis Hecuba, Orestes, et Phoenissae* (Oxford).

Mynors, R. A. B. (1990) *Virgil's* Georgics (Oxford).

BIBLIOGRAPHY

Nauck, J. A. (1886) *Porphyrii Philosophi Platonici Opuscula Selecta*[2] (1st edn. 1860; Leipzig).

  (1889) *Tragicorum Graecorum Fragmenta*[2] (1st edn. 1856; Leipzig; reprinted with a supplement by B. Snell, Hildesheim 1964).

Neri, C. (2003) *Erinna. Testimonianze e frammenti* (Eikasmos Quaderni Bolognesi di Filologia Classica Studi 9; Bologna).

Nickau, K. (1966) *Ammonii qui dicitur liber de adfinium vocabulorum differentia* (Leipzig).

Nisbet, R. G. M., and Hubbard, M. (1970) *A Commentary on Horace: Odes Book I* (Oxford).

  (1978) *A Commentary on Horace: Odes Book II* (Oxford).

Nisbet, R. G. M., and Rudd, N. (2004) *A Commentary on Horace: Odes Book III* (Oxford).

Norden, E. (1957) *P. Vergilius Maro Aeneis Buch VI*[4] (1st edn. Leipzig 1903; Stuttgart).

Oakley, S. P. (1997–2005) *A Commentary on Livy*, Books VI–X (4 vols.; Oxford).

Ogilvie, R. M. (1965) *A Commentary on Livy*, Books I–V (Oxford).

Olson, S. D. (1998) *Aristophanes: Peace* (Oxford).

  (2002) *Aristophanes: Acharnians* (Oxford).

Pack, R. A. (1963) *Artemidorou Daldiani Onirocriticon Libri V* (Leipzig).

Page, D. L. (1938) *Euripides: Medea* (Oxford).

  (1972) *Aeschyli septem quae supersunt tragoediae* (Oxford).

  (1978) *The Epigrams of Rufinus* (Cambridge Classical Texts and Commentaries 21; Cambridge).

Parca, M. G. (1991) *Ptocheia or Odysseus in Disguise at Troy (P. Köln VI 245)* (American Studies in Papyrology 31; Atlanta).

Pearson, A. C. (1917) *The Fragments of Sophocles* (3 vols.; Cambridge).

Pease, A. S. (1973) *M. Tulli Ciceronis De Divinatione Libri Duo* (Darmstadt; reprint of University of Illinois Studies in Language and Literature vol. 6 (1920) 161–500 and vol. 8 (1923) 153–474 [n.v.]).

  (1935) *Publi Vergili Maronis Aeneidos Liber Quartus* (Cambridge, Mass.).

Pendrick, G. J. (2002) *Antiphon the Sophist: the Fragments* (Cambridge Classical Texts and Commentaries 39; Cambridge).

Pfeiffer, R. (1949–53) *Callimachus* (2 vols.; Oxford).

Pignani, A. (1983) *Niceforo Basilace: progimnasmi e monodie* (Byzantina et Neo-Hellenica Neapolitana 10; Naples).

Porson, R. (1798) *Euripidis Orestes* (London).

  (1799) *Euripidis Phoenissae* (London).

  (1817) *Euripidis Medea* (London).

Preiser, C. (2000) *Euripides: Telephos* (Spudasmata 78; Zürich).

Pusey, P. E. (1868) *Sancti Patris Nostri Cyrilli Archiepiscopi Alexandrini in xii Prophetas* (2 vols.; Oxford).

Radt, S. L. (2002–) *Strabons Geographika* (4 vols. to date; Göttingen).

Ramelli, I. (2003) *Anneo Cornuto. Compendio di teologia greca* (Milan).

Rhodes, P. J. (1993) *A Commentary on the Aristotelian* Athenaion Politeia[2] (Oxford; 1st edn. 1981).

Ribbeck, J. K. O. (1871–3) *Tragicorum Romanorum Fragmenta*[2] (1st edn. 1852; 2 vols.; Leipzig).

Richardson, N. J. (1974) *The Homeric* Hymn to Demeter (Oxford).

(1993) *The* Iliad: *a Commentary. Volume VI*: books 21–4 (Cambridge).

Ritschl, F. (1832) *Thomae Magistri Ecloga Vocum Atticarum* (Halle).

Rosati, G. (1996) *P. Ovidii Nasonis Heroidum Epistulae XVIII–XIX. Leander Heroni; Hero Leandro* (Biblioteca Nazionale serie dei classici greci e latini testi con commento filologico 4; Florence).

Rose, V. (1886) *Aristotelis qui ferebantur librorum fragmenta* (Leipzig).

Rosén, H. B. (1987–97) *Herodoti Historiae* (2 vols.; Stuttgart and Leipzig).

Ruhnkenius, D. (1789) *Timaei Sophistae Lexicon vocum Platonicarum*[2] (1st edn. 1754; Leiden).

Russell, D. A. F. M. (1964) 'Longinus': *On the Sublime* (Oxford).

Russell, D. A. F. M., and Wilson, N. G. (1981) *Menander Rhetor* (Oxford).

Russo, J. A., Fernández-Galiano, M., and Heubeck, A. (1992) *A Commentary on Homer's* Odyssey. *Volume III*: books XVII–XXIV (Oxford).

Rutherford, W. G. (1881) *The New Phrynichus: being a Revised Text of the Ecloga of the Grammarian Phrynichus* (London).

Sbardella, L. (2000) *Filita: Testimonianze e frammenti poetici* (Seminari Romani di Cultura Greca Quaderni 3; Roma).

Schaefer, G. H. (1811) *Gregorii Corinthii et aliorum grammaticorum libri de dialectis linguae graecae* (Leipzig).

Scheer, E. (1881–1908) *Lycophronis Alexandra* (2 vols.; Berlin).

Schibli, H. S. (1990) *Pherekydes of Syros* (Oxford).

Schironi, F. (2004) *I frammenti di Aristarco di Samotracia negli etimologici bizantini* (Hypomnemata 152; Göttingen).

Schmidt, M(oritz) (1858–68) *Hesychii Alexandrini Lexicon* (5 vols.; Jena).

(1860) Ἐπιτομὴ τῆς καθολικῆς προσῳδίας Ἡρωδιανοῦ (Jena).

Schrader, H. (1890) *Porphyrii Quaestionum Homericarum ad Odysseam pertinentium reliquiae* (Leipzig).

Schwartz, E. (1887–91) *Scholia in Euripidem* (2 vols.; Berlin).

Seaford, R. (1984) *Euripides*: Cyclops (Oxford).

Sier, K. (1988) *Die lyrischen Partien der Choephoren des Aischylos* (Palingenesia 23; Stuttgart).

Skutsch, O. (1985) *The Annals of Q. Ennius* (Oxford).

Slater, W. J. (1986) *Aristophanis Byzantii Fragmenta* (Sammlung griechischer und lateinischer Grammatiker 6; Berlin and New York).

Smith, O. L. (1976–82) *Scholia Graeca in Aeschylum quae exstant omnia* (1 vol. and 1 fasc.; Stuttgart and Leipzig).

Snell, B. (1937) *Euripides Alexandros und andere Strassburger Papyri mit Fragmenten griechischer Dichtung* (Hermes Einzelschriften 5; Berlin).

Sommerstein, A. H. (1983) *The Comedies of Aristophanes: vol. 4.* Wasps (Warminster).

(1989) *Aeschylus*: Eumenides (Cambridge).

(1996) *The Comedies of Aristophanes: vol. 9.* Frogs (Warminster).

(2001) *The Comedies of Aristophanes: vol. 11.* Wealth (Warminster).

Spanoudakis, K. (2002) *Philetas of Cos* (Mnem. Suppl. 229; Leiden, Boston, Cologne).

Stählin, O. (1905–34) *Clemens Alexandrinus* (4 vols.; Leipzig).

Stockert, W. (1992) *Euripides: Iphigenie in Aulis* (2 vols.; Vienna).

Tarrant, R. J. (1976) *Seneca*: Agamemnon (Cambridge Classical Texts and Commentaries 18; Cambridge).

Theodoridis, C. (1982–) *Photii Patriarchae Lexicon* [A–M only] (2 vols. to date; Berlin and New York).

Thilo, G., and Hagen, H. (1878–1902) *Servii Grammatici qui feruntur in Vergilii Carmina Commentarii* (3 vols.; Leipzig).

Valk, M. van der (1971–87) *Eustathii Commentarii ad Homeri Iliadem pertinentes* (4 vols.; Leiden).

Voigt, E.-M. (1971) *Sappho et Alcaeus: Fragmenta* (Amsterdam).

Wachsmuth, C., and Hense, O. (1884–1912) *Ioannis Stobaei Anthologium* (5 vols.; Berlin).

Walbank, F. W. (1957–79) *A Historical Commentary on Polybius* (3 vols.; Oxford).

Wankel, H. (1976) *Demosthenes: Rede für Ktesiphon über den Kranz* (2 vols.; Heidelberg).

Watson, L. C. (2003) *A Commentary on Horace's* Epodes (Oxford).

Wehrli, F. (1969) *Die Schule des Aristoteles: Texte und Kommentar. Heft VII: Herakleides Pontikos* (Basel and Stuttgart).

West, M. L. (1966) *Hesiod*: Theogony (Oxford).

(1978) *Hesiod*: Works and Days (Oxford).

(1987) *Euripides*: Orestes (Warminster).

(1998) *Aeschylus: Tragoediae* (corrected version of 1990 edn.; Stuttgart and Leipzig).

(1998–2000) *Homerus: Ilias* (2 vols.; Stuttgart, Leipzig, Munich).

West, S. R. (1988) *A Commentary on Homer's* Odyssey. Books I–IV (Oxford).

Wilamowitz-Moellendorff, E. F. W. U. von (1895) *Euripides: Herakles*[2] (2 vols.; 1st edn. 1889; Berlin).

(1896) *Aischylos Orestie. Zweites Stück: Das Opfer am Grabe* (Berlin).

Wilkins, J. (1993) *Euripides*: Heraclidae (Oxford).

Williams, F. J. (1978) *Callimachus* Hymn to Apollo: *a Commentary* (Oxford).

Willink, C. W. (1986) *Euripides:* Orestes (Oxford).

Woodman, A. J., and Martin, R. H. (1996) *The* Annals *of Tacitus.* Book 3 (Cambridge Classical Texts and Commentaries 32; Cambridge).

Wyse, W. (1904) *The Speeches of Isaeus* (Cambridge).

Young, D. C. C. (1971) *Theognis, Ps.-Pythagoras, Ps.-Phocylides, Chares, Anonymi Aulodia, Fragmenta Teliambicum²* (1st edn. 1961; Leipzig).

Zwierlein, O. (1986) *Senecae Tragoediae* (Oxford).

5 WORKS CITED BY AUTHOR'S NAME WITH DATE

Adams, J. N. (1990) 'The uses of *neco* I', *Glotta* 68: 230–55.

Adkins, A. W. H. (1960) *Merit and Responsibility: a Study in Greek Values* (Oxford).
    (1966) 'Aristotle and the best kind of tragedy', *CQ* N.S. 16: 78–102.

Aerts, W. J. (1965) *Periphrastica: an Investigation into the Use of εἶναι and ἔχειν as Auxiliaries or Pseudo-Auxiliaries in Greek from Homer up to the Present Day* (Publications issued under the auspices of the Byzantine-New Greek seminary of the University of Amsterdam 2; Amsterdam).

Ahrens, E. A. J. (1859) *Ueber einige Interpolationen in der Elektra des Sophokles* (Progr. Coburg).

Alexiou, M. (2002) *The Ritual Lament in the Greek Tradition²* (1st edn. 1974; London).

Allan, R. J. (2006) 'Sophocles' voice. Active, middle, and passive in the plays of Sophocles', in de Jong and Rijksbaron (2006) (eds.) 111–26.

Allan, W. (2000) *The* Andromache *and Euripidean Tragedy* (Oxford).

Allen, W. S. (1973) *Accent and Rhythm. Prosodic Features of Latin and Greek: a Study in Theory and Reconstruction* (Cambridge Studies in Linguistics 12; Cambridge).
    (1987) *Vox Graeca: The Pronunciation of Classical Greek³* (1st edn. 1968; Cambridge).

Ambühl, A. (2002) 'Zwischen Tragödie und Roman: Kallimachos' Epigramm auf den Selbstmord der Basilo (20 Pf. = 32 Gow–Page = *AP* 7.517)', in Harder *et al.* (2002) (eds.) 1–26.

Amigues, S. (1977) *Les subordonnées finales par ΟΠΩΣ en attique classique* (Études et commentaires 89; Paris).

Andersen, Ø. (1987) 'Myth, paradigm and "spatial form" in the *Iliad*', in Bremer *et al.* (1987) (eds.) 1–13. [= de Jong (1999) (ed.) iii. 472–85]

Arndt, C. F. G. (1844) *Quaestiones Criticae de locis quibusdam Sophoclis* (Progr. Neubrandenburg).

Arnold, B. (1864) review of Wolff's 1st edition, *Eos: Süddeutsche Zeitschrift für Philologie und Gymnasialwesen* 1: 450–60.
    (1866) *Sophokleische Rettungen* (Munich).

BIBLIOGRAPHY

Arnott, W. G. (1982) 'Off-stage cries and the choral presence: some challenges to theatrical conventions in Euripides', *Antichthon* 16: 35–43.

(2001 a) 'Some orthographical problems in the papyri of later Greek comedy I: πο(ι)εῖν (along with compounds and congeners)', *ZPE* 134: 43–51.

(2001 b) 'Some orthographical problems in the papyri of later Greek comedy II: –ει or –η(ι) as the ending of the second person singular middle and passive in the present and other tenses of verbs in –ω', *ZPE* 135: 36–40.

(2002) 'Some orthographical variants in the papyri of later Greek comedy', in Willi (2002) (ed.) 191–217.

Arnould, D. (1986) 'τήκειν dans la peinture des larmes et du deuil chez Homère et les tragiques', *RPh* 3ᵉ ser. 60: 267–74.

(1990) *Le rire et les larmes dans la littérature grecque d'Homère à Platon* (Collection d'études anciennes 119; Paris).

Aubreton, R. (1949) *Démétrius Triclinius et les recensions médiévales de Sophocle* (Paris).

Aubriot, D. (1994) 'Sur la valeur de quelques prières dans la tragédie grecque', *Journal des savants*, 3–18.

Audollent, A. (1904) *Defixionum tabellae quotquot innotuerunt: tam in Graecis orientis quam in totius occidentis partibus praeter Atticas in Corpore inscriptionum Atticarum editas* (Paris 1904).

Aulotte, R. *et al.* (1970) *Hommages à Marie Delcourt* (Collection Latomus 114; Brussels).

Ausfeld, C. (1903) *De Graecorum precationibus quaestiones* (Jahrb. für klass. Phil. Suppl. 28 pp. 503–47; Leipzig).

Austin, C. F. L., and Reeve, M. D. (1970) 'Notes on Sophocles, Ovid and Euripides', *Maia* 22: 3–18.

Avezzù, G. (2002) (ed.) *Sofocle, Euripide, Hofmannsthal, Yourcenar. Elettra: variazioni sul mito* (Venice).

(2003) (ed.) *Il dramma sofocleo: testo, lingua, interpretazione* (Beiträge zum antiken Drama und seiner Rezeption 13; Stuttgart).

Bagordo, A. (2003) *Reminiszenzen früher Lyrik bei den attischen Tragikern. Beiträge zur Anspielungstechnik und poetischen Tradition* (Zetemata 118; Munich).

Bailey, C. *et al.* (1936) (eds.) *Greek Poetry and Life. Essays Presented to Gilbert Murray on his 70th Birthday, January 2nd 1936* (Oxford).

Bain, D. M. (1977) *Actors and Audience: a Study of Asides and Related Conventions in Greek Drama* (Oxford).

Bakker, E. J. (1997) (ed.) *Grammar as Interpretation: Greek Literature in its Linguistic Contexts* (Mnem. Suppl. 171; Leiden, Cologne, New York).

Bakker, W. F. (1966) *The Greek Imperative: an Investigation into the Aspectual Differences between the Present and Aorist Imperatives in Greek Prayer from Homer up to the Present Day* (Amsterdam).

5 WORKS CITED BY AUTHOR'S NAME WITH DATE

Bal, M. (1978) *De Theorie van Vertellen en Verhalen: Inleiding in de Narratologie* (Couthino, Muiderberg).

(1997) *Narratology: Introduction to the Theory of Narrative*[2] (1st edn. 1985; transl. C. van Boheemen; Toronto).

Bardt, C. *et al.* (1877) *Commentationes philologae in honorem Theodori Mommseni* (Berlin).

Barker, A. (2004) 'Transforming the nightingale: aspects of Athenian musical discourse in the late fifth century', in Murray and Wilson (2004) (eds.) 185–204.

Barner, W. (1971) 'Die Monodie', in Jens (1971) 277–320.

Barnwell, H. T. (1982) *The Tragic Dramas of Corneille and Racine: an Old Parallel Revisited* (Oxford).

Barrett, J. (2002) *Staged Narrative: Poetics and the Messenger in Greek Tragedy* (London, Berkeley, Los Angeles).

Barron, J. P. (1984) 'Ibycus: *Gorgias* and other poems', *BICS* 31: 13–24.

Basson, A. F., and Dominik, W. J. (2003) (eds.) *Literature, Art, History: Studies on Classical Antiquity and Tradition in Honour of W. J. Henderson* (Frankfurt am Main).

Bast, F. J. (1811) *Commentatio Palaeographica*, in Schaefer's edition of Gregory of Corinth, pp. 701–861.

Bastianini, G., and Casanova, A. (2005) (eds.) *Euripide e i papiri. Atti del Convegno Internazionale di Studi, Firenze, 10–11 Giugno 2004* (Studi e Testi di Papirologia N.S. 7; Florence).

Battezzato, L. (2000) 'Synizesis in Euripides and the structure of the iambic trimeter – the case of θεός', *BICS* 44: 41–80.

(2003) 'Linguistica e figure retoriche: *hysteron proteron* e pleonasmo da Omero a Sofocle', in Avezzù (2003) (ed.) 17–48.

Bayfield, M. A. (1901) 'A note on φοναί', *CR* 15: 251–2.

Beare, W. (1927) 'Sophocles, *Electra*, ll. 17–19', *CR* 41: 111–12.

Beck, J. W. *et al.* (1902) *Album Gratulatorium in Honorem Henrici van Herwerden* (Utrecht).

Becker, O. (1937) *Das Bild des Weges und verwandte Vorstellungen im frühgriechischen Denken* (Hermes Einzelschriften 4; Berlin).

Behaghel, O. (1909) 'Beziehungen zwischen Umfang und Reihenfolge von Satzgliedern', *IF* 25 (Festschrift Brugmann): 110–42.

Belger, C. (1879) *Moriz Haupt als academischer Lehrer* (Berlin).

Benardete, S. (1961) 'Sophocles *Electra* 1087', *RhM* n.F. 104: 96.

Benedict, T. F. (1820) *Observationes in Sophoclis septem tragoedias* (Leipzig).

Bentley, R. (1816) 'R. Bentleii Emendatt. Mss. in Sophoclem, Theocritum, Bionem, Moschum, Nicandrum, et Callimachum', *CJ* 13: 244–82.

Benveniste, É. (1969) *Le Vocabulaire des institutions indo-européennes* (2 vols.; Paris).

(1973) *Indo-European Language and Society* (transl. E. Palmer; London).

573

Bergk, T. (1835) review of Dindorf's *Poetae Scenici Graeci* (Leipzig and London 1830), *Zeitschrift für die Alterthumswissenschaft* (sometimes known as 'Zimmermann's Zeitschrift') 1. ser. 2: 945–68.

   (1848) 'Kritik und Erklärung. Sieben Conjecturen zu Sophokles', *RhM* n.F. 6: 145–51.

Bergson, L. (1953) 'The omitted augment in the messengers' speeches of Greek tragedy', *Eranos* 51: 121–8.

   (1956) *L'Épithète ornementale dans Eschyle, Sophocle et Euripide* (Uppsala).

   (1959) 'Episches in den ῥήσεις ἀγγελικαί', *RhM* n.F. 102: 9–32.

Bers, V. (1974) *Enallage and Greek Style* (Mnem. Suppl. 29; Leiden).

   (1984) *Greek Poetic Syntax in the Classical Age* (New Haven and London).

   (1997) *Speech in Speech: Studies in Incorporated* Oratio Recta *in Attic Drama and Oratory* (London, Lanham, Boulder, New York).

Betts, J. H., Hooker, J. T., and Green, J. R. (1986–8) (eds.) *Studies in Honour of T. B. L. Webster* (2 vols.; Bristol).

Beverley, E. J. (1997) *The Dramatic Function of Actors' Monody in Later Euripides* (diss. Oxford).

Bierl, A., and von Möllendorf, P. (1994) (eds.) *Orchestra: Drama, Mythos, Bühne* (Festschrift Flashar; Stuttgart and Leipzig).

Bissinger, M. (1966) *Das Adjektiv ΜΕΓΑΣ in der griechischen Dichtung* (Münchener Studien zur Sprachwissenschaft 10; Munich).

Björck, G. (1946) 'ὄναρ ἰδεῖν. De la perception de rêve chez les anciens', *Eranos* 44: 306–14.

   (1950) *Das Alpha impurum und die tragische Kunstsprache: attische Wort- und Stilstudien* (Acta Societatis Litterarum Humaniorum Regiae Upsaliensis 39.1; Uppsala).

Blanc, A. (1991) 'Le composé στόμαργος et la fureur verbale chez les tragiques grecs', *RPh* 3ᵉ sér. 65: 59–66.

   (1992) 'À propos de l'adjectif ἀντήρης: une origine méconnue du second membre de composé –ήρης', *RPh* 3ᵉ sér. 66: 247–54.

Blaydes, F. H. M. (1899) *Adversaria Critica in Sophoclem* (Halle).

   (1902) *Spicilegium Tragicum. Observationes Criticas in Tragicos Poetas Graecos continens* (Halle).

Blomfield, C. J. (1826) 'Animadversiones quaedam in Euripidis Supplices et Iphigenias', *Museum Criticum* i. 181–93 [orig. 1814, No. 2].

Blomqvist, J. (1979) *Das sogenannte KAI adversativum: zur Semantik einer griechischen Partikel* (Studia Graeca Upsaliensa 13; Uppsala).

Blume, H.-D., and Mann, F. (1983) (eds.) *Platonismus und Christentum. Festschrift für Heinrich Dörrie* (Jahrbuch für Antike und Christentum Ergänzungsband 10; Münster).

Blumenthal, A. von (1934) 'Beobachtungen zu griechischen Dichtern', *Hermes* 69: 454–9.

Blundell, M. W. (1989) *Helping Friends and Harming Enemies. A Study in Sophocles and Greek Ethics* (Cambridge).

Blundell, S., and Williamson, M. (1998) (eds.) *The Sacred and the Feminine in Ancient Greece* (London).

Boeckh, A. (1808) *Graecae tragoediae principum, Aeschyli, Sophoclis, Euripidis, num ea, quae supersunt, et genuina omnia sint, et forma primitiva servata, an eorum familiis aliquid debeat ex iis tribui* (Heidelberg).

Bolton, J. D. P. (1962) *Aristeas of Proconnesus* (Oxford).

Booth, N. B. (1977) 'Sophocles, *Electra* 610–11', *CQ* N.S. 27: 466–7.

Borecky, B. (1965) *Survivals of Some Tribal Ideas in Classical Greek: the Use and the Meaning of* λαγχάνω, δατέομαι *and the Origin of* ἴσον ἔχειν, ἴσον νέμειν, *and Related Idioms* (Acta Universitatis Carolinae Philosophica et Historica Monographia 10; Prague).

Bowersock, G. W., Burkert, W., and Putnam, M. C. J. (1979) (eds.) Arktouros: *Hellenic Studies presented to Bernard M. W. Knox on the Occasion of his 65th Birthday* (Berlin and New York).

Bowman, L. (1997) 'Klutaimnestra's dream: prophecy in Sophokles' *Elektra*', *Mnemosyne* 4th ser. 51: 131–51.

Brandão, J. L. (2001) 'Electra no espelho', in Brasete (2001) (ed.) 115–29.

Brasete, M. F. (2001) (ed.) *Máscaras, Vozes e Gestas: nos caminhos do teatro clássico* (Ágora suplemento 2; Aveiro).

Bravo, B. (1997) Pannychis *e simposio. Feste private notturne di donne e uomini nei testi letterari e nel culto* (Filologia e critica 79; Pisa and Rome).

Bremer, D. (1976) *Licht und Dunkel in der frühgriechischen Dichtung: Interpretationen zur Vorgeschichte der Lichtmetaphysik* (Archiv für Begriffsgeschichte Supplementheft 1; Bonn).

Bremer, J. M. (1977) 'Why messenger speeches?', in Bremer *et al.* (1976) (eds.) 29–48.

Bremer, J. M., de Jong, I. J. F., and Kallf, J. (1987) (eds.) *Homer: Beyond Oral Poetry. Recent Trends in Homeric Interpretation* (Amsterdam).

Bremer, J. M., and Erp Taalman Kip, A. M. van (1994) review of the Sophocles OCT by Lloyd-Jones and Wilson (1990), *Mnemosyne* 4th ser. 47: 236–44.

Bremer, J. M., and Handley, E. W. (1993) (eds.) *Aristophane* (Fondation Hardt Entretiens 38; Geneva).

Bremer, J. M., Radt, S. L., and Ruijgh, C. J. (1976) (eds.) *Miscellanea Tragica in Honorem J. C. Kamerbeek* (Amsterdam).

Bremmer, J. N. (1991) *Profeten, zieners en de macht in Griekenland, Israël en het vroegmoderne Europa* (Utrecht).

  (1993) 'Prophets, seers, and politics in Greece, Israel, and early modern Europe', *Numen* 40: 150–83.

Bremmer, J. N., and Horsfall, N. M. (1987) *Roman Myth and Mythography* (BICS Suppl. 52; London).

Broadhead, H. D. (1961) 'Some textual problems in Sophocles', *BICS* 8: 49–58.

(1968) *Tragica: Elucidations of Passages in Greek Tragedy* (University of Canterbury Publications 8; Christchurch, NZ).

Bruchmann, C. F. H. (1893) *Epitheta deorum quae apud poetas Graecos leguntur* (*Ausführliches Lexikon der griechischen und römischen Mythologie* (ed.W. H. Roscher) Suppl. 1; Leipzig).

Budelmann, F. (1999) *The Language of Sophocles: Communality, Communication and Involvement* (Cambridge).

Bundy, E. L. (1962) 'Studia Pindarica. I: The *Eleventh Olympian Ode*', Univ. Cal. Publ. in Cl. Phil. 18: 1–33. [= (1986) 1–33]

(1986) *Studia Pindarica* (Berkeley).

Burkert, W. (1962) *Weisheit und Wissenschaft. Studien zu Pythagoras, Philolaus und Platon* (Erlanger Beiträge zur Sprach– und Kunstwissenschaft Band 10; Nuremberg).

(1963) 'A note on Aeschylus *Choephori* 205 ff.', *CQ* N.S. 13: 177.

(1966) 'Greek tragedy and sacrificial ritual', *GRBS* 7: 87–121 (transl. S. R. West). [= (2001) 1–36]

(1972) *Lore and Science in Ancient Pythagoreanism* (transl. E. L. Minar, Jr.; Cambridge, Mass.).

(1977) *Griechische Religion der archaischen und klassischen Epoche* (Die Religionen der Menschheit 15; Stuttgart, Berlin, Cologne, Mainz).

(1983) *Homo Necans: the Anthropology of Ancient Greek Sacrificial Ritual and Myth* (transl. P. Bing; London, Berkeley, Los Angeles).

(1984) *Die orientalisierende Epoche in der griechischen Religion und Literatur* (*SB Heidelberg* 1984.1; Heidelberg).

(1985) *Greek Religion* (transl. J. Raffan; Cambridge, Mass.).

(1992) *The Orientalizing Revolution. Near Eastern Influence on Greek Culture in the Early Archaic Age* (transl. M. E. Pinder and W. Burkert; London and Cambridge, Mass.).

(1997) *Homo Necans: Interpretationen altgriechischer Opferriten und Mythen*[2] (1st edn. 1972; Religionsgeschichtliche Versuche und Vorarbeiten 32; Berlin and New York).

(2001) *Savage Energies: Lessons of Myth and Ritual in Ancient Greece* (transl. P. Bing and S. R. West; London and Chicago).

Burnett, A. P. (1998) *Revenge in Attic and Later Tragedy* (Sather Classical Lectures 62; London, Berkeley, Los Angeles).

Burton, R. W. B. (1980) *The Chorus in Sophocles' Tragedies* (Oxford).

Bury, R. G. (1946) 'The Greek fleet at Aulis', *PCPS* 178: 4–6.

Buxton, R. (1982) *Persuasion in Greek Tragedy: A Study of Peitho* (Cambridge).

(1995) *Sophocles*[2] (Greece and Rome New Surveys 16; 1st edn. 1984; Oxford).

Cairns, D. L. (1993) *Aidos: the Psychology and Ethics of Honour and Shame in Ancient Greek Literature* (Oxford).

5 WORKS CITED BY AUTHOR'S NAME WITH DATE

(1994) review of Fisher (1992), *CR* N.S. 44: 76–9.

(2003) 'Ethics, ethology, terminology: Iliadic anger and the cross-cultural study of emotion', *YCS* 32: 11–49.

Cairns, F. (1984) (ed.) *Papers of the Liverpool Latin Seminar: Fourth Volume 1983* (Arca Classical and Medieval Texts, Papers and Monographs 11; Liverpool).

Calder, W. M. III (1963) 'The end of Sophocles' *Electra*', *GRBS* 4: 213–16. [= (2005) 151–5]

(2005) *Theatrokratia. Collected Papers on the Politics and Staging of Greco-Roman Tragedy* (Spudasmata 104; ed. R. Scott Smith; Hildesheim, Zürich, New York).

Calder, W. M. III, and Stern, J. (1970) (eds.) *Pindaros und Bakchylides* (Wege der Forschung 134; Darmstadt).

Cannatà Fera, M., and Grandolini, S. (2000) (eds.) *Poesia e religione in Grecia. Studi in onore di G. Aurelio Privitera* (2 vols.; Naples).

Cantarella, R. *et al.* (1967) *ΚΩΜΩΙΔΟΤΡΑΓΗΜΑΤΑ. Studia Aristophanea viri Aristophanei W. J. W. Koster in honorem* (Amsterdam).

Canter, W. (1566) *Novarum Lectionum Libri Septem²* (1st edn. 1564; Basel).

Carawan, E. M. (1999) 'The edict of Oedipus (*Oedipus Tyrannus* 223–51)', *AJP* 120: 187–222.

Carden, R. (1974) *The Papyrus Fragments of Sophocles* (Texte und Kommentare 7; Berlin and New York).

Carrara, P. (1992) 'Sull' inizio delle Fenicie di Euripide', *ZPE* 102: 43–51.

Carter, J. E. (1902) *Epitheta deorum quae apud poetas Latinos leguntur* (*Ausführliches Lexikon der griechischen und römischen Mythologie* (ed. W. H. Roscher) Suppl. 2; Leipzig).

Carter, L. B. (1986) *The Quiet Athenian* (Oxford).

Casabona, J. (1966) *Recherches sur le vocabulaire des sacrifices en grec: des origines à la fin de l'époque classique* (Publication des annales de la faculté des lettres Aix-en-Provence N.S. 56; Aix-en-Provence).

Casevitz, M. (1985) *Le vocabulaire de la colonisation en grec ancien. Étude lexicologique: les familles de κτίζω et de οἰκέω–οἰκίζω* (Études et commentaires 97; Paris).

Cave, T. (1988) *Recognitions: a Study in Poetics* (Oxford).

Cazzaniga, I. (1950–1) *La saga di Itis nella tradizione letteraria e mitografica greco-romana* (2 vols.; Varese and Milan).

Ceadel, E. B. (1941) 'Resolved feet in the trimeters of Euripides and the chronology of the plays', *CQ* 35: 66–89.

Chadwick, J. (1996) *Lexicographica Graeca: Contributions to the Lexicography of Ancient Greek* (Oxford).

Chantraine, P. (1928) 'Sur le vocabulaire maritime des Grecs', in Meillet (1928) (ed.) 1–25.

(1933) *La formation des noms en grec ancien* (Collection Linguistique 38; Paris).

(1942–53) *Grammaire Homérique* (2 vols.; Collection de Philologie Classique 1 and 4; Paris).

(1956) *Études sur le vocabulaire grec* (Études et commentaires 24; Paris).

(1970) 'A propos d'Euripide, *Médée*, 525: τὴν σὴν στόμαργον γλωσσαλγίαν', in Aulotte *et al.* (1970) 92–5.

(1999) *Dictionnaire étymologique de la langue grecque²* (orig. 1968–80; Paris).

Ciani, M. G. (1974) *Φάος e termini affini nella poesia greca. Introduzione a una fenomenologia della luce* (Università di Padova pubblicazioni della facoltà di lettere e filosofia vol. 51; Florence).

Cobet, C. G. (1856) 'Variae Lectiones', *Mnemosyne* 5: 81–112, 181–204, 233–72, 379–418.

(1858) *Novae Lectiones quibus continentur Observationes Criticae in Scriptores Graecos* (Leiden).

Cole, S. G. (1998) 'Domesticating Artemis', in Blundell and Williamson (1998) (eds.) 27–43.

Collard, C. (1975) 'Formal debates in Euripides' drama', *G&R* 2nd ser. 22: 58–71 [= McAuslan and Walcot (1993) (eds.) 153–66 = Mossman (2003) (ed.) 64–80].

Conomis, N. C. (1964) 'The dochmiacs of Greek drama', *Hermes* 92: 23–50.

Conradt, C. (1894) 'Über den Aufbau einiger Dramen des Sophokles', *Neue Jahrbücher für Philologie und Paedagogik* 149 = *Jahrbücher für classische Philologie* 40: 577–99.

Cooper, G. L. III (1971) *Zur syntaktischen Theorie und Textkritik der attischen Autoren* (Zürich).

(1972) 'In defense of the special dual feminine forms of the article and pronouns τά, ταῖν, ταύτα, ταύταιν κτλ.', *TAPA* 103: 97–125.

Cooper, J. M. (1999) *Reason and Emotion: Essays on Ancient Moral Psychology and Ethical Theory* (Princeton).

Coray, M. (1993) *Wissen und Erkennen bei Sophokles* (Schweizerische Beiträge zur Altertumswissenschaft Heft 24; Basel and Berlin).

Corlu, A. (1966) *Recherches sur les mots relatifs à l'idée de prière, d'Homère aux tragiques* (Études et commentaires 64; Paris).

Corrêa, P. da C. (1998) *Armas e Varões: A Guerra na Lírica de Arquíloco* (São Paulo).

Coulon, V. (1939) 'Observations critiques et exégétiques sur divers passages controversés de Sophocle', *REG* 52: 1–18.

Courbin, P. (1998) 'Le temple d' Apollon Lycien à Argos: quelques suggestions', in Pariente and Touchais (1998) (eds.) 261–6.

Craig, C. P. (1993) *Form as Argument in Cicero's Speeches: a Study of Dilemma* (American Classical Studies 31; Atlanta).

Craik, E. M. (1990) (ed.) *'Owls to Athens'. Essays on Classical Subjects presented to Sir Kenneth Dover* (Oxford).

Croally, N. T. (1994) *Euripidean Polemic: the* Trojan Women *and the Function of Tragedy* (Cambridge).

Cropp, M., Fantham, E., and Scully, S. E. (1986) (eds.) *Greek Tragedy and its Legacy: Essays presented to D. J. Conacher* (Calgary).

Cropp, M., and Fick, G. (1985) *Resolutions and Chronology in Euripides. The Fragmentary Tragedies* (BICS Suppl. 43; London).

Cropp, M., Lee, K. H., and Sansone, D. (1999–2000) (eds.) *Euripides and Tragic Theatre in the Late Fifth Century* (*ICS* 24–5; Champaign).

Crowther, N. B. (1993a) 'More on "drómos" as a technical term in Greek sport', *Nikephoros* 6: 33–7. [= (2004) 241–4]

    (1993b) 'Numbers of contestants in Greek athletic contests', *Nikephoros* 6: 39–52. [= (2004) 171–82]

    (1994a) 'Reflections on Greek equestrian events. Violence and spectator attitudes', *Nikephoros* 7: 121–33. [= (2004) 229–40]

    (1994b) 'The role of heralds and trumpeters at Greek athletic festivals', *Nikephoros* 7: 135–55. [= (2004) 183–202]

    (1999) 'Athlete as warrior in the ancient Greek games. Some reflections', *Nikephoros* 12: 121–30. [= (2004) 313–21]

    (2004) *Athletika. Studies on the Olympic Games and Greek Athletics* (Nikephoros Beihefte 11; Hildesheim).

Cumont, M. F. (1923) 'Il sole vindice dei delitti ed il simbolo delle mani alzate', *Atti della Pontificia Accademia romana di Archeologia (ser. III) Memorie* 1.1: 65–80.

    (1933) 'Deux monuments des cultes solaires', *Syria* 14: 381–95.

Dahlmann, H., and Merkelbach, R. (1959) (eds.) *Studien zur Textgeschichte und Textkritik* (Festschrift Jachmann; Cologne and Opladen).

Dale, A. M. (1936) 'Lyrical clausulae in Sophocles', in Bailey *et al.* (1936) (eds.) 181–201. [= (1969) 1–24]

    (1960) review of Dain's edition of Sophocles, vol. ii (Paris 1958), *CR* N.S. 10: 16–19.

    (1964) 'Observations on dactylic', *WS* 77: 15–36. [= (1969) 185–209]

    (1966) 'The *Electra* of Sophocles', in Kelly (1966) (ed.) 71–7. [≈ (1969) 221–9]

    (1968) *The Lyric Metres of Greek Drama²* (1st edn. 1948; Cambridge).

    (1969) *Collected Papers* (ed. T. B. L. Webster and E. G. Turner; Cambridge).

    (1971–83) *Metrical Analyses of Tragic Choruses* (3 vols.; BICS Suppl. 21.1–3, ed. T. B. L. Webster and E. W. Handley; London).

Damiralis, K. (1888) 'Ein neuer Kodex des Sophokles aus Athen', *Berliner Philologische Wochenschrift* 8: 291.

Daux, G. (1946) 'Note sur Sophocle, Électre, 706 et 724', *BCH* 70: 106–7.

Davidson, J. F. (1988) 'Homer and Sophocles' *Electra*', *BICS* 35: 45–72.

    (1990a) 'The Sophoclean axe', *RhM* n.F. 133: 410.

    (1990b) 'The daughters of Agamemnon (Soph. *El.* 153–63)', *RhM* n.F. 133: 407–9.

(1991) 'Oh brotherly head: Sophocles, *Electra* 1164 and related matters', *QUCC* N.S. 38: 87–96.

(2001) 'Sophocles *Electra* 197–200', *PdelP* 318: 199–202.

(2003) 'Olympia and the chariot-race of Pelops', in Phillips and Pritchard (2003) (eds.) 101–22.

Davidson, J. F., Muecke, F., and Wilson, P. (2006) (eds.) *Greek Drama III. Essays in Honour of Kevin Lee* (BICS Suppl. 87; London).

Davies, J. K. (1997) 'The moral dimension of Pythian Apollo', in A. B. Lloyd (1997) (ed.) 43–64.

Davies, M. (1979) *A Commentary on Stesichorus* (2 vols.; diss. Oxford).

(1981) 'The judgement of Paris and *Iliad* book XXIV', *JHS* 101 : 56–62.

(1985) 'Sophocles' *Antigone* 823ff. as a specimen of "mythological hyperbole"', *Hermes* 113: 247–9.

(1986a) 'Alcaeus, Thetis and Helen', *Hermes* 114: 257–62.

(1986b) 'Who speaks at Sophocles *Antigone* 572?', *Prometheus* 12: 19–24.

(1987) 'Aeschylus's Clytemnestra – sword or axe?', *CQ* N.S. 37: 65–75.

(1988a) 'Stesichorus' *Geryoneis* and its folk-tale origins', *CQ* N.S. 38: 277–90.

(1988b) 'The "Cologne Alcaeus" and paradigmatic allusiveness', *ZPE* 72: 39–42.

(1989a) 'Sisyphus and the invention of religion ("Critias" *TrGF* 1 (43) F 19 = B 25 D–K)', *BICS* 36: 16–32.

(1989b) 'Anticipation and foreshadowing: a use of myth', *SIFC* 3° ser. 7: 7–11.

(1991) 'The end of Sophocles' *O.T.* revisited', *Prometheus* 17: 1–18.

(1997) 'Feasting and food in Homer: realism and stylisation', *Prometheus* 23: 97–107.

(1998) 'Euripides' *Electra*: the recognition scene again', *CQ* N.S. 48: 389–403.

(1999a) '"Leaving out the Erinyes": the history of a misconception', *Prometheus* 25: 117–28.

(1999b) 'The three Electras: Strauss, Hofmannsthal, Sophocles, and the tragic vision', *Antike und Abendland* 45: 36–65.

(1999c) 'Comic priamel and hyperbole in Euripides, *Cyclops* 1–10', *CQ* N.S. 49: 428–32.

(2001) 'The stasimon of Sophocles' *Philoctetes* and the limits of mythological allusion', *SIFC* 3° ser. 19: 53–8.

(forthcoming) 'Comic *Opsimathia* in Aristophanes' *Clouds*'.

(forthcoming 2) 'Some overlooked formulae of *Opsimathia*'.

Davies, M. I. (1969) 'Thoughts on the *Oresteia* before Aischylos', *BCH* 93: 214–60.

Dawe, R. D. (1964) *The Collation and Investigation of Manuscripts of Aeschylus* (Cambridge).

(1968) 'Emendations in Sophocles', *PCPS* N.S. 14: 8–18.

5 WORKS CITED BY AUTHOR'S NAME WITH DATE

(1973) 'Sophocles, "Electra" 1205–10', *PCPS* N.S. 19: 45–6.

(1976) review of Kamerbeek's edition, *Gnomon* 48: 228–34.

(1998) 'EI KAI TPIT' EΣTI . . . Editing Sophocles for the third time', in Most (1998) (ed.) 111–22.

(2002–3) 'On editing Sophocles, Oxford style', *ICS* 27–8: 1–19.

Dawe, R. D., Diggle, J., and Easterling, P. E. (1978) (eds.) *Dionysiaca: Nine Studies in Greek Poetry by Former Pupils Presented to Sir Denys Page on his Seventieth Birthday* (Cambridge).

Dawes, R. (1745) *Miscellanea Critica* (Cambridge).

(1800) *Miscellanea Critica³* (ed.G. C. Harless; Leipzig).

(1827) *Miscellanea Critica⁵* (ed.T. Kidd; Cambridge and London). [n.v.]

Debrunner, A. (1917) *Griechische Wortbildungslehre* (Indogermanische Bibliothek 2. Abt., Sprachwissenschaftliche Gymnasialbibliothek 8; Heidelberg).

Degani, E. (1961) *Aἰών da Omero ad Aristotele* (Università di Padova pubblicazioni della facoltà di lettere e filosofia vol. 37; Padua; 2nd edn. 2001 [n.v.]).

Delcourt, M. (1959) *Oreste et Alcméon. Étude sur la projection légendaire du matricide en Grèce* (Bibliothèque de la Faculté de Philosophie et Lettres de l'Université de Liège fasc. 151; Paris).

De Marco, V. (1937) *De Scholiis in Sophoclis Tragoedias Veteribus* (Reale Accademia Nazionale dei Lincei 6° ser. 6.2; Rome).

Denniston, J. D. (1952) *Greek Prose Style* (prepared for publication by P. H. J. Lloyd-Jones; Oxford).

Descat, R. (1988) 'Aux origines de l'*oikonomia* grecque', *QUCC* N.S. 28: 103–19.

Dettori, E. (1992) *L'interlocuzione difficile: corifeo dialogante nel dramma classico* (Pisa).

Deubner, L. (1941) *Ololuge und Verwandtes* (*APAW* 1; Berlin). [= (1982) 607–34] (1966) *Attische Feste²* (1st edn. Berlin 1932; Vienna).

(1982) *Kleine Schriften zur klassischen Altertumskunde* (Beiträge zur klassischen Philologie 140; Königstein).

De Waele, F. J. M. (1927) *The Magic Staff or Rod in Graeco-Italian Antiquity* (Ghent).

Di Benedetto, V. (2003) 'Spazio scenico e spazio extrascenico alla fine delle tragedie di Sofocle: dissolvenze e rifunzionalizzazioni', in Avezzù (2003) (ed.) 109–24.

Dickey, E. (1996) *Greek Forms of Address: From Herodotus to Lucian* (Oxford).

Dieterich, A. (1891) *De hymnis Orphicis capitula quinque* (diss. Marburg, Elwert). [= (1911) 69–110] (1911) *Kleine Schriften* (Leipzig and Berlin).

Dietrich, B. C. (1965) *Death, Fate and the Gods: the Development of a Religious Idea in Greek Popular Belief and in Homer* (University of London Classical Studies 3; London).

Di Filippo Balestrazzi, E. (1984) 'Apollon Agyieus', *LIMC* II/1: 327–32.

Diggle, J. (1968) 'Notes on the *Agamemnon* and *Persae* of Aeschylus', *CR* N.S. 18: 1–4.

BIBLIOGRAPHY

(1969) 'Marginalia Euripidea', *PCPS* N.S. 15: 30–59. [= (1994) 5–33]

(1972) 'Euripides, *Cyclops* 511–18 (and other passages)', *Maia* 24: 345–8.

(1973) 'The *Supplices* of Euripides', *GRBS* 14: 241–69. [= (1994) 59–89]

(1974) 'On the *Heracles* and *Ion* of Euripides', *PCPS* N.S. 20: 3–36. [= (1994) 90–136]

(1975a) review of S. G. Daitz (ed.) *Euripides*. Hecuba (Leipzig 1973), *JHS* 95: 198–9.

(1975b) review of Kambitsis' *Antiope* (1972), *Gnomon* 47: 288–91. [= (1994) 143–7]

(1976) 'Notes on the *Iphigenia in Tauris* of Euripides', *PCPS* N.S. 22: 42–5. [= (1994) 148–51]

(1977a) 'Notes on the *Electra* of Euripides', *ICS* 2: 110–24. [= (1994) 152–68]

(1977b) review of Collard's *Supplices* (1975), *CR* N.S. 27: 5–6.

(1978) 'On the *Helen* of Euripides' in Dawe *et al.* (1978) (eds.) 159–77. [= (1994) 176–95]

(1981a) *Studies on the Text of Euripides* (Oxford).

(1981b) 'On the *Alcestis* and *Andromache* of Euripides', *ICS* 6: 82–101. [= (1994) 196–215]

(1982a) 'Further notes on the *Heraclidae* of Euripides', *PCPS* N.S. 28: 57–63. [= (1994) 220–8]

(1982b) 'Notes on the *Hecuba* of Euripides', *GRBS* 23: 315–23. [= (1994) 229–38]

(1982c) review of the edition of Aeschylus' *Supplices* by Friis Johansen and Whittle (1980), *CR* N.S. 32: 127–34.

(1982d) review of Burton (1980), *CR* N.S. 32: 12–14.

(1983) 'On the manuscripts and text of Euripides, *Medea*. I. The manuscripts', *CQ* N.S. 33: 339–57. [= (1994) 250–72]

(1984a) 'On the manuscripts and text of Euripides, *Medea*. II. The text', *CQ* N.S. 34: 50–65. [= (1994) 273–97]

(1984b) review of West (1982a), *CR* N.S. 34: 66–71. [= (1994) 313–19 (abbrev.)]

(1987) 'The prophet of Bacchus: *Rhesus* 970–3', *SIFC* 3° ser. 5: 167–72. [= (1994) 320–6]

(1989) 'Notes on the *Phoenissae* of Euripides', *SIFC* 3° ser. 7: 196–206. [= (1994) 341–52]

(1990) 'On the *Orestes* of Euripides', *CQ* N.S. 40: 100–23. [= (1994) 362–99]

(1991) *The Textual Tradition of Euripides'* Orestes (Oxford).

(1993) 'Euripides, *Orestes* 225', in Jocelyn (1993) (ed.) 135–7. [= (1994) 416–20]

(1994) *Euripidea: Collected Essays* (Oxford).

(1995) 'Notes on Euripides, *Hypsipyle*', *Eikasmos* 6: 39–44.

(1995–6) 'Notes on fragments of Aeschylus', *Mus. Crit.* 30–1: 99–104.

(1996a) 'P. Petrie 1.1–2: Euripides, *Antiope* (fr. 223 (Nauck) Kannicht, XLVIII Kambitsis)', *PCPS* N.S. 42: 106–26.

(1996b) 'Critias, *Sisyphus* (fr. 19 Snell, 1 Nauck)', *Prometheus* 22: 103–4.

(1996c) 'Epilegomena Phaethontea', *AC* 65: 189–99.

(1996d) 'Sophocles, *Ichneutae* (fr. 314 Radt)', *ZPE* 112: 3–17.

(1998) 'Euripides, *Bacchae* 1063–1069', *Eikasmos* 9: 41–52. [= López Férez (1999) (ed.) 135–48]

(2002) 'Xenophon, *Anabasis* 3, 1, 6–8 and the limits of "inverse attraction"', *SIFC* 3° ser. 20: 83–6.

(2005) 'Rhythmical prose in the Euripidean hypotheses', in Bastianini and Casanova (2005) (eds.) 27–67.

(forthcoming) 'Housman's Greek'.

Di Gregorio, L. (1967) *Le scene d'annuncio nella tragedia greca* (Scienze filologiche e letteratura 6; Milan).

Dihle, A. (1959) 'Eine Schauspielerinterpolation in der sophokleischen Elektra', in Dahlmann and Merkelbach (1959) (eds.) 47–56.

(1983) 'Vom sonnenhaften Auge', in Blume and Mann (1983) (eds.) 85–91.

Diller, H. (1967) (ed.) *Sophokles* (Wege der Forschung 95; Darmstadt).

Dindorf, K. W. (1836) *Ad Sophoclis tragoedias annotationes* (Oxford).

Dobree, P. P. (1833–43) *Adversaria* (2 vols.; ed. J. Scholefield; Cambridge).

Dodds, E. R. (1951) *The Greeks and the Irrational* (Sather Classical Lectures 25; London, Berkeley, Los Angeles).

(1960) 'Morals and politics in the *Oresteia*', *PCPS* N.S. 6: 19–31. [= (1973) 45–63]

(1973) *The Ancient Concept of Progress and other Essays on Greek Literature and Belief* (Oxford).

Doederlein, J. L. C. W. (1814) *Specimen Novae Editionis Tragoediarum Sophoclearum* (Erlangen).

Dover, K. J. (1963) 'Notes on Aristophanes' *Acharnians*', *Maia* 15: 6–25. [= (1987a) 288–306]

(1968) *Lysias and the Corpus Lysiacum* (Sather Classical Lectures 39; Berkeley and Los Angeles).

(1969) 'Due problemi testuali in Antifonte', *Maia* 21: 123–5. [≈ (1988) 36–7 (English translation)]

(1970) 'Lo stilo di Aristofane', *QUCC* N.S. 9: 7–23. [≈ (1987a) 224–36 (English translation) ≈ Newiger (1975) (ed.) 124–43 (German translation)]

(1972) *Aristophanic Comedy* (Berkeley and Los Angeles).

(1973) 'Some neglected aspects of Agamemnon's dilemma', *JHS* 93: 58–69. [= (1987a) 135–50]

(1974) *Greek Popular Morality in the Time of Plato and Aristotle* (Oxford).

(1976) 'ΗΛΙΟΣ ΚΗΡΥΞ (Soph. *Trach.* 97–102)', in Bremer *et al.* (1976) 49–53. [= (1987a) 186–9]

(1981) 'The colloquial stratum in Attic prose', in Shrimpton and McCargar (1981) (eds.) 15–25. [≈ (1987a) 16–30]

(1983) 'The portrayal of moral evaluation in Greek poetry', *JHS* 103: 35–48. [= (1987a) 77–96]

(1985) 'Some types of abnormal word-order in Attic comedy', *CQ* N.S. 35: 324–43. [= (1987a) 43–66]

(1987a) *Greek and the Greeks. Collected Papers vol. 1: Language, Poetry, Drama* (Oxford).

(1987b) 'Homosexualität in Griechenland und die "Inspiration"', in Duerr (1987) (ed.) 47–63 (transl. C. Groffy).

(1988) *The Greeks and their Legacy. Collected Papers vol. 2: Prose Literature, History, Society, Transmission, Influence* (Oxford).

(1997) *The Evolution of Greek Prose Style* (Oxford).

Duerr, H. P. (1987) (ed.) *Die wilde Seele. Zur Ethnopsychoanalyse von Georges Devereux* (Edition Suhrkamp n.F. 235; Frankfurt am Main).

Dumortier, J. (1975) *Le Vocabulaire médical d'Éschyle et les écrits hippocratiques²* (Paris; 1st edn. 1935).

Earle, M. L. (1903) 'On Sophocles's *Electra*, 683 *sq.*', *CR* 17: 209. [= (1912) 80–1]

(1912) *Classical Papers* (New York).

Easterling, P. E. (1973) 'Repetition in Sophocles', *Hermes* 101: 14–34.

(1977) 'Character in Sophocles', *G&R* 2nd ser. 24: 121–9. [= E. Segal (1983) (ed.) 138–45 = McAuslan and Walcot (1993) (eds.) 58–65]

(1978) 'The second stasimon of *Antigone*', in Dawe *et al.* (1978) (eds.) 141–58.

(1985) 'Anachronism in Greek tragedy', *JHS* 105: 1–10.

(1987) 'Women in tragic space', *BICS* 34: 15–26.

(1989) 'Agamemnon's σκῆπτρον in the *Iliad*', in Mackenzie and Roueché (1989) (eds.) 104–21.

(2005) '*Agamemnon* for the ancients', in Macintosh *et al.* (2005) (eds.) 23–36.

Ebert, J. (1972) *Griechische Epigramme auf Sieger an gymnischen und hippischen Agonen* (*ASAW* 3(2); Berlin).

Egan, R. B. (1983) 'On the relevance of Orestes in Pindar's *Eleventh Pythian*', *Phoenix* 37: 189–200.

Eggert, C. G. (1868) *Quaestiones Sophocleae Criticae Particula Prior* (diss. Munich).

Eitrem, S. (1915) *Opferritus und Voropfer der Griechen und Römer* (Videnskapsselskapets Skrifter II Hist.-filos. klasse 1914. No. 1; Kristiana).

(1916) 'Io', *RE* 9/2: 1732–43.

(1917) 'Varia', *Nordisk Tidsskrift for Filologi* 4° Raekke 6: 157–62.

Ekroth, G. (2002) *The Sacrificial Rituals of Greek Hero-Cults* (Kernos Suppl. 12; Liège).

5 WORKS CITED BY AUTHOR'S NAME WITH DATE

Elliger, W. (1975) *Die Darstellung der Landschaft in der griechischen Dichtung* (Untersuchungen zur antiken Literatur und Geschichte 15; Berlin and New York).

Elmsley, P. (1811) review of R. Porson (ed.) *Euripidis Hecuba* (London 1808), *The Edinburgh Review* vol. 19 (no. 37): 64–95.

Erbse, H. (1981) 'Versumstellungen in der griechischen Tragoedie', *ICS* 6: 34–41.

(1984) *Studien zum Prolog der euripideischen Tragödie* (Untersuchungen zur antiken Literatur und Geschichte 20; Berlin and New York).

Erp Taalman Kip, A. M. van (1990) *Reader and Spectator: Problems in the Interpretation of Greek Tragedy* (Amsterdam).

(1993) 'De omstreden interpretatie van Sophocles' Electra', *Lampas* 26: 4–19.

(1996) 'Truth in tragedy – when are we entitled to doubt a character's words?', *AJP* 117: 517–36.

Errandonea, I. (1955) 'Le chœur dans l'*Électre* de Sophocle', *LÉC* 23: 367–403.

Fahr, W. (1969) Θεοὺς νομίζειν. *Zum Problem der Anfänge des Atheismus bei den Griechen* (Spudasmata 26; Hildesheim and New York).

Fantham, E. (1972) *Comparative Studies in Republican Latin Imagery* (Phoenix Suppl. 10; Toronto).

Farnell, L. R. (1896–1909) *The Cults of the Greek States* (5 vols.; Oxford).

Fauner, M. (1912) *Lyrischen Partien der griechischen Tragödie in Jamben wieder aufgenommen* (diss. Giessen).

Fehling, D. (1968) 'νυκτὸς παῖδες ἄπαιδες (A. Eum. 1034) und das sogenannte Oxymoron in der Tragödie', *Hermes* 96: 142–55.

(1969) *Die Wiederholungsfiguren und ihr Gebrauch bei den Griechen vor Gorgias* (Berlin).

Fehrentz, V. (1993) 'Der antike Agyieus', *Jahrbuch des Deutschen Archäologischen Instituts* 108: 123–96.

Ferrari, F. (1983) *Ricerche sul testo di Sofocle* (Studi di lettere, storia e filosofia 34; Pisa).

Ferrari, W. (1938) 'L'Orestea di Stesicoro', *Athenaeum* N.S. 16: 1–37.

Fialho, M. d. C. Z. (1992) *Luz e Trevas no Teatro de Sófocles* (Estudos da Cultura Clássica 6; Coimbra).

Finglass, P. J. (2005a) 'Euripides, *Phoenissae* 1427–8', *Mnemosyne* 4th ser. 58: 561–4.

(2005b) 'Erinys or Hundred-hander? Pindar, fr. 52i(a).19–21 Snell–Maehler = B3.25–7 Rutherford (*Paean* 8a)', *ZPE* 154: 40–2.

(2005c) 'Is there a *polis* in Sophocles' *Electra*?', *Phoenix* 59: 199–209.

(2007) 'A newly-discovered edition of Sophocles by Peter Elmsley', *GRBS* 47: 101–16.

Finkelberg, M. (2003) 'Motherhood or status? Editorial choices in Sophocles, *Electra* 187', *CQ* N.S. 53: 368–76.

BIBLIOGRAPHY

Fischer, U. (1965) *Der Telosgedanke in den Dramen des Aischylos* (Spudasmata 6; Hildesheim).

Fisher, N. R. E. (1992) *Hybris: a Study in the Values of Honour and Shame in Ancient Greece* (Warminster).

Fitton Brown, A. D. (1956) 'Notes on Sophocles' *Electra*', *CQ* N.S. 6: 38–9.

Fitzpatrick, D. (2001) 'Sophocles' *Tereus*', *CQ* N.S. 51: 90–101.

Focke, F. *et al.* (1929) *Genethliakon Wilhelm Schmid zum siebzigsten Geburtstag am 24. Februar 1929* (Tübinger Beiträge zur Altertumswissenschaft 5; Stuttgart).

Föllinger, S. (1996) *Differenz und Gleichheit. Das Geschlechterverhältnis in der Sicht griechischer Philosophen des 4. bis 1. Jahrhunderts v. Chr.* (Hermes Einzelschriften 74; Stuttgart).

Fontenmoing, A. (1912) (ed.) *Mélanges Henri Weil* (Paris).

Fontenrose, J. (1988) 'The cult of Apollo and the games at Delphi', in Raschke (1988) (ed.) 121–40.

Forbes Irving, P. M. C. (1990) *Metamorphosis in Greek Myths* (Oxford).

Fowler, D. P. (1989) 'First thoughts on closure: problems and prospects', *MD* 22: 75–122. [= (2000) 239–83]

    (1994) 'Postmodernism, romanticism, and classical closure', in de Jong and Sullivan (1994) (eds.) 231–56. [= (2000) 5–33]

    (1997) 'Second thoughts on closure', in Roberts, Dunn and Fowler (1997) (eds.) 3–22. [= (2000) 284–307]

    (2000) *Roman Constructions: Readings in Postmodern Latin* (Oxford).

Fowler, R. L. (1987) 'The rhetoric of desperation', *HSCP* 91: 5–38.

Fraenkel, E(rnst) (1906) *Griechische Denominativa in ihrer geschichtlichen Entwicklung und Verbreitung* (Göttingen).

    (1910–12) *Geschichte der griechischen Nomina agentis auf* –τήρ, –τωρ, –της (–τ–) (Untersuchungen zur indogermanischen Sprach- und Kulturwissenschaft 1; 2 vols.; Strassburg).

Fraenkel, E. D. M. (1912) *De media et nova comoedia quaestiones selectae* (Göttingen).

    (1917–18) 'Lyrische Daktylen', *RhM* n.F. 72: 161–97, 321–52. [= (1964) i. 165–233]

    (1920) 'Zur Form der αἶνοι', *RhM* n.F. 73: 366–70. [= (1964) i. 235–9]

    (1922) *Plautinisches im Plautus* (Philologische Untersuchungen 28; Berlin).

    (1933) 'ΑΠΕΝΘΕΙΑ ΤΛΗΣΙΚΑΡΔΙΟΣ', *Hermes* 68: 242–4.

    (1957) *Horace* (Oxford).

    (1960a) *Elementi plautini in Plauto* (Il Pensiero storico 41; transl. F. Munari; Florence).

    (1960b) 'Eine Anfangsformel attischer Reden', *Glotta* 39: 1–5. [= (1964) i. 505–10]

    (1962) *Beobachtungen zu Aristophanes* (Rome).

    (1963a) 'Attische Scheltreihen', *Glotta* 41: 285–6.

    (1963b) *Zu den Phoenissen des Euripides* (*SB München* 1; Munich).

5 WORKS CITED BY AUTHOR'S NAME WITH DATE

(1964) *Kleine Beiträge zur klassischen Philologie* (2 vols.; Rome).

(1967) 'Zwei Aias-Szenen hinter der Bühne', *MH* 24: 79–86.

(1969) 'οὐδ' αὖ μ' ἐάσεις', *MH* 26: 158.

(1977) *Due seminari romani di Eduard Fraenkel* (ed. L. E. Rossi; Sussidi Eruditi 28; Rome).

Fraser, B. (2001) 'Consider the lilies: prolepsis and the development of complementation', *Glotta* 77: 7–37.

Friis Johansen, H. (1959) *General Reflection in Tragic Rhesis: A Study in Form* (Copenhagen).

(1962) 'Sophocles 1939–59', *Lustrum* 7: 94–342.

(1964) 'Die *Elektra* des Sophokles – Versuch einer neuen Deutung', *C&M* 25: 8–32.

Führer, R. (1967) *Formproblem-Untersuchungen zu den Reden in der frühgriechischen Lyrik* (Zetemata 44; Munich).

Gager, J. G. (1992) (ed.) *Curse Tablets and Binding Spells from the Ancient World* (Oxford and New York).

Gagnepain, J. (1959) *Les Noms grecs en –ος et en –α: Contribution à l'étude du genre en indo-européen* (Études et commentaires 31; Paris).

Gallagher, R. L. (2003) 'Making the stronger argument the weaker: Euripides, *Electra* 518–44', *CQ* N.S. 53: 401–15.

García Romero, F. (2001) *El deporte en los proverbios griegos antiguos* (Nikephoros Beihefte 7; Hildesheim).

Gardiner, C. P. (1987) *The Sophoclean Chorus: a Study of Character and Function* (Iowa City).

Garland, R. (2001) *The Greek Way of Death*² (1st edn. 1985; London).

Garvie, A. F. (1969) *Aeschylus' Supplices: Play and Trilogy* (Cambridge).

(1970) 'The opening of the *Choephori*', *BICS* 17: 79–91.

Gaster, T. H. (1969) *Myth, Legend and Custom in the Old Testament: a comparative study with chapters from Sir James G. Frazer's Folklore in the Old Testament* (London).

Geisser, F. (2002) *Götter, Geister und Dämonen. Unheilsmächte bei Aischylos – zwischen Aberglauben und Theatralik* (Beiträge zur Altertumskunde 179; Munich and Leipzig).

Gellie, G. H. (1972) *Sophocles: a Reading* (Melbourne).

Gent, I. M. van (1858) 'Miscellanea Critica', *Mnemosyne* 7: 219–24.

George, C. H. (2005) *Expressions of Agency in Ancient Greek* (Cambridge).

Gernet, L. (1909) 'ΑΥΘΕΝΤΗΣ', *REG* 22: 13–32.

(1951) 'Sur le symbolisme politique en Grèce ancienne: le foyer commun', *Cahiers internationaux de sociologie* 11: 21–43. [= (1968) 382–402 ≈ (1981) 322–39]

(1955) *Droit et société dans la Grèce ancienne* (Publications de l'Institut de droit romain de l'Université de Paris 13; Paris).

(1968) *Anthropologie de la Grèce antique* (Paris).

(1981) *The Anthropology of Ancient Greece* (transl. J. Hamilton and B. Nagy; London and Baltimore).

Gershenson, D. E. (1991) *Apollo the Wolf God* (JIES Monogr. 8; McLean, Virginia).

Gibert, J. (2003) 'Apollo's sacrifice: the limits of a metaphor in Greek tragedy', *HSCP* 101 : 159–206.

Gigon, O. *et al.* (1946) Phyllobolia *für Peter Von der Mühll zum 60. Geburtstag am 1. August 1945* (Basel).

Gill, C., Postlethwaite, N., and Seaford, R. A. S. (1998) (eds.) *Reciprocity in Ancient Greece* (Oxford).

Ginouvès, R. *et al.* (1994) (eds.) *L'eau, la santé et la maladie dans le monde grec* (BCH Suppl. 28; Athens and Paris).

Gladigow, B. (1967) 'Zum Makarismos des Weisen', *Hermes* 95: 404–33.

Golden, M. (1990) *Children and Childhood in Classical Athens* (London and Baltimore).

(1998) *Sport and Society in Ancient Greece* (Cambridge).

Goldhill, S. D. (1984) 'Two notes on τέλος and related words in the *Oresteia*', *JHS* 104: 169–76.

Goldhill, S. D., and Osborne, R. (1999) (eds.) *Performance Culture and Athenian Democracy* (Cambridge).

Gomperz, T. *et al.* (1909) *Wiener Eranos zur fünfzigsten Versammlung deutscher Philologen und Schulmänner in Graz 1909* (Vienna).

Gonda, J. (1929) Δείκνυμι: *semantische Studie over den Indo-Germaanschen Wortel DEIK–* (Amsterdam).

Goodell, T. D. (1906) 'Bisected trimeters in Attic tragedy', *CPh* 1 : 145–66.

Gould, J. (1973) '*Hiketeia*', *JHS* 93, 74–103. [= (2001) 22–77 (with addenda)]

(1978) 'Dramatic character and "human intelligibility" in Greek tragedy', *PCPS* N.S. 24: 43–67. [= (2001) 78–111]

(2001) *Myth, Ritual, Memory, and Exchange: Essays in Greek Literature and Culture* (Oxford).

Goward, B. (1999) *Telling Tragedy: Narrative Technique in Aeschylus, Sophocles and Euripides* (London).

Graf, F. (1985) *Nordionische Kulte: religionsgeschichtliche und epigraphische Untersuchungen zu den Kulten von Chios, Erythrai, Klazomenai und Phokaia* (Bibliotheca Helvetica Romana 21 ; Rome).

Grant, J. N. (1987) (ed.) *Editing Greek and Latin Texts. Papers given at the Twenty-Third Annual Conference on Editorial Problems, University of Toronto, 6–7 November 1987* (New York).

Green, J. P. (2001) 'Comic cuts: snippets of action on the Greek comic stage', *BICS* 45: 37–64.

Greene, H. W. (1907) 'Soph. *Electr.* 724', *CR* 21 : 136–7.

Greenwood, L. H. G. (1953) *Aspects of Euripidean Tragedy* (Cambridge).

5 WORKS CITED BY AUTHOR'S NAME WITH DATE

Gregor, D. B. (1950) 'Sophocles *Electra* 610–11', *CR* 64: 87–8.

(1957) 'ὦ φίλτατ', *CR* N.S. 7: 14–15.

Grenfell, B. P. (1919) 'The value of papyri for the textual criticism of extant Greek authors', *JHS* 39: 16–36.

Griffin, J. (1980) *Homer on Life and Death* (Oxford).

(1999a) (ed.) *Sophocles Revisited: Essays Presented to Sir Hugh Lloyd-Jones* (Oxford).

(1999b) 'Sophocles and the democratic city', in *Griffin* (1999a) (ed.) 73–94.

Griffith, M. (1974) review of Dale (1971–83) i., *CR* N.S. 24: 211–13.

(1977) *The Authenticity of the Prometheus Bound* (Cambridge).

(1978) 'Euripides *Alkestis* 636–641', *HSCP* 82: 83–6.

(1995) 'Brilliant dynasts: power and politics in the *Oresteia*', *Class. Ant.* 14: 62–129.

(1998) 'The king and eye: the rule of the father in Greek tragedy', *PCPS* N.S. 44: 20–84.

Groeneboom, P. (1898) *Studia praesertim critica et epicritica in Sophoclis Oedipum Regem* (diss. Utrecht).

(1902) 'Ad Sophoclis Electram', in Beck *et al.* (1902) 72–8.

Gronewald, M. (1975) 'Hellenistiche Elegie: Kallimachos? P. Oxy. 14 + P. Mich. Inv. 4761 c', *ZPE* 15: 105–16.

Gross, J. G. A. (1905) *Die Stichomythie in der griechischen Tragödie und Komödie, ihre Anwendung und ihr Ursprung* (Berlin).

Gross, N. P. (1985) *Amatory Persuasion in Antiquity: Studies in Theory and Practice* (London, Newark, Toronto).

Günther, H. C. (1996) *Exercitationes Sophocleae* (Hypomnemata 109; Göttingen).

Gygli-Wyss, B. (1966) *Das nominale Polyptoton im älteren Griechisch* (Ergänzungsheft zur Zeitschrift für vergleichende Sprachforschung auf dem Gebiete der indogermanischen Sprachen 18; Göttingen).

Habicht, C. (1990) 'Euripides *Phoenissae* 1–3 and Aelius Nico of Pergamum', *GRBS* 31: 177–82.

Hähnle, A. (1929) ΓΝΩΡΙΣΜΑΤΑ (Diss. Tübingen).

Hajistephanou, C. E. (1975) *The Use of φύσις and its Cognates in Greek Tragedy with Special Reference to Character Drawing* (Nicosia).

Hale, J. R. (2003) 'Salpinx and salpinktes: trumpet and trumpeter in ancient Greece', in Basson and Dominik (2003) (eds.) 267–72.

Hall, E. M. (1989) *Inventing the Barbarian: Greek Self-Definition through Tragedy* (Oxford).

(1999a) 'Sophocles' *Electra* in Britain', in Griffin (1999a) (ed.) 261–306.

(1999b) 'Actor's song in tragedy', in Goldhill and Osborne (1999) (eds.) 96–122.

Hall, E. M., and Macintosh, F. (2005) *Greek Tragedy and the British Theatre 1660–1914* (Oxford).

BIBLIOGRAPHY

Hall, J. M. (1995) 'How Argive was the "Argive" Heraion? The political and cultic geography of the Argive plain, 900–400 BC', *AJA* 99: 577–613.

(1997) *Ethnic Identity in Greek Antiquity* (Cambridge).

Halliwell, S. (1991) 'The uses of laughter in Greek culture', *CQ* N.S. 41: 279–96.

Hamdorf, F. W. (1964) *Griechische Kultpersonifikationen der vorhellenistischen Zeit* (Mainz).

Hamilton, R. (1978) 'Announced entrances in Greek tragedy', *HSCP* 82: 63–82.

(1987) 'Cries within the tragic skene', *AJP* 108: 585–99.

Hancock, J. L. (1917) *Studies in Stichomythia* (Chicago).

Handley, E. W. (1993) 'Aristophanes and his theatre', in Bremer and Handley (1993) (eds.) 97–117.

Hansen, M. H. (1980) 'Seven hundred *archai* in classical Athens', *GRBS* 21: 151–73.

Hansen, W. (2000) 'The winning of Hippodameia', *TAPA* 130: 19–40.

(2002) *Ariadne's Thread. A Guide to International Tales Found in Classical Literature* (London and Ithaca).

Hanslik, R. (1949) 'Panopeus (2)', *RE* 18/3: 649.

Harder, M. A., Regtuit, R. F., and Wakker, G. C. (2002) (eds.) *Hellenistic Epigrams* (Hellenistica Groningana 6; Leuven, Paris, Sterling Virginia).

Harris, H. A. (1968) 'The starting-gate for chariots at Olympia', *G&R* 2nd ser. 15: 113–26.

Harrison, E. (1933) 'Elmsley's law', *PCPS* 156: 10–11.

(1943) 'Interlinear hiatus in tragic trimeters II', *CR* 57: 61–3.

Harvey, J. (1977) 'A note on Shakespeare and Sophocles', *Essays in Criticism* 27: 259–70.

Haslam, M. W. (1975a) 'Phoenician Women decapitated', in Parsons *et al.* (1975) (eds.) 161–6.

(1975b) 'The authenticity of Euripides, *Phoenissae* 1–2 and Sophocles, *Electra* 1', *GRBS* 16: 149–75.

(1976) 'Interpolations in the *Phoenissae*: papyrus evidence', *CQ* N.S. 26: 4–10.

(1979) 'O suitably-attired-in-leather-boots. Interpolations in Greek tragedy', in Bowersock *et al.* (1979) (eds.) 91–100.

Hasse, E. (1891) *Ueber den Dual bei den attischen Dramatikern* (Beilage zum Programm des Königl. Gymnasiums zu Bartenstein; Bartenstein).

Haupt, M. (1865a) *Ind. Lect. Berol. Aest.* [= (1875–6) ii. 286–96]

(1865b) *Ind. Lect. Berol. Hib.* [= (1875–6) ii. 297–312]

(1875–6) *Opuscula* (ed. E. F. W. U. von Wilamowitz-Moellendorff; 3 vols.; Leipzig).

Headlam, W. G. (1891) *On Editing Aeschylus* (London).

(1902) 'Transposition of words in MSS', *CR* 16: 243–56.

5 WORKS CITED BY AUTHOR'S NAME WITH DATE

Heath, B. (1762) *Notae sive lectiones ad Sophoclem*, in *Notae sive lectiones ad tragicorum Graecorum veterum Aeschyli Sophoclis Euripidis quae supersunt dramata deperditorumque relliquias* (Oxford).

Heath, M. (1987) *The Poetics of Greek Tragedy* (London).

Heer, C. de (1969) *MAKAP – EYΔAIMΩN – OΛBIOΣ – EΥΤΥΧΗΣ. A Study of the Semantic Field denoting Happiness in Ancient Greek to the End of the 5th Century B.C.* (Amsterdam).

Heimsoeth, F. (1865) *Kritische Studien zu den griechischen Tragödien* (Bonn).

(1866) 'Commentatio critica de diversa diversorum mendorum emendatione', *Ind. Schol. Bonn Hib.* iii–xxi.

(1869) 'De necessaria in re critica vigilantia, perseverantia atque audacia', *Ind. Schol. Bonn Hib.* iii–xviii.

(1872a) 'De Madvigii Hauniensis Adversariis Criticis commentatio altera', *Ind. Schol. Bonn Aest.* iii–xxx.

(1872b) 'De Interpolationibus IV', *Ind. Schol. Bonn Hib.* iii–xix.

(1873) 'De Interpolationibus V', *Ind. Schol. Bonn Aest.* iii–xvi.

Heller, J. L. (1974) (ed.) *Serta Turyniana. Studies in Greek Literature and Palaeography in Honor of Alexander Turyn* (London, Urbana, Chicago).

Helly, B. (1990) Ένα ανέκδοτο ψήφισμα της Τρίκκης για τον αξιωματικό του μακεδονικού στρατού Ορθότιμο από την Τυλισσό της Κρήτης', *Θεσσαλικό Ημερολόγιο* 17: 95–114. [transl. T. Papademetriou-Demoula]

(1991) 'Décret de Trikka pour Orthotimos de Tylissos, officier Macédonien', *BCH* 115: 325–43.

Henrichs, A. (1976) 'Despoina Kybele: ein Beitrag zur religiösen Namenkunde', *HSCP* 80: 253–86.

(1983) 'The "sobriety" of Oedipus: Sophocles *OC* 100 misunderstood', *HSCP* 87: 87–100.

(1989) 'Zur Perhorreszierung des Wassers der Styx bei Aischylos und Vergil', *ZPE* 78: 1–29.

(1991) 'Namenlosigkeit und Euphemismus: Zur Ambivalenz der chthonischen Mächte im attischen Drama', in Hofmann (1991) (ed.) 161–201.

(1993) 'The tomb of Aias and the prospect of hero cult in Sophokles', *Class. Ant.* 12: 165–80.

(1994–5) '"Why should I dance?" Choral self-referentiality in Greek tragedy', *Arion* 3.1: 56–111.

(2000) 'Drama and *dromena*: bloodshed, violence, and sacrificial metaphor in Euripides', *HSCP* 100: 173–88.

Hense, K. O. F. (1880) *Studien zu Sophokles* (Leipzig).

Hepding, H. (1922) 'Krisos', *RE* 11/2: 1893.

Hermann, J. G. J. (1816) *Elementa Doctrinae Metricae* (Leipzig).

(1827–77) *Opuscula* (8 vols.; Leipzig).

591

BIBLIOGRAPHY

(1831) review of Dissen's edition of Pindar, *Seebodens und Jahns Jahrbüchern* 1.
    B 1. Hft.: 44–91. [= (1827–77) vi. 3–69]

Herter, H. (1976) 'Hermes: Ursprung und Wesen eines griechischen Gottes',
    RhM n.F. 119: 193–241.

Herwerden, H. van (1862) *Exercitationes Criticae in Poeticis et Prosaicis quibusdam
    Atticorum Monumentis* (The Hague).

    (1868) *Analecta Critica ad Thucydidem, Lysiam, Sophoclem, Aristophanem et Comico-
    rum Graecorum Fragmenta* (Utrecht).

    (1872) *Studia Critica in Poetas Scenicos Graecorum* (Amsterdam).

    (1878) 'Ad poetas scenicos Graecorum', *Mnemosyne* 2nd ser. 6: 264–82.

    (1886) *Excerpta e poetis graecis*² (1st edn. 1873; Utrecht).

    (1887) *Lucubrationes Sophocleae* (Utrecht).

    (1899) 'Varia ad varios', *Mnemosyne* 2nd ser. 27: 378–98.

Hester, D. A. (1981) 'Some deceptive oracles: Sophocles, *Electra* 32–7',
    Antichthon 15: 15–25.

Heubeck, A. (1971) 'Amphiaraos', *Die Sprache* 17: 8–22.

Heubner, H. (1961) 'Elektra oder Chrysothemis?', *RhM* n.F. 104: 152–6.

    (1963) 'Zu Sophokles, *Elektra* 1318 ff.', *Hermes* 91: 377–80.

Hinds, A. E. (1980) 'Binary action in Sophocles', *Hermathena* 129: 51–7.

Hirzel, R. R. (1902) *Der Eid: ein Beitrag zu seiner Geschichte* (Leipzig).

    (1907–10) *Die Talion* (Philologus Suppl. 11.4: 405–82).

Hodkinson, S. (2000) *Property and Wealth in Classical Sparta* (London).

Hofmann, H. (1991) (ed.) *Fragmenta Dramatica: Beiträge zur Interpretation der
    griechischen Tragikerfragmente und ihrer Wirkungsgeschichte* (Festschrift Radt;
    Göttingen).

Holford-Strevens, L. (1999) 'Sophocles at Rome', in Griffin (1999a) (ed.) 219–
    59.

    (2003) *Aulus Gellius: an Antonine Scholar and his Achievement*² (1st edn. London
    1988; Oxford).

Holwerda, D. (1955) *Commentatio de vocis quae est φύσις vi atque usu praesertim in
    graecitate Aristotele anteriore* (Groningen).

Hooker, J. T. (1979) 'The unity of Alcman's Partheneion', *RhM* n.F. 122: 211–
    21. [= (1996) 609–19]

    (1996) *Scripta Minora. Selected Essays on Minoan, Mycenaean, Homeric
    and Classical Greek Subjects* (ed. F. Amory, P. Considine, S. Hooker;
    Amsterdam).

Hopkinson, N. (1982) 'Juxtaposed prosodic variants in Greek and Latin poetry',
    Glotta 60: 162–77.

Hornblower, S. (2004) *Thucydides and Pindar. Historical Narrative and the World of
    Epinikian Poetry* (Oxford).

Horsfall, N. M. (1995a) (ed.) *A Companion to the Study of Virgil* (Mnem. Suppl.
    151; Leiden, Cologne, New York).

5 WORKS CITED BY AUTHOR'S NAME WITH DATE

(1995b) *'Aeneid* book 12: justice and judgement', in Horsfall (1995a) (ed.) 192–216.

Horsley, G. H. R. (1980) *'Sophokles*, Elektra, 1361', *CJ* 75: 299–300.

Horst, P. W. van der (1994) 'Silent prayer in antiquity', *Numen* 41: 1–25.

Hose, M. (1990–1) *Studien zum Chor bei Euripides* (Beiträge zur Altertumskunde 10, 20; 2 vols.; Stuttgart).

(1994) 'Zur Elision des αι im Tragödienvers', *Hermes* 122: 32–43.

Housman, A. E. (1887) 'On Soph. *Electr.* 564, and Eur. *I.T.* 15 and 35', *CR* 1: 240–1. [= (1972) i. 10–13]

(1888) 'σωφρόνη', *CR* 2: 242–5. [= (1972) i. 24–8]

(1892) 'Sophoclea', *JPh* 20: 25–48. [= (1972) i. 209–26]

(1972) *The Classical Papers of A. E. Housman* (3 vols.; ed. J. Diggle and F. R. D. Goodyear; Cambridge).

Hubbard, T. K. (1992) 'Remaking myth and rewriting history: cult tradition in Pindar's *Ninth Nemean*', *HSCP* 94: 77–111.

Hutchinson, G. O. (1999) 'Sophocles and time', in Griffin (1999a) (ed.) 47–72.

Huys, M. (1986) 'The plotting scene in Euripides' *Alexandros*: an interpretation of fr. 23, 23A, 23B, 43 Sn. (cf. hypothesis, ll. 23–25)', *ZPE* 62: 9–36.

(1995) *The Tale of the Hero who was Exposed at Birth in Euripidean Tragedy: a Study of Motifs* (Symbolae Facultatis Litterarum Lovaniensis, ser. A vol. 20; Leuven).

Itsumi, K. (1982) 'The "choriambic dimeter" of Euripides', *CQ* N.S. 32: 59–74.

(1984) 'The glyconic in tragedy', *CQ* N.S. 34: 66–82.

(1991–3) 'Enoplian in tragedy', *BICS* 38: 243–61.

Jachmann, G. (1936) 'Binneninterpolation. I. Teil', Nachrichten von der Gesellschaft der Wissenschaften zu Göttingen, phil.–hist. Klasse, n.F. 1.7: 123–44. [= (1982) 528–49]

(1982) *Textgeschichtliche Studien* (ed. C. Grilka; Beiträge zur klassichen Philologie 143; Königstein).

Jackson, J. (1955) *Marginalia Scaenica* (ed. E. D. M. Fraenkel; Oxford).

Jacobson, H. (1982) 'Ritualistic formulae in Greek dramatic texts', *CQ* N.S. 32: 233–4.

(1983) *The* Exagoge *of Ezekiel* (Cambridge).

Jacoby, F. (1949) *Atthis: The Local Chronicles of Ancient Athens* (Oxford).

Jacquemin, A. (1999) *Offrandes monumentales à Delphes* (Bibliothèque des écoles françaises d'Athènes et de Rome 304; Paris).

Jacquinod, B. (1997) 'Sur le rôle pragmatique de καίτοι', in Rijksbaron (1997) (ed.) 131–49.

Jax, K. (1933) *Die weibliche Schönheit in der griechischen Dichtung* (Innsbruck).

Jaya-Suriya, B. (1966) 'Sophocles, *Electra* 361–4', *CR* N.S. 16: 147.

Jenkyns, R. H. A. (1982) *Three Classical Poets: Sappho, Catullus and Juvenal* (London).

BIBLIOGRAPHY

Jenner, E. A. B. (1986) 'Further speculations on Ibycus and the epinician ode: S 220, S 176, and the "Bellerophon" ode', *BICS* 33: 59–66.

Jens, W. (1971) *Die Bauformen der griechischen Tragödie* (Beihefte zu Poetica 6; Munich).

Jocelyn, H. D. (1966) 'Cicero, *Ad Atticum* i. 18. 1', *CR* N.S. 16: 149–50.

(1993) (ed.) Tria Lustra: *Essays and Notes Presented to John Pinsent* (Liverpool Classical Papers 3; Liverpool).

Jones, J. (1962) *On Aristotle and Greek Tragedy* (London).

Jong, I. J. F. de (1987) *Narrators and Focalisers: the Presentation of the Story in the* Iliad (Amsterdam).

(1991) *Narrative in Drama: the Art of the Euripidean Messenger-Speech* (Mnem. Suppl. 116; Leiden, New York, Copenhagen, Cologne).

(1994) 'πιστὰ τεκμήρια in Soph. *El.* 774', *Mnemosyne* 4th ser. 47 (1994): 679–81.

(1997) 'γάρ introducing embedded narratives', in Rijksbaron (1997) (ed.) 175–85.

(1999) (ed.) *Homer: Critical Assessments* (4 vols.; London and New York).

(2004) 'Sophocles' in de Jong *et al.* (2004) (eds.) 255–68.

Jong, I. J. F. de, and Sullivan, J. P. (1994) (eds.) *Modern Critical Theory and Classical Literature* (Mnem. Suppl. 130; Leiden, Cologne, New York).

Jong, I. J. F. de, and Rijksbaron, A. (2006) (eds.) *Sophocles and the Greek Language. Aspects of Diction, Syntax and Pragmatics* (Mnem. Suppl. 269; Leiden and Boston).

Jong, I. J. F. de, Nünlist, R., and Bowie, A. M. (2004) (eds.) *Narrators, Narratees, and Narrative in Ancient Greek Literature* (Studies in Ancient Greek Narrative 1; Mnem. Suppl. 257; Leiden and Boston).

Jordan, D. R. (1979) 'An appeal to the sun for vengeance (Inscriptions de Délos)', *BCH* 103: 521–5.

Jost, M. (1985) *Sanctuaires et cultes d'Arcadie* (Études peloponnésiennes 9; Paris).

Juffras, D. M. (1991) 'Sophocles' *Electra* 973–85 and tyrannicide', *TAPA* 121: 99–108.

Kaczko, S. (2002) 'ἡμῖν, ἥμιν, ἦμιν da Omero a Sofocle: problemi linguistici e editoriali', *RFIC* 130: 257–98.

Kahn, L. (1979) 'Hermès, la frontière et l'identité ambiguë', *Ktema* 4: 201–11.

Kaibel, G. (1884) 'Sententiarum liber tertius', *Hermes* 19: 246–63.

Kaimio, M. (1970) *The Chorus of Greek Drama within the Light of the Person and Number Used* (Commentationes Humanarum Litterarum 46; Helsinki).

(1977) *Characterisation of Sound in Early Greek Literature* (Commentationes Humanarum Litterarum 53; Helsinki).

(1988) *Physical Contact in Greek Tragedy: a Study of Stage Conventions* (Helsinki).

5 WORKS CITED BY AUTHOR'S NAME WITH DATE

Kamerbeek, J. C. (1972) 'Sophoclea VI: notes on the *Electra*', *Mnemosyne* 4th ser. 25: 28–41.

—— (1974) 'Comments on some passages of Sophocles' *Electra*', in Heller (1974) (ed.) 268–74.

Kannicht, R. (1957) *Untersuchungen zu Form und Funktion des Amoibaion in der attischen Tragödie* (diss. Heidelberg). [n.v.]

—— (1973) review of Korzeniewski (1968), *Gnomon* 45: 113–34. [= (1996) 153–79]

—— (1996) *Paradeigmata: Aufsätze zur griechischen Poesie* (Suppl. zu den *SB Heidelberg* 10; ed. L. Käppel and E. A. Schmidt; Heidelberg).

Kassel, R. (1954) *Quomodo quibus locis apud veteres scriptores graecos infantes atque parvuli pueri inducantur describantur commemorentur* (Würzburg). [= (1991) 1–73]

—— (1958) *Untersuchungen zur griechischen und römischen Konsolationsliteratur* (Zetemata 18; Munich).

—— (1979) 'Ein neues Philemonfragment', *ZPE* 36: 15–21. [= (1991) 303–9]

—— (1991) *Kleine Schriften* (ed. H.-G. Nesselrath; Berlin and New York).

Katsouris, A. G. (1997) Πρόλογος δραματική τεχνική (Ioannina).

Kefalidou, E. (1996) ΝΙΚΗΤΗΣ: Εικονογραφική μελέτη του αρχαίου ελληνικού αθλητισμού (Thessaloniki).

Kells, J. H. (1963) 'Sophocles, *Philoctetes* 1140–5', *CR* N.S. 13: 7–9.

—— (1966) 'Sophocles, *Electra* 1243–57', *CR* N.S. 16: 255–9.

—— (1977) 'The "added oath" in Sophocles' *Electra* again', *BICS* 24: 88.

—— (1986) 'Sophocles' *Electra* revisited', in Betts *et al.* (1986–8) (eds.) i. 153–60.

Kelly, M. (1966) (ed.) *For Service to Classical Studies. Essays in Honour of Francis Letters* (Melbourne, Canberra, Sydney).

Kemmer, E. (1903) *Die polare Ausdrucksweise in der griechischen Literatur* (Beiträge zur historischen Syntax der griechischen Sprache 15; Würzburg).

Kerrigan, J. (1996) *Revenge Tragedy: Aeschylus to Armageddon* (Oxford).

Kessels, A. H. M. (1973) *Studies on the Dream in Greek Literature* (Utrecht).

Kiefner, G. (1964) *Die Versparung: Untersuchungen zu einer Stilfigur der dichterischen Rhetorik am Beispiel der griechischen Tragödie (unter Berücksichtigung des σχῆμα ἀπὸ κοινοῦ)* (Klassisch-philologische Studien 25; Wiesbaden).

Kienzle, E. (1936) *Der Lobpreis von Städten und Ländern in der älteren griechischen Dichtung* (diss. Kallmünz).

Kirkwood, G. M. (1942) 'Two structural features of Sophocles' *Electra*', *TAPA* 73: 86–95.

Kitzinger, R. (1991) 'Why mourning becomes Electra', *Cl. Ant.* 10: 298–327.

Klumbach, H. (1937) *Tarentiner Grabkunst* (Tübinger Forschungen zur Archäologie und Kunstgeschichte 13; Reutlingen).

Knox, B. M. W. (1964) *The Heroic Temper: Studies in Sophoclean Tragedy* (Sather Classical Lectures 35; Berkeley and Los Angeles).

(1968) review of T. H. Banks (transl.) *Sophocles. Four Plays* (London and New York 1966), *JHS* 88: 157–8.

(1983) 'Sophocles and the *polis*', in de Romilly (1983) (ed.) 1–27.

Köhler, W. (1913) *Die Versbrechung bei den griechischen Tragikern* (Darmstadt).

Kõiv, M. (2003) *Ancient Tradition and Early Greek History. The Origins of States in Early-Archaic Sparta, Argos and Corinth* (Tallinn).

Kolster, W. H. (1850) 'Zu Sophokles *Elektra*', *Philologus* 5: 193–224, 601–42.

Kopff, E. C. (1993) review of the Sophocles OCT by Lloyd-Jones and Wilson (1990), and Davies's *Trachiniae* (1990), *AJP* 114: 155–63.

Korzeniewski, D. (1968) *Griechische Metrik* (Darmstadt).

Kossatz-Deissmann, A. (1978) *Dramen des Aischylos auf westgriechischen Vasen* (Schriften zur antiken Mythologie 4; Mainz).

Kovacs, P. D. (1980) 'Shame, pleasure, and honor in Phaedra's great speech (Euripides, *Hippolytus* 375–87)', *AJP* 101 : 287–303.

(1987) 'Treading the circle warily: literary criticism and the text of Euripides', *TAPA* 117: 257–70.

(1993) 'Zeus in Euripides' *Medea*', *AJP* 114: 45–70.

(1994) *Euripidea* (Mnem. Suppl. 132; Leiden, New York, Cologne).

Kraay, C. M. (1976) *Archaic and Classical Greek Coins* (London).

Kranz, W. (1933) *Stasimon: Untersuchungen zu Form und Gehalt der griechischen Tragödie* (Berlin).

Kraus, W. (1957) *Strophengestaltung in der griechischen Tragödie, 1. Aischylos und Sophokles* (*SB Wien* 231.4; Vienna).

Krause, J. (1976) *ALLOTE ALLOS. Untersuchungen zum Motiv des Schicksalswechsels in der griechischen Dichtung bis Euripides* (Tuduv Studien 4; Munich).

Kruse, G. (1927a) 'Loxias', *RE* 13/2: 1532–3.

(1927b) 'Lykeios', *RE* 13/2: 2268–70.

Kugler, L. (1905) *De Sophoclis quae vocantur abusionibus* (Göttingen).

Kuhlmann, P. (1997–8) 'Εἷς als Indefinitpronomen im Griechischen in diachroner Sicht', *Glotta* 74: 76–93.

Kujọrẹ, Ọ (1973) *Greek Polymorphic Presents. A Study of their Development and Functional Tendencies* (Amsterdam).

Kurtz, D. C. (1975) *Athenian White Lekythoi: Patterns and Painters* (Oxford).

Kurtz, D. C., and Boardman, J. (1971) *Greek Burial Customs* (London).

Kvíčala, J. (1864) *Beiträge zur Kritik und Erklärung des Sophokles*, SB Wien 45.391–494.

Lachmann, K. K. F. W. (1822) *De Mensura Tragoediarum Liber Singularis* (Berlin).

Lacombrade, C. (1959) 'En marge de Sophocle: une course de quadriges aux jeux pythiques', *Pallas* 8: 5–14.

Lacroix, L. (1976) 'La légende de Pélops et son iconographie', *BCH* 100: 327–41.

5 WORKS CITED BY AUTHOR'S NAME WITH DATE

Lader, F. (1909) 'Die römische Tragödie *Octavia* und die *Elektra* des Sophokles', in Gomperz *et al.* (1909) 189–99.

Lange, C. C. L. (1859) *De Sophoclis Electrae Stasimo Secundo commentatio* (Giessen). (1860) *De locis nonnullis Sophocleis emendandis commentatio* (Giessen).

Langholf, V. (1971) *Die Gebete bei Euripides und die zeitliche Folge der Tragödien* (Hypomnemata 32; Göttingen).

Lanza, L., and Fort, L. (1991) *Sofocle: Problemi di tradizione indiretta* (Saggi e materiali universitari 16; Padua).

Laroche, E. (1949) *Histoire de la racine NEM– en grec ancien* (Études et commentaires 6; Paris).

Lattimore, R. (1942) *Themes in Greek and Latin Epitaphs* (Illinois Studies in Languages and Literature 28.1–2; Urbana).

Lausberg, H. (1998) *Handbook of Literary Rhetoric* (transl. M. T. Bliss *et al.*; ed. D. E. Orton *et al.*; Leiden, Boston, Cologne).

Lautensach, O. (1899) *Grammatische Studien zu den griechischen Tragikern und Komikern. Augment und Reduplikation* (Hannover and Leipzig).
(1916) 'Grammatische Studien zu den attischen Tragikern und Komikern. Konjunktiv und Optativ', *Glotta* 7: 92–116.

Lee, A. van der (1957) 'Zum literarischen Motiv der Vatersuche', *Verhandelingen der Koninklijke Nederlandse Akademie van Wetenschappen, afd. letterkunde*, Nieuwe Reeks 53/3.

Lee, H. M. (1986) 'Pindar *Olympian* 3.33–34: "the twelve-turned terma" and the length of the four-horse chariot race', *AJP* 107: 162–74.

Leigh, M. (1997) *Lucan: Spectacle and Engagement* (Oxford).

Lejeune, M. (1939) *Les Adverbes grecs en –θεν* (Bordeaux).

Leo, F. (1908) *Der Monolog im Drama. Ein Beitrag zur griechisch-römischen Poetik* (Abhandlungen der königlichen Gesellschaft der Wissenschaften zu Göttingen, phil.–hist. Klasse, n.F. 10.5; Berlin).

Lieshout, R. G. A. van (1980) *Greeks on Dreams* (Utrecht).

Lilley, D. J. (1975) 'Sophocles, *Electra* 610–11', *CQ* N.S. 25: 309–11.

Lilja, S. (1976) *Dogs in Ancient Greek Poetry* (Commentationes Humanarum Litterarum 56; Helsinki).

Linforth, I. M. (1963) 'Electra's day in the tragedy of Sophocles', *Univ. Cal. Publ. in Cl. Phil.* 19: 89–125.

Lloyd, A. B. (1997) (ed.) *What is a God? Studies in the Nature of Greek Divinity* (London).

Lloyd, G. E. R. (1966) *Polarity and Analogy: Two Types of Argumentation in Early Greek Thought* (Cambridge).

Lloyd, M. A. (1992) *The Agon in Euripides* (Oxford).
(1999) 'The tragic aorist', *CQ* N.S. 49: 24–45.
(2006) 'Sophocles in the light of face-threat politeness theory', in De Jong and Rijksbaron (2006) (eds.) 225–39.

BIBLIOGRAPHY

Lloyd-Jones, P. H. J. (1954) 'Sophoclea', *CQ* N.S. 4: 91–5. [= (1990a) 361–7]

  (1959) review of Dain's edition of Sophocles, vol. ii (Paris 1958) *Gnomon* 31: 478–81.

  (1960) 'Three notes on Aeschylus' *Agamemnon*', *RhM* n.F. 103: 76–80. [= (1990a) 305–9]

  (1963) 'The seal of Posidippus', *JHS* 83: 75–99. [= (1990b) 158–95]

  (1964a) 'The *Supplices* of Aeschylus: the new date and old problems', *AC* 33: 356–74. [= (1990a) 262–77 = E. Segal (1983) (ed.) 42–56]

  (1964b) 'Theocritus 14.1 again', *RBPh* 42: 96–7.

  (1965) 'A problem in the Tebtunis *Inachus*-fragment', *CR* N.S. 15: 241–3. [= (1990a) 397–400]

  (1969a) 'Agamemnonea', *HSCP* 73: 97–104. [= (1990a) 310–17]

  (1969b) review of Vögler (1967), *CR* N.S. 19: 36–8.

  (1972a) 'Tycho von Wilamowitz-Moellendorff on the dramatic technique of Sophocles', *CQ* N.S. 22: 214–28. [= (1982) 219–37 = (1990a) 401–18]

  (1972b) 'Notes on Sophocles' *Trachiniae*', *YCS* 22: 263–70. [= (1990a) 390–6]

  (1975) review of Kells's commentary, *CR* N.S. 25: 10–12.

  (1978) review of Dawe's first edition and his *STS* vol. i, *CR* N.S. 28: 214–21.

  (1981) 'Notes on P.Köln III 125 (Aeschylus, *Psychagogoi*?)', *ZPE* 42: 21–2. [= (1990a) 355–6]

  (1982) *Blood for the Ghosts: Classical Influences in the Nineteenth and Twentieth Centuries* (London).

  (1983a) 'Artemis and Iphigeneia', *JHS* 103: 87–102. [= (1990b) 306–30]

  (1983b) review of Moorhouse, *CR* N.S. 33: 171–3.

  (1986) review of Dawe's second edition, *CR* N.S. 36: 10–12.

  (1989) 'The two Electras: Hofmannsthal's *Elektra* as a Goethean drama', *Publications of the English Goethe Society* 59: 16–34 [= (1991) 155–71]

  (1990a) *Greek Epic, Lyric, and Tragedy: the Academic Papers of Sir Hugh Lloyd-Jones* (Oxford).

  (1990b) *Greek Comedy, Hellenistic Literature, Greek Religion, and Miscellanea: the Academic Papers of Sir Hugh Lloyd-Jones* (Oxford).

  (1990c) 'Erinyes, Semnai Theai, Eumenides', in Craik (1990) (ed.) 203–11. [= (2005) 90–9]

  (1991) *Greek in a Cold Climate* (London).

  (1992) 'Helikaon (Sophocles, fr. 10e; fr. 210, 47–53)', *ZPE* 92: 55–8. [= (2005) 106–9]

  (1993a) 'OMMA in Sophocles, *Electra* 902 and *Oedipus Tyrannus* 81' in Most *et al.* (1993) (eds.) 300–4. [= (2005) 110–14]

  (1993b) review of West's Teubner Aeschylus and West (1990), *Gnomon* 65: 1–11. [= (2005) 163–80]

(2005) *The Further Academic Papers of Sir Hugh Lloyd-Jones* (Oxford).

Loenen, D. (1960) 'Eusebeia en de cardinale deugden. Een studie over de functie van eusebeia in het leven der grieken en haar verhouding tot de ethiek', *Mededelingen der Koninklijke Nederlandse Akademie van Wetenschappen, Afd. Letterkunde*, Nieuwe Reeks 23/4: 77–164 [1–94].

Long, A. A. (1964a) 'Sophocles, *Electra* 1251–2', *CR* N.S. 14: 130–2.

(1964b) 'Sophocles *Ajax* 68–70. A reply to Professor Eduard Fraenkel', *MH* 21: 228–31.

(1968) *Language and Thought in Sophocles: A Study of Abstract Nouns and Poetic Technique* (University of London Classical Studies 6; London).

Longman, G. A. (1954) 'Sophocles, *Electra* 1478', *CR* N.S. 4: 192–4.

Loomis, C. G. (1948) *White Magic: an Introduction to the Folklore of Christian Legend* (Mediaeval Academy of America Publications 52; Cambridge, Mass.).

López Férez, J. A. (1999) (ed.) *Desde los poemas homéricos hasta la prosa griega del siglo IV d.C. Veintiséis estudios filológicos* (Estudios de filología griega 4; Madrid).

Loraux, N. (1988) 'De l'amnistie et de son contraire', in Yerushalmi *et al.* (1988) 23–48. [≈ (1997) 146–72 ≈ (1998) 84–109 ≈ (2002) 145–69]

(1997) *La cité divisée: l'oublié dans la mémoire d'Athènes* (Paris).

(1998) *Mothers in Mourning* (transl. C. Pache; London and Ithaca).

(2002) *The Divided City: On Memory and Forgetting in Ancient Athens* (transl. C. Pache with J. Fort; New York).

Lossau, M. (1994) 'Retter-Licht (φόως, φάος) bei Homer und den Tragikern', *Eranos* 92: 85–92.

Lowe, J. C. B. (1973) 'γ᾿ ἄρα, γ᾿ ἄρα and τἄρα', *Glotta* 51: 34–64.

Lowe, N. (2000) *The Classical Plot and the Invention of Western Narrative* (Cambridge).

Ludwich, A. (1884–5) *Aristarchs Homerische Textkritik nach den Fragmenten des Didymos* (Leipzig; 2 vols.).

Maas, P. (1913) 'Zu Aristophanes Thesmophoriazusen', *RhM* n.F. 68: 355–60. [= (1973) 54–8]

(1929) *Griechische Metrik²* (with addenda to 1st edn. 1923; Einleitung in die Altertumswissenschaft (ed. A. Gercke and E. Norden) 1.7; Leipzig and Berlin).

(1938) review of De Marco (1937), *BZ* 38: 200.

(1962) *Greek Metre* (transl. P. H. J. Lloyd-Jones; Oxford).

(1973) *Kleine Schriften* (ed. W. Buchwald; Munich).

Machin, A. (1988) 'Oreste ou l'échec glorieux: Sophocle, *Électre* 741–745', *Pallas* 34: 45–60.

Machin, A., and Perneé, L. (1993) (eds.) *Sophocle: le texte, les personnages. Actes du colloque international d'Aix-en-Provence, 10, 11 et 12 janvier 1992* (Provence).

Macintosh, F., Michelakis, P., Hall, E. M., Taplin, O. P. (2005) (eds.) *Agamemnon in Performance 458 BC to AD 2004* (Oxford).

Mackenzie, M. M., and Roueché, C. (1989) (eds.) *Images of Antiquity. Papers Presented to Joyce Reynolds on the Occasion of her 70th Birthday* (PCPS Suppl. 16; Cambridge).

MacLachlan, B. (1993) *The Age of Grace.* Charis *in Early Greek Poetry* (Princeton, NJ).

MacLeod, L. (2001) *Dolos and Dike in Sophokles' Elektra* (Mnem. Suppl. 219; Leiden, Boston, Cologne).

Mähly, J. (1889) 'Sophokleïsches', in Mähly *et al.* (1889) 22–44.

Mähly, J. *et al.* (1889) *Einladungs-Schrift zur Feier des Dreihundertjährigen Bestandes des Gymnasiums Basel 26.–27. September 1889* (Basel).

Malten, L. (1912) 'Hephaistos', *RE* 8/1: 311–66.

Manakidou, H. P. (1994) Παραστάσεις με άρματα· παρατηρήσεις στην εικονογραφία τους (Thessalonica).

Manieri, A. (1998) *L'Immagine poetica nella teoria degli antichi* (Philologia e Critica 82; Pisa and Rome).

Mantziou, M. (1995) 'The palace door in Sophocles' *Electra*', in Rybowska and Witczak (1995) (eds.) 189–95.

March, J. (1987) *The Creative Poet: Studies on the Treatment of Myths in Greek Poetry* (BICS Suppl. 49; London).

  (2004) '*Electra*: introduction', in the preface to the reprint of Jebb's edition, 31–56.

Marchetti, P. (1994) 'Recherches sur les mythes et la topographie d'Argos. II. Présentation du site. III. Le téménos de Zeus', *BCH* 118: 131–60.

Marcovich, M. (1984) *Three-Word Trimeter in Greek Tragedy* (Beiträge zur klassischen Philologie Heft 158; Königstein).

Markantonatos, A. (2002) *Tragic Narrative: a Narratological Study of Sophocles' Oedipus at Colonus* (Untersuchungen zur antiken Literatur und Geschichte 63; Berlin and New York).

Markantonatos, G. (1976) 'Dramatic irony in the *Electra* of Sophocles', *Platon* 28: 147–50.

Marshall, C. W. (1994) 'The rule of three actors in practice', *Text and Presentation* 15: 53–61.

  (2006) 'How to write a messenger speech (Sophocles, *Electra* 680–762)', in Davidson *et al.* (2006) (eds.) 203–21.

Martin, A. (1898) 'Les jeux pythiques d'après l'*Électre* de Sophocle', in Fontenmoing (1898) (ed.) 273–81.

Martina, A. (1975) *Il riconoscimento di Oreste nelle* Coefore *e nelle due* Elettre (Rome).

Mastronarde, D. J. (1979) *Contact and Discontinuity: Some Conventions of Speech and Action on the Greek Tragic Stage (Univ. Cal. Publ. in Cl. Phil.* 21; Berkeley, Los Angeles, London).

Matthiae, A. H. (1825–7) *Ausführliche griechische Grammatik²* (3 vols.; Leipzig).

Matthiae, I. C. (1832) *Quaestiones Sophocleae* (Leipzig).

5 WORKS CITED BY AUTHOR'S NAME WITH DATE

Matthiessen, K. (1964) *Elektra, Taurische Iphigenie und Helena: Untersuchungen zur Chronologie und zur dramatischen Form im Spätwerk des Euripides* (Hypomnemata 4; Göttingen).

Mauduit, C. (1994) 'Bain et libations: à propos de deux emplois de λουτρά dans l'*Électre* de Sophocle', in Ginouvès *et al.* (1994) (eds.) 131–45.

McAuslan, I., and Walcot, P. (1993) (eds.) *Greek Tragedy* (Greece and Rome studies 2; Oxford).

McDevitt, A. S. (1974) 'Sophocles' *Electra* 495–7', *RhM* n.F. 117: 181–2.

(1981) '*Antilabe* in Sophoclean *kommoi*', *RhM* n.F. 124: 19–28.

(1994) 'Horses for courses: a note on Bacchylides 3.3–4', *Hermes* 122: 502–3.

McInerney, J. (1999) *The Folds of Parnassos. Land and Ethnicity in Ancient Phokis* (Austin).

Medda, E. (1983) *La forma monologica. Ricerche su Omero e Sofocle* (Studi di Lettere, Storia e Filosofia pubblicati dalla Scuola Normale Superiore di Pisa 35; Pisa).

(1993) 'Su alcuni associazioni del docmio con altri metri in tragedia', *SCO* 43: 101–234.

Meillet, A. (1928) (ed.) *Étrennes de linguistique offertes à Benveniste* (Paris).

Meineke, J. A. F. A. (1857) 'Zu Hesychius', *Philologus* 12: 602–33.

(1863a) *Analecta Sophoclea* (in an appendix to his edition of the *OC*; Berlin).

(1863b) 'Beiträge zur Kritik des Aeschylus und Sophokles', *Philologus* 20: 718–20.

Meissner, T. (1995) *S-Stem Nouns and Adjectives in Ancient Greek. A Study in Greek and Indo-European Word Formation* (diss. Oxford).

Mendelsohn, D. (2002) *Gender and the City in Euripides' Political Plays* (Oxford).

Merkelbach, R. (1967) 'Interpolierte Eigennamen', *ZPE* 1: 100–2.

Metlikovitz, A. (1890) 'De Sophoclis codice Laurentiano Plut. XXXI.10', *Dissertationes Philologae Vindobonenses* 2: 213–302.

Meuli, K. (1946) 'Griechische Opferbräuche', in Gigon *et al.* (1946) 185–288. [= (1975b) ii. 907–1021]

(1975a) 'Das Weinen als Sitte', in (1976b) i. 353–85.

(1975b) *Gesammelte Schriften* (2 vols.; ed. T. Gelzer; Basel and Stuttgart).

Meurig Davies, E. L. B. (1949) 'Two notes on Euripides', *CR* 63: 49.

Mewaldt, J. (1929) 'Fundament des Staates', in Focke *et al.* (1929) (ed.) 69–93.

Mikalson, J. D. (1975) *The Sacred and Civil Calendar of the Athenian Year* (Princeton).

(1989) 'Unanswered prayers in Greek tragedy', *JHS* 109: 81–98.

Miller, H. W. (1946) 'ὁ φιλόμηρος Σοφοκλῆς and Eustathius', *CPh* 41: 99–102.

Monk, J. H. (1826) 'Notes on the *Electra* of Sophocles', *Museum Criticum* i. 60–78, 201–15. [orig. 1813–14, Nos. 1 and 2]

Monteil, P. (1963) *La phrase relative en grec ancien. Sa formation, son développement, sa structure des origines à la fin du Ve siècle A.C.* (Études et commentaires 47; Paris).

BIBLIOGRAPHY

Moorhouse, A. C. (1940) 'The construction with MH OY', *CQ* 34: 70–7.

(1948) 'On negativing Greek participles, where the leading verbs are of a type to require μή', *CQ* 42: 35–40.

(1959) *Studies in the Greek Negatives* (Cardiff).

(1965) 'A use of οὐδείς and μηδείς', *CQ* N.S. 15: 31–40.

Moretti, L. (1953) *Iscrizioni agonistiche greche* (Studi pubblicati dall'Istituto italiano per la storia antica 12; Rome).

(1957) *Olympionikai. I vincitori negli antichi agoni olimpici* (Accademia nazionale dei Lincei. Classe di scienze morali, storiche e filologiche 8° ser. 8; Rome).

Morstadt, R. A. (1864) *Beiträge zur Exegese und Kritik der sophokleischen Tragödien Elektra, Aias und Antigone* (Beilage zum Oster–Programm des Gymnasiums zu Schaffhausen; Schaffhausen).

Moser, D.-R. (1977) *Die Tannhäuser-Legende. Eine Studie über Intentionalität und Rezeption katechetischer Volkserzählungen zum Buß-Sakrament* (Supplement-Serie zu Fabula B 4; Berlin and New York).

Mossé, C. (1985) 'ΑΣΤΗ ΚΑΙ ΠΟΛΙΤΙΣ. La dénomination de la femme athénienne dans les plaidoyers démosthéniens', *Ktema* 10: 77–9.

Mossman, J. M. (1994) review of M. A. Lloyd (1992), *CR* N.S. 44: 261–2.

(1995) *Wild Justice: A Study of Euripides' Hecuba* (Oxford).

(2003) (ed.) *Oxford Readings in Classical Studies. Euripides* (Oxford).

Most, G. W. (1985) *The Measures of Praise: Structure and Function in Pindar's Second Pythian and Seventh Nemean Odes* (Hypomnemata 83; Göttingen).

(1994) 'Sophocles, *Electra* 1086–7' in Bierl *et al.* (1994) (eds.) 129–38.

(1998) (ed.) *Editing Texts: Texte edieren* (Aporemata 2; Göttingen).

(2002) 'Three notes on Sophocles' *Oedipus in Colonus* (68–69, 755, 1640)', *Philologus* 146: 252–64.

Most, G. W., Petersmann, H., and Ritter, A. M. (1993) (eds.) *Philanthropia kai Eusebeia: Festschrift für Albrecht Dihle zum 70. Geburtstag* (Göttingen).

Motte, A. (1971) *Prairies et jardins de la Grèce antique. De la religion à la philosophie* (Académie Royale de Belgique: Mémoires de la classe des lettres 61.5; Brussels).

Moussy, C. (1969) *Recherches sur τρέφω et les verbes grecs signifiant «nourrir»* (Études et commentaires 70; Paris).

Müller, C. F. (1866) *De Pedibus Solutis in Dialogorum Senariis Aeschyli, Sophoclis, Euripidis* (Berlin).

Müller, C. W. (1965) *Gleiches zu Gleichem. Ein Prinzip frühgriechischen Denkens* (Klassisch-Philologische Studien 31; Wiesbaden).

Müller, G. (1978) 'Textkritische Vorschläge zu griechischen Dichterstellen', *Hermes* 106: 4–14.

Murray, P., and Wilson, P. (2004) (eds.) *Music and the Muses. The Culture of 'Mousike' in the Classical Athenian City* (Oxford).

Naber, S. A. (1881) 'Sophoclea', *Mnemosyne* N.S. 9: 210–44.

602

5 WORKS CITED BY AUTHOR'S NAME WITH DATE

Nauck, J. A. (1859–62) *Euripideische Studien* (2 vols.; Mémoires de l'Académie Impériale des Sciences de St.-Pétersbourg, VII^c sér., 1.12 and 5.6; St. Petersburg).

(1862) review of Dindorf's Oxford 1860 edition (i.e. 1858–9), *Neue Jahrbücher für Philologie und Paedagogik* 85 = *Jahrbücher für classische Philologie* 8: 153–87.

(1866) 'Kritische Bemerkungen IV', in *Mélanges gréco-romains tirés du Bulletin de l'Académie Impériale des Sciences de St.-Pétersbourg* 2 (St. Petersburg) 639–746. [orig. Nov. 1865].

(1874) 'Kritische Bemerkungen V', in *ib.* 3 (St. Petersburg) 9–102. [orig. Dec. 1867]

(1880) 'Kritische Bemerkungen VIII', in *ib.* 4 (St. Petersburg) 407–508, 579–730. [orig. March 1879, April 1880]

(1890) review of Papageorgius's edition of the Sophoclean scholia, *ib.* 6/1: 21–51.

Nes, D. van (1963) *Die maritime Bildersprache des Aischylos* (diss. Groningen).

Nestle, W. (1930) *Die Struktur des Eingangs in der attischen Tragödie* (Tübinger Beiträge zur Altertumswissenschaft 10; Stuttgart).

Newiger, H.-J. (1969) 'Hofmannsthals "Elektra" und die griechische Tragödie', *Arcadia* 4: 138–63.

(1975) (ed.) *Aristophanes und die alte Komödie* (Wege der Forschung 265; Darmstadt).

Norden, E. (1909) *Die antike Kunstprosa vom VI. Jahrhundert v. Chr. bis in die Zeit des Renaissance*^{2} (1st edn. 1898; Leipzig and Berlin).

(1913) *Agnostos Theos. Untersuchungen zur Formengeschichte religiöser Rede* (Leipzig and Berlin).

(1939) *Aus altrömischen Priesterbüchern* (Acta Regiae Societatis Humaniorum Litterarum Lundensis 29; Oxford, London, Lund, Leipzig, Paris).

(2002) *Dio Ignoto. Ricerche sulla storia della forma del discorso religioso* (transl. C. O. Tommasi Moreschini; Brescia).

Nünlist, R. (1998) *Poetologische Bildersprache in der frühgriechischen Dichtung* (Beiträge zur Altertumskunde 101; Stuttgart and Leipzig).

Oehler, R. (1925) *Mythologische Exempla in der älteren griechischen Dichtung* (Basel).

Olmos, R. (1993) *Catalogo de los Vasos Griegos del Museo Nacional de Bellas Artes de La Habana* (Madrid).

Omont, H. A. (1892–3) *Demosthenis Orationum Codex Σ. Oeuvres complètes de Démosthène* (2 vols.; Paris).

Opstelten, J. C. (1945) *Sophocles en het grieksche pessimisme* (Leiden).

(1952) *Sophocles and Greek Pessimism* (transl. J. A. Ross; Amsterdam).

Orlandos, A. K., and Traglos, I. N. (1986) Λεξικὸν Ἀρχαίων Ἀρχιτεκτονικῶν Ὅρων (Βιβλιοθήκη τῆς ἐν Ἀθηναῖς Ἀρχαιολογικῆς Ἑταιρείας 94; Athens).

Ostwald, M. (1969) *Nomos and the Beginnings of the Athenian Democracy* (Oxford).

BIBLIOGRAPHY

Otterlo, W. A. A. van (1944) *Untersuchungen über Begriff, Anwendung und Entstehung der griechischen Ringkomposition* (Mededeelingen der Nederlandsche Akademie van Wetenschappen, Afdeeling Letterkunde N.R. 7.3; Amsterdam).

Otto, A. (1890) *Die Sprichwörter und sprichwörtlichen Redensarten der Römer* (Leipzig).

Owen, A. S. (1927) 'Τά τ᾽ ὄντα καὶ μέλλοντα. The end of Sophocles' *Electra*', *CR* 50–2.

Padel, R. (1992) *In and Out of the Mind: Greek Images of the Tragic Self* (Princeton, NJ).

Paduano, G. (1968) *La formazione del mondo ideologico e poetico di Euripide. Alcesti – Medea* (Studi di lettere, storia e filosofia pubblicati dalla Scuola Normale Superiore di Pisa 31; Pisa).

——— (2002) 'L'*Elettra* di Hofmannsthal come interpretazione di Sofocle', *SIFC* 3° ser. 20 (Scritti in ricordo di Marcello Gigante): 266–84.

Page, D. L. (1937) 'The chorus of Alcman's *Partheneion*', *CQ* 31: 94–101.

Pallantza, E. (2005) *Der Troische Krieg in der nachhomerischen Literatur bis zum 5. Jahrhundert v. Chr.* (Hermes Einzelschriften 94; Stuttgart).

Papageorgius, P. N. (1887) 'Emendationsvorschläge zu sophokleischen Stellen', *BPhW* 7: 1523–4.

Papathomopoulos, M. (1993) 'De quelques manuscrits de Sophocle revisités', in Machin and Pernée (1993) (eds.) 75–94.

Pariente, A., and Touchais, G. (1998) *Argos et l'Argolide. Topographie et urbanisme* (Recherches franco-helléniques III; Paris).

Parker, L. P. E. (1958) 'Some observations on the incidence of word-end in anapaestic paroemiacs and its application to textual questions', *CQ* N.S. 8: 82–9.

——— (1968) 'Split resolution in Greek dramatic lyric', *CQ* N.S. 18: 241–69.

——— (1976) 'Catalexis', *CQ* N.S. 26: 14–28.

——— (1990) 'Trochee to iamb, iamb to trochee', in Craik (1990) (ed.) 331–48.

——— (1997) *The Songs of Aristophanes* (Oxford).

——— (2001) '*Consilium et ratio*? Papyrus A of Bacchylides and Alexandrian metrical scholarship', *CQ* N.S. 51: 23–52.

Parker, R. C. T. (1983) *Miasma: Pollution and Purification in Early Greek Religion* (Oxford).

——— (1984) 'A note on φόνοι, θυσία and μασχαλισμός', *LCM* 9: 138.

——— (1996) *Athenian Religion: a History* (Oxford).

——— (1997) 'Gods cruel and kind: tragedy and civic ideology', in Pelling (1997) (ed.) 143–60.

——— (1998) 'Pleasing thighs: reciprocity in Greek religion', in Gill *et al.* (1998) (eds.) 105–25.

——— (1999) 'Through a glass darkly: Sophocles and the divine', in Griffin (1999a) (ed.) 11–30.

——— (2005) *Polytheism and Society at Athens* (Oxford).

Parker, V. (1998) 'τύραννος. The semantics of a political concept from Archilochus to Aristotle', *Hermes* 126: 145–72.

Parmentier, L. (1919) 'Notes sur l'Électre de Sophocle', *Rev. Phil.* 43: 66–77.

Parry, H. (1965) 'The second stasimon of Euripides' *Heracles* (637–700)', *AJP* 86: 363–74.

Parsons, P. J. *et al.* (1975) (eds.) *Proceedings of the XIV International Congress of Papyrologists. Oxford, 24–31 July 1974* (Graeco-Roman Memoirs 61; London).

Pasquali, G. (1913) *Quaestiones Callimacheae* (Göttingen). [= (1986) i. 152–301]
    (1986) *Scritti Filologici* (ed. F. Bornmann,G. Pascucci, S. Timpanaro; 2 vols.; Florence).

Patterson, C. (1981) *Pericles' Citizenship Law of 451–50 B.C.* (Arno Press Monographs in Classical Studies; Salem, N.H.).

Pattoni, M. P. (1988) *'L'exemplum* mitico consolatorio: variazioni di un *topos* nella tragedia greca', *SCO* 38: 229–62.
    (2003) 'Sofocle fr. 941 R.: testo e interpretazione', in Avezzù (2003) (ed.) 223–52.

Pearson, A. C. (1919) 'Some glosses in the text of Sophocles', *CQ* 13: 118–26.
    (1923) 'Critical notes on Sophocles and in particular on the *Ajax*', *PCPS* 121–3: 14–29.
    (1929) 'Sophoclea II', *CQ* 23: 87–95.
    (1930) 'Sophoclea IV', *CQ* 24: 154–63.

Pelling, C. B. R. (1990) (ed.) *Characterization and Individuality in Greek Literature* (Oxford).
    (1996) 'The urine and the vine: Astyages' dreams at Herodotus 1.107–8', *CQ* N.S. 46: 68–77.
    (1997) (ed.) *Greek Tragedy and the Historian* (Oxford).

Peppink, S. (1934) 'De Sophoclis codice Vaticano 1332', *Mnemosyne* 3rd ser. 1: 155–9.

Petretto, M. A. (1995) 'Musica e guerra: note sulla Salpinx', *Sandalon* 18: 35–53.

Petropoulou, A. (1979) 'The attribution of Sophocles' *Electra* 1015–16', *AJP* 100: 480–6.

Pettazzoni, R. (1955) *L'onniscienza di Dio* (Turin).
    (1956) *The All-Knowing God: Researches into Early Religion and Culture* (transl. H. J. Rose; London).

Pfaff, C. A. (2003) *The Argive Heraion. Results of Excavations Conducted by the American School of Classical Studies at Athens, volume 1. The Architecture of the Classical Temple of Hera* (Ann Arbor).

Pfeiffer, R. (1933) 'Die Σκύριοι des Sophokles', *Philologus* n.F. 42: 1–15. [= (1960) 85–97]

(1958) 'Ein neues Inachos-Fragment des Sophokles', *SB München* 6, 3–41.
[= Diller (1967) (ed.) 460–99]

(1960) *Ausgewählte Schriften. Aufsätze und Vorträge zur griechischen Dichtung und zum Humanismus* (ed. W. Bühler; Munich).

Pfeiffer-Petersen, S. (1996) *Konfliktstichomythien bei Sophokles: Funktion und Gestaltung* (Serta Graeca: Beiträge zur Erforschung griechischer Texte 5; Wiesbaden).

Phillips, D., and Pritchard, D. (2003) (eds.) *Sport and Festival in the Ancient Greek World* (Swansea).

Piccolomini, E. (1877) 'Sulla trasposizione dei versi 720–722 della Elettra di Sofocle', in C. Bardt *et al.* (1877) 753–8.

Pickard-Cambridge, A. W. (1988) *The Dramatic Festivals of Athens* (rev. of 2nd edn. 1968 by J. Gould and D. M. Lewis; 1st edn. 1953; Oxford).

Pickering, P. E. (2000) 'Verbal repetition in *Prometheus* and Greek tragedy generally', *BICS* 44: 81–101.

(2002) 'Did the Greek ear detect "careless" verbal repetitions?', *CQ* N.S. 53: 490–9.

Pizzani, U. (2000) 'Qualche osservazione sulla terminologia "teratologica" in Omero', in Cannatà Fera and Grandolini (2000) (eds.) ii. 527–39.

Platt, A. (1899) 'Sophoclea', *CR* 13: 147–8.

Plüss, H. T. (1891) *Sophokles' Elektra. Eine Auslegung* (Leipzig).

Poe, J. P. (1989) 'The altar in the fifth-century theater', *Cl. Ant.* 8: 116–39.

(1992) 'Entrance-announcements and entrance speeches in Greek tragedy', *HSCP* 94: 121–56.

(1993) 'The determination of episodes in Greek tragedy', *AJP* 114: 343–96.

Pöhlmann, E. (2001) 'Realität und Fiktion auf der attischen Bühne des 5. und 4. Jh.', *WS* 114: 31–46.

Porson, R. (1812) *Adversaria* (ed. J. H. Monk and C. J. Blomfield; Cambridge).

(1815) *Tracts and Miscellaneous Criticisms of the late Richard Porson, Esq., Regius Greek Professor in the University of Cambridge* (ed. T. Kidd; London).

(1820) *Ricardi Porsoni Notae in Aristophanem* (ed. with additions P. P. Dobree; Cambridge).

Powell, J. U. (1905) 'Notes on passages of Sophocles', *CR* 19: 230.

Prag, A. J. N. W. (1985) *The Oresteia: Iconographic and Narrative Tradition* (Warminster).

(1991) 'Clytemnestra's weapon yet once more', *CQ* N.S. 41: 242–6.

Probert, P. (2003) *A New Short Guide to the Accentuation of Ancient Greek* (Bristol).

Pulleyn, S. J. (1997) *Prayer in Greek Religion* (Oxford).

Purgold, L. (1802) *Observationes Criticae in Sophoclem, Euripidem, Anthologiam Graecam et Ciceronem* (Jena and Leipzig).

Quincey, J. H. (1966) 'Greek expressions of thanks', *JHS* 86: 133–58.

5 WORKS CITED BY AUTHOR'S NAME WITH DATE

Race, W. H. (1981) 'The word καιρός in Greek drama', *TAPA* 111: 197–213.

(1990) *Style and Rhetoric in Pindar's Odes* (American Classical Studies 24; Atlanta).

Radermacher, L. (1949) 'Das Meer und die Toten', Anz. Österr. Akad. Wiss., phil.–hist. Kl. 86, 307–15.

Radke, G. (1959) 'Pylades', *RE* 23/2: 2077–81.

Radt, S. L. (1971) 'Aristoteles und die Tragödie', *Mnemosyne* 4th ser. 24: 189–205. [= (2002) 56–70]

(1974) 'Zu Menanders *Dyskolos*', *Mnemosyne* 4th ser. 25: 137–47. [= (2002) 94–103]

(1983) 'Sophokles in seinen Fragmenten', in de Romilly (1983) (ed.) 185–222. [= (2002) 263–92 = Hofmann (1991) (ed.) 79–109]

(2002) *Noch einmal zu . . . Kleine Schriften von Stefan Radt zu seinem 75. Geburtstag* (ed. M. A. Harder, R. Regtuit and G. Wakker; Mnem. Suppl. 235; Leiden, Cologne, Boston).

Rappold, J. (1876) *Die Gleichnisse bei Aischylos, Sophokles und Euripides. I. Theil* (Klagenfurt).

Raschke, W. J. (1988) (ed.) *The Archaeology of the Olympics: the Olympics and other Festivals in Antiquity* (Wisconsin).

Rau, P. (1967) *Paratragodia. Untersuchung einer komischen Form des Aristophanes* (Zetemata 45; Munich).

Rausa, F. (1992) 'Nemesis a Roma e nelle provincie occidentali', *LIMC* VI/1: 762–70.

Raven, D. S. (1965) 'Metrical development in Sophocles' lyrics', *AJP* 86: 225–39.

Reeve, M. D. (1970) 'Some interpolations in Sophocles', *GRBS* 11: 283–93.

(1973) 'Interpolation in Greek tragedy, III', *GRBS* 14: 145–71.

Rehm, R. (1994) *Marriage to Death: the Conflation of Wedding and Funeral Rituals in Greek Tragedy* (Princeton).

Reiner, E. (1938) *Die rituelle Totenklage der Griechen* (Tübinger Beiträge zur Altertumswissenschaft 30; Stuttgart and Berlin).

Reinhardt, K. (1947) *Sophokles³* (1st edn. 1933; Frankfurt am Main).

(1979) *Sophocles* (transl. H. and D. Harvey; Oxford).

Reisig, C. K. (1816) *Coniectaneorum in Aristophanem Libri Duo* (1st vol.; Leipzig).

Reiske, J. J. (1753) *Animadversiones ad Sophoclem* (Leipzig).

Renehan, R. F. (1975) *Greek Lexicographical Notes* (Hypomnemata 45; Göttingen).

(1976) *Studies in Greek Texts: Critical Observations to Homer, Plato, Euripides, Aristophanes and some other authors* (Hypomnemata 43; Göttingen).

(1985) review article on Bond's commentary on Euripides' *Heracles*, *CPh* 80: 143–75.

(1992) review article on the Sophocles OCT by Lloyd-Jones and Wilson (1990), *CPh* 87: 335–75.

BIBLIOGRAPHY

Reynolds, L. D., and Wilson, N. G. (1991) *Scribes and Scholars: a Guide to the Transmission of Greek and Latin Literature³* (1st edn. 1968; Oxford).

Richards, I. A. (1936) *The Philosophy of Rhetoric* (London and New York).

Richardson, N. J. (1984) 'Recognition scenes in the *Odyssey* and ancient literary criticism', in F. Cairns (1984) (ed.) 219–35.

Richardson, S. (1990) *The Homeric Narrator* (Nashville).

Rijksbaron, A. (1976) 'How does a messenger begin his speech? Some observations on the opening lines of Euripidean messenger speeches', in Bremer *et al.* (1976) (eds.) 293–308.

  (1991) *Grammatical Observations on Euripides'* Bacchae (Amsterdam Studies in Classical Philology 1; Amsterdam).

  (1997) (ed.) *New Approaches to Greek Particles* (Amsterdam Studies in Classical Philology 7; Festschrift Ruijgh; Amsterdam).

  (2006) 'On false historic presents in Sophocles (and Euripides)', in De Jong and Rijksbaron (2006) (eds.) 127–49.

Risch, E. (1972) 'θρόνος, θρόνα und die Komposita vom Typus χρυσόθρονος', *Studii Clasice* 14: 17–24. [= (1981) 354–62]

  (1981) *Kleine Schriften* (ed. A. Etter and M. Looser; Berlin and New York).

Ritchie, W. (1964) *The Authenticity of the* Rhesus *of Euripides* (Cambridge).

Ritter, F. (1861) 'Sieben unechte Schlussstellen in den Tragödien des Sophokles', *Philologus* 17: 422–36.

Roberts, D. H. (1984) *Apollo and his Oracle in the* Oresteia (Hypomnemata 78; Göttingen).

  (1987) 'Parting words: final lines in Sophocles and Euripides', *CQ* N.S. 37: 51–64.

  (1988) 'Sophoclean endings: another story', *Arethusa* 21: 177–96.

  (1993) 'The frustrated mourner: strategies of closure in Greek tragedy', in Rosen and Farrell (1993) (eds.) 573–89.

Roberts, D. H., Dunn, F., and Fowler, D. P. (1997) (eds.) *Classical Closure: Reading the End in Greek and Latin Literature* (Princeton, NJ).

Robinson, D. (1990) 'Homeric φίλος: love of life and limbs, and friendship with one's θυμός', in Craik (1990) (ed.) 97–108.

Rohde, E. (1925a) *Psyche. Seelencult und Unsterblichkeitsglaube der Griechen⁹⁻¹⁰* (2 vols.; orig. 1894; Tübingen).

  (1925b) *Psyche: the Cult of Souls and Belief in Immortality among the Greeks* (transl. of 8th edn. by W. B. Hillis; London).

Roisman, H. (1984) *Loyalty in Early Greek Epic and Tragedy* (Beiträge zur klassischen Philologie 155; Königstein im Taunus).

Romilly, J. de (1983) (ed.) *Sophocle* (Entretiens sur l'antiquité classique 29; Geneva).

Ros, J. G. A. (1938) *Die μεταβολή (variatio) als Stilprinzip des Thukydides* (Nijmegen).

Rosen, R. M., and Farrell, J. (1993) (eds.) *Nomodeiktes: Greek Studies in Honor of Martin Ostwald* (Ann Arbor).

Rossum-Steenbeek, M. van (1998) *Greek Readers' Digests? Studies on a Selection of Subliterary Papyri* (Mnem. Suppl. 175; Leiden, New York, Cologne).

Ruijgh, C. J. (1957) *L'Élément achéen dans la langue épique* (Bibliotheca classica Vangorcumiana 8; Assen).

(1971) *Autour de "τε épique": études sur la syntaxe grecque* (Amsterdam).

(1976) 'Observations sur l'emploi onomastique de κεκλῆσθαι, vis-à-vis de celui de καλεῖσθαι, notamment dans la tragédie attique', in Bremer *et al.* (1976) (eds.) 333–95. [= (1991–6) i. 701–63]

(1989) 'Les anapestes de marche dans la versification grecque et le rythme du mot grec', *Mnemosyne* 4th ser. 42: 308–330. [= (1991–6) ii. 752–74]

(1991–6) *Scripta minora ad linguam graecam pertinentia* (ed. A. Rijksbaron and F. M. J. Waanders; 2 vols.; Amsterdam).

(2006) 'The use of the demonstratives ὅδε, οὗτος and (ἐ)κεῖνος in Sophocles', in De Jong and Rijksbaron (2006) (eds.) 151–61.

Russell, D. A. F. M. (1990) '*Ethos* in oratory and rhetoric', in Pelling (1990) (ed.) 197–212.

Rusten, J. S. (1983) 'γείτων ἥρως: Pindar's prayer to Heracles (*N.* 7.86–101) and Greek popular religion', *HSCP* 87: 289–97.

Rutherford, I. (2001) *Pindar's Paeans: a Reading of the Fragments with a Survey of the Genre* (Oxford).

Rybowska, J., and Witczak, K. T. (1995) (eds.) *In Honorem Annae Mariae Komornicka* (Collectanea Philologica 2; Lódź).

Saïd, S. (1993) 'Tragic Argos', in Sommerstein *et al.* (1993) (eds.) 167–89.

Sandbach, F. H. (1977) 'Sophocles, *Electra* 77–85', *PCPS* N.S. 23: 71–3.

Sansone, D. (1988) 'The survival of the bronze-age demon', *ICS* 13: 1–17.

Scattolin, P. (2003) 'Su alcuni codici degli scoli all' *Elettra* di Sofocle', in Avezzù (2003) (ed.) 307–19.

Schachter, A. (1981–94) *Cults of Boiotia* (4 vols.; BICS Suppl. 38.1–4; London).

Schadewaldt, W. (1926) *Monolog und Selbstgespräch* (Neue philologische Untersuchungen 2; Berlin).

(1932) 'Der Kommos in Aischylos' Choephoren', *Hermes* 67: 312–54. [= (1970) i. 249–84]

(1970) *Hellas und Hesperien*² (2 vols.; 1st edn. 1960; Zürich and Stuttgart).

Schaefer, G. H. (1808) *Meletemata Critica in Dionysii Halicarnassensis Artem Rhetoricam Cap. I–IV*, in *Dionysii Halicarnassensis De Compositione Verborum Liber* (London and Leipzig).

Schaefer, H. (1954) 'Πράκτωρ', *RE* 22/2: 2538–48.

Schauer, M. (2002) *Tragisches Klagen. Form und Funktion der Klagedarstellung bei Aischylos, Sophokles und Euripides* (Classica Monacensia 26; Tübingen).

Schein, S. L. (1979) *The Iambic Trimeter in Aeschylus and Sophocles: a Study in Metrical Form* (Columbia Studies in the Classical Tradition 6; Leiden).

(1982) '*Electra*: a Sophoclean problem play', *Antike und Abendland* 28: 69–80.

(1998) 'Verbal adjectives in Sophocles: necessity and morality', *CPh* 93: 293–307.

Scheltema, H. J. (1949) 'De codice Sophocleo Lugdunensi', *Mnemosyne* 4th ser. 2: 132–7.

Schenkl, K. (1869) review of Nauck's 1867 edition of Sophocles, *Zeitschrift für die österreichischen Gymnasien* 20: 530–40.

Schmalfeld, G. F. A. (1868) *Einige Bemerkungen zur Elektra des Sophokles mit einem Seitenblick auf Shakespeare's Hamlet* (Progr. Eisleben).

Schmidt, F(riedrich) W(ilhelm) (1864) *Analecta Sophoclea et Euripidea* (Neustrelitz).

(1886–7) *Kritische Studien zu den griechischen Dramatikern* (3 vols.; Berlin).

Schmitt, R(üdiger) (1967) *Dichtung und Dichtersprache in indogermanischer Zeit* (Wiesbaden).

Schneidewin, F. H. (1852) 'Sophocl. Electr. 797', *Philologus* 7: 146.

Schulze, W. (1896) review of P. W. Kretschmer, *Die griechischen Vaseninschriften, ihrer Sprache nach untersucht* (Gütersloh 1894), *GGA* 158: 228–56. [= (1934) 692–717]

(1918) 'Beiträge zur Wort- und Sittengeschichte', *SPAW* 320–32, 481–511, 769–91. [= (1934) 148–210]

(1934) *Kleine Schriften* (Göttingen).

Schütz, W. (1964) ΑΣΘΕΝΕΙΑ ΦΥΣΕΩΣ (diss. Heidelberg).

Schwindt, J. P. (1993) *Das Motiv der 'Tagesspanne'. Ein Beitrag zur Ästhetik der Zeitgestaltung im griechisch-römischen Drama* (Studien zur Geschichte und Kultur des Altertums 1/9; Paderborn).

Schwinge, E.-R. (1968) (ed.) *Euripides* (Wege der Forschung 89; Darmstadt).

Schwyzer, E. (1923) 'Deutungsversuche griechischer, besonders homerischer Wörter', *Glotta* 12: 8–29. [= (1983) 464–85]

(1930) 'Lesbisch φαι und altarmenisch *bam bas bay*', *KZ* 57: 242–7 [= (1983) 756–61]

(1940) *Syntaktische Archaismen des Attischen* (*APAW* 7.3–16; Berlin). [= (1983) 443–56]

(1983) *Kleine Schriften* (Innsbrucker Beiträge zur Sprachwissenschaft 45; ed. R. Schmitt; Innsbruck).

Scullion, V. S. (1999–2000) 'Tradition and invention in Euripidean aitiology', in Cropp *et al.* (1999–2000) (eds.) 217–33.

Seaford, R. A. S. (1984) 'The last bath of Agamemnon', *CQ* N.S. 34: 247–54.

(1985) 'The destruction of limits in Sophokles' *Elektra*', *CQ* N.S. 35: 315–23.

(1990) 'The imprisonment of women in Greek tragedy', *JHS* 110: 76–90.

(1994) *Reciprocity and Ritual: Homer and Tragedy in the Developing City-State* (Oxford).

Seager, J. (1813) 'Miscellaneous observations on several ancient and modern authors, no. II', *The Classical Journal* vol. 7 (no. 14): 240–7.

Seebeck, J. (1865) *De Homero Oedipodeae fabulae auctore* (diss. Bonn).

Segal, C. P. (1966) 'The *Electra* of Sophocles', *TAPA* 97: 473–545.

(1968) review of Vögler (1967), *CJ* 64: 137–40.

(1971) *The Theme of the Mutilation of the Corpse in the Iliad* (Mnem. Suppl. 17; Leiden).

(1977) 'Synaesthesia in Sophocles', *YCS* 2: 88–96.

(1981) *Tragedy and Civilization: an Interpretation of Sophocles* (London and Cambridge, Mass.).

(1982) 'Sophocles *Electra* 610–11 again', *CPh* 77: 133–6.

(1983) 'κλέος and its ironies in the *Odyssey*', *AC* 52: 22–47.

(1985) 'Messages to the underworld – an aspect of poetic immortalization in Pindar', *AJP* 106: 199–212. [= (1998) 133–48]

(1998) *Aglaia: The Poetry of Alcman, Sappho, Pindar, Bacchylides and Corinna* (Oxford, Lanham, Boulder, New York).

Segal, E. (1983) (ed.) *Oxford Readings in Greek Tragedy* (Oxford).

Seidensticker, B. (1971) 'Die Stichomythie', in Jens (1971) (ed.) 183–220.

Seidler, J. F. A. (1811–12) *De versibus dochmiacis tragicorum Graecorum* (2 vols.; Leipzig).

Seyffert, A. (1868) *De Electrae Sophocliae versibus aliquot commentatio* (Progr. Brandenburg).

Shackleton Bailey, D. R. (1989) 'Animals not admitted: Martial 4.55.23–4', *TAPA* 119: 285. [= (1997) 275]

(1997) *Selected Classical Papers* (Ann Arbor).

Sheppard, J. T. (1918) 'The tragedy of *Electra*, according to Sophocles', *CQ* 12: 80–8.

(1927) '*Electra* – a defence of Sophocles', *CR* 41: 2–9.

Shipp, G. P. (1979) *Modern Greek Evidence for the Ancient Greek Vocabulary* (Sydney).

Shisler, F. L. (1942) 'The technique of the portrayal of joy in Greek tragedy', *TAPA* 73: 277–92.

(1945) 'The use of stage business to portray emotion in Greek tragedy', *AJP* 66: 377–97.

Shrimpton, G. S., and McCargar, D. J. (1981) (eds.) *Classical Contributions. Studies in Honor of Malcolm Francis McGregor* (Locust Valley, NY).

Sicking, C. M. J. (1997) 'Particles in questions in Plato', in Rijksbaron (1997) (ed.) 151–74.

Sicking, C. M. J., and Stork, P. (1997) 'The grammar of the so-called historical present in ancient Greek', in E. J. Bakker (1997) (ed.) 131–68.

BIBLIOGRAPHY

Sideras, A. (1971) *Aeschylus Homericus: Untersuchungen zu den Homerismen der aischyleischen Sprache* (Hypomnemata 31; Göttingen).

Silk, M. S. (1974) *Interaction in Poetic Imagery, with Special Reference to Early Greek Poetry* (Cambridge).

Simondon, M. (1982) *La mémoire et l'oubli dans la pensée grecque jusqu'à la fin du Ve siècle avant J.-C.* (Paris).

Sirks, J. L. (1861) *Specimen litterarium exhibens Heronis mathematici Alexandrini Metrica nunc primum edita* (Leiden). [n.v.]

Sittl, C. (1890) *Die Gebärden der Griechen und Römer* (Leipzig).

Slater, W. J. (2001) 'Pindar, *Nemean* 7.102 – past and present', *CQ* N.S. 51: 360–7.

Slings, S. R. (1992) 'Written and spoken language: an exercise in the pragmatics of the Greek sentence', *CPh* 87: 95–109.

(1993) 'Figuren en wat daarvoor doorgaat', *Lampas* 26: 20–37.

Smith, B. H. (1968) *Poetic Closure: a Study of How Poems End* (London and Chicago).

Smith, J. S. (1785) 'Notes on reading the *Electra* of Sophocles', in Leeds Brotherton Library, Special Collections MS 533, pp. 29–69. [approximate date: the notes may reflect the lectures of William Collier at Cambridge]

Smith, O. L. (1971–80) 'A note on the Sophocles MS *Vat. Gr.* 1333', *C&M* 32: 35–43.

Sokolowski, F. (1960) 'On the episode of Onchestus in the Homeric Hymn to Apollo', *TAPA* 91: 376–80.

(1962–9) *Lois sacrées des cités grecques* (2 vols.; Paris).

(1979) 'τὰ ἔνπυρα: on the mysteries in the Lydian and Phrygian cults', *ZPE* 34: 65–9.

Solmsen, F. (1932) 'Zur Gestaltung des Intriguenmotivs in den Tragödien des Sophokles und Euripides', *Philologus* 87: 1–17. [= (1968–82) i. 141–57 = Schwinge (1968) (ed.) 326–44]

(1967) 'Electra and Orestes. Three recognitions in Greek tragedy', *Mededelingen der Koninklijke Nederlandse Akademie van Wetenschappen, Afd. Letterkunde*, Nieuwe Reeks 30/2: 31–62. [= (1968–82) iii. 32–63]

(1968–82) *Kleine Schriften* (Collectanea 4; 3 vols.; Hildesheim).

Sommer, L. (1912) *Das Haar in Religion und Aberglauben der griechen* (Diss. Münster).

Sommerstein, A. H. (1989) 'Again Klutaimestra's axe', *CQ* N.S. 39: 296–301.

(1995–6) 'Aeschylus' epitaph', *Mus. Crit.* 30–1: 111–17.

(1997) 'Alternative scenarios in Sophocles' *Electra*', *Prometheus* 23: 193–214.

Sommerstein, A. H., Halliwell, S., Henderson, J., and Zimmermann, B. (1993) (eds.) *Tragedy, Comedy and the Polis. Papers from the Greek Drama Conference Nottingham, 18–20 July 1990* (le Rane Collana di Studi e Testi 11; Bari).

Soteroudes, P. S. (1977–8) 'οἱ στίχοι ἀπὸ τὸν Σοφοκλῆ στὸ χφ αρ. 36 τῆς μονῆς Βατοπεδίου', *Hellenika* 30: 397–9.

Spence, I. G. (1993) *The Cavalry of Classical Greece: a Social and Military History with Particular Reference to Athens* (Oxford).

Spengel, L. (1863) 'Zu Sophocles Electra', *Philologus* 20: 173–4.

Stählin, F. (1924) *Das hellenische Thessalien. Landeskundliche und geschichtliche Beschreibung Thessaliens in der hellenischen und römischen Zeit* (Stuttgart).

Stein, P. (1909) *ΤΕΡΑΣ* (diss. Marburg).

Steinhart, K. A. H. (1843) *Symbolae Criticae* (Progr. Pforta; Naumberg). [n.v.]

Stengel, P. (1920) *Die griechischen Kultusaltertümer*[3] (Handbuch der klassischen Altertumswissenschaft 3 / 5; 1st edn. 1890; Munich).

Stephan, G. (1981) *Die Ausdruckskraft der caesura media im iambischen Trimeter der attischen Tragödie* (Beiträge zur klassischen Philologie Heft 126; Königstein).

Stephanopoulos, T. K. (1988a) 'Tragica I', *ZPE* 73: 207–47.

    (1988b) 'Tragica II', *ZPE* 75: 3–38.

Stevens, P. T. (1937) 'Colloquial expressions in Euripides', *CQ* 31: 182–91.

    (1945) 'Colloquial expressions in Aeschylus and Sophocles', *CQ* 39: 95–105.

    (1976) *Colloquial Expressions in Euripides* (Hermes Einzelschriften 38; Wiesbaden).

    (1978) 'Sophocles: *Electra*, doom or triumph?', *G&R* 2nd ser. 25: 111–20.

Stinton, T. C. W. (1965) 'Two rare verse forms', *CR* N.S. 15: 142–6. [= (1990) 11–16]

    (1977a) 'Notes on Greek tragedy II', *JHS* 1977: 127–53. [= (1990) 271–309]

    (1977b) 'Pause and period in the lyrics of Greek tragedy', *CQ* N.S. 27: 27–66. [= (1990) 310–61]

    (1985) 'Greek tragic texts and the limits of conservatism', *BICS* 32: 35–44. [= (1990) 430–45]

    (1986) 'The scope and limits of allusion in Greek tragedy', in Cropp *et al.* (1986) (eds.) 67–102. [= (1990) 454–92]

    (1990) *Collected Papers on Greek Tragedy* (Oxford).

Stokes, M. C., 'Sophocles, *Electra* 1087; text and context', in Bowersock *et al.* (1979) (eds.) 134–43.

Stolz, F. (1903) 'Zur griechischen und zur lateinischen Sprachgeschichte', *IF* 14: 15–24.

Stone, J. A. (1964) *Sophocles and Racine. A Comparative Study in Dramatic Technique* (Geneva).

Stray, C. (2004) 'From one Museum to another: the *Museum Criticum* (1813–26) and the *Philological Museum* (1831–33)', *Victorian Periodicals Review* 37: 289–314.

Swart, G. (1984) 'Dramatic function of the "agon" scene in the *Electra* of Sophocles', *Acta Classica* 27: 23–9.

Taplin, O. P. (1971) 'Significant actions in Sophocles' *Philoctetes*', *GRBS* 12: 25–44.

(1977a) *The Stagecraft of Aeschylus: the Dramatic Use of Exits and Entrances in Greek Tragedy* (Oxford).

(1977b) 'Did Greek dramatists write stage instructions?', *PCPS* N.S. 23: 121–32.

(1979) 'Yielding to forethought: Sophocles' *Ajax*', in Bowersock *et al.* (1979) (eds.) 122–9.

(1983) 'Sophocles in his theatre', in de Romilly (1983) (ed.) 155–74.

(1984–5) 'Lyric dialogue and dramatic construction in later Sophocles', *Dioniso* 55: 115–22.

(1989) 'Spazio e messa in scena in Sofocle', *Dioniso* 59 fasc. 2: 103–5. [in English]

Tarrant, R. J. (1987) 'The reader as author: collaborative interpolation in Latin poetry', in Grant (1987) (ed.) 121–62.

Taylor, M. W. (1991) *The Tyrant Slayers. The Heroic Image in Fifth Century B. C. Athenian Art and Politics²* (Salem, NH; 1st edn. New York 1981).

Thesleff, H. (1954) *Studies on Intensification in Early and Classical Greek* (Commentationes Humanarum Litterarum 21.1; Helsingfors).

(1955) *Studies on the Greek Superlative* (Commentationes Humanarum Litterarum 21.3; Helsingfors).

Thiersch, B. (1841) *Scholae Tremonienses* (Progr. Dortmund).

Thomas, R. (1997) 'Ethnography, proof and argument in Herodotus' *Histories*', *PCPS* N.S. 43: 128–48.

(2000) *Herodotus in Context: Ethnography, Science and the Art of Persuasion* (Cambridge).

Thompson, D. W. (1936) *A Glossary of Greek Birds²* (St. Andrews University Publications 39; 1st edn. 1895; Oxford and London).

Thompson, E. M., and Jebb, R. C. (1885) *Facsimile of the Laurentian Manuscript of Sophocles* (London).

Thompson, S. (1955–8) *Motif-Index of Folk Literature: a Classification of Narrative Elements in Folktales, Ballads, Myths, Fables, Mediaeval Romances, Exempla, Fabliaux, Jest-Books and Local Legends²* (1st edn. Bloomington, Indiana 1932–6; 6 vols.; Copenhagen).

Thomsen, R. (1980) *King Servius Tullius: a Historical Synthesis* (Humanitas 5; Copenhagen).

Thomson, G. D. (1939) 'The postponement of interrogatives in Attic drama', *CQ* 33: 147–52.

(1953) 'From religion to philosophy', *JHS* 73: 77–83.

(1973) *Aeschylus and Athens: a Study in the Social Origins of Drama⁴* (1st edn. 1941; London).

Tibaldi, A. (1999) 'L'associazione docmio-anapesto in Eur. *Hec.* 154–176 = 197–215, 177–196 e 1056–1108', *SCO* 47: 175–84.

5 WORKS CITED BY AUTHOR'S NAME WITH DATE

Timpanaro, S. (1974) *Il lapsus freudiano. Psicanalisi e critica testuale* (Dimensioni 34; Florence).

(1976) *The Freudian Slip: Psychoanalysis and Textual Criticism* (transl. K. Soper; London).

Todt, B. (1873) 'Bemerkungen zu Sophokles' Elektra', *Philologus* 32: 252–69.

Toepfer, J. G. (1831) *Commentationis Criticae in Sophoclem Specimen* (Progr. Lubben).

Tomlinson, R. A. (1972) *Argos and the Argolid: From the End of the Bronze Age to the Roman Occupation* (London).

Toup, J. (1760–6) *Emendationes in Suidam: in quibus plurima loca veterum Græcorum explicantur* (3 vols.; Oxford).

Tournier, E. (1882) 'Sophocle', *RPh* 6: 113–48. [under the pseudonym 'Y']

Trédé, M. (1992) *Kairos, l'à-propos et l'occasion: le mot et la notion, d'Homère à la fin du IVe siècle avant J.-C.* (Études et commentaires 103; Paris).

(1993) '*Kairos* dans le théâtre de Sophocle et son rôle dans l'action dans l'*Électre* et le *Philoctète*', in Machin and Perneé (1993) (eds.) 201–17.

Trenkner, S. (1960) *Le Style KAI dans le récit attique oral* (Bibliotheca Classica Vangorcumiana 9; orig. 1948; Assen).

Triantis, I. (1992) 'Myrtilos', *LIMC* VI/1: 693–6.

Troxler, H. (1964) *Sprache und Wortschatz Hesiods* (Zürich).

Tsantsanoglou, K., and Parássoglou, G. M. (1987) 'Two gold lamellae from Thessaly', *Hellenica* 38: 3–16.

Tsitsoni, E. (1963) *Untersuchungen der EK-Verbal-Komposita bei Sophokles* (Munich).

Turner, E. G. (1968) *Greek Papyri. An Introduction* (Oxford).

Turyn, A. (1944) 'The manuscripts of Sophocles', *Traditio* 2: 1–41.

(1952) *Studies in the Manuscript Tradition of the Tragedies of Sophocles* (Illinois Studies in Languages and Literature 36.1–2; Urbana).

Usener, H. (1878) 'Grammatische Bemerkungen', *Jahrb. für klass. Phil.* 117: 51–80. [= (1912–14) i. 223–61]

(1896) *Götternamen. Versuch einer Lehre von der religiösen Begriffsbildung* (Bonn).

(1912–14) *Kleine Schriften* (4 vols.; Leipzig and Berlin).

Vahlen, J. (1876) 'De Theocriti carminibus collectis; Emendationes Theocriteae', *Ind. Lect. Berol. Aest.* [= (1907–8) i. 13–22]

(1879) 'De Platonis Philebo', *Ind. Lect. Berol. Aest.* [= (1907–8) i. 77–87]

(1887) 'De Euripidis Electra', *Ind. Lect. Berol. Aest.* [= (1907–8) i. 367–78]

(1891) 'Zu Sophokles' und Euripides' Electra', *Hermes* 26: 351–65. [= (1911–23) ii. 354–68]

(1895) 'Observationes criticae in Sophoclis Electram; De verbo ἀφειδεῖν in Sophoclis Antigona', *Ind. Lect. Berol. Aest.* [= (1907–8) ii. 157–79]

(1895–6) 'De Theocriti Idyllio VII. De formis quibusdam sententiae comparativae', *Ind. Lect. Berol. Hib.* [= (1907–8) ii. 180–202]

(1902) 'De genere quodam dicendi graecis romanisque familiari', *Ind. Lect. Berol. Aest.* [= (1907–8) ii. 431–47]

(1904) 'ὑπόθεσις Electrae Sophocleae; Adnotationes grammaticae in Sophoclis Electram', *Ind. Lect. Berol. Aest.* [= (1907–8) ii. 500–15]

(1907–8) *Opuscula Academica* (2 vols.; Leipzig).

(1911–23) *Gesammelte philologische Schriften* (2 vols.; Leipzig and Berlin).

Valavanis, P. D. (1999) *HYSPLEX: The Starting Mechanism in Ancient Stadia* (*Univ. Cal. Publ. in Cl. Phil.* 36; London, Berkeley, Los Angeles).

Valk, M. van der (1967) 'Observations in connection with Aristophanes', in Cantarella *et al.* (1967) 125–44.

(1982) 'Euripides *Phoenissae* 1–2 and Sophocles *Electra* 1 – again', *GRBS* 23: 234–40.

Vanderpool, E. (1970) 'A *lex sacra* of the Attic deme Phrearrhioi', *Hesperia* 39: 47–53.

Vernant, J.-P. (1963) 'Hestia et Hermès. Sur l'expression religieuse de l'espace et du mouvement chez les Grecs', *L'homme* 3: 12–53. [= (1985) 155–201 ≈ (1983) 127–175]

(1983) *Myth and Thought among the Greeks* (London, Henley, Melbourne and Boston).

(1985) *Mythe et pensée chez les Grecs: études de psychologie historique*[3] (1st edn. 1965; Paris).

Vigneron, J. (1968) *Le Cheval dans l'antiquité gréco-romaine: des guerres médiques aux grandes invasions, contribution à l'histoire des techniques* (Annales de l'Est 35; Nancy).

Viketos, E. (1975) 'Notes on Sophocles', *Hermes* 103: 255–6.

(1987) 'Sophocles, *Electra* 1508–10', *Hermes* 115: 372–3.

Visser, E. (1997) *Homers Katalog der Schiffe* (Stuttgart and Leipzig).

Vlastos, G. (1947) 'Equality and justice in early Greek cosmologies', *CPh* 42: 156–78. [= (1995) i. 57–88]

(1995) *Studies in Greek Philosophy* (2 vols.; ed. D. W. Graham; Princeton, NJ).

Vögler, A. (1967) *Vergleichende Studien zur sophokleischen und euripideischen Elektra* (Bibliothek der klassischen Altertumswissenschaften n.F. 2.19; Heidelberg).

Von der Mühll, P. (1930) *Der Grosse Aias* (Basel). [= (1976) 435–72]

(1962) 'παρεοῦσα im Epigramm des Asklepiades', *MH* 19: 202–3. [= (1976) 286–8]

(1976) *Ausgewählte Kleine Schriften* (Schweizerische Beiträge zur Altertumswissenschaft Heft 12; ed. B. Wyss; Basel).

Vos, H. (1956) *ΘΕΜΙΣ* (Bibliotheca Classica Vangorcumiana 7; Assen).

Waanders, F. M. J. (1983) *The History of τέλος and τελέω in Ancient Greek* (Amsterdam).

Wackernagel, J. (1877) 'Der griechische Verbalakzent', *KZ* 23: 457–70. [= (1953–79) ii. 1058–71]

5 WORKS CITED BY AUTHOR'S NAME WITH DATE

(1889) *Das Dehnungsgesetz der griechischen Komposita* (Basle). [= (1953–79) ii. 897–961]

(1892) 'Über ein Gesetz der indogermanischen Wortstellung', *IF* 1: 333–436. [= (1953–79) i. 1–92]

(1895) 'Miszellen zur griechischen Grammatik', *KZ* 33: 1–62. [= (1953–79) i. 680–741]

(1897) 'Vermischte Beiträge zur griechischen Sprachkunde', *Programm zur Rektoratsfeier der Universität Basel*, 3–62. [= (1953–79) i. 764–823]

(1907) *Hellenistica* (Göttingen).

(1912) 'Über einige antike Anredeformen', *Programm zur akademischen Preisverteilung, Göttingen*, 3–32. [= (1953–79) ii. 970–999]

(1916a) 'Sprachliche Untersuchungen zu Homer', *Glotta* 7: 161–319. [= (1916b) 1–159]

(1916b) *Sprachliche Untersuchungen zu Homer* (Forschungen zur griechischen und lateinischen Grammatik 4; Göttingen).

(1926–8) *Vorlesungen über Syntax: mit besonderer Berücksichtigung von Griechisch, Lateinisch und Deutsch* (2 vols.; Basel).

(1953–79) *Kleine Schriften* (3 vols.; Göttingen).

Wærn, I. (1951) *ΓΗΣ ΟΣΤΕΑ. The Kenning in Pre-Christian Poetry* (Uppsala).

Wagener, A. P. (1931) 'Stylistic qualities of the apostrophe to nature as a dramatic device', *TAPA* 62: 78–100.

Wakefield, G. (1789–95) *Silva Critica: sive in auctores sacros profanosque commentarius philologus* (5 vols.; Cambridge and London).

Wakker, G. (1994) *Conditions and Conditionals: an Investigation of Ancient Greek* (Amsterdam Studies in Classical Philology 3; Amsterdam).

(1997) 'Emphasis and affirmation: some aspects of μήν in tragedy', in Rijksbaron (1997) (ed.) 209–31.

Waldock, A. C. A. (1951) *Sophocles the Dramatist* (Sydney).

Walter, K. (1877) *Emendationum in Sophoclis fabulas specimen* (diss. Leipzig). [n.v.]

Wankel, H. (1983) '"Alle Menschen müssen sterben": Variationen eines Topos der griechischen Literatur', *Hermes* 111: 129–54.

Waś, J. (1983) *Aspects of Realism in Greek Tragedy* (diss. Oxford).

Watkins, C. (1995) *How to Kill a Dragon: Aspects of Indo-European Poetics* (Oxford and New York).

Watson, L. (1991) *Arae: the Curse Poetry of Antiquity* (ARCA Classical and Medieval Texts, Papers and Monographs 26; Leeds).

Watt, W. S. (2004) 'Error Wattianus', *CQ* N.S. 54: 658–60.

Wecklein, N. (1869a) *Ars Sophoclis Emendandi. Accedunt Analecta Euripidea* (Wurzburg).

(1869b) *Curae epigraphicae ad grammaticam graecam et poetas scenicos pertinentes* (Leipzig).

(1922) *Textkritische Studien zu den griechischen Tragikern* (SB München 5; Munich).

617

Wehrli, F. (1931) Λάθε βιώσας. *Studien zur ältesten Ethik bei den Griechen* (Leipzig and Berlin).

Weinreich, O. (1929) 'Gebet und Wunder. Zwei Abhandlungen zur Religions- und Literaturgeschichte. 1. Abhandlung: Primitiver Gebetsegoismus. Ein Beitrag zu Terenz, Andria 232f.', in Focke *et al.* (1929) 169–99.

West, M. L. (1965) 'Alcmanica', *CQ* N.S. 15: 188–202.

   (1969) 'The sayings of Democritus', *CR* N.S. 19: 142.

   (1973) *Textual Criticism and Editorial Technique Applicable to Greek and Latin Texts* (Stuttgart).

   (1977) 'Tragica I', *BICS* 24: 89–103.

   (1978a) 'Tragica II', *BICS* 25: 106–22.

   (1978b) review of Dawe's first edition (1975), *Gnomon* 50: 236–43.

   (1979) 'Tragica III', *BICS* 26: 104–17.

   (1981) 'Tragica V', *BICS* 28: 61–78.

   (1982a) *Greek Metre* (Oxford).

   (1982b) 'Cosmology in the Greek tragedians', *Balkan and Asia Minor Studies* 8 (Research Institute of Civilization, Tokai University, Tokyo): 1–13.

   (1984) 'Tragica VII', *BICS* 31: 171–96.

   (1985) *The Hesiodic Catalogue of Women. Its Nature, Structure, and Origins* (Oxford).

   (1990) *Studies in Aeschylus* (Beiträge zur Altertumskunde 1; Stuttgart).

   (1991) review of the Sophocles OCT by Lloyd-Jones and Wilson (1990), *CR* N.S. 41: 299–301.

   (1992) *Ancient Greek Music* (Oxford).

   (1997) *The East Face of Helicon: West Asiatic Elements in Greek Poetry and Myth* (Oxford).

   (1999) 'Ancestral curses', in Griffin (1999a) (ed.) 31–45.

   (2001) *Studies in the Text and Transmission of the* Iliad (Munich and Leipzig).

   (2004) 'The death of Baldr', *JIES* 32: 1–9.

   (2007) *Indo-European Poetry and Myth* (Oxford).

West, S. R. (1989) 'Laertes revisited', *PCPS* N.S. 35: 113–43.

   (1999) 'Sophocles' *Antigone* and Herodotus Book Three', in Griffin (1999a) (ed.) 109–36.

Wex, F. K. (1837) *Beiträge zur Kritik des sophokleischen Oedipus auf Kolonos nebst Probe einer metrischen Übersetzung* (Schwerin).

Whitman, C. H. (1958) *Homer and the Heroic Tradition* (London and Cambridge, Mass.).

Wijnpersse, W. M. A. van de (1929) *De Terminologie van het Jachtwezen bij Sophocles* (diss. Amsterdam).

Wilamowitz-Moellendorff, E. F. W. U. von (1875) *Analecta Euripidea* (Berlin).

   (1883) 'Die beiden Elektren', *Hermes* 18: 214–63. [= (1935–72) vi. 161–208]

5 WORKS CITED BY AUTHOR'S NAME WITH DATE

(1895) 'Hephaistos', *Nachrichten der kgl. Gesellschaft der Wissenschaften zu Göttingen*, phil.-hist. Klasse, 217–45. [= (1935–72) v.2 5–35]

(1899–1923) *Griechische Tragoedien* (4 vols.; Berlin).

(1921) *Griechische Verskunst* (Berlin).

(1931–2) *Der Glaube der Hellenen* (ed. G. Klaffenbach; 2 vols.; Berlin).

(1935–72) *Kleine Schriften* (6 vols.; Berlin and Amsterdam).

(1974) *In wieweit befriedigen die Schlüsse der erhaltenen griechischen Trauerspiele? Ein ästhetischer Versuch* (ed. W. M. Calder III; Leiden).

Wilamowitz-Moellendorff, T. J. W. von (1917) *Die dramatische Technik des Sophokles* (Philologische Untersuchungen 22; Berlin).

Wilhelm, A. (1915) 'Neue Beiträge zur griechischen Inschriftenkunde 4', *SB Wien* 176.6.

(1974) *Akademieschriften zur griechischen Inschriftenkunde* (Opuscula vol. 8; 3 vols.; ed. W. Peek; Leipzig).

Wilkinson, L. P. (1963) *Golden Latin Artistry* (Cambridge).

Willi, A. (2002) (ed.) *The Language of Greek Comedy* (Oxford).

(2003) *The Languages of Aristophanes: Aspects of Linguistic Variation in Classical Attic Greek* (Oxford).

Williams, B. A. O. (1993) *Shame and Necessity* (Sather Classical Lectures 57: London, Berkeley, Los Angeles).

Williger, E. (1922) *Hagios. Untersuchungen zur Terminologie des Heiligen in den hellenisch-hellenistischen Religionen* (Religionsgeschichtliche Versuche und Vorarbeiten 19.1; Giessen).

(1928) *Sprachliche Untersuchungen zu den Komposita der griechischen Dichter des 5. Jahrhunderts* (Forschungen zur griechischen und lateinischen Grammatik 8; Göttingen).

Willink, C. W. (1989) 'The reunion duo in Euripides' *Helen*', *CQ* N.S. 39: 45–69.

(1990) 'The goddess Εὐλάβεια and pseudo-Euripides in Euripides' *Phoenissae*', *PCPS* N.S. 36: 182–201.

(1997) 'Sophocles, *Electra* 137–9', *CQ* N.S. 47: 299–301.

(2001) 'Critical studies in the *cantica* of Sophocles: I. *Antigone*', *CQ* N.S. 51: 65–89.

(2002) 'Critical studies in the *cantica* of Sophocles: II. *Ajax, Trachiniae, Oedipus Tyrannus*', *CQ* N.S. 52: 50–80.

(2003) 'Critical studies in the *cantica* of Sophocles: III. *Electra, Philoctetes, Oedipus at Colonus*', *CQ* N.S. 53: 75–110.

(2004) 'Further critical notes on Euripides' *Orestes*', *CQ* N.S. 54: 424–40.

Wills, J. (1996) *Repetition in Latin Poetry: Figures of Allusion* (Oxford).

Wilson, J. R. (1967) 'An interpolation in the prologue of Euripides' *Troades*', *GRBS* 8: 205–23.

(1971) 'τόλμα and the meaning of τάλας', *AJP* 92: 292–300.

BIBLIOGRAPHY

(1979) 'ΚΑΙ ΚΕ ΤΙΣ ΩΔ' ΕΡΕΕΙ: an Homeric device in Greek literature', *ICS* 4: 1–15.

(1980) 'ΚΑΙΡΟΣ as "due measure"', *Glotta* 58: 177–204.

(1987) 'Non-temporal οὐκέτι / μηκέτι', *Glotta* 65: 194–8.

Wilson, N. G. (1976) review of Dawe, *STS* i.-ii., *JHS* 96: 171–6.

(1977) 'A note on two manuscripts of Sophocles', *JHS* 97: 168–9.

(1983) 'A mysterious Byzantine scriptorium: Ioannikos and his colleagues', *Scrittura e Civiltà* 7: 161–76.

(1987) 'Variant readings with poor support in the manuscript tradition', *RHT* 17: 1–13.

Winnington-Ingram, R. P. (1954–5) 'The *Electra* of Sophocles: Prolegomena to an interpretation', *PCPS* N.S. 3: 20–6. [≈ (1980) 217–47 (revised and expanded) ≈ E. Segal (1983) (ed.) 210–16 (irritatingly abbreviated) ≈ Diller (1967) (ed.) 400–11 (German translation)]

(1969) 'Euripides, *poiêtês sophos*', *Arethusa* 2: 127–42.

(1979) 'Sophoclea', *BICS* 26: 1–12.

(1980) *Sophocles: An Interpretation* (Cambridge).

Wöhrle, G. (1995) *Hypnos, der Allbezwinger. Eine Studie zum literarischen Bild des Schlafes in der griechischen Antike* (Palingenesia 53; Stuttgart).

Wolf, E. (1910) *Sentenz und Reflexion bei Sophokles. Ein Beitrag zu seiner poetischen Technik* (diss. Tübingen).

Wölfflin, E. von (1881) 'Über die Alliterierenden Verbindungen der lateinischen Sprache', *SB München* 2, 1–94. [= (1933) 225–81]

(1883) 'Die Gemination im lateinischen', *SB München* 3, 422–91. [= (1933) 285–328]

(1933) *Ausgewählte Schriften* (ed. G. Meyer; Leipzig).

Woodard, T. M. (1964) '*Electra* by Sophocles: the dialectical design', *HSCP* 68: 163–205.

(1965) '*Electra* by Sophocles: the dialectical design (part II)', *HSCP* 70: 195–233.

Woodbury, L. E. (1979) 'Gold hair and grey, or the game of love: Anacreon fr. 13.358 *PMG*, 13 Gentili', *TAPA* 109: 277–87. [= (1991) 325–34]

(1991) *Collected Writings* (ed. C. G. Brown *et al.*; Atlanta).

Wright, M. E. (2005) 'The joy of Sophocles' *Electra*', *G&R* 2nd ser. 52: 172–94.

Wuhrmann, W. (1940) *Strukturelle Untersuchungen zu den beiden Elektren und zum euripideischen Orestes* (diss. Zürich).

Wunder, E. (1838) *De Scholiorum in Sophoclis Tragoedias Auctoritate* (Grima).

(1841) *Emendationes in Sophoclis Trachinias* (Grima).

(1843) *Miscellanea Sophoclea* (Grima).

Wüst, E. (1956) 'Erinys', *RE* Suppl. 8: 82–166.

Wyß, K. (1914) *Die Milch im Kultus der Griechen und Römer* (Religionsgeschichtliche Versuche und Vorarbeiten 15.2; Gießen).

5 WORKS CITED BY AUTHOR'S NAME WITH DATE

Yerushalmi, Y. H. *et al.* (1988) *Usages de l'oubli* (Paris).

Young, D(ouglas) C. C. (1964) 'Some types of error in manuscripts of Aeschylus' *Oresteia*', *GRBS* 5: 85–99.

(1965) 'Some types of scribal error in manuscripts of Pindar', *GRBS* 6: 247–73 [= Calder and Stern (1970) (eds.) 96–126]

Young, D(avid) C. (1971) *Pindar* Isthmian 7, *Myth and Exempla* (Mnem. Suppl. 15; Leiden).

(1983) 'Pindar *Pythians* 2 and 3: inscriptional ποτέ and the "poetic epistle"', *HSCP* 87: 32–48.

Zagagi, N. (1980) *Tradition and Originality in Plautus: Studies of the Amatory Motifs in Plautine Comedy* (Hypomnemata 62; Göttingen).

Zakas, A. I. (1890–1) Κριτικαὶ καὶ Ἑρμηνευτικαὶ Παρατηρήσεις εἰς Αἰσχύλον Σοφοκλέα Λυσίαν Πλάτωνα Λυκοῦργον καὶ Δημοσθένην (2 vols.; Athens).

Zieliński, T. (1925) *Tragodumenon Libri Tres* (Cracow).

Zimmermann, B. (1993) review of the Sophocles OCT by Lloyd-Jones and Wilson (1990), *Gnomon* 65: 100–9.

Zink, N. (1962) *Griechische Ausdrucksweisen für warm und kalt im seelischen Bereich* (diss. Heidelberg).

Zippmann, A. (1864) *Atheteseon Sophoclearum Specimen* (diss. Bonn).

Zucker, F. (1955) 'Formen gesteigert affektischer Rede in Sprechversen der griechischen Tragödie', *IF* 62: 63–78. [= (1963) 72–84]

(1963) *Semantica, Rhetorica, Ethica* (Deutsche Akademie der Wissenschaften zu Berlin, Schriften der Sektion für Altertumswissenschaft 38; Berlin).

Zuntz, G. (1955) *The Political Plays of Euripides* (Manchester).

(1971) *Persephone: Three Essays on Religion and Thought in Magna Graecia* (Oxford).

(1984) *Drei Kapitel zur griechischen Metrik* (*SB* Wien 443; Vienna).

Zwierlein, O. (1983) *Prolegomena zu einer kritischen Ausgabe der Tragödien Senecas* (Akademie der Wissenschaften und der Literatur zu Mainz, Geistes- und Socialwissenschaftliche Klasse 6; Wiesbaden).

INDEX OF SUBJECTS

627

635

INDEX OF SUBJECTS

verbs (*cont.*)
number
dual; endings of: 406, 407,
409, 410; first person: 395,
396–7
plural; suggests politeness: 428
middle, future, as passive: 403
–ατο for –ντο: 165
intransitive, of usually
transitive: 311, 388

'weight of griefs': 134
winds, unwanted objects thrown
to: 222
women
ἀνδρεία and: 408, 410

glory of: 403–4
grow old unwedded: 402
restrictions of movement: 191,
386
warlike: 475
work, required for success: 394, 396

Zeus
all-seeing: 155, 294
and εὐσέβεια: 437
angry with evil-doers: 155
in consolations: 155
μέγας: 155
preserves Orestes: 152
thunderbolt as weapon:
357

INDEX OF GREEK

INDEX OF GREEK

INDEX OF GREEK

INDEX LOCORUM

Printed in Great Britain
by Amazon.co.uk, Ltd.,
Marston Gate.